Bond's Franchise Guide

2009 Edition

20th Annual Edition

Robert E. Bond
Publisher

Blair Cavagrotti
Senior Editor

Tiffany Han
Editor

Emily Joyce Hanks
Editor

Source Book Publications
Serving the Franchising Industry
1814 Franklin Street, Suite 603, Oakland, CA 94612
800.841.0873 / 510.839.5471

ISBN-10: 1-887137-65-3
ISBN-13: 978-1-887137-65-2

DISCLAIMER

Bond's Franchise Guide is based on data submitted by the franchisors themselves. Every effort has been made to obtain up-to-date, reliable information. As the information returned has not been independently verified, we assume no responsibility for errors or omissions and reserve the right to include or eliminate listings and otherwise edit and present the data based on our discretion and judgment as to what is useful to the readers of this directory. Inclusion in the publication does not imply endorsement by the editors or the publisher. Errors brought to the attention of the publisher and verified to the satisfaction of the publisher will be corrected in future editions. The publisher specifically disclaims all warranties, including the implied warranties of merchantability and fitness for a specific purpose.

Bond's Franchise Guide was previously published as *The Source Book of Franchise Opportunities*. *The Source Book of Franchise Opportunities* went through seven editions before the name was changed in 1995 to *Bond's Franchise Guide*.

This publication is designed to provide its readers with accurate and authoritative information with regard to the subject matter covered. It is sold with the understanding that neither the author nor the publisher is engaged in rendering legal, accounting or other professional services. If legal advice or other expert assistance is required, the services of a competent professional person should be sought.

From a Declaration of Principles jointly adopted by a Committee of the American Bar Association and a Committee of Publishers.

Cover Design by Joyce Coffland, Artistic Concepts, Oakland, CA.

ISBN-10: 1-887137-65-3
ISBN-13: 978-1-887137-65-2

Printed in the United States of America.
10 9 8 7 6 5 4 3 2 1

Bond's Franchise Guide is available at special discounts for bulk purchase. Special editions or book excerpts can also be created to specifications. For details, contact **Source Book Publications**, 1814 Franklin Street, Suite 603, Oakland, CA 94612. Phone: (800) 841-0873 / (510) 839-5471; Fax: (510) 839-2104.

Preface

At its best, purchasing a franchise is a time-tested, paint-by-the-numbers method of starting a new business. Many of the myriad pitfalls normally encountered by someone starting a new business are avoided and the odds of success are vastly improved. Franchising represents an exceptional blend of operating independence with a proven system that includes a detailed blueprint for starting and managing the business, as well as the critical on-going support. However, purchasing a franchise is clearly not a fool-proof investment that somehow guarantees the investor financial independence.

At its worst, if the evaluation and investment decision is sloppy or haphazard, franchising can be a nightmare. If things don't work out, for whatever reason, you can't simply walk away. You are still responsible for the long-term lease on your retail space, the large bank loan that underwrote your entry into the business and/or the binding, long-term financial obligation to the franchisor. While it is easy to sell a profitable business, an unprofitable business will most likely result in a significant financial loss. If that loss is all equity, that might be an acceptable risk. If, however, you still have obligations to the bank, landlord or others, your hardship is greatly compounded. This says nothing about

the inevitable stress on one's personal life, relationships and self-esteem.

Your ultimate success as a franchisee will be determined by two factors:

1. The homework you do at the front-end to ensure that you are selecting the optimal franchise for your particular needs, experience and financial resources.

2. Your commitment to work hard and play by the rules once you have signed a binding, long-term franchise agreement. For most new franchisees, this involves working 60+ hours per week until you can justify delegating some of the day-to-day responsibilities. It also requires being a team player — not acting as an entrepreneur who does his or her own thing without regard for the system as a whole. A franchise system is only as good as the franchisees make it. This means following the script.

The motivation for writing this annual directory has always been to assist in the evaluation phase of the equation: to provide accurate, in-depth data on the many legitimate companies actively selling franchises. The book is written for the sophisticated businessperson seriously interested in the process of selecting an optimal franchise opportunity: someone willing to commit the time and resources necessary to find the best franchise for his or her particular needs; someone with the wisdom to know that the franchise selection process is exceedingly difficult and filled with potholes; someone keenly aware of the risks — including missed opportunities — of going through the process in a half-hearted way.

We hope we can facilitate the evaluation process by ensuring that the potential franchisee is exposed to the range of options open to him or her and that he or she goes about the selection process in a logical and systematic manner.

৪৩

Over 850 in-depth franchisor profiles are listed on the following pages. These profiles are the result of the detailed questionnaire noted in Appendix A.

No doubt you will be familiar with a large number of the listings. Many are household names. That, incidentally, is one of the primary benefits of franchising. Most people would agree that Express Employment Professionals has a better ring to it than Ace Recruiting. Apart from the proven systems and procedures, you are buying a recognized name along with the reputation that the name enjoys in the marketplace.

৪৩

After you have decided which of the 29 industry groups appeal to you the most, contact all of the companies listed and request a marketing brochure. Thoroughly read their literature and pick out the companies that most interest you and that naturally fit your talents and financial resources. You should be able to narrow your choices down to a manageable list of six or eight franchises that fit these criteria. Initiate an in-depth analysis of and dialogue with each of these franchisors. Concurrently, develop a thorough knowledge of the business and/or services that you are considering. Seek the advice of professionals, even if you are experienced in various elements of the evaluation process. Don't leave any stone unturned.

৪৩

Remember, this is not a game. I cannot overemphasize the fact that, in most cases, you will be making a once-in-a-lifetime investment decision. It is incumbent on you to do it right at the outset. This can only be done by taking your time, properly researching all the options, realistically addressing both the best- and worst-case scenarios, seeking the advice of friends and professionals and, in general, doing the due diligence required. You want to invest in a system that will take advantage of your unique talents and experiences and not take advantage of you in the process! Don't take short-cuts. Listen carefully to what the franchisor and your advisors tell you. Don't think you are so clever or independent that you can't benefit from the advice of outside professionals. Don't assume that the franchisor's required guidelines regarding the amount of investment, experience, temperament, etc., somehow don't apply to you. Don't accept any promises or "understandings" from the franchisor that are not committed in writing in the franchise agreement. Invest the additional time to talk to and/or meet with as many franchisees in the system as you can. The additional front-end investment you make, both in time and money, will pay off handsomely if it saves you from making a marginal, or poor, investment decision. This is one of the few times in business when second chances are rare. Make the extra effort to do it right the first time.

৪৩

Good luck and Godspeed.

Table of Contents

Section Three — Appendix

Section Four — Index

DEFINITIVE FRANCHISOR DATABASE AVAILABLE FOR RENT

SAMPLE FRANCHISOR PROFILE

Name of Franchise:	**EXPRESS EMPLOYMENT PROFESSIONALS**
Address:	8516 Northwest Expy.
City/State/Zip/Postal Code:	Oklahoma City, OK 73162-5145
Country:	U. S. A.
800 Telephone #:	(877) 652-6400
Local Telephone #:	(405) 840-5000
Fax #:	(405) 717-5665
General E-Mail:	franchising@expresspros.com
Internet Address:	www.expressfranchising.com
# Franchised Units:	570
# Company-Owned Units:	2
# Total Units:	572
Company Contact:	Ms. Diane Carter
Contact Title/Position:	Manager of Franchise Admin.
Contact Salutation:	Ms. Carter
President:	Mr. Robert A. Funk
President Title:	Chief Executive Officer
President Salutation:	Mr. Funk
Industry Category (of 48):	17 / Personnel Services
IFA Member:	International Franchise Association
CFA Member:	
Name Lower Case:	Express Employment Professionals
Division Of:	
Stock Symbol:	

KEY FEATURES

• Number of Active North American Franchisors	~ 3,000
% US	~90%
% Canadian	~10%
• Data Fields (See Above)	29
• Industry Categories	48
• % With Toll-Free Telephone Numbers	64%
• % With Fax Numbers	94%
• % With Name of Preferred Contact	95%
• % With Name of President	81%
• % With Number of Total Operating Units	92%
• Guaranteed Accuracy — $0.50 Rebate/Returned Bad Address	
• Converted to Any Popular Database or Contact Management Program	
• Initial Front-End Cost	$1,500
• Quarterly Updates	$150
• Mailing Labels Only — One-Time Use	$800

For More Information, Please Contact
Source Book Publications
1814 Franklin Street, Suite 603, Oakland, CA 94612
(800) 841-0873 • (510) 839-5471 • (510) 839-2104 Fax

There are three stages to the franchise selection process: the investigation, the evaluation and the negotiation stages. This book is intended to assist the reader in the first two stages by providing a framework for developing reasonable financial guidelines upon which to make a well-researched and properly documented investment decision.

Understand at the outset that the entire franchise selection process should take many months and can involve a great deal of frustration. I suggest that you set up a realistic timeline for signing a franchise agreement and that you stick to that schedule. There will be a lot of pressure on you to prematurely complete the selection and negotiation phases. Resist the temptation. The penalties are too severe for a seat-of-the-pants attitude. A decision of this magnitude clearly deserves careful consideration.

Before starting the selection process, briefly review the areas covered below.

Franchise Industry Structure

The franchising industry is made up of two distinct types of franchises. The first, and by far the larger, includes product and trade name franchising. Included in this group are automotive and truck dealers, soft drink bottlers and gasoline service stations. For the most part, these are essentially distributorships.

The second group encompasses business format franchisors. This book only includes information on this latter category.

Layman's Definition of Franchising

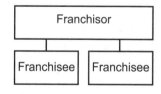

Classic Business Format Model

Business format franchising is a method of market expansion by which one business entity expands the distribution of its products and/or services through independent, third-party operators. Franchising occurs when the operator of a concept or system (the franchisor) grants an independent businessperson (the franchisee) the right to duplicate its entire business format at a particular location, for a specified period of time, under terms and conditions set forth in a contract (the franchise agreement). The franchisee has full access to all of the trademarks, logos, marketing techniques, controls and systems that have made the franchisor successful. In effect, the franchisee acts as a surrogate for a company-owned store in the distribution of the franchisor's goods and/or services. It is important to keep in mind that the franchisor and the franchisee are separate legal entities.

In return for a front-end franchise fee — which usually ranges from $15,000–35,000 — the franchisor is obligated to "set up" the franchisee in business. This generally includes assistance in selecting a location, negotiating a lease, obtaining financing, building and equipping a site and providing the necessary training, operating manuals and start-up assistance. Once the training is completed and the store is open, the new franchisee should have a carbon copy of other units in the system and enjoy the same benefits they do, whether they are company-owned or not.

Business format franchising is unique because it is a long-term relationship characterized by an on-going, mutually beneficial partnership. On-going services include research and development, marketing strategies, advertising campaigns, group buying, periodic field visits, training updates and whatever else is required to make the franchisee competitive and profitable. In effect, the franchisor acts as the franchisee's "back office" support organization. To reimburse the franchisor for this support, the franchisee pays the franchisor an on-going royalty fee, generally 4–8 % of gross sales. In many cases, franchisees also contribute an advertising fee to reimburse the franchisor for expenses incurred in maintaining a national or regional advertising campaign.

To work to maximum advantage, both the franchisor and the franchisees should share common objectives and goals. Both parties must accept the premise that their fortunes are mutually intertwined and that they are each better off working in a co-operative effort rather than toward self-serving goals. Unlike the parent/child relationship that has dominated franchising over much of the past 30

years, franchising is now becoming a true and productive partnership.

The Players

Franchisors

Source Book Publications routinely tracks more than 3,500 U.S. and Canadian franchisors. We believe this represents the number of legitimate, active franchisors in North America at any point in time. Profiles for more than 900 of these franchisors are found in this book, which is published annually by Source Book Publications. Additional copies of this 400+ page directory, considered the definitive directory in the field, are available for $34.95 plus $8.50 for shipping and handling ($45.50 + $12.00 in Canada). Call (800) 841-0873 or fax (510) 839-2104 to place a credit card order, or send a check to Source Book Publications, 1814 Franklin St., Suite 603, Oakland, CA 94612. There is an order form at the end of Chapter 3.

While you may already have your sights on a particular franchise opportunity, it would be short-sighted not to find out as much as you can about both the direct and indirect competition. You might discover that other franchises have similar products or services, but offer superior training and support, a reduced royalty fee or vastly superior financing options. I strongly encourage you to thoroughly utilize *Bond's Franchise Guide* or one of the other franchise directories to fully explore the options open to you.

The Regulatory Agencies

The offer and sale of franchises are regulated at both the federal and state levels. Federal requirements cover all 50 states. In addition, certain states have adopted their own requirements.

In 1979, after many years of debate, the Federal Trade Commission (FTC) implemented Rule 436. The Rule required that franchisors provide prospective franchisees with a disclosure statement (called an offering circular) containing specific information about a company's franchise offering. The Rule had two objectives: to ensure that the potential franchisee has sufficient background information to make an educated investment decision and to provide him or her with adequate time to do so.

The Franchise Rule was substantially updated (and improved) on July 1, 2008 as the FTC tried to make the disclosure document more consistent with various state regulations. Among other things, the Uniform Franchise Offering Circular (UFOC) became the Franchise Disclosure Document (FDD) and Item 19 of the new FDD was renamed from an Earnings Claims Statement to a Financial Performance Representation. Overall the revisions were positive and resulted in considerably more and better information being available to the prospective franchisee. Unfortunately, the revisions did not <u>require</u> all franchisors to provide a Financial Performance Representation from which potential franchisees could better determine the overall profitability of their potential investments.

Certain "registration states" require additional safeguards to protect potential franchisees. Their requirements are generally more stringent than the FTC's requirements. These states include California, Florida, Illinois, Indiana, Maryland, Michigan, Minnesota, New York, North Dakota, Oregon, Rhode Island, South Dakota, Virginia, Washington and Wisconsin. Separate registration is also required in the provinces of Alberta, Ontario and Prince Edward Island, Canada.

The regulations require that the franchisor provide a prospective franchisee with the required information at their first face-to-face meeting or at least 14 days prior to the signing of the franchise agreement, whichever is earlier. Required information includes:

1. The franchisor and any predecessors.
2. Identity and business experience of persons affiliated with the franchisor.
3. Litigation.
4. Bankruptcy.
5. Franchisee's initial fee or other payments.
6. Other fees.
7. Franchisee's estimated initial investment.
8. Obligations of franchisee to purchase or lease from designated sources
9. Obligations of franchisee to purchase or lease in accordance with specifications or from approved suppliers.

10. Financing arrangements.
11. Obligations of franchisor; other supervision, assistance or services.
12. Exclusive area or territory.
13. Trademarks, service marks, trade names, logotypes and commercial symbols.
14. Patents and copyrights.
15. Obligations of the participant in the actual operation of the franchise business.
16. Restrictions on goods and services offered by franchisee.
17. Renewal, termination, repurchase, modification and assignment of the franchise agreement and related information.
18. Arrangements with public figures
19. Actual, average, projected or forecasted franchise sales, profits or earnings.
20. Information regarding franchises of the franchisor.
21. Financial statements.
22. Contracts.
23. Acknowledgement of receipt by respective franchisee.

If you live in a registration state, make sure that the franchisor you are evaluating is, in fact, registered to sell franchises there. If not, and the franchisor has no near-term plans to register in your state, you should consider other options.

Keep in mind that neither the FTC nor any of the states has reviewed the FDD/UFOC to determine whether the information submitted is true or not. They merely require that the franchisor make representations based upon a prescribed format. If the information provided is false, franchisors are subject to civil penalties. However, this may not help a franchisee who cannot undo a very expensive mistake.

It is up to you to read thoroughly and fully understand all elements of the FDD/UFOC. There is no question that it is tedious reading. Know exactly what you can expect from the franchisor and what your own obligations are. Ask yourself: under what circumstances can the relationship be unilaterally terminated by the franchisor? What is your protected territory? Specifically, what front-end assistance will the franchisor provide? You should have a professional review the FDD/UFOC. It would be a shame not to take full advantage of the documentation that is available to you.

The Trade Associations

The **International Franchise Association** (IFA) was established in 1960 as a non-profit trade association to promote franchising as a responsible method of doing business. The IFA currently represents over 1,200 franchisors in the U.S. and around the world. It is recognized as the leading spokesperson for the industry. For most of its 50+ years, the IFA has represented the interests of franchisors only. In recent years, however, it has initiated an aggressive campaign to recruit franchisees and to represent their interests as well. Located at 1501 K St. NW, Suite 350, Washington, DC 20005. TEL (202) 628-8000; FAX (202) 628-0812, www.Franchise.org.

The **Canadian Franchise Association** (CFA), which has some 250+ members, is the Canadian equivalent of the IFA. Information on the CFA can be obtained by writing the group at 5399 Eglinton Avenue W, Suite 116, Toronto, ON M9C 5K6 Canada. TEL (416) 695-2896; (800) 665-4232; FAX (416) 695-1950, www.CFA.ca.

The **American Association of Franchisees & Dealers** (AAFD) is a national non-profit trade association dedicated to defining and promoting *Total Quality Franchising* practices. Focusing on market driven solutions to improve the franchising community, the AAFD promotes *collaborative franchising cultures and practices* through:

- The development and promotion of the *AAFD's Fair Franchising Standards*.

- The AAFD's accreditation program for franchise systems including *AAFD Accredited Contracts* and the prestigious *AAFD Fair Franchising Seal*.

- Support of effective *franchise associations*.

- Education and legal support programs.

- A dynamic vendor program including special *AAFD Branded Programs and Services*.

Information on the AAFD can be obtained by writing at P.O. Box 81887, San Diego, CA 92138. TEL (619) 209-3775; FAX: (619) 209-3777, www.AAFD.org.

Franchising's Role in the Economy

The IFA's Educational Foundation recently released *Volume 2* of the *Economic Impact of Franchised Businesses*. This report, which was prepared by PricewaterhouseCoopers for the IFA's Educational Foundation, documents the important role the franchising industry continues to play in the U.S. economy.

In 2005, more than 900,000 franchised establishments generated over $880 billion of direct economic output, or over 4.4 percent of the private sector economy in the United States. The franchising industry provided jobs for more than 11 million American workers, or just over 8 percent of all U.S. private sector employment. Including the additional economic activity that occurs outside of franchised businesses because of franchising activities, the overall economic contribution of franchised businesses was $2.3 trillion in 2005, or 11 percent of the U.S economy.

These economic activities provided more than 20 million jobs for American workers, over 15 percent of all U.S. private sector employment. From 2001 to 2005, the franchising sector of the economy grew at a faster pace than many other sectors of the economy. Franchising now provides more jobs than many other sectors of the U.S. economy. For example, franchising provides more jobs than the durable goods manufacturing sector or the financial activities sector of the economy. The franchising sector expanded by over 18 percent from 2001 to 2005, adding more than 140,000 new establishments and creating more than 1.2 million new jobs. Direct economic output increased by more than 40 percent from 2001 to 2005, from $624.6 billion to $880.9 billion. Including the impact of additional economic activity that occurs outside of franchised businesses because of franchising activities, the franchising industry added nearly 3 million jobs and over $780 billion of economic output to the U.S. economy. Much more detailed information can be found in the full 600-plus page report, published on the IFA website at www.franchise.org.

Franchise Survival/Failure Rate

In order to promote the industry's attractiveness, most literature on franchising includes the same often-quoted, but very misleading, statistics that leave the impression that franchising is a near risk-free investment.

In the 1970s, the Small Business Administration produced a poorly documented report stating that 38% of all small businesses fail within their first year of operation and 77% fail within their first five years. With franchising, however, comparative failure rates miraculously drop to only three percent after the first year and eight percent after five years. No effort was made to define failure. Instead, "success" was defined as an operating unit still in business under the same name at the same location.

While most people would agree that the failure rates for franchised businesses are substantially lower than those of independent businesses, this assumption is not substantiated by reliable statistics. Part of the problem is definitional. Part is the fact that the industry has a vested interest in perpetuating the myth rather than debunking it.

FRANdata, the industry's pre-eminent research firm, conducted a review several years ago of franchise terminations and renewals It found that 4.4% of all franchisees left their franchise system each year for a variety of reasons, excluding sales to third parties (to be fully meaningful, the data should include sales to third parties and the reasons behind a sale).

The critical issue is to properly define failure and success, and then require franchisors to report changes in ownership based on these universally accepted definitions. A logical starting point in defining success should be whether the franchisee can "make an honest living" as a franchisee. A "success" would occur when the franchisee prefers to continue as a franchisee rather than sell the business. A "failure" would occur when the franchisee is forced to sell his or her business at a loss.

A reasonable measure of franchise success would be to ask franchisees, "would you do it again?" If a legitimate survey were conducted of all franchisees of all systems, my guess is that the answer to this question would indicate a "success rate" well under 70% after a five-year period. Alternatively, one could ask the question, "has the franchise investment met your expectations?" I estimate that fewer than 50% would say "yes" after a five-year period. These are just educated guesses.

The failure rate is unquestionably lower for larger, more mature companies in the industry that have proven their systems and carefully chosen their franchisees. It is substantially higher for smaller, newer companies that have unproven products and are less demanding in whom they accept as a franchisee.

As it now stands, the Franchise Disclosure Document (FDD) only requires the franchisor to provide the potential franchisee with the names of owners who have left the system within the past 12 months. In my opinion, this is a severe shortcoming of the regulatory process. Unless required, franchisors will not willingly provide information about failures to prospective franchisees. There is no question in my mind, however, that franchisors are fully aware of when and why past failures have occurred.

It is patently unfair that a potential investor should not have access to this critical information. To ensure its availability, I propose that the FDD/UFOC be amended to require that franchisors provide franchisee turn-over information for the most recent five-year period. Underlying reasons for a change in ownership would be provided by a departing franchisee on a universal, industry-approved questionnaire filled out during an "exit" interview. The questionnaire would then be returned to some central clearing house.

The only way to make up for this lack of information is to aggressively seek out as many previous and current franchisees as possible. Request past FDDs/UFOCs to get the names of previous owners and then contact them. Whether successful or not, these owners are an invaluable resource. Try to determine the reason for their failure and/or disenchantment. Most failures are the result of poor management or inadequate finances on the part of the departing franchisee. But people do give up franchises for other reasons.

Current franchisees are even better sources of meaningful information. For systems with under 25 units, I strongly encourage you to contact all franchisees. For those having between 25 and 100 units, I recommend talking to at least half. For all others, interview a minimum of 50.

What Makes a Winning Franchise

Virtually every writer on the subject of franchising has his or her own idea of what determines a winning franchise. I believe there are five primary factors.

1. A product or service with clear advantages over the competition. These advantages may include brand recognition, a unique, proprietary product or service, or 30 years of proven experience.

2. A standardized franchise system that has been time-tested. A company that has operated numerous units, both company-owned and franchised, has usually worked out most of the bugs in the system. By the time a system has 30 or more operating units, it should be thoroughly tested.

3. Exceptional franchisor support. This includes not only the initial training program, but the on-going support (research & development, refresher training, [800] help-lines, field representatives who provide on-site training, annual meetings, advertising and promotion, central purchasing, etc.).

4. The financial wherewithal and management experience to carry out any announced growth plans without short-changing its franchisees. Sufficient depth of management is often lacking in younger, high-growth franchises.

5. A strong mutuality of interest between franchisor and franchisees. Unless both parties realize that their relationship is one of long-term partners, the system will probably never achieve its full potential. A few telephone calls to existing and former franchisees can easily determine whether the necessary rapport between franchisor and franchisees exists.

The Negotiation Process

Once you have narrowed your options down to your two or three top choices, you now have to negotiate the best deal you can with the franchisor. In most cases, the franchisor will tell you that the franchise agreement cannot be changed. Think twice before you accept the statement that the contract is non-negotiable. Notwithstanding the legal requirement that all of a franchisor's agreements be substantially the same at any point in time, there are usually a number of variables that are flexible. If the franchisor truly wants you as a franchisee, it may be willing to make concessions not available to the next applicant.

Will the franchisor take a short-term note for all or part of the franchise fee? Can you expand from your initial unit after you have proven yourself? If so, can the franchise fee on a second unit be eliminated or reduced? Can you get a right of first refusal on adjacent territories? Can the term of the agreement be extended from 10 to 15 years? Can you include a franchise cancellation right if the training and/or initial support don't meet your expectations or the franchisor's promises? The list goes on ad infinitum.

To successfully negotiate, you must have a thorough knowledge of the industry, the franchise agreement you are negotiating (as well as agreements of competitive franchise opportunities) and access to experienced professional advice. This can be a lawyer, an accountant or a franchise consultant. Above all else, he or she should have proven experience in negotiating franchise agreements. Franchising is a unique method of doing business. Don't pay someone $100+ per hour to learn the industry. Make him or her demonstrate that he or she has been through the process several times before. Negotiating a long-term agreement of this type is extremely tricky and fraught with pitfalls. The risks are extremely high. Don't think that you can handle the negotiations yourself, or that you can't afford outside counsel. In point of fact, you can't afford not to employ an experienced professional advisor.

The 4 R's of Franchising

At a young age we're taught that the three R's of reading, 'riting, and 'rithmetic are critical to our scholastic success. In franchising, success depends on four R's — realism, research, reserves and resolve.

Realism

At the outset of your investigation, be realistic about your strengths, weaknesses, goals and capabilities. I strongly recommend you take the time necessary to do a personal audit — possibly with the help of outside professionals — before investing your life's savings in a franchise.

Franchising is not a money machine. It involves hard work, dedication, set-backs and long hours. Be realistic about the nature of the business you are buying. What traits will ultimately determine your success? Do you have them? If it is a service-oriented business, will you be able to keep smiling when you know the client is a fool? If it is a fast-food business, will you be able to properly manage a minimum-wage staff? How well will you handle the uncertainties that will invariably arise? Can you make day-to-day decisions based on imperfect information? Can you count on the support of your spouse after you have gone through all of your working capital reserves and the future looks increasingly cloudy?

Be equally realistic about your franchise selection process. Have you thoroughly evaluated all of the alternatives? Have you talked with everyone you can, leaving no stone unturned? Have you carefully and realistically assessed the advantages and disadvantages of the system offered, the unique demographics of your territory, near-term market trends and the financial projections? The selection process is tiring. It is easy to convince yourself that the franchise opportunity in your hand is really the best one for you before you've done all your homework. The penalties for such slothfulness, however, are extreme.

Research

There is no substitute for exhaustive research!

Bond's Franchise Guide contains over 1,000 franchise listings, broken into 45 distinct business categories. This represents a substantial number of options from which to choose. Other directories also cover the industry in varying degrees of thoroughness and accuracy. Spend the time required to come up with an optimal selection. At a minimum, you will probably be in the business for five years. More likely, you will be in it for 10 years or more. Given the long-term commitment, allow yourself the necessary time to ensure you won't regret your decision. Research is a tedious, boring process, but doing it carefully and thoroughly can greatly reduce your risk and exposure. The benefits are immeasurable.

First, determine which industry groups hold your interest. Don't arbitrarily limit yourself to a particular industry in which you have first-hand experience. Next, request information from all of the companies that participate in those industries. The incremental cost of mailing (or calling) an additional 15 or 20 companies for information is insignificant in the big picture. Based on personal experience, you may feel you already know the best franchise. Step back. Assume there is a competing franchise out there with a comparable product or service, comparable management, etc., but which charges a royalty fee of sales that is 2% lower than your intuitive choice. Over a 10-year period, that could add up to a great deal of money. It certainly justifies your requesting initial information.

A thorough analysis of the literature you receive should allow you to reduce the list of prime candidates to six or eight companies. Aggressively evaluate each firm. Talking with current and former franchisees is the single best source of information you can get. Where possible, visit franchise sites. My experience is that franchisees tend to be candid in their level of satisfaction with the franchisor. However, since they don't know you, they may be less candid about their sales, expenses and income. *"How Much Can I Make?"* is another book by Source Book Publications that should assist in filling this void. Published annually, it details historical sales, expense and/or profit data on actual franchise operations, as provided by the franchisors themselves. The earnings claims statements for approximately 100 companies are included, representing the food-service, lodging, retail, and service-based industries. For even further information, go to the library and get studies that forecast industry growth, market saturation, industry problems, technical break-throughs, etc.

Reserves

Like any new business, franchising is replete with uncertainty, uneven cash flows and unforeseen problems. It is an imperfect world that might not bear any relation to the clean pro formas you prepared to justify getting into the business. Any one of these unforeseen contingencies could cause a severe drain on your cash reserves. At the same time, you will have fixed and/or contractual payments that must be met on a current basis regardless of sales: rent, employee salaries, insurance, etc.

Adequate back-up reserves may be in the form of savings, commitments from relatives, bank loans, etc. Just make certain that the funds are available when, and if, you need them. To be absolutely safe, I suggest that you double the level of reserves recommended by the franchisor.

Keep in mind that the most common cause of business failure is inadequate working capital. Plan properly so you don't become a statistic.

Resolve

Let's assume for the time being that you have demonstrated exceptional levels of realism, thoroughly researched your options and lined up ample capital reserves. You have picked an optimal franchise that takes full advantage of your strengths. You are in business and bringing in enough money to achieve a positive cash flow. The future looks bright. Now the fourth R — resolve — comes into play. Remember why you chose franchising in the first place: to take full advantage of a system that had been time-tested in the marketplace. Remember also what makes franchising work so well: the franchisor and franchisees maximize their respective success by working within the system for the common good. Invariably, two obstacles arise.

The first is the physical pain associated with writing that monthly royalty check. Annual sales of $250,000 and a 6% royalty fee result in a monthly royalty check of $1,250 that must be sent to the franchisor. Every month. As a franchisee, you may look for any justification to reduce this sizable monthly outflow. Resist the temptation. Accept the fact that royalty fees are simply another cost of doing business in the franchising industry. They are also a legal obligation that you willingly agreed to pay when you signed the franchise agreement. In effect, they are the dues you agreed to pay to belong to the club.

Although there may be an incentive, don't look for loopholes in the contract that might allow you to sue the franchisor or get out of the relationship. Don't report lower sales than actual in an effort to reduce royalties. If you have received the support that you were promised, continue to play by the rules. Honor your commitment. Let the franchisor enjoy the rewards it has earned from your success.

The second obstacle is the desire to change the system. You need to honor your commitment to be a "franchisee" and to live within the franchise system. What makes franchising successful as far as your customers are concerned is uniformity and consistency of appearance, product/service quality and corporate image. The most damaging thing an individual franchisee can do is suddenly and unilaterally introduce changes into a proven system. While these modifications may work in one market, they only serve to diminish the value of the system as a whole. Imagine what would happen to the national perception of your franchise if every franchisee had the latitude to make unilateral changes in his or her operations. Accordingly, any ideas you have on improving the system should be submitted directly to the franchisor for its evaluation. Accept the franchisor's decision on whether or not to pursue an idea.

If you suspect that you have a penchant for being an entrepreneur, for unrestrained experimenting and tinkering, you are probably not cut out to be a good franchisee. Seriously consider this question before you get into a relationship, instead of waiting until you are locked into an untenable situation.

Additional Resources

During your due diligence effort, there are several other sources of information that are invaluable.

1. www.BlueMauMau.com – the industry's premier community of franchise research, news, blogs and management insights. This website is the most open-ended site for in-depth information about franchising in general and individual franchise systems in particular. Through both in-house investigative reporting and third-party blogs, the site provides an excellent snapshot of the industry at any point in time.

2. www.WorldFranchising.com – the industry's pre-eminent source of current, up-to-date and detailed information about individual franchises. The site has detailed profiles on over 900 individual franchises and over 100 suppliers. Updates on the franchisor profiles in this book can be found on the site.

3. www.UFOCs.com – the site provides access to both historical UFOCs and current FDDs and has over 10,000 current and archived FDDs/UFOCs in inventory. In addition to industry packages of historical Item 19s, the site also provides individual Item 19s for the majority of companies that produce them. To the extent that you wish to streamline the investigative process, it might make sense to purchase a company's FDD well before you spend a great deal of time researching a franchisor. Having access to a company's litigation history and information about their financial strength before you make a significant time commitment could save you many hours of effort.

4. www.FRANdata.com – unquestionably the leader in third-party research on the franchising industry. Their president, Darrell Johnson, is the most widely-quoted independent spokesman for the industry.

5. www.Franchise.org – the website for the International Franchising Association and the voice of the industry in representing the interests of franchising to the public.

An invaluable gauge on historical franchisee success has to do with how various franchise systems have performed in connection with SBA (Small Business Administration) loans. Although the report is not made available to the general public, one can nevertheless gain access to the report through www.BlueMauMau.com. The report is called the SBA Failure Rates by Franchise Brand and can be found at http://www.bluemaumau.org/6812/2008s_sba_loan_failure_rates_franchise_brand.

The report lists all the franchise systems that have received SBA 7(a) and 504 loans between 10/1/2000 and 9/30/2008 It lists the number of loans that were disbursed to that franchisor, the total dollar amount of the loans, the percentage failure rate (number of loans in liquidation or charged off divided by the number of loans disbursed) and, most importantly, the percentage rate that the SBA had to charge off as bad debt (dollar amount charged off divided by the dollar amount disbursed). You can download the report and sort it both alphabetically and by the amount of the charge off percentage. If a company has an above-average charge off percentage, that should certainly raise some red flags. What is not shown, however, is what has happened during the eight-year period. If the franchisor can demonstrate to your satisfaction that the problems occurred years ago and are no longer relevant, that is a good sign. If the franchisor avoids the question, that may well mean that the poor franchisee problems are still prevalent.

Bond's Top 100 Franchises

As the pre-eminent publisher of books on franchising, Source Book Publications is constantly asked, "What are the best franchises?" Given that there are more than 3,000 active North American franchise systems, there clearly is no simple answer. This is especially true given the individual needs, experience and financial wherewithal of a widely divergent pool of prospective franchisees.

To at least partially answer the question, our staff has broken the franchising industry into four major segments — food-service, lodging, retail and service-based franchises. Within each group a rigorous, in-depth analysis was performed on literally hundreds of proven franchise systems to arrive at what we feel are the top 100 franchises in each of these segments. Companies were evaluated on the basis of historical performance, brand identification, market dynamics, franchisee satisfaction, the level of initial training and on-going support, financial stability and other key factors.

The end result of this evaluation process is *Bond's Top 100 Franchises*.

To ensure that we provide the most current information on the dynamics of the industry and its key players, the publication of *Bond's Top 100 Franchises* is an annual effort. Inclusion as a Top 100 company is based solely on merit. There is absolutely no favoritism shown toward any particular franchise. Since we do not permit advertising in our publications, there is also no correlation between the Top 100 selection process and advertising revenues.

Summary

I hope that I have been clear in suggesting that the selection of an optimal franchise is both time and energy-consuming. Done properly, the process may take six to nine months and involve the expenditure of several thousand dollars. The difference between a hasty, gut-feel investigation and an exhaustive, well-thought-out investigation may mean the difference between finding a poorly-conceived, or even fraudulent, franchise and an exceptional one.

There is a strong positive correlation between the efforts put into the investigative process and the ultimate degree of success you enjoy as a franchisee. The process is to investigate, evaluate and negotiate. Don't try to bypass any one of these elements.

The appendix includes the original questionnaire sent to some 3,000+ U.S. and Canadian franchisors. Franchisors who did not respond to the original mailing received a follow-up package roughly one month later. The end result was that roughly 39% of the contacted franchisors returned a completed questionnaire.

The data returned has been condensed into the profiles shown on the following pages. In some cases, an answer has been abbreviated to conserve room and to make the profiles more directly comparable. All of the data is displayed with the objective of providing as much background as possible. In those cases where no answer was provided to a particular question within the questionnaire, an "NR" is used to signify "No Response."

Please take a few minutes to acquaint yourself with the composition of the sample profile. Supplementary comments have been added where some interpretation of the franchisor's response is required.

Keep in mind that all of the profile data is based on questionnaires returned by the franchisors themselves, with no effort to verify its accuracy independently. There is no doubt that franchisors had some latitude to exaggerate their response in order to make themselves appear bigger, more mature and/or more franchisee-oriented than they really are. I am confident that some small percentage did just that. The vast majority, however, would see any such deception as dishonest, counter-productive and a general waste of everyone's time.

EXPRESS EMPLOYMENT PROFESSIONALS has been selected to illustrate how this book uses the collected data.

EXPRESS EMPLOYMENT PROFESSIONALS
8516 Northwest Expy.,
Oklahoma City, OK 73162-5145
Tel: (877) 652-6400   (405) 840-5000

Fax: (405) 717-5665
E-Mail: franchising@expresspros.com
Web Site: www.expressfranchising.com
Ms. Diane Carter, Manager of Franchise Admin.

Express franchise offices provide a full range of business-to-business staffing and HR services. The franchise includes all three service lines in one agreement: temporary/contract staffing, professional search/direct hire, and HR services. Express offers new franchise owners the unique chance to earn money by helping people grow their careers and businesses while impacting the local community. For established staffing business owners, we provide the opportunity to grow your business and advance the services provided. Independent staffing owners that have teamed with Express have benefited from our network of support, allowing them to keep up in this fast paced business.

BACKGROUND: IFA MEMBER
Established: 1983; 1st Franchised: 1985
Franchised Units: 592
Company-Owned Units: 4
Total Units: 596
Dist.:   US-554; CAN-27; O'seas-15
  North America: 49 States, 3 Provinces
  Density: 55 in TX, 49 in CA, 34 in OK
Projected New Units (12 Months):   50
Qualifications: 4, 4, 3, 4, 4, 4
Registered: All States

FINANCIAL/TERMS:
Cash Investment: $130-170K
Total Investment: $153.75-241.5K
Minimum Net Worth: $300K
Fees: Franchise — $35K
                   Royalty — 8-9%; Ad. — 0.6%
Earnings Claim Statement: Yes
Term of Contract (Years):   5/5
Avg. # Of Employees: 3 FT
Passive Ownership: Not Allowed
Encourage Conversions: Yes
Area Develop. Agreements: No
Sub-Franchising Contracts: No
Expand In Territory: Yes
Space Needs: 1,000-1,200 SF

SUPPORT & TRAINING:
Financial Assistance Provided: No
Site Selection Assistance: Yes

Lease Negotiation Assistance: Yes
Co-Operative Advertising: Yes
Franchisee Assoc./Member: No
Size Of Corporate Staff: 200
On-Going Support: A,C,D,E,G,H,I
Training: 2 Weeks in Oklahoma City, OK;
    1 Week in Certified Training Office (In Field).

SPECIFIC EXPANSION PLANS:
US: All United States
Canada: All Except Quebec
Overseas: South Africa, Australia

Address/Contact

1. **Company name, address, telephone and fax numbers.**

Comment: All of the data published in this book were current at the time the completed questionnaire was received or upon subsequent verification by phone. Over a 12-month period between publications, 10–15% of the addresses and/or telephone numbers become obsolete for various reasons. If you are unable to contact a franchisor at the address/telephone number listed, please call Source Book Publications at (800) 841-0873 / (510) 839-5471 or fax us at (510) 839-2104 and we will provide you with the current address and telephone number.

2. **(877) 652-6400   (405) 840-5000.** In many cases, you may find that you cannot access the (800) number from your area. Do not conclude that the company has gone out of business. Simply call the local number.

Comment: An (800) number serves two important functions. The first is to provide an efficient, no-cost way for potential franchisees to contact the franchisor. Making the prospective franchisee foot the bill artificially limits the number of people who might otherwise make the initial contact. The second function is to demonstrate to existing franchisees that the franchisor is doing everything it can to efficiently respond to problems in the field as they occur. Many companies have a restricted (800) line for their franchisees that the general public cannot access. Since you will undoubtedly be talking with the franchisor's staff on a periodic basis, determine whether an (800) line is available to franchisees.

3. **Contact.** You should honor the wishes of the franchisor and address all initial correspondence to the contact listed. It would be counter-productive to try to reach the president directly if the designated contact is the director of franchising.

Comment: The president is the designated contact in approximately half of the company profiles in this book. The reason for this varies among franchisors. The president is the best spokesperson for his or her operation, and no doubt it flatters the franchisee to talk directly with the president, or perhaps there is no one else around. Regardless of the justification, it is important to determine if the operation is a one-man show in which the president does everything or if the president merely feels that having an open line to potential franchisees is the best way for him or her to sense the "pulse" of the company and the market. Convinced that the president can only do so many things well, I would want assurances that, by taking all incoming calls, he or she is not neglecting the day-to-day responsibilities of managing the business.

Description of Business

4. **Description of Business:** The questionnaire provides franchisors with adequate room to differentiate their franchise from the competition. In a minor number of cases, some editing was required.

Comment: In instances where franchisors show no initiative or imagination in describing their operations, you must decide whether this is symptomatic of the company or simply a reflection on the individual who responded to the questionnaire.

Background

5. **IFA.** There are two primary affinity groups associated with the franchising industry — the International Franchise Association (IFA) and the Canadian Franchise Association (CFA). Both the IFA and the CFA are described in Chapter One.

6. **Established: 1983.** Express Employment Professionals was founded in 1983, and, accordingly, has more than 25 years of experience in its primary business. It should be intuitively obvious that a firm that has been in existence for over 25 years has a greater likelihood of being around five years from now than a firm that was founded only last year.

7. **1st Franchised: 1985.** 1985 was the year that Express Employment Professionals' first franchised unit(s) were established.

Comment: Over ten years of continuous operation, both as an operator and as a franchisor, is compelling evidence that a firm has staying power. The number of years a franchisor has been in business is one of the key variables to consider in choosing a franchise. This is not to say that a new franchise should not receive your full attention. Every company has to start from scratch. Ultimately, a prospective franchisee has to be convinced that the franchise has 1) been in operation long enough, or 2) its key management personnel have adequate industry experience to have worked out the bugs normally associated with a new business. In most cases, this experience can only be gained through on-the-job training. Don't be the guinea pig that provides the franchisor with the experience it needs to develop a smoothly running operation.

8. **Franchised Units: 592.** As of 8/14/09, Express Employment Professionals had 592 franchisee-owned and operated units.

9. **Company-Owned Units: 4.** As of 8/14/09, Express Employment Professionals had 8 company-owned or operated units.

Comment: A younger franchise should prove that its concept has worked successfully in several company-owned units before it markets its "system" to an inexperienced franchisee. Without company-owned prototype stores, the new franchisee may well end up being the "testing kitchen" for the franchise concept itself.

If a franchise concept is truly exceptional, why doesn't the franchisor commit some of its resources to take advantage of the investment opportunity? Clearly, a financial decision on the part of the franchisor, the absence of company-owned units should not be a negative in and of itself. This is especially true of proven franchises, which may have previously sold their company-owned operations to franchisees.

Try to determine if there is a noticeable trend in the percentage of company-owned units. If the franchisor is buying back units from franchisees, it may be doing so to preclude litigation. Some firms also "churn" their operating units with some regularity. If the sales pitch is compelling, but the follow-through is not competitive, a franchisor may sell a unit to a new franchisee, wait for him or her to fail, buy it back for $0.60 cents on the dollar, and then sell that same unit to the next unsuspecting franchisee. Each time the unit is resold, the franchisor collects a franchise fee, plus the negotiated discount from the previous franchisee.

Alternatively, an increasing or a high percentage of company-owned units may well mean the company is convinced of the long-term profitability of such an approach. The key is to determine whether a franchisor is building new units from scratch or buying them from failing and/or unhappy franchisees.

10. **Total Units: 596.** As of 8/14/09, Express Employment Professionals had a total of 596 operating units.

Comment: Like a franchisor's longevity, its experience in operating multiple units offers considerable comfort. Those franchisors with over 15–25 operating units have proven that their system works and have probably encountered and overcome most of the problems that plague a new operation. Alternatively, the management of franchises with less than 15 operating units may have gained considerable industry experience before joining the current franchise. It is up to the franchisor to convince you that it is providing you with as risk-free an operation as possible. You don't want to be providing a company with its basic experience in the business.

11. **Distribution: US-554; CAN-27; O'seas-15.** As of 8/14/09, Express Employment Professionals had 554 operating units in the U.S., 27 in Canada and 15 Overseas.

12. **Distribution: North America: 49 States, 2 Provinces.** As of 8/14/09, Express Employment Professionals had operations in 49 states and 2 Canadian provinces.

Comment: It should go without saying that the wider the geographic distribution, the greater the franchisor's level of success. For the most part, such distribution can only come from a large number of operating units. If, however, the franchisor has operations in 15 states, but only 18 total operating units, it is unlikely that it can efficiently service these accounts because of geographic constraints. Other things being equal, a prospective franchisee should vastly prefer a franchisor with 15 units in New York to one with 15 units scattered throughout the U.S., Canada and overseas.

13. **Distribution: Density: TX, CA, OK.** The franchisor was asked, "what three states/provinces have the largest number of operating units." As of 8/14/09, Express Employment Professionals had the largest number of units in Texas, California and Oklahoma.

Comment: For smaller, regional franchises, geographic distribution could be a key variable in deciding whether to buy. If the franchisor has a concentration of units in your immediate geographic area, it is likely you will be well-served.

For those far removed geographically from the franchisor's current areas of operation, however, there can be problems. It is both time consuming and expensive to support a franchisee 2,000 miles away from company headquarters. To the extent that a franchisor can visit four franchisees in one area on one trip, there is no problem. If, however, your operation is the only one west of the Mississippi, you may not receive the on-site assistance you would like. Don't be a missionary who has to rely on his or her own devices to survive. Don't accept a franchisor's idle promises of support. If on-site assistance is important to your ultimate success, get assurances in writing that the necessary support will be forthcoming. Remember, you are buying into a system, and the availability of day-to-day support is one of the key ingredients of any successful franchise system.

14. Projected New Units (12 Months): 50. Express Employment Professionals plans to establish 50 new units over the course of the next 12 months.

Comment: In business, growth has become a highly visible symbol of success. Rapid growth is generally perceived as preferable to slower, more controlled growth. I maintain, however, that the opposite is frequently the case. For a company of Express Employment Professionals' size, adding 50 new units over a 12-month period is both reasonable and achievable. It is highly unlikely, however, that a new franchise with only five operating units can successfully attract, screen, train and bring multiple new units on-stream in a 12-month period. If a franchisor suggests that it can, or even wants to, be properly wary. You must be confident that a company has the financial and management resources necessary to pull off such a Herculean feat. If management is already thin, concentrating on attracting new units will clearly diminish the time it can and should spend supporting you. It takes many months, if not years, to develop and train a second level of management. You don't want to depend upon new hires teaching you systems and procedures they themselves know little or nothing about.

15. Qualifications: 4,4,3,4,4,4. This question was posed to determine which specific evaluation criteria were important to the franchisor. The franchisor was asked the following: "In qualifying a potential franchisee, please rank the following criteria from Unimportant (1) to Very Important (5)." The responses should be self-explanatory:

Financial Net Worth (Rank from 1–5)
General Business Experience (Rank from 1–5)
Specific Industry Experience (Rank from 1–5)
Formal Education (Rank from 1–5)
Psychological Profile (Rank from 1–5)
Personal Interview(s) (Rank from 1–5)

16. Registered refers to the 16 states that require specific formal registration at the state level before the franchisor may offer franchises in that state. State registration and disclosure

to the Federal Trade Commission are separate issues that are discussed in Chapter 1.

Capital Requirements/Rights

17. Cash Investment: $130-170K. On average, an Express Employment Professionals franchisee will have made a cash investment of $130,000–170,000 by the time he or she finally opens the initial operating unit.

Comment: It is important that you be realistic about the amount of cash you can comfortably invest in a business. Stretching beyond your means can have grave and far-reaching consequences. Assume that you will encounter periodic set-backs and that you will have to draw on your reserves. The demands of starting a new business are harsh enough without adding the uncertainties associated with inadequate working capital. Trust the franchisor's recommendations regarding the suggested minimum cash investment. If anything, there is an incentive for setting the recommended level of investment too low, rather than too high. The franchisor will want to qualify you to the extent that you have adequate financing. No legitimate franchisor wants you to invest if there is a chance that you might fail because of a shortage of funds.

Keep in mind that you will probably not achieve a positive cash flow before you've been in business more than six months. In your discussions with the franchisor, be absolutely certain that its calculations include an adequate working capital reserve.

18. Total Investment: $153.75-241.5K. On average, Express Employment Professionals franchisees will invest a total of $153,750 to $241,500, including both cash and debt, by the time the franchise opens its doors.

Comment: The total investment should be the cash investment noted above plus any debt that you will incur in starting up the new business. Debt could be a note to the franchisor for all or part of the franchise fee, an equipment lease, building and facilities leases, etc. Make sure that the total includes all of the obligations that you assume, especially any long-term lease obligations.

Be conservative in assessing what your real exposure is. If you are leasing highly specialized equipment or if you are leasing a single-purpose building, it is naive to think that you will recoup your investment if you have to sell or sub-lease those assets in a buyer's market. If there is any specialized equipment that may have been manufactured to the franchisor's specifications, determine if the franchisor has any form of buy-back provision.

19. **Minimum Net Worth: $300K.** In this case, Express Employment Professionals feels that a potential franchisee should have a minimum net worth of $300,000. Although net worth can be defined in vastly different ways, the franchisor's response should suggest a minimum level of equity that the prospective franchisee should possess. Net worth is the combination of both liquid and illiquid assets. Again, don't think that franchisor-determined guidelines somehow don't apply to you.

20. **Fees (Franchise): $35K.** Express Employment Professionals requires a front-end, one-time-only payment of $35,000 to grant a franchise for a single location. As noted in Chapter One, the franchise fee is a payment to reimburse the franchisor for the incurred costs of setting the franchisee up in business — from recruiting through training and manuals. The fee usually ranges from $15,000–30,000. It is a function of competitive franchise fees and the actual out-of-pocket costs incurred by the franchisor.

Depending upon the franchisee's particular circumstances and how well the franchisor thinks he or she might fit into the system, the franchisor may finance all or part of the franchise fee. (See Section 32 below to see if a franchisor provides any direct or indirect financial assistance.)

The franchise fee is one area in which the franchisor frequently provides either direct or indirect financial support.

Comment: Ideally, the franchisor should do no more than recover its costs on the initial franchise fee. Profits come later in the form of royalty fees, which are a function of the franchisee's sales. Whether the franchise fee is $5,000 or $35,000, the total should be carefully

evaluated. What are competitive fees and are they financed? How much training will you actually receive? Are the fees reflective of the franchisor's expenses? If the fees appear to be non-competitive, address your concerns with the franchisor.

Realize that a $5,000 differential in the one-time franchise fee is a secondary consideration in the overall scheme of things. You are in the relationship for the long-term.

By the same token, don't get suckered in by an extremely low fee if there is any doubt about the franchisor's ability to follow through. Franchisors need to collect reasonable fees to cover their actual costs. If they don't recoup these costs, they cannot recruit and train new franchisees on whom your own future success partially depends.

21. **Fees (Royalty): 8-9%** means that eight to nine percent of gross sales (or other measure, as defined in the franchise agreement) must be periodically paid directly to the franchisor in the form of royalties. This on-going expense is your cost for being part of the larger franchise system and for all of the "back-office" support you receive. In a few cases, the amount of the royalty fee is fixed rather than variable. In others, the fee decreases as the volume of sales (or other measure) increases (i.e., 6% on the first $200,000 of sales, 5% on the next $100,000 and so on). In others, the fee is held at artificially low levels during the start-up phase of the franchisee's business, then increases once the franchisee is better able to afford it.

Comment: Royalty fees represent the mechanism by which the franchisor finally recoups the costs it has incurred in developing its business. It may take many years and many operating units before the franchisor is able to make a true operating profit.

Consider a typical franchisor who might have been in business for three years. With a staff of five, rent, travel, operating expenses, etc., assume it has annual operating costs of $300,000 (including reasonable owner's salaries). Assume also that there are 25 franchised units with average annual sales of $250,000. Each franchise

23

is required to pay a 6% royalty fee. Total annual royalties under this scenario would total only $375,000. The franchisor is making a $75,000 profit. Then consider the personal risk the franchisor took in developing a new business and the initial years of negative cash flows. Alternatively, evaluate what it would cost you, as a sole proprietor, to provide the myriad services included in the royalty payment.

In assessing various alternative investments, the amount of the royalty percentage is a major on-going expense. Assuming average annual sales of $250,000 per annum over a 15 year period, the total royalties at 5% would be $187,500. At 6%, the cumulative fees would be $225,000. You have to be fully convinced that the $37,500 differential is justified. While this is clearly a meaningful number, what you are really evaluating is the quality of management and the competitive advantages of the goods and/or services offered by the franchisor.

22. Fees (Advertising): 0.6%. Most national or regional franchisors require their franchisees to contribute a certain percentage of their sales (or other measure, as determined in the franchise agreement) into a corporate advertising fund. These individual advertising fees are pooled to develop a corporate advertising/marketing effort that produces great economies of scale. The end result is a national or regional advertising program that promotes the franchisor's products and services. Depending upon the nature of the business, this percentage usually ranges from 2–6% and is in addition to the royalty fee.

Comment: One of the greatest advantages of a franchised system is its ability to promote, on a national or regional basis, its products and services. The promotions may be through television, radio, print medias or direct mail. The objective is name recognition and, over time, the assumption that the product and/or service has been "time-tested." An individual business owner could never justify the expense of mounting a major advertising program at the local level. For a smaller franchise that may not yet have an advertising program or fee, it is important to know when an advertising program will start, how it will be monitored and its expected cost.

23. Earnings Claims Statement: Yes. This means that Express Employment Professionals does provide an earnings claims statement to potential franchisees. Unfortunately, only 12–15% of franchisors provide an earnings claims statement in their Franchise Disclosure Document (FDD). The franchising industry's failure to require earnings claims statements does a serious disservice to the potential franchisee. See Chapter Two for comments on the earnings claims statement.

24. Term of Contract (Years): 5/5. Express Employment Professionals' initial franchise period runs for five years. The first renewal period runs for an additional five years. Assuming that the franchisee operates within the terms of the franchise agreement, he or she has ten years within which to develop and, ultimately, sell the business.

Comment: The potential (discounted) value of any business (or investment) is the sum of the operating income that is generated each year plus its value upon liquidation. Given this truth, the length of the franchise agreement and any renewals are extremely important to the franchisee. It is essential that he or she has adequate time to develop the business to its full potential. At that time, he or she will have maximized the value of the business as an on-going concern. The value of the business to a potential buyer, however, is largely a function of how long the franchise agreement runs. If there are only two years remaining before the agreement expires, or if the terms of an extension(s) are vague, the business will be worth only a fraction of the value assigned to a business with 15 years to go. For the most part, the longer the agreement and the subsequent extension, the better. (The same logic applies to a lease. If your sales are largely a function of your location and traffic count, then it is important that you have options to extend the lease under known terms. Your lease should never be longer than the remaining term of your franchise agreement, however.)

Assuming the length of the agreement is acceptable, be clear under what circumstances renewals might not be granted. Similarly, know the circumstances under which a franchise agreement might be prematurely and unilaterally

24

canceled by the franchisor. I strongly recommend you have an experienced lawyer review this section of the franchise agreement. It would be devastating if, after spending years developing your business, there were a loophole in the contract that allowed the franchisor to arbitrarily cancel the relationship.

25. **Avg. # of Employees: 3 FT.** The question was asked, "Including the owner/operator, how many employees are recommended to properly staff the average franchised unit?" In Express Employment Professionals' case, three full-time employees and eight part-time employees are required.

Comment: Most entrepreneurs start a new business based on their intuitive feel that it will be "fun" and that their talents and experience will be put to good use. They will be doing what they enjoy and what they are good at. Times change. Your business prospers. The number of employees increases. You are spending an increasing percentage of your time taking care of personnel problems and less and less on the fun parts of the business. In Chapter One, the importance of conducting a realistic self-appraisal was stressed. If you found that you really are not good at managing people, or you don't have the patience to manage a large minimum wage staff, cut your losses before you are locked into doing just that.

26. **Passive Ownership: Not Allowed.** Depending on the nature of the business, many franchisors are indifferent as to whether you manage the business directly or hire a full-time manager. Others are insistent that, at least for the initial franchise, the franchisee be a full-time owner/operator. Express Employment Professionals does not allow franchisees to hire full-time managers to run their outlets.

Comment: Unless you have a great deal of experience in the business you have chosen or in managing similar businesses, I feel strongly that you should initially commit your personal time and energies to make the system work. After you have developed a full understanding of the business and have competent, trusted staff members who can assume day-to-day operations, then consider delegating these responsibilities. Running the business through a manager can be fraught with peril unless

you have mastered all aspects of the business and there are strong economic incentives and sufficient safeguards to ensure the manager will perform as desired.

27. **Conversions Encouraged: Yes.** This section pertains primarily to sole proprietorships or "mom and pop" operations. To the extent that there truly are centralized operating savings associated with the franchise, the most logical people to join a franchise system are sole practitioners who are working hard but only eking out a living. The implementation of proven systems and marketing clout could significantly reduce operating costs and increase profits.

Comment: The franchisor has the option of 1) actively encouraging such independent operators to become members of the franchise team, 2) seeking out franchisees with limited or no applied experience or 3) going after both groups. Concerned that it will be very difficult to break independent operators of the bad habits they have picked up over the years, many only choose course two. "They will continue to do things their way. They won't, or can't, accept corporate direction," they might say to themselves. Others are simply selective in the conversions they allow. In many cases, the franchise fee is reduced or eliminated for conversions.

28. **Area Development Agreements: No.** This means that Express Employment Professionals does not offer an area development agreement. Area development agreements are more fully described in Chapter One. Essentially, they allow an investor or investment group to develop an entire area or region. The schedule for development is clearly spelled out in the area development agreement. (Note: "Var." means varies and "Neg." means negotiable.)

Comment: Area development agreements represent an opportunity for the franchisor to choose a single franchisee or investment group to develop an entire area. The franchisee's qualifications should be strong and include proven business experience and the financial depth to pull it off. An area development agreement represents a great opportunity for an investor to tie up a large geographical area and develop a concept that may not have proven itself on a national basis. Keep in mind that this is a quantum leap from making an investment in a single franchise and is relevant only to those with development experience and deep pockets.

29. **Sub-Franchising Contracts: No.** Express Employment Professionals does not grant sub-franchising agreements. (See Chapter One for a more thorough explanation.) Like area development agreements, sub-franchising allows an investor or investment group to develop an entire area or region. The difference is that the sub-franchisor becomes a self-contained business, responsible for all relations with franchisees within its area, from initial training to on-going support. Franchisees pay their royalties to the sub-franchisor, who in turn pays a portion to the master franchisor.

Comment: Sub-franchising is used primarily by smaller franchisors who have a relatively easy concept and who are prepared to sell a portion of the future growth of their business to someone for some front-end cash and a percentage of the future royalties they receive from their franchisees.

30. **Expand in Territory: Yes.** Under conditions spelled out in the franchise agreement, Express Employment Professionals will allow its franchisees to expand within their exclusive territory.

Comment: Some franchisors define the franchisee's exclusive territory so tightly that there would never be room to open additional outlets within an area. Others provide a larger area in the hopes that the franchisee will do well and have the incentive to open additional units. There are clearly economic benefits to both parties from having franchisees with multiple units. There is no question that it is in your best interest to have the option to expand once you have proven to both yourself and the franchisor that you can manage the business successfully. Many would concur that the real profits in franchising come from managing multiple units rather than being locked into a single franchise in a single location. Additional fees may or may not be required with these additional units.

31. **Space Needs: 1,000-1,200 SF.** The average Express Employment Professionals' retail outlet

will require 1,000-1,200 square feet.

Comment: Armed with the rough space requirements, you can better project your annual occupancy costs. It should be relatively easy to get comparable rental rates for the type of space required. As annual rent and related expenses can be as high as 15% of your annual sales, be as accurate as possible in your projections.

Franchisor Support and Training Provided

32. **Financial Assistance Provided: No.** This notes that Express Employment Professionals does not provide financial assistance. Some franchisors provide indirect assistance (I), which might include making introductions to the franchisor's financial contacts, providing financial templates for preparing a business plan or actually assisting in the loan application process. In some cases, the franchisor becomes a co-signer on a financial obligation (e.g. equipment lease, space lease, etc.). Other franchisors are (D) directly involved in the process. In this case, the assistance may include a lease or loan made directly by the franchisor. Any loan would generally be secured by some form of collateral. A very common form of assistance is a note for all or part of the initial franchise fee. The level of assistance will generally depend upon the relative strengths of the franchisee.

Comment: The best of all possible worlds is one in which the franchisor has enough confidence in the business and in you to co-sign notes on the building and equipment leases and allow you to pay off the franchise fee over a specified period of time. Depending upon your qualifications, this could happen. Most likely, however, the franchisor will only give you some assistance in raising the necessary capital to start the business. Increasingly, franchisors are testing a franchisee's business acumen by letting him or her assume an increasing level of personal responsibility in securing financing. The objective is to find out early in the process how competent a franchisee really is.

33. **Site Selection Assistance: Yes** means that Express Employment Professionals will assist the franchisee in selecting a site location. While the phrase "location, location, location" may

be hackneyed, its importance should not be discounted, especially when a business depends upon retail traffic counts and accessibility. If a business is home- or warehouse-based, assistance in this area is of negligible or minor importance.

Comment: Since you will be locked into a lease for a minimum of three, and probably five, years, optimal site selection is absolutely essential. Even if you were somehow able to sub-lease and extricate yourself from a bad lease or bad location, the franchise agreement may not allow you to move to another location. Accordingly, it is imperative that you get it right the first time.

If a franchisor is truly interested in your success, it should treat your choice of a site with the same care it would use in choosing a company-owned site. Keep in mind that many firms provide excellent demographic data on existing locations at a very reasonable cost.

34. **Lease Negotiations Assistance: Yes.** Once a site is selected, Express Employment Professionals will be actively involved in negotiating the terms of the lease.

Comment: Given the complexity of negotiating a lease, an increasing number of franchisors are taking an active role in lease negotiations. There are far too many trade-offs that must be considered — terms, percentage rents, tenant improvements, pass-throughs, kick-out clauses, etc. This responsibility is best left to the professionals. If the franchisor doesn't have the capacity to support you directly, enlist the help of a well-recommended broker. The penalties for signing a bad long-term lease are very severe.

35. **Co-operative Advertising: Yes.** This refers to the existence of a joint advertising program in which the franchisor and franchisees each contribute to promote the company's products and/or services (usually within the franchisee's specific territory).

Comment: Co-op advertising is a common and mutually-beneficial effort. By agreeing to split part of the advertising costs, whether for television, radio or direct mail, the franchisor

is not only supporting the franchisee, but guaranteeing itself royalties from the incremental sales. A franchisor that is not intimately involved with the advertising campaign — particularly when it is an important part of the business — may not be fully committed to your overall success.

36. **Franchisee Assoc./Member: No.** This response notes that the Express Employment Professionals system does not include an active association made up of Express Employment Professionals franchisees and that, consequently, the franchisor is not a member of any such franchisee association.

Comment: The empowerment of franchisees has become a major rallying cry within the industry over the past three years. Various states have recently passed laws favoring franchisee rights, and the subject has been widely discussed in congressional staff hearings. Political groups even represent franchisee rights on a national basis. Similarly, the IFA is now actively courting franchisees to become active members. Whether they are equal members remains to be seen.

Franchisees have also significantly increased their clout with respect with the franchisor. If a franchise is to grow and be successful in the long term, it is critical that the franchisor and its franchisees mutually agree they are partners rather than adversaries.

37. **Size of Corporate Staff: 200.** Express Employment Professionals has 200 full-time employees on its staff to support its operating units.

Comment: There are no magic ratios that tell you whether the franchisor has enough staff to provide the proper level of support. It would appear, however, that Express Employment Professionals' staff of 200 is adequate to support 596 operating units. Less clear is whether a staff of three, including the company president and his wife, can adequately support 15 fledgling franchisees in the field.

Many younger franchises may be managed by a skeleton staff, assisted by outside consultants who perform various management functions during the start-up phase. From the perspective

27

of the franchisee, it is essential that the franchisor have actual in-house franchising experience, and that the franchisee not be forced to rely on outside consultants to make the system work. Whereas a full-time, salaried employee will probably have the franchisee's objectives in mind, an outside consultant may easily not have the same priorities. Franchising is a unique form of business that requires specific skills and experience — both of which are markedly different from those required to manage a non-franchised business. If you are thinking about establishing a long-term relationship with a firm just starting out in franchising, you should insist that the franchisor prove that it has an experienced, professional team on board and in place to provide the necessary levels of support to all concerned.

38. On-Going Support: A,C,D,E,G,H,I. Like initial training, the on-going support services provided by the franchisor are of paramount importance. Having a solid and responsive team behind you can certainly make your life much easier and allow you to concentrate your energies on other areas. As is noted below, the franchisors were asked to indicate their support for nine separate on-going services:

Service Provided	Included in Fees	At Add'l. Cost	NA
Central Data Processing	A	a	NA
Central Purchasing	B	b	NA
Field Operations Evaluation	C	c	NA
Field Training	D	d	NA
Initial Store Opening	E	e	NA
Inventory Control	F	f	NA
Franchisee Newsletter	G	g	NA
Regional or National Meetings	H	h	NA
800 Telephone Hotline	I	i	NA

If the franchisor provides the service at no additional cost to the franchisee (as indicated by letters A–I), a capital letter was used to indicate this. If the service is provided, but only at an additional cost, a lower case letter was used. If the franchisor responded with a NA, or failed to note an answer for a particular service, the corresponding letter was omitted from the data sheet.

39. Training: 2 Weeks in Oklahoma City, OK; 1 Week in Certified Training Office (In Field).

Comment: Assuming that the underlying business concept is sound and competitive, adequate training and on-going support are among the most important determinants of your success as a franchisee. The initial training should be as lengthy and as "hands-on" as necessary to allow the franchisee to operate alone and with confidence. Obviously, every potential situation cannot be covered in any training program. But the franchisee should come away with a basic understanding of how the business operates and where to go to resolve problems when they come up. Depending on the business, there should be operating manuals, procedural manuals, company policies, training videos, (800) help-lines, etc. available to franchisees. It may be helpful at the outset to establish how satisfied recent franchisees are with a company's training. I would also have a clear understanding about how often the company updates its manuals and training programs, the cost of sending additional employees through training, etc.

Remember, you are part of an organization that you are paying (in the form of a franchise fee and on-going royalties) to support you. Training is the first step. On-going support is the second step.

Specific Expansion Plans

40. U.S.: All United States. Express Employment Professionals is currently focusing its growth on the entire United States. Alternatively, the franchisor could have listed particular states or regions into which it wished to expand.

41. Canada: All Except Quebec. Express Employment Professionals is currently seeking additional franchisees in all Canadian provinces except for Quebec. Specific markets or provinces could have also been indicated.

42. Overseas: South Africa, Australia. Express Employment Professionals is currently expanding overseas with a focus on South Africa and Australia.

Comment: You will note that many smaller companies with less than 15 operating units suggest that they will concurrently expand throughout the U.S., Canada and internationally. In many cases, these are the same companies that foresee a 50+% growth rate in operating units over the next 12 months. The chances of this happening are negligible. As a prospective franchisee, you should be wary of any company that thinks it can expand throughout the world without a solid base of experience, staff and financial resources. Even if adequate financing is available, the demands on existing management will be extreme. New management cannot adequately fill the void until they are able to fully understand the system and absorb the corporate culture. If management's end objective is expansion for its own sake rather than by design, the existing franchisees will suffer.

Note: The statistics noted in the profiles preceding each company's analysis are the result of data provided by the franchisors themselves by way of a detailed questionnaire. Similarly, the data in the summary comparisons in the Introduction Chapter were taken from the company profile data. The figures used throughout each company's analysis, however, were generally taken from the UFOCs. In many cases, the UFOCs, which are only printed annually, contain information that is somewhat out of date. This is especially true with regard to the number of operating units and the current level of investment. A visit to our website at www.worldfranchising.com should provide current data.

℞

If you have not already done so, please invest some modest time to read Chapter One — 30 Minute Overview.

Recommended Reading Chapter 3

My strong sense is that every potential franchisee should be well-versed in the underlying fundamentals of the franchising industry before he or she commits to the way of life it involves. The better you understand the industry, the better prepared you will be to take maximum advantage of the relationship with your franchisor. There is no doubt that it will also place you in a better position to negotiate the franchise agreement — the conditions of which will dictate every facet of your life as a franchisee for the term of the agreement. The few extra dollars spent on educating yourself could well translate into tens of thousand of dollars in the years ahead.

In addition to general franchising publications, we have included several special interest books that relate to specific, but critical, parts of the start-up and on-going management process—site selection, hiring and managing minimum wage employees, preparing accurate cash flow projections, developing comprehensive business and/or marketing plans, etc.

We have also attempted to make the purchasing process easier by allowing readers to purchase the books directly from Source Book Publications, either via our 800-line at (800) 841-0873 or our website at www.sourcebookpublications.com. All of the books are currently available in inventory and are generally sent the same day an order is received. A 15% discount is available on all orders over $100.00. See page 35 for an order form. Your complete satisfaction is 100% guaranteed on all books.

Background/Evaluation

The Franchise Fraud: How to Protect Yourself Before and After You Invest, Purvin, Jr., BookSurge Publishing. 2008. 332 pp. $18.95.

A primer on the promises and perils of franchising. It's big business, accounting for one-third of America's retail revenue, but franchising is still a risky proposition — at least for the franchisee. This resource exposes the frauds and abuses too many companies perpetrate on their franchisees — everything from unfulfilled pledges of promotional support to oversaturating the market with outlets. It helps potential franchise owners avoid being victimized by explaining, in specific detail, what to look for, what questions to ask, and what agreements to make before signing a contract. Robert Purvin also reveals how to identify and take advantage of the worthwhile franchising opportunities available today.

Grow to Greatness: How to Build a World-Class Franchise System Faster, 2nd Edition, Olson, Franchise Update Media Group. 2008. 237 pp. $29.95.

This breakthrough book, *Grow to Greatness*, has instantly become the must-read, essential guide on how to build a world-class franchise system — faster! This book contains advice and proven, step-by-step systems and processes for emerging and established franchisors, as well as for anyone considering franchising a business.

Franchise Times Guide to Selecting, Buying and Owning a Franchise, Bennett/Babcock/Hamburger, Sterling. 2008. 352 pp. $17.95.

Buying a franchise can be a handy shortcut to the American dream of owning your own business. But there are dangerous pitfalls — and possible drawbacks to even the best franchise deals. Here, for every prospective franchisee, is authoritative advice from a trustworthy source. The experts of *Franchise Times* offer their picks of the top 200 franchisees and 100 up-and-comers, complete with contact information, financial requirements, fees and more. There are practical tips on everything from hiring and marketing to financing your franchise, leasing a retail space (or setting up a home office) and

deciding if you should buy or run a franchise with your spouse. With anecdotes and advice from current franchisees and franchisors, this is a book every would-be entrepreneur should read before signing a contract.

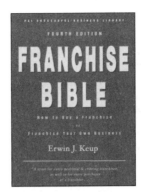

Franchise Bible: How to Buy a Franchise or Franchise Your Own Business, 5th Edition, Keup, Entrepreneur Press. 2000. 337 pp. $22.95.

This recently updated classic is equally useful for prospective franchisees and franchisors alike. The comprehensive guide and workbook explain in detail what the franchise system entails and the precise benefits it offers. The book features the new franchise laws that became effective January 1995. To assist the prospective franchisee in rating a potential franchisor, Keup provides necessary checklists and forms. Also noted are the franchisor's contractual obligations to the franchisee and what the franchisee should expect from the franchisor in the way of services and support.

Tips & Traps When Buying a Franchise, Revised 2nd Edition, Tomzack, Source Book Publications. 1999. 236 pp. $19.95.

Many a novice franchisee is shocked to discover that the road to success in franchising is full of hidden costs, inflated revenue promises, reneged marketing support and worse. In this candid, hard-hitting book, Tomzack steers potential franchisees around the pitfalls and guides them in making a smart, lucrative purchase. Topics include: matching a franchise with personal finances and lifestyle, avoiding the five most common pitfalls, choosing a prime location, asking the right questions, etc.

Databases

Franchisor Database, Source Book Publications. (800) 841-0873 or (510) 839-5471.

Listing of over 3,000 active North American franchisors. 29 fields of information per company: full address, telephone/800/fax numbers, Internet address, email address, contact/title/salutation, president/title/salutation, # of franchised units, # of company-owned units, # total units, IFA/CFA Member, etc. 48 industry categories. Unlimited use. Guaranteed deliverability — $0.50 rebate for any returned mailings. $1,500 for initial database, $150 per quarter for updates.

Directories

Minority Franchise Guide — 2006 Edition, Bond/Hinh/Kimmel, Source Book Publications, 2006. 360 pp. $19.95.

The only minority franchising directory! Contains detailed profiles and company logos of over 500 forward-looking franchisors that encourage and actively support the inclusion of minority franchisees. It also includes a listing of resources available to prospective minority franchisees.

Earnings Claims

"How Much Can I Make?", Bond/Cavagrotti/Sanghera/Hwang/Han, Source Book Publications. 2009. 368 pp. $34.95.

The single most important task for a prospective investor is to prepare a realistic cash flow statement that accurately reflects the economic potential of that business. *"How Much Can I Make?"* is an invaluable insider's guide that details historical sales, expense and/or profit data on actual franchise operations, **as provided by the franchisors themselves**. Whether you plan to buy a franchise or start your own business, these actual performance statistics will ensure that you have a realistic starting point in determining how much you can expect to make in a similar business. 93 current earnings claim statements, in their entirety, are included for the food-service, retail and service-based industries. Unfortunately, less than 20% of franchisors provide such projections/guidelines to prospective franchisees. *"How Much Can I Make?"* includes roughly half of the total universe of earnings claim statements available. The list of companies includes household names such as McDonald's and Baskin-Robbins to newer, smaller franchises with only a few operating units. Any serious investor would be shortsighted not to take full advantage of this extraordinary resource.

Franchise Rankings

Bond's Top 100 Franchises, Bond/Cavagrotti/Kimmel/Han/Hanks/Sanghera, Source Book Publications, 2009. 408 pp. $24.95.

In response to the constantly asked question, *"What are the best franchises?"*, Bond's new book focuses on the top 100 franchises broken down into four major segments — food-service, lodging, retail and service-based franchises. Within each group, a rigorous, in-depth analysis was performed on over 500 systems. Many of the companies selected are household names. Others are rapidly growing, mid-sized firms that are also strong national players. Still others are somewhat smaller systems that demonstrate sound concepts, exceptional management and an aggressive expansion system. Companies were analyzed on the basis of historical performance, brand identification, market dynamics, franchisee satisfaction, the level of training and on-going support, financial stability, etc. Detailed two to four page profiles on each company, as well as key statistics and industry overview. All companies are proven performers and most have a national presence.

Other

The Economics of Franchising, Blair/Lafontaine, Cambridge University Press. 2005. 338 pp. $45.00.

The Economics of Franchising describes how and why franchising works. It also analyzes the economic tensions that contribute to conflict in the franchisor-franchisee relationship. The treatment includes a great deal of empirical evidence on franchising, its importance in various segments of the economy, the terms of franchise contracts, and what we know about how all these have evolved over time, especially in the US market. The economic analysis of the franchisor-franchisee relationship begins with the observation that for franchisors, franchising is a contractual alternative to vertical integration. Subsequently, the tensions that arise between a franchisor and its franchisees, who in fact are owners of independent businesses, are examined in turn. In particular the authors discuss issues related to product quality control, tying arrangements, pricing, location and territories, advertising, and termination and renewals.

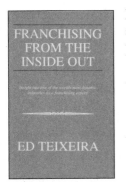

Franchising From the Inside Out, Teixeira, 2005. 177 pp. $19.95.

Franchising From the Inside Out is a valuable resource for those people interested in buying a franchise. This book contains an in-depth explanation of the entire franchise process including how to choose and evaluate a franchise opportunity and detailing the important questions to ask before making that final decision. There are also chapters for franchisees and franchisors currently involved in the franchising industry. The chapters on "Negotiating the Franchise Agreement," "The Laws of Franchising," and "The Secrets to Success" represent examples of the practical advice this book contains.

From Ice Cream to the Internet, Shane, Prentice Hall. 2005. 256 pp. $29.95.

Franchising can offer businesses a powerful new source of growth and improved financial performance. Now, Dr. Scott A. Shane helps businesses systematically asses the pros and cons of franchising, and offers proven best practices for building a successful system. *From Ice Cream to the Internet* focuses squarely on the strategic issues and challenges faced by franchisors. Shane answers key questions such as : What do the winners do differently? How does franchising affect your ability to compete with firms that don't? Shane then presents proven principles for every facet of franchising success: designing the system, recruiting, selecting, managing and supporting franchisees; establishing territories and pricing; managing expansion; and more.

Earnings Claims Packages

2008 Food-Service Earnings Claims Package. $250.00.

The 2008 Food-Service Earnings Claims Package includes 89 recent earnings claims, including Arby's, Baskin-Robbins, El Pollo Loco, Famous Dave's, Great Harvest Bread Co., Mrs. Fields Cookies, Pizza Patron, Pizzeria Uno, Quiznos and TCBY.

2008 Lodging Earnings Claims Package. $90.00.

The 2008 Lodging Earnings Claims Package includes 29 recent earnings claims, including Clarion Hotels, Holiday Inns, Motel 6, Quality Inns, Ramada, Studio 6 and Suburban Lodges.

2008 Retail Earnings Claims Package. $100.00.

The 2008 Retail Earnings Claims Package includes 33 recent earnings claims, including 7-Eleven, Aaron's Sales and Lease Ownership, Color Me Mine, Pearle Vision, Relax The Back, Snap-On Tools and Verlo Mattress Factory Stores.

2008 Service-Based Earnings Claims Package. $350.00.

The 2008 Service-Based Earnings Claims Package includes 143 recent earnings claims, including Allegra Network, Aussie Pet Mobile, Children's Orchard, ComForcare Senior Services, Epcon Communities, FasTracKids, Great Clips, Huntington Learning Centers, Keller Williams Realtors, Link Staffing, Money Mailer, Mr. Rooter, Postal Annex+, Thrifty Car Sales, Weed Man and WSI.

2008 Complete Earnings Claims Package. $525.00.

The 2008 Complete Earnings Claims Package includes 295 recent earnings claims — 89 Food-Service Earnings Claims, 29 Lodging Earnings Claims, 33 Retail Earnings Claims and 143 Service-Based Earnings Claims.

For more detailed information on the contents of the earnings claims packages, please visit either www.sourcebookpublications.com or www.ufocs.com.

The Franchise Bookstore
Order Form

To place an order, please call (800) 841-0873 or (510) 839-5471; or fax this form to (510) 839-2104

Title	Price	Qty.	Total

Basic postage (1 Book)	$8.50
Each additional book add $4.00	
California tax (if CA resident)	
Total due in U.S. dollars	
Deduct 15% if total due is over $100.00	
Net amount due in U.S. dollars	

Please include credit card number and expiration date for all charge card orders. Checks should be made payable to Source Book Publications. All prices are in U.S. dollars.

Mailing Information: All books shipped by USPS Priority Mail (2nd Day Air). Please print clearly and include your phone number in case we need to contact you. Postage and handling rates are for shipping within the U.S. Please call for international rates.

☐ Check enclosed or

Charge my:

☐ MasterCard ☐ VISA ☐ American Express

Card #: _____

Expiration Date: _____

Signature: _____

CVV2 (Security) Code: _____

Name: _____

Company: _____

Address: _____

City: _____

Title: _____

Telephone No.: (___) _____

State/Prov.: _____ Zip: _____

Please send order to:

Source Book Publications

1814 Franklin St., Ste. 603, Oakland, CA 94612

(800) 841-0873 • (510) 839-5471 • (510) 839-2104 Fax

Satisfaction Guaranteed. If not fully satisfied, return for a prompt, 100% refund.

FIVE LARGEST PARTICIPANTS IN SURVEY

Company	# Franchised Units	# Co-Owned Units	# Total Units	Franchise Fee	On-Going Royalty	Total Investment
1. Midas	2,464	91	2,555	$20K	10%	$261.6-350.7K
2. Novus Glass	2,200	6	2,206	$7.5K	5-8%	$38.1-115.5K
3. Thrifty Car Rental	849	151	1,000	Varies	3%	$200-250K
4. Meineke Car Care Centers	901	11	912	$30K	3-7%	$182.8-426.8K
5. AAMCO	879	0	879	$39.5K	7.5%	$50-225K

All of the data provided are proprietary and should not be quoted without acknowledging *Bond's Franchise Guide*.

AAMCO
201 Gibraltar Rd.
Horsham, PA 19044
Tel: (800) 462-2626 (610) 668-2900
Fax: (215) 956-0340
E-Mail: franchise@aamco.com
Web Site: www.aamco.com
Mr. Kevin Gordon, Vice President

AAMCO Transmissions is the world's largest chain of transmission specialists and one of the leaders in total car care services. AAMCO has approximately 900 automotive centers throughout the United States, Canada and Puerto Rico. Established in 1962, AAMCO is proud to have served more than 35 million drivers.

BACKGROUND: IFA MEMBER
Established: 1962;   1st Franchised: 1964
Franchised Units: 879
Company-Owned Units: 0
Total Units: 879
Dist.:   US-806; CAN-34; O'seas-39
  North America: 48 States, 4 Provinces
  Density: 49 in PA, 68 in TX, 71 in FL
Projected New Units (12 Months):   40
Qualifications: 3, 3, 2, 2, 3, 3
FINANCIAL/TERMS:

Cash Investment: $25-125K
Total Investment: $50-225K
Minimum Net Worth: $50-182K
Fees: Franchise - $39,500
  Royalty - 7.5%;   Ad. - Varies, $150/mo
for national
Earnings Claims Statement: Yes
Term of Contract (Years):   15/15
Avg. # Of Employees: 4 FT, 0 PT
Passive Ownership: Not Allowed
Encourage Conversions: Yes
Area Develop. Agreements: No
Sub-Franchising Contracts: No
Expand In Territory: No
Space Needs: NR
SUPPORT & TRAINING:
Financial Assistance Provided: Yes (I)

Site Selection Assistance: Yes
Lease Negotiation Assistance: Yes
Co-Operative Advertising: Yes
Franchisee Assoc./Member: Yes/No
Size Of Corporate Staff: 120
On-Going Support: „C,D,E,f,G,h,I
Training: 3 Weeks Horsham, PA
SPECIFIC EXPANSION PLANS:
US: All United States
Canada: All Canada
Overseas: All Countries

≪ ≫

ABRA AUTO BODY & GLASS

6601 Shingle Creek Pkwy., # 200
Brooklyn Center, MN 55430
Tel: (888) 872-2272 (651) 491-3384
Fax: (651) 351-7075
E-Mail: mwahlin@abraauto.com
Web Site: www.abraauto.com
Mr. Mark Wahlin, VP of Franchise Development

One of the first automobile collision and glass franchises. Operating company and franchised auto body collision and auto glass replacement shops. We offer support with marketing, business management, equipment and material purchases. Investment opportunities for qualifying owners and managers.

BACKGROUND:
Established: 1984; 1st Franchised: 1987
Franchised Units: 24
Company-Owned Units: 68
Total Units: 92
Dist.: US-92; CAN-0; O'seas-0
North America: 12 States, 0 Provinces
Density: 6 in WI, 7 in TN, 28 in MN
Projected New Units (12 Months): 12
Qualifications: 5, 5, 5, 3, 3, 5
FINANCIAL/TERMS:
Cash Investment: $60-100K
Total Investment: $229.6-422.6K
Minimum Net Worth: $500K
Fees: Franchise - $22.5K
Royalty - NR; Ad. - NR
Earnings Claims Statement: Yes
Term of Contract (Years): 10/10
Avg. # Of Employees: FT, 0 PT
Passive Ownership: Allowed
Encourage Conversions: Yes
Area Develop. Agreements: Yes/1
Sub-Franchising Contracts: No
Expand In Territory: Yes
Space Needs: 8,000-15,000 SF
SUPPORT & TRAINING:
Financial Assistance Provided: No

Site Selection Assistance: Yes
Lease Negotiation Assistance: Yes
Co-Operative Advertising: No
Franchisee Assoc./Member: No
Size Of Corporate Staff: 53
On-Going Support: a,B,C,D,E,F,g,h,I
Training: 2-4 Weeks ABRA Training Center, Minneapolis, MN; 6 Weeks On-Site
SPECIFIC EXPANSION PLANS:
US: Central, South, Southeast
Canada: No
Overseas: NR

≪ ≫

ACTIVE GREEN + ROSS

580 Evans Ave.
Toronto, ON M8W 2W1 Canada
Tel: (416) 255-5581
Fax: (416) 255-4793
E-Mail: careers@activegreenross.com
Web Site: www.activegreenross.com
Ms. Rita Chiodo, Franchise Operations

Tire and automotive sales and service. The company currently has locations in Toronto and surrounding area and is one of the largest independent groups of tire and automotive service centers in Canada. Company operations began in 1982. Franchised first outlet in 1983; Training provided for up to 2 months; Dealers elect representatives on Dealer Advisory Committee.

BACKGROUND:
Established: 1982; 1st Franchised: 1983
Franchised Units: 65
Company-Owned Units: 8
Total Units: 73
Dist.: US-0; CAN-73; O'seas-0
North America: 0 States, 1 Provinces
Density: 73 in ON
Projected New Units (12 Months): NR
Qualifications: 4, 4, 4, 4, 4, 4
FINANCIAL/TERMS:
Cash Investment: NR
Total Investment: $115-200K
Minimum Net Worth: $250K
Fees: Franchise - $25K
Royalty - 5%; Ad. - 2.5%
Earnings Claims Statement: No
Term of Contract (Years): 5/5
Avg. # Of Employees: 4 FT, 0 PT
Passive Ownership: Not Allowed
Encourage Conversions: Yes
Area Develop. Agreements: No
Sub-Franchising Contracts: Yes
Expand In Territory: Yes

Space Needs: 3,000-5,000 SF
SUPPORT & TRAINING:
Financial Assistance Provided: Yes (D)
Site Selection Assistance: Yes
Lease Negotiation Assistance: NA
Co-Operative Advertising: No
Franchisee Assoc./Member: Yes/Yes
Size Of Corporate Staff: 9
On-Going Support: ,,,,,,,
Training: Head Office; On-Site
SPECIFIC EXPANSION PLANS:
US: NR
Canada: ON
Overseas: NR

≪ ≫

AERO COLOURS

10824 Nesbitt Ave. S., P.O. Box 385846
Bloomington, MN 55437-5846
Tel: (800) 275-5200 (952) 942-0490
Fax: (952) 372-4826
E-Mail:
Web Site: www.aerocolours.com
Mr. Doug Asher, Director of Franchise Support

AERO COLOURS is an exclusive mobile automotive paint repair process, providing service to dealerships, fleet operations and individual vehicle owners. Our solid support system, complemented by our industry-leading training, allows our franchisees to provide unmatched service. We will show you how to operate, market and grow your own business.

BACKGROUND: IFA MEMBER
Established: 1985; 1st Franchised: 1993
Franchised Units: 217
Company-Owned Units: 1
Total Units: 218
Dist.: US-218; CAN-0; O'seas-2
North America: 28 States, 0 Provinces
Density: 24 in TX, 14 in FL, 55 in CA
Projected New Units (12 Months): 10
Qualifications: 5, 3, 5, 3, 5, 5
FINANCIAL/TERMS:
Cash Investment: $46.4K-155.4K
Total Investment: $66.4K-175.4K
Minimum Net Worth: $100K
Fees: Franchise - $10K-125K
Royalty - 7%; Ad. - 0%
Earnings Claims Statement: No
Term of Contract (Years): 10/10
Avg. # Of Employees: 4-5 FT, 0 PT

Passive Ownership: Allowed
Encourage Conversions: No
Area Develop. Agreements: No
Sub-Franchising Contracts: Yes
Expand In Territory: Yes
Space Needs: NA

SUPPORT & TRAINING:
Financial Assistance Provided: Yes (D)
Site Selection Assistance: NA
Lease Negotiation Assistance: NA
Co-Operative Advertising: No
Franchisee Assoc./Member: Yes/Yes
Size Of Corporate Staff: 5
On-Going Support: A,B,C,D,E,,G,H,I
Training: 10 Days Minneapolis, MN; 10 Days Territory

SPECIFIC EXPANSION PLANS:
US: All United States
Canada: All Canada
Overseas: NR

≪ ≫

AFFILIATED CAR RENTAL
96 Freneau Ave., # 2
Matawan, NJ 07747
Tel: (800) 367-5159 (732) 290-8300
Fax: (732) 290-8305
E-Mail: msmil@sensiblecarrental.com
Web Site: www.sensiblecarrental.com
Mr. Michael S. Miller, National Sales Manager

We offer a rental car program which provides training, insurance and management support.

BACKGROUND:
Established: 1981; 1st Franchised: 1981
Franchised Units: 150
Company-Owned Units: 0
Total Units: 150
Dist.: US-150; CAN-0; O'seas-0
North America: 15 States, 0 Provinces
Density: NR
Projected New Units (12 Months): 20
Qualifications: 2, 3, 4, 2, 2, 5

FINANCIAL/TERMS:
Cash Investment: $30-50K
Total Investment: $45-71.8K
Minimum Net Worth: Varies
Fees: Franchise - $3.5K Min.
Royalty - $10-15/Car; Ad. - 0%
Earnings Claims Statement: No
Term of Contract (Years): Perpetual
Avg. # Of Employees: 1 FT, 2 PT
Passive Ownership: Not Allowed
Encourage Conversions: NA
Area Develop. Agreements: No
Sub-Franchising Contracts: No

Expand In Territory: Yes
Space Needs: NR

SUPPORT & TRAINING:
Financial Assistance Provided: No
Site Selection Assistance: NA
Lease Negotiation Assistance: NA
Co-Operative Advertising: No
Franchisee Assoc./Member: Yes/Yes
Size Of Corporate Staff: 9
On-Going Support: ,,C,D,,F,G,H,I
Training: 2 Days Corporate in NJ

SPECIFIC EXPANSION PLANS:
US: All United States
Canada: No
Overseas: NR

≪ ≫

AIRBAG SERVICE
9675 S. E. 36th St., # 100
Mercer Island, WA 98040
Tel: (800) 224-7224 (206) 275-4105
Fax: (206) 275-4122
E-Mail: marketing@airbagservice.com
Web Site: www.airbagservice.com
Mr. Peter Smith, Sales/Marketing Manager

Automotive service company, specializing in airbag system repair. Our mobile service supplies a needed expertise to the automotive collision repair industry. Specialized software and tools allow us to work on any system right on site for increased efficiency.

BACKGROUND:
Established: 1992; 1st Franchised: 1995
Franchised Units: 40
Company-Owned Units: 1
Total Units: 41
Dist.: US-39; CAN-2; O'seas-0
North America: 20 States, 2 Provinces
Density: 3 in WA, 7 in TX, 4 in CA
Projected New Units (12 Months): 18
Qualifications: 3, 5, 4, 1, 1, 4

FINANCIAL/TERMS:
Cash Investment: $50-100K
Total Investment: $50-125K
Minimum Net Worth: $75K
Fees: Franchise - $25-30K
Royalty - 8.5% Net; Ad. - 2% Net
Earnings Claims Statement: No
Term of Contract (Years): 10/5+
Avg. # Of Employees: 2 FT, 0 PT
Passive Ownership: Discouraged
Encourage Conversions: NA
Area Develop. Agreements: Yes/1
Sub-Franchising Contracts: No
Expand In Territory: Yes

Space Needs: 1,000 SF

SUPPORT & TRAINING:
Financial Assistance Provided: Yes (D)
Site Selection Assistance: No
Lease Negotiation Assistance: No
Co-Operative Advertising: No
Franchisee Assoc./Member: No
Size Of Corporate Staff: 10
On-Going Support: ,,C,D,,,G,H,I
Training: 3 Weeks Seattle, WA

SPECIFIC EXPANSION PLANS:
US: All United States
Canada: No
Overseas: NR

≪ ≫

ATL INTERNATIONAL
8334 Veterans Hwy.
Millersville, MD 21108-2543
Tel: (800) 935-8863 (410) 987-1011
Fax: (410) 987-9080
E-Mail: sales@alltuneandlube.com
Web Site: www.alltuneandlube.com
Mr. Louis Kibler, VP Franchise Development

ALL TUNE AND LUBE is the leader in 'One Stop' total car care. Our full-service centers provide vehicle maintenance and repair, such as engine performance, brakes, ride control and oil changes. Franchise owners also have the option of adding the ATL MOTOR MATE franchise, which specializes in engine installation, and the ALL TUNE TRANSMISSIONS franchise, which provides transmission service. This co-branding concept provides three times the potential at one location.

BACKGROUND:
Established: 1985; 1st Franchised: 1985
Franchised Units: 450
Company-Owned Units: 0
Total Units: 450
Dist.: US-448; CAN-2; O'seas-0
North America: 34 States, 0 Provinces
Density: 35 in TX, 30 in MD, 50 in CA
Projected New Units (12 Months): 450
Qualifications: 3, 4, 1, 2, 1, 4

FINANCIAL/TERMS:
Cash Investment: $25K
Total Investment: $120-130K
Minimum Net Worth: $75K
Fees: Franchise - $25K
Royalty - 7%; Ad. - 8%
Earnings Claims Statement: No
Term of Contract (Years): 15/3x5
Avg. # Of Employees: 4-6 FT, 0 PT
Passive Ownership: Not Allowed

Encourage Conversions: Yes
Area Develop. Agreements: No
Sub-Franchising Contracts: No
Expand In Territory: Yes
Space Needs: 3,000 SF
SUPPORT & TRAINING:
Financial Assistance Provided: Yes (D)
Site Selection Assistance: Yes
Lease Negotiation Assistance: Yes
Co-Operative Advertising: No
Franchisee Assoc./Member: No
Size Of Corporate Staff: 75
On-Going Support: ,B,C,D,E,F,G,H,I
Training: 2 Weeks Corporate Office; 1
   Week Center
SPECIFIC EXPANSION PLANS:
US: All United States
Canada: All Canada
Overseas: All Countries

<< >>

AUTO-LAB DIAGNOSTIC & TUNE-UP CENTERS
705 S. Main St., #200
Plymouth, MI 48170
Tel: (877) 349-4968 (269) 966-0500
Fax: (269) 441-1825
E-Mail: autolabfmc@aol.com
Web Site: www.autolabusa.com
Mr. Bill Downs, VP Sales

Full service automotive repair facility, performing all aspects of auto service and repair. Our specialty is in the diagnostics and repair of computerized and electrical systems. Our goal is to be a professional alternative to auto dealer repair shops.

BACKGROUND:
Established: 1987; 1st Franchised: 1989
Franchised Units: 32
Company-Owned Units: 0
Total Units: 32
Dist.: US-32; CAN-0; O'seas-0
   North America: 2 States, 0 Provinces
   Density: 1 in OH, 25 in MI
Projected New Units (12 Months): 18
Qualifications: 3, 2, 3, 3, 2, 5
FINANCIAL/TERMS:
Cash Investment: $35-75K
Total Investment: $110-175K
Minimum Net Worth: $250K
Fees: Franchise - $19.5K
   Royalty - 6%; Ad. - 3%
Earnings Claims Statement: No
Term of Contract (Years): 15/15
Avg. # Of Employees: 5 FT, 1 PT
Passive Ownership: Discouraged
Encourage Conversions: Yes

Area Develop. Agreements: Yes/1
Sub-Franchising Contracts: No
Expand In Territory: Yes
Space Needs: 3,000+ SF
SUPPORT & TRAINING:
Financial Assistance Provided: No
Site Selection Assistance: Yes
Lease Negotiation Assistance: Yes
Co-Operative Advertising: No
Franchisee Assoc./Member: No
Size Of Corporate Staff: 10
On-Going Support: a,b,C,D,E,,G,H,I
Training: 2 Weeks Grand Rapids, MI; 2-4
   Weeks Battle Creek, MI
SPECIFIC EXPANSION PLANS:
US: MW & E. to Gulf of Mexico
Canada: All Canada
Overseas: All Countries

<< >>

AUTOMOTIVE MAINTENANCE SOLUTIONS
1404 Seventh Ave. E.
Hendersonville, NC 28792
Tel: (866) 845-9611 (828) 696-9611
Fax: (828) 693-0823
E-Mail: amscarcare@hotmail.com
Web Site: www.amscarcare.com
Mr. Paul Sheldrick, President

If you have a love for automobiles, have a desire to develop a positive future, have the tenacity to excel and are willing to work to be the very best. This business is about premium automotive services related to neglected maintenance. This program goes far beyond the quick oil change format. This industry addresses $70 billion a year in unperformed maintenance.

BACKGROUND:
Established: 1962; 1st Franchised: 2002
Franchised Units: 0
Company-Owned Units: 1
Total Units: 1
Dist.: US-1; CAN-0; O'seas-0
   North America: 1 States, Provinces
   Density: 1 in NC
Projected New Units (12 Months): NR
Qualifications: NR
FINANCIAL/TERMS:
Cash Investment: $50-75K
Total Investment: $120-175K
Minimum Net Worth: $150K
Fees: Franchise - $25K
   Royalty - 7%; Ad. - 1 + 2%
Earnings Claims Statement: No
Term of Contract (Years): NR
Avg. # Of Employees: 4 FT, 1 PT

Passive Ownership: Allowed
Encourage Conversions: Yes
Area Develop. Agreements: Yes/1
Sub-Franchising Contracts: No
Expand In Territory: Yes
Space Needs: 2,500 SF
SUPPORT & TRAINING:
Financial Assistance Provided: Yes (D)
Site Selection Assistance: Yes
Lease Negotiation Assistance: Yes
Co-Operative Advertising: No
Franchisee Assoc./Member: No
Size Of Corporate Staff: 4
On-Going Support: ,b,C,d,E,,G,h,I
Training: 2-3 Weeks Franchise Location
SPECIFIC EXPANSION PLANS:
US: NC, SC, GA, FL, TN, AL
Canada: NR
Overseas: NR

<< >>

BIG O TIRES
12650 E. Briarwood Ave., #2D
Centennial, CO 80112-6734
Tel: (800) 622-2446 (303) 728-5500
Fax: (303) 728-5689
E-Mail: franchise@bigotires.com
Web Site: www.bigotires.com
Mr. Bill Thomas, Director Franchise
   Development

BIG O TIRES is the fastest-growing retail tire and under-car service center franchisor in North America. We offer over 30 years' experience and proven success, site selection assistance, comprehensive training and on-going field support, protected territory, exclusive product lines, consistent product supply, unique marketing programs, contemporary building designs, effective advertising support, and proven business systems.

BACKGROUND: IFA MEMBER
Established: 1962; 1st Franchised: 1980
Franchised Units: 545
Company-Owned Units: 1
Total Units: 546
Dist.: US-546; CAN-1; O'seas-0
   North America: 20 States, 1 Provinces
   Density: 65 in CO, 200 in CA, 60 in AZ
Projected New Units (12 Months): 40
Qualifications: 5, 5, 1, 2, 1, 5
FINANCIAL/TERMS:
Cash Investment: $100K-150K
Total Investment: $225.8-543.3K

Minimum Net Worth: $300K
Fees: Franchise - $30K
  Royalty - 2%; Ad. - 4%
Earnings Claims Statement: No
Term of Contract (Years): 10/
Avg. # Of Employees: NR FT, 0 PT
Passive Ownership: Discouraged
Encourage Conversions: Yes
Area Develop. Agreements: Yes/1
Sub-Franchising Contracts: Yes
Expand In Territory: Yes
Space Needs: NR

SUPPORT & TRAINING:
Financial Assistance Provided: Yes (D)
Site Selection Assistance: Yes
Lease Negotiation Assistance: Yes
Co-Operative Advertising: No
Franchisee Assoc./Member: NR
Size Of Corporate Staff: 100
On-Going Support: A,B,C,d,E,F,G,h,I
Training: 7 Weeks Littleton, CO

SPECIFIC EXPANSION PLANS:
US: All United States
Canada: BC and AB
Overseas: NR

BRAKE MASTERS
6179 E. Broadway Blvd.
Tucson, AZ 85711
Tel: (877) 524-7541 (520) 631-7200
Fax: (866) 459-8731
E-Mail: moshei@brakemasters.com
Web Site: www.brakemasters.com
Mr. Moshe Issaharov, Dir. Franchise
  Development

Brake repair, brake-related services, quick oil changes and maintenance services.

BACKGROUND:
Established: 1983; 1st Franchised: 1994
Franchised Units: 46
Company-Owned Units: 52
Total Units: 98
Dist.: US-98; CAN-0; O'seas-0
  North America: 7 States, 0 Provinces
  Density: 9 in NM, 35 in CA, 31 in AZ
Projected New Units (12 Months): NR
Qualifications: NR
FINANCIAL/TERMS:
Cash Investment: $80-100K
Total Investment: $175-600K
Minimum Net Worth: NR
Fees: Franchise - $22.95K
  Royalty - 5%; Ad. - 1%
Earnings Claims Statement: No
Term of Contract (Years): 20/
Avg. # Of Employees: 6 FT, 2 PT

Passive Ownership: Discouraged
Encourage Conversions: Yes
Area Develop. Agreements: Yes/20
Sub-Franchising Contracts: Yes
Expand In Territory: Yes
Space Needs: 4,000 SF
SUPPORT & TRAINING:
Financial Assistance Provided: No
Site Selection Assistance: Yes
Lease Negotiation Assistance: Yes
Co-Operative Advertising: Yes
Franchisee Assoc./Member: No
Size Of Corporate Staff: 30
On-Going Support: „C,D,E,F,,,I
Training: 2 Weeks Location Near
  Franchisee; 2 Weeks Tucson, AZ;
SPECIFIC EXPANSION PLANS:
US: West, SW, NW, Midwest.
Canada: No
Overseas: NR

CARTEX LIMITED
42816 Mound Rd.
Sterling Heights, MI 48314-3256
Tel: (800) 421-7328 (586) 739-4330
Fax: (586) 739-4331
E-Mail: crismar@aol.com
Web Site: www.fabrion.net
Mr. Lawrence P. Klukowski, Chief Executive Officer

CARTEX LIMITED, better known as Fabrion, is a mobile service business, specializing in automotive interior repair. The Fabrion repair process electrostatically repairs auto cloth, velour and carpet. Due to our specialization, we have revolutionized auto upholstery repair. Updating on current (OEM) original equipment materials and providing the tools to match all current patterns being used in auto interiors are our strong points.

BACKGROUND:
Established: 1980; 1st Franchised: 1988
Franchised Units: 105
Company-Owned Units: 0
Total Units: 105
Dist.: US-104; CAN-1; O'seas-0
  North America: 36 States, Provinces
  Density: 13 in CA, 10 in FL, 8 in TX
Projected New Units (12 Months): 20
Qualifications: 3, 3, 3, 3, 3, 3
FINANCIAL/TERMS:
Cash Investment: $23.5-36.5K
Total Investment: $23.5-36.5K
Minimum Net Worth: NA
Fees: Franchise - $23.5-36.5K

Royalty - 7%,min month fee; Ad. - NA
Earnings Claims Statement: No
Term of Contract (Years): 5/5
Avg. # Of Employees: 3 FT, 0 PT
Passive Ownership: Discouraged
Encourage Conversions: Yes
Area Develop. Agreements: No
Sub-Franchising Contracts: No
Expand In Territory: Yes
Space Needs: NA
SUPPORT & TRAINING:
Financial Assistance Provided: Yes (D)
Site Selection Assistance: NA
Lease Negotiation Assistance: NA
Co-Operative Advertising: No
Franchisee Assoc./Member: No
Size Of Corporate Staff: 8
On-Going Support: ,B,C,D,,,G,H,I
Training: 3 Weeks On-Site Under
  Development.
SPECIFIC EXPANSION PLANS:
US: All United States
Canada: All Canada
Overseas: All Countries

CARX AUTO SERVICE
1375 E. Woodfield Rd., # 500
Schaumburg, IL 60173
Tel: (800) 359-2359 + 8927 (847) 273-8920
Fax: (847) 619-3310
E-Mail: kbauer@carx.com
Web Site: www.carx.com
Mr. Kim Bauer, Director Franchise Development

Retail auto repair specialists providing service in brakes, exhaust, road handling, tune-ups, steering systems, air conditioning, tires oil changes and more for all makes of cars and light trucks.

BACKGROUND:
Established: 1971; 1st Franchised: 1971
Franchised Units: 147
Company-Owned Units: 30
Total Units: 177
Dist.: US-177; CAN-0; O'seas-0
  North America: 10 States, 0 Provinces
  Density: 23 in MO, 27 in MN, 59 in IL
Projected New Units (12 Months): 8
Qualifications: 5, 3, 2, 2, 2, 5
FINANCIAL/TERMS:
Cash Investment: $100K
Total Investment: $214K-326K
Minimum Net Worth: $250K
Fees: Franchise - $25K
  Royalty - 5%; Ad. - 5-7%

Earnings Claims Statement: Yes
Term of Contract (Years): 15/5
Avg. # Of Employees: 4 FT, 0 PT
Passive Ownership: Discouraged
Encourage Conversions: Yes
Area Develop. Agreements: Yes/1
Sub-Franchising Contracts: No
Expand In Territory: Yes
Space Needs: 5,000 SF

SUPPORT & TRAINING:
Financial Assistance Provided: Yes (D)
Site Selection Assistance: Yes
Lease Negotiation Assistance: Yes
Co-Operative Advertising: No
Franchisee Assoc./Member: Yes/Yes
Size Of Corporate Staff: 24
On-Going Support: „C,D,E,F,G,H,I
Training: 5 Weeks Headquarters; 2 Weeks Franchisee's Shop

SPECIFIC EXPANSION PLANS:
US: MW, SW
Canada: No
Overseas: NR

◁◁　▷▷

CERTIGARD (PETRO-CANADA)
2489 N. Sheridan Wy.
Mississauga, ON L5K 1A8 Canada
Tel: (888) 541-7632 (905) 804-4555
Fax: (905) 804-4898
E-Mail: hupponen@petro-canada.ca
Web Site: www.petro-canada.ca
Mr. Harvey Hupponen, Network Utilization Manager

Petro-Canada is a major integrated oil and gasoline company in Canada. CERTIGARD is Petro-Canada's franchise organization of automotive repair/service outlets across Canada. In operation since 1987, the CERTIGARD franchisee network is supported by a team of dedicated, corporate specialists. The top sales performers now measure annual sales/bay in excess of $260,000. Competitive pricing; convenient locations; national warranties on repairs, lifetime on certain products.

BACKGROUND:
Established: 1987; 1st Franchised: 1987
Franchised Units: 120
Company-Owned Units: 0
Total Units: 120
Dist.: US-0; CAN-120; O'seas-0
North America: 0 States, 9 Provinces
Density: 53 in ON, 30 in BC, 24 in AB
Projected New Units (12 Months): 6
Qualifications: 4, 5, 4, 3, 3, 4
FINANCIAL/TERMS:

Cash Investment: $40-60K
Total Investment: $75K
Minimum Net Worth: $30K
Fees: Franchise - $25K
  Royalty - 5%; Ad. - 2%
Earnings Claims Statement: No
Term of Contract (Years): 5/5
Avg. # Of Employees: 6 FT, 0 PT
Passive Ownership: Not Allowed
Encourage Conversions: Yes
Area Develop. Agreements: No
Sub-Franchising Contracts: No
Expand In Territory: Yes
Space Needs: 4,000 SF

SUPPORT & TRAINING:
Financial Assistance Provided: No
Site Selection Assistance: Yes
Lease Negotiation Assistance: No
Co-Operative Advertising: No
Franchisee Assoc./Member: Yes/Yes
Size Of Corporate Staff: 25
On-Going Support: „C,D,E,F,G,H,I
Training: 3 Days System Training -- Local Classroom; 3 Days Automation Training (Class & On-Site

SPECIFIC EXPANSION PLANS:
US: No
Canada: All Canada
Overseas: NR

◁◁　▷▷

COLORS ON PARADE
125 Daytona St.
Conway, SC 29526
Tel: (866) 756-4185 (843) 347-8818
Fax: (843) 347-0349
E-Mail: info@colorsonparade.com
Web Site: www.copfran1.com
Ms. Kris Lee, Director of Franchise Development

Colors on Parade is the "original body shop on wheels." Offering same-day on-site repairs of minor surface paint and dent damage, our service is second to none. Colors on Parade offers two home-based franchise opportunities, the Operator Franchise and the Area Developer Franchise. Our system makes the opportunity and dream of owning a business an attainable goal.

BACKGROUND: IFA MEMBER
Established: 1988; 1st Franchised: 1991
Franchised Units: 243
Company-Owned Units: 9
Total Units: 252
Dist.: US-252; CAN-0; O'seas-0
North America: 0 States, 0 Provinces

Density: 19 in TN, 26 in FL, 51 in CA
Projected New Units (12 Months): 50
Qualifications: 3, 3, 2, 3, 5, 5
FINANCIAL/TERMS:
Cash Investment: $10K-200K
Total Investment: $35K-500K
Minimum Net Worth: $25K
Fees: Franchise - $1.5K-18K
  Royalty - 7-30%; Ad. - 1%
Earnings Claims Statement: No
Term of Contract (Years): 10/5
Avg. # Of Employees: 1 FT, 0 PT
Passive Ownership: Discouraged
Encourage Conversions: Yes
Area Develop. Agreements: Yes/15
Sub-Franchising Contracts: Yes
Expand In Territory: Yes
Space Needs: NA

SUPPORT & TRAINING:
Financial Assistance Provided: Yes (D)
Site Selection Assistance: NA
Lease Negotiation Assistance: Yes
Co-Operative Advertising: Yes
Franchisee Assoc./Member: Yes/Yes
Size Of Corporate Staff: 13
On-Going Support: ,b,C,D,E,,G,H,I
Training: 2 Weeks Conway, SC

SPECIFIC EXPANSION PLANS:
US: All United States
Canada: All Canada
Overseas: Mexico

◁◁　▷▷

COTTMAN TRANSMISSION SYSTEMS
201 Gibraltar Rd., # 150
Horsham, PA 19044
Tel: (800) 394-6116 + 120 (215) 643-5885
Fax: (801) 640-7923
E-Mail: barry@cottman.com
Web Site: www.cottman.com
Mr. Barry Auchenbach, VP Franchise Development

Automotive service franchise with centers nationwide. A market leader with opportunities for solid growth. A highly supportive company that offers intensive training, outstanding advertising and on-site support. A forty-year reputation of treating customers with fairness, integrity and honesty. No automotive experience required.

BACKGROUND: IFA MEMBER
Established: 1962; 1st Franchised: 1964
Franchised Units: 405
Company-Owned Units: 6
Total Units: 411
Dist.: US-405; CAN-4; O'seas-2

North America: 43 States, 2 Provinces
Density: TX, PA, NJ
Projected New Units (12 Months): 60
Qualifications: 4, 4, 1, 2, 3, 3

FINANCIAL/TERMS:

Cash Investment: $60K
Total Investment: $165-180K
Minimum Net Worth: $150K
Fees: Franchise - $31.5K
  Royalty - 7.5%; Ad. - $730/Wk.
Earnings Claims Statement: Yes
Term of Contract (Years): 15/15
Avg. # Of Employees: 3 FT, 0 PT
Passive Ownership: Not Allowed
Encourage Conversions: Yes
Area Develop. Agreements: No
Sub-Franchising Contracts: Yes
Expand In Territory: Yes
Space Needs: 3,000 SF

SUPPORT & TRAINING:

Financial Assistance Provided: Yes (D)
Site Selection Assistance: Yes
Lease Negotiation Assistance: Yes
Co-Operative Advertising: No
Franchisee Assoc./Member: No
Size Of Corporate Staff: 70
On-Going Support: „C,D,E,F,G,H,I
Training: 1 Week Franchise Location; 3
  Weeks Home Office

SPECIFIC EXPANSION PLANS:

US: All United States
Canada: All Canada
Overseas: All Countries

≪ ≫

**CREATIVE COLORS
INTERNATIONAL**

19015 S. Jodi Rd., # E
Mokena, IL 60448
Tel: (800) 933-2656 (708) 478-1437
Fax: (708) 478-1636
E-Mail: terri@creativecolorsintl.com
Web Site: www.creativecolorsintl.com
Ms. Terri L. Sniegolski, Senior Vice President

The ULTIMATE in on-site restoration and dyeing of leather, vinyl, fabrics and plastics. Mobile units providing repair and restoration in all markets that have leather, vinyl, fabric, velour, plastics and fiberglass. These markets include car dealerships (new and used), furniture retailers and manufactures, hotels, airports, car rental agencies and company fleet cars.

BACKGROUND: IFA MEMBER
Established: 1990; 1st Franchised: 1991
Franchised Units: 61
Company-Owned Units: 23
Total Units: 84
Dist.: US-81; CAN-1; O'seas-2
  North America: 34 States, 1 Provinces
Density: 9 in OH, 23 in IL, 12 in FL
Projected New Units (12 Months): 10+
Qualifications: 4, 4, 3, 4, 4, 5

FINANCIAL/TERMS:

Cash Investment: $27.5K
Total Investment: $27.5K-71.4K
Minimum Net Worth: $50K
Fees: Franchise - $27.5K
  Royalty - 6%/$175/Mo.; Ad. - 1%
Earnings Claims Statement: Yes
Term of Contract (Years): 10/10
Avg. # Of Employees: 3-4 FT, 0 PT
Passive Ownership: Discouraged
Encourage Conversions: Yes
Area Develop. Agreements: No
Sub-Franchising Contracts: No
Expand In Territory: Yes
Space Needs: NA

SUPPORT & TRAINING:

Financial Assistance Provided: Yes (D)
Site Selection Assistance: Yes
Lease Negotiation Assistance: NA
Co-Operative Advertising: Yes
Franchisee Assoc./Member: Yes/Yes
Size Of Corporate Staff: 13
On-Going Support: A,B,C,D,E,F,G,H,I
Training: 1 Week Franchisee's Territory; 3
  Weeks Headquarters, IL

SPECIFIC EXPANSION PLANS:

US: All United States
Canada: All Canada
Overseas: NR

≪ ≫

DENT DOCTOR

11301 W. Markham St.
Little Rock, AR 72211
Tel: (800) 946-3368 (501) 224-0500
Fax: (501) 224-0507
E-Mail: info@dentdoctor.com
Web Site: www.dentdoctor.com
Mr. Tom Harris, Franchise Sales

DENT DOCTOR gives you a strategy to succeed. Earn extraordinary rewards removing minor dents, door dings and hail damage from vehicles without painting. Customers receive same day service. No automotive experience is required. You can operate from a retail shop along with providing mobile service.

BACKGROUND: IFA MEMBER
Established: 1986; 1st Franchised: 1990
Franchised Units: 23
Company-Owned Units: 3
Total Units: 26
Dist.: US-25; CAN-1; O'seas-0
  North America: 13 States, 1 Provinces
Density: 2 in TX, 2 in TN, 3 in CO
Projected New Units (12 Months): 2
Qualifications: 4, 4, 2, 3, 4, 5

FINANCIAL/TERMS:

Cash Investment: $29.9K-69.9K
Total Investment: $59.9K-99.9K
Minimum Net Worth: $200K
Fees: Franchise - $10-23K
  Royalty - 6%; Ad. - 20K
Earnings Claims Statement: No
Term of Contract (Years): 10/20
Avg. # Of Employees: 4 FT, 0 PT
Passive Ownership: Allowed
Encourage Conversions: Yes
Area Develop. Agreements: Yes/1
Sub-Franchising Contracts: No
Expand In Territory: Yes
Space Needs: 1,200 SF

SUPPORT & TRAINING:

Financial Assistance Provided: No
Site Selection Assistance: Yes
Lease Negotiation Assistance: Yes
Co-Operative Advertising: Yes
Franchisee Assoc./Member: No
Size Of Corporate Staff: 6
On-Going Support: ,B,C,,E,,G,H,I
Training: 1 Week Franchisee's Home Area
  (Optional); 4 Weeks Little Rock, AR

SPECIFIC EXPANSION PLANS:

US: All United States
Canada: All Canada
Overseas: All Countries

≪ ≫

DOLLAR RENT A CAR

5330 E. 31st St.
Tulsa, OK 74135
Tel: (800) 555-9893 (918) 669-0000
Fax: (918) 669-3006
E-Mail: pfritz@dollar.com
Web Site: www.dollar.com
Mr. Peter Fritz, Dir. Franchise Development

DOLLAR RENT A CAR operates and licenses others to operate daily car rental operations. Established over 30 years ago, DOLLAR RENT A CAR now serves the worldwide car rental market.

BACKGROUND:

Established: 1965;   1st Franchised: 1966
Franchised Units: 224
Company-Owned Units: 148
Total Units: 372
Dist.:   US-86; CAN-36; O'seas-250
  North America: 48 States, 0 Provinces
  Density: in TX, in FL, in CA
Projected New Units (12 Months):   24
Qualifications: 5, 5, 4, 4, 4, 5

FINANCIAL/TERMS:

Cash Investment: $100K-2MM
Total Investment: $100K-2MM
Minimum Net Worth: $250K
Fees: Franchise - $12.5K+
  Royalty - 8%;   Ad. - Included
Earnings Claims Statement: No
Term of Contract (Years):   10/10
Avg. # Of Employees: Varies
Passive Ownership: Not Allowed
Encourage Conversions: Yes
Area Develop. Agreements: Yes/1
Sub-Franchising Contracts: No
Expand In Territory: Yes
Space Needs: 1,000+ SF

SUPPORT & TRAINING:

Financial Assistance Provided: Yes (D)
Site Selection Assistance: No
Lease Negotiation Assistance: No
Co-Operative Advertising: No
Franchisee Assoc./Member: No
Size Of Corporate Staff: 400
On-Going Support: a,B,C,D,E,,G,H,I
Training: 3 Days Headquarters Orientation; 2 Weeks On-Site Field Training; 1 Week Automation

SPECIFIC EXPANSION PLANS:

US: Not FL,MA,VT,NH,NV,AR,UT,MT
Canada: 2 Master Fran.
Overseas: Australia, China, Southeast Asia

≪   ≫

EAGLERIDER MOTORCYCLE RENTAL

11860 S. La Cienega Blvd.
Los Angeles, CA 90250-3461
Tel: (800) 501-8687 (310) 536-6777
Fax: (310) 536-6770
E-Mail: rent@eaglerider.com
Web Site: www.eaglerider.com
Mr. Marcelino Orozco, Vice President Franchising

EAGLERIDER is the world's largest motorcycle rental & tour company that specializes in Harley-Davidson motorcycles, ATVs, dirt bike, watercraft and snowmobile rentals. Why buy it when you can rent it?

BACKGROUND:

Established: 1992;   1st Franchised: 1997
Franchised Units: 21
Company-Owned Units: 4
Total Units: 25
Dist.:   US-9; CAN-3; O'seas-13
  North America: 11 States, 0 Provinces
  Density: 4 in TX, 2 in FL, 6 in CA
Projected New Units (12 Months):   10
Qualifications: 3, 2, 4, 2, 3, 5

FINANCIAL/TERMS:

Cash Investment: $69.5-184K
Total Investment: $219.5-684K
Minimum Net Worth: $225K
Fees: Franchise - $30K
  Royalty - 10%;   Ad. - 0%
Earnings Claims Statement: No
Term of Contract (Years):   10/10
Avg. # Of Employees: 2 FT, 2 PT
Passive Ownership: Discouraged
Encourage Conversions: Yes
Area Develop. Agreements: Yes/1
Sub-Franchising Contracts: No
Expand In Territory: Yes
Space Needs: 3,500 SF

SUPPORT & TRAINING:

Financial Assistance Provided: Yes (D)
Site Selection Assistance: Yes
Lease Negotiation Assistance: No
Co-Operative Advertising: No
Franchisee Assoc./Member: No
Size Of Corporate Staff: 31
On-Going Support: A,B,C,d,E,F,G,h,I
Training: 2 Weeks Los Angeles, CA

SPECIFIC EXPANSION PLANS:

US: All United States
Canada: All Canada
Overseas: All Tourist Destinations with 6 months or greater

≪   ≫

ECONO LUBE N' TUNE

128 S. Tryon St.
Charlotte, NC 28202
Tel: (800) 628-0253 (704) 644-8171
Fax: (704) 372-4826
E-Mail: ryank@econolube.com
Web Site: www.econolube.com
Mr. Ryan Keller, VP Franchise Development

Turn-key automotive service franchise.

Lubrications, tune-ups, brake and other general services. Drive-through oil change

BACKGROUND:

Established: 1973;   1st Franchised: 1974
Franchised Units: 182
Company-Owned Units: 18
Total Units: 200
Dist.:   US-200; CAN-0; O'seas-0
  North America: 0 States, 0 Provinces
  Density: NR
Projected New Units (12 Months):   10
Qualifications: 4, 4, 2, 4, 3, 5

FINANCIAL/TERMS:

Cash Investment: $50K-100K
Total Investment: $200K
Minimum Net Worth: $300-500K
Fees: Franchise - $49.5K
  Royalty - 5%/$500; Ad. - 5%/.5% Natl
Earnings Claims Statement: Yes
Term of Contract (Years):   15/5
Avg. # Of Employees: 6-7 FT, 0 PT
Passive Ownership: Discouraged
Encourage Conversions: NA
Area Develop. Agreements: No
Sub-Franchising Contracts: No
Expand In Territory: Yes
Space Needs: NR

SUPPORT & TRAINING:

Financial Assistance Provided: Yes (D)
Site Selection Assistance: NA
Lease Negotiation Assistance: No
Co-Operative Advertising: No
Franchisee Assoc./Member: Yes/Yes
Size Of Corporate Staff: 100
On-Going Support: ,B,C,D,E,F,G,H,I
Training: 1 Week Ontario, CA; 1 Week Cypress, CA

SPECIFIC EXPANSION PLANS:

US: East Coast, VA, NC, SC, GA
Canada: No
Overseas: NR

≪   ≫

EXPRESS OIL CHANGE

1880 Southpark Dr.
Birmingham, AL 35244
Tel: (888) 945-1771 + 114 (205) 945-1771 + 114
Fax: (205) 943-5779
E-Mail: hbarrow@expressoil.com
Web Site: www.expressoil.com
Ms. Heather Barrow, Franchise Develop-

ment Associate

We are among the top ten fast oil change chains in the world. Per unit, sales out-pace our competitors by over 40%. Attractive, state-of-the-art facilities offer expanded, highly profitable services in addition to our ten minute oil change. We also provide transmission service, air conditioning service, brake repair, tire rotation and balancing and miscellaneous light repairs... Most extensive training and franchise support in the industry.

BACKGROUND: IFA MEMBER
Established: 1979; 1st Franchised: 1984
Franchised Units: 103
Company-Owned Units: 68
Total Units: 171
Dist.: US-171; CAN-0; O'seas-0
North America: 11 States, 0 Provinces
Density: 19 in TN, 35 in GA, 89 in AL
Projected New Units (12 Months): 20
Qualifications: 5, 5, 1, 3, 3, 5
FINANCIAL/TERMS:
Cash Investment: $225-$350K
Total Investment: $247K-$1.4MM
Minimum Net Worth: $450K
Fees: Franchise - $27.5K
 Royalty - 5%; Ad. - 3%
Earnings Claims Statement: No
Term of Contract (Years): 10/10
Avg. # Of Employees: 7 FT, 0 PT
Passive Ownership: Not Allowed
Encourage Conversions: Yes
Area Develop. Agreements: Yes
Sub-Franchising Contracts: No
Expand In Territory: Yes
Space Needs: 22,000 SF
SUPPORT & TRAINING:
Financial Assistance Provided: Yes (I)
Site Selection Assistance: Yes
Lease Negotiation Assistance: Yes
Co-Operative Advertising: Yes
Franchisee Assoc./Member: Yes/Yes
Size Of Corporate Staff: 44
On-Going Support: A,B,C,D,E,F,G,H,I
Training: Post-Opening Training; Continuous Training; On-Site; Birmingham, AL Closest Training Center
SPECIFIC EXPANSION PLANS:
US: Southeast
Canada: No
Overseas: NR

⟨⟨ ⟩⟩

GOO GOO 3-MINUTE EXPRESS WASH

6021 Coca Cola Blvd.
Columbus, GA 31909
Tel: (866) 246-6466 (706) 563-6110
Fax: (706) 563-6138
E-Mail: jimwilliamson@googoocarwash.com
Web Site: www.googoocarwash.com
Mr. Jim Williamson, VP Sales

Thank you for your interest in franchise opportunities with Goo-Goo Car Wash. We have been in the business of washing cars since 1945. Based in Columbus, Georgia, we have worked hard to earn our reputation as car wash innovators, always looking for a way to improve our washes and the industry in general. We have washes that span the Southeast and are excited to be experiencing a period of rapid expansion into areas beyond. Our EXPRESS WASH franchises are currently available in all 50 states.

BACKGROUND:
Established: 1945; 1st Franchised: 2002
Franchised Units: 10
Company-Owned Units: 11
Total Units: 21
Dist.: US-21; CAN-0; O'seas-0
North America: 8 States, 0 Provinces
Density: 3 in TN, 4 in GA, 6 in AL
Projected New Units (12 Months): 12
Qualifications: 5, 4, 1, 3, 2, 5
FINANCIAL/TERMS:
Cash Investment: $300-600K
Total Investment: $1.5-3.3MM
Minimum Net Worth: $2MM
Fees: Franchise - $96K
 Royalty - 4%; Ad. - 0
Earnings Claims Statement: No
Term of Contract (Years): 10/5
Avg. # Of Employees: 4 FT, 1 PT
Passive Ownership: Allowed
Encourage Conversions: No
Area Develop. Agreements: Yes
Sub-Franchising Contracts: No
Expand In Territory: Yes
Space Needs: 50,000 SF
SUPPORT & TRAINING:
Financial Assistance Provided: No
Site Selection Assistance: Yes
Lease Negotiation Assistance: Yes
Co-Operative Advertising: No

Franchisee Assoc./Member: No
Size Of Corporate Staff: 15
On-Going Support: ,,C,D,E,F,G,H,I
Training: 2 weeks Columbus, Georgia-Corporate Headquarters; Varies On Site; Varies Birmingham, Alabama
SPECIFIC EXPANSION PLANS:
US: All U.S.
Canada: No
Overseas: NR

⟨⟨ ⟩⟩

GREASE MONKEY INTERNATIONAL

7100 E. Belleview Ave., # 305
Greenwood Village, CO 80111
Tel: (800) 364-0352 (303) 308-1660
Fax: (303) 308-5906
E-Mail: mikeb@greasemonkeyintl.com
Web Site: www.greasemonkeyintl.com
Mr. Michael J. Brunetti, VP Sales, Development, Real Estate

GREASE MONKEY Centers provide convenient vehicle preventive maintenance services. We provide comprehensive technical training for all franchisees, including instruction performing all GREASE MONKEY approved services thoroughly and safely. You will also learn basic accounting, computer marketing and customer satisfaction techniques to help you operate your business.

BACKGROUND:
Established: 1978; 1st Franchised: 1979
Franchised Units: 235
Company-Owned Units: 3
Total Units: 238
Dist.: US-196; CAN-0; O'seas-34
North America: 28 States, 0 Provinces
Density: 13 in WA, 57 in CO, 14 in CA
Projected New Units (12 Months): 20
Qualifications: 5, 4, 2, 2, 3, 5
FINANCIAL/TERMS:
Cash Investment: $200-250K
Total Investment: $850K-1.2MM
Minimum Net Worth: $300K
Fees: Franchise - $28K
 Royalty - 5%; Ad. - 6%
Earnings Claims Statement: Yes
Term of Contract (Years): 15/15

Avg. # Of Employees: 3 FT, 3 PT
Passive Ownership: Discouraged
Encourage Conversions: Yes
Area Develop. Agreements: Yes/1
Sub-Franchising Contracts: No
Expand In Territory: Yes
Space Needs: 1,800 SF

SUPPORT & TRAINING:
Financial Assistance Provided: Yes (D)
Site Selection Assistance: Yes
Lease Negotiation Assistance: Yes
Co-Operative Advertising: No
Franchisee Assoc./Member: Yes/Yes
Size Of Corporate Staff: 45
On-Going Support: A,B,C,D,E,F,G,H,I
Training:1 Week Corporate Headquarters, Denver, CO; 1 Week Market Center

SPECIFIC EXPANSION PLANS:
US: All United States
Canada: No
Overseas: Mexico

≪ ≫

LEE MYLES TRANSMISSIONS & AUTOCARE

650 From Rd., S. Lbby., 4 Fl.
Paramus, NJ 07652
Tel: (800) 533-6953 (201) 262-0555
Fax: (201) 262-5177
E-Mail: info@leemyles.com
Web Site: www.leemyles.com
Mr. Sal Gargone, Franchise Development

We offer and support franchises for LEE MYLES TRANSMISSIONS & AUTO-CARE businesses that provide servicing, repair and replacements of standard and automatic transmission, as well as preventative maintenance and specialty general automotive repair and related services and products.

BACKGROUND: IFA MEMBER
Established: 1947; 1st Franchised: 1964
Franchised Units: 95
Company-Owned Units: 0
Total Units: 95
Dist.: US-95; CAN-0; O'seas-0
North America: 17 States, 0 Provinces
Density: 25 in NY, 12 in NJ, 12 in AZ
Projected New Units (12 Months): 22
Qualifications: 4, 4, 4, 5, 5, 5

FINANCIAL/TERMS:
Cash Investment: $70-90K

Total Investment: $177-206K
Minimum Net Worth: $250K
Fees: Franchise - $30K
 Royalty - 7%; Ad. - Regional Co-ops Set Rates
Earnings Claims Statement: Yes
Term of Contract (Years): 15/15
Avg. # Of Employees: 4 FT, 0 PT
Passive Ownership: Not Allowed
Encourage Conversions: Yes
Area Develop. Agreements: Yes/1
Sub-Franchising Contracts: No
Expand In Territory: Yes
Space Needs: 2,500 - 3,000 SF

SUPPORT & TRAINING:
Financial Assistance Provided: Yes (I)
Site Selection Assistance: Yes
Lease Negotiation Assistance: Yes
Co-Operative Advertising: Yes
Franchisee Assoc./Member: No
Size Of Corporate Staff: 15
On-Going Support: ,,C,D,E,,G,H,I
Training: 1 Week In-Store Training; 1-2 Weeks Corporate Office

SPECIFIC EXPANSION PLANS:
US: All US Exc. AK and HI
Canada: All Canada
Overseas: NR

≪ ≫

LENTZ USA SERVICE CENTERS

1001 Riverview Dr.
Kalamazoo, MI 49048
Tel: (800) 354-2131 (269) 342-2200
Fax: (269) 342-9461
E-Mail: quietcar@LENTZusa.com
Web Site: www.lentzusa.com
Mr. Gary R. Thomas, Franchise Liaison

Vehicle repair service centers. Brakes, mufflers, steering systems and more.

BACKGROUND: IFA MEMBER
Established: 1972; 1st Franchised: 1989
Franchised Units: 12
Company-Owned Units: 11
Total Units: 23
Dist.: US-23; CAN-0; O'seas-0
North America: 2 States, Provinces
Density: 2 in FL, 21 in MI
Projected New Units (12 Months): 6
Qualifications: 4, 3, 1, 3, 4, 5

FINANCIAL/TERMS:
Cash Investment: $35-70K
Total Investment: $112-120K
Minimum Net Worth: $100K
Fees: Franchise - $20K
 Royalty - 0-7%; Ad. - 0%
Earnings Claims Statement: No

Term of Contract (Years): 10/10
Avg. # Of Employees: 3-5 FT, 0 PT
Passive Ownership: Discouraged
Encourage Conversions: Yes
Area Develop. Agreements: Yes/1
Sub-Franchising Contracts: No
Expand In Territory: Yes
Space Needs: 3,600 SF

SUPPORT & TRAINING:
Financial Assistance Provided: Yes (D)
Site Selection Assistance: Yes
Lease Negotiation Assistance: Yes
Co-Operative Advertising: No
Franchisee Assoc./Member: No
Size Of Corporate Staff: 10
On-Going Support: ,B,C,D,E,F,G,,I
Training: 2 Weeks Kalamazoo, MI; 1 Week Franchise Site

SPECIFIC EXPANSION PLANS:
US: All United States
Canada: All Canada
Overseas: Middle East, India, Europe

≪ ≫

LINE-X SPRAY-ON TRUCK BEDLINERS

6 Hutton Centre Dr., # 500
Santa Ana, CA 92707
Tel: (800) 831-3232 (714) 850-1662
Fax: (714) 850-8759
E-Mail: dboeke@linexmail.com
Web Site: www.linex.com
Mr. David Boeke, VP Franchise Development

A LINE-X franchisee operates a retail/ industrial location that applies sprayed on coatings. LINE-X has a number of applications from flooring to industrial applications. LINE-X is in a growing, new and unsaturated market with extraordinary opportunities for minority entrepreneurs.

BACKGROUND:
Established: 1993; 1st Franchised: 1998
Franchised Units: 453
Company-Owned Units: 0
Total Units: 453
Dist.: US-453; CAN-0; O'seas-7
North America: 50 States, 0 Provinces
Density: 15 in WA, 10 in GA, 20 in CA
Projected New Units (12 Months): NR
Qualifications: NR

FINANCIAL/TERMS:
Cash Investment: $40K-100K
Total Investment: $140K-252K
Minimum Net Worth: $20K
Fees: Franchise - $20K
 Royalty - 0%; Ad. - 1.5%

Earnings Claims Statement: No
Term of Contract (Years): 5/15
Avg. # Of Employees: 2 FT, 0 PT
Passive Ownership: Discouraged
Encourage Conversions: No
Area Develop. Agreements: Yes/1
Sub-Franchising Contracts: Yes
Expand In Territory: Yes
Space Needs: 2,500 SF

SUPPORT & TRAINING:

Financial Assistance Provided: No
Site Selection Assistance: Yes
Lease Negotiation Assistance: Yes
Co-Operative Advertising: No
Franchisee Assoc./Member: No
Size Of Corporate Staff: 14
On-Going Support: „C,D,E,,G,H,I
Training: Our Location Up to 5 Days; Up to 7 Days Franchisee's Location

SPECIFIC EXPANSION PLANS:

US: All United States
Canada: All Canada
Overseas: All Countries

<< >>

LUBEPRO'S INTERNATIONAL

1740 S. Bell School Rd.
Cherry Valley, IL 61016
Tel: (800) 654-5823 (815) 332-9200
Fax: (815) 332-9355
E-Mail: rayk@lubepros.com
Web Site: www.lubepros.com
Mr. Ray Keating, Vice President

Our building design, our training program and our unique approach to marketing truly set us ahead of our competitors.

BACKGROUND:

Established: 1978; 1st Franchised: 1985
Franchised Units: 18
Company-Owned Units: 16
Total Units: 34
Dist.: US-34; CAN-0; O'seas-0
 North America: 4 States, 0 Provinces
 Density: 3 in WI, 29 in IL, 1 in TN
Projected New Units (12 Months): 4
Qualifications: 4, 3, 1, 2, 2, 4

FINANCIAL/TERMS:

Cash Investment: $150K
Total Investment: $223-274K
Minimum Net Worth: $400K
Fees: Franchise - $32K
 Royalty - 5%; Ad. - 5%
Earnings Claims Statement: Yes
Term of Contract (Years): 20/10/10
Avg. # Of Employees: 9 FT, 0 PT
Passive Ownership: Allowed
Encourage Conversions: NA

Area Develop. Agreements: No
Sub-Franchising Contracts: No
Expand In Territory: Yes
Space Needs: 1,800 SF

SUPPORT & TRAINING:

Financial Assistance Provided: No
Site Selection Assistance: Yes
Lease Negotiation Assistance: No
Co-Operative Advertising: No
Franchisee Assoc./Member: No
Size Of Corporate Staff: 4
On-Going Support: „C,D,E,,,H,I
Training: 7 Days In-Store; 10 Days Rockford, IL

SPECIFIC EXPANSION PLANS:

US: Central, North Central
Canada: No
Overseas: NR

<< >>

MAACO COLLISION REPAIR AND AUTO PAINTING

8400 Lawson Rd., # 1
Milton, ON L9T 0A4 Canada
Tel: (800) 387-6780 (905) 501-1212
Fax: (905) 875-1248
E-Mail: gdohring@maaco.com
Web Site: www.maaco.ca
Mr. Gary Dohring, Mgr. Franchise Development

There are over 500 MAACO franchise centres in Canada, the U.S. and Puerto Rico. Between them, these franchises repair and paint over 800,000 vehicles a year. Thousands of car owners as well as local and national fleet administrators rely upon their local MAACO centre to maintain their vehicles' appearance. In 2005 MAACO was ranked #1 in Automotive Appearance Services in Entrepreneur magazine's annual Franchise 500.

BACKGROUND:

Established: 1972; 1st Franchised: 1972
Franchised Units: 34
Company-Owned Units: 0
Total Units: 34
Dist.: US-0; CAN-34; O'seas-0
 North America: 0 States, 6 Provinces
 Density: 19 in ON, 3 in BC, 6 in AB
Projected New Units (12 Months): 5
Qualifications: 3, 4, 1, 2, 4, 5

FINANCIAL/TERMS:

Cash Investment: $80K

Total Investment: $350K
Minimum Net Worth: $350K
Fees: Franchise - $30K
 Royalty - 8%; Ad. - $700/Wk.
Earnings Claims Statement: Yes
Term of Contract (Years): 15/5
Avg. # Of Employees: 6-10 FT, 0 PT
Passive Ownership: Not Allowed
Encourage Conversions: No
Area Develop. Agreements: No
Sub-Franchising Contracts: No
Expand In Territory: Yes
Space Needs: 8,000 SF

SUPPORT & TRAINING:

Financial Assistance Provided: No
Site Selection Assistance: Yes
Lease Negotiation Assistance: No
Co-Operative Advertising: No
Franchisee Assoc./Member: Yes/Yes
Size Of Corporate Staff: 8
On-Going Support: A,B,C,D,E,F,G,H,I
Training: 4 Weeks King of Prussia, PA; 3 Weeks In Store; On-Going as Required In Store

SPECIFIC EXPANSION PLANS:

US: No
Canada: All Canada
Overseas: NR

<< >>

MASTER CARE CLEANING SYSTEMS

555 Sixth St., # 327
New Westminster, BC V3L 4Y4 Canada
Tel: (800) 889-2799 (604) 525-8221
Fax: (604) 526-2235
E-Mail: info@mastercare.com
Web Site: www.mastercare.com
Mr. Chris Stone, President

Commercial janitorial services.

BACKGROUND:

Established: 1987; 1st Franchised: 1987
Franchised Units: 159
Company-Owned Units: 1
Total Units: 160
Dist.: US-0; CAN-160; O'seas-0
 North America: 0 States, 1 Provinces
 Density: 108 in BC
Projected New Units (12 Months): 30
Qualifications: 3, 3, 1, 1, 2, 3

FINANCIAL/TERMS:

Cash Investment: $2-75K
Total Investment: $18K
Minimum Net Worth: $25K
Fees: Franchise - $18K
 Royalty - 5-15%; Ad. - 1%
Earnings Claims Statement: No

Term of Contract (Years):	5/5
Avg. # Of Employees:	2 FT, 0 PT
Passive Ownership:	Discouraged
Encourage Conversions:	Yes
Area Develop. Agreements:	Yes/1
Sub-Franchising Contracts:	Yes
Expand In Territory:	Yes
Space Needs:	NR

SUPPORT & TRAINING:

Financial Assistance Provided:	Yes (D)
Site Selection Assistance:	Yes
Lease Negotiation Assistance:	NA
Co-Operative Advertising:	No
Franchisee Assoc./Member:	Yes/Yes
Size Of Corporate Staff:	4
On-Going Support:	A,B,C,D,E,,G,h,I
Training:	1-6 Weeks Head Office

SPECIFIC EXPANSION PLANS:

US:	Master Franchises Only
Canada:	Master Franchise
Overseas:	NR

≪ ≫

MASTER MECHANIC, THE
3250 Ridgeway Dr., # 1
Mississauga, ON L5L 5Y6 Canada
Tel: (800) 383-8523 (905) 820-2552
Fax: (905) 820-2558
E-Mail: hugh@mastermechanic.ca
Web Site: www.mastermechanic.ca
Mr. Hugh Welsford, President

The business provides full-service automotive repair and maintenance services to both retail and commercial clients through its franchisees, with special emphasis on drivability and engine performance. This is an excellent opportunity for existing independent garages looking to rebrand or for those with automotive and/or business experience who are considering the benefits of owning their own business.

BACKGROUND:

Established: 1982;	1st Franchised: 1983
Franchised Units:	36
Company-Owned Units:	1
Total Units:	37
Dist.:	US-0; CAN-37; O'seas-0
North America:	0 States, 1 Provinces
Density:	37 in ON
Projected New Units (12 Months):	4
Qualifications:	4, 4, 4, 3, 4, 5

FINANCIAL/TERMS:

Cash Investment:	$60-80K
Total Investment:	$125K-175K
Minimum Net Worth:	$200K
Fees: Franchise -	$25K
Royalty - 6%;	Ad. - 3%

Earnings Claims Statement:	Yes
Term of Contract (Years):	20/Open
Avg. # Of Employees:	3-5 FT, 1-2 PT
Passive Ownership:	Discouraged
Encourage Conversions:	Yes
Area Develop. Agreements:	Yes
Sub-Franchising Contracts:	Yes
Expand In Territory:	Yes
Space Needs:	3,000-5,000 SF

SUPPORT & TRAINING:

Financial Assistance Provided:	Yes (I)
Site Selection Assistance:	Yes
Lease Negotiation Assistance:	Yes
Co-Operative Advertising:	Yes
Franchisee Assoc./Member:	Yes/Yes
Size Of Corporate Staff:	5
On-Going Support:	,,C,D,E,F,G,H,I
Training:	3 Weeks On-Site; NA Training Shop; 1 Week Classroom

SPECIFIC EXPANSION PLANS:

US:	No
Canada:	ON
Overseas:	NR

≪ ≫

MEINEKE CAR CARE CENTERS
128 S. Tryon St., # 900
Charlotte, NC 28202-5001
Tel: (800) 275-5200 (704) 377-8855
Fax: (704) 372-4826
E-Mail: franchise.info@meineke.com
Web Site: www.meinekefranchise.com
Mr. Dave Schaefers, VP Franchise Development

MEINEKE has been offering superior automotive repair services at discount prices for over 30 years. We are a nationally-recognized brand with a proven system. Brand recognition, comprehensive training and on-going technical and operational support are some of the benefits enjoyed by MEINEKE franchisees.

BACKGROUND: IFA MEMBER

Established: 1972;	1st Franchised: 1972
Franchised Units:	901
Company-Owned Units:	11
Total Units:	912
Dist.:	US-852; CAN-18; O'seas-18
North America:	49 States, 5 Provinces
Density:	56 in TX, 57 in PA, 69 in NY
Projected New Units (12 Months):	69
Qualifications:	4, 3, 3, 2, 2, 5

FINANCIAL/TERMS:

Cash Investment:	$60K
Total Investment:	$182.8K-426.8K
Minimum Net Worth:	$150K
Fees: Franchise -	$30K
Royalty - 3-7%;	Ad. - 8%
Earnings Claims Statement:	Yes
Term of Contract (Years):	15/15
Avg. # Of Employees:	4 FT, 0 PT
Passive Ownership:	Not Allowed
Encourage Conversions:	Yes
Area Develop. Agreements:	Yes
Sub-Franchising Contracts:	No
Expand In Territory:	Yes
Space Needs:	2,880-3,880 SF

SUPPORT & TRAINING:

Financial Assistance Provided:	Yes (I)
Site Selection Assistance:	Yes
Lease Negotiation Assistance:	Yes
Co-Operative Advertising:	No
Franchisee Assoc./Member:	Yes/Yes
Size Of Corporate Staff:	110
On-Going Support:	A,B,C,D,E,,G,H,I
Training:	4 Weeks Charlotte, NC

SPECIFIC EXPANSION PLANS:

US:	All United States
Canada:	All Canada
Overseas:	All Countries

≪ ≫

MERLIN 200,000 MILE SHOPS
1 N. River Ln., # 206
Geneva, IL 60134-2267
Tel: (800) 652-9900 + 124 (630) 208-9900
Fax: (630) 208-8601
E-Mail: mlawson@merlins.com
Web Site: www.merlins.com
Mr. Maria T. Lawson, Coordinator, Market Development

MERLIN is an upscale automotive service chain with one of the highest average sales per shop statistics in the industry. MERLIN specializes in brakes, exhaust, suspension, oil/lubrication, air conditioning, tires and related services. Marketing is based on long-term employee and customer relationships. Candidates must have significant management and sales/customer service experience. Automotive experience is helpful. Special equity assistance is available to candidates with significant automotive experience (FASTRAK), qualified bilingual candidates (TLP), and for employees enrolled in Merlin's Entrepreneur Development Program (EDP). See Website for details on equity assistance.

BACKGROUND: IFA MEMBER
Established: 1975; 1st Franchised: 1975
Franchised Units: 66
Company-Owned Units: 4
Total Units: 70
Dist.:   US-70; CAN-0; O'seas-0
 North America: 6 States, 0 Provinces
 Density: 50 in IL, 5 in GA
Projected New Units (12 Months):   6
Qualifications: 3, 5, 4, 3, 4, 5
FINANCIAL/TERMS:
Cash Investment: $20-50K
Total Investment: $185-210K
Minimum Net Worth: $75K
Fees: Franchise - $26-30K
 Royalty - 4%;   Ad. - 5%
Earnings Claims Statement: Yes
Term of Contract (Years):   20/20
Avg. # Of Employees: 3-4 FT, 1 PT
Passive Ownership: Not Allowed
Encourage Conversions: Yes
Area Develop. Agreements: No
Sub-Franchising Contracts: No
Expand In Territory: Yes
Space Needs: 3,850 SF
SUPPORT & TRAINING:
Financial Assistance Provided: Yes (I)
Site Selection Assistance: Yes
Lease Negotiation Assistance: Yes
Co-Operative Advertising: Yes
Franchisee Assoc./Member: No
Size Of Corporate Staff: 20
On-Going Support: „C,D,E,F,G,H,I
Training: 6 Weeks Corporate Headquarters; As Needed In Shop
SPECIFIC EXPANSION PLANS:
US: IL, MI, GA, WI, IN
Canada: No
Overseas: NR

MIDAS
1300 Arlington Heights Rd.
Itasca, IL 60143-3174
Tel: (800) 365-0007 (630) 438-3000
Fax: (630) 438-3700

E-Mail: midasfranchise@midas.com
Web Site: www.midasfran.com
Ms. Barbara Korus, Franchise Recruitment Coord.

Globally respected with over 2,500 franchised, licensed and company-owned Midas shops throughout the United States, Canada and the world. Ours is a premier brand name in world-class automotive services, offering repair and maintenance services, as well as tires and batteries. Consider the opportunity. A world-famous brand . . . with a 50-year record of success . . . and a commitment to long-term growth through customer service, customer value and customer relationships.

BACKGROUND: IFA MEMBER
Established: 1956; 1st Franchised: 1956
Franchised Units: 2464
Company-Owned Units: 91
Total Units: 2555
Dist.:   US-1559; CAN-209; O'seas-823
 North America: 50 States, 9 Provinces
 Density: NR
Projected New Units (12 Months):   40
Qualifications: 5, 4, 3, 2, 1, 5
FINANCIAL/TERMS:
Cash Investment: $75-100K
Total Investment: $261.6K-350.7K
Minimum Net Worth: $250-300K
Fees: Franchise - $20K
 Royalty - 10%;   Ad. - Incl. Roy.
Earnings Claims Statement: Yes
Term of Contract (Years):   20/20
Avg. # Of Employees: 6 FT, 4 PT
Passive Ownership: Discouraged
Encourage Conversions: Yes
Area Develop. Agreements: No
Sub-Franchising Contracts: No
Expand In Territory: Yes
Space Needs: 4,000-5,000 SF
SUPPORT & TRAINING:
Financial Assistance Provided: Yes (I)
Site Selection Assistance: Yes
Lease Negotiation Assistance: Yes
Co-Operative Advertising: No
Franchisee Assoc./Member: Yes/Yes
Size Of Corporate Staff: 197
On-Going Support: „C,D,e,f,G,H,I
Training: 3 Weeks Palatine, IL; 1-2 Weeks In-Shop Assignment; 1-2 Weeks Self Study
SPECIFIC EXPANSION PLANS:
US: All United States
Canada: All Canada
Overseas: Select Countries

MIGHTY DISTRIBUTING SYSTEM OF AMERICA
650 Engineering Dr.
Norcross, GA 30092-2821
Tel: (800) 829-3900 (770) 448-3900
Fax: (770) 446-8627
E-Mail: franchising@mightyautoparts.com
Web Site: www.mightyfranchise.com
Mr. Barry Teagle, Vice President Franchising

Wholesale distribution of original equipment-quality, MIGHTY-branded auto parts. Franchisees operate in exclusive territories, supplying automotive maintenance and repair facilities with under-car and under-hood products, such as filters, belts, tune-up and brake parts.

BACKGROUND: IFA MEMBER
Established: 1963; 1st Franchised: 1970
Franchised Units: 107
Company-Owned Units: 4
Total Units: 111
Dist.:   US-111; CAN-0; O'seas-0
 North America: 45 States, 0 Provinces
 Density: 9 in TX, 7 in FL, 7 in CA
Projected New Units (12 Months):   10
Qualifications: 5, 4, 3, 3, 3, 4
FINANCIAL/TERMS:
Cash Investment: $70-80K
Total Investment: $150-200K
Minimum Net Worth: $500K
Fees: Franchise - $5K+ $.035/Vcl
 Royalty - 5%;   Ad. - 0.5%
Earnings Claims Statement: Yes
Term of Contract (Years):   10/1
Avg. # Of Employees: 4 FT, 2 PT
Passive Ownership: Not Allowed
Encourage Conversions: Yes
Area Develop. Agreements: No
Sub-Franchising Contracts: No
Expand In Territory: Yes
Space Needs: 3,000 SF
SUPPORT & TRAINING:
Financial Assistance Provided: No
Site Selection Assistance: No
Lease Negotiation Assistance: No
Co-Operative Advertising: Yes
Franchisee Assoc./Member: Yes/Yes
Size Of Corporate Staff: 50
On-Going Support: „,D,,,,,
Training: 1 Week On-the-Job Training; 1 Week Home Office
SPECIFIC EXPANSION PLANS:
US: All United States
Canada: All Canada
Overseas: NR

≪ ≫

MINUTE MUFFLER AND BRAKE

365 Bloor St., E., # 1100
Toronto, ON M4W 3M7 Canada
Tel: (800) 387-1410
Fax: (416) 960-7916
E-Mail: minmuff@agt.net
Web Site: www.minutemuffler.com
Mr. Rick Massey, National Director of
  Franchise Development

Retail exhaust, brake, suspension outlets with 0% royalty, 0% advertising fee. Your 65-70% average gross profit goes in your pocket, not ours. Unsurpassed support systems by actual store owner/operators. Service is our business!!

BACKGROUND:

Established: 1969;   1st Franchised: 1971
Franchised Units: 91
Company-Owned Units: 91
Total Units: 182
Dist.:   US-0; CAN-182; O'seas-0
  North America: 0 States, 0 Provinces
  Density: 18 in ON, 25 in BC, 24 in AB
Projected New Units (12 Months):   12
Qualifications: 4, 3, 2, 3, 3, 5

FINANCIAL/TERMS:

Cash Investment: $50-100K
Total Investment: $150K-250K
Minimum Net Worth: $75-100K
Fees: Franchise - $0-25K
  Royalty - 0%;   Ad. - 0%
Earnings Claims Statement: No
Term of Contract (Years):   On-Going/
Avg. # Of Employees: 3-5 FT, 1 PT
Passive Ownership: Discouraged
Encourage Conversions: Yes
Area Develop. Agreements: No
Sub-Franchising Contracts: Yes
Expand In Territory: Yes
Space Needs: 3,200-3,500 SF

SUPPORT & TRAINING:

Financial Assistance Provided: No
Site Selection Assistance: Yes
Lease Negotiation Assistance: Yes
Co-Operative Advertising: No
Franchisee Assoc./Member: No
Size Of Corporate Staff: 13
On-Going Support: ,B,C,D,e,F,G,h,I
Training: 1-10 Weeks Head Office; 1-2
  Weeks On-Site

SPECIFIC EXPANSION PLANS:

US: No
Canada: All Canada
Overseas: Carribean, South/Central
  America, Europe

≪ ≫

Hottest New Franchise

MIRACLE AUTO
PAINTING & BODY REPAIR

2343 Lincoln Ave.
Hayward, CA 94545
Tel: (877) 647-2253 (510) 887-2211
Fax: (510) 887-3092
E-Mail: jim@miracleautopainting.com
Web Site: www.miracleautopainting.com
Mr. Jim Jordan, Vice President

MIRACLE is a production collision repair and refinishing company that specializes in complete paint jobs. MIRACLE caters to individual vehicle owners, insurance carriers, other body shop facilities and new and used automobile dealers.

BACKGROUND:

Established: 1953;   1st Franchised: 1964
Franchised Units: 20
Company-Owned Units: 3
Total Units: 23
Dist.:   US-23; CAN-0; O'seas-0
  North America: 5 States, 0 Provinces
  Density: 1 in TX, 4 in OK, 16 in CA
Projected New Units (12 Months):   3
Qualifications: 5, 4, 4, 1, 1, 3

FINANCIAL/TERMS:

Cash Investment: $100-125K
Total Investment: $215-275K
Minimum Net Worth: $500K
Fees: Franchise - $35K
  Royalty - 5%;   Ad. - 5%
Earnings Claims Statement: No
Term of Contract (Years):   10/10
Avg. # Of Employees: 8 FT, 2 PT
Passive Ownership: Discouraged
Encourage Conversions: Yes
Area Develop. Agreements: Yes/5
Sub-Franchising Contracts: Yes
Expand In Territory: Yes
Space Needs: 7,500-10,000 SF

SUPPORT & TRAINING:

Financial Assistance Provided: Yes (I)
Site Selection Assistance: Yes
Lease Negotiation Assistance: Yes
Co-Operative Advertising: No
Franchisee Assoc./Member: Yes/Yes
Size Of Corporate Staff: 12
On-Going Support: ,,C,D,E,,G,H,
Training: 10 Days Headquarters; 10 Days
  On-Site

SPECIFIC EXPANSION PLANS:

US: West,Southwest
Canada: No
Overseas: Italy, Romania

≪ ≫

MISTER TRANSMISSION
(INTERNATIONAL)

9675 Yonge St., 2 Fl.
Richmond Hill, ON L4C 1V7 Canada
Tel: (800) 373-8432 (905) 884-1511
Fax: (905) 884-4727
E-Mail: info@mistertransmission.com
Web Site: www.MisterTransmission.com
Mr. Randy Moore, VP Operations

With over 30 years' experience, MISTER TRANSMISSION is the established name for transmission repair service in Canada. We make sales, training, advertising, a computer program, national fleet accounts, site selection and a warranty program available to all franchisees. MISTER TRANSMISSION is Canadian-owned.

BACKGROUND:

Established: 1963;   1st Franchised: 1969
Franchised Units: 85
Company-Owned Units: 0
Total Units: 85
Dist.:   US-0; CAN-85; O'seas-0
  North America: 0 States, 7 Provinces
  Density: 3 in QC, 63 in ON, 14 in BC
Projected New Units (12 Months):   3
Qualifications: 3, 3, 3, 2, 3, 4

FINANCIAL/TERMS:

Cash Investment: $60-80K
Total Investment: $120K-150K
Minimum Net Worth: $300K
Fees: Franchise - $25K
  Royalty - 7%;   Ad. - Varies
Earnings Claims Statement: No
Term of Contract (Years):   10/10
Avg. # Of Employees: 5 FT, 0 PT
Passive Ownership: Discouraged
Encourage Conversions: Yes
Area Develop. Agreements: No
Sub-Franchising Contracts: No
Expand In Territory: No
Space Needs: 2,800 SF

SUPPORT & TRAINING:

Financial Assistance Provided: No
Site Selection Assistance: Yes
Lease Negotiation Assistance: Yes
Co-Operative Advertising: No
Franchisee Assoc./Member: Yes/Yes
Size Of Corporate Staff: 12
On-Going Support: ,,C,D,E,,G,H,I
Training: 1 Week Head Office

SPECIFIC EXPANSION PLANS:

US:	No
Canada:	All Canada
Overseas:	NR

◄◄ ►►

MR. TRANSMISSION

4444 W. 147th St.
Midlothian, IL 60445
Tel: (800) 581-8468 (708) 389-5922
Fax: (708) 389-9882
E-Mail: vgarcia@moranindustries.com
Web Site: www.moranindustries.com
Ms. Viginia Garcia, Franchise Development Manager

It takes experience to build a good reputation and to be considered a pro. Mr. Transmission has been repairing transmissions for fifty years. We work hard to keep our reputation by offering honest professional service and a written nationwide warranty. The three important sources of business for our franchisees are retail sales, fleet accounts, and wholesale accounts.

BACKGROUND: IFA MEMBER

Established: 1956;	1st Franchised: 1956
Franchised Units:	120
Company-Owned Units:	0
Total Units:	120
Dist.:	US-120; CAN-0; O'seas-0
North America:	20 States, 0 Provinces
Density:	18 in TX, 21 in GA, 13 in IL
Projected New Units (12 Months):	5
Qualifications:	5, 3, 2, 3, 2, 3

FINANCIAL/TERMS:

Cash Investment:	$70K
Total Investment:	$142K-179K
Minimum Net Worth:	$250K
Fees: Franchise -	$30K
Royalty - 7%;	Ad. - $100/Mo.
Earnings Claims Statement:	Yes
Term of Contract (Years):	20/20
Avg. # Of Employees:	4-5 FT, 0 PT
Passive Ownership:	Discouraged
Encourage Conversions:	Yes
Area Develop. Agreements:	Yes/5
Sub-Franchising Contracts:	No
Expand In Territory:	Yes
Space Needs:	4,500 SF

SUPPORT & TRAINING:

Financial Assistance Provided:	Yes (I)
Site Selection Assistance:	Yes
Lease Negotiation Assistance:	Yes
Co-Operative Advertising:	Yes
Franchisee Assoc./Member:	Yes/Yes
Size Of Corporate Staff:	25
On-Going Support:	,,C,D,E,,G,H,I

Training: 2 Weeks Midlothian, IL

SPECIFIC EXPANSION PLANS:

US:	All US except HI, ND, RI, SD, WI
Canada:	No
Overseas:	NR

◄◄ ►►

NOVUS GLASS

12800 Hwy., 13 S., # 500
Savage, MN 55378
Tel: (800) 944-6811 (952) 946-0447
Fax: (922) 946-0481
E-Mail: michaelv@novusglass.com
Web Site: www.novusglass.com
Mr. Michael Vogel, Director Franchise Development

NOVUS invented windshield repair.

BACKGROUND: IFA MEMBER

Established: 1972;	1st Franchised: 1985
Franchised Units:	2200
Company-Owned Units:	6
Total Units:	2206
Dist.:	US-540; CAN-46; O'seas-1620
North America:	50 States, 8 Provinces
Density:	48 in WA
Projected New Units (12 Months):	8
Qualifications:	4, 3, 1, 3, 3, 5

FINANCIAL/TERMS:

Cash Investment:	$6.5-115.5K
Total Investment:	$38.1-115.5K
Minimum Net Worth:	$50K
Fees: Franchise -	$7.5K
Royalty - 5-8%;	Ad. - 2% of WS. R volume
Earnings Claims Statement:	No
Term of Contract (Years):	10/each 10
Avg. # Of Employees:	FT, 1-3 PT
Passive Ownership:	Allowed
Encourage Conversions:	Yes
Area Develop. Agreements:	Yes
Sub-Franchising Contracts:	No
Expand In Territory:	Yes
Space Needs:	1,000+ SF

SUPPORT & TRAINING:

Financial Assistance Provided:	Yes (I)
Site Selection Assistance:	Yes
Lease Negotiation Assistance:	No
Co-Operative Advertising:	Yes
Franchisee Assoc./Member:	Yes/No
Size Of Corporate Staff:	35
On-Going Support:	A,,C,D,E,,G,H,I

Training: 10 Days Replacement at Regional Training Center; 5.5 Days Windshield Repair Minneapolis

SPECIFIC EXPANSION PLANS:

US:	All United States
Canada:	All Canada
Overseas:	All Countries

◄◄ ►►

OIL BUTLER INTERNATIONAL

1599 Rte. 22 W.
Union, NJ 07083
Tel: (888) 428-8537 (908) 687-3283
Fax: (908) 687-7617
E-Mail: info@oilbutlerinternational.com
Web Site: www.oilbutlerinternational.com
Mr. Pete Rosin, VP Franchise Development

OIL BUTLER INTERNATIONAL is a mobile oil-change service and windshield repair franchise combining two money-making opportunities in one. Our uniquely designed vehicle provides the corporate image and service your customers will expect from the leader in the field of on-site service. Low-investment, low-overhead, complete training and on-going support.

BACKGROUND:

Established: 1987;	1st Franchised: 1991
Franchised Units:	149
Company-Owned Units:	1
Total Units:	150
Dist.:	US-134; CAN-4; O'seas-12
North America:	22 States, 0 Provinces
Density:	21 in TX, 8 in CO, 14 in CA
Projected New Units (12 Months):	100
Qualifications:	3, 3, 2, 2, 5, 5

FINANCIAL/TERMS:

Cash Investment:	$8-15K
Total Investment:	$9-18K
Minimum Net Worth:	NR
Fees: Franchise -	$4-7K
Royalty - 7%;	Ad. - 2%
Earnings Claims Statement:	No
Term of Contract (Years):	10/5
Avg. # Of Employees:	1 FT, 0 PT
Passive Ownership:	Discouraged
Encourage Conversions:	NA
Area Develop. Agreements:	Yes/1
Sub-Franchising Contracts:	No
Expand In Territory:	Yes
Space Needs:	NR

SUPPORT & TRAINING:

Financial Assistance Provided:	Yes (D)
Site Selection Assistance:	Yes
Lease Negotiation Assistance:	NA
Co-Operative Advertising:	No
Franchisee Assoc./Member:	No
Size Of Corporate Staff:	9
On-Going Support:	,B,C,D,,F,G,H,

Training: 4 Days to 2 Weeks Union, NJ

SPECIFIC EXPANSION PLANS:

US: All United States
Canada: All Canada
Overseas: All Countries

⋖ ⋗

The One You Can Trust.℠

**OIL CAN HENRY'S
INTERNATIONAL**
1200 Naito Pkwy., N.W., # 690
Portland, OR 97209
Tel: (800) 765-6244 (503) 243-6311
Fax: (503) 228-5227
E-Mail: georges@oilcanhenry.com
Web Site: www.oilcanhenry.com
Mr. George Steinfurth, VP Franchise
Development

Automotive lubrication and filter specialist. We work hard, blending the best of
yesterday with the best of today to provide
unbeatable service. The distinctive design
of our crew uniforms and service centers
evoke memories of days past when the
neighbor service station provided friendly,
quality service. While our centers may
remind you of yesteryear, our focus is on
the future. Our technicians are well-trained
to provide a wide variety of valuable maintenance and safety services.

BACKGROUND: IFA MEMBER
Established: 1978; 1st Franchised: 1989
Franchised Units: 70
Company-Owned Units: 12
Total Units: 82
Dist.: US-82; CAN-0; O'seas-0
North America: 9 States, 0 Provinces
Density: 19 in WA, 41 in OR, 11 in CA
Projected New Units (12 Months): 15
Qualifications: 5, 4, 3, 3, 4, 5
FINANCIAL/TERMS:
Cash Investment: $150-250K
Total Investment: $816-1259K
Minimum Net Worth: $500K
Fees: Franchise - $25K
Royalty - 5.5%; Ad. - 1%
Earnings Claims Statement: No
Term of Contract (Years): 15/5+
Avg. # Of Employees: 4-6 FT, 5-9 PT
Passive Ownership: Not Allowed
Encourage Conversions: Yes
Area Develop. Agreements: Yes/1
Sub-Franchising Contracts: No

Expand In Territory: Yes
Space Needs: 15,000 SF
SUPPORT & TRAINING:
Financial Assistance Provided: Yes (I)
Site Selection Assistance: Yes
Lease Negotiation Assistance: Yes
Co-Operative Advertising: Yes
Franchisee Assoc./Member: No
Size Of Corporate Staff: 15
On-Going Support: A,B,C,D,E,F,G,H,I
Training: NA Ongoing; 2 Weeks On-Site;
5 Weeks Portland, OR
SPECIFIC EXPANSION PLANS:
US: WA,OR,CA,AZ,NV,ID,MN,CO
Canada: No
Overseas: NR

⋖ ⋗

PAYLESS CAR RENTAL SYSTEM
2350 34th St., N.
St. Petersburg, FL 33713
Tel: (800) 729-5255 + 148 (727) 321-6352
Fax: (727) 322-6540
E-Mail: franchise@paylesscarrental.com
Web Site: www.paylesscarrental.com
Ms. Kathleen Gassner, Dir. of Franchise
Development

PAYLESS CAR RENTAL SYSTEM, Inc.,
has been a recognized name in the car
rental industry for almost 30 years. Car
rental expertise and an experienced corporate office staff give each franchisee individual assistance and the competitive edge.
We offer the tools to become successful in
the vehicle rental and sales business.

BACKGROUND: IFA MEMBER
Established: 1971; 1st Franchised: 1971
Franchised Units: 103
Company-Owned Units: 5
Total Units: 108
Dist.: US-57; CAN-0; O'seas-51
North America: 15 States, 0 Provinces
Density: 10 in FL, 8 in CA, 5 in AK
Projected New Units (12 Months): 15
Qualifications: 5, 4, 1, 2, 3, 5
FINANCIAL/TERMS:
Cash Investment: $300K+
Total Investment: $260K-6.5MM+
Minimum Net Worth: $500K-$1MM
Fees: Franchise - $20-500K
Royalty - 4-5%; Ad. - 1-3%
Earnings Claims Statement: No
Term of Contract (Years): 5/5

Avg. # Of Employees: Varies
Passive Ownership: Discouraged
Encourage Conversions: Yes
Area Develop. Agreements: Yes/4
Sub-Franchising Contracts: Yes
Expand In Territory: Yes
Space Needs: Varies
SUPPORT & TRAINING:
Financial Assistance Provided: No
Site Selection Assistance: No
Lease Negotiation Assistance: No
Co-Operative Advertising: No
Franchisee Assoc./Member: Yes/Yes
Size Of Corporate Staff: 50
On-Going Support: A,B,C,D,E,,G,h,I
Training: 3-5 Days Franchisee's Location;
3-5 Days Corporate Office
SPECIFIC EXPANSION PLANS:
US: All United States
Canada: All Canada
Overseas: All Countries

⋖ ⋗

POP-A-LOCK
1018 Harding St., # 101
Lafayette, LA 70503-2400
Tel: (877) 233-6211 (337) 233-6211 + 233
Fax: (337) 233-6655
E-Mail: michaelkleimeyer@systemforwa
rd.com
Web Site: www.popalock.com/franchis-
ing.php
Mr. Michael Kleimeyer, Director of Fran-
chise Development

POP-A-LOCK is America's largest lock-
smith, car door unlocking, and roadside
assistance service. We provide fast, professional, guaranteed service using our proprietary tools and opening techniques. We
offer an outstanding community service
through our industry.

BACKGROUND: IFA MEMBER
Established: 1991; 1st Franchised: 1994
Franchised Units: 182
Company-Owned Units: 0
Total Units: 182
Dist.: US-182; CAN-0; O'seas-0
North America: 40 States, 0 Provinces
Density: 22 in TX, 14 in LA, 17 in FL
Projected New Units (12 Months): 38

Qualifications: 4, 5, 1, 3, 3, 4
FINANCIAL/TERMS:
Cash Investment: $30-120K
Total Investment: $100-350K
Minimum Net Worth: $250-400K
Fees: Franchise - $29K+$66/1000 of population
  Royalty - 6%; Ad. - 1%
Earnings Claims Statement: No
Term of Contract (Years): 10/10
Avg. # Of Employees: 2 FT, 2 PT
Passive Ownership: Allowed
Encourage Conversions: NA
Area Develop. Agreements: No
Sub-Franchising Contracts: No
Expand In Territory: Yes
Space Needs: NA
SUPPORT & TRAINING:
Financial Assistance Provided: Yes (I)
Site Selection Assistance: NA
Lease Negotiation Assistance: NA
Co-Operative Advertising: No
Franchisee Assoc./Member: Yes/Yes
Size Of Corporate Staff: 11
On-Going Support: A,b,C,D,e,F,G,h,I
Training: 10 Days + Additional Local
  Lafayette, LA
SPECIFIC EXPANSION PLANS:
US: All United States
Canada: Toronto/GTA
Overseas: Ireland, UK, China

◄◄ ►►

PRACTICAL RENT A CAR
4780 I-55 N., # 300
Jackson, MS 39211
Tel: (800) 424-7722 (601) 713-4333
Fax: (601) 713-4330
E-Mail:
Web Site:
Mr. Jay Mitchell, National Sales Director

Recruit, train and develop operators in the car rental industry as independently owned operations. National insurance program by A+ rated company, automated and voice reservation systems. Centralized purchasing, on-going support, newsletters and training.

BACKGROUND:
Established: 1989; 1st Franchised: 1989
Franchised Units: 134
Company-Owned Units: 0
Total Units: 134
Dist.: US-134; CAN-0; O'seas-0
  North America: 34 States, Provinces
  Density: 10 in OK, 14 in PA, 20 in WA
Projected New Units (12 Months): 100

Qualifications: 5, 3, 2, 3, 4, 5
FINANCIAL/TERMS:
Cash Investment: $10-25K
Total Investment: $25-100K
Minimum Net Worth: $100K
Fees: Franchise - $2.5-100K
  Royalty - Flat/Car; Ad. - 0%
Earnings Claims Statement: No
Term of Contract (Years): 10/10
Avg. # Of Employees: 2 FT, 1 PT
Passive Ownership: Discouraged
Encourage Conversions: Yes
Area Develop. Agreements: No
Sub-Franchising Contracts: No
Expand In Territory: Yes
Space Needs: 1,000 SF
SUPPORT & TRAINING:
Financial Assistance Provided: Yes (D)
Site Selection Assistance: Yes
Lease Negotiation Assistance: Yes
Co-Operative Advertising: No
Franchisee Assoc./Member: Yes/Yes
Size Of Corporate Staff: 8
On-Going Support: a,B,C,d,E,,G,H,I
Training: 4.5 Days Headquarters
SPECIFIC EXPANSION PLANS:
US: All United States
Canada: No
Overseas: All Countries

◄◄ ►►

PRECISION TUNE
AUTO CARE CENTER
748 Miller Dr., S.E.
Leesburg, VA 20175
Tel: (800) 438-8863 (703) 669-2311
Fax: (703) 669-1539
E-Mail: lee.oppenheim@precisionac.com
Web Site: www.precisiontune.com
Mr. Lee Oppenheim, VP Franchise Development

PRECISION TUNE AUTO CARE is America's largest engine performance car care company, specializing in tune-up, quick oil and lube and brake services. Our work is backed by certified technicians and a nationwide warranty. We are your one stop shop for all your auto care needs. We offer a variety of automotive services to fit your cars needs, including services for air conditioning, brake systems, fuel injection, air induction systems, cooling systems, fluid maintenance, tune-ups, as well as other scheduled maintenance services. We provide quality support in site selection, training, marketing, operations, management, business profitability and much more.

BACKGROUND: IFA MEMBER
Established: 1975; 1st Franchised: 1976
Franchised Units: 401
Company-Owned Units: 1
Total Units: 407
Dist.: US-286; CAN-2; O'seas-106
  North America: 29 States, 1 Provinces
  Density: 32 in NC, 32 in GA, 33 in CA
Projected New Units (12 Months): 25
Qualifications: 4, 5, 2, 2, 3, 5
FINANCIAL/TERMS:
Cash Investment: $75-100K
Total Investment: $123-208K
Minimum Net Worth: $150K
Fees: Franchise - $10-25K
  Royalty - 6-7.5%; Ad. - 1.5%
Earnings Claims Statement: Yes
Term of Contract (Years): 10/5
Avg. # Of Employees: 6 FT, 1-2 PT
Passive Ownership: Discouraged
Encourage Conversions: Yes
Area Develop. Agreements: Yes/10
Sub-Franchising Contracts: Yes
Expand In Territory: Yes
Space Needs: 3,000 SF
SUPPORT & TRAINING:
Financial Assistance Provided: Yes (I)
Site Selection Assistance: Yes
Lease Negotiation Assistance: No
Co-Operative Advertising: Yes
Franchisee Assoc./Member: Yes/Yes
Size Of Corporate Staff: 26
On-Going Support: A,B,C,D,E,F,G,H,I
Training: 2 Weeks Leesburg, VA
SPECIFIC EXPANSION PLANS:
US: All United States, except Hawaii
Canada: All Canada
Overseas: All Countries

◄◄ ►►

RENT-A-WRECK (CANADA)
204-7710 Fifth St., S.E.
Calgary, AB T2H 2L9 Canada
Tel: (800) 668-8591 (403) 259-6666
Fax: (403) 259-6776
E-Mail: info@rentawreck.ca
Web Site: www.rent-a-wreck.ca
Ms. Colleen Pickard, Franchise Development Coordinator

Our success is based upon teaching our franchisees how to achieve their professional goals. Our reputation is based upon providing the lowest car and truck rental rates across Canada.

BACKGROUND:
Established: 1976; 1st Franchised: 1977

Franchised Units: 50
Company-Owned Units: 0
Total Units: 50
Dist.: US-0; CAN-50; O'seas-0
  North America: 0 States, 0 Provinces
  Density: 8 in NL, 16 in BC, 11 in AB
Projected New Units (12 Months): 21
Qualifications: 5, 5, 3, 3, 5, 5
FINANCIAL/TERMS:
Cash Investment: $75K+
Total Investment: $80K-200K
Minimum Net Worth: $75K
Fees: Franchise - $15K-30K
  Royalty - 6%; Ad. - 4%
Earnings Claims Statement: No
Term of Contract (Years): 5/5
Avg. # Of Employees: 3 FT, 2 PT
Passive Ownership: Discouraged
Encourage Conversions: Yes
Area Develop. Agreements: No
Sub-Franchising Contracts: No
Expand In Territory: Yes
Space Needs: 1,000 SF
SUPPORT & TRAINING:
Financial Assistance Provided: Yes (D)
Site Selection Assistance: Yes
Lease Negotiation Assistance: Yes
Co-Operative Advertising: No
Franchisee Assoc./Member: Yes/Yes
Size Of Corporate Staff: 9
On-Going Support: ,,C,D,E,F,G,H,I
Training: 2 Weeks Calgary, AB
SPECIFIC EXPANSION PLANS:
US: No
Canada: All Canada
Overseas: NR

◄◄ ►►

RENT-A-WRECK OF AMERICA
105 Main St.
Laurel, MD 20707
Tel: (240) 581-1359
Fax: (240) 581-1395
E-Mail: dtripp@rent-a-wreck.com
Web Site: www.rent-a-wreck.com
Mr. Dale Tripp, Sales Manager

America's # 1 neighborhood car rental company, RENT-A-WRECK has attained the highest ratings in the franchising industry. For 5 successive years, Entrepreneur Magazine rated RENT-A-WRECK # 1 in its category for the prestigious Franchise 500 awards. The annual Success Magazine named RENT-A-WRECK 'one of the best-managed franchises in America.' Success surveyed over 2,800 franchise companies in all industries and ranked RENT-A-WRECK 4th.

BACKGROUND: IFA MEMBER
Established: 1968; 1st Franchised: 1973
Franchised Units: 195
Company-Owned Units: 0
Total Units: 231
Dist.: US-195; CAN-0; O'seas-36
  North America: 49 States, 0 Provinces
  Density: 34 in NY, 31 in NJ, 33 in CA
Projected New Units (12 Months): 12
Qualifications: 5, 5, 2, 3, 3, 3
FINANCIAL/TERMS:
Cash Investment: $50K
Total Investment: $100-362K
Minimum Net Worth: $250K
Fees: Franchise - $15K
  Royalty - $30/Car; Ad. - $7/Car
Earnings Claims Statement: Yes
Term of Contract (Years): 5/5
Avg. # Of Employees: 2 FT, 1 PT
Passive Ownership: Discouraged
Encourage Conversions: No
Area Develop. Agreements: Yes
Sub-Franchising Contracts: No
Expand In Territory: Yes
Space Needs: 1,500 SF
SUPPORT & TRAINING:
Financial Assistance Provided: No
Site Selection Assistance: No
Lease Negotiation Assistance: No
Co-Operative Advertising: Yes
Franchisee Assoc./Member: Yes/Yes
Size Of Corporate Staff: 12
On-Going Support: ,,C,D,e,,G,h,
Training: 1 Week Laurel, MD
SPECIFIC EXPANSION PLANS:
US: All United States
Canada: No
Overseas: All Countries

◄◄ ►►

SENSIBLE CAR RENTAL
96 Freneau Ave., # 2
Matawan, NJ 07747
Tel: (800) 367-5159 (732) 583-8500
Fax: (732) 290-8305
E-Mail: corporate@sensiblecarrental.com
Web Site: www.sensiblecarrental.com
Mr. Charles A. Vitale, VP/General Manager

We offer a rental car program which provides training, insurance and support. Majority of franchisee are used car dealers and other automotive related businesspersons.

BACKGROUND:
Established: 1986; 1st Franchised: 1986

Franchised Units: 140
Company-Owned Units: 0
Total Units: 140
Dist.: US-140; CAN-0; O'seas-0
  North America: 22 States, Provinces
  Density: 10 in MA, 24 in NJ, 25 in NY
Projected New Units (12 Months): 25
Qualifications: 2, 3, 4, 2, 2, 5
FINANCIAL/TERMS:
Cash Investment: $20-25K
Total Investment: $46.4-69.5K
Minimum Net Worth: Varies
Fees: Franchise - $6-10K
  Royalty - $10-15/Car; Ad. - 0%
Earnings Claims Statement: No
Term of Contract (Years): Perpetual
Avg. # Of Employees: 1 FT, 1 PT
Passive Ownership: Not Allowed
Encourage Conversions: NA
Area Develop. Agreements: No
Sub-Franchising Contracts: No
Expand In Territory: Yes
Space Needs: NR
SUPPORT & TRAINING:
Financial Assistance Provided: Yes (D)
Site Selection Assistance: No
Lease Negotiation Assistance: No
Co-Operative Advertising: No
Franchisee Assoc./Member: Yes/Yes
Size Of Corporate Staff: 10
On-Going Support: ,,C,d,,F,G,H,I
Training: 2 Days Matawan, NJ
SPECIFIC EXPANSION PLANS:
US: All United States
Canada: No
Overseas: NR

◄◄ ►►

SHINE FACTORY
121 Ilsley Ave., # PP
Dartmouth, NS B3B 1S4 Canada
Tel: (800) 747-8118 (902) 405-3171
Fax: (902) 405-3484
E-Mail: sfactory@eastlink.ca
Web Site: shinepro.com
Mr. Gary H. Wright, National Sales Manager

A solid, proven program to put entrepreneurs into the automotive protection and detail business.

BACKGROUND:
Established: 1981; 1st Franchised: 1981
Franchised Units: 16
Company-Owned Units: 0
Total Units: 16
Dist.: US-0; CAN-16; O'seas-0
  North America: 0 States, 6 Provinces

Density: 12 in NS, 4 in BC, 12 in AB
Projected New Units (12 Months): 3-4
Qualifications: 4, 4, 3, 3, 3, 5

FINANCIAL/TERMS:

Cash Investment: $100K
Total Investment: $50K
Minimum Net Worth: $60K
Fees: Franchise - $12.5K
  Royalty - 8%; Ad. - 5%
Earnings Claims Statement: No
Term of Contract (Years): 5/5
Avg. # Of Employees: 3 FT, 2 PT
Passive Ownership: Discouraged
Encourage Conversions: Yes
Area Develop. Agreements: Yes/1
Sub-Franchising Contracts: Yes
Expand In Territory: Yes
Space Needs: 4,000 SF

SUPPORT & TRAINING:

Financial Assistance Provided: No
Site Selection Assistance: Yes
Lease Negotiation Assistance: Yes
Co-Operative Advertising: No
Franchisee Assoc./Member: No
Size Of Corporate Staff: 4
On-Going Support: ,,C,D,E,F,,H,I
Training: 2 Weeks Training Center; 2
  Weeks On-Site

SPECIFIC EXPANSION PLANS:

US: No
Canada: All Canada
Overseas: NR

‹‹ ››

**SPEEDEE OIL CHANGE &
TUNE-UP**
1300 Arlington Heights Rd.
Itasca, IL 60143
Tel: (800) 621-0144 + 3075 (630) 438-3000
Fax: (630) 438-3700
E-Mail: jcooper@midas.com
Web Site: www.speedeeoil.com
Mr. Jerry Cooper, N. American Franchise
  Recruitment Mgr.

SPEEDEE offers preventive auto maintenance services, specializing in a 17-point quick oil change, diagnostic tune-up and brake services. Also offered: fuel system cleanings, a/c services, radiator flushes, emission/smog checks andtransmission/ differential services. No appointment necessary. Performed while you wait. Suc-

cessful franchisees are enthusiastic, have a strong commitment to customer service and people management skills. Retail experience preferred.

BACKGROUND:
Established: 1980; 1st Franchised: 1982
Franchised Units: 112
Company-Owned Units: 4
Total Units: 116
Dist.: US-111; CAN-0; O'seas-59
  North America: 15 States, 0 Provinces
  Density: 10 in MA, 22 in LA, 50 in CA
Projected New Units (12 Months): 14
Qualifications: 5, 5, 3, 3, 3, 4

FINANCIAL/TERMS:
Cash Investment: $100-150K
Total Investment: $186-765.5K
Minimum Net Worth: $250K
Fees: Franchise - $30K
  Royalty - 6%; Ad. - 8%
Earnings Claims Statement: No
Term of Contract (Years): 15/5/5/
Avg. # Of Employees: 5 FT, 2 PT
Passive Ownership: Discouraged
Encourage Conversions: Yes
Area Develop. Agreements: Yes
Sub-Franchising Contracts: No
Expand In Territory: Yes
Space Needs: 2,800 SF

SUPPORT & TRAINING:
Financial Assistance Provided: No
Site Selection Assistance: Yes
Lease Negotiation Assistance: Yes
Co-Operative Advertising: Yes
Franchisee Assoc./Member: No
Size Of Corporate Staff: 16
On-Going Support: ,,C,D,E,,G,H,
Training: 1 Week Local Office; 3-Day
  Orientation Headquarters; 2 Weeks
  Shop

SPECIFIC EXPANSION PLANS:
US: All United States
Canada: All Canada
Overseas: All Countries

‹‹ ››

**SPEEDY TRANSMISSION
CENTERS**
74 N.E. Fourth Ave., # 1
Delray Beach, FL 33483
Tel: (800) 336-0310 (561) 274-0445
Fax: (561) 274-6456
E-Mail: speedytrans@mindspring.com
Web Site: www.speedytransmission.com
Mr. Dan Hinson, Franchise Sales

Centers repair, rebuild and recondition automatic and standard transmissions.

Other drive train repair services also available. Training, marketing and operational assistance. Warranties are honored throughout the U.S. and Canada.

BACKGROUND: IFA MEMBER
Established: 1974; 1st Franchised: 1974
Franchised Units: 30
Company-Owned Units: 0
Total Units: 30
Dist.: US-30; CAN-0; O'seas-0
  North America: 6 States, 0 Provinces
  Density: 7 in GA, 18 in FL, 2 in CA
Projected New Units (12 Months): 8
Qualifications: 3, 3, 2, 4, 4, 3

FINANCIAL/TERMS:
Cash Investment: $40K
Total Investment: $80-100K
Minimum Net Worth: NR
Fees: Franchise - $19.5K
  Royalty - 7%; Ad. - $100/Mo.
Earnings Claims Statement: No
Term of Contract (Years): 20/10
Avg. # Of Employees: 4 FT, 1 PT
Passive Ownership: Discouraged
Encourage Conversions: Yes
Area Develop. Agreements: Yes/1
Sub-Franchising Contracts: Yes
Expand In Territory: Yes
Space Needs: 2,400 SF

SUPPORT & TRAINING:
Financial Assistance Provided: Yes (D)
Site Selection Assistance: Yes
Lease Negotiation Assistance: Yes
Co-Operative Advertising: No
Franchisee Assoc./Member: Yes/Yes
Size Of Corporate Staff: 4
On-Going Support: ,,C,D,E,F,G,H,I
Training: 2 Weeks Home Office; 1 Week
  On-Site

SPECIFIC EXPANSION PLANS:
US: Southeast, Northeast
Canada: No
Overseas: Latin America

‹‹ ››

SPOT-NOT CAR WASHES
P. O. Box 1269
Joplin, MO 64802
Tel: (800) 682-7629 (417) 781-6233
Fax: (417) 781-3906
E-Mail: doug@spot-not.com
Web Site: www.spot-not.com
Mr. Doug Myers, Executive Vice President

High-pressure spray brushless automatic car wash, complemented by full-featured, self-service wash bays. Each facility offers canopied, lighted vacuum areas. An all cash business with few employees.

BACKGROUND: IFA MEMBER
Established: 1968;   1st Franchised: 1985
Franchised Units: 36
Company-Owned Units: 0
Total Units: 36
Dist.:   US-36; CAN-0; O'seas-0
   North America: 6 States, Provinces
   Density: 10 in AR, 10 in IL, 8 in IN
Projected New Units (12 Months):   3
Qualifications: NR
FINANCIAL/TERMS:
Cash Investment: $300K
Total Investment: $622K-1.1MM
Minimum Net Worth: NR
Fees: Franchise - $25K
   Royalty - 5%;   Ad. - 1%
Earnings Claims Statement: No
Term of Contract (Years):   10/5/5/
Avg. # Of Employees: 2 FT, 3 PT
Passive Ownership: Discouraged
Encourage Conversions: Yes
Area Develop. Agreements: Yes/1
Sub-Franchising Contracts: No
Expand In Territory: Yes
Space Needs: 40,000 SF
SUPPORT & TRAINING:
Financial Assistance Provided: Yes (D)
Site Selection Assistance: Yes
Lease Negotiation Assistance: Yes
Co-Operative Advertising: No
Franchisee Assoc./Member: No
Size Of Corporate Staff: 18
On-Going Support: „C,D,E,F,G,H,I
Training: 3 Sessions -- 17 Days Joplin,
   MO and OJT Site
SPECIFIC EXPANSION PLANS:
US: Midwest, South and Southwest
Canada: No
Overseas: NR

≪ ≫

SUPERGLASS WINDSHIELD REPAIR

6101 Chancellor Dr., # 200
Orlando, FL 32809
Tel: (888) 771-2700 (407) 240-1920
Fax: (407) 240-3266
E-Mail: david@superglass.net
Web Site: www.sgwr.com
Mr. David A. Casey, President

SUPERGLASS WINDSHIELD REPAIR is the largest repair-only franchisor in the United States, with locations in 43 states. Two weeks of training, including one week in Orlando and one week in the franchisee's exclusive territory, are provided along

with all equipment, uniforms, manuals, printing and bookkeeping systems.

BACKGROUND:
Established: 1992;   1st Franchised: 1993
Franchised Units: 223
Company-Owned Units: 0
Total Units: 223
Dist.:   US-209; CAN-1; O'seas-13
   North America: 43 States, 1 Provinces
   Density: 14 in GA, 13 in FL, 11 in CO
Projected New Units (12 Months):   25
Qualifications: 2, 4, 1, 2, 3, 4
FINANCIAL/TERMS:
Cash Investment: $9.5-11.5K
Total Investment: $9.5-28.5K
Minimum Net Worth: $15K
Fees: Franchise - $5.4K
   Royalty - 3%;   Ad. - 1%/$20 Min.
Earnings Claims Statement: No
Term of Contract (Years):   10/10
Avg. # Of Employees: 2 FT, 0 PT
Passive Ownership: Discouraged
Encourage Conversions: Yes
Area Develop. Agreements: Yes/1
Sub-Franchising Contracts: No
Expand In Territory: Yes
Space Needs: NA
SUPPORT & TRAINING:
Financial Assistance Provided: Yes (D)
Site Selection Assistance: NA
Lease Negotiation Assistance: Yes
Co-Operative Advertising: No
Franchisee Assoc./Member: No
Size Of Corporate Staff: 6
On-Going Support: a,B,C,D,E,F,G,H,I
Training: 5 Days Orlando, FL; 5 Days
   Exclusive Franchisee Territory;
SPECIFIC EXPANSION PLANS:
US: All United States
Canada: All Canada
Overseas: Portugal, Mexico, Brazil

≪ ≫

THRIFTY CAR RENTAL

5310 E. 31st St.
Tulsa, OK 74135
Tel: (800) 532-3401 (918) 669-2219
Fax: (918) 669-2061
E-Mail: franchisesales@thrifty.com
Web Site: www.thrifty.com
Mr. Trey Russell, Director

THRIFTY operates in over 57 countries and territories, with over 1,000 locations

throughout North and South America, Europe, the Middle East, Caribbean, Asia and the Pacific, and is one of the fastest-growing car rental company in Canada and Australia. THRIFTY has a significant presence both in the airport and local car rental markets. Approximately 66% of its business is in the airport market, 34% in the local market.

BACKGROUND:
Established: 1958;   1st Franchised: 1962
Franchised Units: 849
Company-Owned Units: 151
Total Units: 1000
Dist.:   US-374; CAN-135; O'seas-491
   North America: 46 States, 10 Provinces
   Density: 34 in CA, 37 in FL, 59 in ON
Projected New Units (12 Months):   50-75
Qualifications: 5, 5, 5, 3, 3, 5
FINANCIAL/TERMS:
Cash Investment: $150K
Total Investment: $200-250K
Minimum Net Worth: $500K
Fees: Franchise -   Varies
   Royalty - 3%;   Ad. - 2.5-5%
Earnings Claims Statement: No
Term of Contract (Years):   10/5
Avg. # Of Employees: 4-6 FT, 0 PT
Passive Ownership: Not Allowed
Encourage Conversions: Yes
Area Develop. Agreements: No
Sub-Franchising Contracts: No
Expand In Territory: Yes
Space Needs: Varies
SUPPORT & TRAINING:
Financial Assistance Provided: No
Site Selection Assistance: No
Lease Negotiation Assistance: Yes
Co-Operative Advertising: No
Franchisee Assoc./Member: No
Size Of Corporate Staff: 1000
On-Going Support: A,B,C,D,E,F,G,H,I
Training: 5 Days Mentor Program at
   Headquarters in Tulsa, OK
SPECIFIC EXPANSION PLANS:
US: Selected Markets Remaining
Canada: All Canada
Overseas: All Countries

≪ ≫

TILDEN CAR CARE CENTERS

300 Hempstead Tpke., # 110
W. Hempstead, NY 11552

Tel: (800) 845-3367 (516) 746-7911
Fax: (516) 746-1288
E-Mail: jbaskind@tildencarcare.com
Web Site: www.tildencarcare.com
Mr. Jason Baskind, Dir. Franchise Development

We're not just brakes. The total care concept allows you to offer a full menu of automotive services for maximum customer procurement - rather than a limited niche market. You benefit from a management team whose concept system and training were proven and perfected before we even considered offering franchises.

BACKGROUND:
Established: 1923; 1st Franchised: 1996
Franchised Units: 60
Company-Owned Units: 0
Total Units: 60
Dist.:   US-60; CAN-0; O'seas-0
  North America: 13 States, Provinces
  Density: 24 in FL, 5 in GA, 15 in NY
Projected New Units (12 Months):   10
Qualifications: 3, 4, 3, 3, 3, 4
FINANCIAL/TERMS:
Cash Investment: $50-60K
Total Investment: $131-171.5K
Minimum Net Worth: $150K
Fees: Franchise - $25K
  Royalty - 6%/$350/Wk.;   Ad.
- 3%/$175/Wk.
Earnings Claims Statement: No
Term of Contract (Years):   20/20/20
Avg. # Of Employees: 2 FT, 2 PT
Passive Ownership: Discouraged
Encourage Conversions: Yes
Area Develop. Agreements: Yes/1
Sub-Franchising Contracts: No
Expand In Territory: Yes
Space Needs: 3,500+ SF
SUPPORT & TRAINING:
Financial Assistance Provided: Yes (D)
Site Selection Assistance: Yes
Lease Negotiation Assistance: Yes
Co-Operative Advertising: No
Franchisee Assoc./Member: Yes/Yes
Size Of Corporate Staff: 6
On-Going Support: A,B,C,D,E,F,G,H,I
Training: 2 Weeks Home Office
SPECIFIC EXPANSION PLANS:
US: All United States
Canada: All Canada
Overseas: NR

≪ ≫

TUFFY AUTO SERVICE CENTERS
7150 Granite Cir.
Toledo, OH 43617

Tel: (800) 228-8339 (419) 865-6900
Fax: (419) 865-7343
E-Mail: jacobs@tuffy.com
Web Site: www.tuffy.com
Mr. Jim Jacobs, Director of Franchising

TUFFY AUTO SERVICE CENTERS have been ranked by Success and Entrepreneur Magazines as one of the top franchises in the country. We are an upscale automotive repair franchise specializing in brakes, exhaust, shocks, alignments, air conditioning, batteries, starting and charging, lube-oil-filter, and more. We provide initial and on-going operations, technical and marketing support. Excellent sites being developed in IN, IA, WI, VA, FL, OH, ND, SD, NE, IL, NC, SC, GA, and TN.

BACKGROUND: IFA MEMBER
Established: 1970; 1st Franchised: 1971
Franchised Units: 256
Company-Owned Units: 10
Total Units: 266
Dist.:   US-266; CAN-0; O'seas-0
  North America: 18 States, 0 Provinces
  Density: 63 in OH, 67 in MI, 46 in FL
Projected New Units (12 Months):   20
Qualifications: 4, 4, 2, 2, 2, 4
FINANCIAL/TERMS:
Cash Investment: $80-125K
Total Investment: $209-317K
Minimum Net Worth: $300K
Fees: Franchise - $25K
  Royalty - 5%;   Ad. - 5%
Earnings Claims Statement: Yes
Term of Contract (Years):   15/10
Avg. # Of Employees: 4 FT, 1 PT
Passive Ownership: Discouraged
Encourage Conversions: Yes
Area Develop. Agreements: Yes
Sub-Franchising Contracts: Yes
Expand In Territory: Yes
Space Needs: Min. 3,800 SF
SUPPORT & TRAINING:
Financial Assistance Provided: Yes (I)
Site Selection Assistance: Yes
Lease Negotiation Assistance: Yes
Co-Operative Advertising: Yes
Franchisee Assoc./Member: Yes/Yes
Size Of Corporate Staff: 47
On-Going Support: ,,C,D,E,,G,H,I
Training: 2-3 Weeks On-Site at Franchise;
  3-4 Weeks Toledo, OH
SPECIFIC EXPANSION PLANS:
US: Southwest, North Central U.S., FL
Canada: No
Overseas: NR

≪ ≫

**TUNEX AUTOMOTIVE
SPECIALISTS**
12608 S. 125 West
Draper, UT 84020
Tel: (800) 448-8639 (801) 486-8133
Fax: (801) 484-4740
E-Mail: info@tunex.com
Web Site: www.tunex.com
Mr. Scott Mower, Franchise Sales

We offer diagnostic, engine performance, tune-up services and repairs of engine related systems, i.e. ignition, carburetion, fuel injection, emission controls, computer controls, cooling, air conditioning, emission inspections, used-car evaluations, and lubrication services. For maximum customer satisfaction, we always analyze systems for the problem and maintenance requirements, so the customer can make service and repair decisions.

BACKGROUND: IFA MEMBER
Established: 1974; 1st Franchised: 1975
Franchised Units: 30
Company-Owned Units: 2
Total Units: 32
Dist.:   US-31; CAN-0; O'seas-1
  North America: 6 States, 0 Provinces
  Density: 16 in UT, 4 in CO, 1 in AZ
Projected New Units (12 Months):   4
Qualifications: 4, 3, 2, 3, 2, 5
FINANCIAL/TERMS:
Cash Investment: $50-60K
Total Investment: $122.5-163.1K
Minimum Net Worth: $200K
Fees: Franchise - $19K
  Royalty - 5%;   Ad. - $600/Mo.
Earnings Claims Statement: No
Term of Contract (Years):   10/10
Avg. # Of Employees: 4 FT, 0 PT
Passive Ownership: Discouraged
Encourage Conversions: NA
Area Develop. Agreements: Yes/1
Sub-Franchising Contracts: Yes
Expand In Territory: No
Space Needs: 2,750 SF
SUPPORT & TRAINING:
Financial Assistance Provided: Yes (D)
Site Selection Assistance: Yes
Lease Negotiation Assistance: Yes
Co-Operative Advertising: No
Franchisee Assoc./Member: No
Size Of Corporate Staff: 5

On-Going Support: „C,D,E„G,H,I
Training:1 Week Corporate Headquarters;
   On-Site 1 Week
SPECIFIC EXPANSION PLANS:
US: Inter-Mountain, Southwest
Canada: Master Franchise
Overseas: NR

⊰⊰ ⊱⊱

U-SAVE AUTO RENTAL OF AMERICA, INC.

4780 I-55 N., # 300
Jackson, MS 39211
Tel: (800) 438-2300 (601) 713-4333
Fax: (601) 982-9850
E-Mail: info@usave.com
Web Site: www.usave.com
Mr. Robert M. Barton, EVP

U-SAVE has over 194 locations through-out the country and is one of the nation's largest franchise car rental companies. Having primarily serviced the local market for the past 30 years, current expansion plans call for the opening of airport loca-tions in the top 30 markets across the country. U-Save now services 33 airport markets in 14 different states, in addition to 11 international airport locations.

BACKGROUND: IFA MEMBER
Established: 1979;   1st Franchised: 1979
Franchised Units: 194
Company-Owned Units: 0
Total Units: 194
Dist.:   US-174; CAN-5; O'seas-15
  North America: 33 States, 1 Provinces
  Density: 10 in MS, 12 in OH, 16 in SC
Projected New Units (12 Months):   NR
Qualifications: 5, 4, 3, 2, 1, 3
FINANCIAL/TERMS:
Cash Investment: $60-100K
Total Investment: $60-681.3K
Minimum Net Worth: $300K
Fees: Franchise - $20K+
  Royalty - 3-6%;   Ad. - 1-2%
Earnings Claims Statement: No
Term of Contract (Years):   10/10
Avg. # Of Employees: 2 FT, 2 PT
Passive Ownership: Discouraged
Encourage Conversions: Yes
Area Develop. Agreements: Yes
Sub-Franchising Contracts: Yes
Expand In Territory: Yes

Space Needs: 1,500-2,000 SF
SUPPORT & TRAINING:
Financial Assistance Provided: Yes (I)
Site Selection Assistance: No
Lease Negotiation Assistance: No
Co-Operative Advertising: Yes
Franchisee Assoc./Member: Yes/Yes
Size Of Corporate Staff: 50
On-Going Support: a,,C,D,E,f,G,h,
Training: 5 Days Jackson, MS
SPECIFIC EXPANSION PLANS:
US: All United States
Canada: All Canada
Overseas: All Countries

⊰⊰ ⊱⊱

VALVOLINE INSTANT OIL CHANGE

3499 Blazer Pkwy.
Lexington, KY 40509
Tel: (800) 622-6846 (859) 357-7214
Fax: (859) 357-7049
E-Mail: jjtaylor@ashland.com
Web Site: www.viocfranchise.com
Ms. Josie Taylor, Installed Sales Analyst

Offers licenses for the establishment and operation of a business which provides a quick oil change, chassis lubrication and routine maintenance checks on automo-biles. The licensor and/or its affiliates will offer (to qualified prospects) leasing programs for equipment, signage, POS systems and mortgage based financing for land, building.

BACKGROUND:
Established: 1988;   1st Franchised: 1988
Franchised Units: 468
Company-Owned Units: 302
Total Units: 770
Dist.:   US-770; CAN-0; O'seas-0
  North America: 41 States, Provinces
  Density: 57 in MI, 67 in MN, 84 in OH
Projected New Units (12 Months):   45
Qualifications: 5, 4, 2, 3, 5, 5
FINANCIAL/TERMS:
Cash Investment: $400K
Total Investment: $121K-1.3MM
Minimum Net Worth: $600K
Fees: Franchise - $30K
  Royalty - 6%;   Ad. - 2%
Earnings Claims Statement: Yes

Term of Contract (Years):   15/5/5/
Avg. # Of Employees: 4 FT, 2 PT
Passive Ownership: Allowed
Encourage Conversions: Yes
Area Develop. Agreements: No
Sub-Franchising Contracts: No
Expand In Territory: Yes
Space Needs: 15,000 SF
SUPPORT & TRAINING:
Financial Assistance Provided: Yes (D)
Site Selection Assistance: Yes
Lease Negotiation Assistance: Yes
Co-Operative Advertising: No
Franchisee Assoc./Member: No
Size Of Corporate Staff: 84
On-Going Support: A,B,C,D,E,F,G,h,I
Training: 3+ Weeks
  Classroom/OJT/On-Site Training
SPECIFIC EXPANSION PLANS:
US: All United States
Canada: No
Overseas: NR

⊰⊰ ⊱⊱

VICTORY LANE QUICK OIL CHANGE

405 Little Lake Dr.
Ann Arbor, MI 48103
Tel: (734) 996-1196
Fax: (734) 996-4912
E-Mail: customerservice@victorylane.net
Web Site: www.victorylane.net
Mr. Earl W. Farr, Director of Franchising

VICTORY LANE QUICK OIL CHANGE is a low-overhead, high-profit, drive-thru, quick oil change operation. We also perform transmission flush, fuel injec-tion cleaning, serpentine belts, radiator flush and other high-profit services. Most franchisees are multi-shop owners.

BACKGROUND: IFA MEMBER
Established: 1980;   1st Franchised: 1986
Franchised Units: 34
Company-Owned Units: 6
Total Units: 40
Dist.:   US-40; CAN-0; O'seas-0
  North America: 6 States, 0 Provinces
  Density: 21 in OH, 21 in MI, 21 in IN
Projected New Units (12 Months):   10
Qualifications: 3, 2, 1, 1, 1, 5
FINANCIAL/TERMS:
Cash Investment: $40-80K
Total Investment: $80K
Minimum Net Worth: $80K
Fees: Franchise - $20K
  Royalty - 6%;   Ad. - 1%
Earnings Claims Statement: No

ZIEBART INTERNATIONAL
1290 E. Maple Rd.
Troy, MI 48007-1290
Tel: (800) 877-1312 (248) 588-4100
Fax: (248) 588-0718
E-Mail: cdobyns@ziebart.com
Web Site: www.ziebart.com
Mr. Charlie Dobyns, Dir. Franchise Sales

Business format consists of automobile detailing, accessories and protection services. Ultra-modern showrooms maximize the exposure for the services offered by the franchisee. The customer base consists of retail, wholesale and fleet - making ZIEBART # 1 in the world.

BACKGROUND: IFA MEMBER
Established: 1959; 1st Franchised: 1962
Franchised Units: 360
Company-Owned Units: <u>20</u>
Total Units: 380
Dist.: US-150; CAN-50; O'seas-200
  North America: 39 States, 7 Provinces
  Density: in MI, in IN, in IL
Projected New Units (12 Months): 20
Qualifications: 5, 4, 2, 3, 4, 5
FINANCIAL/TERMS:

Term of Contract (Years):	20/20
Avg. # Of Employees:	5 FT, 0 PT
Passive Ownership:	Allowed
Encourage Conversions:	Yes
Area Develop. Agreements:	Yes/1
Sub-Franchising Contracts:	No
Expand In Territory:	Yes
Space Needs:	1,500 SF
SUPPORT & TRAINING:	
Financial Assistance Provided:	Yes (I)
Site Selection Assistance:	Yes
Lease Negotiation Assistance:	Yes
Co-Operative Advertising:	Yes
Franchisee Assoc./Member:	No
Size Of Corporate Staff:	12
On-Going Support:	,B,C,D,E,F,G,H,
Training:	2 Week Corporate Office
SPECIFIC EXPANSION PLANS:	
US:	Midwest
Canada:	No
Overseas:	NR

Cash Investment:	$60K
Total Investment:	$100-161K
Minimum Net Worth:	$200K
Fees: Franchise -	$25K
Royalty - 12.5%;	Ad. - 7.5%
Earnings Claims Statement:	No
Term of Contract (Years):	10/10
Avg. # Of Employees:	2 FT, 3 PT
Passive Ownership:	Discouraged
Encourage Conversions:	Yes
Area Develop. Agreements:	Yes/1
Sub-Franchising Contracts:	No
Expand In Territory:	Yes
Space Needs:	3,000 SF
SUPPORT & TRAINING:	
Financial Assistance Provided:	Yes (I)
Site Selection Assistance:	Yes
Lease Negotiation Assistance:	Yes
Co-Operative Advertising:	Yes
Franchisee Assoc./Member:	Yes/Yes
Size Of Corporate Staff:	100
On-Going Support:	a,B,C,D,E,F,G,h,I
Training:	3-6 Weeks Training at Home Office
SPECIFIC EXPANSION PLANS:	
US:	All United States
Canada:	All Canada
Overseas:	All Countries

FIVE LARGEST PARTICIPANTS IN SURVEY						
Company	# Fran-chised Units	# Co-Owned Units	# Total Units	Franchise Fee	On-Going Royalty	Total Investment
1. Dunkin' Donuts	7,200	0	7,200	$40-80K	5.9%	$240K-1.67MM
2. Auntie Anne's Hand-Rolled Soft Pretzels	929	10	939	$30K	7%	$198-441K
3. Cinnabon	749	0	749	$30K	6%	$192.2-317K
4. Panera Bread Company	356	184	540	$35K	5%	$550-650K
5. Mrs. Fields Cookies	300	300	300	$30K	6%	$179.1-251.1K

All of the data provided are proprietary and should not be quoted without acknowledging *Bond's Franchise Guide*.

ATLANTA BREAD COMPANY
1955 Lake Park Dr., #400
Smyrna, GA 30080
Tel: (800) 398-3728 (770) 432-0933
Fax: (770) 444-9082
E-Mail: bomarra@atlantabread.com
Web Site: www.atlantabread.com
Mr. Barbara O'Marra, Executive Assistant

Let's make some bread together! The concept behind the ATLANTA BREAD COMPANY BAKERY CAFE is simple: an upscale neighborhood caf serving soups, salads, sandwiches, breads and pastries. ATLANTA BREAD COMPANY is riding the crest of the hottest food concept around - and we've experienced over 450% growth in just 12 months. ABC provides a full spectrum of support, from training to real estate assistance. Franchise offer made by offering circular only.

BACKGROUND: IFA MEMBER
Established: 1993;   1st Franchised: 1995
Franchised Units: 167
Company-Owned Units: 2
Total Units: 169
Dist.:   US-169; CAN-0; O'seas-0
  North America: 23 States, 0 Provinces
  Density: SC, NC, GA
Projected New Units (12 Months):   60
Qualifications: 5, 3, 3, 3, 4, 4
FINANCIAL/TERMS:
Cash Investment: $400K

Total Investment: $650K-1MM
Minimum Net Worth: $1MM
Fees: Franchise - $40K
  Royalty - 5%;   Ad. - 2%
Earnings Claims Statement: No
Term of Contract (Years):   10/10
Avg. # Of Employees: 34 FT, 0 PT
Passive Ownership: Discouraged
Encourage Conversions: NA
Area Develop. Agreements: Yes/1
Sub-Franchising Contracts: No
Expand In Territory: Yes
Space Needs: 4,000-4,500 SF
SUPPORT & TRAINING:
Financial Assistance Provided: Yes (D)
Site Selection Assistance: Yes
Lease Negotiation Assistance: Yes

Co-Operative Advertising: No
Franchisee Assoc./Member: No
Size Of Corporate Staff: 34
On-Going Support: ,B,C,D,E,F,,H,I
Training: 7 Weeks Atlanta, GA

SPECIFIC EXPANSION PLANS:
US: All United States
Canada: No
Overseas: NR

≪≪ ≫≫

PRETZEL PERFECT

AUNTIE ANNE'S
HAND-ROLLED SOFT PRETZELS

48-50 W. Chestnut St., # 200
Lancaster, PA 17603
Tel: (717) 442-4766
Fax: (717) 442-4139
E-Mail: lindae@auntieannesinc.com
Web Site: www.auntieannes.com
Ms. Linda Engels, Franchise Support Rep.

Auntie Anne's, Inc. is a franchise organization with a commitment to exceeding our customers' expectations. We've built our company on the quality of our products and strong support for our franchisees, nurturing relationships for the long-term growth of the franchise system. That approach continues to drive our growth. We provide our customers with pretzels, dips, and drinks which are mixed, twisted, and baked to a golden brown in full view of our customers. Each and every one of our pretzels comes with the Pretzel Perfect Guarantee - we guarantee you'll love your pretzel or we'll replace it with one that you do.

BACKGROUND: IFA MEMBER
Established: 1988; 1st Franchised: 1989
Franchised Units: 929
Company-Owned Units: 10
Total Units: 939
Dist.: US-744; CAN-0; O'seas-195
North America: 43 States, 0 Provinces
Density: 50 in NY, 60 in CA, 78 in PA
Projected New Units (12 Months): 50
Qualifications: 4, 2, 2, 2, 3, 5
FINANCIAL/TERMS:
Cash Investment: $198-441K
Total Investment: $198-441K
Minimum Net Worth: $400K
Fees: Franchise - $30K

Royalty - 7%; Ad. - 1%
Earnings Claims Statement: Yes
Term of Contract (Years): 20/Variable
Avg. # Of Employees: 4 FT, 4 PT
Passive Ownership: Allowed
Encourage Conversions: NA
Area Develop. Agreements: No
Sub-Franchising Contracts: No
Expand In Territory: No
Space Needs: 400-600 SF
SUPPORT & TRAINING:
Financial Assistance Provided: Yes (I)
Site Selection Assistance: Yes
Lease Negotiation Assistance: Yes
Co-Operative Advertising: Yes
Franchisee Assoc./Member: Yes/Yes
Size Of Corporate Staff: 150
On-Going Support: ,,C,D,E,,G,H,I
Training: 3 Weeks Gap, PA
SPECIFIC EXPANSION PLANS:
US: All United States
Canada: Yes
Overseas: All Countries

≪≪ ≫≫

BIG APPLE BAGELS

500 Lake Cook Rd., # 475
Deerfield, IL 60015
Tel: (800) 251-6101 (847) 948-7520
Fax: (847) 948-7521
E-Mail: tcervini@babcorp.com
Web Site: www.babcorp.com
Mr. Anthony S. Cervini, Director of Development

Bakery-cafe featuring three brands, fresh-from-scratch Big Apple Bagels and My Favorite Muffin, and freshly roasted Brewster's specialty coffee. Our product offering covers many day parts with a delicious assortment of made-to-order gourmet sandwiches, salads, soups, espresso beverages, and fruit smoothies. Franchisees can develop beyond their stores with corporate catering and gift basket opportunities, as well as wholesaling opportunities within their market area.

BACKGROUND: IFA MEMBER
Established: 1992; 1st Franchised: 1993
Franchised Units: 136
Company-Owned Units: 1

Total Units: 137
Dist.: US-136; CAN-0; O'seas-1
North America: 21 States, 0 Provinces
Density: 19 in WI, 37 in MI, 8 in IL
Projected New Units (12 Months): 10
Qualifications: 3, 4, 3, 3, 3, 5
FINANCIAL/TERMS:
Cash Investment: $60K
Total Investment: $204.8-342.5K
Minimum Net Worth: $250K
Fees: Franchise - $25K
Royalty - 5%; Ad. - 1%
Earnings Claims Statement: No
Term of Contract (Years): 10/10
Avg. # Of Employees: 3 FT, 11 PT
Passive Ownership: Allowed
Encourage Conversions: Yes
Area Develop. Agreements: Yes/1
Sub-Franchising Contracts: No
Expand In Territory: Yes
Space Needs: 1,600-1,900 SF
SUPPORT & TRAINING:
Financial Assistance Provided: No
Site Selection Assistance: Yes
Lease Negotiation Assistance: Yes
Co-Operative Advertising: No
Franchisee Assoc./Member: No
Size Of Corporate Staff: 20
On-Going Support: ,,C,D,E,F,G,H,I
Training: 2 Weeks Milwaukee, WI
SPECIFIC EXPANSION PLANS:
US: All United States
Canada: All Canada
Overseas: All Countries

≪≪ ≫≫

BLUE CHIP COOKIES

157 Barnwood Dr.
Edgewood, KY 41017
Tel: (800) 888-9866 (859) 331-7600
Fax: (859) 331-7604
E-Mail: bluechip@fuse.net
Web Site: www.bluechipcookies.com
Mr. Mark D. Hannahan, President/CEO

BLUE CHIP COOKIES brings pleasure to our customers by making the world's best gourmet cookies and brownies, fresh from scratch, everyday, at every one of our retail locations. We have won numerous awards, and our wonderful cookies and brownies continue to bring joy to young and old alike!

BACKGROUND:
Established: 1983; 1st Franchised: 1986
Franchised Units: 10
Company-Owned Units: 10
Total Units: 20

Dist.:	US-20; CAN-0; O'seas-0
North America:	7 States, 0 Provinces
Density:	5 in OH, 2 in NJ, 5 in CA
Projected New Units (12 Months):	4
Qualifications:	5, 4, 4, 3, 1, 5

FINANCIAL/TERMS:

Cash Investment:	$50-100K
Total Investment:	$120-200K
Minimum Net Worth:	$200K
Fees: Franchise -	$19.5K
Royalty - NR;	Ad. - NR
Earnings Claims Statement:	No
Term of Contract (Years):	10/10
Avg. # Of Employees:	2-3 FT, 4-8 PT
Passive Ownership:	Allowed
Encourage Conversions:	Yes
Area Develop. Agreements:	No
Sub-Franchising Contracts:	No
Expand In Territory:	Yes
Space Needs:	600+ SF

SUPPORT & TRAINING:

Financial Assistance Provided:	No
Site Selection Assistance:	Yes
Lease Negotiation Assistance:	Yes
Co-Operative Advertising:	No
Franchisee Assoc./Member:	No
Size Of Corporate Staff:	6
On-Going Support:	,,C,D,E,,G,H,I
Training:	1-2 Weeks Cincinnati, OH

SPECIFIC EXPANSION PLANS:

US:	All United States
Canada:	No
Overseas:	NR

◄◄ ►►

BREADSMITH

409 E. Silver Spring Dr.
Whitefish Bay, WI 53217
Tel: (888) BREADS-1 (414) 962-1965
Fax: (414) 962-5888
E-Mail: lynn@breadsmith.com
Web Site: www.breadsmith.com
Ms. Lynn Pavlic, Support Specialist

Award-winning, European, hearth-bread bakery, featuring fresh-from-scratch crusty breads, scones, muffins, gourmet jams and oils. Open kitchen concept reveals a six-ton, stone hearth oven imported from Europe used to bake the hand-crafted loaves each morning. BREADSMITH has been ranked by Bon Appetit, Best in 11 cities across the country.

BACKGROUND: IFA MEMBER

Established: 1993;	1st Franchised: 1994
Franchised Units:	35
Company-Owned Units:	1
Total Units:	36

Dist.:	US-36; CAN-0; O'seas-0
North America:	10 States, 0 Provinces
Density:	10 in MI, 7 in IL
Projected New Units (12 Months):	5
Qualifications:	4, 4, 2, 4, 4, 5

FINANCIAL/TERMS:

Cash Investment:	$100-250K
Total Investment:	$200-400K
Minimum Net Worth:	$500K
Fees: Franchise -	$30K
Royalty - 7/6/5%;	Ad. - 0%
Earnings Claims Statement:	Yes
Term of Contract (Years):	15/15
Avg. # Of Employees:	6 FT, 12 PT
Passive Ownership:	Not Allowed
Encourage Conversions:	NA
Area Develop. Agreements:	Yes/1
Sub-Franchising Contracts:	No
Expand In Territory:	Yes
Space Needs:	1,800 SF

SUPPORT & TRAINING:

Financial Assistance Provided:	Yes (D)
Site Selection Assistance:	Yes
Lease Negotiation Assistance:	Yes
Co-Operative Advertising:	No
Franchisee Assoc./Member:	Yes/Yes
Size Of Corporate Staff:	10
On-Going Support:	,,C,D,E,F,G,H,I
Training:	4 Weeks Corporate Store; 1 Week Franchisee Store

SPECIFIC EXPANSION PLANS:

US:	All United States
Canada:	All Canada
Overseas:	NR

◄◄ ►►

BRUEGGER'S

159 Bank St.
Burlington, VT 05401
Tel: (866) 660-4104 (802) 660-4020
Fax: (802) 660-4034
E-Mail: franchise@brueggers.com
Web Site: www.brueggers.com
Mr. Holly Ryan, Franchise Development Assistant

Our mission is to be the dominant, first choice, neighborhood bagel bakery in all markets where we operate.

BACKGROUND: IFA MEMBER

Established: 1983;	1st Franchised: 1993
Franchised Units:	103
Company-Owned Units:	155

Total Units:	258
Dist.:	US-258; CAN-0; O'seas-0
North America:	18 States, 0 Provinces
Density:	25 in OH, 35 in NY, 29 in MA
Projected New Units (12 Months):	25
Qualifications:	4, 3, 5, 1, 4, 5

FINANCIAL/TERMS:

Cash Investment:	$100K
Total Investment:	$330.4K-559.4K
Minimum Net Worth:	$400K
Fees: Franchise -	$25K
Royalty - 5%;	Ad. - 2-4%
Earnings Claims Statement:	Yes
Term of Contract (Years):	10/5
Avg. # Of Employees:	FT, 0 PT
Passive Ownership:	Not Allowed
Encourage Conversions:	Yes
Area Develop. Agreements:	Yes/1
Sub-Franchising Contracts:	No
Expand In Territory:	Yes
Space Needs:	1,500-2,200 SF

SUPPORT & TRAINING:

Financial Assistance Provided:	No
Site Selection Assistance:	Yes
Lease Negotiation Assistance:	No
Co-Operative Advertising:	No
Franchisee Assoc./Member:	No
Size Of Corporate Staff:	20
On-Going Support:	a,b,C,D,E,f,G,H,
Training:	NR

SPECIFIC EXPANSION PLANS:

US:	All United States
Canada:	No
Overseas:	NR

◄◄ ►►

CINDY'S CINNAMON ROLLS

P. O. Box 1480
Fallbrook, CA 92028
Tel: (800) 468-7655 (760) 723-1121
Fax: (760) 723-4143
E-Mail: cindyscin@aol.com
Web Site: http://www.worldfranchising.com
Mr. Thomas Harris, President

Fresh-baked cinnamon rolls and muffins. All shops in major shopping malls. Great family business. All products made in the shop and baked fresh all day.

BACKGROUND:

Established: 1985;	1st Franchised: 1986
Franchised Units:	32
Company-Owned Units:	0
Total Units:	32
Dist.:	US-29; CAN-0; O'seas-3
North America:	14 States, 0 Provinces
Density:	8 in NY, 2 in NJ, 3 in CA

Projected New Units (12 Months): 5
Qualifications: 3, 3, 3, 3, 3, 3
FINANCIAL/TERMS:
Cash Investment: $130K
Total Investment: $130K
Minimum Net Worth: $100K
Fees: Franchise - $25K
 Royalty - 5%; Ad. - 0%
Earnings Claims Statement: No
Term of Contract (Years): 10/10
Avg. # Of Employees: 8 FT, 0 PT
Passive Ownership: Allowed
Encourage Conversions: Yes
Area Develop. Agreements: No
Sub-Franchising Contracts: No
Expand In Territory: Yes
Space Needs: 800 SF
SUPPORT & TRAINING:
Financial Assistance Provided: No
Site Selection Assistance: Yes
Lease Negotiation Assistance: Yes
Co-Operative Advertising: No
Franchisee Assoc./Member: No
Size Of Corporate Staff: 3
On-Going Support: ,B,C,D,E,F,G,H,I
Training: 1 Week New York, NY; 4 Days
 Store
SPECIFIC EXPANSION PLANS:
US: All United States
Canada: All Canada
Overseas: All Countries

◄◄ ►►

CINNABON
200 Glenridge Pt. Pkwy., # 200
Atlanta, GA 30342
Tel: (800) 227-8353 (404) 255-3250
Fax: (404) 255-4978
E-Mail: spando@focusbrands.com
Web Site: www.cinnabon.com
Mr. D'wayne Tanner, VP Franchise Sales/
 Develop.

Maker of the world's most famous cinnamon rolls, Cinnabon serves fresh, aromatic, oven-hot cinnamon rolls, as well as a variety of other baked goods and specialty beverages. Cinnabon currently operates more than 600 franchised locations worldwide, primarily in high traffic venues such as shopping malls, airports, train stations, travel plazas, entertainment venues, academic institutions and military bases.

BACKGROUND: IFA MEMBER
Established: 1985; 1st Franchised: 1986
Franchised Units: 749
Company-Owned Units: 0
Total Units: 749
Dist.: US-749; CAN-26; O'seas-277
 North America: 44 States, 2 Provinces
 Density: 48 in TX, 43 in FL, 129 in CA
Projected New Units (12 Months): 10
Qualifications: 5, 5, 5, 4, 4, 5
FINANCIAL/TERMS:
Cash Investment: $100K
Total Investment: $192.2K-317K
Minimum Net Worth: $300K
Fees: Franchise - $30K
 Royalty - 6%; Ad. - 1.5%
Earnings Claims Statement: Yes
Term of Contract (Years): 20/20
Avg. # Of Employees: 6 FT, 0 PT
Passive Ownership: Not Allowed
Encourage Conversions: Yes
Area Develop. Agreements: Yes/1
Sub-Franchising Contracts: No
Expand In Territory: Yes
Space Needs: 850 SF
SUPPORT & TRAINING:
Financial Assistance Provided: NR
Site Selection Assistance: Yes
Lease Negotiation Assistance: Yes
Co-Operative Advertising: Yes
Franchisee Assoc./Member: Yes/Yes
Size Of Corporate Staff: 52
On-Going Support: ,,,,E,,G,,
Training: 2 Weeks CRT Location
SPECIFIC EXPANSION PLANS:
US: LA, NY, AL, MS, AR, MO
Canada: Yes
Overseas: All Countries

◄◄ ►►

COFFEE TIME DONUTS
77 Progress Ave.
Toronto, ON M1P 2Y7 Canada
Tel: (416) 288-8515
Fax: (416) 288-8895
E-Mail: cioannou@coffeetime.ca
Web Site: www.coffeetime.ca
Mr. Chris Loannou, Director of Franchising

A quick-service restaurant-type donut chain, with great-tasting coffee, muffins, donuts, salads and sandwiches. Fresh, quality products are what set us apart from the competition.

BACKGROUND:
Established: 1982; 1st Franchised: 1986
Franchised Units: 205

Company-Owned Units: 21
Total Units: 226
Dist.: US-0; CAN-226; O'seas-0
 North America: 0 States, 3 Provinces
 Density: 319 in ON, 3 in MB, 1 in AB
Projected New Units (12 Months): 65
Qualifications: 3, 3, 2, 2, 3, 5
FINANCIAL/TERMS:
Cash Investment: NR
Total Investment: $100-360K
Minimum Net Worth: $150K
Fees: Franchise - NR
 Royalty - 4.5%; Ad. - 2%
Earnings Claims Statement: No
Term of Contract (Years): NR/
Avg. # Of Employees: 6 FT, 4 PT
Passive Ownership: Not Allowed
Encourage Conversions: Yes
Area Develop. Agreements: No
Sub-Franchising Contracts: No
Expand In Territory: Yes
Space Needs: NR
SUPPORT & TRAINING:
Financial Assistance Provided: No
Site Selection Assistance: No
Lease Negotiation Assistance: NA
Co-Operative Advertising: No
Franchisee Assoc./Member: No
Size Of Corporate Staff: 50
On-Going Support: ,b,C,D,E,F,G,H,
Training: 3-6 Weeks Scarborough, ON
SPECIFIC EXPANSION PLANS:
US: All United States
Canada: All Canada
Overseas: All Countries

◄◄ ►►

COOKIES BY DESIGN
1865 Summit Ave., # 605
Plano, TX 75074-8147
Tel: (800) 945-2665 (972) 398-9536
Fax: (972) 398-9542
E-Mail: frandevelopment@mgwmail.com
Web Site: www.cookiesbydesign.com/
 index.cfm
Mr. David Patterson, CFO

Unique retail opportunity! Gift bakery, specializing in hand-decorated cookie arrangements and gourmet cookies, decorated for special events, holidays, centerpieces, etc. Clientele include both individual and corporate customers. A wonderfully delicious alternative to flowers or balloons.

BACKGROUND: IFA MEMBER
Established: 1983; 1st Franchised: 1987
Franchised Units: 220
Company-Owned Units: 1
Total Units: 221
Dist.: US-221; CAN-0; O'seas-0
 North America: 42 States, 0 Provinces
 Density: 28 in TX, 21 in FL, 23 in CA
Projected New Units (12 Months): 10
Qualifications: 3, 5, 4, 4, 4, 5
FINANCIAL/TERMS:
Cash Investment: $90-180K
Total Investment: $90-180K
Minimum Net Worth: NR
Fees: Franchise - $25K
 Royalty - 6%; Ad. - 1.5%
Earnings Claims Statement: No
Term of Contract (Years): 5/5
Avg. # Of Employees: 3 FT, 2 PT
Passive Ownership: Discouraged
Encourage Conversions: No
Area Develop. Agreements: Yes/1
Sub-Franchising Contracts: No
Expand In Territory: Yes
Space Needs: 1,200-1,500 SF
SUPPORT & TRAINING:
Financial Assistance Provided: No
Site Selection Assistance: Yes
Lease Negotiation Assistance: Yes
Co-Operative Advertising: Yes
Franchisee Assoc./Member: No
Size Of Corporate Staff: 25
On-Going Support: ,,C,D,E,,G,h,I
Training: 2 Weeks Dallas, TX
SPECIFIC EXPANSION PLANS:
US: All United States
Canada: No
Overseas: NR

≪ ≫

COOKIES IN BLOOM
12700 Hillcrest Rd., # 251
Dallas, TX 75230
Tel: (800) 222-3104 (972) 490-8644
Fax: (972) 490-8646
E-Mail: cibinc@swbell.net
Web Site: www.cookiesinbloom.com
Mr. Robert E. Pinac, Vice President

Exciting retail opportunity featuring cookie gift baking shop, offering hand-decorated cookies, cookie arrangements and gourmet cookies for all holidays and special occasions. We specialize in birthday, baby, thank you, get well and anniversary arrangements for both individual and corporate customers. Instead of flowers,

think COOKIES IN BLOOM.

BACKGROUND:
Established: 1988; 1st Franchised: 1992
Franchised Units: 20
Company-Owned Units: 0
Total Units: 20
Dist.: US-20; CAN-0; O'seas-0
 North America: 14 States, Provinces
 Density: 2 in CA, 2 in FL, 8 in TX
Projected New Units (12 Months): 4
Qualifications: 4, 4, 1, 3, 3, 4
FINANCIAL/TERMS:
Cash Investment: $75-116K
Total Investment: $75-116K
Minimum Net Worth: $100K
Fees: Franchise - $19.5K
 Royalty - 5%; Ad. - 2%
Earnings Claims Statement: No
Term of Contract (Years): 5/5
Avg. # Of Employees: 3 FT, 2 PT
Passive Ownership: Discouraged
Encourage Conversions: No
Area Develop. Agreements: Yes/1
Sub-Franchising Contracts: No
Expand In Territory: Yes
Space Needs: 1,000-1,500 SF
SUPPORT & TRAINING:
Financial Assistance Provided: No
Site Selection Assistance: Yes
Lease Negotiation Assistance: Yes
Co-Operative Advertising: No
Franchisee Assoc./Member: Yes/Yes
Size Of Corporate Staff: 2
On-Going Support: ,b,C,D,E,,G,H,I
Training: 2 Weeks Phoenix, AZ
SPECIFIC EXPANSION PLANS:
US: All United States
Canada: All Canada
Overseas: UK, Australia, New Zealand,
 Mexico

≪ ≫

DUNKIN' DONUTS
130 Royall St.
Canton, MA 02021
Tel: (877) 938-6546
Fax:
E-Mail: pam.gore@dunkinbrands.com
Web Site: www.dunkinfranchising.com
Ms. Pam Gore, Director of Franchising

Founded in 1950, today Dunkin' Donuts is the number one retailer of coffee-by-the-

cup in America, selling 2.7 million cups a day, nearly one billion cups a year. Dunkin' Donuts is also the largest coffee and baked goods chain in the world and sells more donuts, coffee and bagels than any other quick service restaurant in America. Dunkin' Donuts has more than 6,500 shops in 29 countries worldwide. Based in Canton, Massachusetts, Dunkin' Donuts is a subsidiary of Dunkin' Brands, Inc. For more information, visit www.DunkinDonuts.com.

BACKGROUND: IFA MEMBER
Established: 1950; 1st Franchised: 1955
Franchised Units: 7200
Company-Owned Units: 0
Total Units: 7200
Dist.: US-4736; CAN-78; O'seas-1856
 North America: 39 States, 5 Provinces
 Density:359 in NY, 490 in MA, 237 in IL
Projected New Units (12 Months): 350
Qualifications: 5, 4, 2, 2, 5, 4
FINANCIAL/TERMS:
Cash Investment: $750K
Total Investment: $240K-1.67MM
Minimum Net Worth: $1.5MM
Fees: Franchise - $40-80K
 Royalty - 5.9%; Ad. - 5%
Earnings Claims Statement: Yes
Term of Contract (Years): 20/
Avg. # Of Employees: FT, 0 PT
Passive Ownership: Allowed
Encourage Conversions: Yes
Area Develop. Agreements: Yes/1
Sub-Franchising Contracts: No
Expand In Territory: Yes
Space Needs: NR
SUPPORT & TRAINING:
Financial Assistance Provided: Yes (D)
Site Selection Assistance: NA
Lease Negotiation Assistance: Yes
Co-Operative Advertising: No
Franchisee Assoc./Member: Yes/Yes
Size Of Corporate Staff: NR
On-Going Support: ,B,C,,E,,G,H,I
Training: 51 Days Randolph, MA;
 3.5 Days Another Location
SPECIFIC EXPANSION PLANS:
US: All Regions
Canada: PQ, ON
Overseas: All Countries

≪ ≫

GREAT AMERICAN BAGEL, THE
519 N. Cass Ave., # 1W
Westmont, IL 60559
Tel: (888) 224-3563 (630) 963-3393
Fax: (630) 963-7799

E-Mail: greatambgl@aol.com
Web Site: www.greatamericanbagel.com
Mr. Chris Lettieri, President

Bagel bakery and restaurant, specializing in freshly made bagels - made daily from scratch on the store premises. Stores feature monthly specials along with 28 varieties of bagels daily. In addition, each store also prepares it's own fresh cream cheeses!

BACKGROUND:
Established: 1987; 1st Franchised: 1994
Franchised Units: 201
Company-Owned Units: 14
Total Units: 215
Dist.: US-215; CAN-0; O'seas-0
 North America: 10 States, 0 Provinces
 Density: 3 in WA, 2 in IN, 25 in IL
Projected New Units (12 Months): 20
Qualifications: 5, 3, 2, 3, 4, 5

FINANCIAL/TERMS:
Cash Investment: $60-80K
Total Investment: $230-280K
Minimum Net Worth: $250K
Fees: Franchise - $20K
 Royalty - 4%; Ad. - 2%
Earnings Claims Statement: No
Term of Contract (Years): 20/5
Avg. # Of Employees: 3 FT, 9 PT
Passive Ownership: Not Allowed
Encourage Conversions: NA
Area Develop. Agreements: No
Sub-Franchising Contracts: No
Expand In Territory: Yes
Space Needs: 2,000 SF

SUPPORT & TRAINING:
Financial Assistance Provided: No
Site Selection Assistance: Yes
Lease Negotiation Assistance: Yes
Co-Operative Advertising: No
Franchisee Assoc./Member: Yes/Yes
Size Of Corporate Staff: NR
On-Going Support: ,B,C,D,E,,g,h,
Training: 4 Weeks Western Springs, IL

SPECIFIC EXPANSION PLANS:
US: All United States
Canada: No
Overseas: NR

◄◄ ►►

GREAT AMERICAN COOKIES
1346 Oakbrook Dr., # 170
Norcross, GA 30093

Tel: (800) 343-5377 + 2399
Fax: (801) 736-5936
E-Mail: franchiseinfo@nexcenfm.com
Web Site: www.greatamericancookies.com
Mr. Marty Amschler, Dir. Intl. Development

'Share the Fun of Cookies.' Established cookie concept with a great old family recipe, attractive retail price point, unique cookie cake program, available in store formats for traditional and non-traditional venues.

BACKGROUND: IFA MEMBER
Established: 1977; 1st Franchised: 1977
Franchised Units: 299
Company-Owned Units: 0
Total Units: 299
Dist.: US-293; CAN-5; O'seas-6
 North America: 31 States, 3 Provinces
 Density: 22 in FL, 24 in GA, 76 in TX
Projected New Units (12 Months): 25
Qualifications: 5, 3, 1, 1, 3, 5

FINANCIAL/TERMS:
Cash Investment: $122-493K
Total Investment: $167K-296.5K
Minimum Net Worth: $75/250K LIQ
Fees: Franchise - $25K
 Royalty - 6%; Ad. - 1.5%
Earnings Claims Statement: No
Term of Contract (Years): W/ Lease/
Avg. # Of Employees: 3 FT, 2 PT
Passive Ownership: Discouraged
Encourage Conversions: Yes
Area Develop. Agreements: Yes
Sub-Franchising Contracts: No
Expand In Territory: Yes
Space Needs: 200-1,000 SF

SUPPORT & TRAINING:
Financial Assistance Provided: No
Site Selection Assistance: Yes
Lease Negotiation Assistance: Yes
Co-Operative Advertising: No
Franchisee Assoc./Member: Yes/Yes
Size Of Corporate Staff: 135
On-Going Support: ,,C,D,E,,G,H,I
Training: Atlanta, GA

SPECIFIC EXPANSION PLANS:
US: All United States
Canada: Yes
Overseas: NR

◄◄ ►►

GREAT CANADIAN BAGEL, THE
1290 Central Pkwy. W., # 100
Mississauga, ON L5C 4R3 Canada
Tel: (905) 566-1903
Fax: (905) 566-1402

E-Mail: edk@greatcanadianbagel.com
Web Site: www.greatcanadianbagel.com
Mr. Ed Kwiatkowski, President

Canada's largest chain devoted to bagels has elevated the bagel to a new culinary experience. The chain offers a healthy way to enjoy a sandwich, snack or meal, while providing an alternative to higher fat, fast-food establishments. The bagel has become the ideal convenience food of the 90's - low in fat, high in taste, nutritious and now, convenient, thanks to the expansion of THE GREAT CANADIAN BAGEL.

BACKGROUND:
Established: 1993; 1st Franchised: 1994
Franchised Units: 47
Company-Owned Units: 3
Total Units: 50
Dist.: US-0; CAN-50; O'seas-0
 North America: 0 States, 9 Provinces
 Density: 90 in ON, 24 in BC
Projected New Units (12 Months): 20
Qualifications: 5, 4, 3, 3, 2, 5

FINANCIAL/TERMS:
Cash Investment: $100K
Total Investment: $120K
Minimum Net Worth: $10K
Fees: Franchise - $20K
 Royalty - 6%; Ad. - 1.5%
Earnings Claims Statement: Yes
Term of Contract (Years): 10/5
Avg. # Of Employees: 7 FT, 5 PT
Passive Ownership: Discouraged
Encourage Conversions: No
Area Develop. Agreements: No
Sub-Franchising Contracts: Yes
Expand In Territory: Yes
Space Needs: 2,000 SF

SUPPORT & TRAINING:
Financial Assistance Provided: Yes (D)
Site Selection Assistance: Yes
Lease Negotiation Assistance: NA
Co-Operative Advertising: No
Franchisee Assoc./Member: Yes/Yes
Size Of Corporate Staff: 0
On-Going Support: A,B,C,D,E,F,G,h,
Training: 4-6 Weeks Toronto, ON

SPECIFIC EXPANSION PLANS:
US: See The Great American Bagel
Canada: All Canada
Overseas: All Countries

◄◄ ►►

GREAT HARVEST BREAD CO.

28 S. Montana St.
Dillon, MT 59725-2434
Tel: (800) 442-0424 + 252 (406) 683-6842 + 252
Fax: (406) 683-5537
E-Mail: dawne@greatharvest.com
Web Site: www.greatharvest.com
Ms. Dawn Eisenzimer, Dir. New Franchise Devel.

GREAT HARVEST BREAD CO. stores are neighborhood, retail bread bakeries, specializing in the best tasting, made-from-scratch, naturally fresh whole wheat breads you ever had. These unique stores also serve scratch-made cookies, scones, muffins, specialty breads, coffee and an inviting and fun environment for customers.

BACKGROUND:

Established: 1976;   1st Franchised: 1978
Franchised Units: 208
Company-Owned Units: 0
Total Units: 208
Dist.:   US-208; CAN-0; O'seas-0
  North America: 42 States, 0 Provinces
  Density: 13 in CO, 15 in MI, 16 in UT
Projected New Units (12 Months):   18
Qualifications: 4, 4, 3, 4, 5, 4

FINANCIAL/TERMS:

Cash Investment: $70-75K
Total Investment: $108-476K
Minimum Net Worth: $350K
Fees: Franchise - $35K
  Royalty - 5-7%;   Ad. - 0%
Earnings Claims Statement: Yes
Term of Contract (Years):   10/10
Avg. # Of Employees: 3 FT, 6 PT
Passive Ownership: Discouraged
Encourage Conversions: NA
Area Develop. Agreements: Yes/2
Sub-Franchising Contracts: No
Expand In Territory: Yes
Space Needs: 1,800-2,100 (2,099 average) SF

SUPPORT & TRAINING:

Financial Assistance Provided: Yes (I)
Site Selection Assistance: Yes
Lease Negotiation Assistance: Yes
Co-Operative Advertising: No

Franchisee Assoc./Member: Yes/Yes
Size Of Corporate Staff: 30
On-Going Support: „C,D,E,,G,H,I
Training: 3-10 Days Store Opening;
  1 week Host Training or Sandwich
  Training;2 weeksDillon, MT

SPECIFIC EXPANSION PLANS:

US: All United States
Canada: West of Toronto
Overseas: NR

◄◄ ►►

HOUSE OF BREAD

858 Higuera St.
San Luis Obispo, CA 93401
Tel: (800) 545-5146 (805) 542-0257
Fax: (805) 542-0257
E-Mail: bread@houseofbread.com
Web Site: www.houseofbread.com
Ms. Sheila McCann, Chief Executive Officer

Healthy, premium bread bakery, with over 20 varieties of delicious breads - from traditional honey whole wheat to irresistible sourdough pesto artichoke or the decadent triple chocolate bread. HOUSE OF BREAD's unique recipes use no dairy, refined sugar or fat, yet taste incredible.

BACKGROUND:

Established: 1996;   1st Franchised: 1999
Franchised Units: 9
Company-Owned Units: 1
Total Units: 10
Dist.:   US-10; CAN-0; O'seas-0
  North America: 2 States, 0 Provinces
  Density: 7 in CA
Projected New Units (12 Months):   6
Qualifications: 3, 3, 1, 3, 3, 5

FINANCIAL/TERMS:

Cash Investment: $125K-175K
Total Investment: $250K-350K
Minimum Net Worth: $50K
Fees: Franchise - $24K
  Royalty - 6%;   Ad. - 2%
Earnings Claims Statement: No
Term of Contract (Years):   10/10
Avg. # Of Employees: 2 FT, 8 PT
Passive Ownership: Discouraged
Encourage Conversions: No
Area Develop. Agreements: Yes/1
Sub-Franchising Contracts: No
Expand In Territory: Yes
Space Needs: 1,500 SF

SUPPORT & TRAINING:

Financial Assistance Provided: Yes (D)
Site Selection Assistance: Yes
Lease Negotiation Assistance: Yes

Co-Operative Advertising: No
Franchisee Assoc./Member: No
Size Of Corporate Staff: 2
On-Going Support: „C,D,E,F,G,H,I
Training: Minimum 9 Days San Luis
  Obispo, CA; Minimum 7 Days Franchisee Location

SPECIFIC EXPANSION PLANS:

US: All United States
Canada: All Canada
Overseas: All Countries

◄◄ ►►

KOLACHE FACTORY

15730 Park Row, # 150
Houston, TX 77084
Tel: (281) 829-6188
Fax: (281) 829-6813
E-Mail: franchising@kolachefactory.com
Web Site: www.kolachefactory.com
Mr. Aaron Nielsen, Director of Franchise Sales

A quick-service bakery that specializes in making kolaches. Kolaches are ideal for breakfast, lunch or as a snack, with over 25 different varieties to choose from, ranging from sausage to egg to fruit. Our delicious and satisfying meals are sure to please even the pickiest of eaters. Our kolaches have grown in popularity over the last 25 years and business continues to grow. We take great pride in offering the freshest ingredients and our dough is made fresh on-site daily at each one of our locations.

BACKGROUND:

Established: 1986;   1st Franchised: 2000
Franchised Units: 14
Company-Owned Units: 19
Total Units: 33
Dist.:   US-33; CAN-0; O'seas-0
  North America: 5 States, 0 Provinces
  Density: 28 in TX, 2 in IN
Projected New Units (12 Months): 10-20
Qualifications: 5, 4, 3, 3, 4, 4

FINANCIAL/TERMS:

Cash Investment: $30-50K
Total Investment: $350-450K
Minimum Net Worth: $500K
Fees: Franchise - $35K
  Royalty - 6%;   Ad. - 3%

65

Earnings Claims Statement:	Yes
Term of Contract (Years):	10/5
Avg. # Of Employees:	5-7 FT, 1 PT
Passive Ownership:	Not Allowed
Encourage Conversions:	No
Area Develop. Agreements:	Yes
Sub-Franchising Contracts:	No
Expand In Territory:	Yes
Space Needs:	1,600-1,800 SF

SUPPORT & TRAINING:

Financial Assistance Provided:	Yes (I)
Site Selection Assistance:	Yes
Lease Negotiation Assistance:	Yes
Co-Operative Advertising:	Yes
Franchisee Assoc./Member:	No
Size Of Corporate Staff:	9
On-Going Support:	A,,C,D,E,F,,h,I
Training:	4 weeks Houston, TX

SPECIFIC EXPANSION PLANS:

US:	TX, IN, CO, MO, KS
Canada:	No
Overseas:	NR

‹‹ ››

LAMAR'S DONUTS

5601 S. 27th St., # 202
Lincoln, NE 68512
Tel: (402) 420-0203
Fax: (402) 420-0209
E-Mail: franinfo@lamars.com
Web Site: www.lamars.com
Ms. Cheri Emerson, Franchise Sales Inquiries

LAMAR'S DONUTS is a rapidly growing chain of retail donut shops, founded in Kansas City, specializing in 53 varieties of handmade donuts and specialties since 1933, served in an atmosphere rich in hospitality and authenticity. A K.C. institution and Chamber of Commerce tourist attraction, LAMAR's has received acclaim nationwide, creating what critics call "the perfect donut."

BACKGROUND: IFA MEMBER

Established: 1933;	1st Franchised: 1993
Franchised Units:	25
Company-Owned Units:	3
Total Units:	28
Dist.:	US-28; CAN-0; O'seas-0
North America:	7 States, 0 Provinces
Density:	8 in MO, 11 in CO
Projected New Units (12 Months):	4-6
Qualifications:	4, 5, 3, 2, 3, 5

FINANCIAL/TERMS:

Cash Investment:	$150K
Total Investment:	$300-400K
Minimum Net Worth:	$350K

Fees: Franchise -	$28.5K
Royalty - 5%;	Ad. - 4.5%
Earnings Claims Statement:	No
Term of Contract (Years):	10/10
Avg. # Of Employees:	4-6 FT, 5-10 PT
Passive Ownership:	Allowed
Encourage Conversions:	Yes
Area Develop. Agreements:	Yes/1
Sub-Franchising Contracts:	Yes
Expand In Territory:	Yes
Space Needs:	2,000 SF

SUPPORT & TRAINING:

Financial Assistance Provided:	Yes (D)
Site Selection Assistance:	Yes
Lease Negotiation Assistance:	Yes
Co-Operative Advertising:	Yes
Franchisee Assoc./Member:	No
Size Of Corporate Staff:	10
On-Going Support:	a,b,C,D,E,F,G,H,I
Training: 1 Week On-Site in Franchise Store; 3-4 Weeks Training Store in Colorado	

SPECIFIC EXPANSION PLANS:

US:	Central, Midwest, West
Canada:	No
Overseas:	NR

‹‹ ››

MANHATTAN BAGEL COMPANY

555 Zang St.
Lakewood, CO 80228
Tel: (609) 737-7266
Fax: (609) 737-7268
E-Mail: rguckel@einsteinnoah.com
Web Site: www.newworldrestaurantgroup.com
Mr. Kevin Kruse, Vice President - Franchise Development

MANHATTAN BAGEL COMPANY franchises fast casual bagel cafes which serve over 15 varieties of authentic New York bagels, as well as gourmet coffees and deli items, and a full breakfast and lunch menu. Our franchising program includes assistance with site selection, construction, and operations training.

Our comprehensive training includes a detailed operations manual and continuing assistance in baking and food preparation and service, marketing, and merchandising. We typically close each evening by 5 PM promoting a better quality of life for Management and Staff. Contact us to learn more about this established and growing opportunity!

BACKGROUND: IFA MEMBER
Established: 1987;   1st Franchised: 1991

Franchised Units:	68
Company-Owned Units:	1
Total Units:	70
Dist.:	US-0; CAN-0; O'seas-0
North America:	9 States, 0 Provinces
Density:	21 in PA, 7 in NY, 26 in NJ
Projected New Units (12 Months):	6
Qualifications:	4, 4, 5, 3, 1, 5

FINANCIAL/TERMS:

Cash Investment:	$225K
Total Investment:	$483K-849K
Minimum Net Worth:	$450K
Fees: Franchise -	$25K
Royalty - 5%;	Ad. - Up to 5%
Earnings Claims Statement:	Yes
Term of Contract (Years):	10/10
Avg. # Of Employees:	3 FT, 9 PT
Passive Ownership:	Discouraged
Encourage Conversions:	Yes
Area Develop. Agreements:	Yes/2
Sub-Franchising Contracts:	No
Expand In Territory:	Yes
Space Needs:	1,800-2,200 SF

SUPPORT & TRAINING:

Financial Assistance Provided:	No
Site Selection Assistance:	Yes
Lease Negotiation Assistance:	Yes
Co-Operative Advertising:	Yes
Franchisee Assoc./Member:	Yes/Yes
Size Of Corporate Staff:	200
On-Going Support:	,B,C,D,E,F,,H,
Training: 1 Week Corporate Office; 2 Weeks Store	

SPECIFIC EXPANSION PLANS:

US:	All United States
Canada:	No
Overseas:	NR

‹‹ ››

MMMARVELLOUS MMMUFFINS (CANADA)

400 Steeprock Dr.
Toronto, ON M3J2XI Canada
Tel: (800) 827-1039 + 273 (416) 638-3333 + 273
Fax: (416) 236-0054
E-Mail: timothym@timothys.com
Web Site: www.mmmuffins.com
Mr. Tim Martin, Franchise Director

Fresh, high-quality specialty baked goods including over 100 varieties of muffins as well as scones, cinnamon swirls, cookies and streusel cakes. In addition, we offer a selection of gourmet coffee, teas, and fruit juices.

BACKGROUND:
Established: 1979;   1st Franchised: 1980

Franchised Units: 85
Company-Owned Units: 5
Total Units: 90
Dist.: US-0; CAN-88; O'seas-2
  North America: 0 States, 8 Provinces
  Density: 26 in PA, 43 in ON, 13 in BC
Projected New Units (12 Months): 10
Qualifications: 5, 4, 3, 3, 4, 5
FINANCIAL/TERMS:
Cash Investment: $40-60K+
Total Investment: $160K
Minimum Net Worth: $200K
Fees: Franchise - $25K
  Royalty - 7%; Ad. - 1%
Earnings Claims Statement: No
Term of Contract (Years): 10/10
Avg. # Of Employees: 2-3 FT, 4-7 PT
Passive Ownership: Not Allowed
Encourage Conversions: Yes
Area Develop. Agreements: Yes/1
Sub-Franchising Contracts: Yes
Expand In Territory: Yes
Space Needs: 300 SF
SUPPORT & TRAINING:
Financial Assistance Provided: Yes (D)
Site Selection Assistance: Yes
Lease Negotiation Assistance: Yes
Co-Operative Advertising: No
Franchisee Assoc./Member: No
Size Of Corporate Staff: 35
On-Going Support: A,B,C,D,E,F,G,h,
Training: 4 Weeks Toronto, ON
SPECIFIC EXPANSION PLANS:
US: NR
Canada: All Canada
Overseas: Asia, Eastern Europe, Middle
  East, South America

MRS. FIELDS COOKIES
2855 E. Cottonwood Pkwy., # 400
Salt Lake City, UT 84121-7050
Tel: (800) 343-5377 + 2399
Fax: (801) 736-5936
E-Mail: donl@mrsfields.com
Web Site: www.mrsfields.com
Mr. Don Lewandowski, VP of Develop-
  ment Bakery

Premier retail cookie business with
'uncompromising quality,' 94% brand recognition, easy to operate, flexible designs

and store options that operate in traditional and non-traditional venues.

BACKGROUND: IFA MEMBER
Established: 1977; 1st Franchised: 1990
Franchised Units: 300
Company-Owned Units: 300
Total Units: 300
Dist.: US-213; CAN-0; O'seas-77
  North America: 43 States, 0 Provinces
  Density: 30 in MI, 25 in IL, 103 in CA
Projected New Units (12 Months): 38
Qualifications: 4, 4, 2, 2, 2, 5
FINANCIAL/TERMS:
Cash Investment: $100K-200K
Total Investment: $179.1-251.1K
Minimum Net Worth: $150K/75K LIQ
Fees: Franchise - $30K
  Royalty - 6%; Ad. - 1%
Earnings Claims Statement: Yes
Term of Contract (Years): 7/7
Avg. # Of Employees: 3 FT, 2 PT
Passive Ownership: Not Allowed
Encourage Conversions: Yes
Area Develop. Agreements: No
Sub-Franchising Contracts: No
Expand In Territory: Yes
Space Needs: 600-900 SF
SUPPORT & TRAINING:
Financial Assistance Provided: No
Site Selection Assistance: Yes
Lease Negotiation Assistance: Yes
Co-Operative Advertising: No
Franchisee Assoc./Member: Yes/Yes
Size Of Corporate Staff: 100
On-Going Support: A,B,C,D,E,F,G,H,I
Training: Salt Lake City, UT
SPECIFIC EXPANSION PLANS:
US: All United States
Canada: All Canada
Overseas: NR

PANERA BREAD COMPANY
6710 Clayton Rd.
Richmond Heights, MO 63117
Tel: (800) 301-5566 (314) 633-7100
Fax: (314) 633-7200
E-Mail: peter.wright@panerabread.com
Web Site: www.panerabread.com
Mr. Peter Wright, Dir. Franchise Admin-
  istration

Founded in Saint Louis in 1987, SAINT

LOUIS BREAD has expanded into new
markets over the past few years, with
strong consumer acceptance for its unique
concept. Each SAINT LOUIS BREAD
bakery-cafe features a comfortable neighborhood setting where residents can relax
and enjoy a wide range of fresh-baked
sourdough breads, along with other fresh-
baked goods, bagels and hearty made-to-
order sandwiches, salads and soups.

BACKGROUND:
Established: 1987; 1st Franchised: 1993
Franchised Units: 356
Company-Owned Units: 184
Total Units: 540
Dist.: US-540; CAN-0; O'seas-0
  North America: 14 States, 0 Provinces
  Density: 36 in MO, 25 in IL, 8 in GA
Projected New Units (12 Months): 108
Qualifications: 5, 5, 5, 3, 3, 4
FINANCIAL/TERMS:
Cash Investment: $135-165K
Total Investment: $550-650K
Minimum Net Worth: $3MM
Fees: Franchise - $35K
  Royalty - 5%; Ad. - Up to 5%
Earnings Claims Statement: Yes
Term of Contract (Years): 20/Agrmt.
Avg. # Of Employees: 17 FT, 17 PT
Passive Ownership: Not Allowed
Encourage Conversions: No
Area Develop. Agreements: Yes/1
Sub-Franchising Contracts: No
Expand In Territory: No
Space Needs: 3,500 SF
SUPPORT & TRAINING:
Financial Assistance Provided: No
Site Selection Assistance: Yes
Lease Negotiation Assistance: No
Co-Operative Advertising: No
Franchisee Assoc./Member: No
Size Of Corporate Staff: 54
On-Going Support: ,B,C,D,E,F,,H,I
Training: 10 Weeks St. Louis, MO
SPECIFIC EXPANSION PLANS:
US: All United States
Canada: No
Overseas: NR

SAINT CINNAMON BAKE SHOPPE
350 Esna Park Dr.
Markham, ON L3R 1A5 Canada
Tel: (877) 490-5916 (905) 470-1517
Fax: (905) 470-8112
E-Mail: info@saintcinnamon.com
Web Site: www.saintcinnamon.com

Mr. Mark Halpern, Executive Vice President

Largest cinnamon-roll franchise in Canada. The rolls are made and baked daily at each location. The franchisee is given two weeks of intensive training in all aspects of operations.

BACKGROUND:

Established: 1986;	1st Franchised: 1986
Franchised Units:	87
Company-Owned Units:	0
Total Units:	87
Dist.:	US-0; CAN-61; O'seas-26
North America:	0 States, 4 Provinces
Density: 27 in QC, 31 in ON, 2 in NB	
Projected New Units (12 Months):	25
Qualifications:	4, 4, 4, 4, 4, 5

FINANCIAL/TERMS:

Cash Investment:	$40-75K
Total Investment:	$144-265K
Minimum Net Worth:	NR
Fees: Franchise -	$25K
Royalty - 6%;	Ad. - 1-3%
Earnings Claims Statement:	No
Term of Contract (Years):	10/10
Avg. # Of Employees:	2 FT, 5 PT
Passive Ownership:	Not Allowed
Encourage Conversions:	NA
Area Develop. Agreements:	No
Sub-Franchising Contracts:	Yes
Expand In Territory:	Yes
Space Needs:	300-600 SF

SUPPORT & TRAINING:

Financial Assistance Provided:	NR
Site Selection Assistance:	Yes
Lease Negotiation Assistance:	Yes
Co-Operative Advertising:	No
Franchisee Assoc./Member:	No
Size Of Corporate Staff:	7
On-Going Support:	A,B,C,D,e,F,G,h,
Training:	2 Weeks ON

SPECIFIC EXPANSION PLANS:

US:	Yes
Canada:	Yes
Overseas: Middle East, Europe, South & Central America	

≺≺ ≻≻

TREATS INTERNATIONAL
418 Preston St.
Ottawa, ON K1S 4N2 Canada
Tel: (800) 461-4003 (613) 563-4073
Fax: (613) 563-1982
E-Mail: sadams@treats.com
Web Site: www.treats.com
Ms. Shirley Adams, Franchise Relations

Micro-bakery concept, featuring gourmet and specialty coffees and fresh-baked, on-site baked goods, including muffins, cookies and bagels. Three concept variations are available: TREATS BAKERY (~400 SF) serves the base menu offering; TREATS CAF (~1,200 SF) also serves sandwiches (baguettes), soups and salads; TREATS COFFEE EMPORIUM (~1,200 SF) also offers coffee beans, coffee-related merchandise and sandwiches.

BACKGROUND:

Established: 1977;	1st Franchised: 1979
Franchised Units:	97
Company-Owned Units:	3
Total Units:	100
Dist.:	US-5; CAN-95; O'seas-0
North America:	3 States, 9 Provinces
Density: 20 in QC, 70 in ON, 10 in AB	
Projected New Units (12 Months):	12
Qualifications:	3, 3, 3, 2, 3, 5

FINANCIAL/TERMS:

Cash Investment:	$40-50K
Total Investment:	$100-150K
Minimum Net Worth:	$200K
Fees: Franchise -	$25K
Royalty - 7%;	Ad. - 1%
Earnings Claims Statement:	No
Term of Contract (Years):	Lease/
Avg. # Of Employees:	3 FT, 2 PT
Passive Ownership:	Discouraged
Encourage Conversions:	Yes
Area Develop. Agreements:	Yes/1
Sub-Franchising Contracts:	Yes
Expand In Territory:	Yes
Space Needs:	500-1,500 SF

SUPPORT & TRAINING:

Financial Assistance Provided:	No
Site Selection Assistance:	Yes
Lease Negotiation Assistance:	Yes
Co-Operative Advertising:	No
Franchisee Assoc./Member:	No
Size Of Corporate Staff:	15
On-Going Support:	,B,C,D,E,,G,H,I
Training:	2 Weeks Training Center; On-Site

SPECIFIC EXPANSION PLANS:

US:	East Coast
Canada:	All Canada
Overseas:	Chile, Brazil, Middle East

≺≺ ≻≻

For a full explanation of the data provided in the Franchisor Profiles, please refer to *Chapter 2, "How to Use the Data."*

FIVE LARGEST PARTICIPANTS IN SURVEY						
Company	# Fran-chised Units	# Co-Owned Units	# Total Units	Franchise Fee	On-Going Royalty	Total Investment
1. Great Clips	2,738	0	2,738	$25K	6%	$109.4-202.5K
2. SuperCuts	1,010	1,122	2,132	$22.5K	4% Yr. 1; 6% succ. Yrs.	$97-208K
3. Merle Norman Cosmetics	1,936	4	1,940	$0	0%	$28.5K
4. Fantastic Sams	1,324	0	1,324	$25-35K	Varies by Region	$103-230.1K
5. Cost Cutters Family Hair Care	477	367	844	$22.5K; 12,500 after 1st	4% Yr. 1; 6% succ. Yrs.	$94,495-210,295

All of the data provided are proprietary and should not be quoted without acknowledging *Bond's Franchise Guide.*

ALOETTE COSMETICS
4900 Highlands Pkwy.
Smyrna, GA 30082
Tel: (800) 256-3883 (678) 444-2563
Fax: (678) 444-2564
E-Mail: snormand@aloette.com
Web Site: www.aloette.com
Ms. Sharon Normand, Franchise Admin-
    istrator

ALOETTE is a direct marketer of Aloe
Vera-based skin care products. Franchises
provide career opportunities to beauty
consultants who sell the products through
home shows.

BACKGROUND: IFA MEMBER
Established: 1978;   1st Franchised: 1978
Franchised Units: 58
Company-Owned Units: 0
Total Units: 58
Dist.:   US-37; CAN-21; O'seas-0
  North America: 36 States, 10 Provinces
  Density: 3 in QC, 18 in ON, 4 in BC
Projected New Units (12 Months):   10
Qualifications: 1, 2, 5, 2, 1, 2
FINANCIAL/TERMS:
Cash Investment: $10-20K

Total Investment: $55-86.3K
Minimum Net Worth: $10K
Fees: Franchise - $20K
  Royalty - 5%;   Ad. - NA
Earnings Claims Statement: No
Term of Contract (Years):   5/10
Avg. # Of Employees: 3 FT, 0 PT
Passive Ownership: Discouraged
Encourage Conversions: NA
Area Develop. Agreements: No
Sub-Franchising Contracts: No
Expand In Territory: Yes
Space Needs: 1,000 SF

SUPPORT & TRAINING:
Financial Assistance Provided: Yes (D)
Site Selection Assistance: No
Lease Negotiation Assistance: No
Co-Operative Advertising: No
Franchisee Assoc./Member: No
Size Of Corporate Staff: 25
On-Going Support: ,,C,D,E,,,h,
Training: 2 Days Operations Training
    at Franchise; 2 Days Sales Training at
    Franchise
SPECIFIC EXPANSION PLANS:
US: All United States
Canada: ON
Overseas: NR

⋘ ⋙

**BEAUTY BRANDS
SALON-SPA-SUPERSTORE**
4600 Madison Ave., # 400
Kansas City, MO 64112-3002
Tel: (888) 725-6608 (816) 531-2266
Fax: (816) 531-7122
E-Mail: franchising@beautybrands.com
Web Site: www.beautybrands.com
Mr. Steve Eckman, VP Corporate Development

BEAUTY BRANDS SALON/SPA/
SUPERSTORE is the cutting-edge concept that offers consumers a "total beauty" experience. We have brought together a full-service salon and spa and have showcased it in a dynamic 6,000-7,000 square-foot retail environment offering nearly 50,000 units of product representing the top salon brands for hair, skin and nails.

BACKGROUND: IFA MEMBER
Established: 1995;   1st Franchised: 1999
Franchised Units: 2
Company-Owned Units: 45
Total Units: 47
Dist.:   US-47; CAN-0; O'seas-0
North America: 5 States, 0 Provinces
Density: 6 in TX, 4 in KS, 6 in CO
Projected New Units (12 Months):   10
Qualifications: 5, 5, 5, 4, 4, 4
FINANCIAL/TERMS:
Cash Investment: $150K-250K
Total Investment: $594.5K-936K
Minimum Net Worth: $3MM
Fees: Franchise - $25K

Royalty - 1-5%;   Ad. - 1-2%
Earnings Claims Statement: Yes
Term of Contract (Years):   10/10
Avg. # Of Employees: 10 FT, 20 PT
Passive Ownership: Not Allowed
Encourage Conversions: Yes
Area Develop. Agreements: Yes/1
Sub-Franchising Contracts: No
Expand In Territory: Yes
Space Needs: 5,000-7,000 SF
SUPPORT & TRAINING:
Financial Assistance Provided: No
Site Selection Assistance: Yes
Lease Negotiation Assistance: Yes
Co-Operative Advertising: No
Franchisee Assoc./Member: Yes/Yes
Size Of Corporate Staff: 50
On-Going Support: A,B,C,D,E,F,,h,I
Training: 4-6 Weeks Kansas City, MO
SPECIFIC EXPANSION PLANS:
US: All United States
Canada: No
Overseas: NR

⋘ ⋙

CELSIUS TANNERY
12142 State Line Rd.
Leawood, KS 66223
Tel: (866) 826-7400 (913) 451-7000
Fax: (913) 451-7001
E-Mail: jburandt@celsiustan.com
Web Site: www.celsiustan.com
Mr. Jim Burandt, Vice President of Sales

We are the fastest growing indoor tanning franchise chain in the U.S. With the exclusive STS tanning process, we are the first tanning salon franchise inside a big box retailer. We offer motivating and educational instruction in management, sales, and marketing your salon, and help you with professional guidance as well as ongoing administrative and business support. Site location, lease negotiation, construction, financial assistance and a toll-free number for support!

BACKGROUND:
Established: 1995;   1st Franchised: 2000
Franchised Units: 15
Company-Owned Units: 3
Total Units: 18
Dist.:   US-18; CAN-0; O'seas-0
North America: 3 States, Provinces
Density: 10 in KS, 7 in MO, 1 in NE
Projected New Units (12 Months):   8-10
Qualifications: 3, 2, 1, 1, 2, 4
FINANCIAL/TERMS:
Cash Investment: $35-100K

Total Investment: $240-600K
Minimum Net Worth: $150K
Fees: Franchise - $20-35K
   Royalty - 1%/$250 Min.;   Ad.
   - $1,200/Mo.
Earnings Claims Statement: No
Term of Contract (Years):   5/5
Avg. # Of Employees: 3 FT, 5 PT
Passive Ownership: Allowed
Encourage Conversions: Yes
Area Develop. Agreements: Yes/1
Sub-Franchising Contracts: No
Expand In Territory: Yes
Space Needs: 2,000 SF
SUPPORT & TRAINING:
Financial Assistance Provided: Yes (D)
Site Selection Assistance: Yes
Lease Negotiation Assistance: Yes
Co-Operative Advertising: No
Franchisee Assoc./Member: No
Size Of Corporate Staff: 10
On-Going Support: A,B,C,D,E,F,,,I
Training:1 Week Corporate Headquarters;
    3 Weeks On-Site
SPECIFIC EXPANSION PLANS:
US: All United States
Canada: No
Overseas: NR

⋘ ⋙

CITY LOOKS
7201 Metro Blvd.
Minneapolis, MN 55439-2103
Tel: (888) 888-7008 (952) 947-7777
Fax: (952) 947-7900
E-Mail: franchiseleads@regiscorp.com
Web Site: www.regisfranchise.com
Mr. Alan Storry, VP Franchise Development

Conveniently located in nearby malls and strip centers in 10 states, city looks caters to style-conscious clients looking for exceptional customer service and a full array of salon services.

BACKGROUND: IFA MEMBER
Established: 1963;   1st Franchised: 1968
Franchised Units: 22
Company-Owned Units: 0
Total Units: 22
Dist.:   US-22; CAN-1; O'seas-0
North America: 3 States, 1 Provinces
Density: 14 in MN, 3 in MI, 3 in IA
Projected New Units (12 Months):   3
Qualifications: 4, 5, 1, 3, 3, 4
FINANCIAL/TERMS:
Cash Investment: $116.1K-317.6K
Total Investment: $94.5-275K

Minimum Net Worth: $400K + 150K Liquid Assets
Fees: Franchise - $22.5K
Royalty - 2% 1st Yr./6% succ. Yrs.; Ad. - 5%
Earnings Claims Statement: No
Term of Contract (Years): 10/10
Avg. # Of Employees: 6 FT, 3 PT
Passive Ownership: Discouraged
Encourage Conversions: Yes
Area Develop. Agreements: Yes/1
Sub-Franchising Contracts: No
Expand In Territory: Yes
Space Needs: 1,000-1,200 SF

SUPPORT & TRAINING:
Financial Assistance Provided: Yes (I)
Site Selection Assistance: Yes
Lease Negotiation Assistance: Yes
Co-Operative Advertising: No
Franchisee Assoc./Member: Yes/Yes
Size Of Corporate Staff: 900
On-Going Support: ,,C,D,E,,G,h,I
Training: 3-5 Days Franchise Support Office; 5 Days Field Training

SPECIFIC EXPANSION PLANS:
US: All United States
Canada: No
Overseas: NR

◄◄ ►►

COST CUTTERS FAMILY HAIR CARE
7201 Metro Blvd.
Minneapolis, MN 55439-2130
Tel: (888) 888-7008 (952) 947-7777
Fax: (952) 947-7900
E-Mail: franchiseleads@regiscorp.com
Web Site: www.costcutters.com
Mr. Alan Storry, VP Franchise Development

COST CUTTERS FAMILY HAIR CARE is a value-priced, family hair salon chain offering its customers high-quality hair care services and professional products.

BACKGROUND: IFA MEMBER
Established: 1963; 1st Franchised: 1982
Franchised Units: 477
Company-Owned Units: 367
Total Units: 844
Dist.: US-844; CAN-0; O'seas-0
North America: 45 States, 0 Provinces
Density: 150 in WI, 69 in MN, 102 in CO

Projected New Units (12 Months): 20
Qualifications: 5, 5, 1, 4, 2, 5
FINANCIAL/TERMS:
Cash Investment: NR
Total Investment: $94495-210295K
Minimum Net Worth: $300K/100K Liq
Fees: Franchise - $22.5K; 12,500 after 1st
Royalty - 4% Yr.1/6% succ. Yrs.; Ad. - 4%
Earnings Claims Statement: Yes
Term of Contract (Years): 15/15
Avg. # Of Employees: 6 FT, 3 PT
Passive Ownership: Discouraged
Encourage Conversions: Yes
Area Develop. Agreements: Yes/1
Sub-Franchising Contracts: No
Expand In Territory: Yes
Space Needs: 900-1,200 SF

SUPPORT & TRAINING:
Financial Assistance Provided: Yes (D)
Site Selection Assistance: Yes
Lease Negotiation Assistance: Yes
Co-Operative Advertising: No
Franchisee Assoc./Member: No
Size Of Corporate Staff: 900
On-Going Support: ,,C,D,E,,G,h,I
Training: 1 Week On-Site; 3-5 Days Training Minneapolis, MN

SPECIFIC EXPANSION PLANS:
US: All United States
Canada: No
Overseas: NR

◄◄ ►►

EXECUTIVE TANS
165 S. Union Blvd., # 785
Lakewood, CO 80228-2215
Tel: (877) 393-2826 (303) 988-9999
Fax: (303) 988-5390
E-Mail: mike@executivetans.com
Web Site: www.executivetans.com
Mr. Mike Garcia, VP Sales/Marketing

Indoor tanning salons along with related products and services.

BACKGROUND: IFA MEMBER
Established: 1991; 1st Franchised: 1995
Franchised Units: 41
Company-Owned Units: 0
Total Units: 41
Dist.: US-41; CAN-0; O'seas-0
North America: 11 States, 0 Provinces
Density: 18 in CO
Projected New Units (12 Months): 15
Qualifications: 3, 3, 2, 4, 3, 3
FINANCIAL/TERMS:
Cash Investment: $40-60K
Total Investment: $260-500K

Minimum Net Worth: $175K
Fees: Franchise - $25K
Royalty - $795-1,195/Mo.; Ad. - $490-690/Mo.
Earnings Claims Statement: Yes
Term of Contract (Years): 10/5
Avg. # Of Employees: 2 FT, 2 PT
Passive Ownership: Discouraged
Encourage Conversions: Yes
Area Develop. Agreements: No
Sub-Franchising Contracts: No
Expand In Territory: Yes
Space Needs: 1,200-8,000 SF

SUPPORT & TRAINING:
Financial Assistance Provided: Yes (I)
Site Selection Assistance: Yes
Lease Negotiation Assistance: Yes
Co-Operative Advertising: Yes
Franchisee Assoc./Member: No
Size Of Corporate Staff: 8
On-Going Support: ,,,D,E,,G,h,I
Training: 1 Week Corporate Offices; 1 Week Location

SPECIFIC EXPANSION PLANS:
US: All United States
Canada: No
Overseas: NR

FACES

◄◄ ►►

FACES COSMETICS
3010 LBJ Fwy., # 1200
Dallas, Texas 75234
Tel: (877) 343-2237 (972) 888-6081
Fax: (972) 888-6083
E-Mail: jennifer@faces-cosmetics.com
Web Site: www.faces-cosmetics.com
Ms. Jennifer Vaidya, Director International Franchise Development

Founded in 1974, FACES COSMETICS is a retail cosmetic franchise system that has been successfully providing women with premium cosmetics and aesthetic services. FACES is established globally in Canada, Mexico, Europe, Puerto Rico, and is now expanding in the USA. FACES offers one of the largest selections of cosmetics, skincare and anti-aging products and services for make-up, aesthetics and mini-spa treatments. FACES owners become part of the dominant player in the cosmetic industry by offering a truly unique experience that speaks to the needs of all women, from all ages and cultural backgrounds. FACES provides a turn-key package: fully-equipped boutique, complete inventory, training, marketing & advertising programs and ongoing Head-Office support.

BACKGROUND: IFA MEMBER
Established: 1976; 1st Franchised: 1976
Franchised Units: 45
Company-Owned Units: <u>11</u>
Total Units: 56
Dist.:   US-2; CAN-34; O'seas-19
  North America: 0 States, 9 Provinces
  Density: 16 in QC, 12 in ON
Projected New Units (12 Months):   NR
Qualifications: 3, 4, 3, 3, 3, 5
FINANCIAL/TERMS:
Cash Investment: $125K
Total Investment: $219.5K-372.5K
Minimum Net Worth: Varies
Fees: Franchise - $27.5K
  Royalty - 6%;   Ad. - 2%
Earnings Claims Statement: No
Term of Contract (Years):   10/10
Avg. # Of Employees: 1 FT, 3-4 PT
Passive Ownership: Allowed
Encourage Conversions: Yes
Area Develop. Agreements: Yes/1
Sub-Franchising Contracts: Yes
Expand In Territory: Yes
Space Needs: 700-1,000 SF
SUPPORT & TRAINING:
Financial Assistance Provided: No
Site Selection Assistance: Yes
Lease Negotiation Assistance: Yes
Co-Operative Advertising: No
Franchisee Assoc./Member: No
Size Of Corporate Staff: 70
On-Going Support: A,B,,D,E,,G,h,
Training: 2 Weeks Toronto, ON
SPECIFIC EXPANSION PLANS:
US: All United States
Canada: All Canada
Overseas: All Countries in a Master
  Franchisee capacity

<<   >>

Fantastic Sams
HAIR SALONS

Top 100

FANTASTIC SAMS
50 Dunham Rd., 3rd Fl.
Beverly, MA 01915
Tel: (877) 383-3831 (978) 232-5600
Fax: (978) 232-5601

E-Mail: franchise@fantasticsams.com
Web Site: www.fantasticsamsfranchises.com
Ms. Cindy Gaudette, Project Coord., Fran. Devel.

FANTASTIC SAMS is one of the world's largest full-service hair care franchises, with over 1,300 salons in North America. Our full service salons offer quality hair care services for the entire family, including cuts, perms and color. When you join the FANTASTIC SAMS family of franchisees, you'll receive both local and national support through on-going management training, educational programs and national conferences, as well as advertising and other benefits. No hair care experience required.

BACKGROUND: IFA MEMBER
Established: 1974; 1st Franchised: 1976
Franchised Units: 1324
Company-Owned Units: <u>0</u>
Total Units: 1324
Dist.:   US-1312; CAN-12; O'seas-0
  North America: 44 States, 4 Provinces
  Density: 105 in MN, 105 in FL, 224 in CA
Projected New Units (12 Months):   50
Qualifications: 5, 5, 1, 4, 1, 5
FINANCIAL/TERMS:
Cash Investment: $60K
Total Investment: $103-230.1K
Minimum Net Worth: $250K
Fees: Franchise - $25-35K
  Royalty - Varies by Region; Ad. - Varies by Region
Earnings Claims Statement: No
Term of Contract (Years):   10/10
Avg. # Of Employees: 8 FT, 0 PT
Passive Ownership: Allowed
Encourage Conversions: Yes
Area Develop. Agreements: Yes
Sub-Franchising Contracts: No
Expand In Territory: Yes
Space Needs: 1,200 SF
SUPPORT & TRAINING:
Financial Assistance Provided: Yes (I)
Site Selection Assistance: Yes
Lease Negotiation Assistance: Yes
Co-Operative Advertising: No
Franchisee Assoc./Member: No
Size Of Corporate Staff: 40
On-Going Support: ,,C,D,E,,G,H,
Training: On-Going Region;
  5 Days Salon Fundamentals Class
SPECIFIC EXPANSION PLANS:
US: All United States
Canada: All Canada

Overseas: NR

<<   >>

FIRST CHOICE HAIRCUTTERS
6465 Millcreek Dr., # 210
Mississauga, ON L5N 5R6 Canada
Tel: (800) 617-3961 (905) 821-8555
Fax: (905) 567-7000
E-Mail: franchiseleads@regiscorp.com
Web Site: www.regisfranchise.com
Ms. Teresa Partridge, Dir. Franchise Development

We're a cutting edge chain of price-value family hair care salons with over 400 locations across Canada and the US. Since 1980, we've built a strong, growing base of loyal customers -- over 6 million last year alone. And you don't even have to have any hair experience or become a stylist. We'll provide all the training, tools and on-going support you'll need to manage your thriving salon business. At First Choice Haircutters, our philosophy is simple: your success is our success.

BACKGROUND: IFA MEMBER
Established: 1980; 1st Franchised: 1982
Franchised Units: 183
Company-Owned Units: <u>261</u>
Total Units: 444
Dist.:   US-92; CAN-354; O'seas-0
  North America: 3 States, 10 Provinces
  Density: 246 in ON, 40 in OH, 50 in FL
Projected New Units (12 Months):   36
Qualifications: 3, 3, 3, 3, 3, 3
FINANCIAL/TERMS:
Cash Investment: $109.5K-169.5K
Total Investment: $96-167K
Minimum Net Worth: $300K + 100K
Liquid Assets
Fees: Franchise - $22.5K
  Royalty - 5-7%;   Ad. - 3%
Earnings Claims Statement: No
Term of Contract (Years):   10/5
Avg. # Of Employees: 5-7 FT, 2-4 PT
Passive Ownership: Not Allowed
Encourage Conversions: Yes
Area Develop. Agreements: Yes/3
Sub-Franchising Contracts: No
Expand In Territory: Yes
Space Needs: 800-1,000 SF
SUPPORT & TRAINING:
Financial Assistance Provided: Yes (I)
Site Selection Assistance: Yes

Lease Negotiation Assistance: Yes
Co-Operative Advertising: No
Franchisee Assoc./Member: No
Size Of Corporate Staff: 20
On-Going Support: A,B,C,D,E,,G,H,I
Training: 10 Days or more On-Site;
    1 Week Classroom; Annual Staff
    Refresher

SPECIFIC EXPANSION PLANS:
US: Yes
Canada: All Canada except Quebec
Overseas: NR

◄◄ ►►

Top 100 Great Clips®

GREAT CLIPS
7700 France Ave. S., # 425
Minneapolis, MN 55435
Tel: (800) 947-1143 (952) 893-9088
Fax: (952) 844-3443
E-Mail: franchise@greatclips.com
Web Site: www.greatclipsfranchise.com
Mr. Rob Goggins, VP Franchise Development

High-volume haircutting salon, specializing in haircuts for the entire family. What really makes this business concept unique is the fact that it's recession resistant, simple and has steady growth; you will be hard pressed to find a better business that meets all three. Strong, local support to franchisees, excellent training programs.

BACKGROUND: IFA MEMBER
Established: 1982;   1st Franchised: 1983
Franchised Units: 2738
Company-Owned Units: 0
Total Units: 2738
Dist.:   US-2681; CAN-57; O'seas-0
   North America: 45 States, 3 Provinces
   Density: 173 in IL, 183 in CA, 215 in OH
Projected New Units (12 Months):   200
Qualifications: 5, 4, 1, 3, 3, 5
FINANCIAL/TERMS:
Cash Investment: $25K
Total Investment: $109.4-202.5K
Minimum Net Worth: $300K
Fees: Franchise - $25K
   Royalty - 6%;   Ad. - 5%
Earnings Claims Statement: Yes
Term of Contract (Years):   10/10
Avg. # Of Employees: 3 FT, 5 PT
Passive Ownership: Allowed
Encourage Conversions: No
Area Develop. Agreements: Yes

Sub-Franchising Contracts: No
Expand In Territory: Yes
Space Needs: 1,000-1,200 SF
SUPPORT & TRAINING:
Financial Assistance Provided: Yes (I)
Site Selection Assistance: Yes
Lease Negotiation Assistance: Yes
Co-Operative Advertising: Yes
Franchisee Assoc./Member: Yes/Yes
Size Of Corporate Staff: 200
On-Going Support: A,B,C,D,E,f,G,H,I
Training: 2.5 Weeks Local Market; 4 Days
   Minneapolis, MN
SPECIFIC EXPANSION PLANS:
US: All United States
Canada: Western Canada, Toronto
Overseas: NR

◄◄ ►►

HAIRCOLOREXPERTS / HCX
4850 W. Prospect Rd.
Ft. Lauderdale, FL 33309-3048
Tel: (866) HCX-HCX1 (954) 315-4900
Fax: (954) 486-5623
E-Mail: dsacks@haircolorxpress.com
Web Site: www.hcx.com
Ms. Danielle Sacks, Marketing Coordinator

HCX INTERNATIONAL is the newest innovation in hair salons, offering affordable hair color services and custom blended cosmetics at affordable prices in an up-scale salon environment.

BACKGROUND: IFA MEMBER
Established: 2000;   1st Franchised: 2001
Franchised Units: 14
Company-Owned Units: 4
Total Units: 18
Dist.:   US-18; CAN-0; O'seas-0
   North America: 14 States, Provinces
   Density: 10 in FL, 2 in MD, 3 in NJ
Projected New Units (12 Months):   250
Qualifications: 5, 4, 4, 3, 3, 5
FINANCIAL/TERMS:
Cash Investment: $80-100K
Total Investment: $199-299K
Minimum Net Worth: $250K
Fees: Franchise - $15K
   Royalty - 6%;   Ad. - 3%
Earnings Claims Statement: No
Term of Contract (Years):   10/5
Avg. # Of Employees: 15 FT, 1 PT
Passive Ownership: Allowed
Encourage Conversions: Yes
Area Develop. Agreements: Yes/1
Sub-Franchising Contracts: No
Expand In Territory: Yes

Space Needs: 1,200-1,400 SF
SUPPORT & TRAINING:
Financial Assistance Provided: Yes (D)
Site Selection Assistance: Yes
Lease Negotiation Assistance: Yes
Co-Operative Advertising: No
Franchisee Assoc./Member: NR
Size Of Corporate Staff: 42
On-Going Support: A,B,C,D,E,F,G,H,I
Training: 10 Days Ft. Lauderdale, FL
SPECIFIC EXPANSION PLANS:
US: All United States
Canada: All Canada
Overseas: Australia, UK, Canada

◄◄ ►►

LEMON TREE FAMILY HAIR SALON
1 Division Ave.
Levittown, NY 11756-1310
Tel: (800) 345-9156 (516) 735-2828
Fax: (516) 735-1851
E-Mail: lemontree@lemontree.com
Web Site: www.lemontree.com
Ms. Taylor Wagner, Director Salon Relations

LEMON TREE serves the full-service haircare needs of the entire family. We offer affordable prices and quality service and use only quality, name-brand products. We provide our franchisees a strong, hands-on training program.

BACKGROUND: IFA MEMBER
Established: 1975;   1st Franchised: 1976
Franchised Units: 60
Company-Owned Units: 0
Total Units: 60
Dist.:   US-60; CAN-0; O'seas-0
   North America: 5 States, 0 Provinces
   Density: 53 in NY, 2 in NJ, 2 in FL
Projected New Units (12 Months):   10
Qualifications: 2, 2, 1, 2, 1, 5
FINANCIAL/TERMS:
Cash Investment: $25-30K
Total Investment: $44-75K
Minimum Net Worth: $40K
Fees: Franchise - $15K
   Royalty - 6%;   Ad. - $400/Mo.
Earnings Claims Statement: No
Term of Contract (Years):   15/15
Avg. # Of Employees: 5 FT, 3 PT
Passive Ownership: Discouraged
Encourage Conversions: Yes
Area Develop. Agreements: No
Sub-Franchising Contracts: No
Expand In Territory: Yes
Space Needs: 1,200 SF

SUPPORT & TRAINING:

Financial Assistance Provided: Yes (D)
Site Selection Assistance: Yes
Lease Negotiation Assistance: Yes
Co-Operative Advertising: No
Franchisee Assoc./Member: No
Size Of Corporate Staff: 6
On-Going Support: ,B,C,D,E,F,,H,I
Training: 5 Days Main Office; Minimum 5
Days Location of Franchise

SPECIFIC EXPANSION PLANS:

US: Northeast, Southeast
Canada: No
Overseas: NR

◄◄ ►►

MAGICUTS

6465 Millcreek Dr., # 210
Mississauga, ON L5N 5R6 Canada
Tel: (800) 617-3961 (905) 363-4105
Fax: (905) 567-7000
E-Mail: franchiseleads@regiscorp.com
Web Site: www.magicutssalons.com
Ms. Teresa Partridge, Dir. Franchise
Development

We are a contemporary, full service salon with the added convenience of walk-in service. At Magicuts, our clients receive high-end style without the high-end cost. Conveniently located within Zellers department stores and suburban shopping centres across Canada, Magicuts markets to adults, 25 to 54, as well as families with children. The fusion of innovative service and quality with affordable pricing has made Magicuts a highly recognized and profitable brand for 25 years.

BACKGROUND: IFA MEMBER

Established: 1982; 1st Franchised: 1982
Franchised Units: 90
Company-Owned Units: 54
Total Units: 144
Dist.: US-0; CAN-144; O'seas-0
North America: 0 States, 9 Provinces
Density: 82 in ON, 24 in BC
Projected New Units (12 Months): 18
Qualifications: 5, 5, 1, 3, 4, 5

FINANCIAL/TERMS:

Cash Investment: $110.5K-165.5K
Total Investment: $110.5K-165.5K
Minimum Net Worth: $300K + 100K
Liquid Assets
Fees: Franchise - $22.5K

Royalty - 6%; Ad. - 3%
Earnings Claims Statement: No
Term of Contract (Years): 10/5/5
Avg. # Of Employees: 5-7 FT, 2-4 PT
Passive Ownership: Not Allowed
Encourage Conversions: Yes
Area Develop. Agreements: Yes/1
Sub-Franchising Contracts: No
Expand In Territory: Yes
Space Needs: 800-1,000 SF

SUPPORT & TRAINING:

Financial Assistance Provided: Yes (I)
Site Selection Assistance: Yes
Lease Negotiation Assistance: Yes
Co-Operative Advertising: Yes
Franchisee Assoc./Member: No
Size Of Corporate Staff: 20
On-Going Support: ,,C,D,E,,G,H,I
Training: 1 Week Classroom; On-Site

SPECIFIC EXPANSION PLANS:

US: No
Canada: All Canada except Quebec
Overseas: NR

◄◄ ►►

MERLE NORMAN COSMETICS

9130 Bellanca Ave.
Los Angeles, CA 90045-4710
Tel: (800) 421-6648 (310) 641-3000
Fax: (310) 337-2370
E-Mail: claporta@merlenorman.com
Web Site: www.merlenorman.com
Ms. Carol LaPorta, VP Studio Development

MERLE NORMAN COSMETICS is a specialty retail store, selling scientifically developed, state-of-the-art cosmetic products, using the 'free make over' and 'try before you buy' complete customer satisfaction methods of selling.

BACKGROUND: IFA MEMBER

Established: 1931; 1st Franchised: 1989
Franchised Units: 1936
Company-Owned Units: 4
Total Units: 1940
Dist.: US-1830; CAN-90; O'seas-20
North America: 50 States, 1 Provinces
Density:260 in TX, 113 in GA, 99 in AL
Projected New Units (12 Months): 120
Qualifications: 3, 4, 3, 3, 4, 4

FINANCIAL/TERMS:

Cash Investment: NR

Total Investment: $28.5K
Minimum Net Worth: NR
Fees: Franchise - $0
Royalty - 0%; Ad. - 0%
Earnings Claims Statement: Yes
Term of Contract (Years): Unlimited
Avg. # Of Employees: 2 FT, 2-5 PT
Passive Ownership: Discouraged
Encourage Conversions: No
Area Develop. Agreements: No
Sub-Franchising Contracts: No
Expand In Territory: Yes
Space Needs: 450-800 SF

SUPPORT & TRAINING:

Financial Assistance Provided: Yes (I)
Site Selection Assistance: Yes
Lease Negotiation Assistance: Yes
Co-Operative Advertising: Yes
Franchisee Assoc./Member: No
Size Of Corporate Staff: 630
On-Going Support: ,B,C,D,E,F,G,H,I
Training: 2 Weeks Los Angeles, CA

SPECIFIC EXPANSION PLANS:

US: All United States
Canada: All Canada, except Quebec
Overseas: NR

◄◄ ►►

PALM BEACH TAN

13800 Senlac Dr.
Framers Branch, TX 75234
Tel: (866) 728-2450 (972) 406-2400
Fax: (972) 406-2536
E-Mail: roy.sneed@palmbeachtan.com
Web Site: www.palmbeachtan.com
Mr. Roy Sneed, Director of Franchising

PALM BEACH TAN sells UV-free tanning equipment and skincare products to independently operated tanning salons, tanning services and skincare products directly to consumers and tanning salon franchises to independent operating companies.

BACKGROUND: IFA MEMBER

Established: 1990; 1st Franchised: 2001
Franchised Units: 66
Company-Owned Units: 66
Total Units: 132
Dist.: US-40; CAN-0; O'seas-0
North America: 5 States, 0 Provinces
Density: 32 in TX, 4 in NC, 2 in MD
Projected New Units (12 Months): NR
Qualifications: 5, 5, 2, 2, 2, 5

FINANCIAL/TERMS:

Cash Investment: $150-200K
Total Investment: $447-791K
Minimum Net Worth: $1MM

Fees: Franchise - $25K
   Royalty - 2%/4%/6%;   Ad. - 5%
Earnings Claims Statement: Yes
Term of Contract (Years):   10/10
Avg. # Of Employees: 6 FT, 6 PT
Passive Ownership: Allowed
Encourage Conversions: No
Area Develop. Agreements: Yes/1
Sub-Franchising Contracts: No
Expand In Territory: Yes
Space Needs: 3,200 SF

SUPPORT & TRAINING:
Financial Assistance Provided: No
Site Selection Assistance: Yes
Lease Negotiation Assistance: No
Co-Operative Advertising: No
Franchisee Assoc./Member: No
Size Of Corporate Staff: 7
On-Going Support: A,B,C,D,E,F,G,H,
Training: 3 Days Franchisee Organization
   Dallas, TX; 4 Weeks Operator Training
   Dallas, TX

SPECIFIC EXPANSION PLANS:
US: All United States
Canada: No
Overseas: NR

≪ ≫

PLANET BEACH CONTEMPO SPA
5145 Taravella Rd.
Marrero, LA 70072
Tel: (888) 290-8266 (504) 361-5550
Fax: (504) 361-5540
E-Mail: franchise@planetbeach.com
Web Site: www.planetbeach.com
Ms. Rita Zayas, Franchise Development
   Advisor

For the benefit of our customers and the communities we serve, we will remain dedicated to the continued success of each PLANET BEACH CONTEMPO SPA franchise. Our salons provide superior customer service with an alternative, exciting atmosphere. PLANET BEACH CONTEMPO SPA will focus solely on the service of tanning and the sale of retail products that enhance the tanning experience.

BACKGROUND: IFA MEMBER
Established: 1995;   1st Franchised: 1996
Franchised Units: 250
Company-Owned Units: 0
Total Units: 250

Dist.:   US-250; CAN-18; O'seas-1
North America: 31 States, 0 Provinces
Density: 29 in TX, 52 in LA, 21 in CA
Projected New Units (12 Months):   NR
Qualifications: NR

FINANCIAL/TERMS:
Cash Investment: $133K-470K
Total Investment: $133K-170K
Minimum Net Worth: $225K
Fees: Franchise - $30K
   Royalty - 6%;   Ad. - 1%
Earnings Claims Statement: Yes
Term of Contract (Years):   10/5
Avg. # Of Employees: 1 FT, 2 PT
Passive Ownership: Discouraged
Encourage Conversions: No
Area Develop. Agreements: Yes/1
Sub-Franchising Contracts: Yes
Expand In Territory: Yes
Space Needs: 1,000-1,500 SF

SUPPORT & TRAINING:
Financial Assistance Provided: No
Site Selection Assistance: Yes
Lease Negotiation Assistance: Yes
Co-Operative Advertising: No
Franchisee Assoc./Member: Yes/Yes
Size Of Corporate Staff: 65
On-Going Support: A,B,C,d,,,G,h,I
Training: NR

SPECIFIC EXPANSION PLANS:
US: All United States
Canada: NR
Overseas: NR

≪ ≫

PRO-CUTS
7201 Metro Blvd.
Minneapolis, MN 55439-2130
Tel: (888) 888-7008 (952) 947-7777
Fax: (952) 947-7900
E-Mail: franchiseleads@regiscorp.com
Web Site: www.regisfranchise.com
Mr. Alan Storry, VP Franchise Development

PRO-CUTS provides professional haircuts for the whole family at affordable prices in a neighborhood environment. PRO-CUTS exhibits a friendly, yet professional atmosphere. Our franchisees are provided with support and training in ALL phases of operation, as well as on-going training and support for employees.

BACKGROUND: IFA MEMBER

Established: 1982;   1st Franchised: 1983
Franchised Units: 175
Company-Owned Units: 0
Total Units: 175
Dist.:   US-176; CAN-0; O'seas-0
North America: 12 States, 0 Provinces
Density: 130 in TX, 17 in OK, 7 in NM
Projected New Units (12 Months):   10
Qualifications: 4, 5, 1, 3, 3, 4

FINANCIAL/TERMS:
Cash Investment: $90K-196K
Total Investment: $90K-196K
Minimum Net Worth: $300K/100K Liq
Fees: Franchise - $22.5K 1st
   Royalty - 4% 1st Yr./6% succ. Yrs.; Ad.
   - 5%
Earnings Claims Statement: No
Term of Contract (Years):   10/10
Avg. # Of Employees: 6 FT, 2 PT
Passive Ownership: Discouraged
Encourage Conversions: No
Area Develop. Agreements: Yes/1
Sub-Franchising Contracts: No
Expand In Territory: Yes
Space Needs: 900-1,200 SF

SUPPORT & TRAINING:
Financial Assistance Provided: Yes (I)
Site Selection Assistance: Yes
Lease Negotiation Assistance: Yes
Co-Operative Advertising: No
Franchisee Assoc./Member: Yes/Yes
Size Of Corporate Staff: 900
On-Going Support: ,,C,D,E,,,G,h,I
Training: 5 Days Field Training;
   3-5 Days Franchise Support Office

SPECIFIC EXPANSION PLANS:
US: All United States
Canada: No
Overseas: NR

≪ ≫

ROOSTERS MEN'S GROOMING CENTERS
13343 US Hwy., 183 N., # 215
Uastin, TX 78750
Tel: (866) 642-2625 (512) 238-0733
Fax: (512) 238-0716
E-Mail: info@roostersmgc.com
Web Site: www.roostersmgc.com
Mr. Joseph B. Grondin,

ROOSTERS MEN'S GROOMING CENTERS is an upscale, male only, barber and company-licensed establishment. The only franchise to operate on a flat royalty fee. No percentage of gross. No audits, custom design and setup. The best of the best for men and with the career of the stylest the top priority.

BACKGROUND:

Established: 1999; 1st Franchised: 2004

Franchised Units:	20
Company-Owned Units:	4
Total Units:	24
Dist.:	US-24; CAN-0; O'seas-0
North America: 11 States, 0 Provinces	
Density:	8 in TX, 5 in MI
Projected New Units (12 Months):	10
Qualifications:	2, 3, 2, 2, 2, 5

FINANCIAL/TERMS:

Cash Investment:	$70K-80K
Total Investment:	$150K-225K
Minimum Net Worth:	$50K
Fees: Franchise -	$25K
Royalty - 2.5%;	Ad. - 0%
Earnings Claims Statement:	No
Term of Contract (Years):	10/10
Avg. # Of Employees:	6 FT, 3 PT
Passive Ownership:	Discouraged
Encourage Conversions:	Yes
Area Develop. Agreements:	Yes/10
Sub-Franchising Contracts:	No
Expand In Territory:	Yes
Space Needs:	1,200 SF

SUPPORT & TRAINING:

Financial Assistance Provided:	Yes (I)
Site Selection Assistance:	Yes
Lease Negotiation Assistance:	Yes
Co-Operative Advertising:	Yes
Franchisee Assoc./Member:	Yes/Yes
Size Of Corporate Staff:	5
On-Going Support:	,,C,D,E,,G,h,I
Training:	2 Weeks On-Site

SPECIFIC EXPANSION PLANS:

US:	All United States
Canada:	All Canada
Overseas:	All Countries

⊰⊰ ⊱⊱

SNIP N' CLIP HAIRCUT SHOPS

11427 Strong Line Rd.
Lenexa, KS 66215
Tel: (800) 622-6804 + 10 (913) 345-0077
Fax: (913) 345-1554
E-Mail: info@snipnclip.net
Web Site: www.snipnclip.net
Ms. Deb Vielock,

Family haircut shops. Fast service, low price, no appointments. Strip mall shopping centers. Least expensive corporate turnkey.

BACKGROUND:

Established: 1976; 1st Franchised: 1986

Franchised Units:	46
Company-Owned Units:	49

Total Units:	95
Dist.:	US-95; CAN-0; O'seas-0
North America: 12 States, 0 Provinces	
Density:	28 in MO, 38 in KS, 9 in AR
Projected New Units (12 Months):	7
Qualifications:	4, 3, 1, 3, NR, 4

FINANCIAL/TERMS:

Cash Investment:	$60K
Total Investment:	$70-82K
Minimum Net Worth:	$100K
Fees: Franchise -	$10K
Royalty - 5%;	Ad. - 0%
Earnings Claims Statement:	No
Term of Contract (Years):	10/
Avg. # Of Employees:	4 FT, 2 PT
Passive Ownership:	Allowed
Encourage Conversions:	NA
Area Develop. Agreements:	No
Sub-Franchising Contracts:	No
Expand In Territory:	Yes
Space Needs:	1,000 SF

SUPPORT & TRAINING:

Financial Assistance Provided:	Yes (D)
Site Selection Assistance:	Yes
Lease Negotiation Assistance:	Yes
Co-Operative Advertising:	No
Franchisee Assoc./Member:	Yes/Yes
Size Of Corporate Staff:	10
On-Going Support:	,,C,D,E,,G,H,I
Training:	5 Days On-Site

SPECIFIC EXPANSION PLANS:

US:	Midwest, West, Southwest
Canada:	No
Overseas:	NR

⊰⊰ ⊱⊱

SONA MEDSPA INTERNATIONAL

840 Crescent Centre Ct., # 260
Franklin, TN 37067
Tel: (615) 591-5040
Fax: (615) 591-5041
E-Mail: kboughnou@sonamedspa.com
Web Site: www.sonamedspa.com
Ms. Karen Boughnou, Executive Director of Sales

SONA MEDSPA is the premier med-spa franchise in the US. SONA MEDSPA combines state-of-the-art technology with SONA'S patent-pending process called the 'SONA Concept,' which allows laser hair removal and other anti-aging services to be performed in less time, with better results and at fees that are affordable to the general public. All this, offered in an up-scale, spa-like atmosphere.

BACKGROUND: IFA MEMBER

Established: 1997; 1st Franchised: 2002

Franchised Units:	36
Company-Owned Units:	5
Total Units:	41
Dist.:	US-41; CAN-0; O'seas-0
North America: 31 States, 0 Provinces	
Density:	3 in VA, 4 in NC, 4 in CA
Projected New Units (12 Months):	55
Qualifications:	5, 5, 2, 2, 4, 5

FINANCIAL/TERMS:

Cash Investment:	$250K
Total Investment:	$409-825K
Minimum Net Worth:	$750K
Fees: Franchise -	$59.5K Std.
Royalty - 7.75%;	Ad. - 2%
Earnings Claims Statement:	Yes
Term of Contract (Years):	15/15
Avg. # Of Employees:	5 FT, 5 PT
Passive Ownership:	Not Allowed
Encourage Conversions:	Yes
Area Develop. Agreements:	Yes
Sub-Franchising Contracts:	No
Expand In Territory:	Yes
Space Needs:	3,000-4,200 SF

SUPPORT & TRAINING:

Financial Assistance Provided:	Yes (D)
Site Selection Assistance:	Yes
Lease Negotiation Assistance:	Yes
Co-Operative Advertising:	No
Franchisee Assoc./Member:	Yes/Yes
Size Of Corporate Staff:	26
On-Going Support:	,,C,D,E,,G,H,I
Training: 6 Days Laser Center; 4 Days Corporate Office; 6 Days On-Site	

SPECIFIC EXPANSION PLANS:

US:	All United States
Canada:	All Canada
Overseas:	All Countries

⊰⊰ ⊱⊱

SPORT CLIPS

110 Briarwood
Georgetown, TX 78628
Tel: (800) 872-4247 + 240 (512) 868-4601
Fax: (512) 868-4699
E-Mail: beth@sportclips.com
Web Site: www.sportclips.com
Ms. Beth Boecker, Director of Franchise Recruitment

Sports-themed haircutting salons, appealing primarily to men and boys. Unique design, proprietary haircutting system and complete support at the unit level. Retail sale of Paul Mitchell & American Crew hair care products, sports apparel and memorabilia.

BACKGROUND: IFA MEMBER
Established: 1993;   1st Franchised: 1995
Franchised Units: 636
Company-Owned Units: <u>14</u>
Total Units: 650
Dist.:   US-650; CAN-0; O'seas-0
  North America: 36 States, 0 Provinces
  Density: 42 in IL, 48 in CA, 150 in TX
Projected New Units (12 Months):   100
Qualifications: 4, 5, 1, 1, 3, 5
FINANCIAL/TERMS:
Cash Investment: $100K
Total Investment: $150-200K
Minimum Net Worth: $300K
Fees: Franchise - $25K - 1 lic., $39.5K - 2
lic., $49.5K - 3 lic.
  Royalty - ;   Ad. - $300/Wk.
Earnings Claims Statement: Yes
Term of Contract (Years):   5/5
Avg. # Of Employees: 6-8 FT or PT
Passive Ownership: Allowed
Encourage Conversions: No
Area Develop. Agreements: Yes/10
Sub-Franchising Contracts: No
Expand In Territory: Yes
Space Needs: 1,200 SF
SUPPORT & TRAINING:
Financial Assistance Provided: Yes (D)
Site Selection Assistance: Yes
Lease Negotiation Assistance: Yes
Co-Operative Advertising: Yes
Franchisee Assoc./Member: No
Size Of Corporate Staff: 60
On-Going Support: ,,C,D,E,F,G,H,I
Training: 1 Week Locally for Manager;
    1 Week Locally; 5 Days Georgetown,
    TX for Franchisee
SPECIFIC EXPANSION PLANS:
US: All United States
Canada: No
Overseas: NR

<< >>

SUPERCUTS
7201 Metro Blvd.
Minneapolis, MN 55439-2103
Tel: (888) 888-7008 (952) 947-7777
Fax: (952) 947-7900
E-Mail: franchiseleads@regiscorp.com
Web Site: www.regisfranchise.com
Mr. Alan Storry, VP Franchise Develop-
    ment

Our strategy is simple: give men and busy families what they want. That's why SUPERCUTS Salons offer a contemporary and comfortable atmosphere that appeals to those in search of current hairstyles at affordable prices.

BACKGROUND: IFA MEMBER
Established: 1975;   1st Franchised: 1975
Franchised Units: 1010
Company-Owned Units: <u>1122</u>
Total Units: 2132
Dist.:   US-2066; CAN-50; O'seas-16
  North America: 48 States, 1 Provinces
  Density: 164 in TX, 188 in FL, 397 in
CA
Projected New Units (12 Months):   78
Qualifications: 5, 5, 1, 3, 4, 5
FINANCIAL/TERMS:
Cash Investment: $111-239.7K
Total Investment: $97-208K
Minimum Net Worth: $300K/100K Liq
Fees: Franchise - $22.5K
  Royalty - 4% Yr. 1/6% succ. Yrs.;   Ad.
- 4
Earnings Claims Statement: No
Term of Contract (Years):   Evergreen/
Avg. # Of Employees: 5 FT, 4 PT
Passive Ownership: Allowed
Encourage Conversions: Yes
Area Develop. Agreements: Yes/3
Sub-Franchising Contracts: No
Expand In Territory: Yes
Space Needs: 1,000 SF
SUPPORT & TRAINING:
Financial Assistance Provided: Yes (I)
Site Selection Assistance: Yes
Lease Negotiation Assistance: Yes
Co-Operative Advertising: Yes
Franchisee Assoc./Member: Yes/Yes
Size Of Corporate Staff: 900
On-Going Support: ,,C,D,E,,G,H,
Training: Outstanding support in all areas;
    4-5 Days Minneapolis, MN
SPECIFIC EXPANSION PLANS:
US: All United States
Canada: All Canada
Overseas: NR

<< >>

TOP OF THE LINE FRAGRANCES
515 Bath Ave.
Long Branch, NJ 07740
Tel: (800) 929-3083 (732) 229-0014
Fax: (732) 222-1762
E-Mail: info@tolfranchise.com
Web Site: www.tolfranchise.com
Mr. Steven Ciaverelli, Vice President

T.O.L. specializes in the retail sale of designer fragrances at the lowest discounted prices.

BACKGROUND:
Established: 1987;   1st Franchised: 1987
Franchised Units: 3
Company-Owned Units: <u>1</u>
Total Units: 4
Dist.:   US-4; CAN-0; O'seas-0
  North America: 3 States, Provinces
  Density: 2 in FL, 1 in PA, 1 in TN
Projected New Units (12 Months):   3
Qualifications: 5, 3, 3, 1, 1, 4
FINANCIAL/TERMS:
Cash Investment: $150-200K
Total Investment: $150-200K
Minimum Net Worth: $150K
Fees: Franchise - $20K
  Royalty - 5%;   Ad. - NA
Earnings Claims Statement: No
Term of Contract (Years):   10/5
Avg. # Of Employees: 3 FT, 3 PT
Passive Ownership: Discouraged
Encourage Conversions: Yes
Area Develop. Agreements: Yes/1
Sub-Franchising Contracts: No
Expand In Territory: Yes
Space Needs: 700-1,200 SF
SUPPORT & TRAINING:
Financial Assistance Provided: Yes (D)
Site Selection Assistance: Yes
Lease Negotiation Assistance: Yes
Co-Operative Advertising: No
Franchisee Assoc./Member: No
Size Of Corporate Staff: 5
On-Going Support: ,B,C,d,E,F,,,I
Training: 7-10 Days Franchise Location
SPECIFIC EXPANSION PLANS:
US: East
Canada: No
Overseas: NR

<< >>

TROPI-TAN FRANCHISING
5152 Commerce Rd.
Flint, MI 48507-2939
Tel: (866) 818-1826 (810) 230-6789
Fax: (810) 230-1115
E-Mail: theo@tropitan.biz
Web Site: www.tropitan.biz
Mr. Theo Deming, Director of Franchis-
    ing

In business for 20 years, TROPI-TAN

indoor sun-tanning salons are international design and decor award winners. One of the most progressive salon chains, TROPI-TAN salons also feature a full line of tanning lotions, clothing, and related accessories.

BACKGROUND: IFA MEMBER
Established: 1979; 1st Franchised: 1986
Franchised Units: 8
Company-Owned Units: 7
Total Units: 15
Dist.: US-15; CAN-0; O'seas-0
 North America: 1 States, 0 Provinces
 Density: 12 in MI
Projected New Units (12 Months): 25
Qualifications: 3, 3, 1, 3, 3, 5

FINANCIAL/TERMS:
Cash Investment: $50-100K
Total Investment: $191.5-380K
Minimum Net Worth: $150K
Fees: Franchise - $20K
 Royalty - 5%; Ad. - 3%
Earnings Claims Statement: No
Term of Contract (Years): 10/5
Avg. # Of Employees: 1 FT, 3 PT
Passive Ownership: Discouraged
Encourage Conversions: Yes
Area Develop. Agreements: Yes/1
Sub-Franchising Contracts: No
Expand In Territory: Yes
Space Needs: 2,500 SF
SUPPORT & TRAINING:

Financial Assistance Provided: Yes (D)
Site Selection Assistance: Yes
Lease Negotiation Assistance: Yes
Co-Operative Advertising: No
Franchisee Assoc./Member: No
Size Of Corporate Staff: 30
On-Going Support: A,B,C,D,E,F,G,H,I
Training: 80 Hours Corporate Training
 Center; 40 Hours On-Site
SPECIFIC EXPANSION PLANS:
US: All United States
Canada: All Canada
Overseas: All Countries

7

FIVE LARGEST PARTICIPANTS IN SURVEY

Company	# Fran-chised Units	# Co-Owned Units	# Total Units	Franchise Fee	On-Going Royalty	Total Investment
1. Nation-Wide General Rental Centers	487	1	488	$0	0%	$169.5K
2. ATL International	450	0	450	$25K	7%	$120-130K
3. HouseMaster Home Inspections	393	10	403	$27.5K	7.5%	$25-55K
4. American Leak Detection	335	4	339	$29.5K	6-10%	$83.3-233.6K
5. Kitchen Tune-Up	280	0	280	$25K	Varies	$83K-91K

All of the data provided are proprietary and should not be quoted without acknowledging *Bond's Franchise Guide*.

ABC SEAMLESS

3001 Fiechtner Dr.
Fargo, ND 58103
Tel: (800) 732-6577 (701) 293-5952
Fax: (701) 293-3107
E-Mail: theduck@abcseamless.com
Web Site: www.abcsiding.com
Mr. Veryl Vik, VP Franchise Development

Franchisor of seamless steel siding, gutters, soffit and fascia. A portable machine embosses and creates seamless siding profiles of any length on the job site.

BACKGROUND:

Established: 1978; 1st Franchised: 1978
Franchised Units: 129

Company-Owned Units: 19
Total Units: 148
Dist.: US-148; CAN-0; O'seas-0
  North America: 38 States, 0 Provinces
  Density: 16 in WI, 22 in MN, 12 in IL
Projected New Units (12 Months): 10
Qualifications: 5, 4, 5, 4, 4, 4

FINANCIAL/TERMS:

Cash Investment: $20-40K
Total Investment: $73.8-212K
Minimum Net Worth: $150K
Fees: Franchise - $12K
  Royalty - 2-5%; Ad. - 0.05%
Earnings Claims Statement: No
Term of Contract (Years): 10/10
Avg. # Of Employees: 4 FT, 0 PT
Passive Ownership: Discouraged

Encourage Conversions: No
Area Develop. Agreements: Yes/1
Sub-Franchising Contracts: No
Expand In Territory: Yes
Space Needs: NR
SUPPORT & TRAINING:
Financial Assistance Provided: Yes (D)
Site Selection Assistance: NA
Lease Negotiation Assistance: Yes
Co-Operative Advertising: No
Franchisee Assoc./Member: No
Size Of Corporate Staff: 15
On-Going Support: ,,C,D,E,,G,H,I
Training: 2 Weeks Franchisee's Site;
  On-Goin Corporate Location
SPECIFIC EXPANSION PLANS:
US: All United States

Canada: No
Overseas: NR

≪≪ ≫≫

ALTRACOLOR SYSTEMS
113 23rd St.
Kenner, LA 70062
Tel: (800) 678-5220 (504) 454-7233
Fax: (985) 863-9962
E-Mail: altra@altracolor.com
Web Site: www.altracolor.com
Mr. Jeff Richards, President

ALTRACOLOR SYSTEMS is the state-of-the-art mobile, on-site touch-up and spot repair system for automotive paint repair.

BACKGROUND: IFA MEMBER
Established: 1988; 1st Franchised: 1991
Franchised Units: 82
Company-Owned Units: 92
Total Units: 174
Dist.: US-174; CAN-0; O'seas-0
  North America: 27 States, Provinces
  Density: 14 in NC, 13 in SC, 13 in VA
Projected New Units (12 Months): 23
Qualifications: 3, 3, 1, 1, 2, 4
FINANCIAL/TERMS:
Cash Investment: $5-11.7K
Total Investment: $16.9-25.2K
Minimum Net Worth: NA
Fees: Franchise - $9.95K
  Royalty - $95/Wk.; Ad. - 0%
Earnings Claims Statement: Yes
Term of Contract (Years): 15/5
Avg. # Of Employees: 1 FT, 0 PT
Passive Ownership: Not Allowed
Encourage Conversions: Yes
Area Develop. Agreements: Yes/1
Sub-Franchising Contracts: Yes
Expand In Territory: Yes
Space Needs: NA
SUPPORT & TRAINING:
Financial Assistance Provided: Yes (D)
Site Selection Assistance: NA
Lease Negotiation Assistance: NA
Co-Operative Advertising: No
Franchisee Assoc./Member: No
Size Of Corporate Staff: 5
On-Going Support: „C,D,„,G,H,I
Training: 1 Week Metairie, LA
SPECIFIC EXPANSION PLANS:
US: All United States
Canada: No
Overseas: NR

≪≪ ≫≫

AMERICAN ASPHALT SEALCOATING
P. O. Box 600
Chesterland, OH 44026
Tel: (888) 603-7325 (440) 729-8080
Fax: (440) 729-2231
E-Mail: asphaltusa@aol.com
Web Site: www.american-sealcoating.com
Mr. John Jonz, General Manager

Get your share at the billion dollar pavement maintenance industry with our franchise. Residential, commercial and industrial sealcoating and pavement services. 94% of all pavement is asphalt that needs our service. (50 million driveways, 7+ million parking lots, 4 million miles of road.) Our expert training staff and low start-up investment of $38K will get you up and running within 60 days. Your trained crew will perform the work while you manage the business from your home-based office.

BACKGROUND:
Established: 1988; 1st Franchised: 1998
Franchised Units: 10
Company-Owned Units: 1
Total Units: 11
Dist.: US-11; CAN-0; O'seas-0
  North America: 4 States, Provinces
  Density: 4 in OH, 1 in VA
Projected New Units (12 Months): 10
Qualifications: 4, 3, 1, 1, 1, 3
FINANCIAL/TERMS:
Cash Investment: $10-30K
Total Investment: $35-50K
Minimum Net Worth: $50K
Fees: Franchise - $15K
  Royalty - 5-7%; Ad. - 1%
Earnings Claims Statement: No
Term of Contract (Years): 15/15
Avg. # Of Employees: 1-2 FT, 1-2 PT
Passive Ownership: Discouraged
Encourage Conversions: Yes
Area Develop. Agreements: Yes/1
Sub-Franchising Contracts: No
Expand In Territory: Yes
Space Needs: NA
SUPPORT & TRAINING:
Financial Assistance Provided: Yes (D)
Site Selection Assistance: Yes
Lease Negotiation Assistance: Yes
Co-Operative Advertising: No
Franchisee Assoc./Member: No
Size Of Corporate Staff: 6
On-Going Support: ,B,C,d,„,,H,I
Training: NR
SPECIFIC EXPANSION PLANS:
US: All United States

Canada: No
Overseas: NR

≪≪ ≫≫

AMERICAN LEAK DETECTION
888 Research Dr., # 100
Palm Springs, CA 92262
Tel: (800) 755-6697 (760) 320-9991
Fax: (760) 320-1288
E-Mail: jhoward@americanleakdetection.com
Web Site: www.americanleakdetection-franchise.com
Ms. Judy Howard, Director of Franchise Relations

Electronic detection of water, drain, gas, waste, and sewer leaks under concrete slabs of homes, commercial buildings, pools, spas, fountains, etc. with equipment commissioned/ manufactured by company.

BACKGROUND: IFA MEMBER
Established: 1974; 1st Franchised: 1984
Franchised Units: 335
Company-Owned Units: 4
Total Units: 339
Dist.: US-299; CAN-8; O'seas-28
  North America: 40 States, 2 Provinces
  Density: 22 in TX, 37 in FL, 84 in CA
Projected New Units (12 Months): 4
Qualifications: 3, 3, 2, 2, 2, 3
FINANCIAL/TERMS:
Cash Investment: $29.5-80K
Total Investment: $83.3-233.6K
Minimum Net Worth: Varies
Fees: Franchise - $29.5K
  Royalty - 6-10%; Ad. - NA
Earnings Claims Statement: No
Term of Contract (Years): 10/10
Avg. # Of Employees: 1-4 FT, 2 PT
Passive Ownership: Discouraged
Encourage Conversions: NA
Area Develop. Agreements: No
Sub-Franchising Contracts: No
Expand In Territory: Yes
Space Needs: NR
SUPPORT & TRAINING:
Financial Assistance Provided: Yes (D)
Site Selection Assistance: NA
Lease Negotiation Assistance: NA
Co-Operative Advertising: Yes
Franchisee Assoc./Member: No
Size Of Corporate Staff: 34

On-Going Support: a,B,C,D,,f,G,H,I
Training: 6-10 Weeks Palm Springs, CA
SPECIFIC EXPANSION PLANS:
US: Northeast, Midwest
Canada: MB, SK, BC
Overseas: Western Europe, Japan, Mexico, Australia

◄◄ ►►

ARCHADECK

2924 Emerywood Pkwy., # 101
Richmond, VA 23294
Tel: (800) 722-4668 (804) 353-6999
Fax: (804) 358-1878
E-Mail: cgrandpre@outdoorlivingbrands.com
Web Site: www.archadeckfranchise.com
Mr. Chris Grandpre, President & CEO

ARCHADECK, founded in 1980, started the nation's first network specializing in custom-designed and built decks, porches and other outdoor products. Today, there are over 80 locally owned and operated offices in the U.S., Canada, the United Kingdom and Japan. Because construction experience is not required, our franchisees come from a variety of professional backgrounds.

BACKGROUND:
Established: 1980; 1st Franchised: 1984
Franchised Units: 70
Company-Owned Units: 1
Total Units: 71
Dist.: US-71; CAN-2; O'seas-2
North America: 27 States, 2 Provinces
Density: 5 in TX, 4 in NC, 6 in GA
Projected New Units (12 Months): 25
Qualifications: 5, 5, 1, 3, 4, 5
FINANCIAL/TERMS:
Cash Investment: $50K-150K
Total Investment: $89K-200K
Minimum Net Worth: $100K
Fees: Franchise - $28K
Royalty - 6.5%; Ad. - 1%
Earnings Claims Statement: No
Term of Contract (Years): 10/10
Avg. # Of Employees: 1 FT, 1 PT
Passive Ownership: Discouraged
Encourage Conversions: Yes
Area Develop. Agreements: No
Sub-Franchising Contracts: No
Expand In Territory: Yes
Space Needs: NA
SUPPORT & TRAINING:
Financial Assistance Provided: Yes (D)
Site Selection Assistance: NA
Lease Negotiation Assistance: NA

Co-Operative Advertising: No
Franchisee Assoc./Member: Yes/Yes
Size Of Corporate Staff: 25
On-Going Support: ,,C,D,,,G,H,I
Training: 20 Business Days Richmond, VA; 9 Days Location
SPECIFIC EXPANSION PLANS:
US: All United States
Canada: All Canada
Overseas: Europe

◄◄ ►►

BATH FITTER

27 Berard Dr., # 2701
South Burlington, VT 05403-5810
Tel: (877) 422-2322 + 277 (450) 472-0027
Fax: (450) 472-9490
E-Mail: jfasoli@bathfitter.com
Web Site: www.bathfitter.com
Mr. Joe Fasoli, Franchise Sales

Since 1984, BATH FITTER has been installing custom-molded acrylic bathtub liners, shower bases and one-piece, seamless wall surrounds over existing fixtures in just a few hours in countless residential and commercial properties. We provide full training, specialized tools, marketing and technical manuals and on-going support through regular visits to your location. We award exclusive territories with enormous residential and commercial market potential to qualified franchise owners.

BACKGROUND:
Established: 1984; 1st Franchised: 1992
Franchised Units: 180
Company-Owned Units: 39
Total Units: 219
Dist.: US-180; CAN-39; O'seas-0
North America: 34 States, 10 Provinces
Density: 17 in NY, 17 in OH, 18 in FL
Projected New Units (12 Months): 12
Qualifications: 3, 3, 2, 1, 4, 5
FINANCIAL/TERMS:
Cash Investment: NA
Total Investment: $120-175K
Minimum Net Worth: NA
Fees: Franchise - $40K
Royalty - 0%; Ad. - NA
Earnings Claims Statement: Yes
Term of Contract (Years): 5/5
Avg. # Of Employees: 8 FT, 0 PT
Passive Ownership: Not Allowed

Encourage Conversions: No
Area Develop. Agreements: No
Sub-Franchising Contracts: No
Expand In Territory: Yes
Space Needs: 3,500+ SF
SUPPORT & TRAINING:
Financial Assistance Provided: No
Site Selection Assistance: Yes
Lease Negotiation Assistance: NA
Co-Operative Advertising: No
Franchisee Assoc./Member: No
Size Of Corporate Staff: 13
On-Going Support: ,,C,D,E,,,G,h,I
Training: 10 Days Franchisee Site;10 Days Headquarters
SPECIFIC EXPANSION PLANS:
US: All United States
Canada: No
Overseas: NR

◄◄ ►►

BEARCOM BUILDING SERVICES

7022 S. 400 W.
Midvale, UT 84047
Tel: (888) 569-9533 (801) 569-9500
Fax: (801) 569-8400
E-Mail: joseph@bearcomservices.com
Web Site: www.bearcomservices.com
Mr. Joseph Jenkins, President/CEO

We train you on how to get your own janitorial accounts. We support you to help you maintain those accounts. We have software to help you manage your business. You will own and operate a cleaning business (commercial).

BACKGROUND:
Established: 1993; 1st Franchised: 1994
Franchised Units: 60
Company-Owned Units: 0
Total Units: 60
Dist.: US-60; CAN-0; O'seas-0
North America: 1 States, 0 Provinces
Density: 60 in UT
Projected New Units (12 Months): NR
Qualifications: NR
FINANCIAL/TERMS:
Cash Investment: $3K
Total Investment: $12.8K
Minimum Net Worth: $0K
Fees: Franchise - $10K
Royalty - 8%; Ad. - 0%
Earnings Claims Statement: No
Term of Contract (Years): 5/5
Avg. # Of Employees: 2 FT, 3 PT
Passive Ownership: Allowed
Encourage Conversions: No
Area Develop. Agreements: No

Sub-Franchising Contracts: No
Expand In Territory: No
Space Needs: NA

SUPPORT & TRAINING:
Financial Assistance Provided: No
Site Selection Assistance: No
Lease Negotiation Assistance: No
Co-Operative Advertising: No
Franchisee Assoc./Member: No
Size Of Corporate Staff: 4
On-Going Support: a,,,,,,G,,I
Training: 3 Days UT

SPECIFIC EXPANSION PLANS:
US: Utah
Canada: No
Overseas: NR

BORDER MAGIC

1503 Country Rd., 2700 N.
Rantoul, IL 61866-9705
Tel: (877) 892-2954 (217) 892-2954
Fax: (217) 893-3739
E-Mail: bordermagic@illicom.net
Web Site: www.bordermagic.com
Mr. Eldean Bergman, President

Sell and install beautiful, seamless concrete landscape edging that has the look and feel of real brick and stone in your protected territory using the BORDER MAGIC BM 2000 extruder and the BORDER MAGIC proven method. The BM 2000 also extrudes concrete parking lot curbing for schools, restaurants and businesses of all kinds. A turnkey franchise opportunity awaits you as a licensed dealer. Border Magic is also the manufacturer of equipment. Border Magic is the only franchisor in this particular industry.

BACKGROUND:
Established: 1984; 1st Franchised: 2002
Franchised Units: 73
Company-Owned Units: 0
Total Units: 73
Dist.: US-73; CAN-0; O'seas-0
North America: 24 States, 0 Provinces
Density: 9 in OH, 9 in IN, 12 in IL
Projected New Units (12 Months): 15
Qualifications: 3, 2, 2, 1, 2, 3

FINANCIAL/TERMS:
Cash Investment: $30K
Total Investment: $64-105K
Minimum Net Worth: $250K
Fees: Franchise - $25K
  Royalty - $250/Mo.; Ad. - Included in
monthly royalty
Earnings Claims Statement: Yes

Term of Contract (Years): 5/5
Avg. # Of Employees: 3 FT, 0 PT
Passive Ownership: Allowed
Encourage Conversions: NA
Area Develop. Agreements: Yes/1
Sub-Franchising Contracts: Yes
Expand In Territory: Yes
Space Needs: NA

SUPPORT & TRAINING:
Financial Assistance Provided: Yes (I)
Site Selection Assistance: Yes
Lease Negotiation Assistance: NA
Co-Operative Advertising: Yes
Franchisee Assoc./Member: No
Size Of Corporate Staff: 7
On-Going Support: A,B,C,D,,F,G,H,I
Training: Ongoing Rantoul, IL

SPECIFIC EXPANSION PLANS:
US: All United States
Canada: No
Overseas: NR

CALIFORNIA CLOSET COMPANY

1000 Fourth St., # 800
San Rafael, CA 94901-3142
Tel: (800) 274-6754 (415) 256-8500
Fax: (415) 256-8501
E-Mail: franchising@calclosets.com
Web Site: www.californiaclosets.com
Ms. Kathleen Low, Director of Franchise
Operations

CALIFORNIA CLOSETS COMPANY pioneered the custom storage business over 30 years ago. It is now the most famous brand and leader in its industry. Known for innovative design, California Closets commitment is to creating solutions that work specifically for its customer's lifestyle and home. California Closets has exceptional national advertising presence, local marketing tools, sophisticated and successful programs in learning and development for all aspects of operations. Continuous communication through conventions, regional seminars, webinars, franchise intranet site and on-site visits.

BACKGROUND: IFA MEMBER
Established: 1978; 1st Franchised: 1980
Franchised Units: 109
Company-Owned Units: 1
Total Units: 110
Dist.: US-99; CAN-8; O'seas-3
North America: 43 States, 5 Provinces
Density: NR
Projected New Units (12 Months): 4
Qualifications: 5, 5, 1, 3, 1, 5

FINANCIAL/TERMS:
Cash Investment: $125K
Total Investment: $227.9K-741.2K
Minimum Net Worth: $750K
Fees: Franchise - $70K
  Royalty - 6%; Ad. - 3%
Earnings Claims Statement: No
Term of Contract (Years): 10/10
Avg. # Of Employees: 3-25 FT, 0 PT
Passive Ownership: Discouraged
Encourage Conversions: NA
Area Develop. Agreements: No
Sub-Franchising Contracts: No
Expand In Territory: Yes
Space Needs: 1,000-12,000 SF

SUPPORT & TRAINING:
Financial Assistance Provided: Yes (I)
Site Selection Assistance: Yes
Lease Negotiation Assistance: Yes
Co-Operative Advertising: No
Franchisee Assoc./Member: No
Size Of Corporate Staff: 0
On-Going Support: A,B,C,D,E,F,G,H,I
Training: 2 Weeks On-Site

SPECIFIC EXPANSION PLANS:
US: Various U.S. Locations
Canada: No
Overseas: NR

CLOSET FACTORY, THE

12800 S. Broadway
Los Angeles, CA 90061-1116
Tel: (800) 318-8800 (310) 715-1000
Fax: (310) 516-8065
E-Mail: info@closetfactory.com
Web Site: www.closetfactory.com
Mr. John LaBarbara, Chief Executive Officer

Join the industry leader, ranked #1 in custom closets by Entrepreneur Magazine worldwide. Franchisees design, sell, manufacture and install custom closet systems, garage organizers, kitchen pantries, entertainment centers and custom office systems. Operate a large, vertically integrated cash business during normal business hours in an exclusive territory. A complete turn-key business through training and ongoing support. No technical experience is necessary.

BACKGROUND:
Established: 1983; 1st Franchised: 1985
Franchised Units: 90
Company-Owned Units: 27
Total Units: 117
Dist.: US-102; CAN-5; O'seas-10

North America: 39 States, 2 Provinces
Density: 8 in NY, 7 in FL, 14 in CA
Projected New Units (12 Months): 15
Qualifications: 5, 5, 2, 4, 3, 3

FINANCIAL/TERMS:
Cash Investment: $40-50K
Total Investment: $99.5-185K
Minimum Net Worth: $150-350K
Fees: Franchise - $28.5-39.5K
  Royalty - 5.8%; Ad. - 1%
Earnings Claims Statement: No
Term of Contract (Years): 5/5
Avg. # Of Employees: 5-6 FT, 0 PT
Passive Ownership: Allowed
Encourage Conversions: Yes
Area Develop. Agreements: No
Sub-Franchising Contracts: No
Expand In Territory: No
Space Needs: 3,500-4,000 SF

SUPPORT & TRAINING:
Financial Assistance Provided: Yes (D)
Site Selection Assistance: Yes
Lease Negotiation Assistance: Yes
Co-Operative Advertising: No
Franchisee Assoc./Member: No
Size Of Corporate Staff: NR
On-Going Support: ,B,C,D,E,,G,h,
Training: 2 Weeks Corporate
  Headquarters; 4 Weeks On-Site

SPECIFIC EXPANSION PLANS:
US: All United States
Canada: All Canada
Overseas: All Countries

◄◄ ►►

CLOSETS BY DESIGN
11145 Knott Ave., # A
Cypress, CA 90630
Tel: (800) 377-5737 (714) 890-5860
Fax: (714) 901-0424
E-Mail: ccooper@closetsbydesign.com
Web Site: www.closetsbydesign.com
Mr. Jerry Egner, President & CEO

Sell, design, manufacture and install custom closet organizers, garage cabinets, in-home office systems, wall units, pantries and more ...

BACKGROUND: IFA MEMBER
Established: 1982; 1st Franchised: 1998
Franchised Units: 28
Company-Owned Units: 3
Total Units: 31
Dist.: US-31; CAN-0; O'seas-0
North America: 8 States, 0 Provinces
Density: 5 in OH, 3 in NY, 3 in IL
Projected New Units (12 Months): 6
Qualifications: 5, 5, 1, 4, 1, 5

FINANCIAL/TERMS:
Cash Investment: $100-341K
Total Investment: $124.9K-278.4K
Minimum Net Worth: $500K
Fees: Franchise - $36.9K
  Royalty - 6%; Ad. - 3%
Earnings Claims Statement: No
Term of Contract (Years): 5/5
Avg. # Of Employees: 7-50 FT, 0 PT
Passive Ownership: Discouraged
Encourage Conversions: Yes
Area Develop. Agreements: No
Sub-Franchising Contracts: No
Expand In Territory: Yes
Space Needs: 8,000-14,000 SF

SUPPORT & TRAINING:
Financial Assistance Provided: No
Site Selection Assistance: Yes
Lease Negotiation Assistance: No
Co-Operative Advertising: No
Franchisee Assoc./Member: Yes/Yes
Size Of Corporate Staff: 10
On-Going Support: ,,C,D,E,,,h,I
Training: 2 Weeks
  Corporate Headquarters; 1 Week To
  Be Determined; 2 Weeks On-Site

SPECIFIC EXPANSION PLANS:
US: States not currently in.
Canada: ON, BC and PQ
Overseas: NR

◄◄ ►►

DRY-B-LO DESIGNER DECK DRAIN SYSTEM
475 Tribble Gap Rd., # 305
Cumming, GA 30040
Tel: (800) 437-9256 (770) 781-4754
Fax: (770) 886-7408
E-Mail: gmoore@dry-b-lo.com
Web Site: www.dry-b-lo.com
Mr. Grant Moore, President/CEO

DRY-B-LO Designer Deck Drain System is one of the nation's fastest-growing franchise companies in the booming home improvement industry. We currently offer "exclusive territory" opportunities to qualified individuals. Our comprehensive training program provides business management, sales and technical instruction and a strong, on-going support system. No construction or trade experience is required.

BACKGROUND: IFA MEMBER
Established: 1993; 1st Franchised: 1997
Franchised Units: 29
Company-Owned Units: 0
Total Units: 29
Dist.: US-29; CAN-0; O'seas-0
North America: 7 States, Provinces
Density: 5 in GA, 4 in NC, 6 in SC
Projected New Units (12 Months): 15
Qualifications: 4, 4, 2, 4, 1, 5

FINANCIAL/TERMS:
Cash Investment: $65.7-147.8K
Total Investment: $65.7-147.8K
Minimum Net Worth: $250K
Fees: Franchise - $15K and 25K
  Royalty - 7.5%; Ad. - 0%
Earnings Claims Statement: No
Term of Contract (Years): 5/5/5/
Avg. # Of Employees: 3 FT, 0 PT
Passive Ownership: Discouraged
Encourage Conversions: NA
Area Develop. Agreements: No
Sub-Franchising Contracts: No
Expand In Territory: Yes
Space Needs: NA

SUPPORT & TRAINING:
Financial Assistance Provided: Yes (D)
Site Selection Assistance: NA
Lease Negotiation Assistance: NA
Co-Operative Advertising: No
Franchisee Assoc./Member: No
Size Of Corporate Staff: 4
On-Going Support: ,B,C,D,,,G,h,I
Training: 1 Week Atlanta, GA;
  1 Week Denver, CO

SPECIFIC EXPANSION PLANS:
US: All United States
Canada: No
Overseas: NR

◄◄ ►►

EPCON COMMUNITIES
500 Stonehenge Dr.
Dublin, OH 43017
Tel: (800) 783-3838 (614) 761-1010
Fax: (614) 761-2678
E-Mail: dnoreen@epconcommunities.com
Web Site: www.epconcommunities.com
Mr. Dan Noreen, Business Development Manager

We put our franchisees in the home-building business. EPCON Communities provides a comprehensive homebuilding development system targeted at the industry's largest market - active adults. As an EPCON Communities franchisee, you receive not only the rights to build our proven, award-winning floor plans, but also on-going training for yourself and your team. National account purchasing power, standards and specification on building and selling the homes, marketing support, POP materials and support with industry experts.

BACKGROUND: IFA MEMBER
Established: 1985; 1st Franchised: 1995
Franchised Units: 140
Company-Owned Units: 2
Total Units: 142
Dist.: US-142; CAN-0; O'seas-0
  North America: 28 States, 0 Provinces
  Density: 918 in VA, 3620 in OH, 1208 in GA
Projected New Units (12 Months): 20
Qualifications: 5, 5, 3, 3, 3, 5
FINANCIAL/TERMS:
Cash Investment: $~$1MM
Total Investment: $3-5MM
Minimum Net Worth: Varies
Fees: Franchise - $50K
  Royalty - 1.75%; Ad. - $500/month
Earnings Claims Statement: Yes
Term of Contract (Years): 3/Varies
Avg. # Of Employees: 5 FT, 0 PT
Passive Ownership: Not Allowed
Encourage Conversions: NA
Area Develop. Agreements: No
Sub-Franchising Contracts: No
Expand In Territory: Yes
Space Needs: NA
SUPPORT & TRAINING:
Financial Assistance Provided: No
Site Selection Assistance: Yes
Lease Negotiation Assistance: No
Co-Operative Advertising: Yes
Franchisee Assoc./Member: No
Size Of Corporate Staff: 12
On-Going Support: ,,C,D,,,G,H,
Training: 3 Days Sales Training;
  5 Days Orientation; 4 Days Sales/
  Construction - all Columbus, OH
SPECIFIC EXPANSION PLANS:
US: All United States
Canada: No
Overseas: NR

FIVE STAR PAINTING
936 S. 2000 W., # 220
Springville, UT 84663
Tel: (888) 965-STAR (801) 805-6901
Fax:
E-Mail: svaleti@fivestar-painting.com
Web Site: www.fivestar-painting.com
Ms. Amanda Johnson, Franchise Sales
  Manager

Buying a Five Star Painting Franchise isn't an investment in a new job, but a new lifestyle. It's an opportunity to be your own

boss and make positive changes in the lives of the customers you service-changing your own life in the process. The financial independence and personal empowerment that a Five Star Painting Franchise offers isn't for everyone: Just those who want to take control of their future. At Five Star we take great pride in meeting the needs of the ever-changing painting world. We offer an exceptional franchise opportunity to advance your career.

BACKGROUND: IFA MEMBER
Established: 2001; 1st Franchised: 2005
Franchised Units: 70
Company-Owned Units: 1
Total Units: 71
Dist.: US-63; CAN-7; O'seas-1
  North America: 36 States, 2 Provinces
  Density: 4 in NV, 9 in UT, 16 in TX
Projected New Units (12 Months): 50
Qualifications: 4, 3, 2, 2, 3, 4
FINANCIAL/TERMS:
Cash Investment: $20K-$40K
Total Investment: $40-$87K
Minimum Net Worth: $20K-$40K
Fees: Franchise - $20K-$40K
  Royalty - 5%; Ad. - 4.5%
Earnings Claims Statement: No
Term of Contract (Years): 10/10
Avg. # Of Employees: Start up 3 FT, NA PT
Passive Ownership: Discouraged
Encourage Conversions: NA
Area Develop. Agreements: No
Sub-Franchising Contracts: No
Expand In Territory: Yes
Space Needs: NA
SUPPORT & TRAINING:
Financial Assistance Provided: Yes (D)
Site Selection Assistance: NA
Lease Negotiation Assistance: NA
Co-Operative Advertising: Yes
Franchisee Assoc./Member: No
Size Of Corporate Staff: 8
On-Going Support: ,b,C,d,,,G,H,I
Training: 1 week Springville, UT
SPECIFIC EXPANSION PLANS:
US: All US
Canada: All Canada
Overseas: All Overseas

HOUSEMASTER HOME INSPECTIONS
426 Vosseller Ave.
Bound Brook, NJ 08805-1220
Tel: (800) 526-3939 (732) 823-4087
Fax: (732) 469-7405
E-Mail: kim.fanus@housemaster.com
Web Site: www.housemaster.com
Ms. Kimberly Fanus, Franchise Development

Celebrating 30 years in the industry, HouseMaster is the most experienced, respected and innovative home inspection franchise system. Since its inception in 1979, HouseMaster has performed nearly two million home inspections and has grown to almost 400 franchises. Our company culture focuses on franchise relationships and support, technical proficiency, proven marketing methods, aggressive risk management tools and cutting edge technology. You will be impressed with the unsurpassed level of expertise and support that HouseMaster franchisees enjoy. Interviewed by media giants such as the Associated Press, The Today Show, Good Morning America, CNN, HGTV, USA Today and the NY Times, HouseMaster is the authority on home inspections.

BACKGROUND: IFA MEMBER
Established: 1979; 1st Franchised: 1979
Franchised Units: 393
Company-Owned Units: 10
Total Units: 403
Dist.: US-365; CAN-38; O'seas-0
  North America: 45 States, 8 Provinces
  Density: 18 in FL, 20 in NY, 23 in NJ
Projected New Units (12 Months): 20
Qualifications: 4, 3, 2, 2, 5, 5
FINANCIAL/TERMS:
Cash Investment: $18-40K
Total Investment: $25-55K
Minimum Net Worth: $70K
Fees: Franchise - $27.5K
  Royalty - 7.5%; Ad. - 2.25%
Earnings Claims Statement: No
Term of Contract (Years): 5/5
Avg. # Of Employees: Varies
Passive Ownership: Allowed
Encourage Conversions: NA
Area Develop. Agreements: No
Sub-Franchising Contracts: No

Expand In Territory:	Yes
Space Needs:	NA

SUPPORT & TRAINING:

Financial Assistance Provided:	Yes (I)
Site Selection Assistance:	NA
Lease Negotiation Assistance:	NA
Co-Operative Advertising:	Yes
Franchisee Assoc./Member:	Yes/Yes
Size Of Corporate Staff:	13
On-Going Support:	A,B,C,D,E,,G,h,I
Training:	2-3 Weeks Bound Brook, NJ

SPECIFIC EXPANSION PLANS:

US:	All United States
Canada:	All Canada
Overseas:	Australia, UK

<< >>

HYDRO PHYSICS PIPE INSPECTION

1855 W. Union Ave., # N
Englewood, CO 80110
Tel: (800) 781-3164 (303) 783-8855
Fax: (303) 781-0477
E-Mail: hydrophys@aol.com
Web Site: www.hydrophysics-wa.com
Mr. Pete Fitzgerald, Dir. Franchise Development

HYDRO PHYSICS specializes in the video inspection of underground pipes. By seeing exactly what and where the problems are located, we can save our customers thousands of dollars in unnecessary repair costs. We are the only franchise specializing in this type of work.

BACKGROUND:

Established: 1991;	1st Franchised: 1998
Franchised Units:	18
Company-Owned Units:	0
Total Units:	18
Dist.:	US-18; CAN-0; O'seas-0
North America:	4 States, 0 Provinces
Density:	1 in MO, 3 in CO, 3 in WA
Projected New Units (12 Months):	20
Qualifications:	4, 3, 2, 2, 2, 5

FINANCIAL/TERMS:

Cash Investment:	$25K
Total Investment:	$95K
Minimum Net Worth:	$200K
Fees: Franchise -	$29.5K
Royalty - 7.5%;	Ad. - 2%
Earnings Claims Statement:	No
Term of Contract (Years):	10/10
Avg. # Of Employees:	4 FT, 0 PT
Passive Ownership:	Not Allowed
Encourage Conversions:	NA
Area Develop. Agreements:	Yes/10
Sub-Franchising Contracts:	No

Expand In Territory:	Yes
Space Needs:	NR

SUPPORT & TRAINING:

Financial Assistance Provided:	Yes (I)
Site Selection Assistance:	Yes
Lease Negotiation Assistance:	Yes
Co-Operative Advertising:	Yes
Franchisee Assoc./Member:	No
Size Of Corporate Staff:	4
On-Going Support:	,,C,D,,F,G,H,I
Training:	2 Weeks Englewood, CO

SPECIFIC EXPANSION PLANS:

US:	All United States
Canada:	Yes
Overseas:	NR

<< >>

INTELLITURF

P. O. Box 8685
Atlanta, GA 31106
Tel: (800) 490-2971 (404) 392-2783
Fax: (866) 511-9194
E-Mail: info@intelliturf.com
Web Site: intelliturf.com
Mr. Clay Neff, Franchise Development

IntelliTurf is dedicated to the professional design and installation of synthetic putting greens, artificial turf lawn systems, playgrounds or play areas, and recreational landscaping such as croquet and bocce courts. Take your business skills and desire to run your own company and join a proven concept, a growing market, and an established system. Do it with the support of a professional team, who will provide the tools and techniques you need to deliver The Perfect Amenity to your clients.

BACKGROUND: IFA MEMBER

Established: 1998;	1st Franchised: 2007
Franchised Units:	0
Company-Owned Units:	1
Total Units:	1
Dist.:	US-1; CAN-0; O'seas-0
North America:	1 States, 0 Provinces
Density:	1 in GA
Projected New Units (12 Months):	10
Qualifications:	5, 4, 2, 2, 4, 4

FINANCIAL/TERMS:

Cash Investment:	$30-145K
Total Investment:	$65-145K
Minimum Net Worth:	$250K
Fees: Franchise -	$32K

Royalty - .60 per square foot;	Ad. - 1%
Earnings Claims Statement:	No
Term of Contract (Years):	10/5
Avg. # Of Employees:	1 FT, 5 PT
Passive Ownership:	Allowed
Encourage Conversions:	NA
Area Develop. Agreements:	No
Sub-Franchising Contracts:	No
Expand In Territory:	Yes
Space Needs:	NA

SUPPORT & TRAINING:

Financial Assistance Provided:	No
Site Selection Assistance:	Yes
Lease Negotiation Assistance:	No
Co-Operative Advertising:	No
Franchisee Assoc./Member:	No
Size Of Corporate Staff:	3
On-Going Support:	A,B,C,D,E,F,G,h,
Training: 5 to 6 days Corporate Head-	
quarters; 5 to 7 days Your Territory	

SPECIFIC EXPANSION PLANS:

US:	All United States
Canada: Would consider interested parties	
Overseas:	Any with qualified applicants

<< >>

JET-BLACK

990 Loan Oak Rd., # 142
Eagan, MN 55121
Tel: (888) 538-2525 (952) 890-8343
Fax: (952) 890-7022
E-Mail: info@jet-black.com
Web Site: www.jet-black.com
Mr. Nick Kelso, Director Franchising

We provide blacktop driveway sealcoating, hot-rubber crack and joint filling, heat-treat oil spots, grass edging and patching. We beautify and protect driveways.

BACKGROUND: IFA MEMBER

Established: 1987;	1st Franchised: 1993
Franchised Units:	125
Company-Owned Units:	0
Total Units:	125
Dist.:	US-125; CAN-0; O'seas-0
North America:	24 States, 0 Provinces
Density:	NR
Projected New Units (12 Months):	80
Qualifications:	3, 3, 3, 3, 5, 5

FINANCIAL/TERMS:

Cash Investment:	$35K-50K
Total Investment:	$35K-100K
Minimum Net Worth:	$50K
Fees: Franchise -	$15K
Royalty - 8%;	Ad. - NA
Earnings Claims Statement:	Yes
Term of Contract (Years):	15/15
Avg. # Of Employees:	1 FT, 0 PT

Passive Ownership:	Not Allowed
Encourage Conversions:	No
Area Develop. Agreements:	No
Sub-Franchising Contracts:	No
Expand In Territory:	Yes
Space Needs:	NR

SUPPORT & TRAINING:

Financial Assistance Provided:	Yes (D)
Site Selection Assistance:	Yes
Lease Negotiation Assistance:	NA
Co-Operative Advertising:	No
Franchisee Assoc./Member:	Yes/Yes
Size Of Corporate Staff:	3
On-Going Support:	A,B,C,D,E,F,G,H,
Training:	1 Week Burnsville, MN

SPECIFIC EXPANSION PLANS:

US:	All United States
Canada:	All Canada
Overseas:	NR

‹‹ ››

KITCHEN SOLVERS
401 Jay St.
La Crosse, WI 54601-4064
Tel: (800) 845-6779 (608) 791-5516 + 515
Fax: (608) 784-2917
E-Mail: rick@kitchensolvers.com
Web Site: www.kitchensolvers.com
Mr. Rick McGarry, VP Business Development

Specialize or diversify… It's your option. Two different models to choose from. Six different profit centers. We are the most experienced kitchen and bath remodeling franchise in the US. Home-based business with no inventory required. Complete start-up and on-going support. Personalized marketing strategies. Experienced technical training and support.

BACKGROUND:	IFA MEMBER
Established: 1982;	1st Franchised: 1984
Franchised Units:	132
Company-Owned Units:	0
Total Units:	132
Dist.:	US-128; CAN-4; O'seas-0
North America:	32 States, 4 Provinces
Density:	15 in WI, 17 in IL, 12 in IA
Projected New Units (12 Months):	20
Qualifications:	2, 2, 2, 2, NR, 5

FINANCIAL/TERMS:

Cash Investment:	$40-60.2K

Total Investment:	$48-82K
Minimum Net Worth:	$250K
Fees: Franchise -	$27.5-32.0K
Royalty - 6%;	Ad. - 1%
Earnings Claims Statement:	Yes
Term of Contract (Years):	10/10
Avg. # Of Employees:	1 FT, 0 PT
Passive Ownership:	Not Allowed
Encourage Conversions:	Yes
Area Develop. Agreements:	No
Sub-Franchising Contracts:	No
Expand In Territory:	Yes
Space Needs:	NA

SUPPORT & TRAINING:

Financial Assistance Provided:	Yes (D)
Site Selection Assistance:	NA
Lease Negotiation Assistance:	NA
Co-Operative Advertising:	No
Franchisee Assoc./Member:	Yes/Yes
Size Of Corporate Staff:	10
On-Going Support:	a,B,C,D,,,G,h,I
Training:	2 Weeks LaCrosse, WI Corporate Headquarter

SPECIFIC EXPANSION PLANS:

US:	All United States
Canada:	All Canada
Overseas:	NR

‹‹ ››

KITCHEN TUNE-UP
813 Circle Dr.
Aberdeen, SD 57401-2670
Tel: (800) 333-6385 (605) 225-4049
Fax: (605) 308-4206
E-Mail: ktu@kitchentuneup.com
Web Site: www.kitchentuneup.com
Mr. Craig Green, Franchise Director

The housing downturn hasn't hurt the "mini-remodeling" market! We're recession proof. Join Kitchen Tune-Up, the number one ranked kitchen and bath remodeling franchise. You will serve the growing home remodeling industry and enjoy the convenience of working from your home. Retail location business models are also available if you prefer to have a store front. We have been offering franchise opportunities since 1988. We offer "Kitchen Solutions for Any Budget": cabinet & wood restoration, cabinet refacing, custom cabinetry, custom storage solutions and more.

BACKGROUND:	IFA MEMBER
Established: 1975;	1st Franchised: 1988
Franchised Units:	280

Company-Owned Units:	0
Total Units:	280
Dist.:	US-278; CAN-2; O'seas-0
North America:	38 States, 2 Provinces
Density:	11 in FL, 10 in CO, 10 in IL
Projected New Units (12 Months):	40
Qualifications:	4, 5, 1, 3, 2, 4

FINANCIAL/TERMS:

Cash Investment:	$50K
Total Investment:	$83K-91K
Minimum Net Worth:	$150K
Fees: Franchise -	$25K
Royalty - varies;	Ad. - $300/mo
Earnings Claims Statement:	Yes
Term of Contract (Years):	10/10
Avg. # Of Employees:	2-3 FT, 1 PT
Passive Ownership:	Discouraged
Encourage Conversions:	Yes
Area Develop. Agreements:	Yes/10
Sub-Franchising Contracts:	No
Expand In Territory:	Yes
Space Needs:	500-2,500 SF

SUPPORT & TRAINING:

Financial Assistance Provided:	Yes (D)
Site Selection Assistance:	Yes
Lease Negotiation Assistance:	No
Co-Operative Advertising:	Yes
Franchisee Assoc./Member:	Yes/Yes
Size Of Corporate Staff:	14
On-Going Support:	A,B,,D,e,,G,h,I
Training:	4 Days In-The-Field Training; 9 Days Home Office Training; 2-3 Weeks Pre-Training

SPECIFIC EXPANSION PLANS:

US:	All United States
Canada:	Masters Only
Overseas:	NR

‹‹ ››

MIRACLE METHOD SURFACERESTORATION
5020 Mark Dabling Blvd.
Colorado Springs, CO 80918
Tel: (800) 444-8827 (719) 594-9196
Fax: (719) 594-9282
E-Mail: sales@miraclemethod.com
Web Site: www.miraclemethod.com
Mr. Chuck Pistor, President

Make money in the growing remodeling industry by running your own bath and kitchen refinishing business. Save customers money by refinishing instead of replacing. Bathtubs, tile, showers, counter tops and more. Excellent income potential!

BACKGROUND:

Established: 1979;   1st Franchised: 1980
Franchised Units: 120
Company-Owned Units: 0
Total Units: 120
Dist.:   US-110; CAN-0; O'seas-10
  North America: 30 States, 0 Provinces
  Density: 15 in TX, 9 in CO, 20 in CA
Projected New Units (12 Months):   25
Qualifications: 5, 5, 4, 3, 3, 5

FINANCIAL/TERMS:

Cash Investment: $36K
Total Investment: $50K
Minimum Net Worth: $50K
Fees: Franchise - $28K
  Royalty - 5%;   Ad. - 1%
Earnings Claims Statement: Yes
Term of Contract (Years):   5/
Avg. # Of Employees: 5 FT, 1 PT
Passive Ownership: Discouraged
Encourage Conversions: Yes
Area Develop. Agreements: No
Sub-Franchising Contracts: No
Expand In Territory: No
Space Needs: NA

SUPPORT & TRAINING:

Financial Assistance Provided: Yes (D)
Site Selection Assistance: No
Lease Negotiation Assistance: No
Co-Operative Advertising: Yes
Franchisee Assoc./Member: Yes/Yes
Size Of Corporate Staff: 3
On-Going Support: ,,C,D,,,G,H,I
Training: 2 Weeks Company Location

SPECIFIC EXPANSION PLANS:

US: All United States
Canada: All Canada
Overseas: Western Europe

◄◄ ►►

**NATION-WIDE GENERAL
RENTAL CENTERS**

5510 Hwy., 9 N.
Alpharetta, GA 30004
Tel: (800) 227-1643 (770) 664-7765
Fax: (770) 664-0052
E-Mail: office@nation-widerental.com
Web Site: www.nation-widerental.com
Mr. Ike Goodvin, President

We are a full service tool and equipment

rental business, HOMEOWNER-CON-TRACTOR and PARTY since 1976. NO franchise fee and NO royalties. A complete TURN-KEY package of proven equipment, we do business plans and we go to the banks for you - we have a BUY-BACK agreement, exclusive area, insurance, site selection assistance, signs, rental rates guide for each item, accounting system, operations manual, advertising program, and TRAINING program. A great family business, this may be a business opportunity for you - ACT NOW - see our website.

BACKGROUND:

Established: 1976;   1st Franchised: 1976
Franchised Units: 487
Company-Owned Units: 1
Total Units: 488
Dist.:   US-488; CAN-0; O'seas-0
  North America: 38 States, 0 Provinces
  Density: NR
Projected New Units (12 Months):   15
Qualifications: 3, 1, 1, 4, 3, 5

FINANCIAL/TERMS:

Cash Investment: $55K
Total Investment: $169.5K
Minimum Net Worth: NA
Fees: Franchise - $0
  Royalty - 0%;   Ad. - 0%
Earnings Claims Statement: No
Term of Contract (Years):   3+/10+
Avg. # Of Employees: 1-3 FT, 1-2 PT
Passive Ownership: Discouraged
Encourage Conversions: NA
Area Develop. Agreements: Yes/3
Sub-Franchising Contracts: No
Expand In Territory: Yes
Space Needs: 2,000 SF

SUPPORT & TRAINING:

Financial Assistance Provided: Yes (D)
Site Selection Assistance: Yes
Lease Negotiation Assistance: Yes
Co-Operative Advertising: No
Franchisee Assoc./Member: No
Size Of Corporate Staff: 0
On-Going Support: ,b,C,d,,,,,I
Training: One Week GA - KY

SPECIFIC EXPANSION PLANS:

US: All United States
Canada: No
Overseas: NR

◄◄ ►►

PIRTEK USA

501 Haverty Ct.
Rockledge, FL 32955
Tel: (888) 774-7835 (321) 504-4422
Fax: (321) 504-4433
E-Mail: pirtekusa@pirtekusa.com
Web Site: www.pirtekusa.com
Mr. Gwyn O'Kane, Director Franchise
  Development

PIRTEK is the world's leading service provider of hydraulic hoses, couplings, metric and standard fittings, and other accessories for on-site hose replacement. The PIRTEK brand is associated with the highest levels of service, responsiveness, and dependability. Hundreds of service centers and more than 1,000 mobile service vehicles worldwide. Over-the-counter service, fully-equipped mobile service vans for 24-hour emergency on-site service, and preventive maintenance programs help reduce downtime.

BACKGROUND: IFA MEMBER
Established: 1996;   1st Franchised: 1997
Franchised Units: 35
Company-Owned Units: 1
Total Units: 36
Dist.:   US-36; CAN-0; O'seas-0
  North America: 22 States, 0 Provinces
  Density: 2 in TX, 2 in MN, 5 in FL
Projected New Units (12 Months):   10
Qualifications: 5, 3, 2, 2, 2, 4

FINANCIAL/TERMS:

Cash Investment: $100-150K
Total Investment: $500-600K
Minimum Net Worth: $350K
Fees: Franchise - $45K
  Royalty - 4%;   Ad. - 1.5-3%
Earnings Claims Statement: No
Term of Contract (Years):   10/10/10/
Avg. # Of Employees: 6 FT, 0 PT
Passive Ownership: Allowed
Encourage Conversions: NA
Area Develop. Agreements: No
Sub-Franchising Contracts: No
Expand In Territory: Yes
Space Needs: 2,500-3,000 SF

SUPPORT & TRAINING:

Financial Assistance Provided: Yes (D)
Site Selection Assistance: Yes
Lease Negotiation Assistance: Yes
Co-Operative Advertising: No
Franchisee Assoc./Member: Yes/Yes
Size Of Corporate Staff: 35

On-Going Support: „C,D,E,,G,,

Training: 3 Weeks Franchisee Training; 2 Weeks Ops. Mgr./Msst Training; 1 Week Admin. Training in Rockledge, FL.

SPECIFIC EXPANSION PLANS:

US: All United States
Canada: No
Overseas: NR

PRECISION CONCRETE CUTTING

3191 N. Canyon Rd.
Provo, UT 84604
Tel: (800) 833-7770 (801) 373-3990
Fax: (801) 373-6088
E-Mail: matt@pccfranchise.com
Web Site: www.pccfranchise.com
Mr. Matthew Haney, Franchise Development

PRECISION CONCRETE CUTTING specializes in removing trip hazards from sidewalks. Trip hazards occur when tree roots or ground settling causes the slabs of concrete to become uneven. Our proprietary equipment and process allow us to bring sidewalks into full compliance with the Americans With Disabilities Act requirements. Clients include municipalities, school districts, apartment complex owners. No experience necessary.

BACKGROUND:

Established: 1992; 1st Franchised: 2001
Franchised Units: 11
Company-Owned Units: 1
Total Units: 12
Dist.: US-12; CAN-0; O'seas-0
North America: 4 States, 0 Provinces
Density: 2 in WA, 6 in CA, 1 in AZ
Projected New Units (12 Months): NR
Qualifications: NR

FINANCIAL/TERMS:

Cash Investment: $45-50K
Total Investment: $95-105K
Minimum Net Worth: NA
Fees: Franchise - $45K
Royalty - 4%; Ad. - 0%
Earnings Claims Statement: No
Term of Contract (Years): 10/10
Avg. # Of Employees: 2 FT, 2 PT
Passive Ownership: Discouraged
Encourage Conversions: No
Area Develop. Agreements: No
Sub-Franchising Contracts: No
Expand In Territory: No
Space Needs: NA

SUPPORT & TRAINING:

Financial Assistance Provided: No
Site Selection Assistance: Yes
Lease Negotiation Assistance: NA
Co-Operative Advertising: No
Franchisee Assoc./Member: No
Size Of Corporate Staff: 4
On-Going Support: A,B,C,D,,G,,I
Training: 5 Days Provo, UT

SPECIFIC EXPANSION PLANS:

US: South & Southeast
Canada: No
Overseas: NR

PRECISION DOOR SERVICE

2397 S. Washington Ave. Suites
Titusville, FL 32780
Tel: (888) 833-3494 (321) 225-3500
Fax: (321) 225-3513
E-Mail: jwellbeloved@precisiondoor.net
Web Site: www.precisiondoor.net
Mr. Jim T. Wellbeloved, Mgr. Franchise Admin.

PRECISION DOOR SERVICE franchise businesses principally sell garage door repair services. Franchisees also sell and install new garage doors. Business operates 24/7 and provides a lifetime warranty on all parts and labor. Trucks carry parts and supplies to repair every garage door system in the market place.

BACKGROUND: IFA MEMBER

Established: 1997; 1st Franchised: 1999
Franchised Units: 72
Company-Owned Units: 0
Total Units: 72
Dist.: US-72; CAN-0; O'seas-0
North America: 32 States, 0 Provinces
Density: 4 in SC, 7 in FL, 9 in CA
Projected New Units (12 Months): NR
Qualifications: NR

FINANCIAL/TERMS:

Cash Investment: $150-250K
Total Investment: $73.5K-1.0MM
Minimum Net Worth: $150K
Fees: Franchise - $25-800K
Royalty - 1-1.3K.Wk.; Ad. - 0%
Earnings Claims Statement: No
Term of Contract (Years): 10/5/5/5/
Avg. # Of Employees: 3-4 FT, 1 PT
Passive Ownership: Discouraged
Encourage Conversions: No
Area Develop. Agreements: No
Sub-Franchising Contracts: No
Expand In Territory: No
Space Needs: 1,200 - 2,000 SF

SUPPORT & TRAINING:

Financial Assistance Provided: No
Site Selection Assistance: No
Lease Negotiation Assistance: No
Co-Operative Advertising: Yes
Franchisee Assoc./Member: No
Size Of Corporate Staff: 20
On-Going Support: „C,D,E,F,G,H,I
Training: 2 Weeks OH

SPECIFIC EXPANSION PLANS:

US: All United States
Canada: No
Overseas: NR

RAPID RECOVERY

P.O. Box 10845
Glendale, AZ 85318
Tel: (877) 372-7732 (623) 362-3882
Fax: (877) 572-7732
E-Mail: info@raprec.com
Web Site: www.raprec.com
Mr. Les Rhynard, Franchise Contact

Rapid Recovery is the nation's leading refrigerant abatement company. We provide refrigerant abatement services for the HVAC, refrigeration, demolition, and marine industries. Projects range in size from single residential split systems to chilling systems operating on tens of thousands of pounds, to projects with thousands of units. Rapid Recovery's franchise owners are dedicated to high-speed EPA compliant refrigerant abatement as a value added service to their customers.

BACKGROUND:

Established: 2002; 1st Franchised: 2004
Franchised Units: 5
Company-Owned Units: 0
Total Units: 5
Dist.: US-5; CAN-0; O'seas-0
North America: 4 States, 0 Provinces
Density: 2 in CA, 1 in IL, 1 in MD
Projected New Units (12 Months): 3
Qualifications: 3, 3, 2, 2, 3, 5

FINANCIAL/TERMS:

Cash Investment: $60-150K
Total Investment: $85-325K
Minimum Net Worth: $100K
Fees: Franchise - $60-150K
Royalty - 6%; Ad. - NR
Earnings Claims Statement: No

Term of Contract (Years):	5/10
Avg. # Of Employees:	NR
Passive Ownership:	Not Allowed
Encourage Conversions:	NA
Area Develop. Agreements:	No
Sub-Franchising Contracts:	No
Expand In Territory:	No
Space Needs:	NR

SUPPORT & TRAINING:

Financial Assistance Provided:	No
Site Selection Assistance:	NA
Lease Negotiation Assistance:	NA
Co-Operative Advertising:	Yes
Franchisee Assoc./Member:	No
Size Of Corporate Staff:	0
On-Going Support:	A,,,d,,,,H,I
Training:	2 Weeks Peoria, AZ

SPECIFIC EXPANSION PLANS:

US:	All
Canada:	No
Overseas:	NR

◄◄ ►►

RE-BATH CORPORATION

421 W. Alameda Dr.
Tempe, AZ 85282
Tel: (800) 426-4573 (480) 844-2596
Fax: (480) 833-7199
E-Mail: cjohnson@re-bath.com
Web Site: www.re-bath.com
Mr. Cecil Johnson, Director Franchise
    Development

Re-Bath is the World's Largest Bathroom Remodeler and offers Bathtubs and Bathtub Liners, Showers and Shower Base Liners, Wall Surround Systems, Bathtub-to-Shower Conversions, Walk-In Bathtubs, Vanity Cabinets and Tops, Toilets, Shower Spas, Faucets, Mirrors and Accessories.

BACKGROUND: IFA MEMBER

Established: 1979;	1st Franchised: 1991
Franchised Units:	221
Company-Owned Units:	0
Total Units:	221
Dist.:	US-207; CAN-8; O'seas-6
North America:	48 States, 6 Provinces
Density:	8 in NY, 12 in CA, 16 in TX
Projected New Units (12 Months):	40+
Qualifications:	4, 4, 3, 3, 4, 5

FINANCIAL/TERMS:

Cash Investment:	$6-40K

Total Investment:	$33-250K
Minimum Net Worth:	$50K
Fees: Franchise -	$3-40K
Royalty - $28/Unit;	Ad. - 0%
Earnings Claims Statement:	No
Term of Contract (Years):	3/3
Avg. # Of Employees:	7 FT, 0 PT
Passive Ownership:	Not Allowed
Encourage Conversions:	No
Area Develop. Agreements:	No
Sub-Franchising Contracts:	No
Expand In Territory:	Yes
Space Needs:	1,200 SF

SUPPORT & TRAINING:

Financial Assistance Provided:	No
Site Selection Assistance:	Yes
Lease Negotiation Assistance:	Yes
Co-Operative Advertising:	Yes
Franchisee Assoc./Member:	Yes/Yes
Size Of Corporate Staff:	50
On-Going Support:	„C,D,E,F,G,h,I
Training:	5 days in field Arden, NC or Decatur, IL; 5 days in field Phoenix, AZ; 3 days in field Mobile, AL

SPECIFIC EXPANSION PLANS:

US:	All United States
Canada:	All Canada
Overseas:	Europe, Mexico, Latin Am., S. Am., Australia

◄◄ ►►

SCREENMOBILE

72-050A Corporate Way
Thousand Palms, CA 92276
Tel: (866) 540-5800 (760) 343-3500
Fax: (760) 343-7543
E-Mail: salesmail@screenmobile.com
Web Site: www.screenmobile.com
Mr. Monty M. Walker, Director of Sales

SCREENMOBILE provides quality window and door screens. SCREENMOBILE is a mobile outdoor service business offering custom design and installations of high-quality screening products right at the job site on the very first visit.

BACKGROUND:

Established: 1982;	1st Franchised: 1984
Franchised Units:	72
Company-Owned Units:	1
Total Units:	73
Dist.:	US-73; CAN-0; O'seas-0
North America:	21 States, 0 Provinces
Density:	in CO, in CA, in AZ
Projected New Units (12 Months):	5
Qualifications:	3, 1, 1, 1, 3, 5

FINANCIAL/TERMS:

Cash Investment:	NR

Total Investment:	$69.3K
Minimum Net Worth:	$76K
Fees: Franchise -	$25.5K
Royalty - $350-1,000;	Ad. - $150/Mo.
Earnings Claims Statement:	No
Term of Contract (Years):	10/
Avg. # Of Employees:	1 FT, 0 PT
Passive Ownership:	Not Allowed
Encourage Conversions:	No
Area Develop. Agreements:	No
Sub-Franchising Contracts:	No
Expand In Territory:	Yes
Space Needs:	400 SF

SUPPORT & TRAINING:

Financial Assistance Provided:	Yes (D)
Site Selection Assistance:	Yes
Lease Negotiation Assistance:	No
Co-Operative Advertising:	Yes
Franchisee Assoc./Member:	No
Size Of Corporate Staff:	11
On-Going Support:	„C,D,E,F,G,H,I
Training:	10 Days Palm Springs, CA

SPECIFIC EXPANSION PLANS:

US:	All United States
Canada:	No
Overseas:	NR

◄◄ ►►

SEALMASTER

2520 S. Campbell St.
Sandusky, OH 44870
Tel: (800) 395-7325 + 146 (419) 621-8001
Fax: (419) 626-5477
E-Mail: tim@sealmaster.com
Web Site: www.sealmaster.net
Mr. Tim Stephens, Franchise Director

SEALMASTER is now offering manufacturing/sales opportunities in the billion dollar pavement products industry. This is a business-to-business franchise, offering pavement sealers, crack fillers, asphalt repair products, tennis court/running track coatings, traffic striping paints, tools, equipment and more. Turn-key operations available with on-going training and support.

BACKGROUND: IFA MEMBER

Established: 1969;	1st Franchised: 1993
Franchised Units:	25
Company-Owned Units:	2
Total Units:	27
Dist.:	US-27; CAN-0; O'seas-0
North America:	17 States, 0 Provinces
Density:	NR
Projected New Units (12 Months):	6
Qualifications:	5, 3, 2, 2, 3, 4

FINANCIAL/TERMS:

Cash Investment:	$295K-632K
Total Investment:	$295K-632K
Minimum Net Worth:	$300-500K
Fees: Franchise -	$35K
Royalty - 5%;	Ad. - 1.5%
Earnings Claims Statement:	No
Term of Contract (Years):	10/5/5/5/
Avg. # Of Employees:	3 FT, 3 PT
Passive Ownership:	Discouraged
Encourage Conversions:	Yes
Area Develop. Agreements:	No
Sub-Franchising Contracts:	No
Expand In Territory:	No
Space Needs:	7,000-10,000 SF

SUPPORT & TRAINING:

Financial Assistance Provided:	No
Site Selection Assistance:	Yes
Lease Negotiation Assistance:	No
Co-Operative Advertising:	No
Franchisee Assoc./Member:	No
Size Of Corporate Staff:	27
On-Going Support:	A,B,C,D,E,,G,,I
Training:	2 Weeks Corporate Headquarters, OH

SPECIFIC EXPANSION PLANS:

US:	All United States
Canada:	All Canada
Overseas:	All Countries

SHELFGENIE

1642 Powers Ferry Rd., S.E.
Marietta, GA 30067
Tel: (877) 814-3643 (770) 955-4375
Fax: (928) 752-6374
E-Mail: franchise@shelfgenie.com
Web Site: www.shelfgenie.com
Mr. Mike Pollock, Director of Franchise
    Development

Want to glide into a fabulous business opportunity? We're looking for a select group of franchise owners, who want to provide great products and services to customers in their own protected territories. As a franchise owner with ShelfGenie, you'll have a wealth of resources that take away many of the administrative headaches of running your business (phone calls, manufacturing, and installations) along with advanced technologies that help you make informed management decisions.

BACKGROUND: IFA MEMBER

Established: 2000;	1st Franchised: 2008
Franchised Units:	26
Company-Owned Units:	9
Total Units:	35
Dist.:	US-35; CAN-0; O'seas-0
North America:	16 States, 0 Provinces
Density:	9 in TX, 9 in IL, 10 in CA
Projected New Units (12 Months):	25
Qualifications:	3, 3, 1, 3, 4, 5

FINANCIAL/TERMS:

Cash Investment:	$80-128K
Total Investment:	$80-128K
Minimum Net Worth:	$50K
Fees: Franchise -	$40K
Royalty - 4%;	Ad. - 2%
Earnings Claims Statement:	No
Term of Contract (Years):	5/5
Avg. # Of Employees:	0 FT, 4 PT
Passive Ownership:	Discouraged
Encourage Conversions:	Yes
Area Develop. Agreements:	No
Sub-Franchising Contracts:	No
Expand In Territory:	No
Space Needs:	NA

SUPPORT & TRAINING:

Financial Assistance Provided:	Yes (I)
Site Selection Assistance:	No
Lease Negotiation Assistance:	No
Co-Operative Advertising:	No
Franchisee Assoc./Member:	No
Size Of Corporate Staff:	9
On-Going Support:	,,C,D,E,F,G,H,
Training:	8 Days Atlanta, GA

SPECIFIC EXPANSION PLANS:

US:	All United States
Canada:	All Canada
Overseas:	NR

SUPERIOR WALLS OF AMERICA

937 E. Earl Rd.
New Holland, PA 17557-9597
Tel: (800) 452-9255 (717) 351-9255
Fax: (717) 351-9263
E-Mail: lhawthorne@superiorwalls.com
Web Site: www.superiorwalls.com
Mr. Lee B. Hawthorne, Dir. of Risk
    Mgmt/Franchise Recruiter

We provide license agreements to manufacturer, sell and install the patented SUPERIOR WALLS SYSTEM, a pre-cast, insulated, studded, waterproof concrete foundation wall for new residential and light commercial construction.

BACKGROUND: IFA MEMBER

Established: 1985;	1st Franchised: 1999
Franchised Units:	22
Company-Owned Units:	1
Total Units:	23
Dist.:	US-22; CAN-0; O'seas-1
North America:	10 States, 0 Provinces
Density:	2 in WI, 6 in PA, 2 in MI
Projected New Units (12 Months):	3
Qualifications:	5, 4, 5, 3, 2, 3

FINANCIAL/TERMS:

Cash Investment:	$500K
Total Investment:	$2-3MM
Minimum Net Worth:	$500K
Fees: Franchise -	$30K
Royalty - 4%;	Ad. - 0%
Earnings Claims Statement:	No
Term of Contract (Years):	10/10/10/
Avg. # Of Employees:	8 FT, 2 PT
Passive Ownership:	Discouraged
Encourage Conversions:	No
Area Develop. Agreements:	No
Sub-Franchising Contracts:	No
Expand In Territory:	Yes
Space Needs:	~30,000 SF

SUPPORT & TRAINING:

Financial Assistance Provided:	Yes (D)
Site Selection Assistance:	Yes
Lease Negotiation Assistance:	NA
Co-Operative Advertising:	No
Franchisee Assoc./Member:	No
Size Of Corporate Staff:	20
On-Going Support:	,B,c,D,,,G,H,I
Training:	2 Weeks Corporate Office; 3 Weeks Field Location

SPECIFIC EXPANSION PLANS:

US:	All United States
Canada:	All Canada
Overseas:	England, Philippines

SURFACE SPECIALISTS SYSTEMS

621-B Stallings Rd.
Matthews, NC 28105
Tel: (866) 239-8707 (704) 821-3380
Fax: (704) 821-2097
E-Mail: amy@surfacespecialists.com
Web Site: www.surfacespecialists.com
Ms. Amy Irali, Marketing/Sales Director

SURFACE SPECIALISTS franchisees specialize in repairing and refinishing kitchen and bathroom surfaces. These surfaces include acrylic spas, fiberglass tubs and showers, porcelain tubs, cultured marble, Formica countertops, and PVC/ABS (plastic). Become a factory authorized warranty service provider for more than 34 manufacturers nationwide. We are the only franchisor in the industry providing full service to the new construction market. Excellent opportunity of high profit potential at low investment.

BACKGROUND:

Established: 1981;   1st Franchised: 1982
Franchised Units: 44
Company-Owned Units: 0
Total Units: 44
Dist.:   US-43; CAN-1; O'seas-0
  North America: 16 States, 0 Provinces
  Density: 6 in WI, 6 in MN, 4 in FL
Projected New Units (12 Months):   4
Qualifications: 4, 4, 2, 3, 4, 5

FINANCIAL/TERMS:

Cash Investment: $10-15K
Total Investment: $26-38K
Minimum Net Worth: $90K
Fees: Franchise - $21K
  Royalty - 5%;   Ad. - NA
Earnings Claims Statement: Yes
Term of Contract (Years):   10/10
Avg. # Of Employees: 2 FT, 2 PT
Passive Ownership: Discouraged
Encourage Conversions: Yes
Area Develop. Agreements: No
Sub-Franchising Contracts: No
Expand In Territory: Yes
Space Needs: 300 SF

SUPPORT & TRAINING:

Financial Assistance Provided: Yes (D)
Site Selection Assistance: NA
Lease Negotiation Assistance: NA
Co-Operative Advertising: No
Franchisee Assoc./Member: No
Size Of Corporate Staff: 2
On-Going Support: ,B,C,D,,,G,H,I
Training: 15 Days Matthews, NC

SPECIFIC EXPANSION PLANS:

US: All United States
Canada: All Canada
Overseas: NR

◄◄ ►►

UBUILDIT
12006 98th Ave., N.E., # 200
Kirkland, WA 98034
Tel: (800) 992-4357 (425) 821-6200
Fax: (425) 821-6876
E-Mail: franchiseinfo@ubuildit.com
Web Site: www.ubuildit.com
Ms. Kathe Noyes, National Director Franchise Development

For over 10 years, the UBuildIt system has been assisting homeowners to act as their own general contractor for both remodeling and new home construction. By teaming a homeowner with a construction professional, the project is efficiently completed while avoiding the common

pitfalls and saving thousands. Providing subcontractors, bank financing, site visits, etc., UBuildIt is a perfect complementary service for the building professional or entrepreneur looking for a huge untapped niche.

BACKGROUND:

Established: 1988;   1st Franchised: 1998
Franchised Units: 101
Company-Owned Units: 0
Total Units: 101
Dist.:   US-101; CAN-0; O'seas-0
  North America: 18 States, 0 Provinces
  Density: 12 in WA
Projected New Units (12 Months):   30
Qualifications: 4, 5, 4, 3, 4, 5

FINANCIAL/TERMS:

Cash Investment: $50-100K
Total Investment: $125-250K
Minimum Net Worth: $100K
Fees: Franchise - $25K
  Royalty - 5-7%/$300;   Ad.
- 2%/$50/Mo.
Earnings Claims Statement: No
Term of Contract (Years):   10/10
Avg. # Of Employees: 1 FT, 1 PT
Passive Ownership: Not Allowed
Encourage Conversions: Yes
Area Develop. Agreements: No
Sub-Franchising Contracts: No
Expand In Territory: No
Space Needs: 400 SF

SUPPORT & TRAINING:

Financial Assistance Provided: No
Site Selection Assistance: No
Lease Negotiation Assistance: No
Co-Operative Advertising: No
Franchisee Assoc./Member: No
Size Of Corporate Staff: 7
On-Going Support: ,,C,D,E,,,H,I
Training: 2 Weeks Seattle, WA

SPECIFIC EXPANSION PLANS:

US: All United States
Canada: All Canada
Overseas: NR

◄◄ ►►

UNITED STATES SEAMLESS
474 45th St., S.
Fargo, ND 58103
Tel: (800) 615-9318 (701) 241-8888
Fax: (701) 241-9999
E-Mail: info@usseamless.com
Web Site: www.usseamless.com
Mr. David E. Hedman, National Franchise Sales

UNITED STATES SEAMLESS, ranked

the #1 seamless siding franchise in America by Entrepreneur Magazine, is offering protected franchise territories for the sale and installation of seamless steel siding, gutters and vinyl replacement windows. The franchiseoffers 14 solid PVC colors, 12 of which have matching accessories. We also offer 7 colors in the exclusive Mountain Cedar two-tone steel siding coil, which can be produced in the standard profile plus used in our patent pending log cabin siding machine.

BACKGROUND:

Established: 1991;   1st Franchised: 1992
Franchised Units: 87
Company-Owned Units: 0
Total Units: 87
Dist.:   US-87; CAN-0; O'seas-0
  North America: 14 States, 0 Provinces
  Density: 9 in ND, 32 in MN, 10 in IA
Projected New Units (12 Months): 8-12
Qualifications: 5, 5, 4, 3, 4, 5

FINANCIAL/TERMS:

Cash Investment: $20-40K
Total Investment: $49.5-147K
Minimum Net Worth: $40K
Fees: Franchise - $8.5K
  Royalty - $2.5K/Mach.;   Ad.
- $200-500/Mo
Earnings Claims Statement: No
Term of Contract (Years):   15/15
Avg. # Of Employees: 4 FT, 0 PT
Passive Ownership: Not Allowed
Encourage Conversions: No
Area Develop. Agreements: No
Sub-Franchising Contracts: No
Expand In Territory: Yes
Space Needs: 2,000 SF

SUPPORT & TRAINING:

Financial Assistance Provided: Yes (D)
Site Selection Assistance: Yes
Lease Negotiation Assistance: No
Co-Operative Advertising: No
Franchisee Assoc./Member: No
Size Of Corporate Staff: 10
On-Going Support: ,,C,d,,,G,H,I
Training: 1 Week Fargo, ND

SPECIFIC EXPANSION PLANS:

US: All United States
Canada: No
Overseas: NR

◄◄ ►►

FIVE LARGEST PARTICIPANTS IN SURVEY						
Company	# Fran-chised Units	# Co-Owned Units	# Total Units	Franchise Fee	On-Going Royalty	Total Investment
1. Jackson Hewitt Tax Service	5,763	1,000	6763	$25K	15%	$55-99K
2. Liberty Tax Service	3,055	62	3117	$40K	Varies	$56.8-69.9K
3. Fiducial	554	30	584	$12.5-25K	1.5-6%	$44.4-115.5K
4. Action International	550	0	550	$45K	5%	$72.2-84K
5. Resource Associates Corp.	500	0	500	$0K	0%	$1-35K

All of the data provided are proprietary and should not be quoted without acknowledging *Bond's Franchise Guide*.

ACTION INTERNATIONAL
5670 Wynn Rd., # C
Las Vegas, NV 89118-2356
Tel: (888) 483-2828 (702) 795-3188
Fax: (702) 795-3183
E-Mail: actionusa@action-international.com
Web Site: www.action-international.com
Mr. Richard Bernstein, U.S. Sales Manager

ACTION INTERNATIONAL is one of the fastest-growing franchises (#16 Entrepreneur Mag., 2/04) and is the largest business coaching company in the world. The company was established in 1993 in Australia by Brad Sugars. Brad recognized early that most owners of small- to medium-sized businesses were unaware of how to effectively grow their businesses and achieve their goals. He developed a comprehensive system and methodology to assist this group. There are now 550 franchisees in 19 countries.

BACKGROUND: IFA MEMBER
Established: 1993;   1st Franchised: 1997
Franchised Units: 550
Company-Owned Units: 0
Total Units: 550
Dist.:   US-180; CAN-60; O'seas-310
  North America: 25 States, 3 Provinces
  Density: 14 in GA, 22 in NJ, 23 in PA

Projected New Units (12 Months):   180
Qualifications: 4, 3, 3, 3, 4, 5
FINANCIAL/TERMS:
Cash Investment: $72.2-84K
Total Investment: $72.2-84K
Minimum Net Worth: $100K
Fees: Franchise - $45K
  Royalty - 5%;   Ad. - 5%
Earnings Claims Statement: No
Term of Contract (Years):   5/5
Avg. # Of Employees: 1 FT, 0 PT
Passive Ownership: Not Allowed
Encourage Conversions: NA
Area Develop. Agreements: Yes/1
Sub-Franchising Contracts: No
Expand In Territory: Yes
Space Needs: NA
SUPPORT & TRAINING:

Financial Assistance Provided: Yes (D)
Site Selection Assistance: NA
Lease Negotiation Assistance: NA
Co-Operative Advertising: No
Franchisee Assoc./Member: No
Size Of Corporate Staff: 8
On-Going Support: A,B,C,D,E,F,G,H,I
Training: 10 Days Las Vegas, NV
SPECIFIC EXPANSION PLANS:
US: All United States Except CA
Canada: All Canada
Overseas: AU, UK, Ireland, GR, FR, MX, Singapore, India, Mal

⊰⊰ ⊱⊱

ADVENTURES IN ADVERTISING
800 W. Winneconne Ave., P.O. Box 872
Neenah, WI 54957-0872
Tel: (800) 460-7836 (920) 886-3700
Fax: (920) 886-3701
E-Mail: rkollman@aiacorporation.com
Web Site: www.exploreaia.com
Ms. Rebecca Kollmann, Director of Marketing

Adventures in Advertising Franchise, Inc. (AIAFI) is an international network of over 450 individually owned and operated, professional promotional product distributorships. Ranked in Entrepreneur Magazine as the #1 franchise in its category, AIAFI offers unlimited capital to grow your business, a complete training and education program, and support from top industry professionals.

BACKGROUND:
Established: 1979; 1st Franchised: 1994
Franchised Units: 310
Company-Owned Units: 0
Total Units: 310
Dist.: US-310; CAN-55; O'seas-0
North America: 44 States, 0 Provinces
Density: 16 in TX, 18 in FL, 26 in CA
Projected New Units (12 Months): 60
Qualifications: 3, 3, 3, 2, 5, 5
FINANCIAL/TERMS:
Cash Investment: $50K-100K
Total Investment: $30K-65K
Minimum Net Worth: $10K
Fees: Franchise - $35K
Royalty - 4-7%; Ad. - .25-1%
Earnings Claims Statement: No
Term of Contract (Years): 5/5
Avg. # Of Employees: 1-2 FT, 0 PT
Passive Ownership: Discouraged
Encourage Conversions: Yes
Area Develop. Agreements: No
Sub-Franchising Contracts: No

Expand In Territory: Yes
Space Needs: NA
SUPPORT & TRAINING:
Financial Assistance Provided: Yes (D)
Site Selection Assistance: No
Lease Negotiation Assistance: No
Co-Operative Advertising: No
Franchisee Assoc./Member: Yes/Yes
Size Of Corporate Staff: 60
On-Going Support: A,B,C,D,,,G,H,I
Training: NR
SPECIFIC EXPANSION PLANS:
US: All United States
Canada: All Canada
Overseas: NR

⊰⊰ ⊱⊱

ADVICOACH
900 Main St., S. Bldg., #2
Southbury, CT 06488
Tel: (800) 892-1085 (203) 405-2171
Fax: (203) 264-3516
E-Mail: info@baiopportunity.com
Web Site: www.advicoach.com
Ms. Susan Stilwell, VP of Business Development

AdviCoach is now offering Multi-Unit and Individual franchises in the highly rewarding business-to-business Advisory/Coaching field. With more than 24 years of experience, our unique AdviCoach approach creates a coaching environment designed to provide small business owners with Rapid Impact Strategies that drive immediate results in several core areas of business. AdviCoach offers world class training, proven systems and a national network of support.

BACKGROUND: IFA MEMBER
Established: 2002; 1st Franchised: 2006
Franchised Units: 27
Company-Owned Units: 0
Total Units: 27
Dist.: US-27; CAN-0; O'seas-0
North America: 14 States, 0 Provinces
Density: 5 in VA, 2 in MN, 2 in TX
Projected New Units (12 Months): 75-125
Qualifications: 4, 4, 1, 3, 4, 4
FINANCIAL/TERMS:
Cash Investment: $35-70K
Total Investment: $73-86.3K
Minimum Net Worth: $150K

Fees: Franchise - $40K
Royalty - 100K; Ad. - 15
Earnings Claims Statement: No
Term of Contract (Years): 10/10
Avg. # Of Employees: 1 FT, 0 PT
Passive Ownership: Allowed
Encourage Conversions: Yes
Area Develop. Agreements: Yes/10
Sub-Franchising Contracts: No
Expand In Territory: Yes
Space Needs: NA
SUPPORT & TRAINING:
Financial Assistance Provided: No
Site Selection Assistance: NA
Lease Negotiation Assistance: NA
Co-Operative Advertising: No
Franchisee Assoc./Member: No
Size Of Corporate Staff: 25
On-Going Support: ,b,C,D,,,G,h,I
Training: 5 Days Phase Two Academy - Southbury, CT; 6 Days Phase One Academy - Southbury, CT
SPECIFIC EXPANSION PLANS:
US: All
Canada: All
Overseas: All

⊰⊰ ⊱⊱

AMSPIRIT BUSINESS CONNECTIONS
158 W. Johnstown Rd., P. O. Box 30724
Columbus, OH 43230
Tel: (888) 267-7474 (614) 476-5540
Fax: (614) 476-6699
E-Mail: info@amspirit.com
Web Site: www.amspirit.com
Mr. Frank J. Agin, President

AmSpirit Business Connections is a business that establishes chapters of entrepreneurs, sales representatives, and professionals and then empowers their success through the use of a structured meeting format in which these members develop dynamic business relationships and as a result promote the exchange of qualified referrals with each other.

BACKGROUND:
Established: 1997; 1st Franchised: 2006
Franchised Units: 1
Company-Owned Units: 7
Total Units: 8
Dist.: US-8; CAN-0; O'seas-0
North America: 1 States, 0 Provinces
Density: 8 in OH
Projected New Units (12 Months): 7
Qualifications: 2, 5, 3, 1, 4, 4
FINANCIAL/TERMS:

Cash Investment: $25K
Total Investment: $29-46K
Minimum Net Worth: NA
Fees: Franchise - $25K
  Royalty - 30%; Ad. - 0
Earnings Claims Statement: No
Term of Contract (Years): 10/10
Avg. # Of Employees: 2 FT, 2 PT
Passive Ownership: Not Allowed
Encourage Conversions: NA
Area Develop. Agreements: No
Sub-Franchising Contracts: No
Expand In Territory: Yes
Space Needs: NA

SUPPORT & TRAINING:
Financial Assistance Provided: No
Site Selection Assistance: No
Lease Negotiation Assistance: No
Co-Operative Advertising: No
Franchisee Assoc./Member: No
Size Of Corporate Staff: 4
On-Going Support: A,B,c,d,,,,h,I
Training: 3 Days Columbus, OH

SPECIFIC EXPANSION PLANS:
US: Midwest (Ohio, Pennsylvania, Kentucky, West Virginia
Canada: No
Overseas: NR

◄◄ ►►

AUCTION IT TODAY

10327 E. Grand River Ave., # 402
Brighton, MI 48116
Tel: (866) 216-3666 (810) 225-0555
Fax: (810) 225-8231
E-Mail: shoose@auctionittoday.com
Web Site: www.auctionittoday.com
Mr. Scoot Hoose, Director of Operations

Auction It TODAY is the eBay drop-off store franchise built on trust, integrity and maintaining the entrepreneurial spirit of our franchisees. Our fees are highly competitive, allowing many people the opportunity to own their own business. Our franchise support is unparalleled and we offer our franchisees all of the tools necessary to own a successful business. We have three main programs. Full-line retail stores, kiosks (store within an existing retail business) and Area Developers.

BACKGROUND:
Established: 2004; 1st Franchised: 2005
Franchised Units: 96
Company-Owned Units: 1
Total Units: 97
Dist.: US-82; CAN-0; O'seas-0
  North America: 9 States, 0 Provinces

Density: 44 in MI, 4 in IN
Projected New Units (12 Months): NR
Qualifications: 3, 3, 3, 3, 3, 3
FINANCIAL/TERMS:
Cash Investment: $20-60K
Total Investment: $30-100K
Minimum Net Worth: $50K
Fees: Franchise - $14-18K
  Royalty - 4% or $1,200; Ad. - $450
Earnings Claims Statement: No
Term of Contract (Years): 10/10
Avg. # Of Employees: 2-5 FT, 0-3 PT
Passive Ownership: Discouraged
Encourage Conversions: NA
Area Develop. Agreements: Yes/5
Sub-Franchising Contracts: Yes
Expand In Territory: Yes
Space Needs: 1,800 SF

SUPPORT & TRAINING:
Financial Assistance Provided: No
Site Selection Assistance: Yes
Lease Negotiation Assistance: Yes
Co-Operative Advertising: No
Franchisee Assoc./Member: No
Size Of Corporate Staff: 10
On-Going Support: a,b,C,d,E,,G,h,I
Training: 5 Days Brighton, MI

SPECIFIC EXPANSION PLANS:
US: All United States
Canada: No
Overseas: NR

◄◄ ►►

BE▼INCO

BEVINCO

505 Consumers Rd., # 510
Toronto, ON M2J 4V8 Canada
Tel: (888) 238-4626 (416) 490-6266
Fax: (416) 490-6899
E-Mail: globaloffice@bevinco.com
Web Site: www.bevinco.com
Mr. Barry Driedger, President/CEO

Liquor inventory auditing and control service for bars and restaurants. Utilizing our computerized weighing system, franchisees will identify and resolve the shrinkage problems associated with the bar business. On-going weekly accounts make for an excellent executive income.

BACKGROUND: IFA MEMBER
Established: 1987; 1st Franchised: 1990
Franchised Units: 267
Company-Owned Units: 1
Total Units: 268

Dist.: US-195; CAN-27; O'seas-46
  North America: 49 States, 8 Provinces
Density: 10 in TX, 23 in OH, 14 in CA
Projected New Units (12 Months): 50
Qualifications: 3, 4, 4, 3, 3, 3
FINANCIAL/TERMS:
Cash Investment: $40K
Total Investment: $40K
Minimum Net Worth: $40K
Fees: Franchise - $39.9K
  Royalty - $4/Audit; Ad. - $2/Audit
Earnings Claims Statement: No
Term of Contract (Years): 5/5
Avg. # Of Employees: 1-3 FT, 1-3 PT
Passive Ownership: Not Allowed
Encourage Conversions: NA
Area Develop. Agreements: Yes/1
Sub-Franchising Contracts: No
Expand In Territory: No
Space Needs: NR

SUPPORT & TRAINING:
Financial Assistance Provided: Yes (D)
Site Selection Assistance: NA
Lease Negotiation Assistance: NA
Co-Operative Advertising: No
Franchisee Assoc./Member: Yes/Yes
Size Of Corporate Staff: 12
On-Going Support: A,b,,D,,,G,H,I
Training: 5 Days Franchisee's Location; 7 Days Head Office in Toronto

SPECIFIC EXPANSION PLANS:
US: All United States
Canada: All Canada
Overseas: All Countries

◄◄ ►►

BillboardConnection.
Your Source for Successful Advertising

BILLBOARD CONNECTION

2121 Vista Pkwy.
West Palm Beach, FL 33411
Tel: (866) 257-6025 (561) 640-5570
Fax: (561) 640-5580
E-Mail: mprince@ufgcorp.com
Web Site: www.billboardconnection.com
Mr. Michael Prince, Director Franchise Development

Home-based advertising agency, specializing in all outdoor advertising formats, including billboards, malls, airports, transit, stadiums and more. We provide our clients with a complete solution for their outdoor advertising campaign to include design, production and placement. Advantages include: industry contacts provided; no rent; no inventory to carry; no equipment lease payments; no employees; no overhead; recurring income; and protected territory. Keep current position while growing your business.

BACKGROUND: IFA MEMBER
Established: 1997; 1st Franchised: 2005
Franchised Units: 77
Company-Owned Units: 0
Total Units: 77
Dist.: US-66; CAN-6; O'seas-5
North America: 12 States, 1 Provinces
Density: 3 in MD, 3 in FL, 4 in CA
Projected New Units (12 Months): 60
Qualifications: 3, 4, 2, 3, 2, 4
FINANCIAL/TERMS:
Cash Investment: $24.5K
Total Investment: $40K
Minimum Net Worth: $50K
Fees: Franchise - $24.5K
Royalty - 3.5%; Ad. - 0.5%
Earnings Claims Statement: No
Term of Contract (Years): 35/35
Avg. # Of Employees: 0 FT, 0 PT
Passive Ownership: Discouraged
Encourage Conversions: NA
Area Develop. Agreements: No
Sub-Franchising Contracts: No
Expand In Territory: No
Space Needs: NA
SUPPORT & TRAINING:
Financial Assistance Provided: Yes (D)
Site Selection Assistance: NA
Lease Negotiation Assistance: NA
Co-Operative Advertising: Yes
Franchisee Assoc./Member: No
Size Of Corporate Staff: 150
On-Going Support: ,,C,D,E,,G,H,I
Training: 1 week In market training;
1 week West Palm Beach, FL
SPECIFIC EXPANSION PLANS:
US: All United States
Canada: All Canada
Overseas: All Foreign Countries

≪ ≫

**BUSINESS PARTNER
MARKETING COACH**
900 Main St. S., Bldg. #2
Southbury, CT 06488
Tel: (800)289-0086 (724) 863-7888
Fax: (203)264-3516
E-Mail: bviolette@businesspartner.com
Web Site: www.businesspartner.com

Mr./Ms. Bruce Violette, Franchise Director / Founder

Business Partner Marketing Coach simplifies the life of busy business professionals by saving them time and money with a one source resource that satisfies all their marketing needs. Business Partner Marketing Coach provides business owners a full suite of creative marketing services. These services include: Marketing Coaching, Printing, Signs, Trade Show Displays & Graphics, Promotional Products, Corporate Apparel, Website & Graphic Design, Digital Media & E-Myth Business Success Educational Programs.

BACKGROUND: IFA MEMBER
Established: 1996; 1st Franchised: 2002
Franchised Units: 10
Company-Owned Units: 0
Total Units: 0
Dist.: US-10; CAN-0; O'seas-0
North America: 6 States, 0 Provinces
Density: 2 in PA, 3 in FL
Projected New Units (12 Months): 6
Qualifications: 2, 2, 1, 2, 2, 2
FINANCIAL/TERMS:
Cash Investment: $25K
Total Investment: $65-79K
Minimum Net Worth: $50K
Fees: Franchise - $40K
Royalty - 6-10%; Ad. - NA
Earnings Claims Statement: No
Term of Contract (Years): 10/10
Avg. # Of Employees: 0 FT, 0 PT
Passive Ownership: Discouraged
Encourage Conversions: NA
Area Develop. Agreements: Yes/10
Sub-Franchising Contracts: Yes
Expand In Territory: Yes
Space Needs: NA
SUPPORT & TRAINING:
Financial Assistance Provided: Yes (I)
Site Selection Assistance: NA
Lease Negotiation Assistance: NA
Co-Operative Advertising: No
Franchisee Assoc./Member: No
Size Of Corporate Staff: 25
On-Going Support: A,B,C,D,,,G,,I
Training: 11 days Southbury,CT
SPECIFIC EXPANSION PLANS:
US: All States
Canada: All Provinces
Overseas: All Countries

≪ ≫

CFOTODAY
401 St. Francis St.

Tallahassee, FL 32301
Tel: (888) 643-1348 (850) 681-1941
Fax: (850) 561-1374
E-Mail: rbaker@cfotoday.com
Web Site: www.cfotoday.com
Mr. Ron Baker, Vice President

Accounting, tax, payroll and financial services franchise, offering services to small business clients. Reports they can understand and use, professional services at affordable prices.

BACKGROUND:
Established: 1989; 1st Franchised: 1990
Franchised Units: 241
Company-Owned Units: 1
Total Units: 242
Dist.: US-239; CAN-2; O'seas-1
North America: 37 States, 0 Provinces
Density: in NC, in FL, in CA
Projected New Units (12 Months): 10
Qualifications: 3, 5, 5, 3, 2, 4
FINANCIAL/TERMS:
Cash Investment: $24.4-37.4K
Total Investment: $24.4-37.4K
Minimum Net Worth: NR
Fees: Franchise - $24K
Royalty - 6%; Ad. - 2%
Earnings Claims Statement: No
Term of Contract (Years): 10/10
Avg. # Of Employees: 1 FT, 0 PT
Passive Ownership: Allowed
Encourage Conversions: Yes
Area Develop. Agreements: No
Sub-Franchising Contracts: No
Expand In Territory: Yes
Space Needs: 400 SF
SUPPORT & TRAINING:
Financial Assistance Provided: No
Site Selection Assistance: NA
Lease Negotiation Assistance: No
Co-Operative Advertising: No
Franchisee Assoc./Member: No
Size Of Corporate Staff: 7
On-Going Support: ,,c,D,,,G,H,
Training: 5 Days Tallahassee, FL
SPECIFIC EXPANSION PLANS:
US: All United States
Canada: All Canada
Overseas: NR

≪ ≫

COMMISSION EXPRESS
8306 Professional Hill Dr.
Fairfax, VA 22031
Tel: (888) 560-5501 (703) 560-5500
Fax: (703) 560-5502
E-Mail: manager@commissionexpress.

com
Web Site: www.commissionexpress.com
Mr. John L. Stedman, President

We are a true 'white collar' franchise. We offer 'exclusive' territories with professional customers. 9 to 5, no holidays or late nights, a normal life. High profit margin per transaction and a high 80% repeat factor.

BACKGROUND:

Established: 1992;	1st Franchised: 1996
Franchised Units:	55
Company-Owned Units:	1
Total Units:	56
Dist.:	US-56; CAN-0; O'seas-0
North America:	30 States, 0 Provinces
Density:	4 in VA, 4 in FL, 5 in CA
Projected New Units (12 Months):	14
Qualifications:	4, 5, 3, 3, 3, 4

FINANCIAL/TERMS:

Cash Investment:	$34.4-43.7K
Total Investment:	$80-180K
Minimum Net Worth:	$100K
Fees: Franchise -	$10-40K
Royalty - 4.5-9%;	Ad. - 1%
Earnings Claims Statement:	No
Term of Contract (Years):	10/5
Avg. # Of Employees:	1 FT, 0 PT
Passive Ownership:	Discouraged
Encourage Conversions:	NA
Area Develop. Agreements:	No
Sub-Franchising Contracts:	No
Expand In Territory:	Yes
Space Needs:	400 SF

SUPPORT & TRAINING:

Financial Assistance Provided:	Yes (D)
Site Selection Assistance:	Yes
Lease Negotiation Assistance:	No
Co-Operative Advertising:	No
Franchisee Assoc./Member:	No
Size Of Corporate Staff:	4
On-Going Support:	,,C,D,,,G,H,I
Training:	5 Days Fairfax, VA

SPECIFIC EXPANSION PLANS:

US:	All United States
Canada:	All Canada
Overseas:	NR

<< >>

CRESTCOM INTERNATIONAL, LTD.
6900 E. Belleview Ave., 3rd Fl.

Greenwood Village, CO 80111-1619
Tel: (888) 273-7826 (303) 267-8200
Fax: (303) 267-8207
E-Mail: franchiseinfo@crestcom.com
Web Site: www.crestcom.com
Mr. Kelly Krause, Director International Marketing

Crestcom franchisees sell, market and deliver Bullet Proof Manager training. The training focuses on sales, recruiting, customer service and management skills development. It is a unique combination of live and video instruction, which emphasizes involvement, participation, teamwork and leadership development. Thousands of organizations worldwide have benefited from Crestcom's Bullet Proof Manager training, which works with all sizes of organizations, from small, local companies to multi-national giants. The training is currently offered by licensees in more than 50 countries. Various versions of Bullet Proof Manager training are available in more 25 language versions.

BACKGROUND: IFA MEMBER

Established: 1987;	1st Franchised: 1992
Franchised Units:	143
Company-Owned Units:	0
Total Units:	143
Dist.:	US-60; CAN-4; O'seas-79
North America:	25 States, 4 Provinces
Density:	NR
Projected New Units (12 Months):	25
Qualifications:	3, 3, 4, 4, 5, 1

FINANCIAL/TERMS:

Cash Investment:	$59.5K
Total Investment:	$54.8K-89K
Minimum Net Worth:	NR
Fees: Franchise -	$62.5K
Royalty - 1.5%;	Ad. - NA
Earnings Claims Statement:	Yes
Term of Contract (Years):	7/7
Avg. # Of Employees:	2-5 FT, 0 PT
Passive Ownership:	Discouraged
Encourage Conversions:	NA
Area Develop. Agreements:	Yes/10
Sub-Franchising Contracts:	No
Expand In Territory:	Yes
Space Needs:	NR

SUPPORT & TRAINING:

Financial Assistance Provided:	Yes (D)
Site Selection Assistance:	NA
Lease Negotiation Assistance:	NA
Co-Operative Advertising:	No
Franchisee Assoc./Member:	Yes/Yes
Size Of Corporate Staff:	15
On-Going Support:	,,C,D,,,G,H,
Training:	8 Days United States

SPECIFIC EXPANSION PLANS:

US:	All United States
Canada:	All Canada
Overseas:	All Countries

<< >>

CYBERTARY
10016 Foothill Blvd., # 110
Roseville, CA 95747
Tel: (888) CYB-TARY (916) 781-7799
Fax: (916) 781-7717
E-Mail: Franchise@Cybertary.com
Web Site: www.CybertaryFranchise.com
Ms. Patricia Beckman, Founder / CEO

WORK AT HOME! BALANCE YOUR LIFE! Cybertary offers the only national franchise in the booming Virtual Assistant (VA) industry providing "on-demand" administrative support to businesses, entrepreneurs, and busy people. Cybertaries work within a diversely talented nationwide team network to meet the administrative needs of any business. This home-based B2B service offers low overhead and a flexible schedule. Cybertary's proven systems will get your business up and running in as little as six weeks!

BACKGROUND: IFA MEMBER

Established: 2005;	1st Franchised: 2006
Franchised Units:	11
Company-Owned Units:	0
Total Units:	11
Dist.:	US-11; CAN-0; O'seas-0
North America:	0 States, 0 Provinces
Density:	1 in PA, 2 in NC, 5 in CA
Projected New Units (12 Months):	Entire United States
Qualifications:	4, 4, 3, 3, 2, 4

FINANCIAL/TERMS:

Cash Investment:	$30K
Total Investment:	$29-125K
Minimum Net Worth:	$70K
Fees: Franchise -	$27.5K
Royalty - $400;	Ad. - 1% of gross sales
Earnings Claims Statement:	No
Term of Contract (Years):	10/10
Avg. # Of Employees:	1 FT, 0 PT
Passive Ownership:	Discouraged
Encourage Conversions:	NA
Area Develop. Agreements:	Yes/10
Sub-Franchising Contracts:	No
Expand In Territory:	Yes
Space Needs:	NA

SUPPORT & TRAINING:

Financial Assistance Provided: Yes (I)
Site Selection Assistance: Yes
Lease Negotiation Assistance: NA
Co-Operative Advertising: No
Franchisee Assoc./Member: No
Size Of Corporate Staff: 4
On-Going Support: A,,,,E,,G,,
Training: 4 days Cybertary Corporate

SPECIFIC EXPANSION PLANS:
US: CA, WA, OR, MT, ID, UT, NV, AZ, WY, CO, NM, TX, NE
Canada: No
Overseas: NR

⫷⫷ ⫸⫸

DEI FRANCHISE SYSTEMS
888 Seventh Ave., 9th Fl.
New York, NY 10106
Tel: (800) 224-2140 (212) 581-7390 + 223
Fax: (212) 245-7897
E-Mail: franchise@dei-sales.com
Web Site: www.dei-sales.com
Mr. Scott Forman, Franchise Sales

DEI Management offers you an exciting business opportunity - the chance to own your own firm in the $7.6 billion sales training industry. At the same time, you will enjoy the benefits of an outstanding franchising company with a proven selling system.

BACKGROUND:
Established: 1979; 1st Franchised: 2003
Franchised Units: 31
Company-Owned Units: 1
Total Units: 32
Dist.: US-28; CAN-2; O'seas-2
  North America: 18 States, Provinces
Density: 2 in NY
Projected New Units (12 Months): 50
Qualifications: 3, 2, 2, 3, 3, 3

FINANCIAL/TERMS:
Cash Investment: $50K
Total Investment: $60-75K
Minimum Net Worth: NA
Fees: Franchise - $50K
  Royalty - 7%; Ad. - 2+4%=6%
Earnings Claims Statement: No
Term of Contract (Years): 5/5/5/5/
Avg. # Of Employees: 1 FT, 0 PT
Passive Ownership: Discouraged
Encourage Conversions: Yes
Area Develop. Agreements: Yes/1
Sub-Franchising Contracts: No
Expand In Territory: Yes
Space Needs: 900 SF

SUPPORT & TRAINING:
Financial Assistance Provided: No

Site Selection Assistance: Yes
Lease Negotiation Assistance: NA
Co-Operative Advertising: No
Franchisee Assoc./Member: No
Size Of Corporate Staff: 20
On-Going Support: A,B,C,D,E,F,G,H,I
Training: 2 Weeks Homebased; 2 Weeks Headquarters

SPECIFIC EXPANSION PLANS:
US: All United States
Canada: All Canada
Overseas: All Countries

⫷⫷ ⫸⫸

ELECTRONIC TAX FILERS
P. O. Box 2077
Cary, NC 27512-2077
Tel: (800) 945-9277 (919) 469-0651
Fax: (919) 460-5935
E-Mail: rachelwishon@aol.com
Web Site: www.electronictaxfilers.com
Ms. Rachel Wishon, President

We do no tax preparation! Instead, we provide a local, reasonably priced, walk-in retail location where the 51% of the taxpayers who prepare their own returns can obtain electronic filing without being pressured into tax preparation they do not need. We transmit the data from self-pre-pared returns to the IRS and states in order that the taxpayer may receive his refunds in days, not months, via direct deposit into his bank, mail or refund loan.

BACKGROUND:
Established: 1990; 1st Franchised: 1990
Franchised Units: 43
Company-Owned Units: 2
Total Units: 45
Dist.: US-45; CAN-0; O'seas-0
  North America: 15 States, 0 Provinces
Density: 8 in NC
Projected New Units (12 Months): 3
Qualifications: 3, 4, 1, 3, NR, 4

FINANCIAL/TERMS:
Cash Investment: $25K
Total Investment: $25K
Minimum Net Worth: $25K
Fees: Franchise - $13.5K
  Royalty - 12%; Ad. - 3%
Earnings Claims Statement: No
Term of Contract (Years): 3/17
Avg. # Of Employees: 2 FT, 4 PT

Passive Ownership: Not Allowed
Encourage Conversions: No
Area Develop. Agreements: No
Sub-Franchising Contracts: No
Expand In Territory: Yes
Space Needs: 700 SF

SUPPORT & TRAINING:
Financial Assistance Provided: Yes (D)
Site Selection Assistance: Yes
Lease Negotiation Assistance: Yes
Co-Operative Advertising: Yes
Franchisee Assoc./Member: No
Size Of Corporate Staff: 0
On-Going Support: A,,C,D,,,,h,I
Training: As Needed On-Site; 1 Week Cary, NC

SPECIFIC EXPANSION PLANS:
US: Eastern United States
Canada: No
Overseas: NR

⫷⫷ ⫸⫸

Top 100

ENTREPRENEUR'S SOURCE, THE
900 Main St. S., Bldg. # 2
Southbury, CT 06488
Tel: (800) 289-0086 (203) 264-2006
Fax: (203) 264-3516
E-Mail: info@theesource.com
Web Site: www.theesource.com
Ms. Susan Stilwell, Business Development

We provide consulting, education and guidance to people exploring self-employment as an additional career option. Using a unique profiling system, ENTREPRENEUR'S SOURCE consultants help people discover the best options for them.

BACKGROUND: IFA MEMBER
Established: 1984; 1st Franchised: 1997
Franchised Units: 250
Company-Owned Units: 0
Total Units: 250
Dist.: US-248; CAN-2; O'seas-0
  North America: 40 States, 0 Provinces
Density: 19 in IL, 27 in CA
Projected New Units (12 Months): 100
Qualifications: 4, 4, 1, 1, 2, 5

FINANCIAL/TERMS:
Cash Investment: $49K-95K
Total Investment: $72L-85.5K

Minimum Net Worth:	$150K
Fees: Franchise -	$49K
Royalty - 0%;	Ad. - $750/Mo.
Earnings Claims Statement:	No
Term of Contract (Years):	10/10
Avg. # Of Employees:	1 FT, 0 PT
Passive Ownership:	Not Allowed
Encourage Conversions:	Yes
Area Develop. Agreements:	No
Sub-Franchising Contracts:	Yes
Expand In Territory:	Yes
Space Needs:	NR

SUPPORT & TRAINING:

Financial Assistance Provided:	Yes (D)
Site Selection Assistance:	NA
Lease Negotiation Assistance:	NA
Co-Operative Advertising:	No
Franchisee Assoc./Member:	No
Size Of Corporate Staff:	17
On-Going Support:	,,,D,,,,H,I
Training:	8 Days CT. Initial

SPECIFIC EXPANSION PLANS:

US:	All United States
Canada:	All Canada
Overseas:	Most Countries

EXPENSE REDUCTION CONSULTING

5050 Avenida Encinas, # 200
Carlsbad, CA 92008
Tel: (877) 255-2511 (760) 712-3600
Fax: (760) 712-3700
E-Mail: khagerstrom@era-usa.com
Web Site: www.allaboutera.com
Mr. Ken Hagerstrom, President

ERC Franchisees employ a finely tuned methodology that has helped a wide range of companies minimize idirect costs since 1993. This methodology, along with proprietary web-based tools and Knowledge Base, assists ERC Franchisees in increasing their client's bottom lines by decreasing their often elusive indirect costs. Best of all, ERC Franchisees maximize their earning potential by providing their services on a "pay for performance basis," sharing in their clients long-term savings.

BACKGROUND:

Established: 1993;	1st Franchised: 2005
Franchised Units:	7
Company-Owned Units:	1
Total Units:	8
Dist.:	US-8; CAN-0; O'seas-0
North America:	5 States, 0 Provinces
Density:	2 in TX, 2 in FL
Projected New Units (12 Months):	NR
Qualifications:	3, 3, 3, 3, 3, 3

FINANCIAL/TERMS:

Cash Investment:	$34-45K
Total Investment:	$34-45K
Minimum Net Worth:	NR
Fees: Franchise -	$29K
Royalty - 7%;	Ad. - 2%
Earnings Claims Statement:	No
Term of Contract (Years):	7/5
Avg. # Of Employees:	1 FT, 0 PT
Passive Ownership:	Allowed
Encourage Conversions:	NA
Area Develop. Agreements:	Yes/15
Sub-Franchising Contracts:	No
Expand In Territory:	No
Space Needs:	NA

SUPPORT & TRAINING:

Financial Assistance Provided:	No
Site Selection Assistance:	No
Lease Negotiation Assistance:	No
Co-Operative Advertising:	No
Franchisee Assoc./Member:	No
Size Of Corporate Staff:	1
On-Going Support:	A,B,c,d,,,G,,I
Training:	5 Days Ft. Landerdale, FL

SPECIFIC EXPANSION PLANS:

US: All United States except the Dakotas and Maryland	
Canada:	No
Overseas:	NR

FIDUCIAL

10480 Little Patuxent Pkwy., # 300
Columbia, MD 21044
Tel: (800) 323-9000 (410) 910-5860
Fax: (410) 910-5903
E-Mail: howard.margolis@fiducial.com
Web Site: www.fiducial.com
Mr. Howard J. Margolis, Director Field Support/Devel.

A FIDUCIAL franchise is a business which provides small businesses and individuals with back office support and accounting and financial management services, tax services, financial services, business counseling services and payroll services. Franchise offices operate out of commercial spaces furnished in such a manner that clients walking in immediately realize that their business, financial and tax needs will be taken care of by qualified individuals who will be there for them year after year.

BACKGROUND: IFA MEMBER

Established: 1999;	1st Franchised: 1999
Franchised Units:	554
Company-Owned Units:	30
Total Units:	584
Dist.:	US-584; CAN-0; O'seas-0
North America:	48 States, 0 Provinces
Density:	NR
Projected New Units (12 Months):	30
Qualifications:	5, 4, 5, 2, 3, 4

FINANCIAL/TERMS:

Cash Investment:	$60-75K
Total Investment:	$44.4-115.5K
Minimum Net Worth:	$150K
Fees: Franchise -	$12.5-25K
Royalty - 1.5-6%;	Ad. - 2%
Earnings Claims Statement:	No
Term of Contract (Years):	10/5
Avg. # Of Employees:	1-8 FT, 1-2 PT
Passive Ownership:	Discouraged
Encourage Conversions:	Yes
Area Develop. Agreements:	No
Sub-Franchising Contracts:	No
Expand In Territory:	No
Space Needs:	800-3,200 SF

SUPPORT & TRAINING:

Financial Assistance Provided:	Yes (D)
Site Selection Assistance:	Yes
Lease Negotiation Assistance:	No
Co-Operative Advertising:	No
Franchisee Assoc./Member:	No
Size Of Corporate Staff:	82
On-Going Support:	a,b,C,D,,,g,h,I
Training:	10-15 Days Columbia, MD

SPECIFIC EXPANSION PLANS:

US:	All United States
Canada:	No
Overseas:	NR

FOCALPOINT COACHING

5740 S. Eastern Ave., #100
Las Vegas, NV 89119
Tel: (877) 433-6225 (702) 932-3870
Fax: (702) 932-3871
E-Mail: insales@focalpointcoaching.com
Web Site: www.focalpointcoaching.com
Ms. Kristina Raffaniello, Executive Assistant

FocalPoint Coaching, "Powered by Brian Tracy" is part of the lucrative business performance coaching segment of the coaching market. FocalPoint's mission is to boost the performance of organizations by coaching and teaching proven and innovative business strategies and tactics directly to business owners or key leaders. Our franchise opportunity provides expansive tools, systems and a brand our coaches can leverage as they operate a successful business as a FocalPoint Coach.

BACKGROUND: IFA MEMBER

Established: 2004;	1st Franchised: 2006
Franchised Units:	37
Company-Owned Units:	0
Total Units:	37
Dist.:	US-34; CAN-3; O'seas-0
North America:	17 States, 9 Provinces
Density:	5 in TN, 2 in NJ, 5 in FL
Projected New Units (12 Months):	60
Qualifications:	4, 5, 3, 3, 4, 4

FINANCIAL/TERMS:

Cash Investment:	$50K
Total Investment:	$78.5-118.5K
Minimum Net Worth:	$150K
Fees: Franchise -	$40K
Royalty - $1800;	Ad. - 5%
Earnings Claims Statement:	No
Term of Contract (Years):	5/5
Avg. # Of Employees:	1 FT, 0 PT
Passive Ownership:	Not Allowed
Encourage Conversions:	NA
Area Develop. Agreements:	Yes/10
Sub-Franchising Contracts:	No
Expand In Territory:	No
Space Needs:	NA

SUPPORT & TRAINING:

Financial Assistance Provided:	Yes (D)
Site Selection Assistance:	NA
Lease Negotiation Assistance:	NA
Co-Operative Advertising:	Yes
Franchisee Assoc./Member:	No
Size Of Corporate Staff:	7
On-Going Support:	,,C,D,,,G,,I
Training:	6 Days Las Vegas, NV

SPECIFIC EXPANSION PLANS:

US:	All Unites States
Canada:	All Canada
Overseas:	All Countries

⊰⊰ ⊱⊱

INNER CIRCLE INTERNATIONAL, THE

7100 E. Pleasant Valley Rd., # 300
Independence, OH 44131
Tel: (877) 392-6278 (216) 674-0645
Fax: (216) 674-0650
E-Mail: kgolubski@merrymtg.com
Web Site: www.TheInnerCircle.com
Ms. Kylne Golubski, VP Business Devel-

opment

Each Inner Circle is a peer group of 8-10 individuals who own and operate growing companies. An Inner Circle meets once a month for three hours with a proprietary format that focuses on each member as a person and as a business owner. As an Inner Circle franchisee, you facilitate group members as they provide one another with objective, high quality professional counsel as well as direct, no-holds-barred insights.

BACKGROUND:

Established: 1985;	1st Franchised: 1997
Franchised Units:	10
Company-Owned Units:	2
Total Units:	12
Dist.:	US-12; CAN-0; O'seas-0
North America:	7 States, 0 Provinces
Density:	1 in TN, 4 in MN, 1 in MD
Projected New Units (12 Months):	4
Qualifications:	3, 5, 1, 3, 4, 5

FINANCIAL/TERMS:

Cash Investment:	$25K
Total Investment:	$41K-59K
Minimum Net Worth:	$250K
Fees: Franchise -	$25K
Royalty - 15%;	Ad. - 0
Earnings Claims Statement:	No
Term of Contract (Years):	10/10
Avg. # Of Employees:	1 FT, 0 PT
Passive Ownership:	Discouraged
Encourage Conversions:	NA
Area Develop. Agreements:	No
Sub-Franchising Contracts:	No
Expand In Territory:	Yes
Space Needs:	NA

SUPPORT & TRAINING:

Financial Assistance Provided:	No
Site Selection Assistance:	No
Lease Negotiation Assistance:	No
Co-Operative Advertising:	No
Franchisee Assoc./Member:	No
Size Of Corporate Staff:	0
On-Going Support:	,,,D,,,G,h,
Training:	5 Days Minneapolis, MN; 3 Days Franchisee Location

SPECIFIC EXPANSION PLANS:

US:	All United States
Canada:	No
Overseas:	NR

⊰⊰ ⊱⊱

INTELLIGENT OFFICE

4450 Arapahoe Ave.
Boulder, CO 80303-9123
Tel: (880) 800-4987 (303) 415-2510
Fax: (303) 415-2500

E-Mail: scochran@intelligentoffice.com
Web Site: www.intelligentoffice.com
Mr. Sean Cochran, Director Franchise Development

This highly evolved alternative to the traditional office provides a prestigious address, anywhere communications and a live receptionist for businesses, corporate executives and professionals, releasing them from the limitations and expense of a traditional or home office. INTELLIGENT OFFICE offers private offices, conference rooms and professional office services on an as-needed basis and at only a fraction of the cost of a traditional office.

BACKGROUND: IFA MEMBER

Established: 1995;	1st Franchised: 1999
Franchised Units:	44
Company-Owned Units:	3
Total Units:	47
Dist.:	US-40; CAN-3; O'seas-0
North America:	16 States, 1 Provinces
Density:	3 in TX, 9 in FL, 3 in CO
Projected New Units (12 Months):	18
Qualifications:	5, 1, 1, 1, 1, 5

FINANCIAL/TERMS:

Cash Investment:	$200K
Total Investment:	$420K-620K
Minimum Net Worth:	$1MM
Fees: Franchise -	$48K
Royalty - 5%;	Ad. - $250/Mo.
Earnings Claims Statement:	No
Term of Contract (Years):	20/20
Avg. # Of Employees:	3 FT, 2 PT
Passive Ownership:	Not Allowed
Encourage Conversions:	No
Area Develop. Agreements:	Yes/1
Sub-Franchising Contracts:	No
Expand In Territory:	No
Space Needs:	5,000-8,000 SF

SUPPORT & TRAINING:

Financial Assistance Provided:	No
Site Selection Assistance:	Yes
Lease Negotiation Assistance:	Yes
Co-Operative Advertising:	No
Franchisee Assoc./Member:	Yes/Yes
Size Of Corporate Staff:	8
On-Going Support:	,,C,D,E,,G,H,
Training:	1 Week Boulder, CO; 1 Week On-Site; Ongoing remote training and support

SPECIFIC EXPANSION PLANS:

US:	All United States
Canada:	All Canada
Overseas:	All Countries

⊰⊰ ⊱⊱

INTERFACE FINANCIAL GROUP, THE

2182 DuPont Dr., # 221
Irvine, CA 92612-1320
Tel: (800) 387-0860 (905) 475-5701
Fax: (866) 475-8688
E-Mail: dtbanf@interfacefinancial.biz
Web Site: www.interfacefinancial.com
Mr. David T. Banfield, President

Franchise buys quality accounts receivables from client companies at a discount to provide short-term working capital to expanding businesses.

BACKGROUND:
Established: 1971;   1st Franchised: 1991
Franchised Units: 146
Company-Owned Units: 0
Total Units: 146
Dist.:   US-114; CAN-20; O'seas-12
   North America: 34 States, 6 Provinces
   Density: 8 in ON, 17 in CA
Projected New Units (12 Months):   30
Qualifications: 1, 1, 1, 1, 1, 1
FINANCIAL/TERMS:
Cash Investment: $100K+
Total Investment: $100K+
Minimum Net Worth: $150K
Fees: Franchise - $36K
   Royalty - 8%;   Ad. - NR
Earnings Claims Statement: No
Term of Contract (Years):   10/10
Avg. # Of Employees: FT, PT
Passive Ownership: Discouraged
Encourage Conversions: NA
Area Develop. Agreements: Yes/1
Sub-Franchising Contracts: No
Expand In Territory: Yes
Space Needs: NA
SUPPORT & TRAINING:
Financial Assistance Provided: NR
Site Selection Assistance: NA
Lease Negotiation Assistance: NA
Co-Operative Advertising: Yes
Franchisee Assoc./Member: No
Size Of Corporate Staff: 0
On-Going Support: ,,D,E,,G,H,I
Training: 6 Days Total (2 days on-site)
SPECIFIC EXPANSION PLANS:
US: All United States
Canada: All Canada
Overseas: All Countries

<< >>

JACKSON HEWITT TAX SERVICE
3 Sylvan Wy. 3rd Fl.
Parsippany, NJ 07054
Tel: (800) 475-2904 (973) 496-1040
Fax: (973) 496-2760
E-Mail: joinus@jtax.com
Web Site: www.jacksonhewitt.com
Mr. Charlie Harris, SVP Franchise Sales/
   Devel.

JACKSON HEWITT prepares tax returns for customers throughout over 4,000 franchised offices in more than 48 states, including locations within Wal-Mart, Kmart, Staples, etc. Since its founding in 1986, JACKSON HEWITT is the fastest-growing national tax service. Offices are independently owned and operated, offering full-service individual tax preparation, electronic filing, refund anticipation loans (subj. to qualification), and audit representation. A subsidiary of Cendant Corp. since 1998.

BACKGROUND: IFA MEMBER
Established: 1983;   1st Franchised: 1986
Franchised Units: 5763
Company-Owned Units: 1000
Total Units: 6763
Dist.:   US-6763; CAN-0; O'seas-0
   North America: 48 States, 0 Provinces
   Density:480 in TX, 350 in IL, 381 in FL
Projected New Units (12 Months):   350
Qualifications: 5, 5, 3, 4, 4, 5
FINANCIAL/TERMS:
Cash Investment: $25-50K
Total Investment: $55K-99K
Minimum Net Worth: $100K
Fees: Franchise - $25K
   Royalty - 15%;   Ad. - 6%
Earnings Claims Statement: Yes
Term of Contract (Years):   10/10
Avg. # Of Employees: 1 FT, 6 PT
Passive Ownership: Allowed
Encourage Conversions: Yes
Area Develop. Agreements: No
Sub-Franchising Contracts: No
Expand In Territory: Yes
Space Needs: 400-1,000 SF
SUPPORT & TRAINING:
Financial Assistance Provided: Yes (D)
Site Selection Assistance: Yes
Lease Negotiation Assistance: No
Co-Operative Advertising: No
Franchisee Assoc./Member: Yes/Yes
Size Of Corporate Staff: 235
On-Going Support: A,B,C,D,,,G,H,I
Training: 5 Days Parsippany, NJ.
SPECIFIC EXPANSION PLANS:
US: All United States
Canada: No
Overseas: NR

<< >>

LEADERSHIP MANAGEMENT, INC.
4567 Lake Shore Dr.
Waco, TX 76710
Tel: (800) 568-1241
Fax: (254) 757-4600
E-Mail: info@lmi-usa.com
Web Site: www.lmi-bus.com
Mr. Tony Stigliano, VP Development
   Opportunities

Own a professional training dealership that helps companies achieve success. Producing measurable results for clients since 1966; interface with business executives; programs and a process to develop leaders, managers and executives; proven success system; long-term client relationships; national network. Call (800) 365-7437 or send resume.

BACKGROUND:
Established: 1965;   1st Franchised: 1965
Franchised Units: 223
Company-Owned Units: 0
Total Units: 223
Dist.:   US-223; CAN-0; O'seas-0
   North America: 0 States, 0 Provinces
   Density: NR
Projected New Units (12 Months):   12
Qualifications: NR
FINANCIAL/TERMS:
Cash Investment: NR
Total Investment: NA
Minimum Net Worth: NR
Fees: Franchise - $30K
   Royalty - 6%;   Ad. - NA
Earnings Claims Statement: No
Term of Contract (Years):   10/
Avg. # Of Employees: Varies
Passive Ownership: Discouraged
Encourage Conversions: NA
Area Develop. Agreements: No
Sub-Franchising Contracts: No
Expand In Territory: No
Space Needs: NR
SUPPORT & TRAINING:
Financial Assistance Provided: Yes (D)
Site Selection Assistance: NA
Lease Negotiation Assistance: NA
Co-Operative Advertising: No
Franchisee Assoc./Member: No

Size Of Corporate Staff: 25
On-Going Support: ,,C,D,,,,H,I
Training: NR

SPECIFIC EXPANSION PLANS:
US: All United States
Canada: All Canada
Overseas: NR

≺≺ ≻≻

LIBERTY TAX SERVICE
1716 Corporate Landing Pkwy.
Virginia Beach, VA 23454
Tel: (800) 790-3863 (877) 285-4237
Fax: (800) 880-6432
E-Mail: sales@libtax.com
Web Site: www.libertytaxfranchise.com
Ms. Ami Hill, Media Director

We're #1! LIBERTY TAX SERVICE is the fastest-growing international tax service ever, and is ranked as the #1 tax franchise on the latest Entrepreneur magazine "Franchise 500" and #3 overall. Recession or not, there's a growing market of taxpayers, and approximately 63% of them outsource the tax preparation task to paid professionals. LIBERTY's growth is fueled by a proven operating system that has been fine-tuned by the leadership and field support staff's 600 total years of experience. Founder/CEO John Hew

BACKGROUND: IFA MEMBER
Established: 1997; 1st Franchised: 1997
Franchised Units: 3055
Company-Owned Units: 62
Total Units: 3117
Dist.: US-2872; CAN-245; O'seas-0
 North America: 50 States, 0 Provinces
 Density: 189 in FL, 226 in TX, 303 in CA
Projected New Units (12 Months): 300-500
Qualifications: 4, 4, 2, 1, 1, 5

FINANCIAL/TERMS:
Cash Investment: $40K
Total Investment: $56.8-69.9K
Minimum Net Worth: $100K
Fees: Franchise - $40K
 Royalty - Varies; Ad. - 5%
Earnings Claims Statement: No
Term of Contract (Years): 5/5
Avg. # Of Employees: 4-6 FT, 2 PT

Passive Ownership: Discouraged
Encourage Conversions: No
Area Develop. Agreements: Yes/10
Sub-Franchising Contracts: No
Expand In Territory: Yes
Space Needs: 400+ SF

SUPPORT & TRAINING:
Financial Assistance Provided: Yes (I)
Site Selection Assistance: Yes
Lease Negotiation Assistance: Yes
Co-Operative Advertising: No
Franchisee Assoc./Member: No
Size Of Corporate Staff: 407
On-Going Support: A,B,C,D,E,F,G,H,I
Training: 5 Days Virginia Beach, VA
 - Initial, Intermediate, Advanced; 3
 Days Various Cities - Intermediate,
 Advanced

SPECIFIC EXPANSION PLANS:
US: All United States
Canada: Yes
Overseas: NR

≺≺ ≻≻

**MANUFACTURING
MANAGEMENT ASSOCIATES**
700 Commerce Dr., 5 Fl.
Oak Brook, IL 60523-8736
Tel: (800) 574-0308 (630) 574-0300
Fax: (630) 574-0309
E-Mail: franchising@consult-mma.com
Web Site: www.consult-mma.com
Mr. Roger Dykstra, President

Manufacturing consulting: for the small- and medium-size company. Teaching you the market development and sales techniques that made the 'big guys' big. We use your experience and knowledge with our proven methodologies to deliver a quality service.

BACKGROUND:
Established: 1982; 1st Franchised: 1992
Franchised Units: 10
Company-Owned Units: 0
Total Units: 10
Dist.: US-8; CAN-2; O'seas-0
 North America: 6 States, Provinces
 Density: 2 in IL, 2 in IN
Projected New Units (12 Months): 4
Qualifications: 4, 5, 4, 4, 3, 5

FINANCIAL/TERMS:
Cash Investment: $10-15K
Total Investment: $15-25K
Minimum Net Worth: $25-50K
Fees: Franchise - $6-8K
 Royalty - 5%; Ad. - 1%/$500
Earnings Claims Statement: No

Term of Contract (Years): 10/10
Avg. # Of Employees: 1 FT, 0 PT
Passive Ownership: Not Allowed
Encourage Conversions: Yes
Area Develop. Agreements: No
Sub-Franchising Contracts: No
Expand In Territory: Yes
Space Needs: NR

SUPPORT & TRAINING:
Financial Assistance Provided: NR
Site Selection Assistance: Yes
Lease Negotiation Assistance: Yes
Co-Operative Advertising: No
Franchisee Assoc./Member: No
Size Of Corporate Staff: 20
On-Going Support: a,,,,E,,G,H,I
Training: 8-10 Days Chicago, IL

SPECIFIC EXPANSION PLANS:
US: All United States
Canada: All Canada
Overseas: NR

≺≺ ≻≻

MONEY MAILER
12131 Western Ave.
Garden Grove, CA 92841
Tel: (800) 418-3030 (714) 889-4694
Fax: (714) 265-8494
E-Mail: djenkins@moneymailer.com
Web Site: www.moneymailer.com
Mr. Dennis H. Jenkins, VP Franchise
 Licensing

MONEY MAILER is one of America's leading direct mail advertising companies with over 300 franchises in the U.S. and Canada. Over its 27 year history, MONEY MAILER has been at the forefront of introducing innovative direct mail advertising products and programs to the marketplace - helping businesses get and keep more customers and helping consumers save money everyday.

BACKGROUND: IFA MEMBER
Established: 1979; 1st Franchised: 1980
Franchised Units: 270
Company-Owned Units: 6
Total Units: 276
Dist.: US-314; CAN-6; O'seas-1
 North America: 0 States, 0 Provinces
 Density: 21 in NJ, 25 in IL, 44 in CA
Projected New Units (12 Months): 40
Qualifications: 4, 3, 4, 3, 4, 5

FINANCIAL/TERMS:

Cash Investment:	$54K
Total Investment:	$100K
Minimum Net Worth:	Varies
Fees: Franchise -	$37.5-52.5K
Royalty - $1400-1600/mo.;	Ad.
- $930/yr.	
Earnings Claims Statement:	Yes
Term of Contract (Years):	10/10
Avg. # Of Employees:	1 FT, PT
Passive Ownership:	Discouraged
Encourage Conversions:	NA
Area Develop. Agreements:	No
Sub-Franchising Contracts:	No
Expand In Territory:	Yes
Space Needs:	NR

SUPPORT & TRAINING:

Financial Assistance Provided:	No
Site Selection Assistance:	NA
Lease Negotiation Assistance:	NA
Co-Operative Advertising:	Yes
Franchisee Assoc./Member:	Yes/Yes
Size Of Corporate Staff:	300
On-Going Support:	,B,C,D,,,,H,I
Training: 13 Days Field Training in Territory; 1 Week Corporate Headquarters	

SPECIFIC EXPANSION PLANS:

US:	All United States
Canada:	No
Overseas:	NR

MONTHLY COUPONS
268 W. Hospitality Ln., # 205
San Bernardino, CA 92408
Tel: (909) 386-0550
Fax: (909) 386-0551
E-Mail: info@monthlycoupons.com
Web Site: www.monthlycoupons.com
Mr. Michael Gonzales, President

Join the Monthly Coupons Franchise Success Story... Why choose Monthly Coupons? Low Investment: Single franchises are $25,000. Unique Marketing Strategy. Monthly Coupons Training and Support which includes a 12 month Mentor program. Multiple streams of income: produce income from publishing your local coupon magazine plus benefit from an additional stream of income offering wholesale printing. Production Benefits. Low Productions Costs. Monthly Residual Income. Franchise Funding. Nationwide Opportunities.

BACKGROUND: IFA MEMBER
Established: 2001;   1st Franchised: 2007
Franchised Units: 19

Company-Owned Units:	10
Total Units:	29
Dist.:	US-29; CAN-0; O'seas-0
North America:	7 States, 0 Provinces
Density:	3 in GA, 3 in FL, 20 in CA
Projected New Units (12 Months):	60
Qualifications:	5, 3, 5, 3, 3, 5

FINANCIAL/TERMS:

Cash Investment:	$45K
Total Investment:	$45-100K
Minimum Net Worth:	$100K
Fees: Franchise -	$25K
Royalty - 300K;	Ad. - 0
Earnings Claims Statement:	No
Term of Contract (Years):	10/10
Avg. # Of Employees:	1 FT, 0 PT
Passive Ownership:	Not Allowed
Encourage Conversions:	NA
Area Develop. Agreements:	Yes/10
Sub-Franchising Contracts:	No
Expand In Territory:	Yes
Space Needs:	NA

SUPPORT & TRAINING:

Financial Assistance Provided:	No
Site Selection Assistance:	Yes
Lease Negotiation Assistance:	No
Co-Operative Advertising:	No
Franchisee Assoc./Member:	Yes/Yes
Size Of Corporate Staff:	15
On-Going Support:	,,C,D,,,,H,
Training:	varies yearly conventions; 5 days at franchisee location; 5 days Headquarters

SPECIFIC EXPANSION PLANS:

US:	All United States
Canada:	No
Overseas:	NR

MR. PAYROLL
1600 W. Seventh St.
Fort Worth, TX 76102-2500
Tel: (800) 322-3250 (817) 570-1636
Fax: (817) 509-8295
E-Mail: franchise_
mrpay@cashamericaonline.com
Web Site: www.mrpayroll.com
Mr. Scott Carskadon, Franchise Development

MR. PAYROLL provides financial services (check cashing, money orders, bill pay, wire transfer, etc.) to the un-banked

BACKGROUND: IFA MEMBER
Established: 1990;   1st Franchised: 1990

Franchised Units:	137
Company-Owned Units:	5
Total Units:	142

Dist.:	US-142; CAN-0; O'seas-0
North America:	21 States, 0 Provinces
Density:	65 in TX, 8 in NM, 16 in GA
Projected New Units (12 Months):	NR
Qualifications:	NR

FINANCIAL/TERMS:

Cash Investment:	$70-120K
Total Investment:	$30-45K
Minimum Net Worth:	$140K
Fees: Franchise -	$10-30K
Royalty - 10%;	Ad. - 0%
Earnings Claims Statement:	Yes
Term of Contract (Years):	10/10
Avg. # Of Employees:	1 FT, 1 PT
Passive Ownership:	Discouraged
Encourage Conversions:	No
Area Develop. Agreements:	No
Sub-Franchising Contracts:	No
Expand In Territory:	Yes
Space Needs:	48 SF

SUPPORT & TRAINING:

Financial Assistance Provided:	No
Site Selection Assistance:	Yes
Lease Negotiation Assistance:	Yes
Co-Operative Advertising:	No
Franchisee Assoc./Member:	No
Size Of Corporate Staff:	3000
On-Going Support:	A,B,C,D,E,F,G,h,I
Training:	3 Day Operations Training Ft. Worth; 1 Day Mgr. Orientation Ft. Worth; 2 Week Opening

SPECIFIC EXPANSION PLANS:

US:	Northwest Southwest, SE
Canada:	NR
Overseas:	NR

OUR TOWN AMERICA
3845 Gateway Centre Blvd.
Pinellas Park, FL 33782
Tel: (800) 497-8360 (727) 345-0811 + 226
Fax: (727) 345-0338
E-Mail: franchise@ourtownamerica.com
Web Site: www.ourtownamerica.com
Mr. Ingrid Schaad, Franchise Development Consultant

Our Town America is the fastest growing, direct mail new mover program in the U.S. We bring new customers to local businesses by mailing welcome packages to people who have recently moved to the community. Our start up costs are low, our training is thorough and ongoing and we offer a 100% franchise fee money back guarantee!

BACKGROUND: IFA MEMBER
Established: 1972;   1st Franchised: 2005

Franchised Units: 35
Company-Owned Units: 1
Total Units: 36
Dist.: US-36; CAN-0; O'seas-0
North America: 2 States, 0 Provinces
Density: 5 in OH, 7 in FL
Projected New Units (12 Months): 20
Qualifications: 2, 4, 3, 1, 1, 5

FINANCIAL/TERMS:
Cash Investment: $29-40K
Total Investment: $45-60K
Minimum Net Worth: $100K
Fees: Franchise - $29K
Royalty - 5%; Ad. - 2%
Earnings Claims Statement: No
Term of Contract (Years): 10/5
Avg. # Of Employees: 1 FT, 0 PT
Passive Ownership: Not Allowed
Encourage Conversions: NA
Area Develop. Agreements: No
Sub-Franchising Contracts: No
Expand In Territory: No
Space Needs: NA

SUPPORT & TRAINING:
Financial Assistance Provided: Yes (I)
Site Selection Assistance: Yes
Lease Negotiation Assistance: No
Co-Operative Advertising: Yes
Franchisee Assoc./Member: Yes/No
Size Of Corporate Staff: 5
On-Going Support: a,B,C,D,E,,G,H,I
Training: 6 Days Smithtown, NY

SPECIFIC EXPANSION PLANS:
US: All United States
Canada: No
Overseas: NR

◄◄ ►►

PADGETT BUSINESS SERVICES
160 Hawthorne Park
Athens, GA 30606-2147
Tel: (877) 729-8725 + 225 (781) 251-9410
+ 225
Fax: (877) 251-9520
E-Mail: padgett@smallbizpros.com
Web Site: www.smallbizpros.com
Ms. Carol Clark, Franchise Development
Coordinator

America's top-rated and fastest-growing tax and accounting franchise - serving the fastest-growing segment of the economy - America's small business owners. Initial training. Specialized software. On-going support.

BACKGROUND: IFA MEMBER
Established: 1966; 1st Franchised: 1975
Franchised Units: 383
Company-Owned Units: 1
Total Units: 383
Dist.: US-282; CAN-101; O'seas-0
North America: 45 States, 8 Provinces
Density: 38 in QC, 67 in ON, 26 in GA
Projected New Units (12 Months): 50
Qualifications: 3, 3, 4, 4, 2, 4

FINANCIAL/TERMS:
Cash Investment: $100K
Total Investment: $98.5K
Minimum Net Worth: $100K
Fees: Franchise - $27.5K
Royalty - 9-4.5%; Ad. - 0%
Earnings Claims Statement: Yes
Term of Contract (Years): 10/10
Avg. # Of Employees: 1 FT, 2 PT
Passive Ownership: Not Allowed
Encourage Conversions: Yes
Area Develop. Agreements: No
Sub-Franchising Contracts: No
Expand In Territory: Yes
Space Needs: 200-400 SF

SUPPORT & TRAINING:
Financial Assistance Provided: No
Site Selection Assistance: NA
Lease Negotiation Assistance: NA
Co-Operative Advertising: No
Franchisee Assoc./Member: Yes/Yes
Size Of Corporate Staff: 20
On-Going Support: ,,C,D,,,G,H,I
Training: 3 (2.5 Day) Site Visits;
2.5 Weeks Athens, GA

SPECIFIC EXPANSION PLANS:
US: All United States
Canada: All Canada
Overseas: NR

◄◄ ►►

PARTNER ON-CALL NETWORK
730 Sandy Point Ln.
N. Palm Beach, FL 33410
Tel: (561) 776-2515
Fax:
E-Mail: PartnerOnCall@comcast.net
Web Site: www.PartnerOnCall.com
Mr. Ted J. Leverette, President

Mature, proven, unique. If you're thinking about being a coach, consultant or business broker, our franchise will shift your perception and can change your life for the better. The more you know what it is really like to be one of these me-too specialists the more you may want to join our network. Be a "Business BUYER Advocate" and "Partner" On-Call -- so you can realize your dream of owning a consulting business by showing your clients how to realize their dreams of owning a MORE profitable business.

BACKGROUND: IFA MEMBER
Established: 2005; 1st Franchised: 2006
Franchised Units: 8
Company-Owned Units: 0
Total Units: 8
Dist.: US-8; CAN-0; O'seas-0
North America: 7 States, 0 Provinces
Density: 2 in WA, 1 in PA, 1 in KS
Projected New Units (12 Months): NR
Qualifications: 3, 4, 3, 1, 3, 3

FINANCIAL/TERMS:
Cash Investment: $40K
Total Investment: $56-76K
Minimum Net Worth: $100K
Fees: Franchise - $25K
Royalty - 6%; Ad. - 3%
Earnings Claims Statement: No
Term of Contract (Years): 5/5
Avg. # Of Employees: 1 FT, 1 PT
Passive Ownership: Not Allowed
Encourage Conversions: NA
Area Develop. Agreements: No
Sub-Franchising Contracts: No
Expand In Territory: No
Space Needs: NA

SUPPORT & TRAINING:
Financial Assistance Provided: No
Site Selection Assistance: NA
Lease Negotiation Assistance: NA
Co-Operative Advertising: Yes
Franchisee Assoc./Member: No
Size Of Corporate Staff: 3
On-Going Support: ,,,,,G,H,
Training: 3 Days On-call via email &
telephone; 10 Days Franchisee home
study course; 5 Days HQ, FL

SPECIFIC EXPANSION PLANS:
US: All United States
Canada: No
Overseas: NR

◄◄ ►►

PMA FRANCHISE SYSTEMS
1950 Spectrum Cir., # B-310

Marietta, GA 30067
Tel: (800) 466-7822 (770) 916-1668
Fax: (770) 916-1429
E-Mail: bill@pmasearch.com
Web Site: www.pmafranchise.com
Mr. Bill Lins, Director Operations

A national executive search firm specializing in store and mid-level management through vice president level positions in the retail, hospitality and service industries.

BACKGROUND:

Established: 1984; 1st Franchised: 1999
Franchised Units: 5
Company-Owned Units: 2
Total Units: 7
Dist.:   US-7; CAN-0; O'seas-0
  North America: 6 States, 0 Provinces
  Density: 2 in MA, 1 in RI, 1 in CT
Projected New Units (12 Months):   5
Qualifications: NR

FINANCIAL/TERMS:

Cash Investment: $50-60K
Total Investment: $50-60K
Minimum Net Worth: NA
Fees: Franchise - $30K
  Royalty - 10%;   Ad. - 8%
Earnings Claims Statement: Yes
Term of Contract (Years):   10/
Avg. # Of Employees: FT, 0 PT
Passive Ownership: Not Allowed
Encourage Conversions: No
Area Develop. Agreements: Yes/1
Sub-Franchising Contracts: No
Expand In Territory: Yes
Space Needs: 150+ SF

SUPPORT & TRAINING:

Financial Assistance Provided: Yes (I)
Site Selection Assistance: Yes
Lease Negotiation Assistance: Yes
Co-Operative Advertising: Yes
Franchisee Assoc./Member: Yes/Yes
Size Of Corporate Staff: 12
On-Going Support: A,,C,,E,,G,h,I
Training: 4 Weeks Atlanta, GA

SPECIFIC EXPANSION PLANS:

US: All United States
Canada: No
Overseas: NR

◀◀   ▶▶

PROFIT-TELL INTERNATIONAL

201 Ogden Ave.
Hinsdale, IL 60521
Tel: (888) 366-4653 + 131 (630) 655-3700
Fax: (630) 655-3700
E-Mail: info@profit-tell.com

Web Site: www.profit-tell.com
Mr. Tony Corniel, Dir. Franchise Development

PROFIT-TELL is a leader in providing audio marketing solutions to businesses through message-on-hold, enhancement of existing Websites with streaming audio, in-store overhead announcements and more cutting-edge audio marketing solutions. We teach franchisees how to build a solid and loyal customer base with immediate cash flow and no receivables. Our program includes: low investment/low overhead. Every business needs our service. No evenings or weekends.

BACKGROUND: IFA MEMBER

Established: 1993; 1st Franchised: 2002
Franchised Units: 29
Company-Owned Units: 1
Total Units: 30
Dist.:   US-30; CAN-0; O'seas-0
  North America: 11 States, 0 Provinces
  Density: 3 in IL, 14 in CA
Projected New Units (12 Months):   18
Qualifications: NR

FINANCIAL/TERMS:

Cash Investment: $25K
Total Investment: $25-35K
Minimum Net Worth: $125K
Fees: Franchise - $22.5K
  Royalty - 0%;   Ad. - 5%
Earnings Claims Statement: Yes
Term of Contract (Years):   20/20
Avg. # Of Employees: 2 FT, 0 PT
Passive Ownership: Discouraged
Encourage Conversions: NA
Area Develop. Agreements: No
Sub-Franchising Contracts: No
Expand In Territory: Yes
Space Needs: NA

SUPPORT & TRAINING:

Financial Assistance Provided: Yes (D)
Site Selection Assistance: NA
Lease Negotiation Assistance: NA
Co-Operative Advertising: No
Franchisee Assoc./Member: No
Size Of Corporate Staff: 10
On-Going Support: A,B,C,d,,F,G,h,I
Training: 6 Days Hinsdale, IL;
  6 Months Curriculum

SPECIFIC EXPANSION PLANS:

US: All United States
Canada: All Canada
Overseas: NR

◀◀   ▶▶

PROPERTY DAMAGE APPRAISERS

6100 Southwest Blvd., # 200
Fort Worth, TX 76109-3964
Tel: (800) 749-7324 + 49 (817) 731-5555
Fax: (817) 731-5565
E-Mail: katherine.slate@pdaorg.net
Web Site: www.pdahomeoffice.com
Ms. Katherine Slate, AVP Franchise Relations

The industry's largest, franchised appraisal company, with national marketing support, a computerized office management system, training and on-going management assistance. No initial franchise fee is required - only a royalty on completed business. Automobile damage appraising experience a pre-requisite.

BACKGROUND:

Established: 1963; 1st Franchised: 1963
Franchised Units: 250
Company-Owned Units: 0
Total Units: 250
Dist.:   US-250; CAN-0; O'seas-0
  North America: 47 States, 0 Provinces
  Density: 25 in TX, 15 in FL, 21 in CA
Projected New Units (12 Months):   20
Qualifications: 3, 3, 5, 3, NR, 5

FINANCIAL/TERMS:

Cash Investment: $9-23K
Total Investment: $9-23K
Minimum Net Worth: NR
Fees: Franchise - $0
  Royalty - 15%;   Ad. - 0%
Earnings Claims Statement: No
Term of Contract (Years):   3/5
Avg. # Of Employees: 2 FT, 0 PT
Passive Ownership: Not Allowed
Encourage Conversions: Yes
Area Develop. Agreements: No
Sub-Franchising Contracts: No
Expand In Territory: Yes
Space Needs: NR

SUPPORT & TRAINING:

Financial Assistance Provided: No
Site Selection Assistance: Yes
Lease Negotiation Assistance: NA
Co-Operative Advertising: Yes
Franchisee Assoc./Member: No
Size Of Corporate Staff: 36
On-Going Support: A,,C,D,,G,H,I
Training: 1 Week Corporate Headquarters;
  4 Days On-Site

SPECIFIC EXPANSION PLANS:

US: All United States
Canada: No
Overseas: NR

‹‹ ››

PROSHRED

6790 Century Blvd., # 200
Toronto, ON LN5 2V8 Canada
Tel: (877) PROSHRED (416) 204-0071
Fax: (905) 812-9448
E-Mail: john.prittie@proshred.com
Web Site: www.proshred.com
Mr. John Prittie, Chief Executive Officer

PROSHRED invented mobile shredding. The Proshred onsite professional shredding system is the most secure method of destroying confidential documents and other proprietary materials. Government legislation passed to protect customers and the environment has made it imperative that all companies, big and small, as well as home-based employees and businesses, find convenient and effective ways to discard all types of documents and materials containing sensitive information. Proshred is a powerful, long-standing brand supported by an experienced management team.

BACKGROUND: IFA MEMBER
Established: 2002; 1st Franchised: 2002
Franchised Units: 18
Company-Owned Units: 0
Total Units: 18
Dist.: US-18; CAN-0; O'seas-0
North America: 10 States, 0 Provinces
Density: NR
Projected New Units (12 Months): 9
Qualifications: 5, 4, 1, 3, 1, 5
FINANCIAL/TERMS:
Cash Investment: $250K
Total Investment: $178.5K-499.5K
Minimum Net Worth: $750K
Fees: Franchise - $35K
  Royalty - 6.5%; Ad. - 1-3%
Earnings Claims Statement: Yes
Term of Contract (Years): 10/5/5
Avg. # Of Employees: 5 FT, 2 PT
Passive Ownership: Allowed
Encourage Conversions: Yes
Area Develop. Agreements: Yes/1
Sub-Franchising Contracts: No
Expand In Territory: Yes
Space Needs: 2,000 SF
SUPPORT & TRAINING:
Financial Assistance Provided: Yes (I)
Site Selection Assistance: Yes
Lease Negotiation Assistance: Yes

Co-Operative Advertising: Yes
Franchisee Assoc./Member: Yes/Yes
Size Of Corporate Staff: 11
On-Going Support: ,B,C,D,E,F,G,H,I
Training: 10 Days Toronto, ON; 10 Days Local
SPECIFIC EXPANSION PLANS:
US: All United States
Canada: All Canada
Overseas: No

‹‹ ››

RELAY EXPRESS

498 Commercial Dr.
Fairfield, Ohio 45014
Tel: (866) 657-3529 (513) 860-2835
Fax: (513) 860-2869
E-Mail: matt@relayexpress.com
Web Site: www.relayexpress.com
Mr. Matt Seiter, Owner/Franchise Developement

Relay Express is a sameday package delivery service specializing B2B. We do what UPS and FedEx can't do.

BACKGROUND: IFA MEMBER
Established: 1986; 1st Franchised: 2006
Franchised Units: 0
Company-Owned Units: 3
Total Units: 3
Dist.: US-3; CAN-0; O'seas-0
North America: 1 States, 0 Provinces
Density: 3 in OH
Projected New Units (12 Months): 4
Qualifications: 4, 4, 2, 3, 4, 5
FINANCIAL/TERMS:
Cash Investment: $30K
Total Investment: $84-198K
Minimum Net Worth: $250K
Fees: Franchise - $30K
  Royalty - 5%; Ad. - 0-3%
Earnings Claims Statement: No
Term of Contract (Years): 5/5
Avg. # Of Employees: 3 FT, 1 PT
Passive Ownership: Discouraged
Encourage Conversions: Yes
Area Develop. Agreements: No
Sub-Franchising Contracts: No
Expand In Territory: No
Space Needs: 4,000 SF
SUPPORT & TRAINING:
Financial Assistance Provided: No
Site Selection Assistance: Yes
Lease Negotiation Assistance: No
Co-Operative Advertising: Yes
Franchisee Assoc./Member: No
Size Of Corporate Staff: 4
On-Going Support: ,b,C,D,E,,,h,

Training: 2 Weeks Home Office; 1 Week Franchisee Location
SPECIFIC EXPANSION PLANS:
US: All, mainly in the Midwest
Canada: No
Overseas: NR

‹‹ ››

RENAISSANCE EXECUTIVE FORUMS

7855 Ivanhoe Ave., # 300
La Jolla, CA 92037-4500
Tel: (858) 551-6600
Fax: (858) 551-8777
E-Mail: shawna@executiveforums.com
Web Site: www.executiveforums.info
Ms. Shawna Nolan, Director of Franchise Development

RENAISSANCE EXECUTIVE FORUMS bring together top executives from similarly sized, non-competing companies into an advisory board process in which thousands of chief executives throughout the world participate. These CEOs, presidents and owners meet once a month in small groups of approximately eight to fourteen individuals. The meetings provide an environment designed to address the opportunities and challenges they face as individuals and leaders of their respective organizations.

BACKGROUND: IFA MEMBER
Established: 1994; 1st Franchised: 1994
Franchised Units: 50
Company-Owned Units: 0
Total Units: 50
Dist.: US-45; CAN-1; O'seas-11
North America: 20 States, 1 Provinces
Density: 4 in IL, 3 in FL, 7 in CA
Projected New Units (12 Months): 10
Qualifications: 5, 5, 4, 4, 4, 5
FINANCIAL/TERMS:
Cash Investment: $55.4K-73.3K
Total Investment: $75.5K-110K
Minimum Net Worth: $500K
Fees: Franchise - $39.5K
  Royalty - 20%; Ad. - 0%
Earnings Claims Statement: No
Term of Contract (Years): 10/10
Avg. # Of Employees: 1 FT, 0 PT
Passive Ownership: Not Allowed

Encourage Conversions:	NA
Area Develop. Agreements:	No
Sub-Franchising Contracts:	No
Expand In Territory:	Yes
Space Needs:	NA

SUPPORT & TRAINING:

Financial Assistance Provided:	No
Site Selection Assistance:	No
Lease Negotiation Assistance:	No
Co-Operative Advertising:	No
Franchisee Assoc./Member:	Yes/Yes
Size Of Corporate Staff:	15
On-Going Support:	A,B,C,D,,,G,H,
Training:	8 Days La Jolla, CA.

SPECIFIC EXPANSION PLANS:

US:	All United States
Canada:	All Canada
Overseas:	All Countries

⋘ ⋙

RESOURCE ASSOCIATES CORP.

31 Hickory Rd.
Mohnton, PA 19540
Tel: (800) 799-6227 (610) 775-5222
Fax: (610) 775-9686
E-Mail: success@rac-tqi.com
Web Site: www.rac-tqi.com
Mr. William L. Sweney, Vice President of
Development

RESOURCE ASSOCIATES CORP. is a network of independent consultants working in the areas of strategic planning, people development, process improvement, coaching and youth leadership. RESOURCE ASSOCIATES CORP. is a business opportunity, not a franchise.

BACKGROUND:

Established: 1978;	1st Franchised:
Franchised Units:	500
Company-Owned Units:	0
Total Units:	500
Dist.:	US-500; CAN-0; O'seas-0
North America:	45 States, Provinces
Density:	in CA, in NJ, in PA
Projected New Units (12 Months):	100
Qualifications:	3, 5, 1, 1, 1, 5

FINANCIAL/TERMS:

Cash Investment:	$1-35K
Total Investment:	$1-35K
Minimum Net Worth:	NA
Fees: Franchise -	$0K
Royalty - 0%;	Ad. - 0%
Earnings Claims Statement:	No
Term of Contract (Years):	97/
Avg. # Of Employees:	0 FT, 0 PT
Passive Ownership:	Discouraged
Encourage Conversions:	NA

Area Develop. Agreements:	No
Sub-Franchising Contracts:	No
Expand In Territory:	Yes
Space Needs:	NA

SUPPORT & TRAINING:

Financial Assistance Provided:	No
Site Selection Assistance:	NA
Lease Negotiation Assistance:	NA
Co-Operative Advertising:	No
Franchisee Assoc./Member:	No
Size Of Corporate Staff:	30
On-Going Support:	,,,,,G,H,I
Training:	Optional

SPECIFIC EXPANSION PLANS:

US:	All United States
Canada:	All Canada
Overseas:	NR

⋘ ⋙

SALES CONSULTANTS

200 Public Sq., 31 Fl.
Cleveland, OH 44114-2301
Tel: (800) 875-4000 (216) 416-8467
Fax: (216) 696-6612
E-Mail: mary.costanzo@brilliantpeople.com
Web Site: www.mrifranchise.com
Ms. Mary Costanzo, Franchise Sales Rep.

Complete range of recruitment and human resource services for sales, sales management and marketing professionals, including permanent placement, interim staffing; video-conferencing; with coverage on all continents through strategic alliances with leading search firms.

BACKGROUND:	**IFA MEMBER**
Established: 1957;	1st Franchised: 1966
Franchised Units:	170
Company-Owned Units:	17
Total Units:	187
Dist.:	US-187; CAN-0; O'seas-0
North America:	39 States, 0 Provinces
Density:	14 in MI, 15 in FL, 20 in CA
Projected New Units (12 Months):	20
Qualifications:	3, 4, 1, 4, 3, 3

FINANCIAL/TERMS:

Cash Investment:	$113-154K
Total Investment:	$113-154K
Minimum Net Worth:	NA
Fees: Franchise -	$75-80K
Royalty - 7%;	Ad. - 1%
Earnings Claims Statement:	Yes
Term of Contract (Years):	10-20/5
Avg. # Of Employees:	3-4 Total FT, 3-4 Total PT
Passive Ownership:	Discouraged
Encourage Conversions:	Yes

Area Develop. Agreements:	No
Sub-Franchising Contracts:	No
Expand In Territory:	Yes
Space Needs:	600-1,000 SF

SUPPORT & TRAINING:

Financial Assistance Provided:	Yes (D)
Site Selection Assistance:	Yes
Lease Negotiation Assistance:	Yes
Co-Operative Advertising:	No
Franchisee Assoc./Member:	Yes/Yes
Size Of Corporate Staff:	128
On-Going Support:	,,C,D,E,,G,H,I
Training: 3 Weeks Headquarters, Cleveland, OH; 2 Weeks Franchisee's Location;	

SPECIFIC EXPANSION PLANS:

US:	All United States
Canada:	No
Overseas:	NR

⋘ ⋙

SANDLER TRAINING

300 Red Brook Blvd., # 400
Owings Mills, MD 21117
Tel: (800) 669-3537 (410) 653-1993
Fax: (410) 358-7858
E-Mail: rtaylor@sandler.com
Web Site: www.sandler.com
Mr. Ron Taylor, Vice President Franchise
Development

SANDLER TRAINING offers a distinctive style of training to companies and individuals in the fields of sales, management consulting and leadership development through on-going seminars and workshops. SANDLER TRAINING provides intensive training, a unique lead generation program, on-going day-to-day support and protected territories to help you succeed in business.

BACKGROUND:	**IFA MEMBER**
Established: 1969;	1st Franchised: 1983
Franchised Units:	235
Company-Owned Units:	0
Total Units:	235
Dist.:	US-179; CAN-16; O'seas-40
North America:	38 States, 7 Provinces
Density:	13 in PA, 14 in OH, 13 in CA
Projected New Units (12 Months):	20
Qualifications:	3, 5, 5, 3, 1, 5

FINANCIAL/TERMS:

Cash Investment:	$68K
Total Investment:	$80,150-$96,750

Minimum Net Worth: $150K
Fees: Franchise - $68K
  Royalty - $1160/Mo. at Mo. 9; Ad. - NA
Earnings Claims Statement: No
Term of Contract (Years): 5/5/5/5/
Avg. # Of Employees: 1 FT, 1 PT
Passive Ownership: Discouraged
Encourage Conversions: NA
Area Develop. Agreements: No
Sub-Franchising Contracts: No
Expand In Territory: Yes
Space Needs: NA

SUPPORT & TRAINING:

Financial Assistance Provided: No
Site Selection Assistance: Yes
Lease Negotiation Assistance: No
Co-Operative Advertising: No
Franchisee Assoc./Member: Yes/Yes
Size Of Corporate Staff: 35
On-Going Support: ,,,,,g,H,I
Training: 1 Day Home Office/Other;
  8 Days Home Office/Other

SPECIFIC EXPANSION PLANS:

US: All United States
Canada: Yes
Overseas: Europe and South America

◄◄ ►►

**DOCUMENT DESTRUCTION.
DONE RIGHT. ON SITE.**

SHRED-IT

2794 S. Sheridan Way
Oakville, ON L6J 7T4 Canada
Tel: (905) 829-2794
Fax: (905) 829-1999
E-Mail: info@shredit.com
Web Site: www.shredit.com
Mr. Brian MacLean, VP Franchise Devel./
  Ops.

Business service, offering mobile paper
shredding and recycling, serving Fortune
1,000 companies, hospitals, medical facilities, banks, financial institutions, investment and professional firms and the government.

BACKGROUND:

Established: 1988; 1st Franchised: 1992
Franchised Units: 53
Company-Owned Units: 65
Total Units: 118
Dist.: US-81; CAN-12; O'seas-25
  North America: 35 States, 6 Provinces
  Density: 4 in OH, 5 in FL, 8 in CA

Projected New Units (12 Months): 10
Qualifications: 5, 4, 1, 2, 4, 5

FINANCIAL/TERMS:

Cash Investment: $200-250K
Total Investment: $400-500K
Minimum Net Worth: $500K
Fees: Franchise - $75K
  Royalty - 6%; Ad. - 1.5%
Earnings Claims Statement: No
Term of Contract (Years): 10/10/10/
Avg. # Of Employees: 10 FT, 0 PT
Passive Ownership: Not Allowed
Encourage Conversions: NA
Area Develop. Agreements: Yes/10
Sub-Franchising Contracts: No
Expand In Territory: Yes
Space Needs: 1,500 SF

SUPPORT & TRAINING:

Financial Assistance Provided: No
Site Selection Assistance: Yes
Lease Negotiation Assistance: Yes
Co-Operative Advertising: No
Franchisee Assoc./Member: Yes/Yes
Size Of Corporate Staff: 100
On-Going Support: ,,C,D,E,,,H,
Training: 1 Week Oakville, ON; 1 Week
  On-Site

SPECIFIC EXPANSION PLANS:

US: No
Canada: No
Overseas: Asia, E. Europe, S. America

◄◄ ►►

SUNBELT BUSINESS ADVISORS
NETWORK

7100 E. Pleasant Valley Rd., # 300
Independence, OH 44131
Tel: (877) 392-6278 (216) 674-0645
Fax: (216) 674-0650
E-Mail: join-sunbelt@sunbeltnetwork.
com
Web Site: www.sunbeltnetwork.com
Mr. Matt Ottaway, Brand Manager

We offer business brokerage/merger and
acquisition franchises. SUNBELT is the
largest and fastest-growing business brokerage firm in the world. Our success
comes from our name recognition, quality training programs and hands-on assistance. We are the leaders in computerized
office management, networking and Internet technology. We take no percentage
fees. All of our services are covered in our
low semi-annual fee.

BACKGROUND: IFA MEMBER

Established: 1978; 1st Franchised: 1993
Franchised Units: 300

Company-Owned Units: 0
Total Units: 300
Dist.: US-294; CAN-0; O'seas-6
  North America: 38 States, 0 Provinces
  Density: 10 in VA, 10 in NC, 16 in FL
Projected New Units (12 Months): 50
Qualifications: NR

FINANCIAL/TERMS:

Cash Investment: $5-15K
Total Investment: $5-50K
Minimum Net Worth: NA
Fees: Franchise - $5-10K
  Royalty - $3-6K/Yr.; Ad. - 0%
Earnings Claims Statement: No
Term of Contract (Years): On-Going/
Avg. # Of Employees: Independent
Contrac. FT, 0 PT
Passive Ownership: Not Allowed
Encourage Conversions: Yes
Area Develop. Agreements: No
Sub-Franchising Contracts: No
Expand In Territory: Yes
Space Needs: 1,000 SF

SUPPORT & TRAINING:

Financial Assistance Provided: Yes (D)
Site Selection Assistance: NA
Lease Negotiation Assistance: NA
Co-Operative Advertising: No
Franchisee Assoc./Member: Yes/Yes
Size Of Corporate Staff: 9
On-Going Support: ,,C,D,,,G,H,I
Training: 4 Days Various Regional
  Centers

SPECIFIC EXPANSION PLANS:

US: All United States
Canada: All Canada
Overseas: All Countries

◄◄ ►►

SUPERCOUPS

350 Revolutionary Dr.
E. Taunton, MA 02718
Tel: (800) 626-2620 (508) 977-2010
Fax: (508) 977-0644
E-Mail: jbyrne@supercoups.com
Web Site: www.supercoups.com
Ms. Jennifer Byrne, Marketing and Fran-
chise Sales Manager

SUPERCOUPS offers the flexibility,
independence and income potential you
seek combined with the strategies, support and tools you need. Low Investment,
High Potential: With no inventory to buy
and no storefront to lease, our start-up
costs are among the lowest in the industry. Family Friendly: Since sales work
takes place during business hours, you set
your work schedule and determine your

income potential. A Quality Product: Sell an affordable, effective product to a high-growth market. Strong Support System: State-of-the-art production facility; training at headquarters and in your territory; simple, standardized procedures, optimized processes to minimize your cost.

BACKGROUND:　　　IFA MEMBER
Established: 1982;　1st Franchised: 1984
Franchised Units:	136
Company-Owned Units:	22
Total Units:	158
Dist.:	US-158; CAN-0; O'seas-0
North America:	17 States, 0 Provinces
Density:	NR
Projected New Units (12 Months):	50
Qualifications:	5, 5, 4, 3, 1, 5

FINANCIAL/TERMS:
Cash Investment:	$17-26K
Total Investment:	$26-50K
Minimum Net Worth:	$100K
Fees: Franchise -	$17.5-26K
Royalty - ;	Ad. - $500/Yr.
Earnings Claims Statement:	No
Term of Contract (Years):	10/10
Avg. # Of Employees:	1 FT, 0 PT
Passive Ownership:	Not Allowed
Encourage Conversions:	Yes
Area Develop. Agreements:	No
Sub-Franchising Contracts:	No
Expand In Territory:	Yes
Space Needs:	NA

SUPPORT & TRAINING:
Financial Assistance Provided:	No
Site Selection Assistance:	Yes
Lease Negotiation Assistance:	No
Co-Operative Advertising:	Yes
Franchisee Assoc./Member:	Yes/Yes
Size Of Corporate Staff:	140
On-Going Support:	,,C,D,,F,G,H,I
Training:	1 Week Field; 1 Week
Headquarters, Taunton, MA	

SPECIFIC EXPANSION PLANS:
US:	All United States
Canada:	No
Overseas:	NR

◄◄ ►►

THE ALTERNATIVE BOARD
Change Perspective. Improve Business. Enjoy Life.

TAB BOARDS INTERNATIONAL
11031 Sheridan Blvd.
Westminster, CO 80020
Tel: (800) 727-0126 (303) 839-1200

Fax: (303) 839-0012
E-Mail: franchise@thealternativeboard.com
Web Site: www.thealternativeboard.com
Ms. Kristine Vollrath, Franchise Acquisition Manager

THE ALTERNATIVE BOARD (TAB) is seeking entrepreneurs, business consultants or transitioning executives who are looking to start or expand their own business. As a TAB-certified Facilitator, you will chair monthly group meetings of owners, CEOs and presidents of privately owned companies. In addition to facilitating these monthly meetings, you will provide individual coaching sessions using proprietary processes and tools.

BACKGROUND:　　　IFA MEMBER
Established: 1990;　1st Franchised: 1996
Franchised Units:	170
Company-Owned Units:	12
Total Units:	182
Dist.:	US-157; CAN-12; O'seas-1
North America:	39 States, 4 Provinces
Density:	NR
Projected New Units (12 Months):	45
Qualifications:	3, 5, 5, 5, 4, 5

FINANCIAL/TERMS:
Cash Investment:	$47-111K
Total Investment:	$47-111K
Minimum Net Worth:	$300K
Fees: Franchise -	$25-55K
Royalty - 35% or $1.5-4.5K/Mo;	Ad. - 1% or $100-400/Mo
Earnings Claims Statement:	No
Term of Contract (Years):	10/10
Avg. # Of Employees:	1 FT, 0 PT
Passive Ownership:	Not Allowed
Encourage Conversions:	NA
Area Develop. Agreements:	No
Sub-Franchising Contracts:	No
Expand In Territory:	Yes
Space Needs:	NA

SUPPORT & TRAINING:
Financial Assistance Provided:	No
Site Selection Assistance:	NA
Lease Negotiation Assistance:	NA
Co-Operative Advertising:	No
Franchisee Assoc./Member:	Yes/No
Size Of Corporate Staff:	32
On-Going Support:	A,,C,D,,,G,H,I
Training:	6 Days Denver, CO

SPECIFIC EXPANSION PLANS:
US:	All United States
Canada:	All Canada
Overseas:	All Countries

◄◄ ►►

TAX CENTERS OF AMERICA
1611 E. Main St.
Russellville, AR 72801-5328
Tel: (800) 364-2012 (479) 968-4796
Fax: (479) 968-8012
E-Mail: tonia@tcoa.net
Web Site: www.tcoa.net
Mr. Gordon Thornsberry, Franchise Manager

TAX CENTERS OF AMERICA is a tax preparation and electronic filing company with franchises in over 15 states. Our franchisees are provided with all the training and knowledge, and full-time support, to become successful. We are innovative in offering franchise opportunities to individuals desiring to become self-employed and businesses searching for a significant income stream. Franchises have unlimited expansion with our unique satellite system. The entrepreneurial spirit is a fundamental motivation.

BACKGROUND:
Established: 1992;　1st Franchised: 1996
Franchised Units:	113
Company-Owned Units:	2
Total Units:	115
Dist.:	US-115; CAN-0; O'seas-0
North America:	16 States, 0 Provinces
Density:	8 in NE, 10 in LA, 67 in AR
Projected New Units (12 Months):	NR
Qualifications:	NR

FINANCIAL/TERMS:
Cash Investment:	$20-46K
Total Investment:	$20-46K
Minimum Net Worth:	NA
Fees: Franchise -	$15.5K
Royalty - $17/Return;	Ad. - NA
Earnings Claims Statement:	No
Term of Contract (Years):	10/5
Avg. # Of Employees:	4 FT, 2 PT
Passive Ownership:	Discouraged
Encourage Conversions:	No
Area Develop. Agreements:	No
Sub-Franchising Contracts:	No
Expand In Territory:	Yes
Space Needs:	800-1,200 SF

SUPPORT & TRAINING:
Financial Assistance Provided:	No
Site Selection Assistance:	Yes
Lease Negotiation Assistance:	No
Co-Operative Advertising:	No
Franchisee Assoc./Member:	No
Size Of Corporate Staff:	13
On-Going Support:	A,,,d,,,G,h,I
Training:	4 Days Russellville, AR

SPECIFIC EXPANSION PLANS:
US:	All United States

Canada: NR
Overseas: NR

≪ ≫

THE GROWTH COACH
10700 Montgomery Rd., # 300
Cincinnati, OH 45242
Tel: (888) 292-7992 (513) 563-0570
Fax: (513) 563-2691
E-Mail: webinquiry@thegrowthcoach.com
Web Site: www.thegrowthcoach.com
Ms. Amber Kershaw, Sales Support Manager

The Growth Coach, ranked "Top 10 New Franchises" by Entrepreneur Magazine, is the leader in Business Coaching. Small business owners and self-employed professionals will invest in themselves to achieve success. Our Coaches utilize a proven coaching process to help their clients transform their businesses and balance their lives.

BACKGROUND: IFA MEMBER
Established: 2002; 1st Franchised: 2003
Franchised Units: 158
Company-Owned Units: 0
Total Units: 158
Dist.: US-156; CAN-2; O'seas-0
North America: 39 States, 1 Provinces
Density: NR
Projected New Units (12 Months): 60
Qualifications: 3, 3, 1, 3, 3, 4
FINANCIAL/TERMS:
Cash Investment: $7-36.9K
Total Investment: $46.2-75.4K
Minimum Net Worth: $22.9K
Fees: Franchise - $36.9K
Royalty - Varied based on annual
resources; Ad. - $200/Mo.
Earnings Claims Statement: No
Term of Contract (Years): 10/10/10/
Avg. # Of Employees: 1 FT, 0 PT
Passive Ownership: Not Allowed
Encourage Conversions: Yes
Area Develop. Agreements: Yes/1
Sub-Franchising Contracts: No
Expand In Territory: Yes
Space Needs: NA
SUPPORT & TRAINING:
Financial Assistance Provided: Yes (D)

Site Selection Assistance: NA
Lease Negotiation Assistance: NA
Co-Operative Advertising: No
Franchisee Assoc./Member: No
Size Of Corporate Staff: 50
On-Going Support: ,,C,D,E,,G,H,I
Training: 5 Business Days Cincinnati, OH
SPECIFIC EXPANSION PLANS:
US: All United States
Canada: All Canada
Overseas: All Countries

≪ ≫

TRADEBANK INTERNATIONAL
1000 Laval Blvd.
Lawrenceville, GA 30043
Tel: (888) 568-5680 (678) 533-7100
Fax: (678) 533-7113
E-Mail: info@tradebank.com
Web Site: www.tradebank.com
Mr. John P. Davis, Jr., Chief Executive Officer

Tradebank International is one of the world's largest trade exchanges with offices in over 70 cities across the United States, Canada and East Central Europe. Since 1987, we have completed over two million transactions, each helping our clients conserve cash and make their business more profitable. Tradebank franchise owners are responsible for new client acquisition and management throughout their protected territories. Unlimited possibilities.

BACKGROUND: IFA MEMBER
Established: 1987; 1st Franchised: 1995
Franchised Units: 77
Company-Owned Units: 16
Total Units: 93
Dist.: US-63; CAN-18; O'seas-12
North America: 14 States, 3 Provinces
Density: 7 in TN, 8 in GA, 13 in ON
Projected New Units (12 Months): 12
Qualifications: 4, 3, 5, 3, 2, 1
FINANCIAL/TERMS:
Cash Investment: $10K
Total Investment: $10-50K
Minimum Net Worth: $25K
Fees: Franchise - $35-50K
Royalty - 30-40%; Ad. - 0%
Earnings Claims Statement: No

Term of Contract (Years): 5/5/5/
Avg. # Of Employees: 3 FT, PT
Passive Ownership: Discouraged
Encourage Conversions: NA
Area Develop. Agreements: Yes/1
Sub-Franchising Contracts: Yes
Expand In Territory: Yes
Space Needs: 400 SF
SUPPORT & TRAINING:
Financial Assistance Provided: Yes (D)
Site Selection Assistance: NA
Lease Negotiation Assistance: NA
Co-Operative Advertising: Yes
Franchisee Assoc./Member: Yes/Yes
Size Of Corporate Staff: 12
On-Going Support: A,B,C,D,E,,g,h,I
Training: 3 Days Broker; 5 Days Opening;
5 Days Atlanta, GA
SPECIFIC EXPANSION PLANS:
US: All United States
Canada: All Canada
Overseas: All Countries

≪ ≫

VALPAK DIRECT MARKETING
8605 Largo Lakes Dr.
Largo, FL 33773-4912
Tel: (800) 237-6266 + 3200 (727) 399-3121
Fax: (727) 392-0049
E-Mail: chrys_richardson@valpak.com
Web Site: www.valpakfranchising.com
Ms. Chrys Richardson, New Franchise Development Administrator

Valpak Direct Marketing Systems, Inc. ("Valpak") is the largest cooperative direct mail envelope company in the US and is an indirect subsidiary of Atlanta-based Cox Enterprises, Inc. who was named by Advertising Age as the 5th largest media company in the U.S. With almost 200 franchises in the U.S., Canada and Puerto Rico mail over 22 billion coupons to more than 500 million households annually.

BACKGROUND: IFA MEMBER
Established: 1968; 1st Franchised: 1988
Franchised Units: 172
Company-Owned Units: 5
Total Units: 177
Dist.: US-169; CAN-8; O'seas-0
North America: 46 States, 4 Provinces
Density: 13 in VA, 27 in FL, 17 in CA

Projected New Units (12 Months): 10-20
Qualifications: 3, 2, 1, 2, 3, 4
FINANCIAL/TERMS:
Cash Investment: $75-150K
Total Investment: $60.2-104.8K
Minimum Net Worth: $150K
Fees: Franchise - $15-75.5K
  Royalty - 0%; Ad. - 0%
Earnings Claims Statement: Yes
Term of Contract (Years): 10/5
Avg. # Of Employees: Varies
Passive Ownership: Discouraged
Encourage Conversions: Yes
Area Develop. Agreements: No
Sub-Franchising Contracts: No
Expand In Territory: Yes
Space Needs: NA
SUPPORT & TRAINING:
Financial Assistance Provided: Yes (I)
Site Selection Assistance: NA
Lease Negotiation Assistance: NA
Co-Operative Advertising: No
Franchisee Assoc./Member: Yes/Yes
Size Of Corporate Staff: 100
On-Going Support: A,,C,D,E,,G,H,I
Training: 2 Weeks New Owner- Largo,
  FL & in territory; 2 Weeks Sales-
  Largo, FL;4 DaysCoupon University
SPECIFIC EXPANSION PLANS:
US: All United States
Canada: All Canada
Overseas: NR

◄◄ ►►

VITAL DENT
17 Battery Pl., # 205
New York, NY 10004
Tel: (877) 2VITALDENT (212) 967-2400
Fax: (212) 668-5252
E-Mail: expansion@vitaldentus.com
Web Site: www.vitaldent.com
Ms. Hillary Rivman, Public Relations

East River International LLC D/B/A Vital Dent offers our franchisees the opportunity to buy a Dental Office Management Company (the Franchised Business). Vital Dent offers franchisees turn-key businesses, by providing the know-how and the latest technology needed in order to start the Franchised Business from the ground up. The Franchised Business provides dental management services to a Professional Corporation run by a dentist, as well as unique marketing and branding services and human resources.

BACKGROUND: IFA MEMBER
Established: 1989; 1st Franchised: 1995

Franchised Units: 350
Company-Owned Units: 50
Total Units: 400
Dist.: US-24; CAN-0; O'seas-376
  North America: 3 States, 0 Provinces
  Density: 17 in NY, 1 in MA, 6 in FL
Projected New Units (12 Months): NR
Qualifications: 3, 3, 3, 3, 3, 3
FINANCIAL/TERMS:
Cash Investment: $50K
Total Investment: $700K
Minimum Net Worth: $500K
Fees: Franchise - $87.5K
  Royalty - 5%; Ad. - 5%
Earnings Claims Statement: No
Term of Contract (Years): 10/10
Avg. # Of Employees: 8 FT, 0 PT
Passive Ownership: Not Allowed
Encourage Conversions: NA
Area Develop. Agreements: No
Sub-Franchising Contracts: No
Expand In Territory: Yes
Space Needs: 2,000 SF
SUPPORT & TRAINING:
Financial Assistance Provided: No
Site Selection Assistance: No
Lease Negotiation Assistance: No
Co-Operative Advertising: No
Franchisee Assoc./Member: No
Size Of Corporate Staff: 15
On-Going Support: ,B,C,d,E,,,,
Training: NR
SPECIFIC EXPANSION PLANS:
US: No
Canada: No
Overseas: NR

◄◄ ►►

VR BUSINESS BROKERS/
MERGERS & ACQUISITIONS
1 E. Broward Blvd., # 1500
Ft. Lauderdale, FL 33301
Tel: (800) 377-8722 (954) 565-1555 + 24
Fax: (954) 565-6855
E-Mail: vrbb@vrbusinessbrokers.com
Web Site: www.vrbusinessbrokers.com
Ms. JoAnn Lombardi, President

International network of business brokers and intermediaries, specializing in the sale of small to mid-size companies. Extensive training, support and marketing materials make it possible to become a full-time professional in our industry. VR has sold more businesses in North America than

anyone . Of the 11 million businesses in America, 20% change hands every year for you to sell. Since 1979, VR has sold free enterprise. Now it's your turn.

BACKGROUND: IFA MEMBER
Established: 1979; 1st Franchised: 1979
Franchised Units: 120
Company-Owned Units: 0
Total Units: 120
Dist.: US-108; CAN-0; O'seas-12
  North America: 37 States, 0 Provinces
  Density: 4 in TX, 16 in FL, 14 in CA
Projected New Units (12 Months): 25
Qualifications: 4, 4, 1, 2, 3, 3
FINANCIAL/TERMS:
Cash Investment: $25-50K
Total Investment: $65-100K
Minimum Net Worth: $250K
Fees: Franchise - $26.5K
  Royalty - 6%; Ad. - $150/Mo.
Earnings Claims Statement: No
Term of Contract (Years): 10/10
Avg. # Of Employees: 2 FT, 1 PT
Passive Ownership: Allowed
Encourage Conversions: Yes
Area Develop. Agreements: No
Sub-Franchising Contracts: No
Expand In Territory: No
Space Needs: 1,200 SF
SUPPORT & TRAINING:
Financial Assistance Provided: Yes (D)
Site Selection Assistance: Yes
Lease Negotiation Assistance: Yes
Co-Operative Advertising: Yes
Franchisee Assoc./Member: Yes/Yes
Size Of Corporate Staff: 12
On-Going Support: A,B,C,D,E,,G,H,I
Training: 3 Weeks Dallas, TX
SPECIFIC EXPANSION PLANS:
US: All United States
Canada: All Canada
Overseas: All Countries

◄◄ ►►

WE THE PEOPLE
1436 Lancaster Ave.
Berwyn, PA 19312
Tel: (610) 640-6416
Fax: (610) 296-7844
E-Mail: scott.finn@dfg.com
Web Site: www.wethepeopleusa.com
Mr. Scott Finn, Director Franchise Development

Legal Document Service -- alternative to lawyers. We empower people to represent themselves by preparing all the paperwork necessary for them to avoid lawyers in their uncontested legal matters. Fueled by the growing dissatisfaction of millions of Americans with our over-priced, under-responsive legal system, people who need to prepare routine legal paperwork are turning to independent paralegals like WE THE PEOPLE, instead of lawyers.

BACKGROUND: IFA MEMBER
Established: 1985; 1st Franchised: 1996
Franchised Units: 175
Company-Owned Units: <u>22</u>
Total Units: 199
Dist.:   US-199; CAN-0; O'seas-0
  North America: 16 States, 0 Provinces
  Density: 4 in CO, 48 in CA, 3 in AZ
Projected New Units (12 Months):   30

Qualifications: 3, 2, 1, 1, 1, 5
FINANCIAL/TERMS:
Cash Investment: NR
Total Investment: $125-150K
Minimum Net Worth: $250K
Fees: Franchise - $125-150K
  Royalty - 0%;   Ad. - 0%
Earnings Claims Statement: No
Term of Contract (Years):   10/5/2/
Avg. # Of Employees: 1 FT, 0 PT
Passive Ownership: Allowed
Encourage Conversions: Yes
Area Develop. Agreements: Yes/1
Sub-Franchising Contracts: Yes
Expand In Territory: Yes
Space Needs: NR

SUPPORT & TRAINING:
Financial Assistance Provided: No
Site Selection Assistance: Yes
Lease Negotiation Assistance: Yes
Co-Operative Advertising: No
Franchisee Assoc./Member: No
Size Of Corporate Staff: 60
On-Going Support: A,B,C,D,E,F,G,H,
Training: 1 Week Santa Barbara, CA
SPECIFIC EXPANSION PLANS:
US: All United States, NY
Canada: No
Overseas: NR

<< >>

FIVE LARGEST PARTICIPANTS IN SURVEY

Company	# Fran-chised Units	# Co-Owned Units	# Total Units	Franchise Fee	On-Going Royalty	Total Investment
1. Gymboree Play & Music	612	7	619	$45K	6%	$128-267.3K
2. Huntington Learning Center	284	34	318	$43K	8%/$1.5K Min.	$203-393.75K
3. Goddard School	300	0	300	$135K	7%	$650K
4. FasTracKids International Ltd.	275	0	275	$30K	Varies	$32.5-87.5K
5. Little Gym, The	267	0	267	$69.5K	8%	$127.5-294K

All of the data provided are proprietary and should not be quoted without acknowledging *Bond's Franchise Guide.*

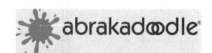

ABRAKADOODLE REMARKABLE ART EDUCATION
1800 Robert Fulton Dr. # 205
Reston, VA 20191
Tel: (703) 860-6570
Fax: (703) 860-6574
E-Mail: info@abrakadoodle.com
Web Site: www.abrakadoodle.com
Ms. Shani Seidel, Director of Franchising

ABRAKADOODLE is a remarkable arts education program for children that combines high-quality Crayola paints, pastels, modeling compounds and other products with imaginative learning activities. The ABRAKADOODLE program has been designed by notable educators and artists.

BACKGROUND: IFA MEMBER
Established: 2001; 1st Franchised: 2004
Franchised Units: 74
Company-Owned Units: 2
Total Units: 76
Dist.: US-76; CAN-0; O'seas-0
North America: 24 States, 0 Provinces
Density: NR
Projected New Units (12 Months): NR
Qualifications: 4, 4, 2, 4, NR, 5
FINANCIAL/TERMS:
Cash Investment: $45K-70K
Total Investment: $48.4K-63.7K
Minimum Net Worth: $100K
Fees: Franchise - $33,900
  Royalty - 8%; Ad. - 1%

Earnings Claims Statement: No
Term of Contract (Years): 10/10
Avg. # Of Employees: 1 FT, Varies PT
Passive Ownership: Not Allowed
Encourage Conversions: NA
Area Develop. Agreements: No
Sub-Franchising Contracts: No
Expand In Territory: Yes
Space Needs: NA
SUPPORT & TRAINING:
Financial Assistance Provided: No
Site Selection Assistance: NA
Lease Negotiation Assistance: NA
Co-Operative Advertising: No
Franchisee Assoc./Member: Yes/Yes
Size Of Corporate Staff: 10
On-Going Support: a,b,c,d,,,,h,
Training: 5 Days Reston, VA

SPECIFIC EXPANSION PLANS:
US: All States Where Registered
Canada: No
Overseas: NR

◄◄ ►►

BABIES 'N' BELLS
4489 Mira Vista Dr.
Frisco, TX 75034-7519
Tel: (888) 418-2229 (972) 335-3535
Fax: (469) 384-0138
E-Mail: franchise.east@babiesnbells.com
Web Site: www.babiesnbells.com
Ms. Cheryl Rogers, Franchise Manager

Balance family and career and work from home! BABIES 'N' BELLS uses state-of-the-art computer printing systems and proprietary design elements to produce custom announcements and invitations for all occasions. BABIES 'N' BELLS has been featured in industry publications, including Entrepreneur Magazine.

BACKGROUND:
Established: 1993;   1st Franchised: 1997
Franchised Units: 65
Company-Owned Units: 34
Total Units: 99
Dist.:   US-99; CAN-0; O'seas-0
  North America: 25 States, Provinces
  Density: 7 in CA, 7 in NY, 10 in TX
Projected New Units (12 Months):   152
Qualifications: 4, 2, 2, 3, 5, NR
FINANCIAL/TERMS:
Cash Investment: $9-20K
Total Investment: $17-29.3K
Minimum Net Worth: NA
Fees: Franchise - $9K
  Royalty - 8%;   Ad. - 2%
Earnings Claims Statement: No
Term of Contract (Years):   5/5
Avg. # Of Employees: 1 FT, 0 PT
Passive Ownership: Not Allowed
Encourage Conversions: NA
Area Develop. Agreements: No
Sub-Franchising Contracts: No
Expand In Territory: Yes
Space Needs: 600 SF
SUPPORT & TRAINING:
Financial Assistance Provided: No
Site Selection Assistance: Yes
Lease Negotiation Assistance: NA
Co-Operative Advertising: No
Franchisee Assoc./Member: No
Size Of Corporate Staff: 8
On-Going Support: A,B,c,d,E,F,G,h,I
Training: 5 Days Dallas, TX
SPECIFIC EXPANSION PLANS:

US: All United States
Canada: No
Overseas: NR

◄◄ ►►

CHILDRENS LIGHTHOUSE LEARNING CENTERS
101 S. Jennings St., # 209
Fort Worth, TX 76104-1112
Tel: (888) 338-4466 (817) 338-4422
Fax: (817) 348-8317
E-Mail: jstone@childrenslighthouse.com
Web Site: www.childrenslighthouse.com
Ms. Jessica Stone, Franchise Administrator

CHILDREN'S LIGHTHOUSE is one of the newest and brightest concepts in the child care industry in the last decade. State-of-the-art 10,000 square foot centers, with keycode entry and cameras in each room so a parent can view their child from anywhere in the world.

BACKGROUND:
Established: 1997;   1st Franchised: 1999
Franchised Units: 7
Company-Owned Units: 9
Total Units: 16
Dist.:   US-16; CAN-0; O'seas-0
  North America: 4 States, 0 Provinces
  Density: 14 in TX, 2 in FL
Projected New Units (12 Months):   6
Qualifications: 4, 4, 3, 3, 3, 4
FINANCIAL/TERMS:
Cash Investment: $275K
Total Investment: $1.8-2.4MM
Minimum Net Worth: $500K
Fees: Franchise - $50K
  Royalty - 7%;   Ad. - 1%
Earnings Claims Statement: Yes
Term of Contract (Years):   25/10
Avg. # Of Employees: 25 FT, 0 PT
Passive Ownership: Allowed
Encourage Conversions: Yes
Area Develop. Agreements: Yes/1
Sub-Franchising Contracts: No
Expand In Territory: Yes
Space Needs: 10,000 SF
SUPPORT & TRAINING:
Financial Assistance Provided: Yes (I)
Site Selection Assistance: Yes
Lease Negotiation Assistance: NA
Co-Operative Advertising: No
Franchisee Assoc./Member: No
Size Of Corporate Staff: 10
On-Going Support: ,,C,D,E,,,,I
Training: 40 Hours Corporate Office Ft. Worth, TX; 80 Hours On-Site

SPECIFIC EXPANSION PLANS:
US: All United States
Canada: All Canada
Overseas: NR

◄◄ ►►

CHILDREN'S ORCHARD
900 Victor's Wy., # 200
Ann Arbor, MI 48108
Tel: (800) 999-5437 (734) 994-9199 + 222
Fax: (734) 994-9323
E-Mail: campaign364@mail.emaximation.com
Web Site: www.childorch.com
Ms. Lisa Morgan, Franchise Development Director

Upscale children's retail/resale stores, featuring clothing, toys, furniture, equipment, books and parenting products. We buy top-brand items from area families by appointment, and re-sell in boutique-style stores, along with top-quality new children's items from nearly 200 suppliers. These are large volume stores selling thousands of items per week.

BACKGROUND: IFA MEMBER
Established: 1980;   1st Franchised: 1985
Franchised Units: 84
Company-Owned Units: 1
Total Units: 85
Dist.:   US-85; CAN-0; O'seas-0
  North America: 22 States, Provinces
  Density: 18 in CA, 14 in MA, 6 in MI
Projected New Units (12 Months):   15
Qualifications: 5, 3, 2, 4, 2, 5
FINANCIAL/TERMS:
Cash Investment: $30-50K
Total Investment: $72.5-158K
Minimum Net Worth: $200K
Fees: Franchise - $22.5K
  Royalty - 5%;   Ad. - 1.0%
Earnings Claims Statement: No
Term of Contract (Years):   10/
Avg. # Of Employees: 1 FT, 3 PT
Passive Ownership: Discouraged
Encourage Conversions: Yes
Area Develop. Agreements: Yes/1
Sub-Franchising Contracts: No
Expand In Territory: No
Space Needs: 1,200-2,000 SF
SUPPORT & TRAINING:
Financial Assistance Provided: Yes (D)
Site Selection Assistance: Yes
Lease Negotiation Assistance: Yes

113

Co-Operative Advertising: No
Franchisee Assoc./Member: Yes/Yes
Size Of Corporate Staff: 15
On-Going Support: ,B,C,D,E,F,G,H,I
Training: 12 Days Training in Ann Arbor, MI

SPECIFIC EXPANSION PLANS:
US: All US Except HI, AK
Canada: No
Overseas: NR

≪ ≫

CHILDREN'S TECHNOLOGY WORKSHOP

109 Vanderhoof Ave., # 101A
Toronto, ON M4G 2H7 Canada
Tel: (866) 704-2267 + 24 (416) 425-2289
Fax: (647) 439-0890
E-Mail: franchise@ctworkshop.com
Web Site: www.ctworkshop.com
Mr. Len Rosen, Director Business Development

CHILDREN'S TECHNOLOGY WORKSHOP develops and delivers interactive, applied, technology programs through camps, after-school workshops, academic supplementary education and special events and birthday parties. Children aged 7-14 learn video game programming, animation and LEGO robotics through individualized activities structured around exciting adventure themes. If your passion includes educating and encouraging children to learn, explore and create using technology, then we want to speak with you.

BACKGROUND: IFA MEMBER
Established: 1997; 1st Franchised: 2004
Franchised Units: 37
Company-Owned Units: 1
Total Units: 38
Dist.: US-24; CAN-10; O'seas-4
North America: 12 States, 2 Provinces
Density: 9 in ON
Projected New Units (12 Months): 24-30
Qualifications: 3, 3, 4, 5, 5, 5
FINANCIAL/TERMS:
Cash Investment: $25K
Total Investment: $105-150K
Minimum Net Worth: $500K
Fees: Franchise - $25K
 Royalty - 6%; Ad. - 3%

Earnings Claims Statement: No
Term of Contract (Years): 7/
Avg. # Of Employees: 1 FT, 0 PT
Passive Ownership: Discouraged
Encourage Conversions: Yes
Area Develop. Agreements: Yes
Sub-Franchising Contracts: Yes
Expand In Territory: Yes
Space Needs: NA
SUPPORT & TRAINING:
Financial Assistance Provided: Yes (I)
Site Selection Assistance: Yes
Lease Negotiation Assistance: NA
Co-Operative Advertising: No
Franchisee Assoc./Member: No
Size Of Corporate Staff: 10
On-Going Support: A,,,,,,G,H,I
Training: 1 Week Toronto, ON
SPECIFIC EXPANSION PLANS:
US: All United States
Canada: All Canada
Overseas: NR

≪ ≫

COMPUTER EXPLORERS

12715 Telge Rd.
Cypress, TX 77429-2289
Tel: (888) 638-8722 (281) 256-4221
Fax: (281) 256-4178
E-Mail: franchisedevelopment@iced.net
Web Site: www.computerexplorers.com
Ms. Jenny Langfeld, Franchise Dev. Support Mgr.

The newest member of the ICED family of franchises provides educational technology training for childcare centers, preschools and elementary schools. Having taught more than three million classes, we seek entrepreneurs who wish to build a thriving business while providing quality computer education and curriculum for children.

BACKGROUND: IFA MEMBER
Established: 1983; 1st Franchised: 1988
Franchised Units: 107
Company-Owned Units: 0
Total Units: 107
Dist.: US-101; CAN-1; O'seas-5
North America: 30 States, 1 Provinces
Density: 6 in NJ, 6 in IL, 6 in CA
Projected New Units (12 Months): NR
Qualifications: 4, NR, NR, NR, NR, NR
FINANCIAL/TERMS:
Cash Investment: $30K
Total Investment: $62.9K-73.3K
Minimum Net Worth: $100K
Fees: Franchise - $35K

Royalty - 8%; Ad. - 1%
Earnings Claims Statement: No
Term of Contract (Years): 15/15
Avg. # Of Employees: 1 FT, 5 PT
Passive Ownership: Not Allowed
Encourage Conversions: NA
Area Develop. Agreements: No
Sub-Franchising Contracts: No
Expand In Territory: No
Space Needs: NA
SUPPORT & TRAINING:
Financial Assistance Provided: No
Site Selection Assistance: NA
Lease Negotiation Assistance: NA
Co-Operative Advertising: No
Franchisee Assoc./Member: Yes/Yes
Size Of Corporate Staff: 0
On-Going Support: ,,c,d,,,g,h,I
Training: 2 Weeks Headquarters
SPECIFIC EXPANSION PLANS:
US: All United States
Canada: No
Overseas: NR

≪ ≫

Hottest New Franchise

CREATIVE TUTORS

6705 Patrick Ln.
Plano, TX 75024
Tel: (877) TUTORS-U (214) 282-6268
Fax: NA
E-Mail: janvb@creativetutors.com
Web Site: www.creativetutors.com
Ms. Jan Van Blarcum, Founder

Owning a Creative Tutors franchise is both financially and personally rewarding! Franchise owners manage and direct tutors that provide services to students Pre-K through 12th grade. Services are provided by certified teachers in the privacy and comfort of the student's home or after school location. By eliminating the high overhead associated with running a traditional "brick and mortar" center, Creative Tutors franchisees can focus their resources on marketing, management and growing their business.

BACKGROUND: IFA MEMBER
Established: 1999; 1st Franchised: 2004
Franchised Units: 10
Company-Owned Units: 0
Total Units: 10

114

Dist.: US-10; CAN-0; O'seas-0
North America: 5 States, 0 Provinces
Density: 1 in UT, 1 in CO, 8 in TX
Projected New Units (12 Months): 50
Qualifications: 3, 2, 3, 3, 3, 5

FINANCIAL/TERMS:

Cash Investment: $35-60K
Total Investment: $35-300K
Minimum Net Worth: $70K
Fees: Franchise - $12-40K
Royalty - 7%; Ad. - 2%
Earnings Claims Statement: No
Term of Contract (Years): 10/10
Avg. # Of Employees: 1 FT, 0 PT
Passive Ownership: Discouraged
Encourage Conversions: NA
Area Develop. Agreements: Yes/10
Sub-Franchising Contracts: No
Expand In Territory: No
Space Needs: NA

SUPPORT & TRAINING:

Financial Assistance Provided: Yes (I)
Site Selection Assistance: Yes
Lease Negotiation Assistance: No
Co-Operative Advertising: Yes
Franchisee Assoc./Member: No
Size Of Corporate Staff: 2
On-Going Support: A,,C,D,E,,,H,I
Training: Weekly Conference Call;
2 Days Quarterly Plano, TX

SPECIFIC EXPANSION PLANS:

US: All United States
Canada: No
Overseas: NR

≪ ≫

DIGIKIDS®

9463 Hwy. 377 S., # 111
Fort Worth, TX 76126
Tel: (888) 344-4543 (817) 249-2126
Fax:
E-Mail: info@digikids-id.com
Web Site: www.digikids-id.com
Ms. Lisa Schmidt, Franchise Development

More than 2,200 children are reported lost or missing each day in the United States. DIGIKIDS® offers a unique, high-tech solution to aid in the recovery of those children. With a DIGIKIDS® franchise, you'll enjoy great earning potential and very low overhead, while providing a much-needed and highly respected service for your community.

BACKGROUND:

Established: 2003; 1st Franchised: 2004
Franchised Units: 31
Company-Owned Units: 0
Total Units: 31
Dist.: US-31; CAN-0; O'seas-0
North America: 18 States, 0 Provinces
Density: 8 in TX, 2 in NC, 4 in FL
Projected New Units (12 Months): 10
Qualifications: 2, 1, 1, 2, 3, 5

FINANCIAL/TERMS:

Cash Investment: $28.7K
Total Investment: $28.7K
Minimum Net Worth: $100K
Fees: Franchise - $28.7K
Royalty - 0%; Ad. - 2%
Earnings Claims Statement: Yes
Term of Contract (Years): 10/10
Avg. # Of Employees: 1 FT, 1 PT
Passive Ownership: Allowed
Encourage Conversions: Yes
Area Develop. Agreements: Yes/5
Sub-Franchising Contracts: No
Expand In Territory: Yes
Space Needs: NA

SUPPORT & TRAINING:

Financial Assistance Provided: Yes (D)
Site Selection Assistance: NA
Lease Negotiation Assistance: NA
Co-Operative Advertising: No
Franchisee Assoc./Member: No
Size Of Corporate Staff: 5
On-Going Support: ,,C,D,E,F,G,H,I
Training: As Agreed On-Site;
2 Days Corporate Headquarters

SPECIFIC EXPANSION PLANS:

US: All United States
Canada: No
Overseas: All Countries

≪ ≫

DRAMA KIDS INTERNATIONAL

3225-B Corporate Ct.
Ellicott City, MD 21042
Tel: (877) 543-7456 (410) 480-2015 + 31
Fax: (410) 480-2026
E-Mail: clare@dramakids.com
Web Site: www.dramakids.com
Ms. Clare Ryan, Director of Franchise Development

DRAMA KIDS and its international affiliates, Helen O'Grady Drama Academy, is the largest after-school drama program in the world, with over 45,000 children currently enrolled. Our award-winning drama curriculum uses a wide variety of fun and creative drama activities that are new each week. We teach skills that are not being taught in most schools today, skills critical for ongoing success in life. Franchise owners enjoy a home-based office and a flexible lifestyle. Drama experience is NOT required.

BACKGROUND: IFA MEMBER

Established: 1979; 1st Franchised: 1989
Franchised Units: 145
Company-Owned Units: 4
Total Units: 149
Dist.: US-34; CAN-0; O'seas-115
North America: 17 States, 0 Provinces
Density: 6 in NY
Projected New Units (12 Months): 15
Qualifications: 3, 3, 1, 4, 3, 5

FINANCIAL/TERMS:

Cash Investment: $17-52K
Total Investment: $17-52K
Minimum Net Worth: $50K
Fees: Franchise - $15-39K
Royalty - 6-11%; Ad. - 1%
Earnings Claims Statement: Yes
Term of Contract (Years): 7/7
Avg. # Of Employees: 1 FT, 2 PT
Passive Ownership: Not Allowed
Encourage Conversions: NA
Area Develop. Agreements: No
Sub-Franchising Contracts: No
Expand In Territory: No
Space Needs: NA

SUPPORT & TRAINING:

Financial Assistance Provided: No
Site Selection Assistance: Yes
Lease Negotiation Assistance: Yes
Co-Operative Advertising: Yes
Franchisee Assoc./Member: Yes/Yes
Size Of Corporate Staff: 6
On-Going Support: ,,C,D,E,F,G,H,I
Training: 1 Week Baltimore, MD

SPECIFIC EXPANSION PLANS:

US: All United States
Canada: No
Overseas: NR

≪ ≫

E.NOPI

50 Passaic St.
Hackensack, NJ 07601
Tel: (888) 835-1212 +203
Fax: (201) 498-1218
E-Mail: eugene.ahn@enopi.com
Web Site: www.enopi.com
Mr. Eugene Ahn, East Coast General
    Manager

E.nopi Learning Centers provide supplementary education for children age 4 to 14 in Math, Reading and Writing. E.nopi has developed a unique product and method of implementation for a market with an established need. The benefits of owning an E.nopi Learning Center include: reasonable work/life balance, proven system (over 30 years of experience), relatively low cost investment, and socially responsible and respected business.

BACKGROUND: IFA MEMBER
Established: 1991;   1st Franchised: 1991
Franchised Units: 106
Company-Owned Units: 2
Total Units: 108
Dist.:   US-102; CAN-6; O'seas-0
  North America: 14 States, 2 Provinces
  Density: 25 in NY, 24 in NJ, 28 in CA
Projected New Units (12 Months):   na
Qualifications: 5, 4, 3, 3, 2, 4
FINANCIAL/TERMS:
Cash Investment: $30K
Total Investment: $52-91K
Minimum Net Worth: $100K
Fees: Franchise - $12K
  Royalty - 15%;   Ad. - 1%
Earnings Claims Statement: No
Term of Contract (Years):   5/5
Avg. # Of Employees: 1 FT, 2 PT
Passive Ownership: Discouraged
Encourage Conversions: Yes
Area Develop. Agreements: Yes/5
Sub-Franchising Contracts: No
Expand In Territory: Yes
Space Needs: 900-1200 SF
SUPPORT & TRAINING:
Financial Assistance Provided: No
Site Selection Assistance: Yes
Lease Negotiation Assistance: No
Co-Operative Advertising: Yes
Franchisee Assoc./Member: No
Size Of Corporate Staff: 24

On-Going Support: „C,D,E,F,G,h,I
Training: 5-6 DaysHackensack, NJ
SPECIFIC EXPANSION PLANS:
US: All United States
Canada: All Provinces
Overseas: NR

≪ ≫

FASTRACKIDS INTERNATIONAL LTD.

6900 E. Belleview Ave., 1st Fl.
Greenwood Village, CO 80111-1619
Tel: (888) 576-6888 (303) 224-0200
Fax: (303) 224-0222
E-Mail: info@fastrackids.com
Web Site: www.fastrackids.com
Mr. Kevin Krause, General Manager

FASTRACKIDS   INTERNATIONAL, a top-rated Enrichment Education franchise, has appointed over 190 licensees in 30 countries. Thousands of children have benefitted from the technologically advanced FASTRACKIDS curriculum. Developed for children ages 6 months to 6 years, FASTRACKIDS is designed to increase thinking and reasoning abilities while enhancing communication skills and self-esteem.

BACKGROUND: IFA MEMBER
Established: 1998;   1st Franchised: 1998
Franchised Units: 275
Company-Owned Units: 0
Total Units: 275
Dist.:   US-65; CAN-17; O'seas-90
  North America: 23 States, 1 Provinces
  Density: NR
Projected New Units (12 Months):   55
Qualifications: 4, 4, 4, 4, 5, 5
FINANCIAL/TERMS:
Cash Investment: $21.5K
Total Investment: $32.5K-87.5K
Minimum Net Worth: NR
Fees: Franchise - $30K
  Royalty - Varies;   Ad. - 0%
Earnings Claims Statement: No
Term of Contract (Years):   5/20
Avg. # Of Employees: 1-5 FT, 0 PT
Passive Ownership: Discouraged
Encourage Conversions: NA
Area Develop. Agreements: Yes/1

Sub-Franchising Contracts: No
Expand In Territory: Yes
Space Needs: 1,600-1,800 SF
SUPPORT & TRAINING:
Financial Assistance Provided: No
Site Selection Assistance: Yes
Lease Negotiation Assistance: Yes
Co-Operative Advertising: Yes
Franchisee Assoc./Member: No
Size Of Corporate Staff: 12
On-Going Support: „C,,,,G,h,I
Training: 5 Days Denver, CO
SPECIFIC EXPANSION PLANS:
US: All United States
Canada: All Canada
Overseas: All Countries

≪ ≫

GODDARD SCHOOL

1016 W. Ninth Ave.
King of Prussia, PA 19406
Tel: (800) 272-4901 (610) 265-8510
Fax: NA
E-Mail: jtravitz@goddardsystems.com
Web Site: www.goddardsystems.com
Mr. Jeff Travitz, Director

The Goddard School, franchised by Goddard Systems, Inc. (GSI), is recognized as the "#1 Franchise Preschool Chain in the U.S." (Entrepreneur, 01/08) and is ranked in the "Top 200 Franchises," (Franchise Times, 10/07). GSI has 290+ schools licensed in 37 states, and is expanding the network throughout the United States and Canada. GSI has achieved its initial goal as the acknowledged leader in franchised childcare and now has its sights on the next level - recognition as the premier childcare provider.

BACKGROUND: IFA MEMBER
Established: 1988;   1st Franchised: 1988
Franchised Units: 330
Company-Owned Units: 0
Total Units: 330
Dist.:   US-330; CAN-0; O'seas-0
  North America: 37 States, 0 Provinces
  Density: 57 in NJ, 41 in OH, 34 in PA
Projected New Units (12 Months):   50
Qualifications: 5, 4, 2, 3, 1, 5
FINANCIAL/TERMS:
Cash Investment: $130K
Total Investment: $650K

Minimum Net Worth: $600K
Fees: Franchise - $135K
  Royalty - 7%;   Ad. - 4% or $2,000
Earnings Claims Statement: Yes
Term of Contract (Years): 15/5
Avg. # Of Employees: 15+ FT, 10+ PT
Passive Ownership: Not Allowed
Encourage Conversions: NA
Area Develop. Agreements: No
Sub-Franchising Contracts: No
Expand In Territory: No
Space Needs: NA

SUPPORT & TRAINING:
Financial Assistance Provided: No
Site Selection Assistance: Yes
Lease Negotiation Assistance: Yes
Co-Operative Advertising: No
Franchisee Assoc./Member: No
Size Of Corporate Staff: 105
On-Going Support: A,,C,D,E,F,G,H,I
Training: 3 Weeks King of Prussia, PA

SPECIFIC EXPANSION PLANS:
US: All United States
Canada: All Canada
Overseas: NR

◄◄ ►►

GYMBOREE PLAY&MUSIC

GYMBOREE PLAY & MUSIC
500 Howard St.
San Francisco, CA 94105
Tel: (800) 520-7529 (415) 278-7000
Fax: (415) 278-7452
E-Mail: cms_gymboree@ifxonline.com
Web Site: www.gymboreeclasses.com
Mr. Stuart Ford, Director, Franchise
  Development

GYMBOREE PLAY & MUSIC has been providing childhood development programs for young children and their parents for more than 30 years. GYMBOREE's core belief is that children should develop at their own pace via physical, mental and creative activities in a fun environment - - with parents by their side. There are more than 600 GYMBOREE locations in 30 countries. Franchisees have access to a wide selection of branded consumer products for resale, and gain a competitive advantage with children's clothing stores.

BACKGROUND: IFA MEMBER
Established: 1976; 1st Franchised: 1978
Franchised Units: 612
Company-Owned Units: 7
Total Units: 619

Dist.: US-245; CAN-15; O'seas-359
  North America: 42 States, 4 Provinces
  Density: 24 in NY, 31 in NJ, 39 in CA
Projected New Units (12 Months): 15
Qualifications: 4, 4, 3, 3, 2, 4

FINANCIAL/TERMS:
Cash Investment: $25K-45K
Total Investment: $128-267.3K
Minimum Net Worth: $250K
Fees: Franchise - $45K
  Royalty - 6%;   Ad. - 2.25%
Earnings Claims Statement: No
Term of Contract (Years): 10/10
Avg. # Of Employees: 1 FT, 3 PT
Passive Ownership: Not Allowed
Encourage Conversions: No
Area Develop. Agreements: No
Sub-Franchising Contracts: No
Expand In Territory: Yes
Space Needs: 2,400 SF

SUPPORT & TRAINING:
Financial Assistance Provided: No
Site Selection Assistance: Yes
Lease Negotiation Assistance: Yes
Co-Operative Advertising: Yes
Franchisee Assoc./Member: Yes/Yes
Size Of Corporate Staff: 19
On-Going Support: ,,,D,,,G,h,I
Training: 8 Days Headquarters

SPECIFIC EXPANSION PLANS:
US: All United States
Canada: All Canada
Overseas: India, Europe

◄◄ ►►

HIGH TOUCH-HIGH TECH
P.O. Box 8495
Asheville, NC 28814
Tel: (800) 444-4968 (828) 277-5611
Fax: 828) 277-5610
E-Mail: support@sciencemadefun.net
Web Site: www.ScienceMadeFun.net
Ms. Terri Connolly, Director, Franchise
  Support & Brand Development

High Touch High Tech provides all the joys of teaching and the rewards of running your own profitable business. High Touch High Tech has been fueling the imaginations of children everywhere, since 1994, by providing FUN, interactive, hands-on science and nature experiences for children. Through discovery style learning and inquiry based dialogue, children are engaged in exciting programs that encourage them to explore the many wonders of science. Our programs spark a child's natural curiosity about science through in-school "field-trips", preschool programs,

afterschool enrichments, summer camp programs, mini-camps and birthday parties. With more than 2 million children participating in our programs annually, High Touch High Tech has emerged as the leader in innovative science programming.

BACKGROUND:
Established: 1992; 1st Franchised: 1994
Franchised Units: 150
Company-Owned Units: 11
Total Units: 161
Dist.: US-135; CAN-9; O'seas-6
  North America: 16 States, 0 Provinces
  Density: 13 in GA, 31 in TX, 34 in FL
Projected New Units (12 Months): 8-10
Qualifications: 5, 5, 3, 5, 3, 3

FINANCIAL/TERMS:
Cash Investment: $27-31K
Total Investment: $42-46K
Minimum Net Worth: NA
Fees: Franchise - $35K
  Royalty - 7%;   Ad. - NA
Earnings Claims Statement: No
Term of Contract (Years): 10/10
Avg. # Of Employees: 1 FT, 2-3 PT
Passive Ownership: Discouraged
Encourage Conversions: NA
Area Develop. Agreements: Yes/10
Sub-Franchising Contracts: No
Expand In Territory: Yes
Space Needs: NA

SUPPORT & TRAINING:
Financial Assistance Provided: Yes (D)
Site Selection Assistance: NA
Lease Negotiation Assistance: NA
Co-Operative Advertising: No
Franchisee Assoc./Member: No
Size Of Corporate Staff: 8
On-Going Support: ,,,d,,,,h,
Training: 5 Days Corporate Office

SPECIFIC EXPANSION PLANS:
US: All United States, Global
Canada: All Canada
Overseas: Europe, Asia, Pacific Region

◄◄ ►►

**HUNTINGTON
LEARNING CENTER**
496 Kinderkamack Rd.
Oradell, NJ 07649-1512
Tel: (800) 653-8400 (201) 261-8400
Fax: (800) 361-9728
E-Mail: franchise@huntingtonlearning.
com

Web Site: www.huntingtonlearning.com/franchise

Mr. Russell Miller, VP Business Development

Offers tutoring to 5-19 year-olds in reading, writing, language development study skills and mathematics, as well as programs to prepare for standardized entrance exams. Instruction is offered in a tutorial setting and is predominately remedial in nature.

BACKGROUND: IFA MEMBER
Established: 1977; 1st Franchised: 1985
Franchised Units: 284
Company-Owned Units: 34
Total Units: 318
Dist.: US-318; CAN-0; O'seas-0
 North America: 41 States, 0 Provinces
 Density: 26 in NY, 37 in FL, 31 in CA
Projected New Units (12 Months): 80
Qualifications: 5, 3, 1, 3, 1, 5
FINANCIAL/TERMS:
Cash Investment: $60K
Total Investment: $203-393.75K
Minimum Net Worth: $250K
Fees: Franchise - $43K
 Royalty - 8%/$1.5K Min.; Ad.
- 2%/$500 Min
Earnings Claims Statement: Yes
Term of Contract (Years): 10/10
Avg. # Of Employees: 2-4 FT, 12-20 PT
Passive Ownership: Not Allowed
Encourage Conversions: Yes
Area Develop. Agreements: Yes/1
Sub-Franchising Contracts: No
Expand In Territory: No
Space Needs: 2,000-2,500 SF
SUPPORT & TRAINING:
Financial Assistance Provided: Yes (I)
Site Selection Assistance: Yes
Lease Negotiation Assistance: Yes
Co-Operative Advertising: Yes
Franchisee Assoc./Member: No
Size Of Corporate Staff: 100
On-Going Support: ,,C,D,E,F,G,h,I
Training: On-Going Regional; 5 Weeks
 Oradell, NJ (Corporate Headquarters)
SPECIFIC EXPANSION PLANS:
US: Contiguous US
Canada: No
Overseas: NR

◄◄ ►►

JACADI

70 West Red Oak Ln.
White Plains, NY 10604
Tel: (914) 697-7684
Fax: (914) 697-7679

E-Mail: info@jacadiusa.com
Web Site: www.jacadiusa.com
Ms. Peggy Waldo, President/CEO

JACADI is a childrenswear retail company whose collections include clothing, shoes, accessories, furniture and nursery items in newborn through size 12 for both boys and girls. The merchandise is a European-style which adapts the latest trends to classic design and allows the customer to mix and match the various styles and color groups. JACADI also strives to give excellent customer service and the highest price/quality ratio.

BACKGROUND: IFA MEMBER
Established: 1988; 1st Franchised: 1992
Franchised Units: 22
Company-Owned Units: 3
Total Units: 25
Dist.: US-25; CAN-0; O'seas-0
 North America: 10 States, 0 Provinces
 Density: 7 in NY, 3 in FL, 8 in CA
Projected New Units (12 Months): 8
Qualifications: 5, 3, 1, 2, 4, 5
FINANCIAL/TERMS:
Cash Investment: $120-250K
Total Investment: $183-313K
Minimum Net Worth: $750K Liquid
Fees: Franchise - $20K
 Royalty - 4%; Ad. - 1%
Earnings Claims Statement: No
Term of Contract (Years): 7/7
Avg. # Of Employees: 2-3 FT, 2-3 PT
Passive Ownership: Not Allowed
Encourage Conversions: NA
Area Develop. Agreements: Yes/1
Sub-Franchising Contracts: No
Expand In Territory: Yes
Space Needs: 1,100 SF
SUPPORT & TRAINING:
Financial Assistance Provided: No
Site Selection Assistance: Yes
Lease Negotiation Assistance: Yes
Co-Operative Advertising: No
Franchisee Assoc./Member: No
Size Of Corporate Staff: 4
On-Going Support: ,B,C,d,E,f,G,h,
Training: 3-5 Days Subsidiary Shop; 3
 Days Franchisee's Shop Before Open-
 ing; On-Going Corporate
SPECIFIC EXPANSION PLANS:
US: All United States
Canada: All Canada
Overseas: All Countries

◄◄ ►►

JUMPBUNCH

302 Annapolis St.
Annapolis, MD 21401
Tel: (866) 826-5645 (410) 703-2300
Fax: (410) 268-0465
E-Mail: tom@jumpbunch.com
Web Site: www.jumpbunch.com
Mr. Thomas Bunchman, CEO

Jumpbunch offers structured sports and fitness programs for children 15 months to 6 years old, as well as for school-age children ages 6-12. The classes are 30 minutes long, once a week, year-round with over 70 activity plans. They are offered as part of a child's day at school, daycare, after-school programs and rec. departments. Jumpbunch is not a gym or facility; rather, we go out into the community to teach our classes.

BACKGROUND:
Established: 1997; 1st Franchised: 2002
Franchised Units: 33
Company-Owned Units: 1
Total Units: 34
Dist.: US-34; CAN-0; O'seas-0
 North America: 11 States, 0 Provinces
 Density: 3 in MD, 2 in GA, 5 in CA
Projected New Units (12 Months): NR
Qualifications: 3, 3, 3, 3, 3, 3
FINANCIAL/TERMS:
Cash Investment: $35K-77K
Total Investment: $35K-77K
Minimum Net Worth: $100K
Fees: Franchise - $15-25K
 Royalty - 8%; Ad. - 2%
Earnings Claims Statement: No
Term of Contract (Years): 5/5
Avg. # Of Employees: 0 FT, 3 PT
Passive Ownership: Discouraged
Encourage Conversions: NA
Area Develop. Agreements: No
Sub-Franchising Contracts: No
Expand In Territory: Yes
Space Needs: NA
SUPPORT & TRAINING:
Financial Assistance Provided: No
Site Selection Assistance: Yes
Lease Negotiation Assistance: No
Co-Operative Advertising: No
Franchisee Assoc./Member: No
Size Of Corporate Staff: 2
On-Going Support: ,b,C,d,,,G,H,I
Training: 2 Days Annapolis, MD
SPECIFIC EXPANSION PLANS:
US: All United States
Canada: No
Overseas: NR

‹‹ ››

KID TO KID

170 S. 1000 E.
Salt Lake City, UT 84102
Tel: (888) 543-2543 (801) 359-0071
Fax: (801) 359-3207
E-Mail: sales@bcfranchise.com
Web Site: www.kidtokid.com
Mr. Nathan Bennett, Director Business
  Development

KID TO KID is an up-scale children's resale store based on the premise that 'kids grow faster than paychecks.' Parents buy and sell better-quality used children's clothing, toys, equipment and accessories. If you enjoy working with people and want to increase your financial security as you grow your own business, call KID TO KID today!

BACKGROUND: IFA MEMBER
Established: 1992;   1st Franchised: 1994
Franchised Units: 56
Company-Owned Units: 2
Total Units: 58
Dist.:   US-53; CAN-0; O'seas-2
  North America: 15 States, 0 Provinces
  Density: 4 in VA, 11 in UT, 15 in TX
Projected New Units (12 Months):   10
Qualifications: 4, 3, 1, 2, 4, 5
FINANCIAL/TERMS:
Cash Investment: $40K-50K
Total Investment: $142K-216K
Minimum Net Worth: $150K
Fees: Franchise - $25K
  Royalty - 5%;   Ad. - 0.5%
Earnings Claims Statement: No
Term of Contract (Years):   10/5
Avg. # Of Employees: 2 FT, 2 PT
Passive Ownership: Discouraged
Encourage Conversions: Yes
Area Develop. Agreements: Yes/1
Sub-Franchising Contracts: Yes
Expand In Territory: No
Space Needs: 2,000 SF
SUPPORT & TRAINING:
Financial Assistance Provided: Yes (D)
Site Selection Assistance: Yes
Lease Negotiation Assistance: Yes
Co-Operative Advertising: No
Franchisee Assoc./Member: No
Size Of Corporate Staff: 5
On-Going Support: ,,C,d,E,f,G,H,

Training: 11 Days Salt Lake City, UT
SPECIFIC EXPANSION PLANS:
US: All United States
Canada: All Canada
Overseas: English & Spanish-Speaking
    Countries

‹‹ ››

Community Begins Here.®
CHILD CARE LEARNING CENTERS

KIDDIE ACADEMY INTERNATIONAL

3415 Box Hill Corporate Center Dr.
Abington, MD 21009
Tel: (800) 554-3343 + 260 (410) 515-0788
  + 260
Fax: (410) 569-2729
E-Mail: sales@kiddieacademy.com
Web Site: www.kiddieacademy.com
Mr. Jim Tisack, VP Franchising

We offer comprehensive training and support without additional cost. KIDDIE ACADEMY's step-by-step program assists with staff recruitment, training, accounting support, site selection, marketing, advertising and curriculum. A true turn-key opportunity that provides on-going support so you can focus on running a successful business.

BACKGROUND: IFA MEMBER
Established: 1981;   1st Franchised: 1992
Franchised Units: 98
Company-Owned Units: 5
Total Units: 103
Dist.:   US-103; CAN-0; O'seas-0
  North America: 24 States, 0 Provinces
  Density: 22 in NJ, 15 in MD, 6 in IL
Projected New Units (12 Months):   25
Qualifications: 4, 4, 2, 3, 2, 4
FINANCIAL/TERMS:
Cash Investment: $150K
Total Investment: $500K-3.7MM
Minimum Net Worth: $500K
Fees: Franchise - $60K
  Royalty - 7%;   Ad. - 2%
Earnings Claims Statement: Yes
Term of Contract (Years):   15/15
Avg. # Of Employees: 10-20 FT, 2 PT
Passive Ownership: Discouraged
Encourage Conversions: Yes
Area Develop. Agreements: Yes
Sub-Franchising Contracts: No

Expand In Territory: Yes
Space Needs: 6,500-12,000 SF
SUPPORT & TRAINING:
Financial Assistance Provided: Yes (D)
Site Selection Assistance: Yes
Lease Negotiation Assistance: Yes
Co-Operative Advertising: Yes
Franchisee Assoc./Member: Yes
Size Of Corporate Staff: 50
On-Going Support: a,B,C,D,E,,G,,I
Training: 2 Weeks Owner Train., Corp.
  HQ; 1 Week Director Train., Corp.
  HQ; 3-5 Day Staff Training
SPECIFIC EXPANSION PLANS:
US: All United States
Canada: No
Overseas: No

‹‹ ››

Education Through Dance
INTERNATIONAL
OFFERS FIVE PROGRAMS:
Kinderdance® (Ages3-8) Kindergym® (Ages 3-5) Kindertots® (Age 2)
Kindercombo® (Ages6-9)   Kindermotion® (Ages 3-12)
All 5 Programs - 1 Franchise!

KINDERDANCE INTERNATIONAL

1333 Gateway Dr., # 1003
Melbourne, FL 32901
Tel: (800) 554-2334 (321) 984-4448
Fax: (321) 984-4490
E-Mail: leads@kinderdance.com
Web Site: www.kinderdance.com
Mr. Richard Maltese, Vice President /
  Franchise Development

KINDERDANCE® is the original Developmental Dance, Motor Skills, Gymnastics, Music and Fitness Program, blended with academics, specifically designed for boys and girls age 2 to 12. KINDERDANCE® franchisees are trained to teach 5 developmentally unique "Education Through Dance and Motor Development" programs: KINDERDANCE®, KINDERGYM®, KINDERTOTS®), KINDERCOMBO™, and KINDERMOTION®, which are designed for boys and girls ages 2-12. Children learn the basics of ballet, tap, gymnastics, motor development

BACKGROUND: IFA MEMBER
Established: 1979;   1st Franchised: 1985
Franchised Units: 114
Company-Owned Units: 1
Total Units: 115
Dist.:   US-109; CAN-2; O'seas-4
  North America: 38 States, 1 Provinces
  Density: 8 in TX, 14 in FL, 12 in CA
Projected New Units (12 Months):   20

Qualifications: 2, 2, 1, 2, 2, 5
FINANCIAL/TERMS:
Cash Investment: $12-40K
Total Investment: $14.9-46.1K
Minimum Net Worth: NA
Fees: Franchise - $12-40K
  Royalty - 6-15%; Ad. - 3%
Earnings Claims Statement: Yes
Term of Contract (Years): 5/5
Avg. # Of Employees: 2 FT, 1-2+ PT
Passive Ownership: Discouraged
Encourage Conversions: Yes
Area Develop. Agreements: Yes/10
Sub-Franchising Contracts: No
Expand In Territory: Yes
Space Needs: NR
SUPPORT & TRAINING:
Financial Assistance Provided: Yes (D)
Site Selection Assistance: NA
Lease Negotiation Assistance: NA
Co-Operative Advertising: Yes
Franchisee Assoc./Member: Yes/Yes
Size Of Corporate Staff: 8
On-Going Support: A,B,C,D,E,F,G,H,I
Training: 6 Days Plus Onsite Melbourne,
  FL and On-Site
SPECIFIC EXPANSION PLANS:
US: All United States
Canada: All Canada
Overseas: Europe, Asia, New Zealand, S.
  America, Mexico, Aus

◄◄ ►►

LEARNING EXPERIENCE, THE
10 Sylvan Way, # 110
Parsippany, NJ 07054
Tel: (888) 865-7775 + 240 (973) 539-5392
+ 240
Fax: (973) 539-2422
E-Mail: jlh@tlecorp.com
Web Site: www.thelearningexperience.com
Ms. Jennifer Hansen, Director Special Pro-
  grams/Mktg.

We build and deliver a complete turn-key,
10,000-15,000 square foot freestanding
child development center. Low upfront
cost, lowest royalty payment in the industry, with a proven franchisor that has over
25 years of direct industry experience. We
want the best for your child, don't you?

BACKGROUND:
Established: 2001; 1st Franchised: 2003
Franchised Units: 60
Company-Owned Units: 35
Total Units: 95
Dist.: US-95; CAN-0; O'seas-0
  North America: 7 States, 0 Provinces
  Density: 6 in NY, 37 in NJ, 9 in MI
Projected New Units (12 Months): 15
Qualifications: 4, 5, 2, 3, 4, 4
FINANCIAL/TERMS:
Cash Investment: $125K
Total Investment: $350-650K
Minimum Net Worth: $400K
Fees: Franchise - $50K
  Royalty - 6%, 5%,4%; Ad. - 1.5%
Earnings Claims Statement: No
Term of Contract (Years): 15/10
Avg. # Of Employees: 10 FT, 12 PT
Passive Ownership: Allowed
Encourage Conversions: Yes
Area Develop. Agreements: Yes/25
Sub-Franchising Contracts: Yes
Expand In Territory: Yes
Space Needs: 10,000-15,000 SF
SUPPORT & TRAINING:
Financial Assistance Provided: Yes (D)
Site Selection Assistance: Yes
Lease Negotiation Assistance: Yes
Co-Operative Advertising: Yes
Franchisee Assoc./Member: Yes/Yes
Size Of Corporate Staff: 60
On-Going Support: A,,C,D,E,F,G,H,I
Training: 3-4 Months Franchise Unit;
  4 Weeks Operating Unit; 2 Weeks Par-
  sippany, NJ
SPECIFIC EXPANSION PLANS:
US: East Coast
Canada: All Canada
Overseas: All Countries

◄◄ ►►

LEARNING EXPRESS
29 Buena Vista St.
Devens, MA 01434
Tel: (888) 825-3619 (843) 352-4222
Fax: (843) 352-4223
E-Mail: wes@learningexpress.com
Web Site: www.learningexpress.com
Mr. Wes McAden, National Sales Direc-
  tor

Largest franchisor of specialty toy stores

in the United states, currently operating in
26 states. Average sales significantly out-
performs independent operators. Comprehensive training and turn-key services
by franchisor.

BACKGROUND: IFA MEMBER
Established: 1987; 1st Franchised: 1990
Franchised Units: 139
Company-Owned Units: 0
Total Units: 139
Dist.: US-139; CAN-0; O'seas-0
  North America: 26 States, 0 Provinces
  Density: 14 in TX, 13 in NJ, 12 in FL
Projected New Units (12 Months): 10-20
Qualifications: 4, 3, 2, 3, 1, 5
FINANCIAL/TERMS:
Cash Investment: $100K-125K
Total Investment: $207.5K-384.5K
Minimum Net Worth: $300K
Fees: Franchise - $35K
  Royalty - 5%; Ad. - NR
Earnings Claims Statement: Yes
Term of Contract (Years): 10/10
Avg. # Of Employees: 2 FT, 8-10 PT
Passive Ownership: Discouraged
Encourage Conversions: NA
Area Develop. Agreements: No
Sub-Franchising Contracts: No
Expand In Territory: Yes
Space Needs: 2,500-3,000 SF
SUPPORT & TRAINING:
Financial Assistance Provided: No
Site Selection Assistance: Yes
Lease Negotiation Assistance: Yes
Co-Operative Advertising: Yes
Franchisee Assoc./Member: Yes/Yes
Size Of Corporate Staff: 25
On-Going Support: ,,C,D,E,F,G,H,I
Training: 4 Weeks On-Site; 8 Days Home
  Office
SPECIFIC EXPANSION PLANS:
US: All United States
Canada: No
Overseas: NR

◄◄ ►►

LITTLE GYM, THE
7001 N. Scottsdale Rd., # 1050
Scottsdale, AZ 85253-3658
Tel: (888) 228-2878 (480) 948-2878
Fax: (480) 948-2765
E-Mail: campaign21482@mail.emaxima-

tion.com
Web Site: www.thelittlegym.com
Mr. J. Ruk Adams, SVP Franchise Development

THE LITTLE GYM child development centers are for children 4 months to 12 years, and offer a unique, integrated approach to child development. THE LITTLE GYM'S highly motivational and individualized programs are curriculum-based and provide physical, social and intellectual development. Classes develop motor skills, build self-esteem and encourage risk-taking through gymnastics, karate, dance, cheer and sports skills development.

BACKGROUND: IFA MEMBER
Established: 1976;   1st Franchised: 1992
Franchised Units: 267
Company-Owned Units: 0
Total Units: 267
Dist.:   US-267; CAN-13; O'seas-35
   North America: 35 States, 4 Provinces
   Density: 30 in TX, 23 in NJ, 26 in CA
Projected New Units (12 Months):   25
Qualifications: 5, 5, 2, 3, 5, 5
FINANCIAL/TERMS:
Cash Investment: $75K
Total Investment: $127.5-294K
Minimum Net Worth: $250K
Fees: Franchise - $69.5K
   Royalty - 8%;   Ad. - 1%
Earnings Claims Statement: Yes
Term of Contract (Years):   10/10/10/
Avg. # Of Employees: 2 FT, 2-3 PT
Passive Ownership: Discouraged
Encourage Conversions: Yes
Area Develop. Agreements: Yes
Sub-Franchising Contracts: No
Expand In Territory: Yes
Space Needs: 3,800-4,300 SF
SUPPORT & TRAINING:
Financial Assistance Provided: Yes (I)
Site Selection Assistance: Yes
Lease Negotiation Assistance: Yes
Co-Operative Advertising: Yes
Franchisee Assoc./Member: No
Size Of Corporate Staff: 35
On-Going Support: ,,C,D,,,G,H,I
Training: 1 Week Internship at Site To Be
   Determined; 3 Weeks Scottsdale, AZ;
SPECIFIC EXPANSION PLANS:
US: All United States
Canada: All Canada
Overseas: Asia, Aus., Europe, Mex., S.
   America, Middle East

<< >>

LITTLE SCIENTISTS

14 Selden St.
Woodbridge, CT 06525-2208
Tel: (800) 322-8386 (203) 732-3522
Fax: (203) 397-2165
E-Mail: dr_heidi@little-scientists.com
Web Site: www.little-scientists.com
Ms. Heidi Van Borkin, VP Franchise
   Development

LITTLE SCIENTISTS is a leader in hands-on science education for children ages 3 to 9. Nearly 200 hands-on lessons make up a innovative science curriculum. The curriculum has been developed by renowned scientists and educators. The market is growing at a remarkable rate. Owning a LITTLE SCIENTIST franchise is a highly profitable endeavor yielding great community benefits.

BACKGROUND:
Established: 1993;   1st Franchised: 1996
Franchised Units: 27
Company-Owned Units: 2
Total Units: 29
Dist.:   US-28; CAN-0; O'seas-1
   North America: 7 States, 0 Provinces
   Density: 2 in NJ, 5 in CT
Projected New Units (12 Months):   14
Qualifications: 3, 5, 4, 4, 5, 5
FINANCIAL/TERMS:
Cash Investment: $25K
Total Investment: $35K
Minimum Net Worth: $50K
Fees: Franchise - $20K
   Royalty - 6%/$250/Mo.;   Ad. - 1%
Earnings Claims Statement: No
Term of Contract (Years):   10/10
Avg. # Of Employees: 2 FT, 6-10 PT
Passive Ownership: Discouraged
Encourage Conversions: Yes
Area Develop. Agreements: Yes/1
Sub-Franchising Contracts: Yes
Expand In Territory: Yes
Space Needs: 500 SF
SUPPORT & TRAINING:
Financial Assistance Provided: Yes (D)
Site Selection Assistance: NA
Lease Negotiation Assistance: NA
Co-Operative Advertising: No
Franchisee Assoc./Member: Yes/Yes
Size Of Corporate Staff: 15
On-Going Support: A,B,C,D,,,G,H,I
Training: 1 Week HQ; 2 Times/Year HQ;
   2-4 Times/Year On Site
SPECIFIC EXPANSION PLANS:
US: All United States
Canada: All Canada
Overseas: All Countries Except Korea

<< >>

MAD SCIENCE GROUP, THE

8360 Bougainville, # 201
Montreal, PQ H4P 2G1 Canada
Tel: (800) 586-5231 + 104 (514) 344-4181
+ 104
Fax: (514) 344-6695
E-Mail: dominicl@madscience.org
Web Site: www.madscience.org
Mr. Dominic Lachapelle, Franchise Sales
   Manager

Your staff provides hands-on, interactive science shows for children ages 4-12. Turn kids onto science! Home based, profitable, rewarding.

BACKGROUND: IFA MEMBER
Established: 1985;   1st Franchised: 1995
Franchised Units: 205
Company-Owned Units: 0
Total Units: 205
Dist.:   US-165; CAN-10; O'seas-30
   North America: 30 States, 8 Provinces
   Density: 10 in NJ, 12 in CA, 4 in BC
Projected New Units (12 Months):   20
Qualifications: 2, 5, 3, 3, 5, 5
FINANCIAL/TERMS:
Cash Investment: $23.5K-50K
Total Investment: $30K-70K
Minimum Net Worth: $23.5K
Fees: Franchise - $23.5K
   Royalty - 8%;   Ad. - 0%
Earnings Claims Statement: Yes
Term of Contract (Years):   10/5
Avg. # Of Employees: 1 FT, 3-5 PT
Passive Ownership: Not Allowed
Encourage Conversions: NA
Area Develop. Agreements: No
Sub-Franchising Contracts: No
Expand In Territory: Yes
Space Needs: NR
SUPPORT & TRAINING:
Financial Assistance Provided: Yes (I)
Site Selection Assistance: NA
Lease Negotiation Assistance: NA
Co-Operative Advertising: No
Franchisee Assoc./Member: Yes/Yes
Size Of Corporate Staff: 30
On-Going Support: A,b,C,D,E,F,G,h,i
Training: 5 Days On-Site; 5 Days Corporate Office, Montreal, PQ

SPECIFIC EXPANSION PLANS:
US: All United States
Canada: All Canada
Overseas: All Countries

MY GYM CHILDREN'S FITNESS CENTER

15300 Ventura Blvd., # 414
Sherman Oaks, CA 91403
Tel: (800) 469-4967 (818) 907-0735
Fax: (818) 907-0735
E-Mail: franchises@my-gym.com
Web Site: www.my-gym.com
Mr. Michael Chalovich, Chief Operating Officer

MY GYM CHILDREN'S FITNESS CENTER's structured, age-appropriate weekly classes incorporates music, dance, relays, games, special rides, gymnastics, sports and other original activities. MY GYM kids have so much fun as they gain strength, balance, gross motor skills, agility, flexibility and social skills. Our programs' biggest benefit is the building of confidence and self esteem. We help design our state-of-the-art facility and assist in every aspect of getting you started.

BACKGROUND: IFA MEMBER
Established: 1983;   1st Franchised: 1994
Franchised Units: 170
Company-Owned Units: _0_
Total Units: 170
Dist.:   US-135; CAN-0; O'seas-3
  North America: 29 States, 0 Provinces
  Density: 8 in IL, 18 in FL, 24 in CA
Projected New Units (12 Months):   40
Qualifications: 2, 3, 3, 3, 4, 5
FINANCIAL/TERMS:
Cash Investment: $30K-60K
Total Investment: $100K-250K
Minimum Net Worth: NA
Fees: Franchise - $49.4K
  Royalty - 6%;   Ad. - 1%
Earnings Claims Statement: No
Term of Contract (Years):   12/12
Avg. # Of Employees: 3 FT, 4 PT
Passive Ownership: Discouraged
Encourage Conversions: NA
Area Develop. Agreements: Yes/1
Sub-Franchising Contracts: No
Expand In Territory: Yes
Space Needs: 2,400 SF
SUPPORT & TRAINING:
Financial Assistance Provided: Yes (D)
Site Selection Assistance: Yes
Lease Negotiation Assistance: Yes

Co-Operative Advertising: No
Franchisee Assoc./Member: No
Size Of Corporate Staff: 15
On-Going Support: ,B,C,D,E,F,,I
Training:19 Days Corporate Headquarters
  in Los Angeles, CA; Regional Pre-and
  Post-Training
SPECIFIC EXPANSION PLANS:
US: All United States
Canada: All Canada
Overseas: All Countries

ONCE UPON A CHILD

4200 Dahlberg Dr., # 100
Minneapolis, MN 55422-4837
Tel: (800) 453-7750 (763) 520-8490
Fax: (763) 520-8501
E-Mail: ouac-franchise-development@ouac.com
Web Site: www.ouac.com
  Franchise Development Dept.,

ONCE UPON A CHILD stores sell and buy used and new children's clothing, toys, furniture, equipment and accessories. Customers have the opportunity to sell their used children's wear to a ONCE UPON A CHILD store when outgrown and to purchase quality used items at prices lower than new merchandise.

BACKGROUND: IFA MEMBER
Established: 1984;   1st Franchised: 1993
Franchised Units: 230
Company-Owned Units: _0_
Total Units: 230
Dist.:   US-227; CAN-24; O'seas-0
  North America: 37 States, 5 Provinces
  Density: 18 in ON, 32 in OH, 16 in IN
Projected New Units (12 Months):   15
Qualifications: 5, 4, 2, 2, 1, 4
FINANCIAL/TERMS:
Cash Investment: $47.5K-75.5K
Total Investment: $158.5K-251.5K
Minimum Net Worth: $200K
Fees: Franchise - $20K
  Royalty - 5%;   Ad. -
Earnings Claims Statement: Yes
Term of Contract (Years):   10/10
Avg. # Of Employees: 3 FT, 2 PT
Passive Ownership: Not Allowed
Encourage Conversions: No
Area Develop. Agreements: No
Sub-Franchising Contracts: No

Expand In Territory: No
Space Needs: 2,500-3,000 SF
SUPPORT & TRAINING:
Financial Assistance Provided: No
Site Selection Assistance: Yes
Lease Negotiation Assistance: Yes
Co-Operative Advertising: No
Franchisee Assoc./Member: No
Size Of Corporate Staff: 97
On-Going Support: ,,C,D,E,F,G,H,I
Training: 5 Days Minneapolis, MN;
  4 Days Minneapolis, MN
SPECIFIC EXPANSION PLANS:
US: All United States
Canada: All Canada
Overseas: NR

PRIMROSE SCHOOLS FRANCHISING COMPANY

3660 Cedarcrest Rd.
Atworth, GA 30101
Tel: (800) 774-6767 (770) 529-4100
Fax: (770) 529-1551
E-Mail: kmusso@primroseschools.com
Web Site: www.primroseschools.com
Ms. Kim Musso, Dir. Franchise Recruitment

Educational child-care franchise, offering a traditional pre-school curriculum and programs while also providing quality childcare services. Site selection assistance, extensive training, operations manuals, building plans, marketing plans and on-going support.

BACKGROUND: IFA MEMBER
Established: 1982;   1st Franchised: 1989
Franchised Units: 200
Company-Owned Units: 1
Total Units: 201
Dist.:   US-201; CAN-0; O'seas-0
  North America: 15 States, 0 Provinces
  Density: 37 in TX, 10 in NC, 37 in GA
Projected New Units (12 Months):   15
Qualifications: 5, 5, 1, 4, 5, 5
FINANCIAL/TERMS:
Cash Investment: $350-500K
Total Investment: $2.8-4.2MM
Minimum Net Worth: $500K
Fees: Franchise - $70K

Royalty - 7%; Ad. - 1%
Earnings Claims Statement: Yes
Term of Contract (Years): 11/10/10/
Avg. # Of Employees: 25 FT, 5 PT
Passive Ownership: Not Allowed
Encourage Conversions: NA
Area Develop. Agreements: No
Sub-Franchising Contracts: No
Expand In Territory: No
Space Needs: 8,500 SF

SUPPORT & TRAINING:
Financial Assistance Provided: Yes (D)
Site Selection Assistance: Yes
Lease Negotiation Assistance: Yes
Co-Operative Advertising: No
Franchisee Assoc./Member: Yes/Yes
Size Of Corporate Staff: 35
On-Going Support: A,,C,D,E,f,G,h,I
Training: 1 Week Home Office; 1 Week
    Existing School; 1 Week Franchisee's
    New School

SPECIFIC EXPANSION PLANS:
US: SW, SE, TX, OH, CO
Canada: No
Overseas: NR

⊰⊰ ⊱⊱

RAINBOW STATION
4551 Cox Rd., # 310
Glen Allen, VA 23060
Tel: (888) 716-1717 (804) 747-5900
Fax: (804) 747-8016
E-Mail: info@rainbowstation.org
Web Site: www.rainbowstation.org
Mr. R. Earl Johnson, Vice President of
Sales

High-end, accredited pre-school and after-school recreation programs with registered nurse on site in sick child care facility (Get Well Place). Programs are accredited by National Association of Early Childhood Programs and based in 18,000 SF of state-of-the-art structures with Standards of Learning based curriculum - fully developed in-house. The pre-school will accommodate 158 children from 0 to pre-school, while the after-school program will accommodate 175 children up to 14 years of age.

BACKGROUND: IFA MEMBER
Established: 1989; 1st Franchised: 1999
Franchised Units: 16
Company-Owned Units: 3
Total Units: 19
Dist.: US-19; CAN-0; O'seas-0
  North America: 2 States, 0 Provinces
  Density: 18 in VA, 10 in TX, 6 in NC

Projected New Units (12 Months): 14
Qualifications: 5, 4, 3, 4, 4, 5
FINANCIAL/TERMS:
Cash Investment: $400K-1MM
Total Investment: $5MM-6.5MM
Minimum Net Worth: $750K
Fees: Franchise - $50K
  Royalty - 6%; Ad. - 1%
Earnings Claims Statement: No
Term of Contract (Years): 10/5
Avg. # Of Employees: 40 FT, 35 PT
Passive Ownership: Not Allowed
Encourage Conversions: No
Area Develop. Agreements: No
Sub-Franchising Contracts: No
Expand In Territory: Yes
Space Needs: 20,000 SF

SUPPORT & TRAINING:
Financial Assistance Provided: Yes (I)
Site Selection Assistance: Yes
Lease Negotiation Assistance: Yes
Co-Operative Advertising: No
Franchisee Assoc./Member: No
Size Of Corporate Staff: 7
On-Going Support: ,B,C,D,E,,G,,I
Training: 2 Weeks Headquarters;
    Approximately 2 Weeks On-Site

SPECIFIC EXPANSION PLANS:
US: All United States
Canada: No
Overseas: NR

⊰⊰ ⊱⊱

STRETCH-N-GROW INTERNATIONAL
14399 87th Ave.
Seminole, FL 33776-1927
Tel: (800) 348-0166 (727) 596-7614
Fax:
E-Mail: info@stretch-n-grow.com
Web Site: www.stretch-n-grow.com
Ms. Karyn Burnier, Franchise Sales

STRETCH-N-GROW is a comprehensive mobile fitness program for children ages 2 1/2 to 8. It is taught primarily in child care facilities. We provide a corporate marketing system and a curriculum package which covers health-related issues and exercise that is age-appropriate, but adaptable to the age ranges above. The investment and time demands are minimal, the rewards, both financial and personal, immense.

BACKGROUND:
Established: 1992; 1st Franchised: 1994
Franchised Units: 173
Company-Owned Units: 0
Total Units: 173

Dist.: US-172; CAN-1; O'seas-0
  North America: 24 States, 1 Provinces
  Density: 10 in TX, 5 in PA, 5 in NY
Projected New Units (12 Months): 12
Qualifications: 3, 3, 4, 4, NR, 5
FINANCIAL/TERMS:
Cash Investment: $7.6-12.6K
Total Investment: $23.6K
Minimum Net Worth: NA
Fees: Franchise - $7.6-12.6K
  Royalty - $100/Mo.; Ad. - $100/Yr.
Earnings Claims Statement: No
Term of Contract (Years): 97/
Avg. # Of Employees: 1 FT, 1-2 PT
Passive Ownership: Discouraged
Encourage Conversions: NA
Area Develop. Agreements: No
Sub-Franchising Contracts: No
Expand In Territory: No
Space Needs: NA

SUPPORT & TRAINING:
Financial Assistance Provided: No
Site Selection Assistance: NA
Lease Negotiation Assistance: NA
Co-Operative Advertising: No
Franchisee Assoc./Member: No
Size Of Corporate Staff: 2
On-Going Support: ,b,,D,,,G,h,I
Training: 3 Days Dallas, TX
SPECIFIC EXPANSION PLANS:
US: All United States
Canada: No
Overseas: Australia

⊰⊰ ⊱⊱

THINKERTOTS
22214 Union Tpke.
Bayside, NY 11364
Tel: (877) TOTS-444 (718) 740-1616
Fax: NR
E-Mail: thinkertots@thinkertots.com
Web Site: www.thinkertots.com
Ms. Lori Barnett, Director of Franchising

Thinkertots provides developmentally enriching programs for children from birth to 5 years. Our focus on the under four market fills the availability gap in educational programs for small children. Thinkertots classes are structured much like pre-school, but seem like playtime to the children, who look forward to these fun sessions. Thinkertots is a franchise that gives you the opportunity to make a difference, while owning your own business.

BACKGROUND:

Established: 1998;	1st Franchised: 2005
Franchised Units:	4
Company-Owned Units:	1
Total Units:	5
Dist.:	US-4; CAN-0; O'seas-0
North America:	2 States, 0 Provinces
Density:	3 in NY
Projected New Units (12 Months):	10
Qualifications:	3, 2, 3, 4, 5, 5

FINANCIAL/TERMS:

Cash Investment:	$15-25K
Total Investment:	$42-163K
Minimum Net Worth:	NR
Fees: Franchise -	$15-25K
Royalty - 6%;	Ad. - 2%
Earnings Claims Statement:	No
Term of Contract (Years):	5/5
Avg. # Of Employees:	2 FT, 0 PT
Passive Ownership:	Not Allowed
Encourage Conversions:	Yes
Area Develop. Agreements:	No
Sub-Franchising Contracts:	No
Expand In Territory:	No
Space Needs:	900 SF

SUPPORT & TRAINING:

Financial Assistance Provided:	No
Site Selection Assistance:	Yes
Lease Negotiation Assistance:	Yes
Co-Operative Advertising:	Yes
Franchisee Assoc./Member:	No
Size Of Corporate Staff:	2
On-Going Support:	A,B,C,D,E,,,H,I
Training:	2 Weeks Headquarters

SPECIFIC EXPANSION PLANS:

US: NY, NJ, CT, MA, NH, VT, PA, GA, TN, AL, MS, FL, OH

Canada:	No
Overseas:	NR

◄◄ ►►

Young Rembrandts

YOUNG REMBRANDTS

23 N. Union St.
Elgin, IL 60123
Tel: (866) 300-6010 (847) 742-6966
Fax: (847) 742-7197
E-Mail: kim@youngrembrandts.com
Web Site: www.youngrembrandts.com
Ms. Kim Swanson, Director Franchise Development

YOUNG REMBRANDTS, the premier instructional drawing program, ensures every child's creative success. All children are enthusiastic, confident artists when they are taught to draw using YOUNG REMBRANDTS' innovative step-by-step method. Our instructors guide students using a well-tested curriculum developed by artists and educators to maximize each child's creative potential. YOUNG REMBRANDTS classes are offered anywhere there is a desire for children to enjoy a positive artistic experience.

BACKGROUND: IFA MEMBER

Established: 1988;	1st Franchised: 2001
Franchised Units:	59
Company-Owned Units:	3
Total Units:	62
Dist.:	US-62; CAN-0; O'seas-0
North America:	24 States, 0 Provinces
Density:	7 in IL, 10 in CA
Projected New Units (12 Months):	NR
Qualifications:	NR

FINANCIAL/TERMS:

Cash Investment:	$31.5K
Total Investment:	$39.9-49.6K
Minimum Net Worth:	$100K
Fees: Franchise -	$31.5K
Royalty - 10%/8%;	Ad. -
Earnings Claims Statement:	No
Term of Contract (Years):	10/
Avg. # Of Employees:	FT, 0 PT
Passive Ownership:	Not Allowed
Encourage Conversions:	NA
Area Develop. Agreements:	Yes/1
Sub-Franchising Contracts:	No
Expand In Territory:	Yes
Space Needs:	NA

SUPPORT & TRAINING:

Financial Assistance Provided:	No
Site Selection Assistance:	NA
Lease Negotiation Assistance:	NA
Co-Operative Advertising:	No
Franchisee Assoc./Member:	Yes/Yes
Size Of Corporate Staff:	15
On-Going Support:	,B,C,,,,,H,
Training:	5 Days Elgin, IL

SPECIFIC EXPANSION PLANS:

US:	All United States Where Registered
Canada:	Yes
Overseas:	NR

◄◄ ►►

For a full explanation
of the data provided
in the Franchisor
Profiles, please refer to
*Chapter 2, "How to Use
the Data."*

FIVE LARGEST PARTICIPANTS IN SURVEY

Company	# Fran- chised Units	# Co- Owned Units	# Total Units	Franchise Fee	On-Going Royalty	Total Investment
1. EmbroidMe	371	0	371	$42.5K	6%	$185K
2. Plato's Closet	220	0	220	$20K	4%	$161.1-316.8K
3. Furla	11	17	28	$25K	2%	$284-480K
4. Educational Outfitters	23	0	23	$29.5K	5%	$200-250K
5. Shoes-n-Feet	8	1	9	$25K	5%	$160-230K

All of the data provided are proprietary and should not be quoted without acknowledging *Bond's Franchise Guide*.

EDUCATIONAL OUTFITTERS
8002 E. Brainerd Rd.
Chattanooga, TN 37421
Tel: (877) 814-1222 (423) 499-5052
Fax: (423) 894-9222
E-Mail: info@educationaloutfitters.com
Web Site: www.educationaloutfitters.com
Mr. Dan Sladek, Franchise Development

EDUCATIONAL OUTFITTERS is a retail franchise, offering school uniforms, embroidery, corporate wear, screenprinting and promotional products through our retail locations. If it needs a logo, we can do it!

BACKGROUND: IFA MEMBER
Established: 1998;   1st Franchised: 2001
Franchised Units: 23
Company-Owned Units: 0
Total Units: 23
Dist.:   US-23; CAN-0; O'seas-0
  North America: 10 States, 0 Provinces
  Density: 3 in TN, 3 in NC, 2 in FL
Projected New Units (12 Months):   20
Qualifications: 5, 5, 1, 4, 3, 5
FINANCIAL/TERMS:
Cash Investment: $100K-175K
Total Investment: $200K-250K

Minimum Net Worth: $400K
Fees: Franchise - $29.5K
  Royalty - 5%;   Ad. - 3%
Earnings Claims Statement: No
Term of Contract (Years):   10/5
Avg. # Of Employees: 3 FT, 5 PT
Passive Ownership: Not Allowed
Encourage Conversions: No
Area Develop. Agreements: No
Sub-Franchising Contracts: No
Expand In Territory: Yes
Space Needs: 3,000 SF
SUPPORT & TRAINING:
Financial Assistance Provided: No
Site Selection Assistance: Yes
Lease Negotiation Assistance: Yes
Co-Operative Advertising: No
Franchisee Assoc./Member: No

Size Of Corporate Staff: 5
On-Going Support: ,B,C,D,E,F,G,h,i
Training: 6 Days Chattanooga, TN;
   6 Days Franchise Location
SPECIFIC EXPANSION PLANS:
US: All United States
Canada: No
Overseas: NR

≪ ≫

EMBROIDME

2121 Vista Pkwy.
West Palm Beach, FL 33411
Tel: (800) 727-6720 (561) 640-5570
Fax: (561) 640-5580
E-Mail: Franchise@embroidme.com
Web Site: www.embroidme.com
Mr. Michael Prince, Director Franchise
   Development

The need for businesses to get noticed through brand recognition and advertising has rapidly increased due to the steady growth of competitive services. As a result, this need to get noticed has propelled the embroidery industry to a $20 billion market. EmbroidMe has been at the forefront of this growth as one of the world's first embroidery and promotional products franchises; successfully franchising the full-service embroidery, screen printing, promotional products and personalized gifts concept for over six years. We have used our experience to develop a business model that have led hundreds of EmbroidMe franchisees to success and helped us grow to become the world's largest embroidery franchise. As part of our family you get the full support and services of the EmbroidMe team - a group that is committed to providing you with the training, consulting, equipment and resources you need to make your EmbroidMe store successful.

BACKGROUND: IFA MEMBER
Established: 2000; 1st Franchised: 2001
Franchised Units: 371
Company-Owned Units: 0
Total Units: 371
Dist.: US-317; CAN-20; O'seas-34
   North America: 37 States, 6 Provinces
   Density: 30 in TX, 22 in FL, 32 in CA
Projected New Units (12 Months): 95
Qualifications: 3, 3, 2, 2, 1, 4

FINANCIAL/TERMS:
Cash Investment: $48K
Total Investment: $185K
Minimum Net Worth: $50K
Fees: Franchise - $42.5K
  Royalty - 6%; Ad. - 1%
Earnings Claims Statement: No
Term of Contract (Years): 35/35
Avg. # Of Employees: 3 FT, 0 PT
Passive Ownership: Discouraged
Encourage Conversions: Yes
Area Develop. Agreements: Yes
Sub-Franchising Contracts: No
Expand In Territory: Yes
Space Needs: 1,300-1,500 SF
SUPPORT & TRAINING:
Financial Assistance Provided: Yes (I)
Site Selection Assistance: Yes
Lease Negotiation Assistance: Yes
Co-Operative Advertising: Yes
Franchisee Assoc./Member: No
Size Of Corporate Staff: 180
On-Going Support: ,,C,D,E,F,G,H,I
Training: 2 Weeks (1 Wk. Technical, 1
   Week Mktng.) Franchisee's Location; 2
   Weeks West Palm Beach, FL
SPECIFIC EXPANSION PLANS:
US: All United States
Canada: All Canada
Overseas: All Countries

≪ ≫

FURLA

389 Fifth Ave., # 700
New York, NY 10016
Tel: (212) 213-1177 + 15
Fax: (212) 685-5910
E-Mail: franchise@furlausa.com
Web Site: www.furlausa.com
Mr. TJ Jones, Manager of Franchising

FURLA designs and sells women's handbags, shoes, belts, small leather goods and related accessories. Our brand is known worldwide through 200+ boutiques around the globe. Our exclusively designed and manufactured products are primarily made in Italy and are priced in better to designer marketplace. Our shops have a distinctive design and are located in upscale retail trade areas.

BACKGROUND: IFA MEMBER
Established: 1998; 1st Franchised: 2001
Franchised Units: 11
Company-Owned Units: 17
Total Units: 28
Dist.: US-29; CAN-1; O'seas-9
   North America: 5 States, 1 Provinces

Density: 3 in NY, 5 in FL, 3 in CA
Projected New Units (12 Months): 10
Qualifications: 3, 4, 2, 3, 5, 5
FINANCIAL/TERMS:
Cash Investment: $150-250K
Total Investment: $284-480K
Minimum Net Worth: $$400K
Fees: Franchise - $25K
  Royalty - 2%; Ad. - 1%
Earnings Claims Statement: No
Term of Contract (Years): 7-10/7-10
Avg. # Of Employees: 3 FT, 3 PT
Passive Ownership: Not Allowed
Encourage Conversions: No
Area Develop. Agreements: No
Sub-Franchising Contracts: No
Expand In Territory: Yes
Space Needs: 900-1,200 SF
SUPPORT & TRAINING:
Financial Assistance Provided: Yes (I)
Site Selection Assistance: Yes
Lease Negotiation Assistance: Yes
Co-Operative Advertising: No
Franchisee Assoc./Member: No
Size Of Corporate Staff: 13
On-Going Support: ,B,C,D,E,,,h,I
Training: 1 Week New York Offices and
   Stores; On-going Store Visits
SPECIFIC EXPANSION PLANS:
US: All United States
Canada: All Canada
Overseas: South America, Caribbean
   Basin, Central America.

≪ ≫

GENT'S FORMAL WEAR

400 E. Wright St.
Pensacola, FL 32501
Tel: (866) 889-GENTS (850) 434-3272
Fax: (850) 439-2177
E-Mail: gentsformalwear@aol.com
Web Site: www.gentsformalwear.com
Mr. Richard Crenshaw, President

Everybody knows that weddings are big business. Love and marriages are relatively resistant to recession. GENTS is a highly attractive and affordable franchise for the individual or couple seeking to enter the business world.

BACKGROUND:
Established: 1980; 1st Franchised: 1991
Franchised Units: 6
Company-Owned Units: 1
Total Units: 7
Dist.: US-7; CAN-0; O'seas-0
   North America: 2 States, 0 Provinces
   Density: 1 in GA, 1 in TN, 1 in FL

Projected New Units (12 Months):   2
Qualifications: 5, 4, 3, 3, 3, 4
FINANCIAL/TERMS:
Cash Investment: $75K
Total Investment: $50-75K
Minimum Net Worth: $100K
Fees: Franchise - $15K
  Royalty - 6%;   Ad. - 0%
Earnings Claims Statement: Yes
Term of Contract (Years):   5/5
Avg. # Of Employees: 1 FT, 2 PT
Passive Ownership: Discouraged
Encourage Conversions: Yes
Area Develop. Agreements: Yes/1
Sub-Franchising Contracts: Yes
Expand In Territory: Yes
Space Needs: 1,000 SF
SUPPORT & TRAINING:
Financial Assistance Provided: No
Site Selection Assistance: Yes
Lease Negotiation Assistance: Yes
Co-Operative Advertising: No
Franchisee Assoc./Member: Yes/Yes
Size Of Corporate Staff: 2
On-Going Support: A,B,C,d,E,F,,h,
Training: 2 Weeks Home Office; 1 Week
  Franchise Location
SPECIFIC EXPANSION PLANS:
US: Southeast
Canada: No
Overseas: NR

◄◄ ►►

PLATO'S CLOSET
4200 Dahlberg Dr., # 100
Minneapolis, MN 55422-4837
Tel: (800) 269-4081 (763) 520-8581
Fax: (763) 520-8501
E-Mail: pc-franchise-
development@platoscloset.com
Web Site: www.platoscloset.com
, Franchise Development

PLATO'S CLOSET stores buy and sell
gently used, brand-name apparel and
accessories for teens and young adults.
Customers have the opportunity to sell
their used items to a PLATO'S CLOSET
store when outgrown and to purchase
quality used clothing and accessories at
prices lower than new merchandise.

BACKGROUND: IFA MEMBER
Established: 1998;   1st Franchised: 1999
Franchised Units: 220

Company-Owned Units: 0
Total Units: 220
Dist.:   US-220; CAN-0; O'seas-0
  North America: 1 States, 0 Provinces
  Density: 23 in OH, 15 in IN, 21 in FL
Projected New Units (12 Months):   30
Qualifications: 5, 4, 2, 2, 1, 4
FINANCIAL/TERMS:
Cash Investment: $48.3-95K
Total Investment: $161.1-316.8K
Minimum Net Worth: $200K
Fees: Franchise - $20K
  Royalty - 4%;   Ad. - $500/Yr.
Earnings Claims Statement: Yes
Term of Contract (Years):   10/10
Avg. # Of Employees: 3 FT, 2 PT
Passive Ownership: Not Allowed
Encourage Conversions: No
Area Develop. Agreements: No
Sub-Franchising Contracts: No
Expand In Territory: No
Space Needs: 2,500-3,000 SF
SUPPORT & TRAINING:
Financial Assistance Provided: No
Site Selection Assistance: Yes
Lease Negotiation Assistance: Yes
Co-Operative Advertising: No
Franchisee Assoc./Member: No
Size Of Corporate Staff: 97
On-Going Support: ,,C,D,E,F,G,H,I
Training: 5 Days Minneapolis, MN; 4
  Days Minneapolis, MN
SPECIFIC EXPANSION PLANS:
US: All United States
Canada: All Canada
Overseas: NR

◄◄ ►►

SHOES-N-FEET
15015 Main St., # 211
Bellevue, WA 98007
Tel: (888) 994-FEET (206) 683-7584
Fax: (425) 562-5005
E-Mail: jb.smith@shoesnfeet.com
Web Site: www.shoesnfeet.com
Ms. JB Smith, Director of Marketing

SHOES-n-FEET takes a long-term
approach and blends strong old-world
tradition with new-world, cutting-edge
innovation in its one-of-a-kind educa-
tion-based foot healthy stores. Servicing
the baby-bloomer generation, SHOES-n-
FEET is uniquely positioned to capitalize
on the accelerating trend towards staying
fit, keeping active and remaining fashion-
able. We provide a professional shoe-fit-
ting solution to each customer. Success-
driven, goal-oriented franshisees wanting

to make a positive difference.

BACKGROUND:
Established: 1998;   1st Franchised: 2003
Franchised Units: 8
Company-Owned Units: 1
Total Units: 9
Dist.:   US-9; CAN-0; O'seas-0
  North America: 3 States, 0 Provinces
  Density: 6 in WA, 1 in NV, 2 in CA
Projected New Units (12 Months):   12
Qualifications: 5, 5, 1, 4, 1, 5
FINANCIAL/TERMS:
Cash Investment: $25K
Total Investment: $160-230K
Minimum Net Worth: $250K
Fees: Franchise - $25K
  Royalty - 5%;   Ad. - 2%
Earnings Claims Statement: No
Term of Contract (Years):   10/10
Avg. # Of Employees: 2-4 FT, 0 PT
Passive Ownership: Discouraged
Encourage Conversions: No
Area Develop. Agreements: Yes
Sub-Franchising Contracts: No
Expand In Territory: Yes
Space Needs: 1,800 SF
SUPPORT & TRAINING:
Financial Assistance Provided: No
Site Selection Assistance: Yes
Lease Negotiation Assistance: Yes
Co-Operative Advertising: Yes
Franchisee Assoc./Member: No
Size Of Corporate Staff: 9
On-Going Support: A,,C,D,E,F,g,,I
Training: Before, At, and After Opening
  Franchise Location; 4 Weeks SHOES-
  n-FEET University;
SPECIFIC EXPANSION PLANS:
US: Western Region and Midwest Region
Canada: Vancouver, BC
Overseas: NR

◄◄ ►►

FIVE LARGEST PARTICIPANTS IN SURVEY						
Company	# Fran-chised Units	# Co-Owned Units	# Total Units	Franchise Fee	On-Going Royalty	Total Investment
1. WSI	1,743	20	1763	$49.7K	10%	$49.7K
2. Computer TroubleShooters	495	0	495	$19.5K	$330/Mo.	$24-34K
3. Quik Internet	240	0	240	$35K	10%	$60-65K
4. Geeks On Call	234	0	234	$25K	11%	$60-100K
5. Rapid Refill Ink International Corp	110	0	110	$30K	6%	$95-199K

All of the data provided are proprietary and should not be quoted without acknowledging *Bond's Franchise Guide.*

COMPUTER RENAISSANCE

3440 W. Cheyenne Ave, # 100
Winter Haven, FL 33880-3419
Tel: (800) 656-3115 (863) 669-1155 + 225
Fax: (800) 869-2780
E-Mail: franchising@compren.com
Web Site: www.compren.com
Mr. Eric Vetter, Director Franchise Support

COMPUTER RENAISSANCE, a full-service retail store specializing in quality used, refurbished and new computer hardware, software and related accessories. Our stores also provide custom-built computers, system upgrades, networking, consulting and superior technical service. With constant upgrades to computers in both the hardware and software fields, you can ensure your spot in a highly innovative industry by becoming part of a continuing market demand.

BACKGROUND: IFA MEMBER
Established: 1988; 1st Franchised: 1993
Franchised Units: 78
Company-Owned Units: 1
Total Units: 79
Dist.: US-79; CAN-0; O'seas-0
  North America: 34 States, 0 Provinces
  Density: 8 in MN, 7 in IN, 11 in FL
Projected New Units (12 Months): 15
Qualifications: 4, 5, 2, 3, 4, 5
FINANCIAL/TERMS:
Cash Investment: $40K-60K
Total Investment: $193K-284K
Minimum Net Worth: $250K
Fees: Franchise - $27.5K
  Royalty - 6%; Ad. - .5%

Earnings Claims Statement: Yes
Term of Contract (Years): 10/10
Avg. # Of Employees: 3 FT, 2 PT
Passive Ownership: Discouraged
Encourage Conversions: Yes
Area Develop. Agreements: No
Sub-Franchising Contracts: No
Expand In Territory: Yes
Space Needs: 1,600 SF
SUPPORT & TRAINING:
Financial Assistance Provided: Yes (D)
Site Selection Assistance: Yes
Lease Negotiation Assistance: Yes
Co-Operative Advertising: No
Franchisee Assoc./Member: Yes/Yes
Size Of Corporate Staff: 15
On-Going Support: ,,C,D,E,F,G,h,I
Training: 2 Weeks Florida
SPECIFIC EXPANSION PLANS:

US: All United States
Canada: No
Overseas: NR

⋖⋖ ⋗⋗

**COMPUTER
TROUBLESHOOTERS**
755 Commerce Dr., # 412
Decatur, GA 30030
Tel: (877) 704-1702 (770) 454-6382
Fax: (770) 234-6162
E-Mail: info@comptroub.com
Web Site: www.comptroub.com
Mr. Chip Reaves, National Director

COMPUTER TROUBLESHOOTERS is the world's largest and best computer service franchise. Over 420 locations in 20 countries provide personal, friendly on-site services to business and residential customers. See www.comptroub.com

BACKGROUND:
Established: 1997; 1st Franchised: 1997
Franchised Units: 495
Company-Owned Units: 0
Total Units: 495
Dist.: US-219; CAN-12; O'seas-244
  North America: 33 States, 3 Provinces
  Density: 16 in TX, 19 in PA, 16 in CA
Projected New Units (12 Months): 30
Qualifications: 2, 3, 4, 3, 3, 3
FINANCIAL/TERMS:
Cash Investment: $24-34K
Total Investment: $24-34K
Minimum Net Worth: $20K
Fees: Franchise - $19.5K
  Royalty - $330/Mo.; Ad. - $70/Mo.
Earnings Claims Statement: No
Term of Contract (Years): 10/10
Avg. # Of Employees: 1 FT, 0 PT
Passive Ownership: Discouraged
Encourage Conversions: Yes
Area Develop. Agreements: Yes/1
Sub-Franchising Contracts: Yes
Expand In Territory: Yes
Space Needs: NA
SUPPORT & TRAINING:
Financial Assistance Provided: Yes (I)
Site Selection Assistance: Yes
Lease Negotiation Assistance: NA
Co-Operative Advertising: No
Franchisee Assoc./Member: No
Size Of Corporate Staff: 5

On-Going Support: ,,d,,,G,h,i
Training: 2-3 Days Atlanta
SPECIFIC EXPANSION PLANS:
US: All United States
Canada: All Canada
Overseas: All Countries

⋖⋖ ⋗⋗

**EXPETEC TECHNOLOGY
SERVICES**
12 Second Ave. S. W.
Aberdeen, SD 57402-0487
Tel: (888) 297-2292 (605) 225-4122
Fax: (605) 225-5176
E-Mail: csommers@expetec.com
Web Site: www.expetec.com
Ms. Carol Sommers, Director of Franchise
  Development

Every business needs IT Assistance. EXPETEC franchisees target all businesses to provide IT services such as Network Security, Business Continuity, Web Services, Network Administration, and Business Solution Bundles.

BACKGROUND: IFA MEMBER
Established: 1992; 1st Franchised 1996
Franchised Units: 30
Company-Owned Units: 1
Total Units: 31
Dist.: US-31; CAN-1; O'seas-0
  North America: 23 States, 0 Provinces
  Density: SD
Projected New Units (12 Months): 70
Qualifications: NR
FINANCIAL/TERMS:
Cash Investment: $100K
Total Investment: $100K
Minimum Net Worth: $100K
Fees: Franchise - $35K
  Royalty - 15%; Ad. - 0
Earnings Claims Statement: No
Term of Contract (Years): 10/
Avg. # Of Employees: 1 FT, 0 PT
Passive Ownership: Discouraged
Encourage Conversions: No
Area Develop. Agreements: No
Sub-Franchising Contracts: No
Expand In Territory: Yes
Space Needs: NR
SUPPORT & TRAINING:
Financial Assistance Provided: No
Site Selection Assistance: No
Lease Negotiation Assistance: No

Co-Operative Advertising: No
Franchisee Assoc./Member: Yes/Yes
Size Of Corporate Staff: 16
On-Going Support: A,,C,D,,,G,H,I
Training: 1-2 Weeks Aberdeen, SD
SPECIFIC EXPANSION PLANS:
US: All United States
Canada: Yes
Overseas: NR

⋖⋖ ⋗⋗

GEEKS ON CALL
814 Kempsville Rd., #106
Norfolk, VA 23502
Tel: (888) 667-4577 + 320 (757) 466-3558
Fax: (866) 516-3513
E-Mail: Michelle.Joyner@geeksoncall.com
Web Site: www.geeksoncallfranchise.com
Ms. Michelle Joyner, Exec. Asst. of Franchise Devel.

On-site computer support includes troubleshooting, virus/spyware removal, repairs, upgrades, wired/wireless networking, one-on-one training and custom-built PCs. Franchisee need only business experience, however, only certified technicians may perform computer services. Mobile business concept. Low overhead, coupled with central dispatching, advertising, marketing campaigns and proven support make GEEKS ON CALL the logical choice. Single and multi-units available. Highly ranked in Entrepreneur Magazine.

BACKGROUND: IFA MEMBER
Established: 1999; 1st Franchised: 2001
Franchised Units: 234
Company-Owned Units: 0
Total Units: 234
Dist.: US-234; CAN-0; O'seas-0
  North America: 0 States, 0 Provinces
  Density: VA, TX, CA
Projected New Units (12 Months): 100
Qualifications: 4, 4, 1, 4, 4, 5
FINANCIAL/TERMS:
Cash Investment: $60K
Total Investment: $60-100K
Minimum Net Worth: $250K
Fees: Franchise - $25K
  Royalty - 11%; Ad. - $150/Wk.
Earnings Claims Statement: No

129

Term of Contract (Years):	10/10
Avg. # Of Employees:	1 FT, 0 PT
Passive Ownership:	Not Allowed
Encourage Conversions:	NA
Area Develop. Agreements:	Yes/10
Sub-Franchising Contracts:	No
Expand In Territory:	No
Space Needs:	NA

SUPPORT & TRAINING:

Financial Assistance Provided:	Yes (I)
Site Selection Assistance:	NA
Lease Negotiation Assistance:	NA
Co-Operative Advertising:	No
Franchisee Assoc./Member:	No
Size Of Corporate Staff:	50
On-Going Support:	,,C,D,,,G,H,I
Training: As needed Franchise Territory; 5 Days Norfolk, VA	

SPECIFIC EXPANSION PLANS:

US:	All United States
Canada:	No
Overseas:	NR

⋖⋖ ⋗⋗

QUIK INTERNET

129 Cbrillo St., # 100
Costa Mesa, CA 92627-3053
Tel: (888) 784-5266 (949) 548-2171
Fax: (949) 548-0569
E-Mail: jack@quik.com
Web Site: www.quik.com
Mr. Jack Reynolds, President

QUIK INTERNET is the world's first and largest Internet services franchise, with over 200 franchises worldwide. Provide highly demanded Internet services in your local community, including Internet access, Web design, on-line marketing and more. Prime territories, low fees - apply today!

BACKGROUND: IFA MEMBER

Established: 1996; 1st Franchised: 1996	
Franchised Units:	240
Company-Owned Units:	0
Total Units:	240
Dist.:	US-80; CAN-4; O'seas-156
North America:	States, Provinces
Density:	CA, FL, TX
Projected New Units (12 Months):	50
Qualifications:	5, 5, 1, 4, 4, 4

FINANCIAL/TERMS:

Cash Investment:	$60-65K
Total Investment:	$60-65K
Minimum Net Worth:	NA
Fees: Franchise -	$35K
Royalty - 10%;	Ad. - 5%
Earnings Claims Statement:	No

Term of Contract (Years):	10/10
Avg. # Of Employees:	1 FT, 0 PT
Passive Ownership:	Not Allowed
Encourage Conversions:	NA
Area Develop. Agreements:	No
Sub-Franchising Contracts:	No
Expand In Territory:	No
Space Needs:	NA

SUPPORT & TRAINING:

Financial Assistance Provided:	No
Site Selection Assistance:	NA
Lease Negotiation Assistance:	NA
Co-Operative Advertising:	No
Franchisee Assoc./Member:	No
Size Of Corporate Staff:	30
On-Going Support:	A,B,C,D,,F,,,
Training:	1 Week Costa Mesa, CA

SPECIFIC EXPANSION PLANS:

US:	All United States
Canada:	All Canada
Overseas:	All Countries

⋖⋖ ⋗⋗

RAPID REFILL INK INTERNATIONAL CORP

18732 Lake Dr., E.
Chanhassen, MN 55317
Tel: (877) 880-4465 (952) 238-1000
Fax: (952) 238-1009
E-Mail: dave.shaw@rapidrefillink.com
Web Site: www.rapidrefillink.com
Mr. Dave Shaw, VP Franchise Development

The leader in low cost inkjet and laser toner cartridges. Fully automated remanufacturing production site with a retail storefront environment. RAPID REFILL INK has a diversified approach to the market and product offering. With the sales strategy and marketing message we have created, we fully anticipate the ability to enter into any market region and quickly gain substantial market share. Our stores offer printer cartridges for an average savings of 50% over OEM!

BACKGROUND: IFA MEMBER

Established: 2002; 1st Franchised: 2004	
Franchised Units:	110
Company-Owned Units:	0
Total Units:	110
Dist.:	US-110; CAN-0; O'seas-0
North America:	38 States, 0 Provinces
Density:	8 in WA, 6 in VA, 12 in OR
Projected New Units (12 Months):	150
Qualifications:	3, 3, 1, 3, 4, 5

FINANCIAL/TERMS:

Cash Investment:	$35K-50K

Total Investment:	$95K-199K
Minimum Net Worth:	$350
Fees: Franchise -	$30K
Royalty - 6%;	Ad. - 4%
Earnings Claims Statement:	No
Term of Contract (Years):	10/10
Avg. # Of Employees:	2-3 FT, 3-4 PT
Passive Ownership:	Discouraged
Encourage Conversions:	NA
Area Develop. Agreements:	No
Sub-Franchising Contracts:	No
Expand In Territory:	Yes
Space Needs:	500-1,500 SF

SUPPORT & TRAINING:

Financial Assistance Provided:	Yes (I)
Site Selection Assistance:	Yes
Lease Negotiation Assistance:	Yes
Co-Operative Advertising:	Yes
Franchisee Assoc./Member:	No
Size Of Corporate Staff:	30
On-Going Support:	A,B,C,D,E,F,G,H,I
Training:	3-13 Days Minneapolis, MN

SPECIFIC EXPANSION PLANS:

US:	All United States
Canada:	No
Overseas:	NR

⋖⋖ ⋗⋗

RESCUECOM CORPORATION

2560 Burnet Ave.
Syracuse, NY 13206
Tel: (800) 737-2837 (315) 433-0002
Fax: (315) 433-5228
E-Mail: joinus@rescuecom.com
Web Site: www.rescuecom.com
Mr. David A. Milman, Chief Executive Officer

For the best computer technical talent, RESCUECOM offers the freedom of business ownership without the requirements (and headaches) of the mundane day to day business functions.

BACKGROUND:

Established: 1997; 1st Franchised: 1999	
Franchised Units:	95
Company-Owned Units:	0
Total Units:	95
Dist.:	US-95; CAN-0; O'seas-0
North America:	3 States, 0 Provinces
Density:	3 in NY, 1 in IL, 1 in CA
Projected New Units (12 Months):	3
Qualifications:	3, 3, 5, 4, 4, 4

FINANCIAL/TERMS:

Cash Investment:	$15-17K
Total Investment:	$29.4-53.2K
Minimum Net Worth:	$30K
Fees: Franchise -	$17K

Royalty - 18%;	Ad. - 2%
Earnings Claims Statement:	Yes
Term of Contract (Years):	5/5
Avg. # Of Employees:	1-3 FT, 2-5 PT
Passive Ownership:	Not Allowed
Encourage Conversions:	Yes
Area Develop. Agreements:	No
Sub-Franchising Contracts:	No
Expand In Territory:	No
Space Needs:	NA

SUPPORT & TRAINING:

Financial Assistance Provided:	Yes (D)
Site Selection Assistance:	Yes
Lease Negotiation Assistance:	Yes
Co-Operative Advertising:	Yes
Franchisee Assoc./Member:	No
Size Of Corporate Staff:	40
On-Going Support:	A,B,C,D,E,F,,H,I
Training:	8 Days Syracuse, NY

SPECIFIC EXPANSION PLANS:

US:	All United States
Canada:	All Canada
Overseas:	Europe

◄◄ ►►

VTS FRANCHISING

10 E. Fifth St.
Deer Park, NY 11729
Tel: (631) 586-7400
Fax: (866) 873-0066
E-Mail: ed@vtsn.com
Web Site: www.vtsn.com
Mr. Ed Teixeira, Chief Operating Officer

Become part of the fast-growing Automatic Vehicle Location (AVL) industry by owning a VTS franchise. With no royalty payments, 5 years of residual monthly income and exclusive territory rights, the VTS franchise is the only franchise in the vehicle tracking industry. New franchisees will receive complete training by VTS direct sales professionals, as well as a rapid start-up kit which includes a laptop, client-relationship software, marketing tools and demonstration hardware.

BACKGROUND: IFA MEMBER

Established: 2002;	1st Franchised: 2007
Franchised Units:	0
Company-Owned Units:	1
Total Units:	1
Dist.:	US-1; CAN-0; O'seas-0
North America:	1 States, 0 Provinces

Density:	1 in NY
Projected New Units (12 Months):	NR
Qualifications:	3, 3, 3, 3, 1, 4

FINANCIAL/TERMS:

Cash Investment:	$45-50K
Total Investment:	$56.5-70K
Minimum Net Worth:	$150K
Fees: Franchise -	$19.5K
Royalty - 0;	Ad. - $250
Earnings Claims Statement:	No
Term of Contract (Years):	10/5
Avg. # Of Employees:	2-4 FT, PT
Passive Ownership:	Discouraged
Encourage Conversions:	Yes
Area Develop. Agreements:	No
Sub-Franchising Contracts:	No
Expand In Territory:	Yes
Space Needs:	NA

SUPPORT & TRAINING:

Financial Assistance Provided:	Yes (D)
Site Selection Assistance:	No
Lease Negotiation Assistance:	No
Co-Operative Advertising:	Yes
Franchisee Assoc./Member:	No
Size Of Corporate Staff:	21
On-Going Support:	,B,C,D,,,G,H,
Training:	10 Days VTS Corporate- Deer Park, NY

SPECIFIC EXPANSION PLANS:

US:	All States
Canada:	No
Overseas:	NR

◄◄ ►►

WSI

5580 Explorer Dr., # 600
Mississauga, ON L4W 4Y1 Canada
Tel: (888) 678-7588 (905) 678-7588
Fax: (905) 678-7242
E-Mail: wsileads@wsicorporate.com
Web Site: www.wsicorporate.com
, Franchise Development Team

Own the Worlds #1 rated Internet and Technology Franchise. WSI is the world's largest & fastest growing Internet services franchise providing affordable internet solutions to small and medium size business. WSI is ranked the #1 Internet and Technology Services Franchise and ranked among the Top 50 Best Global Franchises. Discover WSI Today. Become a part of the network of men and women of all backgrounds who have taken their entrepreneurial spirit, managerial skills

and business development capabilities to a place of amazing profit, professional freedom and personal success.

BACKGROUND: IFA MEMBER

Established: 1995;	1st Franchised: 1996
Franchised Units:	1743
Company-Owned Units:	20
Total Units:	1763
Dist.:	US-804; CAN-69; O'seas-890
North America:	1 States, 1 Provinces
Density:	NR
Projected New Units (12 Months):	400
Qualifications:	2, 2, 3, 3, 4, 5

FINANCIAL/TERMS:

Cash Investment:	$49.7K
Total Investment:	$49.7K
Minimum Net Worth:	$100K
Fees: Franchise -	$49.7K
Royalty - 10%;	Ad. - NA
Earnings Claims Statement:	No
Term of Contract (Years):	5/5
Avg. # Of Employees:	3 FT, 1 PT
Passive Ownership:	Not Allowed
Encourage Conversions:	NA
Area Develop. Agreements:	No
Sub-Franchising Contracts:	No
Expand In Territory:	Yes
Space Needs:	1,600-1,900 SF

SUPPORT & TRAINING:

Financial Assistance Provided:	No
Site Selection Assistance:	NA
Lease Negotiation Assistance:	NA
Co-Operative Advertising:	No
Franchisee Assoc./Member:	Yes/Yes
Size Of Corporate Staff:	100
On-Going Support:	a,b,c,,e,,G,H,I
Training:	1 Week Mississauga, ON

SPECIFIC EXPANSION PLANS:

US:	All United States
Canada:	All Canada
Overseas:	All Countries

◄◄ ►►

131

FIVE LARGEST PARTICIPANTS IN SURVEY

Company	# Fran- chised Units	# Co- Owned Units	# Total Units	Franchise Fee	On-Going Royalty	Total Investment
1. Aaron's Sales & Lease Ownership	478	1,024	1,502	$15-50K	6%	$233.8-607.5K
2. Budget Blinds	1,112	1	1,113	$25K	4-5%	$30-45K
3. Interiors By Decorating Den	435	1	436	$30K	7-9%	$49-70K
4. Badcock Home Furniture & More	278	55	333	$0	0%	$100-300K
5. SGO Designer Glass	312	0	312	$49.5K	5%	$100-125K

All of the data provided are proprietary and should not be quoted without acknowledging *Bond's Franchise Guide*.

A SHADE BETTER
2110 W. 110th St.
Cleveland, OH 44102
Tel: (800) 722-8676 (216) 281-0640
Fax: (216) 961-9736
E-Mail: info@ashadebetter.com
Web Site: www.ashadebetter.com
Mr. James P. Prexta, President

Distinctive retail stores selling beautiful lamp shades, lamps and accessories. Franchisees will also have the opportunity to develop and service the wholesale market in their exclusive territory.

BACKGROUND:
Established: 1988;   1st Franchised: 1993
Franchised Units: 10
Company-Owned Units: 7

Total Units: 17
Dist.:   US-17; CAN-0; O'seas-0
 North America: 7 States, 0 Provinces
 Density: 2 in TX, 5 in OH, 3 in IL
Projected New Units (12 Months):   12
Qualifications: 4, 4, 2, 2, 3, 5
FINANCIAL/TERMS:
Cash Investment: $75-100K
Total Investment: $114-156K
Minimum Net Worth: $300K
Fees: Franchise - $35K
 Royalty - 6%;   Ad. - 1%
Earnings Claims Statement: No
Term of Contract (Years):   5/5/5/5/
Avg. # Of Employees: 2 FT, 2 PT
Passive Ownership: Discouraged
Encourage Conversions: Yes
Area Develop. Agreements: Yes/1

Sub-Franchising Contracts: No
Expand In Territory: Yes
Space Needs: 1,800 SF
SUPPORT & TRAINING:
Financial Assistance Provided: No
Site Selection Assistance: Yes
Lease Negotiation Assistance: Yes
Co-Operative Advertising: No
Franchisee Assoc./Member: No
Size Of Corporate Staff: 6
On-Going Support: ,B,C,D,E,,,h,I
Training: 6 Days Cleveland, OH or Phoe-
 nix, AZ; 6 Days On-Site
SPECIFIC EXPANSION PLANS:
US: Midwest, Southwest
Canada: No
Overseas: NR

‹‹ ››

**AARON'S SALES
& LEASE OWNERSHIP**
309 E. Paces Ferry Rd., N. E.
Atlanta, GA 30305-2377
Tel: (800) 551-6015 (678) 402-3445
Fax: (678) 402-3540
E-Mail: greg.tanner@aaronrents.com
Web Site: www.aaronsfranchise.com
Mr. Greg Tanner, National Director of
   Franchising

AARON'S SALES & LEASE OWNER-
SHIP, North America's largest lease-to-
own retail franchise, is changing the way a
growing and underserved market acquires
necessities like furniture, appliances, electronics and computers. We're NYSE
listed with more than 1,500 showrooms.
We offer franchise owners the expertise,
advantages and support of a well-estab-
lished company.

BACKGROUND: IFA MEMBER
Established: 1955; 1st Franchised: 1992
Franchised Units: 478
Company-Owned Units: 1024
Total Units: 1502
Dist.: US-1480; CAN-22; O'seas-0
   North America: 48 States, 6 Provinces
   Density: NR
Projected New Units (12 Months): 80
Qualifications: 5, 5, 1, 4, 5, 5
FINANCIAL/TERMS:
Cash Investment: NA
Total Investment: $233.8-607.5K
Minimum Net Worth: $450K
Fees: Franchise - $15-50K
   Royalty - 6%; Ad. - 2.5%
Earnings Claims Statement: Yes
Term of Contract (Years): 10/10
Avg. # Of Employees: 6 FT, 0 PT
Passive Ownership: Allowed
Encourage Conversions: Yes
Area Develop. Agreements: Yes
Sub-Franchising Contracts: No
Expand In Territory: Yes
Space Needs: 8,000 SF
SUPPORT & TRAINING:
Financial Assistance Provided: Yes (D)
Site Selection Assistance: Yes
Lease Negotiation Assistance: Yes
Co-Operative Advertising: No
Franchisee Assoc./Member: Yes/Yes
Size Of Corporate Staff: 3500

On-Going Support: A,B,C,D,E,F,,H,I
Training: 2 Weeks Minimum On-Site;
   On-Going Varies; 3 Weeks Corporate
   Headquarters
SPECIFIC EXPANSION PLANS:
US: All United States
Canada: All Canada
Overseas: NR

‹‹ ››

**AWC COMMERCIAL WINDOW
COVERINGS**
825 W. Williamson Wy.
Fullerton, CA 92832
Tel: (800) 252-2280 (714) 879-3880
Fax: (714) 879-8419
E-Mail: jim@awc-cwc.com
Web Site: www.awc-cwc.com
Mr. Jim Cherry, Franchise Director

Mobile non-toxic drapery dry cleaning services provided on location for commercial
customers; as well as sales, installation &
repairs of all types of window coverings
at competitive prices through centralized
buying. Nationwide accounts will be serviced by the franchisees as they are established. Utilizing the customer base, refer-
ences and reputation of the franchisor,
developed over the past 37 years makes
this an exceptional opportunity with endless possibilities and immediate credibility.

BACKGROUND:
Established: 1963; 1st Franchised: 1992
Franchised Units: 6
Company-Owned Units: 4
Total Units: 10
Dist.: US-10; CAN-0; O'seas-0
   North America: 5 States, 0 Provinces
   Density: 1 in NJ, 1 in DC, 6 in CA
Projected New Units (12 Months): 3
Qualifications: 3, 4, 3, 3, 4, 4
FINANCIAL/TERMS:
Cash Investment: $25-50K
Total Investment: $112.5-181.4K
Minimum Net Worth: NA
Fees: Franchise - $25K
   Royalty - 5-12.5%; Ad. - 2.5%
Earnings Claims Statement: No
Term of Contract (Years): 10/10
Avg. # Of Employees: 1 FT, PT As
Needed PT
Passive Ownership: Not Allowed
Encourage Conversions: Yes
Area Develop. Agreements: Yes/1
Sub-Franchising Contracts: No
Expand In Territory: Yes
Space Needs: NA

SUPPORT & TRAINING:
Financial Assistance Provided: Yes (D)
Site Selection Assistance: NA
Lease Negotiation Assistance: Yes
Co-Operative Advertising: No
Franchisee Assoc./Member: No
Size Of Corporate Staff: 8
On-Going Support: A,B,C,D,,F,,h,I
Training: 2 Weeks Plant;
   On-Site On-Going
SPECIFIC EXPANSION PLANS:
US: All United States
Canada: All Canada
Overseas: All Countries

‹‹ ››

**BADCOCK HOME FURNITURE
& MORE**
P. O. Box 497
Mulberry, FL 33860
Tel: (800) 223-2625 (863) 869-7972
Fax: (863) 425-7691
E-Mail: smccorkle@badcock.com
Web Site: www.badcock.com
Mr. Scott McCorkle, Dealer Development
   Coordinator

W.S. BADCOCK Corp. offers dealership
opportunities to qualified individuals.
Dealerships are similar to franchises in
that they are individually owned and operated, but require less capital (no franchise
fee or monthly royalty fees) and allow for
a quicker start-up than a traditional franchise. BADCOCK provides all stores with
total inventory at no cost to the dealer and
all account financing through the parent
company.

BACKGROUND:
Established: 1904; 1st Franchised: 1928
Franchised Units: 278
Company-Owned Units: 55
Total Units: 333
Dist.: US-333; CAN-0; O'seas-0
   North America: 7 States, 0 Provinces
   Density: 35 in SC, 87 in GA, 145 in FL
Projected New Units (12 Months): 8-12
Qualifications: 4, 4, 3, 2, 2, 4
FINANCIAL/TERMS:
Cash Investment: $75-150K
Total Investment: $100-300K
Minimum Net Worth: $300K
Fees: Franchise - $0
   Royalty - 0%; Ad. - .3%
Earnings Claims Statement: Yes

Term of Contract (Years): 10/5/5/
Avg. # Of Employees: 4 FT, 2 PT
Passive Ownership: Discouraged
Encourage Conversions: Yes
Area Develop. Agreements: Yes/1
Sub-Franchising Contracts: No
Expand In Territory: Yes
Space Needs: 18,000-20,000 SF
SUPPORT & TRAINING:
Financial Assistance Provided: Yes (D)
Site Selection Assistance: Yes
Lease Negotiation Assistance: No
Co-Operative Advertising: No
Franchisee Assoc./Member: No
Size Of Corporate Staff: 1100
On-Going Support: A,B,C,D,E,F,G,H,I
Training: 60-90 Days Corporate Office
   and Training Store
SPECIFIC EXPANSION PLANS:
US: GA, MS, SC, NC, TN, AL, VA, WV,
KY
Canada: No
Overseas: NR

≪ ≫

BIRTHFLOWERS.COM
161 Swint Ave.
Milledgeville, GA 31061
Tel: (478) 452-0008
Fax:
E-Mail: birthflowers@yahoo.com
Web Site: www.birthflowers.com
Ms. Linda McKnight, CFO

We give a free ($150 for text books) week-long course on vital business principles and gardening information to entrepreneurs in Georgia to help them decide if a franchised proven system of operations in the landscaping, design/build business is a good fit for them. Scholarships are available. Total cost for this in-home business is low.

BACKGROUND: IFA MEMBER
Established: 1995; 1st Franchised: 2009
Franchised Units: 0
Company-Owned Units: <u>1</u>
Total Units: 1
Dist.: US-1; CAN-0; O'seas-0
 North America: 1 States, 0 Provinces
 Density: 1 in GA
Projected New Units (12 Months): 5
Qualifications: 3, 3, 3, 3, 4, 4
FINANCIAL/TERMS:
Cash Investment: $5K-30K
Total Investment: $9.9K-40K
Minimum Net Worth: $25K
Fees: Franchise - $7K

Royalty - 5.5%; Ad. - 4
Earnings Claims Statement: No
Term of Contract (Years): 5/10
Avg. # Of Employees: 1 FT, 2 PT
Passive Ownership: Discouraged
Encourage Conversions: Yes
Area Develop. Agreements: Yes
Sub-Franchising Contracts: No
Expand In Territory: Yes
Space Needs: 200 SF
SUPPORT & TRAINING:
Financial Assistance Provided: Yes (I)
Site Selection Assistance: NA
Lease Negotiation Assistance: NA
Co-Operative Advertising: No
Franchisee Assoc./Member: Yes/No
Size Of Corporate Staff: 2
On-Going Support: ,,C,D,E,,G,h,
Training: 7 Days Milledgeville, GA
SPECIFIC EXPANSION PLANS:
US: Georgia only
Canada: No
Overseas: NR

≪ ≫

BLIND MAN OF AMERICA
606 Fremont Cir.
Colorado Springs, CO 80919
Tel: (800) 547-9889 (719) 260-8989
Fax: (719) 272-4105
E-Mail: blindmanofamerica@msn.com
Web Site: www.blindmanofamerica.com
Ms. Linda Keller, Vice President

Sell custom-made blinds, shades, shutters and more. Our home-based, mobile showroom concept makes it easy for customers to do business with us. THE BLIND MAN'S unique approach of offering interior as well as exterior window coverings sets us apart from the competition. Not only that, but our territory sizes are normally double that of other window covering franchises. We will teach you everything you need to know, from sales to installation to office management.

BACKGROUND: IFA MEMBER
Established: 1991; 1st Franchised: 1996
Franchised Units: 6
Company-Owned Units: <u>1</u>
Total Units: 7
Dist.: US-7; CAN-0; O'seas-0
 North America: 4 States, Provinces
 Density: 1 in AZ, 4 in CO, 1 in WA
Projected New Units (12 Months): 10
Qualifications: 3, 4, 2, 1, 3, 5
FINANCIAL/TERMS:
Cash Investment: $15-25K

Total Investment: $26.8-50.4K
Minimum Net Worth: $26.8K
Fees: Franchise - $15K
 Royalty - 4.25%; Ad. - 0%
Earnings Claims Statement: No
Term of Contract (Years): 5/5
Avg. # Of Employees: 1-3 FT, 0 PT
Passive Ownership: Not Allowed
Encourage Conversions: No
Area Develop. Agreements: No
Sub-Franchising Contracts: No
Expand In Territory: No
Space Needs: NR
SUPPORT & TRAINING:
Financial Assistance Provided: No
Site Selection Assistance: No
Lease Negotiation Assistance: NA
Co-Operative Advertising: No
Franchisee Assoc./Member: No
Size Of Corporate Staff: 2
On-Going Support: ,B,C,D,,,G,h,I
Training: 2 Weeks Colorado Springs, CO
SPECIFIC EXPANSION PLANS:
US: Midwest and West Coast
Canada: No
Overseas: NR

≪ ≫

BUDGET BLINDS
1927 N. Glassell St.
Orange, CA 92865
Tel: (800) 420-5374 (714) 637-2100
Fax: (714) 637-1400
E-Mail: todd@budgetblinds.com
Web Site: www.budgetblinds.com
Mr. Todd Jackson, Operations Manager

BUDGET BLINDS trains individuals to own and operate a home-based business that sells and installs window coverings, via a well-equipped mobile showroom. What makes our franchise unique is that we actually teach people how to run a business, versus teaching people how to do a job. By business we mean hiring, monitoring and maintaining employees, working from cash flow, profit loss and balance statements, We teach what business owners need to know, not what job operators want to know.

BACKGROUND: IFA MEMBER
Established: 1992; 1st Franchised: 1994
Franchised Units: 1112

Company-Owned Units: 1
Total Units: 1113
Dist.: US-1113; CAN-0; O'seas-0
 North America: 36 States, 0 Provinces
 Density: 15 in GA, 60 in CA, 14 in AZ
Projected New Units (12 Months): 350
Qualifications: 2, 4, 1, 2, 3, 5

FINANCIAL/TERMS:
Cash Investment: $50K
Total Investment: $30-45K
Minimum Net Worth: $30K
Fees: Franchise - $25K
 Royalty - 4-5%; Ad. - $150
Earnings Claims Statement: Yes
Term of Contract (Years): 5/5
Avg. # Of Employees: 1-5 FT, 0 PT
Passive Ownership: Discouraged
Encourage Conversions: Yes
Area Develop. Agreements: No
Sub-Franchising Contracts: No
Expand In Territory: Yes
Space Needs: NR

SUPPORT & TRAINING:
Financial Assistance Provided: Yes 0
Site Selection Assistance: NA
Lease Negotiation Assistance: NA
Co-Operative Advertising: No
Franchisee Assoc./Member: No
Size Of Corporate Staff: 25
On-Going Support: A,B,C,D,,,G,H,
Training: 10 Days Orange, CA

SPECIFIC EXPANSION PLANS:
US: All United States
Canada: All Canada
Overseas: NR

<< >>

CARPET NETWORK
109 Gaither Dr., # 302
Mount Laurel, NJ 08054-1704
Tel: (800) 428-1067 (856) 273-9393
Fax: (856) 273-0160
E-Mail: Franchise@carpetnetwork.com
Web Site: www.carpetnetwork.com
Ms. Jennifer Ostroff, VP Operations/
 Franchise Devel.

Carpet Network is a top-ranked mobile floor & window covering retail model specializing in the residential market but with the ability to cater to Main Street businesses as well as commercial and builder markets. Carpet Network appeals to outgoing and motivated candidates who are looking for a professional but family-like atmosphere; a climate in which they will be nurtured and encouraged to realize their full potential in a $20.9 billion industry that is season-less. Our unique, custom Unicell vehicle carries a vast array of over 10,000 sku's to accommodate our customers' requests. Franchisees utilize proprietary estimating & pricing software on a tablet computer. Our targeted marketing programs will help cultivate middle to high-end clients who invite owners into their homes or businesses. Owners of Carpet Network enjoy a flexible schedule, low overhead, no employees to begin & the ability to work from home. Owners receive training and support that is second to none.

BACKGROUND:
Established: 1991; 1st Franchised: 1992
Franchised Units: 46
Company-Owned Units: 0
Total Units: 46
Dist.: US-46; CAN-0; O'seas-0
 North America: 20 States, 0 Provinces
 Density: 7 in PA, 8 in NJ, 4 in MN
Projected New Units (12 Months): 15
Qualifications: 5, 5, 3, 3, 5, 5

FINANCIAL/TERMS:
Cash Investment: $58.5K
Total Investment: $67.4 - $91.7K
Minimum Net Worth: $100K
Fees: Franchise - $39.5K + start-up costs
of $19K
 Royalty - 7-2% sliding scale; Ad.
- $165/Mo.
Earnings Claims Statement: Yes
Term of Contract (Years): 15/15
Avg. # Of Employees: 1
(Owner-Operated) FT, PT
Passive Ownership: Discouraged
Encourage Conversions: NA
Area Develop. Agreements: No
Sub-Franchising Contracts: No
Expand In Territory: Yes
Space Needs: NA

SUPPORT & TRAINING:
Financial Assistance Provided: Yes (D)
Site Selection Assistance: Yes
Lease Negotiation Assistance: NA
Co-Operative Advertising: No
Franchisee Assoc./Member: Yes/Yes
Size Of Corporate Staff: 7
On-Going Support: ,,C,D,,,G,H,I
Training: 2 Weeks Home Study; 1 Week
 Mt. Laurel, NJ Home Office

SPECIFIC EXPANSION PLANS:
US: All United States

Canada: No
Overseas: NR

<< >>

CLOSET & STORAGE CONCEPTS
1000 Haddonfield-Berlin Rd., # 208
Voorhees, NJ 08043
Tel: (800) 862-1919 (856) 627-5700
Fax: (856) 627-7447
E-Mail: boblewis@closetandstorageconc
epts.com
Web Site: www.closetandstorageconcepts.
com
Mr. Bob Lewis, President

Closet & Storage Concepts designs, manufacturers and installs a wide variety of custom closet, garage, laundry room, home office and storage units. All franchisees receive complete training in all aspects of the operation of the business, both prior to opening and on an on-going basis. Call 1-800-862-1919.

BACKGROUND: IFA MEMBER
Established: 1987; 1st Franchised: 2000
Franchised Units: 14
Company-Owned Units: 3
Total Units: 17
Dist.: US-16; CAN-1; O'seas-0
 North America: 0 States, 0 Provinces
 Density: NR
Projected New Units (12 Months): 5
Qualifications: 3, 4, 1, 3, 4, 5

FINANCIAL/TERMS:
Cash Investment: $50-200K
Total Investment: $44.9K-234K
Minimum Net Worth: $100K
Fees: Franchise - $40K
 Royalty - 5%; Ad. - 0%
Earnings Claims Statement: No
Term of Contract (Years): 10/10
Avg. # Of Employees: 8 FT, 0 PT
Passive Ownership: Discouraged
Encourage Conversions: NA
Area Develop. Agreements: No
Sub-Franchising Contracts: No
Expand In Territory: Yes
Space Needs: 4,000 SF

SUPPORT & TRAINING:
Financial Assistance Provided: Yes (D)

Site Selection Assistance: Yes
Lease Negotiation Assistance: Yes
Co-Operative Advertising: No
Franchisee Assoc./Member: Yes/Yes
Size Of Corporate Staff: 6
On-Going Support: „C,D,E,,G,H,I
Training: 2 Weeks NJ
SPECIFIC EXPANSION PLANS:
US: All United States
Canada: All Canada
Overseas: NR

＜＜ ＞＞

COLOR YOUR CARPET

767 Blanding Blvd., # 112
Orange Park, FL 32065
Tel: (800) 321-6567 (904) 272-6567
Fax:
E-Mail: cdimperio@carpetcolor.com
Web Site: www.coloryourcarpet.com
Ms. Connie D'Imperio, President

No competition! The ONLY on-site, 100% carpet dyeing and color restoration service in the world. Advanced technology provides cost-effective, convenient alternative to costly carpet replacement. Design dyeing, spot dyeing and color matching taught by experts. Large protected territory expansion program.

BACKGROUND:
Established: 1979; 1st Franchised: 1990
Franchised Units: 256
Company-Owned Units: 1
Total Units: 257
Dist.: US-177; CAN-48; O'seas-32
  North America: 14 States, 4 Provinces
  Density: 18 in FL, 12 in AB
Projected New Units (12 Months): 24
Qualifications: 3, 4, 1, 4, 5, 5
FINANCIAL/TERMS:
Cash Investment: $25-35K
Total Investment: $39-49K
Minimum Net Worth: $150K
Fees: Franchise - $15K
  Royalty - 3%; Ad. - 0%
Earnings Claims Statement: Yes
Term of Contract (Years): 5/5
Avg. # Of Employees: 1 FT, 1 PT
Passive Ownership: Allowed
Encourage Conversions: No
Area Develop. Agreements: Yes/1
Sub-Franchising Contracts: Yes
Expand In Territory: Yes
Space Needs: NA
SUPPORT & TRAINING:
Financial Assistance Provided: No
Site Selection Assistance: NA

Lease Negotiation Assistance: NA
Co-Operative Advertising: No
Franchisee Assoc./Member: Yes/Yes
Size Of Corporate Staff: 6
On-Going Support: A,B,C,D,E,F,G,H,I
Training: 1 Week On-the-Job Existing
  Franchisee's Site; 1 Week Orange Park,
  FL; 2 Weeks Home Study
SPECIFIC EXPANSION PLANS:
US: All United States
Canada: All Canada
Overseas: Primarily South America,
  Europe, Asia, Middle East

＜＜ ＞＞

DECOR & YOU

900 Main St. S., Bldg. #2
Southbury, CT 06488
Tel: (800) 477-3326 (203) 264-3500
Fax: (203) 264-5095
E-Mail: admin2@decorandyou.com
Web Site: www.decorandyou.com
Ms. Jeanne Moscariello, Director of Franchising

Decor&You offers franchisees a proven success system of outstanding tools, technology, training and support. Whether your passion is pioneering a new region, developing a team of marketer manager franchisees, building a team of certified decorating professionals, or helping clients realize their decorating dreams, Decor&You has the right fit for you. Call 800-477-3326 x 2131 today for more information.

BACKGROUND: IFA MEMBER
Established: 1994; 1st Franchised: 1998
Franchised Units: 210
Company-Owned Units: 0
Total Units: 210
Dist.: US-210; CAN-0; O'seas-0
  North America: 29 States, 0 Provinces
  Density: 35 in VA, 34 in NJ, 22 in CO
Projected New Units (12 Months): 50
Qualifications: 4, 4, 2, 4, 4, 4
FINANCIAL/TERMS:
Cash Investment: $50K
Total Investment: $100K-250K
Minimum Net Worth: $100K
Fees: Franchise - $25K
  Royalty - 10%; Ad. - 10%
Earnings Claims Statement: No
Term of Contract (Years): 10/10

Avg. # Of Employees: 2 FT, 0 PT
Passive Ownership: Not Allowed
Encourage Conversions: NA
Area Develop. Agreements: Yes/10
Sub-Franchising Contracts: No
Expand In Territory: Yes
Space Needs: NA
SUPPORT & TRAINING:
Financial Assistance Provided: No
Site Selection Assistance: No
Lease Negotiation Assistance: No
Co-Operative Advertising: No
Franchisee Assoc./Member: Yes/Yes
Size Of Corporate Staff: 8
On-Going Support: „C,D,,,G,H,I
Training: 6 Weeks + Home-based/Home
  office; 6 Days Southbury CT DPEC
  Center;4 Days (Grad Semester II) and
  Advanced Training Co Southbury CT
  DPEC Center
SPECIFIC EXPANSION PLANS:
US: All
Canada: No
Overseas: NR

＜＜ ＞＞

DIRECTBUY

8450 Broadway
Merrillville, IN 46410
Tel: (800) 827-6400 + 357 (219) 736-1100
+ 357
Fax: (219) 755-6208
E-Mail: dbowen@directbuy.com
Web Site: www.directbuyfranchising.com
Ms. Debbie Bowen, VP Franchise Development

DirectBuy offers consumers the unparalleled opportunity to buy merchandise at manufacturer's invoice cost. Our hundreds of thousands of members purchase directly from more than 700 manufacturers. No mark-up, no middleman, no kidding. DirectBuy franchise owners enroll members through our time-tested marketing system and service these members with the support of more than 300 specialists at the DirectBuy Corporate Support Center.

BACKGROUND: IFA MEMBER
Established: 1971; 1st Franchised: 1972
Franchised Units: 119
Company-Owned Units: 2
Total Units: 121
Dist.: US-121; CAN-22; O'seas-0
  North America: 25 States, 4 Provinces
  Density: 10 in NY, 11 in FL, 14 in CA
Projected New Units (12 Months): 15
Qualifications: 4, 4, 1, 3, 1, 5

FINANCIAL/TERMS:

Cash Investment: $105K-237K
Total Investment: $0K
Minimum Net Worth: $500K
Fees: Franchise - $75K-155K
　Royalty - 22%; Ad. - NA
Earnings Claims Statement: No
Term of Contract (Years): 12/12
Avg. # Of Employees: 12 FT, 2 PT
Passive Ownership: Discouraged
Encourage Conversions: NA
Area Develop. Agreements: No
Sub-Franchising Contracts: No
Expand In Territory: No
Space Needs: 8,000-12,000 SF

SUPPORT & TRAINING:

Financial Assistance Provided: Yes (D)
Site Selection Assistance: Yes
Lease Negotiation Assistance: Yes
Co-Operative Advertising: No
Franchisee Assoc./Member: No
Size Of Corporate Staff: 500
On-Going Support: A,B,C,D,E,,G,H,
Training: 5 Weeks Operating Franchise;
　4 Weeks Merrillville, IN

SPECIFIC EXPANSION PLANS:

US: All United States
Canada: All Canada
Overseas: NR

<< >>

DESIGNS OF THE INTERIOR

Because every life is uniquely designed.

DOTI DESIGN STORES
236 Ponte Vedra Park Dr. #201
Ponte Vedra Beach, FL 32082
Tel: (888) 382-7488 (847) 713-2622
Fax: (904) 395-9041
E-Mail: info@doti.com
Web Site: www.dotifranchising.com
Mr. Jim Evanger, CEO

Upscale home furnishings and design retail stores. DOTI DESIGN STORES offer "one-stop-shopping" for all furniture, window treatments, accessories, rugs and lights for discriminating home owners. Franchisees do NOT need industry experience - but rather a people management background and leadership ability. Huge $200 billion industry. Learn more at www.doti.com.

BACKGROUND: IFA MEMBER
Established: 1983; 1st Franchised: 1999

Franchised Units: 28
Company-Owned Units: 1
Total Units: 29
Dist.: US-29; CAN-0; O'seas-0
　North America: 6 States, 0 Provinces
　Density: 2 in WI, 6 in IL, 2 in FL
Projected New Units (12 Months): 10
Qualifications: 4, 5, 2, 4, 3, 5

FINANCIAL/TERMS:

Cash Investment: $125K-150K
Total Investment: $275K-422K
Minimum Net Worth: $550K
Fees: Franchise - $36K
　Royalty - 6%; Ad. - 0%
Earnings Claims Statement: Yes
Term of Contract (Years): 5/5/5/5/
Avg. # Of Employees: 9 FT, 1 PT
Passive Ownership: Not Allowed
Encourage Conversions: NA
Area Develop. Agreements: Yes/1
Sub-Franchising Contracts: No
Expand In Territory: Yes
Space Needs: 5,000 SF

SUPPORT & TRAINING:

Financial Assistance Provided: No
Site Selection Assistance: Yes
Lease Negotiation Assistance: Yes
Co-Operative Advertising: No
Franchisee Assoc./Member: No
Size Of Corporate Staff: 6
On-Going Support: ,,C,D,E,F,G,H,I
Training: 4 Days Barrington, IL;
　7 Days On-Site

SPECIFIC EXPANSION PLANS:

US: All United States
Canada: No
Overseas: NR

<< >>

**FLOOR COVERINGS
INTERNATIONAL**
200 Technology Ct., S.E., # 1200
Smyrna, GA 30082
Tel: (800) 955-4324 (770) 874-7600
Fax: (770) 874-7605
E-Mail: djames@floorcoveringsinternational.com
Web Site: www.floorcoveringsinternational.com
Ms. Denise James, Franchise Administrator

FLOOR COVERINGS INTERNATIONAL is the 'Flooring Store at your Door.' FCI is the first and leading mobile 'shop at home' flooring store. Customers can select from over 3,000 styles and colors of flooring right in their own home! All the right ingredients are there

to simplify a buying decision. We offer all the brand names you and your customers will be familiar with. We carry all types of flooring, as well as window blinds.

BACKGROUND: IFA MEMBER
Established: 1988; 1st Franchised: 1989
Franchised Units: 72
Company-Owned Units: 0
Total Units: 72
Dist.: US-78; CAN-3; O'seas-9
　North America: 43 States, 5 Provinces
　Density: 15 in PA, 11 in OH, 9 in IL
Projected New Units (12 Months): 45
Qualifications: 5, 5, 4, 3, 4, 4

FINANCIAL/TERMS:

Cash Investment: $150K
Total Investment: $31.1-41.3K
Minimum Net Worth: $50K
Fees: Franchise - $16K
　Royalty - 5%/$325/Mo.; Ad.
　- 2%/$130/Mo.
Earnings Claims Statement: No
Term of Contract (Years): 10/10
Avg. # Of Employees: 1 FT, 1 PT
Passive Ownership: Discouraged
Encourage Conversions: Yes
Area Develop. Agreements: Yes/1
Sub-Franchising Contracts: No
Expand In Territory: Yes
Space Needs: NR

SUPPORT & TRAINING:

Financial Assistance Provided: Yes (D)
Site Selection Assistance: Yes
Lease Negotiation Assistance: NA
Co-Operative Advertising: No
Franchisee Assoc./Member: Yes/Yes
Size Of Corporate Staff: 15
On-Going Support: A,B,C,D,E,,G,H,I
Training: 2 Weeks Home Study;
　2 Weeks Atlanta, GA

SPECIFIC EXPANSION PLANS:

US: All United States
Canada: All Canada
Overseas: U.K.

<< >>

GARAGETEK
5 Aerial Wy.
Syosset, NY 11791
Tel: (866) 664-2724 (516) 621-4300
Fax: (516) 992-8600

E-Mail: sbarrett@garagetek.com
Web Site: www.garagetek.com
Mr. Skip Barrett, Development Director

GarageTek is the leading international brand for installed garage furnishing systems. With 55 domestic locations and two international locations, GarageTek is the recognized premium brand in the exploding garage organization, home improvement category. We offer spacious exclusive territories, proprietary products and technology and a full training package that has transformed tens of thousands of garages and the lives of our owner operators.

BACKGROUND: IFA MEMBER
Established: 2000; 1st Franchised: 2001
Franchised Units: 55
Company-Owned Units: 2
Total Units: 57
Dist.: US-55; CAN-1; O'seas-1
North America: 27 States, 1 Provinces
Density: NR
Projected New Units (12 Months): NR
Qualifications: 3, 3, 3, 3, 3, 3
FINANCIAL/TERMS:
Cash Investment: $250K
Total Investment: $300K
Minimum Net Worth: $1MM
Fees: Franchise - $50K
Royalty - 6%; Ad. - 4%
Earnings Claims Statement: No
Term of Contract (Years): 10/5/5
Avg. # Of Employees: 4 FT, 0 PT
Passive Ownership: Not Allowed
Encourage Conversions: NA
Area Develop. Agreements: No
Sub-Franchising Contracts: No
Expand In Territory: Yes
Space Needs: 2,500 SF
SUPPORT & TRAINING:
Financial Assistance Provided: Yes (I)
Site Selection Assistance: Yes
Lease Negotiation Assistance: Yes
Co-Operative Advertising: No
Franchisee Assoc./Member: Yes/Yes
Size Of Corporate Staff: 12
On-Going Support: ,B,C,D,,F,G,H,I
Training: 2 Weeks Syosset, NY
SPECIFIC EXPANSION PLANS:
US: Midwest, Southwest, West
Canada: No
Overseas: NR

◄◄ ►►

GOTCHA COVERED BLINDS
1611 N. Stemmons Plwy., # 318
Carrollton, TX 75006

Tel: (877) 777-2544 (972) 466-2544
Fax: (972) 446-6774
E-Mail: garyh@gotchacoveredblinds.com
Web Site: www.gotchacoveredfranchise.com
Mr. Gary Hudson, Franchise Devel. Manager

GOTCHA COVERED BLINDS is listed in Entrepreneur 500 and rated #2 in the window treatment industry. Home-based franchise with complete training and on-going support. Training is 19 weeks originally. Wide open market for growth with exclusive areas.

BACKGROUND: IFA MEMBER
Established: 1995; 1st Franchised: 1999
Franchised Units: 130
Company-Owned Units: 0
Total Units: 130
Dist.: US-130; CAN-0; O'seas-0
North America: 28 States, 0 Provinces
Density: 14 in IL, 13 in FL
Projected New Units (12 Months): 48
Qualifications: NR, NR, NR, NR, 5, NR
FINANCIAL/TERMS:
Cash Investment: $59.5K
Total Investment: $64-89K
Minimum Net Worth: $100K
Fees: Franchise - $59.5K
Royalty - $300/700/1K/Mo.; Ad. - $150/Mo.
Earnings Claims Statement: No
Term of Contract (Years): 10/10
Avg. # Of Employees: 1 FT, 1 PT
Passive Ownership: Allowed
Encourage Conversions: No
Area Develop. Agreements: Yes
Sub-Franchising Contracts: No
Expand In Territory: Yes
Space Needs: NA
SUPPORT & TRAINING:
Financial Assistance Provided: Yes (I)
Site Selection Assistance: Yes
Lease Negotiation Assistance: Yes
Co-Operative Advertising: Yes
Franchisee Assoc./Member: Yes/Yes
Size Of Corporate Staff: 15
On-Going Support: A,B,C,D,E,F,G,H,I
Training: 9 Weeks On-the-Job Franchise Location; 2 Weeks Corporate Office Carrollton, TX
SPECIFIC EXPANSION PLANS:
US: All United States
Canada: No
Overseas: NR

◄◄ ►►

GUARDSMAN FURNITUREPRO
4999 36th St. S. E.
Grand Rapids, MI 49512
Tel: (800) 496-6377 (616) 285-7864
Fax: (616) 285-7882
E-Mail: tziegler@valspar.com
Web Site: www.guardsmanfurniturepro.com
Mr. Tony Ziegler

Partner and profit with a world leader. As a business unit of Lilly Industries, the largest manufacturer of furniture finishes in N. America, GUARDSMAN WOOD-PRO is the premier choice of residential and commercial customers alike for furniture repair and refinishing services. Lilly has been involved in the furniture industry for 130 years, supplying finishes, furniture care products and now furniture repair services. If you want to be in the furniture business, you want to be with us.

BACKGROUND:
Established: 1865; 1st Franchised: 1994
Franchised Units: 123
Company-Owned Units: 0
Total Units: 123
Dist.: US-110; CAN-13; O'seas-0
North America: 36 States, 2 Provinces
Density: 6 in TX, 6 in OH, 9 in MI
Projected New Units (12 Months): 36
Qualifications: 4, 4, 4, 3, 5, 5
FINANCIAL/TERMS:
Cash Investment: $10-25K
Total Investment: $7-25K
Minimum Net Worth: $50K
Fees: Franchise - $7K
Royalty - Fixed; Ad. - Fixed
Earnings Claims Statement: No
Term of Contract (Years): 5/5
Avg. # Of Employees: 1-3 FT, 1-2 PT
Passive Ownership: Discouraged
Encourage Conversions: Yes
Area Develop. Agreements: Yes/1
Sub-Franchising Contracts: Yes
Expand In Territory: Yes
Space Needs: NR
SUPPORT & TRAINING:
Financial Assistance Provided: Yes (D)
Site Selection Assistance: NA
Lease Negotiation Assistance: NA
Co-Operative Advertising: No
Franchisee Assoc./Member: Yes/Yes
Size Of Corporate Staff: 80
On-Going Support: A,,C,D,,,G,H,I
Training: 2 Weeks Grand Rapids, MI
SPECIFIC EXPANSION PLANS:
US: All United States
Canada: All Canada

Overseas: All Countries

‹‹ ››

INTERIORS BY DECORATING DEN

8659 Commerce Dr.
Easton, MD 21601-7425
Tel: (800) 686-6393 (410) 822-9001
Fax: (410) 820-5131
E-Mail: kevina@decoratingden.com
Web Site: www.decoratingden.com
Mr. Kevin Atkinson, VP Program Development

Celebrating our 40th successful year, INTERIORS BY DECORATING DEN is the premier international, shop-at-home interior decorating franchise in the world. Our company-trained interior decorators bring thousands of samples including window coverings, wall coverings, floor coverings, furniture and accessories to their customers' homes in our uniquely equipped COLORVAN. Special business features include: home-based, marketing systems, business systems, training, support and complete sampling.

BACKGROUND: IFA MEMBER
Established: 1969;   1st Franchised: 1970
Franchised Units: 435
Company-Owned Units: 1
Total Units: 436
Dist.:   US-471; CAN-32; O'seas-0
  North America: 0 States, 0 Provinces
  Density: 27 in TX, 28 in NC, 33 in FL
Projected New Units (12 Months):   50
Qualifications: 5, 5, 3, 3, 4, 5
FINANCIAL/TERMS:
Cash Investment: $15K
Total Investment: $49-70K
Minimum Net Worth: $50K
Fees: Franchise - $30K
  Royalty - 7-9%;   Ad. - 4%/$100 Min
Earnings Claims Statement: No
Term of Contract (Years):   10/10
Avg. # Of Employees: 1 FT, 0 PT
Passive Ownership: Not Allowed
Encourage Conversions: Yes
Area Develop. Agreements: Yes/1
Sub-Franchising Contracts: Yes
Expand In Territory: No
Space Needs: NA
SUPPORT & TRAINING:
Financial Assistance Provided: No

Site Selection Assistance: NA
Lease Negotiation Assistance: NA
Co-Operative Advertising: No
Franchisee Assoc./Member: Yes/Yes
Size Of Corporate Staff: 40
On-Going Support: „C,D,E,„G,H,I
Training: 45 Days plus 12 Weeks Local;
  10.5 Days Easton, MD
SPECIFIC EXPANSION PLANS:
US: All United States
Canada: All Canada
Overseas: NR

‹‹ ››

LANGENWALTER CARPET DYEING

1111 S. Richfield Rd.
Placentia, CA 92870-6790
Tel: (800) 422-4370 (714) 528-7610
Fax: (714) 528-7620
E-Mail:
Web Site: www.langdye.com
Mr. John Langenwalter, VP Franchise Development

We offer complete carpet color correction. The franchisees are carpet color correction experts. They can take care of problems such as sun fading, pet stains, bleach spots, chemical stains, etc. Complete color changes are also done to save the customer 85% of carpet replacement costs.

BACKGROUND:
Established: 1975;   1st Franchised: 1981
Franchised Units: 170
Company-Owned Units: 3
Total Units: 173
Dist.:   US-152; CAN-19; O'seas-2
  North America: 25 States, 3 Provinces
  Density: 10 in BC, 75 in CA, 9 in MA
Projected New Units (12 Months):   50
Qualifications: 3, 2, 1, 1, 2, 4
FINANCIAL/TERMS:
Cash Investment: $30K
Total Investment: $30K
Minimum Net Worth: $30K
Fees: Franchise - $18K
  Royalty - $110/Mo.;   Ad. - 0%
Earnings Claims Statement: No
Term of Contract (Years):   3/3
Avg. # Of Employees: 1 FT, 0 PT
Passive Ownership: Not Allowed
Encourage Conversions: No
Area Develop. Agreements: No
Sub-Franchising Contracts: No
Expand In Territory: Yes
Space Needs: NR
SUPPORT & TRAINING:

Financial Assistance Provided: No
Site Selection Assistance: NA
Lease Negotiation Assistance: NA
Co-Operative Advertising: No
Franchisee Assoc./Member: No
Size Of Corporate Staff: 10
On-Going Support: „„„„G,h,I
Training: 5 Days Placentia, CA
SPECIFIC EXPANSION PLANS:
US: All United States
Canada: All Canada
Overseas: All Countries

‹‹ ››

MORE SPACE PLACE

5040 140th Ave., N.
Clearwater, FL 33760-3735
Tel: (888) 731-3051 + 14 (727) 539-1611
Fax: (727) 524-6382
E-Mail: mjuarez@morespaceplace.com
Web Site: www.morespaceplace.com
Mr. Marty Juarez, Vice President Franchising

One of America's Top 100 Franchise Opportunities! (as listed in Bond's Top 100 Franchises, 2004 and 2006). We create beautiful living spaces for our customers. Picture an elegant home office that converts into an extra bedroom. With our professionally installed Murphy bed and custom-designed office, it can happen. With us, you can fashionably design closets, entertainment centers, utility rooms and garages and turn spare bedrooms into multi-purpose rooms.

BACKGROUND:
Established: 1989;   1st Franchised: 1993
Franchised Units: 40
Company-Owned Units: 4
Total Units: 44
Dist.:   US-44; CAN-0; O'seas-0
  North America: 15 States, 0 Provinces
  Density: 4 in TX, 4 in SC, 22 in FL
Projected New Units (12 Months):   12
Qualifications: 4, 4, 1, 3, 2, 5
FINANCIAL/TERMS:
Cash Investment: $40-60K
Total Investment: $133-203K
Minimum Net Worth: $150K
Fees: Franchise - $29.5-22K
  Royalty - 4.5%;   Ad. - 2.5%

Earnings Claims Statement: No
Term of Contract (Years): 10/10
Avg. # Of Employees: 3 FT, 1 PT
Passive Ownership: Discouraged
Encourage Conversions: Yes
Area Develop. Agreements: Yes/10
Sub-Franchising Contracts: No
Expand In Territory: Yes
Space Needs: 1,400-2,000 SF

SUPPORT & TRAINING:
Financial Assistance Provided: Yes (I)
Site Selection Assistance: Yes
Lease Negotiation Assistance: Yes
Co-Operative Advertising: Yes
Franchisee Assoc./Member: No
Size Of Corporate Staff: 55
On-Going Support: ,B,C,D,E,F,G,H,I
Training: 12 Days Headquarters Clearwater, FL; 6 Days On-Site; Free Ongoing

SPECIFIC EXPANSION PLANS:
US: All United States
Canada: No
Overseas: NR

≪ ≫

MOUNTAIN COMFORT FURNISHINGS

P. O. Box 767
Frisco, CO 80443
Tel: (888) 686-2638 (970) 668-3661
Fax: (970) 668-5329
E-Mail: mtncmft@colorado.net
Web Site: www.mountaincomfort.net
Mr. Bill Jarski, President

Franchises for the establishment and operation of a specialty furniture store which sells distinctive mountain life-style furnishings and specialty di¿½cor items. Group buying and marketing benefits. Low yearly license fee.

BACKGROUND:
Established: 1984; 1st Franchised: 1991
Franchised Units: 5
Company-Owned Units: 1
Total Units: 6
Dist.: US-6; CAN-0; O'seas-0
  North America: 0 States, 0 Provinces
  Density: 1 in OR, 3 in CO, 1 in CA
Projected New Units (12 Months): 6
Qualifications: 4, 4, 2, 3, 3, 4

FINANCIAL/TERMS:
Cash Investment: Varies
Total Investment: $190-410.8K
Minimum Net Worth: $150K
Fees: Franchise - $22.5K
  Royalty - $10K/Yr.; Ad. - 0.5%/Mo.
Earnings Claims Statement: No

Term of Contract (Years): 5/5
Avg. # Of Employees: 3 FT, 2 PT
Passive Ownership: Discouraged
Encourage Conversions: Yes
Area Develop. Agreements: No
Sub-Franchising Contracts: No
Expand In Territory: Yes
Space Needs: 3,000-8,000 SF

SUPPORT & TRAINING:
Financial Assistance Provided: Yes (D)
Site Selection Assistance: Yes
Lease Negotiation Assistance: Yes
Co-Operative Advertising: No
Franchisee Assoc./Member: Yes/Yes
Size Of Corporate Staff: 4
On-Going Support: ,b,C,D,E,F,G,H,I
Training: 2+ Weeks Frisco or Vail, CO; 6+ Days Franchise Location

SPECIFIC EXPANSION PLANS:
US: Rocky Mtn. States and NE
Canada: No
Overseas: NR

≪ ≫

NATIONWIDE FLOOR & WINDOW COVERINGS

111 E. Kilbourn Ave., 24 Fl.
Milwaukee, WI 53202-6611
Tel: (800) 366-8088 (414) 765-9900
Fax: (414) 765-1300
E-Mail: ekoepel@floorsandwindows.com
Web Site: www.floorsandwindows.com
Mr. Ed Koepel, Franchise Sales Manager

As a franchisee, you will own two businesses in one: a mobile Window Coverings business and a Mobile Floor Coverings business. Nationwide Floor & Window Coverings offers a unique, mobile shop-at-home service to time-starved customers. One of our distinctive qualities...we cater to the trades- General Contractors, Home Builders, Realtors, Property Managers, and Insurance Companies. At Nationwide Floor & Window Coverings, "We Bring the Showroom to You!"

BACKGROUND:
Established: 1992; 1st Franchised: 1996
Franchised Units: 89
Company-Owned Units: 0
Total Units: 89
Dist.: US-81; CAN-4; O'seas-0
  North America: 31 States, 0 Provinces
  Density: 8 in WI, 6 in CO, 13 in CA
Projected New Units (12 Months): 30
Qualifications: 3, 3, 1, 2, 5, 5

FINANCIAL/TERMS:
Cash Investment: $10-25K

Total Investment: $50K-80K
Minimum Net Worth: $250K
Fees: Franchise - $25K
  Royalty - 5%; Ad. - 4.8K
Earnings Claims Statement: Yes
Term of Contract (Years): 10/10
Avg. # Of Employees: 1-2 FT, 0 PT
Passive Ownership: Not Allowed
Encourage Conversions: Yes
Area Develop. Agreements: No
Sub-Franchising Contracts: No
Expand In Territory: Yes
Space Needs: 0 SF

SUPPORT & TRAINING:
Financial Assistance Provided: No
Site Selection Assistance: Yes
Lease Negotiation Assistance: No
Co-Operative Advertising: No
Franchisee Assoc./Member: No
Size Of Corporate Staff: 16
On-Going Support: ,,C,D,,,G,h,I
Training: 6 Weeks Franchise Market; 2 Weeks Corporate Headquarters

SPECIFIC EXPANSION PLANS:
US: All United States; 27 units
Canada: 3 units
Overseas: NR

≪ ≫

NORWALK - THE FURNITURE IDEA

100 Furniture Pkwy.
Norwalk, OH 44857-9587
Tel: (888) 667-9255 (800) 837-2565 + 6749
Fax: (419) 744-3212
E-Mail: mturbeville@nfcorp.com
Web Site: www.norwalkfurnitureidea.com
Mr. Mike Turbeville, Director of Franchise Development

Custom order living room specialty stores, offering consumers 1,000 fabrics and leathers available in 500 styles, with delivery in just 35 days. Low inventory investment.

BACKGROUND: IFA MEMBER
Established: 1902; 1st Franchised: 1987
Franchised Units: 62
Company-Owned Units: 4
Total Units: 66
Dist.: US-69; CAN-8; O'seas-0
  North America: 30 States, 3 Provinces
  Density: 4 in TX, 13 in FL, 5 in CA
Projected New Units (12 Months): 8
Qualifications: 4, 4, 2, 2, 4, 5

FINANCIAL/TERMS:
Cash Investment: $100-125K
Total Investment: $450-495K

Minimum Net Worth:	$350K
Fees: Franchise -	$35K
Royalty - 0%;	Ad. - 0%
Earnings Claims Statement:	No
Term of Contract (Years):	20/5
Avg. # Of Employees:	10 FT, 1 PT
Passive Ownership:	Not Allowed
Encourage Conversions:	NA
Area Develop. Agreements:	Yes/1
Sub-Franchising Contracts:	No
Expand In Territory:	Yes
Space Needs:	4,500 SF

SUPPORT & TRAINING:

Financial Assistance Provided:	Yes (D)
Site Selection Assistance:	Yes
Lease Negotiation Assistance:	Yes
Co-Operative Advertising:	No
Franchisee Assoc./Member:	Yes/Yes
Size Of Corporate Staff:	11
On-Going Support:	,B,C,d,E,,G,h,I
Training:	3 Weeks Cleveland; 1 Week Atlanta, GA; 2 Weeks Another Store

SPECIFIC EXPANSION PLANS:

US:	All United States
Canada:	Most Provinces
Overseas:	NR

<< >>

PAINT MEDIC

3111 Walden Ave.
Depew, NY 14043
Tel: (866) 446-2277 (905) 732-9770
Fax: (905) 788-1939
E-Mail: moniquefinley@paintmedic.com
Web Site: www.paintmedic.com
Ms. Monique Finley, VP Franchise Development

PAINT MEDIC is an automotive paint touch-up company. Our franchisees and their technicians can quickly, cost-effectively and permanently repair stone chips, scratches, plastic bumper scuffs and other minor paint blemishes. We service new and used car dealerships, rental car agencies, fleet companies and retail consumers. PAINT MEDIC operates from both fixed location retail facilities, as well as on a mobile basis. PAINT MEDIC is ideally suited for someone who loves cars and wants to be his own boss.

BACKGROUND:

Established: 1990;	1st Franchised: 1995
Franchised Units:	22
Company-Owned Units:	2
Total Units:	24
Dist.:	US-2; CAN-22; O'seas-0
North America:	2 States, 3 Provinces
Density:	1 in NY, 20 in ON
Projected New Units (12 Months):	12
Qualifications:	4, 4, 2, 3, 4, 3

FINANCIAL/TERMS:

Cash Investment:	$30-60K
Total Investment:	$30-60K
Minimum Net Worth:	$50K
Fees: Franchise -	$25-50K
Royalty - 5%/$500;	Ad. - NA
Earnings Claims Statement:	No
Term of Contract (Years):	10.10/
Avg. # Of Employees:	3-4 FT, 1-2 PT
Passive Ownership:	Not Allowed
Encourage Conversions:	NA
Area Develop. Agreements:	Yes/1
Sub-Franchising Contracts:	No
Expand In Territory:	Yes
Space Needs:	2,000 SF

SUPPORT & TRAINING:

Financial Assistance Provided:	No
Site Selection Assistance:	Yes
Lease Negotiation Assistance:	Yes
Co-Operative Advertising:	No
Franchisee Assoc./Member:	No
Size Of Corporate Staff:	7
On-Going Support:	,B,C,D,,,G,h,I
Training:	3 Weeks Buffalo, NY; 1 Week Territory

SPECIFIC EXPANSION PLANS:

US:	Focusing on NE
Canada:	All Canada
Overseas:	Master Franchises

<< >>

SGO DESIGNER GLASS

1827 N. Case St.
Orange, CA 92865
Tel: (800) 944-4746 (714) 974-6124
Fax: (714) 974-6529
E-Mail: info@stainedglassoverlay.com
Web Site: www.sgodesignerglass.com
Ms. Amanda Carnegie, Franchise Service Coordinator

We are the leading decorative glass franchisor in the world. Combine our patented technology and proven format into a great business. Design works of SGO, for homes, business and religious institutions. We don't require that you have an artistic or glass industry background. We provide training in all required skills.

BACKGROUND: IFA MEMBER

Established: 1978;	1st Franchised: 1981
Franchised Units:	312
Company-Owned Units:	0
Total Units:	312
Dist.:	US-312; CAN-11; O'seas-145
North America:	39 States, 6 Provinces
Density:	7 in IL, 9 in FL, 29 in CA
Projected New Units (12 Months):	25
Qualifications:	4, 4, 3, 2, 2, 5

FINANCIAL/TERMS:

Cash Investment:	$100K-125K
Total Investment:	$100K-125K
Minimum Net Worth:	$200K
Fees: Franchise -	$49.5K
Royalty - 5%;	Ad. - 2%
Earnings Claims Statement:	Yes
Term of Contract (Years):	10/10
Avg. # Of Employees:	3 FT, 0 PT
Passive Ownership:	Discouraged
Encourage Conversions:	Yes
Area Develop. Agreements:	No
Sub-Franchising Contracts:	No
Expand In Territory:	Yes
Space Needs:	1,100 SF

SUPPORT & TRAINING:

Financial Assistance Provided:	Yes (I)
Site Selection Assistance:	Yes
Lease Negotiation Assistance:	No
Co-Operative Advertising:	No
Franchisee Assoc./Member:	Yes/Yes
Size Of Corporate Staff:	17
On-Going Support:	,,C,D,E,F,G,h,I
Training:	2 x 1 Week Headquarters in Orange, CA

SPECIFIC EXPANSION PLANS:

US:	All United States
Canada:	All Canada
Overseas:	Western Europe

<< >>

SLUMBERLAND INTERNATIONAL

100 S. Owasso Blvd., E.
Little Canada, MN 55117
Tel: (888) 482-7500 (651) 482-7500
Fax: (651) 494-5927
E-Mail: michael.larson@slumberland.com
Web Site: www.slumberland.com
Mr. Michael Larson, Director Franchise Development

SLUMBERLAND is a home furnishings specialty retailer, featuring name-brand mattresses, sleep sofas, reclining chairs, sofas and chairs, daybeds and related bedroom furniture. SLUMBERLAND is a market-driven retailer that outpaces

141

national averages in sales/SF and gross margins.

BACKGROUND: IFA MEMBER
Established: 1967;   1st Franchised: 1978
Franchised Units: 68
Company-Owned Units: <u>35</u>
Total Units: 103
Dist.:   US-103; CAN-0; O'seas-0
 North America: 7 States, 0 Provinces
 Density: 8 in SD, 33 in MN, 12 in IA
Projected New Units (12 Months):   8
Qualifications: NR

FINANCIAL/TERMS:
Cash Investment: $100-300K
Total Investment: $442.5K-1.7MM
Minimum Net Worth: NR
Fees: Franchise - $12.5K
 Royalty - 3%;   Ad. - 2%
Earnings Claims Statement: No
Term of Contract (Years):   10/10
Avg. # Of Employees: 4 FT, 2 PT
Passive Ownership: Discouraged
Encourage Conversions: Yes
Area Develop. Agreements: No
Sub-Franchising Contracts: No
Expand In Territory: Yes
Space Needs: 15,000 SF

SUPPORT & TRAINING:
Financial Assistance Provided: No
Site Selection Assistance: No
Lease Negotiation Assistance: Yes
Co-Operative Advertising: No
Franchisee Assoc./Member: NR
Size Of Corporate Staff: NR
On-Going Support: ,B,c,d,,,G,H,i
Training: 3 Days Headquarters;
  2 Weeks On-Site

SPECIFIC EXPANSION PLANS:
US: Central Midwest
Canada: No
Overseas: NR

≪≪ ≫≫

ULTRASONIC BLIND SERVICES
2706 Artesia Blvd., # F
Redondo Beach, CA 90278
Tel: (866) 617-6642
Fax: (310) 937-2400
E-Mail: sales@ultrasonicblindservices.com

Web Site: ultrasonicblindservices.com
Mr. Brian Sher, VP

Ultrasonic Blind Services is the leader in servicing the multi billion dollar window covering industry. With a proven on-site system and high tech ultrasonic cleaning equipment you can cash in on this lucrative opportunity that is virtually untouched. See for yourself that there is little or no competition with this franchise. You can be cleaning, repairing and selling name brand window coverings right out of your mobile unit. Call now for this rare opportunity. Call Ultrasonic Blind Services.

BACKGROUND: IFA MEMBER
Established: 1989;   1st Franchised: 2004
Franchised Units: 3
Company-Owned Units: <u>2</u>
Total Units: 5
Dist.:   US-5; CAN-0; O'seas-0
 North America: 1 States, 0 Provinces
 Density: 5 in CA
Projected New Units (12 Months):   8
Qualifications: 5, 5, 1, 2, 2, 5

FINANCIAL/TERMS:
Cash Investment: $75K
Total Investment: $130K
Minimum Net Worth: $100K
Fees: Franchise - $35K
 Royalty - 7%;   Ad. - 1%
Earnings Claims Statement: No
Term of Contract (Years):   10/0
Avg. # Of Employees: 1 FT, 0 PT
Passive Ownership: Discouraged
Encourage Conversions: NA
Area Develop. Agreements: No
Sub-Franchising Contracts: No
Expand In Territory: Yes
Space Needs: NA

SUPPORT & TRAINING:
Financial Assistance Provided: No
Site Selection Assistance: NA
Lease Negotiation Assistance: NA
Co-Operative Advertising: No
Franchisee Assoc./Member: No
Size Of Corporate Staff: 2
On-Going Support: ,,C,D,,,G,H,I
Training: 2 Weeks 2706 Artesia Blvd #F

SPECIFIC EXPANSION PLANS:
US: Western
Canada: No
Overseas: NR

≪≪ ≫≫

V2K WINDOW DECOR & MORE
13949 W. Colfax, # 250
Lakewood, CO 80401
Tel: (800) 200-0835 + 331 (303) 202-1120
Fax: (303) 202-5201
E-Mail: franchising@v2k.com
Web Site: www.v2k.com
Mr. Paul Linenberg, Marketing Director

The heart of V2K, and what makes us different from every other franchise on the planet, is our exclusive and proprietary 3D Decor Creator software. This easy-to-use software program separates us from all of our competition because it allows you to perform simple to complex window treatment designs in high-quality 3D right in front of your customer! By showing your customer exactly what their window treatments will look like on their windows, they have the confidence to place the order with you instead of your competition. It's almost an unfair advantage...

BACKGROUND: IFA MEMBER
Established: 1996;   1st Franchised: 2001
Franchised Units: 187
Company-Owned Units: <u>0</u>
Total Units: 187
Dist.:   US-170; CAN-4; O'seas-1
 North America: 44 States, 2 Provinces
 Density: NR
Projected New Units (12 Months):   100
Qualifications: 3, 3, 2, 1, 1, 1

FINANCIAL/TERMS:
Cash Investment: $40-90K
Total Investment: $40-90K
Minimum Net Worth: NA
Fees: Franchise - $39.9K-59.9K
 Royalty - 4-8%;   Ad. - 2%
Earnings Claims Statement: Yes
Term of Contract (Years):   10/5/5/
Avg. # Of Employees: 1 FT, 0 PT
Passive Ownership: Allowed
Encourage Conversions: NA
Area Develop. Agreements: No
Sub-Franchising Contracts: No
Expand In Territory: Yes
Space Needs: NA

SUPPORT & TRAINING:
Financial Assistance Provided: Yes (I)
Site Selection Assistance: NA
Lease Negotiation Assistance: NA
Co-Operative Advertising: Yes
Franchisee Assoc./Member: No
Size Of Corporate Staff: 20

On-Going Support: A,B,C,D,,,G,h,I
Training: 2 Weeks Denver, CO
SPECIFIC EXPANSION PLANS:
US: All United States
Canada: License Agreement
Overseas: NR

‹‹ ››

**VERLO MATTRESS
FACTORY STORES**
201 N. Main St., # 5
Fort Atkinson, WI 53538
Tel: (800) 229-8957 + 101 (920) 568-3100
Fax: (920) 568-3140
E-Mail: info@verlofranchise.com
Web Site: www.verlofranchise.com
Ms. Jennifer Roethe, Franchise Administrator

VERLO MATTRESS FACTORY STORES (R) is the nation's largest CRAFTSMAN DIRECT (R) retailer. Each franchise assembles custom-made mattresses to the customer's specifications. Our business model appeals to the multi-unit master because owners can penetrate markets quickly and cost-effectively.

BACKGROUND: IFA MEMBER
Established: 1958; 1st Franchised: 1981
Franchised Units: 60
Company-Owned Units: 0
Total Units: 60
Dist.: US-60; CAN-0; O'seas-0
  North America: 10 States, 0 Provinces
  Density: 29 in WI, 18 in IL, 4 in FL
Projected New Units (12 Months): 6
Qualifications: 4, 3, 2, 3, 4, 5
FINANCIAL/TERMS:
Cash Investment: $50-100K
Total Investment: $300-500K
Minimum Net Worth: $350K
Fees: Franchise - $50K
  Royalty - 6%; Ad. - $400/Mo.
Earnings Claims Statement: Yes

Term of Contract (Years): 10/10
Avg. # Of Employees: 5 FT, 0 PT
Passive Ownership: Not Allowed
Encourage Conversions: Yes
Area Develop. Agreements: Yes
Sub-Franchising Contracts: No
Expand In Territory: Yes
Space Needs: 3,000-10,000 SF
SUPPORT & TRAINING:
Financial Assistance Provided: Yes (I)
Site Selection Assistance: Yes
Lease Negotiation Assistance: Yes
Co-Operative Advertising: No
Franchisee Assoc./Member: Yes/Yes
Size Of Corporate Staff: 8
On-Going Support: ,,C,D,E,,G,H,i
Training: ;
  5-10 Days Corporate Office;5-7
  DaysOn-Site
SPECIFIC EXPANSION PLANS:
US: All United States except CA, HI
Canada: No
Overseas: NR

‹‹ ››

FIVE LARGEST PARTICIPANTS IN SURVEY

Company	# Fran-chised Units	# Co-Owned Units	# Total Units	Franchise Fee	On-Going Royalty	Total Investment
1. Kumon North America	25,616	31	25,947	$1K, Materials: $1K	$32-36/ subj./mo.	$32.9-131.0K
2. Sylvan Learning Centers	921	198	1,119	$42-48K	8-9%	$188.6-304.6K
3. Berlitz International	80	350	430	$30-50K	10%	$150-300K
4. New Horizons Computer Learning Center	269	5	274	$25-75K	6%	$400-500K
5. Oxford Learning	125	6	131	$39.5K	10%	$125-215K

All of the data provided are proprietary and should not be quoted without acknowledging *Bond's Franchise Guide.*

ACADEMY FOR MATHEMATICS & SCIENCE

30 Glen Cameron Rd., # 200
Thornhill, ON L3T 1N7 Canada
Tel: (800) 809-5555 (905) 709-3233
Fax: (905) 709-3045
E-Mail: info@acadfor.com
Web Site: www.acadfor.com
Mr. Balti Sauer, President/CEO

Licensees provide math, science, English and computer tutoring to school age children from kindergarten to the end of high school. Individualized, self-paced learning is provided in learning centers located in major malls, using a unique audio-visual learning program.

BACKGROUND:
Established: 1993;   1st Franchised: 1993
Franchised Units: 51
Company-Owned Units: 2
Total Units: 53
Dist.:   US-13; CAN-40; O'seas-0
 North America: 0 States, 3 Provinces
 Density: 29 in ON, 6 in BC, 5 in AB
Projected New Units (12 Months):   6
Qualifications: 2, 3, 1, 4, 1, 5
FINANCIAL/TERMS:
Cash Investment: $70-100K

Total Investment: $120-140K
Minimum Net Worth: NA
Fees: Franchise - $35K
 Royalty - 10-12%;   Ad. - 2%
Earnings Claims Statement: No
Term of Contract (Years):   5/5
Avg. # Of Employees: 2 FT, 6 PT
Passive Ownership: Not Allowed
Encourage Conversions: NA
Area Develop. Agreements: Yes/1
Sub-Franchising Contracts: Yes
Expand In Territory: Yes
Space Needs: 1,000 SF
SUPPORT & TRAINING:
Financial Assistance Provided: Yes (D)

Site Selection Assistance: Yes
Lease Negotiation Assistance: Yes
Co-Operative Advertising: No
Franchisee Assoc./Member: Yes/Yes
Size Of Corporate Staff: 14
On-Going Support: „C,D,E,„G,H,I
Training: 1 Week Training Center;
2 Weeks Corporate Office

SPECIFIC EXPANSION PLANS:
US: In Progress
Canada: All Canada
Overseas: All Countries

<< >>

BERLITZ INTERNATIONAL
400 Alexander Park Dr.
Princeton, NJ 08540
Tel: (800) 626-6419 (609) 514-3046
Fax: (609) 514-9675
E-Mail: charles.gilbert@berlitz.com
Web Site: www.berlitz.com
Mr. Charles J. Gilbert, Dir. Worldwide
Franchise

Language instruction, publishing and translation services

BACKGROUND: IFA MEMBER
Established: 1878; 1st Franchised: 1996
Franchised Units: 80
Company-Owned Units: 350
Total Units: 430
Dist.: US-91; CAN-11; O'seas-328
North America: 0 States, 0 Provinces
Density: 18 in NY, 18 in FL, 18 in CA
Projected New Units (12 Months): 50
Qualifications: 4, 5, 2, 3, 4, 5

FINANCIAL/TERMS:
Cash Investment: $150K-300K
Total Investment: $150K-300K
Minimum Net Worth: $300K
Fees: Franchise - $30-50K
Royalty - 10%; Ad. - 2%
Earnings Claims Statement: No
Term of Contract (Years): 10/10
Avg. # Of Employees: 1 FT, 1 PT
Passive Ownership: Discouraged
Encourage Conversions: Yes
Area Develop. Agreements: Yes/1
Sub-Franchising Contracts: No
Expand In Territory: No
Space Needs: 1,500-3,000 SF

SUPPORT & TRAINING:
Financial Assistance Provided: No
Site Selection Assistance: Yes
Lease Negotiation Assistance: Yes
Co-Operative Advertising: No
Franchisee Assoc./Member: No
Size Of Corporate Staff: 7000

On-Going Support: „C,D,E,F,G,H,
Training: 2 Weeks Division Training;
2 Weeks Home Office; 2 Weeks On-
Site

SPECIFIC EXPANSION PLANS:
US: Southeast, West
Canada: NB
Overseas: Africa, Central Asia, Asia

<< >>

CMIT SOLUTIONS
1701 Directors Blvd., # 300
Austin, TX 78744
Tel: (800) 710-2648 (512) 692-3710
Fax: (512) 692-3711
E-Mail: franchise@cmitsolutions.com
Web Site: www.cmitsolutions.com
Ms. Sheri Vandermause, VP Franchise
Development

Offers IT service and computer support to small businesses. Franchise can be home-based, as we service the client at their place of business.

BACKGROUND: IFA MEMBER
Established: 1994; 1st Franchised: 1998
Franchised Units: 87
Company-Owned Units: 0
Total Units: 87
Dist.: US-87; CAN-0; O'seas-0
North America: 32 States, 0 Provinces
Density: NR
Projected New Units (12 Months): 60
Qualifications: 2, 3, 4, 2, 4, 4

FINANCIAL/TERMS:
Cash Investment: $40K-74.2K
Total Investment: $150K-250K
Minimum Net Worth: $200K
Fees: Franchise - $39.5K
Royalty - 6%; Ad. - 2%
Earnings Claims Statement: No
Term of Contract (Years): 10/10
Avg. # Of Employees: 0 FT, 6-10 PT
Passive Ownership: Not Allowed
Encourage Conversions: No
Area Develop. Agreements: Yes/1
Sub-Franchising Contracts: No
Expand In Territory: No
Space Needs: NR

SUPPORT & TRAINING:
Financial Assistance Provided: No
Site Selection Assistance: NA
Lease Negotiation Assistance: NA
Co-Operative Advertising: No

Franchisee Assoc./Member: No
Size Of Corporate Staff: 15
On-Going Support: A,B,C,d,„„H,I
Training: 1 Week Austin, TX

SPECIFIC EXPANSION PLANS:
US: All United States
Canada: No
Overseas: NR

<< >>

EWF INTERNATIONAL
4900 Richmond Sq., # 105
Oklahoma City, OK 73118
Tel: (866) 831-3934 (405) 843-3934
Fax: (405) 843-3933
E-Mail: darcie@ewfinternational.com
Web Site: www.ewfinternational.com
Ms. Darcie Harris, Co-Owner

At EWF INTERNATIONAL, our focus is on professional women who are looking for something more. Our service is peer advisory groups for women executives and business owners. Our clients are professional women with business goals to achieve. Our franchisees quickly become valuable business resources. We offer business management, operational/sales training, ongoing mentoring, and access to our other franchisees who can provide 'been there, done that' assistance. It's the 'more' you've been dreaming of!

BACKGROUND: IFA MEMBER
Established: 1998; 1st Franchised: 2002
Franchised Units: 2
Company-Owned Units: 1
Total Units: 3
Dist.: US-3; CAN-0; O'seas-0
North America: 2 States, Provinces
Density: 2 in OK, 1 in TX
Projected New Units (12 Months): 3
Qualifications: 2, 4, 5, 4, 5, 5

FINANCIAL/TERMS:
Cash Investment: $25-30K
Total Investment: $25-30K
Minimum Net Worth: $40K
Fees: Franchise - $25K
Royalty - 15%; Ad. - 2%
Earnings Claims Statement: Yes
Term of Contract (Years): 5/5
Avg. # Of Employees: 1 FT, 1 PT
Passive Ownership: Not Allowed
Encourage Conversions: No
Area Develop. Agreements: No
Sub-Franchising Contracts: No
Expand In Territory: No
Space Needs: NA

SUPPORT & TRAINING:

Financial Assistance Provided: No
Site Selection Assistance: NA
Lease Negotiation Assistance: NA
Co-Operative Advertising: No
Franchisee Assoc./Member: No
Size Of Corporate Staff: 2
On-Going Support: ,,C,D,,,G,H,I
Training: 1 Week Corporate Headquarters Oklahoma City, OK; Additional Field Training

SPECIFIC EXPANSION PLANS:
US: All United States
Canada: No
Overseas: NR

◄◄ ►►

FOURTH R, THE
11410 N. E. 124th St., # 142
Kirkland, WA 98034-4399
Tel: (425) 765-9969
Fax:
E-Mail: rob@fourthr.com
Web Site: www.fourthr.com
Mr. Robert McCauley, Dir. of Int'l Development

Computers have changed virtually all aspects of our lives. As we move into the information age, many experts agree that computer literacy has become THE FOURTH R in education today. The Fourth R provides PC courseware, assessment software and certification services to leading schools and learning centers throughout the world.

BACKGROUND: IFA MEMBER
Established: 1991; 1st Franchised: 1994
Franchised Units: 41
Company-Owned Units: 1
Total Units: 42
Dist.: US-6; CAN-0; O'seas-36
North America: 4 States, 0 Provinces
Density: NR
Projected New Units (12 Months): 10
Qualifications: 2, 4, 3, 4, 3, 3
FINANCIAL/TERMS:
Cash Investment: $15-25K
Total Investment: $18-38K
Minimum Net Worth: $None
Fees: Franchise - $12-25K
Royalty - $100/Mo./5%Sale; Ad. - 0%
Earnings Claims Statement: No
Term of Contract (Years): 5/5

Avg. # Of Employees: Varies
Passive Ownership: Allowed
Encourage Conversions: Yes
Area Develop. Agreements: Yes/1
Sub-Franchising Contracts: No
Expand In Territory: Yes
Space Needs: 1,800 SF
SUPPORT & TRAINING:
Financial Assistance Provided: Yes (D)
Site Selection Assistance: No
Lease Negotiation Assistance: Yes
Co-Operative Advertising: No
Franchisee Assoc./Member: No
Size Of Corporate Staff: 3
On-Going Support: ,,C,,,,G,H,
Training: 3-4 Days On-Site
SPECIFIC EXPANSION PLANS:
US: No
Canada: All Canada
Overseas: All Countries

◄◄ ►►

FRED ASTAIRE DANCE STUDIOS
10 Bliss Rd.
Longmeadow, MA 01106
Tel: (800) 278-2473 (413) 567-3200
Fax: (413) 565-2455
E-Mail: dancefads@aol.com
Web Site: www.fredastaire.com
Mr. Andy Kreig, Franchise Manager

FRED ASTAIRE DANCE STUDIOS (FADS) provides its franchised community with a 50+ year tradition that gives the individual franchisee worldwide name recognition identified with dance excellence unsurpassed in its industry. The original teaching methods of the great Fred Astaire are still in place today at the company that proudly bears his name. FADS provides its franchisees with extensive business and dance training, and ensures that its franchises operate under the strictest code of ethics.

BACKGROUND:
Established: 1947; 1st Franchised: 1950
Franchised Units: 100
Company-Owned Units: 0
Total Units: 100
Dist.: US-97; CAN-3; O'seas-0
North America: 28 States, 1 Provinces
Density: 12 in OH, 13 in NY, 16 in FL
Projected New Units (12 Months): 8-10
Qualifications: 5, 4, 3, 2, 2, 5
FINANCIAL/TERMS:
Cash Investment: $125K
Total Investment: $138.5-357K
Minimum Net Worth: $150K

Fees: Franchise - $15-35K
Royalty - 7-8%; Ad. - 0.2%/$25Min
Earnings Claims Statement: No
Term of Contract (Years): 5/5
Avg. # Of Employees: 10 FT, 0 PT
Passive Ownership: Discouraged
Encourage Conversions: Yes
Area Develop. Agreements: No
Sub-Franchising Contracts: Yes
Expand In Territory: Yes
Space Needs: 2,500 Min. SF
SUPPORT & TRAINING:
Financial Assistance Provided: Yes (D)
Site Selection Assistance: Yes
Lease Negotiation Assistance: Yes
Co-Operative Advertising: No
Franchisee Assoc./Member: No
Size Of Corporate Staff: 9
On-Going Support: A,b,c,d,E,f,G,h,I
Training: 8 Hours Dance or Management (Franchisee's Site); 16 Hours Management (Existing Site)

SPECIFIC EXPANSION PLANS:
US: All United States
Canada: All Canada
Overseas: Under Trade Name Megadance International

◄◄ ►►

JOHN CASABLANCAS MODELING AND CAREER CENTERS
648 Trade Center Blvd.
Chesterfield, MO 63005
Tel: (970) 454-0253
Fax: (970) 454-0254
E-Mail: charyn.u@imestl.com
Web Site: www.jcasablancas.com
Ms. Charyn Parker Urban, Dir. Franchise Development

Our franchised schools and in-house modeling agencies provide cutting-edge professional modeling, personal image development and TV/Film acting programs and workshops. Created by John Casablancas, founder of Elite Model Management.

BACKGROUND: IFA MEMBER
Established: 1979; 1st Franchised: 1979
Franchised Units: 46
Company-Owned Units: 0
Total Units: 46
Dist.: US-38; CAN-1; O'seas-7

North America: 26 States, 1 Provinces
Density: 5 in FL
Projected New Units (12 Months): 2
Qualifications: 5, 5, 4, 4, 5, 5

FINANCIAL/TERMS:

Cash Investment: $135K-298K
Total Investment: $135K-298K
Minimum Net Worth: NR
Fees: Franchise - $50K
Royalty - 7%; Ad. - 3%
Earnings Claims Statement: No
Term of Contract (Years): 10/10
Avg. # Of Employees: 4 FT, 6-8 PT
Passive Ownership: Not Allowed
Encourage Conversions: Yes
Area Develop. Agreements: No
Sub-Franchising Contracts: No
Expand In Territory: Yes
Space Needs: 1,800-2,500 SF

SUPPORT & TRAINING:

Financial Assistance Provided: No
Site Selection Assistance: Yes
Lease Negotiation Assistance: Yes
Co-Operative Advertising: Yes
Franchisee Assoc./Member: No
Size Of Corporate Staff: 8
On-Going Support: ,,C,D,E,,G,h,
Training: 3 Days Field; 2-3 Days MO

SPECIFIC EXPANSION PLANS:

US: All United States
Canada: All Canada
Overseas: Far East, Europe, Latin
America

≺≺ ≻≻

KIDZART

1902 E. Common St., # 400
New Braunfels, TX 78130
Tel: (800) 379-8302 (830) 626-1959
Fax: (830) 626-0260
E-Mail: shell@kidzart.com
Web Site: www.kidzart.com
Ms. Shell Herman, Chief Executive Officer

KidzArt's drawing-based fine arts programs emphasize creativity, individuality and building confidence for all ages groups. You don't have to be an artist to own and operate a KidzArt franchise! While art education is all but eliminated from many schools around the country, KidzArt is providing a viable solution with after school fine arts programs, as well as programs that serve all ages. KidzArt programs and locations are simple to establish and businesses love to partner with us. Our rave reviews and national recognition from parents, teachers, educational

administrators and community leaders will support you in your efforts. With KidzArt your opportunities are endless. And that's just the beginning.

BACKGROUND: IFA MEMBER
Established: 1998; 1st Franchised: 2002
Franchised Units: 61
Company-Owned Units: 0
Total Units: 61
Dist.: US-61; CAN-0; O'seas-0
North America: 29 States, 0 Provinces
Density: 4 in NC, 9 in CA, 10 in AZ
Projected New Units (12 Months): NR
Qualifications: 3, 5, 2, 3, 4, 5

FINANCIAL/TERMS:

Cash Investment: $50K-75K
Total Investment: $50K-75K
Minimum Net Worth: $200K
Fees: Franchise - $32K
Royalty - 8%/$250 Min.; Ad. - 1%
Earnings Claims Statement: No
Term of Contract (Years): 10/10
Avg. # Of Employees: 2 FT, 4-15 PT
Passive Ownership: Not Allowed
Encourage Conversions: No
Area Develop. Agreements: No
Sub-Franchising Contracts: No
Expand In Territory: No
Space Needs: NA

SUPPORT & TRAINING:

Financial Assistance Provided: No
Site Selection Assistance: Yes
Lease Negotiation Assistance: NA
Co-Operative Advertising: No
Franchisee Assoc./Member: Yes/Yes
Size Of Corporate Staff: 7
On-Going Support: ,,C,D,E,,G,h,I
Training: 4 Days New Braunfels, TX

SPECIFIC EXPANSION PLANS:

US: All States Exc. Registration
Canada: NR
Overseas: NR

≺≺ ≻≻

KUMON NORTH AMERICA

300 Frank W. Burr Blvd., 5 Fl.
Teaneck, NJ 07666-6703
Tel: (866) 633-0740 (201) 928-0444
Fax: (201) 692-3130
E-Mail: dklein@kumon.com
Web Site: www.kumon.com
Mr. Deven Klein, Vice President of Franchising

Premiere supplemental education franchise where you'll find success, one child at a time.

BACKGROUND: IFA MEMBER
Established: 1958; 1st Franchised: 1958
Franchised Units: 25616
Company-Owned Units: 31
Total Units: 25947
Dist.: US-1453; CAN-344; O'seas-24150
North America: 50 States, 9 Provinces
Density:110 in TX, 93 in NY, 241 in CA
Projected New Units (12 Months): 120
Qualifications: 3, 3, 3, 5, 4, 4

FINANCIAL/TERMS:

Cash Investment: NR
Total Investment: $32.9-131.0K
Minimum Net Worth: $50-100K
Fees: Franchise - $1K, Materials:$1K
Royalty - $32-36/subj.,/mo.; Ad. - NA
Earnings Claims Statement: Yes
Term of Contract (Years): 3/5
Avg. # Of Employees: 1 FT, 1-3 PT
Passive Ownership: Not Allowed
Encourage Conversions: NA
Area Develop. Agreements: No
Sub-Franchising Contracts: No
Expand In Territory: No
Space Needs: 1,000 SF

SUPPORT & TRAINING:

Financial Assistance Provided: NR
Site Selection Assistance: Yes
Lease Negotiation Assistance: No
Co-Operative Advertising: Yes
Franchisee Assoc./Member: Yes/Yes
Size Of Corporate Staff: 400
On-Going Support: ,,C,D,E,F,G,H,I
Training: National Training Dept. Oakbrook Terrace, IL.; 8-11 Days Total Start-Up

SPECIFIC EXPANSION PLANS:

US: All United States
Canada: All Canada
Overseas: All Countries

≺≺ ≻≻

LEARNINGRX

5085 List Dr., # 200
Colorado Springs, CO 80919
Tel: (800) 679-1569 (719) 264-8808
Fax: (719) 522-0434
E-Mail: kelly@learningrx.com
Web Site: www.learningrx.com
Ms. Kelly Harms, Franchise Development Coordinator

LearningRx is a franchise at the forefront of finding and correcting the root of learning problems (cognitive skills). Studies show that 88% of learning problems have weak cognitive skills as a primary cause. Over 15,000 students have improved their learning skills (attention, memory, reasoning, visual or auditory processing, or processing speed) by an average of over 4 grade levels within 24 weeks of using these innovative programs. LearningRx also offers enhancement training for adults and athletes.

BACKGROUND: IFA MEMBER
Established: 1986; 1st Franchised: 2003
Franchised Units: 58
Company-Owned Units: 2
Total Units: 60
Dist.: US-60; CAN-0; O'seas-0
North America: 17 States, 0 Provinces
Density: 8 in TX, 7 in FL
Projected New Units (12 Months): 48
Qualifications: 3, 3, 3, 3, 4, 4
FINANCIAL/TERMS:
Cash Investment: $17K-50K
Total Investment: $73K-150K
Minimum Net Worth: $250K
Fees: Franchise - $29K
Royalty - 10%; Ad. - 2.5%
Earnings Claims Statement: Yes
Term of Contract (Years): 10/10
Avg. # Of Employees: 3 FT, 20 PT
Passive Ownership: Discouraged
Encourage Conversions: NA
Area Develop. Agreements: Yes/3
Sub-Franchising Contracts: No
Expand In Territory: Yes
Space Needs: 1,200-1,800 SF
SUPPORT & TRAINING:
Financial Assistance Provided: No
Site Selection Assistance: Yes
Lease Negotiation Assistance: No
Co-Operative Advertising: No
Franchisee Assoc./Member: No
Size Of Corporate Staff: 17
On-Going Support: A,,C,,,,G,H,
Training: 2 Weeks plus On-Site
SPECIFIC EXPANSION PLANS:
US: 44
Canada: No
Overseas: NR

⋘ ⋙

**NEW HORIZONS COMPUTER
LEARNING CENTER**
1900 S. State College Blvd., # 120
Anaheim, CA 92806
Tel: (714) 940-8188
Fax: (714) 938-6008
E-Mail: craig.brubeck@newhorizons.com
Web Site: www.newhorizons.com
Mr. Craig Brubeck, VP North American
Franchise Development

NEW HORIZONS COMPUTER LEARNING CENTERS, Inc. is the world's largest independent IT training company, meeting the needs of more than 2.4 million students each year. NEW HORIZONS offers a variety of flexible training choices: instructor-led classes, Web-based training, computer-based training, computer labs, certification exam preparation tools and 24-hour, 7-day-a-week help-desk support.

BACKGROUND: IFA MEMBER
Established: 1982; 1st Franchised: 1992
Franchised Units: 269
Company-Owned Units: 5
Total Units: 274
Dist.: US-139; CAN-1; O'seas-116
North America: 42 States, 1 Provinces
Density: 6 in NY, 9 in FL, 14 in CA
Projected New Units (12 Months): 10
Qualifications: 5, 5, 2, 3, 3, 5
FINANCIAL/TERMS:
Cash Investment: $250-450K
Total Investment: $400-500K
Minimum Net Worth: $500K
Fees: Franchise - $25-75K
Royalty - 6%; Ad. - 1%
Earnings Claims Statement: No
Term of Contract (Years): 10/5
Avg. # Of Employees: 15 FT, 0 PT
Passive Ownership: Discouraged
Encourage Conversions: Yes
Area Develop. Agreements: Yes/1
Sub-Franchising Contracts: Yes
Expand In Territory: Yes
Space Needs: 4,000-5,000 SF
SUPPORT & TRAINING:
Financial Assistance Provided: Yes (D)
Site Selection Assistance: Yes
Lease Negotiation Assistance: Yes
Co-Operative Advertising: No
Franchisee Assoc./Member: Yes/Yes

Size Of Corporate Staff: 200
On-Going Support: ,B,C,D,E,,G,H,
Training: 2 Weeks Headquarters;
1 Week Franchise Location; 2 Days
Regional
SPECIFIC EXPANSION PLANS:
US: All United States
Canada: All Canada
Overseas: All Countries

⋘ ⋙

ONLINE TRADING ACADEMY
18004 Sky Park Circle S., # 140
Irvine, CA 92612
Tel: (888) 841-8418 (949) 608-6020
Fax: (949) 608-6026
E-Mail: ralph@tradingacademy.com
Web Site: www.tradingacademy.com
Mr. Ralph Loberger, VP Franchise Development

We are the global brand leader in direct access trading education for: stocks, futures and options. All students earn tuition rebates from a choice of five (5) brokers. Our classes are delivered via Web, CDROM and classroom experiences. OTA won the Voyager Award from Technology Investor Magazine for Education Excellence.

BACKGROUND:
Established: 1997; 1st Franchised: 2004
Franchised Units: 10
Company-Owned Units: 1
Total Units: 11
Dist.: US-7; CAN-1; O'seas-3
North America: 6 States, 1 Provinces
Density: 2 in TX, 1 in NY, 2 in CA
Projected New Units (12 Months): 12
Qualifications: 3, 4, 2, 4, 5, 5
FINANCIAL/TERMS:
Cash Investment: $50-100K
Total Investment: $200-250K
Minimum Net Worth: $200K
Fees: Franchise - $65-190K
Royalty - 10%; Ad. - 3%
Earnings Claims Statement: No
Term of Contract (Years): 10/5
Avg. # Of Employees: 2 FT, 3 PT
Passive Ownership: Discouraged
Encourage Conversions: Yes
Area Develop. Agreements: Yes
Sub-Franchising Contracts: No
Expand In Territory: Yes
Space Needs: 3,000 SF
SUPPORT & TRAINING:
Financial Assistance Provided: Yes (D)
Site Selection Assistance: Yes

Lease Negotiation Assistance: Yes
Co-Operative Advertising: No
Franchisee Assoc./Member: No
Size Of Corporate Staff: 12
On-Going Support: a,,C,D,E,,G,H,I
Training: 2 Weeks Plus 2 Weeks
Instructors at Irvine, CA
SPECIFIC EXPANSION PLANS:
US: All United States
Canada: All Canada
Overseas: Europe First, then Asia

≺≺ ≻≻

OXFORD LEARNING
97B S. Livingston Ave.
Livingston, NJ 07039
Tel: (888) 559-2212 (519) 473-1460
Fax: (519) 473-6447
E-Mail: franchise@oxfordlearning.com
Web Site: www.oxfordlearning.com
Ms. Lenka Whitehead, COO

Join the leaders in supplemental education. Our proprietary curriculum developed over the past 20 years, ensures that your students will make impressive academic gains while developing higher self-esteem. Successful, confident students and happy parents mean referrals and a growing business. We will assist you every step of the way, providing the proven training, marketing, and business expertise you will need. Excellent territories available.

BACKGROUND: IFA MEMBER
Established: 1984; 1st Franchised: 1991
Franchised Units: 125
Company-Owned Units: 6
Total Units: 131
Dist.: US-45; CAN-83; O'seas-2
North America: 14 States, 7 Provinces
Density: 52 in ON, 9 in NJ
Projected New Units (12 Months): 30
Qualifications: 4, 3, 2, 3, 4, 5
FINANCIAL/TERMS:
Cash Investment: $60-90K
Total Investment: $125-215K
Minimum Net Worth: $200K
Fees: Franchise - $39.5K
Royalty - 10%; Ad. - 3%
Earnings Claims Statement: No
Term of Contract (Years): 10/10
Avg. # Of Employees: 3 FT, 5 PT

Passive Ownership: Not Allowed
Encourage Conversions: No
Area Develop. Agreements: Yes/1
Sub-Franchising Contracts: No
Expand In Territory: Yes
Space Needs: 1,600-2,000 SF
SUPPORT & TRAINING:
Financial Assistance Provided: No
Site Selection Assistance: Yes
Lease Negotiation Assistance: Yes
Co-Operative Advertising: Yes
Franchisee Assoc./Member: Yes/Yes
Size Of Corporate Staff: 30
On-Going Support: ,,C,D,E,F,G,H,I
Training: 2 Weeks London, ON
SPECIFIC EXPANSION PLANS:
US: All United States
Canada: All Canada
Overseas: India, Hong Kong, Japan, Germany, Korea, Caribbean

≺≺ ≻≻

Hottest New Franchise

SPIRIT OF MATH SCHOOLS
120A Willowdale Ave.
Toronto, Ontario M2N 4Y2 Canada
Tel: (866) 767-6284 (416) 223-1985
Fax: (416) 964-1902
E-Mail: franchise@spiritofmath.com
Web Site: www.spiritofmath.com
Mr. Darrin Langen, Director of Franchise Operations

Spirit of Math provides a unique opportunity for you to offer a complete, unique and well documented system of after school math classes for highly motivated students. It is not a tutoring program. Students come once a week from September to June and are taught in a classroom setting by highly qualified teachers using proprietary curriculum. Advanced Thinking, Academic Excellence, Award-Winning Program. A franchise opportunity that really adds up!

BACKGROUND:
Established: 1992; 1st Franchised: 2004
Franchised Units: 6
Company-Owned Units: 11
Total Units: 17
Dist.: US-0; CAN-17; O'seas-0
North America: 0 States, 2 Provinces
Density: 11 in ON, 1 in MB

Projected New Units (12 Months): 10
Qualifications: 4, 4, 5, 4, 3, 4
FINANCIAL/TERMS:
Cash Investment: $32K-70K
Total Investment: Varies
Minimum Net Worth: $200K
Fees: Franchise - $35K
Royalty - 9%; Ad. - 1%
Earnings Claims Statement: No
Term of Contract (Years): 5/5
Avg. # Of Employees: 0 FT, 4 PT
Passive Ownership: Not Allowed
Encourage Conversions: No
Area Develop. Agreements: No
Sub-Franchising Contracts: No
Expand In Territory: Yes
Space Needs: 1600 - 2100 SF
SUPPORT & TRAINING:
Financial Assistance Provided: No
Site Selection Assistance: Yes
Lease Negotiation Assistance: Yes
Co-Operative Advertising: No
Franchisee Assoc./Member: No
Size Of Corporate Staff: 12
On-Going Support: A,,C,d,E,,G,h,i
Training: 10 days Local; 5 days Toronto
SPECIFIC EXPANSION PLANS:
US: New York, New Jersey, Connecticut, Rhode Island, MA
Canada: Ontario, Alberta, B.C.
Overseas: NR

≺≺ ≻≻

Top 100

SYLVAN LEARNING CENTERS
1001 Fleet St.
Baltimore, MD 21202-4382
Tel: (800) 627-4276 + 8729 (410) 843-8000
Fax: (410) 843-6265
E-Mail: greg.helwig@educate.com
Web Site: www.sylvanfranchise.com
Mr. Greg Helwig, VP System Development

SYLVAN is the leading provider of educational services to families, schools and industry. SYLVAN services pre-kindergarten through adult-levels from more than 1,100 SYLVAN LEARNING CENTERS worldwide.

BACKGROUND: IFA MEMBER
Established: 1979; 1st Franchised: 1980

149

Franchised Units: 921
Company-Owned Units: 198
Total Units: 1119
Dist.: US-1030; CAN-79; O'seas-10
  North America: 49 States, 6 Provinces
  Density: 68 in TX, 71 in FL, 107 in CA
Projected New Units (12 Months): 50
Qualifications: 4, 4, 3, 4, 4, 5

FINANCIAL/TERMS:

Cash Investment: $101.1-171.3K
Total Investment: $188.6-304.6K
Minimum Net Worth: $250K
Fees: Franchise - $42-48K
  Royalty - 8-9%; Ad. - 5-13%
Earnings Claims Statement: Yes
Term of Contract (Years): 10/10
Avg. # Of Employees: 2 FT, 5 PT
Passive Ownership: Not Allowed
Encourage Conversions: Yes
Area Develop. Agreements: Yes/1
Sub-Franchising Contracts: No
Expand In Territory: Yes
Space Needs: 1,500-2,500 SF

SUPPORT & TRAINING:

Financial Assistance Provided: Yes (D)
Site Selection Assistance: Yes
Lease Negotiation Assistance: Yes
Co-Operative Advertising: Yes
Franchisee Assoc./Member: Yes/Yes
Size Of Corporate Staff: 300
On-Going Support: ,,C,D,E,,G,H,I
Training: Online, Intranet, Zee TV and
  other means; 5 Days Various Other
  Locations; 6 Days Baltimore, MD

SPECIFIC EXPANSION PLANS:

US: All United States
Canada: All Canada
Overseas: Asia, Europe, S. America, Cent.
  America, Mid. East

⫷ ⫸

**WHIZARD ACADEMY FOR MATH-
EMATICS & ENGLISH**
30 Glen Cameron Rd., # 200
Thornhill, ON L3T 1N7 Canada
Tel: (800) 809-5555 (905) 709-3233
Fax: (905) 709-3045
E-Mail: balti@acadfor.com
Web Site: www.whizardmath.com
Mr. Balti Sauer, President/CEO

Licensees provide math, science and English tutoring to school age children from
kindergarten to the end of high school.
Individualized, self-paced learning is provided in learning centers located in malls
and strip plazas, using a unique audio-
visual learning program.

BACKGROUND:

Established: 1992; 1st Franchised: 1993
Franchised Units: 48
Company-Owned Units: 4
Total Units: 52
Dist.: US-0; CAN-0; O'seas-0
  North America: 2 States, 4 Provinces
  Density: 33 in ON, 5 in BC, 8 in AB
Projected New Units (12 Months): 5
Qualifications: 3, 3, 3, 3, 3, 3

FINANCIAL/TERMS:

Cash Investment: $100-130K
Total Investment: $100-130K
Minimum Net Worth: NA
Fees: Franchise - $35K
  Royalty - 10-12%; Ad. - 2%
Earnings Claims Statement: No
Term of Contract (Years): 5/5
Avg. # Of Employees: 2 FT, 6 PT
Passive Ownership: Not Allowed
Encourage Conversions: NA
Area Develop. Agreements: Yes/10
Sub-Franchising Contracts: Yes
Expand In Territory: Yes
Space Needs: 1,000 SF

SUPPORT & TRAINING:

Financial Assistance Provided: No
Site Selection Assistance: Yes
Lease Negotiation Assistance: Yes
Co-Operative Advertising: Yes
Franchisee Assoc./Member: Yes/Yes
Size Of Corporate Staff: 14
On-Going Support: ,,C,D,E,,G,H,I
Training: 1 Week Training Center

SPECIFIC EXPANSION PLANS:

US: All United States
Canada: No
Overseas: NR

⫷ ⫸

WOODY'S WOOD SHOPS
1814 Franklin St., # 820
Oakland, CA 94612
Tel: (510) 839-5462
Fax: (510) 839-2104
E-Mail: alouie@worldfranchising.com
Web Site: www.woodyswood.com
Mr. McKee F. Bermuda, President

WOODY'S WOOD SHOPS offer instruction and use of virtually all shop tools in
a fully outfitted wood shop. After detailed
instruction and testing, members have full
use of shop and related facilities. Open 15
hours/day, 7 days/week. Also sell small
tools and all power equipment at cost
plus 5%. Members pay front-end fees plus
dues.

BACKGROUND:

Established: 1978; 1st Franchised: 1980
Franchised Units: 28
Company-Owned Units: 14
Total Units: 42
Dist.: US-36; CAN-6; O'seas-0
  North America: 7 States, 2 Provinces
  Density: 3 in WA, 8 in OR, 16 in CA
Projected New Units (12 Months): 4
Qualifications: NR

FINANCIAL/TERMS:

Cash Investment: $72K
Total Investment: $85-185K
Minimum Net Worth: NR
Fees: Franchise - $22K
  Royalty - 6%; Ad. - 2%
Earnings Claims Statement: Yes
Term of Contract (Years): 15/15
Avg. # Of Employees: 1 FT, 4 PT
Passive Ownership: Discouraged
Encourage Conversions: Yes
Area Develop. Agreements: Yes/1
Sub-Franchising Contracts: Yes
Expand In Territory: No
Space Needs: 2,800-3,400 SF

SUPPORT & TRAINING:

Financial Assistance Provided: Yes (D)
Site Selection Assistance: Yes
Lease Negotiation Assistance: Yes
Co-Operative Advertising: No
Franchisee Assoc./Member: NR
Size Of Corporate Staff: 21
On-Going Support: A,,C,D,,,g,H,i
Training: 3 Weeks Headquarters;
  2 Weeks On-Site

SPECIFIC EXPANSION PLANS:

US: All United States
Canada: ON Only
Overseas: NR

⫷ ⫸

FIVE LARGEST PARTICIPANTS IN SURVEY

Company	# Fran-chised Units	# Co-Owned Units	# Total Units	Franchise Fee	On-Going Royalty	Total Investment
1. McDonald's	25,801	6,357	32,158	$45K	12.5%	$588K-1.8MM
2. Subway Restaurants	30,300	0	30,300	$15K (10K Intl.)	8%	$108.3-300K
3. Burger King Corporation	10,144	1,079	11,223	$50K	4.5%	$294-2.8M
4. Domino's Pizza	5,796	656	6,462	$3.2K	5.5%	$118.5-460.3K
5. KFC	4,287	1023	5,310	$25K	4% or $600/Mo.	$1.2-1.7MM

All of the data provided are proprietary and should not be quoted without acknowledging *Bond's Franchise Guide.*

A & W RESTAURANTS

P. O. Box 34550, 1900 Colonel Sanders Ln.
Louisville, KY 40213
Tel: (866) 2YUM-YUM
Fax: (502) 874-8848
E-Mail: 2yumyum@yum.com
Web Site: www.yumfranchises.com
Ms. Sarah Kramer, Franchise Specialist

A & W has been a successful, all-American icon for more than 80 years. Since repositioning A & W as the home of 'All American Food' with a menu of burgers, hot dogs, coney dogs, french fries, onion rings, and our signature A & W Root Beer and Root Beer floats, we have entered the ranks of the most rapidly growing quick-service restaurants in the world. Opportunities to develop are now even greater with our new co-branded restaurants that combine A & W and our sister brand, LONG JOHN SILVER'S.

BACKGROUND: IFA MEMBER
Established: 1919; 1st Franchised: 1925
Franchised Units: 468
Company-Owned Units: 17

Total Units: 485
Dist.:   US-485; CAN-0; O'seas-0
  North America: 48 States, 0 Provinces
  Density: NR
Projected New Units (12 Months):   300
Qualifications: 5, 5, 3, 4, 5, 5
FINANCIAL/TERMS:
Cash Investment: NR
Total Investment: $1.0-1.2MM
Minimum Net Worth: $1MM
Fees: Franchise - $30-50K
  Royalty - 6% Gr. Receipts; Ad. - 4% Gr. Rec.
Earnings Claims Statement: Yes
Term of Contract (Years):   20/
Avg. # Of Employees: 50-60 Total FT, 50-60 Total PT

151

Passive Ownership:	Allowed
Encourage Conversions:	Yes
Area Develop. Agreements:	No
Sub-Franchising Contracts:	No
Expand In Territory:	Yes
Space Needs:	1,200+ SF

SUPPORT & TRAINING:

Financial Assistance Provided:	No
Site Selection Assistance:	Yes
Lease Negotiation Assistance:	Yes
Co-Operative Advertising:	No
Franchisee Assoc./Member:	Yes/Yes
Size Of Corporate Staff:	300
On-Going Support:	,,C,D,E,F,G,H,I
Training:	NR

SPECIFIC EXPANSION PLANS:

US:	All United States
Canada:	No
Overseas:	All Countries

⋘ ⋙

ARBY'S
1155 Perimeter Ctr. W.
Atlanta, GA 30338
Tel: (800) 487-2729 (678) 514-4100
Fax: (678) 514-5346
E-Mail: challiday@arbys.com
Web Site: www.arbys.com
Ms. Cindy Halliday, Franchise Development Marketing Manager

Arby's serves slow roasted, freshly sliced roast beef, Market Fresh sandwiches, wraps and salads as well as Arby's Chicken Naturals.

BACKGROUND: IFA MEMBER

Established: 1964;	1st Franchised: 1965
Franchised Units:	2542
Company-Owned Units:	1162
Total Units:	3704
Dist.:	US-3704; CAN-118; O'seas-9
North America:	48 States, 8 Provinces
Density: 288 in OH, 191 in MI, 175 in FL	
Projected New Units (12 Months):	132
Qualifications:	5, 5, 4, 3, 3, 5

FINANCIAL/TERMS:

Cash Investment:	$180.7K-544.4K
Total Investment:	$336.5K-2.5MM
Minimum Net Worth:	NR

Fees: Franchise -	$37.5K
Royalty - 4%; Ad. - 4.2% (mkts may vary)	
Earnings Claims Statement:	Yes
Term of Contract (Years):	20/Varies
Avg. # Of Employees:	FT, 30 PT
Passive Ownership:	Allowed
Encourage Conversions:	Yes
Area Develop. Agreements:	Yes/1
Sub-Franchising Contracts:	No
Expand In Territory:	Yes
Space Needs:	2,500-3,500 SF

SUPPORT & TRAINING:

Financial Assistance Provided:	No
Site Selection Assistance:	Yes
Lease Negotiation Assistance:	No
Co-Operative Advertising:	Yes
Franchisee Assoc./Member:	Yes/Yes
Size Of Corporate Staff:	400
On-Going Support:	,B,C,D,E,,G,H,I
Training: 7 Weeks MTP-Certified Training Locations	

SPECIFIC EXPANSION PLANS:

US:	Yes
Canada:	Yes
Overseas:	NR

⋘ ⋙

ARIZONA PIZZA COMPANY
350 S. E. 15th Ave.
Pompano Beach, FL 33060
Tel: (954) 942-9424
Fax: (954) 783-5177
E-Mail: fdiintl@bellsouth.net
Web Site: www.arizonapizza.com
Ms. Linda Biciocchi, Director

Full service, casual dining restaurant, offering eat-in and take-out service. A full-service bar attracts singles, couples, males and females. Our wood-fired pizza oven is the central focus. We feature gourmet and traditional pasta entrees, plus appetizers, salads, wraps, calzones and other popular items, e.g. hamburgers, sandwiches. Cable TV sets at the tables attracts families and is a favorite for the children.

BACKGROUND:

Established: 2002;	1st Franchised: 2003
Franchised Units:	4
Company-Owned Units:	1
Total Units:	5
Dist.:	US-5; CAN-0; O'seas-0
North America:	3 States, 0 Provinces
Density: 1 in MO, 1 in FL, 3 in MA	
Projected New Units (12 Months):	6
Qualifications:	4, 4, 4, 3, 3, 5

FINANCIAL/TERMS:

Cash Investment:	$200K
Total Investment:	$390-890K
Minimum Net Worth:	$600K
Fees: Franchise -	$35K
Royalty - 4%;	Ad. - 2-4%
Earnings Claims Statement:	No
Term of Contract (Years):	10/10
Avg. # Of Employees:	10 FT, 10 PT
Passive Ownership:	Allowed
Encourage Conversions:	Yes
Area Develop. Agreements:	Yes/5
Sub-Franchising Contracts:	No
Expand In Territory:	Yes
Space Needs:	3,200-4,200 SF

SUPPORT & TRAINING:

Financial Assistance Provided:	Yes (I)
Site Selection Assistance:	Yes
Lease Negotiation Assistance:	Yes
Co-Operative Advertising:	No
Franchisee Assoc./Member:	No
Size Of Corporate Staff:	10
On-Going Support:	,,C,D,E,F,,,
Training: 3-4 Weeks Corporate Location in MA	

SPECIFIC EXPANSION PLANS:

US:	All United States
Canada:	No
Overseas:	NR

⋘ ⋙

ARTHUR TREACHER'S FISH & CHIPS
14 Penn Plz., #1305
New York, NY 10122
Tel: (212) 359-3600 +133
Fax: (212) 359-3601
E-Mail:
Web Site: www.arthurtreachers.com
Mr. Bob Ritter, Director of Franchise Development

In 1969, ARTHUR TREACHER'S purchased the original fish and chips recipe from a London restaurant called Malin's of Bow (dating back to the 1860s), and with it, the original fish and chips recipe. Since then, we've adjusted the menu to accommodate American tastes and expanded it to include shrimp, clams, fried chicken and side orders including tasty hush puppies and our unique coleslaw. All of which makes ARTHUR TREACHER'S DISH & CHIPS the English meal perfect for today's all-American appetite.

BACKGROUND: IFA MEMBER

Established: 1969;	1st Franchised: 1969
Franchised Units:	199
Company-Owned Units:	5

Total Units: 204
Dist.: US-203; CAN-0; O'seas-1
  North America: 21 States, 0 Provinces
  Density: 26 in OH, 71 in NY, 77 in FL
Projected New Units (12 Months): 50
Qualifications: 5, 4, 4, 2, 3, 5

FINANCIAL/TERMS:
Cash Investment: $75K-100K
Total Investment: $150K-300K
Minimum Net Worth: $250K
Fees: Franchise - $30K
  Royalty - 5%; Ad. - 3%
Earnings Claims Statement: No
Term of Contract (Years): 10/10
Avg. # Of Employees: 3 FT, 8 PT
Passive Ownership: Discouraged
Encourage Conversions: Yes
Area Develop. Agreements: Yes/1
Sub-Franchising Contracts: No
Expand In Territory: Yes
Space Needs: 500-2,000 SF

SUPPORT & TRAINING:
Financial Assistance Provided: Yes (D)
Site Selection Assistance: Yes
Lease Negotiation Assistance: Yes
Co-Operative Advertising: No
Franchisee Assoc./Member: Yes/Yes
Size Of Corporate Staff: 50
On-Going Support: A,B,C,D,E,F,G,H,I
Training: 10 Days Long Island, NY

SPECIFIC EXPANSION PLANS:
US: All United States
Canada: All Canada
Overseas: All Countries

◄◄ ►►

BACK YARD BURGERS
500 Church St., #200
Nashville, TN 37219
Tel: (800) 854-6939 (615) 620-2300
+1203
Fax: (615) 620-2301
E-Mail: rzeising@backyardburgers.com
Web Site: www.backyardburgers.com
Mr. Reid Zeising, Chairman of the Board

BACK YARD BURGERS operates and franchises quick casual restaurants, serving 1/3 lb. gourmet hamburgers, boneless, skinless chicken fillet sandwiches, fresh lemonade, hand-dipped shakes and malts and other menu items. Our theme emphasizes charbroiled, fresh, great-tasting food as the customers would cook in their own back yard.

BACKGROUND: IFA MEMBER
Established: 1987; 1st Franchised: 1988
Franchised Units: 128

Company-Owned Units: <u>44</u>
Total Units: 172
Dist.: US-172; CAN-0; O'seas-0
  North America: 17 States, 0 Provinces
  Density: 32 in TN, 10 in NC, 12 in AR
Projected New Units (12 Months): 15
Qualifications: 4, 4, 3, 2, 1, 3

FINANCIAL/TERMS:
Cash Investment: $300K-500K
Total Investment: $600K-2MM
Minimum Net Worth: $300K
Fees: Franchise - $25K
  Royalty - 4%; Ad. - 1%
Earnings Claims Statement: No
Term of Contract (Years): 10/5
Avg. # Of Employees: 8 FT, 22 PT
Passive Ownership: Discouraged
Encourage Conversions: Yes
Area Develop. Agreements: Yes/1
Sub-Franchising Contracts: No
Expand In Territory: Yes
Space Needs: 2,500 SF

SUPPORT & TRAINING:
Financial Assistance Provided: Yes (D)
Site Selection Assistance: Yes
Lease Negotiation Assistance: Yes
Co-Operative Advertising: No
Franchisee Assoc./Member: Yes/Yes
Size Of Corporate Staff: 30
On-Going Support: ,B,C,D,E,F,G,H,
Training: 8 Weeks Corporate Headquarters

SPECIFIC EXPANSION PLANS:
US: SE, MW, Mid-Atlantic, SW
Canada: No
Overseas: NR

◄◄ ►►

BAJA SOL TORTILLA GRILL
2922 Upper 55th St.
Inver Grove Heights, MN 55076
Tel: (612) 280-1467
Fax: (952) 944-2001
E-Mail: franchise@baja-sol.com
Web Site: www.baja-sol.com
Ms. Melanie Hall,

BAJA SOL TORTILLA GRILL is a growing casual fresh Mexican restaurant concept, featuring fresh-made tortillas and an extensive salsa bar.

BACKGROUND:
Established: 1995; 1st Franchised: 1999
Franchised Units: 7
Company-Owned Units: <u>5</u>
Total Units: 12
Dist.: US-12; CAN-0; O'seas-0
  North America: 1 States, 0 Provinces

Density: 12 in MN
Projected New Units (12 Months): NR
Qualifications: NR

FINANCIAL/TERMS:
Cash Investment: NA
Total Investment: $$230K-$1203K
Minimum Net Worth: NA
Fees: Franchise - $30K
  Royalty - 5; Ad. - 1.5%
Earnings Claims Statement: No
Term of Contract (Years): 10/10
Avg. # Of Employees: 12 FT, PT
Passive Ownership: Not Allowed
Encourage Conversions: Yes
Area Develop. Agreements: Yes/1
Sub-Franchising Contracts: No
Expand In Territory: Yes
Space Needs: 2,500 SF

SUPPORT & TRAINING:
Financial Assistance Provided: No
Site Selection Assistance: Yes
Lease Negotiation Assistance: Yes
Co-Operative Advertising: No
Franchisee Assoc./Member: No
Size Of Corporate Staff: 9
On-Going Support: ,,C,D,E,,,,
Training: 20 Days Minneapolis, MN

SPECIFIC EXPANSION PLANS:
US: MN and other states (TBD).
Canada: NR
Overseas: NR

◄◄ ►►

BIG TOWN HERO
912 S. W. Third Ave.
Portland, OR 97204
Tel: (503) 228-4376
Fax: (503) 228-8778
E-Mail: rick@bth.com
Web Site: www.bth.com
Mr. Rick Olson, Director of Franchising

Sub sandwich franchise. We bake our bread from scratch everyday. We have the "Ultimate Sandwich" and the "Ultimate Franchise."

BACKGROUND:
Established: 1982; 1st Franchised: 1987
Franchised Units: 36
Company-Owned Units: <u>0</u>
Total Units: 36
Dist.: US-36; CAN-0; O'seas-0
  North America: 3 States, Provinces
  Density: 1 in CA, 34 in OR, 1 in WA
Projected New Units (12 Months): 12
Qualifications: 5, 4, 3, 1, 1, 5

FINANCIAL/TERMS:
Cash Investment: $25-70K

153

Total Investment:	$25-125K
Minimum Net Worth:	$100K
Fees: Franchise -	$14.5K
Royalty - 6%;	Ad. - $300/Mo.
Earnings Claims Statement:	No
Term of Contract (Years):	5/5
Avg. # Of Employees:	1 FT, 4 PT
Passive Ownership:	Not Allowed
Encourage Conversions:	No
Area Develop. Agreements:	Yes/1
Sub-Franchising Contracts:	No
Expand In Territory:	Yes
Space Needs:	1,500 SF

SUPPORT & TRAINING:

Financial Assistance Provided:	No
Site Selection Assistance:	Yes
Lease Negotiation Assistance:	Yes
Co-Operative Advertising:	No
Franchisee Assoc./Member:	No
Size Of Corporate Staff:	6
On-Going Support:	„C,D,E,F,G,h,
Training:	3 Weeks Portland, OR

SPECIFIC EXPANSION PLANS:

US:	NW, SW
Canada:	No
Overseas:	NR

‹‹ ››

BLIMPIE SUBS & SALADS
9311 E. Via De Ventura
Scottsdale, AZ 85258
Tel: (866) 452-4252 (480) 362-4800
Fax: (480) 362-4792
E-Mail: rjjohnson@kahalacorp.com
Web Site: http://www.kahalacorp.com/
Mr. Ted Milburn, Franchise Director

Since 1964 Blimpie has been serving fresh-sliced, high-quality meats and cheeses on fresh-baked bread. Blimpie also offers an assortment of fresh-made salads and other quality products.

BACKGROUND: IFA MEMBER

Established: 1964;	1st Franchised: 1971
Franchised Units:	1089
Company-Owned Units:	1
Total Units:	1090
Dist.:	US-1090; CAN-0; O'seas-0
North America: 50 States, 0 Provinces	
Density: 106 in NY, 131 in GA, 166 in FL	
Projected New Units (12 Months):	NR
Qualifications:	4, 3, 2, 2, 2, 5

FINANCIAL/TERMS:

Cash Investment:	$50K
Total Investment:	$145.85-397.8K
Minimum Net Worth:	$250K
Fees: Franchise -	$18K
Royalty - 6%;	Ad. - 4%
Earnings Claims Statement:	No
Term of Contract (Years):	10/10
Avg. # Of Employees:	4 FT, 8 PT
Passive Ownership:	Allowed
Encourage Conversions:	Yes
Area Develop. Agreements:	Yes
Sub-Franchising Contracts:	Yes
Expand In Territory:	Yes
Space Needs:	1,200-1,400 SF

SUPPORT & TRAINING:

Financial Assistance Provided:	No
Site Selection Assistance:	Yes
Lease Negotiation Assistance:	Yes
Co-Operative Advertising:	Yes
Franchisee Assoc./Member:	Yes/Yes
Size Of Corporate Staff:	250
On-Going Support:	„C,D,E,F,G,H,I
Training:	1 Week Scottsdale, AZ;
1 Week Local Franchise	

SPECIFIC EXPANSION PLANS:

US:	All United States
Canada:	All Canada
Overseas:	All Countries

‹‹ ››

Top 100

BOJANGLES' FAMOUS CHICKEN N BISCUITS
9432 Southern Pine Blvd.
Charlotte, NC 28273-5553
Tel: (800) 366-9921 (704) 527-2675
Fax: (704) 523-6803
E-Mail: cbailey@bojangles.com
Web Site: www.bojanglesfranchise.com
Mr. Chris Bailey, Dir. Franchise Development

BOJANGLES' OPERATES DURING ALL 3 DAY-PARTS. Breakfast items are available all day long. Restaurants operate in traditional locations and non-traditional locations in convenience stores.

BACKGROUND: IFA MEMBER

Established: 1977;	1st Franchised: 1979
Franchised Units:	286
Company-Owned Units:	158

Total Units:	444
Dist.:	US-440; CAN-0; O'seas-4
North America: 10 States, 0 Provinces	
Density: 36 in GA, 90 in SC, 246 in NC	
Projected New Units (12 Months):	50
Qualifications:	5, 4, 5, 3, 3, 5

FINANCIAL/TERMS:

Cash Investment:	$500K
Total Investment:	$300K-1.5M
Minimum Net Worth:	$1M
Fees: Franchise -	$12-25K
Royalty - 4%;	Ad. - 1%
Earnings Claims Statement:	Yes
Term of Contract (Years):	20/10
Avg. # Of Employees:	20 FT, 25 PT
Passive Ownership:	Discouraged
Encourage Conversions:	Yes
Area Develop. Agreements:	Yes/5
Sub-Franchising Contracts:	No
Expand In Territory:	Yes
Space Needs:	3,000+ SF

SUPPORT & TRAINING:

Financial Assistance Provided:	No
Site Selection Assistance:	Yes
Lease Negotiation Assistance:	No
Co-Operative Advertising:	Yes
Franchisee Assoc./Member:	Yes/Yes
Size Of Corporate Staff:	118
On-Going Support:	„C,D,E,F,G,H,I
Training:	6 Weeks Training in Training
Units	

SPECIFIC EXPANSION PLANS:

US:	Southeast
Canada:	No
Overseas:	NR

‹‹ ››

BREADEAUX PIZZA
P. O. Box 6158, Fairleigh Station
St. Joseph, MO 64506
Tel: (800) 835-6534 (816) 364-1088
Fax: (816) 364-3739
E-Mail: matt@breadeauxpizza.com
Web Site: www.breadeauxpizza.com
Mr. Matt Gilliland, Director of Franchise Sales

BREADEAUX PIZZA is a growing regional chain, stressing quality and service. Our acclaimed pizza is made with a double raised crust that is chewy and sweet like fine french bread and our meat toppings have no fillers or additives. We also

154

offer pastas, subs, baked potatoes, hot wings and salads to give customers plenty of variety. Our customers say 'Best Pizza in Town.'

BACKGROUND:

Established: 1985;   1st Franchised: 1985
Franchised Units: 98
Company-Owned Units: 3
Total Units: 101
Dist.:   US-97; CAN-4; O'seas-0
  North America: 10 States, 1 Provinces
  Density: 27 in MO, 6 in KS, 37 in IA
Projected New Units (12 Months):   10
Qualifications: 3, 5, 2, 2, 3, 5

FINANCIAL/TERMS:

Cash Investment: $30-80K
Total Investment: $69.5-310K
Minimum Net Worth: $50K
Fees: Franchise - $15K
  Royalty - 5%;   Ad. - 3%
Earnings Claims Statement: No
Term of Contract (Years):   15/15
Avg. # Of Employees: 2 FT, 12 PT
Passive Ownership: Discouraged
Encourage Conversions: Yes
Area Develop. Agreements: Yes/10
Sub-Franchising Contracts: Yes
Expand In Territory: Yes
Space Needs: 1,200-2,500 SF

SUPPORT & TRAINING:

Financial Assistance Provided: Yes (I)
Site Selection Assistance: Yes
Lease Negotiation Assistance: Yes
Co-Operative Advertising: Yes
Franchisee Assoc./Member: Yes/Yes
Size Of Corporate Staff: 10
On-Going Support: A,B,C,D,E,F,G,H,I
Training: 1 Week Franchisee Location;
  2 Weeks Corporate Headquarters

SPECIFIC EXPANSION PLANS:

US: Midwest
Canada: All Canada
Overseas: NR

BROWN'S CHICKEN & PASTA
489 W. Fullerton Ave.
Elmhurst, IL 60126
Tel: (630) 617-8800
Fax:
E-Mail: frankportillo@brownschicken. com
Web Site: www.brownschicken.com
Mr. Frank Portillo, Jr., President

High-quality, quick-service franchisor of BROWN'S CHICKEN & PASTA RES-TAURANTS. Featuring various fresh-made side dishes. Stores can have take-out, dine-in and drive-up service. Our products, service and franchisee support exceed both customer and franchisee expectations. Expanded into corporate and home catering. Oven-baked chicken and full-service grill and pan pasta catering.

BACKGROUND:

Established: 1965;   1st Franchised: 1965
Franchised Units: 70
Company-Owned Units: 24
Total Units: 94
Dist.:   US-94; CAN-0; O'seas-0
  North America: 3 States, 0 Provinces
  Density: 80 in IL, 5 in FL
Projected New Units (12 Months):   3-5
Qualifications: 3, 3, 2, 3, 5, 5

FINANCIAL/TERMS:

Cash Investment: $25K
Total Investment: $150-160K
Minimum Net Worth: $200K
Fees: Franchise - $25K
  Royalty - 5%;   Ad. - 4%
Earnings Claims Statement: Yes
Term of Contract (Years):   15/5
Avg. # Of Employees: 3 FT, 12 PT
Passive Ownership: Not Allowed
Encourage Conversions: Yes
Area Develop. Agreements: Yes/1
Sub-Franchising Contracts: No
Expand In Territory: No
Space Needs: 1,500 SF

SUPPORT & TRAINING:

Financial Assistance Provided: No
Site Selection Assistance: Yes
Lease Negotiation Assistance: Yes
Co-Operative Advertising: No
Franchisee Assoc./Member: Yes/Yes
Size Of Corporate Staff: 12
On-Going Support: ,B,C,D,E,F,G,H,I
Training: 6 Weeks Oakbrook, IL
  Corporate Office

SPECIFIC EXPANSION PLANS:

US: FL, IL, IN
Canada: No
Overseas: Russia, Asia

BUCK'S PIZZA
P. O. Box 405
DuBois, PA 15801
Tel: (800) 310-8848 (814) 371-3076
Fax: (814) 371-4214
E-Mail: lance@buckspizza.com
Web Site: www.buckspizza.com
Mr. Lance Benton, Sales and Marketing

The pizza business is a 31 billion dollar a year business. The dining out business is a 540 billion dollar a year business. Buck's Pizza does carry out, delivery and Sports Pubs. Pizza, wings, hand made gourmet pastas, hoagies, stromboli and mouthwatering chicken tenders go great in both venues. You will be proud to serve the most delicious food in the industry.

My name is Lance Benton, president and founder of Buck's Pizza. Regardless of whether you've visited one of our shops across the United States, or if you're just beginning to discover Buck's Pizza, I hope you find our website interesting and informative. Here you'll find vast, but not time consuming amounts of information ranging from The Buck's Story, how to order dinner tonight for your family using the online ordering option, how to become a successful franchisee in your neighborhood, as well as exactly what we mean when we say "Good. Better. Buck's."

BACKGROUND:

Established: 1994;   1st Franchised: 1994
Franchised Units: 70
Company-Owned Units: 0
Total Units: 70
Dist.:   US-70; CAN-0; O'seas-0
  North America: 15 States, 0 Provinces
  Density: 15 in TX, 8 in SC, 8 in GA
Projected New Units (12 Months):   12
Qualifications: 3, 4, 5, 3, 3, 5

FINANCIAL/TERMS:

Cash Investment: $50-80K
Total Investment: $125-200K
Minimum Net Worth: $50-80K
Fees: Franchise - $20K
  Royalty - 5%;   Ad. - 2%
Earnings Claims Statement: No
Term of Contract (Years):   10/10
Avg. # Of Employees: 8 FT, 20 PT
Passive Ownership: Discouraged
Encourage Conversions: Yes
Area Develop. Agreements: Yes/1
Sub-Franchising Contracts: Yes
Expand In Territory: Yes
Space Needs: 5,000 SF

SUPPORT & TRAINING:

Financial Assistance Provided: Yes (D)
Site Selection Assistance: Yes
Lease Negotiation Assistance: Yes
Co-Operative Advertising: No
Franchisee Assoc./Member: No
Size Of Corporate Staff: 10
On-Going Support: ,,C,d,E,F,,h,I
Training: 10-14 Days On-Site; 1-2 Days
  Headquarters

SPECIFIC EXPANSION PLANS:

US: All United States

Canada:	No
Overseas:	NR

≪≪ ≫≫

BUFFALO WILD WINGS
GRILL & BAR

5500 Wayzata Blvd., # 1600
Minneapolis, MN 55416-1470
Tel: (800) 499-9586 (952) 593-9943
Fax: (952) 593-9787
E-Mail: cchalupnik@buffalowildwings.com
Web Site: www.buffalowildwings.com
Ms. Carolyne Chalupnik, Director of Franchise Sales

Sports theme, family friendly restaurant, world-famous buffalo wings with 12 proprietary sauces, great burgers & sandwiches, full bar, 40+ TV's, National Trivia Network.

BACKGROUND: IFA MEMBER
Established: 1982; 1st Franchised: 1992	
Franchised Units:	359
Company-Owned Units:	196
Total Units:	555
Dist.:	US-555; CAN-0; O'seas-0
North America:	38 States, 0 Provinces
Density:	10 in TX, 70 in OH, 20 in IN
Projected New Units (12 Months):	50
Qualifications:	5, 4, 4, 3, 3, 5

FINANCIAL/TERMS:
Cash Investment:	$300K-500K
Total Investment:	$800K-2.4MM
Minimum Net Worth:	$800K/Store
Fees: Franchise -	$40K
Royalty - 5%;	Ad. - 3-5%
Earnings Claims Statement:	Yes
Term of Contract (Years):	15/10/5/
Avg. # Of Employees:	3 FT, 50 PT
Passive Ownership:	Not Allowed
Encourage Conversions:	Yes
Area Develop. Agreements:	Yes/1
Sub-Franchising Contracts:	No
Expand In Territory:	Yes
Space Needs:	5,000-6,000 SF

SUPPORT & TRAINING:
Financial Assistance Provided:	Yes (D)
Site Selection Assistance:	Yes
Lease Negotiation Assistance:	Yes
Co-Operative Advertising:	No
Franchisee Assoc./Member:	Yes/Yes

Size Of Corporate Staff:	65
On-Going Support:	A,B,C,D,E,F,G,H,I
Training:	5 Weeks Store/Classroom

SPECIFIC EXPANSION PLANS:
US:	All United States
Canada:	No
Overseas:	NR

≪≪ ≫≫

BUFFALO'S SOUTHWEST CAFE

707 Whitlock Ave., # H-13
Marietta, GA 30064-3033
Tel: (800) 459-4647 (770) 420-1800
Fax: (770) 420-1811
E-Mail: franchise@buffaloscafe.com
Web Site: www.buffaloscafe.com
Ms. Teri Teague, Director of Franchise Development

At the value-end of the casual dining segment, our menu appeals to singles, families, groups... We feature Southwest entrees, world-famous wings, salads, burgers, full bar, party platters, take-out and catering. Our interior, featuring artifacts and antiques from the Old West, hardwood floor and rustic metal ceiling, adds to the overall Southwest dining experience.

BACKGROUND:
Established: 1984; 1st Franchised: 1989	
Franchised Units:	38
Company-Owned Units:	0
Total Units:	38
Dist.:	US-38; CAN-0; O'seas-1
North America:	6 States, 0 Provinces
Density:	5 in SC, 3 in NC, 32 in GA
Projected New Units (12 Months):	6
Qualifications:	4, 4, 4, 3, 3, 4

FINANCIAL/TERMS:
Cash Investment:	$400K-1.2MM
Total Investment:	$1.3MM
Minimum Net Worth:	$2.0MM
Fees: Franchise -	$35K
Royalty - 5%;	Ad. - 2%
Earnings Claims Statement:	No
Term of Contract (Years):	10/10
Avg. # Of Employees:	30 FT, 10 PT
Passive Ownership:	Discouraged
Encourage Conversions:	No
Area Develop. Agreements:	Yes/1
Sub-Franchising Contracts:	No
Expand In Territory:	Yes
Space Needs:	4,700 SF

SUPPORT & TRAINING:
Financial Assistance Provided:	Yes (D)
Site Selection Assistance:	Yes
Lease Negotiation Assistance:	Yes
Co-Operative Advertising:	No

Franchisee Assoc./Member:	No
Size Of Corporate Staff:	16
On-Going Support:	„C,D,E,„G,h,I
Training:	2 Days Owner Orientation; 2 Days Atlanta, GA; 28 Days Corporate Facility

SPECIFIC EXPANSION PLANS:
US:	All United States
Canada:	All Canada
Overseas:	All Countries

≪≪ ≫≫

BURGER KING CORPORATION

5505 Blue Lagoon Dr.
Miami, FL 33126
Tel: (866) 546-4252
Fax: (305) 378-7721
E-Mail: franchiseinquiry@whopper.com
Web Site: www.burgerking.com
Ms. Silvie Jordan, VP Franchise Development

Our Vision: We proudly serve the best burgers in the business, plus a variety of real, authentic foods - all freshly prepared - just the way you want it! BURGER KING® Corporation operates more than 11,220 restaurants in all 50 states and in 60 countries around the world. 90% of the BURGER KING® restaurants are owned and operated by independent franchisees, many of them family-owned operations that have been in business for decades.

BACKGROUND: IFA MEMBER
Established: 1954; 1st Franchised: 1961	
Franchised Units:	10144
Company-Owned Units:	1079
Total Units:	11223
Dist.:	US-7679; CAN-460; O'seas-3084
North America:	50 States, 9 Provinces
Density:	NR
Projected New Units (12 Months):	NR
Qualifications:	NR

FINANCIAL/TERMS:
Cash Investment:	Varies
Total Investment:	$294K-2.8M
Minimum Net Worth:	$1.5MM
Fees: Franchise -	$50K
Royalty - 4.5%;	Ad. - 4%
Earnings Claims Statement:	Yes
Term of Contract (Years):	20/

Avg. # Of Employees: 15 FT, 35 PT
Passive Ownership: Allowed
Encourage Conversions: Yes
Area Develop. Agreements: No
Sub-Franchising Contracts: No
Expand In Territory: Yes
Space Needs: 3,600 SF

SUPPORT & TRAINING:
Financial Assistance Provided: Yes (D)
Site Selection Assistance: Yes
Lease Negotiation Assistance: Yes
Co-Operative Advertising: No
Franchisee Assoc./Member: Yes/Yes
Size Of Corporate Staff: 928
On-Going Support: ,B,C,D,E,F,,H,
Training: 400 Hours Restaurant;
300 Hours Classroom

SPECIFIC EXPANSION PLANS:
US: All United States
Canada: All Canada
Overseas: All Countries

◄◄ ►►

BURGER KING RESTAURANTS OF CANADA, INC.

401 The West Mall, 7th Fl.
Toronto, ON M9C5J4 Canada
Tel: (416) 626-7444
Fax: (416) 626-6691
E-Mail: jweinman@whopper.com
Web Site: www.burgerking.ca
Mr. Jeff Weinman, Senior Development Manager

The flame-broiled WHOPPER sandwich, our signature burger, has driven our growth to over 11,500 restaurants worldwide! These are exciting times at Burger King with the launch of several new menu items. Burger King's new line of Salads, Chicken Fries, BK Stackers and the launch of our Breakfast Value Menu has generated much enthusiasm from the public. Burger King is focusing on recruitment of multi-unit operators with foodservice experience for most parts of Canada but will consider single unit operators in selected markets. Single unit operators must have a minimum net worth of $800,000 of which at least $400,000 must be unencumbered or liquid. The financial requirements of multi-unit operators will be based on the expansion potential of the operator and territory.

BACKGROUND: IFA MEMBER
Established: 1954; 1st Franchised: 1969
Franchised Units: 198
Company-Owned Units: 122

Total Units: 320
Dist.: US-0; CAN-320; O'seas-0
North America: 0 States, 10 Provinces
Density: 65 in QC, 142 in ON, 35 in BC
Projected New Units (12 Months): 8
Qualifications: 5, 4, 3, 3, 1, 5

FINANCIAL/TERMS:
Cash Investment: $150K-400K
Total Investment: $750K-1.1MM
Minimum Net Worth: $800K
Fees: Franchise - $55K
Royalty - 4%; Ad. - 4%
Earnings Claims Statement: No
Term of Contract (Years): 20/20
Avg. # Of Employees: 15 FT, 35 PT
Passive Ownership: Allowed
Encourage Conversions: Yes
Area Develop. Agreements: No
Sub-Franchising Contracts: No
Expand In Territory: Yes
Space Needs: 3,000-3,200 SF

SUPPORT & TRAINING:
Financial Assistance Provided: No
Site Selection Assistance: Yes
Lease Negotiation Assistance: Yes
Co-Operative Advertising: No
Franchisee Assoc./Member: Yes/Yes
Size Of Corporate Staff: 70
On-Going Support: ,,C,D,E,F,,H,
Training: 300 Hours Classroom;
400 Hours Restaurant

SPECIFIC EXPANSION PLANS:
US: No
Canada: All Canada
Overseas: NR

◄◄ ►►

CALIFORNIA TORTILLA

20 Courthouse Sq., # 206
Rockville, MD 20850
Tel: (888) 545-3232 (301) 545-0035
Fax: (301) 545-0051
E-Mail: franchising@californiatortilla.com
Web Site: www.californiatortilla.com
Mr. Bob Phillips, President

This popular eatery features quick, friendly (some would say downright spunky) service and a mouthwatering menu of freshly prepared items, such as fajitas, quesadillas,

tacos and burritos, including their best selling Blackened Chicken Caesar, Honey Lime and Crunchy BBQ Ranch Burritos. CALIFORNIA TORTILLA is also known for its quirky promotions such as the Monday Night Mystery Price Burrito Wheel, Freeze Pop Day, Jungle Noise Day and Pop Tart Day, as well as Taco Talk - their popular burrito newsletter read by people nationwide.

BACKGROUND:
Established: 1995; 1st Franchised: 2004
Franchised Units: 25
Company-Owned Units: 3
Total Units: 28
Dist.: US-28; CAN-0; O'seas-0
North America: 4 States, 0 Provinces
Density: 2 in VA, 12 in MD, 2 in DC
Projected New Units (12 Months): 15
Qualifications: 4, 5, 4, 3, 4, 5

FINANCIAL/TERMS:
Cash Investment: $250K-350K
Total Investment: $387K-625K
Minimum Net Worth: $1MM
Fees: Franchise - $25K
Royalty - 5%; Ad. - 2%
Earnings Claims Statement: Yes
Term of Contract (Years): 10/10
Avg. # Of Employees: 10 FT, 15 PT
Passive Ownership: Discouraged
Encourage Conversions: Yes
Area Develop. Agreements: Yes/3
Sub-Franchising Contracts: No
Expand In Territory: No
Space Needs: 2,500 SF

SUPPORT & TRAINING:
Financial Assistance Provided: No
Site Selection Assistance: Yes
Lease Negotiation Assistance: Yes
Co-Operative Advertising: Yes
Franchisee Assoc./Member: Yes/Yes
Size Of Corporate Staff: 11
On-Going Support: ,B,C,D,E,F,G,H,
Training: 4 Weeks Potomac, MD

SPECIFIC EXPANSION PLANS:
US: Mid-Atlantic Region
Canada: No
Overseas: NR

◄◄ ►►

CAPTAIN D'S

1717 Elm Hill Pike, # A-1
Nashville, TN 37210
Tel: (800) 550-4877 (615) 231-2188
Fax: (615) 231-2734
E-Mail: bill_nelson@captainds.com
Web Site: www.captainds.com
Mr. Bill Nelson, VP of Franchise Operations

Captain D's restaurants offer high-quality seafood in a fast food environment. The menu features our signature hand-battered fried fish. We also offer premium-quality grilled, baked, and broiled fish, as well as shrimp, chicken, and home-style side dishes with selected desserts.

BACKGROUND: IFA MEMBER
Established: 1969; 1st Franchised: 1969
Franchised Units: 262
Company-Owned Units: 291
Total Units: 553
Dist.: US-551; CAN-0; O'seas-2
  North America: 25 States, 0 Provinces
  Density: 71 in AL, 79 in TN, 99 in GA
Projected New Units (12 Months): 5
Qualifications: 5, 3, 4, 3, 3, 5
FINANCIAL/TERMS:
Cash Investment: $300K
Total Investment: $1.1MM
Minimum Net Worth: $750K
Fees: Franchise - $25K
  Royalty - 4.5%; Ad. - 4.85%
Earnings Claims Statement: Yes
Term of Contract (Years): 20/20
Avg. # Of Employees: 3-5 FT, 20 PT
Passive Ownership: Allowed
Encourage Conversions: No
Area Develop. Agreements: Yes/3
Sub-Franchising Contracts: No
Expand In Territory: Yes
Space Needs: 2,700 SF
SUPPORT & TRAINING:
Financial Assistance Provided: No
Site Selection Assistance: Yes
Lease Negotiation Assistance: No
Co-Operative Advertising: Yes
Franchisee Assoc./Member: No
Size Of Corporate Staff: 75
On-Going Support: ,B,C,D,E,,,h,
Training: 6 Weeks Field training in
  certified cooperating store

SPECIFIC EXPANSION PLANS:
US: Yes
Canada: No
Overseas: NR

≪ ≫

CARL'S JR.

6307 Carpinteria Ave., # A
Carpinteria, CA 93013
Tel: (866) 253-7655 (805) 745-7842
Fax: (714) 780-6320
E-Mail: nrudis@ckr.com
Web Site: www.ckr.com
Ms. Natasha Rudis, Franchise Coordinator

Over the last 60 years Carl's Jr.® has built a reputation as America's premier burger chain, and is known as the place to go for big, juicy, delicious charbroiled burgers. Today, there are more than 1,100 Carl's Jr.® restaurants worldwide, with more than 300 dual-branded Carl's Jr.®/Green Burrito® restaurants.

BACKGROUND: IFA MEMBER
Established: 1961; 1st Franchised: 1984
Franchised Units: 782
Company-Owned Units: 421
Total Units: 1203
Dist.: US-1080; CAN-0; O'seas-123
  North America: 14 States, 0 Provinces
  Density: 49 in CO, 725 in CA, 64 in AZ
Projected New Units (12 Months): NR
Qualifications: 4, 4, 4, 2, 2, 5
FINANCIAL/TERMS:
Cash Investment: $300K
Total Investment: $1.3-1.8MM
Minimum Net Worth: $1MM
Fees: Franchise - $35K
  Royalty - 4%; Ad. - 5.5%
Earnings Claims Statement: Yes
Term of Contract (Years): 20/5
Avg. # Of Employees: 33 FT, PT
Passive Ownership: Not Allowed
Encourage Conversions: Yes
Area Develop. Agreements: Yes/1
Sub-Franchising Contracts: No
Expand In Territory: Yes
Space Needs: 2,450 SF
SUPPORT & TRAINING:
Financial Assistance Provided: No
Site Selection Assistance: Yes
Lease Negotiation Assistance: No

Co-Operative Advertising: No
Franchisee Assoc./Member: No
Size Of Corporate Staff: 300
On-Going Support: ,,C,D,E,F,G,H,I
Training: NR
SPECIFIC EXPANSION PLANS:
US: Yes
Canada: Yes
Overseas: NR

≪ ≫

CHARLEY'S GRILLED SUBS

2500 Farmers Dr., # 140
Columbus, OH 43235-5706
Tel: (800) 437-8325 (614) 923-4700
Fax: (614) 923-4701
E-Mail: franchising@charleys.com
Web Site: www.charleys.com
Mr. Ted Chang, Dir. Regional Development

CHARLEY'S GRILLED SUBS is a progressive quick-service restaurant with over 300 locations across the United States and Canada. The heart of CHARLEY'S menu consists of freshly grilled Steak and Chicken Subs, fresh-cut fries and freshly squeezed lemonade. CHARLEY'S open kitchen environment and freshly prepared products are unique in the fast-food industry.

BACKGROUND: IFA MEMBER
Established: 1986; 1st Franchised: 1991
Franchised Units: 327
Company-Owned Units: 23
Total Units: 350
Dist.: US-319; CAN-3; O'seas-28
  North America: 39 States, 1 Provinces
  Density: 28 in OH, 28 in FL, 30 in CA
Projected New Units (12 Months): 60
Qualifications: 4, 5, 2, 2, 2, 5
FINANCIAL/TERMS:
Cash Investment: $100
Total Investment: $127.5-513.5K
Minimum Net Worth: $300K
Fees: Franchise - $19.5K
  Royalty - 5% or $250/Wk.; Ad. - 0.25%
Earnings Claims Statement: Yes
Term of Contract (Years): 10/10
Avg. # Of Employees: FT, 12-15 PT
Passive Ownership: Discouraged
Encourage Conversions: Yes
Area Develop. Agreements: No

Sub-Franchising Contracts:	No
Expand In Territory:	Yes
Space Needs:	NR

SUPPORT & TRAINING:

Financial Assistance Provided:	Yes (I)
Site Selection Assistance:	Yes
Lease Negotiation Assistance:	Yes
Co-Operative Advertising:	No
Franchisee Assoc./Member:	Yes/Yes
Size Of Corporate Staff:	35
On-Going Support:	„C,D,e,,G,h,
Training:	3 Weeks Columbus, OH

SPECIFIC EXPANSION PLANS:

US:	All United States
Canada:	ON
Overseas:	All Countries

CHECKERS DRIVE-IN RESTAURANTS

4300 W. Cypress St., # 600
Tampa, FL 33607-4159
Tel: (888) 913-9135 (813) 283-7017
Fax: (813) 283-7439
E-Mail: millerd@checkers.com
Web Site: www.checkers.com
Mr. Donald Miller, Director of Franchising

Quick-service, fast-food restaurant (double drive-thru). Total below reflect ownership of both CHECKERS and RALLY'S brands.

BACKGROUND: IFA MEMBER

Established: 1986;	1st Franchised: 1986
Franchised Units:	600
Company-Owned Units:	205
Total Units:	805
Dist.:	US-797; CAN-0; O'seas-3
North America:	40 States, 0 Provinces
Density: 85 in GA, 191 in FL, 32 in AL
Projected New Units (12 Months):	35
Qualifications:	5, 4, 5, 4, 4, 4

FINANCIAL/TERMS:

Cash Investment:	$150K-400K
Total Investment:	$476.7K-617.2K
Minimum Net Worth:	$250K
Fees: Franchise -	$30K
Royalty - 4%;	Ad. - 0.25%+4.75%
Earnings Claims Statement:	No
Term of Contract (Years):	20/Agrmt.
Avg. # Of Employees:	4 FT, 20 PT
Passive Ownership:	Not Allowed

Encourage Conversions:	No
Area Develop. Agreements:	Yes/1
Sub-Franchising Contracts:	No
Expand In Territory:	Yes
Space Needs:	21,000 SF

SUPPORT & TRAINING:

Financial Assistance Provided:	No
Site Selection Assistance:	Yes
Lease Negotiation Assistance:	NA
Co-Operative Advertising:	No
Franchisee Assoc./Member:	Yes/Yes
Size Of Corporate Staff:	NR
On-Going Support:	A,B,C,D,E,F,G,H,I
Training:	4-6 Weeks Tampa, FL

SPECIFIC EXPANSION PLANS:

US:	All United States
Canada:	All Canada
Overseas:	All Countries

CHEEBURGER CHEEBURGER RESTAURANTS

15951 McGregor Blvd., # 2C
Fort Myers, FL 33908
Tel: (800) 487-6211 (941) 437-1611
Fax: (941) 437-1512
E-Mail: slundy@cheeburger.com
Web Site: www.cheeburger.com
Mr. Mike Santel, Director Franchise Development

Full-service, gourmet, specialty-sandwich restaurant, serving high-quality, freshly prepared products and featuring burgers in various sizes, fresh-cut fries and big, thick milk shakes.

BACKGROUND: IFA MEMBER

Established: 1982;	1st Franchised: 1986
Franchised Units:	45
Company-Owned Units:	1
Total Units:	46
Dist.:	US-46; CAN-0; O'seas-0
North America:	14 States, 0 Provinces
Density:	8 in MD, 16 in FL
Projected New Units (12 Months):	15
Qualifications:	5, 5, 3, 3, 4, 5

FINANCIAL/TERMS:

Cash Investment:	$200-400K
Total Investment:	$400-600K
Minimum Net Worth:	$500K
Fees: Franchise -	$29.5K
Royalty - 5%;	Ad. - 1%
Earnings Claims Statement:	No
Term of Contract (Years):	10/5
Avg. # Of Employees:	10 FT, 20 PT
Passive Ownership:	Not Allowed
Encourage Conversions:	Yes
Area Develop. Agreements:	Yes/1

Sub-Franchising Contracts:	No
Expand In Territory:	Yes
Space Needs:	1,600-3,000 SF

SUPPORT & TRAINING:

Financial Assistance Provided:	No
Site Selection Assistance:	Yes
Lease Negotiation Assistance:	Yes
Co-Operative Advertising:	No
Franchisee Assoc./Member:	Yes/Yes
Size Of Corporate Staff:	5
On-Going Support:	„C,D,E,F,G,H,I
Training:	NR

SPECIFIC EXPANSION PLANS:

US:	All United States
Canada:	No
Overseas:	NR

CHESTER'S INTERNATIONAL

3500 Colonade Pkwy., # 325
Birmingham, AL 35213
Tel: (800) 288-1555 (334) 272-3528
Fax: (205) 298-0332
E-Mail: info@chestersinternational.com
Web Site: www.chestersinternational.com
Mr. Ian Byrd, Director of Franchise Development

CHESTER'S offers consumers a high-quality chicken product, cooked to perfection, with a unique taste and style. The Company's secret is a breading recipe and process that has been successful for more than 30 years. CHESTER'S uses only chicken that is specially marinated and offers double-breaded bone-in, tender and potato wedges as well as sandwiches, salads and breakfast. Great opportunity to enter the QSR industry with flexible locations and store design. * 1,449 units are non-franchised.

BACKGROUND: IFA MEMBER

Established: 1952;	1st Franchised: 2002
Franchised Units:	47
Company-Owned Units:	0
Total Units:	47
Dist.:	US-47; CAN-225; O'seas-50
North America:	47 States, 11 Provinces
Density:	NR
Projected New Units (12 Months):	49
Qualifications:	3, 3, 2, 2, 3, 4

FINANCIAL/TERMS:

Cash Investment:	$50K-100K
Total Investment:	$60K-400.4K
Minimum Net Worth:	$100K
Fees: Franchise -	$5-15K
Royalty - NR;	Ad. -
Earnings Claims Statement:	No

159

Term of Contract (Years): 7-10/7-10
Avg. # Of Employees: 2 FT, 4 PT
Passive Ownership: Allowed
Encourage Conversions: Yes
Area Develop. Agreements: Yes/1
Sub-Franchising Contracts: No
Expand In Territory: Yes
Space Needs: 400-1,400 SF
SUPPORT & TRAINING:
Financial Assistance Provided: Yes (D)
Site Selection Assistance: Yes
Lease Negotiation Assistance: No
Co-Operative Advertising: No
Franchisee Assoc./Member: No
Size Of Corporate Staff: 13
On-Going Support: „C,D,E,„H,I
Training: 1 Week Birmingham, AL;
4 Days Franchisee Location
SPECIFIC EXPANSION PLANS:
US: All United States
Canada: All Canada
Overseas: All Countries

<< >>

CHICKEN DELIGHT (CANADA)
395 Berry St.
Winnipeg, MB R3J 1N6 Canada
Tel: (204) 885-7570
Fax: (204) 831-6176
E-Mail: lmillar@chickendelight.com
Web Site: www.chickendelight.com
Mr. Larry Millar, Marketing Manager

CHICKEN DELIGHT has been in business for 50 years, featuring our famous pressure-fried chicken, BBQ ribs and fresh dough pizzas. We cater to the fast-food market with dine-in, take-out, delivery and drive-thru. Our focus on 3 staple products for take-out and delivery broadens your market potential.

BACKGROUND:
Established: 1952; 1st Franchised: 1952
Franchised Units: 35
Company-Owned Units: 15
Total Units: 50
Dist.: US-10; CAN-38; O'seas-2
North America: 2 States, 4 Provinces
Density: 33 in MB, 1 in ON, 3 in SK
Projected New Units (12 Months): 3
Qualifications: 4, 5, 3, 4, 3, 5
FINANCIAL/TERMS:
Cash Investment: $70-100K
Total Investment: $275-600K
Minimum Net Worth: $70K
Fees: Franchise - $25K
Royalty - 5%; Ad. - 3%
Earnings Claims Statement: No

Term of Contract (Years): 10/10
Avg. # Of Employees: 6 FT, 6 PT
Passive Ownership: Discouraged
Encourage Conversions: Yes
Area Develop. Agreements: Yes/1
Sub-Franchising Contracts: No
Expand In Territory: Yes
Space Needs: 1,600 SF
SUPPORT & TRAINING:
Financial Assistance Provided: No
Site Selection Assistance: Yes
Lease Negotiation Assistance: Yes
Co-Operative Advertising: No
Franchisee Assoc./Member: No
Size Of Corporate Staff: 20
On-Going Support: „C,D,e,F,G,h,
Training: Minimum 1 Month Winnipeg, MB
SPECIFIC EXPANSION PLANS:
US: All United States
Canada: All Canada
Overseas: Any Master License

<< >>

CHURCH'S CHICKEN
980 Hammond Dr., Bldg. # 2, # 1100
Atlanta, GA 30328-6161
Tel: (800) 639-3495 (770) 350-3800
Fax: (770) 554-0973
E-Mail: pperry@churchs.com
Web Site: www.churchs.com
Mr. Douglas Pendergast, EVP & Chief Franchise Officer

Founded in San Antonio, Texas, in 1952, Church's Chicken is a highly recognized brand name in the QSR sector and is one of the largest quick-service chicken concepts in the world. Church's Chicken serves freshly prepared, high quality, flavorful chicken and tenders with signature sides and hand-made from scratch biscuits at low prices and differentiates from its competitors in care and attention given in preparation of food, and is positioned as the Value Leader in the Chicken QSR category. As of February 2007, the Church's system had 1,600+ locations worldwide in 18 countries, with system sales exceeding $1 billion.

BACKGROUND: IFA MEMBER

Established: 1952; 1st Franchised: 1967
Franchised Units: 1337
Company-Owned Units: 277
Total Units: 1614
Dist.: US-1217; CAN-18; O'seas-382
North America: 28 States, 0 Provinces
Density: 433 in TX, 88 in GA, 74 in CA
Projected New Units (12 Months): 111
Qualifications: 5, 5, 4, 3, 3, 5
FINANCIAL/TERMS:
Cash Investment: $300K
Total Investment: $335-1113.5K
Minimum Net Worth: $1MM
Fees: Franchise - $15K
Royalty - 5%; Ad. - 5%
Earnings Claims Statement: No
Term of Contract (Years): 20/10
Avg. # Of Employees: 15 FT, 6 PT
Passive Ownership: Discouraged
Encourage Conversions: Yes
Area Develop. Agreements: Yes/1
Sub-Franchising Contracts: Yes
Expand In Territory: Yes
Space Needs: 850-1,850 SF
SUPPORT & TRAINING:
Financial Assistance Provided: No
Site Selection Assistance: Yes
Lease Negotiation Assistance: No
Co-Operative Advertising: Yes
Franchisee Assoc./Member: Yes/Yes
Size Of Corporate Staff: 157
On-Going Support: ,B,C,D,E,,G,H,I
Training: 4 Weeks Regional
SPECIFIC EXPANSION PLANS:
US: All United States
Canada: All Canada
Overseas: Asia, Middle East, Russia, China

<< >>

CHURRO STATION
2 Fifer Ave., #110
Corte Madera, CA 94925
Tel: (415) 927-7141
Fax: (415) 927-7197
E-Mail: franchiseinfo@churrostation.com
Web Site: www.churrostation.com
Ms. Karol Caballero, Dir. Franchise Development

Who loves churros? I love churros and so will you. The first quick-service retailer in the US to serve authentic, freshly made churros and rellenos (filled churros). Be the first to bring CHURRO STATION to your community! CHURRO STATION not only offers authentic, freshly made churros, but a variety of other mouth-watering Hispanic specialties and made-to-order sandwiches. Today, churros mark the beginning of a new food revolution. Strong franchise opportunities for single & multiple locations.

BACKGROUND:

Established: 2003;	1st Franchised: 2005
Franchised Units:	4
Company-Owned Units:	1
Total Units:	5
Dist.:	US-5; CAN-0; O'seas-0
North America:	1 States, 0 Provinces
Density:	4 in CA, 1 in AZ
Projected New Units (12 Months):	8
Qualifications:	4, 3, 2, 2, 3, 5

FINANCIAL/TERMS:

Cash Investment:	$25K
Total Investment:	$100-172K
Minimum Net Worth:	$70K
Fees: Franchise -	$25K
Royalty - 5%;	Ad. - 3%
Earnings Claims Statement:	No
Term of Contract (Years):	10/10
Avg. # Of Employees:	3 FT, 1 PT
Passive Ownership:	Allowed
Encourage Conversions:	NA
Area Develop. Agreements:	Yes/10
Sub-Franchising Contracts:	No
Expand In Territory:	Yes
Space Needs:	800 SF

SUPPORT & TRAINING:

Financial Assistance Provided:	Yes (I)
Site Selection Assistance:	Yes
Lease Negotiation Assistance:	No
Co-Operative Advertising:	No
Franchisee Assoc./Member:	No
Size Of Corporate Staff:	4
On-Going Support:	,B,C,D,E,F,,
Training:	5 days Corporate Office

SPECIFIC EXPANSION PLANS:

US:	8
Canada:	No
Overseas:	NR

◂◂ ▸▸

COUSINS SUBS
N83 W13400 Leon Rd.
Menomenee Falls, WI 53051
Tel: (800) 238-9736 (262) 250-2822
Fax: (262) 364-2984
E-Mail: betterfranchise@cousinssubs.com
Web Site: www.cousinsfranchise.com
Mr. Mark Cairns, Director of Franchise
    Sales

Over 33 years of excellence describes our Eastern-Style submarine sandwich concept. Our COUSINS SUBS niche is offering a quality submarine sandwich 25% larger than most of our competitiors. Hot and cold subs are highlighted by our freshly baked bread, delicious soups and garden salads made to order! The value and portability of our products promote leveraging outside sales to bottom line profitability. We have high expectations for 2009 and invite you to learn more about our exciting franchise opportunities. We offer single unit and multi-unit franchises.

BACKGROUND: IFA MEMBER

Established: 1972;	1st Franchised: 1985
Franchised Units:	136
Company-Owned Units:	15
Total Units:	151
Dist.:	US-151; CAN-0; O'seas-0
North America:	6 States, 0 Provinces
Density:	128 in WI, 6 in MN, 11 in AZ
Projected New Units (12 Months):	15
Qualifications:	5, 4, 3, 3, 3, 4

FINANCIAL/TERMS:

Cash Investment:	$80K-100K
Total Investment:	$195.7K-311.3K
Minimum Net Worth:	$300K
Fees: Franchise -	$25K ($12,500 through 2009)
Royalty - 6%;	Ad. - 2%
Earnings Claims Statement:	Yes
Term of Contract (Years):	10/10
Avg. # Of Employees:	2 FT, 12 PT
Passive Ownership:	Allowed
Encourage Conversions:	Yes
Area Develop. Agreements:	Yes/1
Sub-Franchising Contracts:	Yes
Expand In Territory:	Yes
Space Needs:	1,250-1,600 SF

SUPPORT & TRAINING:

Financial Assistance Provided:	Yes (D)
Site Selection Assistance:	Yes
Lease Negotiation Assistance:	Yes
Co-Operative Advertising:	Yes
Franchisee Assoc./Member:	No
Size Of Corporate Staff:	40
On-Going Support:	,,C,D,E,,,h,I
Training:	10 Days Franchisee Store; 30 Days Training Store; 3 Days Head-quarters

SPECIFIC EXPANSION PLANS:

US:	IL, MI, MN, WI, AZ
Canada:	No
Overseas:	NR

◂◂ ▸▸

D'ANGELO GRILLED SANDWICHES
600 Providence Hwy.
Dedham, MA 02026
Tel: (888) 374-2830 (781) 467-1668
Fax: (781) 329-8796
E-Mail: mwoodman@papaginos.com
Web Site: www.dangelosfranchising.com
Ms. Mimi Woodman, Franchise Support
    Specialist

D'Angelo Grilled Sandwiches in New England's leading sandwich chain. What separates us from the competition is how D'Angelo's distinctive sandwiches are prepared all three ways; grilled, toasted or cold. With 40 years of success, we've grown to more than 200 locations, serving over 1 million guests monthly. D'Angelo's average unit sales exceeded $770,000 this past fiscal year. Join us and become the next D'Angelo success story!

BACKGROUND: IFA MEMBER

Established: 1967;	1st Franchised: 1988
Franchised Units:	50
Company-Owned Units:	150
Total Units:	200
Dist.:	US-200; CAN-0; O'seas-0
North America:	7 States, 0 Provinces
Density:	23 in RI, 24 in NH, 117 in MA
Projected New Units (12 Months):	12
Qualifications:	5, 3, 3, 2, 1, 5

FINANCIAL/TERMS:

Cash Investment:	$115K
Total Investment:	$390-555K
Minimum Net Worth:	$350K
Fees: Franchise -	$20K
Royalty - 6%;	Ad. - 3%
Earnings Claims Statement:	Yes
Term of Contract (Years):	20/10
Avg. # Of Employees:	6 FT, 12 PT
Passive Ownership:	Discouraged
Encourage Conversions:	Yes
Area Develop. Agreements:	Yes/1
Sub-Franchising Contracts:	No
Expand In Territory:	Yes
Space Needs:	2,000 SF

SUPPORT & TRAINING:

Financial Assistance Provided: No
Site Selection Assistance: Yes
Lease Negotiation Assistance: Yes
Co-Operative Advertising: Yes
Franchisee Assoc./Member: No
Size Of Corporate Staff: 100
On-Going Support: ,,C,D,E,,G,H,I
Training: 4 Weeks Training restuarants;
  2 Weeks Corporate Office

SPECIFIC EXPANSION PLANS:
US: MA, CT, RI, NH, ME, VT, FL
Canada: No
Overseas: NR

<< >>

DEL TACO
25521 Commercentre Dr., 2nd Fl.
Lake Forest, CA 92630-8872
Tel: (949) 462-7319
Fax: (949) 462-7311
E-Mail: bill_nelson@captainds.com
Web Site: www.deltaco.com
Mr. Bill Nelson, VP of Franchise Operations

Mexican-American fast-food restaurant. Second largest Mexican brand in U. S. sales.

BACKGROUND: IFA MEMBER
Established: 1964; 1st Franchised: 1967
Franchised Units: 221
Company-Owned Units: 285
Total Units: 506
Dist.: US-506; CAN-0; O'seas-0
  North America: 13 States, 0 Provinces
  Density: 35 in NV, 355 in CA, 47 in AZ
Projected New Units (12 Months): 28
Qualifications: 5, 3, 5, 2, 3, 5
FINANCIAL/TERMS:
Cash Investment: $300K
Total Investment: $1MM
Minimum Net Worth: $750K
Fees: Franchise - $25K
  Royalty - 5%; Ad. - 4%
Earnings Claims Statement: Yes
Term of Contract (Years): 20/15
Avg. # Of Employees: 2 FT, 24 PT
Passive Ownership: Allowed
Encourage Conversions: No
Area Develop. Agreements: Yes/1
Sub-Franchising Contracts: No
Expand In Territory: Yes
Space Needs: 2,100 SF

SUPPORT & TRAINING:
Financial Assistance Provided: No
Site Selection Assistance: Yes
Lease Negotiation Assistance: No
Co-Operative Advertising: No
Franchisee Assoc./Member: No
Size Of Corporate Staff: 110
On-Going Support: ,,C,,E,,G,H,
Training:1 Week Corporate Headquarters;
  4 Weeks Certified Training Restaurant;
SPECIFIC EXPANSION PLANS:
US: Yes
Canada: No
Overseas: NR

<< >>

DICKEY'S BARBECUE PIT RESTAURANTS
4514 Cole Ave., # 1000
Dallas, TX 75205
Tel: (866) 340-6188 (972) 248-9899
Fax: (972) 248-8667
E-Mail: rdickeyjr@dickeys.com
Web Site: www.dickeys.com
Mr. Roland Dickey, Vice President

Fast casual barbecue restaurant. Simple, efficient operating system. Am,ple training and on-going support. Unique counter service and drive-thru, quick-serve concept with great food - and great sales. We have a great family of franchisees that are about half minority operators. We are growing fast. Come join us and join in the profit.

BACKGROUND: IFA MEMBER
Established: 1941; 1st Franchised: 1994
Franchised Units: 61
Company-Owned Units: 6
Total Units: 67
Dist.: US-67; CAN-0; O'seas-0
  North America: 5 States, 0 Provinces
  Density: 53 in TX, 1 in NJ, 2 in CO
Projected New Units (12 Months): 20
Qualifications: 5, 4, 1, 4, 1, 5
FINANCIAL/TERMS:
Cash Investment: $150-350K
Total Investment: $508K-1.8MM
Minimum Net Worth: $500K
Fees: Franchise - $25/30K
  Royalty - 4%; Ad. - 4%
Earnings Claims Statement: Yes
Term of Contract (Years): 10/20
Avg. # Of Employees: 14 FT, 0 PT
Passive Ownership: Discouraged
Encourage Conversions: Yes
Area Develop. Agreements: No
Sub-Franchising Contracts: No

Expand In Territory: No
Space Needs: 3,000 SF
SUPPORT & TRAINING:
Financial Assistance Provided: No
Site Selection Assistance: Yes
Lease Negotiation Assistance: Yes
Co-Operative Advertising: No
Franchisee Assoc./Member: No
Size Of Corporate Staff: 12
On-Going Support: ,B,C,D,E,F,G,H,I
Training: 30 Days Dallas, TX
SPECIFIC EXPANSION PLANS:
US: All United States
Canada: All Canada
Overseas: Europe, Pacific Rim

<< >>

DIFFERENT TWIST PRETZEL CO., THE
6052 Rte. 8, P.O. Box 334
Bakerstown, PA 15007
Tel: (724) 443-8010
Fax: (724) 443-7287
E-Mail: apmaggio@differenttwistpretzel.com
Web Site: www.differenttwistpretzel.com
Mr. August P. Maggio, President

Serving hand-rolled, fresh-baked soft pretzels in 10 different flavors. (Licensor)

BACKGROUND:
Established: 1992; 1st Franchised: 1992
Franchised Units: 23
Company-Owned Units: 2
Total Units: 25
Dist.: US-18; CAN-1; O'seas-6
  North America: 8 States, Provinces
  Density: 3 in KY, 3 in PA, 4 in WV
Projected New Units (12 Months): 20
Qualifications: 4, 4, 1, 2, 1, 4
FINANCIAL/TERMS:
Cash Investment: $40-80K
Total Investment: $40-80K
Minimum Net Worth: $50K
Fees: Franchise - $5K
  Royalty - 5%; Ad. -
Earnings Claims Statement: Yes
Term of Contract (Years): 10/10
Avg. # Of Employees: 3 FT, 3 PT
Passive Ownership: Allowed
Encourage Conversions: Yes
Area Develop. Agreements: Yes/1
Sub-Franchising Contracts: Yes
Expand In Territory: Yes
Space Needs: 150-400 SF
SUPPORT & TRAINING:
Financial Assistance Provided: Yes (D)
Site Selection Assistance: Yes

Lease Negotiation Assistance:	Yes
Co-Operative Advertising:	No
Franchisee Assoc./Member:	No
Size Of Corporate Staff:	12
On-Going Support:	,b,,D,e,,,,
Training:	1 Week On-Site

SPECIFIC EXPANSION PLANS:

US:	All United States
Canada:	All Canada
Overseas:	All Countries

◄◄ ►►

DINNER A'FARE, THE

1820 N. Brown Rd., # 65
Lawrenceville, GA 30043
Tel: (888) 838-8177 (678) 621-8412
Fax: (866) 221-7924
E-Mail: franchising@dinnerafare.com
Web Site: www.dinnerafare.com
Mr. Ryan Hembree, Director of Franchise
　Development

The Dinner A'Fare is the leading innovator in the meal assembly arena. We feature large functional territories, a comprehensive training program, unparalleled franchise support, and an aggressive marketing campaign. Our franchise owners enjoy the opportunity to compete with other companies as we feature only the highest quality recipes and ingredients. Our distinction is our fresh ingredients and family friendly recipes.

BACKGROUND:

Established: 2004;	1st Franchised: 2004
Franchised Units:	25
Company-Owned Units:	1
Total Units:	26
Dist.:	US-26; CAN-0; O'seas-0
North America:	2 States, 0 Provinces
Density:	3 in GA, 2 in CA
Projected New Units (12 Months):	10
Qualifications:	3, 4, 2, 4, 4, 5

FINANCIAL/TERMS:

Cash Investment:	$30K
Total Investment:	$125K-225K
Minimum Net Worth:	$100K
Fees: Franchise -	$30K
Royalty - 5%;	Ad. - NA
Earnings Claims Statement:	No
Term of Contract (Years):	15/10
Avg. # Of Employees:	2 FT, 2 PT
Passive Ownership:	Not Allowed
Encourage Conversions:	NA
Area Develop. Agreements:	No
Sub-Franchising Contracts:	No
Expand In Territory:	Yes
Space Needs:	1,500 SF

SUPPORT & TRAINING:

Financial Assistance Provided:	Yes (I)
Site Selection Assistance:	Yes
Lease Negotiation Assistance:	Yes
Co-Operative Advertising:	Yes
Franchisee Assoc./Member:	No
Size Of Corporate Staff:	3
On-Going Support:	,,C,D,E,F,G,h,I
Training:9 Days Corporate Training (GA);	
8 Days On-Site Training (at location)	

SPECIFIC EXPANSION PLANS:

US:	All United States
Canada:	No
Overseas:	NR

◄◄ ►►

DOMINO'S PIZZA

30 Frank Lloyd Wright Dr., P.O. Box 997
Ann Arbor, MI 48106-0997
Tel: (800) 564-4918 (734) 930-3044
Fax: (734) 668-0342
E-Mail: mike.mettler@dominos.com
Web Site: www.dominos.com
Mr. Mike Mettler, Director of Franchise
　Recruiting & Sales

DOMINO'S PIZZA is the recognized world leader in pizza delivery, with more than 43 years of experience. We operate a network of more than 7,000 stores in the US and 50 countries around the world.

BACKGROUND:　　IFA MEMBER

Established: 1960;	1st Franchised: 1967
Franchised Units:	5796
Company-Owned Units:	656
Total Units:	6462
Dist.:	US-6462; CAN-233; O'seas-1790
North America:	50 States, 0 Provinces
Density:	215 in NY, 250 in DC, 264 in CA
Projected New Units (12 Months):	NR
Qualifications:	NR

FINANCIAL/TERMS:

Cash Investment:	$75K
Total Investment:	$118.5K-460.3K
Minimum Net Worth:	NR
Fees: Franchise -	$3.2K
Royalty - 5.5%;	Ad. - 3%
Earnings Claims Statement:	No
Term of Contract (Years):	10/10
Avg. # Of Employees:	FT, 0 PT

Passive Ownership:	Not Allowed
Encourage Conversions:	No
Area Develop. Agreements:	Yes/1
Sub-Franchising Contracts:	No
Expand In Territory:	Yes
Space Needs:	1,200 SF

SUPPORT & TRAINING:

Financial Assistance Provided:	No
Site Selection Assistance:	Yes
Lease Negotiation Assistance:	Yes
Co-Operative Advertising:	No
Franchisee Assoc./Member:	Yes/Yes
Size Of Corporate Staff:	NR
On-Going Support:	,B,C,D,E,,G,H,I
Training:	6-8 Weeks Local/Regional

SPECIFIC EXPANSION PLANS:

US:	All United States
Canada:	NR
Overseas:	NR

◄◄ ►►

DUKE SANDWICH COMPANY

1001 Poinsett Hwy.
Greenville, SC 29609
Tel: (877) 308-2343 (864) 331-0703
Fax: (864) 232-0706
E-Mail: franchise@dukesandwich.com
Web Site: www.dukesandwich.com
Ms. Jennifer Stephens, Marketing/Relations Director

We are a family-owned and operated sandwich company with superb sandwich spreads, a superior business system and nearly 90 years of quality, tradition and experience.

BACKGROUND:　　IFA MEMBER

Established: 1917;	1st Franchised: 2004
Franchised Units:	7
Company-Owned Units:	3
Total Units:	10
Dist.:	US-10; CAN-0; O'seas-0
North America:	1 States, 0 Provinces
Density:	3 in SC
Projected New Units (12 Months):	NR
Qualifications:	4, 3, 3, 3, 3, 4

FINANCIAL/TERMS:

Cash Investment:	$60-100K
Total Investment:	$90-240K
Minimum Net Worth:	$400K
Fees: Franchise -	$25K

Royalty - 6%; Ad. - 2%
Earnings Claims Statement: No
Term of Contract (Years): 5/20
Avg. # Of Employees: 0 FT, 4 PT
Passive Ownership: Not Allowed
Encourage Conversions: Yes
Area Develop. Agreements: Yes/1
Sub-Franchising Contracts: No
Expand In Territory: Yes
Space Needs: 1,800-2,400 SF

SUPPORT & TRAINING:
Financial Assistance Provided: No
Site Selection Assistance: Yes
Lease Negotiation Assistance: No
Co-Operative Advertising: No
Franchisee Assoc./Member: No
Size Of Corporate Staff: 5
On-Going Support: A,,C,D,E,,G,H,I
Training: 3-4 Weeks Headquarters or
Specified Training Site

SPECIFIC EXPANSION PLANS:
US: Southeast
Canada: No
Overseas: NR

EAST OF CHICAGO PIZZA COMPANY

512 E. Tiffin St.
Willard, OH 44890
Tel: (800) 940-0086 (419) 935-3033
Fax: (419) 935-3278
E-Mail: mbruno@eastofchicago.com
Web Site: www.eastofchicago.com
Mr. Mike Bruno, Vice President

EAST OF CHICAGO PIZZA COMPANY is a young, determined franchising company that utilizes buffet restaurants and delivery/carry-out restaurants to achieve market dominance. Established in 1990, EOC has grown to over 100 units, with plans to expand. Combining proven marketing and operational systems, with ideal franchisee strategic partnerships, EOC meets demands of customers with unique products, which, when combined with superior customer service, creates an atmosphere of tremendous customer loyalty/repeat business.

BACKGROUND:
Established: 1990; 1st Franchised: 1991
Franchised Units: 137
Company-Owned Units: 4
Total Units: 141
Dist.: US-141; CAN-0; O'seas-0
North America: 5 States, 0 Provinces
Density: 1 in FL, 119 in OH, 20 in IN

Projected New Units (12 Months): 10-15
Qualifications: 4, 3, 3, 3, 4, 4
FINANCIAL/TERMS:
Cash Investment: $50K
Total Investment: $142-251K
Minimum Net Worth: $250K
Fees: Franchise - $20K
Royalty - 5%; Ad. - 2%
Earnings Claims Statement: Yes
Term of Contract (Years): 10/10
Avg. # Of Employees: 10 FT, 10 PT
Passive Ownership: Not Allowed
Encourage Conversions: Yes
Area Develop. Agreements: Yes/1
Sub-Franchising Contracts: Yes
Expand In Territory: Yes
Space Needs: 1,200-3,000 SF

SUPPORT & TRAINING:
Financial Assistance Provided: No
Site Selection Assistance: Yes
Lease Negotiation Assistance: No
Co-Operative Advertising: Yes
Franchisee Assoc./Member: Yes/Yes
Size Of Corporate Staff: 20
On-Going Support: A,B,C,D,E,F,G,H,
Training: 4 Weeks Willard, OH

SPECIFIC EXPANSION PLANS:
US: All United States
Canada: No
Overseas: All Countries

anything but routine®

EINSTEIN BROS. BAGELS

555 Zang St.
Lakewood, CO 80228
Tel: (877) 244-2233 (303) 568-8000
Fax: (303) 568-8259
E-Mail: kkruse@einsteinnoah.com
Web Site: www.einsteinbros.com/franchising
Mr. Kevin Kruse, VP Franchise Development

Einstein Bros. Bagels is taking our award-winning concept into the franchise arena for the first time. Beginning in the Southeastern U.S., we are bringing our established brand and loyal customer base into new markets with a spiffy new neighborhood store prototype. Join a leader in the

quick casual bakery segment that offers craveable cuisine at breakfast, lunch or anytime. Start today by visiting our website at www.einsteinbros.com/franchising.

BACKGROUND: IFA MEMBER
Established: 1995; 1st Franchised: 2006
Franchised Units: 0
Company-Owned Units: 340
Total Units: 340
Dist.: US-340; CAN-0; O'seas-0
North America: 28 States, 0 Provinces
Density: 30 in IL, 50 in FL, 30 in CO
Projected New Units (12 Months): 5
Qualifications: 3, 3, 3, 3, 3, 3
FINANCIAL/TERMS:
Cash Investment: $500K
Total Investment: $426.5-757.8K
Minimum Net Worth: $1.1MM
Fees: Franchise - $30K
Royalty - 5%; Ad. - 3-5%
Earnings Claims Statement: Yes
Term of Contract (Years): 10/10
Avg. # Of Employees: 5 FT, 15 PT
Passive Ownership: Not Allowed
Encourage Conversions: Yes
Area Develop. Agreements: Yes/10
Sub-Franchising Contracts: No
Expand In Territory: Yes
Space Needs: 2200 - 2600 SF
SUPPORT & TRAINING:
Financial Assistance Provided: No
Site Selection Assistance: Yes
Lease Negotiation Assistance: Yes
Co-Operative Advertising: No
Franchisee Assoc./Member: No
Size Of Corporate Staff: 200
On-Going Support: ,,,,,,,,
Training: 8 Weeks Golden, CO
SPECIFIC EXPANSION PLANS:
US: 8
Canada: No
Overseas: NR

EL POLLO LOCO

3535 Harbor Blvd., #100
Costa Mesa, CA 92626
Tel: (800) 997-6556
Fax: (714) 599-5000
E-Mail: sgillie@elpolloloco.com

Web Site: www.elpolloloco.com

Mr. Scott Gillie, Director Franchise Development

EL POLLO LOCO is the nation's leading quick-service restaurant chain specializing in flame-grilled chicken. Offering a fresh, healthy alternative to traditional fast food, EL POLLO LOCO serves its famous citrus-marinated, flame-grilled chicken with warm tortillas, fresh salsas and a variety of accompaniments. Fresh Mexican entrees (signature grilled burritos, Pollo Bowls, Pollo Salads, chicken quesadillas, etc.) also served. All feature the delicious citrus-marinated, flame-grilled chicken that put EL POLLO LOCO on the map.

BACKGROUND: IFA MEMBER

Established: 1980;	1st Franchised: 1984
Franchised Units:	172
Company-Owned Units:	<u>134</u>
Total Units:	306
Dist.:	US-306; CAN-0; O'seas-0
North America:	0 States, 0 Provinces
Density:	13 in NV, 299 in CA, 11 in AZ
Projected New Units (12 Months):	26
Qualifications:	5, 5, 5, 3, 3, 5

FINANCIAL/TERMS:

Cash Investment:	$250K
Total Investment:	$502K-1.1MM
Minimum Net Worth:	$1.5MM
Fees: Franchise -	$40K
Royalty - 4%;	Ad. - 5%
Earnings Claims Statement:	Yes
Term of Contract (Years):	20/
Avg. # Of Employees:	8 FT, 17 PT
Passive Ownership:	Discouraged
Encourage Conversions:	Yes
Area Develop. Agreements:	Yes
Sub-Franchising Contracts:	No
Expand In Territory:	Yes
Space Needs:	2,400 SF

SUPPORT & TRAINING:

Financial Assistance Provided:	No
Site Selection Assistance:	Yes
Lease Negotiation Assistance:	No
Co-Operative Advertising:	No
Franchisee Assoc./Member:	Yes/Yes
Size Of Corporate Staff:	142
On-Going Support:	A,,C,D,E,F,G,H,I
Training:	7 Weeks Southern CA

SPECIFIC EXPANSION PLANS:

US:	All United States
Canada:	No
Overseas:	NR

◄◄ ►►

ERBERT & GERBERT'S SUBS CLUBS

ERBERT & GERBERT'S SUBS & CLUBS

205 E. Grand Ave

Eau Claire, WI 54701

Tel: (800) 283-5241 (715) 833-1375

Fax: (715) 833-8523

E-Mail: info@erbertandgerberts.com

Web Site: www.erbertandgerberts.com

Mr. Kevin Schippers, President/CEO

ERBERT AND GERBERT'S SUBS & CLUBS offer the gourmet sandwich product in the fast-food niche. Growing rapidly, the market is wide open for this top-quality, service-oriented company. Immaculate shops and outstanding service complement the gourmet product.

BACKGROUND:

Established: 1987;	1st Franchised: 1992
Franchised Units:	25
Company-Owned Units:	<u>1</u>
Total Units:	26
Dist.:	US-26; CAN-0; O'seas-0
North America:	3 States, Provinces
Density:	11 in MN, 1 in ND, 14 in WI
Projected New Units (12 Months):	10
Qualifications:	4, 5, 1, 3, 4, 5

FINANCIAL/TERMS:

Cash Investment:	$30-35K
Total Investment:	$194-356K
Minimum Net Worth:	$250K
Fees: Franchise -	$25K
Royalty - 6%;	Ad. - 2%
Earnings Claims Statement:	Yes
Term of Contract (Years):	15/5
Avg. # Of Employees:	2-3 FT, 10 PT
Passive Ownership:	Discouraged
Encourage Conversions:	Yes
Area Develop. Agreements:	Yes/1
Sub-Franchising Contracts:	No
Expand In Territory:	No
Space Needs:	1,000-2,000 SF

SUPPORT & TRAINING:

Financial Assistance Provided:	Yes (D)
Site Selection Assistance:	Yes
Lease Negotiation Assistance:	Yes
Co-Operative Advertising:	No
Franchisee Assoc./Member:	Yes/Yes
Size Of Corporate Staff:	10
On-Going Support:	,,C,D,E,,G,H,I
Training:	3 Weeks Home Office;
	1 Week On-Site during Opening

SPECIFIC EXPANSION PLANS:

US:	All U.S.,Primarily Midwest
Canada:	No
Overseas:	NR

◄◄ ►►

Top 100

FAMIGLIA PIZZERIA

FAMOUS FAMIGLIA

199 Main St., 8th Fl.

White Plains, NY 10601

Tel: (914) 328-4444

Fax: (914) 328-4479

E-Mail: info@famousfamiglia.com

Web Site: www.famousfamiglia.com

Mr. Giorgio Kolaj, Executive Vice President

FAMOUS FAMIGLIA is an award-winning national pizza brand with leading sales in the pizza segment. Operating nationwide, FAMOUS FAMIGLIA has earned several leading industry awards for its unsurpassed product quality and customer service. Expansion plans include high-profile markets and locations such as: leading airports, shopping plazas, universities, casinos, military bases, cinemas, etc. With a successful franchise program in place, a number of high-caliber locations nationwide are available.

BACKGROUND: IFA MEMBER

Established: 1986;	1st Franchised: 2002
Franchised Units:	80
Company-Owned Units:	<u>20</u>
Total Units:	100
Dist.:	US-95; CAN-0; O'seas-5
North America:	26 States, 0 Provinces
Density:	14 in PA, 15 in NJ, 39 in NY
Projected New Units (12 Months):	32
Qualifications:	4, 4, 3, 1, 4, 5

FINANCIAL/TERMS:

Cash Investment:	$200K
Total Investment:	$250-700K
Minimum Net Worth:	$1MM
Fees: Franchise -	$35K
Royalty - 6%;	Ad. - 1%
Earnings Claims Statement:	No
Term of Contract (Years):	10/5-10
Avg. # Of Employees:	4 FT, 8 PT
Passive Ownership:	Discouraged
Encourage Conversions:	Yes
Area Develop. Agreements:	Yes/10
Sub-Franchising Contracts:	Yes
Expand In Territory:	Yes
Space Needs:	600-1,200 SF

SUPPORT & TRAINING:

Financial Assistance Provided:	No
Site Selection Assistance:	Yes
Lease Negotiation Assistance:	Yes

Co-Operative Advertising: Yes
Franchisee Assoc./Member: No
Size Of Corporate Staff: 18
On-Going Support: A,B,C,D,E,F,G,H,I
Training: 2-4 Weeks Corporate
  Headquarters, NY

SPECIFIC EXPANSION PLANS:
US: All United States
Canada: All Canada
Overseas: All Countries

≺≺ ≻≻

FARMER BOYS HAMBURGERS

3452 University Ave.
Riverside, CA 92501
Tel: (888) 930-3276 (951) 275-9900
Fax: (951) 275-9930
E-Mail: dtucker@farmerboys.com
Web Site: www.farmerboys.com
Mr. Don Tucker, Director of Franchise
  Development

FARMER BOYS RESTAURANTS fill a unique food service niche by offering greater choice to both fast food and traditional sit-down restaurant customers. Concept offers over 100 fresh breakfast, lunch or dinner items, prepared and cooked to order in 5 - 7 minutes - with a choice of sit-down, take-out or drive-thru service.

BACKGROUND: IFA MEMBER
Established: 1981; 1st Franchised: 1997
Franchised Units: 47
Company-Owned Units: 15
Total Units: 62
Dist.: US-62; CAN-0; O'seas-0
  North America: 1 States, 0 Provinces
  Density: 56 in CA
Projected New Units (12 Months): 10
Qualifications: 4, 4, 3, 3, 1, 5
FINANCIAL/TERMS:
Cash Investment: $350K-600K
Total Investment: $1.2MM-1.2MM
Minimum Net Worth: $750K
Fees: Franchise - $45K
  Royalty - 5%; Ad. - 3%
Earnings Claims Statement: Yes
Term of Contract (Years): 20/20
Avg. # Of Employees:7-10 FT, 10-15 PT
Passive Ownership: Not Allowed
Encourage Conversions: No
Area Develop. Agreements: Yes
Sub-Franchising Contracts: No

Expand In Territory: Yes
Space Needs: 3,000-3,200 SF
SUPPORT & TRAINING:
Financial Assistance Provided: Yes (I)
Site Selection Assistance: Yes
Lease Negotiation Assistance: Yes
Co-Operative Advertising: Yes
Franchisee Assoc./Member: Yes/Yes
Size Of Corporate Staff: 25
On-Going Support: „C,D,E,F,G,H,I
Training: 10 Weeks Company-Operated
  Unit

SPECIFIC EXPANSION PLANS:
US: Western United States
Canada: No
Overseas: NR

≺≺ ≻≻

FAST EDDIE'S

102 - 129 Wellington St.
Brantford, ON N3R 4R6 Canada
Tel: (877) HOT-FRYS (519) 758-0111
Fax: (519) 758-1393
E-Mail: fasteddies@fasteddies.ca
Web Site: www.fasteddies.ca
Ms. Nicki Straza, Franchise Director

FAST EDDIE'S is a hamburger-based, fast-food, double-drive-thru restaurant with no inside seating. We have 100% pure-beef, quality hamburgers with shakes and fries to go. Try our crazy fries!

BACKGROUND:
Established: 1989; 1st Franchised: 2000
Franchised Units: 6
Company-Owned Units: 4
Total Units: 10
Dist.: US-0; CAN-10; O'seas-0
  North America: States, 1 Provinces
  Density: 10 in ON
Projected New Units (12 Months): 2
Qualifications: 5, 5, 4, 3, 3, 5
FINANCIAL/TERMS:
Cash Investment: $60-100K
Total Investment: $200-400K
Minimum Net Worth: $200-300K
Fees: Franchise - $25K
  Royalty - 4%; Ad. - 2%
Earnings Claims Statement: Yes
Term of Contract (Years): 1-/5
Avg. # Of Employees: 3 FT, 15 PT
Passive Ownership: Not Allowed
Encourage Conversions: No
Area Develop. Agreements: No
Sub-Franchising Contracts: No
Expand In Territory: Yes
Space Needs: 900 SF
SUPPORT & TRAINING:

Financial Assistance Provided: Yes (D)
Site Selection Assistance: Yes
Lease Negotiation Assistance: Yes
Co-Operative Advertising: No
Franchisee Assoc./Member: Yes/Yes
Size Of Corporate Staff: 18
On-Going Support: „C,D,E,F,,,
Training: 2 Weeks Brantford, ON
SPECIFIC EXPANSION PLANS:
US: No
Canada: Ontario
Overseas: NR

≺≺ ≻≻

FATBURGER

1218 Third St. Promenade
Santa Monica, CA 90401-1308
Tel: (310) 319-1850
Fax: (310) 319-1863
E-Mail: mwilkins@fatburger.com
Web Site: www.fatburger.com
Ms. Michelle Wilkins, Director Franchise
  Relations

The classic hamburger stand, serving cooked-to-order burgers at an open grill since 1952. Also serving grilled chicken-breast sandwiches, freshly made onion rings and real milkshakes in a fun environment with a unique R & B jukebox.

BACKGROUND: IFA MEMBER
Established: 1952; 1st Franchised: 1980
Franchised Units: 33
Company-Owned Units: 25
Total Units: 58
Dist.: US-58; CAN-0; O'seas-0
  North America: 7 States, Provinces
  Density: 39 in CA, 10 in NV
Projected New Units (12 Months): 8
Qualifications: 4, 5, 3, 2, 5, 5
FINANCIAL/TERMS:
Cash Investment: $750K+
Total Investment: $370-730K
Minimum Net Worth: $1.25MM
Fees: Franchise - $40K
  Royalty - 6%; Ad. - 2%
Earnings Claims Statement: Yes
Term of Contract (Years): 15/10/10/
Avg. # Of Employees: 16-40 FT, 0 PT
Passive Ownership: Allowed
Encourage Conversions: Yes
Area Develop. Agreements: Yes/1

Sub-Franchising Contracts:	No
Expand In Territory:	No
Space Needs:	1,800-2,000 SF

SUPPORT & TRAINING:

Financial Assistance Provided:	No
Site Selection Assistance:	Yes
Lease Negotiation Assistance:	Yes
Co-Operative Advertising:	No
Franchisee Assoc./Member:	No
Size Of Corporate Staff:	30
On-Going Support:	,,C,D,E,,,H,
Training:	8 Weeks Certified Training
Centers; 7-10 Days On-Site	

SPECIFIC EXPANSION PLANS:

US:	All United States
Canada:	All Canada
Overseas:	NR

◄◄ ►►

FIGARO'S

1500 Liberty St., S. E.
Salem, OR 97302
Tel: (888) 344-2767 (503) 371-9318
Fax: (503) 363-5364
E-Mail: franchisedev@figaros.com
Web Site: www.figaros.com
Mr. Ron Berger, Chairman/CEO

Take the best pizza anywhere! Make it available to consumers either baked or 'take-and-bake;' for in-store dining, take-out, or delivery; add superior world-class store designs, systems, and marketing, and you have the opportunity Figaro's Pizza offers you today. Be the Boss. Instead of making a lot of money for everyone else, the time is right to make it yourself, building your own assets and equity. You deserve it. And we have just the right vehicle to make the move.

BACKGROUND: IFA MEMBER

Established: 1981; 1st Franchised: 1986	
Franchised Units:	89
Company-Owned Units:	0
Total Units:	89
Dist.:	US-87; CAN-0; O'seas-2
North America:	20 States, 0 Provinces
Density:	9 in WI, 10 in CA, 43 in OR
Projected New Units (12 Months):	15
Qualifications:	5, 3, 2, 1, 1, 3

FINANCIAL/TERMS:

Cash Investment:	$150K

Total Investment:	$101K-$1338K
Minimum Net Worth:	$150K
Fees: Franchise -	$35K
Royalty - 5%;	Ad. - 3%
Earnings Claims Statement:	Yes
Term of Contract (Years):	5/5
Avg. # Of Employees:	2-3 FT, 8-12 PT
Passive Ownership:	Allowed
Encourage Conversions:	No
Area Develop. Agreements:	Yes/5
Sub-Franchising Contracts:	Yes
Expand In Territory:	No
Space Needs:	1,100 SF

SUPPORT & TRAINING:

Financial Assistance Provided:	Yes (I)
Site Selection Assistance:	Yes
Lease Negotiation Assistance:	Yes
Co-Operative Advertising:	Yes
Franchisee Assoc./Member:	No
Size Of Corporate Staff:	12
On-Going Support:	,B,C,D,E,F,G,H,I
Training:	14 Days Training School - 3
Options; 3 - 5 Days Mentorship; 9 - 11 Days Store Opening	

SPECIFIC EXPANSION PLANS:

US:	All except Maryland and Hawaii
Canada:	All Canada
Overseas:	All Countries

◄◄ ►►

FOUNDED BY FIREMEN

FIREHOUSE SUBS

3410 Kori Rd.
Jacksonville, FL 32257
Tel: (800) 388-3473 (904) 886-8300
Fax: (904) 886-2111
E-Mail: gdelks@firehousesubs.com
Web Site: www.firehousesubs.com
Mr. Greg Delks, Director of Franchise Development

FIREHOUSE SUBS has expended considerable time and effort developing a sandwich restaurant system specializing in serving large portion, steaming hot submarine-style sandwiches in a unique firehouse atmosphere and decor, at an economical price.

BACKGROUND: IFA MEMBER

Established: 1994; 1st Franchised: 1994	
Franchised Units:	318
Company-Owned Units:	30
Total Units:	348
Dist.:	US-348; CAN-0; O'seas-0
North America:	10 States, 0 Provinces

Density:	26 in SC, 32 in GA, 121 in FL
Projected New Units (12 Months):	90
Qualifications:	NR

FINANCIAL/TERMS:

Cash Investment:	$70K-200K
Total Investment:	$221.1K-464.7K
Minimum Net Worth:	NR
Fees: Franchise -	$20K
Royalty - 6%;	Ad. - 3%
Earnings Claims Statement:	Yes
Term of Contract (Years):	10/5
Avg. # Of Employees:	3-5 FT, 15-20 PT
Passive Ownership:	Not Allowed
Encourage Conversions:	No
Area Develop. Agreements:	Yes
Sub-Franchising Contracts:	No
Expand In Territory:	Yes
Space Needs:	1,400+ SF

SUPPORT & TRAINING:

Financial Assistance Provided:	No
Site Selection Assistance:	Yes
Lease Negotiation Assistance:	Yes
Co-Operative Advertising:	Yes
Franchisee Assoc./Member:	No
Size Of Corporate Staff:	45
On-Going Support:	,B,C,D,E,F,G,H,I
Training: 6 Weeks Various Regional Centers; 2 Weeks Jacksonville, FL Final Training	

SPECIFIC EXPANSION PLANS:

US:	All United States
Canada:	No
Overseas:	NR

◄◄ ►►

FOUR STAR PIZZA

P. O. Box W
Claysville, PA 15323
Tel: (800) 628-3398 (412) 484-9235
Fax: (724) 484-9235
E-Mail: fourstarza@aol.com
Web Site: www.fourstarpizza.net
Mr. David Roderick, President

Four Star Pizza is looking for aggressive, hard-driving entrepreneur as a four star franchisee you will feature a popular premium quality product, a great location, and an unbeatable, low start-up cost. Add a dash of entrepreneurial spirit and you're on your way to an exciting and profitable future.

BACKGROUND:

Established: 1981; 1st Franchised: 1985	
Franchised Units:	14
Company-Owned Units:	0
Total Units:	14
Dist.:	US-14; CAN-0; O'seas-0

North America: 5 States, 0 Provinces
Density: in PA, in OH, in MO
Projected New Units (12 Months): 6
Qualifications: 3, 4, 2, 3, 1, 5
FINANCIAL/TERMS:
Cash Investment: NR
Total Investment: $47.5-142K
Minimum Net Worth: NR
Fees: Franchise - $7K
  Royalty - 5%; Ad. - 1%
Earnings Claims Statement: No
Term of Contract (Years): 10/10
Avg. # Of Employees: 3 FT, 4-10 PT
Passive Ownership: Discouraged
Encourage Conversions: Yes
Area Develop. Agreements: Yes/1
Sub-Franchising Contracts: No
Expand In Territory: Yes
Space Needs: 800-1,200 SF
SUPPORT & TRAINING:
Financial Assistance Provided: Yes (D)
Site Selection Assistance: No
Lease Negotiation Assistance: Yes
Co-Operative Advertising: No
Franchisee Assoc./Member: No
Size Of Corporate Staff: 3
On-Going Support: ,B,C,D,E,,,H,I
Training: 1-2 Weeks Varied Location
SPECIFIC EXPANSION PLANS:
US: PA, VA, OH, WV, MD
Canada: No
Overseas: NR

≪ ≫

FOX'S PIZZA DEN
3243 Old Frankstown Rd.
Pittsburgh, PA 15239
Tel: (800) 899-3697 (724) 733-7888
Fax: (724) 325-5479
E-Mail: foxs@alltel.net
Web Site: www.foxspizza.com
Mr. James R. Fox, President

FOX'S PIZZA DEN believes in one philosophy - you earned it, you keep it! FOX'S royalties are $200 a month - no percentages of sales. FOX'S PIZZA DENS offers the finest pizza, specialty sandwiches, salads and sides and our house special - the 'wedgie.'

BACKGROUND:
Established: 1971; 1st Franchised: 1974
Franchised Units: 265
Company-Owned Units: 0
Total Units: 265
Dist.: US-265; CAN-0; O'seas-0
North America: 26 States, 0 Provinces
Density: 32 in WV, 118 in PA, 24 in OH

Projected New Units (12 Months): 30
Qualifications: 2, 4, 4, 2, 2, 5
FINANCIAL/TERMS:
Cash Investment: $68-150K
Total Investment: $68-150K
Minimum Net Worth: NA
Fees: Franchise - $8K
  Royalty - $200/Mo.; Ad. - 0%
Earnings Claims Statement: No
Term of Contract (Years): 5/5
Avg. # Of Employees: 2-3 FT, 8-10 PT
Passive Ownership: Discouraged
Encourage Conversions: Yes
Area Develop. Agreements: Yes/1
Sub-Franchising Contracts: Yes
Expand In Territory: Yes
Space Needs: 1,000-2,000 SF
SUPPORT & TRAINING:
Financial Assistance Provided: Yes (I)
Site Selection Assistance: Yes
Lease Negotiation Assistance: No
Co-Operative Advertising: Yes
Franchisee Assoc./Member: No
Size Of Corporate Staff: 8
On-Going Support: ,B,C,D,E,F,G,H,I
Training: 7 Days On-Site
SPECIFIC EXPANSION PLANS:
US: All United States
Canada: No
Overseas: NR

≪ ≫

FRESH CITY
145 Rosemary St., # C
Needham, MA 02494
Tel: (888) FRESH55 (781) 453-0200
Fax: (781) 453-8686
E-Mail: jpainter@freshfoodconcepts.com
Web Site: www.freshcity.com
Ms. Joan Painter, Director of Franchising

FRESH CITY, one of Nation's Restaurant News' 'Hot Concept' award winners, 'Ones to Watch' by QSR Magazine and 'Keepin' it Fresh' by Chain Leader, provides comfortable Fast, Fresh, Casual and Fresh Fusion cuisine. Several cooking and fusion stations provide guests with an international diversity of menu offerings, including hot and cold wraps, Asian noodles, salads, distinct sandwiches, smoothies, lattes and more - to dine in, take out or have catered.

BACKGROUND: IFA MEMBER
Established: 1998; 1st Franchised: 2003
Franchised Units: 9
Company-Owned Units: 9
Total Units: 18

Dist.: US-18; CAN-0; O'seas-0
North America: 3 States, 0 Provinces
Density: 1 in NH, 13 in MA, 2 in CT
Projected New Units (12 Months): 5
Qualifications: 5, 4, 4, 4, 1, 5
FINANCIAL/TERMS:
Cash Investment: $726K-1.1MM
Total Investment: $1.75-3MM
Minimum Net Worth: $3.5MM
Fees: Franchise - $25K
  Royalty - 5%; Ad. - 1.5% + 1.5%
Earnings Claims Statement: Yes
Term of Contract (Years): 10/10
Avg. # Of Employees: 5 FT, 10-20 PT
Passive Ownership: Not Allowed
Encourage Conversions: Yes
Area Develop. Agreements: Yes/1
Sub-Franchising Contracts: No
Expand In Territory: No
Space Needs: 3,000-3,500 SF
SUPPORT & TRAINING:
Financial Assistance Provided: No
Site Selection Assistance: Yes
Lease Negotiation Assistance: Yes
Co-Operative Advertising: No
Franchisee Assoc./Member: No
Size Of Corporate Staff: 12
On-Going Support: A,B,C,D,E,F,G,H,I
Training: 9 Weeks Needham, MA
SPECIFIC EXPANSION PLANS:
US: NY, NJ, PA, CT, IL, SE, Mid-Atlantic
Canada: No
Overseas: NR

≪ ≫

Hottest New Franchise
FROOTS
Fresh Smoothies, Salads & Wraps

FROOTS SMOOTHIES
4380 Oakes Rd., # 800
Davie, FL 33314
Tel: (877) FROOTS-1 (954) 791-4793
Fax: (954) 241-6009
E-Mail: tatiana@froots.com
Web Site: www.froots.com
Ms. Tatiana Molina, Sales Facilitator

Froot Smoothies provides a healthy alternative to traditional fast food fare. Our smoothies are made with only all natural ingredients - exactly like you would make at home! In addition to our fantastic smoothies and fresh squeezed juices, we offer a full menu of healthy gourmet wraps, salads, soups and breads.

BACKGROUND: IFA MEMBER

Established: 2001; 1st Franchised: 2004
Franchised Units: 36
Company-Owned Units: 0
Total Units: 36
Dist.:   US-36; CAN-0; O'seas-4
  North America: 1 States, 0 Provinces
  Density: 9 in FL
Projected New Units (12 Months):   70
Qualifications: 5, 5, 2, 3, 1, 4
FINANCIAL/TERMS:
Cash Investment: $100K
Total Investment: $77.35-285K
Minimum Net Worth: $200K
Fees: Franchise - $25K
  Royalty - 6%;   Ad. - 2%
Earnings Claims Statement: No
Term of Contract (Years):   15/15
Avg. # Of Employees: 3 FT, 6 PT
Passive Ownership: Discouraged
Encourage Conversions: Yes
Area Develop. Agreements: Yes/15
Sub-Franchising Contracts: No
Expand In Territory: Yes
Space Needs: 350 - 1,800 (1,000 - 1,400
  preferred) SF
SUPPORT & TRAINING:
Financial Assistance Provided: Yes (I)
Site Selection Assistance: Yes
Lease Negotiation Assistance: Yes
Co-Operative Advertising: No
Franchisee Assoc./Member: Yes/No
Size Of Corporate Staff: 11
On-Going Support: A,B,C,D,E,F,G,H,I
Training: 23 Days Hollywood, FL
SPECIFIC EXPANSION PLANS:
US: Yes
Canada: Yes
Overseas: NR

⤡ ⤢

FRULLATI CAFE & BAKERY

9311 E. Via De Ventura
Scottsdale, AZ 85260
Tel: (866) 4KAHALA (480) 362-4800
Fax: (480) 362-4792
E-Mail: rjjohnson@kahalacorp.com
Web Site: www.kahalacorp.com
Ms. Nicole Rayborn, Franchise Director

FRULLATI CAFE & BAKERY, the fresh
franchise alternative in fast food. Featuring
something fresh for every taste, FRULLA-
TI's lite fare menu includes: fruit smoothies, soups, deli sandwiches, healthy snacks,
fresh baked bread, salads and gourmet
coffee. If the taste of success by owning
one or a chain of FRULLATI CAFEs
sounds appetizing, here's the opportunity
for you. We have FRULLATI CAFE &

BAKERY franchise opportunities coming
to your neighborhood.

BACKGROUND: IFA MEMBER
Established: 1992;   1st Franchised: 1992
Franchised Units: 46
Company-Owned Units: 1
Total Units: 47
Dist.:   US-47; CAN-0; O'seas-6
  North America: 14 States, 0 Provinces
  Density: 19 in TX, 8 in IL
Projected New Units (12 Months):   28
Qualifications: 5, 4, NR, 3, NR, 5
FINANCIAL/TERMS:
Cash Investment: $150.85-511.3K
Total Investment: $150.85-511.3K
Minimum Net Worth: $150K
Fees: Franchise - $30K
  Royalty - 6%;   Ad. - 4%
Earnings Claims Statement: Yes
Term of Contract (Years):   10/10
Avg. # Of Employees: 3 FT, 5 PT
Passive Ownership: Discouraged
Encourage Conversions: Yes
Area Develop. Agreements: Yes/1
Sub-Franchising Contracts: No
Expand In Territory: Yes
Space Needs: 600 SF
SUPPORT & TRAINING:
Financial Assistance Provided: No
Site Selection Assistance: Yes
Lease Negotiation Assistance: Yes
Co-Operative Advertising: No
Franchisee Assoc./Member: Yes/Yes
Size Of Corporate Staff: 250
On-Going Support: ,,C,D,E,,G,H,I
Training: 1 Week Scottsdale, AZ;
  1 Week Local Franchise
SPECIFIC EXPANSION PLANS:
US: All United States
Canada: No
Overseas: NR

⤡ ⤢

GODFATHER'S PIZZA

9140 W. Dodge Rd., # 300
Omaha, NE 68114
Tel: (800) 456-8347 (402) 391-1452
Fax: (402) 255-2685
E-Mail: brucec@godfathers.com
Web Site: www.godfathers.com
Mr. Bruce N. Cannon, Vice President of
  Franchising

GODFATHER'S PIZZA is consistently
recognized by consumers and independent research as having a superior quality
product. Couple this with consistent operations, innovative new products, attention

to service and full support services and
GODFATHER'S PIZZA is positioned to
retain its reputation for high quality and
service.

BACKGROUND:
Established: 1973;   1st Franchised: 1974
Franchised Units: 480
Company-Owned Units: 111
Total Units: 591
Dist.:   US-590; CAN-1; O'seas-0
  North America: 38 States, Provinces
  Density: 60 in IA, 39 in MN, 67 in WA
Projected New Units (12 Months):   27
Qualifications: 5, 5, 5, 3, NR, NR
FINANCIAL/TERMS:
Cash Investment: $55-120K
Total Investment: $82.5-358K
Minimum Net Worth: $200K
Fees: Franchise - $20K
  Royalty - 5%;   Ad. - 0%
Earnings Claims Statement: No
Term of Contract (Years):   ·   15/10
Avg. # Of Employees: 6 FT, 20 PT
Passive Ownership: Discouraged
Encourage Conversions: Yes
Area Develop. Agreements: Yes/1
Sub-Franchising Contracts: No
Expand In Territory: Yes
Space Needs: 3,500 SF
SUPPORT & TRAINING:
Financial Assistance Provided: No
Site Selection Assistance: Yes
Lease Negotiation Assistance: No
Co-Operative Advertising: No
Franchisee Assoc./Member: Yes/Yes
Size Of Corporate Staff: 92
On-Going Support: ,,D,,G,,I
Training: 35 Days Omaha, NE
SPECIFIC EXPANSION PLANS:
US: All United States
Canada: No
Overseas: NR

⤡ ⤢

GOLDEN CHICK

11488 Luna Rd., # 100B
Dallas, TX 75234-9430
Tel: (972) 831-0911
Fax: (972) 831-0401
E-Mail: gcinfo@goldenchick.com
Web Site: www.goldenchick.com
Mr. Kelly Creighton, President

GOLDEN CHICK is a fast-food chicken
restaurant, offering indoor dining, drive-
thru, carry-out and delivery service.
GC's menu consists of fresh, golden
fried chicken, roasted chicken, golden

169

tenders, fried catfish, fresh-baked yeast rolls,country-style biscuits, gravy, french fries, coleslaw, mashed potatoes, corn on the cob, green beans, mac & cheese, sandwiches and fountain soft drinks.

BACKGROUND:

Established: 1967; 1st Franchised: 1972	
Franchised Units:	80
Company-Owned Units:	7
Total Units:	87
Dist.:	US-87; CAN-0; O'seas-0
North America:	2 States, 0 Provinces
Density:	3 in OK, 84 in TX
Projected New Units (12 Months):	6
Qualifications:	4, 4, 5, 2, 2, 5

FINANCIAL/TERMS:

Cash Investment:	$50-200K
Total Investment:	$400-750K
Minimum Net Worth:	$100K
Fees: Franchise -	$20K
Royalty - 4%;	Ad. - 1%
Earnings Claims Statement:	No
Term of Contract (Years):	20/NA
Avg. # Of Employees:	15 FT, 0 PT
Passive Ownership:	Not Allowed
Encourage Conversions:	Yes
Area Develop. Agreements:	Yes
Sub-Franchising Contracts:	No
Expand In Territory:	Yes
Space Needs:	1,800 SF

SUPPORT & TRAINING:

Financial Assistance Provided:	No
Site Selection Assistance:	Yes
Lease Negotiation Assistance:	No
Co-Operative Advertising:	No
Franchisee Assoc./Member:	No
Size Of Corporate Staff:	12
On-Going Support:	a,B,C,D,E,F,G,H,
Training:	6 Weeks Dallas, TX

SPECIFIC EXPANSION PLANS:

US:	South, Southwest
Canada:	No
Overseas:	NR

⋘ ⋙

GREAT STEAK
9311 E. Via De Ventura
Scottsdale, AZ 85258
Tel: (866) 4KAHALA (480) 362-4800
Fax: (480) 362-4792

E-Mail: jdpalumbo@kahalacorp.com
Web Site: www.thegreatsteak.com
Mr. John Palumbo, Franchise Director

As the tagline states, Great Steak serves "America's Premier Cheesesteak." For more than 25 years, Great Steak has carried on the tradition of this hearty, affordable and all-American meal. Always cooked to order on an exhibition-style grill, Great Steak cheesesteaks are made with sirloin steak and topped with the customer's choice of cheese and toppings and served on a freshly baked bun. The menu at Great Steak has grown from a single Cheesesteak sandwich to 14 core entrées, including the popular Chicken Philly and Super Steak sandwiches. Also on the menu are Great Steak's famous fries—large, golden brown and overflowing from their signature cups. The Great Steak concept appeals to both men and women between the ages of 18-45.

BACKGROUND:

Established: 1982; 1st Franchised: 1985	
Franchised Units:	199
Company-Owned Units:	1
Total Units:	200
Dist.:	US-192; CAN-0; O'seas-8
North America:	31 States, 0 Provinces
Density:	20 in OH, 27 in IL, 40 in CA
Projected New Units (12 Months):	24
Qualifications:	4, 4, 3, 2, 3, 4

FINANCIAL/TERMS:

Cash Investment:	$75-150K
Total Investment:	$161.2-511.25K
Minimum Net Worth:	$320K
Fees: Franchise -	$30K
Royalty - 6%;	Ad. - 2%
Earnings Claims Statement:	No
Term of Contract (Years):	10/10
Avg. # Of Employees:	2 FT, 12-15 PT
Passive Ownership:	Allowed
Encourage Conversions:	Yes
Area Develop. Agreements:	Yes
Sub-Franchising Contracts:	Yes
Expand In Territory:	Yes
Space Needs:	600-2,000 SF

SUPPORT & TRAINING:

Financial Assistance Provided:	No
Site Selection Assistance:	Yes
Lease Negotiation Assistance:	Yes
Co-Operative Advertising:	No
Franchisee Assoc./Member:	No
Size Of Corporate Staff:	250
On-Going Support:	a,B,C,D,E,F,G,H,I
Training:	1 Week Local Franchise; 1 Week Scottsdale, AZ

SPECIFIC EXPANSION PLANS:

US:	All United States
Canada:	All Canada
Overseas:	NR

⋘ ⋙

Top 100

GREAT WRAPS

4 Executive Park E., # 315
Atlanta, GA 30329
Tel: (888) 489-7277 (404) 248-9900 + 16
Fax: (404) 248-0180
E-Mail: franchise@greatwraps.com
Web Site: www.greatwraps.com
Ms. Sunny Kincheloe, Director of Franchise Development

GREAT WRAPS is the #1 Hot Wrapped Sandwich & Grilled Sub Franchise, and is experiencing rapid growth. That's because we offer a franchise opportunity that is unique and proven . . . and provides tremendous growth potential. We feature a powerful menu that is fresher and tastier than traditional fast food . . . and our Great Wraps Spice Bar lets customers custom-flavor their fries. No one else offers this level of choice. Our operation is extremely efficient, and is so simple to learn, you don't even need prior food experience.

BACKGROUND: IFA MEMBER

Established: 1978; 1st Franchised: 1986	
Franchised Units:	70
Company-Owned Units:	2
Total Units:	72
Dist.:	US-72; CAN-0; O'seas-0
North America:	20 States, 0 Provinces
Density:	7 in VA, 10 in FL, 25 in GA
Projected New Units (12 Months):	15
Qualifications:	5, 3, 3, 3, 4, 4

FINANCIAL/TERMS:

Cash Investment:	$70-80K
Total Investment:	$230-338K
Minimum Net Worth:	$250K
Fees: Franchise -	$22.5K
Royalty - 5.5%;	Ad. - .5%
Earnings Claims Statement:	No
Term of Contract (Years):	15/10
Avg. # Of Employees:	5 FT, 6 PT
Passive Ownership:	Discouraged
Encourage Conversions:	Yes
Area Develop. Agreements:	No
Sub-Franchising Contracts:	Yes
Expand In Territory:	Yes
Space Needs:	600-2,000 SF

SUPPORT & TRAINING:

Financial Assistance Provided: Yes (I)
Site Selection Assistance: Yes
Lease Negotiation Assistance: Yes
Co-Operative Advertising: Yes
Franchisee Assoc./Member: Yes/Yes
Size Of Corporate Staff: 8
On-Going Support: ,,C,D,E,,G,H,
Training: 2 Weeks Atlanta, GA

SPECIFIC EXPANSION PLANS:

US: NE, SE, SW, MW
Canada: No
Overseas: NR

≪ ≫

GRECO PIZZA RESTAURANTS

P. O. Box 1040
Truro, NS B2N 5G9 Canada
Tel: (902) 897-8418
Fax: (902) 895-7635
E-Mail: g.gallant@greco.ca
Web Site: www.greco.ca
Mr. Guy Gallant, VP Business Development

Atlantic Canada's largest home delivery pizza chain, specializing in pizza, donair products, oven sub sandwiches and pita-wrapped sandwiches.

BACKGROUND:

Established: 1977; 1st Franchised: 1977
Franchised Units: 60
Company-Owned Units: 1
Total Units: 61
Dist.: US-0; CAN-61; O'seas-0
North America: 0 States, 4 Provinces
Density: 23 in NS, 5 in NL, 21 in NB
Projected New Units (12 Months): 5
Qualifications: NR

FINANCIAL/TERMS:

Cash Investment: $40K
Total Investment: $150-180K
Minimum Net Worth: $40K
Fees: Franchise - $20K
Royalty - 5%; Ad. - 3%
Earnings Claims Statement: No
Term of Contract (Years): 10/5/5/
Avg. # Of Employees: 5 FT, 10 PT
Passive Ownership: Discouraged
Encourage Conversions: Yes
Area Develop. Agreements: Yes/1
Sub-Franchising Contracts: Yes
Expand In Territory: Yes
Space Needs: 1,200 SF

SUPPORT & TRAINING:

Financial Assistance Provided: No
Site Selection Assistance: Yes
Lease Negotiation Assistance: Yes

Co-Operative Advertising: No
Franchisee Assoc./Member: NR
Size Of Corporate Staff: 19
On-Going Support: a,b,C,D,E,F,G,h,I
Training: 4 Weeks Correspondence;
2 Days Headquarters; 3 Weeks On-Site

SPECIFIC EXPANSION PLANS:

US: No
Canada: PQ, Atlantic CAN
Overseas: NR

≪ ≫

HAPPY JOE'S PIZZA & ICE CREAM PARLOR

2705 Happy Joe Dr.
Bettendorf, IA 52722
Tel: (800) 640-2834 (563) 332-8811
Fax: (563) 332-5822
E-Mail: tima@happyjoes.com
Web Site: www.happyjoes.com
Mr. Tim Anderson, Director of Franchising

Pizza and ice cream in a fun atmosphere. Birthday party packages available. Very involved with special programs for youth in the community. Diversified pizza, pasta, sandwiches, salad bar and ice cream menu, candy, soft drinks and beer. Several parlors offer Family Fun Centers with redemption games and adventure-style golf.

BACKGROUND:

Established: 1972; 1st Franchised: 1973
Franchised Units: 58
Company-Owned Units: 7
Total Units: 65
Dist.: US-65; CAN-0; O'seas-0
North America: 6 States, 1 Provinces
Density: 33 in IA, 16 in IL, 7 in WI
Projected New Units (12 Months): 3
Qualifications: 5, 4, 3, 3, 3, 4

FINANCIAL/TERMS:

Cash Investment: $300K
Total Investment: $300K-1.5MM
Minimum Net Worth: $200K
Fees: Franchise - $25K
Royalty - 4.5%; Ad. - 1%
Earnings Claims Statement: No
Term of Contract (Years): 15/10
Avg. # Of Employees: 4 FT, 30 PT
Passive Ownership: Discouraged
Encourage Conversions: Yes
Area Develop. Agreements: Yes/1
Sub-Franchising Contracts: No
Expand In Territory: Yes
Space Needs: 3,500 SF

SUPPORT & TRAINING:

Financial Assistance Provided: Yes (D)

Site Selection Assistance: Yes
Lease Negotiation Assistance: Yes
Co-Operative Advertising: No
Franchisee Assoc./Member: Yes/Yes
Size Of Corporate Staff: 30
On-Going Support: ,B,C,D,E,,G,h,
Training: 6-12 Weeks IA

SPECIFIC EXPANSION PLANS:

US: Midwest
Canada: No
Overseas: NR

≪ ≫

Top 100

HARDEE'S

6307 Carpinteria Ave., # A
Carpinteria, CA 93013
Tel: (866) 253-7655 (805) 745-7842
Fax: (714) 780-6320
E-Mail: nrudis@ckr.com
Web Site: www.ckr.com
Ms. Natasha Rudis, Franchise Coordinator

The Hardee's® brand is one of America's Premier Burger Brands and is the Home of the Thickburger®. Established in 1961, Hardee's® operates or franchises over 1,900 quick service restaurants in 30 U.S. states and 9 countries. The Hardee's® menu consists of charbroiled "Made-to-order" Thickburgersâ,,¢, Made from Scratch® biscuits. Hand-Scooped Shakes and Maltsâ,,¢, and a distinctive variety of charbroiled and crispy chicken sandwiches.

BACKGROUND: IFA MEMBER

Established: 1961; 1st Franchised: 1962
Franchised Units: 1427
Company-Owned Units: 481
Total Units: 1908
Dist.: US-1710; CAN-0; O'seas-198
North America: 30 States, 0 Provinces
Density: 151 in TN, 183 in VA, 235 in NC
Projected New Units (12 Months): NR
Qualifications: 4, 4, 4, 2, 2, 5

FINANCIAL/TERMS:

Cash Investment: $300K
Total Investment: $1.2-1.6MM
Minimum Net Worth: $1MM
Fees: Franchise - $35K
Royalty - 4%; Ad. - 5% Min.
Earnings Claims Statement: No

Term of Contract (Years):	20/5
Avg. # Of Employees:	15 FT, PT
Passive Ownership:	Not Allowed
Encourage Conversions:	Yes
Area Develop. Agreements:	No
Sub-Franchising Contracts:	No
Expand In Territory:	Yes
Space Needs:	2,447 SF

SUPPORT & TRAINING:

Financial Assistance Provided:	No
Site Selection Assistance:	Yes
Lease Negotiation Assistance:	No
Co-Operative Advertising:	Yes
Franchisee Assoc./Member:	No
Size Of Corporate Staff:	300
On-Going Support:	„C,D,E,F,G,H,I
Training:	12 Weeks Training

SPECIFIC EXPANSION PLANS:

US:	Midwest/Eastern US
Canada:	No
Overseas:	NR

◄◄ ►►

HO-LEE-CHOW
5415 Dundas St., #110
Toronto, ON M9B 1B5 Canada
Tel: (800) HO-LEE-CHOW (416) 778-8028 + 2006
Fax: (416) 778-6818
E-Mail: holeechow@holeechow.com
Web Site: www.holeechow.com
Ms. Lucy Moody, Franchise Department

Great Chinese food delivered fast and fresh. Each entree in our restaurants is cooked-to-order with no added MSG or preservatives. Each order is delivered in under 45 minutes. All locations are brightly lit and have our open kitchen concept so customers can view their food being cooked in the most pristine kitchens.

BACKGROUND:

Established: 1989;	1st Franchised: 1989
Franchised Units:	18
Company-Owned Units:	3
Total Units:	21
Dist.:	US-0; CAN-21; O'seas-0
North America:	0 States, 1 Provinces
Density:	21 in ON
Projected New Units (12 Months):	15
Qualifications:	3, 3, 1, 2, 3, 5

FINANCIAL/TERMS:

Cash Investment:	$50-75K

Total Investment:	$175K
Minimum Net Worth:	$100K
Fees: Franchise -	$Included
Royalty - 6%;	Ad. - 3%
Earnings Claims Statement:	Yes
Term of Contract (Years):	5/15
Avg. # Of Employees:	3 FT, 1 PT
Passive Ownership:	Discouraged
Encourage Conversions:	Yes
Area Develop. Agreements:	Yes/1
Sub-Franchising Contracts:	Yes
Expand In Territory:	Yes
Space Needs:	900 SF

SUPPORT & TRAINING:

Financial Assistance Provided:	Yes (D)
Site Selection Assistance:	Yes
Lease Negotiation Assistance:	Yes
Co-Operative Advertising:	No
Franchisee Assoc./Member:	Yes/Yes
Size Of Corporate Staff:	50
On-Going Support:	A,B,C,D,E,F,G,H,I
Training:	1 Week Head Office in Toronto, ON; 4 Weeks On-Site

SPECIFIC EXPANSION PLANS:

US:	All United States
Canada:	ON
Overseas:	NR

◄◄ ►►

HUNGRY HOWIE'S PIZZA & SUBS
30300 Stephenson Hwy., # 200
Madison Heights, MI 48071-1600
Tel: (800) 624-8122 (248) 414-3300 + 223
Fax: (248) 414-3301
E-Mail: franchiseinfo@hungryhowies.com
Web Site: www.hungryhowies.com
Mr. Bob Cuffaro, Dir. Franchise Development

HUNGRY HOWIE'S, the innovator of the award-winning Flavored-Crust Pizza, is the nation's 9th largest carry-out / delivery pizza company. Menu offerings include 8 varieties of Flavored-Crust pizzas, delicious oven-baked subs and fresh and crispy salads.

BACKGROUND: IFA MEMBER

Established: 1973;	1st Franchised: 1982
Franchised Units:	565
Company-Owned Units:	0
Total Units:	565
Dist.:	US-565; CAN-1; O'seas-0
North America:	19 States, 1 Provinces
Density:	180 in MI, 180 in FL, 15 in CA
Projected New Units (12 Months):	20
Qualifications:	4, 3, 2, 3, 4, 5

FINANCIAL/TERMS:

Cash Investment:	$50K
Total Investment:	$100K-150K
Minimum Net Worth:	$150K
Fees: Franchise -	$15K
Royalty - 5%;	Ad. - 3%
Earnings Claims Statement:	No
Term of Contract (Years):	20/20
Avg. # Of Employees:	4 FT, 8 PT
Passive Ownership:	Discouraged
Encourage Conversions:	Yes
Area Develop. Agreements:	Yes/1
Sub-Franchising Contracts:	Yes
Expand In Territory:	Yes
Space Needs:	1,200 SF

SUPPORT & TRAINING:

Financial Assistance Provided:	Yes (D)
Site Selection Assistance:	Yes
Lease Negotiation Assistance:	Yes
Co-Operative Advertising:	No
Franchisee Assoc./Member:	No
Size Of Corporate Staff:	20
On-Going Support:	,B,C,D,E,F,G,h,
Training:	5 Weeks Madison Heights, MI

SPECIFIC EXPANSION PLANS:

US:	All United States
Canada:	No
Overseas:	NR

◄◄ ►►

JERRY'S SUBS & PIZZA
15942 Shady Grove Rd.
Gaithersburg, MD 20877-1315
Tel: (800) 990-9176 + 155 (301) 921-8777 + 155
Fax: (301) 948-3508
E-Mail: robbinb@jerrysusa.com
Web Site: www.jerrysusa.com
Ms. Robbin E. Brinkhoff, Dir. Franchise Development

High-volume, high-traffic locations are selected, featuring our 'overstuffed' subs and NY-style pizza. Decor is bright and up-scale and provides a warm, friendly environment.

BACKGROUND:

Established: 1954;	1st Franchised: 1980
Franchised Units:	99
Company-Owned Units:	1
Total Units:	100
Dist.:	US-100; CAN-0; O'seas-0
North America:	5 States, 0 Provinces
Density:	30 in VA, 63 in MD, 3 in DC

172

Projected New Units (12 Months):   15
Qualifications: 4, 2, 1, 1, 4, 2
FINANCIAL/TERMS:
Cash Investment: $65-75K
Total Investment: $300-400K
Minimum Net Worth: $250K
Fees: Franchise - $25K
   Royalty - 6%;   Ad. - 3%
Earnings Claims Statement: No
Term of Contract (Years):   20/Open
Avg. # Of Employees: FT, 0 PT
Passive Ownership: Discouraged
Encourage Conversions: Yes
Area Develop. Agreements: Yes
Sub-Franchising Contracts: No
Expand In Territory: Yes
Space Needs: 1,500-2,000 SF
SUPPORT & TRAINING:
Financial Assistance Provided: Yes (D)
Site Selection Assistance: Yes
Lease Negotiation Assistance: Yes
Co-Operative Advertising: No
Franchisee Assoc./Member: No
Size Of Corporate Staff: 25
On-Going Support: ,,C,D,E,F,G,H,I
Training: 6 Weeks Aspen Hill, MD
SPECIFIC EXPANSION PLANS:
US: East Coast
Canada: No
Overseas: NR

◄◄ ►►

JERSEY MIKE'S SUBS
2251 Landmark Pl.
Manasquan, NJ 08736
Tel: (800) 321-7676 (732) 223-4044
Fax: (732) 223-0777
E-Mail: info@jerseymikes.com
Web Site: www.jerseymikes.com
Ms. Josephine Capozzi, VP Franchise
   Relations

JERSEY MIKE'S is a submarine sandwich franchise company which is voted
â€œBest Subâ€ in virtually every market
served. They have stayed true to their
original recipes to serve premium quality
authentic subs. They bake bread daily in
the store. Roast beefs are cooked on premises. Meats and cheeses are sliced in front
of the customer and the subs are topped
with fresh sliced onions, lettuce, tomatoes,
with red wine vinegar, olive oil and spices.
The company's mission is to bring its customers the highest quality, freshest made
sub in the industry and give back to the
communities in which it operates. **Note:
Operating Units figures are as of year end
2008 - FDD

BACKGROUND:
Established: 1956;   1st Franchised: 1986
Franchised Units: 353
Company-Owned Units: 14
Total Units: 367
Dist.:   US-367; CAN-0; O'seas-0
   North America: 27 States, 0 Provinces
   Density: 34 in OH, 34 in CA, 89 in NC
Projected New Units (12 Months):   NR
Qualifications: NR
FINANCIAL/TERMS:
Cash Investment: NR
Total Investment: $133,226-$384,333
Minimum Net Worth: NR
Fees: Franchise - $18.5K
   Royalty - 6.5%;   Ad. - 3.5%
Earnings Claims Statement: No
Term of Contract (Years):   10/10
Avg. # Of Employees: 7 FT, 8 PT
Passive Ownership: Discouraged
Encourage Conversions: No
Area Develop. Agreements: Yes
Sub-Franchising Contracts: No
Expand In Territory: Yes
Space Needs: 1,500 SF
SUPPORT & TRAINING:
Financial Assistance Provided: No
Site Selection Assistance: Yes
Lease Negotiation Assistance: Yes
Co-Operative Advertising: Yes
Franchisee Assoc./Member: No
Size Of Corporate Staff: 50
On-Going Support: ,,C,D,E,,G,H,
Training: 8-12 Weeks Regionally and at
   Home Office
SPECIFIC EXPANSION PLANS:
US: All United States
Canada: NR
Overseas: NR

◄◄ ►►

JIMBOY'S TACOS
1830 Sierra Gardens Dr., # 80
Roseville, CA 95661
Tel: (800) 546-2697 (916) 788-9770
Fax: (916) 788-9776
E-Mail: jlanni@jimboys.com
Web Site: www.jimboys.com
Mr. John Lanni, Director Franchise Mar-
   keting

JIMBOY'S TACOS - famous, award-winning tacos. Maintaining a proven conept
through 50 years of commitment to
excellent food and service. Cooked fresh
daily using high-quality ingredients. Our
franchisees are given a very thorough and
extensive hands-on classroom training
program. Strong on-going, in-store support. Franchisees required to attend our
classroom training every other month at
our corporate office. We offer free-standing concepts with drive-up windows, also
end-cap concepts in strip centers.

BACKGROUND:
Established: 1954;   1st Franchised: 1965
Franchised Units: 38
Company-Owned Units: 2
Total Units: 40
Dist.:   US-40; CAN-0; O'seas-0
   North America: 2 States, Provinces
   Density: 33 in CA, 7 in NV
Projected New Units (12 Months):   8
Qualifications: 5, 4, 3, 3, 4, 5
FINANCIAL/TERMS:
Cash Investment: Varies
Total Investment: $203-587K
Minimum Net Worth: NR
Fees: Franchise - $36K
   Royalty - 4%;   Ad. - 3%
Earnings Claims Statement: No
Term of Contract (Years):   15/5/5/
Avg. # Of Employees: 4-10 FT, 6-12 PT
Passive Ownership: Discouraged
Encourage Conversions: Yes
Area Develop. Agreements: No
Sub-Franchising Contracts: No
Expand In Territory: Yes
Space Needs: 2,000 SF
SUPPORT & TRAINING:
Financial Assistance Provided: No
Site Selection Assistance: Yes
Lease Negotiation Assistance: Yes
Co-Operative Advertising: No
Franchisee Assoc./Member: No
Size Of Corporate Staff: 7
On-Going Support: ,B,C,D,E,,G,H,I
Training: 96 Hours Corporate Training
   Rest. Folsom, CA; 32 Hours Corpo-
   rate Office, Roseville, CA
SPECIFIC EXPANSION PLANS:
US: California, Nevada
Canada: No
Overseas: NR

◄◄ ►►

JIMMY JOHN'S GOURMET SANDWICHES

2212 Fox Dr.
Champaign, IL 61820
Tel: (800) 546-6904 (217) 356-9900
Fax: (217) 359-2956
E-Mail: bmorena@jimmyjohns.com
Web Site: www.jimmyjohns.com
Mr. Bob Morena, Director Franchise Development

World's greatest gourmet sandwich shop. All the sandwiches are made on fresh-baked french bread or 7-grain honey wheat bread. We only use the highest-quality meats available with garden fresh veggies that are brought in and sliced each morning.

BACKGROUND: IFA MEMBER

Established: 1983; 1st Franchised: 1993
Franchised Units: 560
Company-Owned Units: 19
Total Units: 579
Dist.: US-579; CAN-0; O'seas-0
North America: 30 States, 0 Provinces
Density: 36 in WI, 61 in MI, 131 in IL
Projected New Units (12 Months): 140
Qualifications: 5, 4, 2, 4, 4, 5

FINANCIAL/TERMS:

Cash Investment: $80K
Total Investment: $290K-386.5K
Minimum Net Worth: $300K
Fees: Franchise - $30-35K
  Royalty - 6%; Ad. - 4.5%
Earnings Claims Statement: Yes
Term of Contract (Years): 10/10
Avg. # Of Employees: 2 FT, 25 PT
Passive Ownership: Not Allowed
Encourage Conversions: NA
Area Develop. Agreements: Yes/10
Sub-Franchising Contracts: No
Expand In Territory: Yes
Space Needs: 800-1,200 SF

SUPPORT & TRAINING:

Financial Assistance Provided: No
Site Selection Assistance: Yes
Lease Negotiation Assistance: Yes
Co-Operative Advertising: Yes
Franchisee Assoc./Member: Yes/Yes
Size Of Corporate Staff: 40
On-Going Support: ,,C,D,E,F,G,H,I
Training: 3 Weeks Champaign, IL;

4 Weeks (apprenticeship) Varies

SPECIFIC EXPANSION PLANS:

US: All United States
Canada: All Canada
Overseas: All Countries

‹‹ ››

JODY MARONI'S SAUSAGE KINGDOM

2011 Ocean Front Walk
Venice, CA 90291
Tel: (800) 428-8364 (310) 348-1500
Fax: (310) 348-1510
E-Mail: info@jodymaroni.com
Web Site: www.jodymaroni.com
Mr. Paul Kramer, Director of Franchise Develop.

Born on the boardwalk of Venice Beach in Southern California, Jody Maroni's Sausage Kingdom has been serving the world's greatest sausage for over 25 years. With locations across the country, Jody Maroni's can be seen in entertainment centers, malls, tourism areas, transportation centers, downtown business districts and anywhere people gather for food and fun. Opportunities also exist in street locations in a "hot dog stand" environment as a nostalgic free-standing building or end-cap space.

BACKGROUND:

Established: 1979; 1st Franchised: 1996
Franchised Units: 17
Company-Owned Units: 1
Total Units: 18
Dist.: US-18; CAN-0; O'seas-0
North America: 8 States, 0 Provinces
Density: 3 in OH, 2 in NV, 8 in CA
Projected New Units (12 Months): NR
Qualifications: 3, 3, 3, 3, 3, 3

FINANCIAL/TERMS:

Cash Investment: $20-120K
Total Investment: $75-400K
Minimum Net Worth: $300K
Fees: Franchise - $25K
  Royalty - 5%; Ad. - 0
Earnings Claims Statement: Yes
Term of Contract (Years):10/consecutive
Avg. # Of Employees: 6 FT, 4 PT
Passive Ownership: Discouraged
Encourage Conversions: NA
Area Develop. Agreements: Yes/5
Sub-Franchising Contracts: No
Expand In Territory: Yes
Space Needs: 150-1,500 SF

SUPPORT & TRAINING:

Financial Assistance Provided: No

Site Selection Assistance: Yes
Lease Negotiation Assistance: Yes
Co-Operative Advertising: No
Franchisee Assoc./Member: No
Size Of Corporate Staff: 8
On-Going Support: ,B,C,D,E,,,H,I
Training: 6 Days Los Angeles, CA;
  3 Days On-Site Store location

SPECIFIC EXPANSION PLANS:

US: AR, CA & NV - Single & multi-unit
Franchisees & Ar
Canada: No
Overseas: NR

‹‹ ››

JOHNNY BRUSCO'S NEW YORK STYLE PIZZA

189 Chappell Rd.
Fayetteville, GA 30215
Tel: (404) 729-4900
Fax: (770) 478-5021
E-Mail: franchiseinfo@jnysp.com
Web Site: www.johnnyspizza.com
Mr. Bruce Jackson, President

Johnny Brusco's and Johnny's Pizza are true New York Style Pizzerias, specializing in authentic hand-tossed NY Style Pizza, a variety of salads, appetizers, Italian Dinners, calzones, and stromboli. A sit-down, full-service restaurant that caters to customer service and a memorable dining experience. Family-friendly establishment where kids are comfortable and parents can enjoy their favorite beverages.The atmosphere and décor reflects both the neighborhood and its surrounding interests. Truly your "neighbo

BACKGROUND:

Established: 1977; 1st Franchised: 1995
Franchised Units: 62
Company-Owned Units: 0
Total Units: 62
Dist.: US-62; CAN-0; O'seas-0
North America: 4 States, 0 Provinces
Density: 6 in TN, 51 in GA, 1 in TX
Projected New Units (12 Months): 9-12
Qualifications: 3, 4, 2, 3, 4, 5

FINANCIAL/TERMS:

Cash Investment: $75-250K
Total Investment: $175-275K
Minimum Net Worth: $300K
Fees: Franchise - $27K
  Royalty - 4-5%; Ad. - 2%
Earnings Claims Statement: No
Term of Contract (Years): 10/10
Avg. # Of Employees: 8 FT, 8 PT
Passive Ownership: Discouraged

Encourage Conversions: Yes
Area Develop. Agreements: Yes/10
Sub-Franchising Contracts: No
Expand In Territory: No
Space Needs: 2,100-2,400 SF

SUPPORT & TRAINING:
Financial Assistance Provided: Yes (I)
Site Selection Assistance: Yes
Lease Negotiation Assistance: Yes
Co-Operative Advertising: Yes
Franchisee Assoc./Member: Yes/Yes
Size Of Corporate Staff: 6
On-Going Support: ,B,C,D,E,F,,H,I
Training: 4 Weeks minimum Memphis, TN; 4 Weeks minimum Atlanta, GA; 4 Weeks minimum Dallas, TX

SPECIFIC EXPANSION PLANS:
US: Southeast US; AL, GA, FL, NC, SC, TN, TX
Canada: No
Overseas: NR

≪ ≫

JUICE IT UP!

17915 Sky Park Circle, # J
Irvine, CA 92614
Tel: (888) 705-8423 (949) 475-0146
Fax: (949) 475-0137
E-Mail: carols@juiceitup.com
Web Site: www.juiceitup.com
Ms. Carol Skinner, Franchise System Manager

JUICE IT UP! is a privately held corporation founded in California in 1995. JUICE IT UP! has successfully established itself as a leader in the juice and smoothie bar industry by providing great customer service and products. With over 90 locations and growing, JUICE IT UP! offers a unique and exciting franchise opportunity to entrepreneurially minded individuals. JUICE IT UP! is an approved SBA franchisor.

BACKGROUND: IFA MEMBER
Established: 1995; 1st Franchised: 1998
Franchised Units: 121
Company-Owned Units: 2
Total Units: 123
Dist.: US-123; CAN-0; O'seas-0
North America: 7 States, 0 Provinces
Density: 80 in CA, 5 in AZ
Projected New Units (12 Months): NR
Qualifications: NR

FINANCIAL/TERMS:

Cash Investment: $50K-80K
Total Investment: $237K-349K
Minimum Net Worth: $250K
Fees: Franchise - $25K
Royalty - 6%; Ad. - 2%
Earnings Claims Statement: No
Term of Contract (Years): 10/5/5/
Avg. # Of Employees: 1 FT, 8 PT
Passive Ownership: Discouraged
Encourage Conversions: No
Area Develop. Agreements: Yes/10
Sub-Franchising Contracts: Yes
Expand In Territory: Yes
Space Needs: 1,200 SF

SUPPORT & TRAINING:
Financial Assistance Provided: No
Site Selection Assistance: Yes
Lease Negotiation Assistance: Yes
Co-Operative Advertising: Yes
Franchisee Assoc./Member: Yes/Yes
Size Of Corporate Staff: 20
On-Going Support: ,,C,D,E,,G,H,I
Training: 1 Week Franchisee Store; 2 Days Corporate Office; 1-2 Weeks Corporate Store

SPECIFIC EXPANSION PLANS:
US: All United States
Canada: No
Overseas: NR

≪ ≫

KFC

P. O. Box 34550, 1900 Colonel Sanders Ln.
Louisville, KY 40213
Tel: (866) 2YUM-YUM
Fax: (502) 874-8848
E-Mail: 2yumyum@yum.com
Web Site: www.yumfranchises.com
Ms. Sarah Kramer, Franchise Specialist

World's largest quick-service restaurant with a chicken-dominant menu. KFC offers full-service restaurants and non-traditional express units for captive markets.

BACKGROUND: IFA MEMBER
Established: 1939; 1st Franchised: 1952
Franchised Units: 4287
Company-Owned Units: 1023
Total Units: 5310
Dist.: US-5310; CAN-0; O'seas-0

North America: 50 States, 10 Provinces
Density: in TX, in IL, in CA
Projected New Units (12 Months): 100
Qualifications: 5, 4, 5, 3, 3, 5

FINANCIAL/TERMS:
Cash Investment: NR
Total Investment: $1.2-1.7MM
Minimum Net Worth: $1MM
Fees: Franchise - $25K
Royalty - 4% or $600/Mo.; Ad. - 5%
Earnings Claims Statement: No
Term of Contract (Years): 20/
Avg. # Of Employees: 2 FT, 22 PT
Passive Ownership: Not Allowed
Encourage Conversions: No
Area Develop. Agreements: No
Sub-Franchising Contracts: No
Expand In Territory: Yes
Space Needs: 2,000-3,000 SF

SUPPORT & TRAINING:
Financial Assistance Provided: No
Site Selection Assistance: Yes
Lease Negotiation Assistance: No
Co-Operative Advertising: No
Franchisee Assoc./Member: Yes/Yes
Size Of Corporate Staff: 820
On-Going Support: ,,C,d,E,,G,h,I
Training: 10-16 Weeks Training

SPECIFIC EXPANSION PLANS:
US: All United States
Canada: All Canada
Overseas: All Countries

≪ ≫

KOYA JAPAN

3465 Thimens Blvd.
St. Laurent, QC H4R 1V5 Canada
Tel: (888) 569-2872 (204) 783-4433
Fax: (204) 783-1749
E-Mail: info@koyajapan.com
Web Site: www.koyajapan.com
Ms. Linda Mikulik, Operations Manager

Delicious Japanese food served fast from the freshest of ingredients and complimented by or unique sauce. What makes us successful is our cooking techniques, each meal is made to order in full view of the customer. KOYA JAPAN -- where freshness sizzles before your eyes.

BACKGROUND:
Established: 1979; 1st Franchised: 1985
Franchised Units: 25
Company-Owned Units: 0
Total Units: 25
Dist.: US-0; CAN-25; O'seas-0
North America: 0 States, 6 Provinces
Density: 5 in ON, 6 in MB, 7 in BC

Projected New Units (12 Months): 12
Qualifications: 4, 4, 3, 2, 3, 5
FINANCIAL/TERMS:
Cash Investment: $50% of Total
Total Investment: $175K-500K
Minimum Net Worth: $100K
Fees: Franchise - $30K-40K
  Royalty - 6-7%; Ad. - 2%
Earnings Claims Statement: No
Term of Contract (Years): Up to 10/
Avg. # Of Employees: 3 FT, 1 PT
Passive Ownership: Allowed
Encourage Conversions: Yes
Area Develop. Agreements: Yes/1
Sub-Franchising Contracts: No
Expand In Territory: Yes
Space Needs: 300-400 SF
SUPPORT & TRAINING:
Financial Assistance Provided: No
Site Selection Assistance: Yes
Lease Negotiation Assistance: Yes
Co-Operative Advertising: No
Franchisee Assoc./Member: No
Size Of Corporate Staff: 3
On-Going Support: „C,d,E,,,,I
Training: Up to 1 Month Operating
  Location; Up to 1 Month On-Site; 2-3
  Days Head Office
SPECIFIC EXPANSION PLANS:
US: All United States
Canada: All Canada
Overseas: Bahrain, United Arab Emirates,
  Kuwait, Quatar, Sau

KRYSTAL COMPANY, THE
1 Union Sq., 9 Fl.
Chattanooga, TN 37402-2505
Tel: (800) 458-5841 (423) 757-5645
Fax: (423) 757-5610
E-Mail: awright@krystalco.com
Web Site: www.krystal.com
Mr. Alan Wright, VP Franchise Division

The KRYSTAL COMPANY, a 'cultural icon' in the Southeast, is a unique brand with 72 years of success as a niche franchisor, we provide quality service and thoughtful leadership to our franchise partners. We are an innovative, forward-looking franchisor who is looking for highly motivated operators. We offer a

protected development territory, requiring a minimum 3-restaurant development agreement, minimum liquidity of $650K and a net worth of $1.2 million. KRYSTAL, fresh, hot, small and square.

BACKGROUND: IFA MEMBER
Established: 1932; 1st Franchised: 1991
Franchised Units: 149
Company-Owned Units: 233
Total Units: 382
Dist.: US-382; CAN-0; O'seas-0
  North America: 15 States, 0 Provinces
  Density:105 in TN, 104 in GA, 53 in AL
Projected New Units (12 Months): 25
Qualifications: 5, 4, 5, 2, 2, 5
FINANCIAL/TERMS:
Cash Investment: $250K-300K
Total Investment: $900K-1MM
Minimum Net Worth: $1.2MM
Fees: Franchise - $32.5K
  Royalty - 4.5%; Ad. - 4%
Earnings Claims Statement: No
Term of Contract (Years): 20/20
Avg. # Of Employees: 12-15 FT, 15 PT
Passive Ownership: Allowed
Encourage Conversions: Yes
Area Develop. Agreements: No
Sub-Franchising Contracts: No
Expand In Territory: Yes
Space Needs: 1,300-2,200 SF
SUPPORT & TRAINING:
Financial Assistance Provided: No
Site Selection Assistance: Yes
Lease Negotiation Assistance: No
Co-Operative Advertising: No
Franchisee Assoc./Member: Yes/Yes
Size Of Corporate Staff: 100
On-Going Support: A,B,C,D,E,F,G,H,I
Training: 4 Weeks Company Store;
  1 Week Corporate Computer Center
SPECIFIC EXPANSION PLANS:
US: SE,TX,OK,VA,NC,SC,WV,FL
Canada: No
Overseas: NR

LARRY'S GIANT SUBS
8616 Baymeadows Rd.
Jacksonville, FL 32256
Tel: (800) 358-6870 (904) 739-2498
Fax: (904) 739-1218
E-Mail: bigone@larryssubs.com
Web Site: www.larryssubs.com
Mr. Mitchell Raikes, Vice President

Upscale submarine sandwich franchise, featuring top-quality foods, such as USDA choice roast beef, oven-roasted turkey,

white-meat chicken salad, store decor, custom table tops, laser logo steel chairs and huge ape display.

BACKGROUND:
Established: 1982; 1st Franchised: 1986
Franchised Units: 88
Company-Owned Units: 3
Total Units: 91
Dist.: US-91; CAN-0; O'seas-0
  North America: 6 States, Provinces
  Density: 53 in FL, 28 in GA, 2 in TX
Projected New Units (12 Months): 15
Qualifications: 3, 3, 3, 3, 3, 5
FINANCIAL/TERMS:
Cash Investment: $25-40K
Total Investment: $110-170K
Minimum Net Worth: $150K
Fees: Franchise - $19K
  Royalty - 6%; Ad. - 2%
Earnings Claims Statement: No
Term of Contract (Years): 10/10
Avg. # Of Employees: 6 FT, 10 PT
Passive Ownership: Discouraged
Encourage Conversions: No
Area Develop. Agreements: Yes/1
Sub-Franchising Contracts: Yes
Expand In Territory: Yes
Space Needs: 1,400 SF
SUPPORT & TRAINING:
Financial Assistance Provided: No
Site Selection Assistance: Yes
Lease Negotiation Assistance: Yes
Co-Operative Advertising: No
Franchisee Assoc./Member: No
Size Of Corporate Staff: 10
On-Going Support: A,B,C,D,E,F,G,H,I
Training: 30 Days Corporate Office;
  1-2 Weeks Franchise Store
SPECIFIC EXPANSION PLANS:
US: Southeast
Canada: No
Overseas: NR

LEDO PIZZA SYSTEM
2001 Tidewater Colony Way, # 203
Annapolis, MD 21401-2194
Tel: (410) 721-6887
Fax: (410) 266-6888
E-Mail: ledomarketing@ledomarketing.com
Web Site: www.ledopizza.com
Mr. Will Robinson, Director of Marketing

Ledo Pizza is a full service dining experience with a menu that features fresh salads, pastas, sandwiches, and our critically acclaimed Ledo Pizza.

BACKGROUND: IFA MEMBER
Established: 1955; 1st Franchised: 1989
Franchised Units: 51
Company-Owned Units: 0
Total Units: 51
Dist.: US-51; CAN-0; O'seas-0
North America: 5 States, Provinces
Density: 41 in MD, 2 in PA, 7 in VA
Projected New Units (12 Months): NR
Qualifications: NR
FINANCIAL/TERMS:
Cash Investment: $50-150K
Total Investment: $119-419K
Minimum Net Worth: Varies
Fees: Franchise - $20K
Royalty - 5%; Ad. - 2%
Earnings Claims Statement: No
Term of Contract (Years): 5/15
Avg. # Of Employees: 15 FT, 30 PT
Passive Ownership: Discouraged
Encourage Conversions: No
Area Develop. Agreements: No
Sub-Franchising Contracts: No
Expand In Territory: Yes
Space Needs: 1,800+ SF
SUPPORT & TRAINING:
Financial Assistance Provided: No
Site Selection Assistance: Yes
Lease Negotiation Assistance: Yes
Co-Operative Advertising: No
Franchisee Assoc./Member: Yes/Yes
Size Of Corporate Staff: 12
On-Going Support: ,B,C,D,E,F,G,H,
Training: NR
SPECIFIC EXPANSION PLANS:
US: NE, SE
Canada: NR
Overseas: NR

◄◄ ►►

LITTLE CAESARS

2211 Woodward Ave.
Detroit, MI 48201
Tel: (800) 553-5776 (313) 983-6469
Fax: (313) 983-6435
E-Mail: usdevelopment@LCECorp.com
Web Site: www.littlecaesars.com
Mr. Dan Ducharme, Director of Franchise Development

After 50 years in business, Little Caesars is the fastest growing pizza chain in the United States, with consistent growth for many years. The efficient operating system enables franchisees build-out costs to remain modest while keeping the high quality standards our strong brand requires. Prime markets are available, and franchisee candidates are offered an opportunity for independence with a proven system. Visit LittleCaesars.com to see why we are The Best Kept Secret!

BACKGROUND: IFA MEMBER
Established: 1959; 1st Franchised: 1962
Franchised Units: Confidential
Company-Owned Units: Confidential
Total Units: Confidential
Dist.: Confidential
North America: Confidential
Density: Confidential
Projected New Units (12 Months): NA
Qualifications: 4, 2, 2, 2, 4, 5
FINANCIAL/TERMS:
Cash Investment: $50K
Total Investment: $197.1-559.5K
Minimum Net Worth: $150K
Fees: Franchise - $15-20K
Royalty - 6%; Ad. - 0.25%
Earnings Claims Statement: No
Term of Contract (Years): 10/10
Avg. # Of Employees: 1 FT, 30 PT
Passive Ownership: Not Allowed
Encourage Conversions: Yes
Area Develop. Agreements: Yes/5
Sub-Franchising Contracts: No
Expand In Territory: Yes
Space Needs: 1400 SF
SUPPORT & TRAINING:
Financial Assistance Provided: Yes (I)
Site Selection Assistance: Yes
Lease Negotiation Assistance: Yes
Co-Operative Advertising: Yes
Franchisee Assoc./Member: Yes/No
Size Of Corporate Staff: 300
On-Going Support: ,B,C,D,E,F,G,H,I
Training: 6 Weeks Detroit, MI
SPECIFIC EXPANSION PLANS:
US: All United States
Canada: All Provinces
Overseas: China, India, Mex., Aus., S. Korea, Eur., Caribbean

◄◄ ►►

LITTLE KING

11811 I St.
Omaha, NE 68137
Tel: (800) 788-9478 (402) 330-8019
Fax: (402) 330-3221
E-Mail: bob@littleking.us
Web Site: www.littleking.us
Mr. Robert B. Wertheim, President

Deli and sub restaurant, featuring fresh, fast-food concept - sandwiches. Products are prepared in full view of customers, breads are all baked fresh on premises. All meats are sliced fresh to order. Top-of-the-line food quality, utilizing major nationally known brands. Concept is adaptable to various locations and configurations.

BACKGROUND:
Established: 1968; 1st Franchised: 1978
Franchised Units: 18
Company-Owned Units: 0
Total Units: 18
Dist.: US-18; CAN-0; O'seas-0
North America: 5 States, 0 Provinces
Density: 2 in SD, in NE, 3 in IA
Projected New Units (12 Months): 5-7
Qualifications: 5, 4, 4, 4, 1, 5
FINANCIAL/TERMS:
Cash Investment: $50-70K
Total Investment: $145-200K
Minimum Net Worth: $250-350K
Fees: Franchise - $19.5K
Royalty - 6%; Ad. - 4%
Earnings Claims Statement: No
Term of Contract (Years): 10/10
Avg. # Of Employees: 1-3 FT, 6-9 PT
Passive Ownership: Discouraged
Encourage Conversions: Yes
Area Develop. Agreements: Yes/10
Sub-Franchising Contracts: No
Expand In Territory: Yes
Space Needs: 1,200-1,800 SF
SUPPORT & TRAINING:
Financial Assistance Provided: Yes (D)
Site Selection Assistance: Yes
Lease Negotiation Assistance: Yes
Co-Operative Advertising: Yes
Franchisee Assoc./Member: No
Size Of Corporate Staff: 2
On-Going Support: ,,C,,E,F,G,H,I
Training: As Needed Follow Up Training; 8 Days On-Site; 15 Days Omaha, NE Headquarters
SPECIFIC EXPANSION PLANS:
US: All United States
Canada: No
Overseas: NR

◄◄ ►►

LONG JOHN SILVER'S
P. O. Box 34550, 1900 Colonel Sanders Ln.
Louisville, KY 40213
Tel: (866) 2YUM-YUM
Fax: (502) 874-8848
E-Mail: 2yumyum@yum.com
Web Site: www.yumfranchises.com
Ms. Leigh Anne Lochner, Franchise Specialist

LONG JOHN SILVER'S is the largest, quick-service seafood restaurant chain in the world. We continue to aggressively grow with new units and sales. Opportunities are available in new and existing markets and with our sister brand, A & W in our new co-brand facilities.

BACKGROUND: IFA MEMBER
Established: 1969; 1st Franchised: 1969
Franchised Units: 661
Company-Owned Units: 460
Total Units: 1121
Dist.: US-1121; CAN-0; O'seas-0
North America: 0 States, 0 Provinces
Density: in TX, in OH, in IN
Projected New Units (12 Months): NR
Qualifications: 5, 5, 3, 4, 5, 5
FINANCIAL/TERMS:
Cash Investment: NR
Total Investment: $1.1MM-1.7MM
Minimum Net Worth: $1MM
Fees: Franchise - $20K
Royalty - 6% Gr. Receipts; Ad. - 4% Gr. Rec.
Earnings Claims Statement: Yes
Term of Contract (Years): 20/
Avg. # Of Employees: FT, PT
Passive Ownership: Discouraged
Encourage Conversions: NA
Area Develop. Agreements: No
Sub-Franchising Contracts: No
Expand In Territory: Yes
Space Needs: NR
SUPPORT & TRAINING:
Financial Assistance Provided: No
Site Selection Assistance: Yes
Lease Negotiation Assistance: No
Co-Operative Advertising: No
Franchisee Assoc./Member: Yes/Yes
Size Of Corporate Staff: 0
On-Going Support: ,C,D,E,,G,h,I

Training: 10-16 Weeks Training
SPECIFIC EXPANSION PLANS:
US: All United States
Canada: No
Overseas: NR

◄◄ ►►

MANCHU WOK (USA)
P.O. Box 625
Deerfield Beach, FL 33443-0625
Tel: (800) 361-8864 + 112 (954) 427-2163
Fax: (954) 427-2337
E-Mail: mariellen_clark@manchuwok.com
Web Site: www.manchuwok.com
Ms. Mariellen Clark, Franchise Administrator

MANCHU WOK is one of the largest Chinese quick service franchises in North America. MANCHU WOK operates in over 200 food court locations in large regional malls, airports, colleges, theme parks, office buildings, hospitals and the military.

BACKGROUND: IFA MEMBER
Established: 1980; 1st Franchised: 1988
Franchised Units: 160
Company-Owned Units: 55
Total Units: 215
Dist.: US-165; CAN-42; O'seas-2
North America: 28 States, 10 Provinces
Density: 15 in TX, 45 in ON, 23 in CA
Projected New Units (12 Months): 40
Qualifications: 4, 4, 4, 3, 4, 4
FINANCIAL/TERMS:
Cash Investment: $75K-120K
Total Investment: $260K-400K
Minimum Net Worth: $300K
Fees: Franchise - $30K
Royalty - 7%; Ad. - 1%
Earnings Claims Statement: Yes
Term of Contract (Years): 10/
Avg. # Of Employees: 2-3 FT, 6-10 PT
Passive Ownership: Discouraged
Encourage Conversions: Yes
Area Develop. Agreements: Yes/1
Sub-Franchising Contracts: No
Expand In Territory: Yes
Space Needs: 800 SF
SUPPORT & TRAINING:
Financial Assistance Provided: Yes (I)

Site Selection Assistance: Yes
Lease Negotiation Assistance: Yes
Co-Operative Advertising: No
Franchisee Assoc./Member: Yes/Yes
Size Of Corporate Staff: 100
On-Going Support: ,B,C,D,E,F,G,H,I
Training: 3-4 Weeks Corporate Site and Classroom
SPECIFIC EXPANSION PLANS:
US: Central, Southwest, West
Canada: All Canada
Overseas: NR

◄◄ ►►

MARCO'S PIZZA
5252 Monroe St.
Toledo, OH 43623
Tel: (800) 262-7267 (419) 885-7000
Fax: (419) 885-5215
E-Mail: dallen@marcos.com
Web Site: www.marcos.com
Ms. Debbie Allen, Franchise Compliance Officer

MARCO'S PIZZA offers pizza, hot sub sandwiches, Cheezybread, salad and soft drinks. There are 3 crust style - hand spun, pan and crispy thin, and 3 types of crust flavors - garlic butter, parmesan, and roma seasoning. MARCO'S PIZZA offers carry-out and fast, hot delivery.

BACKGROUND: IFA MEMBER
Established: 1978; 1st Franchised: 1978
Franchised Units: 175
Company-Owned Units: 27
Total Units: 202
Dist.: US-202; CAN-0; O'seas-0
North America: 4 States, 0 Provinces
Density: 98 in OH, 22 in MI, 7 in IN
Projected New Units (12 Months): 34
Qualifications: 5, 4, 3, 4, 3, 5
FINANCIAL/TERMS:
Cash Investment: $100K-110K
Total Investment: $175K-320K
Minimum Net Worth: $100K
Fees: Franchise - $15K
Royalty - 3-5%; Ad. - 1%
Earnings Claims Statement: No
Term of Contract (Years): 10/10
Avg. # Of Employees: 4 FT, 15 PT
Passive Ownership: Not Allowed

Encourage Conversions: NA
Area Develop. Agreements: Yes/1
Sub-Franchising Contracts: No
Expand In Territory: Yes
Space Needs: 1,300-1,400 SF
SUPPORT & TRAINING:
Financial Assistance Provided: Yes (D)
Site Selection Assistance: Yes
Lease Negotiation Assistance: Yes
Co-Operative Advertising: No
Franchisee Assoc./Member: Yes/Yes
Size Of Corporate Staff: 40
On-Going Support: ,B,C,D,E,F,,H,I
Training: 2 Weeks Toledo, OH; 6 Weeks Store
SPECIFIC EXPANSION PLANS:
US: Midwest
Canada: No
Overseas: NR

MAUI TACOS

1775 The Exchange, # 600
Atlanta, GA 30339
Tel: (888) 628-4822 + 102 (770) 226-8226 + 102
Fax: (770) 541-2300
E-Mail:
Web Site: www.mauitacos.com
Mr. Robert Sitkoff, President

Fast-casual "Maui-Mex" restaurant featuring Mexican Foods created by internationally recognized chef Mark Ellmao, using pineapple and lime juice marinade with island spices. Char-grilled chicken, steak, and lean beef burritos topped with unique salsas is our mainstay. This food experience is like a vacation in Maui.

BACKGROUND: IFA MEMBER
Established: 1993; 1st Franchised: 1998
Franchised Units: 10
Company-Owned Units: 1
Total Units: 11
Dist.: US-11; CAN-0; O'seas-0
North America: 2 States, 0 Provinces
Density: 8 in HAWAII, 3 in GA
Projected New Units (12 Months): 20
Qualifications: 4, 4, 3, 3, 4, 4
FINANCIAL/TERMS:
Cash Investment: $60-125K
Total Investment: $180-375K
Minimum Net Worth: $300K
Fees: Franchise - $20K
Royalty - 6%; Ad. - 4%
Earnings Claims Statement: Yes
Term of Contract (Years): 20/20
Avg. # Of Employees: 4 FT, 10 PT

Passive Ownership: Discouraged
Encourage Conversions: Yes
Area Develop. Agreements: Yes/1
Sub-Franchising Contracts: Yes
Expand In Territory: Yes
Space Needs: 2,000 SF
SUPPORT & TRAINING:
Financial Assistance Provided: Yes (D)
Site Selection Assistance: Yes
Lease Negotiation Assistance: Yes
Co-Operative Advertising: No
Franchisee Assoc./Member: Yes/Yes
Size Of Corporate Staff: 6
On-Going Support: A,B,C,D,E,F,G,h,I
Training: 160 Hours Atlanta, GA
SPECIFIC EXPANSION PLANS:
US: All United States
Canada: All Canada
Overseas: All Countries

MAUI WOWI HAWAIIAN COFFEES AND SMOOTHIES

5445 DTC Pkwy., # 1050
Greenwood Village, CO 80111
Tel: (877) 849-6992 + 130 (303) 781-7800
Fax: (303) 781-2438
E-Mail: info@mauiwowi.com
Web Site: www.mauiwowi.com
Ms. Angela Brazda, Development Coordinator

Ranked as # 175 in Inc 500, with over 350 locations, MAUI WOWI HAWAIIAN is the #1 largest smoothie/coffee franchise in the world. With 24/7 support and extensive training, MAUI WOWI HAWAIIAN offers a simple, profitable and flexible business business model. MAUI WOWI HAWAIIAN has thousands of locations and events throughout the country waiting for a MAUI WOWI HAWAIIAN franchise owner. Because of our flexibility, low investment and variety of business models, MAUI WOWI HAWAIIAN is the fastest-growing franchise.

BACKGROUND: IFA MEMBER
Established: 1983; 1st Franchised: 1997
Franchised Units: 500
Company-Owned Units: 0
Total Units: 500
Dist.: US-500; CAN-0; O'seas-0
North America: 47 States, 0 Provinces
Density: NR

Projected New Units (12 Months): 250-300
Qualifications: 2, 2, 1, 1, 1, 5
FINANCIAL/TERMS:
Cash Investment: $50K+
Total Investment: $75-300K
Minimum Net Worth: $250K
Fees: Franchise - $29.5-59.5K
Royalty - 0%; Ad. - 12%
Earnings Claims Statement: Yes
Term of Contract (Years): 10/
Avg. # Of Employees: 2 FT, 0 PT
Passive Ownership: Allowed
Encourage Conversions: Yes
Area Develop. Agreements: Yes/1
Sub-Franchising Contracts: No
Expand In Territory: Yes
Space Needs: 100 SF
SUPPORT & TRAINING:
Financial Assistance Provided: Yes (I)
Site Selection Assistance: Yes
Lease Negotiation Assistance: Yes
Co-Operative Advertising: Yes
Franchisee Assoc./Member: No
Size Of Corporate Staff: 150
On-Going Support: ,,C,D,E,F,G,H,I
Training: 5 Days Denver, CO
SPECIFIC EXPANSION PLANS:
US: All United States
Canada: All Canada
Overseas: All Countries

MCDONALD'S

2915 Jorie Blvd.
Oak Brook, IL 60523-2114
Tel: (888) 800-7257 (630) 623-6264
Fax: (630) 623-5658
E-Mail: john.kujawa@us.mcd.com
Web Site: www.mcdonalds.com
Mr. Bob Villa, National Franchise Manager

Quick-service restaurant.

BACKGROUND: IFA MEMBER
Established: 1955; 1st Franchised: 1955
Franchised Units: 25801
Company-Owned Units: 6357
Total Units: 32158
Dist.:US-13918; CAN-1416; O'seas-16824
North America: 50 States, 6 Provinces
Density: 851 in TX, 1136 in FL, 1333 in

CA

Projected New Units (12 Months):	NR
Qualifications:	3, 5, 3, 3, 4, 4

FINANCIAL/TERMS:

Cash Investment:	$300K
Total Investment:	$588K-1.8MM
Minimum Net Worth:	NR
Fees: Franchise -	$45K
Royalty - 12.5%;	Ad. - 4%
Earnings Claims Statement:	No
Term of Contract (Years):	20/20
Avg. # Of Employees:	FT, 50 PT
Passive Ownership:	Not Allowed
Encourage Conversions:	NA
Area Develop. Agreements:	No
Sub-Franchising Contracts:	No
Expand In Territory:	Yes
Space Needs:	2,000 SF

SUPPORT & TRAINING:

Financial Assistance Provided:	No
Site Selection Assistance:	NA
Lease Negotiation Assistance:	NA
Co-Operative Advertising:	Yes
Franchisee Assoc./Member:	Yes/Yes
Size Of Corporate Staff:	0
On-Going Support:	,,C,D,E,,G,H,I
Training:	NR

SPECIFIC EXPANSION PLANS:

US:	All United States
Canada:	All Canada
Overseas:	All Countries

◄◄ ►►

MICHEL'S BAGUETTE (CANADA)
400 Steeprock Dr.
Toronto, ON M3J 2X1 Canada
Tel: (877) 7-BAKERY (416) 236-0055 + 273
Fax: (416) 236-0054
E-Mail: franchise@mmmuffins.com
Web Site: www.michelsbaguette.com
Franchise Development

European bakery/cafi¿½, featuring authentic European breads, rolls, and pastries. In addition, we offer gourmet soups, salads, sandwiches, and hot entrees. We also serve a variety of beverages including espresso, gourmet coffee, teas and fruit juices. In addition to our full store, we have a "grab 'n' go" version as well.

BACKGROUND:

Established: 1980;	1st Franchised: 1994
Franchised Units:	9
Company-Owned Units:	4
Total Units:	13
Dist.:	US-0; CAN-13; O'seas-0
North America:	0 States, 3 Provinces

Density:	13 in ON, 1 in BC, 3 in AB
Projected New Units (12 Months):	10
Qualifications:	5, 4, 3, 3, 4, 5

FINANCIAL/TERMS:

Cash Investment:	$300K+
Total Investment:	$350K-650K
Minimum Net Worth:	$500K
Fees: Franchise -	$40K
Royalty - 6%;	Ad. - 0.5%
Earnings Claims Statement:	No
Term of Contract (Years):	10/10
Avg. # Of Employees:	10 FT, 8-12 PT
Passive Ownership:	Not Allowed
Encourage Conversions:	Yes
Area Develop. Agreements:	Yes/1
Sub-Franchising Contracts:	Yes
Expand In Territory:	Yes
Space Needs:	4,000 SF

SUPPORT & TRAINING:

Financial Assistance Provided:	No
Site Selection Assistance:	Yes
Lease Negotiation Assistance:	Yes
Co-Operative Advertising:	No
Franchisee Assoc./Member:	No
Size Of Corporate Staff:	35
On-Going Support:	A,B,C,D,E,F,G,h,
Training:	3 Months Toronto, ON or Dallas, TX

SPECIFIC EXPANSION PLANS:

US:	NR
Canada:	All Canada
Overseas:	Middle East, Europe, South America

◄◄ ►►

MILIO'S SANDWICHES
5585 Guliford Rd.
Madison, WI 53711
Tel: (608) 277-9000
Fax: (608) 277-9363
E-Mail: mliataud@milios.com
Web Site: www.milios.com
Mr. Mike Liautaud, President

What makes the typical Milio's franchise so terrific? The secreti¿½s in the sub! We start with the highest quality meats and cheeses. Add onions, lettuce and tomatoes. Even our bread is baked fresh daily, right in each store. Our franchise program simplifies business ownership for qualified, motivated individuals.We are currently looking for new franchises throughout

Minnesota, Wisconsin, Iowa, Illinois and Nebraska; fulfill your dream of owning your own business with this tremendous franchise opportunity.

BACKGROUND: IFA MEMBER

Established: 1989;	1st Franchised: 2005
Franchised Units:	9
Company-Owned Units:	34
Total Units:	43
Dist.:	US-43; CAN-0; O'seas-0
North America:	3 States, 0 Provinces
Density:	28 in WI, 11 in MN, 6 in IA
Projected New Units (12 Months):	7
Qualifications:	5, 3, 1, 1, 5, 5

FINANCIAL/TERMS:

Cash Investment:	$50K
Total Investment:	$100K-350K
Minimum Net Worth:	$250K
Fees: Franchise -	$25K
Royalty - 6%;	Ad. - 3.5%
Earnings Claims Statement:	Yes
Term of Contract (Years):	10/5
Avg. # Of Employees:	3 FT, 6-10 PT
Passive Ownership:	Not Allowed
Encourage Conversions:	Yes
Area Develop. Agreements:	No
Sub-Franchising Contracts:	No
Expand In Territory:	Yes
Space Needs:	800-1,600 SF

SUPPORT & TRAINING:

Financial Assistance Provided:	No
Site Selection Assistance:	Yes
Lease Negotiation Assistance:	Yes
Co-Operative Advertising:	No
Franchisee Assoc./Member:	Yes/Yes
Size Of Corporate Staff:	20
On-Going Support:	A,B,C,D,E,F,,H,I
Training:	250 HoursMadison, WI

SPECIFIC EXPANSION PLANS:

US:	WI, MN, IA, IL, NE
Canada:	No
Overseas:	NR

◄◄ ►►

MOE'S ITALIAN SANDWICHES
15 Constitution Dr., # 140
Bedford, NH 03110
Tel: (800) 588-6637 (603) 472-8008
Fax: (603) 218-6018
E-Mail: info@moesitaliansandwiches.com
Web Site: www.moesitaliansandwiches.com
Mr. Stanley R. DeLoid, President

High-quality sandwiches and soups, featuring our flagship sandwich 'The Original Moe.' We have a simple concept that has over 40 years of heritage in New England.

Low overhead, turnkey system. Very flexible.

BACKGROUND:
Established: 1959; 1st Franchised: 1993
Franchised Units: 12
Company-Owned Units: 0
Total Units: 12
Dist.:   US-12; CAN-0; O'seas-0
  North America: 3 States, Provinces
  Density: 1 in MA, 2 in ME, 9 in NH
Projected New Units (12 Months):   2-5
Qualifications: 4, 4, 3, 3, 4, 5
FINANCIAL/TERMS:
Cash Investment: $30-50K
Total Investment: $60-100K
Minimum Net Worth: $250K
Fees: Franchise - $10K
  Royalty - 5%;   Ad. - 2%
Earnings Claims Statement: No
Term of Contract (Years):   10/5
Avg. # Of Employees: 2 FT, 4 PT
Passive Ownership: Discouraged
Encourage Conversions: Yes
Area Develop. Agreements: No
Sub-Franchising Contracts: No
Expand In Territory: Yes
Space Needs: 1,000-1,400 SF
SUPPORT & TRAINING:
Financial Assistance Provided: Yes (D)
Site Selection Assistance: Yes
Lease Negotiation Assistance: Yes
Co-Operative Advertising: No
Franchisee Assoc./Member: No
Size Of Corporate Staff: 2
On-Going Support: ,,C,D,E,F,G,H,I
Training: 2 Weeks Store - Various
  Locations; 3 Day Class
SPECIFIC EXPANSION PLANS:
US: NE. Expansion Outside 2002
Canada: No
Overseas: NR

⋘ ⋙

Mr. Goodcents®
Subs & Pastas

MR. GOODCENTS SUBS & PASTAS
8997 Commerce Dr.
DeSoto, KS 66018
Tel: (800) 648-2368 (913) 583-8400 + 231
Fax: (913) 583-3500
E-Mail: frandev@mrgoodcents.com
Web Site: www.mrgoodcents.com
Mr. Peter Grams, Director of Franchising

Quick-service lunch and dinner restaurant, serving freshly sliced submarine sandwiches served on bread baked daily on premises, hot pasta dishes, delicious soups and fresh salads, quick-service restaurant for dine-in, carry-out, delivery or catering. continue to grow well into the next century. TRUCK OPTIONS specializes in this field and is already considered the market leader.

BACKGROUND: IFA MEMBER
Established: 1989;   1st Franchised: 1990
Franchised Units: 120
Company-Owned Units: 1
Total Units: 121
Dist.:   US-121; CAN-0; O'seas-0
  North America: 13 States, 0 Provinces
  Density: 54 in MO, 43 in KS, 8 in AZ
Projected New Units (12 Months):   NR
Qualifications: 4, 4, 3, 2, 1, 5
FINANCIAL/TERMS:
Cash Investment: $40K-50K
Total Investment: $150K-200K
Minimum Net Worth: NR
Fees: Franchise - $15K
  Royalty - 5%;   Ad. - 3.5%
Earnings Claims Statement: Yes
Term of Contract (Years):   10/10
Avg. # Of Employees: 1-3 FT, 10-20 PT
Passive Ownership: Not Allowed
Encourage Conversions: Yes
Area Develop. Agreements: Yes/10
Sub-Franchising Contracts: No
Expand In Territory: Yes
Space Needs: 1,500-2,000 SF
SUPPORT & TRAINING:
Financial Assistance Provided: Yes (D)
Site Selection Assistance: Yes
Lease Negotiation Assistance: Yes
Co-Operative Advertising: Yes
Franchisee Assoc./Member: No
Size Of Corporate Staff: 30
On-Going Support: A,B,C,D,E,F,G,H,I
Training: 30 Days DeSoto, KS
SPECIFIC EXPANSION PLANS:
US: All United States
Canada: No
Overseas: NR

⋘ ⋙

MR. HERO
7010 Engle Rd., # 100
Middleburg Heights, OH 44130
Tel: (888) 860-5082 (440) 625-3080
Fax: (440) 625-3081
E-Mail: rkrieger@mrhero.com
Web Site: www.mrhero.com
Mr. Christopher Bejbl, Executive Director
  of Development

MR. HEROï¿½, known for cheesesteaks, burgers and subs, is an exciting alternative to the typical quick-service restaurant. The MR. HEROï¿½ difference centers on the food! MR HEROï¿½ has grilled food offerings, such as the signature Romanburgers, the Grilled Chicken Philly, Hot Buttered Cheesesteaks and Potato Waffer Fries. The extensive menu also boasts an assortment of deli subs, fresh salads, pasta and an array of sides and desserts. MR. HERO ï¿½ is Keepin' It Fresh!

BACKGROUND: IFA MEMBER
Established: 1965;   1st Franchised: 1970
Franchised Units: 86
Company-Owned Units: 5
Total Units: 91
Dist.:   US-91; CAN-0; O'seas-0
  North America: 1 States, 0 Provinces
  Density: 91 in OH
Projected New Units (12 Months):   2
Qualifications: 5, 4, 4, 4, 5, 5
FINANCIAL/TERMS:
Cash Investment: $75-100K
Total Investment: $120-310K
Minimum Net Worth: $250K
Fees: Franchise - $18K
  Royalty - 5.5%;   Ad. - 5%
Earnings Claims Statement: No
Term of Contract (Years):   20/20
Avg. # Of Employees: 4 FT, 4 PT
Passive Ownership: Discouraged
Encourage Conversions: Yes
Area Develop. Agreements: Yes/1
Sub-Franchising Contracts: No
Expand In Territory: Yes
Space Needs: 1,500 SF
SUPPORT & TRAINING:
Financial Assistance Provided: No
Site Selection Assistance: Yes
Lease Negotiation Assistance: Yes
Co-Operative Advertising: No
Franchisee Assoc./Member: No
Size Of Corporate Staff: 12
On-Going Support: A,B,C,D,E,F,,H,I
Training: 4 Weeks Cleveland, OH
SPECIFIC EXPANSION PLANS:
US: NE, E
Canada: No
Overseas: NR

⋘ ⋙

MR. JIM'S PIZZA
4276 Kellway Cir.
Addison, TX 75001
Tel: (800) 583-5960 (972) 267-5467
Fax: (972) 267-5463
E-Mail: randy@mrjimspizza.net

Web Site: www.mrjimspizza.net
Mr. Randall Wooley, Executive Director

Specializing in delivery and take-out operations. Low start-up cost of under $90,000, including franchise fee. Dallas, Ft. Worth's largest locally owned pizza franchise.

BACKGROUND:
Established: 1974;   1st Franchised: 1976
Franchised Units: 64
Company-Owned Units: 0
Total Units: 64
Dist.:   US-64; CAN-0; O'seas-0
 North America: States, Provinces
 Density: 2 in LA, 58 in TX, 2 in VA
Projected New Units (12 Months):   6
Qualifications: 4, 4, 5, 2, 3, 4
FINANCIAL/TERMS:
Cash Investment: $50K
Total Investment: $56-108K
Minimum Net Worth: $100K
Fees: Franchise - $10K
 Royalty - 5%;   Ad. - 0%
Earnings Claims Statement: No
Term of Contract (Years):   15/15
Avg. # Of Employees: 5 FT, 15 PT
Passive Ownership: Discouraged
Encourage Conversions: Yes
Area Develop. Agreements: Yes/1
Sub-Franchising Contracts: No
Expand In Territory: Yes
Space Needs: 1,100 SF
SUPPORT & TRAINING:
Financial Assistance Provided: No
Site Selection Assistance: Yes
Lease Negotiation Assistance: Yes
Co-Operative Advertising: No
Franchisee Assoc./Member: No
Size Of Corporate Staff: 6
On-Going Support: ,B,C,D,E,,G,H,
Training: NR
SPECIFIC EXPANSION PLANS:
US: All Except FL, MI
Canada: No
Overseas: NR

◄◄ ►►

**MR. MIKE'S STEAKHOUSE
AND BAR**
1500 W. Georgia St., # 1290
Vancouver, BC V6G 2Z9 Canada
Tel: (800) 668-6453 (604) 684-6984 + 229
Fax: (604) 684-6937
E-Mail: franchise@mrmikes.ca
Web Site: www.mrmikes.ca
Ms. Blair Kennedy, Vice President

Founded in 1960, MR. MIKE'S WEST

COAST GRILL is a full-service casual dining restaurant experience. Our primary focus is beef. We provide "affordable indulgence" of premium spirits and quality grilled entrees in a refreshing restaurant environment that is relaxed and inviting. A full support franchise system. Proven results, a fresh approach - all uniquely West Coast.

BACKGROUND:
Established: 1960;   1st Franchised: 2003
Franchised Units: 12
Company-Owned Units: 3
Total Units: 15
Dist.:   US-0; CAN-15; O'seas-0
 North America: 0 States, 2 Provinces
 Density: 7 in BC, 1 in AB
Projected New Units (12 Months):   2
Qualifications: 5, 5, 3, 2, 2, 5
FINANCIAL/TERMS:
Cash Investment: $300-700K
Total Investment: $1.2MM-2.4MM
Minimum Net Worth: $300K
Fees: Franchise - $50K
 Royalty - 5%;   Ad. - 2%
Earnings Claims Statement: No
Term of Contract (Years):   10/5
Avg. # Of Employees: 10 FT, 30 PT
Passive Ownership: Discouraged
Encourage Conversions: Yes
Area Develop. Agreements: No
Sub-Franchising Contracts: No
Expand In Territory: No
Space Needs: 3,500-5,000 SF
SUPPORT & TRAINING:
Financial Assistance Provided: Yes (D)
Site Selection Assistance: Yes
Lease Negotiation Assistance: Yes
Co-Operative Advertising: No
Franchisee Assoc./Member: No
Size Of Corporate Staff: 10
On-Going Support: A,B,C,D,E,F,G,H,I
Training: 8-12 Weeks Corporate Store;
 2 Weeks On-Site
SPECIFIC EXPANSION PLANS:
US: No
Canada: BC
Overseas: NR

◄◄ ►►

NATHAN'S FAMOUS
1400 Old Country Rd.
Westbury, NY 11590
Tel: (800) NATHANS (516) 338-8500 + 205
Fax: (516) 338-7220
E-Mail: rwatts@nathansfamous.com
Web Site: www.nathansfamous.com

Mr. Randy K. Watts, VP Franchise Operations

Fast-food restaurant, featuring premium-quality, all beef hot dogs, fresh-cut fries, plus a large variety of menu items - 9 prototypes, ranging from carts, counter modules, food courts and full-service restaurants. Franchise license and area development opportunities available worldwide.

BACKGROUND:
Established: 1916;   1st Franchised: 1975
Franchised Units: 250
Company-Owned Units: 6
Total Units: 256
Dist.:   US-256; CAN-0; O'seas-0
 North America: 37 States, 0 Provinces
 Density: 27 in NY, 19 in NJ, 17 in FL
Projected New Units (12 Months):   35
Qualifications: 5, 3, 4, 2, 3, 5
FINANCIAL/TERMS:
Cash Investment: $10K-100K
Total Investment: $90K-1MM
Minimum Net Worth: $400K
Fees: Franchise - $15-30K
 Royalty - 4.5%;   Ad. - 2.5%
Earnings Claims Statement: No
Term of Contract (Years):   20/15
Avg. # Of Employees: 6-7 FT, 10-15 PT
Passive Ownership: Discouraged
Encourage Conversions: Yes
Area Develop. Agreements: Yes/1
Sub-Franchising Contracts: Yes
Expand In Territory: Yes
Space Needs: 500-2,500 SF
SUPPORT & TRAINING:
Financial Assistance Provided: Yes (D)
Site Selection Assistance: Yes
Lease Negotiation Assistance: Yes
Co-Operative Advertising: No
Franchisee Assoc./Member: No
Size Of Corporate Staff: 42
On-Going Support: ,B,C,D,E,F,G,H,I
Training: 2-4 Weeks Long Island, NY and
 in Store
SPECIFIC EXPANSION PLANS:
US: All United States
Canada: PQ, ON
Overseas: Europe, Asia

◄◄ ►►

NATURE'S TABLE
300 S. Orange Ave.
Orlando, FL 32801
Tel: (800) 222-6090 (407) 481-2544 + 7
Fax: (407) 843-6057
E-Mail: b.ward@naturestable.com
Web Site: www.naturestable.com

Ms. Brittany Ward, Franchise Sales

NATURE'S TABLE is an expanding Florida-based chain with 20 years of experience. Our menu features healthy food such as vegetarian chili, homemade soups, harvest salads, frozen yogurt, smoothies and a variety of sandwiches.

BACKGROUND:

Established: 1977; 1st Franchised: 1985	
Franchised Units:	73
Company-Owned Units:	3
Total Units:	76
Dist.:	US-76; CAN-0; O'seas-0
North America:	1 States, 0 Provinces
Density:	59 in FL
Projected New Units (12 Months):	9
Qualifications:	5, 3, 3, 3, 5, 4

FINANCIAL/TERMS:

Cash Investment:	$100-175K
Total Investment:	$100-175K
Minimum Net Worth:	$100K
Fees: Franchise -	$25K
Royalty - 5%;	Ad. - 1%
Earnings Claims Statement:	No
Term of Contract (Years):	10/5
Avg. # Of Employees:	2 FT, 2-4 PT
Passive Ownership:	Allowed
Encourage Conversions:	NA
Area Develop. Agreements:	Yes/1
Sub-Franchising Contracts:	No
Expand In Territory:	No
Space Needs:	500-750 SF

SUPPORT & TRAINING:

Financial Assistance Provided:	No
Site Selection Assistance:	Yes
Lease Negotiation Assistance:	Yes
Co-Operative Advertising:	No
Franchisee Assoc./Member:	Yes/Yes
Size Of Corporate Staff:	7
On-Going Support:	,B,C,D,E,F,G,,I
Training: 2 Weeks Orlando, FL; On-Site	

SPECIFIC EXPANSION PLANS:

US:	Southeast United States
Canada:	No
Overseas:	NR

≪ ≫

NEW YORK FRIES

1220 Yonge St., # 400
Toronto, ON M4T 1W1 Canada
Tel: (416) 963-5005
Fax: (416) 963-4920
E-Mail: mail@newyorkfries.com
Web Site: www.newyorkfries.com
Mr. Bob Okamoto, Business Develop. Manager

Exceptional product and simplicity of operations make NEW YORK FRIES an outstanding opportunity. Specializing in fresh-cut fries and hot dogs, our concept is simply. Our standards are high. We start with fresh potatoes, hand-cut on site everyday. We cook them in 100% vegetable oil in our special process. Winner, Canada's Best managed Companies award, requalified winner 2001. Winner of numerous advertising awards. Runner-up, Franchisor of the Year award, Canadian Franchise Association 1994.

BACKGROUND:

Established: 1984; 1st Franchised: 1984	
Franchised Units:	160
Company-Owned Units:	15
Total Units:	175
Dist.:	US-0; CAN-171; O'seas-4
North America:	States, 9 Provinces
Density:	24 in AB, 27 in BC, 94 in ON
Projected New Units (12 Months):	10-12
Qualifications:	4, 5, 4, 3, 1, 5

FINANCIAL/TERMS:

Cash Investment:	$50-75K
Total Investment:	$125-175K
Minimum Net Worth:	Varies
Fees: Franchise -	$30K
Royalty - 6%;	Ad. - 2%
Earnings Claims Statement:	No
Term of Contract (Years):	10/5/5/
Avg. # Of Employees:	2-3 FT, 5-6 PT
Passive Ownership:	Allowed
Encourage Conversions:	NA
Area Develop. Agreements:	Yes/1
Sub-Franchising Contracts:	No
Expand In Territory:	Yes
Space Needs:	350 SF

SUPPORT & TRAINING:

Financial Assistance Provided:	No
Site Selection Assistance:	Yes
Lease Negotiation Assistance:	Yes
Co-Operative Advertising:	No
Franchisee Assoc./Member:	Yes/Yes
Size Of Corporate Staff:	16
On-Going Support:	,B,C,D,E,,G,h,
Training:	7-10 Days Toronto, ON; 5-10 Week On-Site

SPECIFIC EXPANSION PLANS:

US:	No
Canada:	All Canada
Overseas:	England, Pacific Rim

≪ ≫

Papa Gino's®

PAPA GINO'S PIZZERIA

600 Providence Hwy.
Dedham, MA 02026
Tel: (888) 374-2830 (781) 467-1668
Fax: (781) 329-8796
E-Mail: franchising@papaginos.com
Web Site: www.papaginosfranchising.com
Ms. Mimi Woodman, Franchise Support Specialist

Papa Gino's Pizzeria is New England's premier Italian restaurant chain in the QSR industry. We offer a variety of authentic Italian specialties to compliment our classic and specialty pizzas. Papa Gino's is visited by more than 13 million guests annually. With a new inviting decor, Papa Gino's is attracting customers like never before. You can get Papa's unique flavor at 170 restaurants. With 40 years of successful experience, Papa Gino's is offering franchises throughout New England. Other East coast markets may be considered, requiring 20 units. Join us and be part of Papa Gino's growth and success!

BACKGROUND: IFA MEMBER

Established: 1968; 1st Franchised: 2007	
Franchised Units:	0
Company-Owned Units:	170
Total Units:	170
Dist.:	US-170; CAN-0; O'seas-0
North America:	6 States, 0 Provinces
Density:	9 in RI, 16 in NH, 113 in MA
Projected New Units (12 Months):	15
Qualifications:	5, 3, 3, 2, 1, 5

FINANCIAL/TERMS:

Cash Investment:	$165K
Total Investment:	$606.1-856K
Minimum Net Worth:	$550K
Fees: Franchise -	$20K
Royalty - 6%;	Ad. - 3%
Earnings Claims Statement:	Yes
Term of Contract (Years):	20/10
Avg. # Of Employees:	15 FT, 20 PT
Passive Ownership:	Discouraged
Encourage Conversions:	Yes
Area Develop. Agreements:	Yes
Sub-Franchising Contracts:	No
Expand In Territory:	Yes
Space Needs:	3,000 SF

SUPPORT & TRAINING:

Financial Assistance Provided:	Yes (I)
Site Selection Assistance:	Yes
Lease Negotiation Assistance:	Yes
Co-Operative Advertising:	Yes

Franchisee Assoc./Member: No
Size Of Corporate Staff: 100
On-Going Support: ,B,C,D,E,,G,H,I
Training: 6 Weeks Training restuarants;
2 Weeks Corporate Office
SPECIFIC EXPANSION PLANS:
US: MA, CT, RI, NH, ME, VT, FL
Canada: No
Overseas: NR

◄◄ ►►

PAPA JOHN'S INTERNATIONAL
2002 Papa John's Blvd.
Louisville, KY 40299
Tel: (502) 261-4825
Fax: (502) 261-4140
E-Mail: erin_snyder@papajohns.com
Web Site: www.papajohns.com
Erin Snyder, Int. Franchise Qual. Specialist

Papa John's International, headquartered in Louisville, KY., is the world's third-largest pizza company, owning and franchising over 3,400 restaurants in all 50 states and 29 countries. For nine out of the last ten years, consumers have rated Papa John's #1 in customer satisfaction among all national pizza chains and #1 seven out of the last ten years among all national Quick Service Restaurant (QSR) chains in the highly regarded American Customer Satisfaction Index (ACSI).

BACKGROUND:
Established: 1984; 1st Franchised: 1985
Franchised Units: 2641
Company-Owned Units: 652
Total Units: 3293
Dist.: US-2776; CAN-19; O'seas-0
North America: 50 States, 7 Provinces
Density:211 in TX, 247 in FL, 207 in CA
Projected New Units (12 Months): 120
Qualifications: 5, 5, 4, 3, 4, 5
FINANCIAL/TERMS:
Cash Investment: Varies
Total Investment: $195K+/Unit
Minimum Net Worth: $250K-2MM
Fees: Franchise - $25K/Unit
Royalty - 5%; Ad. - 2.82%
Earnings Claims Statement: No
Term of Contract (Years): 10/10
Avg. # Of Employees: 8 FT, 18 PT

Passive Ownership: Allowed
Encourage Conversions: NA
Area Develop. Agreements: Yes
Sub-Franchising Contracts: No
Expand In Territory: Yes
Space Needs: 1,000-1,400 SF
SUPPORT & TRAINING:
Financial Assistance Provided: No
Site Selection Assistance: Yes
Lease Negotiation Assistance: No
Co-Operative Advertising: Yes
Franchisee Assoc./Member: Yes/No
Size Of Corporate Staff: 13990
On-Going Support: a,b,C,D,E,,G,h,I
Training: 1 Week
Papa John's University, Louisville, KY; Varies Mentoring; Varied Location; 5 Weeks Mgmt. Training: Varied Location
SPECIFIC EXPANSION PLANS:
US: All United States
Canada: Yes
Overseas: NR

◄◄ ►►

PAPA MURPHY'S
8000 N.E. Parkway Dr., # 350
Vancouver, WA 98662
Tel: (800) 257-7272 (360) 449-4016
Fax: (360) 397-6864
E-Mail: rhondam@papamurphys.com
Web Site: www.papamurphys.com
Ms. Rhonda McGrew, Manager Business Development

PAPA MURPHY'S produces a great pizza made from top-quality ingredients. Letting customers bake it themselves is smart business. Put the 2 together and you get the largest, fastest-growing Take 'N' Bake franchise in the world. PAPA MURPHY'S now has 1,150 stores with another 100 stores expected to open in 2009.

BACKGROUND: IFA MEMBER
Established: 1981; 1st Franchised: 1982
Franchised Units: 1098
Company-Owned Units: 52
Total Units: 1150
Dist.: US-1132; CAN-18; O'seas-0
North America: 33 States, 2 Provinces
Density:95 in OR, 140 in WA, 150 in CA
Projected New Units (12 Months): 100
Qualifications: 4, 3, 2, 3, 3, 5

FINANCIAL/TERMS:
Cash Investment: $80K
Total Investment: $172-353K
Minimum Net Worth: $250K
Fees: Franchise - $25K
Royalty - 5%; Ad. - 2%
Earnings Claims Statement: Yes
Term of Contract (Years): 10/5
Avg. # Of Employees: 2 FT, 8-10 PT
Passive Ownership: Not Allowed
Encourage Conversions: Yes
Area Develop. Agreements: Yes
Sub-Franchising Contracts: No
Expand In Territory: Yes
Space Needs: 1,200-1,400 SF
SUPPORT & TRAINING:
Financial Assistance Provided: Yes (I)
Site Selection Assistance: Yes
Lease Negotiation Assistance: Yes
Co-Operative Advertising: Yes
Franchisee Assoc./Member: Yes/Yes
Size Of Corporate Staff: 150
On-Going Support: ,,C,D,E,,G,H,I
Training: 5 Days Corporate Office; 5 Weeks Store; 3 Days/30 Hours Closest Training Store
SPECIFIC EXPANSION PLANS:
US: Midwest, Central, South
Canada: Yes
Overseas: NR

◄◄ ►►

PAPA'S PIZZA TO GO
4465 Commerce Dr., # 101
Buford, GA 30518-9913
Tel: (770) 614-6676
Fax: (770) 614-9095
E-Mail: papa2go@bellsouth.net
Web Site: www.papaspizzatogo.com
Ms. Kathy Underwood, Dir. Operations/ Franchise Sale

Two business models - one for small town USA and one for metro markets. Small town - to go only to small buffets of limited serving hours. Metro markets - all day, every day with game room for kids.

BACKGROUND:
Established: 1986; 1st Franchised: 1986
Franchised Units: 72
Company-Owned Units: 13
Total Units: 85
Dist.: US-85; CAN-0; O'seas-0
North America: States, Provinces
Density: in GA, in NC, in TN
Projected New Units (12 Months): NR
Qualifications: NR
FINANCIAL/TERMS:

Cash Investment:	$40-130K
Total Investment:	$130-350K
Minimum Net Worth:	$90K
Fees: Franchise -	$9.5-12.5K
Royalty - 5%;	Ad. - 5%
Earnings Claims Statement:	Yes
Term of Contract (Years):	10/10
Avg. # Of Employees:	3 FT, 7 PT
Passive Ownership:	Allowed
Encourage Conversions:	No
Area Develop. Agreements:	No
Sub-Franchising Contracts:	No
Expand In Territory:	Yes
Space Needs:	1,000-4,200 SF

SUPPORT & TRAINING:

Financial Assistance Provided:	No
Site Selection Assistance:	Yes
Lease Negotiation Assistance:	Yes
Co-Operative Advertising:	No
Franchisee Assoc./Member:	No
Size Of Corporate Staff:	12
On-Going Support:	,B,C,D,E,F,G,H,
Training:	10 Days Cherryville, NC;
10 Days Calhoune, GA	

SPECIFIC EXPANSION PLANS:

US:	Southeast
Canada:	NR
Overseas:	NR

≪ ≫

PENN STATION/EAST COAST SUBS

8276 Beechmont Ave.
Cincinnati, OH 45255-3153
Tel: (513) 474-5957
Fax: (513) 474-7116
E-Mail:
Web Site: www.penn-station.com
Mr. Mark Partusch, Dir. Sales/Development

Retail sale of authentic 'East Coast-style' submarines, including the original Philadelphia cheesesteak, all prepared fresh before the customer. Fresh-cut fries, flash fried in peanut oil, and fresh-squeezed lemonade.

BACKGROUND:

Established: 1985;	1st Franchised: 1987
Franchised Units:	79
Company-Owned Units:	4
Total Units:	83
Dist.:	US-83; CAN-0; O'seas-0
North America:	4 States, 0 Provinces
Density: 41 in OH, 13 in KY, 14 in IN	
Projected New Units (12 Months):	25
Qualifications:	3, 5, 3, 4, 4, 5

FINANCIAL/TERMS:

Cash Investment:	$40-82.5K
Total Investment:	$182.8-328.7K
Minimum Net Worth:	Varies
Fees: Franchise -	$17.5K
Royalty - 4-7.5%;	Ad. - 1%
Earnings Claims Statement:	Yes
Term of Contract (Years):	5/5/5/5/
Avg. # Of Employees:	11 FT, 10 PT
Passive Ownership:	Allowed
Encourage Conversions:	No
Area Develop. Agreements:	Yes/1
Sub-Franchising Contracts:	No
Expand In Territory:	Yes
Space Needs:	1,600-1,800 SF

SUPPORT & TRAINING:

Financial Assistance Provided:	No
Site Selection Assistance:	Yes
Lease Negotiation Assistance:	Yes
Co-Operative Advertising:	No
Franchisee Assoc./Member:	Yes/Yes
Size Of Corporate Staff:	13
On-Going Support:	,,C,D,E,F,G,H,
Training:	2 Weeks Penn Station
in Cincinnati, OH; 2-3 Days On-Site	
Training Prior to Grand Opening	

SPECIFIC EXPANSION PLANS:

US:	Midwest, Southeast, South
Canada:	No
Overseas:	NR

≪ ≫

PHILLY CONNECTION

120 Interstate N. Pkwy., E., # 112
Atlanta, GA 30339-2103
Tel: (800) 886-8826 (770) 952-6152
Fax: (770) 952-3168
E-Mail: info@phillyconnection.com
Web Site: www.phillyconnection.com
Mr. John D. Pollock, SVP Franchise Development

Quick service restaurant and ice cream parlor. "The Cheesesteak Champion" serves fresh, high quality products prepared to order in front of customers. On premises, take out, drive though, delivery. May operate in strip shopping centers, convenience stores, free-standing buildings and "end cap" space. Franchisor helps in site location, lease negotiation, equipment purchasing, grand opening, initial and on-

going training, toll free helpline.

BACKGROUND: IFA MEMBER

Established: 1984;	1st Franchised: 1987
Franchised Units:	175
Company-Owned Units:	1
Total Units:	176
Dist.:	US-176; CAN-0; O'seas-0
North America:	7 States, 0 Provinces
Density: 19 in TX, 68 in GA, 10 in FL	
Projected New Units (12 Months):	40
Qualifications:	4, 3, 3, 2, 2, 3

FINANCIAL/TERMS:

Cash Investment:	$35-50K
Total Investment:	$130-198.5K
Minimum Net Worth:	$150K
Fees: Franchise -	$20K
Royalty - 6%;	Ad. - 4%
Earnings Claims Statement:	No
Term of Contract (Years):	10/5
Avg. # Of Employees:	2 FT, 10 PT
Passive Ownership:	Discouraged
Encourage Conversions:	Yes
Area Develop. Agreements:	Yes/1
Sub-Franchising Contracts:	No
Expand In Territory:	No
Space Needs:	1,100-1,600 SF

SUPPORT & TRAINING:

Financial Assistance Provided:	Yes (D)
Site Selection Assistance:	Yes
Lease Negotiation Assistance:	Yes
Co-Operative Advertising:	No
Franchisee Assoc./Member:	No
Size Of Corporate Staff:	15
On-Going Support:	,,C,,E,,,,I
Training:	80 Hours Atlanta, GA

SPECIFIC EXPANSION PLANS:

US:	SE,TX,IL,VA,KY,IN,OH,NJ Only
Canada:	No
Overseas:	NR

≪ ≫

PIZZA DELIGHT

2425 Matheson Blvd. E.
Mississauga, ON L4W 5K4 Canada
Tel: (888) 440-3232 (905) 361-6619
Fax: (905) 361-2633
E-Mail: franchise@pizzadelight.ca
Web Site: www.pizzadelight.com
Mr. Larry Santolini, Vice President of Franchising

PIZZA DELIGHT is a family/mid-scale dining brand, featuring pizza, pasta, salads and rotisserie chicken. Started in 1968 in Shediac, New Brunswick, PIZZA DELIGHT is now the largest family restaurant chain in Atlantic Canada.

BACKGROUND:
Established: 1968;   1st Franchised: 1969
Franchised Units: 104
Company-Owned Units: 2
Total Units: 106
Dist.:   US-0; CAN-106; O'seas-0
  North America: 0 States, 6 Provinces
  Density: 25 in ON, 82 in GA
Projected New Units (12 Months):   15
Qualifications: 5, 3, 2, 2, 4, 5
FINANCIAL/TERMS:
Cash Investment: $50-150K
Total Investment: $125K-150K
Minimum Net Worth: $250K
Fees: Franchise - $40K
  Royalty - 6%;   Ad. - 3%
Earnings Claims Statement: No
Term of Contract (Years):   10/10
Avg. # Of Employees: 5-10 FT, 5-10 PT
Passive Ownership: Not Allowed
Encourage Conversions: Yes
Area Develop. Agreements: Yes/1
Sub-Franchising Contracts: Yes
Expand In Territory: Yes
Space Needs: 1,000-4,000 SF
SUPPORT & TRAINING:
Financial Assistance Provided: Yes (D)
Site Selection Assistance: Yes
Lease Negotiation Assistance: Yes
Co-Operative Advertising: No
Franchisee Assoc./Member: No
Size Of Corporate Staff: 25
On-Going Support: a,B,C,D,E,F,G,H,i
Training: 12 Days Head Office;
  10 Days On-the-Job Training; 3 Days a
  year Continuous Training
SPECIFIC EXPANSION PLANS:
US: No
Canada: Quebec, Alberta
Overseas: NR

⏪ ⏩

PIZZA FACTORY
P. O. Box 989, 49430 Rd. 426, # D
Oakhurst, CA 93644
Tel: (800) 654-4840 (559) 683-3377
Fax: (559) 683-6879
E-Mail: pfinc@sierratel.com
Web Site: www.pizzafactoryinc.com
Ms. Nikki Van Velson, Operations Director

'We Toss 'em, They're Awesome.' PIZZA FACTORY has a proven track record with 107 restaurants in 12 states, The franchisee has a strong support system which includes site location, lease negotiating, on-site training and on-going support from headquarters. Call for brochure. Serving

homemade pizza, pasta, sandwiches, beer and wine.

BACKGROUND:
Established: 1979;   1st Franchised: 1985
Franchised Units: 116
Company-Owned Units: 0
Total Units: 116
Dist.:   US-108; CAN-0; O'seas-8
  North America: 12 States, 0 Provinces
  Density: 17 in WA, 10 in ID, 61 in CA
Projected New Units (12 Months):   10
Qualifications: 5, 4, 4, 2, 2, 3
FINANCIAL/TERMS:
Cash Investment: $65-80K
Total Investment: $70-262K
Minimum Net Worth: $150K
Fees: Franchise - $20K
  Royalty - 5%;   Ad. - 2%
Earnings Claims Statement: No
Term of Contract (Years):   20/
Avg. # Of Employees: 3 FT, 12-15 PT
Passive Ownership: Allowed
Encourage Conversions: Yes
Area Develop. Agreements: Yes/1
Sub-Franchising Contracts: No
Expand In Territory: Yes
Space Needs: 200-1,500 Var SF
SUPPORT & TRAINING:
Financial Assistance Provided: No
Site Selection Assistance: Yes
Lease Negotiation Assistance: Yes
Co-Operative Advertising: No
Franchisee Assoc./Member: NR
Size Of Corporate Staff: 7
On-Going Support: „C,D,E,„G,H,I
Training: 325 Hours Training Stores
SPECIFIC EXPANSION PLANS:
US: All United States
Canada: All Canada
Overseas: All Countries; China

⏪ ⏩

PIZZA INN
3550 Plano Pkwy.
The Colony, TX 75056
Tel: (800) 284-3466 (469) 384-5000
Fax: (469) 384-5054
E-Mail: franchising@pizzainn.com
Web Site: www.pizzainn.com
Mr. Michael Iglesias, VP Franchise Development

For Pizza Out, it's PIZZA INN! Our variety of great pizzas, pasta, salad, sandwiches and dessert pizza options will bring customers to your door! PIZZA INN has franchise opportunities for single and multiple locations in the Southeast US. We

offer a reasonable, well-structured franchise program with a comprehensive training program and on-going marketing and operational support for our Buffet, Delivery/Carry-Out and Express restaurants. Join our team-we're right beside you.

BACKGROUND: IFA MEMBER
Established: 1958;   1st Franchised: 1963
Franchised Units: 320
Company-Owned Units: 2
Total Units: 322
Dist.:   US-322; CAN-0; O'seas-73
  North America: 19 States, 0 Provinces
  Density: 114 in TX, 55 in NC, 26 in MS
Projected New Units (12 Months):   NR
Qualifications: NR
FINANCIAL/TERMS:
Cash Investment: $30-150K
Total Investment: $80-693K
Minimum Net Worth: $80-300K
Fees: Franchise - $5-25K
  Royalty - 4-5%;   Ad. - 1%
Earnings Claims Statement: No
Term of Contract (Years):   5/10/20/
Avg. # Of Employees: Varies
Passive Ownership: Allowed
Encourage Conversions: No
Area Develop. Agreements: Yes/1
Sub-Franchising Contracts: Yes
Expand In Territory: Yes
Space Needs: Varies
SUPPORT & TRAINING:
Financial Assistance Provided: No
Site Selection Assistance: Yes
Lease Negotiation Assistance: Yes
Co-Operative Advertising: No
Franchisee Assoc./Member: Yes/Yes
Size Of Corporate Staff: 0
On-Going Support: „C,D,E,F,G,h,I
Training: 5 days Express Class, The
  Colony, TX; 24 Days MIT Class The
  Colony, TX;
SPECIFIC EXPANSION PLANS:
US: Southeast and Southwest
Canada: No
Overseas: NR

⏪ ⏩

PIZZA NOVA TAKE OUT
2247 Midland Ave.
Scarborough, ON M1P 4R1 Canada
Tel: (416) 439-0051
Fax: (416) 299-3558
E-Mail: frank@pizzanova.com
Web Site: www.pizzanova.com
Mr. Frank Macri, Franchise Director

PIZZA NOVA specializes in traditional

Italian pizza, pastas and chicken wings. All menu items are prepared fresh daily and are available for take-out or delivery. We pride ourselves on quality and service.

BACKGROUND:

Established: 1963; 1st Franchised: 1966	
Franchised Units:	134
Company-Owned Units:	3
Total Units:	137
Dist.:	US-7; CAN-120; O'seas-7
North America:	1 States, 1 Provinces
Density:	80 in ON
Projected New Units (12 Months):	10
Qualifications:	4, 4, 4, 2, 4, 5

FINANCIAL/TERMS:

Cash Investment:	$40K
Total Investment:	$250K-275K
Minimum Net Worth:	NR
Fees: Franchise -	$20K
Royalty - 6%;	Ad. - 4%
Earnings Claims Statement:	Yes
Term of Contract (Years):	5/5
Avg. # Of Employees:	4 FT, 6 PT
Passive Ownership:	Not Allowed
Encourage Conversions:	Yes
Area Develop. Agreements:	No
Sub-Franchising Contracts:	No
Expand In Territory:	Yes
Space Needs:	800-1,100 SF

SUPPORT & TRAINING:

Financial Assistance Provided:	No
Site Selection Assistance:	Yes
Lease Negotiation Assistance:	Yes
Co-Operative Advertising:	No
Franchisee Assoc./Member:	Yes/Yes
Size Of Corporate Staff:	18
On-Going Support:	A,B,C,D,E,F,G,H,
Training:	NR

SPECIFIC EXPANSION PLANS:

US:	NR
Canada:	ON
Overseas:	All Countries

≪ ≫

PIZZA PATRON
10999 Petal St., # 200
Dallas, TX 75238
Tel: (972) 613-8000
Fax: (972) 613-8014
E-Mail: info@pizzapatron.com
Web Site: www.pizzapatron.com

Mr. Guillermo Estrada, Director Business Development

Pizza Patron is leading the industry by developing our brand exclusively in Latino communities. Founded in 1986, Pizza Patron has a proven business model with a strong and fully-developed brand identity. The stores feature a vivd color palette and resonate with festive Latin influence. Locations are community-based and the food is offered at an unparalleled value. Our signature brand focus makes Pizza Patron a truly unique opportunity.

BACKGROUND:

Established: 1986; 1st Franchised: 2003	
Franchised Units:	59
Company-Owned Units:	5
Total Units:	64
Dist.:	US-64; CAN-0; O'seas-0
North America:	5 States, 0 Provinces
Density:	43 in TX, 2 in CA, 8 in AZ
Projected New Units (12 Months):	NR
Qualifications:	3, 3, 3, 3, 3, 3

FINANCIAL/TERMS:

Cash Investment:	$35-50K
Total Investment:	$125.5-182.5K
Minimum Net Worth:	$150K
Fees: Franchise -	$20K
Royalty - 5%;	Ad. - 2%
Earnings Claims Statement:	Yes
Term of Contract (Years):	10/10
Avg. # Of Employees:	5 FT, 3 PT
Passive Ownership:	Not Allowed
Encourage Conversions:	NA
Area Develop. Agreements:	Yes/1
Sub-Franchising Contracts:	No
Expand In Territory:	Yes
Space Needs:	1,200 SF

SUPPORT & TRAINING:

Financial Assistance Provided:	No
Site Selection Assistance:	Yes
Lease Negotiation Assistance:	Yes
Co-Operative Advertising:	No
Franchisee Assoc./Member:	No
Size Of Corporate Staff:	9
On-Going Support:	,b,c,d,e,f,,h,
Training:	3 Weeks Dallas, TX

SPECIFIC EXPANSION PLANS:

US:	All United States
Canada:	No
Overseas:	NR

≪ ≫

PIZZA PIZZA INTERNATIONAL
580 Jarvis St.
Toronto, ON M4Y 2H9 Canada
Tel: (800) 263-5556 (416) 967-1010

Fax: (416) 967-9865
E-Mail: dmason@pizzapizza.ca
Web Site: www.pizzapizza.ca
Mr. Dennis Mason, Franchise Sales Representative

In business over 34 years and established as Ontario's market leader in QSR sector specializing in pizza, chicken and oven-baked sandwiches. Offering state-of-the-art order processing systems, top-ranked training programs and marketing strategies that are second to none.

BACKGROUND:

Established: 1967; 1st Franchised: 1974	
Franchised Units:	322
Company-Owned Units:	0
Total Units:	322
Dist.:	US-0; CAN-322; O'seas-0
North America:	0 States, 2 Provinces
Density:	6 in QC, 318 in ON
Projected New Units (12 Months):	7
Qualifications:	3, 1, 4, 3, 4, 5

FINANCIAL/TERMS:

Cash Investment:	$50-100K
Total Investment:	$50K-150K
Minimum Net Worth:	$200K
Fees: Franchise -	$30K
Royalty - 6%;	Ad. - 6%
Earnings Claims Statement:	No
Term of Contract (Years):	5/5
Avg. # Of Employees:	4 FT, 6 PT
Passive Ownership:	Discouraged
Encourage Conversions:	NA
Area Develop. Agreements:	No
Sub-Franchising Contracts:	No
Expand In Territory:	Yes
Space Needs:	2,300 SF

SUPPORT & TRAINING:

Financial Assistance Provided:	Yes (D)
Site Selection Assistance:	Yes
Lease Negotiation Assistance:	NA
Co-Operative Advertising:	No
Franchisee Assoc./Member:	No
Size Of Corporate Staff:	200
On-Going Support:	A,B,C,D,E,F,G,h,I
Training:	12 Weeks Toronto, Ontario

SPECIFIC EXPANSION PLANS:

US:	NR
Canada:	Ontario
Overseas:	NR

≪ ≫

PIZZA RANCH, THE
1121 Main St., P.O. Box 823
Hull, IA 51239
Tel: (800) 321-3401 (712) 439-1150
Fax: (712) 439-1125

E-Mail: jmoss@pizzaranch.com
Web Site: www.pizzaranch.com
Mr. John Moss, Director Advert./Marketing

THE PIZZA RANCH is a family restaurant, specializing in pizza, pasta and chicken.

BACKGROUND:
Established: 1981;   1st Franchised: 1984
Franchised Units: 95
Company-Owned Units: 0
Total Units: 95
Dist.:   US-95; CAN-0; O'seas-0
  North America: 6 States, 0 Provinces
  Density: 16 in SD, 20 in MN, 40 in IA
Projected New Units (12 Months):   12
Qualifications: 3, 3, 3, 3, 2, 5
FINANCIAL/TERMS:
Cash Investment: $20-50K
Total Investment: $200-500K
Minimum Net Worth: $25K
Fees: Franchise - $10K
  Royalty - 4%;   Ad. - $1.7-2.2K
Earnings Claims Statement: No
Term of Contract (Years):   10/10/10/
Avg. # Of Employees: 2 FT, 20 PT
Passive Ownership: Allowed
Encourage Conversions: Yes
Area Develop. Agreements: Yes/1
Sub-Franchising Contracts: Yes
Expand In Territory: Yes
Space Needs: 4,000 SF
SUPPORT & TRAINING:
Financial Assistance Provided: Yes (D)
Site Selection Assistance: Yes
Lease Negotiation Assistance: Yes
Co-Operative Advertising: No
Franchisee Assoc./Member: No
Size Of Corporate Staff: 15
On-Going Support: „C,D,E,F,G,H,I
Training: 2 Weeks Sioux Center, IA;
  1 Week On-Site
SPECIFIC EXPANSION PLANS:
US: Midwest
Canada: No
Overseas: NR

◄◄ ►►

POPEYES CHICKEN & BISCUITS
5555 Glenridge Connector, N.E., # 300
Atlanta, GA 30342-4759
Tel: (800) 639-3780 (404) 459-4450

Fax: (404) 459-4523
E-Mail: popeyesfranchising@afce.com
Web Site: www.popeyesfranchising.com
Mr. John Feilmeier, Director, New Business Development

POPEYES CHICKEN & BISCUITS, the world's second-largest chicken chain, is owned by AFC Enterprises, Inc., one of the world's largest restaurant parent companies and the winner of the 1997 MUFSO Operator of the Year and Golden Chain awards. POPEYES is famous for its New Orleans-style chicken, buttermilk biscuits and signature side items. The brand name has a presence in 41 states and 20 countries worldwide. 1

BACKGROUND: IFA MEMBER
Established: 1972;   1st Franchised: 1973
Franchised Units: 1725
Company-Owned Units: 80
Total Units: 1805
Dist.:   US-1490; CAN-12; O'seas-257
  North America: 41 States, 2 Provinces
  Density: NR
Projected New Units (12 Months):   120
Qualifications: 5, 4, 5, 3, NR, 3
FINANCIAL/TERMS:
Cash Investment: $250-750K
Total Investment: $1.2-1.5MM
Minimum Net Worth: $1.2MM
Fees: Franchise - $20K
  Royalty - 5%;   Ad. - 3%
Earnings Claims Statement: No
Term of Contract (Years):   20/10
Avg. # Of Employees: 15-25 FT, 25 PT
Passive Ownership: Discouraged
Encourage Conversions: Yes
Area Develop. Agreements: Yes/1
Sub-Franchising Contracts: No
Expand In Territory: Yes
Space Needs: 2,200 SF
SUPPORT & TRAINING:
Financial Assistance Provided: Yes (D)
Site Selection Assistance: Yes
Lease Negotiation Assistance: Yes
Co-Operative Advertising: No
Franchisee Assoc./Member: Yes/Yes
Size Of Corporate Staff: NR
On-Going Support: ,B,C,D,E,F,G,H,I
Training: 4 Weeks Atlanta, GA
SPECIFIC EXPANSION PLANS:
US: All United States
Canada: All Canada
Overseas: All Countries

◄◄ ►►

PORT OF SUBS
5365 Mae Anne Ave., # A-29
Reno, NV 89523-1840
Tel: (800) 245-0245 + 1324 (775) 747-0555 + 1324
Fax: (775) 747-1510
E-Mail: jlarsen@portofsubs.com
Web Site: www.portofsubs.com
Mr. John R. Larsen, CEO

Port of Subs is an established fast-casual submarine sandwich chain with over 30 years of proven operating systems. Port of Subs specializes in fresh, quality, deli-style products and sandwiches. We serve breakfast, lunch and dinner, and offer catering and special event planning. We offer an assortment of made-to-order submarine type sandwiches, hot sandwiches, salads, pastries, party platters, beverages and other quick service food items for the on-premises consumption or take-out.

BACKGROUND: IFA MEMBER
Established: 1972;   1st Franchised: 1984
Franchised Units: 130
Company-Owned Units: 26
Total Units: 156
Dist.:   US-156; CAN-0; O'seas-0
  North America: 5 States, 0 Provinces
  Density: 69 in NV, 45 in CA, 11 in AZ
Projected New Units (12 Months):   25
Qualifications: NR
FINANCIAL/TERMS:
Cash Investment: $80K
Total Investment: $199.3-328.3K
Minimum Net Worth: $250K
Fees: Franchise - $16K
  Royalty - 5.5%;   Ad. - 1%
Earnings Claims Statement: No
Term of Contract (Years):   10/10
Avg. # Of Employees: 2-3 FT, 6-7 PT
Passive Ownership: Discouraged
Encourage Conversions: Yes
Area Develop. Agreements: Yes/1
Sub-Franchising Contracts: No
Expand In Territory: Yes
Space Needs: 1,200-1,500 SF
SUPPORT & TRAINING:
Financial Assistance Provided: No
Site Selection Assistance: Yes
Lease Negotiation Assistance: Yes
Co-Operative Advertising: No
Franchisee Assoc./Member: Yes/Yes
Size Of Corporate Staff: 27
On-Going Support: A,B,C,D,E,F,G,H,I
Training: 3 Weeks Reno, NV

SPECIFIC EXPANSION PLANS:

US:	W,NW,SW
Canada:	No
Overseas:	NR

◄◄ ►►

PRETZEL TWISTER, THE

3705 Mason Rd.
New Hill, NC 27562
Tel: (888) 638-8806 (919) 387-8929
Fax: (919) 363-6945
E-Mail: bwang@pretzeltwister.com
Web Site: www.pretzeltwister.com
Mr. Bobby Wang, President

THE PRETZEL TWISTER is a gourmet, hand-rolled soft pretzel franchise. Other products sold are fresh, hand-squeezed lemonade, frozen fruit smoothies and soft drinks. The pretzels are served fresh and hot and are available in a wide variety of flavors.

BACKGROUND:

Established: 1992; 1st Franchised: 1993	
Franchised Units:	45
Company-Owned Units:	0
Total Units:	45
Dist.:	US-43; CAN-2; O'seas-0
North America:	14 States, 3 Provinces
Density:	3 in SC, 9 in NC, 14 in FL
Projected New Units (12 Months):	NR
Qualifications:	NR

FINANCIAL/TERMS:

Cash Investment:	NR
Total Investment:	$105-162.5K
Minimum Net Worth:	NR
Fees: Franchise -	$22.5K
Royalty - 5%;	Ad. - .5-1%
Earnings Claims Statement:	No
Term of Contract (Years):	NR/
Avg. # Of Employees:	FT, 0 PT
Passive Ownership:	Allowed
Encourage Conversions:	No
Area Develop. Agreements:	No
Sub-Franchising Contracts:	No
Expand In Territory:	Yes
Space Needs:	300-900 SF

SUPPORT & TRAINING:

Financial Assistance Provided:	No
Site Selection Assistance:	Yes
Lease Negotiation Assistance:	Yes
Co-Operative Advertising:	No
Franchisee Assoc./Member:	No

Size Of Corporate Staff:	0
On-Going Support:	„C,D,E,,G,h,I
Training:	NR

SPECIFIC EXPANSION PLANS:

US:	All United States
Canada:	No
Overseas:	NR

◄◄ ►►

PRETZELMAKER

1346 Oakbrook Dr., # 170
Norcross, GA 30093
Tel: (800) 343-5377 + 2399
Fax: (801) 736-5936
E-Mail: franchiseinfo@nexcenfm.com
Web Site: www.pretzelmaker.com
Mr. Marty Amschler, Dir. Intl. Development

The 'World's Best Soft Pretzels,' hand-rolled and served hot with high consumer acceptance and precision portion control. May be operated in both traditional and non-traditional venues.

BACKGROUND: IFA MEMBER

Established: 1991; 1st Franchised: 1992	
Franchised Units:	359
Company-Owned Units:	0
Total Units:	359
Dist.:	US-302; CAN-54; O'seas-3
North America:	42 States, 7 Provinces
Density:	30 in NY, 14 in IA, 22 in CA
Projected New Units (12 Months):	11
Qualifications:	4, 4, 3, 2, 2, 5

FINANCIAL/TERMS:

Cash Investment:	$10-30K
Total Investment:	$107-238.5K
Minimum Net Worth:	$150K/75K LIQ
Fees: Franchise -	$25K
Royalty - 7%;	Ad. - 1.5%
Earnings Claims Statement:	No
Term of Contract (Years):	7/7
Avg. # Of Employees:	3 FT, 2 PT
Passive Ownership:	Discouraged
Encourage Conversions:	Yes
Area Develop. Agreements:	Yes
Sub-Franchising Contracts:	No
Expand In Territory:	Yes
Space Needs:	200-850 SF

SUPPORT & TRAINING:

Financial Assistance Provided:	No
Site Selection Assistance:	Yes
Lease Negotiation Assistance:	Yes

Co-Operative Advertising:	No
Franchisee Assoc./Member:	Yes/Yes
Size Of Corporate Staff:	135
On-Going Support:	„C,D,E,F,G,H,
Training:	5 Days Atlanta, GA

SPECIFIC EXPANSION PLANS:

US:	All United States
Canada:	All Canada
Overseas:	NR

◄◄ ►►

PRETZELS PLUS

639 Frederick St.
Hanover, PA 17331
Tel: (800) 559-7927 (717) 633-7927
Fax: (717) 633-5078
E-Mail: beline@pretzelsplus.com
Web Site: www.pretzelsplus.com
Mr. Bradley L. Eline, President

PRETZELS PLUS stores sell soft, hand-rolled pretzels, soups and hearty sandwiches made on our famous pretzel dough rolls. Our mall-based stores provide ample seating for about twenty people in the cafe-styled environment. With our sandwich menu along with our pretzels, we're definitely a twist above the competition.

BACKGROUND:

Established: 1990; 1st Franchised: 1991	
Franchised Units:	28
Company-Owned Units:	0
Total Units:	28
Dist.:	US-28; CAN-0; O'seas-0
North America:	9 States, 0 Provinces
Density:	5 in VA, 13 in PA, 3 in NC
Projected New Units (12 Months):	24
Qualifications:	5, 2, 1, 1, 2, 2

FINANCIAL/TERMS:

Cash Investment:	$70-90K
Total Investment:	$70-90K
Minimum Net Worth:	NA
Fees: Franchise -	$12K
Royalty - 4%;	Ad. - 0%
Earnings Claims Statement:	No
Term of Contract (Years):	10/10
Avg. # Of Employees:	5 FT, 4 PT
Passive Ownership:	Allowed
Encourage Conversions:	Yes
Area Develop. Agreements:	No
Sub-Franchising Contracts:	No
Expand In Territory:	Yes
Space Needs:	1,000 SF

SUPPORT & TRAINING:

Financial Assistance Provided:	No
Site Selection Assistance:	Yes
Lease Negotiation Assistance:	No
Co-Operative Advertising:	No

Franchisee Assoc./Member: No
Size Of Corporate Staff: 3
On-Going Support: ,B,,D,E,,,,I
Training: NR
SPECIFIC EXPANSION PLANS:
US: Eastern United States
Canada: All Canada
Overseas: NR

≪ ≫

PUDGIE'S FAMOUS CHICKEN

5 Dakota Dr., # 302
Lake Success, NY 11042
Tel: (800) 783-4437 (516) 358-0600 + 133
Fax: (516) 358-5076
E-Mail:
Web Site: www.trufoods.com
Mr. Alan J. Bernstein, Concept Director

Skinless fried chicken. Please see our Website at www.trufoods.com for more information.

BACKGROUND: IFA MEMBER
Established: 1981; 1st Franchised: 1981
Franchised Units: 27
Company-Owned Units: 4
Total Units: 31
Dist.: US-30; CAN-0; O'seas-1
 North America: 3 States, 0 Provinces
 Density: 24 in NY, 5 in NJ, 2 in CT
Projected New Units (12 Months): 20
Qualifications: 5, 4, 4, 2, 3, 5
FINANCIAL/TERMS:
Cash Investment: $75-100K
Total Investment: $150K-300K
Minimum Net Worth: $250K
Fees: Franchise - $30K
 Royalty - 5%; Ad. - 3%
Earnings Claims Statement: Yes
Term of Contract (Years): 10/10
Avg. # Of Employees: 4 FT, 6 PT
Passive Ownership: Discouraged
Encourage Conversions: Yes
Area Develop. Agreements: Yes/1
Sub-Franchising Contracts: No
Expand In Territory: Yes
Space Needs: 1,000-1,200 SF
SUPPORT & TRAINING:
Financial Assistance Provided: Yes (D)
Site Selection Assistance: Yes
Lease Negotiation Assistance: Yes
Co-Operative Advertising: No
Franchisee Assoc./Member: Yes/Yes
Size Of Corporate Staff: 50

On-Going Support: A,B,C,D,E,F,G,H,I
Training: 1 Week - 10 Days Long Island, NY
SPECIFIC EXPANSION PLANS:
US: Northeast, Southeast
Canada: No
Overseas: NR

≪ ≫

MEXICAN GRILL

QDOBA MEXICAN GRILL

4865 Ward Rd., # 500
Wheat Ridge, CO 80033
Tel: (720) 898-2300
Fax: (720) 898-2396
E-Mail: jdikos@qdoba.com
Web Site: www.qdoba.com
Ms. Gail Hill, Franchise Development Coord.

Qdoba is chosen by the world's toughest restaurant critics: successful franchisees. We've attracted successful multi-unit franchisees from Papa John's, Burger King, Applebee's, Johnny Rockets', Hooters and Village Inn, as well as a former president of KFC and a former CEO of Church's and Rally's. Why? Qdoba has a unique position among its Fast Casual Mexican competitors. Qdoba has attractive sales-to-investment ratio. Qdoba has multiple years of double-digit same-store sales growth.

BACKGROUND:
Established: 1995; 1st Franchised: 1996
Franchised Units: 335
Company-Owned Units: 132
Total Units: 467
Dist.: US-467; CAN-0; O'seas-0
 North America: 40 States, 0 Provinces
 Density: 25 in WI, 26 in MI, 53 in CO
Projected New Units (12 Months): 90
Qualifications: 3, 3, 3, 3, 3, 3
FINANCIAL/TERMS:
Cash Investment: $250K
Total Investment: $493K-727K
Minimum Net Worth: $2MM
Fees: Franchise - $30K
 Royalty - 5%; Ad. - 0.8%
Earnings Claims Statement: No
Term of Contract (Years): 10/10
Avg. # Of Employees: 10 FT, 5 PT
Passive Ownership: Discouraged
Encourage Conversions: NA
Area Develop. Agreements: Yes

Sub-Franchising Contracts: No
Expand In Territory: Yes
Space Needs: 2,300 SF
SUPPORT & TRAINING:
Financial Assistance Provided: No
Site Selection Assistance: Yes
Lease Negotiation Assistance: Yes
Co-Operative Advertising: No
Franchisee Assoc./Member: No
Size Of Corporate Staff: 109
On-Going Support: ,,C,D,E,,G,H,I
Training: 4 Weeks Operator + 2 Addtl Mgmt. in Denver, CO; 2 Days Franchise Orientation in Wheat Ridge, CO
SPECIFIC EXPANSION PLANS:
US: All but AK, IN, NC, ND, SC, WI
Canada: No
Overseas: NR

≪ ≫

MMMM...TOASTY!

QUIZNOS SUB

1001 17th St., # 200
Denver, CO 80202
Tel: (800) 335-4782 (720) 359-3300
Fax: (720) 359-3393
E-Mail: hhubbell@quiznos.com
Web Site: www.quiznos.com
Ms. Hedi Hubbell, International Brand Expansion Manager

Toasted subs are the key to QUIZNOS SUB's success. QUIZNOS SUB is dedicated to growing the brand by building financially successful franchises and serving the best sub sandwich in the market.

BACKGROUND: IFA MEMBER
Established: 1981; 1st Franchised: 1991
Franchised Units: 1950
Company-Owned Units: 15
Total Units: 1965
Dist.: US-1965; CAN-310; O'seas-47
 North America: 50 States, 9 Provinces
 Density: 311 in TX, 687 in CA
Projected New Units (12 Months): 400
Qualifications: 5, 4, 2, 2, 2, 5
FINANCIAL/TERMS:
Cash Investment: $70K
Total Investment: $184.5K-265K
Minimum Net Worth: $125K
Fees: Franchise - $25K
 Royalty - 7%; Ad. - 4%
Earnings Claims Statement: No

Term of Contract (Years): 15/
Avg. # Of Employees: 15-20 FT, 0 PT
Passive Ownership: Discouraged
Encourage Conversions: Yes
Area Develop. Agreements: Yes/1
Sub-Franchising Contracts: Yes
Expand In Territory: Yes
Space Needs: 1,200-1,800 SF
SUPPORT & TRAINING:
Financial Assistance Provided: Yes (I)
Site Selection Assistance: Yes
Lease Negotiation Assistance: Yes
Co-Operative Advertising: Yes
Franchisee Assoc./Member: Yes/Yes
Size Of Corporate Staff: 608
On-Going Support: ,,,,E,,G,H,I
Training: 1 Week Corporate Office
    Denver, CO; 3 Weeks Regional Market
SPECIFIC EXPANSION PLANS:
US: All US, Limited in MD and S. CA.
Canada: All Canada
Overseas: Europe

◄◄ ►►

RANCH*1
9311 E. Via De Ventura
Scottsdale, AZ 85258
Tel: (866) 4KAHALA (480) 362-4800
Fax: (480) 362-4792
E-Mail: rjjohnson@kahalacorp.com
Web Site: www.kahalacorp.com
Ms. Lori Merrall, Franchise Director

Up-scale - QSR features - fresh, never-frozen, grilled chicken sandwiches, salads, pasta and wraps.

BACKGROUND: IFA MEMBER
Established: 1990; 1st Franchised: 1994
Franchised Units: 35
Company-Owned Units: 1
Total Units: 36
Dist.: US-36; CAN-0; O'seas-0
North America: 3 States, 0 Provinces
Density: in NY, in MD, in CA
Projected New Units (12 Months): 25
Qualifications: 4, 4, 5, 1, 3, 4
FINANCIAL/TERMS:
Cash Investment: $148K-518K
Total Investment: $148K-518K
Minimum Net Worth: $200K
Fees: Franchise - $40K
    Royalty - 5%; Ad. - 3%
Earnings Claims Statement: No
Term of Contract (Years): 15/5
Avg. # Of Employees: 3 FT, 20 PT
Passive Ownership: Discouraged
Encourage Conversions: Yes
Area Develop. Agreements: Yes/1

Sub-Franchising Contracts: No
Expand In Territory: No
Space Needs: 1,500-2,000 SF
SUPPORT & TRAINING:
Financial Assistance Provided: Yes 0
Site Selection Assistance: Yes
Lease Negotiation Assistance: No
Co-Operative Advertising: No
Franchisee Assoc./Member: Yes/No
Size Of Corporate Staff: 34
On-Going Support: ,,C,D,E,F,G,H,I
Training: 6 Weeks New York Ranch *1;
    2 Weeks On-Site
SPECIFIC EXPANSION PLANS:
US: All United States
Canada: All Canada
Overseas: Europe, Asia

◄◄ ►►

ROBEKS FRUIT SMOOTHIES AND HEALTHY EATS
1230 E. Rosecrans Ave., # 400
Manhattan Beach, CA 90266
Tel: (866) 476-2357 (310) 727-0500 + 237
Fax: (310) 844-1587
E-Mail: franchising@robeks.com
Web Site: www.robeks.com
Mr. Ron Basinger, VP Franchising

At ROBEKS, our passion is to help people lead active and healthy lifestyles by offering the highest-quality nutritional food products and supplements. Our blended-to-order pure fruit smoothies, freshly squeezed juices and other healthy eats provide more nutritious alternatives to traditional fast food. ROBEKS is rapidly expanding across the US to meet this accelerating demand for healthier products.

BACKGROUND: IFA MEMBER
Established: 1996; 1st Franchised: 2001
Franchised Units: 165
Company-Owned Units: 1
Total Units: 166
Dist.: US-166; CAN-0; O'seas-0
North America: 10 States, 0 Provinces
Density: 4 in OH, 48 in CA, 6 in AZ
Projected New Units (12 Months): 49
Qualifications: 5, 5, 3, 3, 3, 5
FINANCIAL/TERMS:
Cash Investment: $100K
Total Investment: $227K-360K

Minimum Net Worth: $250K
Fees: Franchise - $25K
    Royalty - 7%; Ad. - 2.5%
Earnings Claims Statement: Yes
Term of Contract (Years): 10/5/5/
Avg. # Of Employees: 1 FT, 6-14 PT
Passive Ownership: Not Allowed
Encourage Conversions: No
Area Develop. Agreements: Yes/1
Sub-Franchising Contracts: No
Expand In Territory: Yes
Space Needs: 800-1,200 SF
SUPPORT & TRAINING:
Financial Assistance Provided: Yes (I)
Site Selection Assistance: Yes
Lease Negotiation Assistance: Yes
Co-Operative Advertising: No
Franchisee Assoc./Member: Yes/Yes
Size Of Corporate Staff: 29
On-Going Support: ,,C,D,E,,G,H,I
Training: 5 Days In-Store; 5 Days Los
    Angeles, CA; 5 Days Regional
SPECIFIC EXPANSION PLANS:
US: All United States Exc. SD and ND
Canada: No
Overseas: NR

◄◄ ►►

ROTELLI PIZZA & PASTA
4611 Johnson Rd., # 1
Coconut Creek, FL 33070
Tel: (877) 768-3554 (954) 601-0500
Fax: (954) 601-0501
E-Mail: info@rotellipizzapasta.com
Web Site: www.rotellipizzapasta.com
Mr. Jeffrey R. Smith, Chief Operating Officer

ROTELLI is a fast-casual pizza and pasta restaurant that offers superior yet affordable products, prepared fresh to order, and artistically presented in a warm, up-scale environment. Whether it's dine-in, take-out or delivery, our menu contains productswith mass appeal that are made from only the finest, freshest ingredients and include traditional and gourmet pizza, fresh pasta made to order. Our stores can range from 1,800-2,500 square feet and are generally located in high traffic shopping plazas.

BACKGROUND: IFA MEMBER
Established: 1999; 1st Franchised: 1999
Franchised Units: 42
Company-Owned Units: 0
Total Units: 42
Dist.: US-41; CAN-0; O'seas-1
North America: 5 States, 0 Provinces

Density: 3 in PA, 1 in NC, 15 in FL
Projected New Units (12 Months): 15
Qualifications: 3, 4, 2, 3, 2, 4

FINANCIAL/TERMS:

Cash Investment: $100-150K
Total Investment: $300-450K
Minimum Net Worth: $100K
Fees: Franchise - $25K
  Royalty - 6.0%; Ad. - 3%
Earnings Claims Statement: No
Term of Contract (Years): 20/10
Avg. # Of Employees: 30 FT, 0 PT
Passive Ownership: Discouraged
Encourage Conversions: Yes
Area Develop. Agreements: Yes/1
Sub-Franchising Contracts: No
Expand In Territory: Yes
Space Needs: NR

SUPPORT & TRAINING:

Financial Assistance Provided: No
Site Selection Assistance: Yes
Lease Negotiation Assistance: Yes
Co-Operative Advertising: No
Franchisee Assoc./Member: No
Size Of Corporate Staff: 6
On-Going Support: a,B,C,d,E,F,G,h,I
Training: 4-6 Weeks Instore at Area
  Developer; 10 Days Boca Raton, FL

SPECIFIC EXPANSION PLANS:

US: All United States
Canada: No
Overseas: NR

◄◄ ►►

ROUND TABLE PIZZA RESTAURANT

1320 Willow Pass Rd., # 600
Concord, CA 94520
Tel: (925) 969-3900
Fax: (925) 969-3978
E-Mail: krogers@roundtablepizza.com
Web Site: www.roundtablepizza.com
Ms. Kim Rogers, Franchise Sales Manager

ROUND TABLE FRANCHISE CORP. offers franchisees the opportunity to establish and operate a ROUND TABLE PIZZA RESTAURANT, which provides the public with pizza and related products in a wholesome, family restaurant setting. ROUND TABLE PIZZA is the nation's fourth largest pizza franchise chain, providing restaurant, take-out and delivery service.

BACKGROUND:

Established: 1959; 1st Franchised: 1962
Franchised Units: 517
Company-Owned Units: 19

Total Units: 536
Dist.: US-519; CAN-0; O'seas-17
  North America: 11 States, 0 Provinces
  Density: NR
Projected New Units (12 Months): 10
Qualifications: NR

FINANCIAL/TERMS:

Cash Investment: $135K
Total Investment: $420-496K
Minimum Net Worth: $450K
Fees: Franchise - $25K
  Royalty - 4%; Ad. - 4%
Earnings Claims Statement: No
Term of Contract (Years): 10/10
Avg. # Of Employees: 5-7 FT, 10-15 PT
Passive Ownership: Discouraged
Encourage Conversions: Yes
Area Develop. Agreements: Yes/1
Sub-Franchising Contracts: Yes
Expand In Territory: Yes
Space Needs: 2,800 SF

SUPPORT & TRAINING:

Financial Assistance Provided: No
Site Selection Assistance: Yes
Lease Negotiation Assistance: Yes
Co-Operative Advertising: No
Franchisee Assoc./Member: NR
Size Of Corporate Staff: 70
On-Going Support: ,,C,D,E,,G,H,I
Training: 2 Weeks Headquarters;
  2 Weeks Field

SPECIFIC EXPANSION PLANS:

US: Northwest, Southwest
Canada: No
Overseas: All Countries

◄◄ ►►

ROY ROGERS RESTAURANTS

321 Ballenger Center Dr., # 201
Frederick, MD 21703
Tel: (301) 695-8563
Fax: (301) 695-5066
E-Mail: franchise@royrogersrestaurants.com
Web Site: www.royrogersrestaurants.com
Ms. Dee Dee Barsy, Franchise Administrator

ROY ROGERS is a quick-service restaurant that is a "cut above" fast food, with a cult-like following. Our concept focuses on quality, variety and choice, targeted primarily for an adult audience. Our favor-

ite foods include the "Big Three" - roast beef, chicken and burgers. Our "Choose Any Side" option includes french fries, baked and mashed potatoes, cole slaw, tossed salad and baked beans. The ROY ROGERS Fixin's Bar includes multiple complimentary condiments. Guests customize their own sandwiches.

BACKGROUND: IFA MEMBER
Established: 1968; 1st Franchised: 2003
Franchised Units: 36
Company-Owned Units: 16
Total Units: 52
Dist.: US-52; CAN-0; O'seas-0
  North America: 9 States, 0 Provinces
  Density: 10 in NY, 8 in NJ, 18 in MD
Projected New Units (12 Months): 3
Qualifications: 4, 5, 4, 3, 3, 5

FINANCIAL/TERMS:

Cash Investment: $250-300K
Total Investment: $915K-1.5MM
Minimum Net Worth: $1.4MM
Fees: Franchise - $30K
  Royalty - 5%; Ad. - 2%
Earnings Claims Statement: Yes
Term of Contract (Years): 15/5
Avg. # Of Employees: 10-12 FT, 25-30 PT
Passive Ownership: Discouraged
Encourage Conversions: Yes
Area Develop. Agreements: No
Sub-Franchising Contracts: No
Expand In Territory: Yes
Space Needs: 3,200-3,700 SF

SUPPORT & TRAINING:

Financial Assistance Provided: No
Site Selection Assistance: Yes
Lease Negotiation Assistance: No
Co-Operative Advertising: No
Franchisee Assoc./Member: No
Size Of Corporate Staff: 26
On-Going Support: ,B,C,D,E,F,,H,I
Training: 8-10 Weeks Corporate Training
  Store; 7 Days Corporate Offices

SPECIFIC EXPANSION PLANS:

US: MD,DC,VA,DE,NJ,CT,MA,OH
Canada: No
Overseas: NR

◄◄ ►►

RUSSO'S NEW YORK PIZZERIA

5727 Westheimer Rd., # B

Houston, TX 77057
Tel: (832) 251-0220
Fax: (832) 251-8718
E-Mail: franchise@nypizzeria.com
Web Site: www.nypizzeria.com
Mr. Anthony Russo, President and
  Founder

From homemade pasta and calzones to New York-style pizza and coal-fired pizza, New York Pizzeria will help you attract loyal customers day after day. From the freshest ingredients to the right equipment (including brick and coal-fired pizza ovens), it doesn't get more authentic than this. Our traditional Italian decor and neighborhood pizzeria simplicity creates a home-style ambiance that attracts an upscale customer base.

BACKGROUND: IFA MEMBER
Established: 1978; 1st Franchised: 1992
Franchised Units: 22
Company-Owned Units: 5
Total Units: 27
Dist.: US-27; CAN-0; O'seas-0
  North America: 2 States, 0 Provinces
  Density: 27 in TX, 1 in TN
Projected New Units (12 Months): 15
Qualifications: 5, 2, 2, 3, 4, 5
FINANCIAL/TERMS:
Cash Investment: $85-200K
Total Investment: $295-950K
Minimum Net Worth: $750K
Fees: Franchise - $35K
  Royalty - 7%; Ad. - 2%
Earnings Claims Statement: Yes
Term of Contract (Years): 10/5
Avg. # Of Employees: 10 FT, 6 PT
Passive Ownership: Discouraged
Encourage Conversions: No
Area Develop. Agreements: No
Sub-Franchising Contracts: No
Expand In Territory: Yes
Space Needs: NA
SUPPORT & TRAINING:
Financial Assistance Provided: Yes (I)
Site Selection Assistance: Yes
Lease Negotiation Assistance: Yes
Co-Operative Advertising: Yes
Franchisee Assoc./Member: No
Size Of Corporate Staff: 4
On-Going Support: a,,c,d,E,F,,H,I
Training: 4 to 8 Weeks Corporate Store,
  Houston, TX
SPECIFIC EXPANSION PLANS:
US: All United States
Canada: All Canada
Overseas: All Countries

<< >>

SCHLOTZSKYS DELI
301 Congress Ave., # 1100
Austin, TX 78701
Tel: (800) 846-2867 (512) 236-3600
Fax: (512) 236-3650
E-Mail: franchise@schlotzskys.com
Web Site: www.schlotzskys.com
Mr. Darrell King, Licensing Manager

SCHLOTZSKY'S is a leader in the fast casual upscale specialty franchised restaurant category, serving a menu of sandwiches, pizza, soups and salads and featuring SCHLOTZSKY'S baked-fresh-daily sourdough bread. New SCHLOTZSKY'S restaurants are defining fast casual dining, with its appealing architecture, original products and speed of service.

BACKGROUND: IFA MEMBER
Established: 1971; 1st Franchised: 1977
Franchised Units: 354
Company-Owned Units: 21
Total Units: 375
Dist.: US-352; CAN-0; O'seas-23
  North America: 35 States, 0 Provinces
  Density: 154 in TX, 13 in GA, 15 in AZ
Projected New Units (12 Months): 22
Qualifications: 5, 5, 4, 3, 3, 5
FINANCIAL/TERMS:
Cash Investment: $200
Total Investment: $519-729.5K
Minimum Net Worth: $600
Fees: Franchise - $30K
  Royalty - 6%; Ad. - 4%
Earnings Claims Statement: Yes
Term of Contract (Years): 20/10
Avg. # Of Employees: 5 FT, 20 PT
Passive Ownership: Discouraged
Encourage Conversions: Yes
Area Develop. Agreements: No
Sub-Franchising Contracts: No
Expand In Territory: Yes
Space Needs: 2,400-3,500 SF
SUPPORT & TRAINING:
Financial Assistance Provided: No
Site Selection Assistance: Yes
Lease Negotiation Assistance: Yes
Co-Operative Advertising: Yes
Franchisee Assoc./Member: Yes/No
Size Of Corporate Staff: 70
On-Going Support: ,,C,D,E,F,G,H,I
Training: 3 Weeks Austin, TX

SPECIFIC EXPANSION PLANS:
US: All United States
Canada: No
Overseas: NR

<< >>

SCOOTER'S PLACE
221 Bonita Ave., # 240
Piedmont, CA 94611
Tel: (510) 839-5471
Fax: (510) 839-2104
E-Mail: rob@worldfranchising.com
Web Site: www.scootersplace.com
Mr. Fisher F. Scooter, President

SCOOPERS ICE CREAM is a made-fresh-daily concept at each location. Using only the finest ingredients in a homemade, low over-run, high-butterfat, gourmet ice cream. As many as 100 flavors and yogurts and sherbets are made fresh at your location.

BACKGROUND:
Established: 1982; 1st Franchised: 1986
Franchised Units: 28
Company-Owned Units: 10
Total Units: 38
Dist.: US-29; CAN-4; O'seas-5
  North America: 5 States, 1 Provinces
  Density: 1 in TN, 2 in KY, 7 in CA
Projected New Units (12 Months): 3
Qualifications: NR
FINANCIAL/TERMS:
Cash Investment: $25-45K
Total Investment: $35-75K
Minimum Net Worth: NR
Fees: Franchise - $12K
  Royalty - 4%; Ad. - 1%
Earnings Claims Statement: Yes
Term of Contract (Years): 10/10
Avg. # Of Employees: 2 FT, 3 PT
Passive Ownership: Discouraged
Encourage Conversions: Yes
Area Develop. Agreements: Yes/1
Sub-Franchising Contracts: No
Expand In Territory: No
Space Needs: 1,500-1,800 SF
SUPPORT & TRAINING:
Financial Assistance Provided: Yes (D)
Site Selection Assistance: Yes
Lease Negotiation Assistance: Yes
Co-Operative Advertising: No
Franchisee Assoc./Member: NR
Size Of Corporate Staff: 5
On-Going Support: A,,C,D,,,G,H,I
Training: 4 Weeks Headquarters;
  2 Weeks On-Site
SPECIFIC EXPANSION PLANS:

US: All United States
Canada: BC, ON
Overseas: NR

<< >>

SHAKEY'S RESTAURANTS
2200 W. Valley Blvd.
Alhambra, CA 91803
Tel: (888) 444-6686 (626) 576-0737
Fax: (626) 284-6870
E-Mail: info@shakeys.com
Web Site: www.shakeys.com
Dr. Joe Remsa, EVP & COO

SHAKEY'S offers a wide selection of freshly-prepared foods, consisting of a variety of pizzas, chicken and pasta and more than 50 freshly-prepared lunch and dinner items. SHAKEY'S features both pizza and fried chicken and the Bunch of Lunch all-you-can-eat buffet. Serves beer and wine and every store has a game room with approximately 15 redemption games. 64 restaurants in the US and 250 worldwide. Current prototype store has 6,000 SF and seats 200 customers. Average check was $7.25 in 2003.

BACKGROUND: IFA MEMBER
Established: 1954;   1st Franchised: 1957
Franchised Units: 55
Company-Owned Units: 16
Total Units: 71
Dist.:   US-71; CAN-0; O'seas-0
  North America: 7 States, 0 Provinces
  Density: 56 in CA
Projected New Units (12 Months):   10
Qualifications: 4, 4, 4, 2, 2, 5
FINANCIAL/TERMS:
Cash Investment: $25K-250K
Total Investment: $461K-1684.5K
Minimum Net Worth: NR
Fees: Franchise - $25K
  Royalty - 5%;   Ad. - 6%-5% Local
Earnings Claims Statement: No
Term of Contract (Years):   10/5/5/
Avg. # Of Employees:10-24 FT, 45% PT
Passive Ownership: Discouraged
Encourage Conversions: No
Area Develop. Agreements: Yes/1
Sub-Franchising Contracts: No
Expand In Territory: Yes
Space Needs: 4,000-6,000 SF
SUPPORT & TRAINING:
Financial Assistance Provided: No

Site Selection Assistance: Yes
Lease Negotiation Assistance: Yes
Co-Operative Advertising: No
Franchisee Assoc./Member: Yes/Yes
Size Of Corporate Staff: 6
On-Going Support: ,B,C,D,E,F,G,h,
Training: 6 Weeks CA
SPECIFIC EXPANSION PLANS:
US: All United States
Canada: No
Overseas: NR

<< >>

SILVER MINE SUBS
925 E. Harmony Rd., # 500
Fort Collins, CO 80525
Tel: (888) 321-6463 (970) 266-2600 + 2
Fax: (970) 267-3538
E-Mail: kdudek@silverminesubs.com
Web Site: www.silverminesubs.com
Mr. Keith Dudek, President/CEO/CIO

Our concept distinguishes itself with a lighthearted "Old Colorado" mining theme, which is reflected in our restaurant decor and sandwich names. The Silver Mine Subs menu focuses on legendary, fresh-made hot and cold sub sandwiches. Simple extras give our concept wider appeal: delicious wraps, salads, soup, chili, cookies and brownies. We deliver not just foot, but an experience. Our locations all offer dine-in, carryout and delivery service. Hours -- 10AM-3AM. Great advertising and solid marketing.

BACKGROUND: IFA MEMBER
Established: 1996;   1st Franchised: 2002
Franchised Units: 22
Company-Owned Units: 1
Total Units: 23
Dist.:   US-23; CAN-0; O'seas-0
  North America: 7 States, 0 Provinces
  Density: 2 in IL, 10 in CO, 3 in AZ
Projected New Units (12 Months):   8
Qualifications: 4, 4, 3, 3, 3, 4
FINANCIAL/TERMS:
Cash Investment: $75-100K
Total Investment: $211.8-352.3K
Minimum Net Worth: $200K
Fees: Franchise - $20K
  Royalty - 6%;   Ad. - 4%

Earnings Claims Statement: Yes
Term of Contract (Years):   10/NR
Avg. # Of Employees: 3-5 FT, 9-10 PT
Passive Ownership: Not Allowed
Encourage Conversions: NA
Area Develop. Agreements: Yes
Sub-Franchising Contracts: No
Expand In Territory: Yes
Space Needs: 1,200 SF
SUPPORT & TRAINING:
Financial Assistance Provided: No
Site Selection Assistance: Yes
Lease Negotiation Assistance: Yes
Co-Operative Advertising: No
Franchisee Assoc./Member: No
Size Of Corporate Staff: 7
On-Going Support: a,B,C,D,E,F,G,,
Training: 3 Weeks Corporate
  Headquarters
SPECIFIC EXPANSION PLANS:
US: All United States
Canada: No
Overseas: NR

<< >>

SMOOTHIE KING
121 Park Pl.
Covington, LA 70001
Tel: (800) 577-4200 (985) 635-6973
Fax: (985) 635-6987
E-Mail: franchise@smoothieking.com
Web Site: www.smoothieking.com
Mr. Michael C. Powers, EVP New Business Develop.

SMOOTHIE KING is the original nutritional smoothie bar and health marketplace since 1973. Our brand is recognized by Entrepreneur Magazine as being # 1 in our category for 15 consecutive years and has steadily grown to 390 stores. Brand loyalty and recognition, corporate support and innovation are some reasons why SMOOTHIE KING is in the front of the industry.

BACKGROUND: IFA MEMBER
Established: 1973;   1st Franchised: 1989
Franchised Units: 520
Company-Owned Units: 1
Total Units: 521
Dist.:   US-494; CAN-0; O'seas-27
  North America: 35 States, 0 Provinces

Density: 112 in TX, 80 in LA, 54 in FL
Projected New Units (12 Months): 75
Qualifications: 4, 4, 3, 3, 5, 4

FINANCIAL/TERMS:

Cash Investment: $50-60K
Total Investment: $148-299K
Minimum Net Worth: $100K
Fees: Franchise - $25K
 Royalty - 6%; Ad. - 1%
Earnings Claims Statement: No
Term of Contract (Years): 10/5/5/5/
Avg. # Of Employees: 2 FT, 6 PT
Passive Ownership: Discouraged
Encourage Conversions: Yes
Area Develop. Agreements: No
Sub-Franchising Contracts: No
Expand In Territory: Yes
Space Needs: 800-1,000 SF

SUPPORT & TRAINING:

Financial Assistance Provided: NR
Site Selection Assistance: Yes
Lease Negotiation Assistance: Yes
Co-Operative Advertising: Yes
Franchisee Assoc./Member: No
Size Of Corporate Staff: 50
On-Going Support: „C,D,E,F,G,h,I
Training: 7 Days New Orleans, LA

SPECIFIC EXPANSION PLANS:

US: All United States
Canada: No
Overseas: All Countries

◄◄ ►►

SNAPPY TOMATO PIZZA

7230 Turfway Rd.
Florence, KY 41042
Tel: (888) 463-7627 (859) 525-4680
Fax: (859) 525-4686
E-Mail: bwitte@snappytomato.com
Web Site: www.snappytomato.com
Mr. Bret Witte, Director of Marketing

We offer the best in pizza, subs and salads. We have a variety of concepts to offer to our franchisee. We are the pizza of choice in the new millennia.

BACKGROUND:

Established: 1982; 1st Franchised: 1985
Franchised Units: 53
Company-Owned Units: 2
Total Units: 55
Dist.: US-42; CAN-4; O'seas-9
 North America: 7 States, 1 Provinces
 Density: 5 in TN, 17 in KY, 5 in FL
Projected New Units (12 Months): 20
Qualifications: 3, 3, 3, 2, 1, 3

FINANCIAL/TERMS:

Cash Investment: $20-30K

Total Investment: $70-150K
Minimum Net Worth: NR
Fees: Franchise - $15K
 Royalty - 5.5%/$200; Ad. - 2.5%
Earnings Claims Statement: Yes
Term of Contract (Years): 15/15
Avg. # Of Employees: 2 FT, 10 PT
Passive Ownership: Discouraged
Encourage Conversions: Yes
Area Develop. Agreements: Yes/1
Sub-Franchising Contracts: Yes
Expand In Territory: Yes
Space Needs: 400-2,000 SF

SUPPORT & TRAINING:

Financial Assistance Provided: No
Site Selection Assistance: Yes
Lease Negotiation Assistance: Yes
Co-Operative Advertising: No
Franchisee Assoc./Member: No
Size Of Corporate Staff: 5
On-Going Support: A,B,C,D,E,,G,H,I
Training: 3 Days to 2 Weeks KY, TN or
 FL

SPECIFIC EXPANSION PLANS:

US: SE, SE, Mid-Atl., Midwest
Canada: All Canada
Overseas: Japan, China, Caribbean,
 Middle East

◄◄ ►►

SONIC DRIVE-IN

300 Johnny Bench Dr.
Oklahoma City, OK 73104
Tel: (800) 569-6656 (405) 225-5000
Fax: (405) 225-5963
E-Mail: lcoffman@sonicdrivein.com
Web Site: www.sonicdrivein.com
Mr. David Vernon, VP Franchise Sales

SONIC DRIVE-INS offer made-to-order hamburgers and other sandwiches, and feature signature items, such as extra-long cheese coneys, hand-breaded onion rings, tater tots, fountain favorites, including cherry limeades, slushes and a full ice-cream dessert menu.

BACKGROUND: IFA MEMBER
Established: 1953; 1st Franchised: 1959
Franchised Units: 2850
Company-Owned Units: 625
Total Units: 3475
Dist.: US-3468; CAN-0; O'seas-7

North America: 37 States, 0 Provinces
Density: 739 in TX, 191 in TN, 234 in
OK
Projected New Units (12 Months): 185
Qualifications: 5, 5, 5, 2, 2, 4

FINANCIAL/TERMS:

Cash Investment: $434-545K
Total Investment: $900K-2.2MM
Minimum Net Worth: $2MM
Fees: Franchise - $30K
 Royalty - 1-5%; Ad. - 4%
Earnings Claims Statement: No
Term of Contract (Years): 20/10
Avg. # Of Employees: 35 FT, 0 PT
Passive Ownership: Not Allowed
Encourage Conversions: No
Area Develop. Agreements: Yes
Sub-Franchising Contracts: No
Expand In Territory: Yes
Space Needs: 1,450 SF

SUPPORT & TRAINING:

Financial Assistance Provided: Yes (I)
Site Selection Assistance: Yes
Lease Negotiation Assistance: Yes
Co-Operative Advertising: Yes
Franchisee Assoc./Member: Yes/Yes
Size Of Corporate Staff: 210
On-Going Support: ,B,C,D,E,F,G,H,I
Training: 1 Week Oklahoma City, OK;
 11 Weeks Local Market

SPECIFIC EXPANSION PLANS:

US: SW, SE, West, Midwest
Canada: No
Overseas: Mexico, Puerto Rico

◄◄ ►►

SOPHIE'S CUBAN CUISINE

420 Lexington Ave., # 300
New York, NY 10170
Tel: (888) 282-8226 (212) 922-9535
Fax: (212) 479-2551
E-Mail: sluna@sophiescuban.com
Web Site: www.sophiescuban.com
Mr. Jim McKenna, Chief Development Officer

Sophie's Cuban Cuisine began in 1997 in downtown Manhattan with an American Dream. Manuela Luna and her three daughters, Patricia, Sofia, and Mila, risked everything to start a restaurant dedicated to having the tastiest lunch with the best service in New York City. Their Cuban chef, Eduardo Mergado, created authentic Cuban meals and sandwiches that have been receiving rave reviews for ten years. Those who join us will be proud to be a Sophie's Cuban Cuisine franchisee!

BACKGROUND:

Established: 1997; 1st Franchised: 2006	
Franchised Units:	0
Company-Owned Units:	<u>6</u>
Total Units:	6
Dist.:	US-6; CAN-0; O'seas-0
North America:	1 States, 0 Provinces
Density:	6 in NY
Projected New Units (12 Months):	NR
Qualifications:	3, 3, 3, 3, 3, 3

FINANCIAL/TERMS:

Cash Investment:	$100-150K
Total Investment:	$365-611K
Minimum Net Worth:	$1MM-1.5MM
Fees: Franchise -	$25K
Royalty - 5%;	Ad. - 2%
Earnings Claims Statement:	No
Term of Contract (Years):	10/10
Avg. # Of Employees:	18 FT, 8-10 PT
Passive Ownership:	Not Allowed
Encourage Conversions:	NA
Area Develop. Agreements:	No
Sub-Franchising Contracts:	No
Expand In Territory:	No
Space Needs:	NA

SUPPORT & TRAINING:

Financial Assistance Provided:	No
Site Selection Assistance:	Yes
Lease Negotiation Assistance:	Yes
Co-Operative Advertising:	No
Franchisee Assoc./Member:	No
Size Of Corporate Staff:	7
On-Going Support:	,,C,D,E,,,,
Training:	8-9 Weeks New York City

SPECIFIC EXPANSION PLANS:

US:	No
Canada:	No
Overseas:	NR

≪ ≫

SPICY PICKLE, INC.
90 Madison St., # 700
Denver, CO 80206
Tel: (800) 711-1902 (303) 297-1902
Fax: (303) 297-1903
E-Mail: marc@spicypickle.com
Web Site: www.spicypickle.com
Mr. Tony Walker, COO

Spicy Pickle restaurants serve high quality meats and fine Italian artisan breads along with a wide choice of 10 different cheeses, 21 toppings and 15 proprietary spreads to create delicious panini and sub sandwiches with flavors from around the world. We also serve a pizzetti neopolitan style thin crust pizza and hand-tossed salads and soups. Spicy Pickle serves the fast growing "fast casual" market where customers demand more than "fast food," but without the price point of "casual dining." The hallmark o

BACKGROUND:

Established: 1999; 1st Franchised: 2003	
Franchised Units:	63
Company-Owned Units:	<u>2</u>
Total Units:	65
Dist.:	US-65; CAN-0; O'seas-0
North America:	0 States, 0 Provinces
Density:	2 in NV, 14 in CO, 2 in CA
Projected New Units (12 Months):	20
Qualifications:	3, 3, 3, 3, 3, 3

FINANCIAL/TERMS:

Cash Investment:	$100-150K
Total Investment:	$300-350K
Minimum Net Worth:	$500K
Fees: Franchise -	$35K
Royalty - 5%;	Ad. - 2%
Earnings Claims Statement:	Yes
Term of Contract (Years):	10/10
Avg. # Of Employees:	3 FT, 9 PT
Passive Ownership:	Discouraged
Encourage Conversions:	Yes
Area Develop. Agreements:	Yes/5
Sub-Franchising Contracts:	Yes
Expand In Territory:	Yes
Space Needs:	1,800 SF

SUPPORT & TRAINING:

Financial Assistance Provided:	No
Site Selection Assistance:	Yes
Lease Negotiation Assistance:	Yes
Co-Operative Advertising:	Yes
Franchisee Assoc./Member:	No
Size Of Corporate Staff:	18
On-Going Support:	A,B,C,D,E,F,G,,
Training:	4 Weeks Denver, CO

SPECIFIC EXPANSION PLANS:

US:	S. CA, Ohio Valley, NW U.S., East Coast
Canada:	Yes
Overseas:	NR

≪ ≫

STEAK ESCAPE
222 Neilston St.
Columbus, OH 43215
Tel: (866) 247-8325 (614) 224-0300
Fax: (614) 224-6460
E-Mail: lallen@steakescape.com
Web Site: www.steakescape.com
Mr. Shane Pratt, VP Franchise Development

STEAK ESCAPE prides itself on serving delicious grilled sandwiches, freshly cut fries and freshly squeezed lemonade. All of these items are created from fresh ingredients and are prepared in full view of customers using our own unique method of exhibition-style cooking. STEAK ESCAPE's signature item is The Genuine Philadelphia Cheesesteak Sandwich. Today we have opportunities available in free-standing locations, strip center locations and in mall locations!

BACKGROUND:

Established: 1982; 1st Franchised: 1983	
Franchised Units:	165
Company-Owned Units:	<u>0</u>
Total Units:	165
Dist.:	US-164; CAN-0; O'seas-1
North America:	35 States, 0 Provinces
Density:	14 in OH, 16 in CO, 18 in CA
Projected New Units (12 Months):	40-45
Qualifications:	4, 4, 3, 1, 3, 4

FINANCIAL/TERMS:

Cash Investment:	$70-250K
Total Investment:	$180-1.25MM
Minimum Net Worth:	$100K
Fees: Franchise -	$25K
Royalty - 6-5%;	Ad. - 0.5%
Earnings Claims Statement:	No
Term of Contract (Years):	20/Varies
Avg. # Of Employees:	4 FT, 12 PT
Passive Ownership:	Allowed
Encourage Conversions:	Yes
Area Develop. Agreements:	Yes/1
Sub-Franchising Contracts:	Yes
Expand In Territory:	Yes
Space Needs:	300-2,400 SF

SUPPORT & TRAINING:

Financial Assistance Provided:	Yes (D)
Site Selection Assistance:	Yes
Lease Negotiation Assistance:	Yes
Co-Operative Advertising:	No
Franchisee Assoc./Member:	Yes/Yes
Size Of Corporate Staff:	28
On-Going Support:	A,B,C,D,e,F,G,H,I
Training:	3 Weeks Columbus, OH

SPECIFIC EXPANSION PLANS:

US:	All United States
Canada:	All Canada
Overseas:	Western Hemisphere

≪ ≫

STEAK-OUT CHAR-BROILED DELIVERY
3901 Governors Lake Dr., # 500
Norcross, GA 30071-1130
Tel: (877) 878-3257 (678) 533-6000
Fax: (678) 291-0222
E-Mail: msavula@steakout.com
Web Site: www.steakout.com
Mr. Michael Savula, Vice President

STEAK-OUT franchising specializes in home and office deliveries of charbroiled steaks, chicken and burgers - other menu items include salads and desserts. The only full meal delivery service expanding nationwide. Customers absolutely love our combination of quality food and delivery service. America's finest delivery.

BACKGROUND: IFA MEMBER
Established: 1986;   1st Franchised: 1987
Franchised Units: 51
Company-Owned Units: 2
Total Units: 53
Dist.:   US-53; CAN-0; O'seas-0
 North America: 18 States, 0 Provinces
 Density: 12 in TN, 8 in GA, 18 in AL
Projected New Units (12 Months):   12
Qualifications: 4, 5, 3, 3, 3, 5
FINANCIAL/TERMS:
Cash Investment: $75-100K
Total Investment: $271-453K
Minimum Net Worth: $300K+
Fees: Franchise - $25K
 Royalty - 5%;   Ad. - 2%
Earnings Claims Statement: Yes
Term of Contract (Years):   10/10
Avg. # Of Employees: 2 FT, 25-30 PT
Passive Ownership: Discouraged
Encourage Conversions: Yes
Area Develop. Agreements: Yes
Sub-Franchising Contracts: No
Expand In Territory: Yes
Space Needs: 1,600 SF
SUPPORT & TRAINING:
Financial Assistance Provided: Yes (I)
Site Selection Assistance: Yes
Lease Negotiation Assistance: Yes
Co-Operative Advertising: No
Franchisee Assoc./Member: No
Size Of Corporate Staff: 18
On-Going Support: ,,C,D,E,,G,H,I
Training: 4-5 Weeks Training Center in
 Columbia, SC
SPECIFIC EXPANSION PLANS:
US: SE, MW
Canada: No
Overseas: NR

◄◄ ►►

STRAW HAT PIZZA
18 Crow Canyon Ct., # 270
San Ramon, CA 94583-1669

Tel: (087) STRAWHAT (925) 837-3400
Fax: (925) 820-1080
E-Mail: info@strawhatpizza.com
Web Site: www.strawhatpizza.com
Mr. Jonathan Fornaci, President

STRAW HAT PIZZA is a cooperative owned by a membership made up of individual store owners. Royalty fees are very low and more than offset by purchasing, insurance and marketing advantages. Stores operate under a detailed system, yet are allowed a great deal of flexibility. Store owners participate in the operation of the parent company.

BACKGROUND: IFA MEMBER
Established: 1959;   1st Franchised: 1969
Franchised Units: 53
Company-Owned Units: 0
Total Units: 53
Dist.:   US-53; CAN-0; O'seas-0
 North America: 2 States, 0 Provinces
 Density: 2 in NV, 43 in CA
Projected New Units (12 Months):   8
Qualifications: 4, 4, 3, 3, 4, 4
FINANCIAL/TERMS:
Cash Investment: $100-200K
Total Investment: $200-700K
Minimum Net Worth: $300K
Fees: Franchise - $25K
 Royalty - 5%;   Ad. - 3%
Earnings Claims Statement: No
Term of Contract (Years):   10/5
Avg. # Of Employees: 3-5 FT, 8-15 PT
Passive Ownership: Discouraged
Encourage Conversions: Yes
Area Develop. Agreements: No
Sub-Franchising Contracts: No
Expand In Territory: Yes
Space Needs: 4,000 SF
SUPPORT & TRAINING:
Financial Assistance Provided: Yes (I)
Site Selection Assistance: Yes
Lease Negotiation Assistance: Yes
Co-Operative Advertising: Yes
Franchisee Assoc./Member: No
Size Of Corporate Staff: 6
On-Going Support: ,,C,D,,F,G,h,
Training: 4 Weeks Vallejo, CA
SPECIFIC EXPANSION PLANS:
US: West
Canada: No
Overseas: NR

◄◄ ►►

STUFT PIZZA
50855 Washington St., # 210
La Quinta, CA 92253-2891

Tel: (760) 777-1660
Fax: (760) 777-1660
E-Mail: noelle@stuftpizza.com
Web Site: www.stuftpizza.com
Ms. Noelle Bertram, VP Sales/Marketing

Take-outs to full service with pasta and micro-brewery.

BACKGROUND:
Established: 1976;   1st Franchised: 1985
Franchised Units: 26
Company-Owned Units: 1
Total Units: 27
Dist.:   US-27; CAN-0; O'seas-0
 North America: 2 States, Provinces
 Density: 26 in CA, 1 in OR
Projected New Units (12 Months):   5
Qualifications: 4, 3, 2, 3, 3, 4
FINANCIAL/TERMS:
Cash Investment: $75-150K
Total Investment: $150-750K
Minimum Net Worth: $250K
Fees: Franchise - $25K
 Royalty - 3%;   Ad. - 0%
Earnings Claims Statement: No
Term of Contract (Years):   10/10
Avg. # Of Employees: 3 FT, 8+ PT
Passive Ownership: Discouraged
Encourage Conversions: Yes
Area Develop. Agreements: Yes/1
Sub-Franchising Contracts: Yes
Expand In Territory: Yes
Space Needs: 1,800+ SF
SUPPORT & TRAINING:
Financial Assistance Provided: NR
Site Selection Assistance: Yes
Lease Negotiation Assistance: Yes
Co-Operative Advertising: No
Franchisee Assoc./Member: No
Size Of Corporate Staff: 4
On-Going Support: ,,C,D,E,,G,H,
Training: 2 Weeks San Clemente, CA
SPECIFIC EXPANSION PLANS:
US: West
Canada: No
Overseas: NR

◄◄ ►►

SUB STATION II
425 N. Main St.
Sumter, SC 29150
Tel: (800) 779-2970 (803) 773-4711
Fax: (803) 775-2220
E-Mail: franchises@substationii.com
Web Site: www.substationii.com
Ms. Susan H. Vaden, Vice President

SUB STATION II is a chain of submarine sandwich franchises. We currently have 90 stores located in 9 states. Our sandwich shops offer a variety of over 25 submarine sandwiches, along with specialty sandwiches and salads. We have developed an efficient method of preparing each sandwich to the customer's specifications. The emphasis is on high-quality food and cleanliness. We provide our franchisee's with training and on-going support, layout, etc.

BACKGROUND:

Established: 1975;   1st Franchised: 1976
Franchised Units: 82
Company-Owned Units: 2
Total Units: 84
Dist.:   US-84; CAN-0; O'seas-0
 North America: 9 States, 0 Provinces
 Density: 40 in SC, 20 in NC, 15 in CA
Projected New Units (12 Months):   15
Qualifications: 5, 4, 2, 3, 2, 4

FINANCIAL/TERMS:

Cash Investment: $40-70K
Total Investment: $75-150K
Minimum Net Worth: $200K
Fees: Franchise - $10.5K
 Royalty - 4%;   Ad. - 2%
Earnings Claims Statement: No
Term of Contract (Years):   10/10
Avg. # Of Employees: 4 FT, 8 PT
Passive Ownership: Allowed
Encourage Conversions: Yes
Area Develop. Agreements: No
Sub-Franchising Contracts: Yes
Expand In Territory: Yes
Space Needs: 1,500 SF

SUPPORT & TRAINING:

Financial Assistance Provided: Yes (D)
Site Selection Assistance: Yes
Lease Negotiation Assistance: Yes
Co-Operative Advertising: No
Franchisee Assoc./Member: No
Size Of Corporate Staff: 8
On-Going Support: ,B,C,D,E,,G,h,
Training: 7-10 Days Corporate Store;
 7-10 Days Franchisee Location

SPECIFIC EXPANSION PLANS:

US: Southeast, Southern CA
Canada: No
Overseas: NR

SUBS PLUS

173 Queenston St.
St. Catharines, ON L2R 3A2 Canada
Tel: (888) 549-7777 (905) 641-3696
Fax: (905) 641-3696
E-Mail: franchise@subsplus.ca
Web Site: www.subsplus.ca

Mr. Robert Dumas, President

SUBS PLUS isn't just another fast food franchise. Cakes and pastries baked fresh on the premises add extra delicious flavor to an already appetizing business opportunity.   And no baking experience is necessary! We will train you in the skills required to successfully operate your own SUBS PLUS franchise.

BACKGROUND:

Established: 1985;   1st Franchised: 1991
Franchised Units: 4
Company-Owned Units: 1
Total Units: 5
Dist.:   US-0; CAN-5; O'seas-0
 North America: States, 1 Provinces
 Density: 5 in ON
Projected New Units (12 Months):   6
Qualifications: 5, 2, 2, 3, 5, 5

FINANCIAL/TERMS:

Cash Investment: $30-60K
Total Investment: $140-160K
Minimum Net Worth: $100K
Fees: Franchise - $20K
 Royalty - 5%;   Ad. - 3%
Earnings Claims Statement: No
Term of Contract (Years):   10/10
Avg. # Of Employees: 1 FT, 8 PT
Passive Ownership: Not Allowed
Encourage Conversions: Yes
Area Develop. Agreements: Yes/1
Sub-Franchising Contracts: No
Expand In Territory: Yes
Space Needs: 1,500 SF

SUPPORT & TRAINING:

Financial Assistance Provided: Yes (D)
Site Selection Assistance: Yes
Lease Negotiation Assistance: Yes
Co-Operative Advertising: No
Franchisee Assoc./Member: No
Size Of Corporate Staff: 5
On-Going Support: ,B,C,D,E,,h,I
Training: 6-8 Weeks Head Office;
 3 Weeks On-Site

SPECIFIC EXPANSION PLANS:

US: NR
Canada: ON
Overseas: NR

SUBWAY RESTAURANTS

325 Bic Dr.
Milford, CT 06461

Tel: (800) 888-4848 (203) 877-4281
Fax: (203) 876-6688
E-Mail: franchise@subway.com
Web Site: www.subway.com
Mr. Pete Gartner, Sales Manager

For more than 40 years, SUBWAY RESTAURANTS has been offering entrepreneurs an opportunity to build and succeed in their own business through a proven, well-structured franchise system. SUBWAY is the world's largest submarine sandwich franchise and the largest restaurant chain in N. America. In 2006, Entrepreneur Magazine again chose SUBWAY as the overall number one franchise opportunity, making it the 14th time in the past 18 years. Over 25,000 independently-owned and operated location in 83 countries.

BACKGROUND: IFA MEMBER

Established: 1965;   1st Franchised: 1974
Franchised Units: 30300
Company-Owned Units: 0
Total Units: 30300
Dist.: US-20160; CAN-2151; O'seas-3678
 North America: 50 States, 12 Provinces
 Density: in TX, in FL, in CA
Projected New Units (12 Months):
1,000+
Qualifications: 5, 4, 3, 4, 3, 3

FINANCIAL/TERMS:

Cash Investment: $Not Required
Total Investment: $108.3-300K
Minimum Net Worth: $Not Required
Fees: Franchise - $15K (10K Intl.)
 Royalty - 8%;   Ad. - 4.5%
Earnings Claims Statement: No
Term of Contract (Years):   20/20
Avg. # Of Employees: 2-3 FT, 6-10 PT
Passive Ownership: Not Allowed
Encourage Conversions: NA
Area Develop. Agreements: Yes/20
Sub-Franchising Contracts: No
Expand In Territory: Yes
Space Needs: 300-2,000 SF

SUPPORT & TRAINING:

Financial Assistance Provided: Yes (D)
Site Selection Assistance: Yes
Lease Negotiation Assistance: Yes
Co-Operative Advertising: No
Franchisee Assoc./Member: Yes/Yes
Size Of Corporate Staff: 700
On-Going Support: A,B,C,D,E,F,G,H,I
Training: 2 Weeks Montreal, PQ; 2 Weeks
 Miami, FL; 2 Weeks Milford, CT

SPECIFIC EXPANSION PLANS:

US: All United States
Canada: All Canada
Overseas: All Countries

TACO BELL

1900 Colonel Sanders Ln.
Louisville, KY 40213
Tel: (866) 2YUM-YUM (502) 874-8300
Fax: (502) 874-8848
E-Mail: 2yumyum@yum.com
Web Site: www.yumfranchises.com
Ms. Leigh Anne Lochner, Franchise Coordinator

TACO BELL has been the world's largest Mexican quick-service franchise for the past 38 years.

BACKGROUND: IFA MEMBER
Established: 1962; 1st Franchised: 1964
Franchised Units: 3803
Company-Owned Units: 1267
Total Units: 5070
Dist.: US-4028; CAN-300; O'seas-702
  North America: 50 States, 0 Provinces
  Density: 151 in OH, 150 in FL, 232 in CA
Projected New Units (12 Months): NR
Qualifications: NR
FINANCIAL/TERMS:
Cash Investment: NR
Total Investment: $1.2-1.7M
Minimum Net Worth: $1MM
Fees: Franchise - $45K
  Royalty - 5.5%; Ad. - 4.5%
Earnings Claims Statement: No
Term of Contract (Years): 20/
Avg. # Of Employees: FT, 0 PT
Passive Ownership: Discouraged
Encourage Conversions: No
Area Develop. Agreements: No
Sub-Franchising Contracts: No
Expand In Territory: Yes
Space Needs: NR
SUPPORT & TRAINING:
Financial Assistance Provided: Yes (D)
Site Selection Assistance: Yes
Lease Negotiation Assistance: Yes
Co-Operative Advertising: Yes
Franchisee Assoc./Member: No
Size Of Corporate Staff: 0
On-Going Support: ,,,,,,,,
Training: 18 Weeks Approved Training

Restaurant
SPECIFIC EXPANSION PLANS:
US: All United States
Canada: All Canada
Overseas: All Countries

TACO JOHN'S INTERNATIONAL

808 W. 20th St.
Cheyenne, WY 82001
Tel: (800) 854-0819 + 9701 (307) 635-0101 + 9701
Fax: (307) 638-0603
E-Mail: bmiller@tacojohns.com
Web Site: www.tacojohns.com
Dr. Brett D. Miller, Director of Development

Mexican fast-food restaurant franchisor.

BACKGROUND:
Established: 1969; 1st Franchised: 1969
Franchised Units: 410
Company-Owned Units: 10
Total Units: 420
Dist.: US-420; CAN-0; O'seas-0
  North America: 26 States, 0 Provinces
  Density: 39 in SD, 71 in MN, 61 in IA
Projected New Units (12 Months): 28
Qualifications: 4, 5, 3, 3, 1, 5
FINANCIAL/TERMS:
Cash Investment: $150K
Total Investment: $550-979K
Minimum Net Worth: $400K
Fees: Franchise - $25K
  Royalty - 4%; Ad. - 3.5%
Earnings Claims Statement: No
Term of Contract (Years): 20/10
Avg. # Of Employees: 15-25 FT, 0 PT
Passive Ownership: Discouraged
Encourage Conversions: Yes
Area Develop. Agreements: Yes/1
Sub-Franchising Contracts: No
Expand In Territory: Yes
Space Needs: 1,200-2,300 SF
SUPPORT & TRAINING:
Financial Assistance Provided: No
Site Selection Assistance: No
Lease Negotiation Assistance: Yes
Co-Operative Advertising: Yes
Franchisee Assoc./Member: Yes/Yes
Size Of Corporate Staff: 60
On-Going Support: ,,C,D,E,,,G,H,I
Training: 4 Weeks Cheyenne, Wyoming
SPECIFIC EXPANSION PLANS:

US: Upper Midwest, Central US
Canada: No
Overseas: NR

TACO MAKER, THE

P.O. Box 362888
San Juan, PR 00936-2888
Tel: (801) 476-9780
Fax: (787) 793-3130
E-Mail: cbudet@fransglobal.com
Web Site: www.tacomaker.com
Mr. Carlos Budet, EVP & COO

The Taco Maker is an international Mexican fast food franchise specializing in quick, friendly service and a complete menu with fresh, made-from-scratch ingredients. Centralized purchasing, marketing, operational support and progressive store design provide for a very comprehensive and fun investment opportunity. The Taco Maker family features two additional concepts: Jake's Over the Top and Mayan Jamma Juice. Jake's offers a unique line of charbroiled burgers and its "Avalanche" shake rises two to three

BACKGROUND:
Established: 1978; 1st Franchised: 1978
Franchised Units: 55
Company-Owned Units: 7
Total Units: 62
Dist.: US-62; CAN-0; O'seas-0
  North America: 32 States, 0 Provinces
  Density: 10 in WA, 13 in UT, 5 in NY
Projected New Units (12 Months): 20
Qualifications: 4, 4, 5, 2, 4, 4
FINANCIAL/TERMS:
Cash Investment: $50-75K
Total Investment: $300-500K
Minimum Net Worth: NR
Fees: Franchise - $19-22.5K
  Royalty - 5-7%; Ad. - 3%/4%
Earnings Claims Statement: No
Term of Contract (Years): 15/15
Avg. # Of Employees: 2-6 FT, 5-20 PT
Passive Ownership: Discouraged
Encourage Conversions: Yes
Area Develop. Agreements: Yes/15
Sub-Franchising Contracts: Yes
Expand In Territory: Yes
Space Needs: 200-3,000 SF
SUPPORT & TRAINING:
Financial Assistance Provided: Yes (I)
Site Selection Assistance: Yes
Lease Negotiation Assistance: Yes
Co-Operative Advertising: Yes
Franchisee Assoc./Member: No

Size Of Corporate Staff: 30
On-Going Support: ,B,C,D,E,F,,,I
Training: 21 Days UT
SPECIFIC EXPANSION PLANS:
US: All United States
Canada: All Canada
Overseas: All Countries

<< >>

TACO PALACE
814 E. Hwy. 60, P.O. Box 87
Monett, MO 65708
Tel: (417) 235-6595
Fax: (573) 216-1739
E-Mail: matt@tacopalace.com
Web Site: www.tacopalace.com
Mr. Matt Deves, VP

Our concept is targeted at people that normally could not afford the cost and expense that other franchises require. Our low overhead concept translates to more profit to the franchisee. We offer more flexibility. Fresh Tex-Mex food at "down to earth" prices!

BACKGROUND:
Established: 1985; 1st Franchised: 1999
Franchised Units: 8
Company-Owned Units: 2
Total Units: 10
Dist.: US-9; CAN-1; O'seas-0
North America: 9 States, 0 Provinces
Density: in TX, in OK, 3 in MO
Projected New Units (12 Months): 6
Qualifications: NR
FINANCIAL/TERMS:
Cash Investment: $69K
Total Investment: $132-170K
Minimum Net Worth: $50-65K
Fees: Franchise - $33.5K
Royalty - 0%; Ad. - 0%
Earnings Claims Statement: Yes
Term of Contract (Years): Unlimited/
Avg. # Of Employees: 8 FT, 2 PT
Passive Ownership: Allowed
Encourage Conversions: Yes
Area Develop. Agreements: Yes
Sub-Franchising Contracts: Yes
Expand In Territory: Yes
Space Needs: 1,000+ SF
SUPPORT & TRAINING:
Financial Assistance Provided: No
Site Selection Assistance: Yes
Lease Negotiation Assistance: Yes
Co-Operative Advertising: No
Franchisee Assoc./Member: No
Size Of Corporate Staff: 4
On-Going Support: ,,C,D,E,F,,

Training: 10-20 Days Franchisee's Location; Unlimited Days Monett, MO
SPECIFIC EXPANSION PLANS:
US: All United States
Canada: All Canada
Overseas: All Countries

<< >>

TACO VILLA
3710 Chesswood Dr., # 220
North York, ON M3J 2W4 Canada
Tel: (416) 636-9348
Fax: (416) 636-9162
E-Mail: tacovilla@on.aibn.com
Web Site: www.tacovillaonline.com
Ms. Wendy MacKinnon, Franchise Director

TACO VILLA is a quick-service Mexican-food concept. With over 16 years' experience, we offer franchisees a dynamic design concept, full turn-key operation, proven menu and procedures, full training and marketing. We provide today's consumer with a high-quality, high-value food experience. TACO VILLA continues to expand.

BACKGROUND:
Established: 1983; 1st Franchised: 1985
Franchised Units: 20
Company-Owned Units: 1
Total Units: 21
Dist.: US-0; CAN-21; O'seas-0
North America: States, 1 Provinces
Density: 21 in ON
Projected New Units (12 Months): 10-15
Qualifications: 5, 3, 2, 3, 4, 4
FINANCIAL/TERMS:
Cash Investment: $40-50K
Total Investment: $140-150K
Minimum Net Worth: $150K
Fees: Franchise - $20K
Royalty - 6%; Ad. - 2%
Earnings Claims Statement: No
Term of Contract (Years): 10/10
Avg. # Of Employees: 3 FT, 5 PT
Passive Ownership: Not Allowed
Encourage Conversions: Yes
Area Develop. Agreements: No
Sub-Franchising Contracts: Yes
Expand In Territory: Yes
Space Needs: 350-400 SF
SUPPORT & TRAINING:
Financial Assistance Provided: Yes (D)
Site Selection Assistance: Yes
Lease Negotiation Assistance: Yes
Co-Operative Advertising: No
Franchisee Assoc./Member: NR

Size Of Corporate Staff: 7
On-Going Support: A,B,C,D,E,,G,,I
Training: 1 Week Head Office;
3 Weeks In Store
SPECIFIC EXPANSION PLANS:
US: Eastern Seaboard, New Eng.
Canada: All Canada
Overseas: NR

<< >>

TACONE / THE COUNTER
950 Flower St., # 105
Los Angeles, CA 90015
Tel: (877) 482-2663 (213) 236-0950
Fax: (213) 236-0951
E-Mail: craig@tacone.com
Web Site: www.tacone.com
Mr. Craig Albert, President

Franchisor of quick-service restaurants serving fresh soups, sandwiches, salads, smoothies and catering.

BACKGROUND:
Established: 1995; 1st Franchised: 1998
Franchised Units: 60
Company-Owned Units: 0
Total Units: 60
Dist.: US-60; CAN-0; O'seas-0
North America: 6 States, Provinces
Density: 9 in CA
Projected New Units (12 Months): NR
Qualifications: NR
FINANCIAL/TERMS:
Cash Investment: $75K
Total Investment: $200-350K
Minimum Net Worth: $100K
Fees: Franchise - $25K
Royalty - 6%; Ad. - 1%
Earnings Claims Statement: No
Term of Contract (Years): 10/
Avg. # Of Employees: 1 FT, 5-7 PT
Passive Ownership: Allowed
Encourage Conversions: No
Area Develop. Agreements: Yes/1
Sub-Franchising Contracts: Yes
Expand In Territory: Yes
Space Needs: 400-1,500 SF
SUPPORT & TRAINING:
Financial Assistance Provided: Yes (D)
Site Selection Assistance: Yes
Lease Negotiation Assistance: Yes
Co-Operative Advertising: No
Franchisee Assoc./Member: Yes/Yes
Size Of Corporate Staff: 10
On-Going Support: A,B,C,D,E,F,G,H,I
Training: 3 Weeks Corporate Training in Downtown Los Angeles, CA
SPECIFIC EXPANSION PLANS:

US:	All United States
Canada:	NR
Overseas:	NR

◄◄ ►►

TACOTIME
9311 E. Via De Ventura
Scottsdale, AZ 85258
Tel: (866) 4KAHALA (480) 362-4800
Fax: (480) 362-4792
E-Mail: rjjohnson@kahalacorp.com
Web Site: www.kahalacorp.com
Ms. Nicole Rayborn, Franchise Director

TacoTime continues to provide and improve our system for quick-service Mexican restaurants that have stood the test of time for 40 years. TacoTime quality, focus on customer service, franchisee support and existing new products make us the innovative leader of high-quality Mexican food.

BACKGROUND: IFA MEMBER
Established: 1960; 1st Franchised: 1962
Franchised Units: 170
Company-Owned Units: 0
Total Units: 170
Dist.: US-170; CAN-119; O'seas-6
   North America: 14 States, 0 Provinces
   Density: 46 in UT, 46 in OR, 26 in ID
Projected New Units (12 Months): 12
Qualifications: 5, 4, 3, 4, 5, 5
FINANCIAL/TERMS:
Cash Investment: $100K
Total Investment: $145-721.3K
Minimum Net Worth: $250K
Fees: Franchise - $30K
   Royalty - 6; Ad. - 4%
Earnings Claims Statement: No
Term of Contract (Years): 10/10
Avg. # Of Employees: 4-5 FT, 15 PT
Passive Ownership: Not Allowed
Encourage Conversions: Yes
Area Develop. Agreements: Yes
Sub-Franchising Contracts: Yes
Expand In Territory: Yes
Space Needs: 1,400-2,500 SF
SUPPORT & TRAINING:
Financial Assistance Provided: No
Site Selection Assistance: Yes
Lease Negotiation Assistance: Yes
Co-Operative Advertising: Yes
Franchisee Assoc./Member: Yes/Yes
Size Of Corporate Staff: 250
On-Going Support: ,,C,D,E,F,G,h,I
Training: 1 Week Scottsdale, AZ;
   1 Week Local Franchise
SPECIFIC EXPANSION PLANS:

US:	All United States
Canada:	Western Province
Overseas:	Master Licensing Agreement
	-- Asia

◄◄ ►►

THUNDERCLOUD SUBS
1102 W. Sixth St.
Austin, TX 78703
Tel: (800) 256-7895 (512) 479-8805
Fax: (512) 479-8806
E-Mail: thunder@onr.com
Web Site: www.thundercloud.com
Mr. David E. Cohen, Director of Franchising

Fresh, fast and healthy sub sandwiches, salads, soup, etc. in a casual atmosphere without the fast-food look. A distinctive trademark, system and product, each store having a unique decor that ties in to the local community. Definitely not a cookie cutter franchise. We train our people to capture the essence of the THUNDERCLOUD experience. The customer service and atmosphere play a large part in overall customer satisfaction. We offer a great value.

BACKGROUND:
Established: 1975; 1st Franchised: 1989
Franchised Units: 15
Company-Owned Units: 10
Total Units: 25
Dist.: US-25; CAN-0; O'seas-0
   North America: 2 States, 0 Provinces
   Density: 24 in TX
Projected New Units (12 Months): 8-12
Qualifications: 4, 4, 3, 3, 4, 5
FINANCIAL/TERMS:
Cash Investment: $25-50K
Total Investment: $60-100K
Minimum Net Worth: $100K
Fees: Franchise - $10K
   Royalty - 4%; Ad. - Varies
Earnings Claims Statement: No
Term of Contract (Years): 10+8/4/4/
Avg. # Of Employees: 2 FT, 6-12 PT
Passive Ownership: Discouraged
Encourage Conversions: Yes
Area Develop. Agreements: Yes/1
Sub-Franchising Contracts: No
Expand In Territory: Yes
Space Needs: 1,000-1,500 SF
SUPPORT & TRAINING:
Financial Assistance Provided: No
Site Selection Assistance: Yes
Lease Negotiation Assistance: Yes

Co-Operative Advertising: No
Franchisee Assoc./Member: No
Size Of Corporate Staff: 5
On-Going Support: ,,C,D,E,F,G,h,I
Training: 1-2 Weeks Corporate Headquarters in Austin; 5-10 Days Franchisee's Store
SPECIFIC EXPANSION PLANS:

US:	Primarily Southwest
Canada:	No
Overseas:	NR

◄◄ ►►

TOGO'S EATERY
18 N. San Pedro St.
San Jose, CA 95110
Tel: (800) 777-9983 (408) 280-6569
Fax: (866) 394-4902
E-Mail: franchisesales@togos.com
Web Site: www.togosfranchise.com
Ms. Lidia Larson, Franchise Sales Manager

Togo's was opened in Northern California in the early 1970s by a guy who didn't have a business plan. He just made reasonably priced sandwiches the way he liked them – made to order in a deli style format and stuffed with fresh, wholesome ingredients. Soon there were lines out the door and Togo's was well on its way to becoming California's most loved sandwich shop. Now, nearly 40 years later, Togo's is still crafting the best sandwiches, on the West Coast, with over 240 franchise restaurants serving over a million guests per month. Our bread is baked every day, especially for us, and we've added our own selection of hearty soups, fresh salads and specialty wraps worthy of the Togo's name.

BACKGROUND: IFA MEMBER
Established: 1971; 1st Franchised: 1977
Franchised Units: 237
Company-Owned Units: 6
Total Units: 243
Dist.: US-243; CAN-0; O'seas-0
   North America: 0 States, 0 Provinces
   Density: 239 in CA
Projected New Units (12 Months): 12
Qualifications: 5, 5, 4, 4, 4, 5
FINANCIAL/TERMS:
Cash Investment: $150K

Total Investment: $222-489K
Minimum Net Worth: $300K
Fees: Franchise - $40K
  Royalty - 5%;   Ad. - 2% currently, but can go up to 5%
Earnings Claims Statement: Yes
Term of Contract (Years): 20/
Avg. # Of Employees: 5 FT, 8 PT
Passive Ownership: Discouraged
Encourage Conversions: No
Area Develop. Agreements: Yes
Sub-Franchising Contracts: No
Expand In Territory: Yes
Space Needs: 1,200-1,400 SF

SUPPORT & TRAINING:
Financial Assistance Provided: No
Site Selection Assistance: Yes
Lease Negotiation Assistance: Yes
Co-Operative Advertising: Yes
Franchisee Assoc./Member: Yes/Yes
Size Of Corporate Staff: 24
On-Going Support: ,B,C,D,E,F,G,H,I
Training: 5 Weeks CA

SPECIFIC EXPANSION PLANS:
US: CA, WA, OR, NV, AZ
Canada: No
Overseas: NR

‹‹ ››

TOPPER'S PIZZA
333 W. Center St.
Whitewater, WI 53190
Tel: (888) 586-7737 (262) 473-6666
Fax: (262) 473-6697
E-Mail: siversen@toppers.com
Web Site: www.toppers.com
Mr. Scott Iversen, Director Franchise Sales

TOPPER'S PIZZA's vision is to provide customers with a unique, high-end pizza AND fast, free delivery. Our menu is superior because we use fresh, hand-prepared ingredients. We cut our own vegetables and sell only the highest-quality meats and real Wisconsin cheeses. We prepare our dough and sauce fresh, from scratch, in each store's kitchen. The cornerstone of our menu is variety. We have developed efficient systems that can be easily taught. Solid strategy and systematized business formula.

BACKGROUND: IFA MEMBER
Established: 1993; 1st Franchised: 2000
Franchised Units: 27
Company-Owned Units: 5
Total Units: 32
Dist.: US-32; CAN-0; O'seas-0
  North America: 3 States, 0 Provinces
  Density: 9 in WI, 3 in NC, 4 in MN
Projected New Units (12 Months): 6
Qualifications: 4, 3, 2, 2, 2, 5

FINANCIAL/TERMS:
Cash Investment: $75-125K
Total Investment: $258.6-422.9K
Minimum Net Worth: $350K
Fees: Franchise - $20K
  Royalty - 5%; Ad. - 1%
Earnings Claims Statement: Yes
Term of Contract (Years): 5/5
Avg. # Of Employees:5-10 FT, 20-30 PT
Passive Ownership: Discouraged
Encourage Conversions: Yes
Area Develop. Agreements: No
Sub-Franchising Contracts: No
Expand In Territory: Yes
Space Needs: 1,500 SF

SUPPORT & TRAINING:
Financial Assistance Provided: No
Site Selection Assistance: Yes
Lease Negotiation Assistance: Yes
Co-Operative Advertising: No
Franchisee Assoc./Member: Yes/Yes
Size Of Corporate Staff: 7
On-Going Support: A,B,C,D,E,F,G,H,I
Training: 30 Days Whitewater/Madison, WI

SPECIFIC EXPANSION PLANS:
US: WI,MN,IL,IA,IN,MI,OH,NC,SC
Canada: No
Overseas: NR

‹‹ ››

TROPICAL SMOOTHIE CAFE
4100 Legendary Dr., # 250
Destin, FL 32541
Tel: (888) 292-2522 (850) 269-9850
Fax: (850) 837-4563
E-Mail: scole@tropicalsmoothie.com
Web Site: www.tropicalsmoothie.com
Mr. Scott Cole, Director of Franchise Development

At Tropical Smoothie, we believe in serving only the highest quality products to create the ultimate refreshing nutritional beverage. We offer over 40 flavors of smoothies with exact recipes to create the perfect smoothie for everyone. In addition to smoothies we offer high quality gourmet wraps, sandwiches and specialty coffee.

BACKGROUND: IFA MEMBER
Established: 1997; 1st Franchised: 1997
Franchised Units: 270
Company-Owned Units: 1
Total Units: 271
Dist.: US-269; CAN-0; O'seas-2
  North America: 22 States, 0 Provinces
  Density: 15 in VA, 68 in FL
Projected New Units (12 Months): 55
Qualifications: 3, 4, 2, 2, 5, 5

FINANCIAL/TERMS:
Cash Investment: $70-80K
Total Investment: $249-380K
Minimum Net Worth: $100-150K
Fees: Franchise - $20K
  Royalty - 6%; Ad. - 1+2%
Earnings Claims Statement: No
Term of Contract (Years): 20/10
Avg. # Of Employees: 2 FT, 10 PT
Passive Ownership: Discouraged
Encourage Conversions: Yes
Area Develop. Agreements: Yes/30
Sub-Franchising Contracts: Yes
Expand In Territory: Yes
Space Needs: 1,600 SF

SUPPORT & TRAINING:
Financial Assistance Provided: Yes (D)
Site Selection Assistance: Yes
Lease Negotiation Assistance: Yes
Co-Operative Advertising: Yes
Franchisee Assoc./Member: No
Size Of Corporate Staff: 11
On-Going Support: A,B,C,D,E,F,G,H,I
Training: 2 Weeks Local Stores;
  1 Week Corporate Office; 1 Week Store Opening

SPECIFIC EXPANSION PLANS:
US: All United States
Canada: All Canada
Overseas: All Countries

‹‹ ››

TROPICANA SMOOTHIES, JUICES & MORE!
4175 Veterans Hwy., # 303
Ronkonkoma, NY 11779
Tel: (800) 528-0727 + 1
Fax: (631) 737-9792

E-Mail: joearancio@aol.com
Web Site: www.tropsmoothies.com
Mr. Joe Arancio, VP Business Development

TROPICANA SMOOTHIES, JUICES & MORE! is a co-branding concept with premium-quality smoothies, nationally-branded ice cream and frozen yogurt. Concept will be sold as exclusive Territory Development Agreements for markets with a minimum of 500,000 population, with a development commitment of 5 stores in 10 years for established food-service and retail owners/operators.

BACKGROUND:

Established: 1949; 1st Franchised: 2004	
Franchised Units:	8
Company-Owned Units:	2
Total Units:	10
Dist.:	US-10; CAN-0; O'seas-0
North America:	7 States, Provinces
Density:	2 in IL, 2 in NV
Projected New Units (12 Months):	12
Qualifications:	5, 5, 4, 4, 4, 5

FINANCIAL/TERMS:

Cash Investment:	$100-150K
Total Investment:	$175-225K/Unit
Minimum Net Worth:	$500K
Fees: Franchise -	$75K/Territory
Royalty - 6%;	Ad. - 1%
Earnings Claims Statement:	No
Term of Contract (Years):	10/10
Avg. # Of Employees:	3-4 FT, 2-4 PT
Passive Ownership:	Not Allowed
Encourage Conversions:	Yes
Area Develop. Agreements:	No
Sub-Franchising Contracts:	No
Expand In Territory:	Yes
Space Needs:	600-900 SF

SUPPORT & TRAINING:

Financial Assistance Provided:	No
Site Selection Assistance:	Yes
Lease Negotiation Assistance:	Yes
Co-Operative Advertising:	No
Franchisee Assoc./Member:	No
Size Of Corporate Staff:	100
On-Going Support:	,B,C,D,E,,G,H,I
Training:	Las Vegas, NV

SPECIFIC EXPANSION PLANS:

US:	All United States
Canada:	All Canada
Overseas:	NR

TUBBY'S SUB SHOPS
35807 Moravian
Clinton Township, MI 48035
Tel: (800) 752-0644 (586) 792-2369
Fax: (586) 792-4250
E-Mail: jennifer@tubby.com
Web Site: www.tubby.com
Ms. Jennifer Ciampa, Franchise Development Legal Asst.

Deli-style and grilled-to-perfection submarine sandwiches, along with soups, healthy salads, various side items, including fries and freshly-baked desserts and bread.

BACKGROUND:

Established: 1968; 1st Franchised: 1978	
Franchised Units:	70
Company-Owned Units:	2
Total Units:	72
Dist.:	US-72; CAN-0; O'seas-0
North America:	2 States, 0 Provinces
Density:	86 in MI, 1 in FL
Projected New Units (12 Months):	10
Qualifications:	5, 3, 2, 2, 3, 4

FINANCIAL/TERMS:

Cash Investment:	$75K
Total Investment:	$50-150K
Minimum Net Worth:	$500K
Fees: Franchise -	$12.5-15K
Royalty - 6%or $200/Wk.;	Ad. - 4%/$150/Wk.
Earnings Claims Statement:	Yes
Term of Contract (Years):	10/5
Avg. # Of Employees:	2-4 FT, 3-5 PT
Passive Ownership:	Allowed
Encourage Conversions:	Yes
Area Develop. Agreements:	Yes
Sub-Franchising Contracts:	No
Expand In Territory:	Yes
Space Needs:	1,200-1,500 SF

SUPPORT & TRAINING:

Financial Assistance Provided:	Yes (I)
Site Selection Assistance:	Yes
Lease Negotiation Assistance:	No
Co-Operative Advertising:	No
Franchisee Assoc./Member:	No
Size Of Corporate Staff:	15
On-Going Support:	A,b,C,D,E,,G,,I
Training:	3 Weeks/120 Hours Clinton Township, MI

SPECIFIC EXPANSION PLANS:

US:	Michigan Only
Canada:	No
Overseas:	NR

◄◄ ►►

VILLA PIZZA/COZZOLI'S
25 Washington St.
Morristown, NJ 07960
Tel: (973) 285-4800
Fax: (973) 401-0121
E-Mail: atorine@villaenterprises.com
Web Site: www.villaenterprises.com
Mr. Adam Torine, VP Business Development

Quick-service pizza and Italian restaurant chain, primarily located in regional malls and outlet centers either in food courts or in-line locations. We use only the freshest cheeses, seasonings, vegetables, homemade sauces and other ingredients.Our large, tantalizing food display offers customers a wide variety of homemade dishes.

BACKGROUND:

Established: 1964; 1st Franchised: 1999	
Franchised Units:	75
Company-Owned Units:	140
Total Units:	215
Dist.:	US-204; CAN-0; O'seas-11
North America:	38 States, 0 Provinces
Density:	23 in TX, 24 in FL, 12 in CA
Projected New Units (12 Months):	25
Qualifications:	4, 4, 5, 3, 3, 4

FINANCIAL/TERMS:

Cash Investment:	$80-100K
Total Investment:	$297-572K
Minimum Net Worth:	$300K
Fees: Franchise -	$25K
Royalty - 6%;	Ad. - 0%
Earnings Claims Statement:	Yes
Term of Contract (Years):	10/10
Avg. # Of Employees:	2 FT, 4-7 PT
Passive Ownership:	Not Allowed
Encourage Conversions:	Yes
Area Develop. Agreements:	Yes
Sub-Franchising Contracts:	No
Expand In Territory:	Yes
Space Needs:	650-2,500 SF

SUPPORT & TRAINING:

Financial Assistance Provided:	Yes (I)
Site Selection Assistance:	Yes
Lease Negotiation Assistance:	Yes
Co-Operative Advertising:	No
Franchisee Assoc./Member:	No
Size Of Corporate Staff:	45
On-Going Support:	,,C,D,E,F,G,,I
Training:	NR

SPECIFIC EXPANSION PLANS:

US:	All United States
Canada:	All Canada
Overseas:	England, Italy, Spain, Kuwait,

Russia

‹‹ ››

VIRGINIA BARBEQUE
1814 Country Rd.
Beaverdam, VA 23015
Tel: (800) 429-9965 (804) 448-9877
Fax: (804) 448-4611
E-Mail: rick@virginiabbq.com
Web Site: www.virginiabbq.com
Mr. Richard Ivery, President/CEO

Virginia Barbeque is a quick service restaurant franchise with the most simple systems for operating our restaurants. Our low initial investments and small (1,500 avg. sq. ft.) locations keep fixed costs down. Virginia Barbeque has been named as Best Barbeque in all regions we have locations, Richmond and Fredericksburg areas of Virginia.

BACKGROUND:

Established: 2000;	1st Franchised: 2004
Franchised Units:	6
Company-Owned Units:	1
Total Units:	7
Dist.:	US-7; CAN-0; O'seas-0
North America:	1 States, 0 Provinces
Density:	7 in VA
Projected New Units (12 Months):	NR
Qualifications:	3, 3, 3, 3, 3, 3

FINANCIAL/TERMS:

Cash Investment:	$25K
Total Investment:	$36-202K
Minimum Net Worth:	$125K
Fees: Franchise -	$15K
Royalty - 6%;	Ad. - 2%
Earnings Claims Statement:	No
Term of Contract (Years):	10/5
Avg. # Of Employees:	4 FT, 3 PT
Passive Ownership:	Discouraged
Encourage Conversions:	NA
Area Develop. Agreements:	No
Sub-Franchising Contracts:	Yes
Expand In Territory:	Yes
Space Needs:	1,200-1,500 SF

SUPPORT & TRAINING:

Financial Assistance Provided:	No
Site Selection Assistance:	Yes
Lease Negotiation Assistance:	Yes
Co-Operative Advertising:	No
Franchisee Assoc./Member:	No

Size Of Corporate Staff:	3
On-Going Support:	,B,C,D,E,,G,H,I
Training:	2 Weeks Richmond, VA

SPECIFIC EXPANSION PLANS:

US:	All United States
Canada:	No
Overseas:	NR

‹‹ ››

VOCELLI PIZZA
1005 S. Bee St.
Pittsburgh, PA 15220
Tel: (800) VOCELLI + 26 (412) 919-2100
Fax: (412) 937-9204
E-Mail: bmontanari@vocellipizza.com
Web Site: www.vocellipizza.com
Mr. Bob Montanari, VP Franchising

VOCELLI PIZZA provides delivery and carry-out service of pizza, subs, wings, breadsticks and drinks. Streamlined operations and a compact menu provide for low start-up costs and ease of operation. On-going support at every level is provided, including a marketing effort with a national focus.

BACKGROUND:

Established: 1988;	1st Franchised: 1993
Franchised Units:	137
Company-Owned Units:	23
Total Units:	160
Dist.:	US-160; CAN-0; O'seas-0
North America:	5 States, 0 Provinces
Density:	6 in WV, 11 in VA, 83 in PA
Projected New Units (12 Months):	15
Qualifications:	5, 4, 4, 2, 2, 4

FINANCIAL/TERMS:

Cash Investment:	$49-75K
Total Investment:	$113-233K
Minimum Net Worth:	$75K
Fees: Franchise -	$15K
Royalty - 4%;	Ad. - 1%
Earnings Claims Statement:	Yes
Term of Contract (Years):	10/5
Avg. # Of Employees:	8 FT, 12 PT
Passive Ownership:	Not Allowed
Encourage Conversions:	Yes
Area Develop. Agreements:	Yes/1
Sub-Franchising Contracts:	No
Expand In Territory:	Yes
Space Needs:	1,200 SF

SUPPORT & TRAINING:

Financial Assistance Provided:	No
Site Selection Assistance:	Yes
Lease Negotiation Assistance:	No
Co-Operative Advertising:	No
Franchisee Assoc./Member:	No

Size Of Corporate Staff:	38
On-Going Support:	,B,C,D,E,F,G,H,I
Training:	4 Weeks Corporate Office;
	1 Week On-Site during Opening

SPECIFIC EXPANSION PLANS:

US:	OH, PA, WV, VA
Canada:	No
Overseas:	NR

‹‹ ››

WE'RE ROLLING PRETZEL COMPANY
P. O. Box 6106, 2500 W. State St.
Alliance, OH 44601
Tel: (888) 549-7655 (330) 823-0575
Fax: (330) 821-8908
E-Mail: kkrabill@wererolling.com
Web Site: www.wererolling.com
Mr. Kevin Krabill, President

WE'RE ROLLING PRETZEL COMPANY offers fresh, hand-made soft pretzels, pretzel rods, pretzel sandwiches and a variety of beverages. By serving an expanded menu, creating a strong system to open and operate stores, and recruiting, training, and supporting dedicated franchisees, WE'RE ROLLING PRETZEL COMPANY can effectively meet the needs of a variety of customers.

BACKGROUND: IFA MEMBER

Established: 1996;	1st Franchised: 2000
Franchised Units:	47
Company-Owned Units:	8
Total Units:	55
Dist.:	US-55; CAN-0; O'seas-0
North America:	6 States, 0 Provinces
Density:	5 in PA, 37 in OH, 6 in KY
Projected New Units (12 Months):	15
Qualifications:	3, 3, 3, 2, 2, 5

FINANCIAL/TERMS:

Cash Investment:	$20-50K
Total Investment:	$65-154K
Minimum Net Worth:	$100K
Fees: Franchise -	$15K
Royalty - 5%;	Ad. - 1%
Earnings Claims Statement:	No
Term of Contract (Years):	5/5
Avg. # Of Employees:	3 FT, 3 PT
Passive Ownership:	Allowed
Encourage Conversions:	Yes
Area Develop. Agreements:	Yes/5
Sub-Franchising Contracts:	No
Expand In Territory:	Yes
Space Needs:	400-1,000 SF

SUPPORT & TRAINING:

Financial Assistance Provided: No
Site Selection Assistance: Yes
Lease Negotiation Assistance: Yes
Co-Operative Advertising: No
Franchisee Assoc./Member: Yes/Yes
Size Of Corporate Staff: 5
On-Going Support: „C,D,E,F,G,H,I
Training: 1 Week On-Site; 4 Days Corporate Store; 3 Days Corporate Office

SPECIFIC EXPANSION PLANS:

US: All United States
Canada: No
Overseas: NR

‹‹ ››

WIENERSCHNITZEL / TASTEE FREEZ

4440 Von Karman Ave., # 222
Newport Beach, CA 92660
Tel: (949) 851-2619
Fax:
E-Mail: kpeters@galardigroup.com
Web Site: www.wienerschnitzel.com
Mr. Ken Peters,

WIENERSCHNITZEL is the world's largest quick service hot dog restaurant chain with over 350 locations selling 90 million hot dogs annually. Wienerschnitzel new franchise licenses are available in most areas of CA, OR, WA, AZ, NV, NM, UT and TX. Other Western states will be considered for development, if the prospective franchisee has a market development plan approved by Galardi Group Franchise. Other geographical areas in which Wienerschnitzel has an existing presence will be considered on a case by case basis.

BACKGROUND: IFA MEMBER

Established: 1961; 1st Franchised: 1965
Franchised Units: 371
Company-Owned Units: 0
Total Units: 371
Dist.: US-370; CAN-0; O'seas-1
  North America: 11 States, 0 Provinces
  Density: 51 in TX, 228 in CA, 14 in AZ
Projected New Units (12 Months): 20
Qualifications: 4, 3, 3, 2, 1, 4

FINANCIAL/TERMS:

Cash Investment: $100K

Total Investment: $135K-1.2MM
Minimum Net Worth: $1MM
Fees: Franchise - $32K
  Royalty - 5%; Ad. - 3-5%
Earnings Claims Statement: No
Term of Contract (Years): 20/1-20
Avg. # Of Employees: 1-3 FT, 15-30 PT
Passive Ownership: Discouraged
Encourage Conversions: Yes
Area Develop. Agreements: No
Sub-Franchising Contracts: No
Expand In Territory: Yes
Space Needs: 20,000 SF

SUPPORT & TRAINING:

Financial Assistance Provided: No
Site Selection Assistance: Yes
Lease Negotiation Assistance: No
Co-Operative Advertising: Yes
Franchisee Assoc./Member: Yes/Yes
Size Of Corporate Staff: 48
On-Going Support: A,B,C,D,E,F,G,H,I
Training: NR

SPECIFIC EXPANSION PLANS:

US: SW, W, NW
Canada: No
Overseas: NR

‹‹ ››

WILLIAMS CHICKEN

2831 E. Ledbetter Dr.
Dallas, TX 75216
Tel: (214) 371-1430 + 304
Fax: (214) 372-4231
E-Mail: twilliams@williamsfriedchicken.com
Web Site: www.williamsfriedchicken.com
Mr. Tim Williams, Director of Franchising

Quick-service restaurant- Fried chicken

BACKGROUND:

Established: 1987; 1st Franchised: 1990
Franchised Units: 40
Company-Owned Units: 12
Total Units: 52
Dist.: US-52; CAN-0; O'seas-0
  North America: 0 States, 0 Provinces
  Density: 50 in TX, 1 in MS, 1 in LA
Projected New Units (12 Months): NR
Qualifications: 3, 3, 3, 3, 3, 3

FINANCIAL/TERMS:

Cash Investment: $150-200K
Total Investment: $400-600K
Minimum Net Worth: $200K
Fees: Franchise - $25K
  Royalty - 5%; Ad. - 3%
Earnings Claims Statement: Yes
Term of Contract (Years): 10/10

Avg. # Of Employees: 5 FT, 4 PT
Passive Ownership: Discouraged
Encourage Conversions: NA
Area Develop. Agreements: Yes/3
Sub-Franchising Contracts: No
Expand In Territory: Yes
Space Needs: 3,500-4,000 SF

SUPPORT & TRAINING:

Financial Assistance Provided: No
Site Selection Assistance: Yes
Lease Negotiation Assistance: Yes
Co-Operative Advertising: Yes
Franchisee Assoc./Member: No
Size Of Corporate Staff: 6
On-Going Support: ,B,C,D,,F,,H,
Training: 6 Weeks Dallas, TX

SPECIFIC EXPANSION PLANS:

US: TX, LA, AL, MS
Canada: No
Overseas: NR

‹‹ ››

WING ZONE

900 Circle 75 Pkwy., # 930
Atlanta, GA 30339
Tel: (877) 333-9464 + 16 (404) 875-5045 + 16
Fax: (404) 875-6631
E-Mail: clint@wingzone.com
Web Site: www.wingzone.com
Mr. Clint Lee, Director of Franchise Development

Delivery & Take-out of 15 taste-tempting flavors of fresh, cooked-to-order Buffalo wings. We also feature chicken fingers, grilled or fried chicken sandwiches, half-pound burgers, salads, sides, appetizers and desserts -- all delivered hot and fresh to your door. A great opportunity in urban and suburban markets, near apartments, campuses, military bases, hospitals and offices.

BACKGROUND: IFA MEMBER

Established: 1991; 1st Franchised: 1999
Franchised Units: 96
Company-Owned Units: 4
Total Units: 100
Dist.: US-95; CAN-0; O'seas-5
  North America: 24 States, 0 Provinces
  Density: 10 in NC, 10 in VA, 18 in FL
Projected New Units (12 Months): 24
Qualifications: 5, 5, 3, 4, 3, 5

FINANCIAL/TERMS:

Cash Investment:	$100K
Total Investment:	$246-317K
Minimum Net Worth:	$250
Fees: Franchise -	$25K
Royalty - 5%;	Ad. - 2%
Earnings Claims Statement:	Yes
Term of Contract (Years):	10/10
Avg. # Of Employees:	5 FT, 10 PT
Passive Ownership:	Not Allowed
Encourage Conversions:	No
Area Develop. Agreements:	Yes/10
Sub-Franchising Contracts:	No
Expand In Territory:	Yes
Space Needs:	1,200 SF

SUPPORT & TRAINING:

Financial Assistance Provided:	Yes (I)
Site Selection Assistance:	Yes
Lease Negotiation Assistance:	Yes
Co-Operative Advertising:	No
Franchisee Assoc./Member:	Yes/Yes
Size Of Corporate Staff:	15
On-Going Support:	A,B,C,D,E,F,G,H,I
Training:	21 Days Atlanta, GA

SPECIFIC EXPANSION PLANS:

US:	SE, NE, MW, SW
Canada:	Near Border
Overseas:	NR

◄◄ ►►

WINGSTOP RESTAURANTS
1101 E. Arapaho Rd., # 150
Richardson, TX 75081
Tel: (972) 686-6500
Fax: (972) 686-6502
E-Mail: bruce@wingstop.com
Web Site: www.wingstop.com
Mr. Bruce Evans, Sr. Dir. Franchise Sales

The Arlington Morning News wrote: ' With the somewhat rough-and-ready air of an early century barnstormers' aircraft hanger, WINGSTOP treads the line between neighborhood hang and a casual, laid-back dinner-snack spot. The place's signature chicken wings, however, are righteously assertive, distinctive and anything but bland . . .' WINGSTOP is fun! WINGSTOP is focused! WINGSTOP is growing fast!

BACKGROUND: IFA MEMBER

Established: 1994;	1st Franchised: 1998
Franchised Units:	270

Company-Owned Units:	0
Total Units:	270
Dist.:	US-270; CAN-0; O'seas-0
North America:	13 States, 0 Provinces
Density:	in TX, in LA, in FL
Projected New Units (12 Months):	90
Qualifications:	2, 3, 2, 2, 1, 5

FINANCIAL/TERMS:

Cash Investment:	$60-70K
Total Investment:	$250K
Minimum Net Worth:	$100K
Fees: Franchise -	$20K
Royalty - 5%;	Ad. - 2%
Earnings Claims Statement:	Yes
Term of Contract (Years):	10/10
Avg. # Of Employees:	2 FT, 4 PT
Passive Ownership:	Discouraged
Encourage Conversions:	NA
Area Develop. Agreements:	No
Sub-Franchising Contracts:	No
Expand In Territory:	Yes
Space Needs:	1,200-1,500 SF

SUPPORT & TRAINING:

Financial Assistance Provided:	Yes (D)
Site Selection Assistance:	Yes
Lease Negotiation Assistance:	Yes
Co-Operative Advertising:	No
Franchisee Assoc./Member:	Yes/Yes
Size Of Corporate Staff:	16
On-Going Support:	A,B,C,D,E,,,H,
Training:	2 Weeks Corporate Store;
	1 Week Franchise Store

SPECIFIC EXPANSION PLANS:

US:	All United States
Canada:	All Canada
Overseas:	All Countries

◄◄ ►►

WORLDLY WRAPS
1814 Franklin St., # 820
Oakland, CA 94612
Tel: (510) 839-5462
Fax: (510) 839-2104
E-Mail: kristy@worldfranchising.com
Web Site: www.worldfranchising.com
Ms. Peyton F. Hamilton, President

Truly the world's best wraps! 17 different varieties. Also, smoothies and health drinks. Low start-up cost. Exceptional training and on-going support. This is a new market that has not yet been tapped. Take advantage of our concept and our growth program. Option to expand within territory.

BACKGROUND:

Established: 1994;	1st Franchised: 1995
Franchised Units:	24

Company-Owned Units:	6
Total Units:	30
Dist.:	US-30; CAN-0; O'seas-0
North America:	6 States, 0 Provinces
Density:	4 in TN, 10 in KY, 2 in IN
Projected New Units (12 Months):	4
Qualifications:	NR

FINANCIAL/TERMS:

Cash Investment:	$90-120K
Total Investment:	$200-280K
Minimum Net Worth:	$100K
Fees: Franchise -	$19.5K
Royalty - 6%;	Ad. - 1%
Earnings Claims Statement:	No
Term of Contract (Years):	10/10
Avg. # Of Employees:	2 FT, 8 PT
Passive Ownership:	Not Allowed
Encourage Conversions:	Yes
Area Develop. Agreements:	Yes/1
Sub-Franchising Contracts:	No
Expand In Territory:	No
Space Needs:	3,000-4,000 SF

SUPPORT & TRAINING:

Financial Assistance Provided:	Yes (D)
Site Selection Assistance:	Yes
Lease Negotiation Assistance:	Yes
Co-Operative Advertising:	No
Franchisee Assoc./Member:	NR
Size Of Corporate Staff:	21
On-Going Support:	A,B,C,D,E,F,G,H,I
Training:	8 Weeks Headquarters;
	3 Weeks Pre-Opening

SPECIFIC EXPANSION PLANS:

US:	South, Southeast
Canada:	No
Overseas:	NR

◄◄ ►►

Z PIZZA
50 Newport Center Dr., # 630
Newport Beach, CA 92660
Tel: (800) 422-2435 (949) 719-3800
Fax: (949) 721-4053
E-Mail: zpizza@zpizza.com
Web Site: www.zpizza.com
Mr. Chris Bright, President

Gourmet pizza, pasta, salads and sandwiches in a very up-scale California style. 1,000 square feet seating for 20 to 50 guests. Start-up costs under $150,000. Over 50 units in development.

BACKGROUND:

Established: 1986;	1st Franchised: 1997
Franchised Units:	10
Company-Owned Units:	12
Total Units:	22
Dist.:	US-22; CAN-0; O'seas-0

North America: 4 States, Provinces
Density: in CA, in NV
Projected New Units (12 Months): 15
Qualifications: 4, 4, 4, 2, 4, 4

FINANCIAL/TERMS:

Cash Investment: $50K
Total Investment: $150K
Minimum Net Worth: $50K
Fees: Franchise - $25K
Royalty - 5%; Ad. - 1%
Earnings Claims Statement: No
Term of Contract (Years): 20/10
Avg. # Of Employees: 3 FT, 10 PT
Passive Ownership: Allowed
Encourage Conversions: Yes
Area Develop. Agreements: Yes/1
Sub-Franchising Contracts: No
Expand In Territory: Yes
Space Needs: 1,000 SF

SUPPORT & TRAINING:

Financial Assistance Provided: Yes (D)
Site Selection Assistance: Yes
Lease Negotiation Assistance: Yes
Co-Operative Advertising: No
Franchisee Assoc./Member: No
Size Of Corporate Staff: 5
On-Going Support: ,B,C,D,E,F,G,H,I
Training: Orange County, CA

SPECIFIC EXPANSION PLANS:

US: All United States
Canada: All Canada
Overseas: NR

≪ ≫

ZERO'S SUBS
620 N. Brand Blvd., # 405
Glendale, CA 91203
Tel: (800) 588-0782 (818) 545-9130
Fax: (818) 545-9132
E-Mail: zeros@zeros.com
Web Site: www.zeros.com
Ms. Elizabeth Fitzpatrick, Director of
Operations

Zero's Subs is a fast casual franchise which offers high quality foods such as hot oven-baked subs, chicken wings, pizza, salads and wraps. Zero's provides unparalleled support to build your business: assistance with site selection, lease negotiation, build-out, operations, marketing, training and education.

BACKGROUND: IFA MEMBER

Established: 1967; 1st Franchised: 1994
Franchised Units: 70
Company-Owned Units: 0
Total Units: 70
Dist.: US-70; CAN-0; O'seas-0
North America: 11 States, 0 Provinces
Density: 6 in CA, 6 in NC, 43 in VA
Projected New Units (12 Months): 20
Qualifications: 4, 4, 3, 3, 3, 5

FINANCIAL/TERMS:

Cash Investment: $100K
Total Investment: $150-250K
Minimum Net Worth: $250K
Fees: Franchise - $20K
Royalty - 5%; Ad. - 2%
Earnings Claims Statement: No
Term of Contract (Years): 15/15
Avg. # Of Employees: 1 FT, 2 PT
Passive Ownership: Discouraged
Encourage Conversions: Yes
Area Develop. Agreements: Yes/25
Sub-Franchising Contracts: Yes
Expand In Territory: Yes
Space Needs: 1,500 SF

SUPPORT & TRAINING:

Financial Assistance Provided: Yes (I)
Site Selection Assistance: Yes
Lease Negotiation Assistance: Yes
Co-Operative Advertising: No
Franchisee Assoc./Member: No
Size Of Corporate Staff: 8
On-Going Support: ,,C,d,E,F,G,,I
Training:2 Weeks Franchisee's New Store;
2 Weeks Virginia Beach, VA or CA

SPECIFIC EXPANSION PLANS:

US: West Coast, East Coast, SW
Canada: All Canada
Overseas: Asia, Europe

≪ ≫

ZOUP! FRESH SOUP COMPANY
28290 Franklin Rd.
Southfield, MI 48034
Tel: (888) 778-7687 (248) 663-1111
Fax: (248) 663-9880
E-Mail: franchise@zoup.com
Web Site: www.zoup.com
Mr. Richard Zimmer, Franchise Department

ZOUP! FRESH SOUP COMPANY, named one of Inc. Magazine's '500 fastest-growing companies,' is the country's leading quick-casual soup restaurant - defining the category with its fresh, handcrafted and all-natural soups, sandwiches and salads. Best known for 'taking soup to the next level,' ZOUP! has used its 'everything matters' philosophy to build the state-of-the-art infrastructure, systems and support programs that make franchisees successful. Offering geographic areas to motivated people.

BACKGROUND: IFA MEMBER

Established: 1997; 1st Franchised: 2003
Franchised Units: 12
Company-Owned Units: 7
Total Units: 19
Dist.: US-19; CAN-0; O'seas-0
North America: 3 States, 0 Provinces
Density: 14 in MI
Projected New Units (12 Months): 12
Qualifications: 4, 4, 2, 3, 4, 5

FINANCIAL/TERMS:

Cash Investment: $150-300K
Total Investment: $192.5-381K
Minimum Net Worth: $300K
Fees: Franchise - $25K
Royalty - 5%; Ad. - 1%
Earnings Claims Statement: Yes
Term of Contract (Years): 10/5
Avg. # Of Employees: 6 FT, 6 PT
Passive Ownership: Discouraged
Encourage Conversions: Yes
Area Develop. Agreements: Yes/1
Sub-Franchising Contracts: No
Expand In Territory: Yes
Space Needs: 2,000 SF

SUPPORT & TRAINING:

Financial Assistance Provided: Yes (I)
Site Selection Assistance: Yes
Lease Negotiation Assistance: Yes
Co-Operative Advertising: Yes
Franchisee Assoc./Member: No
Size Of Corporate Staff: 8
On-Going Support: A,B,C,D,E,F,G,H,I
Training: 1-2 Days Corporte Office;
1 Week More New-Site Opening; 10-
14 Days Training Store

SPECIFIC EXPANSION PLANS:

US: MI, OH, IL, PA, IN, WI, NJ, IA, MO, MN
Canada: No
Overseas: NR

≪ ≫

ZYNG ASIAN GRILL
P.O. Box 72108
Montreal, QC H3J 226 Canada
Tel: (888) EAT-ZYNG (514) 288-8800

Fax: (514) 939-8808
E-Mail: info@zyng.com
Web Site: www.zyng.com
Mr. Chris Kassab, Director of Operations

Zyng Asian Grill is a fun-filled full service restaurant serving pan-Asian food. We offer healthy and flavorful dishes that tend to focus on a larger portion of vegetables. Our Asian Market Bowl allows the guest to create their own meal from start to finish.

BACKGROUND:

Established: 1998;	1st Franchised: 1999
Franchised Units:	12
Company-Owned Units:	0
Total Units:	12
Dist.:	US-0; CAN-4; O'seas-0

North America:	0 States, 0 Provinces
Density:	3 in QC, 2 in ON, 2 in NC
Projected New Units (12 Months):	NR
Qualifications:	3, 3, 3, 3, 3, 3

FINANCIAL/TERMS:

Cash Investment:	$150-300K
Total Investment:	$300K-500K
Minimum Net Worth:	NR
Fees: Franchise -	$25K
Royalty - 5-6%;	Ad. - 1-2%
Earnings Claims Statement:	No
Term of Contract (Years):	10/5
Avg. # Of Employees:	NR
Passive Ownership:	Discouraged
Encourage Conversions:	NA
Area Develop. Agreements:	Yes/5
Sub-Franchising Contracts:	Yes

Expand In Territory:	Yes
Space Needs:	3,000 SF

SUPPORT & TRAINING:

Financial Assistance Provided:	No
Site Selection Assistance:	Yes
Lease Negotiation Assistance:	Yes
Co-Operative Advertising:	Yes
Franchisee Assoc./Member:	Yes/Yes
Size Of Corporate Staff:	4
On-Going Support:	,,C,D,E,,,,I
Training:	NR

SPECIFIC EXPANSION PLANS:

US:	All United States
Canada:	No
Overseas:	NR

<< >>

FIVE LARGEST PARTICIPANTS IN SURVEY

Company	# Fran-chised Units	# Co-Owned Units	# Total Units	Franchise Fee	On-Going Royalty	Total Investment
1. Dairy Queen	5,900	70	5,970	$20-35K	4-6%	$345K-1.6M
2. Baskin-Robbins	4,700	0	4,700	$40K	5-5.9%	$145.7-527.8K
3. Cold Stone Creamery	1,221	44	1,265	$42K	6%	$294.3-438.9K
4. Yogen Fruz Canada Limited	1,100	1	1,101	$25K	6%	$150-280K
5. TCBY	900	0	900	$25K	4%	$142-347.2K

All of the data provided are proprietary and should not be quoted without acknowledging *Bond's Franchise Guide*.

ALL AMERICAN DELI & ICE CREAM SHOPS
812 SW Washington St., # 1100
Portland, OR 97205-3222
Tel: (800) 311-3930 (503) 224-6199
Fax: (503) 224-5042
E-Mail: franchise@allamericanrestaurants.com
Web Site: www.allamericanrestaurants.com
Mr. Barry McVay, Franchise Development Manager

Multi-concept franchise for better utilization of labor and overhead expenses with higher unit volumes vs. single product QSRs. Majority of stores located in regional malls. Upscale interior design.

Choose deli, ice cream or specialty coffee - one, two or three concepts - all under one simple franchise and one investment structure.

BACKGROUND:
Established: 1986; 1st Franchised: 1987
Franchised Units: 36
Company-Owned Units: 0
Total Units: 36
Dist.:   US-36; CAN-0; O'seas-0
 North America: 6 States, 0 Provinces
 Density: 5 in WA, 14 in OR, 3 in NV
Projected New Units (12 Months):   6
Qualifications: 4, 4, 2, 4, 3, 5
FINANCIAL/TERMS:
Cash Investment: $50-90K
Total Investment: $131K-396K

Minimum Net Worth: $250K
Fees: Franchise - $25K
 Royalty - 5%;   Ad. - 1%
Earnings Claims Statement: No
Term of Contract (Years):   10/10
Avg. # Of Employees: 1 FT, 5 PT
Passive Ownership: Discouraged
Encourage Conversions: Yes
Area Develop. Agreements: Yes/1
Sub-Franchising Contracts: No
Expand In Territory: Yes
Space Needs: 1,400 SF
SUPPORT & TRAINING:
Financial Assistance Provided: Yes (D)
Site Selection Assistance: Yes
Lease Negotiation Assistance: Yes
Co-Operative Advertising: No
Franchisee Assoc./Member: Yes/Yes

Size Of Corporate Staff: 4
On-Going Support: ,B,C,D,E,F,G,,I
Training: 1 Week Corporate Office
    Portland, OR; 2 Weeks Onsite (Store)
SPECIFIC EXPANSION PLANS:
US: West and Inter-Mountain States Only
Canada: No
Overseas: NR

◄◄ ►►

BAHAMA BUCK'S ORIGINAL SHAVED ICE CO.

465 E. Chilton Dr., # 5
Chandler, AZ 85225
Tel: (480) 539-6952
Fax: (480) 539-6953
E-Mail: azlee1@aol.com
Web Site: www.bahamabucks.com
Mr. Blake Buchanan, President

BAHAMA BUCK'S offers a unique, low-cost opportunity for anyone interested in a fun, family oriented business. We concentrate on offering quality products and great customer service. Set in a tropical atmosphere, BAHAMA BUCK'S offers 61 flavors of soft, creamy shaved ice, plus over 14 non-alcoholic tropical drinks. Store layouts and sizes vary and are extremely flexible, but typically range from 1200-1500 square feet.

BACKGROUND:
Established: 1990; 1st Franchised: 1992
Franchised Units: 6
Company-Owned Units: 3
Total Units: 9
Dist.: US-9; CAN-0; O'seas-0
    North America: 2 States, 0 Provinces
    Density: 5 in TX, 5 in AZ
Projected New Units (12 Months): 6
Qualifications: 4, 3, 1, 3, 4, 4
FINANCIAL/TERMS:
Cash Investment: $35K
Total Investment: $60-140K
Minimum Net Worth: $120K
Fees: Franchise - $15K
    Royalty - 6%; Ad. - 1%
Earnings Claims Statement: No
Term of Contract (Years): 10/10
Avg. # Of Employees: 1 FT, 12 PT
Passive Ownership: Allowed
Encourage Conversions: Yes
Area Develop. Agreements: Yes/1
Sub-Franchising Contracts: No
Expand In Territory: Yes
Space Needs: 1,000-1,500 SF
SUPPORT & TRAINING:
Financial Assistance Provided: Yes (D)

Site Selection Assistance: Yes
Lease Negotiation Assistance: Yes
Co-Operative Advertising: No
Franchisee Assoc./Member: No
Size Of Corporate Staff: 5
On-Going Support: ,B,C,d,E,,G,H,I
Training: 60-80 Hours Tempe, AZ;
    2 Days On-Site
SPECIFIC EXPANSION PLANS:
US: Southwest, South
Canada: No
Overseas: NR

◄◄ ►►

BASKIN-ROBBINS

130 Royall St.
Canton, MA 02021
Tel: (800) 777-9983 (818) 996-9361
Fax: (818) 996-5163
E-Mail: franchiseinfo@dunkinbrands.com
Web Site: www.dunkinbrandsfranchising.com
Mr. James Franks, Director of Franchising

BASKIN-ROBBINS develops, operates and franchises retail stores that sell ice cream, frozen yogurt and other approved services. In some markets, BASKIN-ROBBINS, together with TOGO'S and/or DUNKIN' DONUTS, offers multiple brand combinations of the three brands. TOGO'S, BASKIN-ROBBINS and DUNKIN' DONUTS are all subsidiaries of Dunkin' Brands, Inc.

BACKGROUND: IFA MEMBER
Established: 1950; 1st Franchised: 1950
Franchised Units: 4700
Company-Owned Units: 0
Total Units: 4700
Dist.: US-2286; CAN-620; O'seas-1594
    North America: 41 States, 0 Provinces
    Density:181 in NY, 195 in IL, 554 in CA
Projected New Units (12 Months): 27
Qualifications: NR
FINANCIAL/TERMS:
Cash Investment: $100K
Total Investment: $145.7-527.8K
Minimum Net Worth: $300K
Fees: Franchise - $40K
    Royalty - 5-5.9%; Ad. - 5%
Earnings Claims Statement: Yes
Term of Contract (Years): 20/

Avg. # Of Employees: NA FT, 0 PT
Passive Ownership: Allowed
Encourage Conversions: No
Area Develop. Agreements: Yes/1
Sub-Franchising Contracts: No
Expand In Territory: Yes
Space Needs: NR
SUPPORT & TRAINING:
Financial Assistance Provided: Yes (D)
Site Selection Assistance: NA
Lease Negotiation Assistance: Yes
Co-Operative Advertising: No
Franchisee Assoc./Member: Yes/Yes
Size Of Corporate Staff: NR
On-Going Support: ,B,C,D,,,G,H,I
Training: 51 Days Randolph, MA;
    3.5 Days Another Location
SPECIFIC EXPANSION PLANS:
US: All Regions
Canada: All Canada
Overseas: All Countries

◄◄ ►►

BEN & JERRY'S

30 Community Dr.
South Burlington, VT 05403-6809
Tel: (802) 846-1500
Fax: (802) 846-1538
E-Mail: franchise.info@benjerry.com
Web Site: www.benjerry.com
Ms. Kim Fanus, Franchise Sales Coordinator

BEN & JERRY'S was started in 1978 in a renovated gas station in Burlington, VT, by childhood friends Ben Cohen and Jerry Greenfield. They soon became popular for their funky, chunky flavors, made from fresh Vermont milk and cream. The scoop shops feature a fun environment with a varied menu including cakes, gifts, baked goods and coffee drinks created from ice cream, frozen yogurt and sorbet flavors. Community involvement is an important element in being a successful BEN & JERRY'S franchisee.

BACKGROUND: IFA MEMBER
Established: 1978; 1st Franchised: 1981
Franchised Units: 750
Company-Owned Units: 7
Total Units: 757
Dist.: US-757; CAN-20; O'seas-200
    North America: 39 States, 5 Provinces
    Density: 22 in NY, 26 in FL, 50 in CA

Projected New Units (12 Months): 45
Qualifications: 5, 4, 5, 3, 4, 5
FINANCIAL/TERMS:
Cash Investment: $80K-120K
Total Investment: $175K-440K
Minimum Net Worth: $350K
Fees: Franchise - $32K
 Royalty - 3%; Ad. - 4%
Earnings Claims Statement: No
Term of Contract (Years): 10/10
Avg. # Of Employees: 2 FT, 10 PT
Passive Ownership: Not Allowed
Encourage Conversions: Yes
Area Develop. Agreements: Yes
Sub-Franchising Contracts: No
Expand In Territory: No
Space Needs: 1,000 SF
SUPPORT & TRAINING:
Financial Assistance Provided: Yes (I)
Site Selection Assistance: Yes
Lease Negotiation Assistance: Yes
Co-Operative Advertising: No
Franchisee Assoc./Member: Yes/Yes
Size Of Corporate Staff: 30
On-Going Support: „C,D,E,F,G,H,I
Training: 8 Days VT
SPECIFIC EXPANSION PLANS:
US: Various Markets
Canada: No
Overseas: Call International Division

⤶⤶ ⤷⤷

BRUSTER'S OLD-FASHIONED
ICE CREAM & YOGURT
730 Mulberry St.
Bridgewater, PA 15009
Tel: (724) 774-4250
Fax: (724) 774-0666
E-Mail: lori@brusters.net
Web Site: www.brusters.com
Ms. Lori Molnar, Franchise Development

BRUSTER'S ICE CREAM features fresh, delicious homemade ice cream which is made fresh daily on-site at each of our stores. Quality products and exceptional customer service are our main goals. Our products feature only the best ingredients - whole nuts, cherries and the best caramels and fudges. Homemade waffle cones are a great complement to our homemade ice cream.

BACKGROUND:
Established: 1989; 1st Franchised: 1993
Franchised Units: 85
Company-Owned Units: 4
Total Units: 89
Dist.: US-89; CAN-0; O'seas-0

North America: 8 States, 0 Provinces
 Density: 21 in PA, 2 in OH, 15 in GA
Projected New Units (12 Months): 30
Qualifications: 3, 2, 1, 1, 4, 4
FINANCIAL/TERMS:
Cash Investment: $150K
Total Investment: $150-761K
Minimum Net Worth: $None
Fees: Franchise - $30K
 Royalty - 5%; Ad. - Up to 3%
Earnings Claims Statement: No
Term of Contract (Years): 10/10/10/
Avg. # Of Employees: 2-3 FT, 25 PT
Passive Ownership: Discouraged
Encourage Conversions: No
Area Develop. Agreements: Yes/1
Sub-Franchising Contracts: No
Expand In Territory: Yes
Space Needs: 988 SF
SUPPORT & TRAINING:
Financial Assistance Provided: No
Site Selection Assistance: Yes
Lease Negotiation Assistance: Yes
Co-Operative Advertising: No
Franchisee Assoc./Member: No
Size Of Corporate Staff: 10
On-Going Support: ,B,C,D,E,,G,H,
Training: 4 Weeks Western PA or Atlanta, GA
SPECIFIC EXPANSION PLANS:
US: Eastern United States
Canada: No
Overseas: NR

⤶⤶ ⤷⤷

CARVEL CORPORATION
200 Glenridge Point Pkwy., # 200
Atlanta, GA 30342-1450
Tel: (800) 227-8353 (404) 255-3250
Fax: (404) 255-4978
E-Mail: spando@focusbrands.com
Web Site: www.carvel.com
Mr. D'Wayne Tanner, VP Franchise Sales/ Develop.

The nation's first retail ice cream franchise, CARVEL is the leading manufacturer of uniquely shaped ice cream cakes, and a leading provider of premium soft serve and hand-dipped ice cream products. Since the company's founding in 1934, CARVEL has become one of the best-loved and most recognized names in the industry. With products made fresh daily in the store, CARVEL has more than 540

franchised and foodservice locations, as well as its famous ice cream cakes in over 8,400 supermarket outlets.

BACKGROUND: IFA MEMBER
Established: 1934; 1st Franchised: 1950
Franchised Units: 512
Company-Owned Units: 20
Total Units: 532
Dist.: US-532; CAN-0; O'seas-34
 North America: 25 States, 0 Provinces
 Density: 211 in NY, 58 in NJ, 47 in FL
Projected New Units (12 Months): 60
Qualifications: 5, 5, 3, 3, 3, 5
FINANCIAL/TERMS:
Cash Investment: $100K
Total Investment: $230.6K-390.1K
Minimum Net Worth: $300K
Fees: Franchise - $30K
 Royalty - $1.93/Gal.; Ad. - $1.71/Gal.
Earnings Claims Statement: Yes
Term of Contract (Years): 20/
Avg. # Of Employees: 2 FT, 6 PT
Passive Ownership: Not Allowed
Encourage Conversions: Yes
Area Develop. Agreements: No
Sub-Franchising Contracts: No
Expand In Territory: Yes
Space Needs: 1,200-1,500 SF
SUPPORT & TRAINING:
Financial Assistance Provided: Yes (I)
Site Selection Assistance: Yes
Lease Negotiation Assistance: No
Co-Operative Advertising: Yes
Franchisee Assoc./Member: Yes/Yes
Size Of Corporate Staff: 100
On-Going Support: ,B,C,D,E,,G,H,I
Training: 10 Days Atlanta, GA
SPECIFIC EXPANSION PLANS:
US: All Exc.WA,OR,ID,UT,MT,WY,ND, SD,KS,MS,NM
Canada: All Canada
Overseas: South and Central America, Asia, Middle East, Europe

⤶⤶ ⤷⤷

COLD STONE CREAMERY
9311 E. Via De Ventura
Scottsdale, AZ 85258
Tel: (866) 452-4252 (480) 362-4800
Fax: (480) 362-4792
E-Mail: jgoldstein@kahalacorp.com
Web Site: www.coldstonecreamery.com

Ms. Tammi Hillier, Franchise Director

Welcome to a franchise opportunity that can only be described as delectable. Cold Stone Creamery was listed #14 overall and #1 in the ice cream and frozen desserts category on Entrepreneur magazine's 2007 "Franchise 500". It takes a very special person to be awarded a Cold Stone Creamery Franchise. That's because we consider our store owners our partners who will share in the continued success of Cold Stone Creamery. Our phenomenal success has only been possible because of our amazing franchisee community.

BACKGROUND: IFA MEMBER
Established: 1988;   1st Franchised: 1995
Franchised Units: 1221
Company-Owned Units: 44
Total Units: 1265
Dist.:   US-1265; CAN-6; O'seas-147
    North America: 47 States, 0 Provinces
    Density: 55 in AZ, 86 in FL, 278 in CA
Projected New Units (12 Months):   136
Qualifications: 2, 3, 1, 1, 3, 5
FINANCIAL/TERMS:
Cash Investment: $100K
Total Investment: $294.3K-438.9K
Minimum Net Worth: $125K
Fees: Franchise - $42K
    Royalty - 6%;   Ad. - 3%
Earnings Claims Statement: No
Term of Contract (Years):   10/5/5/5/
Avg. # Of Employees: 3 FT, 9 PT
Passive Ownership: Discouraged
Encourage Conversions: No
Area Develop. Agreements: No
Sub-Franchising Contracts: No
Expand In Territory: Yes
Space Needs: 1,000 SF
SUPPORT & TRAINING:
Financial Assistance Provided: No
Site Selection Assistance: Yes
Lease Negotiation Assistance: Yes
Co-Operative Advertising: Yes
Franchisee Assoc./Member: No
Size Of Corporate Staff: 250
On-Going Support: „C,D,E,,G,H,
Training: Combination of In-Store
    Training & at Headquarters Scottsdale,
    AZ
SPECIFIC EXPANSION PLANS:
US: All United States
Canada: All Canada
Overseas: All Countries

⋘   ⋙

CULVERS FROZEN CUSTARD
540 Water St.
Prairie du Sac, WI 53578
Tel: (608) 644-2130
Fax: (608) 644-2626
E-Mail: garyrudsinski@culvers.com
Web Site: www.culvers.com
Mr. Gary L. Rudsinski, Franchise Development Manager

The first Culver's opened on July 18, 1984 in Sauk City, Wisconsin, and paved the way for a truly unique quick-service restaurant. Craig Culver, his wife, Lea, and his parents, George and Ruth, set a heightened standard for quality and freshness. The Culver family believes that the "owner/operator" concept is the cornerstone for success. In a sense, the idea was for one entrepreneurial family - the Culver's - to help spawn many more individual entrepreneurs, each of whom would have ownership in and operate

BACKGROUND: IFA MEMBER
Established: 1984;   1st Franchised: 1987
Franchised Units: 394
Company-Owned Units: 8
Total Units: 402
Dist.:   US-402; CAN-0; O'seas-0
    North America: 15 States, 0 Provinces
    Density: 112 in WI, 45 in MN, 70 in IL
Projected New Units (12 Months):   40
Qualifications: 5, 3, 3, 3, 1, 5
FINANCIAL/TERMS:
Cash Investment: $300K-500K
Total Investment: $500K-2.9M
Minimum Net Worth: $700K
Fees: Franchise - $55K
    Royalty - 4%;   Ad. - 2%
Earnings Claims Statement: Yes
Term of Contract (Years):   15/10
Avg. # Of Employees: 18 FT, 52 PT
Passive Ownership: Not Allowed
Encourage Conversions: Yes
Area Develop. Agreements: No
Sub-Franchising Contracts: No
Expand In Territory: No
Space Needs: 3,700-5,300 SF
SUPPORT & TRAINING:
Financial Assistance Provided: No
Site Selection Assistance: Yes
Lease Negotiation Assistance: No
Co-Operative Advertising: No
Franchisee Assoc./Member: No

Size Of Corporate Staff: 98
On-Going Support: „C,D,E,F,G,H,
Training: 16 Weeks South Central, WI
SPECIFIC EXPANSION PLANS:
US: Midwest, TX, AZ
Canada: No
Overseas: NR

⋘   ⋙

DAIRY QUEEN
7505 Metro Blvd.
Minneapolis, MN 55439
Tel: (800) 285-8515 (952) 830-0200
Fax: (952) 830-0450
E-Mail: development@idq.com
Web Site: www.dairyqueen.com
Mr. Thomas Dambrine, Dir. Intl. Development

A subsidiary of Berkshire Hathaway, Inc., DAIRY QUEEN offers several franchise concepts and development programs from single unit to multi-unit agreements. Our concepts are designed for various location types -- from free-standing restaurants to regional shopping malls. With over sixty years and 6000 units we offer great experience and brand recognition.

BACKGROUND:
Established: 1940;   1st Franchised: 1940
Franchised Units: 5900
Company-Owned Units: 70
Total Units: 5970
Dist.:   US-5970; CAN-635; O'seas-294
    North America: 49 States, 12 Provinces
    Density: 629 in TX, 282 in OH, 287 in
IL
Projected New Units (12 Months):   100
Qualifications: 5, 4, 5, 3, NR, 4
FINANCIAL/TERMS:
Cash Investment: $345K-1.6M
Total Investment: $345K-1.6M
Minimum Net Worth: $750K
Fees: Franchise - $20-35K
    Royalty - 4-6%;   Ad. - 3-6%
Earnings Claims Statement: No
Term of Contract (Years):   20/10
Avg. # Of Employees: Varies
Passive Ownership: Allowed
Encourage Conversions: Yes
Area Develop. Agreements: Yes/1
Sub-Franchising Contracts: Yes

Expand In Territory: No
Space Needs: 40,000 SF
SUPPORT & TRAINING:
Financial Assistance Provided: No
Site Selection Assistance: Yes
Lease Negotiation Assistance: Yes
Co-Operative Advertising: No
Franchisee Assoc./Member: Yes/Yes
Size Of Corporate Staff: 470
On-Going Support: „C,D,E„G,H,I
Training: 4 Weeks Existing Restaurants;
1-2 Weeks Headquarters; 1-2 Weeks
On-Site
SPECIFIC EXPANSION PLANS:
US: All United States
Canada: BC, AB, ON
Overseas: Mexico

⧏ ⧐

DIPPIN' DOTS

1640 McCracken Blvd., # 100
Paducah, KY 42001
Tel: (270) 575-6990
Fax: (270) 575-6997
E-Mail: franchiseinfo@dippindots.com
Web Site: www.dippindots.com
Ms. Vanessa Reeves, Franchise Development Manager

DIPPIN' DOTS are those tiny beads of ice cream that are super-cold, creamy, and delicious. Here's your invitation to look at our exciting alternative to traditional ice cream, yogurt, and flavored ice products.

BACKGROUND: IFA MEMBER
Established: 1988; 1st Franchised: 1999
Franchised Units: 445
Company-Owned Units: 2
Total Units: 447
Dist.: US-447; CAN-0; O'seas-0
North America: 42 States, 0 Provinces
Density: 49 in TX, 29 in FL, 37 in CA
Projected New Units (12 Months): NR
Qualifications: 5, 4, 2, 3, 3, 5
FINANCIAL/TERMS:
Cash Investment: $80.4K-235.3K
Total Investment: $80.4K-235.3K
Minimum Net Worth: $250K
Fees: Franchise - $12.5K
Royalty - 4%; Ad. - .05%
Earnings Claims Statement: No
Term of Contract (Years): 5/5/5/
Avg. # Of Employees: 1 FT, 0 PT
Passive Ownership: Discouraged
Encourage Conversions: No
Area Develop. Agreements: No
Sub-Franchising Contracts: No
Expand In Territory: Yes

Space Needs: 800-1,400 SF
SUPPORT & TRAINING:
Financial Assistance Provided: No
Site Selection Assistance: Yes
Lease Negotiation Assistance: Yes
Co-Operative Advertising: No
Franchisee Assoc./Member: No
Size Of Corporate Staff: 15
On-Going Support: „C,D,E„G,H,
Training:2 Days On-Site; 3 Days Paducah, KY
SPECIFIC EXPANSION PLANS:
US: All United States
Canada: No
Overseas: NR

⧏ ⧐

HAPPY & HEALTHY PRODUCTS

1600 S. Dixie Hwy., # 200
Boca Raton, FL 33432
Tel: (800) 764-6114 (561) 367-0739 + 13
Fax: (561) 368-5267
E-Mail: franchiseinfo@happyandhealthy.com
Web Site: www.happyandhealthy.com
Ms. Susan Scotts, SVP Sales & Marketing

A low investment fun, flexible full or part-time home-based distribution business for the wholesale and retail sale of Fruitfull frozen fruit bars and other delicious novelties. Super Grand, Grand and Standard franchisees will receive complete training with 15-20 minimum initial accounts provided. Ranked #1 Franchise by Entrepreneur Magazine's 2006 Franchise 500 in Miscellaneous Food Businesses, we take no royalties and offer low overhead. No employees or previous sales experience necessary.

BACKGROUND: IFA MEMBER
Established: 1991; 1st Franchised: 1993
Franchised Units: 75
Company-Owned Units: 0
Total Units: 75
Dist.: US-75; CAN-2; O'seas-5
North America: 39 States, 0 Provinces
Density: 6 in TX, 6 in NJ, 7 in FL
Projected New Units (12 Months): 12
Qualifications: 3, 2, 2, 2, 4, 5
FINANCIAL/TERMS:
Cash Investment: $32-68K
Total Investment: $32-68K
Minimum Net Worth: NA

Fees: Franchise - $21K
Royalty - 0%; Ad. - $500/Yr.
Earnings Claims Statement: No
Term of Contract (Years): 10/5
Avg. # Of Employees: 1 FT, 1 PT
Passive Ownership: Discouraged
Encourage Conversions: No
Area Develop. Agreements: No
Sub-Franchising Contracts: No
Expand In Territory: Yes
Space Needs: NA
SUPPORT & TRAINING:
Financial Assistance Provided: No
Site Selection Assistance: NA
Lease Negotiation Assistance: NA
Co-Operative Advertising: No
Franchisee Assoc./Member: No
Size Of Corporate Staff: 10
On-Going Support: „C,D„F,G,H,I
Training: 1 or 2 Weeks Franchise MSA
SPECIFIC EXPANSION PLANS:
US: All Except MD,LA,ME,ND,SD
Canada: No
Overseas: NR

⧏ ⧐

ICE CREAM CHURN

210 Shields Ct.
Markham, ON L3R 8V2 Canada
Tel: (800) 528-0727 (905) 479-8762
Fax: (905) 479-3275
E-Mail: aaron@yogenfruz.com
Web Site: www.yogenfruz.com
Ms. Aaron Serruya, President

ICE CREAM CHURN's concept is to add an old-fashioned ice cream parlor within another existing location, such as delis, bakeries, video stores, convenience stores, truckstops. ICE CREAM CHURN sets up location, trains employees, installs exterior signs and supports location with on-going promotions and training. 32 flavors of ice cream and yogurt are available. Master franchise available. New mall kiosk also available!

BACKGROUND:
Established: 1973; 1st Franchised: 1979
Franchised Units: 470
Company-Owned Units: 0
Total Units: 470
Dist.: US-460; CAN-0; O'seas-10
North America: 32 States, 0 Provinces
Density: 117 in FL, 83 in AR, 42 in AL
Projected New Units (12 Months): 100
Qualifications: NR
FINANCIAL/TERMS:
Cash Investment: $5-35K

Total Investment: $5-35K
Minimum Net Worth: NR
Fees: Franchise - $5K
. Royalty - $1.40/Tub; Ad. - $0.25/Tub
Earnings Claims Statement: No
Term of Contract (Years): 10/5
Avg. # Of Employees: 1 FT, 0 PT
Passive Ownership: Allowed
Encourage Conversions: Yes
Area Develop. Agreements: No
Sub-Franchising Contracts: Yes
Expand In Territory: Yes
Space Needs: 135 SF

SUPPORT & TRAINING:
Financial Assistance Provided: Yes (D)
Site Selection Assistance: Yes
Lease Negotiation Assistance: Yes
Co-Operative Advertising: No
Franchisee Assoc./Member: No
Size Of Corporate Staff: 7
On-Going Support: ,,D,E,F,G,,I
Training: NR

SPECIFIC EXPANSION PLANS:
US: Seeking Master Franchisees
Canada: All Canada
Overseas: All Countries

<< >>

MAGGIEMOOS
1346 Oakbrook Dr., # 170
Norcross, GA 30093
Tel: (800) 949-8114 + 122 (410) 740-2100
+ 122
Fax: (410) 521-4310
E-Mail: franchiseinfo@nexcenfm.com
Web Site: www.maggiemoos.com
Mr. Marty Amschler, Dir. Intl. Development

Unique and exciting retail shop, featuring homemade, super-premium ice cream, non-fat ice cream, custom-made cones, sorbet, smoothies, plus a line of specialty merchandise. We make our ice cream fresh in the store and serve it in fresh- baked waffle cones. Featuring over 40 mix-ins and folded in on a frozen granite mixing table to create 1,000s of great combos. Association with a marketable spokes character - MAGGIE MOO - in a fun, contemporary store design.

BACKGROUND: IFA MEMBER
Established: 1996; 1st Franchised: 1996
Franchised Units: 172
Company-Owned Units: 0
Total Units: 172
Dist.: US-168; CAN-0; O'seas-4
North America: 35 States, 0 Provinces
Density: 13 in NJ, 13 in MD, 16 in VA
Projected New Units (12 Months): 30
Qualifications: 4, 5, 3, 2, 3, 5

FINANCIAL/TERMS:
Cash Investment: $75K
Total Investment: $219K-335.5K
Minimum Net Worth: $250K
Fees: Franchise - $25K
Royalty - 6%; Ad. - 2%
Earnings Claims Statement: No
Term of Contract (Years): 10/5/5/
Avg. # Of Employees: 3 FT, 8 PT
Passive Ownership: Discouraged
Encourage Conversions: Yes
Area Develop. Agreements: Yes/1
Sub-Franchising Contracts: No
Expand In Territory: Yes
Space Needs: 900-1,400 SF

SUPPORT & TRAINING:
Financial Assistance Provided: No
Site Selection Assistance: Yes
Lease Negotiation Assistance: Yes
Co-Operative Advertising: No
Franchisee Assoc./Member: Yes/Yes
Size Of Corporate Staff: 150
On-Going Support: ,,C,D,E,F,G,h,I
Training:6 Days Grand Opening On-Site;
10 Days Atlanta, GA

SPECIFIC EXPANSION PLANS:
US: All United States
Canada: No
Overseas: NR

<< >>

MARBLE SLAB CREAMERY
1346 Oakbrook Dr., # 170
Norcross, GA 30093
Tel: (713) 780-3601
Fax: (713) 780-0264
E-Mail: franchiseinfo@nexcenfm.com
Web Site: www.marbleslab.com
Mr. Marty Amschler, Director of Franchising

Retail ice cream stores, featuring super-premium homemade ice cream, cones baked fresh daily, frozen yogurt, frozen pies and cakes, homemade cookies and brownies and specialty coffees. Ice cream is custom-designed for customer on frozen marble slab and made daily in the store.

BACKGROUND: IFA MEMBER
Established: 1983; 1st Franchised: 1984
Franchised Units: 366
Company-Owned Units: 0
Total Units: 366
Dist.: US-299; CAN-51; O'seas-19
North America: 30 States, 4 Provinces
Density: 40 in FL, 60 in CA, 150 in TX
Projected New Units (12 Months): 120
Qualifications: 5, 3, 1, 3, 3, 5

FINANCIAL/TERMS:
Cash Investment: $75K
Total Investment: $220K-381.5K
Minimum Net Worth: $250K
Fees: Franchise - $25K
Royalty - 6%; Ad. - 2%
Earnings Claims Statement: No
Term of Contract (Years): 10/10
Avg. # Of Employees: 2 FT, 8 PT
Passive Ownership: Discouraged
Encourage Conversions: Yes
Area Develop. Agreements: Yes
Sub-Franchising Contracts: No
Expand In Territory: Yes
Space Needs: 500-1,800 SF

SUPPORT & TRAINING:
Financial Assistance Provided: No
Site Selection Assistance: Yes
Lease Negotiation Assistance: Yes
Co-Operative Advertising: No
Franchisee Assoc./Member: Yes/Yes
Size Of Corporate Staff: 135
On-Going Support: ,,C,D,E,,,H,
Training: 10 Days Franchisor Location;
6 Days Franchisee Site

SPECIFIC EXPANSION PLANS:
US: All United States
Canada: All Canada
Overseas: All Countries

<< >>

RITA'S ITALIAN ICE
1210 N. Brook Dr., # 310
Trevose, PA 19053

214

Tel: (800) 677-7482 (215) 876-9300
Fax: (866) 449-0974
E-Mail: Franchise_sales@ritascorp.com
Web Site: www.ritasice.com
Ms. Lauriena Borstein, Manager of Franchise Development

Rita's is the largest Italian Ice chain in the nation. With a 25 year proven business model, Rita's offers a variety of frozen treats including its famous Italian Ice, Old Fashioned Frozen Custard, and layered Gelati as well as its signature Misto and Blendini creations.

BACKGROUND: IFA MEMBER
Established: 1984;   1st Franchised: 1989
Franchised Units: 549
Company-Owned Units: 1
Total Units: 550
Dist.:   US-550; CAN-0; O'seas-0
  North America: 23 States, 0 Provinces
  Density:228 in PA, 108 in NJ, 80 in MD
Projected New Units (12 Months):   30
Qualifications: 3, 3, 3, 3, 3, 5
FINANCIAL/TERMS:
Cash Investment: $75K
Total Investment: $198.4K-385.4K
Minimum Net Worth: $250K
Fees: Franchise - $35K
  Royalty - 6.5%;   Ad. - 2.5%
Earnings Claims Statement: Yes
Term of Contract (Years):   10/10
Avg. # Of Employees: 2 FT, 15 PT
Passive Ownership: Discouraged
Encourage Conversions: No
Area Develop. Agreements: No
Sub-Franchising Contracts: No
Expand In Territory: Yes
Space Needs: 1,000-1,200 SF
SUPPORT & TRAINING:
Financial Assistance Provided: Yes (I)
Site Selection Assistance: Yes
Lease Negotiation Assistance: Yes
Co-Operative Advertising: Yes
Franchisee Assoc./Member: No
Size Of Corporate Staff: 80
On-Going Support: „C,D,E,F,G,H,I
Training: 4 Days On-Site;10 Days
  Corporate Office
SPECIFIC EXPANSION PLANS:
US: East of Mississippi
Canada: No
Overseas: NR

≪ ≫

RITTER'S FROZEN CUSTARD
3755 E. 82nd St., # 325
Indianapolis, IN 46240

Tel: (317) 819-0700
Fax: (317) 819-0261
E-Mail: RFCfranchising@aol.com
Web Site: www.ritters.com
Mr. Robert Ritter, President/CEO

Our mission is to serve a product and experience that people constantly claim as their favorite ice cream ever. The RITTER'S brand has captured the imagination and fanatic loyalties of customers and franchisees alike. As a RITTER'S franchisee, you'll receive comprehensive training, including the importance of our philosophy and brand position. We have systems in place to help maximize franchisee sales, profits and net worth. Our core values have resulted in a diverse and successful franchise system.

BACKGROUND: IFA MEMBER
Established: 1990;   1st Franchised: 1995
Franchised Units: 40
Company-Owned Units: 4
Total Units: 44
Dist.:   US-44; CAN-0; O'seas-0
  North America: 8 States, 0 Provinces
  Density: 7 in OH, 5 in MI, 20 in IN
Projected New Units (12 Months):   NR
Qualifications: NR
FINANCIAL/TERMS:
Cash Investment: $55K-80K
Total Investment: $220K-300K
Minimum Net Worth: $200K
Fees: Franchise - $25K
  Royalty - 5%;   Ad. - 2%
Earnings Claims Statement: Yes
Term of Contract (Years):   10/10
Avg. # Of Employees: 4 FT, 15 PT
Passive Ownership: Discouraged
Encourage Conversions: No
Area Develop. Agreements: Yes/1
Sub-Franchising Contracts: No
Expand In Territory: Yes
Space Needs: 1,200-1,500 SF
SUPPORT & TRAINING:
Financial Assistance Provided: No
Site Selection Assistance: Yes
Lease Negotiation Assistance: Yes
Co-Operative Advertising: No
Franchisee Assoc./Member: Yes/Yes
Size Of Corporate Staff: 12
On-Going Support: A,B,C,D,E,F,G,H
Training: 3 Weeks Indianapolis, IN;
  3 Weeks Port Orange, FL
SPECIFIC EXPANSION PLANS:
US: East of Mississippi River
Canada: No
Overseas: NR

≪ ≫

SHAKE'S FROZEN CUSTARD
244 W. Dickson St.
Fayetteville, AR 72701-5221
Tel: (479) 587-9115
Fax: (479) 587-0780
E-Mail: to@shakesfrozencustard.com
Web Site: www.shakesfrozencustard.com
Mr. Todd Osborne, Vice President Operations/CFO

SHAKE'S FROZEN CUSTARD is where friends gather, couples fall in love, and people of all ages come to enjoy the vibrant nostalgic atmosphere of the 50's. Featuring an extensive menu consisting of our one-of-a-kind, delicious frozen custard and a wide variety of innovative concepts, SHAKE'S is a rapidly growing franchise system. With intensive training and continuous support, we will always ensure your business is operating to its maximum potential.

BACKGROUND:
Established: 1991;   1st Franchised: 1999
Franchised Units: 37
Company-Owned Units: 2
Total Units: 39
Dist.:   US-39; CAN-0; O'seas-0
  North America: 8 States, Provinces
  Density: 12 in AR, 8 in MO, 7 in TX
Projected New Units (12 Months):   25
Qualifications: 4, 4, 2, 1, 3, 5
FINANCIAL/TERMS:
Cash Investment: $50-250K
Total Investment: $166-800K
Minimum Net Worth: $250K
Fees: Franchise - $30K
  Royalty - 5%;   Ad. - 3%
Earnings Claims Statement: Yes
Term of Contract (Years):   15/5
Avg. # Of Employees: 3 FT, 12 PT
Passive Ownership: Discouraged
Encourage Conversions: No
Area Develop. Agreements: Yes/1
Sub-Franchising Contracts: No
Expand In Territory: Yes
Space Needs: 1,200 SF
SUPPORT & TRAINING:
Financial Assistance Provided: Yes (D)

Site Selection Assistance: Yes
Lease Negotiation Assistance: Yes
Co-Operative Advertising: No
Franchisee Assoc./Member: Yes/Yes
Size Of Corporate Staff: 10
On-Going Support: A,B,C,D,E,F,G,h,
Training: 2 Weeks Fayetteville, AR
SPECIFIC EXPANSION PLANS:
US: South, SE, SW, Midwest
Canada: No
Overseas: NR

≺≺ ≻≻

TASTEE-FREEZ

7700 Irvine Center Dr., # 550
Irvine, CA 92618
Tel: (800) 764-9339
Fax: (949) 851-2618
E-Mail: kpeters@galardigroup.com
Web Site: www.tastee-freez.com
Mr. Ken Peters, Director of Franchise
    Sales

Restaurant franchise with the flexibility to offer a full menu from chicken, burgers and fries plus hand-dipped and soft serve ice cream treats to offering a very streamlined soft serve treats-only menu for a co-brand or limited space location.

BACKGROUND:
Established: 1950; 1st Franchised: 1965
Franchised Units: 57
Company-Owned Units: 0
Total Units: 57
Dist.: US-57; CAN-0; O'seas-0
  North America: 0 States, 0 Provinces
  Density: NR
Projected New Units (12 Months): 40-50
Qualifications: 3, 3, 3, 3, 3, 3
FINANCIAL/TERMS:
Cash Investment: $150K
Total Investment: $350-750K
Minimum Net Worth: NA
Fees: Franchise - $5-15K
  Royalty - 4-5%; Ad. - 1%
Earnings Claims Statement: No
Term of Contract (Years): 10/10
Avg. # Of Employees: Varies
Passive Ownership: Discouraged
Encourage Conversions: Yes
Area Develop. Agreements: No
Sub-Franchising Contracts: No
Expand In Territory: Yes
Space Needs: NR
SUPPORT & TRAINING:
Financial Assistance Provided: No
Site Selection Assistance: No
Lease Negotiation Assistance: No

Co-Operative Advertising: No
Franchisee Assoc./Member: No
Size Of Corporate Staff: 7
On-Going Support: ,B,C,D,E,F,G,H,
Training: NR
SPECIFIC EXPANSION PLANS:
US: All United States
Canada: No
Overseas: NR

≺≺ ≻≻

TASTI D-LITE

341 Cool Springs Blvd., # 420
Franklin, TN 37067
Tel: (866) 424-4640 (615) 550-3012
Fax: (615) 550-3018
E-Mail: info@tastidlite.com
Web Site: www.tastidlite.com
Ms. Nikki Sells, V.P. Franchise Development

Tasti D-Lite Now more than ever, people need a little Tasti D-Lite... check out this fast-growing good-for-you frozen dessert concept. Simple and fun to operate, featuring a low-cal, low-fat, low-carb product that's been the talk of New York for more than 20 years. Unlike other light concepts, it has a rich texture and a creamy delicious taste. So healthy, it becomes a daily habit! The world's leading guilt-free food franchise. The right opportunity. At the right time.

BACKGROUND: IFA MEMBER
Established: 1987; 1st Franchised: 2008
Franchised Units: 34
Company-Owned Units: 4
Total Units: 38
Dist.: US-36; CAN-0; O'seas-2
  North America: 5 States, 0 Provinces
  Density: 56 in NY, 4 in NJ
Projected New Units (12 Months): 52
Qualifications: 2, 2, 1, 3, 1, 2
FINANCIAL/TERMS:
Cash Investment: $70K
Total Investment: $240.5-440K
Minimum Net Worth: $250K
Fees: Franchise - $30K
  Royalty - 5%; Ad. - 2%
Earnings Claims Statement: No
Term of Contract (Years): 10/10

Avg. # Of Employees: 2 FT, 4 PT
Passive Ownership: Discouraged
Encourage Conversions: Yes
Area Develop. Agreements: Yes/10
Sub-Franchising Contracts: No
Expand In Territory: No
Space Needs: 1,000 SF
SUPPORT & TRAINING:
Financial Assistance Provided: Yes (I)
Site Selection Assistance: Yes
Lease Negotiation Assistance: Yes
Co-Operative Advertising: Yes
Franchisee Assoc./Member: No
Size Of Corporate Staff: 28
On-Going Support: ,,C,D,e,,,h,I
Training: 1 Week New York, NY;
    1 Week Nashville, TN
SPECIFIC EXPANSION PLANS:
US: All United States
Canada: All Canada
Overseas: All Countries

≺≺ ≻≻

TCBY

2855 E. Cottonwood Pkwy., # 400
Salt Lake City, UT 84121-7050
Tel: (800) 343-5377 (801) 736-5600
Fax: (801) 736-1654
E-Mail: jmanning@mrsfields.com
Web Site: www.tcbyfranchise.com
Ms. Vanessa Hepworth Hogan, Franchise
    Marketing Manager

TCBY shops offer yogurt, sorbet and ice cream products, as well as a complete line of pies and cakes. TCBY Systems, LLC offers franchises for traditional locations, and for 'combined concept' locations, wherein TCBY shops are operated within another business.

BACKGROUND: IFA MEMBER
Established: 1981; 1st Franchised: 1982
Franchised Units: 900
Company-Owned Units: 0
Total Units: 900
Dist.: US-714; CAN-0; O'seas-186
  North America: 50 States, 2 Provinces
  Density: 107 in TX, 136 in FL, 96 in CA
Projected New Units (12 Months): 74
Qualifications: 5, 3, 2, 2, 2, 4
FINANCIAL/TERMS:
Cash Investment: $100-300K
Total Investment: $142-347.2K
Minimum Net Worth: $150K/75K LIQ

Fees: Franchise - $25K
    Royalty - 4%; Ad. - 3%
Earnings Claims Statement: Yes
Term of Contract (Years): 10/10
Avg. # Of Employees: 2 FT, 8 PT
Passive Ownership: Discouraged
Encourage Conversions: Yes
Area Develop. Agreements: No
Sub-Franchising Contracts: No
Expand In Territory: Yes
Space Needs: 100-1,600 SF

SUPPORT & TRAINING:
Financial Assistance Provided: No
Site Selection Assistance: Yes
Lease Negotiation Assistance: Yes
Co-Operative Advertising: No
Franchisee Assoc./Member: Yes/Yes
Size Of Corporate Staff: 100
On-Going Support: ,,C,D,E,,G,H,I
Training: Salt Lake City, Utah

SPECIFIC EXPANSION PLANS:
US: All United States
Canada: All Canada
Overseas: NR

YOGEN FRUZ CANADA LIMITED
210 Shields Ct.
Markham, ON L3R 8V2 CANADA
Tel: (905) 479-8762
Fax: (905) 479-5235
E-Mail: info@yogenfruz.com

Web Site: www.yogenfruz.com
Mr. Aaron Serruya, President

We offer a wide range of possibilities for customizing a frozen dessert shop for your market. Franchisees are selected on the basis of their commitment to the values of caring and responsive service. Our partners are important to us. Through our franchise owner network, we can assist new and existing franchisees with support services for operations, marketing, and training. The franchisee's input is of tremendous value on business and product development. We are committed to franchising, maintaining a highly collaborative relationship with our franchisees and making franchising decisions based on what's best for our customers. We will seize every opportunity to innovate and lead the industry on behalf of our customers.

BACKGROUND:
Established: 1986; 1st Franchised: 1987
Franchised Units: 1100
Company-Owned Units: 1
Total Units: 1101
Dist.: US-186; CAN-257; O'seas-276
    North America: 17 States, 10 Provinces
    Density: 375 in ON, in FL, in AB
Projected New Units (12 Months): 500
Qualifications: 5, 4, 1, 1, 3, 5

FINANCIAL/TERMS:
Cash Investment: $100-150K

Total Investment: $150-280K
Minimum Net Worth: $350K
Fees: Franchise - $25K
    Royalty - 6%; Ad. - 3%
Earnings Claims Statement: No
Term of Contract (Years): 10/10
Avg. # Of Employees: 3 FT, 6-7 PT
Passive Ownership: Not Allowed
Encourage Conversions: Yes
Area Develop. Agreements: Yes/20
Sub-Franchising Contracts: Yes
Expand In Territory: Yes
Space Needs: 200-1,200 SF

SUPPORT & TRAINING:
Financial Assistance Provided: No
Site Selection Assistance: Yes
Lease Negotiation Assistance: Yes
Co-Operative Advertising: Yes
Franchisee Assoc./Member: No
Size Of Corporate Staff: 17
On-Going Support: ,B,C,D,E,f,G,H,
Training: 7 Days Arizona (Phoenix)
    - Restaurant;
    7 Days Toronto, ON - Kiosk;5 Days-
    Las Vegas, NV - Parlour

SPECIFIC EXPANSION PLANS:
US: All United States
Canada: All Canada
Overseas: All Countries

For a full explanation
of the data provided
in the Franchisor
Profiles, please refer to
*Chapter 2, "How to Use
the Data."*

FIVE LARGEST PARTICIPANTS IN SURVEY						
Company	# Fran-chised Units	# Co-Owned Units	# Total Units	Franchise Fee	On-Going Royalty	Total Investment
1. Jazzercise	5,752	1	5,753	$700	20%	$3-33.1K
2. Miracle-Ear	1,200	30	1,230	$28-60K	$46.50/ Unit	$88-200K
3. Anytime Fitness	1,100	10	1,110	$18K	$419/mo	$35-$249K
4. Pearle Vision	402	499	901	$30K	7%	$250-500K
5. Home Instead Senior Care	800	1	801	$25.5K	5%	$34-47K

All of the data provided are proprietary and should not be quoted without acknowledging *Bond's Franchise Guide.*

**ALWAYS BEST CARE
SENIOR SERVICES**

1406 Blue Oaks Rd.
Roseville, CA 95747
Tel: (888) 430-2273 (916) 266-6454
Fax: (916) 848-0268
E-Mail: mgewecke@abc-seniors.com
Web Site: www.alwaysbestcare.com
Mr. Mark Gewecke, Franchise Development

Always Best Care Senior Services is the only Senior Care Franchise to offer:- Two Revenue Streams- Assisted Living Placement and In-Home Care Services - Exclusive Insurance program - Two weeks of one-on-one training in addition to 90 days of training modules - Exclusive care provider retention and recruitment program - Been in business for over 13 years- longest in industry - 24/7 customer support to our franchisees - Full blown website – not just a landing page - Over 12 National Contracts for our franchisees - Over 4,000 Assisted Living Contracts - Virtual Office- all in one web based software system

BACKGROUND: IFA MEMBER
Established: 1996;   1st Franchised: 2007

Franchised Units: 27
Company-Owned Units: 1
Total Units: 28
Dist.:   US-28; CAN-0; O'seas-0
  North America: 7 States, 0 Provinces
  Density: 3 in OH, 9 in CA
Projected New Units (12 Months):   75
Qualifications: 5, 5, 3, 2, 3, 4
FINANCIAL/TERMS:
Cash Investment: $38-$43K
Total Investment: $38-$43K
Minimum Net Worth: $50K
Fees: Franchise - $34.5K
  Royalty - 6%;   Ad. - 0%
Earnings Claims Statement: No
Term of Contract (Years):   10/5
Avg. # Of Employees: 3 FT, 0 PT

Passive Ownership: Discouraged
Encourage Conversions: NA
Area Develop. Agreements: Yes/10
Sub-Franchising Contracts: No
Expand In Territory: Yes
Space Needs: NA
SUPPORT & TRAINING:
Financial Assistance Provided: Yes (I)
Site Selection Assistance: NA
Lease Negotiation Assistance: NA
Co-Operative Advertising: No
Franchisee Assoc./Member: No
Size Of Corporate Staff: 13
On-Going Support: ,,,D,,,G,H,
Training: One-on-one with sales trainer
takes about 90 days Per and post train-
ing modules; 1 week At Franchise
location; 1 week Corporate
SPECIFIC EXPANSION PLANS:
US: All US
Canada: No
Overseas: NR

◄◄ ►►

ANYTIME FITNESS
12181 Margo Ave. S.
Hastings, Minnesota 55033
Tel: (800) 704-5004 (651) 438-5000
Fax: (651) 438-5099
E-Mail: leads@anytimefitness.com
Web Site: www.anytimefitness.com
Mr. Mark Daly, National Media Director

Anytime Fitness is the #1 co-ed fitness
club chain in the world. We've boiled our
business model down to the core essen-
tials which members expect. Our loyal
family of preferred vendors supply our
franchisees with quality products at the
best available prices. Financial and real
estate support available. More than half
of our franchisees own multiple clubs.
Enjoy the freedom of spending time with
your friends and family - and the knowledge that you're making your community a
better place to live.

BACKGROUND: IFA MEMBER
Established: 2002; 1st Franchised: 2002
Franchised Units: 1100
Company-Owned Units: 10
Total Units: 1110
Dist.: US-1087; CAN-11; O'seas-12
North America: 48 States, 4 Provinces
Density: 60 in WI, 115 in MN, 55 in LA

Projected New Units (12 Months): 400
Qualifications: 3, 2, 2, 2, 3, 4
FINANCIAL/TERMS:
Cash Investment: $10K
Total Investment: $35K-$249K
Minimum Net Worth: $10K
Fees: Franchise - $18K
Royalty - $419/mo; Ad. - $150/mo
Earnings Claims Statement: Yes
Term of Contract (Years): 5/5
Avg. # Of Employees: 1 FT, 2 PT
Passive Ownership: Allowed
Encourage Conversions: Yes
Area Develop. Agreements: Yes/2
Sub-Franchising Contracts: Yes
Expand In Territory: Yes
Space Needs: 4,000 SF
SUPPORT & TRAINING:
Financial Assistance Provided: Yes (D)
Site Selection Assistance: Yes
Lease Negotiation Assistance: Yes
Co-Operative Advertising: Yes
Franchisee Assoc./Member: Yes/Yes
Size Of Corporate Staff: 80
On-Going Support: A,B,C,D,E,F,G,H,I
Training: 1 week Hastings, MN
SPECIFIC EXPANSION PLANS:
US: All 50 states
Canada: All Canadian provinces
Overseas: India, China, Japan, Aus, Eur.,
Mid. E., Latin Am.

◄◄ ►►

ARISTOCARE
698 E. Wetmore Rd. #200
Tucson, AZ 85705
Tel: (866) 731-2273 (520) 731-2273
Fax: (520) 529-0862
E-Mail: info@aristocare.net
Web Site: www.aristocare.net
Ms. Marilyn Jacobson, Franchise Sales

Today the rapidly-growing senior population is fueling the demand for in-home
health services. This demand has created explosive growth in the senior care
industry. The ARISTOCARE private duty
home care system is a full-service medical
business, providing two income streams
for non-medical and medical care senior
services. ARISTOCARE provides excellent ownership opportunities. No previous
experience in home health care is necessary. Comprehensive 2 week training provided.

BACKGROUND: IFA MEMBER
Established: 1999; 1st Franchised: 2003
Franchised Units: 2

Company-Owned Units: 3
Total Units: 5
Dist.: US-5; CAN-0; O'seas-0
North America: 2 States, 0 Provinces
Density: 3 in AZ
Projected New Units (12 Months): 5
Qualifications: 4, 4, 1, 3, 3, 5
FINANCIAL/TERMS:
Cash Investment: $50K-60K
Total Investment: $148-259K
Minimum Net Worth: $250K
Fees: Franchise - $36K
Royalty - 5%-7%; Ad. -
Earnings Claims Statement: No
Term of Contract (Years): 10/5
Avg. # Of Employees: 2 FT, 1 PT
Passive Ownership: Allowed
Encourage Conversions: No
Area Develop. Agreements: No
Sub-Franchising Contracts: No
Expand In Territory: Yes
Space Needs: 600 SF
SUPPORT & TRAINING:
Financial Assistance Provided: NR
Site Selection Assistance: Yes
Lease Negotiation Assistance: No
Co-Operative Advertising: Yes
Franchisee Assoc./Member: No
Size Of Corporate Staff: 15
On-Going Support: A,b,C,D,E,,G,H,I
Training: 1 Week On-Site; 2 Weeks
Tucson, AZ Corporate Office
SPECIFIC EXPANSION PLANS:
US: All United States
Canada: Yes
Overseas: NR

◄◄ ►►

**BLITZ, THE, 20-MINUTE TOTAL
FITNESS FOR MEN**
980 E. Santa Fe
Gardner, KS 66030
Tel: (866) 968-2548 (913) 856-2424
Fax: (309) 424-3558
E-Mail: info@timetoblitz.com
Web Site: www.timetoblitz.com
Mr. Scott T. Smith, Founder

The world's largest and fastest-growing fitness franchise for men. THE BLITZ combines strength training with cardio boxing

and martial art techniques, all inside "The BLITZ Ring" 20-minute circuit. Your low investment could yield high returns. Great opportunity for those looking for more independence.

BACKGROUND: IFA MEMBER
Established: 2002;   1st Franchised: 2002
Franchised Units: 201
Company-Owned Units: 1
Total Units: 202
Dist.:   US-70; CAN-40; O'seas-92
  North America: 25 States, Provinces
  Density: NR
Projected New Units (12 Months):   NR
Qualifications: NR
FINANCIAL/TERMS:
Cash Investment: $29.9K
Total Investment: $38-60K
Minimum Net Worth: $300K
Fees: Franchise - $29.9K
  Royalty - $395/Mo.;   Ad. - 0%
Earnings Claims Statement: No
Term of Contract (Years):   7/5
Avg. # Of Employees: 1 FT, 1 PT
Passive Ownership: Discouraged
Encourage Conversions: No
Area Develop. Agreements: Yes/1
Sub-Franchising Contracts: No
Expand In Territory: Yes
Space Needs: 1,800 SF
SUPPORT & TRAINING:
Financial Assistance Provided: No
Site Selection Assistance: Yes
Lease Negotiation Assistance: Yes
Co-Operative Advertising: No
Franchisee Assoc./Member: No
Size Of Corporate Staff: 15
On-Going Support: a,B,C,D,E,f,G,h,I
Training: 4 Days Gardner, KS
  Headquarters
SPECIFIC EXPANSION PLANS:
US: All United States
Canada: All Canada
Overseas: All Countries

⫷⫸ ⫷⫸

CARING SENIOR SERVICE
201 E. Park Ave.
San Antonio, TX 78212
Tel: (866) 528-7905 NA
Fax: (210) 227-6569
E-Mail: dbehrens@caringinc.com

Web Site: www.caringfranchise.com
Mr. Carl Jeffers, National Marketing Director

Caring Senior Service offers non-medical services and safety care products to seniors who need assistance with daily living activities. We give individuals the opportunity to develop a lucrative business in a thriving industry while making positive changes in the lives of seniors and their families. Our turnkey business with a low-cost operating model minimizes start-up costs and our operational support center provides continued business support and development, so you can focus on growing your business.

BACKGROUND:
Established: 1991;   1st Franchised: 2002
Franchised Units: 9
Company-Owned Units: 18
Total Units: 27
Dist.:   US-27; CAN-0; O'seas-0
  North America: 9 States, 0 Provinces
  Density: 13 in TX, 3 in AL, 3 in IL
Projected New Units (12 Months):   12
Qualifications: 3, 5, 3, 3, 3, 5
FINANCIAL/TERMS:
Cash Investment: $32.5-37.5K
Total Investment: $50-75K
Minimum Net Worth: NA
Fees: Franchise - $32.5K
  Royalty - 5%;   Ad. - 5%
Earnings Claims Statement: Yes
Term of Contract (Years):   10/10
Avg. # Of Employees: 3 FT, 0 PT
Passive Ownership: Discouraged
Encourage Conversions: Yes
Area Develop. Agreements: No
Sub-Franchising Contracts: No
Expand In Territory: Yes
Space Needs: 550 SF
SUPPORT & TRAINING:
Financial Assistance Provided: No
Site Selection Assistance: Yes
Lease Negotiation Assistance: Yes
Co-Operative Advertising: No
Franchisee Assoc./Member: No
Size Of Corporate Staff: 18
On-Going Support: A,,C,d,E,,,h,
Training: 1 Week San Antonio, TX
SPECIFIC EXPANSION PLANS:
US: CA,NV,UT,AZ,NM,TX,AR,LA,MS, AL,TN,KY,GA,SC,NC
Canada: All Canada
Overseas: NR

⫷⫸ ⫷⫸

COMFORCARE SENIOR SERVICES
2510 Telegraph Rd., # 100
Bloomfield Hills, MI 48302
Tel: (800) 886-4044 (248) 745-9700
Fax: (248) 745-9763
E-Mail: home@comforcare.com
Web Site: www.comforcare.com/franchise
Ms. Brigitte Betser, Director of Sales & Support

Non-medical home care services for seniors and physically challenged individuals of all ages. Turnkey home care franchise operations for aspiring professionals. The broadest array of non-medical home care services in the field. Largest protected territories in the industry - up to 400,000 at no additional cost. Daily support of new franchises.

BACKGROUND: IFA MEMBER
Established: 1996;   1st Franchised: 2001
Franchised Units: 93
Company-Owned Units: 1
Total Units: 94
Dist.:   US-94; CAN-0; O'seas-0
  North America: 26 States, 0 Provinces
  Density: 6 in TX, 6 in NJ, 13 in CA
Projected New Units (12 Months):   24
Qualifications: 5, 4, 2, 3, 3, 5
FINANCIAL/TERMS:
Cash Investment: $45.5K-52.5K
Total Investment: $69.5K-89.5K
Minimum Net Worth: NR
Fees: Franchise - $35K
  Royalty - 5-3% (Decl.);   Ad. - 0%
Earnings Claims Statement: No
Term of Contract (Years):   10/10
Avg. # Of Employees: 12 FT, 0 PT
Passive Ownership: Discouraged
Encourage Conversions: Yes
Area Develop. Agreements: Yes/1
Sub-Franchising Contracts: No
Expand In Territory: Yes
Space Needs: 250-450 SF
SUPPORT & TRAINING:
Financial Assistance Provided: Yes (I)
Site Selection Assistance: Yes
Lease Negotiation Assistance: Yes
Co-Operative Advertising: Yes
Franchisee Assoc./Member: No
Size Of Corporate Staff: 12

On-Going Support: A,B,C,D,E,,G,H,I
Training: 1 Week Bloomfield Hills, MI
SPECIFIC EXPANSION PLANS:
US: All United States
Canada: No
Overseas: NR

‹‹ ››

COMFORT KEEPERS

6640 Poe Ave., # 200
Dayton, OH 45414-2600
Tel: (888) 329-1368 (937) 264-1933
Fax: (937) 264-3103
E-Mail: admin@comfortkeepers.com
Web Site: www.comfortkeepers.com
Mr. Larry France, Manager, Franchise
    Development, Western USA

COMFORT KEEPERS is the service leader with 95% client satisfaction. We provide non-medical, in-home care, such as companionship, meal preparation, light housekeeping, grocery and clothing shopping, grooming and assistance with recreational activities for the elderly and others who need assistance in daily living.

BACKGROUND: IFA MEMBER
Established: 1998; 1st Franchised: 1999
Franchised Units: 617
Company-Owned Units: 0
Total Units: 617
Dist.: US-568; CAN-29; O'seas-20
    North America: 47 States, 3 Provinces
    Density: 43 in OH, 55 in FL, 73 in CA
Projected New Units (12 Months): 30
Qualifications: 5, 5, 2, 3, 3, 4
FINANCIAL/TERMS:
Cash Investment: $74K
Total Investment: $74K
Minimum Net Worth: $200K
Fees: Franchise - $32.5K
    Royalty - 5/4/3%; Ad. - 0%
Earnings Claims Statement: Yes
Term of Contract (Years): 10/10
Avg. # Of Employees: 2 FT, 4-5 PT
Passive Ownership: Not Allowed
Encourage Conversions: Yes
Area Develop. Agreements: No
Sub-Franchising Contracts: No
Expand In Territory: Yes
Space Needs: 400-700 SF
SUPPORT & TRAINING:
Financial Assistance Provided: Yes (I)

Site Selection Assistance: No
Lease Negotiation Assistance: No
Co-Operative Advertising: No
Franchisee Assoc./Member: Yes/Yes
Size Of Corporate Staff: 35
On-Going Support: ,,C,D,,,G,h,I
Training:8 Days & Ongoing Dayton, OH
SPECIFIC EXPANSION PLANS:
US: All United States
Canada: Yes
Overseas: NR

‹‹ ››

CONTOURS EXPRESS

156 Imperial Wy.
Nicholasville, KY 40356
Tel: (877) 227-2282 (859) 885-6441
Fax: (214) 242-2240
E-Mail: info@contoursexpress.com
Web Site: www.contoursexpress.com
Mr. Bill Helton, President

CONTOURS EXPRESS is a fitness center, designed especially for women, based on the concept of circuit training. A cue tape, with high energy music, keeps club members moving through our 16-piece circuit that alternates between strength-training machines and aerobic stations. Unlike other clubs designed for women, CONTOURS EXPRESS uses actual weight-bearing machines (vs. less efficient hydraulic machines). Franchisees also derive profits from their own pro shop and our line of weight loss supplements.

BACKGROUND: IFA MEMBER
Established: 1998; 1st Franchised: 1999
Franchised Units: 315
Company-Owned Units: 0
Total Units: 315
Dist.: US-288; CAN-25; O'seas-295
    North America: 40 States, 5 Provinces
    Density: 58 in MI, 26 in FL, 30 in CA
Projected New Units (12 Months): 200
Qualifications: NR
FINANCIAL/TERMS:
Cash Investment: $15K-30K
Total Investment: $34K-49K
Minimum Net Worth: $75K
Fees: Franchise - $18K
    Royalty - $395/Mo.; Ad. - 0%
Earnings Claims Statement: No
Term of Contract (Years): 10/5
Avg. # Of Employees: 1 FT, 1 PT
Passive Ownership: Allowed
Encourage Conversions: No
Area Develop. Agreements: No

Sub-Franchising Contracts: Yes
Expand In Territory: Yes
Space Needs: 1,200 SF
SUPPORT & TRAINING:
Financial Assistance Provided: Yes (I)
Site Selection Assistance: Yes
Lease Negotiation Assistance: Yes
Co-Operative Advertising: Yes
Franchisee Assoc./Member: Yes/Yes
Size Of Corporate Staff: 22
On-Going Support: ,,,,E,,G,h,I
Training: 5 Days Nicholasville, KY
SPECIFIC EXPANSION PLANS:
US: All United States
Canada: All Canada
Overseas: All Countries

‹‹ ››

COUNTRY PLACE LIVING

1527 W. State Hwy. 114, # 500-354
Grapevine, TX 76051
Tel: (817) 545-5353 (817) 545-5353
Fax: (866) 360-0060
E-Mail: franchise@countryplaceliving.com
Web Site: www.CountryPlaceLiving.com
Ms. Cynthia Gartman, President & COO

Country Place Living offers franchises for assisted living and group home residences. Our residences are places where seniors truly feel at home and maintain their dignity. We specialize in small group residences consisting of either 18 apartments (Country Place Senior Living) or 8 bedrooms (Country Place Home Plus.) Country Place Senior Living is designed for active seniors, while Country Place Home Plus is created especially for those seniors who may need additional specialized care.

BACKGROUND: IFA MEMBER
Established: 1981; 1st Franchised: 2007
Franchised Units: 1
Company-Owned Units: 8
Total Units: 9
Dist.: US-9; CAN-0; O'seas-0
    North America: 1 States, 0 Provinces
    Density: 9 in KS
Projected New Units (12 Months): 3
Qualifications: 4, 4, 1, 3, 5, 5
FINANCIAL/TERMS:
Cash Investment: $150K - 500K

Total Investment: $600K - 2.3MM
Minimum Net Worth: $250K
Fees: Franchise - $37500
　Royalty - 5%; Ad. - 1/2%
Earnings Claims Statement: Yes
Term of Contract (Years): 10/10
Avg. # Of Employees: 8 - 13 FT, 0 PT
Passive Ownership: Allowed
Encourage Conversions: No
Area Develop. Agreements: No
Sub-Franchising Contracts: No
Expand In Territory: No
Space Needs: .75 acre to 1.5 acres SF

SUPPORT & TRAINING:
Financial Assistance Provided: Yes (I)
Site Selection Assistance: Yes
Lease Negotiation Assistance: NA
Co-Operative Advertising: No
Franchisee Assoc./Member: No
Size Of Corporate Staff: 6
On-Going Support: ,B,C,D,E,,G,h,
Training: 12 Days Wichita, KS; 2 1/2
　Days Dallas, TX; 3-5 Days Franchisee
　Location

SPECIFIC EXPANSION PLANS:
US: All states except for WA, CA, HI
Canada: No
Overseas: NR

◄◄　►►

DIET CENTER
395 Springside Dr.
Akron, OH 44333-2496
Tel: (800) 656-3294 (330) 655-5861
Fax: (330) 666-2197
E-Mail: info@dietcenterworldwide.com
Web Site: www.dietcenterworldwide.com
Mr. Grayden Webb, Dir. Franchise Development

DIET CENTER offers innovative weight management programs.

BACKGROUND:
Established: 1972; 1st Franchised: 1972
Franchised Units: 325
Company-Owned Units: 0
Total Units: 325
Dist.: US-313; CAN-11; O'seas-1
　North America: 44 States, 4 Provinces
　Density: 28 in NY, 19 in NC, 18 in CA
Projected New Units (12 Months): 8-10
Qualifications: 3, 3, 3, 2, 3, 5

FINANCIAL/TERMS:
Cash Investment: $16.4-34.9K
Total Investment: $16.4-34.9K
Minimum Net Worth: $50-75K
Fees: Franchise - $15K
　Royalty - 8%/$100/Wk.; Ad.

- 8%/$500/Mo.
Earnings Claims Statement: No
Term of Contract (Years): 5/5
Avg. # Of Employees: 2 FT, 1 PT
Passive Ownership: Discouraged
Encourage Conversions: Yes
Area Develop. Agreements: No
Sub-Franchising Contracts: No
Expand In Territory: Yes
Space Needs: 700-1,200 SF

SUPPORT & TRAINING:
Financial Assistance Provided: No
Site Selection Assistance: Yes
Lease Negotiation Assistance: Yes
Co-Operative Advertising: No
Franchisee Assoc./Member: No
Size Of Corporate Staff: 40
On-Going Support: ,,C,D,E,,G,H,I
Training: 3 Weeks Akron, OH

SPECIFIC EXPANSION PLANS:
US: All United States
Canada: All Canada
Overseas: NR

◄◄　►►

FOOT SOLUTIONS
2359 Windy Hill Rd., # 400
Marietta, GA 30067
Tel: (866) 338-2597 (770) 955-0099
Fax: (770) 953-6270
E-Mail: fscorp@footsolutions.com
Web Site: www.footsolutionsfranchise.com
Ms. Debbie Fiorentino, Franchise Sales Administrator

Foot Solutions is the world's largest and #1 ranked Health and Wellness Specialty Retail Franchise. Focusing on the 40 Plus Market; Foot Solutions specializes in proper shoe fit and support using topographical foot mapping and gait analysis for producing custom insoles (orthotics). â€œUsing our certified experts and state-of-the-art-technology, we help our clients look, feel and perform better through customized Foot Solutions. If you enjoy helping people and want to own your own business, Foot Solutions may be the opportunity for you!

BACKGROUND: IFA MEMBER

Established: 2000; 1st Franchised: 2000
Franchised Units: 198
Company-Owned Units: 2
Total Units: 200
Dist.: US-200; CAN-22; O'seas-21
　North America: 40 States, 4 Provinces
　Density: 15 in TX, 19 in FL, 26 in CA
Projected New Units (12 Months): 50
Qualifications: 3, 3, 1, 2, 3, 4

FINANCIAL/TERMS:
Cash Investment: $50-65K
Total Investment: $213,400-$250,000
Minimum Net Worth: $300-500K
Fees: Franchise - $35K
　Royalty - 5%; Ad. - NA
Earnings Claims Statement: No
Term of Contract (Years): 20/10/10/
Avg. # Of Employees: 2-3 FT, 0 PT
Passive Ownership: Allowed
Encourage Conversions: Yes
Area Develop. Agreements: Yes/1
Sub-Franchising Contracts: No
Expand In Territory: Yes
Space Needs: 1,200-2,000 SF

SUPPORT & TRAINING:
Financial Assistance Provided: Yes (I)
Site Selection Assistance: Yes
Lease Negotiation Assistance: Yes
Co-Operative Advertising: Yes
Franchisee Assoc./Member: Yes/Yes
Size Of Corporate Staff: 50
On-Going Support: ,,C,D,E,,G,H,I
Training: 1 Week Field; 2 1/2 Weeks
　Marietta, GA

SPECIFIC EXPANSION PLANS:
US: All United States
Canada: All Canada
Overseas: All Countries

◄◄　►►

GRISWOLD SPECIAL CARE
717 Bethlehem Pk., # 300
Erdenheim, PA 19038
Tel: (888) 777-7630 (215) 402-0200
Fax: (215) 402-0202
E-Mail: meghan@griswoldspecialcare.com
Web Site: www.griswoldspecialcare.com
Ms. Meghan M. Surdenas, Manager of Development

GRISWOLD SPECIAL CARE refers Caregivers with a wide range of professional experience who care for older adults, people recovering from illness or surgery, and those living with conditions like Arthritis, Alzheimer's disease, Multiple Sclerosis, ALS, and Cancer. Caregiver services include personal care (bathing, continence care, dressing, mouth care), homemaking (cooking, light housekeeping, laundry), and companionship (shopping, errands, friendly conversation). Caregivers work with people who live in their own homes, in hospitals, nursing homes, or assisted living facilities. Services are available on an hourly, overnight, or live-in basis 24 hours per day, seven days a week. Senior care is a hot industry with a growing demand over the next 20 years, as the population of older adults increases dramatically. With low overhead and no inventory or expensive landlord leases, home care is an affordable opportunity that lets you make a difference in your community.

BACKGROUND: IFA MEMBER
Established: 1982;   1st Franchised: 1984
Franchised Units: 95
Company-Owned Units: 9
Total Units: 104
Dist.:   US-103; CAN-0; O'seas-1
  North America: 18 States, 0 Provinces
  Density: 10 in OH, 17 in NJ, 20 in PA
Projected New Units (12 Months):   NR
Qualifications: 5, 4, 2, 4, 4, 5
FINANCIAL/TERMS:
Cash Investment: $33-60K
Total Investment: $33-60K
Minimum Net Worth: $250K
Fees: Franchise - $33K
  Royalty - 3-5%;   Ad. - $100 gross
billings/mo** NTE $300
Earnings Claims Statement: Yes
Term of Contract (Years):   7/5
Avg. # Of Employees: 3-5 (in office) FT, PT
Passive Ownership: Not Allowed
Encourage Conversions: No
Area Develop. Agreements: Yes
Sub-Franchising Contracts: No
Expand In Territory: Yes
Space Needs: minimum 150 SF
SUPPORT & TRAINING:
Financial Assistance Provided: No
Site Selection Assistance: Yes
Lease Negotiation Assistance: NA
Co-Operative Advertising: Yes
Franchisee Assoc./Member: No
Size Of Corporate Staff: 15
On-Going Support: ,,C,D,,,G,H,
Training: 1-2 Days Franchisee's Location;
  1-2 Days Franchisee's Location; 5

Days Corporate Office
SPECIFIC EXPANSION PLANS:
US: 20-30 offices
Canada: Possibly
Overseas: NR

⋘ ⋙

HEMORRHOID CLINIC, THE
P. O. Box 12488
Oakland, CA 94604
Tel: (510) 839-5471
Fax: (510) 839-2104
E-Mail: rob@worldfranchising.com
Web Site: www.nohemies.com
Ms. Leslie F. Antonius, President

Highly efficient and automated out-patient clinics for hemorrhoid and related rectal procedures. Proprietary laser techniques developed by Dr. Anning insure painless, 20-minute procedure and minimal recuperative discomfort. Lucrative business that takes advantage of the fact that 1 in 8 adults requires rectal surgery. 12 week training at headquarters clinic. All procedures on video. Excellent opportunity to work with the best!

BACKGROUND:
Established: 1987;   1st Franchised: 1988
Franchised Units: 32
Company-Owned Units: 1
Total Units: 33
Dist.:   US-27; CAN-3; O'seas-3
  North America: 10 States, 2 Provinces
  Density: 2 in KY, 2 in MS, 5 in OH
Projected New Units (12 Months):   2
Qualifications: NR
FINANCIAL/TERMS:
Cash Investment: $80-125K
Total Investment: $140-225K
Minimum Net Worth: NR
Fees: Franchise - $25K
  Royalty - 6%;   Ad. - 1%
Earnings Claims Statement: Yes
Term of Contract (Years):   10/10
Avg. # Of Employees: 3 FT, 4 PT
Passive Ownership: Not Allowed
Encourage Conversions: Yes
Area Develop. Agreements: Yes/1
Sub-Franchising Contracts: Yes
Expand In Territory: Yes
Space Needs: 1,500-2,000 SF
SUPPORT & TRAINING:
Financial Assistance Provided: Yes (D)
Site Selection Assistance: Yes
Lease Negotiation Assistance: Yes
Co-Operative Advertising: No
Franchisee Assoc./Member: NR

Size Of Corporate Staff: 12
On-Going Support: ,,C,D,E,,G,H,I
Training: 12 Weeks Anning Clinic;
  3 Weeks On-Site; On-Going Video
  Training Procedures
SPECIFIC EXPANSION PLANS:
US: All United States
Canada: ON Only
Overseas: NR

⋘ ⋙

Home Care | Assistance

HOME CARE ASSISTANCE
360 Bryant St., # 201
Palo Alto, CA 94301
Tel: (866) 454-8346 (650) 462-6900
Fax: (650) 462-6907
E-Mail: jj@homecareassistance.com
Web Site: www.homecareassistance.com
Mr. Jim Johnson, Franchise Devel. Director

Home Care Assistance 1-866-4-LiveIn is unparalleled in the home senior care market. We are known in the industry as the "live-in" specialists" and tend to attract and attain longer hour cases than anyone else. Our business model appeals to customers with higher measures of affluence and caregivers with more seniority and experience. Even within markets that have established competition our business model will enable you to be a successful business owner, quickly growing a business that can achieve and sustain incredible earnings. After all, senior home care is one of the fastest growing market segments with the potential for significant financial rewards.

BACKGROUND: IFA MEMBER
Established: 2002;   1st Franchised: 2004
Franchised Units: 42
Company-Owned Units: 3
Total Units: 42
Dist.:   US-41; CAN-1; O'seas-0
  North America: 2 States, 0 Provinces
  Density: 3 in PA, 4 in NJ, 3 in TX
Projected New Units (12 Months):   25
Qualifications: 4, 4, 2, 3, 3, 4
FINANCIAL/TERMS:
Cash Investment: $50-150K
Total Investment: $50-150K
Minimum Net Worth: $100K
Fees: Franchise - $25K
  Royalty - 5%;   Ad. - .75%
Earnings Claims Statement: Yes

Term of Contract (Years): 15/10
Avg. # Of Employees: 2 FT, PT
Passive Ownership: Allowed
Encourage Conversions: No
Area Develop. Agreements: Yes
Sub-Franchising Contracts: No
Expand In Territory: Yes
Space Needs: 700 SF
SUPPORT & TRAINING:
Financial Assistance Provided: No
Site Selection Assistance: Yes
Lease Negotiation Assistance: NA
Co-Operative Advertising: Yes
Franchisee Assoc./Member: No
Size Of Corporate Staff: 12
On-Going Support: A,B,C,D,,,G,H,I
Training: 1 Week Palo Alto, CA
SPECIFIC EXPANSION PLANS:
US: All United States
Canada: Yes
Overseas: All Countries

≪ ≫

HOME HELPERS/ DIRECT LINK
10700 Montgomery Rd., # 300
Cincinnati, OH 45242
Tel: (800) 216-4196 (513) 563-8339
Fax: (513) 563-2691
E-Mail: webinquiry@homehelpers.cc
Web Site: www.homehelpers.cc
Ms. Amber Kershaw, Sales Support Manager

Home Helpers is ranked "#1 Senior Care Franchise" in North America and "Best of the Best" by Entrepreneur magazine four years in a row! This is a rewarding business providing non-medical and personal care for: Seniors, New Moms, those recuperating from illness or injury, and those with lifelong challenges.

BACKGROUND: IFA MEMBER
Established: 1997; 1st Franchised: 1997
Franchised Units: 780
Company-Owned Units: 0
Total Units: 780
Dist.: US-775; CAN-5; O'seas-0
North America: 47 States, 3 Provinces
Density: NR
Projected New Units (12 Months): 100
Qualifications: 3, 3, 1, 2, 3, 4
FINANCIAL/TERMS:

Cash Investment: $7-33.9K
Total Investment: $46.2K-84.8K
Minimum Net Worth: $19.9K
Fees: Franchise - $33.9K
  Royalty - 6-4% Varies; Ad. - $200
Earnings Claims Statement: No
Term of Contract (Years): 10/10/10/
Avg. # Of Employees: 1 FT, 0 PT
Passive Ownership: Allowed
Encourage Conversions: Yes
Area Develop. Agreements: Yes/1
Sub-Franchising Contracts: No
Expand In Territory: Yes
Space Needs: NA
SUPPORT & TRAINING:
Financial Assistance Provided: Yes (I)
Site Selection Assistance: NA
Lease Negotiation Assistance: NA
Co-Operative Advertising: Yes
Franchisee Assoc./Member: No
Size Of Corporate Staff: 50
On-Going Support: ,,C,D,,,G,H,I
Training: 5 Business Days Cincinnati, OH
SPECIFIC EXPANSION PLANS:
US: All United States
Canada: All Canada
Overseas: All Countries

≪ ≫

HOME INSTEAD SENIOR CARE
13330 California St., # 200
Omaha, NE 68154
Tel: (888) 484-5759 (402) 498-4466
Fax: (402) 498-5757
E-Mail: franinfo@homeinstead.com
Web Site: www.homeinstead.com
Mr. Tim Connelly, Director of Franchise Development

HOME INSTEAD SENIOR CARE is the world's largest, most successful, non-medical companionship and home care franchise. Entrepreneur and other leading business publications have ranked us one of the top opportunities in all of franchising. The elderly market we serve is the fastest-growing segment of the population. Services such as companionship, light housework, errands and meal preparation assist the elderly in remaining in their homes rather than being institutionalized.

BACKGROUND: IFA MEMBER
Established: 1994; 1st Franchised: 1995
Franchised Units: 800
Company-Owned Units: 1
Total Units: 801
Dist.: US-613; CAN-10; O'seas-181
North America: 49 States, 3 Provinces

Density: 24 in TX, 27 in FL, 53 in CA
Projected New Units (12 Months): 70
Qualifications: 4, 3, 1, 3, 1, 5
FINANCIAL/TERMS:
Cash Investment: $39K-52K
Total Investment: $34-47K
Minimum Net Worth: Varies
Fees: Franchise - $25.5K
  Royalty - 5%; Ad. - 0%
Earnings Claims Statement: No
Term of Contract (Years): 10/10
Avg. # Of Employees: 2 FT, 45 PT
Passive Ownership: Discouraged
Encourage Conversions: Yes
Area Develop. Agreements: No
Sub-Franchising Contracts: No
Expand In Territory: Yes
Space Needs: 500-700 SF
SUPPORT & TRAINING:
Financial Assistance Provided: No
Site Selection Assistance: Yes
Lease Negotiation Assistance: No
Co-Operative Advertising: No
Franchisee Assoc./Member: Yes/Yes
Size Of Corporate Staff: 65
On-Going Support: ,B,C,D,E,F,G,H,I
Training: 3 Days Field Visit Franchise
  Office; 1 Week Corporate Headquarters
SPECIFIC EXPANSION PLANS:
US: All United States
Canada: All Canada
Overseas: All Countries

≪ ≫

HOMEWATCH CAREGIVERS
7100 E. Belleview Ave., #303
Greenwood Village, CO 80111
Tel: (800) 777-9770 (303) 758-5111
Fax: (303) 758-1724
E-Mail: franchise@homewatch-intl.com
Web Site: www.homewatch-intl.com &
www.homewatchcaregivers.com
Ms. Dawn Wilson, Sales Coordinator

Homewatch CareGivers is the largest and most experienced full-service home care franchise that enables our franchisees to capture the largest market share possible. Our 29 years of medical and non-medical experience translates to success. In addition to the widest range of home care services, we offer the most individual revenue streams of any home care franchise, including Minor Medical Services - Nursing Services - Care Management Services - Transportation Services - Temporary Medical Staffing Services - Telehealth with Remote Care Monitoring - Veteran's Outreach Program - Medical Tourism Partnerships - our exclusive Pathways to Memory® Alzheimer's Program - our exclusive Work/Life Home Care® Back-Up Care Program.

BACKGROUND: IFA MEMBER
Established: 1980;   1st Franchised: 1996
Franchised Units: 173
Company-Owned Units: <u>3</u>
Total Units: 176
Dist.:   US-157; CAN-12; O'seas-7
   North America: 33 States, 2 Provinces
   Density: 10 in TX, 11 in CO, 22 in CA
Projected New Units (12 Months):   44
Qualifications: 5, 4, 2, 2, 2, 5
FINANCIAL/TERMS:
Cash Investment: $60K
Total Investment: $90-140K
Minimum Net Worth: $250K
Fees: Franchise - $35K
   Royalty - 5%;   Ad. - 1%
Earnings Claims Statement: Yes
Term of Contract (Years):   10/10
Avg. # Of Employees: 3-4 FT, 25-50 PT
Passive Ownership: Discouraged
Encourage Conversions: Yes
Area Develop. Agreements: Yes/2
Sub-Franchising Contracts: No
Expand In Territory: Yes
Space Needs: 700 SF
SUPPORT & TRAINING:
Financial Assistance Provided: Yes (I)
Site Selection Assistance: NA
Lease Negotiation Assistance: NA
Co-Operative Advertising: No
Franchisee Assoc./Member: Yes/Yes
Size Of Corporate Staff: 25
On-Going Support: ,,C,D,e,,G,h,I
Training: Weekly Teleconferences;
   5 Days Corporate Office; 4 Weeks
   Prior to Corp. Office Training Via
   Phone
SPECIFIC EXPANSION PLANS:
US: All United States except HI & UT
Canada: All Canada
Overseas: NR

◀◀   ▶▶

IKOR
415 McFarlan Rd., #200
Kennett Square, PA 19348
Tel: (877) IKOR-USA (610) 444-1454
Fax: (610) 444-9001
E-Mail: ikor@ikorusa.com
Web Site: www.ikorusa.com
Ms. Jennifer Corneliussen, COO

IKOR provides advocacy directed to the life issue facing the elderly / disabled and their families - the missing element in eldercare. IKOR provides RN assessment, strategic planning, implementation, and ongoing quality assurance enabling families to address the day to day concerns. IKOR also provides basic bill pay services and financial support. IKOR meets the needs of persons with no family, family at a distance, or when family is in conflict in making the decisions. In addition to core advocacy services, IKOR also provides professional guardianship of person / estate by the court appointment.

BACKGROUND:
Established: 1991;   1st Franchised: 2008
Franchised Units: 0
Company-Owned Units: <u>1</u>
Total Units: 1
Dist.:   US-1; CAN-0; O'seas-0
   North America: 2 States, 0 Provinces
   Density: 1 in PA
Projected New Units (12 Months):   10
Qualifications: 3, 5, 3, 5, 3, 5
FINANCIAL/TERMS:
Cash Investment: $53790-84630
Total Investment: $53790-84630
Minimum Net Worth: $87K
Fees: Franchise - $35K
   Royalty - 8%;   Ad. - 2%
Earnings Claims Statement: No
Term of Contract (Years):   10/5
Avg. # Of Employees: 5 FT, 5 PT
Passive Ownership: Discouraged
Encourage Conversions: No
Area Develop. Agreements: No
Sub-Franchising Contracts: No
Expand In Territory: No
Space Needs: 1,800 SF
SUPPORT & TRAINING:
Financial Assistance Provided: No
Site Selection Assistance: Yes

Lease Negotiation Assistance: Yes
Co-Operative Advertising: No
Franchisee Assoc./Member: No
Size Of Corporate Staff: 5
On-Going Support: A,,C,d,E,f,G,h,I
Training: 3 Weeks Kennett Square, PA
SPECIFIC EXPANSION PLANS:
US: Yes
Canada: No
Overseas: NR

◀◀   ▶▶

INTRIVAH HEALTH AND WELLNESS
2012 Eighth Ave.
Altoona, PA 16602
Tel: (800) 941-9251 (814) 941-9250
Fax: (814) 941-8260
E-Mail: info@intrivah.com
Web Site: www.intrivah.com
Mr. Michael McConnell, Vice President Franchising

INTRIVAH is an innovative, cutting-edge fitness and nutrition center with superb methodologies, an outstanding business system and a dynamic franchise opportunity. Consultants develop personalized wellness programs for people of all fitness levels in a safe, non-intimidating environment. INTRIVAH is an exciting franchise with a healthy future.

BACKGROUND:
Established: 2002;   1st Franchised: 2004
Franchised Units: 1
Company-Owned Units: <u>1</u>
Total Units: 2
Dist.:   US-2; CAN-0; O'seas-0
   North America: 1 States, 0 Provinces
   Density: 2 in PA
Projected New Units (12 Months):   10
Qualifications: 3, 2, 4, 3, 4, 5
FINANCIAL/TERMS:
Cash Investment: $50-80K
Total Investment: $134-225K
Minimum Net Worth: $150K
Fees: Franchise - $30K
   Royalty - 5%;   Ad. - 2%
Earnings Claims Statement: No
Term of Contract (Years):   5/5
Avg. # Of Employees: 2 FT, 1 PT
Passive Ownership: Not Allowed
Encourage Conversions: NA

Area Develop. Agreements: Yes/1
Sub-Franchising Contracts: No
Expand In Territory: No
Space Needs: 3,000 SF
SUPPORT & TRAINING:
Financial Assistance Provided: Yes (I)
Site Selection Assistance: Yes
Lease Negotiation Assistance: No
Co-Operative Advertising: Yes
Franchisee Assoc./Member: No
Size Of Corporate Staff: 3
On-Going Support: ,,C,d,E,,,h,I
Training: 10-14 Days Altoona, PA
SPECIFIC EXPANSION PLANS:
US: All United States
Canada: No
Overseas: NR

⊰⊰ ⊱⊱

JAZZERCISE

2460 Impala Dr.
Carlsbad, CA 92008
Tel: (800) FIT IS IT (760) 476-1750
Fax: (760) 602-7180
E-Mail: jazzinc@jazzercise.com
Web Site: www.jazzercise.com
Ms. Nancy Guetzke, Franchise Coordinator

JAZZERCISE is the world's leading international dance fitness franchisor, with a multi-media division and mail-order catalog business at 1-800-FIT-IS-IT, specializing in active wear and accessories.

BACKGROUND:
Established: 1969; 1st Franchised: 1983
Franchised Units: 5752
Company-Owned Units: 1
Total Units: 5753
Dist.: US-4792; CAN-101; O'seas-860
  North America: 50 States, 5 Provinces
  Density: 343 in TX, 296 in OH, 626 in CA
Projected New Units (12 Months): 600
Qualifications: 1, 2, 4, 2, 5, 5
FINANCIAL/TERMS:
Cash Investment: $1.5-3K
Total Investment: $3-33.1K
Minimum Net Worth: NA
Fees: Franchise - $700
  Royalty - 20%; Ad. - NA
Earnings Claims Statement: No
Term of Contract (Years): 5/5
Avg. # Of Employees: FT, 0 PT
Passive Ownership: Allowed
Encourage Conversions: NA
Area Develop. Agreements: No
Sub-Franchising Contracts: No

Expand In Territory: Yes
Space Needs: 3,000 SF
SUPPORT & TRAINING:
Financial Assistance Provided: No
Site Selection Assistance: No
Lease Negotiation Assistance: No
Co-Operative Advertising: No
Franchisee Assoc./Member: No
Size Of Corporate Staff: 125
On-Going Support: ,,C,D,,,G,H,I
Training: 3 Days Various Locations;
;
SPECIFIC EXPANSION PLANS:
US: All United States
Canada: All Canada
Overseas: All Countries

⊰⊰ ⊱⊱

JENNY CRAIG WEIGHT LOSS AND MANAGEMENT CENTRES

5770 Fleet St.
Carlsbad, CA 92008
Tel: (888) 848-8885 (760) 696-4000
Fax: (760) 696-4708
E-Mail: franchising@jennycraig.com
Web Site: www.jennycraig.com/franchise
Ms. Tracy Heiser, Franchise Development Coordinator

We change lives! JENNY CRAIG provides dynamic, safe and effective weight loss and lasting management solutions, tailored to individuals who desire to look better, feel better and live healthier. The JENNY CRAIG program is a long-term solution that helps clients lose weight, create a healthy relationship with food, build an active lifestyle and develop a balanced approach to living.

BACKGROUND: IFA MEMBER
Established: 1983; 1st Franchised: 1983
Franchised Units: 110
Company-Owned Units: 493
Total Units: 603
Dist.: US-485; CAN-34; O'seas-121
  North America: 46 States, 3 Provinces
  Density: NR
Projected New Units (12 Months): 20
Qualifications: 5, 5, 4, 4, 5, 5
FINANCIAL/TERMS:
Cash Investment: $100-150K
Total Investment: $165.6-440.5K
Minimum Net Worth: $300K
Fees: Franchise - $25K
  Royalty - 7%; Ad. - 10%
Earnings Claims Statement: Yes
Term of Contract (Years): 10/10
Avg. # Of Employees: 4 FT, 0 PT

Passive Ownership: Discouraged
Encourage Conversions: NA
Area Develop. Agreements: Yes/1
Sub-Franchising Contracts: No
Expand In Territory: Yes
Space Needs: 1,200-1,500 SF
SUPPORT & TRAINING:
Financial Assistance Provided: No
Site Selection Assistance: Yes
Lease Negotiation Assistance: Yes
Co-Operative Advertising: No
Franchisee Assoc./Member: No
Size Of Corporate Staff: 250
On-Going Support: A,B,C,D,E,F,,H,I
Training: 2-3 Weeks Corporate Office;
  2 Weeks In-Centre
SPECIFIC EXPANSION PLANS:
US: All United States
Canada: All Canada
Overseas: NR

⊰⊰ ⊱⊱

Hottest New Franchise

KNUCKLEHEADS
The coolest gym in town!

KNUCKLEHEADS GYM

2080 Newbury Rd., # C
Newbury Park, CA 91320
Tel: (866) 4KNUCKLE (805) 499-1554
Fax: (805) 499-3293
E-Mail: knuckleheadsgym@verizon.net
Web Site: www.knuckleheadsgym.com
Mr. Andy Kaplan, Sr. VP of Franchising

The Knuckleheads Gym Franchise Opportunity - Knuckleheads Gym is a kid-friendly, colorful, well organized, and safe environment that provides Futuristic Fitness Training for children. Our selection of specialized exercise equipment uses computer-generated devices, including virtual reality games and activity simulators. This means there is something for every child to enjoy. Best of all, the interactive nature of our state-of-the-art equipment actually makes kids enthusiastic about exercising!

BACKGROUND: IFA MEMBER
Established: 2006; 1st Franchised: 2008
Franchised Units: 0
Company-Owned Units: 2
Total Units: 2
Dist.: US-2; CAN-0; O'seas-0
  North America: 2 States, 0 Provinces
  Density: 1 in NY, 1 in CA
Projected New Units (12 Months): 12

Qualifications: 5, 4, 4, 3, 4, 5

FINANCIAL/TERMS:

Cash Investment: $125K
Total Investment: $178,900-$282,000
Minimum Net Worth: $500K
Fees: Franchise - $30K
  Royalty - 8; Ad. - 2
Earnings Claims Statement: No
Term of Contract (Years): 5/5
Avg. # Of Employees: 1-2 FT, 2-4 PT
Passive Ownership: Not Allowed
Encourage Conversions: Yes
Area Develop. Agreements: No
Sub-Franchising Contracts: No
Expand In Territory: Yes
Space Needs: 1800 SF

SUPPORT & TRAINING:

Financial Assistance Provided: Yes (I)
Site Selection Assistance: Yes
Lease Negotiation Assistance: Yes
Co-Operative Advertising: No
Franchisee Assoc./Member: No
Size Of Corporate Staff: 5
On-Going Support: „C,D,E,f,,h,
Training: 50 hours Onsite training;
  50 hours CA or NY

SPECIFIC EXPANSION PLANS:

US: California, Tri-state NY Area
Canada: No
Overseas: NR

◄◄ ►►

L A WEIGHT LOSS CENTERS

3959 Welsh Rd., # 302
Willow Grove, PA 19090
Tel: (888) 258-7099 (215) 346-8762
Fax: (215) 346-8929
E-Mail: franchise@la-weightloss.com
Web Site: www.laweightloss.com
Mr. Tim Britt, SVP Franchise Development

L A WEIGHT LOSS CENTERS combine personalized meal plans, using everyday foods, with professional one-on-one counseling and a line of proprietary products to create one of the hottest new business opportunities. This center-based weight loss program features the industry's leading marketing, training and operations systems.

BACKGROUND: IFA MEMBER
Established: 1989; 1st Franchised: 1998
Franchised Units: 60
Company-Owned Units: 0
Total Units: 60
Dist.: US-25; CAN-30; O'seas-5
  North America: NR
  Density: 11 in AB, 4 in ND
Projected New Units (12 Months): NR
Qualifications: 3, 5, 1, 3, 3, 4

FINANCIAL/TERMS:

Cash Investment: $60K-115K
Total Investment: $84.6K-149.8K
Minimum Net Worth: $200K
Fees: Franchise - $20K
  Royalty - 7%; Ad. -
Earnings Claims Statement: No
Term of Contract (Years): 10/10
Avg. # Of Employees: 5 FT, 0 PT
Passive Ownership: Not Allowed
Encourage Conversions: NA
Area Develop. Agreements: Yes/1
Sub-Franchising Contracts: No
Expand In Territory: Yes
Space Needs: 1,200 SF

SUPPORT & TRAINING:

Financial Assistance Provided: Yes (D)
Site Selection Assistance: Yes
Lease Negotiation Assistance: Yes
Co-Operative Advertising: No
Franchisee Assoc./Member: No
Size Of Corporate Staff: 1460
On-Going Support: A,B,C,D,E,,G,H,I
Training:1 Week Corporate Headquarters;
  2 Weeks Center; 2 Weeks Classroom

SPECIFIC EXPANSION PLANS:

US: Specific Cities Only
Canada: Yes
Overseas: S. America, Mexico, W. Europe, UK

◄◄ ►►

LIBERTY FITNESS FOR WOMEN

1701 Directors Blvd., # 110
Austin, TX 78744
Tel: (888) 521-2592 (512) 623-3660
Fax: (512) 623-3661
E-Mail: franchisedevelopment@libertyfitness.com
Web Site: www.libertyfitness.com
Mr. Josh Burzynski, Franchise Development Coordinator

Liberty Fitness, one of the fastest growing 30-minute fitness franchises, addresses the whole woman through the total body approach of fitness, nutrition and wellness. Recently ranked 3rd in the woman's only fitness category by Entrepreneur Magazine's Franchise 500, Liberty Fitness offers multiple and recurring revenues streams.

BACKGROUND: IFA MEMBER
Established: 2002; 1st Franchised: 2002
Franchised Units: 40
Company-Owned Units: 0
Total Units: 40
Dist.: US-40; CAN-0; O'seas-0
  North America: 0 States, 0 Provinces
  Density: 3 in OH, 4 in GA, 14 in CA
Projected New Units (12 Months): NR
Qualifications: NR

FINANCIAL/TERMS:

Cash Investment: $30.5-44.5K
Total Investment: $108-160K
Minimum Net Worth: $250K
Fees: Franchise - $30.6K
  Royalty - 5%; Ad. - $300/mo.
Earnings Claims Statement: No
Term of Contract (Years): 10/10
Avg. # Of Employees: 1 FT, 4-5 PT
Passive Ownership: Allowed
Encourage Conversions: No
Area Develop. Agreements: Yes/10
Sub-Franchising Contracts: No
Expand In Territory: Yes
Space Needs: 2,000+ SF

SUPPORT & TRAINING:

Financial Assistance Provided: Yes (I)
Site Selection Assistance: Yes
Lease Negotiation Assistance: Yes
Co-Operative Advertising: Yes
Franchisee Assoc./Member: No
Size Of Corporate Staff: 9
On-Going Support: ,B,C,D,E,,G,H,
Training: 2-3 Days; 1 Week Corporate
  Headquarters;

SPECIFIC EXPANSION PLANS:

US: All United States
Canada: No
Overseas: NR

◄◄ ►►

LOA FITNESS FOR WOMEN

500 E. Broward Blvd., # 1650
Ft. Lauderdale, FL 33394-3000
Tel: (800) 833-5239 (954) 326-1306
Fax: (954) 527-5436
E-Mail: jmajirsky@ladyofamerica.com
Web Site: www.loafitnessforwomen.com
Mr. Jim Majirsky, Director Franchise Sales

Owning a LOA Fitness For Women Center sets you apart from the competition. We take great pride in our units. As the world's largest full service Workout and Fitness centers focused on women, we are truly unique. From our training staff, group exercise programs, and message therapy, LOA Fitness Centers have been developed in every way with the woman in mind. Clean, comfortable, and safe, we have been offering an outstanding workout environment to our members for nearly 25 years!

BACKGROUND: IFA MEMBER
Established: 1984;   1st Franchised: 1989
Franchised Units: 385
Company-Owned Units: 9
Total Units: 394
Dist.:   US-364; CAN-4; O'seas-30
  North America: 45 States, 1 Provinces
  Density: 34 in CA, 36 in TX, 40 in FL
Projected New Units (12 Months):   12
Qualifications: 5, 5, 4, 4, 5, 5
FINANCIAL/TERMS:

Cash Investment: $100K
Total Investment: $187-452K
Minimum Net Worth: $250K
Fees: Franchise - $30K
  Royalty - 8%;   Ad. - $195
Earnings Claims Statement: No
Term of Contract (Years):   10/2
Avg. # Of Employees: 4 FT, 3 PT
Passive Ownership: Discouraged
Encourage Conversions: Yes
Area Develop. Agreements: Yes/1
Sub-Franchising Contracts: No
Expand In Territory: Yes
Space Needs: 3,500-6,000 SF
SUPPORT & TRAINING:

Financial Assistance Provided: Yes (I)
Site Selection Assistance: Yes
Lease Negotiation Assistance: Yes
Co-Operative Advertising: Yes
Franchisee Assoc./Member: Yes/Yes
Size Of Corporate Staff: 21
On-Going Support: ,,C,D,E,,G,h,I
Training: 1 Week Home Office in Ft. Lauderdale, FL; 1-3 Weeks Membership pre-sale prior to opening at location;1 WeekGrand opening at location
SPECIFIC EXPANSION PLANS:

US: All United States
Canada: All Canada
Overseas: All Countries

◄◄   ►►

MEDSONIX
2626 S. Rainbow Blvd., # 109
Las Vegas, NV 89146
Tel: (866) 565-6337 NR
Fax: (702) 873-6880
E-Mail: bruce@medsonix.com
Web Site: www.medsonix.com
Mr. Bruce Benson, VP

Medsonix has a new medical breakthrough technology that is FDA registered, holds a US Patent, also two University studies completed. This Therapy is a non-invasive and drug free method of dealing with wellness issues by using our acoustic wave system.

BACKGROUND:
Established: 2001;   1st Franchised: 2006
Franchised Units: 1
Company-Owned Units: 1
Total Units: 2
Dist.:   US-2; CAN-0; O'seas-0
  North America: 2 States, 0 Provinces
  Density: 1 in NY, 1 in CA
Projected New Units (12 Months):   NR
Qualifications: 3, 3, 3, 3, 3, 3
FINANCIAL/TERMS:

Cash Investment: $125K
Total Investment: $125K
Minimum Net Worth: $150K
Fees: Franchise - $80K
  Royalty - 12%;   Ad. - 0
Earnings Claims Statement: No
Term of Contract (Years):   10/20
Avg. # Of Employees: 2 FT, 0 PT
Passive Ownership: Allowed
Encourage Conversions: NA
Area Develop. Agreements: Yes
Sub-Franchising Contracts: No
Expand In Territory: No
Space Needs: 800 SF
SUPPORT & TRAINING:

Financial Assistance Provided: No
Site Selection Assistance: Yes
Lease Negotiation Assistance: Yes
Co-Operative Advertising: No
Franchisee Assoc./Member: No
Size Of Corporate Staff: 3
On-Going Support: A,,,D,E,,,,I
Training: 1 Day Las Vegas, NV
SPECIFIC EXPANSION PLANS:

US: All United States
Canada: No
Overseas: NR

◄◄   ►►

MIRACLE-EAR
5000 Cheshire Ln., N.

Plymouth, MN 55446
Tel: (800) 234-7714 + 4048 (763) 268-4000
Fax: (763) 268-4254
E-Mail: carl.fulton@amplifon.com
Web Site: www.miracle-ear.com
Mr. Carl Fulton, Franchise Development Manager

Manufacturer and world's largest retailer of hearing systems, with 1,287 offices nationally. MIRACLE-EAR also has master franchisors in 20 foreign countries.

BACKGROUND: IFA MEMBER
Established: 1948;   1st Franchised: 1984
Franchised Units: 1200
Company-Owned Units: 30
Total Units: 1230
Dist.:   US-1230; CAN-0; O'seas-20
  North America: 50 States, 0 Provinces
  Density: 39 in TX, 74 in FL, 96 in CA
Projected New Units (12 Months):   125
Qualifications: 4, 4, 2, 3, 4, 4
FINANCIAL/TERMS:

Cash Investment: $25K-50K
Total Investment: $88K-200K
Minimum Net Worth: $100K
Fees: Franchise - $28-60K
  Royalty - $46.50/Unit;   Ad.
  - $26/Inquiry
Earnings Claims Statement: No
Term of Contract (Years):   5/5
Avg. # Of Employees: 2 FT, 1 PT
Passive Ownership: Not Allowed
Encourage Conversions: NA
Area Develop. Agreements: Yes/1
Sub-Franchising Contracts: No
Expand In Territory: Yes
Space Needs: 750 SF
SUPPORT & TRAINING:

Financial Assistance Provided: NR
Site Selection Assistance: NA
Lease Negotiation Assistance: No
Co-Operative Advertising: No
Franchisee Assoc./Member: No
Size Of Corporate Staff: 3
On-Going Support: A,,C,D,E,,G,h,I
Training: 2 Weeks Corporate Headquarters; 10 Weeks On-Site
SPECIFIC EXPANSION PLANS:

US: West,Midwest
Canada: No
Overseas: All Countries

◄◄   ►►

PEARLE VISION

4000 Luxottica Pl.
Mason, OH 45040
Tel: (800) 732-7531 (513) 765-3462
Fax: (513) 492-3462
E-Mail: mlichten@luxotticaretail.com
Web Site: www.pearlevision.com
Mr. Ray Kirmeyer, Manager Franchise
  Development

PEARLE VISION, the largest optical franchisor, offers the ability for qualified individuals to benefit from PEARLE's strong name recognition and operating systems developed over the past 36 years. We have been franchising for 16 years.

BACKGROUND: IFA MEMBER
Established: 1961; 1st Franchised: 1980
Franchised Units: 402
Company-Owned Units: <u>499</u>
Total Units: 901
Dist.: US-813; CAN-103; O'seas-36
  North America: 43 States, 2 Provinces
  Density: 48 in TX, 65 in PA, 53 in IL
Projected New Units (12 Months): 25
Qualifications: 5, 4, 5, 3, 2, 4
FINANCIAL/TERMS:
Cash Investment: $35-125K
Total Investment: $250-500K
Minimum Net Worth: Varies
Fees: Franchise - $30K
  Royalty - 7%; Ad. - 8%
Earnings Claims Statement: No
Term of Contract (Years): 10/10
Avg. # Of Employees: Varies
Passive Ownership: Not Allowed
Encourage Conversions: Yes
Area Develop. Agreements: No
Sub-Franchising Contracts: No
Expand In Territory: Yes
Space Needs: 1,800-2,400 SF
SUPPORT & TRAINING:
Financial Assistance Provided: No
Site Selection Assistance: No
Lease Negotiation Assistance: No
Co-Operative Advertising: Yes
Franchisee Assoc./Member: Yes/Yes
Size Of Corporate Staff: 250
On-Going Support: a,B,C,D,E,F,G,h,
Training: Varies Dramatically Skill
  Assessment of Franchisee
SPECIFIC EXPANSION PLANS:
US: All U.S. Except CA
Canada: No
Overseas: NR

≪ ≫

PERSONAL TRAINING INSTITUTE

500 N. Broadway
Jericho, NY 11753
Tel: (877) PTI-WORK (516) 342-9064
+ 12
Fax:
E-Mail: ekaplan@personaltraininginstitute.com
Web Site: www.ptifranchise.com
Mr. Cliff Nonnenmacher, VP Franchise
  Development

Personal Training Institute combines fitness and nutrition to help its clients reach their goals. PTI's program centers around a custom-tailored 30 minute strength training session with a personal trainer. As part of the program the client meets with a licensed nutritionist who helps them develop good eating habits. Over the past 18 years PTI has developed a very strong business model that is easy to operate. We are looking for passionate, business-minded, financially-qualified individuals.

BACKGROUND: IFA MEMBER
Established: 1987; 1st Franchised: 2005
Franchised Units: 10
Company-Owned Units: <u>7</u>
Total Units: 17
Dist.: US-14; CAN-0; O'seas-0
  North America: 2 States, 0 Provinces
  Density: 13 in NY, 1 in ME
Projected New Units (12 Months): 25
Qualifications: 2, 4, 3, 1, 1, 5
FINANCIAL/TERMS:
Cash Investment: $40-50K
Total Investment: $120-220K
Minimum Net Worth: $0K
Fees: Franchise - $19.5K
  Royalty - 5%; Ad. - 2%
Earnings Claims Statement: No
Term of Contract (Years): 10/5
Avg. # Of Employees: 1 FT, 8 PT
Passive Ownership: Allowed
Encourage Conversions: NA
Area Develop. Agreements: Yes/10
Sub-Franchising Contracts: No
Expand In Territory: No
Space Needs: 2,000 SF
SUPPORT & TRAINING:
Financial Assistance Provided: Yes (I)
Site Selection Assistance: Yes
Lease Negotiation Assistance: Yes
Co-Operative Advertising: Yes
Franchisee Assoc./Member: Yes/No
Size Of Corporate Staff: 5

On-Going Support: a,B,C,D,E,,G,H,I
Training: 10 Days Smithtown, NY
SPECIFIC EXPANSION PLANS:
US: All United States
Canada: No
Overseas: NR

≪ ≫

RELAX THE BACK

6 Centerpointe Dr., # 350
La Palma, CA 90623
Tel: (800) 290-2225 (714) 523-2870
Fax: (714) 523-2980
E-Mail: rociom@relaxtheback.com
Web Site: www.relaxtheback.com
Mr./Ms. Rocio Meza, Coord., Franchise
  Development

North America's largest specialty retailer of ergonomic and back care products. We are in the comfort business, many of our products are designed to relieve or eliminate back and neck pain.

BACKGROUND: IFA MEMBER
Established: 1984; 1st Franchised: 1989
Franchised Units: 126
Company-Owned Units: <u>0</u>
Total Units: 126
Dist.: US-122; CAN-4; O'seas-0
  North America: 35 States, 1 Provinces
  Density: 12 in TX, 11 in FL, 27 in CA
Projected New Units (12 Months): 20
Qualifications: 4, 4, 3, 3, 2, 5
FINANCIAL/TERMS:
Cash Investment: $85K-100K
Total Investment: $198K-371.5K
Minimum Net Worth: $450K
Fees: Franchise - $49.5K
  Royalty - 4-5%; Ad. - 2%
Earnings Claims Statement: Yes
Term of Contract (Years): 10/10
Avg. # Of Employees: 3 FT, 1 PT
Passive Ownership: Discouraged
Encourage Conversions: NA
Area Develop. Agreements: Yes
Sub-Franchising Contracts: No
Expand In Territory: No
Space Needs: 2,600 SF
SUPPORT & TRAINING:
Financial Assistance Provided: Yes (I)
Site Selection Assistance: Yes
Lease Negotiation Assistance: Yes
Co-Operative Advertising: Yes
Franchisee Assoc./Member: Yes/Yes

Size Of Corporate Staff: 32
On-Going Support: ,,C,D,E,,G,H,I
Training: 1 Week On-Site;
   10 Days Corp HQ
SPECIFIC EXPANSION PLANS:
US: All United States
Canada: All Canada
Overseas: NR

RIGHT AT HOME
11949 Q St., # 100
Omaha, NE 68137
Tel: (877) 697-7537 (402) 697-7537
Fax: (402) 697-0289
E-Mail: dcarlson@rightathome.net
Web Site: www.rightathome.net
Ms. Sharon Thomsen, Franchise Development Coordinator

RIGHT AT HOME offers one of the most exciting opportunities in franchising today. RIGHT AT HOME offers in-home senior care and supplemental staffing for the healthcare industry. You double your opportunity with the same franchise system.

BACKGROUND: IFA MEMBER
Established: 1995; 1st Franchised: 2000
Franchised Units: 150
Company-Owned Units: 1
Total Units: 151
Dist.: US-151; CAN-0; O'seas-0
North America: 35 States, 0 Provinces
Density: NR
Projected New Units (12 Months): 50
Qualifications: 3, 4, 1, 1, 1, 5
FINANCIAL/TERMS:
Cash Investment: $50K-60K
Total Investment: $40K-70K
Minimum Net Worth: $100K
Fees: Franchise - $30K
  Royalty - 5%; Ad. - 0%
Earnings Claims Statement: Yes
Term of Contract (Years): 10/5/5/5/
Avg. # Of Employees: FT, 0 PT
Passive Ownership: Discouraged
Encourage Conversions: No
Area Develop. Agreements: No
Sub-Franchising Contracts: No
Expand In Territory: Yes
Space Needs: 700 SF
SUPPORT & TRAINING:

Financial Assistance Provided: No
Site Selection Assistance: Yes
Lease Negotiation Assistance: No
Co-Operative Advertising: Yes
Franchisee Assoc./Member: No
Size Of Corporate Staff: 18
On-Going Support: ,,C,D,,,G,H,I
Training: 2 Weeks Omaha, NE
SPECIFIC EXPANSION PLANS:
US: All United States except RI, ND, HI
Canada: No
Overseas: NR

SENIOR HELPERS
8601 LaSalle Rd., # 208
Towson, MD 21286
Tel: (800) 760-6389 (410) 453-6172
Fax: (815) 346-9545
E-Mail: pross@seniorhelpers.com
Web Site: www.seniorhelpers.com
Mr. Jason Wiedder, Director of Franchise Development

Senior Helpers is the fastest growing in-home senior care franchise in the US. Dominate your local market with our state-of-the-art marketing blueprint, large territories focused on the true senior market of 75 years of age, RN on staff, and all software included. By the year 2030, over 70,000,000 people in the US will be seniors, that is one out of every 5 persons living in the US. Our franchises are offered industry leading training and technology platforms to provide the best support available.

BACKGROUND: IFA MEMBER
Established: 2001; 1st Franchised: 2005
Franchised Units: 208
Company-Owned Units: 1
Total Units: 209
Dist.: US-209; CAN-0; O'seas-0
North America: 17 States, 0 Provinces
Density: 5 in VA, 4 in GA, 13 in CA
Projected New Units (12 Months): 50
Qualifications: 4, 5, 4, 4, 1, 5
FINANCIAL/TERMS:
Cash Investment: $60K-80K
Total Investment: $60K-80K
Minimum Net Worth: $60K
Fees: Franchise - $35K
  Royalty - 5%; Ad. - .5%

Earnings Claims Statement: Yes
Term of Contract (Years): 15/5
Avg. # Of Employees: 0 FT, 1 PT
Passive Ownership: Not Allowed
Encourage Conversions: NA
Area Develop. Agreements: No
Sub-Franchising Contracts: No
Expand In Territory: Yes
Space Needs: NA
SUPPORT & TRAINING:
Financial Assistance Provided: No
Site Selection Assistance: Yes
Lease Negotiation Assistance: Yes
Co-Operative Advertising: Yes
Franchisee Assoc./Member: No
Size Of Corporate Staff: 7
On-Going Support: ,,C,D,E,,G,h,
Training: 2 Days Franchisee On-Site
  - Initial; 5 Days Corporate Office
  - Batlimore;1 Day Franchise On-Site
  - 90 Days
SPECIFIC EXPANSION PLANS:
US: All States
Canada: No
Overseas: NR

WOMEN'S HEALTH BOUTIQUE
12715 Telge Rd.
Cypress, TX 77429-2289
Tel: (888) 280-2053 (281) 256-4100
Fax: (281) 256-4178
E-Mail: w-h-bsales@w-h-b.com
Web Site: www.w-h-b.com
Mr. Donald Averitt, VP Franchise Sales

WOMEN'S HEALTH BOUTIQUE provides products and services for women with special needs. A caring and compassionate staff creates a comfortable environment for individuals buying maternity and post-mastectomy products and personal care items, including compression therapy, turbans and wigs.

BACKGROUND: IFA MEMBER
Established: 1988; 1st Franchised: 1993
Franchised Units: 13
Company-Owned Units: 1
Total Units: 14
Dist.: US-14; CAN-0; O'seas-0
North America: 6 States, 0 Provinces
Density: 4 in TX, 2 in MI, 2 in CA
Projected New Units (12 Months): NR

Qualifications:	4, 4, 3, 2, 5, 5	Encourage Conversions:	NA
FINANCIAL/TERMS:		Area Develop. Agreements:	No
Cash Investment:	$35K	Sub-Franchising Contracts:	No
Total Investment:	$215.3-247.4K	Expand In Territory:	Yes
Minimum Net Worth:	$200K	Space Needs:	1,500 SF
Fees: Franchise -	$20K	**SUPPORT & TRAINING:**	
Royalty - 4-7%;	Ad. - 0%	Financial Assistance Provided:	Yes (D)
Earnings Claims Statement:	No	Site Selection Assistance:	Yes
Term of Contract (Years):	15/	Lease Negotiation Assistance:	Yes
Avg. # Of Employees:	2 FT, 0 PT	Co-Operative Advertising:	No
Passive Ownership:	Not Allowed	Franchisee Assoc./Member:	Yes/Yes

Size Of Corporate Staff:	NR
On-Going Support:	,,C,D,E,,G,H,I
Training:	3 Weeks Headquarters
SPECIFIC EXPANSION PLANS:	
US:	All United States
Canada:	No
Overseas:	NR

◄◄   ►►

FIVE LARGEST PARTICIPANTS IN SURVEY

Company	# Fran-chised Units	# Co-Owned Units	# Total Units	Franchise Fee	On-Going Royalty	Total Investment
1. Choice Hotels International	5,827	0	5,827	$25-50K	2.75-5.1%	$2.3-12.6MM
2. InterContinental Hotels Group (IHG®)	4,186	16	4,202	Minimum $50K	5%	Varies
3. Hampton Inn/Hampton Inn & Suites	1,652	31	1,683	$50K	5% Gross Rm. Rev	$3.7-13.1MM
4. Carlson Hotels Worldwide	958	37	995	$35K-75K	4-5%	$3-100MM
5. Motel 6	312	651	963	$25K	4%	$2.3-$3.2MM

All of the data provided are proprietary and should not be quoted without acknowledging *Bond's Franchise Guide.*

AMERICINN INTERNATIONAL, LLC
250 Lake Dr. E.
Chanhassen, MN 55317-9364
Tel: (800) 856-0951 (952) 294-5000
Fax: (952) 294-5001
E-Mail: jkennedy@americinn.com
Web Site: www.americinn.com
Mr. Jon D. Kennedy, SVP Franchise Development

The AmericInn Lodging System is one of the fastest growing limited service lodging chains. The success and solid growth of the AmericInn Lodging System is due to its unique AmericInn SoundGuard construction, product and market niche.

AmericInn competes across the mid-scale without food and beverage segments and is dedicated to the concept of providing the best lodging value for its guests. **AmericInn International, LLC, 250 Lake Drive East, Chanhassen, Minnesota 55317; MNReg No.F-1492. This advertisement is not an offering. An offering can only be made by a prospectus first filed with the Department of Law of the State of New York. Such filing does not constitute approval by the Department of Law. These franchises have been registered under the franchise investment law of the state of California. Such registration does not constitute approval, recommendation or endorsement by the commissioner of

corporations nor a finding by the commissioner that the information provided herein is true, complete and not misleading.

BACKGROUND: IFA MEMBER
Established: 1984;   1st Franchised: 1984
Franchised Units: 230
Company-Owned Units: 0
Total Units: 230
Dist.:   US-230; CAN-0; O'seas-0
  North America: 24 States, 0 Provinces
  Density: 45 in WI, 38 in MN, 27 in IA
Projected New Units (12 Months):   200
Qualifications: 5, 5, 4, 4, 4, NR
FINANCIAL/TERMS:
Cash Investment: $900K-1.5MM

Total Investment:	$5MM-10MM
Minimum Net Worth:	$1MM
Fees: Franchise -	$35K
Royalty - 5%;	Ad. - 2%
Earnings Claims Statement:	No
Term of Contract (Years):	20/
Avg. # Of Employees:	20 FT, 9 PT
Passive Ownership:	Allowed
Encourage Conversions:	NA
Area Develop. Agreements:	No
Sub-Franchising Contracts:	No
Expand In Territory:	Yes
Space Needs:	70,000+ SF

SUPPORT & TRAINING:

Financial Assistance Provided:	Yes (D)
Site Selection Assistance:	Yes
Lease Negotiation Assistance:	Yes
Co-Operative Advertising:	No
Franchisee Assoc./Member:	Yes/Yes
Size Of Corporate Staff:	75
On-Going Support:	A,B,C,D,E,F,G,h,i
Training:	1 Week Varies

SPECIFIC EXPANSION PLANS:

US:	All United States
Canada:	All Canada
Overseas:	All Countries

◄◄ ►►

CARLSON HOTELS WORLDWIDE

701 Carlson Pkwy., MS 8205
Minnetonka, MN 55305
Tel: (800) 336-3301 NR
Fax: NR
E-Mail: jrussenberger@carlson.com
Web Site: www.carlson.com
Ms. Janelle Russenberger, Development Associate

Carlson Hotels Worldwide is one of the world's major hotel companies, encompassing five brands and operating in more than 995 locations in 74 countries. Brands include: Regent International Hotels, Radisson Hotels & Resorts, Park Plaza Hotels & Resorts, Country Inns & Suites by Carlson, and Park Inn Hotels. These operations include most of the major segments in the hotel industry, ranging from luxury to limited service.

BACKGROUND: IFA MEMBER

Established: 1938;	1st Franchised: 1938
Franchised Units:	958
Company-Owned Units:	37
Total Units:	995
Dist.:	US-592; CAN-39; O'seas-364

North America:	43 States, 7 Provinces
Density:	39 in WI, 43 in GA, 51 in MN
Projected New Units (12 Months):	NR
Qualifications:	5, 5, 5, 3, 5, 5

FINANCIAL/TERMS:

Cash Investment:	$1-20MM
Total Investment:	$3-100MM
Minimum Net Worth:	NA
Fees: Franchise -	$35K-75K
Royalty - 4-5%;	Ad. - 2-2.5%
Earnings Claims Statement:	Yes
Term of Contract (Years):	15-20/NR
Avg. # Of Employees:	Varies
Passive Ownership:	Allowed
Encourage Conversions:	NA
Area Develop. Agreements:	No
Sub-Franchising Contracts:	No
Expand In Territory:	No
Space Needs:	NA

SUPPORT & TRAINING:

Financial Assistance Provided:	No
Site Selection Assistance:	No
Lease Negotiation Assistance:	No
Co-Operative Advertising:	No
Franchisee Assoc./Member:	Yes/Yes
Size Of Corporate Staff:	0
On-Going Support:	,B,C,D,E,,G,H,I
Training:	5 Days Minneapolis, MN; varies A hotel site;

SPECIFIC EXPANSION PLANS:

US:	All United States
Canada:	All Canada
Overseas:	All Countries

◄◄ ►►

CHOICE HOTELS INTERNATIONAL

CHOICE HOTELS INTERNATIONAL

10750 Columbia Pike
Silver Spring, MD 20901-4427
Tel: (866) 560-9871 (301) 592-5041
Fax: (301) 592-5058
E-Mail: emerging_markets@choicehotels.com
Web Site: www.choicehotels.com
Mr. Brian Parker, Dir. Emerging Mkts./ Bus. Devel

Choice Hotels® is the leading hotel franchisor with over 65 years experience in developing brands and services that optimize hotel performance. Our single focus is on enhancing the return on investment for our owners and growing our brands strategically. Brands include Comfort Inn®, Comfort Suites®, Quality®, Sleep Inn®, Clarion®, MainStay Suites®, Suburban Extended Stay®, Econo Lodge®, Rodeway Inn® and our newest upscale, all-suites brand Cambria Suites®. We offer brands for conversion and new build opportunities. *Source of operating units data: 4th quarter 2008 operating unit numbers. *Your fees/terms may fall outside the ranges listed. Please contact Choice Hotels at (800) 547-0007 to receive the latest FDD for the brand(s) you are interested in or visit choicehotelsfranchise.com for more details.

BACKGROUND: IFA MEMBER

Established: 1940;	1st Franchised: 1940
Franchised Units:	5827
Company-Owned Units:	0
Total Units:	5827
Dist.:	US-4716; CAN-275; O'seas-836
North America:	50 States, 10 Provinces
Density:	258 in FL, 358 in CA, 365 in TX
Projected New Units (12 Months):	NR
Qualifications:	4, 4, 4, 2, 1, 1

FINANCIAL/TERMS:

Cash Investment:	$20-30% Costs
Total Investment:	$2.3-12.6M
Minimum Net Worth:	Varies
Fees: Franchise -	$25-50K
Royalty - 2.75-5.1%;	Ad. - 1.75% Rev.
Earnings Claims Statement:	Yes
Term of Contract (Years):	20/5
Avg. # Of Employees:	Varies
Passive Ownership:	Allowed
Encourage Conversions:	Yes
Area Develop. Agreements:	No
Sub-Franchising Contracts:	No
Expand In Territory:	Yes
Space Needs:	31,000-33,000 SF

SUPPORT & TRAINING:

Financial Assistance Provided:	Yes (D)
Site Selection Assistance:	Yes
Lease Negotiation Assistance:	Yes
Co-Operative Advertising:	No
Franchisee Assoc./Member:	Yes/Yes
Size Of Corporate Staff:	1500
On-Going Support:	A,B,C,D,,F,G,h,I
Training:	NR

SPECIFIC EXPANSION PLANS:

US:	All United States
Canada:	All Canada
Overseas:	All Countries

◄◄ ►►

COUNTRY INNS & SUITES BY CARLSON

701 Carlson Pkwy., MS 8254
Minnetonka, MN 55305
Tel: (800) 336-3301 (763) 212-6615
Fax: (763) 212-3350
E-Mail: jrussenberger@carlson.com
Web Site: www.countryinns.com
Ms. Janelle Russenberger, Development
    Associate

Country Inns & Suites by Carlson℠ is a highly successful mid-tier lodging chain offering excellent value at more than 492 locations with 39,421 guestrooms worldwide. Country Inns & Suites locations feature traditional architecture and furnishings, and each hotel welcomes guests with a sophisticated residential interior design including hardwood flooring, lobby fireplace and decorative ceiling borders.

BACKGROUND: IFA MEMBER
Established: 1986;   1st Franchised: 1987
Franchised Units: 483
Company-Owned Units: 2
Total Units: 492
Dist.:   US-462; CAN-14; O'seas-16
    North America: 42 States, 7 Provinces
    Density: 31 in IL, 41 in MN, 47 in GA
Projected New Units (12 Months):   40
Qualifications: 5, 5, 5, 3, 5, 5
FINANCIAL/TERMS:
Cash Investment: Varies
Total Investment: $4.2-6.54MM
Minimum Net Worth: NA
Fees: Franchise - $45K
    Royalty - 4.5%;   Ad. - 2.5%
Earnings Claims Statement: Yes
Term of Contract (Years):   15/NA
Avg. # Of Employees: Varies
Passive Ownership: Allowed
Encourage Conversions: Yes
Area Develop. Agreements: No
Sub-Franchising Contracts: No
Expand In Territory: No
Space Needs: Varies
SUPPORT & TRAINING:
Financial Assistance Provided: No
Site Selection Assistance: No
Lease Negotiation Assistance: No
Co-Operative Advertising: No
Franchisee Assoc./Member: Yes/Yes

Size Of Corporate Staff: 100
On-Going Support: ,B,C,D,E,,G,H,I
Training: 3 Days On-Site;
    3 Days New Franchisee; 1 Week Minneapolis, MN (Brand Orientation)
SPECIFIC EXPANSION PLANS:
US: All United States
Canada: All Canada
Overseas: Europe, Asia, South and
    Central America

<< >>

DOUBLETREE

9336 Civic Center Dr.
Beverly Hills, CA 90210
Tel: (800) 286-0645 (310) 205-7696
Fax: (310) 205-7655
E-Mail: bill_fortier@hilton.com
Web Site: www.doubletreefranchise.com
Mr. Bill Fortier, SVP Franchise Development

With a growing collection of contemporary, upscale accommodations in more than 200 gateway cities, metropolitan areas and vacation destinations worldwide, Doubletree Hotels, Guest Suites and Resorts are distinctively designed properties that provide true comfort to today's business and leisure travelers. From the millions of delighted hotel guests who are welcomed with the brand's legendary, warm chocolate chip cookies at check-in to the advantages of the award-winning Hilton HHonors® guest reward program, each Doubletree guest receives a satisfying stay wherever their travels take them. Doubletree is part of Hilton Hotels Corporation, the leading global hospitality company with more than 3,000 hotels and 500,000 rooms in 74 countries and territories, with more than 135,000 team members worldwide. The company owns, manages or franchises some of the best known and highly regarded hotel brands including Hilton®, Conrad® Hotels & Resorts, Doubletree®, Embassy Suites Hotels®, Hampton Inn®, Hampton Inn & Suites®, Hilton Garden Inn®, Hilton Grand Vacations™, Homewood Suites by Hilton®, the Waldorf Astoria™ and the Waldorf Astoria Collection™, as well as the recently launched Home2 Suites by Hilton™.

BACKGROUND: IFA MEMBER
Established: 1989;   1st Franchised: 1989
Franchised Units: 166
Company-Owned Units: 50
Total Units: 216
Dist.:   US-200; CAN-2; O'seas-14
    North America: 40 States, 2 Provinces
    Density: 12 in TX, 19 in FL, 30 in CA
Projected New Units (12 Months):   NR
Qualifications: 5, 5, 5, 3, 1, 3
FINANCIAL/TERMS:
Cash Investment: $75K
Total Investment: $33.8-56.7MM
Minimum Net Worth: $70K/Rm.
Fees: Franchise - $75K Min.
    Royalty - 5% Gross Rm. Rev; Ad. - 4%
Gross Rm
Earnings Claims Statement: No
Term of Contract (Years):   22/10-20
Avg. # Of Employees: 100 FT, 0 PT
Passive Ownership: Allowed
Encourage Conversions: Yes
Area Develop. Agreements: Yes/1
Sub-Franchising Contracts: No
Expand In Territory: Yes
Space Needs: 90-100 Rooms SF
SUPPORT & TRAINING:
Financial Assistance Provided: Yes (I)
Site Selection Assistance: No
Lease Negotiation Assistance: No
Co-Operative Advertising: Yes
Franchisee Assoc./Member: No
Size Of Corporate Staff: 2332
On-Going Support: ,B,C,D,E,,G,H,I
Training: Pprior to certification for opening General Manager Training
SPECIFIC EXPANSION PLANS:
US: All United States
Canada: All Canada
Overseas: Mexico, Latin America,
    Europe, Asia, All Countries

<< >>

EMBASSY SUITES HOTELS

9336 Civic Center Dr.
Beverly Hills, CA 90210
Tel: (800) 286-0645 (310) 205-7690
Fax: (310) 205-7655
E-Mail: bill_fortier@hilton.com
Web Site: www.embassyfranchise.com
Mr. Bill Fortier, SVP Franchise Development

Embassy Suites Hotels defines the upscale, all-suite segment and today has more than 200 hotels, with an additional 60 properties in the development pipeline. With spacious two-room suites, engaging team members and an inviting atrium environment, guests are allowed to put their feet up and feel right at home. Embassy Suites Hotels is part of Hilton Hotels Corporation, the leading global hospitality company with more than 3,000 hotels and 500,000 rooms in 74 countries and territories, with more than 135,000 team members worldwide. The company owns, manages or franchises some of the best known and highly regarded hotel brands including Hilton®, Conrad® Hotels & Resorts, Doubletree®, Embassy Suites Hotels®, Hampton Inn®, Hampton Inn & Suites®, Hilton Garden Inn®, Hilton Grand Vacations™, Homewood Suites by Hilton®, the Waldorf Astoria™ and the Waldorf Astoria Collection™, as well as the recently launched Home2 Suites by Hilton™.

BACKGROUND: IFA MEMBER
Established: 1983;   1st Franchised: 1983
Franchised Units: 127
Company-Owned Units: <u>72</u>
Total Units: 199
Dist.:   US-191; CAN-2; O'seas-6
   North America: 38 States, 1 Provinces
   Density: 18 in FL, 20 in TX, 29 in CA
Projected New Units (12 Months):   NR
Qualifications: 5, 5, 5, 3, 1, 3
FINANCIAL/TERMS:
Cash Investment: $75K
Total Investment: $19.9MM-34.2MM
Minimum Net Worth: $70K/Rm.
Fees: Franchise - $75K
   Royalty - 5% Gross Rm. Rev;   Ad. - 4% GrRmRev
Earnings Claims Statement: No
Term of Contract (Years):   22/10-20
Avg. # Of Employees: 75 FT, 0 PT
Passive Ownership: Allowed
Encourage Conversions: Yes
Area Develop. Agreements: No
Sub-Franchising Contracts: No
Expand In Territory: Yes
Space Needs: 153,000 SF
SUPPORT & TRAINING:
Financial Assistance Provided: Yes (I)
Site Selection Assistance: No
Lease Negotiation Assistance: Yes
Co-Operative Advertising: Yes
Franchisee Assoc./Member: No
Size Of Corporate Staff: 2332
On-Going Support: ,,C,D,E,,G,h,I
Training: 2 Weeks Memphis, TN

SPECIFIC EXPANSION PLANS:
US: All United States
Canada: All Canada
Overseas: Mexico, Latin America,
    Europe, Asia, All Countries

≪ ≫

HAMPTON INN/HAMPTON INN & SUITES
9336 Civic Center Dr.
Beverly Hills, CA 90210
Tel: (800) 286-0645 (310) 205-7696
Fax: (310) 205-7655
E-Mail: bill_fortier@hilton.com
Web Site: www.hamptonfranchise.com
Mr. Bill Fortier, SVP Franchise Development

Hampton, which includes Hampton Inn, Hampton by Hilton and Hampton Inn & Suites hotels, is a mid-priced leader in the lodging segment. Hampton is part of Hilton Hotels Corporation, the leading global hospitality company with more than 3,000 hotels and 500,000 rooms in 74 countries and territories, with more than 135,000 team members worldwide. The company owns, manages or franchises some of the best known and highly regarded hotel brands including Hilton®, Conrad® Hotels & Resorts, Doubletree®, Embassy Suites Hotels®, Hampton Inn®, Hampton Inn & Suites®, Hilton Garden Inn®, Hilton Grand Vacations™, Homewood Suites by Hilton®, the Waldorf Astoria™ and the Waldorf Astoria Collection™, as well as the recently launched Home2 Suites by Hilton™.

BACKGROUND: IFA MEMBER
Established: 1983;   1st Franchised: 1983
Franchised Units: 1652
Company-Owned Units: <u>31</u>
Total Units: 1683
Dist.:   US-1641; CAN-26; O'seas-16
   North America: 49 States, 5 Provinces
   Density:88 in NC, 125 in FL, 132 in TX
Projected New Units (12 Months):   NR
Qualifications: 5, 5, 5, 3, 1, 3
FINANCIAL/TERMS:
Cash Investment: $50K
Total Investment: $3.7-13.1MM
Minimum Net Worth: $40K/Rm.

Fees: Franchise - $50K
   Royalty - 5% Gross Rm. Rev;   Ad. - 4% Gross Rm
Earnings Claims Statement: No
Term of Contract (Years):   22/10-20
Avg. # Of Employees: 25 FT, 0 PT
Passive Ownership: Allowed
Encourage Conversions: Yes
Area Develop. Agreements: No
Sub-Franchising Contracts: No
Expand In Territory: Yes
Space Needs: 1.5-3 Acres SF
SUPPORT & TRAINING:
Financial Assistance Provided: Yes (I)
Site Selection Assistance: Yes
Lease Negotiation Assistance: No
Co-Operative Advertising: Yes
Franchisee Assoc./Member: No
Size Of Corporate Staff: 2332
On-Going Support: ,,C,D,E,,G,H,I
Training: 2 Weeks GM in Memphis, TN;
   3 Days New Owner;
SPECIFIC EXPANSION PLANS:
US: All United States
Canada: All Canada
Overseas: Mexico & Latin America

≪ ≫

HAWTHORN SUITES HOTELS INTERNATIONAL
13 Corporate Sq., # 250
Atlanta, GA 30329
Tel: (404) 235-5804
Fax: (404) 235-7460
E-Mail: hawthorn.franchise@usfsi.com
Web Site: www.hawthorn.com
Mr. Chick Armstrong, VP Franchise Sales & Development

HAWTHORN SUITES is one of the fastest-growing hotel brands in the upper extended stay market. With 112 hotels open and 28 under development as of 3/30/2004, HAWTHORN continues to expand in both primary and tertiary markets. In November, 2000, HAWTHORN SUITES paretn company, U. S. Franchise Systems, was purchased by business interests of the Pritzker family. This acquisition bolstered our already strong leadership by providing powerful strategic and financial advantages.

BACKGROUND: IFA MEMBER
Established: 1986;   1st Franchised: 1986
Franchised Units: 106
Company-Owned Units: <u>0</u>
Total Units: 106
Dist.:   US-109; CAN-1; O'seas-1

North America: 32 States, 0 Provinces
Density: 23 in TX, 5 in FL, 9 in CA
Projected New Units (12 Months): 25
Qualifications: 4, 4, 4, 2, 2, 3

FINANCIAL/TERMS:
Cash Investment: $600K-1.5MM
Total Investment: $5.6-7.5MM
Minimum Net Worth: NA
Fees: Franchise - $40K
 Royalty - 5%; Ad. - 2.5%
Earnings Claims Statement: Yes
Term of Contract (Years): 20/10
Avg. # Of Employees: 15-20 FT, 0 PT
Passive Ownership: Allowed
Encourage Conversions: Yes
Area Develop. Agreements: No
Sub-Franchising Contracts: No
Expand In Territory: Yes
Space Needs: NR

SUPPORT & TRAINING:
Financial Assistance Provided: Yes (D)
Site Selection Assistance: Yes
Lease Negotiation Assistance: No
Co-Operative Advertising: No
Franchisee Assoc./Member: Yes/Yes
Size Of Corporate Staff: 96
On-Going Support: „C,D,„G,h,I
Training: 5 Days Training in Atlanta, GA;
 5 Days Sales Training in Atlanta, GA

SPECIFIC EXPANSION PLANS:
US: All United States
Canada: All Canada
Overseas: Europe, South America, Latin
 America.

≺≺ ≻≻

HILTON
9336 Civic Center Dr.
Beverly Hills, CA 90210
Tel: (800) 286-0645 (310) 278-4321
Fax: (310) 205-7655
E-Mail: bill_fortier@hilton.com
Web Site: www.hiltonfranchise.com
Mr. Bill Fortier, SVP Franchise Development

With more than 500 hotels and resorts on six continents, Hilton continues to be an innovative leader in the full-service hospitality segment and one of the most recognized global names in the industry. Hilton's belief that Travel Should Take

You Places® celebrates a commitment to the guest experience and to the idea that travel can and should be transformative. Hilton's variety of services, amenities and programs are designed to give guests more choice and control over their stays so they can be at their best, 24/7 whether they travel for business or leisure. Each unique Hilton hotel and resort was designed to reflect the sense of place of its location; each team member chosen to reflect the local culture and community. The Hilton brand is part of Hilton Hotels Corporation, the leading global hospitality company with more than 3,000 hotels and 500,000 rooms in 74 countries and territories, with more than 135,000 team members worldwide. The company owns, manages or franchises some of the best known and highly regarded hotel brands including Hilton®, Conrad® Hotels & Resorts, Doubletree®, Embassy Suites Hotels®, Hampton Inn®, Hampton Inn & Suites®, Hilton Garden Inn®, Hilton Grand Vacations™, Homewood Suites by Hilton®, the Waldorf Astoria™ and the Waldorf Astoria Collection™, as well as the recently launched Home2 Suites by Hilton™.

BACKGROUND: IFA MEMBER
Established: 1919; 1st Franchised: 1969
Franchised Units: 232
Company-Owned Units: 294
Total Units: 526
Dist.: US-450; CAN-14; O'seas-262
 North America: 41 States, 4 Provinces
 Density: 26 in TX, 29 in FL, 36 in CA
Projected New Units (12 Months): NR
Qualifications: 5, 5, 5, 3, 1, 3

FINANCIAL/TERMS:
Cash Investment: $85K
Total Investment: $53.3-90.1MM
Minimum Net Worth: $70K/Rm.
Fees: Franchise - $85K Min.
 Royalty - 5% Gross Rm. Rev; Ad. - 4% GrRmRev
Earnings Claims Statement: No
Term of Contract (Years): 22/10-20
Avg. # Of Employees: 150 FT, 0 PT
Passive Ownership: Allowed
Encourage Conversions: Yes
Area Develop. Agreements: No
Sub-Franchising Contracts: No
Expand In Territory: Yes
Space Needs: 135,000 SF

SUPPORT & TRAINING:
Financial Assistance Provided: Yes (D)
Site Selection Assistance: NA
Lease Negotiation Assistance: No

Co-Operative Advertising: Yes
Franchisee Assoc./Member: No
Size Of Corporate Staff: 2332
On-Going Support: „C,D,E,„G,H,I
Training: 3 Days Beverly Hills, CA;
 4 Days Dallas, TX; 3 Days Regional Office

SPECIFIC EXPANSION PLANS:
US: All United States
Canada: All Canada
Overseas: Mexico, Latin America, Europe, Asia, All Countries

≺≺ ≻≻

HILTON GARDEN INN
9336 Civic Center Dr.
Beverly Hills, CA 90210
Tel: (800) 286-0645 (310) 205-7696
Fax: (310) 205-7655
E-Mail: bill_fortier@hilton.com
Web Site: www.hiltongardeninnfranchise.com
Mr. Bill Fortier, SVP Franchise Development

Hilton Garden Inn is the award-winning, mid-priced brand that continually strives to ensure today's busy travelers have everything they need to be most productive on the road — from complimentary wired and Wi-Fi Internet access in all guestrooms and PrinterOn remote printing to the hotel's complimentary 24-hour business center to the Garden Sleep System® bed. So whether on the road for personal or business reasons, Hilton Garden Inn offers the amenities and services for travelers to sleep deep, stay fit, eat well, work smart and treat themselves while away from home. Hilton Garden Inn is part of Hilton Hotels Corporation, the leading global hospitality company with more than 3,000 hotels and 500,000 rooms in 74 countries and territories, with more than 135,000 team members worldwide. The company owns, manages or franchises some of the best known and highly regarded hotel brands including Hilton®, Conrad® Hotels & Resorts, Doubletree®, Embassy Suites Hotels®, Hampton Inn®, Hampton Inn & Suites®, Hilton Garden Inn®, Hilton Grand Vacations™, Homewood Suites by Hilton®, the Waldorf Astoria™ and the Waldorf Astoria Collection™, as well as the recently launched

Home2 Suites by Hilton™.

BACKGROUND: IFA MEMBER
Established: 1996; 1st Franchised: 1996
Franchised Units: 449
Company-Owned Units: 14
Total Units: 463
Dist.: US-433; CAN-17; O'seas-13
 North America: 44 States, 4 Provinces
 Density: 34 in FL, 35 in TX, 36 in CA
Projected New Units (12 Months): NR
Qualifications: 5, 5, 5, 3, 1, 3
FINANCIAL/TERMS:
Cash Investment: $60K
Total Investment: $11.2-20.1MM
Minimum Net Worth: $50K/Rm.
Fees: Franchise - $60K Min.
 Royalty - 5% Gross Rm.; Ad. - 4.3%
Gross Rm
Earnings Claims Statement: No
Term of Contract (Years): 22/10-20
Avg. # Of Employees: 35-50 FT, 10-15 PT
Passive Ownership: Allowed
Encourage Conversions: Yes
Area Develop. Agreements: No
Sub-Franchising Contracts: No
Expand In Territory: Yes
Space Needs: 90-250 Rooms SF
SUPPORT & TRAINING:
Financial Assistance Provided: Yes (I)
Site Selection Assistance: Yes
Lease Negotiation Assistance: No
Co-Operative Advertising: Yes
Franchisee Assoc./Member: No
Size Of Corporate Staff: 2332
On-Going Support: a,b,C,d,E,,G,H,
Training: 3 Days Owner Orientation,
 Beverly Hills, CA
SPECIFIC EXPANSION PLANS:
US: All United States
Canada: All Canada
Overseas: Mexico, Latin America,
 Europe, Asia, All Countries

≪ ≫

HOMEWOOD SUITES BY HILTON
9336 Civic Center Dr.
Beverly Hills, CA 90210
Tel: (800) 286-0645 (310) 205-7696
Fax: (310) 205-7655
E-Mail: bill_fortier@hilton.com

Web Site: www.homewoodfranchise.com
Mr. Bill Fortier, SVP Franchise Development

The Homewood Suites by Hilton brand offers spacious suites and home-like amenities, including an on-site Suite Shop® convenience store, complimentary grocery shopping services (guests pay for groceries), a complete business center, and laundry services at most locations. The innovative brand is a guest favorite among both business and leisure travelers, consistently taking the top spot on key satisfaction studies. Homewood Suites by Hilton is part of Hilton Hotels Corporation, the leading global hospitality company with more than 3,000 hotels and 500,000 rooms in 74 countries and territories, with more than 135,000 team members worldwide. The company owns, manages or franchises some of the best known and highly regarded hotel brands including Hilton®, Conrad® Hotels & Resorts, Doubletree®, Embassy Suites Hotels®, Hampton Inn®, Hampton Inn & Suites®, Hilton Garden Inn®, Hilton Grand Vacations™, Homewood Suites by Hilton®, the Waldorf Astoria™ and the Waldorf Astoria Collection™, as well as the recently launched Home2 Suites by Hilton™.

BACKGROUND: IFA MEMBER
Established: 1988; 1st Franchised: 1988
Franchised Units: 231
Company-Owned Units: 43
Total Units: 274
Dist.: US-265; CAN-8; O'seas-1
 North America: 42 States, 2 Provinces
 Density: 17 in CA, 24 in FL, 38 in TX
Projected New Units (12 Months): NR
Qualifications: 5, 5, 5, 3, 1, 3
FINANCIAL/TERMS:
Cash Investment: $60K
Total Investment: $10.1-17.8MM
Minimum Net Worth: $50K/Rm.
Fees: Franchise - $60K Min.
 Royalty - 4% Gross Rm. Rev; Ad. - 4% GrRmRev
Earnings Claims Statement: No
Term of Contract (Years): 22/10-20
Avg. # Of Employees: 25 FT, 0 PT
Passive Ownership: Allowed
Encourage Conversions: Yes
Area Develop. Agreements: No
Sub-Franchising Contracts: No
Expand In Territory: Yes
Space Needs: 110,000 SF
SUPPORT & TRAINING:
Financial Assistance Provided: Yes (I)

Site Selection Assistance: No
Lease Negotiation Assistance: Yes
Co-Operative Advertising: Yes
Franchisee Assoc./Member: No
Size Of Corporate Staff: 2332
On-Going Support: ,,C,D,E,,G,h,I
Training: 2 Weeks Memphis, TN
SPECIFIC EXPANSION PLANS:
US: All United States
Canada: All Canada
Overseas: Mexico, Latin America,
 Europe, Asia, All Countries

≪ ≫

HOSPITALITY INTERNATIONAL
1726 Montreal Cir.
Tucker, GA 30084
Tel: (800) 247-4677 (770) 270-1180
Fax: (770) 270-1077
E-Mail: sales@hifranchise.com
Web Site: www.bookroomsnow.com
Ms. Amy Foy, VP Franchise Development

Hotel franchisor of MASTER HOSTS INNS AND RESORTS, RED CARPET INN, SCOTTISH INNS, PASSPORT INN, DOWNTOWNER INNS, with over 252 franchised properties. HOSPITALITY INTERNATIONAL is proud of the fact that approximately 75% of its current franchisees are minorities. The company is actively pursuing the addition of new minority-owned franchises in all of the U.S.

BACKGROUND:
Established: 1982; 1st Franchised: 1982
Franchised Units: 251
Company-Owned Units: 0
Total Units: 251
Dist.: US-251; CAN-0; O'seas-0
 North America: 32 States, 0 Provinces
 Density: 18 in TN, 39 in GA, 30 in FL
Projected New Units (12 Months): 25
Qualifications: 3, 5, 4, 3, 2, 5
FINANCIAL/TERMS:
Cash Investment: $70-200K
Total Investment: $1.0-5.0MM
Minimum Net Worth: Varies
Fees: Franchise - $2.5-5K
 Royalty - 3-4%; Ad. - 2%
Earnings Claims Statement: No
Term of Contract (Years): 5/
Avg. # Of Employees: 6 FT, 3 PT
Passive Ownership: Allowed
Encourage Conversions: Yes
Area Develop. Agreements: No
Sub-Franchising Contracts: No
Expand In Territory: No

Space Needs: 288/Guest SF

SUPPORT & TRAINING:

Financial Assistance Provided: Yes (D)
Site Selection Assistance: Yes
Lease Negotiation Assistance: Yes
Co-Operative Advertising: No
Franchisee Assoc./Member: Yes/Yes
Size Of Corporate Staff: 36
On-Going Support: ,B,C,D,E,,G,H,I
Training: 2 Days Tucker, GA

SPECIFIC EXPANSION PLANS:

US: All United States
Canada: All Canada
Overseas: Mexico, Asia, South America

≪ ≫

INTERCONTINENTAL HOTELS GROUP (IHG®)

3 Ravinia Dr., # 100
Atlanta, GA 30346-2118
Tel: (866) 933-8356 (770) 604-5000
Fax: (770) 604-2584
E-Mail: development@ihg.com
Web Site: www.ihg.com
Mr. Brown Kessler, VP Franchise Sales/
Develop.

IHG is the world's largest hotel company by number of rooms. The company operates or franchises more than 4,200 hotels and 600,000 guest rooms in nearly 100 countries. IHG offers franchises with the following brands: InterContinental® Hotels & Resorts, Crowne Plaza®, Hotel Indigo®, Holiday Inn® Hotels and Resorts, Holiday Inn Express®, Staybridge Suites® and Candlewood Suites®. Notes: Operating Units chart represents all IHG hotel brands. Geographic Distribution chart is as of March 31, 2009 and represents all IHG hotel brands. Fees listed are for a 100 room Holiday Inn; please contact IHG directly for fee information on our other brands, www.ihg.com/development. Financial requirements chart represents fees for a typical Holiday Inn brand hotel. Training chart represents all IHG hotel brands. Expansion Plans chart represents all IHG hotel brands.

BACKGROUND: IFA MEMBER

Established: 1946; 1st Franchised: 1954
Franchised Units: 4186
Company-Owned Units: 16
Total Units: 4202
Dist.: US-3141; CAN-157; O'seas-904

North America: 50 States, 1 Provinces
Density: NR
Projected New Units (12 Months): NR
Qualifications: 5, 4, 4, NR, NR, NR

FINANCIAL/TERMS:

Cash Investment: Varies
Total Investment: Varies
Minimum Net Worth: NA
Fees: Franchise - $Minimum $50K
Royalty - 5%; Ad. - 2.5%
Earnings Claims Statement: Yes
Term of Contract (Years): Varies, Avg. 10/10
Avg. # Of Employees: Varies per brand FT, 0 PT
Passive Ownership: Allowed
Encourage Conversions: Yes
Area Develop. Agreements: No
Sub-Franchising Contracts: No
Expand In Territory: No
Space Needs: Varies per brand SF

SUPPORT & TRAINING:

Financial Assistance Provided: No
Site Selection Assistance: Yes
Lease Negotiation Assistance: No
Co-Operative Advertising: Yes
Franchisee Assoc./Member: Yes/Yes
Size Of Corporate Staff: 1000
On-Going Support: ,,C,D,E,,,H,I
Training: 4-5 Days Regional;
4-5 Days Atlanta

SPECIFIC EXPANSION PLANS:

US: All United States
Canada: All Canada
Overseas: All Countries

≪ ≫

MICROTEL INNS & SUITES

13 Corporate Sq., # 250
Atlanta, GA 30329-1906
Tel: (888) 771-7171 (404) 235-7412
Fax: (404) 235-7460
E-Mail: franchise.info@usfsi.com
Web Site: www.microtelinn.com
Mr. Mike Muir, SVP Sales/Development

MICROTEL INNS & SUITES is one of the fastest-growing, all-new construction budget hotel franchise brands in the economy/budget segment and has establishe a reputation for customer satisfaction in

the minds of travel consumers around the country. MICROTEL is the proven leader in the economy/budget hotel market. Our concept involves offering the traveling public a high-quality product at a value rate while keeping operating and development costs to a minimum. All MICRO-TEL INNS are 100% new construction.

BACKGROUND: IFA MEMBER

Established: 1995; 1st Franchised: 1995
Franchised Units: 300
Company-Owned Units: 0
Total Units: 300
Dist.: US-300; CAN-0; O'seas-10
North America: 38 States, 0 Provinces
Density: 20 in TX, 26 in NC, 19 in GA
Projected New Units (12 Months): 35
Qualifications: 3, 4, 4, 2, 2, 3

FINANCIAL/TERMS:

Cash Investment: $500K-1MM
Total Investment: $2.1MM-4.8MM
Minimum Net Worth: NA
Fees: Franchise - $35K
Royalty - 4,5,6%; Ad. - 3,2.5,2%
Earnings Claims Statement: Yes
Term of Contract (Years): 20/10
Avg. # Of Employees: 11 FT, 0 PT
Passive Ownership: Allowed
Encourage Conversions: No
Area Develop. Agreements: No
Sub-Franchising Contracts: No
Expand In Territory: Yes
Space Needs: NR

SUPPORT & TRAINING:

Financial Assistance Provided: Yes (D)
Site Selection Assistance: Yes
Lease Negotiation Assistance: No
Co-Operative Advertising: No
Franchisee Assoc./Member: Yes/Yes
Size Of Corporate Staff: 96
On-Going Support: ,,C,D,E,,G,h,I
Training: 4 Weeks Mana./Staff On-Site;
1 Week Classroom Atlanta, GA; 3
Days Reservation Marion, IL

SPECIFIC EXPANSION PLANS:

US: All United States
Canada: All Canada
Overseas: Europe, South America

≪ ≫

MOTEL 6

4001 International Pkwy.
Carrollton, TX 75007
Tel: (888) 842-2942 (972) 360-2547
Fax: (972) 360-5567
E-Mail: franchisesales@accor-na.com
Web Site: www.motel6.com
Mr. Dean Savas, SVP Franchising

Accor Hotels is one of the largest owner/operators of economy lodging in the United States. Accor North America is a division of Accor, with 150,000 people in 100 countries, employing approximately 470 people at the corporate offices including the call centers. Approximately 13,000 are employed at Motel 6 and Studio 6 combined.

BACKGROUND: IFA MEMBER
Established: 1962; 1st Franchised: 1996
Franchised Units: 312
Company-Owned Units: 651
Total Units: 963
Dist.: US-948; CAN-15; O'seas-0
 North America: 49 States, 1 Provinces
 Density:48 in AZ, 137 in TX, 188 in CA
Projected New Units (12 Months): 55
Qualifications: 4, 4, 1, 1, 1, 3
FINANCIAL/TERMS:
Cash Investment: $100-500K
Total Investment: $2.3-$3.2MM
Minimum Net Worth: $1.5MM
Fees: Franchise - $25K
 Royalty - 4%; Ad. - 3.5%
Earnings Claims Statement: Yes
Term of Contract (Years): NA/10
Avg. # Of Employees: 2-4 FT, 4-10 PT
Passive Ownership: Allowed
Encourage Conversions: Yes
Area Develop. Agreements: No
Sub-Franchising Contracts: No
Expand In Territory: Yes
Space Needs: 1.5 Acres SF
SUPPORT & TRAINING:
Financial Assistance Provided: No
Site Selection Assistance: No
Lease Negotiation Assistance: No
Co-Operative Advertising: Yes
Franchisee Assoc./Member: Yes/Yes
Size Of Corporate Staff: 450
On-Going Support: A,b,C,d,e,,,h,I
Training: 7 business days Manager

Training Dallas, TX; 1-3 days; 2 days On-Site Opening Training; Computer Trainings; 2 Days Carrollton, TX for Owner's Orientation
SPECIFIC EXPANSION PLANS:
US: All United States
Canada: All Canada
Overseas: NR

PARK INN

701 Carlson Pkwy., MS 8254
Minnetonka, MN 55305
Tel: (800) 336-3301 (763) 212-6615
Fax: (763) 212-3350
E-Mail: jrussenberger@carlson.com
Web Site: www.parkinn.com
Ms. Janelle Russenberger, Development Associate

Park Inn® is a unique hotel brand offering a relaxed environment in the economy category and is poised for aggressive global growth. Park Inn provides a hotel experience that serves a wide range of guests in both suburban and leisure destinations. There are currently 98 Park Inn locations with 17,166 rooms in 24 countries, and 11 in North America.

BACKGROUND: IFA MEMBER
Established: 2000; 1st Franchised: 2000
Franchised Units: 98
Company-Owned Units: 0
Total Units: 98
Dist.: US-7; CAN-4; O'seas-87
 North America: 7 States, 4 Provinces
 Density: 1 in OH, 1 in NC, 1 in NM
Projected New Units (12 Months): 5
Qualifications: 5, 5, 5, 3, 5, 5
FINANCIAL/TERMS:
Cash Investment: Varies
Total Investment: $1.58 - 4.35MM
Minimum Net Worth: NA
Fees: Franchise - $35K
 Royalty - 4.5%; Ad. - 2%
Earnings Claims Statement: Yes
Term of Contract (Years): 15/NA
Avg. # Of Employees: Varies
Passive Ownership: Allowed
Encourage Conversions: Yes
Area Develop. Agreements: No
Sub-Franchising Contracts: No
Expand In Territory: No
Space Needs: Varies
SUPPORT & TRAINING:
Financial Assistance Provided: No
Site Selection Assistance: No
Lease Negotiation Assistance: No

Co-Operative Advertising: No
Franchisee Assoc./Member: Yes/Yes
Size Of Corporate Staff: 100
On-Going Support: ,B,C,D,E,,G,H,I
Training: 3 Days On-Site;
 3 Days New Franchisee; 1 Week Minneapolis, MN (Brand Orientation)
SPECIFIC EXPANSION PLANS:
US: All United States
Canada: All Canada
Overseas: Europe, Asia, South and Central America

RADISSON HOTELS & RESORTS

701 Carlson Pkwy., MS 8254
Minnetonka, MN 55305
Tel: (800) 336-3301 (763) 212-3475
Fax: (763) 212-3240
E-Mail: jrussenberger@carlson.com
Web Site: www.radisson.com
Ms. Janelle Russenberger, Development Associate

Radisson Hotels & Resorts® - One of the world's leading full-service hotel companies, Radisson Hotels & Resorts currently encompasses 415 properties with 90,000 guestrooms in 69 countries. Radisson is focused on being the hotel of choice with business and leisure travelers by understanding the independent mindset and changing needs of today's frequent travelers who want more control over their hotel experience. Radisson Hotels & Resorts is continuing to evolve the brand, introducing new product and service standards to address key guest needs and distinguish the hotels within the full-service category.

BACKGROUND: IFA MEMBER
Established: 1983; 1st Franchised: 1983
Franchised Units: 405
Company-Owned Units: 12
Total Units: 417
Dist.: US-141; CAN-22; O'seas-254
 North America: 35 States, 7 Provinces
 Density: 9 in FL, 15 in TX, 16 in CA
Projected New Units (12 Months): 20
Qualifications: 5, 5, 5, 3, 5, 5
FINANCIAL/TERMS:
Cash Investment: Varies
Total Investment: $2.96-7.3M
Minimum Net Worth: NA
Fees: Franchise - $75K
 Royalty - 5%; Ad. - 2%
Earnings Claims Statement: Yes
Term of Contract (Years): 20/NA
Avg. # Of Employees: Varies

Passive Ownership: Allowed
Encourage Conversions: Yes
Area Develop. Agreements: No
Sub-Franchising Contracts: No
Expand In Territory: No
Space Needs: Varies

SUPPORT & TRAINING:

Financial Assistance Provided: No
Site Selection Assistance: No
Lease Negotiation Assistance: No
Co-Operative Advertising: No
Franchisee Assoc./Member: Yes/Yes
Size Of Corporate Staff: 100
On-Going Support: „C,D,E,„G,H,I
Training: 1 Week Minneapolis,
     MN (Brand Orientation); 3 Days New
     Franchisee; 3 Days On-Site

SPECIFIC EXPANSION PLANS:

US: All United States
Canada: All Canada
Overseas: Europe, Asia, South and
     Central America

≪ ≫

RAMADA FRANCHISE SYSTEMS

1 Sylvan Way
Parsippany, NJ 07054
Tel: (800) 758-8999 (973) 428-9700
Fax: (973) 753-8724
E-Mail: gus.stamoutsos@wyndhamworld
wide.com
Web Site: www.ramada.com
Mr. Gus E. Stamoutsos, Senior Vice President

RAMADA is proud to have nearly 900 properties in the United States and Canada. The RAMADA brand was created in Flagstaff, AZ in 1954. In 1990, the brand was acquired by Cendant Corporation, formerly HFS Inc. RAMADA FRANCHISE SYSTEMS is a subsidiary of Cendant Corporation (NYSE: CD).

BACKGROUND: IFA MEMBER
Established: 1954;   1st Franchised: 1990
Franchised Units: 871
Company-Owned Units: 0
Total Units: 871
Dist.:   US-802; CAN-69; O'seas-0
  North America: 48 States, 8 Provinces
  Density: 64 in TX, 67 in FL, 90 in CA
Projected New Units (12 Months):   NR
Qualifications: 3, 2, 4, 1, 1, 5
FINANCIAL/TERMS:

Cash Investment: $384K-8.3MM
Total Investment: $380.7K-10.2M
Minimum Net Worth: NA
Fees: Franchise - $35Kor $350/RM
  Royalty - 4%;   Ad. - 4.5%
Earnings Claims Statement: Yes
Term of Contract (Years):   15-20/
Avg. # Of Employees: 75% FT, 25% PT
Passive Ownership: Allowed
Encourage Conversions: Yes
Area Develop. Agreements: No
Sub-Franchising Contracts: No
Expand In Territory: No
Space Needs: 18.-2.4 Acres SF

SUPPORT & TRAINING:

Financial Assistance Provided: Yes (D)
Site Selection Assistance: No
Lease Negotiation Assistance: No
Co-Operative Advertising: No
Franchisee Assoc./Member: Yes/Yes
Size Of Corporate Staff: NR
On-Going Support: ,B,C,D,,,G,h,I
Training: 3-6 Days On-Site Property
     Opening/Training

SPECIFIC EXPANSION PLANS:

US: All United States
Canada: All Canada
Overseas: NR

≪ ≫

RED ROOF INNS

605 S. Front St.
Columbus, OH 43215
Tel: (615) 744-211
Fax: (615) 885-5328
E-Mail: rwallace@redroof.com
Web Site: www.redroof.com
Mr. Rob Wallace, Sr. VP Franchising

Red Roof Inn was incorporated by founder James R. Trueman in 1972. Its first Inn opened in Columbus, Ohio, with a single room rate of $8.50 in 1973. Today, Red Roof Inn has more than 325 locations, serves millions of guests each year and employs over 6,000 people. Over the last 30 years, the lodging company's commitment to quality growth has contributed to the creation of the Red Roof Inn identity, which represents value, consistency, and excellent service. Red Roof Inn will con-

tinue to grow through franchising, acquisitions and new development.

BACKGROUND: IFA MEMBER
Established: 1972;   1st Franchised: 1996
Franchised Units: 128
Company-Owned Units: 221
Total Units: 349
Dist.:   US-349; CAN-0; O'seas-0
  North America: 43 States, 0 Provinces
  Density: 21 in TX, 35 in OH, 22 in FL
Projected New Units (12 Months):   15
Qualifications: 4, 4, 1, 1, 1, 3
FINANCIAL/TERMS:

Cash Investment: $100-500K
Total Investment: $2.7-3.1MM
Minimum Net Worth: $1.5MM
Fees: Franchise - $30K
  Royalty - 4.5%;   Ad. - 4%
Earnings Claims Statement: Yes
Term of Contract (Years):   15/20/10
Avg. # Of Employees: 2-4 FT, 4-10 PT
Passive Ownership: Allowed
Encourage Conversions: Yes
Area Develop. Agreements: No
Sub-Franchising Contracts: No
Expand In Territory: No
Space Needs: 15,000+ SF

SUPPORT & TRAINING:

Financial Assistance Provided: No
Site Selection Assistance: No
Lease Negotiation Assistance: No
Co-Operative Advertising: Yes
Franchisee Assoc./Member: Yes/Yes
Size Of Corporate Staff: 130
On-Going Support: A,b,C,D,e,,G,h,I
Training: 2 Weeks Columbus, OH for
     Manager Orientation; 2 Days Columbus, OH for Owner's Orientation
SPECIFIC EXPANSION PLANS:

US: All United States
Canada: All Canada
Overseas: NR

≪ ≫

STUDIO 6

4001 International Pkwy.
Carrollton, TX 75007
Tel: (888) 842-2942 (972) 360-2547
Fax: (972) 360-5567
E-Mail: franchisesales@accor-na.com

Web Site: www.staystudio6.com
Mr. Dean Savas, Sr. VP Franchising

Accor Hotels is one of the largest owner/ operators of economy lodging in the United States. Accor North America is a division of Accor, with 150,000 people in 100 countries, employing approximately 470 people at the corporate offices including the call centers. Approximately 13,000 are employed at Motel 6 and Studio 6 combined.

BACKGROUND: IFA MEMBER
Established: 1998; 1st Franchised: 1998
Franchised Units: 12
Company-Owned Units: 40
Total Units: 52
Dist.: US-51; CAN-1; O'seas-0
 North America: 15 States, 1 Provinces
 Density: 4 in GA, 4 in FL, 25 in TX
Projected New Units (12 Months): 5
Qualifications: 4, 4, 1, 1, 1, 3
FINANCIAL/TERMS:
Cash Investment: $100-500K
Total Investment: $2.9-4.1MM
Minimum Net Worth: $1.5MM
Fees: Franchise - $25K
 Royalty - 5%; Ad. - 2%
Earnings Claims Statement: Yes
Term of Contract (Years): 15/20/10
Avg. # Of Employees: 2-4 FT, 4-10 PT
Passive Ownership: Allowed
Encourage Conversions: Yes
Area Develop. Agreements: No
Sub-Franchising Contracts: No
Expand In Territory: Yes
Space Needs: 1.5 Acres Min SF
SUPPORT & TRAINING:
Financial Assistance Provided: Yes (D)
Site Selection Assistance: No

Lease Negotiation Assistance: No
Co-Operative Advertising: No
Franchisee Assoc./Member: Yes/Yes
Size Of Corporate Staff: 470
On-Going Support: A,b,C,d,e,,G,h,I
Training: 7 business days Carrollton, TX
 for Managers' Orientation;
 2 Days Carrollton, TX for Owner's
 Orientation;
SPECIFIC EXPANSION PLANS:
US: All United States
Canada: All Canada
Overseas: NR

◄◄ ►►

US FRANCHISE SYSTEMS
13 Corporate Sq., # 250
Atlanta, GA 30329
Tel: (404) 321-4045
Fax: (404) 321-4482
E-Mail: charles.watson@usfsi.com
Web Site: www.usfsi.com
Mr. Roy E. Flora, COO

Hotel franchisor of MICROTEL INNS & SUITES and HAWTHORN SUITES. MICROTEL -- all new construction, budget. HAWTHORN -- upper mid-priced all-suites brand. USFS is known as the "fair franchisor" with the most 2-sided agreement, lower than average fee structure, and no-hidden fees. Brands range from low-capital requirements (MICROTEL) to upper-middle (HAWTHORN).

BACKGROUND:

Established: 1995; 1st Franchised: 1995
Franchised Units: 382
Company-Owned Units: 0
Total Units: 382
Dist.: US-368; CAN-1; O'seas-13
 North America: 49 States, 0 Provinces
 Density: NR
Projected New Units (12 Months): 20
Qualifications: 4, 4, 4, 3, 3, 4
FINANCIAL/TERMS:
Cash Investment: $600K-1MM
Total Investment: $2-7MM
Minimum Net Worth: NA
Fees: Franchise - $40K
 Royalty - 5-6%; Ad. - 2.5%
Earnings Claims Statement: Yes
Term of Contract (Years): 20/10
Avg. # Of Employees: 10-25 FT, 0 PT
Passive Ownership: Allowed
Encourage Conversions: Yes
Area Develop. Agreements: No
Sub-Franchising Contracts: No
Expand In Territory: Yes
Space Needs: 45,000 SF
SUPPORT & TRAINING:
Financial Assistance Provided: Yes (I)
Site Selection Assistance: No
Lease Negotiation Assistance: Yes
Co-Operative Advertising: No
Franchisee Assoc./Member: Yes/Yes
Size Of Corporate Staff: 150
On-Going Support: ,,C,D,E,,G,H,I
Training: As Needed On-Site;
 3-4 Days Atlanta, GA;
SPECIFIC EXPANSION PLANS:
US: All United States
Canada: All Canada
Overseas: All Countries

◄◄ ►►

241

FIVE LARGEST PARTICIPANTS IN SURVEY

Company	# Fran-chised Units	# Co-Owned Units	# Total Units	Franchise Fee	On-Going Royalty	Total Investment
1. Jani-King International	13,000	27	13,027	$8-33K	10%	$2.9-40K
2. Coverall Health-Based Cleaning System	9,603	0	9,603	$10-$32.2K	5%	$10,612-$37,345
3. Jan-Pro Cleaning Systems	8,091	2	8,093	$1-30K	14%	$5-60K
4. Chem-Dry Carpet & Upholstery Cleaning	4,500	0	4,500	$13K	$350/Mo.	$28-250K
5. ServiceMaster Clean	4,488	0	4,488	$16.9-49K	4-10%	$16.9-43K

All of the data provided are proprietary and should not be quoted without acknowledging *Bond's Franchise Guide.*

**AEROWEST & WESTAIR
SANITATION SERVICES**
3882 Del Amo Blvd., # 3602
Torrance, CA 90503
Tel: (888) 663-6726 (310) 793-4242
Fax: (310) 793-4250
E-Mail: info@westsanitation.com
Web Site: www.westsanitation.com
Mr. Graham H. Emery, President

AEROWEST & WESTAIR franchisees provide a specialized restroom fixture service to kill unpleasant odors, provide a light fragrance in the restroom and leave the urinals and toilets sanitary. The services do not involve any janitorial work, only the 28-day service of dispensers. WEST supplies full administrative support (billing, collections, reports). (Products are supplied to franchisees at WEST's cost.)

BACKGROUND: IFA MEMBER
Established: 1983; 1st Franchised: 1983
Franchised Units: 48
Company-Owned Units: 20
Total Units: 68
Dist.: US-68; CAN-0; O'seas-0
North America: 30 States, 0 Provinces

Density: 11 in TX, 9 in IL, 14 in CA
Projected New Units (12 Months): 10
Qualifications: 2, 1, 4, 3, 2, 4
FINANCIAL/TERMS:
Cash Investment: $3-10K
Total Investment: $3-40K
Minimum Net Worth: $0
Fees: Franchise - $4K
  Royalty - 8%; Ad. - 4%
Earnings Claims Statement: Yes
Term of Contract (Years): 5/1
Avg. # Of Employees: 1 FT, 0 PT
Passive Ownership: Discouraged
Encourage Conversions: Yes
Area Develop. Agreements: No
Sub-Franchising Contracts: No
Expand In Territory: No

Space Needs: NA

SUPPORT & TRAINING:
Financial Assistance Provided: Yes (D)
Site Selection Assistance: NA
Lease Negotiation Assistance: NA
Co-Operative Advertising: No
Franchisee Assoc./Member: No
Size Of Corporate Staff: 14
On-Going Support: A,B,,D,,,G,H,
Training: 7-10 Working Days Near
  Existing Franchisee

SPECIFIC EXPANSION PLANS:
US: OR, MD, FL, VA
Canada: No
Overseas: NR

≪ ≫

**AIRE SERV HEATING
& AIR CONDITIONING**
1020 N. University Parks Dr.
Waco, TX 76707
Tel: (800) 583-2662 (254) 759-5850
Fax: (800) 209-7621
E-Mail: info@servicefranchiseopportun
ities.com
Web Site: www.servicefranchiseopportu-
nities.com
Mr. Pat Humburg, Lead Development
  Manager

Established in 1992, Aire Serv is a global franchise organization providing installation, maintenance and repair of heating, ventilation, air conditioning and indoor air quality systems. Recognized by Entrepreneur magazine among its "Franchise 500," Aire Serv franchisees provide these services to both residential and commercial customers at more than 100 locations worldwide. Aire Serv is part of The Dwyer Group family of companies, which also includes Rainbow International, Mr. Rooter, Mr. Electric, Mr. App

BACKGROUND: IFA MEMBER
Established: 1992; 1st Franchised: 1994
Franchised Units: 124
Company-Owned Units: 0
Total Units: 124
Dist.: US-121; CAN-1; O'seas-2
  North America: 31 States, 2 Provinces
  Density: 15 in TX, 8 in FL, 16 in CA
Projected New Units (12 Months): 59
Qualifications: 4, 3, 5, 3, 2, 4

FINANCIAL/TERMS:
Cash Investment:$22K/100K population
Total Investment: $35K+
Minimum Net Worth: Varies
Fees: Franchise - $22 per 100K
population
  Royalty - 4-7%; Ad. - 2%
Earnings Claims Statement: No
Term of Contract (Years): 10/5
Avg. # Of Employees: Varies
Passive Ownership: Discouraged
Encourage Conversions: Yes
Area Develop. Agreements: Yes/10
Sub-Franchising Contracts: No
Expand In Territory: Yes
Space Needs: Varies

SUPPORT & TRAINING:
Financial Assistance Provided: Yes (D)
Site Selection Assistance: NA
Lease Negotiation Assistance: NA
Co-Operative Advertising: Yes
Franchisee Assoc./Member: Yes/Yes
Size Of Corporate Staff: 7
On-Going Support: A,B,,D,E,F,G,H,I
Training: 3 Days, On-going On-Site; 5
  Days Corporate Office

SPECIFIC EXPANSION PLANS:
US: All United States
Canada: No
Overseas: NR

≪ ≫

AIRE-MASTER OF AMERICA
1821 N. Hwy. CC, P.O. Box 2310
Nixa, MO 65714
Tel: (800) 784-2691 (417) 725-2691
Fax: (417) 725-5737
E-Mail: gparker@airemaster.com
Web Site: www.airemaster.com
Mr. Greg Parker, Business Director

AIRE-MASTER is a unique system of odor control and restroom fixture cleaning. Unlike the majority of 'air-fresheners' on the market, AIRE-MASTER deodorizers and deodorant products actually eliminate odors by oxidation. You don't need prior experience in the odor control/sanitary supply industry to qualify for a franchise. Customer base is built by making sales calls and providing good customer service. Complete training. We are FDA approved and manufacture deodorants, cleaning products and hand soaps. Ninth year in a row on Entrepreneur Magazines Franchise 500. Ranked #1 Restroom Maintenance Franchise.

BACKGROUND:

Established: 1958; 1st Franchised: 1976
Franchised Units: 81
Company-Owned Units: 4
Total Units: 85
Dist.: US-83; CAN-2; O'seas-0
  North America: 40 States, 2 Provinces
  Density: 7 in MO, 5 in ID, 5 in FL
Projected New Units (12 Months): 14
Qualifications: 5, 5, 5, 5, 5, 5

FINANCIAL/TERMS:
Cash Investment: $33K
Total Investment: $33K-83K
Minimum Net Worth: NR
Fees: Franchise - $29K
  Royalty - 5%; Ad. - 0%
Earnings Claims Statement: No
Term of Contract (Years): 20/3
Avg. # Of Employees: 2-3 FT, 0 PT
Passive Ownership: Discouraged
Encourage Conversions: Yes
Area Develop. Agreements: Yes/0
Sub-Franchising Contracts: No
Expand In Territory: No
Space Needs: NA

SUPPORT & TRAINING:
Financial Assistance Provided: Yes (D)
Site Selection Assistance: NA
Lease Negotiation Assistance: Yes
Co-Operative Advertising: No
Franchisee Assoc./Member: Yes/Yes
Size Of Corporate Staff: 70
On-Going Support: a,B,C,D,E,,G,h,I
Training: 5 Days Franchisee's Location;
  5 Days Headquarters, Nixa, MO

SPECIFIC EXPANSION PLANS:
US: All United States
Canada: All Canada
Overseas: NR

≪ ≫

ANAGO CLEANING SYSTEMS
3111 N. University Dr. # 625
Coral Springs, FL 33065
Tel: (800) 213-5857 (954) 752-3111
Fax: (954) 752-1200
E-Mail: jwalker@anagousa.net
Web Site: www.anagousa.com
Ms. Judy Walker, VP Marketing

We are the digital generation of cleaning franchises. We provide you with customers!!! Plus invoicing and collection services. We provide complete training, progressive business development, equipment package and start-up. Master franchises available for select locations, as well as local unit franchises.

BACKGROUND:

243

Established: 1995; 1st Franchised: 1995
Franchised Units: 800
Company-Owned Units: 0
Total Units: 800
Dist.:   US-800; CAN-0; O'seas-0
  North America: 15 States, 0 Provinces
  Density: 41 in OH, 54 in IL, 169 in FL
Projected New Units (12 Months):   200
Qualifications: 3, 3, 3, 2, 2, 2

FINANCIAL/TERMS:

Cash Investment: $2K-50K
Total Investment: $10K-50K
Minimum Net Worth: $2-100K
Fees: Franchise - $4.5-150K
  Royalty - 5%;   Ad. - 2%
Earnings Claims Statement: No
Term of Contract (Years):   10/10
Avg. # Of Employees: 1-2 FT, 4 PT
Passive Ownership: Discouraged
Encourage Conversions: Yes
Area Develop. Agreements: Yes/1
Sub-Franchising Contracts: Yes
Expand In Territory: Yes
Space Needs: 1,500 SF

SUPPORT & TRAINING:

Financial Assistance Provided: Yes (D)
Site Selection Assistance: Yes
Lease Negotiation Assistance: Yes
Co-Operative Advertising: No
Franchisee Assoc./Member: No
Size Of Corporate Staff: 10
On-Going Support: ,,C,,E,,G,H,I
Training: 2 Weeks Master in FL Corp.
  Office; 75 Hours Unit Franchise -
  Master Office

SPECIFIC EXPANSION PLANS:

US: All United States
Canada: All Canada
Overseas: All Countries

⋖⋖ ⋗⋗

ANDY ONCALL

921 E. Main St.
Chattanooga, TN 37408
Tel: (877) 263-9662 (423) 242-0401
Fax: (423) 622-0580
E-Mail: clay@andyoncall.com
Web Site: www.andyoncall.com
Mr. H. Clay Thompson, Director Franchise Development

Homeowners spend over $200 billion annually on home improvements and repair. ANDY ONCALL taps into this growing market. Franchise owners do not actually perform home repairs. They advertise to consumers, recruit craftsmen, schedule orders and oversee the day-to-day operation of the business. ANDY ONCALL is in the business of connecting craftsmen who are looking for work with homeowners who need minor home repairs. We locate, qualify and supervise handymen for residential and commercial markets. Franchisees of ANDY ONCALL Franchising, Inc. are eligible for expedited and streamlined SBA loan processing through the SBA's Franchise Registry Program, www.franchiseregistry.com

BACKGROUND: IFA MEMBER
Established: 1993; 1st Franchised: 1999
Franchised Units: 58
Company-Owned Units: 0
Total Units: 58
Dist.:   US-58; CAN-0; O'seas-0
  North America: 23 States, 0 Provinces
  Density: 5 in TN, 5 in NC, 5 in IL
Projected New Units (12 Months):   12
Qualifications: 5, 5, 3, 3, 4, 5

FINANCIAL/TERMS:

Cash Investment: $39.6K-55.5K
Total Investment: $56.2K-79.1K
Minimum Net Worth: $100K
Fees: Franchise - $26K
  Royalty - 5%;   Ad. - 0%
Earnings Claims Statement: No
Term of Contract (Years):   10/10
Avg. # Of Employees: 1 FT, 1 PT
Passive Ownership: Not Allowed
Encourage Conversions: No
Area Develop. Agreements: No
Sub-Franchising Contracts: No
Expand In Territory: Yes
Space Needs: 1,000 SF

SUPPORT & TRAINING:

Financial Assistance Provided: Yes (D)
Site Selection Assistance: Yes
Lease Negotiation Assistance: Yes
Co-Operative Advertising: No
Franchisee Assoc./Member: No
Size Of Corporate Staff: 10
On-Going Support: A,B,C,D,E,,G,H,I
Training: 8 Days Chattanooga, TN

SPECIFIC EXPANSION PLANS:

US: All United States
Canada: No
Overseas: NR

⋖⋖ ⋗⋗

BATHMASTER BMR

4498 Trepanier Rd.
Peachland, BC V0H 1X3 Canada
Tel: (877) 767-2336 (250) 767-2336
Fax: (250) 767-2718
E-Mail: sales@bathmaster.com
Web Site: www.bathmaster.com

Mr. Trevor Dixon, President

Quality bathtub, tile reglazing, acrylic bathtub liners, tub walls, porcelain restoration and countertop resurfacing with superior materials. Transform dull, worn, unsightly fixtures to a brilliant new finish in just a few hours. This system leaves no mess or odor behind and offers same day use. This franchise includes equipment, training and on-going support. We do it all!

BACKGROUND:

Established: 1989; 1st Franchised: 1994
Franchised Units: 26
Company-Owned Units: 0
Total Units: 26
Dist.:   US-1; CAN-26; O'seas-0
  North America: 0 States, 5 Provinces
  Density: 2 in SK, 12 in ON, 6 in BC
Projected New Units (12 Months):   5
Qualifications: 3, 2, 4, 3, 4, 3

FINANCIAL/TERMS:

Cash Investment: $5K-10K
Total Investment: $36K
Minimum Net Worth: NA
Fees: Franchise - $7K
  Royalty - 5%/$200/Mo.;   Ad. - 2%
Earnings Claims Statement: No
Term of Contract (Years):   5/5
Avg. # Of Employees: 1 FT, 0 PT
Passive Ownership: Discouraged
Encourage Conversions: Yes
Area Develop. Agreements: No
Sub-Franchising Contracts: No
Expand In Territory: Yes
Space Needs: 300 SF

SUPPORT & TRAINING:

Financial Assistance Provided: No
Site Selection Assistance: NA
Lease Negotiation Assistance: No
Co-Operative Advertising: No
Franchisee Assoc./Member: Yes/Yes
Size Of Corporate Staff: 2
On-Going Support: ,B,C,D,,F,G,H,I
Training: 15 Days Minimum Peachland,
  BC

SPECIFIC EXPANSION PLANS:

US: All United States
Canada: All Canada
Overseas: NR

⋖⋖ ⋗⋗

BONUS BUILDING CARE
P. O. Box 300

Indianola, OK 74442
Tel: (800) 931-1102 (918) 823-4990
Fax: (918) 823-4994
E-Mail: franchiseofficer@bonusbuilding
care.com
Web Site: www.bonusbuildingcare.com
Mr. Perry White, President

World's best investment opportunity in commercial cleaning. National rankings include: Entrepreneur Franchise 500 #20 (2008), Franchise Business Review, Franchisee Satisfaction #2 (2008), Franchise Market Magazine #5 (2008). You are offered customers, training, insurance, financing, clerical and procedural assistance as well as opportunities for expansion. Total investment, which can be partially financed by Bonus, is $9K to $41.9K

BACKGROUND: IFA MEMBER
Established: 1996;   1st Franchised: 1996
Franchised Units: 2444
Company-Owned Units: <u>40</u>
Total Units: 2484
Dist.:   US-2484; CAN-0; O'seas-0
   North America: 18 States, 0 Provinces
   Density: 461 in TX, 595 in TN, 253 in MO
Projected New Units (12 Months):   100
Qualifications: 1, 1, 2, 2, 3, 3
FINANCIAL/TERMS:
Cash Investment: Varies
Total Investment: $9-41.9K
Minimum Net Worth: NA
Fees: Franchise - $7.5K
   Royalty - 10%;   Ad. - 0%
Earnings Claims Statement: No
Term of Contract (Years):   10/10
Avg. # Of Employees: Varies
Passive Ownership: Discouraged
Encourage Conversions: Yes
Area Develop. Agreements: No
Sub-Franchising Contracts: Yes
Expand In Territory: Yes
Space Needs: NA
SUPPORT & TRAINING:
Financial Assistance Provided: Yes (D)
Site Selection Assistance: NA
Lease Negotiation Assistance: NA
Co-Operative Advertising: No
Franchisee Assoc./Member: Yes/Yes
Size Of Corporate Staff: 17
On-Going Support: ,,C,D,,G,,I
Training: As Needed Self-Study;
   Minimum 5 Hours Classroom; Minimum 20 Hours - unlimited On-Site
SPECIFIC EXPANSION PLANS:
US: All United States
Canada: All Canada

Overseas: All Countries

◄◄ ►►

BUILDING SERVICES OF AMERICA
11900 W. 87th St., # 135
Lenexa, KS 66215
Tel: (913) 599-6200
Fax: (913) 599-4441
E-Mail: howard@buildingservicesofame
rica.com
Web Site: www.buildingservicesofamerica.
com
Mr. Howard Capps, President

Franchised commercial cleaning.

BACKGROUND:
Established: 1992;   1st Franchised: 1991
Franchised Units: 35
Company-Owned Units: <u>1</u>
Total Units: 36
Dist.:   US-36; CAN-0; O'seas-0
   North America: 2 States, Provinces
   Density: 15 in KS, 21 in MO
Projected New Units (12 Months):   6
Qualifications: 2, 2, 1, 2, 2, 2
FINANCIAL/TERMS:
Cash Investment: $1.5-15K
Total Investment: $7.5-20K
Minimum Net Worth: $0K
Fees: Franchise - $1.5-15K
   Royalty - 8%;   Ad. - 0%
Earnings Claims Statement: No
Term of Contract (Years):   10/10
Avg. # Of Employees: Varies
Passive Ownership: Not Allowed
Encourage Conversions: NA
Area Develop. Agreements: No
Sub-Franchising Contracts: No
Expand In Territory: Yes
Space Needs: NR
SUPPORT & TRAINING:
Financial Assistance Provided: Yes (D)
Site Selection Assistance: No
Lease Negotiation Assistance: No
Co-Operative Advertising: No
Franchisee Assoc./Member: Yes/Yes
Size Of Corporate Staff: 7
On-Going Support: A,,C,D,,G,H,
Training: 1-2 Weeks Corporate Office
SPECIFIC EXPANSION PLANS:
US: All United States
Canada: No
Overseas: NR

◄◄ ►►

CAPITAL CARPET CLEANING & DYE
22410 Woodward Ave.
Ferndale, MI 48220
Tel: (586) 677-6378
Fax: (248) 542-4566
E-Mail:
Web Site: www.chemmasters.com
Mr. Michael Woods, President

CAPITAL CARPET CLEANING was developed out of an unquestionable need in the carpet and upholstery cleaning industry to provide a superior, ultra-high powered, carpet and upholstery cleaning system.

BACKGROUND:
Established: 1983;   1st Franchised: 1990
Franchised Units: 12
Company-Owned Units: <u>2</u>
Total Units: 14
Dist.:   US-14; CAN-0; O'seas-0
   North America: 3 States, Provinces
   Density: 3 in CA, 7 in FL, 4 in MN
Projected New Units (12 Months):   10
Qualifications: 1, 3, 1, 3, 3, 5
FINANCIAL/TERMS:
Cash Investment: $0-5K
Total Investment: $35-45K
Minimum Net Worth: NR
Fees: Franchise - $1-10K
   Royalty - 0%;   Ad. - 0%
Earnings Claims Statement: No
Term of Contract (Years):   5/5
Avg. # Of Employees: 1 FT, 1 PT
Passive Ownership: Allowed
Encourage Conversions: Yes
Area Develop. Agreements: No
Sub-Franchising Contracts: No
Expand In Territory: Yes
Space Needs: NR
SUPPORT & TRAINING:
Financial Assistance Provided: Yes (D)
Site Selection Assistance: Yes
Lease Negotiation Assistance: Yes
Co-Operative Advertising: No
Franchisee Assoc./Member: No
Size Of Corporate Staff: 2
On-Going Support: ,,C,D,E,,G,H,
Training: 2 Weeks FL
SPECIFIC EXPANSION PLANS:
US: All United States
Canada: All Canada
Overseas: All Countries

◄◄ ►►

CERTIRESTORE
310 N. Pacific Ave.

Fargo, ND 58102
Tel: (888) 50-CERTI (701) 277-1005
Fax: (701) 277-0534
E-Mail: bmitchell@certirestore.com
Web Site: www.certirestore.com
Mr. Robert Mitchell, Vice President

CERTIRESTORE Certified Furniture Restoration is a shop-based, full-service furniture restoration and repair franchise opportunity. We focus on providing professional furniture restoration to commercial clients, moving and insurance companies, restaurants, etc. - everyone who owns furniture needs our services. CERTIRESTORE provides protected territories. We provide the tools, supplies, equipment, support and hands-on training. 12-day shop training class. Chemical-free finish removal system.

BACKGROUND:

Established: 1989;	1st Franchised: 2004
Franchised Units:	27
Company-Owned Units:	0
Total Units:	27
Dist.:	US-26; CAN-1; O'seas-0
North America:	12 States, 1 Provinces
Density:	4 in WI, 6 in MN
Projected New Units (12 Months):	19
Qualifications:	2, 3, 2, 2, 3, 3

FINANCIAL/TERMS:

Cash Investment:	$39.5K
Total Investment:	$53-83K
Minimum Net Worth:	NA
Fees: Franchise -	$49.5K
Royalty - 5-8%;	Ad. - 1%
Earnings Claims Statement:	No
Term of Contract (Years):	10/10
Avg. # Of Employees:	1-2 FT, 1-3 PT
Passive Ownership:	Discouraged
Encourage Conversions:	Yes
Area Develop. Agreements:	Yes/0
Sub-Franchising Contracts:	No
Expand In Territory:	Yes
Space Needs:	2,000-3,000 SF

SUPPORT & TRAINING:

Financial Assistance Provided:	Yes (I)
Site Selection Assistance:	Yes
Lease Negotiation Assistance:	Yes
Co-Operative Advertising:	No
Franchisee Assoc./Member:	No
Size Of Corporate Staff:	4
On-Going Support:	„C,D,E,„G,H,I
Training:	12 Days Hands-On Training Fargo, ND

SPECIFIC EXPANSION PLANS:

US:	17, All United States
Canada:	2
Overseas:	NR

<< >>

**CHEM-DRY CARPET
& UPHOLSTERY CLEANING**
1530 N. 1000 W.
Logan, UT 84321
Tel: (877) 307-8233 (435) 755-0099
Fax: (435) 755-0021
E-Mail: leadin@chemdry.com
Web Site: www.chemdry.com
Ms. Chelsey Sanders, Franchise Development Director

Discover your potential with Chem-Dry: America's #1 Carpet and Upholstery Cleaning Franchise, and a partner of The Home Depot.

BACKGROUND: IFA MEMBER

Established: 1977;	1st Franchised: 1978
Franchised Units:	4500
Company-Owned Units:	0
Total Units:	4500
Dist.:	US-2547; CAN-124; O'seas-1331
North America:	50 States, 11 Provinces
Density:	166 in TX, 146 in FL, 421 in CA
Projected New Units (12 Months):	2200
Qualifications:	4, 3, 1, 1, 1, 5

FINANCIAL/TERMS:

Cash Investment:	$12K-40.8K
Total Investment:	$28K-250K
Minimum Net Worth:	$10K
Fees: Franchise -	$13K
Royalty - $350/Mo.;	Ad. - 0%
Earnings Claims Statement:	No
Term of Contract (Years):	5/5
Avg. # Of Employees:	1 FT, 0 PT
Passive Ownership:	Discouraged
Encourage Conversions:	NA
Area Develop. Agreements:	No
Sub-Franchising Contracts:	No
Expand In Territory:	No
Space Needs:	NA

SUPPORT & TRAINING:

Financial Assistance Provided:	Yes (D)
Site Selection Assistance:	NA
Lease Negotiation Assistance:	No
Co-Operative Advertising:	Yes
Franchisee Assoc./Member:	No
Size Of Corporate Staff:	70
On-Going Support:	„C,D,„,G,H,I
Training:	5 Days Logan, UT

SPECIFIC EXPANSION PLANS:

US:	Northeast,Cenrtral,Southeast

Canada:	All Canada
Overseas:	Most Countries

<< >>

**CHEMSTATION
INTERNATIONAL**
3400 Encrete Ln.
Dayton, OH 45439
Tel: (800) 554-8265 (937) 294-8265
Fax: (937) 297-6641
E-Mail: jpurks@chemstation.com
Web Site: www.chemstation.com
Mr. Jeff Purks, Vice President

CHEMSTATION is an affiliation of manufacturing centers which offer their customers the unique service of custom manufactured cleaning chemicals delivered in bulk to refillable containers that eliminate the waste and inefficiencies of drums.

BACKGROUND: IFA MEMBER

Established: 1977;	1st Franchised: 1984
Franchised Units:	49
Company-Owned Units:	5
Total Units:	54
Dist.:	US-54; CAN-0; O'seas-0
North America:	27 States, 0 Provinces
Density:	5 in OH, 3 in MI, 3 in IN
Projected New Units (12 Months):	4
Qualifications:	5, 4, 3, 2, 1, 5

FINANCIAL/TERMS:

Cash Investment:	$187K-277K
Total Investment:	$500K-750K
Minimum Net Worth:	NR
Fees: Franchise -	$45K
Royalty - 4%;	Ad. - 2%/$5K Max.
Earnings Claims Statement:	No
Term of Contract (Years):	10/5
Avg. # Of Employees:	10 FT, 0 PT
Passive Ownership:	Discouraged
Encourage Conversions:	NA
Area Develop. Agreements:	No
Sub-Franchising Contracts:	No
Expand In Territory:	Yes
Space Needs:	6,000 SF

SUPPORT & TRAINING:

Financial Assistance Provided:	No
Site Selection Assistance:	Yes
Lease Negotiation Assistance:	Yes
Co-Operative Advertising:	No
Franchisee Assoc./Member:	Yes/Yes
Size Of Corporate Staff:	41
On-Going Support:	A,B,C,D,E,F,G,H,I
Training:	1 Week and On-Going Dayton,

OH

SPECIFIC EXPANSION PLANS:

US:	West, NY, Northeast
Canada:	All Canada
Overseas:	All Countries

⟪ ⟫

Top 100

CLEANING AUTHORITY, THE

7230 Lee DeForest Dr., # 200
Columbia, MD 21046
Tel: (866) 682-6243 (410) 740-1900
Fax: (866) 685-6243
E-Mail: iric@thecleaningauthority.com
Web Site: www.the cleaningauthority.com
Mr. Iric Wexler, VP Development

The Cleaning Authority utilizes innovative methods to develop large, successful residential cleaning businesses. Business owners implement an ambitious and effective customer acquisition program. This program, employee management and client satisfaction systems, drives the cased based, residual income model. The Cleaning Authority's business model combines simple business fundamentals with solid systems, and an unprecedented support infrastructure, towards tremendous income potential.

BACKGROUND: IFA MEMBER

Established: 1977;	1st Franchised: 1996
Franchised Units:	185
Company-Owned Units:	1
Total Units:	186
Dist.:	US-186; CAN-0; O'seas-0
North America:	39 States, 0 Provinces
Density:	14 in TX, 13 in MI, 15 in FL
Projected New Units (12 Months):	25
Qualifications:	4, 4, 1, 3, 3, 4

FINANCIAL/TERMS:

Cash Investment:	$30K
Total Investment:	$113K
Minimum Net Worth:	$200K
Fees: Franchise -	$30K-50K
Royalty - 4-6%;	Ad. - 1%
Earnings Claims Statement:	Yes
Term of Contract (Years):	10/5
Avg. # Of Employees:	18 FT, 0 PT
Passive Ownership:	Not Allowed
Encourage Conversions:	No
Area Develop. Agreements:	No

Sub-Franchising Contracts:	No
Expand In Territory:	Yes
Space Needs:	1000 SF

SUPPORT & TRAINING:

Financial Assistance Provided:	Yes (I)
Site Selection Assistance:	Yes
Lease Negotiation Assistance:	No
Co-Operative Advertising:	No
Franchisee Assoc./Member:	No
Size Of Corporate Staff:	20
On-Going Support:	A,B,C,D,,,G,H,I
Training:	2 weeks Corporate Office

SPECIFIC EXPANSION PLANS:

US:	All
Canada:	No
Overseas:	NR

⟪ ⟫

CLEANNET USA

9861 Broken Land Pkwy., # 208
Columbia, MD 21046
Tel: (800) 735-8838 (410) 720-6444
Fax: (410) 720-5307
E-Mail: elugo@cleannetusa.com
Web Site: www.cleannetusa.com
Mr. Ed Lugo, Franchise Sales

Full-service, turn-key commercial office cleaning franchise, offering guaranteed customer accounts, complete training, brand new equipment, supplies, local office support, quality control backup, billing/invoicing and services provided. Company also sells master licenses for markets with metropolitan populations of 500,000 and up.

BACKGROUND:

Established: 1987;	1st Franchised: 1988
Franchised Units:	2591
Company-Owned Units:	6
Total Units:	2597
Dist.:	US-2597; CAN-0; O'seas-0
North America:	13 States, 0 Provinces
Density:	195 in PA, 308 in NJ, 366 in MD
Projected New Units (12 Months):	400
Qualifications:	4, 3, 2, 1, 3, 4

FINANCIAL/TERMS:

Cash Investment:	$0-25K
Total Investment:	$3.9-35.6K
Minimum Net Worth:	$0-100K
Fees: Franchise -	$2-25.5K
Royalty - 3%;	Ad. - 0%
Earnings Claims Statement:	No
Term of Contract (Years):	10/10
Avg. # Of Employees:	2 FT, 10 PT
Passive Ownership:	Discouraged
Encourage Conversions:	NA

Area Develop. Agreements:	Yes/1
Sub-Franchising Contracts:	Yes
Expand In Territory:	Yes
Space Needs:	2,000 SF

SUPPORT & TRAINING:

Financial Assistance Provided:	Yes (D)
Site Selection Assistance:	Yes
Lease Negotiation Assistance:	Yes
Co-Operative Advertising:	No
Franchisee Assoc./Member:	No
Size Of Corporate Staff:	75
On-Going Support:	A,B,C,D,E,,G,H,I
Training:	8 Days to 2 Weeks Company
	Offices; 4 Days to 3 Weeks Job Site or
	Master Offices

SPECIFIC EXPANSION PLANS:

US:	All United States
Canada:	All Canada
Overseas: South Africa, Korea, Southeast	
Asia, Europe, Australia	

⟪ ⟫

**CLINTAR GROUNDSKEEPING
SERVICES**

70 Esna Park Dr., # 1
Markham, ON L3R 1E3 Canada
Tel: (800) 361-3542 (905) 943-9530
Fax: (905) 943-9529
E-Mail: rwilton@clintar.com
Web Site: www.clintar.com
Mr. Robert C. Wilton, President

Company provides a full-service, year-round grounds care service to Fortune 500 clients and government agencies. The average size business is $1,500,000. It provides landscape maintenance services, power sweeping, and snow and ice control services.

BACKGROUND:

Established: 1973;	1st Franchised: 1984
Franchised Units:	18
Company-Owned Units:	0
Total Units:	18
Dist.:	US-0; CAN-18; O'seas-0
North America:	0 States, 1 Provinces
Density:	18 in ON
Projected New Units (12 Months):	5
Qualifications:	4, 5, 2, 3, 4, 5

FINANCIAL/TERMS:

Cash Investment:	$50-75K
Total Investment:	$90-150K
Minimum Net Worth:	$250K
Fees: Franchise -	$40K
Royalty - 8%;	Ad. - 0%
Earnings Claims Statement:	No
Term of Contract (Years):	10/5
Avg. # Of Employees:	10 FT, 15 PT

Passive Ownership:	Not Allowed
Encourage Conversions:	Yes
Area Develop. Agreements:	Yes/1
Sub-Franchising Contracts:	Yes
Expand In Territory:	Yes
Space Needs:	3,000 SF

SUPPORT & TRAINING:

Financial Assistance Provided:	Yes (I)
Site Selection Assistance:	Yes
Lease Negotiation Assistance:	Yes
Co-Operative Advertising:	Yes
Franchisee Assoc./Member:	Yes/Yes
Size Of Corporate Staff:	13
On-Going Support:	a,B,C,D,E,F,,H,I

Training: 2 Weeks and ongoing Toronto, ON

SPECIFIC EXPANSION PLANS:

US:	Northwest (Great Lakes Area)
Canada:	All Canada
Overseas:	NR

◄◄ ►►

CORPORATE CLEANING GROUP

39201 Schoolcraft, # B5
Livonia, MI 48150
Tel: (734) 522-1144
Fax: (734) 522-0044
E-Mail: lisa@corporatecleaninggroup.
com
Web Site: www.corporatecleaninggroup.
com
Mr. Devin Dollar, Chief Executive Officer

Corporate Cleaning Group is an exciting company that specializes in janitorial services. What sets the Corporate Cleaning Group apart from our competitors is our expertise and specialization in premium niche markets. Corporate Cleaning Group pursues top-level customers in the area of churches, schools, medical and other specialty areas. In the cleaning industry, the number of prospects is infinite, something that can easily become over-whelming, leading to complete paralysis of sales initiative.

BACKGROUND: IFA MEMBER

Established: 1993;	1st Franchised: 2007
Franchised Units:	2
Company-Owned Units:	2
Total Units:	4
Dist.:	US-4; CAN-0; O'seas-0
North America:	2 States, 0 Provinces

Density:	2 in MO, 2 in MI
Projected New Units (12 Months):	6
Qualifications:	3, 5, 1, 1, 3, 4

FINANCIAL/TERMS:

Cash Investment:	$30K
Total Investment:	$50K-75K
Minimum Net Worth:	$200K-500K
Fees: Franchise -	$30K
Royalty - 5%;	Ad. - 1%
Earnings Claims Statement:	No
Term of Contract (Years):	15/15

Avg. # Of Employees: depends on how many accounts

Passive Ownership:	Discouraged
Encourage Conversions:	Yes
Area Develop. Agreements:	No
Sub-Franchising Contracts:	No
Expand In Territory:	No
Space Needs:	NA

SUPPORT & TRAINING:

Financial Assistance Provided:	Yes (D)
Site Selection Assistance:	NA
Lease Negotiation Assistance:	NA
Co-Operative Advertising:	No
Franchisee Assoc./Member:	No
Size Of Corporate Staff:	7
On-Going Support:	,,C,D,,,,H

Training: Sales and Operation On-Going Franshisee; Sales 1 Week Franchisee Location;1 Week Detroit

SPECIFIC EXPANSION PLANS:

US: OK,MO,MI,NE,OH,IL,MN,WI,TX, PA,IA,IN,AR,KS,SD

Canada:	No
Overseas:	NR

◄◄ ►►

COTTAGECARE

6323 W. 110th St.
Overland Park, KS 66211
Tel: (800) 469-6303 (913) 469-8778
Fax: (913) 469-0822
E-Mail: mnagel@cottagecare.com
Web Site: www.cottagecare.com
Ms. Molly Nagel, Franchise Licensing Representative

Big business approach to housecleaning. We do the marketing and sign up new customers for you! You retain customers and manage the business, not clean houses. Jumbo exclusive territories are 4 times larger than industry standards,leading to 'Jumbo' sales.

BACKGROUND:

Established: 1988;	1st Franchised: 1989
Franchised Units:	45
Company-Owned Units:	3

Total Units:	48
Dist.:	US-41; CAN-7; O'seas-0
North America:	20 States, 3 Provinces
Density:	5 in AB, 4 in KS
Projected New Units (12 Months):	15
Qualifications:	4, 4, 2, 2, 1, 5

FINANCIAL/TERMS:

Cash Investment:	$46K
Total Investment:	$46K
Minimum Net Worth:	NA
Fees: Franchise -	$7K
Royalty - 5.5%;	Ad. - As Needed
Earnings Claims Statement:	Yes
Term of Contract (Years):	10/10
Avg. # Of Employees:	1 FT, 16 PT
Passive Ownership:	Discouraged
Encourage Conversions:	No
Area Develop. Agreements:	Yes/1
Sub-Franchising Contracts:	Yes
Expand In Territory:	Yes
Space Needs:	400 SF

SUPPORT & TRAINING:

Financial Assistance Provided:	Yes (D)
Site Selection Assistance:	Yes
Lease Negotiation Assistance:	Yes
Co-Operative Advertising:	No
Franchisee Assoc./Member:	No
Size Of Corporate Staff:	10
On-Going Support:	,,C,D,,,G,H,

Training: 2 Weeks Overland Park, KS Headquarters

SPECIFIC EXPANSION PLANS:

US:	All United States
Canada:	All Canada
Overseas:	NR

◄◄ ►►

COUSTIC-GLO INTERNATIONAL

7115 Ohms Ln., # 7111
Minneapolis, MN 55439
Tel: (800) 333-8523 (612) 835-1338
Fax: (612) 835-1395
E-Mail: cgiinc@aol.com
Web Site: www.causticglo.com
Mr. Scott L. Smith, Marketing

Building restoration products which enable you to clean and restore all types of ceiling and wall areas. Very specialized market which is growing as buildings age and the indoor environmental concerns continue to grow nationwide.

BACKGROUND: IFA MEMBER

Established: 1975;	1st Franchised: 1984
Franchised Units:	31
Company-Owned Units:	0
Total Units:	31
Dist.:	US-31; CAN-26; O'seas-26

North America: 0 States, 0 Provinces
Density: 5 in TX, 12 in GA, 6 in FL
Projected New Units (12 Months): 50
Qualifications: 4, 4, 3, 3, 3, 3
FINANCIAL/TERMS:
Cash Investment: $12K
Total Investment: $17.6K-20.3K
Minimum Net Worth: $20K
Fees: Franchise - $12K
    Royalty - 5%; Ad. - 1%
Earnings Claims Statement: Yes
Term of Contract (Years): 10/5
Avg. # Of Employees: 1 FT, 0 PT
Passive Ownership: Allowed
Encourage Conversions: NA
Area Develop. Agreements: Yes/1
Sub-Franchising Contracts: Yes
Expand In Territory: Yes
Space Needs: NA
SUPPORT & TRAINING:
Financial Assistance Provided: Yes (D)
Site Selection Assistance: NA
Lease Negotiation Assistance: NA
Co-Operative Advertising: No
Franchisee Assoc./Member: Yes/Yes
Size Of Corporate Staff: 20
On-Going Support: ,B,C,D,,,G,H,I
Training: 2 Weeks On-Location
SPECIFIC EXPANSION PLANS:
US: All United States
Canada: All Canada
Overseas: All Countries

◄◄ ►►

**COVERALL HEALTH-BASED
CLEANING SYSTEM**
5201 Congress Ave., # 275
Boca Raton, FL 33487
Tel: (800) 537-3371 (561) 922-2500
Fax: (561) 922-2423
E-Mail: jack.caughey@coverall.com
Web Site: www.coverall.com
Mr. Jack Caughey, Business Development

Commercial cleaning franchise which includes comprehensive training, equipment, billing and collection services, and an initial customer base. With an affordable down payment as low as $3,950, COVERALL HEALTH-BASED CLEANING SYSTEM provides a combination of business programs and support systems that focus on meeting the franchisees and customers alike. Master and territory franchises are also available.

BACKGROUND: IFA MEMBER
Established: 1985; 1st Franchised: 1985
Franchised Units: 9603
Company-Owned Units: 0
Total Units: 9603
Dist.: US-8917; CAN-286; O'seas-400
 North America: 32 States, 3 Provinces
 Density: 718 in OH, 729 in CA, 757 in FL
Projected New Units (12 Months): 1736
Qualifications: 3, 3, 2, 2, 3, 5
FINANCIAL/TERMS:
Cash Investment: $2,000-$27,200
Total Investment: $$10,612-$37,345
Minimum Net Worth: $10,612
Fees: Franchise - $10,000-$32,200
    Royalty - 5%; Ad. - 0%
Earnings Claims Statement: No
Term of Contract (Years): 20/20
Avg. # Of Employees: 1-2 FT, 2-3 PT
Passive Ownership: Allowed
Encourage Conversions: Yes
Area Develop. Agreements: No
Sub-Franchising Contracts: Yes
Expand In Territory: Yes
Space Needs: NA
SUPPORT & TRAINING:
Financial Assistance Provided: Yes (D)
Site Selection Assistance: NA
Lease Negotiation Assistance: NA
Co-Operative Advertising: No
Franchisee Assoc./Member: No
Size Of Corporate Staff: 90
On-Going Support: A,B,,D,,,G,H,I
Training: 30 - 40 Hours Local Regional
    Support Center
SPECIFIC EXPANSION PLANS:
US: All United States
Canada: All Canada
Overseas: All Countries

◄◄ ►►

CRACK TEAM, THE
11694 Lackland Rd.
St. Louis, MO 63146
Tel: (866) 905-5200 (314) 426-0900
Fax: (314) 426-0915
E-Mail: franchise@thecrackteam.com
Web Site: www.thecrackteam.com
Ms. Elizabeth Johnson, Franchise Support
    Coordinator

THE CRACK TEAM offers a unique specialty service repairing concrete. Cracked and leaking concrete can be repaired permanently, quickly and inexpensively using our proven materials.

BACKGROUND: IFA MEMBER
Established: 1985; 1st Franchised: 2001
Franchised Units: 28
Company-Owned Units: 0
Total Units: 28
Dist.: US-28; CAN-0; O'seas-0
 North America: 15 States, 0 Provinces
 Density: 3 in IL, 3 in MI, 8 in MO
Projected New Units (12 Months): 24
Qualifications: 5, 3, 1, 2, 2, 3
FINANCIAL/TERMS:
Cash Investment: $75K
Total Investment: $66-89K
Minimum Net Worth: $150-175K
Fees: Franchise - $35K
    Royalty - 6%; Ad. - 2%
Earnings Claims Statement: No
Term of Contract (Years): 10/10
Avg. # Of Employees: 2 FT, 0 PT
Passive Ownership: Discouraged
Encourage Conversions: No
Area Develop. Agreements: No
Sub-Franchising Contracts: No
Expand In Territory: No
Space Needs: 300 SF
SUPPORT & TRAINING:
Financial Assistance Provided: No
Site Selection Assistance: Yes
Lease Negotiation Assistance: NA
Co-Operative Advertising: No
Franchisee Assoc./Member: No
Size Of Corporate Staff: 8
On-Going Support: A,B,C,D,E,F,G,h,I
Training: NR
SPECIFIC EXPANSION PLANS:
US: Midwest, East Coast
Canada: All Canada
Overseas: NR

◄◄ ►►

CRITTER CONTROL
9435 E. Cherry Bend Rd.
Traverse City, MI 49684
Tel: (800) 699-1953 (734) 453-6300
Fax: (231) 947-9440
E-Mail: culver@crittercontrol.com
Web Site: www.crittercontrol.com
Mr. Charlie Culver, Chief Operating Officer

Urban Wildlife Management Specialists. The nation's leading wildlife control firm. Humane animal removal, prevention and repairs of animal damage.

BACKGROUND: IFA MEMBER
Established: 1982; 1st Franchised: 1987
Franchised Units: 100
Company-Owned Units: 3
Total Units: 103
Dist.: US-103; CAN-2; O'seas-0
North America: 36 States, 2 Provinces
Density: 6 in OH, 11 in MI, 7 in FL
Projected New Units (12 Months): 14
Qualifications: 2, 3, 3, 3, 3, 4
FINANCIAL/TERMS:
Cash Investment: $5K-8K
Total Investment: $18K-36K
Minimum Net Worth: NR
Fees: Franchise - $15-24K
Royalty - 6-16%; Ad. - 1-2%
Earnings Claims Statement: Yes
Term of Contract (Years): 10/10
Avg. # Of Employees: 2 FT, 1 PT
Passive Ownership: Discouraged
Encourage Conversions: NA
Area Develop. Agreements: No
Sub-Franchising Contracts: No
Expand In Territory: Yes
Space Needs: NA
SUPPORT & TRAINING:
Financial Assistance Provided: Yes (D)
Site Selection Assistance: Yes
Lease Negotiation Assistance: NA
Co-Operative Advertising: No
Franchisee Assoc./Member: Yes/Yes
Size Of Corporate Staff: 8
On-Going Support: ,,C,D,,,G,H,I
Training: 1 Week Columbus, OH
SPECIFIC EXPANSION PLANS:
US: All United States
Canada: All Canada
Overseas: NR

◄◄ ►►

CULLIGAN
9399 W. Higgins Rd. #110
Rosemont, IL 60018
Tel: (800) 285-5426 (847) 205-6000
Fax: (847) 205-6005
E-Mail: tvitacco@culligan.com
Web Site: www.culligan.com
Mr. Tom Vitacco, VP Franchising

CULLIGAN is looking for franchisees to start a business selling 5 gallon bottles of water for delivery to homes and offices. CULLIGAN is a manufacturer of water conditioners, filters and drinking water devices.

BACKGROUND: IFA MEMBER
Established: 1936; 1st Franchised: 1940
Franchised Units: 586

Company-Owned Units: 68
Total Units: 654
Dist.: US-654; CAN-48; O'seas-0
North America: 50 States, 0 Provinces
Density: 35 in WI, 40 in MN, 40 in IA
Projected New Units (12 Months): 8
Qualifications: 5, 5, 2, 3, 4, 4
FINANCIAL/TERMS:
Cash Investment: $103-225K
Total Investment: $103-225K
Minimum Net Worth: $250K
Fees: Franchise - $5K
Royalty - 3-5%; Ad. - 0%
Earnings Claims Statement: No
Term of Contract (Years): 10/10
Avg. # Of Employees: 6 FT, 0 PT
Passive Ownership: Discouraged
Encourage Conversions: Yes
Area Develop. Agreements: No
Sub-Franchising Contracts: No
Expand In Territory: No
Space Needs: 2,500 SF
SUPPORT & TRAINING:
Financial Assistance Provided: No
Site Selection Assistance: No
Lease Negotiation Assistance: No
Co-Operative Advertising: No
Franchisee Assoc./Member: Yes/Yes
Size Of Corporate Staff: 200
On-Going Support: ,,C,D,,,G,H,I
Training: 1 Week Chicago, IL;
1 Week On-Site
SPECIFIC EXPANSION PLANS:
US: All United States
Canada: All Canada
Overseas: Mexico, South America

◄◄ ►►

DREAMMAKER BATH & KITCHEN REMODELING
1020 N. University Parks Dr.
Waco, TX 76707
Tel: (800) 583-9099 (254) 745-2477
Fax: (254) 745-2588
E-Mail: karen.cagle@dwyergroup.com
Web Site: www.dreammaker-remodel.com
Ms. Karen Cagle, Vice President of Franchising

DREAMMAKER BATH & KITCHEN is a full-service kitchen, bath and interior remodeling franchise. DREAMMAKER

provides proven business systems, brand name and image, group buying power and remodeling options to help you grow your business and experience the strong margins and quality of life you deserve. Support includes training, research and development, marketing and one-on-one coaching.

BACKGROUND: IFA MEMBER
Established: 1970; 1st Franchised: 1971
Franchised Units: 180
Company-Owned Units: 0
Total Units: 180
Dist.: US-110; CAN-0; O'seas-70
North America: 50 States, 0 Provinces
Density: 5 in IL, 8 in TX, 14 in CA
Projected New Units (12 Months): 30
Qualifications: 4, 3, 5, 2, 2, 5
FINANCIAL/TERMS:
Cash Investment: $88-315K
Total Investment: $112-339K
Minimum Net Worth: $100K
Fees: Franchise - $35K
Royalty - 6-3%; Ad. - 2-1%
Earnings Claims Statement: No
Term of Contract (Years): 10/10
Avg. # Of Employees: 4 FT, 0 PT
Passive Ownership: Discouraged
Encourage Conversions: Yes
Area Develop. Agreements: No
Sub-Franchising Contracts: No
Expand In Territory: Yes
Space Needs: 700-2,500 SF
SUPPORT & TRAINING:
Financial Assistance Provided: Yes (D)
Site Selection Assistance: Yes
Lease Negotiation Assistance: Yes
Co-Operative Advertising: No
Franchisee Assoc./Member: Yes/Yes
Size Of Corporate Staff: 14
On-Going Support: ,B,C,D,E,,G,H,I
Training: 8 Days Headquarters, Waco, TX
- Basic Business; 5 Days Tech. Training after 12 Months
SPECIFIC EXPANSION PLANS:
US: All United States
Canada: All Except PQ
Overseas: NR

◄◄ ►►

DUCTBUSTERS
2030 Main St.
Dunedin, FL 34698
Tel: (800) 786-3828 (727) 787-7087
Fax: (727) 442-3380
E-Mail: iaqtomy@aol.com
Web Site: www.ductbusters.com
Mr. Dan Wantz, Franchise Director

DUCTBUSTERS is the largest franchisor of duct-cleaning businesses selling exclusively to air conditioning contractors. You receive a protected territory, full use of the nationally registered name and logo, the Busterlink computer software, training for production-sales-and management, 14-volume training and reference manuals, equipment recommendations and continual on-going support.

BACKGROUND:

Established: 1989; 1st Franchised: 1992
Franchised Units: 29
Company-Owned Units: 1
Total Units: 30
Dist.:   US-27; CAN-0; O'seas-3
  North America: 8 States, 0 Provinces
  Density: 2 in TX, 3 in LA, 17 in FL
Projected New Units (12 Months):   16
Qualifications: 3, 4, 5, 2, 3, 5

FINANCIAL/TERMS:

Cash Investment: $7.5K
Total Investment: $2.5-50K
Minimum Net Worth: NA
Fees: Franchise - $7.5-24K
  Royalty - 7%;   Ad. - 0%
Earnings Claims Statement: No
Term of Contract (Years):   10/5
Avg. # Of Employees: 6 FT, 0 PT
Passive Ownership: Discouraged
Encourage Conversions: Yes
Area Develop. Agreements: No
Sub-Franchising Contracts: No
Expand In Territory: Yes
Space Needs: NR

SUPPORT & TRAINING:

Financial Assistance Provided: Yes (D)
Site Selection Assistance: NA
Lease Negotiation Assistance: NA
Co-Operative Advertising: No
Franchisee Assoc./Member: No
Size Of Corporate Staff: 6
On-Going Support: A,B,C,D,,F,,H,I
Training: 5 Days Clearwater, FL;
  2 Days Franchisee's Facilities

SPECIFIC EXPANSION PLANS:

US: All United States
Canada: All Canada
Overseas: All Countries

◄◄ ►►

DURACLEAN INTERNATIONAL
220 Campus Dr.
Arlington Heights, IL 60004-1485
Tel: (800) 251-7070 + 130 (847) 704-7100 + 122
Fax: (847) 704-7101

E-Mail: info@duraclean.com
Web Site: www.duraclean.com
Ms. Danielle Canup, Director of Administration

DURACLEAN offers distinct services, markets and revenue center packages to fit your needs for independence and growth. Carpet cleaning, ceiling and wall cleaning, upholstery and drapery cleaning, mold remediation, fire/water damage restoration, janitorial, pressure washing,hard surface floor care, duct cleaning and ultrasonic cleaning are all services that we offer. We are the most diversified cleaning franchise in the world.

BACKGROUND: IFA MEMBER
Established: 1930; 1st Franchised: 1945
Franchised Units: 374
Company-Owned Units: 20
Total Units: 394
Dist.:   US-222; CAN-6; O'seas-168
  North America: 50 States, 0 Provinces
  Density: 34 in IL, 38 in FL, 30 in CA
Projected New Units (12 Months):   30
Qualifications: 4, 4, 3, 3, 3, 3

FINANCIAL/TERMS:

Cash Investment: $51K-91.5K
Total Investment: $51K-91.5K
Minimum Net Worth: NR
Fees: Franchise - $17.5K
  Royalty - 2-8%;   Ad. - 0%
Earnings Claims Statement: No
Term of Contract (Years):   5/5
Avg. # Of Employees: Varies
Passive Ownership: Discouraged
Encourage Conversions: Yes
Area Develop. Agreements: No
Sub-Franchising Contracts: No
Expand In Territory: Yes
Space Needs: NA

SUPPORT & TRAINING:

Financial Assistance Provided: Yes (D)
Site Selection Assistance: NA
Lease Negotiation Assistance: NA
Co-Operative Advertising: Yes
Franchisee Assoc./Member: Yes/Yes
Size Of Corporate Staff: 25
On-Going Support: ,,C,D,,,G,H,I
Training: 2 Days On-Site Cleaning;
  5 Days Success Institute, Corp. Office;
  Home Study Program

SPECIFIC EXPANSION PLANS:

US: All United States
Canada: All Canada
Overseas: All Countries

◄◄ ►►

ENVIRO MASTERS LAWN CARE
P. O. Box 74
Caledon East, ON L7C 3L8 Canada
Tel: (905) 584-9592
Fax: (905) 584-0402
E-Mail: martin@enviromasters.com
Web Site: www.enviromasters.com
Mr. Martin Fielding, President

Enjoy the Great Outdoors! and be part of a great new approach to lawn care. Organic and environmentally considerate. Home based. Excellent opportunity. Protected territories. Repeat business. Full training and marketing support. Business, turf management and in-field training. Master rights are now available in the U.S.

BACKGROUND:

Established: 1987; 1st Franchised: 1991
Franchised Units: 50
Company-Owned Units: 2
Total Units: 52
Dist.:   US-0; CAN-52; O'seas-0
  North America: 0 States, 0 Provinces
  Density: NR
Projected New Units (12 Months):   6
Qualifications: 3, 2, 1, 2, 3, 3

FINANCIAL/TERMS:

Cash Investment: $40-50K
Total Investment: $40-50K
Minimum Net Worth: $50K
Fees: Franchise - $35-40K
  Royalty - 5%;   Ad. - 2%
Earnings Claims Statement: No
Term of Contract (Years):   10/10
Avg. # Of Employees: 1 FT, 1 PT
Passive Ownership: Discouraged
Encourage Conversions: Yes
Area Develop. Agreements: Yes/1
Sub-Franchising Contracts: Yes
Expand In Territory: No
Space Needs: NR

SUPPORT & TRAINING:

Financial Assistance Provided: Yes (D)
Site Selection Assistance: Yes
Lease Negotiation Assistance: NA
Co-Operative Advertising: Yes
Franchisee Assoc./Member: No
Size Of Corporate Staff: 4
On-Going Support: ,B,C,D,E,F,G,H,I
Training: 1-2 Weeks Caledon East, ON

SPECIFIC EXPANSION PLANS:

US: All United States
Canada: All Canada
Overseas: All Countries

◄◄ ►►

FABRIZONE CLEANING SYSTEMS

3135 Universal Dr., # 6
Mississauga, ON L4X 2E2 Canada
Tel: (888) 781-1123 (416) 201-1010
Fax: (905) 602-7821
E-Mail: headoffice@fabrizone.com
Web Site: www.fabrizone.com
Mr. Jerry Cunningham, Franchise Development

FABRI-ZONE offers a full-service affiliate concept to start with a turn-key system with an environmentally sensitive cleaning program, a patented dry cleaning and purification carpet cleaning process. Steam finishing process cleans upholstery and draperies. 14 profit centers mean high returns for affiliates. Recommended by carpet manufacturers.

BACKGROUND:

Established: 1981;   1st Franchised: 1984
Franchised Units: 39
Company-Owned Units: 1
Total Units: 40
Dist.:   US-7; CAN-30; O'seas-3
North America: States, Provinces
Density: NR
Projected New Units (12 Months):   8
Qualifications: 3, 4, 1, 4, 4, 4

FINANCIAL/TERMS:

Cash Investment: $6K
Total Investment: $14K
Minimum Net Worth: NR
Fees: Franchise -   Varies
  Royalty - $150/Mo.;   Ad. - 0%
Earnings Claims Statement: No
Term of Contract (Years):   3/3
Avg. # Of Employees: 2 FT, 4 PT
Passive Ownership: Not Allowed
Encourage Conversions: Yes
Area Develop. Agreements: Yes/1
Sub-Franchising Contracts: No
Expand In Territory: No
Space Needs: NA

SUPPORT & TRAINING:

Financial Assistance Provided: Yes (D)
Site Selection Assistance: NA
Lease Negotiation Assistance: NA
Co-Operative Advertising: No
Franchisee Assoc./Member: No
Size Of Corporate Staff: 20
On-Going Support: ,B,C,d,e,,G,H,I
Training: 8 Days Toronto, ON

SPECIFIC EXPANSION PLANS:

US: All United States
Canada: All Canada
Overseas: All Countries

FISH WINDOW CLEANING SERVICES

200 Enchanted Pkwy.
Manchester, MO 63021
Tel: (877) 707-3474 (636) 530-7334
Fax: (636) 530-7856
E-Mail: nathan@fishwindowcleaning.com
Web Site: www.fishwindowcleaning.com
Mr. Nathan Merrick, VP Franchise Development

There is no glass ceiling when it comes to the potential you will have to grow your own unique service business in a large protected territory, specializing in year-round commercial and residential low-rise window cleaning. You can have the satisfaction of owning a business that requires no night or weekend work, backed by a franchisor with 31 years of experience.

BACKGROUND: IFA MEMBER

Established: 1978;   1st Franchised: 1998
Franchised Units: 230
Company-Owned Units: 2
Total Units: 232
Dist.:   US-232; CAN-0; O'seas-0
North America: 40 States, 0 Provinces
Density: NR
Projected New Units (12 Months):   25
Qualifications: 4, 4, 1, 2, 3, 5

FINANCIAL/TERMS:

Cash Investment: $59.5-133.5K
Total Investment: $59.5-133.5K
Minimum Net Worth: $100-200K
Fees: Franchise - $21.9-51.9K
  Royalty - 8-6%;   Ad. - 1%
Earnings Claims Statement: Yes
Term of Contract (Years):   10/5
Avg. # Of Employees: 3-12 FT, 0 PT
Passive Ownership: Discouraged
Encourage Conversions: Yes
Area Develop. Agreements: No
Sub-Franchising Contracts: No
Expand In Territory: Yes
Space Needs: NA

SUPPORT & TRAINING:

Financial Assistance Provided: Yes (I)
Site Selection Assistance: Yes
Lease Negotiation Assistance: Yes
Co-Operative Advertising: No
Franchisee Assoc./Member: Yes/Yes
Size Of Corporate Staff: 20

On-Going Support: A,B,C,D,E,,G,H,I
Training: Franchisee Territory;
  Corporate Headquarters

SPECIFIC EXPANSION PLANS:

US: All United States
Canada: No
Overseas: NR

FOLIAGE DESIGN SYSTEMS

7048 Narcoossee Rd.
Orlando, FL 32822
Tel: (800) 933-7351 (407) 245-7776
Fax: (407) 245-7533
E-Mail: john@foliagedesign.com
Web Site: www.foliagedesign.com
Mr. John S. Hagood, Chairman

FOLIAGE DESIGN SYSTEMS is one of the largest interior plant maintenance companies in the U. S., according to Interiorscape Magazine. FOLIAGE DESIGN franchisees learn the business from the ground up in an intensive training program followed by training sessions in the field. Franchisees are taught design, sales and maintenance of interior foliage plants.

BACKGROUND:

Established: 1971;   1st Franchised: 1980
Franchised Units: 38
Company-Owned Units: 3
Total Units: 41
Dist.:   US-41; CAN-0; O'seas-0
North America: 18 States, 0 Provinces
Density: 4 in SC, 3 in MS, 13 in FL
Projected New Units (12 Months):   3
Qualifications: 4, 5, 3, 3, 1, 5

FINANCIAL/TERMS:

Cash Investment: $20K
Total Investment: $44-64K
Minimum Net Worth: NR
Fees: Franchise - $20K/min.pop.400,000
  Royalty - 6%;   Ad. - 0%
Earnings Claims Statement: No
Term of Contract (Years):   10/
Avg. # Of Employees: 4 FT, 2 PT
Passive Ownership: Discouraged
Encourage Conversions: No
Area Develop. Agreements: Yes/1
Sub-Franchising Contracts: No
Expand In Territory: Yes
Space Needs: 200 SF

SUPPORT & TRAINING:

Financial Assistance Provided: No
Site Selection Assistance: Yes
Lease Negotiation Assistance: No
Co-Operative Advertising: No
Franchisee Assoc./Member: No

Size Of Corporate Staff: 8
On-Going Support: ,B,C,D,,F,G,H,I
Training: 3-5 Days Field;
8-10 Days Headquarters
SPECIFIC EXPANSION PLANS:
US: All United States
Canada: All Canada
Overseas: Europe, Asia, Mexico, South
America

<< >>

FRESH COAT
10700 Montgomery Rd., # 300
Cincinnati, OH 45242
Tel: (800) 317-7089 (513) 587-4974
Fax: (513) 563-2691
E-Mail: webinquiry@freshcoatpainters.
com
Web Site: www.freshcoatpainters.com
Ms. Amber Kershaw, Sales Support Manager

Ranked "Top 25 New Franchise" by Entrepreneur and "Top 55 Fastest-Growing" by Franchise Times in 2009. You'll use 5 great revenue streams in the $100 billion home services industry to grow and manage your organization while the painters you hire do the painting. This is a great home-based opportunity for mid-managers and executives in an industry with promising growth potential. Own this exciting, year-round, recession resistant business with low start-up costs and low overhead.

BACKGROUND: IFA MEMBER
Established: 2004; 1st Franchised: 2005
Franchised Units: 73
Company-Owned Units: 0
Total Units: 73
Dist.: US-71; CAN-2; O'seas-0
North America: 24 States, 1 Provinces
Density: NR
Projected New Units (12 Months): 60
Qualifications: 3, 4, 1, 2, 2, 4
FINANCIAL/TERMS:
Cash Investment: $7-27.9K
Total Investment: $36.4-58.9K
Minimum Net Worth: $15.9K
Fees: Franchise - $27.9K
Royalty - 6%; Ad. - $200/Mo.
Earnings Claims Statement: No
Term of Contract (Years): 10/10/10/

Avg. # Of Employees: 2 FT, 0 PT
Passive Ownership: Allowed
Encourage Conversions: Yes
Area Develop. Agreements: Yes/1
Sub-Franchising Contracts: No
Expand In Territory: Yes
Space Needs: NA
SUPPORT & TRAINING:
Financial Assistance Provided: Yes (D)
Site Selection Assistance: NA
Lease Negotiation Assistance: NA
Co-Operative Advertising: No
Franchisee Assoc./Member: No
Size Of Corporate Staff: 50
On-Going Support: ,,C,,,,G,H,I
Training: 5 Days Cincinnati, OH
SPECIFIC EXPANSION PLANS:
US: All United States
Canada: All Canada
Overseas: All Countries

<< >>

  FURNITURE MEDIC®

FURNITURE MEDIC
3839 Forest Hill-Irene Rd.
Memphis, TN 38125-2502
Tel: (800) 255-9687 (901) 597-8600
Fax: (901) 597-8660
E-Mail: dmessenger@smclean.com
Web Site: www.furnituremedicfranchise.
com
Mr. David Messenger, VP Market Expansion

FURNITURE MEDIC is a division of The ServiceMaster Company. It is the largest furniture and wood repair and restoration company in the world with over 500 franchises. Furniture Medic has unique products and processes which enable much of the work to be done on-site, reducing costs and saving time for its residential and commercial customers. Financing is provided for the initial franchise fees, start-up equipment and vehicles to qualified candidates through ServiceMaster Acceptance Company.

BACKGROUND: IFA MEMBER
Established: 1992; 1st Franchised: 1992
Franchised Units: 595
Company-Owned Units: 0
Total Units: 595
Dist.: US-420; CAN-71; O'seas-104
North America: 47 States, 10 Provinces
Density: 22 in VA, 38 in FL, 27 in CA

Projected New Units (12 Months): 50
Qualifications: 4, 4, 2, 3, 3, 5
FINANCIAL/TERMS:
Cash Investment: $15-25K
Total Investment: $37-81.9K
Minimum Net Worth: $50K
Fees: Franchise - $24.5K
Royalty - 7%/$250 Min.; Ad. - 1%/$50 Min.
Earnings Claims Statement: No
Term of Contract (Years): 5/5
Avg. # Of Employees: 1 FT, 1 PT
Passive Ownership: Not Allowed
Encourage Conversions: Yes
Area Develop. Agreements: No
Sub-Franchising Contracts: No
Expand In Territory: Yes
Space Needs: NR
SUPPORT & TRAINING:
Financial Assistance Provided: Yes (D)
Site Selection Assistance: NA
Lease Negotiation Assistance: No
Co-Operative Advertising: Yes
Franchisee Assoc./Member: Yes/Yes
Size Of Corporate Staff: 21
On-Going Support: A,B,,,,G,h,I
Training: 3 Weeks Memphis, TN
SPECIFIC EXPANSION PLANS:
US: Most metropolitan markets in US.
Canada: All Canada
Overseas: All Countries

<< >>

GLASS DOCTOR
1020 N. University Parks Dr.
Waco, TX 76707
Tel: (800) 280-9858 (254) 759-5850
Fax: (800) 209-7621
E-Mail: info@servicefranchiseopportun
ities.com
Web Site: www.servicefranchiseopportu-
nities.com
Ms. Sherri Jurls, Vice President of Franchising

From windows to windshields to store-fronts, Glass Doctor® can handle any glass repair or replacement need. Glass Doctor also offers custom glass services, such as tub and shower enclosures, entry door glass and mirrors. Established in 1962 with one shop in Seattle, Wash., today Glass Doctor offers complete glass repair, replacement and services to the residential, automotive, and commercial markets at more than 360 locations in the United States and Canada. Glass Doctor began franchising in 1977 and joined The Dwyer Group, Inc., an international franchisor of service industry companies, in 1998. Now there are more than 170 Glass Doctor franchise owners across the United States and Canada. New franchise owners are trained at the nation's only full-service glass training facility, Glass Doctor University, at the company headquarters in Waco, Texas. The Dwyer Group® family of companies also includes Aire Serv Heating and Air Conditioning®, Mr. Appliance®, Mr. Electric®, Mr. Rooter® and Rainbow International Restoration and Cleaning®.

BACKGROUND: IFA MEMBER
Established: 1962; 1st Franchised: 1974
Franchised Units: 171
Company-Owned Units: 0
Total Units: 171
Dist.: US-168; CAN-3; O'seas-0
  North America: 46 States, 2 Provinces
  Density: 12 in FL, 13 in CA, 15 in TX
Projected New Units (12 Months): 60
Qualifications: 4, 4, 2, 2, 3, 5
FINANCIAL/TERMS:
Cash Investment: $50-100K
Total Investment: $119.7-$301.7K
Minimum Net Worth: Varies
Fees: Franchise - $24K/100KPop + $220/1,000 add'l pop over minimum
  Royalty - 4-7%; Ad. - 2%
Earnings Claims Statement: Yes
Term of Contract (Years): 10/10
Avg. # Of Employees: 4 FT, 0 PT
Passive Ownership: Discouraged
Encourage Conversions: Yes
Area Develop. Agreements: No
Sub-Franchising Contracts: No
Expand In Territory: Yes
Space Needs: 1,500 SF
SUPPORT & TRAINING:
Financial Assistance Provided: Yes (I)
Site Selection Assistance: No
Lease Negotiation Assistance: No
Co-Operative Advertising: No
Franchisee Assoc./Member: Yes/No
Size Of Corporate Staff: 20
On-Going Support: A,B,C,D,E,F,G,h,I
Training:11 days optional Flat Glass Tech Basic / Commercial / Residential;
  5 days optional Auto Glass Tech Basic / Certification; 2 weeks required Basic Franchisee Training
SPECIFIC EXPANSION PLANS:
US: All United States
Canada: All Canada
Overseas: NR

GROUT DOCTOR
7923 E. Palm Ln.
Mesa, AZ 85207
Tel: (877) 476-8800 (480) 924-2100
Fax: (877) 615-2173
E-Mail: sales@groutdoctor.com
Web Site: www.groutdoctor.com
Ms. Robin Rotella, Director Franchise Development

Ceramic tile sales continue to increase, indicating a huge demand for the aftermarket care of tile and grout. As the largest and most recognized name in the business since 1992, The Grout Doctor franchise is ideally positioned to harness the demand in this multi-million dollar industry. All franchisees are trained to become highly qualified grout, tile and stone care specialists. The Grout Doctor offers an uncomplicated and affordable path to personal independence and unlimited income potential!

BACKGROUND: IFA MEMBER
Established: 1992; 1st Franchised: 2001
Franchised Units: 57
Company-Owned Units: 0
Total Units: 57
Dist.: US-57; CAN-0; O'seas-0
  North America: 20 States, 0 Provinces
  Density: 9 in FL, 7 in AZ
Projected New Units (12 Months): 10
Qualifications: 4, 3, 1, 2, 5, 3
FINANCIAL/TERMS:
Cash Investment: $19-34K
Total Investment: $19-34K
Minimum Net Worth: NA
Fees: Franchise - $19K
  Royalty - varies; Ad. - 0
Earnings Claims Statement: Yes
Term of Contract (Years): 7/7
Avg. # Of Employees: FT, PT
Passive Ownership: Not Allowed
Encourage Conversions: NA
Area Develop. Agreements: Yes/3
Sub-Franchising Contracts: No
Expand In Territory: Yes
Space Needs: NA
SUPPORT & TRAINING:
Financial Assistance Provided: No
Site Selection Assistance: NA
Lease Negotiation Assistance: NA

Co-Operative Advertising: No
Franchisee Assoc./Member: No
Size Of Corporate Staff: 10
On-Going Support: A,B,C,d,E,,G,h,I
Training: ;
  50 Hours Mesa, AZ (Phoenix);50 HoursSt. Charles, IL (Chicago)
SPECIFIC EXPANSION PLANS:
US: All United States
Canada: No
Overseas: NR

HANDYMAN CONNECTION
10250 Alliance Rd., # 100
Cincinnati, OH 45242
Tel: (800) 466-5530 + 116 (513) 771-3003
Fax: (513) 771-6439
E-Mail: lvonderhaar@handymanconnection.com
Web Site: www.handymanconnection.com
Ms. Lisa Vonderhaar, Company Administrator

HANDYMAN CONNECTION specializes in the small to medium size home repair and remodeling industry. We offer a turnkey package that includes marketing, advertising and a complete training program.

BACKGROUND: IFA MEMBER
Established: 1990; 1st Franchised: 1993
Franchised Units: 163
Company-Owned Units: 1
Total Units: 164
Dist.: US-137; CAN-24; O'seas-0
  North America: 33 States, 0 Provinces
  Density: 6 in TX, 17 in FL, 40 in CA
Projected New Units (12 Months): 15
Qualifications: 4, 4, 2, 3, 2, 5
FINANCIAL/TERMS:
Cash Investment: $80-90K
Total Investment: $65-125K
Minimum Net Worth: $250K
Fees: Franchise - $25-40K
  Royalty - 7%; Ad. - 2%
Earnings Claims Statement: Yes
Term of Contract (Years): 10/5/5/
Avg. # Of Employees: 3 FT, 0 PT
Passive Ownership: Discouraged
Encourage Conversions: NA
Area Develop. Agreements: No
Sub-Franchising Contracts: No
Expand In Territory: Yes

Space Needs: 750-1,500 SF

SUPPORT & TRAINING:

Financial Assistance Provided: Yes (I)

Site Selection Assistance: NA

Lease Negotiation Assistance: No

Co-Operative Advertising: No

Franchisee Assoc./Member: Yes/Yes

Size Of Corporate Staff: 14

On-Going Support: „C,D,E,,G,h,I

Training: 1 Week Franchisee Location; 2 Weeks Headquarters (Cincinnati, OH)

SPECIFIC EXPANSION PLANS:

US: All United States

Canada: All Canada

Overseas: All Countries

‹‹ ››

HANDYMAN MATTERS

12567 Cedar St., # 150

Lakewood, CO 80228

Tel: (866) 808-8401 (303) 984-0177

Fax: (303) 942-5933

E-Mail: careyann@handymanmatters.com

Web Site: www.handymanmatters.com

Ms. Careyann Larson, Director of Franchise Development

Hanydman Matters has taken the traditional handyman repair and restore business and has created a very tech savvy handyman service that is one-stop shopping for the consumer. Our system works as a home-based business that offers you as the owner the ability to generate multiple revenue streams of income from day one.

BACKGROUND: IFA MEMBER

Established: 1997; 1st Franchised: 2001

Franchised Units: 132

Company-Owned Units: 0

Total Units: 132

Dist.: US-127; CAN-1; O'seas-2

North America: 33 States, 1 Provinces

Density: 12 in TX, 8 in FL, 11 in CA

Projected New Units (12 Months): 50

Qualifications: 3, 4, 2, 2, 3, 5

FINANCIAL/TERMS:

Cash Investment: $90-150K

Total Investment: $64-106K

Minimum Net Worth: $175K

Fees: Franchise - $30-50K

Royalty - 6%; Ad. - 1%

Earnings Claims Statement: Yes

Term of Contract (Years): 10/10

Avg. # Of Employees: NR

Passive Ownership: Allowed

Encourage Conversions: NA

Area Develop. Agreements: No

Sub-Franchising Contracts: No

Expand In Territory: Yes

Space Needs: 500 or fewer SF

SUPPORT & TRAINING:

Financial Assistance Provided: Yes (I)

Site Selection Assistance: Yes

Lease Negotiation Assistance: Yes

Co-Operative Advertising: Yes

Franchisee Assoc./Member: Yes/Yes

Size Of Corporate Staff: 20

On-Going Support: „C,D,E,,G,h,I

Training: 1 Week Advanced Program; 1 Week On-Site; 1 Week Denver, CO

SPECIFIC EXPANSION PLANS:

US: All United States

Canada: All Canada

Overseas: All Countries

‹‹ ››

HANDYPRO HANDYMAN

995 S. Main St.

Plymouth, MI 48170-2048

Tel: (800) 942-6394 (734) 254-9160

Fax: (734) 254-9171

E-Mail: handypro@comcast.net

Web Site: www.handypro.com

Mr. Kim Madeleine, Dir. Franchise Development

Professional handyman service. Specializing in minor home repairs and improvements. Our business is focused on top-quality customer service.

BACKGROUND:

Established: 1996; 1st Franchised: 2000

Franchised Units: 4

Company-Owned Units: 1

Total Units: 5

Dist.: US-5; CAN-0; O'seas-0

North America: 4 States, 0 Provinces

Density: 1 in TX, 1 in MN, 2 in MI

Projected New Units (12 Months): 13

Qualifications: 4, 4, 2, 3, 4, 5

FINANCIAL/TERMS:

Cash Investment: $36.5-65.5K

Total Investment: $29K

Minimum Net Worth: $36.5K

Fees: Franchise - $25K

Royalty - $600-1,500/Mo.; Ad. - 1%

Earnings Claims Statement: No

Term of Contract (Years): 7/7

Avg. # Of Employees: 10 FT, 1 PT

Passive Ownership: Discouraged

Encourage Conversions: NA

Area Develop. Agreements: No

Sub-Franchising Contracts: No

Expand In Territory: Yes

Space Needs: NA

SUPPORT & TRAINING:

Financial Assistance Provided: No

Site Selection Assistance: Yes

Lease Negotiation Assistance: Yes

Co-Operative Advertising: No

Franchisee Assoc./Member: Yes/Yes

Size Of Corporate Staff: 3

On-Going Support: A,b,C,D,E,,G,H,I

Training: 1 Week Corporate Office; 30 Hours/Year On-Site

SPECIFIC EXPANSION PLANS:

US: All United States

Canada: No

Overseas: NR

‹‹ ››

HEAVEN'S BEST CARPET/ UPHOLST. CLEANING

247 N. 1st E., P.O. Box 607

Rexburg, ID 83440

Tel: (800) 359-2095 (208) 359-1106

Fax: (208) 359-1236

E-Mail: mcoinc@heavensbest.com

Web Site: www.heavensbest.com

Mr. Cody Howard, Chief Executive Officer

Unique low moisture cleaning process. There is no better franchise opportunity than this. Our franchisees are happy, our customers are happy. Our franchise is very affordable. Call for our free video.

BACKGROUND:

Established: 1983; 1st Franchised: 1983

Franchised Units: 1289

Company-Owned Units: 0

Total Units: 1289

Dist.: US-1263; CAN-10; O'seas-16

North America: 28 States, 0 Provinces

Density: 36 in IA, 42 in NC, 267 in CA

Projected New Units (12 Months): 100

Qualifications: NR

FINANCIAL/TERMS:

Cash Investment: $14.5-28K

Total Investment:	$28-64K
Minimum Net Worth:	$10K
Fees: Franchise -	$14
Royalty - $80/Mo.;	Ad. -
Earnings Claims Statement:	No
Term of Contract (Years):	5/5
Avg. # Of Employees:	1 FT, 0 PT
Passive Ownership:	Allowed
Encourage Conversions:	Yes
Area Develop. Agreements:	No
Sub-Franchising Contracts:	Yes
Expand In Territory:	Yes
Space Needs:	NA

SUPPORT & TRAINING:

Financial Assistance Provided:	Yes (D)
Site Selection Assistance:	NA
Lease Negotiation Assistance:	NA
Co-Operative Advertising:	No
Franchisee Assoc./Member:	Yes/Yes
Size Of Corporate Staff:	9
On-Going Support:	A,B,,,,F,G,H,I
Training:	4 Days Rexburg, ID

SPECIFIC EXPANSION PLANS:

US:	All United States
Canada:	All Canada
Overseas:	All Countries

HOME CLEANING CENTERS OF AMERICA

4851 W. 134th St., # D
Leawood, KS 66209
Tel: (800) 767-1118 (913) 327-5227
Fax: (913) 327-5272
E-Mail: mcalhoon@homecleaningcenters.com
Web Site: www.homecleaningcenters.com
Mr. Mike Calhoon, President

Very large franchise zones. Quality Quality Quality. Owners do not clean houses. Every corporate policy is made by the franchise owners. Each and every owner is hand picked - having money is not enough. Corporate 'Mission Statement' is to have the largest grossing, highest-quality offices in the industry.

BACKGROUND:	IFA MEMBER
Established: 1981;	1st Franchised: 1984
Franchised Units:	41
Company-Owned Units:	0
Total Units:	41
Dist.:	US-41; CAN-0; O'seas-0
North America:	9 States, 0 Provinces
Density:	7 in MO, 4 in KS, 4 in CO

Projected New Units (12 Months):	3
Qualifications:	3, 3, 1, 3, 5, 5

FINANCIAL/TERMS:

Cash Investment:	$20-25K
Total Investment:	$30-40K
Minimum Net Worth:	NA
Fees: Franchise -	$12.5K
Royalty - 4.5-5%;	Ad. - 0%
Earnings Claims Statement:	Yes
Term of Contract (Years):	10/10
Avg. # Of Employees:	12 FT, 0 PT
Passive Ownership:	Discouraged
Encourage Conversions:	No
Area Develop. Agreements:	No
Sub-Franchising Contracts:	No
Expand In Territory:	Yes
Space Needs:	500 SF

SUPPORT & TRAINING:

Financial Assistance Provided:	No
Site Selection Assistance:	Yes
Lease Negotiation Assistance:	Yes
Co-Operative Advertising:	No
Franchisee Assoc./Member:	Yes/Yes
Size Of Corporate Staff:	2
On-Going Support:	,b,C,D,E,F,G,H,I
Training:	5 Days Denver, CO; 5 Days St. Louis, MO

SPECIFIC EXPANSION PLANS:

US:	All United States
Canada:	No
Overseas:	NR

HOUSE DOCTORS HANDYMAN SERVICE

575 Chamber Dr.
Milford, OH 45150
Tel: (800) 319-3359 (513) 831-0100
Fax: (513) 813-0610
E-Mail: salesleads@housedoctors.com
Web Site: www.housedoctors.com
Mr. Steve M. Cohen, President

There's big money in house calls. Millions of dollars are being spent every day on those odd jobs around the house that people don't have the time or skill to do. You don't need a screwdriver or hammer to own this franchise. Financing and training provided.

BACKGROUND:	IFA MEMBER

Established: 1995;	1st Franchised: 1995
Franchised Units:	113
Company-Owned Units:	0
Total Units:	113
Dist.:	US-224; CAN-0; O'seas-1
North America:	42 States, 0 Provinces
Density:	10 in OH, 9 in IN, 9 in IL
Projected New Units (12 Months):	30
Qualifications:	2, 3, 2, 2, 4, 5

FINANCIAL/TERMS:

Cash Investment:	$50K
Total Investment:	$70K-120K
Minimum Net Worth:	$26K
Fees: Franchise -	$12-30K
Royalty - 6%;	Ad. - 3%
Earnings Claims Statement:	No
Term of Contract (Years):	10/10/10/
Avg. # Of Employees:	3 FT, 2 PT
Passive Ownership:	Discouraged
Encourage Conversions:	Yes
Area Develop. Agreements:	Yes/1
Sub-Franchising Contracts:	No
Expand In Territory:	No
Space Needs:	NA

SUPPORT & TRAINING:

Financial Assistance Provided:	Yes (D)
Site Selection Assistance:	NA
Lease Negotiation Assistance:	NA
Co-Operative Advertising:	No
Franchisee Assoc./Member:	No
Size Of Corporate Staff:	12
On-Going Support:	A,B,C,D,E,,G,H,I
Training:	1 Week Cincinnati, OH

SPECIFIC EXPANSION PLANS:

US:	All United States
Canada:	All Canada
Overseas:	All Countries

JAN-PRO CLEANING SYSTEMS

11605 Haynes Bridge Rd. # 425
Alpharetta, GA 30009
Tel: (866) 355-1064 (678) 336-1811
Fax: (678) 336-1782
E-Mail: brad.smith@jan-pro.com
Web Site: www.jan-pro.com
Mr. Bradford M. Smith, VP of Franchise Licensing

Jan-Pro provides one of today's exceptional business opportunities, allowing you to enter one of the fastest-growing industries by safely becoming your own boss through the guidance and support of an established franchise organization.

BACKGROUND: IFA MEMBER
Established: 1991; 1st Franchised: 1995
Franchised Units: 8091
Company-Owned Units: 2
Total Units: 8093
Dist.: US-8080; CAN-8; O'seas-3
North America: 39 States, 2 Provinces
Density: 274 in GA, 478 in FL, 556 in CA
Projected New Units (12 Months): 12
Masters and over 2,000 units
Qualifications: 3, 2, 1, 1, 1, 1

FINANCIAL/TERMS:
Cash Investment: $1-30K
Total Investment: $5-60K
Minimum Net Worth: $50K
Fees: Franchise - $1-30K
Royalty - 14%; Ad. - 0%
Earnings Claims Statement: No
Term of Contract (Years): 5/5
Avg. # Of Employees: 0 FT, 0 PT
Passive Ownership: Discouraged
Encourage Conversions: Yes
Area Develop. Agreements: Yes/15
Sub-Franchising Contracts: Yes
Expand In Territory: Yes
Space Needs: 0 SF

SUPPORT & TRAINING:
Financial Assistance Provided: Yes (D)
Site Selection Assistance: Yes
Lease Negotiation Assistance: Yes
Co-Operative Advertising: No
Franchisee Assoc./Member: Yes/No
Size Of Corporate Staff: 15
On-Going Support: A,B,C,D,E,F,G,H,I
Training: 5 weeks Regional & Local

SPECIFIC EXPANSION PLANS:
US: All United States
Canada: All Canada
Overseas: All except England and Ireland

⫷⫷ ⫸⫸

JANI-KING INTERNATIONAL
16885 Dallas Pkwy.
Addison, TX 75001-5215
Tel: (800) 552-5264 (972) 991-0900
Fax: (972) 764-3651
E-Mail: info@janiking.com
Web Site: www.janiking.com
Mr. Robert Kindred, Director Public Relations

JANI-KING INTERNATIONAL is the world's largest commercial cleaning franchisor, with locations in 19 countries and over 125 regions in the U. S. and abroad. Our franchise opportunity includes initial customer contracts, training, continuous local support, administrative and accounting assistance, an equipment leasing program and national advertising. If you are searching for a flexible business opportunity, look no further.

BACKGROUND: IFA MEMBER
Established: 1969; 1st Franchised: 1974
Franchised Units: 13000
Company-Owned Units: 27
Total Units: 13027
Dist.: US-12148; CAN-351; O'seas-528
North America: 39 States, 7 Provinces
Density: 880 in TX, 307 in FL, 737 in CA
Projected New Units (12 Months): 1,500
Qualifications: 2, 2, 1, 2, 2, 3

FINANCIAL/TERMS:
Cash Investment: $2.9-33K
Total Investment: $2.9-40K
Minimum Net Worth: $2.9-33K
Fees: Franchise - $8-33K
Royalty - 10%; Ad. - 0%
Earnings Claims Statement: Yes
Term of Contract (Years): 20/20
Avg. # Of Employees: FT, 0 PT
Passive Ownership: Allowed
Encourage Conversions: NA
Area Develop. Agreements: Yes/1
Sub-Franchising Contracts: Yes
Expand In Territory: Yes
Space Needs: NR

SUPPORT & TRAINING:
Financial Assistance Provided: No
Site Selection Assistance: NA
Lease Negotiation Assistance: NA
Co-Operative Advertising: No
Franchisee Assoc./Member: Yes/Yes
Size Of Corporate Staff: 65
On-Going Support: A,B,C,D,,,G,H,I
Training: 2 Weeks Local Regional Office

SPECIFIC EXPANSION PLANS:
US: All United States
Canada: All Canada
Overseas: All Countries

⫷⫷ ⫸⫸

JANTIZE AMERICA
8801 JM Keynes Dr., # 450
Charlotte, NC 28262
Tel: (704) 503-7141
Fax: (704) 405-5989
E-Mail: jerryg@jantize.com

Web Site: www.jantize.com
Mr. Paul Dorsey, VP Franchise Sales

This system is one of the best franchise models in business today. It allows you to develop a large business within a short period of time with an extremely high success rate. Our Area Developer/Master Franchise business is a multi-unit development business that offers the opportunity for you to develop and grow our system in a defined geographic territory.

Our business model is consistently ranked as one of the fastest growing and most successful opportunities in the world for the following reasons: Low Cost Start Up, Recurring Royalty Revenues, Unlimited Growth Potential, Industry Size of $128 Billion and Growing, Recession Resistant and YOU have the benefit of Proven business practices from the Franchisor.

BACKGROUND:
Established: 1986; 1st Franchised: 1988
Franchised Units: 145
Company-Owned Units: 0
Total Units: 145
Dist.: US-145; CAN-0; O'seas-0
North America: 7 States, 0 Provinces
Density: 21 in FL, 87 in NC, 13 in MI
Projected New Units (12 Months): 5
Qualifications: 4, 4, 3, 2, 2, 5

FINANCIAL/TERMS:
Cash Investment: $75K
Total Investment: $125-225K
Minimum Net Worth: $50-150K
Fees: Franchise - $75K
Royalty - 9%; Ad. - 0%
Earnings Claims Statement: No
Term of Contract (Years): 10/10
Avg. # Of Employees: 3-20 FT, 0 PT
Passive Ownership: Discouraged
Encourage Conversions: Yes
Area Develop. Agreements: Yes/0
Sub-Franchising Contracts: Yes
Expand In Territory: Yes
Space Needs: 500-1000 SF

SUPPORT & TRAINING:
Financial Assistance Provided: Yes (D)
Site Selection Assistance: Yes
Lease Negotiation Assistance: No
Co-Operative Advertising: Yes
Franchisee Assoc./Member: No
Size Of Corporate Staff: 8
On-Going Support: a,,,D,E,,G,H,I
Training: 3 Days Franchisee Location;
3-6 Days Headquarters

SPECIFIC EXPANSION PLANS:
US: All United States

Canada: All Canada
Overseas: NR

≪ ≫

MAIDS HOME SERVICES, THE
4820 Dodge St.
Omaha, NE 68132-3111
Tel: (800) 843-6243 (402) 558-5555
Fax: (402) 558-1437
E-Mail: kbenning@maids.com
Web Site: www.maids.com
Ms. Kristin Benning, Director Franchise
  Development

Distinguished as the number one residential cleaning franchise in 2007, 2008 and 2009, and the Fastest Growing residential cleaning franchise four years running by Entrepreneur magazine, The Maids Home Services is the quality leader in the industry. The Maids was founded in 1979 and began franchising in 1980. We currently have 165 Franchise Partners operating over 1,000 territories in the US and Canada. Franchise partners benefit from a time-tested cleaning system and business model based on leading-edge technology. The Maids provides the most comprehensive package of training, support, and exclusive territory in the industry. We provide extensive training, including seven weeks of pre-training and 10 days of classroom and field training. We are in touch and involved with the new franchisee a minimum of 195 days within the first year. With The Maids, you can build a great business and achieve the lifestyle you desire, all with nights, weekends and holidays off. The Maids Home Services is looking for individuals to join its franchise system. We are looking for people who want an executive experience. With The Maids you are working ON the business, not IN the business. Our franchise partners are not cleaning homes, and are building their business Monday through Friday- no nights, no weekends, and no holidays. The Maids ideal franchise candidate will have good management and business skills, and most importantly, great people skills.

BACKGROUND: IFA MEMBER
Established: 1979; 1st Franchised: 1980
Franchised Units: 1027

Company-Owned Units: <u>26</u>
Total Units: 1053
Dist.: US-1023; CAN-30; O'seas-0
  North America: 39 States, 4 Provinces
  Density: 77 in MA, 78 in TX, 107 in CA
Projected New Units (12 Months): 80
Qualifications: 5, 5, 1, 2, 1, 5
FINANCIAL/TERMS:
Cash Investment: $100K-$150K
Total Investment: $175-$225K
Minimum Net Worth: $350K
Fees: Franchise - $10K + $.95 per QHH
  Royalty - 3.9-6.9%; Ad. - 2%
Earnings Claims Statement: Yes
Term of Contract (Years): 20/20
Avg. # Of Employees: 2 FT, 6 to start
(maids) PT
Passive Ownership: Discouraged
Encourage Conversions: Yes
Area Develop. Agreements: No
Sub-Franchising Contracts: No
Expand In Territory: Yes
Space Needs: 1,000 - 1,200 SF
SUPPORT & TRAINING:
Financial Assistance Provided: Yes (D)
Site Selection Assistance: Yes
Lease Negotiation Assistance: No
Co-Operative Advertising: Yes
Franchisee Assoc./Member: No
Size Of Corporate Staff: 35
On-Going Support: A,B,C,D,E,F,G,h,I
Training: 9 days Corporate Training -
  Omaha, NE; 2-3 days Power Training
  - Franchisee location;7 weeks Foun-
  dation Training (Pre-Training) Done
  from Franch
SPECIFIC EXPANSION PLANS:
US: All United States
Canada: All except SK and QC
Overseas: NR

≪ ≫

MARBLELIFE
5470 E. Loop 820, S., # 110
Fort Worth, TX 76119-6515
Tel: (800) 627-4569 (817) 478-4437
Fax: (817) 478-6954
E-Mail: jfreitag@marblelife.com
Web Site: www.marblelife.com
Mr. John Freitag, Franchise Director

Specializes in the restoration, preservation and maintenance services for natural stones and other surfaces.

BACKGROUND:
Established: 1987; 1st Franchised: 1993
Franchised Units: 49
Company-Owned Units: <u>0</u>

Total Units: 49
Dist.: US-39; CAN-1; O'seas-9
  North America: 38 States, 1 Provinces
  Density: 3 in CA, 3 in FL, 3 in TX
Projected New Units (12 Months): 10
Qualifications: 4, 4, 2, 2, 2, 4
FINANCIAL/TERMS:
Cash Investment: $50K+
Total Investment: $15-100K
Minimum Net Worth: Varies
Fees: Franchise - $5K/100K Pop.
  Royalty - 6%; Ad. - 2%
Earnings Claims Statement: No
Term of Contract (Years): 10/10
Avg. # Of Employees: 3+ FT, 0 PT
Passive Ownership: Discouraged
Encourage Conversions: Yes
Area Develop. Agreements: Yes/1
Sub-Franchising Contracts: No
Expand In Territory: No
Space Needs: NA
SUPPORT & TRAINING:
Financial Assistance Provided: Yes (D)
Site Selection Assistance: NA
Lease Negotiation Assistance: No
Co-Operative Advertising: No
Franchisee Assoc./Member: Yes/Yes
Size Of Corporate Staff: 12
On-Going Support: ,,C,D,E,,G,H,I
Training: 2 Weeks Grand Prairie, TX
SPECIFIC EXPANSION PLANS:
US: All United States
Canada: All Canada
Overseas: All Europe and Middle East

≪ ≫

**MILLICARE COMMERCIAL
CARPET CARE**
201 Lukken Industrial Dr., W.
LaGrange, GA 30240-5913
Tel: (877) 812-8803 (706) 880-3054
Fax: (706) 880-3279
E-Mail: fred.salitore@milliken.com
Web Site: www.millicare.com
Mr. Fred Salitore, Director Franchise Network

Buy into experience and professionalism. MILLICARE ENVIRONMENTAL SERVICES is currently seeking to select people to become franchisees in select cities in North America. The MILLICARE system includes a variety of services provided to commercial facility managers including carpet maintenance, carpet recycling, panel and upholstery cleaning and entryway systems. Franchisees receive world-class training, sales and marketing programs from a strong, experienced global franchisor.

BACKGROUND: IFA MEMBER
Established: 1976; 1st Franchised: 1996
Franchised Units: 80
Company-Owned Units: 0
Total Units: 80
Dist.: US-80; CAN-6; O'seas-7
North America: 3 States, 1 Provinces
Density: NR
Projected New Units (12 Months): 15-20
Qualifications: 5, 4, 3, 3, 4, 5
FINANCIAL/TERMS:
Cash Investment: $50K
Total Investment: $94K-128K
Minimum Net Worth: $150K
Fees: Franchise - $15-25K
Royalty - 6%; Ad. - 2%
Earnings Claims Statement: No
Term of Contract (Years): 5/5
Avg. # Of Employees: 1-20 FT, 0 PT
Passive Ownership: Allowed
Encourage Conversions: No
Area Develop. Agreements: Yes/1
Sub-Franchising Contracts: No
Expand In Territory: Yes
Space Needs: 2,000 SF
SUPPORT & TRAINING:
Financial Assistance Provided: Yes (D)
Site Selection Assistance: No
Lease Negotiation Assistance: NA
Co-Operative Advertising: No
Franchisee Assoc./Member: Yes/Yes
Size Of Corporate Staff: 6
On-Going Support: ,,C,D,E,,G,H,I
Training: 3 Days La Grange, GA;
3 Days Model Franchise Location,
DE; 2 Days Franchisee's Location
SPECIFIC EXPANSION PLANS:
US: All Major 2ndary Metro Areas
Canada: Toronto,Montreal
Overseas: Mexico

≪≪ ≫≫

MINT CONDITION
1057 521 Corporate Center Dr., # 165
Fort Mill, SC 29707
Tel: (803) 548-6121
Fax: (803) 548-4578
E-Mail: admin@mintconditioninc.com
Web Site: www.mintconditioninc.com
Mr. Ron Colello, Director of Operations

Commercial cleaning franchising that can be started for as little as $1000.00. This is a very flexible program that can be started part-time or full-time. Cleaning accounts are provided as part of the program. Our franchises are provided with a "Green Cleaning System" allowing them to pro-

vide their customers the highest quality service.

BACKGROUND: IFA MEMBER
Established: 1996; 1st Franchised: 1996
Franchised Units: 123
Company-Owned Units: 1
Total Units: 124
Dist.: US-124; CAN-0; O'seas-0
North America: 5 States, 0 Provinces
Density: 14 in SC, 70 in NC, 11 in GA
Projected New Units (12 Months): 45
Qualifications: 1, 1, 2, 2, 3, 5
FINANCIAL/TERMS:
Cash Investment: $1K
Total Investment: $4,890-45,400
Minimum Net Worth: NA
Fees: Franchise - $3K-22K
Royalty - 9%; Ad. - 0
Earnings Claims Statement: No
Term of Contract (Years): 10/5
Avg. # Of Employees: 0-5 FT, 0 PT
Passive Ownership: Not Allowed
Encourage Conversions: No
Area Develop. Agreements: No
Sub-Franchising Contracts: No
Expand In Territory: Yes
Space Needs: NA
SUPPORT & TRAINING:
Financial Assistance Provided: Yes (D)
Site Selection Assistance: NA
Lease Negotiation Assistance: NA
Co-Operative Advertising: No
Franchisee Assoc./Member: No
Size Of Corporate Staff: 6
On-Going Support: ,,C,D,,,G,,
Training: 9 hours of classroom training
Regional office
SPECIFIC EXPANSION PLANS:
US: NC, SC, GA, PA, NJ
Canada: No
Overseas: NR

≪≪ ≫≫

**MODERNISTIC CARPET &
UPHOLSTERY CLEANING CO.**
1460 Rankin St.
Troy, MI 48083
Tel: (800) 609-1000 (866) 917-1700
Fax: (248) 589-2660
E-Mail: jmcbride@modernistic.com
Web Site: www.modernistic.com
Ms. Joyce McBride, Franchising

We are a full-service carpet and upholstery cleaning company, established in 1972 and the largest of its kind in Michigan. We rank in the top 5 nationally among all independent companies, we grant larger territories

and we are looking for qualified people to represent our brand name in major U.S. markets.

BACKGROUND:
Established: 1972; 1st Franchised: 1999
Franchised Units: 4
Company-Owned Units: 0
Total Units: 4
Dist.: US-4; CAN-0; O'seas-0
North America: 1 States, Provinces
Density: 4 in MI
Projected New Units (12 Months): 8-15
Qualifications: 3, 4, 2, 3, 3, 4
FINANCIAL/TERMS:
Cash Investment: $50K
Total Investment: $50-100K
Minimum Net Worth: $50K
Fees: Franchise - $12-40K
Royalty - 6%; Ad. - 14%
Earnings Claims Statement: No
Term of Contract (Years): Life/
Avg. # Of Employees: 2 FT, 0 PT
Passive Ownership: Discouraged
Encourage Conversions: Yes
Area Develop. Agreements: Yes/1
Sub-Franchising Contracts: Yes
Expand In Territory: Yes
Space Needs: NA
SUPPORT & TRAINING:
Financial Assistance Provided: Yes (D)
Site Selection Assistance: Yes
Lease Negotiation Assistance: Yes
Co-Operative Advertising: No
Franchisee Assoc./Member: Yes/Yes
Size Of Corporate Staff: 70
On-Going Support: ,B,C,D,E,,G,h,I
Training: 2 Weeks Troy, MI; 1 Week On-Site
SPECIFIC EXPANSION PLANS:
US: 43 States Where Registered
Canada: No
Overseas: NR

≪≪ ≫≫

TOP 100

MR. APPLIANCE CORPORATION
1010 N. University Parks Dr., P.O. Box 3146
Waco, TX 76707
Tel: (800) 290-1422 (254) 759-5850
Fax: (800) 209-7621
E-Mail: info@servicefranchiseopportunities.com
Web Site: www.servicefranchiseopportu-

nities.com

Ms. Pat Humburg, Lead Development Manager

Mr. Appliance is North America's largest appliance repair franchise system. Established in 1996, its franchises provide full-service residential and light commercial appliance repair. Mr. Appliance has more than 150 locations throughout the United States and Canada and is consistently ranked among the top home service franchises by Entrepreneur magazine and other industry experts. Mr. Appliance is a subsidiary of The Dwyer Group, Inc. For more information, visit www.mrappliance.com.

BACKGROUND: IFA MEMBER
Established: 1996; 1st Franchised: 1996
Franchised Units: 157
Company-Owned Units: 0
Total Units: 157
Dist.: US-150; CAN-7; O'seas-0
North America: 41 States, 4 Provinces
Density: 10 in FL, 17 in CA, 18 in TX
Projected New Units (12 Months): 50
Qualifications: 4, 4, 2, 2, 3, 5
FINANCIAL/TERMS:
Cash Investment: $40-90K
Total Investment: $40-90K
Minimum Net Worth: Varies
Fees: Franchise - $22K
Royalty - 4-7%; Ad. - 2%
Earnings Claims Statement: No
Term of Contract (Years): 10/10
Avg. # Of Employees: Varies
Passive Ownership: Discouraged
Encourage Conversions: Yes
Area Develop. Agreements: No
Sub-Franchising Contracts: No
Expand In Territory: Yes
Space Needs: NR
SUPPORT & TRAINING:
Financial Assistance Provided: Yes (I)
Site Selection Assistance: NA
Lease Negotiation Assistance: NA
Co-Operative Advertising: No
Franchisee Assoc./Member: No
Size Of Corporate Staff: 15
On-Going Support: A,,C,D,E,F,G,H,I
Training: 1 Week & Ongoing Waco, TX
SPECIFIC EXPANSION PLANS:
US: All United States
Canada: All Canada
Overseas: Master Franchise Only

◄◄ ►►

MR. ELECTRIC CORP.
1020 N. University Parks Dr., P.O. Box 3146
Waco, TX 76707
Tel: (800) 805-0575 (254) 759-5850
Fax: (800) 209-7621
E-Mail: info@servicefranchiseopportunities.com
Web Site: www.servicefranchiseopportunities.com
Ms. Pat Humburg, Lead Development Manager

Established in 1994, Mr. Electric is a global franchise organization providing electrical installation and repair services. Recognized by Entrepreneur magazine among its "Franchise 500," Mr. Electric franchisees provide these services to both residential and commercial customers at 160 locations worldwide. Mr. Electric is part of The Dwyer Group family of companies, which also includes Rainbow International, Mr. Rooter, Aire Serv, Mr. Appliance, and Glass Doctor.

BACKGROUND: IFA MEMBER
Established: 1994; 1st Franchised: 1994
Franchised Units: 215
Company-Owned Units: 0
Total Units: 215
Dist.: US-150; CAN-5; O'seas-60
North America: 42 States, 2 Provinces
Density: 7 in OH, 12 in TX, 12 in FL
Projected New Units (12 Months): 36
Qualifications: 4, 4, 2, 2, 3, 5
FINANCIAL/TERMS:
Cash Investment: $30.2-68K
Total Investment: $69-162K
Minimum Net Worth: Varies
Fees: Franchise - $22K/100KPop
Royalty - 4-7%; Ad. - 2%
Earnings Claims Statement: No
Term of Contract (Years): 10/10
Avg. # Of Employees: 4 FT, 1 PT
Passive Ownership: Discouraged
Encourage Conversions: Yes
Area Develop. Agreements: No
Sub-Franchising Contracts: No
Expand In Territory: Yes
Space Needs: 500-1,000 SF
SUPPORT & TRAINING:
Financial Assistance Provided: Yes (D)
Site Selection Assistance: NA
Lease Negotiation Assistance: NA

Co-Operative Advertising: No
Franchisee Assoc./Member: No
Size Of Corporate Staff: 14
On-Going Support: A,B,C,D,E,F,G,H,I
Training: 3 Business Days On-Site in Business; 5 Business Days Corporate Offices
SPECIFIC EXPANSION PLANS:
US: All United States
Canada: Yes
Overseas: Most Latin American and Asian Countries

◄◄ ►►

MR. HANDYMAN
3948 Ranchero Dr.
Ann Arbor, MI 48108-2775
Tel: (800) 289-4600 + 540 (734) 822-6800 + 540
Fax: (734) 822-6888
E-Mail: tburns@mrhandyman.com
Web Site: www.mrhandyman.com
Mr. T. Burns, Licensing Coordinator

Seeking a business with tremendous consumer demand? Stop right here. MR. HANDYMAN is the solution to today's fix-it problems for millions of time-starved families. An affordable investment gives you a franchise catering to 100 million homeowners and commercial customers needing property maintenance and repair. Technicians do the work. You manage the business.

BACKGROUND: IFA MEMBER
Established: 1996; 1st Franchised: 2000
Franchised Units: 300
Company-Owned Units: 0
Total Units: 300
Dist.: US-300; CAN-0; O'seas-0
North America: 37 States, 0 Provinces
Density: NR
Projected New Units (12 Months): 33
Qualifications: 3, 3, 1, 3, 4, 5
FINANCIAL/TERMS:
Cash Investment: $50K-70K
Total Investment: $110K-125K
Minimum Net Worth: $250K
Fees: Franchise - $15K
Royalty - 7%; Ad. - 1.25%
Earnings Claims Statement: Yes
Term of Contract (Years): 10/10

Avg. # Of Employees:	6 FT, 0 PT
Passive Ownership:	Not Allowed
Encourage Conversions:	Yes
Area Develop. Agreements:	No
Sub-Franchising Contracts:	No
Expand In Territory:	Yes
Space Needs:	200 SF

SUPPORT & TRAINING:

Financial Assistance Provided:	Yes (I)
Site Selection Assistance:	NA
Lease Negotiation Assistance:	NA
Co-Operative Advertising:	No
Franchisee Assoc./Member:	No
Size Of Corporate Staff:	10
On-Going Support:	„C,D,E,„G,h,I
Training:	5 Days Home Office;
5 Days Field; 6 Months Right Start Program	

SPECIFIC EXPANSION PLANS:

US:	All United States
Canada:	All Canada
Overseas:	All Countries

◄◄ ►►

MR. ROOTER

1020 N. University Parks Dr.
Waco, TX 76707
Tel: (800) 298-6855 (254) 745-2400
Fax: (800) 209-7621
E-Mail: billy.young@mrrooter.com
Web Site: www.servicefranchiseopportunities.com
Mr. Billy Young, Director of Franchise Development

Established in 1970, Mr. Rooter is an all-franchised, full-service plumbing and drain cleaning company with approximately 300 franchises worldwide. Recognized by Entrepreneur magazine among its "Franchise 500" and Franchise Times Top 200, Mr. Rooter franchisees provide services to both residential and commercial customers. Mr. Rooter began franchising in 1974 and is part of The Dwyer Group family of companies, which also includes Rainbow International, Aire Serv, Mr. Electric, Mr. Appliance, and Glass Docto

BACKGROUND: IFA MEMBER

Established: 1970;	1st Franchised: 1974
Franchised Units:	361
Company-Owned Units:	0
Total Units:	361

Dist.:	US-241; CAN-19; O'seas-101
North America:	47 States, 7 Provinces
Density:	15 in OH, 18 in TX, 32 in CA
Projected New Units (12 Months):	40
Qualifications:	5, 3, 3, 2, 3, 5

FINANCIAL/TERMS:

Cash Investment:	$40-79K
Total Investment:	$54,950-$150,750
Minimum Net Worth:	$100K
Fees: Franchise -	$24K/100KPop
Royalty - 4-7%;	Ad. - 2%
Earnings Claims Statement:	Yes
Term of Contract (Years):	10/10
Avg. # Of Employees:	Varies
Passive Ownership:	Not Allowed
Encourage Conversions:	Yes
Area Develop. Agreements:	No
Sub-Franchising Contracts:	No
Expand In Territory:	Yes
Space Needs:	NA

SUPPORT & TRAINING:

Financial Assistance Provided:	Yes (D)
Site Selection Assistance:	NA
Lease Negotiation Assistance:	NA
Co-Operative Advertising:	No
Franchisee Assoc./Member:	No
Size Of Corporate Staff:	25
On-Going Support:	A,,C,D,,,G,H,
Training:	5 Days Waco, TX

SPECIFIC EXPANSION PLANS:

US:	Uncovered Areas
Canada:	Selected Areas
Overseas:	NR

◄◄ ►►

NATURALAWN OF AMERICA

1 E. Church St.
Frederick, MD 21701
Tel: (800) 989-5444 + 211 (301) 694-5440
Fax: (301) 846-0320
E-Mail: franchise@nl-amer.com
Web Site: www.nl-amer.com
Mr. Randy Loeb, VP Franchise Development

NATURALAWN of America is the only nationwide lawn care franchise offering an environmentally friendly lawn care service incorporating natural, organic-based fertilizers and biological controls. Our franchise owners provide residential and commercial customers with fertilization, weed control, insect control, disease control and lawn diagnosis services using safer and healthier products, eliminating the need for harsh chemicals and pesticides.

BACKGROUND:

Established: 1987;	1st Franchised: 1989
Franchised Units:	60
Company-Owned Units:	4
Total Units:	64
Dist.:	US-64; CAN-0; O'seas-0
North America:	27 States, 0 Provinces
Density:	5 in VA, 5 in PA, 6 in MD
Projected New Units (12 Months):	10-12
Qualifications:	4, 4, 1, 4, 3, 5

FINANCIAL/TERMS:

Cash Investment:	$50K
Total Investment:	$108-155K
Minimum Net Worth:	$250K
Fees: Franchise -	$29.5K
Royalty - 7-9%;	Ad. - 0%
Earnings Claims Statement:	Yes
Term of Contract (Years):	5/10
Avg. # Of Employees:	1-3 FT, 0 PT
Passive Ownership:	Not Allowed
Encourage Conversions:	Yes
Area Develop. Agreements:	No
Sub-Franchising Contracts:	Yes
Expand In Territory:	Yes
Space Needs:	1,200 SF

SUPPORT & TRAINING:

Financial Assistance Provided:	Yes (D)
Site Selection Assistance:	Yes
Lease Negotiation Assistance:	Yes
Co-Operative Advertising:	No
Franchisee Assoc./Member:	No
Size Of Corporate Staff:	14
On-Going Support:	A,B,C,D,E,F,G,h,I
Training:	1 Week Home Office;
1 Week Field Office; 1 Week OnSite	

SPECIFIC EXPANSION PLANS:

US:	All United States
Canada:	All Canada
Overseas:	NR

◄◄ ►►

NUTRI-LAWN, ECOLOGY-FRIENDLY LAWN CARE

202-2077 Dundas St. E.
Mississauga, ON L4X 1M2 Canada
Tel: (800) 396-6096 (416) 620-7100
Fax: (416) 620-7771
E-Mail: kalon@nutrilawn.com
Web Site: www.nutri-lawn.com

Mr. Ian Sharp, President

NUTRI-LAWN offers ecology-friendly lawn care to meet increasing consumer demand. We focus on organic fertilization and reduced control product usage through our spot treating and our natural and safe lawn care product line. We create large lawn care operations through our proven program and systems.

BACKGROUND: IFA MEMBER
Established: 1985; 1st Franchised: 1987
Franchised Units: 29
Company-Owned Units: 2
Total Units: 31
Dist.: US-2; CAN-29; O'seas-0
North America: 2 States, 8 Provinces
Density: 17 in ON, 7 in BC
Projected New Units (12 Months): 3-5
Qualifications: 5, 4, 1, 3, 3, 5
FINANCIAL/TERMS:
Cash Investment: $40K-60K
Total Investment: $120K-150K
Minimum Net Worth: $250K
Fees: Franchise - $40K
Royalty - 6%; Ad. - 1% US)
Earnings Claims Statement: No
Term of Contract (Years): 5/5
Avg. # Of Employees: 1 FT, 0 PT
Passive Ownership: Not Allowed
Encourage Conversions: Yes
Area Develop. Agreements: Yes/1
Sub-Franchising Contracts: No
Expand In Territory: Yes
Space Needs: NR
SUPPORT & TRAINING:
Financial Assistance Provided: No
Site Selection Assistance: Yes
Lease Negotiation Assistance: Yes
Co-Operative Advertising: No
Franchisee Assoc./Member: Yes/Yes
Size Of Corporate Staff: 5
On-Going Support: ,B,C,D,E,,G,H,
Training: 1 Week Toronto, ON; 1 Week At Location
SPECIFIC EXPANSION PLANS:
US: Northeast, Northwest, Midwest
Canada: All Canada
Overseas: No

⋖⋖ ⋗⋗

OCTOCLEAN
5225 Canyon Crest Dr., # 71-339
Riverside, CA 92507
Tel: (866) OCTOCLN (951) 683-5859
Fax: (951) 779-0270
E-Mail: chuck@octoclean.com
Web Site: www.octoclean.com

Mr. Charles Stowe, Chief Executive Officer

OCTOCLEAN is a dynamic, innovative janitorial franchise system. We have developed an exciting opportunity for all kinds of people to simply and quickly start their own commercial janitorial business. Low start-up, guaranteed accounts, and extensive training and support make OCTOCLEAN an attractive option for those looking for the security and growth potential option for those looking for the security and growth potential of an established franchise opportunity.

BACKGROUND:
Established: 1992; 1st Franchised: 2000
Franchised Units: 162
Company-Owned Units: 0
Total Units: 162
Dist.: US-162; CAN-0; O'seas-0
North America: 1 States, 0 Provinces
Density: 74 in CA
Projected New Units (12 Months): 60
Qualifications: 2, 1, 1, 1, 3, 5
FINANCIAL/TERMS:
Cash Investment: $1.5-2K
Total Investment: $8-57.5K
Minimum Net Worth: $10K
Fees: Franchise - $8K
Royalty - 5%; Ad. - 0%
Earnings Claims Statement: Yes
Term of Contract (Years): 5/5/5/
Avg. # Of Employees: 1 FT, 1 PT
Passive Ownership: Discouraged
Encourage Conversions: NA
Area Develop. Agreements: Yes/1
Sub-Franchising Contracts: Yes
Expand In Territory: Yes
Space Needs: NA
SUPPORT & TRAINING:
Financial Assistance Provided: Yes (D)
Site Selection Assistance: NA
Lease Negotiation Assistance: NA
Co-Operative Advertising: No
Franchisee Assoc./Member: No
Size Of Corporate Staff: 12
On-Going Support: ,B,C,D,,,G,H,I
Training: 7 Days Riverside, CA
SPECIFIC EXPANSION PLANS:
US: California
Canada: No
Overseas: NR

⋖⋖ ⋗⋗

OMEX INTERNATIONAL
3905 Hartzdale Dr., # 506
Camp Hill, PA 17011

Tel: (800) 827-6639 (717) 737-7311
Fax: (717) 737-9271
E-Mail: gboarman@omexcorp.com
Web Site: www.omexcorp.com
Mr. Gerald Boarman, President

OMEX provides commercial contract cleaning services to first class office facilities including Fortune 500 companies, large office buildings, banks and medical clinics. Seeking prospects with good management, sales or business backgrounds determined to succeed and willing to follow our system. Low investment! Low royalties! Major territories! Free franchise renewal!

BACKGROUND:
Established: 1979; 1st Franchised: 1994
Franchised Units: 20
Company-Owned Units: 1
Total Units: 21
Dist.: US-18; CAN-3; O'seas-0
North America: 12 States, 2 Provinces
Density: 4 in PA
Projected New Units (12 Months): NR
Qualifications: NR
FINANCIAL/TERMS:
Cash Investment: $40K
Total Investment: $40.4-70.6K
Minimum Net Worth: $150K
Fees: Franchise - $15-25K
Royalty - 4%; Ad. - NA
Earnings Claims Statement: No
Term of Contract (Years): 10/5
Avg. # Of Employees: Varies
Passive Ownership: Discouraged
Encourage Conversions: Yes
Area Develop. Agreements: No
Sub-Franchising Contracts: No
Expand In Territory: Yes
Space Needs: 800-1,200 SF
SUPPORT & TRAINING:
Financial Assistance Provided: No
Site Selection Assistance: Yes
Lease Negotiation Assistance: Yes
Co-Operative Advertising: No
Franchisee Assoc./Member: No
Size Of Corporate Staff: 12
On-Going Support: A,B,C,D,E,,G,H,I
Training: 1 Week Franchisee's Territory; 1 Week Corporate Headquarters
SPECIFIC EXPANSION PLANS:
US: All United States
Canada: All Canada
Overseas: NR

⋖⋖ ⋗⋗

OPENWORKS

4742 N. 24th St., # 300
Phoenix, AZ 85016-4347
Tel: (800) 777-6736 (602) 224-0440
Fax: (602) 468-3788
E-Mail: info@openworksweb.com
Web Site: www.openworksweb.com
Ms. Susan Abbott, Marketing Coordinator

OPENWORKS has been granting commercial cleaning franchises since 1983. Our program is centered around on-going training and support in addition to guaranteed initial customers. All franchises include a customer base, equipment and advanced business training. Contact us today for more information.

BACKGROUND: IFA MEMBER
Established: 1983; 1st Franchised: 1983
Franchised Units: 332
Company-Owned Units: 4
Total Units: 336
Dist.: US-336; CAN-0; O'seas-0
North America: 4 States, 0 Provinces
Density: 33 in CA, 143 in WA, 147 in AZ
Projected New Units (12 Months): 100
Qualifications: 3, 3, 1, 2, 4, 4
FINANCIAL/TERMS:
Cash Investment: $6.5-150K
Total Investment: $14-150K
Minimum Net Worth: $10-500K
Fees: Franchise - $5-150K
Royalty - 10%; Ad. - 1%
Earnings Claims Statement: No
Term of Contract (Years): 10/10
Avg. # Of Employees: 3+ FT, 0 PT
Passive Ownership: Discouraged
Encourage Conversions: Yes
Area Develop. Agreements: Yes/1
Sub-Franchising Contracts: Yes
Expand In Territory: Yes
Space Needs: NR
SUPPORT & TRAINING:
Financial Assistance Provided: Yes (D)
Site Selection Assistance: No
Lease Negotiation Assistance: Yes
Co-Operative Advertising: No
Franchisee Assoc./Member: No
Size Of Corporate Staff: 30
On-Going Support: A,B,C,D,E,,G,H,I
Training: 4 Weeks Regional Office;
2 Weeks Regional Office (Janitorial)
SPECIFIC EXPANSION PLANS:
US: All United States
Canada: All Canada
Overseas: All Countries

◄◄ ►►

PESTMASTER FRANCHISE NETWORK

137 E. South St.
Bishop, CA 93514
Tel: (800) 525-3268 (760) 873-8100
Fax: (760) 873-3268
E-Mail: pfn@pestmaster.com
Web Site: www.pestmaster.com
Ms. Adrienne Chandler, Franchise Manager

PESTMASTER is flexible. We offer proven programs to ensure growth, starting with training and on-going support. You'll benefit from a protected marketing territory, reduced insurance rates, as well as valuable discounts on equipment and supplies. Unlike other franchises, PESTMASTER offers a contracts department, which will consistently seek out government and commercial jobs for bid.

BACKGROUND: IFA MEMBER
Established: 1990; 1st Franchised: 1992
Franchised Units: 21
Company-Owned Units: 11
Total Units: 32
Dist.: US-32; CAN-0; O'seas-0
North America: 6 States, 0 Provinces
Density: 3 in TX, 2 in FL, 18 in CA
Projected New Units (12 Months): 4
Qualifications: 3, 4, 5, 2, 3, 4
FINANCIAL/TERMS:
Cash Investment: $27.5K-35K
Total Investment: $29K-80.5K
Minimum Net Worth: $30K
Fees: Franchise - $15-30K
Royalty - 5-7%; Ad. - 0.5%
Earnings Claims Statement: No
Term of Contract (Years): 10/20
Avg. # Of Employees: 0 FT, 2-4 PT
Passive Ownership: Discouraged
Encourage Conversions: Yes
Area Develop. Agreements: No
Sub-Franchising Contracts: No
Expand In Territory: Yes
Space Needs: 500 SF
SUPPORT & TRAINING:
Financial Assistance Provided: No
Site Selection Assistance: Yes
Lease Negotiation Assistance: No
Co-Operative Advertising: No
Franchisee Assoc./Member: Yes/Yes
Size Of Corporate Staff: 12
On-Going Support: a,,c,D,,,h,I
Training: 3-5 Days Bishop, CA;
2-5 Days Franchise Site
SPECIFIC EXPANSION PLANS:
US: All United States
Canada: No

Overseas: NR

◄◄ ►►

PROFESSIONAL CARPET SYSTEMS

4211 Atlantic Ave.
Raleigh, NC 27604
Tel: (800) 925-5055 (919) 875-8871
Fax: (919) 875-9855
E-Mail: fthompson@procarpetsys.com
Web Site: www.procarpetsys.com
Mr. Fritz D. Thompson, President

PROFESSIONAL CARPET SYSTEMS is the leader in "on-site" carpet re-dyeing, servicing thousands of apartment complexes, hotels and motels worldwide. Services also include carpet cleaning, rejuvenation, repair, water and flood damage restoration and "guaranteed odor control." A total carpet care concept serving commercial and residential customers.

BACKGROUND:
Established: 1978; 1st Franchised: 1979
Franchised Units: 58
Company-Owned Units: 0
Total Units: 58
Dist.: US-51; CAN-4; O'seas-3
North America: 26 States, 2 Provinces
Density: in NC, 7 in NC, 7 in FL
Projected New Units (12 Months): 6
Qualifications: NR
FINANCIAL/TERMS:
Cash Investment: $20K
Total Investment: $40K
Minimum Net Worth: NR
Fees: Franchise - $14.7K
Royalty - 6%; Ad. - 0%
Earnings Claims Statement: No
Term of Contract (Years): 5/5
Avg. # Of Employees: 1 With Truck FT, 0 PT
Passive Ownership: Discouraged
Encourage Conversions: Yes
Area Develop. Agreements: No
Sub-Franchising Contracts: No
Expand In Territory: Yes
Space Needs: NR
SUPPORT & TRAINING:
Financial Assistance Provided: Yes (I)
Site Selection Assistance: Yes
Lease Negotiation Assistance: NA
Co-Operative Advertising: No
Franchisee Assoc./Member: No
Size Of Corporate Staff: 8
On-Going Support: A,B,C,D,,F,G,H,I
Training: 2 Weeks Headquarters
SPECIFIC EXPANSION PLANS:

263

US: All United States
Canada: All Canada
Overseas: All Countries

<< >>

PUROCLEAN

6001 Hiatus Rd., # 13
Tamarac, FL 33321
Tel: (800) 775-7876 (954) 722-6618
Fax: (800) 995-8527
E-Mail: sales@puroclean.com
Web Site: www.puroclean.com
Mr. C. Monty Smith, VP Sales & Development

Service Business Opportunity - PuroClean Franchisees, known as the "Paramedics of Property Damage", offer emergency restoration services to insurance companies and property owners for water damage, mold, smoke, fire clean up, and biohazard events. PuroClean was identified by FRANdata as one of the fastest-growing U.S. franchise concepts, ranking 53rd in the nation. As a PuroClean franchise owner, you have an opportunity to profit from the huge potential of the disaster restoration claims industry -- an indu

BACKGROUND: IFA MEMBER
Established: 1990; 1st Franchised: 1991
Franchised Units: 282
Company-Owned Units: 0
Total Units: 282
Dist.: US-277; CAN-5; O'seas-0
  North America: 41 States, 1 Provinces
  Density: 17 in NC, 23 in CA, 26 in FL
Projected New Units (12 Months): 85-100
Qualifications: 5, 5, 1, 3, 2, 5
FINANCIAL/TERMS:
Cash Investment: $35K
Total Investment: $69K-93K
Minimum Net Worth: $Not Required
Fees: Franchise - $45K
  Royalty - 10-8%; Ad. - 2%
Earnings Claims Statement: Yes
Term of Contract (Years): 20/10
Avg. # Of Employees: 2 FT, 2 PT
Passive Ownership: Discouraged
Encourage Conversions: Yes
Area Develop. Agreements: No
Sub-Franchising Contracts: No
Expand In Territory: Yes
Space Needs: Varies
SUPPORT & TRAINING:

Financial Assistance Provided: Yes (D)
Site Selection Assistance: No
Lease Negotiation Assistance: No
Co-Operative Advertising: No
Franchisee Assoc./Member: Yes/Yes
Size Of Corporate Staff: 35
On-Going Support: „C,D,„G,H,I
Training: 5 Days Franchise Location;
  15 Days Ft. Lauderdale, FL
SPECIFIC EXPANSION PLANS:
US: Southeast, Midwest, West
Canada: All Canada
Overseas: NR

<< >>

RAINBOW INTERNATIONAL
RESTORATION & CLEANING

1020 N. University Parks Dr.
Waco, TX 76707-0146
Tel: (800) 280-9963 (254) 759-5850
Fax: (800) 209-7621
E-Mail: info@servicefranchiseopportunities.com
Web Site: www.servicefranchiseopportunities.com
Ms. Pat Humburg, Marketing Manager

Established in 1981, Rainbow International Restoration & Cleaning is a global franchise organization providing residential and commercial restoration and cleaning services. Recognized by Entrepreneur magazine among its "Franchise 500," Rainbow International franchisees offer a broad range of damage restoration services (ranging from water, smoke and fire damage to carpet and upholstery cleaning and deodorization) to 330 locations worldwide. The new Rapid Structural Drying Network of Rainbow International ha

BACKGROUND: IFA MEMBER
Established: 1980; 1st Franchised: 1981
Franchised Units: 179
Company-Owned Units: 0
Total Units: 179
Dist.: US-165; CAN-7; O'seas-7
  North America: 40 States, 2 Provinces
  Density: 30 in TX, 12 in OH, 9 in CA
Projected New Units (12 Months): 58
Qualifications: 3, 3, 1, 1, 3, 5
FINANCIAL/TERMS:

Cash Investment: $45K
Total Investment: $103.9-165.1K
Minimum Net Worth: $175K
Fees: Franchise - $22K
  Royalty - 4-7%; Ad. - 2%
Earnings Claims Statement: No
Term of Contract (Years): 10/10
Avg. # Of Employees: 8 FT, PT
Passive Ownership: Discouraged
Encourage Conversions: Yes
Area Develop. Agreements: No
Sub-Franchising Contracts: No
Expand In Territory: Yes
Space Needs: NR
SUPPORT & TRAINING:
Financial Assistance Provided: Yes (D)
Site Selection Assistance: Yes
Lease Negotiation Assistance: No
Co-Operative Advertising: Yes
Franchisee Assoc./Member: Yes/Yes
Size Of Corporate Staff: 600
On-Going Support: „C,D,E,„G,h,I
Training: 4 Days (eight monthly, yearly)
  Waco, TX
SPECIFIC EXPANSION PLANS:
US: All United States
Canada: All Canada
Overseas: Japan, Middle East, Europe,
  Latin America

<< >>

RECEIL IT CEILING
RESTORATION

175-B Liberty St.
Copiaque, NY 11726-1207
Tel: (800) 234-5464 (631) 842-0099
Fax: (631) 980-7668
E-Mail: info@receilit.com
Web Site: www.receilit.com
Mr. Glenn Scheel, President

RECEIL IT provides expert restoration and/or cleaning in commercial locations (schools, hospitals, supermarkets, office building, department stores, etc.) of drop ceilings and acoustical tiles using proprietary coatings and cleaners. Work is done at a fraction of the cost and time necessary for ceiling replacement. Your RECEIL IT franchise can be run as a small, home-based operation with minimal personnel or built into a large profile operation.

BACKGROUND: IFA MEMBER
Established: 1992; 1st Franchised: 2003

Franchised Units:	2
Company-Owned Units:	1
Total Units:	3
Dist.:	US-3; CAN-0; O'seas-0
North America:	2 States, Provinces
Density:	1 in CA, 2 in NY
Projected New Units (12 Months):	4
Qualifications:	3, 3, 2, 3, 4, 5

FINANCIAL/TERMS:

Cash Investment:	$38.9-58.9K
Total Investment:	$50-70K
Minimum Net Worth:	Varies
Fees: Franchise -	$17.5K
Royalty - 7%;	Ad. - 0%
Earnings Claims Statement:	No
Term of Contract (Years):	10/5
Avg. # Of Employees:	2 FT, 0 PT
Passive Ownership:	Not Allowed
Encourage Conversions:	No
Area Develop. Agreements:	No
Sub-Franchising Contracts:	No
Expand In Territory:	No
Space Needs:	NA

SUPPORT & TRAINING:

Financial Assistance Provided:	No
Site Selection Assistance:	NA
Lease Negotiation Assistance:	NA
Co-Operative Advertising:	No
Franchisee Assoc./Member:	No
Size Of Corporate Staff:	4
On-Going Support:	a,B,C,D,,,,H,I
Training:	5-6 Days Copiague, NY

SPECIFIC EXPANSION PLANS:

US:	NY, NJ, PA, CT
Canada:	No
Overseas:	NR

◄◄ ►►

ROTO-ROOTER
300 Ashworth Rd.
West Des Moines, IA 50265-3786
Tel: (800) 575-7737 (515) 223-1343
Fax: (515) 223-6109
E-Mail: mike.higgins@rotorootercorp.com
Web Site: www.rotorooter.com
Mr. Michael Higgins, Dir. Franchise Development

World's largest plumbing repair and sewer and drain cleaning company, providing service to residential, commercial and municipal customers.

BACKGROUND: IFA MEMBER

Established: 1935;	1st Franchised: 1936
Franchised Units:	500
Company-Owned Units:	100
Total Units:	600
Dist.:	US-577; CAN-23; O'seas-0
North America:	50 States, 5 Provinces
Density:	28 in TX, 24 in FL, 44 in CA
Projected New Units (12 Months):	2
Qualifications:	3, 4, 5, 2, 2, 2

FINANCIAL/TERMS:

Cash Investment:	$25K-90K
Total Investment:	$25K-30K
Minimum Net Worth:	NA
Fees: Franchise -	$10K
Royalty - Varies;	Ad. - Varies
Earnings Claims Statement:	No
Term of Contract (Years):	10/10
Avg. # Of Employees:	FT, 0 PT
Passive Ownership:	Discouraged
Encourage Conversions:	Yes
Area Develop. Agreements:	No
Sub-Franchising Contracts:	No
Expand In Territory:	Yes
Space Needs:	NR

SUPPORT & TRAINING:

Financial Assistance Provided:	Yes (D)
Site Selection Assistance:	NA
Lease Negotiation Assistance:	NA
Co-Operative Advertising:	No
Franchisee Assoc./Member:	Yes/Yes
Size Of Corporate Staff:	25
On-Going Support:	,B,,,,,G,h,I
Training:	NA

SPECIFIC EXPANSION PLANS:

US:	No
Canada:	No
Overseas:	All Countries

◄◄ ►►

ROTO-STATIC INTERNATIONAL
90 Delta Park Blvd., # A
Brampton, ON L6T 5E7 Canada
Tel: (905) 458-7002
Fax: (905) 458-8650
E-Mail: success@rotostatic.com
Web Site: www.rotostatic.com
Ms. Pauline Wallace, Franchise Director

Profit from offering 6 services, including a unique system of carpet cleaning, , using Static Attraction principle, water damage restoration and odor removal services. Complete training in head office. On-going support systems. A company with a proven past.

BACKGROUND:
Established: 1977; 1st Franchised: 1977

Franchised Units:	141
Company-Owned Units:	0
Total Units:	141
Dist.:	US-0; CAN-141; O'seas-0
North America:	States, 9 Provinces
Density:	in BC, in ON, in QC
Projected New Units (12 Months):	10
Qualifications:	NR

FINANCIAL/TERMS:

Cash Investment:	$5-20K
Total Investment:	$45-60K
Minimum Net Worth:	NR
Fees: Franchise -	$15K
Royalty - 5%;	Ad. - 2%
Earnings Claims Statement:	No
Term of Contract (Years):	10/10
Avg. # Of Employees:	1-2 FT, 0 PT
Passive Ownership:	Not Allowed
Encourage Conversions:	No
Area Develop. Agreements:	Yes/1
Sub-Franchising Contracts:	Yes
Expand In Territory:	No
Space Needs:	NR

SUPPORT & TRAINING:

Financial Assistance Provided:	Yes (D)
Site Selection Assistance:	NA
Lease Negotiation Assistance:	NA
Co-Operative Advertising:	No
Franchisee Assoc./Member:	Yes/Yes
Size Of Corporate Staff:	7
On-Going Support:	,,C,D,E,F,G,H,I
Training:	4 Days Toronto, ON

SPECIFIC EXPANSION PLANS:

US:	All United States
Canada:	All Canada
Overseas:	U.K., Germany, France,
	Australia, Japan, Mexico, S

◄◄ ►►

SCOTTS LAWN SERVICE
14111 Scottslawn Rd.
Marysville, OH 43041
Tel: (800) 221-1760 (937) 644-7297
Fax: (937) 644-7422
E-Mail: jim.miller@scotts.com
Web Site: www.scotts.com
Mr. Jim Miller, Director of Franchising

SCOTTS, the leading marketer of home lawn and garden products, has entered the lawn service business, the result ... SCOTTS LAWN SERVICE. As a franchise system, we offer very strong brand name awareness, powerful sales and marketing programs, extensive training and premium products.

BACKGROUND:
Established: 1998; 1st Franchised: 1998

Franchised Units:	51
Company-Owned Units:	<u>50</u>
Total Units:	101
Dist.:	US-101; CAN-0; O'seas-0
North America:	States, Provinces
Density:	3 in GA, 4 in OH
Projected New Units (12 Months):	15
Qualifications:	4, 3, 3, 2, 2, 5

FINANCIAL/TERMS:

Cash Investment:	$30-60K
Total Investment:	$85.7-405.9K
Minimum Net Worth:	$100-500K
Fees: Franchise -	$30-250K
Royalty - 6-10%;	Ad. - 0%
Earnings Claims Statement:	Yes
Term of Contract (Years):	10/10
Avg. # Of Employees:	2+ FT, 0 PT
Passive Ownership:	Discouraged
Encourage Conversions:	Yes
Area Develop. Agreements:	No
Sub-Franchising Contracts:	No
Expand In Territory:	Yes
Space Needs:	400 SF

SUPPORT & TRAINING:

Financial Assistance Provided:	Yes (D)
Site Selection Assistance:	NA
Lease Negotiation Assistance:	No
Co-Operative Advertising:	No
Franchisee Assoc./Member:	No
Size Of Corporate Staff:	25
On-Going Support:	,B,C,D,E,F,,H,I
Training:	NR

SPECIFIC EXPANSION PLANS:

US:	All United States
Canada:	All Canada
Overseas:	NR

◄◄ ►►

SCREEN MACHINE

4173 First St.
Livermore, CA 94551
Tel: (877) 505-1985 (925) 443-9981
Fax: (925) 443-9983
E-Mail: screens@screen-machine.com
Web Site: www.screen-machine.com
Mr. Jeff Flannigan, Director of Sales

A mobile repair and replacement service for window and door screens. Unique mobile workshop complete with all tools, materials and supplies including a portable generator and chop saw, allows franchisees to quickly take care of customers screen repairs at the customer's home. Very limited competition. High profit margins, low material costs.

BACKGROUND: IFA MEMBER
Established: 1986; 1st Franchised: 1988

Franchised Units:	22
Company-Owned Units:	<u>1</u>
Total Units:	23
Dist.:	US-23; CAN-0; O'seas-0
North America:	1 States, Provinces
Density:	23 in CA
Projected New Units (12 Months):	5
Qualifications:	3, 2, 1, 1, 4, 4

FINANCIAL/TERMS:

Cash Investment:	$20-30K
Total Investment:	$44-73K
Minimum Net Worth:	$50K
Fees: Franchise -	$25K
Royalty - 5%;	Ad. - 0%
Earnings Claims Statement:	No
Term of Contract (Years):	10/10
Avg. # Of Employees:	1 FT, 3 PT
Passive Ownership:	Discouraged
Encourage Conversions:	Yes
Area Develop. Agreements:	Yes/1
Sub-Franchising Contracts:	Yes
Expand In Territory:	Yes
Space Needs:	800 SF

SUPPORT & TRAINING:

Financial Assistance Provided:	Yes (D)
Site Selection Assistance:	NA
Lease Negotiation Assistance:	No
Co-Operative Advertising:	No
Franchisee Assoc./Member:	No
Size Of Corporate Staff:	3
On-Going Support:	,,c,d,,,G,h,I
Training:	7 Days Walnut Creek, CA

SPECIFIC EXPANSION PLANS:

US:	SE, SW
Canada:	No
Overseas:	NR

◄◄ ►►

Top 100

SERVICEMASTER CLEAN

3839 Forest Hill-Irene Rd.
Memphis, TN 38125
Tel: (800) 786-9687 (901) 597-7500
Fax: (901) 597-7580
E-Mail: dmessenger@smclean.com
Web Site: www.ownafranchise.com
Mr. David Messenger, Vice President

SERVICEMASTER CLEAN is a division of The ServiceMaster Company. With over 55 years of franchising experience and over 4,000 franchises, SERVICEMASTER CLEAN continues to grow each year and offers franchise opportunities in three distinct categories: 1) Commercial Cleaning services 2) Residential carpet and upholstery cleaning & 3) Disaster Restoration services. Financing is provided for the initial franchise fee, start-up equipment & vehicles to qualified candidates through ServiceMaster Acceptance Co.

BACKGROUND: IFA MEMBER
Established: 1947; 1st Franchised: 1952

Franchised Units:	4488
Company-Owned Units:	<u>0</u>
Total Units:	4488
Dist.:	US-2914; CAN-176; O'seas-1398
North America:	50 States, 10 Provinces
Density:	139 in OH, 200 in IL, 155 in CA
Projected New Units (12 Months):	150
Qualifications:	5, 3, 2, 2, 3, 5

FINANCIAL/TERMS:

Cash Investment:	$12K
Total Investment:	$16.9-43K
Minimum Net Worth:	$50K
Fees: Franchise -	$16.9-49K
Royalty - 4-10%;	Ad. - 0.5-1%
Earnings Claims Statement:	No
Term of Contract (Years):	5/5
Avg. # Of Employees:	3 FT, 2 PT
Passive Ownership:	Discouraged
Encourage Conversions:	Yes
Area Develop. Agreements:	No
Sub-Franchising Contracts:	Yes
Expand In Territory:	Yes
Space Needs:	NA

SUPPORT & TRAINING:

Financial Assistance Provided:	Yes (D)
Site Selection Assistance:	No
Lease Negotiation Assistance:	No
Co-Operative Advertising:	Yes
Franchisee Assoc./Member:	Yes/Yes
Size Of Corporate Staff:	200
On-Going Support:	A,B,C,D,,F,G,H,I
Training:	1 Week Location; 2 Weeks Memphis, TN

SPECIFIC EXPANSION PLANS:

US:	All United States
Canada:	All Canada
Overseas:	All Countries

◄◄ ►►

SERVICE-TECH CORPORATION

7589 First Pl.
Cleveland, OH 44146-6711
Tel: (800) 992-9302 (440) 735-1505
Fax: (440) 735-1433
E-Mail: stccleve@aol.com
Web Site: www.service-techcorp.com
Mr. Alan J. Sutton, President

Indoor air quality. Opportunity to join 36

years of experience in solving the growing concerns of indoor air pollution. Services offered include air duct cleaning, kitchen exhaust cleaning, vacuum cleaning and specialized cleaning, plus more, to industrial and commercial customers.

BACKGROUND:

Established: 1960; 1st Franchised: 1988	
Franchised Units:	2
Company-Owned Units:	4
Total Units:	6
Dist.:	US-6; CAN-0; O'seas-0
North America:	4 States, 0 Provinces
Density:	3 in OH, 1 in MI, 1 in FL
Projected New Units (12 Months):	3
Qualifications:	4, 3, 2, 3, 3, 5

FINANCIAL/TERMS:

Cash Investment:	$20-50K
Total Investment:	$59-89K
Minimum Net Worth:	NR
Fees: Franchise -	$19K
Royalty - 4-6%;	Ad. - 1%
Earnings Claims Statement:	No
Term of Contract (Years):	10/10+
Avg. # Of Employees:	4 FT, 2 PT
Passive Ownership:	Not Allowed
Encourage Conversions:	NA
Area Develop. Agreements:	No
Sub-Franchising Contracts:	No
Expand In Territory:	Yes
Space Needs:	2,000 SF

SUPPORT & TRAINING:

Financial Assistance Provided:	Yes (D)
Site Selection Assistance:	NA
Lease Negotiation Assistance:	NA
Co-Operative Advertising:	No
Franchisee Assoc./Member:	NR
Size Of Corporate Staff:	35
On-Going Support:	,B,C,D,E,,,H,I
Training:	2 Weeks Headquarters;
1 Week Franchisee Location	

SPECIFIC EXPANSION PLANS:

US:	All United States
Canada:	No
Overseas:	NR

◄◄ ►►

SERVPRO
801 Industrial Dr.
Gallatin, TN 37066
Tel: (800) 826-9586 (615) 451-0200
Fax: (615) 451-1602
E-Mail: franchise@servpronet.com

Web Site: www.servpro.com
Mr. Kevin Brown, Dir. Franchise Expansion

A completely diversified cleaning and restoration business, with multiple income opportunities. The insurance restoration market (fire, smoke and water damages) is our main focus. We also specialize in commercial and residential cleaning. SERVPRO teaches effective management, marketing and technical skills. We are seeking qualified individuals with the desire to own their own business and become part of the SERVPRO team. If you want to be the best, join the best team. Call 1-800-826-9586.

BACKGROUND:

Established: 1967; 1st Franchised: 1969	
Franchised Units:	1430
Company-Owned Units:	0
Total Units:	1430
Dist.:	US-1430; CAN-0; O'seas-0
North America:	47 States, 0 Provinces
Density: 87 in TX, 106 in FL, 157 in CA	
Projected New Units (12 Months):	95
Qualifications:	3, 4, 1, 3, 4, 4

FINANCIAL/TERMS:

Cash Investment:	$60-70K
Total Investment:	$102,250-$161,150
Minimum Net Worth:	$150K
Fees: Franchise -	$40K
Royalty - 3-10%;	Ad. - 3%
Earnings Claims Statement:	No
Term of Contract (Years):	5/5
Avg. # Of Employees:	5-10 FT, 2-4 PT
Passive Ownership:	Not Allowed
Encourage Conversions:	Yes
Area Develop. Agreements:	No
Sub-Franchising Contracts:	No
Expand In Territory:	No
Space Needs:	1,500+ SF

SUPPORT & TRAINING:

Financial Assistance Provided:	Yes (D)
Site Selection Assistance:	Yes
Lease Negotiation Assistance:	No
Co-Operative Advertising:	Yes
Franchisee Assoc./Member:	No
Size Of Corporate Staff:	200
On-Going Support:	,,C,D,E,,G,H,I
Training: 1 Week Franchisee's Location;	
2.5 Weeks Gallatin, TN	

SPECIFIC EXPANSION PLANS:

US:	All United States
Canada:	No
Overseas:	NR

◄◄ ►►

SPARKLE WASH
26851 Richmond Rd.
Bedford Heights, OH 44146
Tel: (800) 321-0770 (216) 464-4212
Fax: (216) 464-8869
E-Mail: sales@sparklewash.com
Web Site: www.sparklewash.com
Mr. Tom Yuhas, VP Franchise Development

SPARKLE WASH provides mobile power-cleaning and restoration, providing broad market opportunities to our franchisees for the commercial, industrial, residential and fleet markets. SPARKLE WASH franchisees can also provide special services, including wood restoration, all using our environmentally friendly products.

BACKGROUND: IFA MEMBER

Established: 1965; 1st Franchised: 1967	
Franchised Units:	105
Company-Owned Units:	1
Total Units:	106
Dist.:	US-95; CAN-0; O'seas-79
North America:	32 States, 0 Provinces
Density:	13 in PA, 13 in OH, 8 in NY
Projected New Units (12 Months):	10
Qualifications:	3, 3, 1, 2, 4, 5

FINANCIAL/TERMS:

Cash Investment:	$40-75K
Total Investment:	$80-120K
Minimum Net Worth:	$60K
Fees: Franchise -	$15K
Royalty - 3-5%;	Ad. - 0%
Earnings Claims Statement:	Yes
Term of Contract (Years):	Continual/
Avg. # Of Employees:	2 FT, 2 PT
Passive Ownership:	Allowed
Encourage Conversions:	Yes
Area Develop. Agreements:	No
Sub-Franchising Contracts:	No
Expand In Territory:	Yes
Space Needs:	NR

SUPPORT & TRAINING:

Financial Assistance Provided:	Yes (D)
Site Selection Assistance:	NA
Lease Negotiation Assistance:	NA
Co-Operative Advertising:	No
Franchisee Assoc./Member:	Yes/Yes
Size Of Corporate Staff:	15
On-Going Support:	,B,C,D,,,G,H,I
Training:	1 Week Headquarters;
3 Days Franchisee Location; 3 Days	
National/Regional Meetings	

SPECIFIC EXPANSION PLANS:

US:	All United States

Canada: All Canada
Overseas: All Countries

‹‹ ››

SPRING-GREEN
America's *Neighborhood* Lawn Care Team.

Top 100

SPRING-GREEN LAWN CARE

11909 Spaulding School Dr.
Plainfield, IL 60544-9501
Tel: (800) 777-8608 (815) 436-8777
Fax: (815) 436-9056
E-Mail: franinfo@spring-green.com
Web Site: www.springgreenfranchise.com
Mr. Mark Potocki, Franchise Development Manager

SPRING-GREEN delivers lawn and tree care services nationwide. Our service is centered on the beautification of middle class and affluent neighborhoods and communities. Our customers include both residential and commercial establishments. SPRING-GREEN services include lawn, tree and shrub fertilization as well as disease and perimeter pest control. SPRING-GREEN has been beautifying the environment for more than 30 years as your national lawn care team.

BACKGROUND: IFA MEMBER
Established: 1977; 1st Franchised: 1977
Franchised Units: 92
Company-Owned Units: 26
Total Units: 118
Dist.: US-118; CAN-0; O'seas-0
North America: 25 States, 0 Provinces
Density: 10 in NC, 15 in WI, 30 in IL
Projected New Units (12 Months): 15
Qualifications: 4, 3, 1, 3, 2, 4
FINANCIAL/TERMS:
Cash Investment: $30K
Total Investment: $131K-165K
Minimum Net Worth: $160K
Fees: Franchise - $30K
Royalty - 10-8%; Ad. - 2%
Earnings Claims Statement: Yes
Term of Contract (Years): 10/10
Avg. # Of Employees: NA FT, NA PT
Passive Ownership: Not Allowed
Encourage Conversions: Yes
Area Develop. Agreements: No
Sub-Franchising Contracts: No
Expand In Territory: No
Space Needs: NA
SUPPORT & TRAINING:
Financial Assistance Provided: Yes (I)
Site Selection Assistance: NA

Lease Negotiation Assistance: NA
Co-Operative Advertising: No
Franchisee Assoc./Member: Yes/Yes
Size Of Corporate Staff: 22
On-Going Support: ,,C,D,E,F,G,h,i
Training: 1 Week Training at Corp. HQ;
Ongoing On-Line Pre-Training; Min. 2
Days Each 3 Annual On-Site Visits
SPECIFIC EXPANSION PLANS:
US: All Exc. AK,AZ,CA,CT,NY,NV,ND,
HI,MA,ME,MS,NM,RI,VT
Canada: No
Overseas: NR

‹‹ ››

STEAM BROTHERS PROFESSIONAL CLEANING & RESTORATION

2124 E. Sweet Ave.
Bismarck, ND 58504
Tel: (800) 767-5064 (701) 222-1263
Fax: (701) 222-1372
E-Mail: steambrothers@gcentral.com
Web Site: www.steambrothers.com
Mr. Adam Leier, President

Residential and commercial - carpet, upholstery, drapery, wall and ceiling cleaning; furnace air duct cleaning; water, smoke and fire clean-up. Named one of the Top 100 home-based franchises in 1995.

BACKGROUND:
Established: 1977; 1st Franchised: 1983
Franchised Units: 24
Company-Owned Units: 0
Total Units: 24
Dist.: US-24; CAN-0; O'seas-0
North America: 5 States, 0 Provinces
Density: 3 in SD, 7 in ND, 9 in MN
Projected New Units (12 Months): 2-5
Qualifications: 3, 2, 1, 3, 4, 5
FINANCIAL/TERMS:
Cash Investment: $16-22.5K
Total Investment: $22.5-53.5K
Minimum Net Worth: NA
Fees: Franchise - $16K
Royalty - 5-6.5%; Ad. - NA
Earnings Claims Statement: No
Term of Contract (Years): 10/10
Avg. # Of Employees: 3 FT, 0 PT
Passive Ownership: Discouraged
Encourage Conversions: Yes
Area Develop. Agreements: No
Sub-Franchising Contracts: No
Expand In Territory: No
Space Needs: NR
SUPPORT & TRAINING:
Financial Assistance Provided: Yes (D)

Site Selection Assistance: Yes
Lease Negotiation Assistance: Yes
Co-Operative Advertising: No
Franchisee Assoc./Member: Yes/Yes
Size Of Corporate Staff: 2
On-Going Support: ,B,C,D,E,F,G,H,I
Training: 5 Days Home Office;
3-5 Days Franchise Location
SPECIFIC EXPANSION PLANS:
US: Upper Midwest States
Canada: No
Overseas: NR

‹‹ ››

STEAMATIC

3333 Quorum Dr., # 280
Fort Worth, TX 76137
Tel: (800) 544-1303 (817) 332-1575
Fax: (817) 332-5349
E-Mail: bsims@steamatic.com
Web Site: www.steamatic.com
Mr. Bill Sims, President

The total cleaning and disaster recover franchise, serving the residential, commercial and industrial markets. Emphasis is on combating problems associated with indoor air pollution, such as cleaning/sanitation of the HVAC system, air ducts, coils, carpet cleaning, etc. Emphasis also on water and fire damage restoration of residential/commercial buildings. Plus, general cleaning of residential and commercial properties.

BACKGROUND: IFA MEMBER
Established: 1967; 1st Franchised: 1968
Franchised Units: 400
Company-Owned Units: 0
Total Units: 400
Dist.: US-361; CAN-60; O'seas-38
North America: 43 States, 10 Provinces
Density: 56 in TX, 26 in IL, 43 in CA
Projected New Units (12 Months): 12
Qualifications: NR
FINANCIAL/TERMS:
Cash Investment: $25-80K
Total Investment: $55-150K
Minimum Net Worth: NR
Fees: Franchise - $7-24K
Royalty - 8-5%; Ad. - 0%
Earnings Claims Statement: No
Term of Contract (Years): 10/5
Avg. # Of Employees: 5-40 FT, 3-10 PT
Passive Ownership: Discouraged
Encourage Conversions: Yes
Area Develop. Agreements: No
Sub-Franchising Contracts: No
Expand In Territory: No

Space Needs:	NA

SUPPORT & TRAINING:

Financial Assistance Provided:	Yes (I)
Site Selection Assistance:	NA
Lease Negotiation Assistance:	NA
Co-Operative Advertising:	No
Franchisee Assoc./Member:	Yes/Yes
Size Of Corporate Staff:	32
On-Going Support:	A,B,C,D,E,F,G,H,I
Training:	3 Weeks Ft. Worth, TX

SPECIFIC EXPANSION PLANS:

US:	All United States
Canada:	All Canada
Overseas:	All Countries

◄◄ ►►

SWISHER HYGIENE

6849 Fairview Rd.
Charlotte, NC 28210-3363
Tel: (800) 444-4138 (704) 364-7707
Fax: (800) 444-4565
E-Mail: jlane@swisherhygiene.com
Web Site: www.swisheronline.com
Mr. Jeffrey Lane, VP Business Development

SWISHER HYGIENE is the world's largest commercial restroom hygiene franchise. This unique niche franchise offers limited competition with high profit returns. Complete training and an extensive support program are provided. Franchisees provide a weekly service that is a combination of a sanitary cleaning and product supply.

BACKGROUND: IFA MEMBER

Established: 1981;	1st Franchised: 1990
Franchised Units:	71
Company-Owned Units:	42
Total Units:	113
Dist.:	US-97; CAN-8; O'seas-8
North America:	40 States, 4 Provinces
Density:	6 in MI, 8 in FL, 12 in CA
Projected New Units (12 Months):	20
Qualifications:	4, 4, 4, 3, 4, 3

FINANCIAL/TERMS:

Cash Investment:	$135-175K
Total Investment:	$135-175K
Minimum Net Worth:	NA
Fees: Franchise -	$15-85K
Royalty - 6%;	Ad. - 2%
Earnings Claims Statement:	No
Term of Contract (Years):	10/5
Avg. # Of Employees:	5 FT, 0 PT
Passive Ownership:	Discouraged
Encourage Conversions:	NA
Area Develop. Agreements:	No
Sub-Franchising Contracts:	No

Expand In Territory:	Yes
Space Needs:	900-1,200 SF

SUPPORT & TRAINING:

Financial Assistance Provided:	Yes (D)
Site Selection Assistance:	No
Lease Negotiation Assistance:	No
Co-Operative Advertising:	No
Franchisee Assoc./Member:	No
Size Of Corporate Staff:	55
On-Going Support:	A,B,C,D,,,G,H,I
Training:	1 Week Charlotte, NC

SPECIFIC EXPANSION PLANS:

US:	All United States
Canada:	All Canada
Overseas:	All Countries

◄◄ ►►

SYNLAWN®

artificial grass never looked more natural.

SYNLAWN

2680 Lakeland Rd.
Dalton, GA 30721
Tel: (866) 796-5296 (706) 876-5531
Fax: (866) 796-5297
E-Mail:
Web Site: www.synlawn.com
Mr. George Neagle, VP of Sales & Marketing

Take advantage of the emerging artificial grass landscape market with a SYNLawn® Franchise. The SYNLawn® Franchise opportunity offers start-up and add-on business models with exclusive branded products backed by manufacturer's warranty, retail and national programs, plus extensive sales, marketing and operations training to help support and grow your business.

BACKGROUND:

Established: 2009;	1st Franchised: 2009
Franchised Units:	0
Company-Owned Units:	0
Total Units:	0
Dist.:	US-0; CAN-0; O'seas-0
North America:	0 States, 0 Provinces
Density:	NR
Projected New Units (12 Months):	20
Qualifications:	5, 4, 3, 4, 4, 5

FINANCIAL/TERMS:

Cash Investment:	NR
Total Investment:	$156-382K
Minimum Net Worth:	NR
Fees: Franchise -	$35K
Royalty - 6%;	Ad. - 2%
Earnings Claims Statement:	No

Term of Contract (Years): 5/20 (4-5 Year Terms)

Avg. # Of Employees:	6 FT, PT
Passive Ownership:	Not Allowed
Encourage Conversions:	Yes
Area Develop. Agreements:	No
Sub-Franchising Contracts:	No
Expand In Territory:	No
Space Needs:	1,200 SF

SUPPORT & TRAINING:

Financial Assistance Provided:	No
Site Selection Assistance:	Yes
Lease Negotiation Assistance:	No
Co-Operative Advertising:	Yes
Franchisee Assoc./Member:	No
Size Of Corporate Staff:	0
On-Going Support:	a,,C,D,E,f,,h,I
Training:	2 Weeks On-Site Training; 2 Weeks Las Vegas, NV; 2 Weeks Dalton, GA

SPECIFIC EXPANSION PLANS:

US:	Yes
Canada:	No
Overseas:	NR

◄◄ ►►

TOWER CLEANING SYSTEMS

P. O. Box 2468
Southeastern, PA 19399
Tel: (800) 355-4000 (610) 278-9000
Fax: (610) 275-7662
E-Mail: towerclean@aol.com
Web Site: www.toweronline.com
Mr. Chuck Lomagro, Vice President

TOWER CLEANING was rated in the top 100 franchises by "Entrepreneur"; "Inc. Magazine" says we are one of the country's fastest-growing franchises of 1997. We feature a tested, proven program with your initial clients already obtained; full start-up package, complete step-by-step and on-going training; professional administrative support (customer relations, accounting, invoicing, on-going marketing).

BACKGROUND:

Established: 1988;	1st Franchised: 1990
Franchised Units:	449
Company-Owned Units:	0
Total Units:	449
Dist.:	US-449; CAN-0; O'seas-0
North America:	19 States, 0 Provinces
Density:	128 in WA, 183 in PA, 138 in NJ
Projected New Units (12 Months):	500
Qualifications:	3, 3, 3, 2, 1, 5

FINANCIAL/TERMS:

Cash Investment:	$1.5-25K
Total Investment:	$3.4-34K
Minimum Net Worth:	$10K
Fees: Franchise -	$4-33.6K
Royalty - 3%;	Ad. - 0%
Earnings Claims Statement:	No
Term of Contract (Years):	10/10
Avg. # Of Employees:	1-5 FT, 0 PT
Passive Ownership:	Allowed
Encourage Conversions:	Yes
Area Develop. Agreements:	Yes/1
Sub-Franchising Contracts:	No
Expand In Territory:	Yes
Space Needs:	NA

SUPPORT & TRAINING:

Financial Assistance Provided:	Yes (D)
Site Selection Assistance:	NA
Lease Negotiation Assistance:	NA
Co-Operative Advertising:	No
Franchisee Assoc./Member:	No
Size Of Corporate Staff:	50
On-Going Support:	A,B,C,D,,,G,H,I
Training:	1 Week Local Office; 2-3 Days On-Site

SPECIFIC EXPANSION PLANS:

US:	All United States
Canada:	All Canada
Overseas:	NR

TRULY NOLEN PEST CONTROL

3636 E. Speedway Blvd.
Tucson, AZ 85716-4018
Tel: (800) 458-3664 (206) 419-0742
Fax: (520) 322-4010
E-Mail: truly@truly.com
Web Site: www.trulynolen.com
Mr. Truly Bill Nolen, Director

Pest, lawn, termite, inspection based upon a unique and memorably established business system.

BACKGROUND: IFA MEMBER

Established: 1938;	1st Franchised: 1996
Franchised Units:	13
Company-Owned Units:	65
Total Units:	78
Dist.:	US-78; CAN-0; O'seas-0
North America: 13 States, 0 Provinces	
Density: 42 in FL, 8 in CA, 19 in AZ	
Projected New Units (12 Months):	4
Qualifications:	2, 2, 2, 2, 2, 5

FINANCIAL/TERMS:

Cash Investment:	$5-300K
Total Investment:	$25-300K
Minimum Net Worth:	$25K
Fees: Franchise -	$45K
Royalty - 7%;	Ad. - 0%

Earnings Claims Statement:	No
Term of Contract (Years):	5/
Avg. # Of Employees:	10 FT, 1 PT
Passive Ownership:	Discouraged
Encourage Conversions:	Yes
Area Develop. Agreements:	No
Sub-Franchising Contracts:	No
Expand In Territory:	Yes
Space Needs:	NR

SUPPORT & TRAINING:

Financial Assistance Provided:	No
Site Selection Assistance:	No
Lease Negotiation Assistance:	No
Co-Operative Advertising:	No
Franchisee Assoc./Member:	No
Size Of Corporate Staff:	25
On-Going Support:	,,C,D,,,,h,I
Training:	1 Week Pompano Beach, FL; On-Site as Determined

SPECIFIC EXPANSION PLANS:

US:	All United States
Canada:	All Canada
Overseas:	NR

U. S. LAWNS

4407 Vineland Rd., # D-15
Orlando, FL 33811
Tel: (866) 781-4875 (407) 246-1630
Fax: (407) 246-1623
E-Mail: franchise@uslawns.net
Web Site: www.uslawns.com
Mr. Brandon Moxam, Director of Franchise Recruiting

Train and support franchisees in a commercial landscape market.

BACKGROUND: IFA MEMBER

Established: 1986;	1st Franchised: 1986
Franchised Units:	208
Company-Owned Units:	0
Total Units:	208
Dist.:	US-208; CAN-0; O'seas-0
North America: 25 States, 0 Provinces	
Density:	34 in FL
Projected New Units (12 Months):	30
Qualifications:	4, 4, 2, 2, 2, 5

FINANCIAL/TERMS:

Cash Investment:	$25K
Total Investment:	$50-85K
Minimum Net Worth:	$70K

Fees: Franchise -	$29K
Royalty - 4%;	Ad. - 3%
Earnings Claims Statement:	No
Term of Contract (Years):	10/10
Avg. # Of Employees:	12-20 FT, 0 PT
Passive Ownership:	Not Allowed
Encourage Conversions:	Yes
Area Develop. Agreements:	No
Sub-Franchising Contracts:	No
Expand In Territory:	Yes
Space Needs:	NA

SUPPORT & TRAINING:

Financial Assistance Provided:	Yes (D)
Site Selection Assistance:	NA
Lease Negotiation Assistance:	No
Co-Operative Advertising:	Yes
Franchisee Assoc./Member:	Yes/Yes
Size Of Corporate Staff:	40
On-Going Support:	,,C,D,E,,G,H,
Training:	6 Days Orlando, FL; 5 Days Location

SPECIFIC EXPANSION PLANS:

US:	All United States
Canada:	No
Overseas:	NR

UNICLEAN SYSTEMS

1010 W. Queens Rd., # 200
North Vancouver, BC V7R 4S9 Canada
Tel: (604) 986-4750
Fax: (604) 987-6838
E-Mail: info@unicleansystems.com
Web Site: www.unicleansystems.com
Mr. Jack B. Karpowicz, President

Commercial office cleaning on a long-term contract basis.

BACKGROUND:

Established: 1976;	1st Franchised: 1981
Franchised Units:	398
Company-Owned Units:	1
Total Units:	399
Dist.:	US-52; CAN-347; O'seas-0
North America: 12 States, 5 Provinces	
Density: 35 in QC, 89 in ON, 167 in BC	
Projected New Units (12 Months):	20
Qualifications:	2, 3, 2, 2, 4, 5

FINANCIAL/TERMS:

Cash Investment:	$5.5-16.5K
Total Investment:	$5.5-16.5K
Minimum Net Worth:	NA
Fees: Franchise -	$1.5K
Royalty - 15%;	Ad. - 0-5%
Earnings Claims Statement:	No
Term of Contract (Years):	3/3
Avg. # Of Employees:	NA FT, 0 PT
Passive Ownership:	Discouraged

270

Encourage Conversions: No
Area Develop. Agreements: Yes/1
Sub-Franchising Contracts: Yes
Expand In Territory: Yes
Space Needs: NA

SUPPORT & TRAINING:
Financial Assistance Provided: Yes (D)
Site Selection Assistance: NA
Lease Negotiation Assistance: No
Co-Operative Advertising: No
Franchisee Assoc./Member: No
Size Of Corporate Staff: 8
On-Going Support: A,b,c,D,,,G,H,
Training: 1-2 Weeks Home Office, North Vancouver, BC

SPECIFIC EXPANSION PLANS:
US: All United States
Canada: All Except AB
Overseas: NR

≪ ≫

VANGUARD CLEANING SYSTEMS
655 Mariners Island Blvd., # 303
San Mateo, CA 94404
Tel: (800) 564-6422 + 414 (650) 287-2414
Fax: (650) 591-1545
E-Mail: wgreene@vanguardcleaning.com
Web Site: www.vanguardcleaning.com
Mr. Will Greene, Business Development Director

VANGUARD CLEANING SYSTEMS has been successfully franchising in the commercial cleaning industry since 1984. VANGUARD is currently seeking unit and master franchisees in the United States and Canada. Currently, Vanguard has 1,287 franchises and 40 regional offices.

BACKGROUND: IFA MEMBER
Established: 1984; 1st Franchised: 1984
Franchised Units: 1524
Company-Owned Units: 0
Total Units: 1524
Dist.: US-1466; CAN-58; O'seas-0
North America: 26 States, 1 Provinces
Density: 351 in CA
Projected New Units (12 Months): 659
Qualifications: 2, 2, 3, 1, 3, 5

FINANCIAL/TERMS:
Cash Investment: $1.5-35K
Total Investment: $7-35K

Minimum Net Worth: $1.5-35K
Fees: Franchise - $7-35K
  Royalty - 5%; Ad. -
Earnings Claims Statement: No
Term of Contract (Years): 10/10
Avg. # Of Employees: FT, 1 PT
Passive Ownership: Discouraged
Encourage Conversions: Yes
Area Develop. Agreements: No
Sub-Franchising Contracts: Yes
Expand In Territory: Yes
Space Needs: NA

SUPPORT & TRAINING:
Financial Assistance Provided: Yes (D)
Site Selection Assistance: NA
Lease Negotiation Assistance: NA
Co-Operative Advertising: No
Franchisee Assoc./Member: No
Size Of Corporate Staff: 26
On-Going Support: A,,C,D,,,G,H,I
Training: 2 Weeks+ Local Regional Office

SPECIFIC EXPANSION PLANS:
US: All United States
Canada: All Canada
Overseas: NR

≪ ≫

WEED MAN
11 Grand Marshall Dr.
Toronto, ON M1B 5N6 Canada
Tel: (888) 321-9333 (416) 269-5754 + 114
Fax: (416) 269-8233
E-Mail: info@weedmanusa.com
Web Site: www.weedmanusa.com
Ms Jennifer Lemcke, COO

Professional lawn care services.

BACKGROUND: IFA MEMBER
Established: 1970; 1st Franchised: 1976
Franchised Units: 355
Company-Owned Units: 0
Total Units: 355
Dist.: US-233; CAN-118; O'seas-4
North America: 29 States, 10 Provinces
Density: 16 in WI, 34 in OH, 35 in MI
Projected New Units (12 Months): 24
Qualifications: 3, 4, 1, 3, 5, 4

FINANCIAL/TERMS:
Cash Investment: $44K
Total Investment: $118K
Minimum Net Worth: $125K
Fees: Franchise - $20-34K
  Royalty - 10.2K/Vehcl.; Ad. - 20%

Royalty
Earnings Claims Statement: No
Term of Contract (Years): 10/10
Avg. # Of Employees: 3 FT, 2 PT
Passive Ownership: Discouraged
Encourage Conversions: Yes
Area Develop. Agreements: No
Sub-Franchising Contracts: Yes
Expand In Territory: Yes
Space Needs: NR

SUPPORT & TRAINING:
Financial Assistance Provided: No
Site Selection Assistance: Yes
Lease Negotiation Assistance: No
Co-Operative Advertising: Yes
Franchisee Assoc./Member: Yes/Yes
Size Of Corporate Staff: 5
On-Going Support: ,B,C,D,,,G,,
Training: 2 Weeks Toronto, ON

SPECIFIC EXPANSION PLANS:
US: All United States
Canada: No
Overseas: NR

≪ ≫

WE DO LINES
79 Danbury Rd, # A-1
Ridgefield, CT 06877
Tel: (516) 320-4750
Fax: (631) 424-2514
E-Mail: sbarrett@wedolines.com
Web Site: www.wedolines.com
Mr. Skip Barrett, VP Franchise Sales

We Do Lines USA, LLC is the nation's first parking lot marking franchise. We Do Lines franchisees enjoy exclusive territories, extensive training, state-of-the-art equipment, and cutting-edge technology support to assist them in the operation of their franchises. In addition, We Do Lines corporate services an array of national and regional accounts and works hand-in-glove with our franchisees to ensure our clients' consistent, professional installations and outstanding customer service.

BACKGROUND:
Established: 2008; 1st Franchised: 2009
Franchised Units: 3
Company-Owned Units: 1
Total Units: 4
Dist.: US-4; CAN-0; O'seas-0
North America: 2 States, 0 Provinces

Density:	4 in CT
Projected New Units (12 Months):	24
Qualifications:	3, 4, 2, 2, 3, 4

FINANCIAL/TERMS:

Cash Investment:	$73-96K
Total Investment:	$73-96K
Minimum Net Worth:	$250K
Fees: Franchise -	$25K
Royalty - 8%	Ad. - 5%
Earnings Claims Statement:	No
Term of Contract (Years):	10/5
Avg. # Of Employees:	1 FT, 1 PT
Passive Ownership:	Not Allowed
Encourage Conversions:	NA
Area Develop. Agreements:	Yes/10
Sub-Franchising Contracts:	No
Expand In Territory:	Yes
Space Needs:	NA

SUPPORT & TRAINING:

Financial Assistance Provided:	No
Site Selection Assistance:	NA
Lease Negotiation Assistance:	NA
Co-Operative Advertising:	No
Franchisee Assoc./Member:	No
Size Of Corporate Staff:	7
On-Going Support:	a,B,c,d,,F,G,h,I
Training:	2 Weeks Ridgefield, CT;
2 Weeks Field	

SPECIFIC EXPANSION PLANS:

US:	Maine to Virginia
Canada:	No
Overseas:	No

≪≫

WINDOW GANG

405 Arendall St.
Morehead City, NC 28557
Tel: (877) WIN-GANG (252) 726-1463
Fax: (252) 726-2837
E-Mail: tim@windowgang.com
Web Site: www.windowgang.com
Mr. Tim McCullen, President

Residential/commercial window, gutter, pressure and blind cleaning company. Large, extensive markets.

BACKGROUND:

Established: 1986;	1st Franchised: 1996
Franchised Units:	151
Company-Owned Units:	0
Total Units:	151
Dist.:	US-151; CAN-0; O'seas-0

North America:	10 States, Provinces
Density:	46 in NC, 24 in SC, 23 in VA
Projected New Units (12 Months):	NR
Qualifications:	NR

FINANCIAL/TERMS:

Cash Investment:	$25-50K
Total Investment:	$25-50K
Minimum Net Worth:	$50K
Fees: Franchise -	$25K+
Royalty - 6%;	Ad. - 0%
Earnings Claims Statement:	No
Term of Contract (Years):	10/10
Avg. # Of Employees:	5 FT, 5 PT
Passive Ownership:	Discouraged
Encourage Conversions:	No
Area Develop. Agreements:	No
Sub-Franchising Contracts:	No
Expand In Territory:	Yes
Space Needs:	1,000 SF

SUPPORT & TRAINING:

Financial Assistance Provided:	No
Site Selection Assistance:	Yes
Lease Negotiation Assistance:	Yes
Co-Operative Advertising:	No
Franchisee Assoc./Member:	No
Size Of Corporate Staff:	3
On-Going Support:	,B,C,D,E,,G,h,
Training:	5-10 Days Beaufort, NC

SPECIFIC EXPANSION PLANS:

US:	All United States
Canada:	NR
Overseas:	NR

≪≫

We Clean Windows and a Whole Lot More!

WINDOW GENIE

4686 Mission Ln.
Cincinnati, OH 45223
Tel: (800) 700-0022 (513) 541-3351
Fax: (513) 541-3421
E-Mail: rik@windowgenie.com
Web Site: www.windowgenie.com
Mr. Richard (Rik) Nonelle, President

The home services leader, specializing in 6 distinct categories: Window Cleaning, Window Tinting, Pressure Washing, Window Blinds, Tile and Grout Cleaning and Gutter Protection. With protected territories and tremendous market appeal, Window Genie is perfectly positioned to service time-starved homeowners.

BACKGROUND: IFA MEMBER

Established: 1994;	1st Franchised: 1998
Franchised Units:	47
Company-Owned Units:	0
Total Units:	47
Dist.:	US-47; CAN-0; O'seas-0
North America:	18 States, 0 Provinces
Density:	7 in OH, 4 in PA, 7 in IL
Projected New Units (12 Months):	19
Qualifications:	4, 4, 1, 3, 3, 5

FINANCIAL/TERMS:

Cash Investment:	$40-50K
Total Investment:	$45-75K
Minimum Net Worth:	Varies
Fees: Franchise -	$19.5K
Royalty - 3-6%;	Ad. - 1%
Earnings Claims Statement:	No
Term of Contract (Years):	10/5
Avg. # Of Employees:	2 FT, 2 PT
Passive Ownership:	Discouraged
Encourage Conversions:	Yes
Area Develop. Agreements:	No
Sub-Franchising Contracts:	No
Expand In Territory:	Yes
Space Needs:	NA

SUPPORT & TRAINING:

Financial Assistance Provided:	No
Site Selection Assistance:	NA
Lease Negotiation Assistance:	NA
Co-Operative Advertising:	No
Franchisee Assoc./Member:	No
Size Of Corporate Staff:	3
On-Going Support:	,,C,D,E,F,G,H,I
Training:	5 Days Corporate, Cincinnati,
OH; 5 Days On-Site	

SPECIFIC EXPANSION PLANS:

US:	All United States
Canada:	No
Overseas:	NR

≪≫

FOUR LARGEST PARTICIPANTS IN SURVEY

Company	# Fran- chised Units	# Co- Owned Units	# Total Units	Franchise Fee	On-Going Royalty	Total Investment
1. Party Land	400	0	400	$35K	5%	$249-329K
2. Complete Music	168	1	169	$18-28.4K	8%	$30.4-48.7K
3. Plan Ahead Events	40	0	40	$24.5K	$300/ month (first year)	$28-32K
4. Sweet Beginnings Wedding Consulting & Event Planners	16	2	18	$10-20K	$300	$29-44K

All of the data provided are proprietary and should not be quoted without acknowledging *Bond's Franchise Guide*.

COMPLETE MUSIC

7877 L St.
Omaha, NE 68127
Tel: (800) 843-3866 (402) 339-0001
Fax: (402) 898-1777
E-Mail: ericm@cmusic.com
Web Site: www.cmusic.com
Mr. Eric Mass, Chief Executive Officer

COMPLETE MUSIC is the leader in disc jockey entertainment, providing dance music for over 1 million people each year. The uniqueness of this business allows owners, who need not be entertainers, to use their skills in management to hire and book their own musically trained DJ's for all types of special events.

BACKGROUND:

Established: 1972; 1st Franchised: 1982
Franchised Units: 168
Company-Owned Units: 1
Total Units: 169
Dist.: US-165; CAN-4; O'seas-0
North America: 31 States, 2 Provinces
Density: 21 in TX, 11 in NE, 8 in CO
Projected New Units (12 Months): 6-12
Qualifications: 3, 4, 1, 4, 1, 3
FINANCIAL/TERMS:
Cash Investment: $9.5-24.5K
Total Investment: $30.4-48.7K
Minimum Net Worth: NA
Fees: Franchise - $18-28.4K
  Royalty - 8%; Ad. - 4%
Earnings Claims Statement: Yes
Term of Contract (Years): Lifetime/10
Avg. # Of Employees: 2 FT, 5-40 PT
Passive Ownership: Discouraged
Encourage Conversions: Yes
Area Develop. Agreements: No

Sub-Franchising Contracts: No
Expand In Territory: Yes
Space Needs: NA

SUPPORT & TRAINING:
Financial Assistance Provided: Yes (D)
Site Selection Assistance: Yes
Lease Negotiation Assistance: Yes
Co-Operative Advertising: No
Franchisee Assoc./Member: Yes/Yes
Size Of Corporate Staff: 5
On-Going Support: ,B,c,D,E,F,G,h,i
Training: 9 Days Omaha, NE;
   4 Days On-Site

SPECIFIC EXPANSION PLANS:
US: All United States
Canada: All Canada
Overseas: NR

⪻ ⪼

PARTY LAND
5215 Militia Hill Rd.
Plymouth Meeting, PA 19462-1216
Tel: (800) 778-9563 (610) 941-6200
Fax: (610) 941-6301
E-Mail: jbarry@partyland.com
Web Site: www.partyland.com
Mr. John L. Barry, VP Franchise Sales

World's largest international retail party supply franchise, specializing in service, selection and savings. The official party store for the 'new millennium.'

BACKGROUND:
Established: 1986; 1st Franchised: 1988
Franchised Units: 400
Company-Owned Units: 0
Total Units: 400
Dist.: US-360; CAN-4; O'seas-36
   North America: 23 States, 3 Provinces
   Density: 8 in TX, 20 in PA, 3 in CO
Projected New Units (12 Months): 20
Qualifications: 5, 4, 2, 1, 5, 5

FINANCIAL/TERMS:
Cash Investment: $80K
Total Investment: $249-329K
Minimum Net Worth: $250K
Fees: Franchise - $35K
   Royalty - 5%; Ad. - 4%
Earnings Claims Statement: No
Term of Contract (Years): 20/10
Avg. # Of Employees: 2 FT, 6 PT
Passive Ownership: Allowed
Encourage Conversions: Yes
Area Develop. Agreements: Yes/1
Sub-Franchising Contracts: Yes
Expand In Territory: No
Space Needs: NR

SUPPORT & TRAINING:

Financial Assistance Provided: Yes (D)
Site Selection Assistance: Yes
Lease Negotiation Assistance: Yes
Co-Operative Advertising: No
Franchisee Assoc./Member: Yes/Yes
Size Of Corporate Staff: 30
On-Going Support: A,B,C,D,E,F,G,H,I
Training: 1 Week Party Land University

SPECIFIC EXPANSION PLANS:
US: All United States
Canada: All Canada
Overseas: All Countries

⪻ ⪼

PLAN AHEAD EVENTS
2121 Vista Pkwy.
West Palm Beach, FL 33411
Tel: (800) 466-2812 (561) 868-1478
Fax: (561) 478-4340
E-Mail: franchise@planaheadevents.com
Web Site: www.planaheadevents.com
Mr. Michael Prince, Director Franchise
   Development

Plan Ahead Events is a home-based, full-service event management company serving clients worldwide. We offer creative solutions for meetings, conventions, trade shows, special events, and incentive travel, and will handle all the details for planning your event, from concept to completion.

Touted as one of the top "50 Best Jobs in America" by CNN/Money Magazine in April 2006 and reported by Entrepreneur.com as a $500 billion industry worldwide, event planning is one of the most exciting business opportunities available. With the trend toward Corporate America learning to outsource most of their meeting planning functions, there is no doubt that investing in a Plan Ahead Events franchise is the right choice for you. Join the only franchise in the event planning industry that was inducted into the Entrepreneur Magazine Franchise 500 in its first year of operation.

BACKGROUND: IFA MEMBER
Established: 2007; 1st Franchised: 2007
Franchised Units: 40
Company-Owned Units: 0
Total Units: 40

Dist.: US-37; CAN-1; O'seas-2
   North America: 20 States, 1 Provinces
   Density: 3 in GA, 3 in VA, 6 in FL
Projected New Units (12 Months): 65
Qualifications: NR

FINANCIAL/TERMS:
Cash Investment: $28-32K
Total Investment: $28-32K
Minimum Net Worth: $30K
Fees: Franchise - $24.5K
   Royalty - $300/month (first year); Ad.
   - $100/month (first year)
Earnings Claims Statement: No
Term of Contract (Years): 35/
Avg. # Of Employees: 1 FT, PT
Passive Ownership: Not Allowed
Encourage Conversions: NA
Area Develop. Agreements: No
Sub-Franchising Contracts: No
Expand In Territory: No
Space Needs: NA

SUPPORT & TRAINING:
Financial Assistance Provided: No
Site Selection Assistance: NA
Lease Negotiation Assistance: NA
Co-Operative Advertising: No
Franchisee Assoc./Member: No
Size Of Corporate Staff: 150
On-Going Support: ,,C,,,,G,H,I
Training: 1 week Franchisee's area;
   1 week WPB HQ

SPECIFIC EXPANSION PLANS:
US: All except MD, ND, SD, ME
Canada: No
Overseas: NR

⪻ ⪼

SWEET BEGINNINGS WEDDING CONSULTING & EVENT PLANNERS
105 - 1037 W. Broadway
Vancouver, BC V6H 1E3 Canada
Tel: (866) 730-5553 (604) 738-9552
Fax: (604) 876-6460
E-Mail: rob@asweetbeginning.com
Web Site: www.asweetbeginning.com
Mr. Rob Lancit, CEO

Sweet Beginnings is a full-service wedding consulting and event-planning franchise that also offers full decor and chair-cover rental services for events ranging from small gatherings to extravagant galas. Sweet

Beginnings' packages are individually tailored to each client's budget and style. In addition, Sweet Beginnings provides event planning for Christmas parties, grand openings, reunions, fashion shows, school events, birthday and anniversary parties, Bar/Bat Mitzvahs and other events.

BACKGROUND: IFA MEMBER
Established: 1997; 1st Franchised: 2004
Franchised Units: 16
Company-Owned Units: 2
Total Units: 18
Dist.: US-2; CAN-16; O'seas-0
North America: 2 States, 3 Provinces
Density: 2 in ON, 1 in CA, 8 in BC
Projected New Units (12 Months): 6

Qualifications: 3, 3, 3, 3, 3, 4
FINANCIAL/TERMS:
Cash Investment: $25-35K
Total Investment: $29-44K
Minimum Net Worth: $35K
Fees: Franchise - $10-20K
Royalty - $300; Ad. - $75
Earnings Claims Statement: No
Term of Contract (Years): 5/5
Avg. # Of Employees: 0 FT, 2 PT
Passive Ownership: Allowed
Encourage Conversions: NA
Area Develop. Agreements: Yes/10
Sub-Franchising Contracts: No
Expand In Territory: Yes
Space Needs: NA

SUPPORT & TRAINING:
Financial Assistance Provided: Yes (I)
Site Selection Assistance: NA
Lease Negotiation Assistance: NA
Co-Operative Advertising: No
Franchisee Assoc./Member: No
Size Of Corporate Staff: 4
On-Going Support: „C,D,,F,G,H,
Training: 3-4 days On-Site; 4-5 days
Corporate Office
SPECIFIC EXPANSION PLANS:
US: CA, FL, AZ, NV
Canada: ALL
Overseas: ALL

◄◄ ►►

For a full explanation
of the data provided
in the Franchisor
Profiles, please refer to
*Chapter 2, "How to Use
the Data."*

FIVE LARGEST PARTICIPANTS IN SURVEY

Company	# Fran- chised Units	# Co- Owned Units	# Total Units	Franchise Fee	On-Going Royalty	Total Investment
1. Management Recruiters/Sales Consultants	1,068	32	1,100	$84.9K	7%	$110-145K
2. Spherion	155	523	678	$25K	3-6%/25%	$98-164K
3. Express Employment Professionals	592	4	596	$35K	8-9%	$153,750-$241,500
4. Interim HomeStyle Services	267	22	289	$10K	5%	$35-70K
5. Labor Finders International	256	29	285	$20K	3%	$116-198K

All of the data provided are proprietary and should not be quoted without acknowledging *Bond's Franchise Guide.*

@WORK PERSONNEL SERVICES
3215 John Sevier Hwy.
Knoxville, TN 37920
Tel: (800) 383-0804 (865) 609-6911
Fax: (865) 573-1171
E-Mail: rmitchell@atwork.com
Web Site: www.atwork.com
Mr. Robert Mitchell, SVP Franchise Sales

@WORK PERSONNEL SERVICES announces its new 3-for-1 Franchise Program. For the cost of one franchise, @WORK offers temporary help, staff leasing and permanent placement programs for its franchisees. Here are some benefits of becoming a member of @WORK's network: franchise fee - $11,500; training fee - $2,500; sliding volume discount sale for royalty and service fees. Call our franchise sales department today to receive our information package.

BACKGROUND: IFA MEMBER
Established: 1987; 1st Franchised: 1992
Franchised Units: 50
Company-Owned Units: 4
Total Units: 54
Dist.: US-54; CAN-0; O'seas-0
 North America: 12 States, 0 Provinces
 Density: 15 in TN, 3 in NC, 2 in ME
Projected New Units (12 Months): 24
Qualifications: 3, 2, 3, 2, 3, 3
FINANCIAL/TERMS:
Cash Investment: $75K-$140K

Total Investment: $75K-$140K
Minimum Net Worth: $75K
Fees: Franchise - $1K
 Royalty - 8%; Ad. - 0%
Earnings Claims Statement: No
Term of Contract (Years): 10/5
Avg. # Of Employees: 3 FT, 1 PT
Passive Ownership: Discouraged
Encourage Conversions: Yes
Area Develop. Agreements: No
Sub-Franchising Contracts: No
Expand In Territory: Yes
Space Needs: 800 SF
SUPPORT & TRAINING:
Financial Assistance Provided: Yes (D)
Site Selection Assistance: Yes

Lease Negotiation Assistance: No
Co-Operative Advertising: No
Franchisee Assoc./Member: No
Size Of Corporate Staff: 15
On-Going Support: A,,C,D,,,,H,I
Training: 4-5 Days Corporate Office
SPECIFIC EXPANSION PLANS:
US: All United States
Canada: No
Overseas: NR

⋖⋖ ⋗⋗

ACCOUNTANTS INC.
111 Anza Blvd., # 400
Burlingame, CA 94010-1932
Tel: (800) 491-9411 (619) 741-8901
Fax: (619) 741-3556
E-Mail: franchise@accountantsinc.com
Web Site: www.accountantsinc.com
Ms. Christy Williams, Franchise Operations Director

Temporary and full time placement of accounting and finance professionals.

BACKGROUND: IFA MEMBER
Established: 1986; 1st Franchised: 1994
Franchised Units: 15
Company-Owned Units: <u>17</u>
Total Units: 32
Dist.: US-32; CAN-0; O'seas-0
North America: 13 States, 0 Provinces
Density: 3 in WA, 21 in CA
Projected New Units (12 Months): 5
Qualifications: 4, 5, 1, 1, 1, 5
FINANCIAL/TERMS:
Cash Investment: $174.5-224K
Total Investment: $174.5-224K
Minimum Net Worth: $145-200K
Fees: Franchise - $30K
Royalty - 7.5-10%/4K; Ad. - 2.5
w/Co-Op
Earnings Claims Statement: Yes
Term of Contract (Years): 10/10
Avg. # Of Employees: 6 FT, 0 PT
Passive Ownership: Not Allowed
Encourage Conversions: No
Area Develop. Agreements: No
Sub-Franchising Contracts: No
Expand In Territory: Yes
Space Needs: NR
SUPPORT & TRAINING:
Financial Assistance Provided: No
Site Selection Assistance: Yes
Lease Negotiation Assistance: Yes
Co-Operative Advertising: No
Franchisee Assoc./Member: No
Size Of Corporate Staff: 35
On-Going Support: ,,,,E,,,h,I

Training: Burlingame, CA;
Franchisee's Location
SPECIFIC EXPANSION PLANS:
US: All United States
Canada: No
Overseas: NR

⋖⋖ ⋗⋗

AHEAD HUMAN RESOURCES
2209 Heather Ln.
Louisville, KY 40218
Tel: (877) 485-5858 (502) 485-1000
Fax: (502) 485-0801
E-Mail: bellisb@aheadhr.com
Web Site: www.aheadhr.com
Mr. Bill Bellis, CEO

AHEAD HR brings a totally unique concept to the human resource franchise industry. SEE OUR WEBSITE! We're offering an industry-leading, top-flight temporary staffing franchise AND a PEO/HR outsourcing franchise, which is one-of-a-kind in the nation. If you want to be on the cutting edge of THE growth industry, SEE OUR WEBSITE!

BACKGROUND: IFA MEMBER
Established: 1995; 1st Franchised: 2000
Franchised Units: 8
Company-Owned Units: <u>1</u>
Total Units: 9
Dist.: US-9; CAN-0; O'seas-0
North America: 6 States, 0 Provinces
Density: 2 in WI, 2 in KY, 2 in CT
Projected New Units (12 Months): 23
Qualifications: 5, 5, 3, 3, 2, 5
FINANCIAL/TERMS:
Cash Investment: $17.7-23.7K
Total Investment: $105K-171.6K
Minimum Net Worth: Varies
Fees: Franchise - $17.7-23.7K
Royalty - Varies; Ad. - Varies
Earnings Claims Statement: No
Term of Contract (Years): 5/5
Avg. # Of Employees: 1 FT, 1 PT
Passive Ownership: Discouraged
Encourage Conversions: No
Area Develop. Agreements: No
Sub-Franchising Contracts: No
Expand In Territory: Yes
Space Needs: 100-1,500 SF

SUPPORT & TRAINING:
Financial Assistance Provided: No
Site Selection Assistance: No
Lease Negotiation Assistance: No
Co-Operative Advertising: No
Franchisee Assoc./Member: Yes/Yes
Size Of Corporate Staff: 22
On-Going Support: A,,C,D,,,,,I
Training: 2 Weeks Louisville, KY
SPECIFIC EXPANSION PLANS:
US: All United States
Canada: No
Overseas: NR

⋖⋖ ⋗⋗

AMERICAN RECRUITERS
6400 N. Andrews Ave., # 100
Ft. Lauderdale, FL 33309-2075
Tel: (800) 493-9201 (954) 492-4592
Fax: (954) 958-3925
E-Mail: roy@arcimail.com
Web Site: www.americanrecruiters.com
Mr. Roy Lantz, Vice President of Franchising

AMERICAN RECRUITERS offers retained and contingent executive search services, personnel placement and human resources consulting and training services. We provide exceptional training services and a state-of-the-art recruiting information system to get franchises up and running quickly. We also provide a universal database of clients, job orders and candidates which is uniquely shared by all franchises.

BACKGROUND:
Established: 1982; 1st Franchised: 1999
Franchised Units: 6
Company-Owned Units: <u>2</u>
Total Units: 8
Dist.: US-8; CAN-0; O'seas-0
North America: 8 States, Provinces
Density: 2 in FL, 1 in GA, 2 in VA
Projected New Units (12 Months): 12
Qualifications: 4, 5, 3, 3, 2, 5
FINANCIAL/TERMS:
Cash Investment: $75-100K
Total Investment: $100-150K
Minimum Net Worth: $250K
Fees: Franchise - $50K
Royalty - 7%; Ad. - NA
Earnings Claims Statement: No
Term of Contract (Years): 5/5
Avg. # Of Employees: 4-6 FT, 0 PT
Passive Ownership: Not Allowed
Encourage Conversions: NA
Area Develop. Agreements: No

Sub-Franchising Contracts: No
Expand In Territory: Yes
Space Needs: NA
SUPPORT & TRAINING:
Financial Assistance Provided: No
Site Selection Assistance: Yes
Lease Negotiation Assistance: Yes
Co-Operative Advertising: No
Franchisee Assoc./Member: Yes/Yes
Size Of Corporate Staff: 50
On-Going Support: A,,C,d,e,,G,H,I
Training:15 Business Days Ft. Lauderdale, FL
SPECIFIC EXPANSION PLANS:
US: East Coast
Canada: No
Overseas: NR

≼≼ ≽≽

ATC HEALTHCARE SERVICES
1983 Marcus Ave., # E122
New Hyde Park, NY 11042-1016
Tel: (800) 444-4633 (516) 750-1694
Fax: (516) 750-1783
E-Mail: ibraun@atchealthcare.com
Web Site: www.atchealthcare.com
Mr. Irv Braun, Director of Business Development

ATC HEALTHCARE SERVICES provide temporary staffing

BACKGROUND: IFA MEMBER
Established: 1984; 1st Franchised: 1995
Franchised Units: 33
Company-Owned Units: 4
Total Units: 37
Dist.: US-37; CAN-0; O'seas-0
North America: 0 States, 0 Provinces
Density: 3 in PA, 4 in OH, 5 in CA
Projected New Units (12 Months): 9
Qualifications: 4, 4, 5, 4, 3, 5
FINANCIAL/TERMS:
Cash Investment: $30-75K
Total Investment: $100K
Minimum Net Worth: $125K
Fees: Franchise - $29.5K
  Royalty - Varies; Ad. - 0%
Earnings Claims Statement: No
Term of Contract (Years): 10/5/5/
Avg. # Of Employees: 3 FT, 2 PT
Passive Ownership: Allowed
Encourage Conversions: Yes
Area Develop. Agreements: Yes/1
Sub-Franchising Contracts: No
Expand In Territory: Yes
Space Needs: 1,000 SF
SUPPORT & TRAINING:
Financial Assistance Provided: Yes (D)

Site Selection Assistance: Yes
Lease Negotiation Assistance: Yes
Co-Operative Advertising: No
Franchisee Assoc./Member: No
Size Of Corporate Staff: 35
On-Going Support: A,B,C,D,E,,G,H,
Training:1 Week Corporate Headquarters
SPECIFIC EXPANSION PLANS:
US: All United States
Canada: All Canada
Overseas: NR

≼≼ ≽≽

CAREERS USA
6501 Congress Ave., # 200
Boca Raton, Fl 33487-2829
Tel: (888) 227-3377 (561) 995-7000
Fax: (561) 995-7001
E-Mail: franchising@careersusa.com
Web Site: www.careersusa.com
Ms. Trudy Feldman, EVP Franchise Development

CAREERS USA provides temporary, temp to hire, and permanent personnel to businesses and corporations in your market area. CAREERS USA's proprietary computer software program computes the franchisee's temporary payroll, taxes and insurance. You, the franchisee, can download and analyze your sales, margins, rates, cash flow, etc. CAREERS USA finances 100% of your temporary payroll and 100% of your accounts receivable, helping you eliminate cash flow problems. Territories available nationally.

BACKGROUND: IFA MEMBER
Established: 1981; 1st Franchised: 1989
Franchised Units: 9
Company-Owned Units: 17
Total Units: 26
Dist.: US-26; CAN-0; O'seas-0
North America: 8 States, 0 Provinces
Density: 5 in PA, 3 in NJ, 6 in FL
Projected New Units (12 Months): 12
Qualifications: 3, 4, 2, 3, 3, 4
FINANCIAL/TERMS:
Cash Investment: $14.5K
Total Investment: $110.5K-154.5K
Minimum Net Worth: $150K
Fees: Franchise - $14.5K
  Royalty - 7%/Varies; Ad. - NA
Earnings Claims Statement: No
Term of Contract (Years): 10/5
Avg. # Of Employees: 3 FT, 0 PT
Passive Ownership: Discouraged
Encourage Conversions: Yes
Area Develop. Agreements: No

Sub-Franchising Contracts: No
Expand In Territory: Yes
Space Needs: 1,000-1,200 SF
SUPPORT & TRAINING:
Financial Assistance Provided: No
Site Selection Assistance: Yes
Lease Negotiation Assistance: Yes
Co-Operative Advertising: No
Franchisee Assoc./Member: No
Size Of Corporate Staff: 38
On-Going Support: A,b,C,D,E,,G,H,I
Training: 1 Week Your Center Location;
  2 Weeks Boca Raton, FL Headquarters
SPECIFIC EXPANSION PLANS:
US: All United States
Canada: All Canada
Overseas: All Countries

≼≼ ≽≽

DALE CARNEGIE TRAINING
290 Motor Pkwy.
Hauppauge, NY 11788-5105
Tel: (631) 415-9378
Fax: (631) 415-9358
E-Mail: joe_garcia@dalecarnegie.com
Web Site: www.dalecarnegie.com
Mr. Joseph Garcia, Senior Vice President Franchising

If you're committed to being the premier, local human resources development partner of a business with global reach and recognition, then DALE CARNEGIE TRAINING is an exceptional opportunity for you. DALE CARNEGIE TRAINING services thousands of organizations throughout the world in 74 countries and 24 languages, providing effective business solutions that can be tailored to meet a client's specific needs.

BACKGROUND: IFA MEMBER
Established: 1912; 1st Franchised: 1999
Franchised Units: 204
Company-Owned Units: 3
Total Units: 207
Dist.: US-97; CAN-5; O'seas-105
North America: 0 States, 0 Provinces
Density: NR
Projected New Units (12 Months): 7-10
Qualifications: 4, 5, 2, 4, 2, 5
FINANCIAL/TERMS:
Cash Investment: $100K
Total Investment: $150-200K
Minimum Net Worth: $200K
Fees: Franchise - $25K
  Royalty - 12%; Ad. - 3%-US
Earnings Claims Statement: No
Term of Contract (Years): 15/10

Avg. # Of Employees: 3 FT, 10 PT
Passive Ownership: Not Allowed
Encourage Conversions: NA
Area Develop. Agreements: Yes/1
Sub-Franchising Contracts: No
Expand In Territory: Yes
Space Needs: NA

SUPPORT & TRAINING:

Financial Assistance Provided: No
Site Selection Assistance: NA
Lease Negotiation Assistance: NA
Co-Operative Advertising: Yes
Franchisee Assoc./Member: Yes/Yes
Size Of Corporate Staff: 70
On-Going Support: 0,B,C,D,E,,G,H,
Training: As Needed On-Site and Head-
  quarters; Varies On-Site; 7-10 Days
  Headquarters

SPECIFIC EXPANSION PLANS:

US: No
Canada: No
Overseas: Japan, Poland, Denmark,
  Portugal, Australia, Turkey

≪ ≫

EXPRESS EMPLOYMENT PROFESSIONALS

8516 N. W. Expy.
Oklahoma City, OK 73162-5145
Tel: (877) 652-6400 (405) 840-5000
Fax: (405) 717-5665
E-Mail: franchising@expresspros.com
Web Site: www.expressfranchising.com
Mr. Fred Bartliff, VP of Franchising

Express franchise offices provide a full range of business-to-business staffing and HR services. The franchise includes all three service lines in one agreement: temporary/contract staffing, professional search/direct hire, and HR services. Express offers new franchise owners the unique chance to earn money by helping people grow their careers and businesses while impacting the local community. For established staffing business owners, we provide the opportunity to grow your business and advance the services provided. Independent staffing owners that have teamed with Express have benefited from our network of support, allowing them to keep up in this fast paced business.

BACKGROUND: IFA MEMBER

Established: 1983; 1st Franchised: 1985

Franchised Units: 592
Company-Owned Units: 4
Total Units: 596
Dist.: US-554; CAN-27; O'seas-15
  North America: 49 States, 3 Provinces
  Density: 55 in TX, 34 in OK, 49 in CA
Projected New Units (12 Months): 50
Qualifications: 4, 4, 3, 4, 4, 4

FINANCIAL/TERMS:

Cash Investment: $130-170K
Total Investment: $153,750-$241,500
Minimum Net Worth: $300K
Fees: Franchise - $35K
  Royalty - 8-9%; Ad. - 0.6%
Earnings Claims Statement: Yes
Term of Contract (Years): 5/5
Avg. # Of Employees: 3 FT, 0 PT
Passive Ownership: Not Allowed
Encourage Conversions: Yes
Area Develop. Agreements: No
Sub-Franchising Contracts: No
Expand In Territory: Yes
Space Needs: 1,000-1,200 SF

SUPPORT & TRAINING:

Financial Assistance Provided: No
Site Selection Assistance: Yes
Lease Negotiation Assistance: Yes
Co-Operative Advertising: Yes
Franchisee Assoc./Member: No
Size Of Corporate Staff: 200
On-Going Support: A,,C,D,E,,G,H,I
Training: 2 Weeks Oklahoma City, OK;
  1 Week Certified Training Office (In
  Field)

SPECIFIC EXPANSION PLANS:

US: All United States
Canada: All Except Quebec
Overseas: South Africa and Australia

≪ ≫

FPC (FORTUNE PERSONNEL CONSULTANTS)

1140 Avenue of the Americas, 5th Fl.
New York, NY 10036-2711
Tel: (800) 886-7839 (212) 302-1141
Fax: (212) 302-2422
E-Mail: jpdusold@fpcnational.com
Web Site: www.fpcnational.com
Mr. JP Dusold, Manager of Franchise
  Development

As one of the largest and most successful executive recruiting firms in the world, FPC (F-O-R-T-U-N-E PERSONNEL CONSULTANTS) has set a distinguished standard of leadership and integrity in the executive placement industry. Franchisees enjoy all of today's technologies, along with good old-fashioned service.

Intensive training and unparalleled support by industry experienced professionals securely places qualified candidates in their own professional business. Extensive on-going training, mentoring and coaching.

BACKGROUND:

Established: 1959; 1st Franchised: 1973
Franchised Units: 70
Company-Owned Units: 0
Total Units: 70
Dist.: US-69; CAN-1; O'seas-0
  North America: 28 States, 0 Provinces
  Density: 7 in NJ, 7 in MA, 7 in FL
Projected New Units (12 Months): 12-15
Qualifications: 4, 3, 3, 4, 2, 4

FINANCIAL/TERMS:

Cash Investment: $93-138K
Total Investment: $93-138K
Minimum Net Worth: $250K
Fees: Franchise - $40K
  Royalty - 7%; Ad. - 1%
Earnings Claims Statement: Yes
Term of Contract (Years): 20/10
Avg. # Of Employees: 3-5 FT, 1-2 PT
Passive Ownership: Not Allowed
Encourage Conversions: NA
Area Develop. Agreements: No
Sub-Franchising Contracts: No
Expand In Territory: Yes
Space Needs: 1,000 SF

SUPPORT & TRAINING:

Financial Assistance Provided: Yes (D)
Site Selection Assistance: Yes
Lease Negotiation Assistance: Yes
Co-Operative Advertising: No
Franchisee Assoc./Member: Yes/Yes
Size Of Corporate Staff: 10
On-Going Support: A,B,C,D,E,F,G,H,I
Training: 5 Days Franchise Location;
  2 Weeks Home Office, New York, NY

SPECIFIC EXPANSION PLANS:

US: All United States
Canada: All Canada
Overseas: NR

≪ ≫

INTERIM HOMESTYLE SERVICES

1601 Sawgrass Corporate Pkwy.
Sunrise, FL 33323
Tel: (800) 338-7786 + 2699 (954) 858-2699
Fax: (954) 858-2720
E-Mail: johnmarquez@interimhealthcare.com
Web Site: www.interimhealthcare.com
Mr. John Marquez, Senior Director

INTERIM HOMESTYLE SERVICES is the brand name for non-medical services provided by INTERIM HEALTHCARE, the country's oldest health care franchise organization. Interim franchise owners have one of the highest records of stability with an average collective of 20 years.

BACKGROUND:

Established: 1956;   1st Franchised: 1966
Franchised Units: 267
Company-Owned Units: 22
Total Units: 289
Dist.:   US-289; CAN-0; O'seas-0
  North America: 39 States, Provinces
  Density: 24 in FL, 27 in NC, 26 in OH
Projected New Units (12 Months):   5
Qualifications: 5, 5, 2, 3, 3, 5

FINANCIAL/TERMS:

Cash Investment: $35-70K
Total Investment: $35-70K
Minimum Net Worth: $100K
Fees: Franchise - $10K
  Royalty - 5%;   Ad. - 0.25%
Earnings Claims Statement: No
Term of Contract (Years):   5/10
Avg. # Of Employees: 3 FT, 0 PT
Passive Ownership: Discouraged
Encourage Conversions: Yes
Area Develop. Agreements: No
Sub-Franchising Contracts: No
Expand In Territory: Yes
Space Needs: 1,000-1,20060 SF

SUPPORT & TRAINING:

Financial Assistance Provided: Yes (D)
Site Selection Assistance: Yes
Lease Negotiation Assistance: Yes
Co-Operative Advertising: No
Franchisee Assoc./Member: Yes/Yes
Size Of Corporate Staff: 100
On-Going Support: A,B,C,D,E,,G,H,I
Training: 1 Week Sunrise, FL;
  ;

SPECIFIC EXPANSION PLANS:

US: All United States
Canada: No
Overseas: Latin America, Mexico, Europe

≪ ≫

**LABOR FINDERS
INTERNATIONAL**
11426 N. Jog Rd.
Palm Beach Gardens, FL 33418
Tel: (800) 864-7749 + 3 (561) 273-8222

Fax: (561) 273-8163
E-Mail: franchise@laborfinders.com
Web Site: www.laborfinders.com
Mr. Bill Watson, Dir. Franchise Development

Labor Finders is the oldest and largest industrial staffing franchise in the nation. We offer a specialized labor staffing service that supplies highly productive skilled, semi-skilled and unskilled workers to companies in construction, industrial and commercial business segments. The strength of Labor Finders continues to come from the commitment of our franchisees toward customer satisfaction. Our franchisee family understands that success depends on exceptional service, respect for all employees and concern for their safety, and appreciation for team members and their personal contributions. We always strive to better support and serve our franchise family in achieving these goals.

BACKGROUND: IFA MEMBER

Established: 1975;   1st Franchised: 1980
Franchised Units: 256
Company-Owned Units: 29
Total Units: 285
Dist.:   US-285; CAN-0; O'seas-0
  North America: 52 States, 0 Provinces
  Density: 27 in GA, 57 in FL, 33 in CA
Projected New Units (12 Months):   15
Qualifications: 4, 4, 2, 3, 4, 4

FINANCIAL/TERMS:

Cash Investment: $75K-125K
Total Investment: $116K-198K
Minimum Net Worth: $200K
Fees: Franchise - $20K
  Royalty - 3%;   Ad. - 0%
Earnings Claims Statement: No
Term of Contract (Years):   10/10
Avg. # Of Employees: 2 FT, PT
Passive Ownership: Allowed
Encourage Conversions: Yes
Area Develop. Agreements: Yes/10
Sub-Franchising Contracts: No
Expand In Territory: Yes
Space Needs: 1,000-1,200 SF

SUPPORT & TRAINING:

Financial Assistance Provided: Yes (D)
Site Selection Assistance: Yes
Lease Negotiation Assistance: No
Co-Operative Advertising: No
Franchisee Assoc./Member: Yes/Yes
Size Of Corporate Staff: 24
On-Going Support: ,,C,D,E,,G,h,I
Training: 1 Week On-Site;
  2 Weeks Operating Unit;1 WeekClassroom

SPECIFIC EXPANSION PLANS:

US: All United States
Canada: All Canada
Overseas: NR

≪ ≫

LINK STAFFING SERVICES
1800 Bering Dr., # 800
Houston, TX 77057-3151
Tel: (800) 848-5465 (713) 784-4400 + 1065
Fax: (713) 784-4454
E-Mail: franchise@linkstaffing.com
Web Site: www.linkstaffing.com
Mr. Brandon Campbell, Director, Franchise Development

Link Staffing is a sales-driven, relationship-building, community-based industrial temporary labor staffing franchise. Link can provide for a wide range of positions including skilled crafts and trades, light industrial and general labor employees. Link also services positions in office, clerical and administration. Link Staffing provides valued services for its clients such as long and short term assignments, temporary to full time, payroll functions, on-site management, customized new employee orientations for the work site and a comprehensive screening process. Link also offers risk management services like client site evaluations, employee safety programs, and pre-employment, post accident and random drug screening.

BACKGROUND: IFA MEMBER

Established: 1980;   1st Franchised: 1994
Franchised Units: 48
Company-Owned Units: 10
Total Units: 58
Dist.:   US-58; CAN-0; O'seas-0
  North America: 13 States, 0 Provinces
  Density: 7 in FL, 8 in CA, 23 in TX
Projected New Units (12 Months):   10
Qualifications: 4, 4, 2, 3, 4, 5

FINANCIAL/TERMS:

Cash Investment: $62K-82K
Total Investment: $85K-158K
Minimum Net Worth: $150K-200K
Fees: Franchise - $17K
  Royalty - Varies;   Ad. - 0%
Earnings Claims Statement: Yes

Term of Contract (Years): 10/5/5/5/5
Avg. # Of Employees: 2-3 FT, 0 PT
Passive Ownership: Discouraged
Encourage Conversions: Yes
Area Develop. Agreements: No
Sub-Franchising Contracts: No
Expand In Territory: Yes
Space Needs: 1,200-1,500 SF

SUPPORT & TRAINING:
Financial Assistance Provided: Yes (D)
Site Selection Assistance: Yes
Lease Negotiation Assistance: Yes
Co-Operative Advertising: Yes
Franchisee Assoc./Member: Yes/Yes
Size Of Corporate Staff: 30
On-Going Support: A,B,C,D,E,,G,H,I
Training: 5 Days (Sales) Support Center, TX; 10 Days Field Training; 5 Days (Operations) Support Center, TX

SPECIFIC EXPANSION PLANS:
US: All United States
Canada: No
Overseas: NR

◄◄ ►►

LLOYD PERSONNEL SYSTEMS
445 Broadhollow Rd., # 119
Melville, NY 11747-3601
Tel: (888) 292-6678 + 708 (631) 777-7600 + 708
Fax: (631) 777-7620
E-Mail: jbanks@lloydstaffing.com
Web Site: www.lloydstaffing.com
Mr. Jason Banks, VP Franchise Operations

Since 1971, we have successfully served thousands of employers, job seekers and temporary employees. Our blended service concept truly embodies the entire staffing scope, including temporary personnel, consultants, direct hire placement and executive search. And because we recognize that the field of human resources has significantly changed its structure and focus over the years, we've added several complimentary and compatible staffing components to enhance the support we provide.

BACKGROUND: IFA MEMBER
Established: 1971; 1st Franchised: 1986
Franchised Units: 6
Company-Owned Units: 6
Total Units: 12
Dist.: US-12; CAN-0; O'seas-0
North America: 0 States, 0 Provinces
Density: 5 in NY, 2 in NJ, 2 in CT
Projected New Units (12 Months): 3

Qualifications: 4, 5, 4, 3, 3, 5
FINANCIAL/TERMS:
Cash Investment: $85-110K
Total Investment: $94.5-159.8K
Minimum Net Worth: $300K
Fees: Franchise - $20K
  Royalty - 60/40-7%; Ad. - NA
Earnings Claims Statement: No
Term of Contract (Years): 10/10
Avg. # Of Employees: 4 FT, 0 PT
Passive Ownership: Not Allowed
Encourage Conversions: No
Area Develop. Agreements: No
Sub-Franchising Contracts: No
Expand In Territory: Yes
Space Needs: 1,500 SF

SUPPORT & TRAINING:
Financial Assistance Provided: Yes (D)
Site Selection Assistance: Yes
Lease Negotiation Assistance: Yes
Co-Operative Advertising: No
Franchisee Assoc./Member: No
Size Of Corporate Staff: 162
On-Going Support: A,,C,D,E,,g,h,I
Training: 1 Week Your Location; 2 Weeks Melville, NY

SPECIFIC EXPANSION PLANS:
US: All U.S.
Canada: No
Overseas: NR

◄◄ ►►

**MANAGEMENT RECRUITERS/
SALES CONSULTANTS**
200 Public Sq., 30 Fl.
Cleveland, OH 44114-2301
Tel: (800) 875-4000 (216) 416-8211
Fax: (216) 696-6612
E-Mail: natasha.gibson@mrinetwork.com
Web Site: www.mrinetwork.com
Ms. Raine Austen, Franchise Sales Representative

Complete range of recruitment and human resource services, including: permanent executive, mid-management, professional, marketing, sales management and sales placement; contract professional and sales staffing; video-conferencing; permanent and contract office support personnel; with coverage on all continents. Franchises are available throughout the U.S. and internationally.

BACKGROUND: IFA MEMBER
Established: 1957; 1st Franchised: 1965
Franchised Units: 1068
Company-Owned Units: 32
Total Units: 1100

Dist.: US-946; CAN-0; O'seas-154
North America: 50 States, 0 Provinces
Density: 60 in NC, 64 in FL, 62 in CA
Projected New Units (12 Months): 80
Qualifications: 3, 4, 1, 4, 3, 3
FINANCIAL/TERMS:
Cash Investment: $110-145K
Total Investment: $110-145K
Minimum Net Worth: NA
Fees: Franchise - $84.9K
  Royalty - 7%; Ad. - 0.5%
Earnings Claims Statement: Yes
Term of Contract (Years): 10-20/5
Avg. # Of Employees: 3-4 FT, 1-2 PT
Passive Ownership: Discouraged
Encourage Conversions: Yes
Area Develop. Agreements: No
Sub-Franchising Contracts: No
Expand In Territory: Yes
Space Needs: 600-1,000 SF

SUPPORT & TRAINING:
Financial Assistance Provided: Yes (D)
Site Selection Assistance: Yes
Lease Negotiation Assistance: Yes
Co-Operative Advertising: No
Franchisee Assoc./Member: Yes/Yes
Size Of Corporate Staff: 105
On-Going Support: a,b,C,D,E,,G,H,I
Training: 4 Weeks Cleveland, OH; 5 Days Franchisee's Location

SPECIFIC EXPANSION PLANS:
US: All United States
Canada: Yes
Overseas: NR

◄◄ ►►

NURSEFINDERS
1701 E. Lamar Blvd., # 200
Arlington, TX 76006
Tel: (800) 445-0459 (817) 460-1181
Fax: (817) 462-9139
E-Mail: ed.mcguinness@nursefinders.com
Web Site: www.nursefinders.com
Mr. Ed McGuinness, Vice President of Franchising

Largest provider in United States of temporary medical staffing to hospitals and other health care facilities. Ranked Number 1 in category by Entrepreneur Magazine. We also provide the full spectrum of home health care.

BACKGROUND:
Established: 1974; 1st Franchised: 1978
Franchised Units: 54
Company-Owned Units: 68
Total Units: 122
Dist.: US-122; CAN-0; O'seas-0

North America: 31 States, 0 Provinces
Density: 8 in IL, 14 in FL, 7 in CA
Projected New Units (12 Months): 10
Qualifications: NR

FINANCIAL/TERMS:

Cash Investment: $50-100K
Total Investment: $110-200K
Minimum Net Worth: $250K
Fees: Franchise - $19.6K
Royalty - 7%; Ad. - 0%
Earnings Claims Statement: No
Term of Contract (Years): 10/5/5/
Avg. # Of Employees: 5 FT, 100 PT
Passive Ownership: Discouraged
Encourage Conversions: Yes
Area Develop. Agreements: Yes/1
Sub-Franchising Contracts: No
Expand In Territory: Yes
Space Needs: 1,500-2,000 SF

SUPPORT & TRAINING:

Financial Assistance Provided: Yes (D)
Site Selection Assistance: Yes
Lease Negotiation Assistance: Yes
Co-Operative Advertising: No
Franchisee Assoc./Member: No
Size Of Corporate Staff: 62
On-Going Support: A,B,C,D,E,,G,h,I
Training: 2 Weeks Arlington, TX; 1 Week
Company Office; 2 Weeks On-Site

SPECIFIC EXPANSION PLANS:

US: All United States
Canada: No
Overseas: NR

≪ ≫

PRIDESTAFF

6780 N. West Ave., # 103
Fresno, CA 93711-1393
Tel: (800) 774-3316 (559) 432-7780 + 116
Fax: (559) 432-4371
E-Mail: jblocker@pridestaff.com
Web Site: www.pridestaff.com
Ms. Jane Blocker, EVP/Chief Operating
Officer

We specialize in supplemental staffing (temporary help), outsourcing and full-time placement. PRIDESTAFF fills administrative, clerical, customer service, data entry, word processing and light industrial positions. The staffing industry is one of the fastest-growing industries in the United States.

BACKGROUND:

Established: 1974; 1st Franchised: 1994
Franchised Units: 20
Company-Owned Units: 7
Total Units: 27

Dist.: US-27; CAN-0; O'seas-0
North America: 13 States, 0 Provinces
Density: 4 in IL, 12 in CA, 4 in AZ
Projected New Units (12 Months): NR
Qualifications: NR

FINANCIAL/TERMS:

Cash Investment: $75-100K
Total Investment: $80.4-126.9K
Minimum Net Worth: NA
Fees: Franchise - $12.5K
Royalty - 65%Gross Margin; Ad. - NA
Earnings Claims Statement: No
Term of Contract (Years): 10/5/5/5/
Avg. # Of Employees: 2 FT, 0 PT
Passive Ownership: Not Allowed
Encourage Conversions: No
Area Develop. Agreements: No
Sub-Franchising Contracts: No
Expand In Territory: Yes
Space Needs: 1,200 SF

SUPPORT & TRAINING:

Financial Assistance Provided: No
Site Selection Assistance: Yes
Lease Negotiation Assistance: Yes
Co-Operative Advertising: No
Franchisee Assoc./Member: No
Size Of Corporate Staff: 16
On-Going Support: A,,C,D,E,,G,H,I
Training: 1 Week Fresno, CA;
1 Week Branch Office

SPECIFIC EXPANSION PLANS:

US: All United States
Canada: NR
Overseas: NR

≪ ≫

REMEDY INTELLIGENT STAFFING

3820 State St.
Santa Barbara, CA 93105
Tel: (800) 688-6162 (949) 425-7600
Fax: (949) 425-7992
E-Mail: franchise@remedystaff.com
Web Site: www.remedystaff.com
Mr. Irwin Much, President, Franchise Division

A national full-service staffing company, providing contingent workers in the disciplines of law, accounting, professional office auditing, clerical and light industrial. Fully automated office, with exclusive, validated behavioral testing. Entire back-office support and exclusive territories.

BACKGROUND: IFA MEMBER
Established: 1965; 1st Franchised: 1987
Franchised Units: 100
Company-Owned Units: 130
Total Units: 230
Dist.: US-230; CAN-0; O'seas-0
North America: 40 States, 0 Provinces
Density: 18 in TX, 24 in FL, 88 in CA
Projected New Units (12 Months): 30
Qualifications: 4, 4, 4, 3, 4, 5

FINANCIAL/TERMS:

Cash Investment: $30-60K
Total Investment: $95-150K
Minimum Net Worth: $250K
Fees: Franchise - $25K
Royalty - Varies; Ad. - 0%
Earnings Claims Statement: No
Term of Contract (Years): 15/10
Avg. # Of Employees: 5 FT, 1 PT
Passive Ownership: Discouraged
Encourage Conversions: Yes
Area Develop. Agreements: Yes/1
Sub-Franchising Contracts: No
Expand In Territory: Yes
Space Needs: 1,400 SF

SUPPORT & TRAINING:

Financial Assistance Provided: No
Site Selection Assistance: Yes
Lease Negotiation Assistance: Yes
Co-Operative Advertising: No
Franchisee Assoc./Member: Yes/Yes
Size Of Corporate Staff: 160
On-Going Support: A,,C,D,E,,G,,I
Training: 2 Weeks Home Office;
1 Week On-Site

SPECIFIC EXPANSION PLANS:

US: All Except CA,WA,OR,NM,CO
Canada: All Canada
Overseas: NR

≪ ≫

SANFORD ROSE ASSOCIATES

1305 Mall of Georgia Blvd., # 160
Buford, GA 30519
Tel: (800) 731-7724 (330) 670-9797 + 102
Fax: (330) 670-9798
E-Mail: rjcarter@sanfordrose.com
Web Site: www.sanfordrose.com
Mr. Marty Thallman, VP Franchise Development

We represent companies and institutions around the world in finding high-quality executives, managers and professionals for important position openings through our proprietary Dimensional Search process.

BACKGROUND: IFA MEMBER
Established: 1959; 1st Franchised: 1970

Franchised Units: 67
Company-Owned Units: 0
Total Units: 67
Dist.: US-64; CAN-0; O'seas-3
  North America: 25 States, 0 Provinces
  Density: 5 in KY, 7 in OH, 10 in CA
Projected New Units (12 Months): 10
Qualifications: 4, 5, 4, 4, 4, 5

FINANCIAL/TERMS:
Cash Investment: $92.1-127.5K
Total Investment: $92.1-127.5K
Minimum Net Worth: $350K
Fees: Franchise - $65K
  Royalty - 7-5%; Ad. - 0.5%
Earnings Claims Statement: No
Term of Contract (Years): 10/5
Avg. # Of Employees: 3 FT, 1 PT
Passive Ownership: Not Allowed
Encourage Conversions: Yes
Area Develop. Agreements: No
Sub-Franchising Contracts: No
Expand In Territory: No
Space Needs: 600-1,000 SF

SUPPORT & TRAINING:
Financial Assistance Provided: No
Site Selection Assistance: Yes
Lease Negotiation Assistance: Yes
Co-Operative Advertising: No
Franchisee Assoc./Member: Yes/Yes
Size Of Corporate Staff: 6
On-Going Support: ,,C,D,,,G,H,I
Training: 13 Days Corporate
  Headquarters; 1.5 Days On-Site

SPECIFIC EXPANSION PLANS:
US: All United States
Canada: All Canada
Overseas: All Countries

≪ ≫

SNELLING STAFFING SERVICES
12801 N. Central Expy., # 600
Dallas, TX 75243
Tel: (800) 766-5556 (972) 776-1434
Fax: (972) 383-3893
E-Mail: david.lamb@snelling.com
Web Site: www.snelling.com
Mr. David Lamb, VP Franchise Development

SNELLING helps you live the American dream - To Own Your Own Business. Our full-service staffing franchise offers temporary, temp-to-hire and career placement opportunities to both people needing jobs and companies needing good people. SNELLING has been helping others achieve the success they desire for neary 50 years and has one of the most recognized names in the industry. We offer: a proven operating system; comprehensive training and on-going support; fully computerized payroll financing, etc.

BACKGROUND: IFA MEMBER
Established: 1951; 1st Franchised: 1956
Franchised Units: 140
Company-Owned Units: 44
Total Units: 184
Dist.: US-184; CAN-0; O'seas-0
  North America: 43 States, 0 Provinces
  Density: 32 in TX, 18 in MI, 17 in FL
Projected New Units (12 Months): 10
Qualifications: 5, 5, 1, 3, 1, 5

FINANCIAL/TERMS:
Cash Investment: $50-100K
Total Investment: $104-184K
Minimum Net Worth: $400K
Fees: Franchise - $25K
  Royalty - % Gr. Margin; Ad. - 0.5-2%
Earnings Claims Statement: No
Term of Contract (Years): 10/10
Avg. # Of Employees: 2-3 FT, 0 PT
Passive Ownership: Not Allowed
Encourage Conversions: Yes
Area Develop. Agreements: No
Sub-Franchising Contracts: No
Expand In Territory: Yes
Space Needs: 1,000-1,200 SF

SUPPORT & TRAINING:
Financial Assistance Provided: Yes (I)
Site Selection Assistance: Yes
Lease Negotiation Assistance: Yes
Co-Operative Advertising: No
Franchisee Assoc./Member: Yes/Yes
Size Of Corporate Staff: 110
On-Going Support: A,,C,D,E,,G,H,I
Training: 8 Days Snelling University

SPECIFIC EXPANSION PLANS:
US: Yes
Canada: No
Overseas: NR

≪ ≫

SPHERION
925 N. Point Pkwy., # 100
Alpharetta, GA 30005
Tel: (800) 903-0082 (678) 867-3702
Fax: (678) 867-3190
E-Mail: robertamarcantonio@spherion.com
Web Site: www.spherion.com
Ms. Roberta Marcantonio, VP Market Expansion

SPHERION franchise opportunities provide individuals a chance to join an exciting and rewarding industry: temporary staffing. We placed millions of workers in flexible and full-time jobs during our nearly 60 years in business. Continuous innovation and decades of growth have helped SPHERION become an industry leader. Entrepreneur Magazine ranked SPHERION Best Staffing Service for five straight years. Our franchisees contribute their talent, commitment and passion to building our brand.

BACKGROUND: IFA MEMBER
Established: 1946; 1st Franchised: 1956
Franchised Units: 155
Company-Owned Units: 523
Total Units: 678
Dist.: US-646; CAN-32; O'seas-0
  North America: 46 States, 8 Provinces
  Density: 27 in OH, 29 in FL, 29 in CA
Projected New Units (12 Months): 10
Qualifications: 5, 4, 1, 3, 4, 4

FINANCIAL/TERMS:
Cash Investment: $100-170K
Total Investment: $98-164K
Minimum Net Worth: $100K
Fees: Franchise - $25K
  Royalty - 3-6%/25%; Ad. - 0.25%
Earnings Claims Statement: Yes
Term of Contract (Years): 10/5
Avg. # Of Employees: 3 FT, 0 PT
Passive Ownership: Not Allowed
Encourage Conversions: Yes
Area Develop. Agreements: No
Sub-Franchising Contracts: No
Expand In Territory: Yes
Space Needs: 1,500 SF

SUPPORT & TRAINING:
Financial Assistance Provided: No
Site Selection Assistance: Yes
Lease Negotiation Assistance: Yes
Co-Operative Advertising: Yes
Franchisee Assoc./Member: No
Size Of Corporate Staff: 525
On-Going Support: A,B,C,D,E,,G,H,I
Training: Addl. Self-Paced Instruction;
  Over 112 Hours In-Office Instruction

SPECIFIC EXPANSION PLANS:
US: Targeted Cities in US.
Canada: No
Overseas: NR

≪ ≫

TALENT TREE
9703 Richmond Ave., # 216

Houston, TX 77042-4620
Tel: (800) 999-1515 + 7304 (713) 361-7304
Fax: (713) 974-6507
E-Mail: franchise@talenttree.com
Web Site: www.talenttree.com
Mr. Mark Dermott, SVP Franchise Group

TALENT TREE offers full-service staffing franchise opportunities with the placement of clerical, administrative, technical support and light industrial staff. Franchisees are offered intensive on-going training and hands-on support by industry experts. Our franchisees have the advantage of our proven system and innovative, proprietary programs.

BACKGROUND: IFA MEMBER
Established: 1976; 1st Franchised: 1990
Franchised Units: 13

Company-Owned Units:	<u>43</u>
Total Units:	56
Dist.:	US-56; CAN-0; O'seas-0
North America:	30 States, 0 Provinces
Density:	13 in TX, 13 in GA, 30 in CA
Projected New Units (12 Months):	3-5
Qualifications:	4, 4, 5, 1, 2, 4

FINANCIAL/TERMS:

Cash Investment:	$100-150K
Total Investment:	$120-170K
Minimum Net Worth:	$150-250K
Fees: Franchise -	$20K
Royalty - Varies;	Ad. - 0%
Earnings Claims Statement:	No
Term of Contract (Years):	10/5
Avg. # Of Employees:	2 FT, 0 PT
Passive Ownership:	Allowed
Encourage Conversions:	Yes
Area Develop. Agreements:	Yes/1
Sub-Franchising Contracts:	No

Expand In Territory:	Yes
Space Needs:	1,000 SF

SUPPORT & TRAINING:

Financial Assistance Provided:	Yes (D)
Site Selection Assistance:	Yes
Lease Negotiation Assistance:	Yes
Co-Operative Advertising:	No
Franchisee Assoc./Member:	No
Size Of Corporate Staff:	180
On-Going Support:	A,B,C,D,E,,,H,I
Training:	3-4 Weeks Corporate Office;
	1st 120 Days and as Needed Franchise

SPECIFIC EXPANSION PLANS:

US:	All United States
Canada:	No
Overseas:	NR

	FIVE LARGEST PARTICIPANTS IN SURVEY					
Company	# Fran-chised Units	# Co-Owned Units	# Total Units	Franchise Fee	On-Going Royalty	Total Investment
1. Aussie Pet Mobile	448	13	461	$35-75K	5%	$200K
2. Bark Busters - Home Dog Training	420	0	420	$37.5K	8%	$71.1-96K
3. Wild Birds Unlimited	285	0	285	$18K	4%	$90-140K
4. Pet Supplies Plus	225	0	225	$25K	$2,000 per month, + 2% of Sales over $1 Million	$450-500K
5. Petland	130	5	135	$25K	4.5%	$180-500K

All of the data provided are proprietary and should not be quoted without acknowledging *Bond's Franchise Guide.*

Top 100

AUSSIE PET MOBILE
34189 Pacific Coast Hwy., # 203
Dana Point, CA 92629-2814
Tel: (949) 234-0680
Fax: (949) 234-0688

E-Mail: dlouy@aussiepetmobile.com
Web Site: www.aussiepetmobile.com
Mr. David Louy, VP Franchise Sales

AUSSIE PET MOBILE is an internationally proven franchise system of mobile pet grooming with new U.S. headquarters in Orange County, CA. We pride ourselves on our innovative Mercedes van design, heated hydrobath and a 15-step grooming maintenance process. No experience is required. The AUSSIE PET MOBILE franchise package includes a comprehensive training course. Franchisees enjoy a protected territory with regional and national advertising support. Single unit owner-operator and multi-unit programs available.

BACKGROUND: IFA MEMBER
Established: 1996;   1st Franchised: 1997
Franchised Units: 448
Company-Owned Units: <u>13</u>
Total Units: 461
Dist.:   US-425; CAN-3; O'seas-20
  North America: 28 States, 1 Provinces

Density: 27 in TX, 34 in FL, 90 in CA
Projected New Units (12 Months): NR
Qualifications: 4, 4, 1, 3, 4, 5
FINANCIAL/TERMS:
Cash Investment: $62K-125K
Total Investment: $200K
Minimum Net Worth: $100K-250K
Fees: Franchise - $35-75K
Royalty - 5%; Ad. - 3%
Earnings Claims Statement: Yes
Term of Contract (Years): 10/10
Avg. # Of Employees: Varies FT, Varies PT
Passive Ownership: Allowed
Encourage Conversions: Yes
Area Develop. Agreements: No
Sub-Franchising Contracts: No
Expand In Territory: Yes
Space Needs: NR
SUPPORT & TRAINING:
Financial Assistance Provided: Yes (D)
Site Selection Assistance: NA
Lease Negotiation Assistance: NA
Co-Operative Advertising: Yes
Franchisee Assoc./Member: Yes/Yes
Size Of Corporate Staff: 40
On-Going Support: A,B,C,D,E,F,G,H,I
Training: 3 Days Advanced Employees;
5 Days Franchisees; 2 Weeks Employees
SPECIFIC EXPANSION PLANS:
US: All United States
Canada: All Canada
Overseas: UK, Europe, Mexico, Asia,
Worldwide

<< >>

BARK BUSTERS - HOME DOG TRAINING
250 W. Lehow Ave., #B
Englewood, CO 80110
Tel: (877) 300-2275 (303) 471-4935
Fax: (720) 283-2819
E-Mail: franchises@barkbusters.com
Web Site: www.barkbusters.com
Ms. Joan Trinka, Director of Franchise
Development

Bark Busters is the world's largest, most trusted dog training company, started in Australia in 1989 and came to the United States in 2000. As a world leader in natural home dog training, Bark Busters has trained over 350,000 dogs worldwide using its dog-friendly, natural methods. With 220+ franchised offices in 40 U.S. states and more than 320 offices in nine countries, Bark Busters is continuing its mission to build a global network of dog behavioral therapists to enhance responsible dog ownership and reduce the possibility of maltreatment, abandonment, and euthanasia of companion dogs. Great lifestyle! fulfilling profession! $40+ billion market!

BACKGROUND: IFA MEMBER
Established: 1989; 1st Franchised: 2000
Franchised Units: 420
Company-Owned Units: 0
Total Units: 420
Dist.: US-255; CAN-25; O'seas-80
North America: 40 States, 1 Provinces
Density: 17 in TX, 16 in IL, 22 in CA
Projected New Units (12 Months): 75
Qualifications: 3, 3, 1, 2, 3, 4
FINANCIAL/TERMS:
Cash Investment: $57K-71.1K
Total Investment: $71.1K-96K
Minimum Net Worth: $100-150K
Fees: Franchise - $37.5K
Royalty - 8%; Ad. - 2%
Earnings Claims Statement: Yes
Term of Contract (Years): 5/5
Avg. # Of Employees: 1 FT, 0 PT
Passive Ownership: Not Allowed
Encourage Conversions: NA
Area Develop. Agreements: No
Sub-Franchising Contracts: No
Expand In Territory: No
Space Needs: 10 x 10 in home office SF
SUPPORT & TRAINING:
Financial Assistance Provided: Yes (I)
Site Selection Assistance: NA
Lease Negotiation Assistance: NA
Co-Operative Advertising: Yes
Franchisee Assoc./Member: No
Size Of Corporate Staff: 23
On-Going Support: A,B,C,D,E,,G,h,I
Training: 3 Weeks Denver, CO
SPECIFIC EXPANSION PLANS:
US: All United States
Canada: All Canada
Overseas: NR

<< >>

GLOBAL RYAN'S PET FOODS
294 Walker Dr., # 2
Brampton, ON L6T 4Z2 Canada
Tel: (866) 463-4124 (905) 790-9023
Fax: (905) 790-7059

E-Mail: franchises@franchisebancorp.com
Web Site: www.globalpetfoods.com
Ms. Lisa Morrison,

A specialty pet food store featuring a full line of natural and wholesome foods for the pet along with a great selection of pet care accessories. Global Ryan's Pet Foods is the health food store for the pet. Including our own private label brand "Nature's Harvest", we offer a complete collection of products to satisfy all your pet care needs.

BACKGROUND:
Established: 1976; 1st Franchised: 1976
Franchised Units: 66
Company-Owned Units: 3
Total Units: 69
Dist.: US-0; CAN-69; O'seas-0
North America: 0 States, 0 Provinces
Density: 59 in ON, 2 in NS, 3 in AB
Projected New Units (12 Months): 16
Qualifications: 3, 3, 3, 3, 3, 3
FINANCIAL/TERMS:
Cash Investment: $60K
Total Investment: $125-135K
Minimum Net Worth: NR
Fees: Franchise - $25K
Royalty - 3-4%; Ad. - 1%
Earnings Claims Statement: No
Term of Contract (Years): 10/10
Avg. # Of Employees: varies FT, varies PT
Passive Ownership: Not Allowed
Encourage Conversions: NA
Area Develop. Agreements: Yes/0
Sub-Franchising Contracts: No
Expand In Territory: No
Space Needs: 1,500 SF
SUPPORT & TRAINING:
Financial Assistance Provided: No
Site Selection Assistance: Yes
Lease Negotiation Assistance: Yes
Co-Operative Advertising: Yes
Franchisee Assoc./Member: No
Size Of Corporate Staff: 20
On-Going Support: ,,C,D,E,,G,H,I
Training: Operating Locations; Training Center
SPECIFIC EXPANSION PLANS:
US: No
Canada: All Canada
Overseas: NR

<< >>

PETLAND
250 Riverside St.

Chillicothe, OH 45601-5606
Tel: (800) 221-5935 (740) 775-2464
Fax: (740) 775-2575
E-Mail: jwhitman@petland.com
Web Site: www.petland.com
Mr. Jim Whitman, Franchise Development
   Coordinator

PETLAND is a full-service, pet retail store that features live animals, including tropical fish, marine fish, small mammals, reptiles, amphibians, tropical, domestically bred birds, puppies and kittens. The PETLAND concept also features over 4,000 merchandise items to support the pets sold to or already in the homes of its customers. Over 1,500 merchandise items are PETLAND brands, sold exclusively through PETLAND retail stores.

BACKGROUND:
Established: 1967; 1st Franchised: 1973
Franchised Units: 130
Company-Owned Units: 5
Total Units: 135
Dist.: US-110; CAN-46; O'seas-6
  North America: 32 States, 5 Provinces
  Density: 19 in OH, 11 in IL, 14 in FL
Projected New Units (12 Months): 18
Qualifications: 3, 5, 1, 3, 4, 5
FINANCIAL/TERMS:
Cash Investment: $60-120K
Total Investment: $180-500K
Minimum Net Worth: $250K
Fees: Franchise - $25K
  Royalty - 4.5%; Ad. - NA
Earnings Claims Statement: No
Term of Contract (Years): 20/20
Avg. # Of Employees: 5 FT, 7 PT
Passive Ownership: Discouraged
Encourage Conversions: Yes
Area Develop. Agreements: No
Sub-Franchising Contracts: No
Expand In Territory: Yes
Space Needs: 5,000 SF
SUPPORT & TRAINING:
Financial Assistance Provided: Yes (D)
Site Selection Assistance: Yes
Lease Negotiation Assistance: Yes
Co-Operative Advertising: No
Franchisee Assoc./Member: No
Size Of Corporate Staff: 38
On-Going Support: ,B,C,D,E,F,G,H,I
Training: 1.5 Weeks Training Store,
  Chillicothe, OH; 1 Week Classroom; 2
  Weeks New Store Location
SPECIFIC EXPANSION PLANS:
US: All United States
Canada: All Canada
Overseas: Western Europe, Australia,

South America

◄◄ ►►

PETS ARE INN

5100 Edina Blvd., # 206
Minneapolis, MN 55439
Tel: (800) 248-PETS (952) 944-8298
Fax: (952) 829-3828
E-Mail: jplatt@petsareinn.com
Web Site: www.petsareinn.com
Mr. Jim Platt, President

When a family goes on vacation, they prefer to have their pet cared for in a loving - caring - home environment. We are looking for individuals that recognize the need for PETS ARE INN in their area. An individual that has a proven track record as a professional in other areas but has made a conscious decision to change career paths - to be involved in business and in the community. Our unique niche in the hospitality/travel industry provides our customers and their pets with worry free services.

BACKGROUND:
Established: 1982; 1st Franchised: 1992
Franchised Units: 18
Company-Owned Units: 0
Total Units: 18
Dist.: US-18; CAN-0; O'seas-0
  North America: 0 States, 0 Provinces
  Density: 2 in WA, 3 in TX, 6 in MN
Projected New Units (12 Months): 4
Qualifications: 5, 4, 3, 5, 5, 4
FINANCIAL/TERMS:
Cash Investment: $20K
Total Investment: $35-65K
Minimum Net Worth: $
Fees: Franchise - $15K
  Royalty - 5-10%; Ad. - 1%
Earnings Claims Statement: Yes
Term of Contract (Years): 10/10
Avg. # Of Employees: 2 FT, 4 PT
Passive Ownership: Not Allowed
Encourage Conversions: NA
Area Develop. Agreements: No
Sub-Franchising Contracts: No
Expand In Territory: No
Space Needs: NR
SUPPORT & TRAINING:
Financial Assistance Provided: No
Site Selection Assistance: Yes
Lease Negotiation Assistance: Yes
Co-Operative Advertising: No
Franchisee Assoc./Member: No
Size Of Corporate Staff: 5
On-Going Support: A,B,C,D,E,,G,H,I

Training: 5 Days Minneapolis, MN
SPECIFIC EXPANSION PLANS:
US: Central Time Zone
Canada: No
Overseas: NR

◄◄ ►►

PET SUPPLIES PLUS

22710 Haggerty Rd., # 100
Farmington Hills, MI 48335
Tel: (866) 477-7747 (248) 374-1900
Fax: (248) 374-7900
E-Mail: mlauten@petsuppliesplus.com
Web Site: www.petsuppliesplus.com
Mr. Mark Lauten, VP Franchise Development

Join the growing $40 Billion specialty Pet Supply industry! Pet Supplies "Plus" is the nation's largest franchised specialty pet supply retailer, with over 230 stores in 23 states. Our smaller store sizes provide a more convenient shopping experience for our customers, while allowing us to enter trade areas where our big-box warehouse style competitors can't. Even though our stores are smaller, we carry a larger variety of products, at retail prices that will often meet, or beat, our competitors.

BACKGROUND:
Established: 1988; 1st Franchised: 1991
Franchised Units: 225
Company-Owned Units: 0
Total Units: 225
Dist.: US-225; CAN-0; O'seas-0
  North America: 23 States, 0 Provinces
  Density: 55 in MI, 19 in NY, 46 in OH
Projected New Units (12 Months): 20 to 30
Qualifications: 4, 3, 2, 3, 4, 5
FINANCIAL/TERMS:
Cash Investment: $250K
Total Investment: $450-500K
Minimum Net Worth: $500K
Fees: Franchise - $25K
  Royalty - $2,000 per month, +2% of
Sales over $1 Million; Ad. - $2,500 per
month minimum
Earnings Claims Statement: No
Term of Contract (Years): 5/5

Avg. # Of Employees: 3-5 FT, 10-12 PT
Passive Ownership: Discouraged
Encourage Conversions: Yes
Area Develop. Agreements: Yes/5
Sub-Franchising Contracts: No
Expand In Territory: Yes
Space Needs: 8,000 to 10,000 SF
SUPPORT & TRAINING:
Financial Assistance Provided: No
Site Selection Assistance: Yes
Lease Negotiation Assistance: No
Co-Operative Advertising: No
Franchisee Assoc./Member: No
Size Of Corporate Staff: 30
On-Going Support: ,,C,d,E,,,h,
Training: 2 to 4 weeks Livonia, MI
SPECIFIC EXPANSION PLANS:
US: Yes, Eastern United States
Canada: No
Overseas: No

≪≪ ≫≫

RUFFIN'S PET CENTRES

109 Industrial Dr.
Dunnville, ON N1A 2X5 Canada
Tel: (905) 774-7079
Fax: (905) 774-1096
E-Mail: franchise@ruffinspet.com
Web Site: www.ruffinspet.com
Mr. Mark Reynolds, President

RUFFIN'S PET CENTER is a unique combination of a traditional pet store and a discount, pet-food outlet. The union of these two types of stores increases the strength of both. The high traffic of a pet store increases the on-going pet food sales. This strong concept, combined with great office support, equals a successful franchise.

BACKGROUND:
Established: 1981; 1st Franchised: 1987
Franchised Units: 13
Company-Owned Units: 0
Total Units: 13
Dist.: US-0; CAN-13; O'seas-0
  North America: 0 States, 1 Provinces
  Density: 14 in ON, in
Projected New Units (12 Months): 3
Qualifications: 4, 2, 1, 1, 2, 4
FINANCIAL/TERMS:
Cash Investment: $
Total Investment: $85K-105K
Minimum Net Worth: Varies
Fees: Franchise - $20K
  Royalty - 4%; Ad. - 1%
Earnings Claims Statement: No
Term of Contract (Years): 5/5
Avg. # Of Employees: 1 FT, 3 PT

Passive Ownership: Not Allowed
Encourage Conversions: Yes
Area Develop. Agreements: No
Sub-Franchising Contracts: No
Expand In Territory: No
Space Needs: 1,500 SF
SUPPORT & TRAINING:
Financial Assistance Provided: No
Site Selection Assistance: Yes
Lease Negotiation Assistance: Yes
Co-Operative Advertising: No
Franchisee Assoc./Member: No
Size Of Corporate Staff: 3
On-Going Support: ,B,C,D,E,f,G,H,
Training:1 Week Operating Store Close to Franchise; 1-2 Weeks Head Office; 1-2 Weeks On-Site
SPECIFIC EXPANSION PLANS:
US: No
Canada: ON
Overseas: NR

≪≪ ≫≫

WILD BIRD CENTERS OF AMERICA

7370 MacArthur Blvd.
Glen Echo, MD 20812-1200
Tel: (800) 945-3247 (301) 229-9585
Fax: (301) 320-6154
E-Mail: inforeq@wildbird.com
Web Site: www.wildbird.com
Mr. George H. Petrides, Jr., Director Franchise Development

A WBCA franchise is more than a store; it is a valued community resource. The story of THE WILD BIRD CENTERS OF AMERICA, Inc. is one of enthusiasm about wild birds and a professional approach to the birding market. The customer enjoys friendly, personal service in a peaceful environment with the feel of a relaxing backyard. The owner provides this service with the help of highly efficient systems and support.

BACKGROUND: IFA MEMBER
Established: 1985; 1st Franchised: 1989
Franchised Units: 84
Company-Owned Units: 0
Total Units: 84
Dist.: US-84; CAN-0; O'seas-0

North America: 31 States, 0 Provinces
Density: 8 in VA, 10 in MD, 8 in CA
Projected New Units (12 Months): 15
Qualifications: 5, 4, 2, 4, 2, 5
FINANCIAL/TERMS:
Cash Investment: $30-50K
Total Investment: $94.9-152.3K
Minimum Net Worth: $150K
Fees: Franchise - $18K
  Royalty - 3-4%; Ad. - .5%
Earnings Claims Statement: Yes
Term of Contract (Years): 10/
Avg. # Of Employees: 1 FT, 2 PT
Passive Ownership: Discouraged
Encourage Conversions: No
Area Develop. Agreements: No
Sub-Franchising Contracts: No
Expand In Territory: No
Space Needs: 1,500-2,400 SF
SUPPORT & TRAINING:
Financial Assistance Provided: Yes (I)
Site Selection Assistance: Yes
Lease Negotiation Assistance: Yes
Co-Operative Advertising: Yes
Franchisee Assoc./Member: Yes/Yes
Size Of Corporate Staff: 15
On-Going Support: ,,C,d,E,F,G,h,I
Training: 1 Day On-Site; 6 Days Home Office
SPECIFIC EXPANSION PLANS:
US: All United States
Canada: All Canada
Overseas: NR

≪≪ ≫≫

Top 100

WILD BIRDS UNLIMITED

11711 N. College Ave., # 146
Carmel, IN 46032-5634
Tel: (888) 730-7108 (317) 571-7100 + 135
Fax: (317) 208-4050
E-Mail: pickettp@wbu.com
Web Site: www.wbu.com
Mr. Paul Pickett, VP of Franchise Development

WILD BIRDS UNLIMITED is North America's original and largest group of retail stores catering to the backyard birdfeeding and nature enthusiast. We currently have over 300 stores in the U.S. and Canada. Stores provide birdseed, feeders, houses, optics and nature-related gifts. Additionally, stores provide extensive educational programs regarding backyard birdfeeding. Franchisees are provided an all-inclusive support system.

BACKGROUND: IFA MEMBER
Established: 1981;   1st Franchised: 1983
Franchised Units: 285
Company-Owned Units: 0
Total Units: 285
Dist.:   US-272; CAN-13; O'seas-0
  North America: 42 States, 3 Provinces
  Density: 16 in OH, 20 in NC, 15 in MI
Projected New Units (12 Months):   15
Qualifications: 5, 5, 1, 3, 2, 5
FINANCIAL/TERMS:
Cash Investment: $25-35K

Total Investment: $90-140K
Minimum Net Worth: $150K
Fees: Franchise - $18K
  Royalty - 4%;   Ad. - .5%
Earnings Claims Statement: Yes
Term of Contract (Years):   10/5
Avg. # Of Employees: 2 (including owner) FT, 4 PT
Passive Ownership: Not Allowed
Encourage Conversions: NA
Area Develop. Agreements: No
Sub-Franchising Contracts: No
Expand In Territory: Yes
Space Needs: 1,300-1,600 SF
SUPPORT & TRAINING:
Financial Assistance Provided: Yes (I)

Site Selection Assistance: Yes
Lease Negotiation Assistance: Yes
Co-Operative Advertising: No
Franchisee Assoc./Member: Yes/Yes
Size Of Corporate Staff: 0
On-Going Support: „C,D,E,F,G,H,I
Training: 1 Day Store Site;
    8 Days Carmel, IN;
SPECIFIC EXPANSION PLANS:
US: All United States
Canada: All Canada
Overseas: NR

≪ ≫

FIVE LARGEST PARTICIPANTS IN SURVEY						
Company	# Fran-chised Units	# Co-Owned Units	# Total Units	Franchise Fee	On-Going Royalty	Total Investment
1. TSS Photography	228	1	229	$18.2-39.7K	0	$37.8-73.2K
2. MotoPhoto	65	1	66	$35K	6%	$225-275K
3. Glamour Shots	64	1	65	$15K	0%	$235-300K
4. CLIX	29	1	30	$21-29.5K	6%	$36.2-381K
5. The Visual Image	17	3	20	$23.5K	0%	$35-40K

All of the data provided are proprietary and should not be quoted without acknowledging *Bond's Franchise Guide*.

CLIX
501 Johnson Ferry Rd., # 250
Marietta, GA 30068
Tel: (888) 2GO-CLIX (678) 213-2549
Fax: (770) 234-4288
E-Mail: franchise@getyourclix.com
Web Site: www.clixfranchise.com
Mr. Kevin Lovejoy, Vice President

CLIX is an innovative, Award-Winning franchise opportunity in the exciting world of digital portrait photography and imaging. We were the pioneer in the digital revolution and have been providing an all-digital, instant delivery product to customers since 1999! CLIX provides franchisees multiple and interconnected and expanding revenue streams through a storefront location, an On-Location Event Photography business, or both!

BACKGROUND: IFA MEMBER
Established: 1999; 1st Franchised: 2005
Franchised Units: 29
Company-Owned Units: 1
Total Units: 30
Dist.: US-30; CAN-0; O'seas-0
North America: 15 States, 0 Provinces
Density: 3 in VA, 6 in NY, 4 in CA
Projected New Units (12 Months): 24

Qualifications: 5, 4, 1, 1, 3, 5
FINANCIAL/TERMS:
Cash Investment: $36.2K-381K
Total Investment: $36.2K-381K
Minimum Net Worth: $75K
Fees: Franchise - $21-29.5K
  Royalty - 6%; Ad. - 2%
Earnings Claims Statement: Yes
Term of Contract (Years): 10/10
Avg. # Of Employees: 1-2 FT, 2-3 PT
Passive Ownership: Discouraged
Encourage Conversions: Yes
Area Develop. Agreements: Yes/1
Sub-Franchising Contracts: No
Expand In Territory: Yes
Space Needs: 1,300-1,600 SF
SUPPORT & TRAINING:

Financial Assistance Provided: Yes (I)
Site Selection Assistance: Yes
Lease Negotiation Assistance: Yes
Co-Operative Advertising: Yes
Franchisee Assoc./Member: No
Size Of Corporate Staff: 14
On-Going Support: „C,D,E,,G,h,I
Training: 1 Week Franchisee Location
    Upon Opening; 3 Weeks Rochester,
    NY

SPECIFIC EXPANSION PLANS:
US: All United States
Canada: No
Overseas: NR

DISCOUNT IMAGING

206 Texas Ave.
Monroe, LA 71201
Tel: (800) 987-8258 (318) 324-8977
Fax: (318) 324-1211
E-Mail: paulm@discountimaging.com
Web Site: www.discountimaging.com
Mr. Paul Moreau, President

Single source providers of printer, fax and copier supplies and service to businesses of all types. Program features proprietary product line, purchasing power and other support services.

BACKGROUND: IFA MEMBER
Established: 1995; 1st Franchised: 1998
Franchised Units: 4
Company-Owned Units: 2
Total Units: 6
Dist.: US-6; CAN-0; O'seas-0
    North America: 5 States, 0 Provinces
    Density: 1 in FL, 2 in AR, 1 in AL
Projected New Units (12 Months): 2
Qualifications: 4, 3, 2, 1, 4, 5
FINANCIAL/TERMS:
Cash Investment: $10K-25K
Total Investment: $50K-100K
Minimum Net Worth: $75K
Fees: Franchise - $25K
    Royalty - 3-6%; Ad. - 0%
Earnings Claims Statement: No
Term of Contract (Years): 10/5
Avg. # Of Employees: 4 FT, 1 PT
Passive Ownership: Discouraged
Encourage Conversions: No
Area Develop. Agreements: No
Sub-Franchising Contracts: No
Expand In Territory: Yes
Space Needs: NR
SUPPORT & TRAINING:
Financial Assistance Provided: Yes (D)
Site Selection Assistance: Yes

Lease Negotiation Assistance: No
Co-Operative Advertising: No
Franchisee Assoc./Member: No
Size Of Corporate Staff: 6
On-Going Support: „C,d,E,F,G,h,I
Training: 2 Weeks Corporate;
    4 Weeks On-Site
SPECIFIC EXPANSION PLANS:
US: South, Southeast
Canada: All Canada
Overseas: NR

GLAMOUR SHOTS

1300 Metropolitan Ave.
Oklahoma City, OK 73108-2082
Tel: (800) 336-4550 + 133 (405) 951-7133
Fax: (405) 951-6838
E-Mail: jeff.hudson@glamourshots.com
Web Site: www.glamourshots.com
Mr Jeff Hudson, Franchise Sales

GLAMOUR SHOTS is more than you ever pictured. We are the industry leader in high-fashion photography. We provide pre-opening assistance, comprehensive training, operational training and systems and regional field consultants, as well as solid, on-going support. Come join the leader!

BACKGROUND: IFA MEMBER
Established: 1989; 1st Franchised: 1989
Franchised Units: 64
Company-Owned Units: 1
Total Units: 65
Dist.: US-64; CAN-1; O'seas-1
    North America: 42 States, 1 Provinces
    Density: 25 in TX, 21 in FL, 14 in CA
Projected New Units (12 Months): 25
Qualifications: 5, 1, 1, 2, 2, 5
FINANCIAL/TERMS:
Cash Investment: $75K
Total Investment: $235-300K
Minimum Net Worth: $200K
Fees: Franchise - $15K
    Royalty - 0%; Ad. - $357/Mo.
Earnings Claims Statement: No
Term of Contract (Years): 10/10
Avg. # Of Employees: FT, 0 PT
Passive Ownership: Not Allowed
Encourage Conversions: Yes
Area Develop. Agreements: Yes/1
Sub-Franchising Contracts: No
Expand In Territory: Yes
Space Needs: 800-1,200 SF
SUPPORT & TRAINING:
Financial Assistance Provided: Yes (D)
Site Selection Assistance: Yes

Lease Negotiation Assistance: Yes
Co-Operative Advertising: No
Franchisee Assoc./Member: Yes/Yes
Size Of Corporate Staff: NR
On-Going Support: A,B,C,D,E,F,G,H,
Training: 1 Week National Training
    Center; 4 Weeks Training Store; As
    Needed Your Location
SPECIFIC EXPANSION PLANS:
US: All United States
Canada: All Canada
Overseas: All Countries

GRINS 2 GO

6969 Corte Santa Fe, #A
San Diego, CA 92121
Tel: (866) GO-GRINS (858) 558-4948
Fax: (858) 558-4947
E-Mail: franchiserecruitment@grins2go.com
Web Site: www.grins2go.com
Mr. Harish Babla, President/CEO

Grins 2 Go® is an innovative franchise so unique that it may be the picture perfect opportunity you've been waiting for. Our unique approach to technology, customer service and photographic styles is what sets us apart from the competition — we know it's not just what we do but how we do it. Our On Location unit is a stylish and highly visible Van. This home-based/Mobile business has a low investment, low overhead and is totally innovative and fun! Nothing like this exists! And, now your timing couldn't be better. You have the chance to get in on the ground floor of this cutting-edge franchise organization.

BACKGROUND: IFA MEMBER
Established: 2004; 1st Franchised: 2004
Franchised Units: 11
Company-Owned Units: 0
Total Units: 11
Dist.: US-11; CAN-0; O'seas-0
    North America: 6 States, 0 Provinces
    Density: 6 in CA
Projected New Units (12 Months): 50
Qualifications: 4, 3, 1, 2, 3, 5
FINANCIAL/TERMS:
Cash Investment: $30-35K
Total Investment: $114-142K

Minimum Net Worth: $150K
Fees: Franchise - $27.5K
  Royalty - 7%;   Ad. - 2%
Earnings Claims Statement: No
Term of Contract (Years): 10/10
Avg. # Of Employees: 2 FT, 1 PT
Passive Ownership: Discouraged
Encourage Conversions: NA
Area Develop. Agreements: Yes/10
Sub-Franchising Contracts: No
Expand In Territory: No
Space Needs: NA

SUPPORT & TRAINING:
Financial Assistance Provided: Yes (I)
Site Selection Assistance: NA
Lease Negotiation Assistance: NA
Co-Operative Advertising: Yes
Franchisee Assoc./Member: No
Size Of Corporate Staff: 4
On-Going Support: ,b,C,D,,,,h,I
Training: 2 Weeks San Diego

SPECIFIC EXPANSION PLANS:
US: All United States
Canada: All Canada
Overseas: All

◄◄ ►►

MOTOPHOTO
7086 Corporate Way
Dayton, OH 45459-4294
Tel: (800) 733-6686 (937) 291-1900 + 291
Fax: (937) 291-2005
E-Mail: franchise@motophoto.com
Web Site: www.motophoto.com
Mr. Ron Mohney, President

MOTOPHOTO is a crisp, up-scale, "clicks and mortar" specialty retailer in the exploding digital photography and digital portrait studio marketplaces. Consumers and Prosumers experience the MOTOPHOTO difference through precisely blending the versatility of digital products and services with the convenience of in-store, kiosk, or on-line interactions. Nearly a quarter century of franchising experience translates to superior franchisee training and exceptional ongoing business support.

BACKGROUND: IFA MEMBER
Established: 1981;   1st Franchised: 1982
Franchised Units: 65
Company-Owned Units: 1
Total Units: 66
Dist.:   US-66; CAN-0; O'seas-0
  North America: 19 States, 0 Provinces

Density: 2 in VA, 2 in OK, 12 in NJ
Projected New Units (12 Months): 0
Qualifications: 4, 4, 1, 2, 4, 4

FINANCIAL/TERMS:
Cash Investment: $40K-60K
Total Investment: $225K-275K
Minimum Net Worth: $250K
Fees: Franchise - $35K
  Royalty - 6%;   Ad. - 0.5%
Earnings Claims Statement: No
Term of Contract (Years): 10/10
Avg. # Of Employees: 3 FT, 3 PT
Passive Ownership: Discouraged
Encourage Conversions: Yes
Area Develop. Agreements: No
Sub-Franchising Contracts: No
Expand In Territory: No
Space Needs: 1,200-1,400 SF

SUPPORT & TRAINING:
Financial Assistance Provided: Yes (I)
Site Selection Assistance: Yes
Lease Negotiation Assistance: Yes
Co-Operative Advertising: Yes
Franchisee Assoc./Member: No
Size Of Corporate Staff: 9
On-Going Support: ,,C,D,E,,,h,I
Training: 3-5 Days Regional
  Training Center; 1 Week Franchisee's
  Store; 9 Days Dayton, OH

SPECIFIC EXPANSION PLANS:
US: Florida only
Canada: ON
Overseas: NR

◄◄ ►►

www.portraitavenue.com

PORTRAIT AVENUE, LLC
7086 Corporate Way, # 200
Dayton, OH 45459-4294
Tel: (937) 219-1900
Fax: (937) 291-2005
E-Mail: info@portraitavenue.com
Web Site: www.portraitavenue.com
Mr. Harry D. Loyle, President & CEO

Bring a smile to the faces of children and families. Portrait Avenue® is an upscale regional mall-based family portrait studio that uses a unique customer experience to create lasting memories. Our marketing tells the story and our complete training allows you to deliver a personalized portrait session, engaging your customers with distinct "portrait themes" and deliv-

ering custom designed products. Join our franchise family and enjoy the pride and benefits of providing a high quality consumer experience.

BACKGROUND: IFA MEMBER
Established: 2003;   1st Franchised: 2008
Franchised Units: 0
Company-Owned Units: 3
Total Units: 3
Dist.:   US-3; CAN-0; O'seas-0
  North America: 1 States, 0 Provinces
  Density: 3 in OH
Projected New Units (12 Months): 12
Qualifications: 3, 3, 2, 2, 4, 5

FINANCIAL/TERMS:
Cash Investment: $50K
Total Investment: $200K
Minimum Net Worth: $225K
Fees: Franchise - $32K
  Royalty - 7%;   Ad. - 6%
Earnings Claims Statement: Yes
Term of Contract (Years): 10/5
Avg. # Of Employees: 3 FT, 3 PT
Passive Ownership: Not Allowed
Encourage Conversions: NA
Area Develop. Agreements: No
Sub-Franchising Contracts: No
Expand In Territory: No
Space Needs: 1,400 SF

SUPPORT & TRAINING:
Financial Assistance Provided: Yes (I)
Site Selection Assistance: Yes
Lease Negotiation Assistance: Yes
Co-Operative Advertising: No
Franchisee Assoc./Member: No
Size Of Corporate Staff: 9
On-Going Support: A,B,C,D,E,,,h,I
Training: 3 Weeks Dayton, OH;
  3 Days Franchisee Site

SPECIFIC EXPANSION PLANS:
US: All United States
Canada: No
Overseas: NR

◄◄ ►►

TSS Photography

TSS PHOTOGRAPHY
2150 Boggs Rd., # 200
Duluth, GA 30096
Tel: (800) 321-9127 (678) 740-0800
Fax: (678) 740-0808
E-Mail: theresa@tssphotography.com
Web Site: www.tssphotographyfranchise.

com

Ms. Theresa Huszka, Director of Franchise Sales Development

TSS Photography has been the leader in youth, sports & school photography for 26 years. We specialize in team picture days, sports photography, school photography, special events and tournament photos. It has been said that when you do what you love, you'll never have to work another day in your life. And our franchise owners love what they do. They especially love controlling their own destiny, the flexibility of scheduling their own time, and calling their own shots. Please visit www.tssphotography.com for more information.

BACKGROUND: IFA MEMBER
Established: 1983; 1st Franchised: 1984
Franchised Units: 228
Company-Owned Units: 1
Total Units: 229
Dist.: US-222; CAN-0; O'seas-7
 North America: 42 States, 0 Provinces
 Density: 18 in CA, 17 in FL, 17 in TX
Projected New Units (12 Months): 20
Qualifications: 3, 3, 1, 1, 3, 4
FINANCIAL/TERMS:
Cash Investment: $35-75K
Total Investment: $37.8-73.2K
Minimum Net Worth: $
Fees: Franchise - $18.2-39.7K
 Royalty - 0; Ad. - 0
Earnings Claims Statement: No
Term of Contract (Years): 10/10
Avg. # Of Employees: 1-2 FT, 1-2 PT
Passive Ownership: Discouraged
Encourage Conversions: Yes
Area Develop. Agreements: No
Sub-Franchising Contracts: Yes
Expand In Territory: Yes
Space Needs: 100 SF

SUPPORT & TRAINING:
Financial Assistance Provided: No
Site Selection Assistance: NA
Lease Negotiation Assistance: NA
Co-Operative Advertising: No
Franchisee Assoc./Member: No
Size Of Corporate Staff: 35
On-Going Support: A,B,C,D,,,G,h,I
Training: 16 Hours Photography (Infield) - Franchisee's Territory; 24 Hours Sales & Marketing - Franchisee's Territory; 8 Hours Initial Photography - Franchisee's Territory
SPECIFIC EXPANSION PLANS:
US: All U.S.
Canada: No
Overseas: NR

VISUAL IMAGE, THE
100 E. Brockman Way
Sparta, TN 38583
Tel: (800) 344-0323 (931) 836-2800
Fax: (931) 836-6279
E-Mail: tamara@childcarephotography.com
Web Site: www.thevisualimageinc.com
Ms. Tamara Young, Office Manager

VISUAL IMAGE combines the advantages of high mark-up photography with the low overhead of home-based business. Because we do all our photography on location, you save the high cost of retail space and the confinement of retail hours! We go to pre-schools and pet shops and take portraits for busy, working parents. Because we do studio-quality portraiture, preschools love our work and invite us back season after season. Creative, fulfilling work, financial and physical rewards.

BACKGROUND:
Established: 1984; 1st Franchised: 1994
Franchised Units: 17
Company-Owned Units: 3
Total Units: 20
Dist.: US-20; CAN-0; O'seas-0
 North America: 12 States, Provinces
 Density: 4 in FL, 2 in NC, 4 in TN
Projected New Units (12 Months): 3
Qualifications: 3, 4, 1, 1, 3, 5
FINANCIAL/TERMS:
Cash Investment: $30-40K
Total Investment: $35-40K
Minimum Net Worth: $50K
Fees: Franchise - $23.5K
 Royalty - 0%; Ad. - 0%
Earnings Claims Statement: Yes
Term of Contract (Years): 3/5
Avg. # Of Employees: 1 FT, 1 PT
Passive Ownership: Discouraged
Encourage Conversions: NA
Area Develop. Agreements: No
Sub-Franchising Contracts: No
Expand In Territory: Yes
Space Needs: NA
SUPPORT & TRAINING:
Financial Assistance Provided: Yes (D)
Site Selection Assistance: NA
Lease Negotiation Assistance: NA
Co-Operative Advertising: No
Franchisee Assoc./Member: Yes/Yes
Size Of Corporate Staff: 3
On-Going Support: ,B,C,D,,,G,h,I
Training: 1 Week Home Base; 1 Week Training Center; 1 Week Training Center/Your Location
SPECIFIC EXPANSION PLANS:
US: All United States
Canada: No
Overseas: NR

For a full explanation of the data provided in the Franchisor Profiles, please refer to *Chapter 2, "How to Use the Data."*

FIVE LARGEST PARTICIPANTS IN SURVEY

Company	# Fran- chised Units	# Co- Owned Units	# Total Units	Franchise Fee	On-Going Royalty	Total Investment
1. Cartridge World	1,650	0	1,650	$30K	6%	$104-196K
2. Minuteman Press International	975	0	975	$44.5K	6%	$100-150K
3. Kwik Kopy Printing Canada Corporation	870	0	870	$29.5K	7%	$130-1MM
4. Proforma	650	0	650	$19.5K	6-8%	$32K
5. Allegra Print & Imaging	600	0	600	$30K	3.6-6%	$207-315.5K

All of the data provided are proprietary and should not be quoted without acknowledging *Bond's Franchise Guide.*

ALLEGRA PRINT & IMAGING
21680 Haggerty Rd. #105S
Northville, MI 48167
Tel: (888) 258-2730 (248) 596-8600
Fax: (248) 596-8601
E-Mail: kennethr@allegranetwork.com
Web Site: www.allegranetwork.com
Mr. Ken Root, Development Coordinator

As one of the largest printing and sign franchises in the world, ALLEGRA NET-WORK links more than 600 locations in the US, Canada and Japan. This January marks the 20th year that ALLEGRA has ranked among Entrepreneur Mag's Annual 500. ALLEGRA NETWORK's premier brand, ALLEGRA PRINT & IMAGING offers full-service print and graphic communications services including full-color printing, graphic design, digital color copying, mailing services, high sped output, online file transfer and many other services.

BACKGROUND: IFA MEMBER
Established: 1976; 1st Franchised: 1977
Franchised Units: 600
Company-Owned Units: 0
Total Units: 600
Dist.: US-557; CAN-38; O'seas-5

North America: 42 States, 1 Provinces
Density: 31 in MN, 63 in MI, 34 in IL
Projected New Units (12 Months): 36
Qualifications: 5, 3, 1, 2, 2, 2
FINANCIAL/TERMS:
Cash Investment: $40K-200K
Total Investment: $207-315.5K
Minimum Net Worth: $200K
Fees: Franchise - $30K
  Royalty - 3.6-6%; Ad. - 1%
Earnings Claims Statement: No
Term of Contract (Years): 20/20
Avg. # Of Employees: 3 FT, 1 PT
Passive Ownership: Not Allowed
Encourage Conversions: Yes
Area Develop. Agreements: No
Sub-Franchising Contracts: Yes
Expand In Territory: Yes

Space Needs: 1,200 SF

SUPPORT & TRAINING:

Financial Assistance Provided:	Yes (D)
Site Selection Assistance:	Yes
Lease Negotiation Assistance:	Yes
Co-Operative Advertising:	Yes
Franchisee Assoc./Member:	Yes/Yes
Size Of Corporate Staff:	50
On-Going Support:	,,C,D,E,F,G,h,I
Training:	2 Weeks Home Office;
1 Week On-Site	

SPECIFIC EXPANSION PLANS:

US:	All United States
Canada:	All Canada
Overseas:	NR

‹‹ ››

alphagraphics®

DESIGN ▪ COPY ▪ PRINT ▶ COMMUNICATE

Top 100

ALPHAGRAPHICS

268 S. State St., # 300
Salt Lake City, UT 84111-2048
Tel: (800) 528-4885 (801) 595-7268
Fax: (801) 533-7968
E-Mail: franchiseleads@alphagraphics.com
Web Site: www.alphagraphics.com
Ms. Jenny Langfeld, Franchise Development Support Manager

At AlphaGraphics, we work with people to plan, produce and manage their visual communications, enabling them to achieve their goals more effectively and confidently. Established in 1970 in Tucson, Arizona, the AlphaGraphics network is comprised of nearly 260 business centers located throughout the U.S. and in nine other countries. Our business centers offer complete visual communications solutions. Our trained and experienced team members provide expert consultation for every element of your communication project, including design, copying, printing, digital archiving, finishing, mailing services, oversized printing and promotional items.

BACKGROUND: IFA MEMBER

Established: 1970;	1st Franchised: 1980
Franchised Units:	260
Company-Owned Units:	0
Total Units:	260
Dist.:	US-228; CAN-0; O'seas-32
North America:	38 States, 0 Provinces
Density:	23 in IL, 24 in AZ, 31 in TX
Projected New Units (12 Months):	30+
Qualifications:	4, 5, 1, 3, 3, 5

FINANCIAL/TERMS:

Cash Investment:	$100K
Total Investment:	$415K
Minimum Net Worth:	$450K
Fees: Franchise -	$35K
Royalty - 1.5-8%;	Ad. - 2.5%
Earnings Claims Statement:	Yes
Term of Contract (Years):	15/10
Avg. # Of Employees:	5 FT, 0 PT
Passive Ownership:	Not Allowed
Encourage Conversions:	Yes
Area Develop. Agreements:	No
Sub-Franchising Contracts:	No
Expand In Territory:	Yes
Space Needs:	1,200 SF

SUPPORT & TRAINING:

Financial Assistance Provided:	Yes (D)
Site Selection Assistance:	Yes
Lease Negotiation Assistance:	Yes
Co-Operative Advertising:	Yes
Franchisee Assoc./Member:	No
Size Of Corporate Staff:	89
On-Going Support:	,,C,D,E,,G,H,I
Training:	3 Weeks Franchisee's Location

SPECIFIC EXPANSION PLANS:

US:	All United States
Canada:	All Canada
Overseas:	Spain, Italy, France, Germany, Benelux, Austria

‹‹ ››

american wholesale® thermographers

AMERICAN WHOLESALE THERMOGRAPHERS / AWT

12715 Telge Rd.
Cypress, TX 77429-2289
Tel: (888) 280-2053 (281) 256-4100
Fax: (281) 256-4178
E-Mail: awtsales@awt.com
Web Site: www.awt.com
Mr. Donald Averitt, VP Franchise Sales

AMERICAN WHOLESALE THERMOGRAPHERS / AWT provides wholesale raised letter printing to retail printers, print brokers, copy centers and business service centers. Our superior customer service and proprietary automated workflow system allow a 24-hour turnaround on most orders.

BACKGROUND: IFA MEMBER

Established: 1980;	1st Franchised: 1981
Franchised Units:	16
Company-Owned Units:	0

Total Units:	16
Dist.:	US-13; CAN-3; O'seas-
North America:	13 States, 2 Provinces
Density:	2 in OK, 3 in ON, 2 in VA
Projected New Units (12 Months):	NR
Qualifications:	NR

FINANCIAL/TERMS:

Cash Investment:	$75K
Total Investment:	$350.4-458.9K
Minimum Net Worth:	$
Fees: Franchise -	$30K
Royalty - 7%;	Ad. -
Earnings Claims Statement:	No
Term of Contract (Years):	25/25
Avg. # Of Employees:	9 FT, 4 PT
Passive Ownership:	Not Allowed
Encourage Conversions:	No
Area Develop. Agreements:	No
Sub-Franchising Contracts:	No
Expand In Territory:	Yes
Space Needs:	2,500-3,000 SF

SUPPORT & TRAINING:

Financial Assistance Provided:	Yes (D)
Site Selection Assistance:	Yes
Lease Negotiation Assistance:	Yes
Co-Operative Advertising:	No
Franchisee Assoc./Member:	Yes/Yes
Size Of Corporate Staff:	NR
On-Going Support:	,B,C,D,E,,G,h,I
Training:	2 Weeks Headquarters;
1 Week On-Site	

SPECIFIC EXPANSION PLANS:

US:	All United States
Canada:	All Canada
Overseas:	NR

‹‹ ››

BUSINESS CARDS TOMORROW

3000 N.E. 30th Pl., 5th Fl.
Ft. Lauderdale, FL 33306
Tel: (800) 627-9998 + 343 (954) 563-1224 + 343
Fax: (954) 565-0742
E-Mail: bob.dolan@bctonline.net
Web Site: www.bct-net.com
Mr. Bob Dolan, VP Franchise Sales

Join the 24-year old industry-leading wholesale, manufacturing franchise with the competitive advantage. We are recession-resistant, high-volume, quick-turn around, wholesale only manufacturers, specializing in next-day delivery of thermographed and offset-printed products and rubber stamps to retail printers, mailing centers, office supply stores and other retailers. Comprehensive training, excellent support and nationally praised.

295

BACKGROUND: IFA MEMBER
Established: 1975; 1st Franchised: 1977
Franchised Units: 82
Company-Owned Units: 3
Total Units: 85
Dist.: US-77; CAN-7; O'seas-1
  North America: 38 States, 5 Provinces
  Density: 5 in NY, 7 in FL, 16 in CA
Projected New Units (12 Months): 2
Qualifications: 4, 4, 3, 3, 3, 5
FINANCIAL/TERMS:
Cash Investment: $115-151K
Total Investment: $354-441K
Minimum Net Worth: $250K
Fees: Franchise - $35K
  Royalty - 6%; Ad. - NA
Earnings Claims Statement: No
Term of Contract (Years): 25/10
Avg. # Of Employees: 10 FT, 6 PT
Passive Ownership: Not Allowed
Encourage Conversions: Yes
Area Develop. Agreements: No
Sub-Franchising Contracts: No
Expand In Territory: No
Space Needs: 4,000+ SF
SUPPORT & TRAINING:
Financial Assistance Provided: Yes (D)
Site Selection Assistance: Yes
Lease Negotiation Assistance: Yes
Co-Operative Advertising: No
Franchisee Assoc./Member: Yes/Yes
Size Of Corporate Staff: 32
On-Going Support: a,B,C,d,E,,G,h,I
Training: 2 Weeks Ft. Lauderdale, FL;
  1 Week Pre-Opening at New-Site
SPECIFIC EXPANSION PLANS:
US: NJ, NE
Canada: No
Overseas: NR

◄◄ ►►

CARTRIDGE WORLD
6460 Hollis St.
Emeryville, CA 94608
Tel: (866) 473-5623 (510) 594-9900
Fax: (510) 594-9991
E-Mail: dshelton@cartridgeworld.com
Web Site: www.cartridgeworldusa.com
Mr. Jake Brown, Senior Vice President

CARTRIDGE WORLD is the leader in printer cartridge refilling. Our business strategy combines the skilled process of refilling printer cartridges for inkjet and laser printers, photocopy and fax machines with knowledgeable and fast customer service, convenient retail locations and large savings to the customer. CARTRIDGE WORLD, which dominates its market, has become one of the fastest-growing franchise concepts in the world. Named #1 in its market by Entrepreneur Magazine.

BACKGROUND: IFA MEMBER
Established: 1997; 1st Franchised: 2002
Franchised Units: 1650
Company-Owned Units: 0
Total Units: 1650
Dist.: US-630; CAN-16; O'seas-1004
  North America: 47 States, 5 Provinces
  Density: 38 in TX, 39 in IL, 58 in CA
Projected New Units (12 Months): 150
Qualifications: 4, 5, 3, 3, 2, 5
FINANCIAL/TERMS:
Cash Investment: $30K
Total Investment: $104-196K
Minimum Net Worth: $250-350K
Fees: Franchise - $30K
  Royalty - 6%; Ad. - 2%
Earnings Claims Statement: No
Term of Contract (Years): 10/10
Avg. # Of Employees: 1 FT, 1 PT
Passive Ownership: Discouraged
Encourage Conversions: Yes
Area Develop. Agreements: No
Sub-Franchising Contracts: Yes
Expand In Territory: Yes
Space Needs: 1,000-1,200 SF
SUPPORT & TRAINING:
Financial Assistance Provided: Yes (I)
Site Selection Assistance: Yes
Lease Negotiation Assistance: Yes
Co-Operative Advertising: Yes
Franchisee Assoc./Member: Yes/Yes
Size Of Corporate Staff: 50
On-Going Support: ,,C,D,E,F,G,H,I
Training: 2 Weeks Emeryville, CA;
  2 Weeks In-Store Field Training
SPECIFIC EXPANSION PLANS:
US: All United States
Canada: All Canada
Overseas: All Countries

◄◄ ►►

COPY CLUB
12715 Telge Rd.
Cypress, TX 77429-2289
Tel: (888) 280-2053 (281) 256-4100
Fax: (281) 256-4178
E-Mail: ccsales@copyclub.com
Web Site: www.copyclub.com
Mr. Donald Averitt, VP Franchise Sales

High-traffic, high-visibility, digital printing and copying center. We offer copying, bindery and graphic design to corporations, small businesses and home offices. Outside sales consultants generate high-volume repeat business in a fast-paced, technology-driven environment.

BACKGROUND: IFA MEMBER
Established: 1992; 1st Franchised: 1994
Franchised Units: 20
Company-Owned Units: 0
Total Units: 20
Dist.: US-20; CAN-0; O'seas-0
  North America: 4 States, Provinces
  Density: 10 in CA, 7 in TX, in
Projected New Units (12 Months): NR
Qualifications: NR
FINANCIAL/TERMS:
Cash Investment: $110K
Total Investment: $311.2-439.4K
Minimum Net Worth: $
Fees: Franchise - $30K
  Royalty - 7%; Ad. - 0%
Earnings Claims Statement: No
Term of Contract (Years): 25/25
Avg. # Of Employees: 8 FT, 5 PT
Passive Ownership: Allowed
Encourage Conversions: No
Area Develop. Agreements: No
Sub-Franchising Contracts: Yes
Expand In Territory: Yes
Space Needs: 3,000 SF
SUPPORT & TRAINING:
Financial Assistance Provided: Yes (D)
Site Selection Assistance: Yes
Lease Negotiation Assistance: Yes
Co-Operative Advertising: No
Franchisee Assoc./Member: Yes/Yes
Size Of Corporate Staff: NR
On-Going Support: ,,C,D,E,,G,h,I
Training: 3 Weeks Headquarters
SPECIFIC EXPANSION PLANS:
US: All United States
Canada: No
Overseas: NR

◄◄ ►►

Design & Print Centres

KWIK KOPY BUSINESS CENTERS
12715 Telge Rd.
Cypress, TX 77429-2289
Tel: (888) 280-2053 (281) 256-421

Fax: (281) 256-4178
E-Mail: franchisedevelopment@iced.net
Web Site: www.kkbconline.com
Mr. Donald Averitt, VP Franchise Development

KWIK KOPY BUSINESS CENTERS use a high-tech approach to provide a full range of printing, copying, pack-and-ship and cargo services for business and retail customers. We have an extensive network of vendor partners and are members of the worldwide ICED family of more than 1,000 franchises.

BACKGROUND: IFA MEMBER
Established: 2001; 1st Franchised: 2001
Franchised Units: 17
Company-Owned Units: 0
Total Units: 17
Dist.: US-17; CAN-0; O'seas-0
  North America: 8 States, 0 Provinces
  Density: 4 in TX, 2 in NC, in
Projected New Units (12 Months): NR
Qualifications: NR
FINANCIAL/TERMS:
Cash Investment: $74K
Total Investment: $224K-250K
Minimum Net Worth: $250K
Fees: Franchise - $25K
  Royalty - 7%; Ad. - 0%
Earnings Claims Statement: No
Term of Contract (Years): 15/
Avg. # Of Employees: 2 FT, 1 PT
Passive Ownership: Not Allowed
Encourage Conversions: No
Area Develop. Agreements: No
Sub-Franchising Contracts: No
Expand In Territory: Yes
Space Needs: 1,500-2,000 SF
SUPPORT & TRAINING:
Financial Assistance Provided: Yes (D)
Site Selection Assistance: Yes
Lease Negotiation Assistance: Yes
Co-Operative Advertising: No
Franchisee Assoc./Member: Yes/Yes
Size Of Corporate Staff: NR
On-Going Support: ,B,C,D,E,,G,h,I
Training: 4 Weeks Training
SPECIFIC EXPANSION PLANS:
US: All United States
Canada: All Canada
Overseas: All Countries

⋘ ⋙

KWIK KOPY PRINTING CANADA CORPORATION
1550 16th Ave., # 4
Richmond Hill, ON L4B 3K9 Canada

Tel: (800) 387-9725 (416) 798-7007
Fax: (905) 780-0575
E-Mail: kkpcc@kwikkopy.ca
Web Site: www.kwikkopy.ca
Mr. Brett Harding, Franchise Development Department

Full-service print franchise, on-site printing, digital imaging, high speed and design. Canada's most successful print franchise. Strong support and training programs -- no industry experience necessary -- over 600 outlets worldwide, in 12 countries.

BACKGROUND:
Established: 1979; 1st Franchised: 1979
Franchised Units: 870
Company-Owned Units: 0
Total Units: 870
Dist.: US-440; CAN-70; O'seas-0
  North America: 0 States, 9 Provinces
  Density: 49 in ON, 5 in BC, 4 in AB
Projected New Units (12 Months): 3
Qualifications: 3, 4, 1, 3, 4, 5
FINANCIAL/TERMS:
Cash Investment: $60K
Total Investment: $130K-1MM
Minimum Net Worth: $200K
Fees: Franchise - $29.5K
  Royalty - 7%; Ad. - 3%
Earnings Claims Statement: No
Term of Contract (Years): 10/10
Avg. # Of Employees: 2 FT, 0 PT
Passive Ownership: Not Allowed
Encourage Conversions: Yes
Area Develop. Agreements: Yes/1
Sub-Franchising Contracts: No
Expand In Territory: Yes
Space Needs: 1,500-2,000 SF
SUPPORT & TRAINING:
Financial Assistance Provided: Yes (D)
Site Selection Assistance: Yes
Lease Negotiation Assistance: Yes
Co-Operative Advertising: No
Franchisee Assoc./Member: Yes/Yes
Size Of Corporate Staff: 15
On-Going Support: ,,C,D,E,,G,h,I
Training: 1 Week Toronto, ON;
  3 Weeks Houston, TX; 1 Week On-Site
SPECIFIC EXPANSION PLANS:
US: No
Canada: All Canada
Overseas: Middle East, India, Asian Pacific Rim, Africa

⋘ ⋙

LAZERQUICK
29900 S.W. Kinsman, # 200

Wilsonville, OR 97070
Tel: (800) 477-2679 (503) 682-1322
Fax: (503) 682-1670
E-Mail: ahoeck@lazerquick.com
Web Site: www.lazerquick.com
Mr. Allan Hoeckendors, Dir. Franchise Development

LAZERQUICK centers are complete, one-stop printing and copying centers. All centers feature state-of-the-art electronic publishing, digital graphics and imaging services that support our range of quality, fast-service offset printing, high-speed copying and related bindery and finishing services. The LAZERQUICK franchise is based on value and performance. Affiliates benefit from our unique and innovative programs.

BACKGROUND:
Established: 1968; 1st Franchised: 1990
Franchised Units: 24
Company-Owned Units: 21
Total Units: 45
Dist.: US-45; CAN-0; O'seas-0
  North America: 7 States, 0 Provinces
  Density: 13 in WA, 29 in OR, 1 in CA
Projected New Units (12 Months): 6
Qualifications: 4, 3, 2, 3, 3, 5
FINANCIAL/TERMS:
Cash Investment: $51.8-82.5K
Total Investment: $172.5-275K
Minimum Net Worth: NA
Fees: Franchise - $25K
  Royalty - 3-5%/$500; Ad. - 1.5%/$250
Earnings Claims Statement: Yes
Term of Contract (Years): 7/7/7/
Avg. # Of Employees: 2 FT, 2 PT
Passive Ownership: Not Allowed
Encourage Conversions: Yes
Area Develop. Agreements: Yes/1
Sub-Franchising Contracts: No
Expand In Territory: No
Space Needs: 1,400-1,800 SF
SUPPORT & TRAINING:
Financial Assistance Provided: Yes (D)
Site Selection Assistance: Yes
Lease Negotiation Assistance: Yes
Co-Operative Advertising: No
Franchisee Assoc./Member: No
Size Of Corporate Staff: 32
On-Going Support: ,,C,D,E,,G,,I
Training: 5-7 Weeks Corporate Headquarters
SPECIFIC EXPANSION PLANS:
US: All United States
Canada: All Exc. AB,PQ
Overseas: NR

MINUTEMAN PRESS INTERNATIONAL

61 Executive Blvd.
Farmingdale, NY 11735
Tel: (800) 645-3006 (631) 249-1370
Fax: (631) 249-5618
E-Mail: info@mpihq.com
Web Site: www.minutemanpress.com
Mr. Mike Miller, Franchise Development

MINUTEMAN PRESS currently has over 900 full-service printing and graphic centers throughout the world. As a MINUTEMAN PRESS owner, you will have a unique place in the industry, having the capability to serve virtually all the printing needs a business may be faced with. No experience necessary. Award-winning training school. On-going technical marketing and business management support through our network of 27 regional offices. Repeatedly named the # 1 printing franchise by Entrepreneur Magazine.

BACKGROUND: IFA MEMBER
Established: 1973; 1st Franchised: 1975
Franchised Units: 975
Company-Owned Units: 0
Total Units: 975
Dist.: US-975; CAN-68; O'seas-128
North America: 46 States, 5 Provinces
Density: 51 in TX, 52 in NY, 89 in CA
Projected New Units (12 Months): 50
Qualifications: 3, 3, 1, 1, 3, 5
FINANCIAL/TERMS:
Cash Investment: $30K-50K
Total Investment: $100K-150K
Minimum Net Worth: $
Fees: Franchise - $44.5K
Royalty - 6%; Ad. - 0%
Earnings Claims Statement: Yes
Term of Contract (Years): 35/35
Avg. # Of Employees: 3 FT, 0 PT
Passive Ownership: Discouraged
Encourage Conversions: Yes
Area Develop. Agreements: No
Sub-Franchising Contracts: No
Expand In Territory: Yes
Space Needs: 1,000 SF
SUPPORT & TRAINING:
Financial Assistance Provided: Yes (D)
Site Selection Assistance: Yes
Lease Negotiation Assistance: Yes
Co-Operative Advertising: Yes

Franchisee Assoc./Member: No
Size Of Corporate Staff: 160
On-Going Support: ,,C,D,E,F,G,H,I
Training: As Needed On-Site; 2.5 Weeks Framingdale, NY
SPECIFIC EXPANSION PLANS:
US: All United States
Canada: All Canada
Overseas: U.K., S. Africa, Australia

PROFORMA

8800 E. Pleasant Valley Rd.
Cleveland, OH 44131
Tel: (800) 825-1525 + 3840 (216) 520-8400
Fax: (216) 520-8474
E-Mail: boravec@proforma.com
Web Site: www.ConnectWithProforma.com
Mr. Greg Muzzillo, Founder & Co-CEO

Proforma is the leading business-to-business franchise opportunity in the $150 billion print and promotional product industry. We support over 600 franchise owners in the U.S. and Canada who have over $350 million in annual sales. Proforma is a great opportunity for individuals who enjoy direct sales to middle-market, upper-market and Fortune 500 companies. Franchise owners concentrate on building sales and profits while Proforma's Support Center handles the back office support. There is no inventory, equipment of retail storefront required, the franchise can be operated from a home-based or small leased office space environment.

BACKGROUND: IFA MEMBER
Established: 1978; 1st Franchised: 1986
Franchised Units: 650
Company-Owned Units: 0
Total Units: 650
Dist.: US-608; CAN-42; O'seas-0
North America: 47 States, 5 Provinces
Density: 42 in TX, 47 in OH, 66 in CA
Projected New Units (12 Months): 80
Qualifications: 2, 2, 1, 1, 1, 3
FINANCIAL/TERMS:
Cash Investment: $19.5K
Total Investment: $32K
Minimum Net Worth: $0
Fees: Franchise - $19.5K
Royalty - 6-8%; Ad. - .5-1%

Earnings Claims Statement: Yes
Term of Contract (Years): 0/0
Avg. # Of Employees: 1 FT, 0 PT
Passive Ownership: Not Allowed
Encourage Conversions: Yes
Area Develop. Agreements: No
Sub-Franchising Contracts: No
Expand In Territory: No
Space Needs: NA
SUPPORT & TRAINING:
Financial Assistance Provided: Yes (D)
Site Selection Assistance: NA
Lease Negotiation Assistance: NA
Co-Operative Advertising: No
Franchisee Assoc./Member: No
Size Of Corporate Staff: 100
On-Going Support: A,,C,D,,F,G,h,i
Training: 1 Week Cleveland, OH
SPECIFIC EXPANSION PLANS:
US: All United States
Canada: All Canada
Overseas: NR

Signal Graphics

SIGNAL GRAPHICS BUSINESS CENTERS

852 Broadway, # 300
Denver, CO 80203
Tel: (800) 852-6336 + 234 (303) 779-6789 + 234
Fax: (303) 779-8445
E-Mail: info@signalgraphics.com
Web Site: www.signalgraphics.com
Ms. Kari Skoket, Dir. Franchise Development

Welcome to SIGNAL GRAPHICS! For over 25 years, SIGNAL GRAPHICS has been developing entrepreneurs. Our business centers enable owners to market printing, copying, graphic design and promotional products. Your store will be a resource center for products such as business cards, stationery, envelopes, brochures, booklets, flyers and labels. You will have the latest technology in computers and digital copiers. Join us in this exciting and gratifying business.

BACKGROUND:
Established: 1974; 1st Franchised: 1982
Franchised Units: 32
Company-Owned Units: 3
Total Units: 36
Dist.: US-36; CAN-0; O'seas-0
North America: 15 States, 0 Provinces

Density: 15 in CO
Projected New Units (12 Months): 10
Qualifications: NR
FINANCIAL/TERMS:
Cash Investment: $40-60K
Total Investment: $159-201K
Minimum Net Worth: $200K
Fees: Franchise - $25K
Royalty - 5% with royalty rebate program; Ad. - $200/Mo. or 1%
Earnings Claims Statement: No
Term of Contract (Years): 20/
Avg. # Of Employees: 2 FT, 1 PT
Passive Ownership: Allowed
Encourage Conversions: Yes
Area Develop. Agreements: No
Sub-Franchising Contracts: No
Expand In Territory: Yes
Space Needs: 1200 SF
SUPPORT & TRAINING:
Financial Assistance Provided: Yes (I)
Site Selection Assistance: Yes
Lease Negotiation Assistance: Yes
Co-Operative Advertising: No
Franchisee Assoc./Member: Yes/Yes
Size Of Corporate Staff: 6
On-Going Support: „C,D,E,,G,H,I
Training: 1 Week On-Site; 2 Weeks Headquarters
SPECIFIC EXPANSION PLANS:
US: All United States
Canada: No
Overseas: NR

≪ ≫

SIGNS NOW
6976 Professional Pkwy., E.
Sarasota, FL 34240
Tel: (800) 356-3373 (941) 373-1958
Fax: (941) 388-9507
E-Mail: phill@signsnow.com
Web Site: www.signsnow.com
Mr. Phil LeBlanc, Dir. Franchise Development

For over 20 years, SIGNS NOW has been a leading franchisor of signage and digital graphics centers and we remain a top innovator in providing high quality visual communication solutions. Signs Now is also a part of Allegra Network, LLC, one of the largest print and graphics franchisors in the world.

BACKGROUND: IFA MEMBER
Established: 1983; 1st Franchised: 1986
Franchised Units: 220
Company-Owned Units: 0
Total Units: 220
Dist.: US-201; CAN-10; O'seas-5
North America: 41 States, 6 Provinces
Density: 16 in NC, 20 in IL, 24 in FL
Projected New Units (12 Months): 20
Qualifications: 3, 3, 3, 3, 3, 3
FINANCIAL/TERMS:
Cash Investment: $50-75K
Total Investment: $190K-300K
Minimum Net Worth: $200K
Fees: Franchise - $30K
Royalty - 6%; Ad. - 2%
Earnings Claims Statement: No
Term of Contract (Years): 20/20
Avg. # Of Employees: 3 FT, 0 PT
Passive Ownership: Not Allowed
Encourage Conversions: Yes
Area Develop. Agreements: No
Sub-Franchising Contracts: No
Expand In Territory: Yes
Space Needs: 1,800-2,400 SF
SUPPORT & TRAINING:
Financial Assistance Provided: Yes (I)
Site Selection Assistance: Yes
Lease Negotiation Assistance: Yes
Co-Operative Advertising: Yes
Franchisee Assoc./Member: Yes/Yes
Size Of Corporate Staff: 16
On-Going Support: „C,D,E,F,G,H,I
Training: 2 Weeks Actual Center; 3 Weeks Sarasota, FL
SPECIFIC EXPANSION PLANS:
US: All United States
Canada: No
Overseas: NR

≪ ≫

SIR SPEEDY
26722 Plaza Dr.
Mission Viejo, CA 92691-6390
Tel: (800) 854-3321 (949) 348-5000
Fax: (949) 348-5010
E-Mail: success@sirspeedy.com
Web Site: www.sirspeedy.com
Mr. Robert Miller, Director Franchise Development

We are the world's largest franchised network of printing and marketing service providers. We target the communication needs of small- and medium-sized businesses by partnering with them to help them achieve their business growth objectives. Whether acquiring, retaining, or reactivating customers, or maintaining brand integrity and increasing ROI, Sir Speedy can assist them with a full range of print communications and marketing support.

We continually expand our products and services, using state-of-the-art digital technology for business communications, online ordering, Web-to-print solutions, personalized printing, and a complete suite of additional printing, integrated marketing, and marketing communication services.

BACKGROUND: IFA MEMBER
Established: 1968; 1st Franchised: 1968
Franchised Units: 463
Company-Owned Units: 0
Total Units: 463
Dist.: US-428; CAN-4; O'seas-31
North America: 42 States, 2 Provinces
Density: 20 in IL, 39 in FL, 43 in CA
Projected New Units (12 Months): 20
Qualifications: 5, 4, 1, 3, 3, 5
FINANCIAL/TERMS:
Cash Investment: $100-175K
Total Investment: $275-300K
Minimum Net Worth: $300K
Fees: Franchise - $25K
Royalty - 4-6%; Ad. - 1-2%
Earnings Claims Statement: Yes
Term of Contract (Years): 20/10
Avg. # Of Employees: 5+ FT, 0 PT
Passive Ownership: Discouraged
Encourage Conversions: Yes
Area Develop. Agreements: No
Sub-Franchising Contracts: No
Expand In Territory: Yes
Space Needs: 1,500 to 2,500 SF
SUPPORT & TRAINING:
Financial Assistance Provided: Yes (D)
Site Selection Assistance: Yes
Lease Negotiation Assistance: Yes
Co-Operative Advertising: No
Franchisee Assoc./Member: No
Size Of Corporate Staff: 62
On-Going Support: „C,D,E,F,G,H,I
Training: 6 Weeks Franchisee's Site; 2 Weeks Mission Viejo, CA
SPECIFIC EXPANSION PLANS:
US: All United States
Canada: ON
Overseas: Most Countries

≪ ≫

FOUR LARGEST PARTICIPANTS IN SURVEY

Company	# Franchised Units	# Co-Owned Units	# Total Units	Franchise Fee	On-Going Royalty	Total Investment
1. Coffee News	821	0	821	$4K	$20-75/ Wk.	$8.5K
2. Bingo Bugle Newspaper	64	0	64	$1.5-10K	10%	$5.1-11.5K
3. Perfect Wedding Guide, The	41	9	50	$25-35K	6%	$53.9-129.4K
4. EasyChair Media	1	5	6	$20K	0%	$32.7-36.7K

All of the data provided are proprietary and should not be quoted without acknowledging *Bond's Franchise Guide.*

BINGO BUGLE NEWSPAPER
P. O. Box 527
Vashon Island, WA 98070-0527
Tel: (800) 327-6437 (206) 463-5656
Fax: (206) 463-5630
E-Mail: tara@bingobugle.com
Web Site: www.bingobugle.com
Ms. Tara Snowden, President

THE BINGO BUGLE is North America's largest network of newspapers devoted to bingo & gaming. Circulation over 1 million copies monthly. Listed in Entrepreneur's Annual Franchise 500 as one of the lowest cost franchise opportunities. Franchise fees range from $1,500 to $7,000. Complete training and support. Modest investment. Call 1-800-327-6437 for details.

BACKGROUND:

Established: 1981;   1st Franchised: 1983
Franchised Units: 64
Company-Owned Units: 0
Total Units: 64
Dist.:   US-59; CAN-5; O'seas-0
  North America: 30 States, 2 Provinces
  Density: 6 in NY, 5 in FL, 12 in CA
Projected New Units (12 Months):   6
Qualifications: 2, 4, 4, 2, 2, 1
FINANCIAL/TERMS:
Cash Investment: $1.5-6K
Total Investment: $5.1-11.5K
Minimum Net Worth: $
Fees: Franchise - $1.5-10K
  Royalty - 10%;   Ad. - 0%
Earnings Claims Statement: No
Term of Contract (Years):   5/5
Avg. # Of Employees: 0 FT, 0 PT
Passive Ownership: Allowed

Encourage Conversions: No
Area Develop. Agreements: No
Sub-Franchising Contracts: No
Expand In Territory: No
Space Needs: NA
SUPPORT & TRAINING:
Financial Assistance Provided: No
Site Selection Assistance: NA
Lease Negotiation Assistance: No
Co-Operative Advertising: No
Franchisee Assoc./Member: Yes/Yes
Size Of Corporate Staff: 2
On-Going Support: ,,,,,,,,
Training: 2.5 Days Seattle, WA
SPECIFIC EXPANSION PLANS:
US: Northeast, Central US, NC
Canada: All Canada
Overseas: NR

≪ ≫

Coffee News

COFFEE NEWS

120 Linden St.
Bangor, ME 04401
Tel: (207) 941-0860
Fax: (207) 941-1050
E-Mail: bill@coffeenewsusa.com
Web Site: www.coffeenewsusa.com
Mr. William A. Buckley, President

COFFEE NEWS is an international, fun-filled weekly publication produced and delivered free of charge by local franchisors to restaurants, coffee shops and the hospitality industry. Each issue contains short stories, trivia, horoscopes, interesting facts and jokes, plus a local event section edited by the franchisee. Income is derived from the sale of ads to small businesses in each community.

BACKGROUND:
Established: 1994; 1st Franchised: 1996
Franchised Units: 821
Company-Owned Units: 0
Total Units: 821
Dist.:   US-549; CAN-146; O'seas-126
    North America: 40 States, 10 Provinces
    Density: 43 in FL, 50 in MI, 80 in TX
Projected New Units (12 Months):   100
Qualifications: 1, 5, 5, 3, 3, 3
FINANCIAL/TERMS:
Cash Investment: $8.5K
Total Investment: $8.5K
Minimum Net Worth: $None
Fees: Franchise - $4K
    Royalty - $20-75/Wk.;   Ad. - 0%
Earnings Claims Statement: No
Term of Contract (Years):   4/4
Avg. # Of Employees: 3 FT, 0 PT
Passive Ownership: Discouraged
Encourage Conversions: NA
Area Develop. Agreements: No
Sub-Franchising Contracts: No
Expand In Territory: Yes
Space Needs: NA
SUPPORT & TRAINING:
Financial Assistance Provided: No
Site Selection Assistance: Yes
Lease Negotiation Assistance: No
Co-Operative Advertising: No
Franchisee Assoc./Member: No
Size Of Corporate Staff: 5
On-Going Support: ,,,,,G,,
Training: Quarterly Sales Meetings in ME

SPECIFIC EXPANSION PLANS:
US: All United States
Canada: All Canada
Overseas: All Countries

≪ ≫

EASYCHAIR MEDIA

800 Third St.
Windsor, CO 80550-5424
Tel: (800) 741-6308 (970) 686-5805
Fax: (800) 438-2150
E-Mail: kristie@easychairmedia.com
Web Site: www.easychairmedia.com
Ms. Kristie Melendez, General Manager

EASYCHAIR MEDIA produces a quality community-based, 4-color glossy lifestyle magazine that targets the best local buyers and brings solid results to satisfied advertisers. We offer results-oriented advertising, with a proven product that makes sense in today's community-oriented economy. EASYCHAIR MEDIA can do any and/or all design, edit content, printing, labeling and mailing of a magazine tailored for your market, community and publishing requirements. All at very affordable prices.

BACKGROUND:
Established: 2000; 1st Franchised: 2003
Franchised Units: 1
Company-Owned Units: 5
Total Units: 6
Dist.:   US-6; CAN-0; O'seas-0
    North America: 1 States, 0 Provinces
    Density: in NY, 5 in CO, in
Projected New Units (12 Months): 10-20
Qualifications: 3, 4, 4, 2, 3, 3
FINANCIAL/TERMS:
Cash Investment: $10-20K
Total Investment: $32.7-36.7K
Minimum Net Worth: $100K+
Fees: Franchise - $20K
    Royalty - 0%;   Ad. - 0%
Earnings Claims Statement: No
Term of Contract (Years):   10/10
Avg. # Of Employees: 1 FT, 1-2 PT
Passive Ownership: Allowed
Encourage Conversions: NA
Area Develop. Agreements: Yes/1
Sub-Franchising Contracts: No
Expand In Territory: Yes
Space Needs: NA
SUPPORT & TRAINING:
Financial Assistance Provided: No
Site Selection Assistance: Yes
Lease Negotiation Assistance: NA
Co-Operative Advertising: No

Franchisee Assoc./Member: No
Size Of Corporate Staff: 5
On-Going Support: ,b,C,D,,,G,h,I
Training: 2-3 Weeks Franchisee Site
SPECIFIC EXPANSION PLANS:
US: All United States
Canada: No
Overseas: Mexico Only

≪ ≫

PERFECT WEDDING GUIDE,
THE

39 Skyline Dr., # 1001
Lake Mary, FL 32746-6249
Tel: (888) 222-7433 (407) 936-0380
Fax: (888) 933-3404
E-Mail: kristy@pwg.com
Web Site: www.pwg.com
Ms. Kristy Miller, Senior Project Manager

THE PERFECT WEDDING GUIDE is a comprehensive buyers' guide to wedding and honeymoon products and services. As the owner of a PERFECT WEDDING GUIDE, you will publish a magazine that thousands of people will read every day. With the guidance of the nation's premier wedding magazine publisher, you will own and manage your own business!

BACKGROUND: IFA MEMBER
Established: 1991;   1st Franchised: 1999
Franchised Units: 41
Company-Owned Units: 9
Total Units: 50
Dist.:   US-50; CAN-1; O'seas-0
    North America: 22 States, 0 Provinces
    Density: 2 in TX, 4 in FL
Projected New Units (12 Months):   24
Qualifications: 4, 3, 3, 3, 5, 5
FINANCIAL/TERMS:
Cash Investment: $53.9-129.4K
Total Investment: $53.9-129.4K
Minimum Net Worth: $50K
Fees: Franchise - $25-35K
    Royalty - 6%;   Ad. - 1%
Earnings Claims Statement: No
Term of Contract (Years):   10/10
Avg. # Of Employees: 2 FT, 0 PT
Passive Ownership: Discouraged
Encourage Conversions: No
Area Develop. Agreements: No
Sub-Franchising Contracts: No
Expand In Territory: Yes
Space Needs: NA
SUPPORT & TRAINING:
Financial Assistance Provided: Yes (D)
Site Selection Assistance: NA
Lease Negotiation Assistance: NA

Co-Operative Advertising: No
Franchisee Assoc./Member: No
Size Of Corporate Staff: 7
On-Going Support: a,b,C,d,,F,g,H,I
Training: 5 Days Longwood, FL;
    5 Days Franchise Territory

SPECIFIC EXPANSION PLANS:
US: All United States
Canada: All Canada
Overseas: NR

◄◄ ►►

Five Largest Participants in Survey

Company	# Fran-chised Units	# Co-Owned Units	# Total Units	Franchise Fee	On-Going Royalty	Total Investment
1. Century 21 Real Estate	8,501	0	8,501	$25K	6%	$22-523K
2. RE/MAX International	5,226	28	5,253	$12.5-25K	Varies	$20-200K
3. Coldwell Banker Real Estate	2,181	722	2,903	$25K	6%	$169-502K
4. ERA Franchise Systems	2,762	28	2,790	$25K	NR	$47.5-210K
5. Help-U-Sell Real Estate	835	0	835	$19.5-29.5K	6%	$45.5-148.5K

All of the data provided are proprietary and should not be quoted without acknowledging *Bond's Franchise Guide.*

AMERICA'S PROPERTY INSPECTIONS (API)

1293 Middle Country Rd.
Middle Island, NY 11953
Tel: (888) 518-5038 NR
Fax: (631) 205-5303
E-Mail: APIHomeInspect@aol.com
Web Site: www.APIFranchise.com
Mr. Ed Neyland, President

At API we want more than just selling you a franchise; we want to help you build a better future. Our main goal at API is to teach you to be the best Home and Building Inspector in the business. With our unbeatable start-up packages, on-going support, marketing and training, API is the clear choice for your home inspection business.

BACKGROUND: IFA MEMBER
Established: 1991; 1st Franchised: 1992
Franchised Units: 120
Company-Owned Units: 3
Total Units: 123
Dist.: US-123; CAN-0; O'seas-0
 North America: 37 States, 0 Provinces
 Density: 15 in NY, 8 in FL, 6 in CA
Projected New Units (12 Months): 50
Qualifications: 3, 2, 1, 1, 2, 3
FINANCIAL/TERMS:
Cash Investment: $16K
Total Investment: $16-25K
Minimum Net Worth: NR

Fees: Franchise - $25K
 Royalty - 5%; Ad. - 1%
Earnings Claims Statement: No
Term of Contract (Years): 10/5
Avg. # Of Employees: 1 FT, 0 PT
Passive Ownership: Discouraged
Encourage Conversions: NA
Area Develop. Agreements: No
Sub-Franchising Contracts: No
Expand In Territory: Yes
Space Needs: NA
SUPPORT & TRAINING:
Financial Assistance Provided: Yes (D)
Site Selection Assistance: Yes
Lease Negotiation Assistance: No
Co-Operative Advertising: No

Franchisee Assoc./Member:	Yes/Yes
Size Of Corporate Staff:	8
On-Going Support:	,,,D,,,,,I
Training:	2 Weeks Middle Island, NY

SPECIFIC EXPANSION PLANS:

US:	All United States
Canada:	No
Overseas:	NR

◄◄ ►►

AMERISPEC HOME INSPECTION SERVICE

3839 Forest Hill Irene Rd.
Memphis, TN 38125
Tel: (800) 426-2270 (901) 597-8508
Fax: (901) 597-8520
E-Mail: sales@amerispec.com
Web Site: www.amerispecfranchise.com
Ms. Dinah Coopwood, Sales Coordinator

AMERISPEC delivers productivity enhancing tools to our owners like feature-rich personal Websites, branded email accounts, secure web delivery for reports and contact management software specifically designed to manage a home inspection business. A private intranet permits two-way communication with and among our owners. Consider our extensive training, the acclaimed and recognized 'AMERISPEC REPORT,' our on-going educational support and the package is complete.

BACKGROUND:	IFA MEMBER
Established: 1987;	1st Franchised: 1988
Franchised Units:	389
Company-Owned Units:	0
Total Units:	389
Dist.:	US-315; CAN-74; O'seas-0
North America:	48 States, 8 Provinces
Density:	17 in IL, 26 in FL, 40 in CA
Projected New Units (12 Months):	25
Qualifications:	3, 3, 3, 3, 1, 5

FINANCIAL/TERMS:

Cash Investment:	$10-15K
Total Investment:	$26.5-64.5K
Minimum Net Worth:	$40K
Fees: Franchise -	$20-30K
Royalty - 7%;	Ad. - 3%
Earnings Claims Statement:	No
Term of Contract (Years):	10/10
Avg. # Of Employees:	1 FT, 2 PT
Passive Ownership:	Allowed
Encourage Conversions:	Yes

Area Develop. Agreements:	No
Sub-Franchising Contracts:	No
Expand In Territory:	Yes
Space Needs:	NA

SUPPORT & TRAINING:

Financial Assistance Provided:	Yes (D)
Site Selection Assistance:	NA
Lease Negotiation Assistance:	NA
Co-Operative Advertising:	Yes
Franchisee Assoc./Member:	No
Size Of Corporate Staff:	45
On-Going Support:	,,C,D,E,,G,h,I
Training:	2 Weeks Memphis, TN

SPECIFIC EXPANSION PLANS:

US:	All United States
Canada:	All Canada
Overseas:	NR

◄◄ ►►

ASSIST-2-SELL

1610 Meadow Wood Ln.
Reno, NV 89502
Tel: (800) 528-7816 (775) 688-6060
Fax: (775) 823-8823
E-Mail: info@assist2sell.com
Web Site: www.assist2sell.com
Mr. Ryan Elliott,

America's "Full Service with $avings" discount real estate franchise. Real estate license required. The future of real estate will focus around a 'menu of services' concept. Lower commissions will be the norm. Don't be left behind: catch our vision and step into the future.

BACKGROUND:

Established: 1987;	1st Franchised: 1993
Franchised Units:	619
Company-Owned Units:	1
Total Units:	620
Dist.:	US-612; CAN-8; O'seas-0
North America:	46 States, 5 Provinces
Density:	91 in FL, 21 in CO, 89 in CA
Projected New Units (12 Months):	170
Qualifications:	4, 4, 5, 2, 1, 1

FINANCIAL/TERMS:

Cash Investment:	$25K
Total Investment:	$62K
Minimum Net Worth:	NA
Fees: Franchise -	$5K
Royalty - 5%;	Ad. - 1.5%
Earnings Claims Statement:	No
Term of Contract (Years):	5/5
Avg. # Of Employees:	3 FT, 0 PT
Passive Ownership:	Not Allowed
Encourage Conversions:	Yes
Area Develop. Agreements:	No
Sub-Franchising Contracts:	No

Expand In Territory:	No
Space Needs:	1,000 SF

SUPPORT & TRAINING:

Financial Assistance Provided:	No
Site Selection Assistance:	Yes
Lease Negotiation Assistance:	Yes
Co-Operative Advertising:	Yes
Franchisee Assoc./Member:	No
Size Of Corporate Staff:	36
On-Going Support:	,,c,d,,,G,h,I
Training:	5 Days Reno, NV

SPECIFIC EXPANSION PLANS:

US:	All United States
Canada:	All Canada
Overseas:	NR

◄◄ ►►

Hottest New Franchise

BETTER HOMES AND GARDENS REAL ESTATE

1 Campus Dr.
Parsippany, NJ 07054
Tel: (866) 616-4244 (973) 407-2000
Fax: (973) 407-8801
E-Mail: help@bhgrealestate.com
Web Site: www.bhgrealestate.com
Mr. Tim Henderson, Executive Vice President

Better Homes and Gardens® Real Estate offers a full range of services to brokers, sales associates and home buyers and sellers. Using innovative technology, sophisticated business systems and the broad appeal of a lifestyle brand, Better Homes and Gardens Real Estate embodies the future of the real estate industry while remaining grounded in the tradition of home. Better Homes and Gardens Real Estate LLC is a subsidiary of Realogy Corporation, a global provider of real estate and relocation services. The Better Homes and Gardens name has been a staple of American life since its inception in 1924.

BACKGROUND:

Established: 2007;	1st Franchised: 2008
Franchised Units:	54
Company-Owned Units:	0
Total Units:	54
Dist.:	US-54; CAN-0; O'seas-0
North America:	8 States, 0 Provinces
Density:	7 in PA, 18 in NH, 7 in ME
Projected New Units (12 Months):	NR

Qualifications: 4, 4, 5, 4, 4, 4

FINANCIAL/TERMS:

Cash Investment: $35-90K
Total Investment: $48-90K
Minimum Net Worth: $500K
Fees: Franchise - $35K
  Royalty - 6%; Ad. - 0% - Currently, subject to change
Earnings Claims Statement: Yes
Term of Contract (Years): 10/10
Avg. # Of Employees: Varies FT, PT
Passive Ownership: Discouraged
Encourage Conversions: Yes
Area Develop. Agreements: No
Sub-Franchising Contracts: No
Expand In Territory: Yes
Space Needs: 1800-3500 SF

SUPPORT & TRAINING:

Financial Assistance Provided: Yes (I)
Site Selection Assistance: No
Lease Negotiation Assistance: No
Co-Operative Advertising: Yes
Franchisee Assoc./Member: Yes/Yes
Size Of Corporate Staff: 15
On-Going Support: A,B,C,D,E,,G,H,I
Training: NR

SPECIFIC EXPANSION PLANS:

US: All United States
Canada: All Canada
Overseas: All Countries

≪ ≫

BETTER HOMES REALTY

1777 Botelho Dr., # 390
Walnut Creek, CA 94596-8181
Tel: (800) 642-4428 (925) 937-9001
Fax: (925) 988-2770
E-Mail: catherine@bhrcorp.com
Web Site: www.bhr.com
Ms. Catherine Prevost, Manager Franchise Sales

Established identity, legal hot line support, no institutional advertising fee, franchise cap each calendar year, excellent corporate support, free renewal, corporate advertising, hands-on regional support and turnkey marketing solutions, technology, and training.

BACKGROUND:

Established: 1964; 1st Franchised: 1969
Franchised Units: 43
Company-Owned Units: 0
Total Units: 43
Dist.: US-43; CAN-0; O'seas-0
  North America: 1 States, 0 Provinces
  Density: 43 in CA
Projected New Units (12 Months): 10

Qualifications: 3, 3, 3, 2, 1, 1

FINANCIAL/TERMS:

Cash Investment: $10-60K
Total Investment: $61.5K
Minimum Net Worth: NA
Fees: Franchise - $9.95K
  Royalty - 6% w/Cap/4.5%; Ad. - 0%
Earnings Claims Statement: Yes
Term of Contract (Years): 5/5
Avg. # Of Employees: NA FT, 0 PT
Passive Ownership: Allowed
Encourage Conversions: Yes
Area Develop. Agreements: No
Sub-Franchising Contracts: Yes
Expand In Territory: Yes
Space Needs: NA

SUPPORT & TRAINING:

Financial Assistance Provided: Yes (D)
Site Selection Assistance: NA
Lease Negotiation Assistance: NA
Co-Operative Advertising: No
Franchisee Assoc./Member: No
Size Of Corporate Staff: 7
On-Going Support: ,,C,D,,,G,H,I
Training: 0.5-1 Day Varies

SPECIFIC EXPANSION PLANS:

US: West
Canada: No
Overseas: NR

≪ ≫

BRICKKICKER, THE

849 N. Ellsworth St.
Naperville, IL 60563
Tel: (888) 339-5425 (630) 420-9900
Fax: (630) 420-2270
E-Mail: jallen@brickkicker.com
Web Site: www.brickkicker.com
Mr. James Allen, Dir. Marketing Services

Home and building inspections. Operating our own business since 1989 gives us a unique insight into the entrepreneurial aspects required to be an impact player in the industry. We've packaged our experience into a dynamic, aggressive program, including a heavy emphasis on 'live,' on-the-job training. Every BRICKKICKER benefits from the roll up our sleeves attitude in which we operate.

BACKGROUND:

Established: 1989; 1st Franchised: 1995
Franchised Units: 120
Company-Owned Units: 20
Total Units: 140
Dist.: US-140; CAN-0; O'seas-0
  North America: 7 States, 0 Provinces
  Density: 8 in WI, 16 in MI, 7 in IN

Projected New Units (12 Months): 45
Qualifications: 3, 4, 2, 3, 3, 4

FINANCIAL/TERMS:

Cash Investment: $9.4-24.9K
Total Investment: $19.4-39.9K
Minimum Net Worth: $10K
Fees: Franchise - $6.9-12.9K
  Royalty - 6%; Ad. - 2%
Earnings Claims Statement: No
Term of Contract (Years): 7/20
Avg. # Of Employees: 1 FT, 0 PT
Passive Ownership: Discouraged
Encourage Conversions: Yes
Area Develop. Agreements: No
Sub-Franchising Contracts: No
Expand In Territory: Yes
Space Needs: NR

SUPPORT & TRAINING:

Financial Assistance Provided: Yes (D)
Site Selection Assistance: NA
Lease Negotiation Assistance: NA
Co-Operative Advertising: No
Franchisee Assoc./Member: Yes/Yes
Size Of Corporate Staff: 7
On-Going Support: ,B,C,D,E,,G,H,I
Training: 10 Days Naperville, IL;
  3 Days On-Site

SPECIFIC EXPANSION PLANS:

US: All United States
Canada: All Canada
Overseas: NR

≪ ≫

CENTURY 21 CANADA

1199 W. Pender St., # 700
Vancouver, BC V6E 2R1
Tel: (604) 562-7219
Fax: (604) 606-2125
E-Mail: corporate@century21.ca
Web Site: www.century21.ca
Mr. C. Brain Rushton, Senior Vice President Franchise Sales & Developmen

Century 21 Canada Limited Partnership is a real estate franchisor with exclusive rights to the Century 21 brand in Canada and is part of the world's largest residential real estate sales organization. Century 21 provides comprehensive training, management, administrative and marketing support for the Century 21 System, which is comprised of more than 7,700 independently owned and operated franchised broker offices in 39 countries and territories.

BACKGROUND:
Established: 1976;   1st Franchised: 1976
Franchised Units: 400
Company-Owned Units: 0
Total Units: 400
Dist.:   US-0; CAN-400; O'seas-0
  North America: 0 States, 0 Provinces
  Density: 51 in QC, 170 in ON, 45 in AB
Projected New Units (12 Months):   NR
Qualifications: 3, 3, 3, 3, 3, 3
FINANCIAL/TERMS:
Cash Investment: $50K
Total Investment: $50K-100K
Minimum Net Worth: $25K
Fees: Franchise - $10.5K-21K
  Royalty - varies;   Ad. - varies
Earnings Claims Statement: No
Term of Contract (Years):   5/5
Avg. # Of Employees: 10 FT, 2 PT
Passive Ownership: Allowed
Encourage Conversions: NA
Area Develop. Agreements: No
Sub-Franchising Contracts: No
Expand In Territory: Yes
Space Needs: 3,000 SF
SUPPORT & TRAINING:
Financial Assistance Provided: No
Site Selection Assistance: No
Lease Negotiation Assistance: No
Co-Operative Advertising: No
Franchisee Assoc./Member: Yes/No
Size Of Corporate Staff: 42
On-Going Support: ,B,,D,,,G,H,I
Training: 5 Days Parsippany, NJ;
  2 Days local office
SPECIFIC EXPANSION PLANS:
US: All United States, NW & SW or NJ
specifically
Canada: No
Overseas: NR

◄◄ ►►

CENTURY 21 REAL ESTATE
1 Campus Dr.
Parsippany, NJ 07054
Tel: (877) 221-2765 (973) 359-7221
Fax: (973) 359-5527
E-Mail: franchise.information@realogy.com
Web Site: www.century21.com

Mr. Tim Henderson, Executive Vice President

With more than 120,000 broker and sales associates worldwide, the Century 21 Real Estate System is the world's largest residential real estate organization, providing comprehensive training, management, administrative and marketing support for its members.

BACKGROUND: IFA MEMBER
Established: 1971;   1st Franchised: 1972
Franchised Units: 7705
Company-Owned Units: 0
Total Units: 7705
Dist.:   US-3456; CAN-0; O'seas-4249
  North America: 50 States, 0 Provinces
  Density: 242 in TX, 275 in FL, 433 in CA
Projected New Units (12 Months):   NR
Qualifications: 4, 4, 5, 4, 4, 4
FINANCIAL/TERMS:
Cash Investment: $10-25K
Total Investment: $22-523K
Minimum Net Worth: $75K
Fees: Franchise - $25K
  Royalty - 6%;   Ad. - 2%
Earnings Claims Statement: No
Term of Contract (Years):   10/
Avg. # Of Employees: Varies
Passive Ownership: Not Allowed
Encourage Conversions: Yes
Area Develop. Agreements: No
Sub-Franchising Contracts: No
Expand In Territory: Yes
Space Needs: 1000 SF
SUPPORT & TRAINING:
Financial Assistance Provided: No
Site Selection Assistance: No
Lease Negotiation Assistance: No
Co-Operative Advertising: Yes
Franchisee Assoc./Member: Yes/Yes
Size Of Corporate Staff: 444
On-Going Support: A,b,C,D,E,,G,H,I
Training: 3-7 Sessions Telephone;
  5 Days Parsippany, NJ; 1 Day On-Site
SPECIFIC EXPANSION PLANS:
US: All United States
Canada: All Canada
Overseas: All Countries

◄◄ ►►

COLDWELL BANKER COMMERCIAL
1 Campus Dr.
Parsippany, NJ 07054-0656
Tel: (800) 222-2162 (973) 428-4700
Fax: (973) 796-0199
E-Mail: commercial@coldwellbanker.com
Web Site: www.coldwellbankercommercial.com
Mr. Tim Henderson, Executive Vice President

COLDWELL BANKER COMMERCIAL is one of the largest commercial franchise operations, with affiliates offering clients comprehensive buying, selling, leasing, acquisition, disposition and management services.

BACKGROUND: IFA MEMBER
Established: 1906;   1st Franchised: 1996
Franchised Units: 244
Company-Owned Units: 1
Total Units: 245
Dist.:   US-244; CAN-19; O'seas-19
  North America: 32 States, 4 Provinces
  Density: 19 in TX, 23 in FL, 40 in CA
Projected New Units (12 Months):   NR
Qualifications: 4, 4, 5, 4, 4, 4
FINANCIAL/TERMS:
Cash Investment: $30-101K
Total Investment: $250K+
Minimum Net Worth: $250K
Fees: Franchise - $20K
  Royalty - 6%;   Ad. - 2%
Earnings Claims Statement: No
Term of Contract (Years):   10/10
Avg. # Of Employees: Varies
Passive Ownership: Not Allowed
Encourage Conversions: Yes
Area Develop. Agreements: No
Sub-Franchising Contracts: No
Expand In Territory: Yes
Space Needs: 1,000 SF
SUPPORT & TRAINING:
Financial Assistance Provided: Yes (I)
Site Selection Assistance: Yes
Lease Negotiation Assistance: Yes
Co-Operative Advertising: Yes
Franchisee Assoc./Member: Yes/Yes
Size Of Corporate Staff: 25
On-Going Support: A,,C,D,E,,G,H,I
Training: Varies Internet;
  1-2 Days On-Site; 2 Days Parsippany
SPECIFIC EXPANSION PLANS:
US: All United States

Canada: All Canada
Overseas: All Countries

◄◄ ►►

COLDWELL BANKER
REAL ESTATE
1 Campus Dr.
Parsippany, NJ 07054
Tel: (973) 359-5757
Fax: (973) 359-5908
E-Mail: franchise.information@realogy.com
Web Site: www.coldwellbanker.com
Mr. Tim Henderson, Executive Vice President

For 103 years, the COLDWELL BANKER (TM) organization has been the premiere provider of full-service real estate. With approximately 3,200 independently and company owned and operated residential real estate offices with approximately 100,000 sales associates globally, the company is an industry leader.

BACKGROUND: IFA MEMBER
Established: 1906; 1st Franchised: 1982
Franchised Units: 2181
Company-Owned Units: 722
Total Units: 2903
Dist.: US-2903; CAN-0; O'seas-605
North America: 50 States, 0 Provinces
Density: 131 in NY, 148 in TX, 208 in CA
Projected New Units (12 Months): NR
Qualifications: 4, 4, 5, 4, 4, 4
FINANCIAL/TERMS:
Cash Investment: NR
Total Investment: $169-502K
Minimum Net Worth: $25K
Fees: Franchise - $25K
Royalty - 6%; Ad. - 2.5%
Earnings Claims Statement: No
Term of Contract (Years): 10/10
Avg. # Of Employees: Varies
Passive Ownership: Not Allowed
Encourage Conversions: Yes
Area Develop. Agreements: No
Sub-Franchising Contracts: No
Expand In Territory: Yes
Space Needs: 1,000 SF
SUPPORT & TRAINING:
Financial Assistance Provided: No
Site Selection Assistance: No

Lease Negotiation Assistance: No
Co-Operative Advertising: No
Franchisee Assoc./Member: Yes/Yes
Size Of Corporate Staff: 100
On-Going Support: A,,C,D,E,,G,H,I
Training: 1-2 Days On-Site;
4 Days Parsippany, NJ; Varies Internet
SPECIFIC EXPANSION PLANS:
US: All United States
Canada: All Canada
Overseas: All Countries

◄◄ ►►

CRITERIUM ENGINEERS
(CANADA)
22 Monument Sq., # 600
Portland, ME 04101
Tel: (800) 242-1969 (207) 828-1969
Fax: (207) 775-4405
E-Mail: phollander@criterium-engineers.com
Web Site: www.criterium-engineers.com
Mr. Peter E. Hollander, Executive Vice President

CRITERIUM ENGINEERS is a consulting franchise available to licensed professional engineers. Company specializes in building inspection and evaluation services for buyers, investors, corporations, attorneys, insurance companies, lenders and government. Services include pre-purchase inspections, insurance investigations, due diligence, maintenance planning, expert testimony, reserve studies, environmental assessments, design and construction review.

BACKGROUND:
Established: 1957; 1st Franchised: 1958
Franchised Units: 72
Company-Owned Units: 0
Total Units: 72
Dist.: US-70; CAN-2; O'seas-0
North America: 37 States, Provinces
Density: 4 in CA, 3 in NJ, 3 in PA
Projected New Units (12 Months): 6
Qualifications: NR
FINANCIAL/TERMS:
Cash Investment: $6K
Total Investment: $30K
Minimum Net Worth: NR
Fees: Franchise - $26.5K
Royalty - 6%; Ad. - 1%
Earnings Claims Statement: Yes
Term of Contract (Years): 5/5/5/
Avg. # Of Employees: 2 FT, 2 PT
Passive Ownership: Not Allowed
Encourage Conversions: NA

Area Develop. Agreements: No
Sub-Franchising Contracts: No
Expand In Territory: Yes
Space Needs: 300 SF
SUPPORT & TRAINING:
Financial Assistance Provided: Yes (D)
Site Selection Assistance: NA
Lease Negotiation Assistance: No
Co-Operative Advertising: No
Franchisee Assoc./Member: NR
Size Of Corporate Staff: 10
On-Going Support: ,B,C,D,,,G,H,I
Training: 1 Week Headquarters;
;
SPECIFIC EXPANSION PLANS:
US: All Legally Permitted
Canada: All Canada
Overseas: All Countries

◄◄ ►►

ERA FRANCHISE SYSTEMS
1 Campus Dr.
Parsippany, NJ 07054
Tel: (800) 869-1260 (973) 428-9700
Fax: (973) 496-7354
E-Mail: franchise.information@realogy.com
Web Site: www.era.com
Mr. Tim Henderson, Executive Vice President

A network of approximately 2,600 offices and approximately 32,000 brokers and sales associates in the U. S. and 49 other countries and territories. As the innovator of the popular ERA® Sellers Security® Plan and the ERA® Answers Book, ERA Real Estate has been developing quality products and services to members and consumers alike since 1971.

BACKGROUND: IFA MEMBER
Established: 1971; 1st Franchised: 1972
Franchised Units: 2762
Company-Owned Units: 28
Total Units: 2790
Dist.: US-925; CAN-0; O'seas-1837
North America: 50 States, 0 Provinces
Density: 64 in NY, 95 in CA, 100 in FL
Projected New Units (12 Months): NR
Qualifications: 4, 4, 5, 4, 4, 4
FINANCIAL/TERMS:

Cash Investment:	Varies
Total Investment:	$47.5-210K
Minimum Net Worth:	$75K
Fees: Franchise -	$25K
Royalty - NR;	Ad. - 2%
Earnings Claims Statement:	No
Term of Contract (Years):	10/
Avg. # Of Employees:	Varies
Passive Ownership:	Not Allowed
Encourage Conversions:	Yes
Area Develop. Agreements:	No
Sub-Franchising Contracts:	No
Expand In Territory:	Yes
Space Needs:	1,000 SF

SUPPORT & TRAINING:

Financial Assistance Provided:	No
Site Selection Assistance:	No
Lease Negotiation Assistance:	No
Co-Operative Advertising:	No
Franchisee Assoc./Member:	Yes/Yes
Size Of Corporate Staff:	52
On-Going Support:	A,,C,D,E,,G,H,I
Training:	1 Week Parsippany, NJ;
2-3 Days On-Site	

SPECIFIC EXPANSION PLANS:

US:	All U.S.
Canada:	All Canada
Overseas:	All Countries

HELP-U-SELL REAL ESTATE
900 W. Castleton Rd.
Castle Rock, CO 80109
Tel: (800) 366-1177 (303) 814-1400
Fax: (303) 814-3400
E-Mail: info@helpusell.com
Web Site: www.helpusellfranchise.com
Mr. Ron McCoy, Director Franchise Sales

HELP-U-SELL Real Estate is the nation's first and largest fee-for-service real estate franchise. Rated as one of the best and fastest-growing franchises, HELP-U-SELL is revitalizing the real estate industry with programs that allow consumers to save money and real estate professionals to achieve higher profits. With hundreds of offices throughout the country and rapidly increasing numbers, HELP-U-SELL Real Estate dominates in the state-of-the-art fee-for-services category.

BACKGROUND: IFA MEMBER
Established: 1976; 1st Franchised: 1976
Franchised Units: 835

Company-Owned Units:	0
Total Units:	835
Dist.:	US-835; CAN-0; O'seas-0
North America:	46 States, 0 Provinces
Density:	79 in FL, 390 in CA, 48 in AZ
Projected New Units (12 Months):	200
Qualifications:	4, 4, 5, 3, 3, 4

FINANCIAL/TERMS:

Cash Investment:	$20K
Total Investment:	$45.5-148.5K
Minimum Net Worth:	NA
Fees: Franchise -	$19.5-29.5K
Royalty - 6%;	Ad. - 1.5%
Earnings Claims Statement:	No
Term of Contract (Years):	5/5
Avg. # Of Employees:	2-10 FT, 0 PT
Passive Ownership:	Discouraged
Encourage Conversions:	Yes
Area Develop. Agreements:	Yes/1
Sub-Franchising Contracts:	Yes
Expand In Territory:	Yes
Space Needs:	1,000 SF

SUPPORT & TRAINING:

Financial Assistance Provided:	No
Site Selection Assistance:	Yes
Lease Negotiation Assistance:	No
Co-Operative Advertising:	Yes
Franchisee Assoc./Member:	Yes/Yes
Size Of Corporate Staff:	25
On-Going Support:	,,c,D,e,,G,h,I
Training:	4 Days San Diego, CA

SPECIFIC EXPANSION PLANS:

US:	All United States
Canada:	All Canada
Overseas:	NR

<< >>

HOMETEAM INSPECTION SERVICE, THE
575 Chamber Dr.
Milford, OH 45150
Tel: (800) 598-5297 (513) 831-1300
Fax: (513) 831-6010
E-Mail: salesleads@hometeaminspection.com
Web Site: www.hometeaminspection.com
Mr. Dennis Malik, Franchise Development

Ranked #1 fastest-growing home inspection franchise in North America. Unique and field-proven marketing system that produces leads and appointments. Exclusive, protected territory. Extensive and continuous training. Sales hotline to build your business. Financing provided.

BACKGROUND: IFA MEMBER
Established: 1991; 1st Franchised: 1992

Franchised Units:	308
Company-Owned Units:	0
Total Units:	308
Dist.:	US-248; CAN-5; O'seas-0
North America:	48 States, 2 Provinces
Density:	20 in OH, 16 in MI, 29 in FL
Projected New Units (12 Months):	29
Qualifications:	2, 3, 2, 3, 3, 5

FINANCIAL/TERMS:

Cash Investment:	$30K
Total Investment:	$40K-80K
Minimum Net Worth:	NA
Fees: Franchise -	$11.9-29.9K
Royalty - 6%;	Ad. - 3%
Earnings Claims Statement:	No
Term of Contract (Years):	10/10/10/
Avg. # Of Employees:	1 FT, 0 PT
Passive Ownership:	Discouraged
Encourage Conversions:	NA
Area Develop. Agreements:	No
Sub-Franchising Contracts:	No
Expand In Territory:	Yes
Space Needs:	NA

SUPPORT & TRAINING:

Financial Assistance Provided:	Yes (D)
Site Selection Assistance:	NA
Lease Negotiation Assistance:	NA
Co-Operative Advertising:	No
Franchisee Assoc./Member:	Yes/Yes
Size Of Corporate Staff:	20
On-Going Support:	A,B,C,D,,,G,H,I
Training:	2 Weeks Corporate
Headquarters, Cincinnati, OH	

SPECIFIC EXPANSION PLANS:

US:	All United States
Canada:	All Canada
Overseas:	NR

<< >>

HOMEVESTORS OF AMERICA
10670 N. Central Expy., # 700
Dallas, TX 75231
Tel: (888) 495-5220 (972) 761-0046
Fax: (972) 534-1508
E-Mail: franchiseinquiry@homevestors.com
Web Site: www.homevestors.com
Mr. Jason Killough, Director Franchise Development

HOMEVESTORS franchise owners are real estate investors that specialize in buying and selling single-family houses. The franchise provides a system to buy houses wholesale, financing to purchase houses, training and other services.

BACKGROUND: IFA MEMBER
Established: 1989; 1st Franchised: 1996
Franchised Units: 265
Company-Owned Units: 0
Total Units: 265
Dist.: US-265; CAN-0; O'seas-0
  North America: 35 States, 0 Provinces
  Density: 44 in TX, 21 in GA, 43 in FL
Projected New Units (12 Months): 68
Qualifications: 4, 4, 3, 2, 4, 5
FINANCIAL/TERMS:
Cash Investment: $165-200K
Total Investment: $200-370K
Minimum Net Worth: NR
Fees: Franchise - $49K
  Royalty - $775/Transaction; Ad.
- $200/Transaction
Earnings Claims Statement: No
Term of Contract (Years): 5/5
Avg. # Of Employees: 3 FT, PT
Passive Ownership: Discouraged
Encourage Conversions: Yes
Area Develop. Agreements: No
Sub-Franchising Contracts: No
Expand In Territory: No
Space Needs: 600 SF
SUPPORT & TRAINING:
Financial Assistance Provided: Yes (I)
Site Selection Assistance: Yes
Lease Negotiation Assistance: No
Co-Operative Advertising: Yes
Franchisee Assoc./Member: No
Size Of Corporate Staff: 82
On-Going Support: A,,C,D,E,,G,H,
Training: 10 Days Dallas, TX;
  10 Days Franchise Location
SPECIFIC EXPANSION PLANS:
US: In 35 states
Canada: No
Overseas: NR

◄◄ ►►

INSPECT-IT 1ST PROPERTY INSPECTION

7100 E. Pleasant Valley Rd., # 300
Independence, OH 44131
Tel: (877) 392-6278 (216) 674-0645
Fax: (216) 674-0650
E-Mail: kgolubski@inspectit1st.com
Web Site: www.inspectit1st.com
Ms. Kylene Golubski, VP Business Development

Before you buy, before you sell, INSPECT-IT 1ST. Providing state-of-the-art home inspections since 1991. Consistently recognized by Entrepreneur Magazine as

one of their Top 500 franchises. 13 years and 60,000 inspections. We provide you with all you need: initial training, digitally-enhanced inspection reports, on-going marketing support and programs, business development CD, support center and more.

BACKGROUND: IFA MEMBER
Established: 1991; 1st Franchised: 1998
Franchised Units: 67
Company-Owned Units: 0
Total Units: 67
Dist.: US-67; CAN-0; O'seas-0
  North America: 0 States, 0 Provinces
  Density: 7 in FL, 4 in CA, 10 in AZ
Projected New Units (12 Months): NR
Qualifications: NR
FINANCIAL/TERMS:
Cash Investment: $27K
Total Investment: $36.5K-59K
Minimum Net Worth: NA
Fees: Franchise - $24.9-27.9K
  Royalty - 6%/$200; Ad. - 2%/$50
Earnings Claims Statement: Yes
Term of Contract (Years): 10/10
Avg. # Of Employees: 1-3 FT, 0 PT
Passive Ownership: Discouraged
Encourage Conversions: No
Area Develop. Agreements: Yes/1
Sub-Franchising Contracts: Yes
Expand In Territory: Yes
Space Needs: NA
SUPPORT & TRAINING:
Financial Assistance Provided: No
Site Selection Assistance: NA
Lease Negotiation Assistance: NA
Co-Operative Advertising: No
Franchisee Assoc./Member: No
Size Of Corporate Staff: 5
On-Going Support: ,B,c,D,E,,G,H,I
Training: 2 Weeks Arizona
SPECIFIC EXPANSION PLANS:
US: All United States
Canada: NR
Overseas: NR

◄◄ ►►

Hottest New Franchise

LEASE COACH, THE

4445 Calgary Trl., # 820 Terrace Plz.
Edmonton, AB T6H 5R7 Canada
Tel: (800) 738-9202 (780) 448-2645
Fax: (780) 448-2670

E-Mail: dalewillerton@TheLeaseCoach.com
Web Site: www.TheLeaseCoach.com
Mr. Jeff Grandfield, Franchise Development

Commercial lease consulting services for tenants. Services include document reviews, lease negotiating, site selection etc.

BACKGROUND: IFA MEMBER
Established: 1993; 1st Franchised: 2006
Franchised Units: 4
Company-Owned Units: 1
Total Units: 5
Dist.: US-3; CAN-2; O'seas-0
  North America: 3 States, 2 Provinces
  Density: 1 in TX, 1 in OH, 2 in AB
Projected New Units (12 Months): 24
Qualifications: 3, 4, 4, 3, 3, 5
FINANCIAL/TERMS:
Cash Investment: $25K-35K
Total Investment: $25K-50K
Minimum Net Worth: $25K
Fees: Franchise - $11.8K
  Royalty - 2.2 - 3.2K; Ad. - 0
Earnings Claims Statement: No
Term of Contract (Years): 10/5
Avg. # Of Employees: 0-1 FT, 0-1 PT
Passive Ownership: Not Allowed
Encourage Conversions: NA
Area Develop. Agreements: No
Sub-Franchising Contracts: No
Expand In Territory: Yes
Space Needs: NA
SUPPORT & TRAINING:
Financial Assistance Provided: No
Site Selection Assistance: NA
Lease Negotiation Assistance: NA
Co-Operative Advertising: Yes
Franchisee Assoc./Member: No
Size Of Corporate Staff: 3
On-Going Support: a,,,,,,g,h,i
Training: 1 week Edmonton, Alberta
SPECIFIC EXPANSION PLANS:
US: All of U.S.
Canada: British Columbia, Saskatchewan, Manitoba, Quebec,
Overseas: NR

◄◄ ►►

NATIONAL PROPERTY INSPECTIONS

NATIONAL PROPERTY INSPECTIONS (NPI)

9375 Burt St., # 201

Omaha, NE 68114
Tel: (800) 333-9807 + 24 (402) 333-9807 + 24
Fax: (800) 933-2508
E-Mail: info@npiweb.com
Web Site: www.npiweb.com
Ms. Julie Erickson, Director of Franchise Sales

Nationally acclaimed residential and commercial property inspection franchise. Low start-up costs. Exclusive territories. Expansion encouraged. Intensive, interactive, 2-week classroom training , 1-week field training. On-going marketing and technical support. Fee includes state-of-the-art computer package and most everything needed to start your business. GLOBAL PROPERTY INSPECTIONS (GPI) is the operating entity in Canada.

BACKGROUND:
Established: 1987; 1st Franchised: 1987
Franchised Units: 250
Company-Owned Units: 0
Total Units: 250
Dist.:   US-239; CAN-11; O'seas-0
  North America: 43 States, 4 Provinces
  Density: 13 in PA, 22 in FL, 24 in CA
Projected New Units (12 Months):   40
Qualifications: 3, 3, 4, 3, 4, 4
FINANCIAL/TERMS:
Cash Investment: $23.8K
Total Investment: $23.8K
Minimum Net Worth: NR
Fees: Franchise - $23.8K
  Royalty - 8%;   Ad. - 0%
Earnings Claims Statement: No
Term of Contract (Years):   10/
Avg. # Of Employees: 1 FT, 0 PT
Passive Ownership: Discouraged
Encourage Conversions: Yes
Area Develop. Agreements: No
Sub-Franchising Contracts: No
Expand In Territory: Yes
Space Needs: NR
SUPPORT & TRAINING:
Financial Assistance Provided: Yes (D)
Site Selection Assistance: NA
Lease Negotiation Assistance: NA
Co-Operative Advertising: No
Franchisee Assoc./Member: No
Size Of Corporate Staff: 11
On-Going Support: ,,,D,,,G,H,I
Training: 2 Weeks Omaha, NE
  in NPI Corporate Office; 1 Week Field
  Training near Franchisee's Home
SPECIFIC EXPANSION PLANS:
US: All United States
Canada: All Canada

Overseas: NR

PILLAR TO POST
14502 N. Dale Mabry Hwy., # 200
Tampa, FL 33618
Tel: (877) 963-3129 (813) 962-4461
Fax: (813) 963-0506
E-Mail: franchise.
development@pillartopost.com
Web Site: www.pillartopost.com
Mr. Gordon Williams, Director Franchise Development

Program directed by specialists with over 50 years of experience. Territory development from preferred aggressive multi-inspector business levels to moderate single inspector levels available. PILLAR TO POST provides the most recognized opportunity in the home inspection industry. Imaginative, highly successful marketing designed for top performance in business development. Promotional materials, IT support, innovative website and on-going, cooperative team building operational assistance are provided.

BACKGROUND: IFA MEMBER
Established: 1994; 1st Franchised: 1994
Franchised Units: 500
Company-Owned Units: 0
Total Units: 500
Dist.:   US-393; CAN-107; O'seas-0
  North America: 44 States, 8 Provinces
  Density: 20 in NY, 20 in NJ, 30 in FL
Projected New Units (12 Months):   10
Qualifications: 3, 3, 3, 3, 3, 3
FINANCIAL/TERMS:
Cash Investment: $20-46K
Total Investment: $24.5K-64.5K
Minimum Net Worth: $100K
Fees: Franchise - $20-46K
  Royalty - 7%;   Ad. - 4%
Earnings Claims Statement: No
Term of Contract (Years):   5/5/5
Avg. # Of Employees: 2 FT, 0 PT
Passive Ownership: Not Allowed
Encourage Conversions: NA
Area Develop. Agreements: No
Sub-Franchising Contracts: Yes
Expand In Territory: Yes
Space Needs: Home-Based
SUPPORT & TRAINING:

Financial Assistance Provided: No
Site Selection Assistance: NA
Lease Negotiation Assistance: No
Co-Operative Advertising: Yes
Franchisee Assoc./Member: No
Size Of Corporate Staff: 20
On-Going Support: A,B,C,D,,,G,h,I
Training: 2 Weeks Mississauga, ON
SPECIFIC EXPANSION PLANS:
US: All United States
Canada: All Canada
Overseas: NR

PROFESSIONAL HOUSE DOCTORS
1406 E. 14th St.
Des Moines, IA 50316-2406
Tel: (800) 288-7437 (515) 265-6667
Fax: (515) 278-2070
E-Mail: info@prohousedr.com
Web Site: www.prohousedr.com
Mr. Dane J. Shearer, President

Environmental and building science specialists providing home and building inspections, radon testing and mitigation, plus over 20 other specialized services.

BACKGROUND:
Established: 1982; 1st Franchised: 1991
Franchised Units: 6
Company-Owned Units: 1
Total Units: 7
Dist.:   US-7; CAN-0; O'seas-0
  North America: 1 States, 0 Provinces
  Density: 7 in IA,
Projected New Units (12 Months):   2
Qualifications: 3, 3, 2, 2, 4, 5
FINANCIAL/TERMS:
Cash Investment: $20K
Total Investment: $20K
Minimum Net Worth: $100K
Fees: Franchise - $18.5K
  Royalty - 6%;   Ad. - 2%
Earnings Claims Statement: No
Term of Contract (Years):   5/5
Avg. # Of Employees: 1 FT, 1 PT
Passive Ownership: Not Allowed
Encourage Conversions: NA
Area Develop. Agreements: No
Sub-Franchising Contracts: No
Expand In Territory: Yes
Space Needs: Minimal SF
SUPPORT & TRAINING:
Financial Assistance Provided: Yes (D)
Site Selection Assistance: Yes
Lease Negotiation Assistance: NA
Co-Operative Advertising: Yes

Franchisee Assoc./Member: Yes/Yes
Size Of Corporate Staff: 0
On-Going Support: A,B,C,D,E,F,G,H,I
Training: 2 Weeks Corporate Office
SPECIFIC EXPANSION PLANS:
US: All United States
Canada: No
Overseas: NR

PROSPECTION

7100 E. Pleasant Valley Rd., # 300
Independence, OH 44131
Tel: (877) 392-6278 + 10 (216) 674-0645
+ 10
Fax: (216) 674-0650
E-Mail: inquiry@pro-spection.com
Web Site: www.prospectionusa.com
Ms. Kylene Golubski, VP Business Planning/Devel.

Benefits of PROSPECTION include large territories, lower franchise fees, interest-free financing, training and more. You also have access to our team of marketing, technology and business development experts. Compare us to other inspection franchises and then contact us for a cost/benefit analysis. PROSPECTION is a subsidiary of Merrymeeting Inc. (MMI) an investment firm specializing in the acquisition and development of franchise systems. Through its multiple franchises, MMI operates 800+ units.

BACKGROUND: IFA MEMBER
Established: 2003; 1st Franchised: 2003
Franchised Units: 15
Company-Owned Units: 0
Total Units: 15
Dist.: US-15; CAN-0; O'seas-0
  North America: 5 States, 0 Provinces
  Density: 2 in TX, 4 in UT
Projected New Units (12 Months): 25
Qualifications: 3, 2, 1, 1, 1, 5
FINANCIAL/TERMS:
Cash Investment: $3-4K
Total Investment: $15.2-38.5K
Minimum Net Worth: $None
Fees: Franchise - $6K or 12K
  Royalty - 7%; Ad. - 2%
Earnings Claims Statement: No
Term of Contract (Years): 7/7
Avg. # Of Employees: 1 FT, 0 PT
Passive Ownership: Allowed

Encourage Conversions: Yes
Area Develop. Agreements: No
Sub-Franchising Contracts: No
Expand In Territory: Yes
Space Needs: NR
SUPPORT & TRAINING:
Financial Assistance Provided: Yes (D)
Site Selection Assistance: NA
Lease Negotiation Assistance: NA
Co-Operative Advertising: No
Franchisee Assoc./Member: No
Size Of Corporate Staff: 25
On-Going Support: A,B,,D,,,G,h,I
Training: 7 Days 8 Different Locations;
  6 Hours Online
SPECIFIC EXPANSION PLANS:
US: All US except NV, OR, MA, CT, PA, AZ, LA, NJ, NC
Canada: No
Overseas: NR

The Real Estate Leaders

RE/MAX INTERNATIONAL

5075 S. Syracuse St.
Denver, CO 80237-2712
Tel: (800) 525-7452 (303) 770-5531
Fax: (303) 796-3599
E-Mail: petergilmour@remax.net
Web Site: www.remax.com
Mr. Peter Gilmour, Sr. VP Intl. Franchise Sales and Brokerage

The RE/MAX real estate franchise network is a global system of more than 7,000 offices worldwide, engaging more than 110,000 members. RE/MAX sales associates lead the industry in professional designations, experience and production while providing real estate services in residential, commercial, referral, relocation and asset management. For more information visit www.remax.com.

BACKGROUND: IFA MEMBER
Established: 1973; 1st Franchised: 1975
Franchised Units: 5226
Company-Owned Units: 28
Total Units: 5253
Dist.: US-4337; CAN-655; O'seas-2039
  North America: 50 States, 12 Provinces
  Density: 314 in TX, 281 in ON, 410 in CA
Projected New Units (12 Months): 700

Qualifications: 3, 4, 5, 1, 4, 4
FINANCIAL/TERMS:
Cash Investment: $20K-200K
Total Investment: $20K-200K
Minimum Net Worth: Varies
Fees: Franchise - $12.5-25K
  Royalty - Varies; Ad. - Varies
Earnings Claims Statement: No
Term of Contract (Years): 5/5
Avg. # Of Employees: 2-4 FT, 1 PT
Passive Ownership: Discouraged
Encourage Conversions: Yes
Area Develop. Agreements: No
Sub-Franchising Contracts: No
Expand In Territory: Yes
Space Needs: Varies
SUPPORT & TRAINING:
Financial Assistance Provided: Yes (D)
Site Selection Assistance: Yes
Lease Negotiation Assistance: Yes
Co-Operative Advertising: No
Franchisee Assoc./Member: No
Size Of Corporate Staff: 500
On-Going Support: ,,C,D,,,G,h,I
Training: 40+ Hours Headquarters in
  Denver, CO
SPECIFIC EXPANSION PLANS:
US: All United States
Canada: Yes
Overseas: NR

REALTY EXECUTIVES INTERNATIONAL

2398 E. Camelback Rd., # 900
Phoenix, AZ 85016
Tel: (800) 252-3366 (602) 957-0747
Fax: (602) 224-5542
E-Mail: billpowers@realtyexecutives.com
Web Site: www.realtyexecutives.com
Mr. William A. Powers, Chief Operating Officer

The originators of the 100% Commission Concept. Awarding franchises to use the REALTY EXECUTIVES' name.

BACKGROUND:
Established: 1965; 1st Franchised: 1987
Franchised Units: 70
Company-Owned Units: 0
Total Units: 70
Dist.: US-64; CAN-3; O'seas-3
  North America: 45 States, 5 Provinces
  Density: NR
Projected New Units (12 Months): 150
Qualifications: 4, 5, 5, 2, 3, 4
FINANCIAL/TERMS:
Cash Investment: $25K

Total Investment:	$25-82.5K
Minimum Net Worth:	$30-50K
Fees: Franchise -	$15K
Royalty - $35-50/Agent/Mo;	Ad.
- $5-10/Agent	
Earnings Claims Statement:	No
Term of Contract (Years):	5/5
Avg. # Of Employees:	1 FT, 0 PT
Passive Ownership:	Allowed
Encourage Conversions:	Yes
Area Develop. Agreements:	Yes/1
Sub-Franchising Contracts:	Yes
Expand In Territory:	Yes
Space Needs:	NR

SUPPORT & TRAINING:

Financial Assistance Provided:	No
Site Selection Assistance:	No
Lease Negotiation Assistance:	No
Co-Operative Advertising:	No
Franchisee Assoc./Member:	No
Size Of Corporate Staff:	12
On-Going Support:	,,,,,G,h,I
Training: 4 Days Company Headquarters in Phoenix	

SPECIFIC EXPANSION PLANS:

US:	All United States
Canada:	All Canada
Overseas:	All Countries

SOTHEBY'S INTERNATIONAL REALTY
1 Campus Dr.
Parsippany, NJ 07054
Tel: (866) 899-4747 (973) 407-8010
Fax:
E-Mail: franchise.information@realogy.com
Web Site: www.sothebysrealty.com
Mr. Tim Henderson, Executive Vice President

Founded in 1976 to provide independent brokerages with a powerful marketing and referral program for luxury listings, the Sotheby's International Realty network was designed to connect the finest independent real estate companies to the most prestigious clientele in the world. In February 2004, Realogy Corporation (then Cendant Corporation), the world's leading real estate brokerage francisor, entered into a long-term strategic alliance with Sotheby's Holdings, Inc. (LSE: STBA).

BACKGROUND:	IFA MEMBER
Established: 2004;	1st Franchised: 2004
Franchised Units:	480
Company-Owned Units:	44
Total Units:	524
Dist.:	US-339; CAN-11; O'seas-185
North America:	36 States, 3 Provinces
Density:	30 in NY, 34 in NJ, 28 in CA
Projected New Units (12 Months): Varies	
Qualifications:	4, 4, 5, 4, 4, 4

FINANCIAL/TERMS:

Cash Investment:	$51.5-146K
Total Investment:	$153.5-566K
Minimum Net Worth:	$150K
Fees: Franchise -	$25K
Royalty - 6%;	Ad. - 2%
Earnings Claims Statement:	Yes
Term of Contract (Years):	10/Varies
Avg. # Of Employees:	Varies
Passive Ownership:	Allowed
Encourage Conversions:	Yes
Area Develop. Agreements:	No
Sub-Franchising Contracts:	No
Expand In Territory:	Yes
Space Needs:	1800-3500 SF

SUPPORT & TRAINING:

Financial Assistance Provided:	No
Site Selection Assistance:	No
Lease Negotiation Assistance:	No
Co-Operative Advertising:	Yes
Franchisee Assoc./Member:	Yes/Yes
Size Of Corporate Staff:	28
On-Going Support:	A,B,C,D,E,,G,h,I
Training:	Varies

SPECIFIC EXPANSION PLANS:

US:	All United States
Canada:	All Canada
Overseas:	All Countries

WIN HOME INSPECTION
6500 6th Ave., N.W.
Seattle, WA 98117-5099
Tel: (800) 967-8127 (206) 728-8100
Fax: (206) 441-3655
E-Mail: joinwin@wini.com
Web Site: www.winfranchise.com
Franchise Development

WIN Home Inspection - the # 1 premium home inspection service in North America. Get your share of the more than 4 million home inspections performed each year. We know home inspections. With more than 13 years in the industry, we give you the independence of being your own boss with the support of a powerful nationwide network of more than 200 franchisees in 33 states. We offer an unparalleled track record of success. Exclusive territories and the most extensive training, technology and support.

BACKGROUND:	IFA MEMBER
Established: 1993;	1st Franchised: 1994
Franchised Units:	223
Company-Owned Units:	0
Total Units:	223
Dist.:	US-223; CAN-0; O'seas-0
North America:	33 States, 0 Provinces
Density:	30 in WA, 19 in NY, 53 in CA
Projected New Units (12 Months):	26
Qualifications:	5, 5, 2, 2, 5, 5

FINANCIAL/TERMS:

Cash Investment:	$28-49K
Total Investment:	$27-52K
Minimum Net Worth:	NA
Fees: Franchise -	$17-26K
Royalty - 7%/$300 Min.; Ad. - 3%/$125 Min	
Earnings Claims Statement:	No
Term of Contract (Years):	10/10
Avg. # Of Employees:	1 FT, 0 PT
Passive Ownership:	Discouraged
Encourage Conversions:	Yes
Area Develop. Agreements:	Yes/10
Sub-Franchising Contracts:	No
Expand In Territory:	Yes
Space Needs:	NA

SUPPORT & TRAINING:

Financial Assistance Provided:	Yes (D)
Site Selection Assistance:	Yes
Lease Negotiation Assistance:	NA
Co-Operative Advertising:	No
Franchisee Assoc./Member:	Yes/Yes
Size Of Corporate Staff:	15
On-Going Support:	,,C,D,,,G,h,I
Training: 2 Weeks Seattle, WA; 2 Weeks Pre-Training at Home	

SPECIFIC EXPANSION PLANS:

US:	Most of United States
Canada:	No
Overseas:	NR

FIVE LARGEST PARTICIPANTS IN SURVEY

Company	# Franchised Units	# Co-Owned Units	# Total Units	Franchise Fee	On-Going Royalty	Total Investment
1. Applebee's International	1,201	383	1,584	$35K/Unit	4%	$1.74-3.17MM
2. Denny's	1,281	263	1,544	$40K	4%	$1-$2.6MM
3. CiCi's Pizza	620	19	639	$30K	4%	$418-659.2K
4. Friendly's Restaurants	206	314	520	$30-35K	4%	$499K-1.94MM
5. Golden Corral Family Steakhouse	378	105	483	$50K	4%	$2-6MM

All of the data provided are proprietary and should not be quoted without acknowledging *Bond's Franchise Guide*.

ALAMO DRAFTHOUSE CINEMAS
1717 W. 6th St., # 351
Austin, Texas 78703
Tel: (512) 219-7800
Fax: (512) 692-1933
E-Mail: franchise@drafthouse.com
Web Site: www.Drafthouse.com
Ms. Allison Marshall, Franchise Relations
    Manager

The first Alamo Drafthouse Cinema opened its doors in 1997. A unique combination of movie theater and restaurant, the Alamo shows the best first-run and independent films and offers an extensive menu of fresh, handmade dishes and a wide selection of beer and wine. Entertainment Weekly voted the Alamo, "The number one theater in the country, doing it right". Come join the Alamo team!

BACKGROUND: IFA MEMBER
Established: 1997;   1st Franchised: 2003
Franchised Units: 4
Company-Owned Units: 3
Total Units: 7
Dist.:   US-7; CAN-0; O'seas-0
  North America: 1 States, 0 Provinces
  Density: 7 in TX
Projected New Units (12 Months):   3
Qualifications: 5, 5, 4, 3, 4, 5

FINANCIAL/TERMS:
Cash Investment: $1.25-2.25MM
Total Investment: $1.6MM
Minimum Net Worth: $1MM
Fees: Franchise - $75K
  Royalty - 5%;   Ad. - 1%
Earnings Claims Statement: Yes
Term of Contract (Years):   10/10
Avg. # Of Employees: 7 FT, 60 PT
Passive Ownership: Allowed
Encourage Conversions: Yes
Area Develop. Agreements: Yes/5
Sub-Franchising Contracts: No
Expand In Territory: Yes
Space Needs: 28 SF
SUPPORT & TRAINING:

Financial Assistance Provided:	No
Site Selection Assistance:	Yes
Lease Negotiation Assistance:	Yes
Co-Operative Advertising:	Yes
Franchisee Assoc./Member:	No
Size Of Corporate Staff:	8
On-Going Support:	a,,C,D,E,,g,H,
Training:	Four weeks Austin, TX; Two weeks On-site

SPECIFIC EXPANSION PLANS:

US:	Continental US
Canada:	No
Overseas:	NR

◄◄ ►►

APPLEBEE'S INTERNATIONAL

4551 W. 107th St., # 100
Overland Park, KS 66207
Tel: (913) 967-4000
Fax: (913) 967-4135
E-Mail: dave.goebel@applebees.com
Web Site: www.applebees.com
Mr. Dave Goebel, President/COO

Everyone's favorite neighbor is definitely APPLEBEE'S neighborhood grill and bar. This distinguished casual-dining restaurant has a comfortable individuality which reflects the neighborhood in which it is located, making the APPLEBEE'S concept appealing wherever it is built.

BACKGROUND: IFA MEMBER

Established: 1980;	1st Franchised: 1988
Franchised Units:	1201
Company-Owned Units:	383
Total Units:	1584
Dist.:	US-1571; CAN-5; O'seas-8
North America:	47 States, 3 Provinces
Density:	48 in OH, 62 in FL, 54 in CA
Projected New Units (12 Months):	125
Qualifications:	5, 5, 5, NR, NR, 5

FINANCIAL/TERMS:

Cash Investment:	$1MM-50% Liq.
Total Investment:	$1.74-3.17MM
Minimum Net Worth:	NR
Fees: Franchise -	$35K/Unit
Royalty - 4%;	Ad. - 3%
Earnings Claims Statement:	No
Term of Contract (Years):	20/
Avg. # Of Employees:	75-100 FT, 0 PT
Passive Ownership:	Not Allowed
Encourage Conversions:	No
Area Develop. Agreements:	Yes/1
Sub-Franchising Contracts:	No
Expand In Territory:	Yes
Space Needs:	5,000-5,400 SF

SUPPORT & TRAINING:

Financial Assistance Provided:	No

Site Selection Assistance:	Yes
Lease Negotiation Assistance:	Yes
Co-Operative Advertising:	No
Franchisee Assoc./Member:	Yes/Yes
Size Of Corporate Staff:	300
On-Going Support:	A,B,C,D,E,,G,H,I
Training:	8-12 Weeks Certified Training Unit; 3 Days Headquarters

SPECIFIC EXPANSION PLANS:

US:	NY, LA, HI, AK
Canada:	All Canada
Overseas:	All Countries

◄◄ ►►

BAKER BROTHERS
AMERICAN DELI

5500 Greenville Ave., #1102
Dallas, TX 75206
Tel: (214) 696-8780
Fax: (214) 696-8809
E-Mail: info@bakerbrosdeli.com
Web Site: www.bakerbrosdeli.com
Mr. Ralph Kinder, Director Franchise Development

Bridging the gap between the typical sandwich chains and full-service casual dining, Baker Brothers is an upscale, fast-casual deli, featuring specialty sandwiches, award-winning salads, gourmet pizzas and more. Baker Brothers is currently seeking franchise partners willing and able to open 3-5 units. We are currently seeking franchisees in all states. Baker Brothers is a business investment and franchisees are not expected to be owner/operators.

BACKGROUND:

Established: 1999;	1st Franchised: 2000
Franchised Units:	8
Company-Owned Units:	7
Total Units:	15
Dist.:	US-15; CAN-0; O'seas-0
North America:	3 States, 0 Provinces
Density:	2 in SC, 12 in TX, 1 in KY
Projected New Units (12 Months):	6-8
Qualifications:	5, 5, 5, 3, 3, 5

FINANCIAL/TERMS:

Cash Investment:	$250K
Total Investment:	$430.5-656K
Minimum Net Worth:	$1.5MM
Fees: Franchise -	$25K
Royalty - 5%;	Ad. - 0
Earnings Claims Statement:	Yes
Term of Contract (Years):	10/10
Avg. # Of Employees:	3 FT, 15 PT
Passive Ownership:	Allowed
Encourage Conversions:	NA
Area Develop. Agreements:	Yes/3

Sub-Franchising Contracts:	No
Expand In Territory:	Yes
Space Needs:	2,500-3,500 SF

SUPPORT & TRAINING:

Financial Assistance Provided:	No
Site Selection Assistance:	Yes
Lease Negotiation Assistance:	Yes
Co-Operative Advertising:	No
Franchisee Assoc./Member:	No
Size Of Corporate Staff:	7
On-Going Support:	,,C,D,,F,G,H,
Training:	8 weeks Dallas, TX

SPECIFIC EXPANSION PLANS:

US:	All United States
Canada:	No
Overseas:	NR

◄◄ ►►

BEEF O'BRADY'S FAMILY
SPORTS PUBS

5510 W. LaSalle St., # 200
Tampa, FL 33607
Tel: (800) 728-8878 (813) 226-2333 + 206
Fax: (813) 226-0030
E-Mail: nick@beefobradys.com
Web Site: www.beefobradys.com
Mr. Nick Vojnovic, President

BEEF O'BRADY'S FAMILY SPORTS PUBS are family-friendly, community-oriented, casual sports pubs. BEEF's features their signature crispy buffalo-style chicken wings, great burgers, sandwiches, salads and kids' meals. Large selection of beers and wines - no hard liquor. Satellite TV. Our concept is built on the owner/operator model, where the day-to-day operations in every BEEF's is conducted by the owner. The concept is simple enough to operate that most of our partners have no prior restaurant experience. Our home office team consists of experienced restaurant operators who support our franchise partners at all levels of operations.

BACKGROUND: IFA MEMBER

Established: 1985;	1st Franchised: 1998
Franchised Units:	227
Company-Owned Units:	4
Total Units:	231
Dist.:	US-231; CAN-0; O'seas-0
North America:	19 States, 0 Provinces
Density:	11 in SC, 23 in GA, 130 in FL
Projected New Units (12 Months):	55
Qualifications:	3, 4, 2, 2, 4, 4

FINANCIAL/TERMS:

Cash Investment:	$125K-250K
Total Investment:	$375K-600K
Minimum Net Worth:	$250K
Fees: Franchise -	$35K
Royalty - 4%;	Ad. - 1.5%
Earnings Claims Statement:	No
Term of Contract (Years):	10/5/5/
Avg. # Of Employees:	15 FT, 10 PT
Passive Ownership:	Not Allowed
Encourage Conversions:	Yes
Area Develop. Agreements:	Yes/3
Sub-Franchising Contracts:	No
Expand In Territory:	Yes
Space Needs:	3,000 SF

SUPPORT & TRAINING:

Financial Assistance Provided:	Yes (D)
Site Selection Assistance:	Yes
Lease Negotiation Assistance:	Yes
Co-Operative Advertising:	No
Franchisee Assoc./Member:	No
Size Of Corporate Staff:	28
On-Going Support:	„C,D,E,,G,H,I
Training:	9 Weeks Approved Location

SPECIFIC EXPANSION PLANS:

US:	SE and Midwest
Canada:	No
Overseas:	NR

⋖⋖ ⋗⋗

BIG BOY RESTAURANT & BAKERY

1 Big Boy Dr.
Warren, MI 48091
Tel: (800) 837-3003 (586) 759-6000
Fax: (586) 757-4737
E-Mail: franchiseinfo@bigboy.com
Web Site: www.bigboy.com
Mr. Dave Knitter, VP Franchising

Full-service family restaurant with over 60 years of success. BIG BOY'S comprehensive menu features a daily breakfast and fruit buffet, soup, salad and fruit bar, in-store bakery and award-winning desserts, in addition to traditional favorites. Industry leader in managed profitability.

BACKGROUND: IFA MEMBER
Established: 1936; 1st Franchised: 1952
Franchised Units: 427
Company-Owned Units: <u>28</u>
Total Units: 455
Dist.: US-455; CAN-0; O'seas-100
North America: 17 States, 0 Provinces
Density:102 in OH, 142 in MI, 25 in KY
Projected New Units (12 Months): 7
Qualifications: 5, 5, 4, 3, 4, 5
FINANCIAL/TERMS:

Cash Investment:	$450K-600K
Total Investment:	$1.6MM-2.6MM
Minimum Net Worth:	$750K
Fees: Franchise -	$40K
Royalty - 3%;	Ad. - 3%
Earnings Claims Statement:	Yes
Term of Contract (Years):	20/
Avg. # Of Employees:	10 FT, 25 PT
Passive Ownership:	Discouraged
Encourage Conversions:	Yes
Area Develop. Agreements:	Yes/1
Sub-Franchising Contracts:	No
Expand In Territory:	Yes
Space Needs:	5,200 SF

SUPPORT & TRAINING:

Financial Assistance Provided:	Yes (D)
Site Selection Assistance:	Yes
Lease Negotiation Assistance:	Yes
Co-Operative Advertising:	No
Franchisee Assoc./Member:	Yes/Yes
Size Of Corporate Staff:	165
On-Going Support:	A,B,C,D,E,F,G,H,I
Training:	6-8 Weeks In-Unit;
	1-2 Weeks Corporate Headquarters

SPECIFIC EXPANSION PLANS:

US:	All United States
Canada:	All Canada
Overseas:	All Countries

⋖⋖ ⋗⋗

BOSTON PIZZA INTERNATIONAL, INC.

5500 Parkwood Wy.
Richmond, BC V6V 2M4 Canada
Tel: (604) 270-1108
Fax: (604) 270-4168
E-Mail: wickstromc@bostonpizza.com
Web Site: www.bostonpizza.com
Ms. Colleen Wickstrom, Executive Administrative Assistant

BOSTON PIZZA is Canada's most successful casual dining pizza and pasta franchise operation, with over 260 locations in North America and system-wide sales in excess of 500 million. Boston Pizza appeals to four sectors: families at early evening, business people at lunch, after movies and takeout and delivery.

BACKGROUND: IFA MEMBER
Established: 1964; 1st Franchised: 1968
Franchised Units: 351
Company-Owned Units: <u>9</u>
Total Units: 360
Dist.: US-37; CAN-226; O'seas-0

North America:	16 States, 9 Provinces
Density:	52 in ON, 54 in BC, 79 in AB
Projected New Units (12 Months):	80
Qualifications:	5, 5, 3, 3, 4, 5

FINANCIAL/TERMS:

Cash Investment:	$600K
Total Investment:	$1.8-2.2MM
Minimum Net Worth:	$1.5MM
Fees: Franchise -	$40K
Royalty - 5-7%;	Ad. - 3.5%
Earnings Claims Statement:	Yes
Term of Contract (Years):	10/10
Avg. # Of Employees:	40 FT, 40 PT
Passive Ownership:	Not Allowed
Encourage Conversions:	No
Area Develop. Agreements:	Yes/1
Sub-Franchising Contracts:	No
Expand In Territory:	Yes
Space Needs:	5,750-6500 SF

SUPPORT & TRAINING:

Financial Assistance Provided:	Yes (I)
Site Selection Assistance:	Yes
Lease Negotiation Assistance:	Yes
Co-Operative Advertising:	Yes
Franchisee Assoc./Member:	Yes/Yes
Size Of Corporate Staff:	123
On-Going Support:	,B,C,D,E,F,G,H,I
Training:	5-6 Weeks Corporate Training Center; 2 Weeks Richmond, BC, Head Office

SPECIFIC EXPANSION PLANS:

US:	All United States
Canada:	All Canada
Overseas:	NR

⋖⋖ ⋗⋗

CAMILLE'S SIDEWALK CAFE

8801 S. Yale, # 400
Tulsa, OK 74137
Tel: (800) 230-7004 (703) 549-5332
Fax: (703) 549-0740
E-Mail: staceyg@fransmart.com
Web Site: www.camillescafe.com
Ms. Stacey Gallagher, Marketing Manager

CAMILLE'S SIDEWALK CAFE is one of the quickest-growing cafes in the US today, opening a new unit nearly every other week. Serving gourmet sandwiches, Italian panini, fresh soups and salads, smoothies, gourmet coffees and espresso, as well as pastries and baked goods, CAMILLE'S is poised to meet any customer's cravings from the health-conscious to the small child. Low start-up costs, simple operations. Simple to run, no bakeries, hoods, fryers or grease traps. Easily replicable.

BACKGROUND: IFA MEMBER
Established: 1996;   1st Franchised: 1999
Franchised Units: 50
Company-Owned Units: <u>1</u>
Total Units: 51
Dist.:   US-51; CAN-0; O'seas-0
   North America: 18 States, Provinces
   Density: 6 in IL, 7 in OK, 8 in TX
Projected New Units (12 Months):   75
Qualifications: 5, 3, 4, 3, 4, 5
FINANCIAL/TERMS:
Cash Investment: $250K
Total Investment: $210-470K
Minimum Net Worth: $500K
Fees: Franchise - $25K
   Royalty - 5%;   Ad. - 1%
Earnings Claims Statement: No
Term of Contract (Years):   20/10
Avg. # Of Employees: 15 FT, 10 PT
Passive Ownership: Allowed
Encourage Conversions: Yes
Area Develop. Agreements: Yes/1
Sub-Franchising Contracts: No
Expand In Territory: Yes
Space Needs: 2,500 SF
SUPPORT & TRAINING:
Financial Assistance Provided: Yes (D)
Site Selection Assistance: Yes
Lease Negotiation Assistance: Yes
Co-Operative Advertising: No
Franchisee Assoc./Member: Yes/Yes
Size Of Corporate Staff: 25
On-Going Support: a,B,C,D,e,F,G,H,I
Training: 3 Weeks Tulsa, OK;
   1 Week Franchisee Store Location
SPECIFIC EXPANSION PLANS:
US: All United States
Canada: No
Overseas: NR

◄◄ ►►

CAPTAIN TONY'S PIZZA & PASTA EMPORIUM

2607 S. Woodland Blvd., # 300
Deland, FL 32720
Tel: (800) 332-8669 (386) 736-9855
Fax: (386) 736-7237
E-Mail: captain-tonys@wati.com
Web Site: www.captain-tonys.wati.com
Mr. Michael J. Martella, President

We have pizza, pasta, etc. for take-out, delivery and dining-in.

BACKGROUND:

Established: 1985;   1st Franchised: 1985
Franchised Units: 12
Company-Owned Units: <u>0</u>
Total Units: 12
Dist.:   US-10; CAN-0; O'seas-2
   North America: 0 States, 0 Provinces
   Density: 3 in OH, 2 in CA
Projected New Units (12 Months):   NR
Qualifications: 3, 3, 2, 3, 3, 5
FINANCIAL/TERMS:
Cash Investment: $25-75K
Total Investment: $65-250K
Minimum Net Worth: $250K
Fees: Franchise - $10-20K
   Royalty - 4.5% $500/Wk cap;   Ad. - 0%
Earnings Claims Statement: No
Term of Contract (Years):   20/
Avg. # Of Employees: FT, 0 PT
Passive Ownership: Discouraged
Encourage Conversions: Yes
Area Develop. Agreements: No
Sub-Franchising Contracts: No
Expand In Territory: No
Space Needs: 1,200 SF
SUPPORT & TRAINING:
Financial Assistance Provided: Yes (D)
Site Selection Assistance: Yes
Lease Negotiation Assistance: Yes
Co-Operative Advertising: No
Franchisee Assoc./Member: No
Size Of Corporate Staff: NR
On-Going Support: ,,,D,E,,,,I
Training: 3 Weeks Orlando, FL
SPECIFIC EXPANSION PLANS:
US: All United States
Canada: No
Overseas: All Countries

◄◄ ►►

CICI'S PIZZA

1080 W. Bethel Rd.
Coppell, TX 75019-4427
Tel: (972) 745-9318 (972) 745-9316
Fax: (972) 745-4204
E-Mail: jsheahan@cicispizza.com
Web Site: www.cicispizza.com
Mr. Jim Sheahan, VP Franchise Sales

CiCi's Pizza is a whole new pizza experience. Our gourmet buffet is an all-you-ca-eat extravaganza of pastas, salads, des-

serts and 16 kinds of unbelievably delicious, fresh-from-the-oven pizza -- all for just $4.49 (Unless you're three or under, and then you eat for free!) Our ingredients are fresh, from the vine-ripened tomatoes we use in our sauces to the pizza dough we bake everyday, from our 100% whole milk mozzarella to our fresh veggies that never ever come from a can. CiCi's is proud to offer qulaity and quantity together, for a super-affordable price!

BACKGROUND: IFA MEMBER
Established: 1985;   1st Franchised: 1988
Franchised Units: 620
Company-Owned Units: <u>19</u>
Total Units: 639
Dist.:   US-639; CAN-0; O'seas-0
   North America: 28 States, 0 Provinces
   Density:
Projected New Units (12 Months):   93
Qualifications: 5, 4, 1, 1, 3, 5
FINANCIAL/TERMS:
Cash Investment: $83.6K-131.8K
Total Investment: $418K-659.2K
Minimum Net Worth: NR
Fees: Franchise - $30K
   Royalty - 4%;   Ad. - 3%/$2.3K/Mo
Earnings Claims Statement: Yes
Term of Contract (Years):   10/1-10
Avg. # Of Employees: 8 FT, 15 PT
Passive Ownership: Not Allowed
Encourage Conversions: No
Area Develop. Agreements: Yes/1
Sub-Franchising Contracts: No
Expand In Territory: Yes
Space Needs: 4,200 SF
SUPPORT & TRAINING:
Financial Assistance Provided: Yes (D)
Site Selection Assistance: Yes
Lease Negotiation Assistance: Yes
Co-Operative Advertising: No
Franchisee Assoc./Member: No
Size Of Corporate Staff: 48
On-Going Support: ,,C,D,E,F,G,H,
Training: 8-12 Weeks Dallas, TX.
SPECIFIC EXPANSION PLANS:
US: South, Southeast, N. Central,
Midwest, S. West
Canada: No
Overseas: NR

◄◄ ►►

COUNTRY KITCHEN INTERNATIONAL

801 Deming Wy.
Madison, WI 53717-1918
Tel: (888) 359-3235 (608) 833-9633
Fax: (608) 826-9080

E-Mail: cmocco@countrykitchen.net
Web Site: www.countrykitchenrestaurants.com
Mr. Charles L. Mocco, Sr. Dir. Franchise Development

COUNTRY KITCHEN INTERNATIONAL, rated the # 1 family dining restaurant franchise, develops, operates and franchises COUNTRY KITCHEN RESTAURANTS, one of the most aggressive and growth-oriented family dining chains in the U. S. They have developed an outstanding reputation for the depth of their support system at all levels.

BACKGROUND:

Established: 1939;	1st Franchised: 1965
Franchised Units:	117
Company-Owned Units:	28
Total Units:	145
Dist.:	US-145; CAN-0; O'seas-0
North America:	26 States, 0 Provinces
Density:	42 in WI, 23 in MO, 21 in MN
Projected New Units (12 Months):	NR
Qualifications:	5, 5, 5, 3, 3, 4

FINANCIAL/TERMS:

Cash Investment:	$150-300K
Total Investment:	$670K - 1.6MM
Minimum Net Worth:	$300K
Fees: Franchise -	$40K
Royalty - 4%;	Ad. - Up to 3%
Earnings Claims Statement:	No
Term of Contract (Years):	20/5/5/
Avg. # Of Employees:	20 FT, 20 PT
Passive Ownership:	Allowed
Encourage Conversions:	Yes
Area Develop. Agreements:	Yes/0
Sub-Franchising Contracts:	Yes
Expand In Territory:	Yes
Space Needs:	NR

SUPPORT & TRAINING:

Financial Assistance Provided:	No
Site Selection Assistance:	Yes
Lease Negotiation Assistance:	No
Co-Operative Advertising:	Yes
Franchisee Assoc./Member:	No
Size Of Corporate Staff:	26
On-Going Support:	„C,D,E,F,G,H,I
Training:	6 to 10 Weeks Training Location, varies by region

SPECIFIC EXPANSION PLANS:

US:	All United States
Canada:	No
Overseas:	NR

◄◄   ►►

COYOTE CANYON

111 E. Third St.
Taylor, TX 76574
Tel: (620) 669-9372
Fax: (620) 669-0531
E-Mail: madisonj@stockadecompanies.com
Web Site: www.coyotecanyonbuffet.com
Mr. Madison Jobe, VP Franchise Development

COYOTE CANYON is an 'all you can eat' steak buffet, featuring a self-service salad bar, a hot food buffet, a dessert bar and a display bakery at one affordable price, which also includes your drink.

BACKGROUND: IFA MEMBER

Established: 1999;	1st Franchised: 1999
Franchised Units:	8
Company-Owned Units:	0
Total Units:	8
Dist.:	US-8; CAN-0; O'seas-0
North America:	5 States, 0 Provinces
Density:	2 in TX, 2 in KS
Projected New Units (12 Months):	2
Qualifications:	5, 4, 4, 3, 2, 4

FINANCIAL/TERMS:

Cash Investment:	$148K-496K
Total Investment:	$419K-3.1MM
Minimum Net Worth:	$1MM
Fees: Franchise -	$20K
Royalty - 3%;	Ad. - 1%
Earnings Claims Statement:	Yes
Term of Contract (Years):	15/15
Avg. # Of Employees:	20 FT, 50 PT
Passive Ownership:	Discouraged
Encourage Conversions:	Yes
Area Develop. Agreements:	Yes/0
Sub-Franchising Contracts:	No
Expand In Territory:	Yes
Space Needs:	10,000 SF

SUPPORT & TRAINING:

Financial Assistance Provided:	No
Site Selection Assistance:	Yes
Lease Negotiation Assistance:	No
Co-Operative Advertising:	No
Franchisee Assoc./Member:	No
Size Of Corporate Staff:	25
On-Going Support:	,B,C,D,E,,G,h,
Training:	6-8 Weeks Training

SPECIFIC EXPANSION PLANS:

US:	All United States
Canada:	No
Overseas:	NR

◄◄   ►►

DENNY'S

203 E. Main St.
Spartanburg, SC 29319-9912
Tel: (800) 304-0222 (864) 597-8000
Fax: (713) 849-0722
E-Mail: franchisedevelopment@dennys.com
Web Site: www.dennys.com

For over 50 years, Denny's has been the trusted leader in family dining. We enjoy a brand awareness of almost 100%! We cheerfully serve over 26 million customers a month in our 1500+ restaurants worldwide. We are proud to serve America's most loved foods 24 hours a day, 7 days a week. If you are an experienced restaurateur or businessman, we invite you to contact us and learn more about growth opportunities within our great brand.

BACKGROUND: IFA MEMBER

Established: 1953;	1st Franchised: 1963
Franchised Units:	1281
Company-Owned Units:	263
Total Units:	1544
Dist.:	US-1205; CAN-49; O'seas-27
North America:	48 States, 5 Provinces
Density:	130 in FL, 141 in TX, 311 in CA
Projected New Units (12 Months):	37
Qualifications:	5, 5, 5, 3, NR, 5

FINANCIAL/TERMS:

Cash Investment:	$350-$400K
Total Investment:	$1M-$2.6M
Minimum Net Worth:	$1M
Fees: Franchise -	$40K
Royalty - 4%;	Ad. - 4%
Earnings Claims Statement:	Yes
Term of Contract (Years):	20/N/A
Avg. # Of Employees:	50 FT, 25 PT
Passive Ownership:	Discouraged
Encourage Conversions:	Yes
Area Develop. Agreements:	Yes/0
Sub-Franchising Contracts:	No
Expand In Territory:	Yes
Space Needs:	4,200 SF

SUPPORT & TRAINING:

Financial Assistance Provided:	No
Site Selection Assistance:	Yes
Lease Negotiation Assistance:	No
Co-Operative Advertising:	Yes
Franchisee Assoc./Member:	Yes/Yes
Size Of Corporate Staff:	250

On-Going Support: „C,D,e,,G,,I
Training: 10 - 13 weeks at the nearest certified training restaurant
SPECIFIC EXPANSION PLANS:
US: All United States
Canada: All Canada
Overseas: All Overseas

≪ ≫

EATZA PIZZA BUFFET
4800 N. Scottsdale Rd., # 3000
Scottsdale, AZ 85251-7631
Tel: (800) 596-8464 (480) 941-5200
Fax: (480) 941-5202
E-Mail: rcordova@eatzapizza.com
Web Site: www.eatzapizza.com
Mr. Ronn Cordova, Franchise Devel. Director

EATZA PIZZA is an all-you-can-eat pizza, pasta, salad and dessert family buffet restaurant. The combination of a great concept, lower than average investment requirements, outstanding systems and franchisee support makes for the ultimate recipe for success!

BACKGROUND: IFA MEMBER
Established: 1999; 1st Franchised: 1999
Franchised Units: 49
Company-Owned Units: 13
Total Units: 62
Dist.: US-62; CAN-0; O'seas-0
North America: 5 States, 0 Provinces
Density: 2 in WA, 4 in UT, 14 in AZ
Projected New Units (12 Months): 13
Qualifications: 3, 4, 4, 3, 5, 5
FINANCIAL/TERMS:
Cash Investment: $55.5-104K
Total Investment: $185.1-347.5K
Minimum Net Worth: $250K
Fees: Franchise - $25K
Royalty - 5%; Ad. - 4%
Earnings Claims Statement: No
Term of Contract (Years): 10/10
Avg. # Of Employees: 2-4 FT, 12-24 PT
Passive Ownership: Not Allowed
Encourage Conversions: No
Area Develop. Agreements: Yes/1
Sub-Franchising Contracts: Yes
Expand In Territory: Yes
Space Needs: 5,200 SF
SUPPORT & TRAINING:

Financial Assistance Provided: Yes (D)
Site Selection Assistance: Yes
Lease Negotiation Assistance: Yes
Co-Operative Advertising: No
Franchisee Assoc./Member: No
Size Of Corporate Staff: 9
On-Going Support: ,B,C,D,e,F,G,H,I
Training: 3 Weeks Phoenix, AZ
SPECIFIC EXPANSION PLANS:
US: West,Great Lakes,Upper/Central US
Canada: No
Overseas: NR

≪ ≫

EDO JAPAN
4838 32nd St. S. E.
Calgary, AB T2B 2S6 Canada
Tel: (888) 336-9888 (403) 215-8823
Fax: (403) 215-8801
E-Mail: edo@edojapan.com
Web Site: www.edojapan.com
Mr. Mike Mielnichuk, Franchisee Recruitment

Edo Japan originated the concept of serving Japanese style fast food, cooked on Teppanyaki grills. Customers experience food that is fresh and nutritious cooked with style and flair right before our eyes. This original and creative idea has made Edo Japan one of the most popular and successful franchise chains in North America. Edo Japan's franchise restaurants are presently experiencing explosive growth and excellent returns with both our food court and street front concepts.

BACKGROUND:
Established: 1979; 1st Franchised: 1986
Franchised Units: 90
Company-Owned Units: 2
Total Units: 92
Dist.: US-20; CAN-72; O'seas-0
North America: 8 States, 5 Provinces
Density: 15 in ON, 10 in BC, 37 in AB
Projected New Units (12 Months): 4-10
Qualifications: 5, 4, 4, 3, 4, 5
FINANCIAL/TERMS:
Cash Investment: NR
Total Investment: $250-375K
Minimum Net Worth: NR
Fees: Franchise - $25K
Royalty - 6%; Ad. - 1-3%
Earnings Claims Statement: No
Term of Contract (Years): Lease/
Avg. # Of Employees: FT, 4-15 PT
Passive Ownership: Discouraged
Encourage Conversions: NA
Area Develop. Agreements: Yes/1

Sub-Franchising Contracts: Yes
Expand In Territory: Yes
Space Needs: 350-1,500 SF
SUPPORT & TRAINING:
Financial Assistance Provided: No
Site Selection Assistance: Yes
Lease Negotiation Assistance: Yes
Co-Operative Advertising: No
Franchisee Assoc./Member: No
Size Of Corporate Staff: 10
On-Going Support: „C,D,E,F,G,H,
Training: 14 Days Opening Assistance On-Site; 3 Weeks Calgary, AB
SPECIFIC EXPANSION PLANS:
US: No
Canada: All Canada
Overseas: NR

≪ ≫

FAMOUS DAVE'S
12701 Whitewater Dr., # 200
Minnetonka, MN 55343
Tel: (800) 210-4040 + 1343 (952) 294-1300
Fax: (952) 294-0242
E-Mail: jim.schwitzer@famousdaves.com
Web Site: www.famousdaves.com
Mr. Jim Schwitzer, Director Franchise Sales

FAMOUS DAVE'S develops, owns, operates and franchises barbecue-style restaurants. We feature award-winning barbecued and grilled meats and other unique menu items in a fun environment.

BACKGROUND: IFA MEMBER
Established: 1994; 1st Franchised: 1999
Franchised Units: 130
Company-Owned Units: 46
Total Units: 176
Dist.: US-176; CAN-0; O'seas-0
North America: 38 States, 0 Provinces
Density: 11 in CA, 13 in IL, 21 in MN
Projected New Units (12 Months): 12
Qualifications: 5, 4, 5, 3, 3, 5
FINANCIAL/TERMS:
Cash Investment: $300K-1MM
Total Investment: $905K-4.51MM
Minimum Net Worth: $750K Liq.
Fees: Franchise - $40K
Royalty - 5%; Ad. - 1%
Earnings Claims Statement: Yes

Term of Contract (Years): 20/10
Avg. # Of Employees: 20 FT, 45 PT
Passive Ownership: Discouraged
Encourage Conversions: Yes
Area Develop. Agreements: Yes/0
Sub-Franchising Contracts: No
Expand In Territory: Yes
Space Needs: 4,000-6,000 SF

SUPPORT & TRAINING:
Financial Assistance Provided: Yes (I)
Site Selection Assistance: Yes
Lease Negotiation Assistance: Yes
Co-Operative Advertising: Yes
Franchisee Assoc./Member: Yes/Yes
Size Of Corporate Staff: 81
On-Going Support: A,B,C,D,E,,G,H,I
Training: 35 Days Minimum Varies

SPECIFIC EXPANSION PLANS:
US: Yes
Canada: Yes
Overseas: NR

≪ ≫

FRIENDLY'S RESTAURANTS
1855 Boston Rd.
Wilbraham, MA 01095-1002
Tel: (800) 576-8088 (413) 543-2400
Fax: (413) 543-2820
E-Mail: laurel.adams@friendlys.com
Web Site: www.friendlys.com
Ms. Laurel Adams, Franchise Development Manager

FRIENDLY'S is a full-service restaurant chain with ice cream a key point of difference. FRIENDLY'S has experienced growth in every year since 2000. The franchisee will receive support, including training, marketing, site selection, restaurant openings and on-going operational assistance.

BACKGROUND: IFA MEMBER
Established: 1935; 1st Franchised: 1997
Franchised Units: 206
Company-Owned Units: 314
Total Units: 520
Dist.: US-520; CAN-0; O'seas-0
North America: 16 States, 0 Provinces
Density:66 in PA, 115 in NY, 122 in MA
Projected New Units (12 Months): 10
Qualifications: NR

FINANCIAL/TERMS:
Cash Investment: $400-500K

Total Investment: $499K-1.94MM
Minimum Net Worth: $1.5MM-650Liq
Fees: Franchise - $30-35K
    Royalty - 4%; Ad. - 3%
Earnings Claims Statement: Yes
Term of Contract (Years): 20/10-20
Avg. # Of Employees: 40 FT, 35 PT
Passive Ownership: Not Allowed
Encourage Conversions: Yes
Area Develop. Agreements: Yes/1
Sub-Franchising Contracts: No
Expand In Territory: Yes
Space Needs: 4,500 SF

SUPPORT & TRAINING:
Financial Assistance Provided: No
Site Selection Assistance: Yes
Lease Negotiation Assistance: No
Co-Operative Advertising: No
Franchisee Assoc./Member: No
Size Of Corporate Staff: 325
On-Going Support: A,b,C,d,E,F,G,h,
Training: 12 Weeks Corporate Training Center

SPECIFIC EXPANSION PLANS:
US: SE, NE, Mid-Atlantic
Canada: No
Overseas: NR

≪ ≫

FUDDRUCKERS
5700 Mopac Expy. S., # C300
Austin, TX 78749
Tel: (512) 275-0421
Fax: (512) 275-0670
E-Mail: kelly.noriega@fuddruckers.com
Web Site: www.fuddruckers.com
Ms. Kelly Noriega, Administrative Sales Assistant

It's an exciting time at FUDDRUCKERS. Our relentless commitment to freshness makes us "Home of the World's Greatest Hamburgers". Our in-house butcher shops and bakeries provide our guests with the freshest products available. FUDDRUCKERS' menu includes not only our famous 1/3 and 1/2 pound hamburgers but now features a 1-lb. burger. We have also added Big Bowl salads, new Steakhouse Platters and fantastic desserts like our Brownie Blast Sundae. We also have a new 50's and 60's rock and roll image.

BACKGROUND: IFA MEMBER
Established: 1980; 1st Franchised: 1983
Franchised Units: 121
Company-Owned Units: 107
Total Units: 228
Dist.: US-207; CAN-1; O'seas-20
North America: 30 States, 1 Provinces
Density: 12 in VA, 44 in TX, 16 in CA
Projected New Units (12 Months): 30
Qualifications: 5, 5, 4, 3, 2, 5

FINANCIAL/TERMS:
Cash Investment: $550K
Total Investment: $740K-1.48MM
Minimum Net Worth: $1.5MM
Fees: Franchise - $50K
    Royalty - 5%; Ad. - 0-4%
Earnings Claims Statement: Yes
Term of Contract (Years): 10 & 20/
Avg. # Of Employees: 15 FT, 30 PT
Passive Ownership: Discouraged
Encourage Conversions: Yes
Area Develop. Agreements: Yes/1
Sub-Franchising Contracts: No
Expand In Territory: Yes
Space Needs: 6,200-7,000 SF

SUPPORT & TRAINING:
Financial Assistance Provided: No
Site Selection Assistance: Yes
Lease Negotiation Assistance: No
Co-Operative Advertising: No
Franchisee Assoc./Member: · No
Size Of Corporate Staff: 70
On-Going Support: ,,C,D,E,,G,H,
Training: 6-8 Weeks Regional Training Locations

SPECIFIC EXPANSION PLANS:
US: All United States
Canada: All Canada
Overseas: All Countries

≪ ≫

GARFIELD'S RESTAURANT & PUB
1220 S. Santa Fe Ave.
Edmond, OK 73003-5904
Tel: (405) 705-5000
Fax: (405) 705-5004
E-Mail: heidiv@eats-inc.com
Web Site: www.eats-inc.com
Ms. Heidi Valenzuela, Franchise Marketing Manager

A friendly casual dining restaurant serving an American menu of convenience, quality and value.

BACKGROUND:
Established: 1984; 1st Franchised: 1987
Franchised Units: 11

Company-Owned Units: <u>47</u>
Total Units: 58
Dist.: US-58; CAN-0; O'seas-0
  North America: 26 States, Provinces
  Density: 8 in IN, 4 in MO, 6 in OK
Projected New Units (12 Months): 12
Qualifications: 5, 3, 5, 3, 3, 5

FINANCIAL/TERMS:
Cash Investment: $300-500K
Total Investment: $1.2-2.0MM
Minimum Net Worth: $1MM
Fees: Franchise - $30K
  Royalty - 4%; Ad. - 3.5%
Earnings Claims Statement: No
Term of Contract (Years): 20/5
Avg. # Of Employees: 50 FT, 25 PT
Passive Ownership: Not Allowed
Encourage Conversions: Yes
Area Develop. Agreements: Yes/1
Sub-Franchising Contracts: No
Expand In Territory: Yes
Space Needs: 4,500-5,000 SF

SUPPORT & TRAINING:
Financial Assistance Provided: No
Site Selection Assistance: Yes
Lease Negotiation Assistance: No
Co-Operative Advertising: No
Franchisee Assoc./Member: Yes/Yes
Size Of Corporate Staff: 48
On-Going Support: a,,C,D,E,,,,
Training: 8 Weeks Edmond, OK

SPECIFIC EXPANSION PLANS:
US: All United States
Canada: No
Overseas: NR

⋘ ⋙

GOLDEN CORRAL FAMILY STEAKHOUSE
5151 Glenwood Ave.
Raleigh, NC 27612
Tel: (800) 284-5673 (919) 881-4479
Fax: (919) 881-5252
E-Mail: abagwell@goldencorral.net
Web Site: www.goldencorralfranchise.com
Ms. Annette Bagwell, Franchise Sales

Golden Corral family restaurants feature 'steaks, buffet and bakery.' The 'Golden Choice Buffet' offers 150 hot and cold items, including all you care to eat steak. A special feature is 'The Brass Bell Bakery' which prepares made-from-scratch rolls, cookies, muffins, brownies and pizza. Steak, chicken and fish entrees are also available. Value-driven concept with a $7.80 per person check average in 2004. Open lunch and dinner - 7 days; Breakfast Buffet - weekends or holidays.

BACKGROUND: IFA MEMBER
Established: 1973; 1st Franchised: 1986
Franchised Units: 378
Company-Owned Units: <u>105</u>
Total Units: 483
Dist.: US-483; CAN-0; O'seas-0
  North America: 38 States, 0 Provinces
  Density: in TXOKNC
Projected New Units (12 Months): 25
Qualifications: NR

FINANCIAL/TERMS:
Cash Investment: $500K
Total Investment: $2-6MM
Minimum Net Worth: $1.5MM
Fees: Franchise - $50K
  Royalty - 4%; Ad. - 2%
Earnings Claims Statement: Yes
Term of Contract (Years): 15/5
Avg. # Of Employees: 80 FT, 40 PT
Passive Ownership: Not Allowed
Encourage Conversions: No
Area Develop. Agreements: Yes/0
Sub-Franchising Contracts: No
Expand In Territory: Yes
Space Needs: 7,780-11,900 SF

SUPPORT & TRAINING:
Financial Assistance Provided: No
Site Selection Assistance: Yes
Lease Negotiation Assistance: No
Co-Operative Advertising: Yes
Franchisee Assoc./Member: No
Size Of Corporate Staff: 200
On-Going Support: ,,C,D,E,,G,,
Training: 12 Weeks Headquarters and Field

SPECIFIC EXPANSION PLANS:
US: All United States
Canada: No
Overseas: NR

⋘ ⋙

GRANDY'S
401 E. Corporate Dr., # 244
Lewisville, TX 75057
Tel: (877) 457-8145 (972) 434-9241
Fax: (972) 317-8174

E-Mail: mwhitehurst@grandys.com
Web Site: www.grandys.com
Mr. Monty Whitehurst, Chief Operating Officer

GRANDY'S is one of America's most distinctive quick-service chains. GRANDY'S offers an unparalleled opportunity for potential franchisees. Our unique niche in the market, coupled with a solid 30-year history and our menu of delicious Home-style Food, including country-style breakfasts, chicken fried steaks, southern fried chicken and grilled chicken and a variety of homestyle vegetables - provide a great recipe for success.

BACKGROUND: IFA MEMBER
Established: 1973; 1st Franchised: 1977
Franchised Units: 90
Company-Owned Units: <u>30</u>
Total Units: 120
Dist.: US-120; CAN-0; O'seas-0
  North America: 9 States, 0 Provinces
  Density: 60 in TX, 9 in OK, 6 in IN
Projected New Units (12 Months): 6
Qualifications: 5, 5, 4, 3, 4, 4

FINANCIAL/TERMS:
Cash Investment: $150-350K
Total Investment: $500K-1.2MM
Minimum Net Worth: $350K
Fees: Franchise - $30K
  Royalty - 5%; Ad. - Up to 2.5%
Earnings Claims Statement: No
Term of Contract (Years): 15/10
Avg. # Of Employees: 6 FT, 15 PT
Passive Ownership: Allowed
Encourage Conversions: Yes
Area Develop. Agreements: Yes/1
Sub-Franchising Contracts: No
Expand In Territory: Yes
Space Needs: 2,700 SF

SUPPORT & TRAINING:
Financial Assistance Provided: No
Site Selection Assistance: Yes
Lease Negotiation Assistance: Yes
Co-Operative Advertising: No
Franchisee Assoc./Member: Yes/Yes
Size Of Corporate Staff: 25
On-Going Support: ,B,C,D,E,,G,h,
Training: 6-8 Weeks Lewisville, TX

SPECIFIC EXPANSION PLANS:
US: TX,OK,AR,FL,GA,IN,LA,NC,SC
Canada: All Canada
Overseas: All Countries

⋘ ⋙

GROUND ROUND GRILL & BAR

500 US Rte. 1
Freeport, ME 04032
Tel: (800) 229-7005 (207) 865-4433
Fax: (207) 865-2227
E-Mail: mbotti@groundround.com
Web Site: www.groundround.com
Ms. Monica Botti, Franchise Sales & Comm. Manager

THE GROUND ROUND GRILL & BAR has a solid plan for success. Whether you wish to diversify or add to your portfolio, we are currently developing exciting franchise opportunities in the country's most desirable markets. The GROUND ROUND is a proven casual dining concept that profits from its vision, commitment and energy. Call or click today and start building a growth plan that can really pay dividends.

BACKGROUND:

Established: 1969; 1st Franchised: 1970	
Franchised Units:	50
Company-Owned Units:	0
Total Units:	50
Dist.:	US-50; CAN-0; O'seas-0
North America:	24 States, 0 Provinces
Density:	7 in PA, 7 in NY, 6 in MA
Projected New Units (12 Months):	5
Qualifications:	5, 5, 4, 3, 3, 4

FINANCIAL/TERMS:

Cash Investment:	$200-400K
Total Investment:	$1.0-1.9MM
Minimum Net Worth:	NA
Fees: Franchise -	$40K
Royalty - 3.5%;	Ad. - 2%
Earnings Claims Statement:	Yes
Term of Contract (Years):	20/10
Avg. # Of Employees:	15 FT, 52 PT
Passive Ownership:	Not Allowed
Encourage Conversions:	Yes
Area Develop. Agreements:	Yes/1
Sub-Franchising Contracts:	No
Expand In Territory:	No
Space Needs:	4,600 Min. SF

SUPPORT & TRAINING:

Financial Assistance Provided:	No
Site Selection Assistance:	Yes
Lease Negotiation Assistance:	No
Co-Operative Advertising:	No
Franchisee Assoc./Member:	Yes/Yes
Size Of Corporate Staff:	7
On-Going Support:	,,C,d,e,,G,h,
Training: 6-10 Weeks Regional Training Unit	

SPECIFIC EXPANSION PLANS:

US:	NE, MW, Atl. States, Grt Lks
Canada:	No
Overseas:	NR

⊰⊰ ⊱⊱

HAMBURGER MARY'S BAR & GRILLE

P. O. Box 456
Corona Del Mar, CA 92625
Tel: (888) 834-6279 (949) 729-8000
Fax: (949) 675-9979
E-Mail: hamburgermary@cox.net
Web Site: www.hamburgermarys.net
Mr. Darren Woolsey, Vice President

Hamburger Mary's Bar & Grille is the only and the largest restaurant franchise catering to the Gay and Lesbian community (as well as the general public). With over 32 years of successful operations, we have totally re-organized under HMI to become a major franchise. 14 franchised stores have been sold across the U.S. Our Owner's Manual, Bar Guide/Recipe book, Ad program and In-store training program are just a few of the plus features offered. Eat, Drink .. and be Mary!

BACKGROUND:

Established: 1972; 1st Franchised: 1997	
Franchised Units:	14
Company-Owned Units:	1
Total Units:	15
Dist.:	US-15; CAN-0; O'seas-0
North America:	8 States, 0 Provinces
Density:	1 in OH, 5 in CA, 1 in AZ
Projected New Units (12 Months):	NR
Qualifications:	NR

FINANCIAL/TERMS:

Cash Investment:	$50K (Fee)
Total Investment:	$200-950K
Minimum Net Worth:	$250K
Fees: Franchise -	$65K
Royalty - 5%;	Ad. - 2%
Earnings Claims Statement:	No
Term of Contract (Years):	15/5/5/5/
Avg. # Of Employees:	35-40 FT, 5-10 PT
Passive Ownership:	Not Allowed
Encourage Conversions:	No
Area Develop. Agreements:	Yes/0
Sub-Franchising Contracts:	Yes
Expand In Territory:	Yes
Space Needs:	4,000+ SF

SUPPORT & TRAINING:

Financial Assistance Provided:	No
Site Selection Assistance:	Yes
Lease Negotiation Assistance:	Yes
Co-Operative Advertising:	No
Franchisee Assoc./Member:	No
Size Of Corporate Staff:	3
On-Going Support:	,B,C,D,E,f,,H,I
Training: 2 Weeks Orange County (CA) Corp. Restaurant	

SPECIFIC EXPANSION PLANS:

US:	All United States
Canada:	No
Overseas:	Australia, Europe

⊰⊰ ⊱⊱

HAPPI HOUSE

1361 S. Winchester Blvd., # 109
San Jose, CA 95128
Tel: (877) HAPPI-411 408-866-5966
Fax: 408-866-5970
E-Mail: hhgeneral@happihouse.com
Web Site: www.happihouse.com
Mr. Joshua Richman, President & CEO

A Happi House Teriyaki restaurant is a unique quick service Asian bistro that is one of today's hottest franchise concepts. With a diverse menu featuring teriyaki, tempura, salads, noodle & rice bowls, sandwiches, and snacks, Happi House serves one of the fastest growing restaurant segments - yet is surprisingly easy to operate. Originating in San Jose, CA Happi House has been a successful part of California for over 30 years. Happi House's revolutionary system & favorable costs make it a great choice.

BACKGROUND: IFA MEMBER

Established: 1976; 1st Franchised: 1990	
Franchised Units:	0
Company-Owned Units:	6
Total Units:	6
Dist.:	US-6; CAN-0; O'seas-0
North America:	1 States, 0 Provinces
Density:	6 in CA
Projected New Units (12 Months):	3
Qualifications:	5, 4, 3, 2, 3, 4

FINANCIAL/TERMS:

Cash Investment:	$100K-200K
Total Investment:	$427K - 598.5K
Minimum Net Worth:	$400K

Fees: Franchise -	$30K
Royalty - 4%;	Ad. - 2%
Earnings Claims Statement:	Yes
Term of Contract (Years):	10/5
Avg. # Of Employees:	4 FT, 12 PT
Passive Ownership:	Allowed
Encourage Conversions:	Yes
Area Develop. Agreements:	No
Sub-Franchising Contracts:	No
Expand In Territory:	Yes
Space Needs:	1,500 - 2,500 SF

SUPPORT & TRAINING:

Financial Assistance Provided:	Yes (I)
Site Selection Assistance:	Yes
Lease Negotiation Assistance:	Yes
Co-Operative Advertising:	Yes
Franchisee Assoc./Member:	No
Size Of Corporate Staff:	6
On-Going Support:	A,B,C,D,E,F,G,h,I
Training:	5 weeks Operating Happi House

SPECIFIC EXPANSION PLANS:

US:	Western States
Canada:	No
Overseas:	NR

◅◅ ▻▻

HARD TIMES CAFE
1404 King St.
Alexandria, VA 22314
Tel: (703) 683-8545
Fax: (703) 837-0057
E-Mail:
Web Site: www.hardtimes.com
Mr. Rich Kelly, Chief Executive Officer

Authentic western-style chili parlor. Featuring chili, burgers and beer.

BACKGROUND:

Established: 1980;	1st Franchised: 1992
Franchised Units:	10
Company-Owned Units:	4
Total Units:	14
Dist.:	US-14; CAN-0; O'seas-0
North America:	3 States, 0 Provinces
Density:	6 in VA, 2 in NC, 6 in MD
Projected New Units (12 Months):	NR
Qualifications:	NR

FINANCIAL/TERMS:

Cash Investment:	$100-200K
Total Investment:	$400-500K
Minimum Net Worth:	$250K
Fees: Franchise -	$30K
Royalty - 4%;	Ad. - 1%
Earnings Claims Statement:	No
Term of Contract (Years):	10/10
Avg. # Of Employees:	6 FT, 20 PT
Passive Ownership:	Not Allowed
Encourage Conversions:	No

Area Develop. Agreements:	Yes/1
Sub-Franchising Contracts:	Yes
Expand In Territory:	Yes
Space Needs:	NR

SUPPORT & TRAINING:

Financial Assistance Provided:	No
Site Selection Assistance:	Yes
Lease Negotiation Assistance:	Yes
Co-Operative Advertising:	No
Franchisee Assoc./Member:	No
Size Of Corporate Staff:	10
On-Going Support:	a,,C,D,E,F,G,H,I
Training:	4 Weeks Washington, DC Area

SPECIFIC EXPANSION PLANS:

US:	East Coast, Mid-Atlantic
Canada:	NR
Overseas:	NR

◅◅ ▻▻

HARVEY'S RESTAURANTS
199 Four Valley Dr.
Vaughn, ON L4K 0B8 Canada
Tel: (905) 760-2244
Fax: (866) 230-9355
E-Mail: HarveysFranchising@cara.com
Web Site: www.harveys.ca
Ms. Joanne Fisher, Franchise Associate

Foodservice. Quick-service restaurants.

BACKGROUND:

Established: 1959;	1st Franchised: 1962
Franchised Units:	143
Company-Owned Units:	135
Total Units:	278
Dist.:	US-0; CAN-278; O'seas-0
North America:	0 States, 0 Provinces
Density:	QC, ON, AB
Projected New Units (12 Months):	5
Qualifications:	5, 4, 3, 3, 1, 5

FINANCIAL/TERMS:

Cash Investment:	$250K
Total Investment:	$150K-200K
Minimum Net Worth:	$300K
Fees: Franchise -	$10K
Royalty - 5%;	Ad. - 4%
Earnings Claims Statement:	Yes
Term of Contract (Years):	20/5x4
Avg. # Of Employees:	3 FT, 40 PT
Passive Ownership:	Not Allowed
Encourage Conversions:	No
Area Develop. Agreements:	No
Sub-Franchising Contracts:	No

Expand In Territory:	Yes
Space Needs:	2,600 SF

SUPPORT & TRAINING:

Financial Assistance Provided:	No
Site Selection Assistance:	Yes
Lease Negotiation Assistance:	Yes
Co-Operative Advertising:	No
Franchisee Assoc./Member:	Yes/Yes
Size Of Corporate Staff:	200
On-Going Support:	,B,C,D,E,,,h,I
Training:	8 Weeks Toronto, ON

SPECIFIC EXPANSION PLANS:

US:	No
Canada:	All Canada
Overseas:	NR

◅◅ ▻▻

HUDDLE HOUSE RESTAURANTS
2969 E. Ponce de Leon Ave.
Decatur, GA 30030
Tel: (800) 868-5700 (404) 377-5700
Fax: (404) 377-0497
E-Mail: franchise@huddlehouse.com
Web Site: www.huddlehouse.com
Ms. Brianne Skinner, Franchise Development Admin.

HUDDLE HOUSE RESTAURANTS are open 24 hours a day, serving delicious meals, cooked to order - a place where hungry folks gather to enjoy good food, good friends and good hospitality. HUDDLE HOUSE RESTAURANTS offer any meal, any time from our broad menu of breakfast, lunch and dinner entrees, featuring, 'Big House' platters, which are our signature 'Big Meals for Big Appetites.'

BACKGROUND: IFA MEMBER

Established: 1964;	1st Franchised: 1966
Franchised Units:	361
Company-Owned Units:	21
Total Units:	382
Dist.:	US-382; CAN-0; O'seas-0
North America:	14 States, 0 Provinces
Density:	60 in SC, 166 in GA, 34 in AL
Projected New Units (12 Months):	40
Qualifications:	5, 5, 4, 3, 3, 4

FINANCIAL/TERMS:

Cash Investment:	$200K
Total Investment:	$300-750K
Minimum Net Worth:	$250K
Fees: Franchise -	$20K
Royalty - 4%;	Ad. - 1%
Earnings Claims Statement:	Yes
Term of Contract (Years):	15/5x3
Avg. # Of Employees:	18 FT, 6 PT
Passive Ownership:	Discouraged

Encourage Conversions:	Yes
Area Develop. Agreements:	Yes/1
Sub-Franchising Contracts:	No
Expand In Territory:	Yes
Space Needs:	2,000 SF

SUPPORT & TRAINING:

Financial Assistance Provided:	No
Site Selection Assistance:	Yes
Lease Negotiation Assistance:	Yes
Co-Operative Advertising:	No
Franchisee Assoc./Member:	Yes/Yes
Size Of Corporate Staff:	120
On-Going Support:	,b,C,D,E,f,,h,I
Training:	7 Weeks Metro Atlanta, GA

SPECIFIC EXPANSION PLANS:

US:	Southeast, Midwest
Canada:	No
Overseas:	NR

◄◄ ►►

**JOHNNY ROCKETS, THE
ORIGINAL HAMBURGER**

25550 Commercentre Dr., # 200
Lake Forest, CA 92630-8855
Tel: (949) 643-6134
Fax: (949) 643-6200
E-Mail: cwells@johnnyrockets.com
Web Site: www.johnnyrockets.com
Ms. Crystal Wells, Franchise Sales Assistant

Johnny Rockets is an international retro diner chain that provides the food and friendliness of feel-good Americana. On June 6, 1986, the first Johnny Rockets opened on Melrose Avenue in Los Angeles, offering guests friendly service and great food in an atmosphere that is fun and nostalgic. Every Johnny Rockets restaurant boasts great-tasting food from a menu of all-American favorites including juicy hamburgers, hand-dipped shakes & malts and freshly-baked apple pie. Guests also enjoy an all-American diner look and feel, servers who know the secret behind getting ketchup out of the bottle, tabletop jukeboxes that belt out tunes for a nickel and authentic decor. Johnny Rockets is the place where every Guest can enjoy all-American favorites served with a smile!

BACKGROUND: IFA MEMBER

Established: 1986;	1st Franchised: 1989
Franchised Units:	232
Company-Owned Units:	52
Total Units:	284
Dist.:	US-260; CAN-3; O'seas-25
North America:	28 States, 3 Provinces
Density:	13 in NY, 24 in FL, 43 in CA
Projected New Units (12 Months):	NR
Qualifications:	NR

FINANCIAL/TERMS:

Cash Investment:	$250K-500K
Total Investment:	$636.5K-875K
Minimum Net Worth:	$1MM+
Fees: Franchise -	$49K
Royalty - 5% of gross sale; Ad. - 3% of Gross	
Earnings Claims Statement:	No
Term of Contract (Years):	10/5
Avg. # Of Employees:	1 Server/12 Guests FT, 0 PT
Passive Ownership:	Allowed
Encourage Conversions:	No
Area Develop. Agreements:	Yes/0
Sub-Franchising Contracts:	No
Expand In Territory:	Yes
Space Needs:	500-2,400 SF

SUPPORT & TRAINING:

Financial Assistance Provided:	No
Site Selection Assistance:	Yes
Lease Negotiation Assistance:	Yes
Co-Operative Advertising:	No
Franchisee Assoc./Member:	No
Size Of Corporate Staff:	40
On-Going Support:	,,C,D,E,,G,H,I
Training:	6 Weeks 1 of 6 Locations

SPECIFIC EXPANSION PLANS:

US:	All United States
Canada:	Yes
Overseas:	All Countries

◄◄ ►►

**LA SALSA FRESH
MEXICAN GRILL**

5900 Katella Blvd.
Cypress, CA 90630
Tel: (562) 391-2400
Fax: (562) 391-2403
E-Mail: jwalkermobile@comcast.net
Web Site: www.lasalsa.com
Mr. James R. Walker, Chief Development Officer

A fast, casual restaurant chain, specializing in hand-crafted Mexican favorites and appealing to health-conscious individuals with discriminating taste.

BACKGROUND: IFA MEMBER

Established: 1979;	1st Franchised: 1989
Franchised Units:	41
Company-Owned Units:	53
Total Units:	94
Dist.:	US-94; CAN-0; O'seas-0
North America:	10 States, 0 Provinces
Density:	3 in FL, 5 in AZ, 70 in CA
Projected New Units (12 Months):	25
Qualifications:	4, 4, 4, 2, 2, 5

FINANCIAL/TERMS:

Cash Investment:	$300K
Total Investment:	$431-612K
Minimum Net Worth:	$500K
Fees: Franchise -	$50K
Royalty - 5%;	Ad. - 1%
Earnings Claims Statement:	No
Term of Contract (Years):	10/
Avg. # Of Employees:	12 FT, 4 PT
Passive Ownership:	Not Allowed
Encourage Conversions:	Yes
Area Develop. Agreements:	Yes/0
Sub-Franchising Contracts:	No
Expand In Territory:	Yes
Space Needs:	600-2000 SF

SUPPORT & TRAINING:

Financial Assistance Provided:	No
Site Selection Assistance:	Yes
Lease Negotiation Assistance:	Yes
Co-Operative Advertising:	Yes
Franchisee Assoc./Member:	Yes/Yes
Size Of Corporate Staff:	0
On-Going Support:	,,C,D,E,,G,H,I
Training:	NR

SPECIFIC EXPANSION PLANS:

US:	All United States
Canada:	All Canada
Overseas:	NR

◄◄ ►►

LION AND ROSE PUB, THE

16109 University Oak
San Antonio, TX 78249
Tel: (210) 798-5301
Fax: (210) 524-7731
E-Mail: franchise@thelionandrose.com
Web Site: www.thelionandrose.com
Mr. James MacKay, VP of Operations

The Lion and Rose Pub isn't just a great place for a meal or a cold brew! It's also a great opportunity for owning and operating your own business. Our concept serves the exciting pub concept niche in a unique way. With rich, deep wood tones, luxurious seating, cozy nooks and corners, a big common area with a hefty wooden bar, a fantastic menu, a full bar and the best beers from around the world, the Lion and Rose has something for everyone.

BACKGROUND: IFA MEMBER
Established: 2004;   1st Franchised: 2006
Franchised Units: 1
Company-Owned Units: 4
Total Units: 5
Dist.:   US-5; CAN-0; O'seas-0
  North America: 1 States, 0 Provinces
  Density: 2 in TX
Projected New Units (12 Months):   16
Qualifications: 4, 4, 3, 3, 5, 5
FINANCIAL/TERMS:
Cash Investment: $500K-750K
Total Investment: $297K-1.2MM
Minimum Net Worth: $500K
Fees: Franchise - $25K
  Royalty - 5%;   Ad. - 2%
Earnings Claims Statement: No
Term of Contract (Years):   10/5
Avg. # Of Employees: 30 FT, 0 PT
Passive Ownership: Discouraged
Encourage Conversions: Yes
Area Develop. Agreements: Yes/0
Sub-Franchising Contracts: No
Expand In Territory: Yes
Space Needs: 5,000 SF
SUPPORT & TRAINING:
Financial Assistance Provided: Yes (I)
Site Selection Assistance: Yes
Lease Negotiation Assistance: No
Co-Operative Advertising: Yes
Franchisee Assoc./Member: No
Size Of Corporate Staff: 4
On-Going Support: ,B,C,D,E,,,h,
Training: 300 Hours San Antonio, TX
SPECIFIC EXPANSION PLANS:
US: Texas and the Southwest
Canada: No
Overseas: NR

⨞⨞ ⨞⨞

MAID-RITE
2951 86th St.
Des Moines, IA 50322
Tel: (515) 276-5448
Fax: (515) 276-5449
E-Mail: tburt@maid-rite.com

Web Site: www.maid-rite.com
Ms. Tania Burt, Executive VP

Maid-Rite Sandwich Shoppes were founded in 1926 in Iowa. We are famous for our fresh ground beef loose meat sandwiches, seasoned to perfection and served on a warm bun. Our menu also includes Broaster Chicken, Blue Bunny Ice Cream, Godfather's Pizza, and Seattle's Best Coffee. We are an affordable franchise choice that provides franchisee assistance for a turn-key restaurant. We have a training school for franchisees to assist in learning all aspects of restaurant operations and customer service.

BACKGROUND: IFA MEMBER
Established: 1926;   1st Franchised: 1928
Franchised Units: 74
Company-Owned Units: 2
Total Units: 76
Dist.:   US-76; CAN-0; O'seas-0
  North America: 10 States, 0 Provinces
  Density: 10 in MO, 17 in IL, 39 in IA
Projected New Units (12 Months):   24
Qualifications: 4, 4, 3, 3, 3, 5
FINANCIAL/TERMS:
Cash Investment: $50-100K
Total Investment: $125K-300K
Minimum Net Worth: $250K
Fees: Franchise - $35K
  Royalty - 4%;   Ad. - 3%
Earnings Claims Statement: No
Term of Contract (Years):   10/Two 10
Additional Term
Avg. # Of Employees: 2 FT, 10 PT
Passive Ownership: Allowed
Encourage Conversions: NA
Area Develop. Agreements: Yes/0
Sub-Franchising Contracts: Yes
Expand In Territory: Yes
Space Needs: 600-1,800 square feet SF
SUPPORT & TRAINING:
Financial Assistance Provided: No
Site Selection Assistance: Yes
Lease Negotiation Assistance: Yes
Co-Operative Advertising: No
Franchisee Assoc./Member: No
Size Of Corporate Staff: 40
On-Going Support: ,B,C,D,E,F,G,H,I
Training: 1-4 Weeks Manager;
  1-2 Weeks Owner; 1-3 Weeks On-Site
  Opening Assistance
SPECIFIC EXPANSION PLANS:
US: Midwest & FL, CA, CO, NV, AZ, TX
Canada: No
Overseas: NR

⨞⨞ ⨞⨞

MANNY AND OLGA'S PIZZA
13707 Northgate Dr.
Silver Spring, MD 20906
Tel: (866) 320-6542 (301) 588-2500
Fax: (301) 924-0081
E-Mail: bobby@mannyandolgas.com
Web Site: www.mannyandolgas.com
Mr. Bobby Athanasakis, President

MANNY AND OLGA'S PIZZA offers a full menu of pizza, subs, salads, pasta, wings, gyros and desserts - everything made fresh daily. Delivery or carry-out.

BACKGROUND:
Established: 1983;   1st Franchised: 1998
Franchised Units: 1
Company-Owned Units: 4
Total Units: 5
Dist.:   US-5; CAN-0; O'seas-0
  North America: 3 States, Provinces
  Density:
Projected New Units (12 Months):   4
Qualifications: 5, 2, 1, 3, 3, 3
FINANCIAL/TERMS:
Cash Investment: $65K
Total Investment: $120-220K
Minimum Net Worth: $100K
Fees: Franchise - $25K
  Royalty - 5%;   Ad. - 4%
Earnings Claims Statement: No
Term of Contract (Years):   5/5
Avg. # Of Employees: 3 FT, 3 PT
Passive Ownership: Not Allowed
Encourage Conversions: Yes
Area Develop. Agreements: Yes/1
Sub-Franchising Contracts: Yes
Expand In Territory: Yes
Space Needs: 700 SF
SUPPORT & TRAINING:
Financial Assistance Provided: No
Site Selection Assistance: Yes
Lease Negotiation Assistance: Yes
Co-Operative Advertising: No
Franchisee Assoc./Member: No
Size Of Corporate Staff: 8
On-Going Support: ,,,,E,,,,
Training: 5 Weeks Silver Spring, MD
SPECIFIC EXPANSION PLANS:
US: Northeast
Canada: No
Overseas: NR

⨞⨞ ⨞⨞

MAX & ERMA'S RESTAURANTS
4849 Evanswood Dr.
Columbus, OH 43229
Tel: (614) 431-5800

Fax: (614) 854-7957
E-Mail: rob@max-ermas.com
Web Site: www.maxandermas.com
Mr. Rob Lindeman, President

MAX & ERMA'S RESTAURANTS is famous for gourmet burgers, overstuffed sandwiches, homemade pasta dishes, char-grilled chicken specialties, super salads and taste-tempting munchies. Friendly service and a casual atmosphere make MAX & ERMA'S a fun, unique place to take friends and family. We work hard every day to help our guests enjoy their total dining experience so they can't wait to come back. And, we believe that experience starts with our food. We use only the freshest, highest-quality ingredients.

BACKGROUND:
Established: 1972;   1st Franchised: 1997
Franchised Units: 22
Company-Owned Units: 78
Total Units: 100
Dist.:   US-100; CAN-0; O'seas-0
  North America: 11 States, 0 Provinces
  Density: 11 in PA, 44 in OH, 13 in MI
Projected New Units (12 Months):   10
Qualifications: 3, 4, 4, 2, 3, 5
FINANCIAL/TERMS:
Cash Investment: $400-500K
Total Investment: $800K-2.7MM
Minimum Net Worth: $3MM
Fees: Franchise - $40K
  Royalty - 4%;   Ad. - 2%
Earnings Claims Statement: No
Term of Contract (Years):   20/10
Avg. # Of Employees: 40 FT, 50 PT
Passive Ownership: Allowed
Encourage Conversions: Yes
Area Develop. Agreements: Yes/1
Sub-Franchising Contracts: No
Expand In Territory: Yes
Space Needs: 5,500-6,250 SF
SUPPORT & TRAINING:
Financial Assistance Provided: No
Site Selection Assistance: Yes
Lease Negotiation Assistance: Yes
Co-Operative Advertising: No
Franchisee Assoc./Member: No
Size Of Corporate Staff: 75
On-Going Support: ,B,C,D,E,F,G,H,
Training: 2-3 Week Opening Training;
  2-6 Weeks Staff Training; 14 Weeks
  Manager Training
SPECIFIC EXPANSION PLANS:
US: All United States
Canada: No
Overseas: NR

MCALISTER'S DELI
731 S. Pear Orchard Rd., # 51
Ridgeland, MS 39157-4800
Tel: (888) 855-3354 (601) 952-1100
Fax: (601) 952-1138
E-Mail: franchising@mcalistersdeli.com
Web Site: www.mcalistersdeli.com
Mr. Patrick K. Walls, Chief Franchise Officer

Fast, casual restaurant, featuring a complete menu of gourmet deli foods, including hot and cold deli sandwiches, super-stuffed baked potatoes, salads, soups, desserts, MCALISTER'S famous sweet tea and other food and beverage products.

BACKGROUND: IFA MEMBER
Established: 1989;   1st Franchised: 1994
Franchised Units: 288
Company-Owned Units: 31
Total Units: 319
Dist.:   US-319; CAN-0; O'seas-0
  North America: 18 States, 0 Provinces
  Density: 24 in TX, 18 in TN, 26 in MS
Projected New Units (12 Months):   45
Qualifications: 5, 5, 4, 3, 1, 3
FINANCIAL/TERMS:
Cash Investment: $300K-500K
Total Investment: $400K-1.5MM
Minimum Net Worth: $1MM
Fees: Franchise - $40K
  Royalty - 5%;   Ad. - 2%
Earnings Claims Statement: Yes
Term of Contract (Years):   10/5/5/5/
Avg. # Of Employees: 5 FT, 35 PT
Passive Ownership: Allowed
Encourage Conversions: Yes
Area Develop. Agreements: Yes/0
Sub-Franchising Contracts: No
Expand In Territory: No
Space Needs: 3,600 SF
SUPPORT & TRAINING:
Financial Assistance Provided: Yes (D)
Site Selection Assistance: Yes
Lease Negotiation Assistance: Yes
Co-Operative Advertising: No
Franchisee Assoc./Member: Yes/Yes
Size Of Corporate Staff: 54
On-Going Support: a,B,C,D,E,F,G,H,I
Training: 10 Days Franchisee Location;
  8 Weeks Jackson, MS
SPECIFIC EXPANSION PLANS:

US: All United States
Canada: All Canada
Overseas: NR

MELTING POT RESTAURANTS, THE
8810 Twin Lakes Blvd.
Tampa, FL 33614
Tel: (800) 783-0867 + 108 (813) 881-0055
Fax: (813) 367-0076
E-Mail: dstone@meltingpot.com
Web Site: www.meltingpot.com
Mr. Dan Stone, Director Franchise Sales

The largest fondue-based restaurant system in the world. Franchise provides numerous areas of expertise and assistance to new and established owners. Large percentage of existing owners become multi-unit operators. A unique dining format that is often referred to as a "fun and gotta be experienced" event. Go to write-up for more information.

BACKGROUND: IFA MEMBER
Established: 1975;   1st Franchised: 1984
Franchised Units: 135
Company-Owned Units: 5
Total Units: 140
Dist.:   US-140; CAN-0; O'seas-0
  North America: 34 States, 0 Provinces
  Density: 7 in TX, 23 in FL, 13 in CA
Projected New Units (12 Months):   12
Qualifications: 5, 5, 2, 2, 4, 5
FINANCIAL/TERMS:
Cash Investment: $250K-300K
Total Investment: $877K-1.54MM
Minimum Net Worth: $700K
Fees: Franchise - $35K
  Royalty - 4.5%;   Ad. - .5%
Earnings Claims Statement: Yes
Term of Contract (Years):   10/10
Avg. # Of Employees: 55 FT, 0 PT
Passive Ownership: Not Allowed
Encourage Conversions: Yes
Area Develop. Agreements: Yes/0
Sub-Franchising Contracts: No
Expand In Territory: Yes
Space Needs: 4,000-6,000 SF
SUPPORT & TRAINING:
Financial Assistance Provided: Yes (I)

Site Selection Assistance: Yes
Lease Negotiation Assistance: Yes
Co-Operative Advertising: Yes
Franchisee Assoc./Member: No
Size Of Corporate Staff: 55
On-Going Support: A,b,C,D,E,F,G,h,I
Training: 6-10 Weeks Tampa, FL
SPECIFIC EXPANSION PLANS:
US: All US Except MT,WY, WV
Canada: Yes
Overseas: Asia, Mexico, Middle East, Europe

<< >>

MONTANA MIKE'S STEAKHOUSE
113 E. Third St.
Taylor, TX 76574
Tel: (620) 669-9372
Fax: (620) 669-0531
E-Mail: madisonj@stockadecompanies.com
Web Site: www.stockadecompanies.com
Mr. Madison Jobe, VP Franchise Development

Montana Mike's Steakhouse is a sit-down, full-service restaurant serving alcohol and a bar area. We are known for very large portions at affordable prices. Open for lunch and dinner daily.

BACKGROUND: IFA MEMBER
Established: 1999; 1st Franchised: 1999
Franchised Units: 23
Company-Owned Units: 2
Total Units: 25
Dist.: US-25; CAN-0; O'seas-0
North America: 8 States, 0 Provinces
Density: 4 in TX, 8 in KS
Projected New Units (12 Months): 5
Qualifications: 5, 4, 4, 3, 2, 4
FINANCIAL/TERMS:
Cash Investment: $148K-439K
Total Investment: $439K-2.7MM
Minimum Net Worth: $1MM
Fees: Franchise - $20K
Royalty - 3%; Ad. - 1%
Earnings Claims Statement: Yes
Term of Contract (Years): 15/15
Avg. # Of Employees: 20 FT, 50 PT
Passive Ownership: Discouraged
Encourage Conversions: Yes
Area Develop. Agreements: Yes/0
Sub-Franchising Contracts: No
Expand In Territory: Yes
Space Needs: 7,000 SF
SUPPORT & TRAINING:
Financial Assistance Provided: No
Site Selection Assistance: Yes

Lease Negotiation Assistance: No
Co-Operative Advertising: No
Franchisee Assoc./Member: No
Size Of Corporate Staff: 25
On-Going Support: ,B,C,D,E,,G,h,
Training: 6-8 Weeks Training
SPECIFIC EXPANSION PLANS:
US: All United States
Canada: No
Overseas: NR

<< >>

PEPE'S MEXICAN RESTAURANT
1325 W. 15th St.
Chicago, IL 60608
Tel: (312) 733-2500
Fax: (312) 733-2564
E-Mail: bobptak@pepes.com
Web Site: www.pepes.com
Mr. Robert Ptak, President

A full-service Mexican restaurant, serving a complete line of Mexican food, with liquor, beer and wine. Complete training and help in remodeling, site selection, equipment purchasing and running the restaurant provided.

BACKGROUND:
Established: 1967; 1st Franchised: 1968
Franchised Units: 55
Company-Owned Units: 0
Total Units: 55
Dist.: US-55; CAN-0; O'seas-0
North America: 3 States, Provinces
Density: 44 in IL, 11 in IN
Projected New Units (12 Months): 4
Qualifications: 3, 3, 2, 2, 1, 4
FINANCIAL/TERMS:
Cash Investment: $30-100K
Total Investment: $75-300K
Minimum Net Worth: NR
Fees: Franchise - $15K
Royalty - 4%; Ad. - 3%
Earnings Claims Statement: Yes
Term of Contract (Years): 20/
Avg. # Of Employees: 8 FT, 5 PT
Passive Ownership: Discouraged
Encourage Conversions: Yes
Area Develop. Agreements: Yes/1
Sub-Franchising Contracts: No
Expand In Territory: No
Space Needs: 3,000 SF
SUPPORT & TRAINING:
Financial Assistance Provided: No
Site Selection Assistance: Yes
Lease Negotiation Assistance: Yes
Co-Operative Advertising: No
Franchisee Assoc./Member: NR

Size Of Corporate Staff: 15
On-Going Support: ,B,C,D,E,F,G,H,
Training: 4 Weeks Headquarters
SPECIFIC EXPANSION PLANS:
US: Midwest
Canada: No
Overseas: NR

<< >>

Top 100

PERKINS RESTAURANT & BAKERY
6075 Poplar Ave., # 800
Memphis, TN 38119-4717
Tel: (800) 877-7375 (901) 766-6400
Fax: (901) 766-6482
E-Mail: franchise@prkmc.com
Web Site: www.perkinsrestaurants.com
Ms. Linda Jones, Franchise Development

Since 1958, Perkins Restaurant & Bakery has offered quality, tasty, affordable food for breakfast, lunch and dinner. Our brand heritage and ability to adapt to trends make Perkins a leader in the family dining segment. We are seeking experienced restaurants operators to meet our expansion goals in key markets across the country. We provide professional support services in training, design & construction, marketing, operations, quality assurance and R&D.

BACKGROUND: IFA MEMBER
Established: 1958; 1st Franchised: 1965
Franchised Units: 316
Company-Owned Units: 163
Total Units: 479
Dist.: US-299; CAN-17; O'seas-0
North America: 34 States, 4 Provinces
Density: 53 in PA, 76 in MN, 59 in FL
Projected New Units (12 Months): NR
Qualifications: 5, 4, 5, 3, 3, 5
FINANCIAL/TERMS:
Cash Investment: $500K
Total Investment: $1.2-2.6M
Minimum Net Worth: $1.5M
Fees: Franchise - $20K
Royalty - 4%; Ad. - 3%
Earnings Claims Statement: Yes
Term of Contract (Years): 20/
Avg. # Of Employees: 6 FT, 64 PT
Passive Ownership: Discouraged
Encourage Conversions: Yes

Area Develop. Agreements:	Yes/5
Sub-Franchising Contracts:	No
Expand In Territory:	Yes
Space Needs:	5,000 SF

SUPPORT & TRAINING:

Financial Assistance Provided:	No
Site Selection Assistance:	Yes
Lease Negotiation Assistance:	Yes
Co-Operative Advertising:	Yes
Franchisee Assoc./Member:	No
Size Of Corporate Staff:	0
On-Going Support:	„C,D,E,F,,h,I

Training: Varies New Product Roll Out Training in Franchisee's Location; Varies University of Perkins at Various Location;VariesManagement Team Training at Various Locations

SPECIFIC EXPANSION PLANS:

US: All except WA, OR, CA, NV, AZ, NM, MA, ME, RI
Canada: All Canada
Overseas: NR

PONDEROSA/BONANZA STEAKHOUSES

6500 International Pkwy., # 1000
Plano, TX 75093
Tel: (800) 527-6832 (321) 773-2788
Fax: (321) 773-2675
E-Mail: etaylor@metrogroup.com
Web Site: www.ponderosasteakhouses.com
Mr. Eric Taylor

PONDEROSA and BONANZA FAMILY STEAKHOUSES serve great-tasting, family priced steaks and entrees, accompanied by a large variety of all-you-can-eat salad items, soups, appetizers, hot vegetables, breads, sundae and dessert bar and other tasty food. All steaks and entrees come with the salad bar, buffet and dessert bar at no extra cost.

BACKGROUND:

Established: 1965;	1st Franchised: 1966
Franchised Units:	398
Company-Owned Units:	85
Total Units:	483
Dist.:	US-417; CAN-8; O'seas-58
North America:	31 States, Provinces
Density:	32 in IN, 36 in MI, 60 in OH
Projected New Units (12 Months):	5
Qualifications:	5, 5, 4, 4, 4, 5

FINANCIAL/TERMS:

Cash Investment:	$750K
Total Investment:	$1.3-2.1MM
Minimum Net Worth:	$3MM

Fees: Franchise -	$40K
Royalty - 4%;	Ad. - 4%
Earnings Claims Statement:	No
Term of Contract (Years):	20/
Avg. # Of Employees:	10 FT, 50 PT
Passive Ownership:	Not Allowed
Encourage Conversions:	No
Area Develop. Agreements:	No
Sub-Franchising Contracts:	No
Expand In Territory:	Yes
Space Needs:	6,000-8,000 SF

SUPPORT & TRAINING:

Financial Assistance Provided:	No
Site Selection Assistance:	No
Lease Negotiation Assistance:	No
Co-Operative Advertising:	No
Franchisee Assoc./Member:	Yes/Yes
Size Of Corporate Staff:	125
On-Going Support:	A,B,C,D,E,F,G,H,I

Training: 9 Weeks Certified Training Restaurant

SPECIFIC EXPANSION PLANS:

US: All United States
Canada: ON,QB,NB,BC,AB
Overseas: Brazil, Canada, China, Hong Kong, Japan, Venezuela

RED HOT & BLUE

1701 Clarendon Blvd., # 105
Arlington, VA 22209
Tel: (800) 723-0745 (703) 276-8833
Fax: (703) 528-4789
E-Mail: dknutsen@rhbri.com
Web Site: www.redhotandblue.com
Mr. Dave Knutsen, Dir. Franchise Operations

RED HOT & BLUE restaurants serve Memphis-style ribs, pork, beef, chicken plus salads, burgers and a full menu in a casual dining environment, featuring blues memorabilia and recorded blues music. Service is Southern hospitality.

BACKGROUND:

Established: 1988;	1st Franchised: 1991
Franchised Units:	32
Company-Owned Units:	6
Total Units:	38
Dist.:	US-38; CAN-0; O'seas-0
North America:	10 States, 0 Provinces
Density:	5 in VA, 5 in TX, 6 in NC
Projected New Units (12 Months):	6
Qualifications:	5, 5, 5, 4, 3, 5

FINANCIAL/TERMS:

Cash Investment:	$347.7-868K
Total Investment:	$397.75K
Minimum Net Worth:	$1MM

Fees: Franchise -	$35K
Royalty - 5%;	Ad. - $375/Mo.
Earnings Claims Statement:	No
Term of Contract (Years):	20/10
Avg. # Of Employees:	30 FT, 20 PT
Passive Ownership:	Not Allowed
Encourage Conversions:	Yes
Area Develop. Agreements:	Yes/1
Sub-Franchising Contracts:	No
Expand In Territory:	No
Space Needs:	2,400-5,000 SF

SUPPORT & TRAINING:

Financial Assistance Provided:	No
Site Selection Assistance:	Yes
Lease Negotiation Assistance:	No
Co-Operative Advertising:	No
Franchisee Assoc./Member:	Yes/Yes
Size Of Corporate Staff:	18
On-Going Support:	„C,D,E,f,G,h,

Training: 3 Weeks Home Office; 2 Weeks On-Site

SPECIFIC EXPANSION PLANS:

US: All United States
Canada: All Canada
Overseas: NR

SALSA 2 GO

2431 Aloma Ave. #124
Winter Park, FL 32792
Tel: (888) SALSA2GO (407) 657-0363
Fax: (407) 657-7262
E-Mail: maryann@starfranchisesystems.com
Web Site: www.mysalsa2go.com
Ms. Maryann Kilgallon, President

Everybody loves Salsa! Salsa 2 Go is a quick service food concept, featuring fresh tex-mex cuisine. Our Salsa, tacos and nachos are like no other, we simply offer the best. Our unique "stations" are placed in sports stadiums, shopping malls, college campuses and other high traffic areas.

BACKGROUND: IFA MEMBER

Established: 2003;	1st Franchised: 2007
Franchised Units:	0
Company-Owned Units:	2
Total Units:	2
Dist.:	US-2; CAN-0; O'seas-0
North America:	1 States, 0 Provinces
Density:	2 in FL,
Projected New Units (12 Months):	NR
Qualifications:	3, 3, 3, 3, 3, 3

FINANCIAL/TERMS:

Cash Investment:	$20K
Total Investment:	$40-150K
Minimum Net Worth:	$150K

Fees: Franchise - $20K
   Royalty - 5%; Ad. - 2%
Earnings Claims Statement: No
Term of Contract (Years): 5/0
Avg. # Of Employees: 2 FT, 6 PT
Passive Ownership: Discouraged
Encourage Conversions: NA
Area Develop. Agreements: Yes/7
Sub-Franchising Contracts: No
Expand In Territory: Yes
Space Needs: 120 SF

SUPPORT & TRAINING:
Financial Assistance Provided: No
Site Selection Assistance: No
Lease Negotiation Assistance: No
Co-Operative Advertising: No
Franchisee Assoc./Member: No
Size Of Corporate Staff: 1
On-Going Support: a,b,C,D,E,F,G,H,I
Training: 3 Days Franchise Location;
   5 Days Corporate Office

SPECIFIC EXPANSION PLANS:
US: Florida, SE
Canada: No
Overseas: NR

≪ ≫

SANDWICH TREE RESTAURANTS
535 Thurlow St.
Vancouver, BC V6E 3L2 Canada
Tel: (604) 220-4566
Fax: (604) 684-2542
E-Mail:
Web Site: www.sandwichtree.ca
Mr. Tony Cardarelli, Director Operations

Famous for our custom sandwiches, creative salads, hearty soups, catering and much more, SANDWICH TREE is a limited-hours operation located in shopping centers, commercial towers and industrial centres. Our quality food, served in our attractive surroundings, makes SANDWICH TREE a number one investment opportunity.

BACKGROUND:
Established: 1978; 1st Franchised: 1979
Franchised Units: 31
Company-Owned Units: 0
Total Units: 31
Dist.: US-0; CAN-31; O'seas-0
   North America: 0 States, 6 Provinces
   Density: in ONNSBC
Projected New Units (12 Months): 4
Qualifications: NR

FINANCIAL/TERMS:
Cash Investment: $35-55K
Total Investment: $90-120K

Minimum Net Worth: NR
Fees: Franchise - $10-17.5K
   Royalty - 5%; Ad. - 3%
Earnings Claims Statement: Yes
Term of Contract (Years): 5/5
Avg. # Of Employees: 4 FT, 7 PT
Passive Ownership: Discouraged
Encourage Conversions: Yes
Area Develop. Agreements: Yes/1
Sub-Franchising Contracts: Yes
Expand In Territory: Yes
Space Needs: 300+ SF

SUPPORT & TRAINING:
Financial Assistance Provided: Yes (D)
Site Selection Assistance: Yes
Lease Negotiation Assistance: Yes
Co-Operative Advertising: No
Franchisee Assoc./Member: NR
Size Of Corporate Staff: 6
On-Going Support: a,B,C,D,E,F,G,H,I
Training: 2 Weeks Headquarters

SPECIFIC EXPANSION PLANS:
US: No
Canada: All Canada
Overseas: All Countries

≪ ≫

SIRLOIN STOCKADE
113 E. Third St.
Taylor, TX 76574
Tel: (620) 669-9372 + 229
Fax: (620) 669-0531
E-Mail: madisonj@stockadecompanies.com
Web Site: www.sirloinstockade.com
Mr. Madison Jobe, VP Franchise Development

SIRLOIN STOCKADE features a selection of top-quality steaks, chicken and fish, a self-service salad bar, hot food buffet and display bakery at affordable prices. Free-standing buildings of approximately 8,000-10,000 square feet, seating 300+ and 70,000 square feet of land required.

BACKGROUND: IFA MEMBER
Established: 1966; 1st Franchised: 1968
Franchised Units: 51
Company-Owned Units: 1
Total Units: 52
Dist.: US-32; CAN-0; O'seas-16
   North America: 10 States, 0 Provinces

Density: 10 in TX, 8 in KS, 4 in IN
Projected New Units (12 Months): 6
Qualifications: 5, 4, 4, 3, 2, 4

FINANCIAL/TERMS:
Cash Investment: $148-496K
Total Investment: $419K-3.1MM
Minimum Net Worth: $1MM
Fees: Franchise - $20K
   Royalty - 3%; Ad. - 1%
Earnings Claims Statement: Yes
Term of Contract (Years): 15/15
Avg. # Of Employees: 20 FT, 50 PT
Passive Ownership: Discouraged
Encourage Conversions: Yes
Area Develop. Agreements: Yes/0
Sub-Franchising Contracts: No
Expand In Territory: Yes
Space Needs: 8,000-10,000 SF

SUPPORT & TRAINING:
Financial Assistance Provided: No
Site Selection Assistance: Yes
Lease Negotiation Assistance: No
Co-Operative Advertising: No
Franchisee Assoc./Member: No
Size Of Corporate Staff: 25
On-Going Support: ,,C,D,E,,G,h,
Training: 6-8 Weeks Training

SPECIFIC EXPANSION PLANS:
US: All United States
Canada: No
Overseas: Mexico

≪ ≫

SKYLINE CHILI
4180 Thunderbird Ln.
Fairfield, OH 45014-2235
Tel: (800) 443-4371 (513) 874-1188
Fax: (513) 874-3591
E-Mail: pmlewis@skylinechili.com
Web Site: www.skylinechili.com
Mr. Phillip Lewis, Jr., SVP Franchise Development

Fast-casual restaurant concept that delivers great Cincinnati style chili in the speed of fast food. Sit down unit with table service that is ideal for owner/operators. Concept has a fanatical following by consumers and is one of the simplest restaurant concepts to run.

BACKGROUND: IFA MEMBER

Established: 1949;   1st Franchised: 1965
Franchised Units: 98
Company-Owned Units: <u>37</u>
Total Units: 135
Dist.:   US-135; CAN-0; O'seas-0
  North America: 5 States, 0 Provinces
  Density: 94 in OH, 19 in KY, 6 in IN
Projected New Units (12 Months):   12
Qualifications: 5, 4, 4, 3, 4, 5
FINANCIAL/TERMS:
Cash Investment: $200-250K
Total Investment: $450K-1.2MM
Minimum Net Worth: $400-500K
Fees: Franchise - $20K
  Royalty - 4%;   Ad. - 4%
Earnings Claims Statement: Yes
Term of Contract (Years):   20/20
Avg. # Of Employees: 15 FT, 20 PT
Passive Ownership: Discouraged
Encourage Conversions: Yes
Area Develop. Agreements: Yes/1
Sub-Franchising Contracts: No
Expand In Territory: Yes
Space Needs: 2,800 SF
SUPPORT & TRAINING:
Financial Assistance Provided: No
Site Selection Assistance: Yes
Lease Negotiation Assistance: Yes
Co-Operative Advertising: No
Franchisee Assoc./Member: Yes/Yes
Size Of Corporate Staff: 40
On-Going Support: a,B,C,D,E,,G,,I
Training: 6-8 Weeks Cincinnati, OH
SPECIFIC EXPANSION PLANS:
US: OH, KY, IN, MI, FL, PA, WV
Canada: No
Overseas: NR

≺≺ ≻≻

STRINGS ITALIAN CAFE
11344 Coloma Rd., # 545
Gold River, CA 95670
Tel: (916) 635-3990
Fax: (916) 631-9775
E-Mail: al@stringscafe.com
Web Site: www.stringscafe.com
Mr. Al DeCaprio, President

STRINGS ITALIAN CAFE is a full-service, casual restaurant, with a menu focusing on a variety of pasta entrees, pizza,
salads, desserts and espresso. A central
kitchen/commissary provides most of the
product requirements.

BACKGROUND:
Established: 1987;   1st Franchised: 1989
Franchised Units: 17
Company-Owned Units: <u>3</u>

Total Units: 20
Dist.:   US-18; CAN-2; O'seas-0
  North America: 3 States, 1 Provinces
  Density: in QCNVCA
Projected New Units (12 Months):   4
Qualifications: 4, 4, 5, 3, 3, 4
FINANCIAL/TERMS:
Cash Investment: $100K
Total Investment: $325K
Minimum Net Worth: $400K
Fees: Franchise - $37.5K
  Royalty - 5%;   Ad. - 2%
Earnings Claims Statement: No
Term of Contract (Years):   10/5
Avg. # Of Employees: 4-6 FT, 15 PT
Passive Ownership: Discouraged
Encourage Conversions: Yes
Area Develop. Agreements: Yes/1
Sub-Franchising Contracts: No
Expand In Territory: Yes
Space Needs: 2,500 SF
SUPPORT & TRAINING:
Financial Assistance Provided: No
Site Selection Assistance: Yes
Lease Negotiation Assistance: Yes
Co-Operative Advertising: No
Franchisee Assoc./Member: No
Size Of Corporate Staff: 12
On-Going Support: ,,C,D,E,F,G,H,
Training: 6 Weeks Gold River, CA;
  3 Weeks On-Site
SPECIFIC EXPANSION PLANS:
US: All United States
Canada: No
Overseas: NR

≺≺ ≻≻

TERIYAKI EXPERIENCE
700 Kerr St.
Oakville, ON L6K 3W3
Tel: (800) 555-5726 (480) 502-2006
Fax: (905) 337-0331
E-Mail: jarancio@teriyakiexperience.com
Web Site: www.teriyakiexperience.com
Mr. Joe Arancio, VP US Development

Asian inspired quick service restaurants
located in major mall food courts, street
fronts, strip centers, airports, universities,
hospitals, theme parks, supermarkets and
other similar high traffic settings. Healthy,
nutritious and delicious meals, prepared
fast and fresh before your eyes. Cooked in

water, not oil.

BACKGROUND: IFA MEMBER
Established: 1986;   1st Franchised: 1987
Franchised Units: 130
Company-Owned Units: <u>0</u>
Total Units: 130
Dist.:   US-8; CAN-105; O'seas-21
  North America: 9 States, 7 Provinces
  Density: 14 in QC, 80 in ON, 5 in BC
Projected New Units (12 Months):   25
Qualifications: 5, 2, 2, 2, 3, 4
FINANCIAL/TERMS:
Cash Investment: $50-100K
Total Investment: $230-330K
Minimum Net Worth: $300K
Fees: Franchise - $25K
  Royalty - 6%;   Ad. - 3%
Earnings Claims Statement: Yes
Term of Contract (Years):   8-10/5-10
Avg. # Of Employees: 3 FT, 6 PT
Passive Ownership: Discouraged
Encourage Conversions: Yes
Area Develop. Agreements: Yes/10
Sub-Franchising Contracts: Yes
Expand In Territory: Yes
Space Needs: 400-1,800 SF
SUPPORT & TRAINING:
Financial Assistance Provided: Yes (I)
Site Selection Assistance: Yes
Lease Negotiation Assistance: Yes
Co-Operative Advertising: Yes
Franchisee Assoc./Member: No
Size Of Corporate Staff: 40
On-Going Support: A,B,C,D,E,,G,H,I
Training: 9-10 Days Store;
  1 Week During your Grand Opening;
  3-4 Days Company Headquarters
SPECIFIC EXPANSION PLANS:
US: All United States
Canada: All Canada
Overseas: All Countries

≺≺ ≻≻

TONY ROMA'S FAMOUS FOR RIBS
9304 Forest Ln., # 200
Dallas, TX 75243-8953
Tel: (800) 286-7662 (214) 343-7800
Fax: (214) 343-2680
E-Mail: kenm@romacorp.com
Web Site: www.tonyromas.com
Mr. Kenneth L. Myres, VP Franchise
  Development

At TONY ROMA'S, we are committed to 'World Wide - World Class.' With intense guest focus, high integrity and Great Food! Providing for a great business opportunity. We started out with one restaurant in Miami FL, and today there are 280 TONY ROMA'S on six continents. We owe our phenomenal growth to one thing - Great People! TONY ROMA'S franchisee partners are a cut above the rest and we are always looking for more people to join our success.

BACKGROUND: IFA MEMBER
Established: 1972; 1st Franchised: 1980
Franchised Units: 197
Company-Owned Units: 56
Total Units: 253
Dist.: US-135; CAN-40; O'seas-81
  North America: 42 States, 3 Provinces
  Density: 37 in CA, 14 in AB
Projected New Units (12 Months): NR
Qualifications: 5, 5, 5, 4, 4, 5
FINANCIAL/TERMS:
Cash Investment: Varies
Total Investment: $1.06M
Minimum Net Worth: $3MM
Fees: Franchise - $20K
  Royalty - 4%; Ad. - .5%
Earnings Claims Statement: No
Term of Contract (Years): 20/10
Avg. # Of Employees: FT, 0 PT
Passive Ownership: Allowed
Encourage Conversions: Yes
Area Develop. Agreements: Yes/1
Sub-Franchising Contracts: No
Expand In Territory: Yes
Space Needs: 6,500 SF
SUPPORT & TRAINING:
Financial Assistance Provided: No
Site Selection Assistance: Yes
Lease Negotiation Assistance: No
Co-Operative Advertising: No
Franchisee Assoc./Member: No
Size Of Corporate Staff: 35
On-Going Support: „C,D,E,„,h,I
Training: NR
SPECIFIC EXPANSION PLANS:
US: All United States
Canada: All Canada
Overseas: All Countries

UNO CHICAGO GRILL
100 Charles Park Rd.
Boston, MA 02132-4985
Tel: (877) 855-8667 (617) 218-5200
Fax: (617) 218-5376
E-Mail: randy.clifton@unos.com
Web Site: www.unos.com
Mr. Jack Crawford, SVP Franchising

A full-service casual theme restaurant with a brand name signature product - UNO's Original Chicago Deep Dish Pizza. A full varied menu with broad appeal featuring steak, shrimp and pasta. A flair for fun including a bar and comfortable décor in a facility that attracts guests of all ages.

BACKGROUND: IFA MEMBER
Established: 1943; 1st Franchised: 1979
Franchised Units: 84
Company-Owned Units: 102
Total Units: 186
Dist.: US-182; CAN-0; O'seas-4
  North America: 32 States, 0 Provinces
  Density: 15 in VA, 31 in NY, 30 in MA
Projected New Units (12 Months): 16
Qualifications: 5, 5, 5, 3, 4, 4
FINANCIAL/TERMS:
Cash Investment: $500-800K
Total Investment: $850K-2.5MM
Minimum Net Worth: $3MM
Fees: Franchise - $40K
  Royalty - 5%; Ad. - 1%
Earnings Claims Statement: Yes
Term of Contract (Years): 20/10
Avg. # Of Employees: 40 FT, 40 PT
Passive Ownership: Allowed
Encourage Conversions: Yes
Area Develop. Agreements: Yes/1
Sub-Franchising Contracts: No
Expand In Territory: Yes
Space Needs: 5,800 SF
SUPPORT & TRAINING:
Financial Assistance Provided: Yes (I)
Site Selection Assistance: Yes
Lease Negotiation Assistance: Yes
Co-Operative Advertising: Yes
Franchisee Assoc./Member: Yes/Yes
Size Of Corporate Staff: 135
On-Going Support: 0,B,C,D,E,F,G,H,I
Training: 2 Weeks On-Site Staff Training;
  12 Weeks Training Restaurant
SPECIFIC EXPANSION PLANS:
US: All United States

Canada: All Canada
Overseas: Asia, South and Central America, Europe

WALL STREET DELI SYSTEMS
14 Penn Plz., # 1305
New York, NY 10122
Tel: (212) 359-3600
Fax: (212) 359-3601
E-Mail:
Web Site: www.wallstreetdeli.com
Franchise Development

Sandwich shop offering fresh salads, coffee and hot entrees. Located at commercial parks and non-traditional locations, such as airports, hospitals, college campuses and office buildings. Quality of life is very appealing to potential franchisees. Monday through Friday, 7 AM - 3 PM. We promote a captive audience.

BACKGROUND: IFA MEMBER
Established: 1967; 1st Franchised: 1997
Franchised Units: 30
Company-Owned Units: 30
Total Units: 60
Dist.: US-60; CAN-0; O'seas-0
  North America: 13 States, 0 Provinces
  Density: 5 in TX, 5 in CA, 9 in AL
Projected New Units (12 Months): 25
Qualifications: 5, 4, 4, 3, 2, 1
FINANCIAL/TERMS:
Cash Investment: $65-467.4K
Total Investment: $75-467.4K
Minimum Net Worth: $200K
Fees: Franchise - $30K
  Royalty - 5%; Ad. - 1%
Earnings Claims Statement: Yes
Term of Contract (Years): 10/10
Avg. # Of Employees: 6 FT, 4 PT
Passive Ownership: Discouraged
Encourage Conversions: Yes
Area Develop. Agreements: Yes/1
Sub-Franchising Contracts: Yes
Expand In Territory: Yes
Space Needs: Varies
SUPPORT & TRAINING:
Financial Assistance Provided: No
Site Selection Assistance: Yes
Lease Negotiation Assistance: Yes
Co-Operative Advertising: No
Franchisee Assoc./Member: Yes/Yes
Size Of Corporate Staff: NR
On-Going Support: A,B,C,D,E,F,G,H,
Training: Training is On-Site;
  10 Days Follow-up in Washington, DC
SPECIFIC EXPANSION PLANS:

US: All United States
Canada: No
Overseas: NR

◄◄ ►►

**WESTERN SIZZLIN'S WOOD
GRILL BUFFET**

1338 Plantation Rd.
Roanoke, VA 24012
Tel: (800) 247-8325 (540) 345-3195
Fax: (540) 345-0831
E-Mail: jplunkett@western-sizzlin.com
Web Site: www.western-sizzlin.com
Mr. Jerry Plunkett, Franchise Administration

WESTERN SIZZLIN' restaurants operate a full line of steak-chicken-seafood entrees, as well as a full expanded food bar, featuring proteins, vegetables and bakery items, along with an expanded salad bar. Our focus is on making a quality statement with excellent price/value. Also offering franchises for Great American Buffet and Western Sizzlin's Buffet.

BACKGROUND: IFA MEMBER
Established: 1962; 1st Franchised: 1976
Franchised Units: 120
Company-Owned Units: 6
Total Units: 126
Dist.: US-126; CAN-0; O'seas-0
  North America: 19 States, 0 Provinces
  Density: 17 in NC, 18 in MS, 28 in AR
Projected New Units (12 Months): 4
Qualifications: 5, 4, 2, 3, 2, 5
FINANCIAL/TERMS:
Cash Investment: NR
Total Investment: $1.1-4.5MM
Minimum Net Worth: $500K
Fees: Franchise - $30K
  Royalty - 2% Gross; Ad. - $250/Mo.
Earnings Claims Statement: Yes

Term of Contract (Years): 20/10
Avg. # Of Employees: 25 FT, 50 PT
Passive Ownership: Not Allowed
Encourage Conversions: Yes
Area Develop. Agreements: Yes/1
Sub-Franchising Contracts: No
Expand In Territory: Yes
Space Needs: 7,500-8,500 SF
SUPPORT & TRAINING:
Financial Assistance Provided: No
Site Selection Assistance: Yes
Lease Negotiation Assistance: No
Co-Operative Advertising: No
Franchisee Assoc./Member: Yes/Yes
Size Of Corporate Staff: 20
On-Going Support: „C,D,E,F,G,h,I
Training: 8 Weeks Training
SPECIFIC EXPANSION PLANS:
US: All United States
Canada: No
Overseas: NR

◄◄ ►►

FIVE LARGEST PARTICIPANTS IN SURVEY

Company	# Fran-chised Units	# Co-Owned Units	# Total Units	Franchise Fee	On-Going Royalty	Total Investment
1. 7-Eleven, Inc.	35,141	462	35,603	Varies by Store	Gross Profit Split	Varies
2. General Nutrition Centers	2,034	3,747	5,781	$40K	6%	$133-182K
3. Circle K	458	2,627	3,085	$15K	4%	$546K-1.35MM
4. Sunoco APlus	270	500	770	$30K	Varies	$300-600K
5. Candy Bouquet International	577	0	577	$3.6-29K	0%	$8K-50K

All of the data provided are proprietary and should not be quoted without acknowledging *Bond's Franchise Guide.*

7-ELEVEN, INC.
2711 N. Haskell Ave., 34th Fl.
Dallas, TX 75204-2911
Tel: (800) 255-0711 (214) 828-7764
Fax: (214) 841-6776
E-Mail: jwebbj01@7-11.com
Web Site: www.7-eleven.com
Ms. Joanne Webb-Joyce, Dir. National
    Franchise Sales

7-ELEVEN stores were born from the simple concept of giving people 'what they want, when and where they want it.' This idea gave rise to the entire convenience store industry. While this formula still works today, customers' needs are changing at an accelerating pace. We are meeting this challenge with an infrastructure of daily distribution of fresh perishables, regional production of fresh foods and pastries and an information system that greatly improves ordering and merchandising decisions.

BACKGROUND: IFA MEMBER
Established: 1927;   1st Franchised: 1964
Franchised Units: 35141
Company-Owned Units: 462
Total Units: 35603
Dist.: US-6378; CAN-462; O'seas-28763
    North America: 31 States, 5 Provinces
    Density: 636 in VA, 565 in FL, 1292 in CA
Projected New Units (12 Months):   200
Qualifications: 4, 4, 3, 3, 5, 5
FINANCIAL/TERMS:
Cash Investment: Varies by Store
Total Investment: Varies
Minimum Net Worth: $15K
Fees: Franchise -   Varies by Store
    Royalty - Gross Profit Split;   Ad. -
Earnings Claims Statement: Yes
Term of Contract (Years):   15/15

Avg. # Of Employees:	5 FT, 5 PT
Passive Ownership:	Not Allowed
Encourage Conversions:	Yes
Area Develop. Agreements:	No
Sub-Franchising Contracts:	No
Expand In Territory:	No
Space Needs:	2,400 SF

SUPPORT & TRAINING:

Financial Assistance Provided:	Yes (I)
Site Selection Assistance:	NA
Lease Negotiation Assistance:	NA
Co-Operative Advertising:	No
Franchisee Assoc./Member:	Yes/Yes
Size Of Corporate Staff:	1000
On-Going Support:	A,B,C,D,E,F,G,H,I
Training:	2 Weeks Franchisee's store;
	4 Weeks Various Training Stores
	throughout US

SPECIFIC EXPANSION PLANS:

US:	NW,SW,MW,NE, Great Lakes,
Southeast	
Canada:	No
Overseas:	NR

◄◄ ►►

ARABICA COFFEEHOUSE

7010 Engle Rd., # 100
Middleburg Heights, OH 44130
Tel: (888) 860-5082 (440) 824-0945
Fax: (440) 625-3081
E-Mail: rkrieger@mrhero.com
Web Site: www.arabicacoffeeinc.com
Mr. Bob Kreiger, Director Franchise
Development

Built to reflect the personality of the community, an ARABICA COFFEEHOUSE is more than a place to enjoy 50 flavors of coffee, specialty drinks, unique teas, health-conscious sandwiches, decadent pastries and desserts. Superior food and beverages in well-appointed, comfortable surroundings is a perfect venue for any purpose.

BACKGROUND:

Established: 1994;	1st Franchised: 1994
Franchised Units:	9
Company-Owned Units:	0
Total Units:	9
Dist.:	US-9; CAN-0; O'seas-0
North America:	1 States, 0 Provinces
Density:	9 in OH,
Projected New Units (12 Months):	1
Qualifications:	5, 4, 4, 4, 4, 5

FINANCIAL/TERMS:

Cash Investment:	$75K
Total Investment:	$126-363K
Minimum Net Worth:	$300K

Fees: Franchise -	$22.5K
Royalty - 5.5%;	Ad. - 2.5%
Earnings Claims Statement:	No
Term of Contract (Years):	10/10
Avg. # Of Employees:	4 FT, 8 PT
Passive Ownership:	Discouraged
Encourage Conversions:	Yes
Area Develop. Agreements:	Yes/1
Sub-Franchising Contracts:	No
Expand In Territory:	Yes
Space Needs:	2,000 SF

SUPPORT & TRAINING:

Financial Assistance Provided:	No
Site Selection Assistance:	Yes
Lease Negotiation Assistance:	Yes
Co-Operative Advertising:	No
Franchisee Assoc./Member:	No
Size Of Corporate Staff:	12
On-Going Support:	„C,D,E,F,G,H,I
Training:	3 Weeks Cleveland, OH

SPECIFIC EXPANSION PLANS:

US:	OH
Canada:	No
Overseas:	NR

◄◄ ►►

BAD ASS COFFEE OF HAWAII

166 W. 2700 S.
Salt Lake City, UT 84115
Tel: (888) 422-3277 (801) 463-1966
Fax: (801) 463-2606
E-Mail: haroldh@badasscoffee.com
Web Site: www.badasscoffee.com
Mr. Harold J. Hill, Director of Franchising

The BAD ASS COMPANY is the premier destination when you go to get yourself or a friend some of the world's best coffee and to experience the friendly aloha spirit while immersed in a unique, exciting, inviting Hawaiian atmosphere.

BACKGROUND:

Established: 1989;	1st Franchised: 1999
Franchised Units:	54
Company-Owned Units:	0
Total Units:	54
Dist.:	US-48; CAN-4; O'seas-6
North America:	1 States, 0 Provinces
Density:	
Projected New Units (12 Months):	10
Qualifications:	5, 3, 3, 3, 1, 2

FINANCIAL/TERMS:

Cash Investment:	$50K
Total Investment:	$150-200K
Minimum Net Worth:	$500K
Fees: Franchise -	$35K
Royalty - 6%;	Ad. - 2%
Earnings Claims Statement:	No
Term of Contract (Years):	5/20
Avg. # Of Employees:	3 FT, 4 PT
Passive Ownership:	Discouraged
Encourage Conversions:	Yes
Area Develop. Agreements:	No
Sub-Franchising Contracts:	No
Expand In Territory:	Yes
Space Needs:	1,500 SF

SUPPORT & TRAINING:

Financial Assistance Provided:	No
Site Selection Assistance:	Yes
Lease Negotiation Assistance:	Yes
Co-Operative Advertising:	No
Franchisee Assoc./Member:	No
Size Of Corporate Staff:	6
On-Going Support:	„C,D,E,F,G,H,I
Training:	5 days Salt Lake City, UT;
	5 days In franchise location

SPECIFIC EXPANSION PLANS:

US:	All United States
Canada:	All Canada
Overseas:	All Countries

◄◄ ►►

CANDY BOUQUET INTERNATIONAL

423 E.Third St.
Little Rock, AR 72201
Tel: (877) 226-3901 (501) 375-9990
Fax: (501) 375-9998
E-Mail: yumyum@candybouquet.com
Web Site: www.candybouquet.com
Ms. Gina McNabb, Executive Vice President

CANDY BOUQUET franchises are as unique as the people who own them. All franchises offer floral-like arrangements that are crafted from candies and the finest of chocolates. Each bouquet includes a burst of accessories, bright cellophane accents and a unique container. CANDY BOUQUETS are fun to give, fun to receive and fun to eat. They are perfect as corporate gifts and can be shipped anywhere.

BACKGROUND: IFA MEMBER
Established: 1989;   1st Franchised: 1993
Franchised Units: 577
Company-Owned Units: 0
Total Units: 577
Dist.:   US-585; CAN-37; O'seas-48
  North America: 49 States, 8 Provinces
  Density: 46 in TX, 31 in CA, 48 in AR
Projected New Units (12 Months):   239
Qualifications: 5, 5, 5, 5, 5, 5
FINANCIAL/TERMS:
Cash Investment: $4K-30K
Total Investment: $8K-50K
Minimum Net Worth: NR
Fees: Franchise - $3.6-29K
  Royalty - 0%;   Ad. - 0%
Earnings Claims Statement: No
Term of Contract (Years):   5/5
Avg. # Of Employees: 1 FT, 2 PT
Passive Ownership: Not Allowed
Encourage Conversions: NA
Area Develop. Agreements: Yes/1
Sub-Franchising Contracts: Yes
Expand In Territory: Yes
Space Needs: ~1,000 SF
SUPPORT & TRAINING:
Financial Assistance Provided: No
Site Selection Assistance: Yes
Lease Negotiation Assistance: No
Co-Operative Advertising: No
Franchisee Assoc./Member: No
Size Of Corporate Staff: 27
On-Going Support: ,b,c,D,e,,G,h,I
Training: 5 Days Little Rock, AR
SPECIFIC EXPANSION PLANS:
US: All United States
Canada: All Canada
Overseas: All Countries

◄◄ ►►

CANDY EXPRESS
10480 Little Patuxent Pkwy., # 400
Columbia, MD 21044
Tel: (800) 511-4438 (410) 964-5500
Fax: (410) 964-6404
E-Mail: jrosenberg@candyexpress.com
Web Site: www.candyexpress.com
Mr. Joel Rosenberg, President

The number-one ranked retail candy store franchise, offering over 1,000 varieties of candy and confections in a self-serve format. This international franchise company provides franchisees with a total turn-key opportunity that is profitable and easy to operate.

BACKGROUND:
Established: 1989;   1st Franchised: 1989
Franchised Units: 37
Company-Owned Units: 5
Total Units: 42
Dist.:   US-34; CAN-0; O'seas-8
  North America: 17 States, 0 Provinces
  Density: 4 in VA, 6 in MD, 5 in GA
Projected New Units (12 Months):   15
Qualifications: 5, 2, 1, 1, 2, 3
FINANCIAL/TERMS:
Cash Investment: $25-75K
Total Investment: $125-175K
Minimum Net Worth: $200K
Fees: Franchise - $25K
  Royalty - 6%;   Ad. - 1%
Earnings Claims Statement: No
Term of Contract (Years):   10/10
Avg. # Of Employees: 1 FT, 3 PT
Passive Ownership: Allowed
Encourage Conversions: Yes
Area Develop. Agreements: Yes/1
Sub-Franchising Contracts: Yes
Expand In Territory: Yes
Space Needs: 1,000 SF
SUPPORT & TRAINING:
Financial Assistance Provided: Yes (D)
Site Selection Assistance: Yes
Lease Negotiation Assistance: Yes
Co-Operative Advertising: No
Franchisee Assoc./Member: Yes/Yes
Size Of Corporate Staff: 10
On-Going Support: A,B,C,D,E,F,G,H,
Training: 2 Weeks MD
SPECIFIC EXPANSION PLANS:
US: All United States
Canada: All Canada
Overseas: All Countries

◄◄ ►►

CIRCLE K
1130 W. Warner Rd., DC-07
Tempe, AZ 85284
Tel: (800) 813-7677 (714) 337-3404
Fax: (602) 728-5248
E-Mail: ddwilliams@circlek.com
Web Site: www.circlek.com
Mr. Daniel D. Williams, Director Franchise
  Development

The Circle K Franchise Program offers Superior business systems, extensive train-

ing and effective promotional tools. Our ongoing business support and our heritage brand is, in fact, the Circle K advantage. With our recognized image and popular proprietary products, Circle K attracts a loyal customer base.

BACKGROUND: IFA MEMBER
Established: 1951;   1st Franchised: 1999
Franchised Units: 458
Company-Owned Units: 2627
Total Units: 3085
Dist.:   US-3085; CAN-0; O'seas-3612
  North America: 29 States, 0 Provinces
  Density: 488 in FL, 348 in CA, 553 in
AZ
Projected New Units (12 Months):   200
Qualifications: 5, 4, 5, 3, 3, 5
FINANCIAL/TERMS:
Cash Investment: $100K-250K
Total Investment: $546K-1.35MM
Minimum Net Worth: $300K
Fees: Franchise - $15K
  Royalty - 4%;   Ad. - 2%
Earnings Claims Statement: Yes
Term of Contract (Years):   10/10
Avg. # Of Employees: 8 FT, 4 PT
Passive Ownership: Discouraged
Encourage Conversions: Yes
Area Develop. Agreements: Yes/5
Sub-Franchising Contracts: No
Expand In Territory: Yes
Space Needs: 1,500-3,000 SF
SUPPORT & TRAINING:
Financial Assistance Provided: Yes (D)
Site Selection Assistance: Yes
Lease Negotiation Assistance: No
Co-Operative Advertising: No
Franchisee Assoc./Member: No
Size Of Corporate Staff: 1200
On-Going Support: ,,C,D,E,F,G,H,I
Training: 2 Weeks Phoenix, AZ
SPECIFIC EXPANSION PLANS:
US: All United States
Canada: No
Overseas: Asia

◄◄ ►►

COFFEE BEANERY
3429 Pierson Pl.
Flushing, MI 48433-2413
Tel: (800) 728-2326 (810) 733-1020

Fax: (810) 733-1536
E-Mail: franchiseinfo@beanerysupport.com
Web Site: www.coffeebeanery.com
Mr. Kurt Shaw, VP Franchise Sales

The cornerstone and foundation of the business is the exceptional quality of its own hand-roasted coffee, which is also flavored and packaged at the corporate warehouse in Michigan. Stores may offer indoor/outdoor seating, lite-fair breakfast and lunch items as well as wi-fi. Our customers enjoy the best coffee and assorted products available from a network of over 100 locations in the USA.

BACKGROUND: IFA MEMBER
Established: 1976;   1st Franchised: 1985
Franchised Units: 93
Company-Owned Units: 1
Total Units: 94
Dist.:   US-100; CAN-0; O'seas-17
  North America: 23 States, 0 Provinces
  Density: 7 in NY, 10 in NJ, 24 in MI
Projected New Units (12 Months):   12
Qualifications: 5, 5, 4, 3, 4, 5
FINANCIAL/TERMS:
Cash Investment: $150K
Total Investment: $350-450K
Minimum Net Worth: $500K
Fees: Franchise - $27.5K
  Royalty - 6%;   Ad. - 2%
Earnings Claims Statement: No
Term of Contract (Years):   5,10,15+/15
Avg. # Of Employees: 2-3 FT, 10-15 PT
Passive Ownership: Discouraged
Encourage Conversions: Yes
Area Develop. Agreements: Yes/2
Sub-Franchising Contracts: No
Expand In Territory: Yes
Space Needs: 100-1,500 SF
SUPPORT & TRAINING:
Financial Assistance Provided: Yes (I)
Site Selection Assistance: Yes
Lease Negotiation Assistance: Yes
Co-Operative Advertising: Yes
Franchisee Assoc./Member: Yes/Yes
Size Of Corporate Staff: 40
On-Going Support: „C,D,E,F,G,H,I
Training: 4 Weeks Corporate Office +
  Local Training Facility
SPECIFIC EXPANSION PLANS:
US: All United States
Canada: No
Overseas: Cyprus, Greece

≺≺ ≻≻

CONNOISSEUR, THE
201 Torrance Blvd.
Redondo Beach, CA 90277
Tel: (877) 261-3111 (310) 374-9768
Fax: (310) 372-9097
E-Mail: info@giftsofwine.com
Web Site: www.giftsofwine.com
Mr. Sandy French, President

Personalized gifts of fine wines, champagnes, gourmet, crystal and special occasion items.

BACKGROUND:
Established: 1975;   1st Franchised: 1989
Franchised Units: 7
Company-Owned Units: 1
Total Units: 8
Dist.:   US-8; CAN-0; O'seas-0
  North America: 5 States, 0 Provinces
  Density: 1 in IL, 2 in CO, 2 in CA
Projected New Units (12 Months):   25
Qualifications: NR
FINANCIAL/TERMS:
Cash Investment: $175K
Total Investment: $175K
Minimum Net Worth: NR
Fees: Franchise - $29.5K
  Royalty - 6%;   Ad. - 1%
Earnings Claims Statement: No
Term of Contract (Years):   10/10
Avg. # Of Employees: 1 FT, 2 PT
Passive Ownership: Discouraged
Encourage Conversions: No
Area Develop. Agreements: Yes/1
Sub-Franchising Contracts: Yes
Expand In Territory: Yes
Space Needs: 2,000 SF
SUPPORT & TRAINING:
Financial Assistance Provided: No
Site Selection Assistance: Yes
Lease Negotiation Assistance: Yes
Co-Operative Advertising: No
Franchisee Assoc./Member: NR
Size Of Corporate Staff: 4
On-Going Support: A,B,C,D,E,F,,H
Training: 1 Week Headquarters
SPECIFIC EXPANSION PLANS:
US: All United States
Canada: No
Overseas: NR

≺≺ ≻≻

FRUIT FLOWERS
3720 W. Chester Pike
Newtown Square, PA 19073
Tel: (866) 203-7848 (610) 353-8844
Fax: (610) 359-9188
E-Mail: ied@fruitflowers.com

Web Site: www.fruitflowers.com
Mr. Melvin Messinger, Vice President of
  Franchising

We are offering a franchised retail business which features the creation and delivery of sculptured fruit and vegetable bouquets. Our bouquets are provided for our customers who share our passion for sight, smell and taste of fruit and vegetables.

BACKGROUND: IFA MEMBER
Established: 1984;   1st Franchised: 1993
Franchised Units: 27
Company-Owned Units: 2
Total Units: 29
Dist.:   US-29; CAN-0; O'seas-0
  North America: 16 States, 0 Provinces
  Density: 4 in PA, 2 in NJ, 4 in FL
Projected New Units (12 Months):   12
Qualifications: 5, 3, 1, 1, 3, 3
FINANCIAL/TERMS:
Cash Investment: $50K
Total Investment: $150-250K
Minimum Net Worth: $200K
Fees: Franchise - $35K
  Royalty - 4.5%;   Ad. - 1%
Earnings Claims Statement: Yes
Term of Contract (Years):   10/10
Avg. # Of Employees: 1 FT, 4 PT
Passive Ownership: Allowed
Encourage Conversions: NA
Area Develop. Agreements: Yes/10
Sub-Franchising Contracts: No
Expand In Territory: Yes
Space Needs: 1,500 SF
SUPPORT & TRAINING:
Financial Assistance Provided: No
Site Selection Assistance: Yes
Lease Negotiation Assistance: Yes
Co-Operative Advertising: No
Franchisee Assoc./Member: No
Size Of Corporate Staff: 9
On-Going Support: „C,D,E,,G,h,
Training: 2 Weeks Newton Square, PA
SPECIFIC EXPANSION PLANS:
US: All United States
Canada: All Canada
Overseas: All Countries

≺≺ ≻≻

GNC

GENERAL NUTRITION CENTERS
300 Sixth Ave., 4th Fl.
Pittsburgh, PA 15222-2514
Tel: (800) 766-7099 (412) 338-2503

Fax: (412) 402-7105
E-Mail: livewell@gncfranchising.com
Web Site: www.gncfranchising.com
Mr. Bruce Pollock, Sr. Dir. Franchise Development

GNC is the leading specialty retailer of vitamins, minerals, herbs and sports nutrition supplements and is uniquely positioned to capitalize on the accelerating self-care trend. As the leading provider of products and information for personal health enhancement, the company holds the largest specialty-retail share of the nutritional supplement market. GNC was ranked America's #1 retail franchise for 17 consecutive years.

BACKGROUND:
Established: 1935; 1st Franchised: 1988
Franchised Units: 2034
Company-Owned Units: <u>3747</u>
Total Units: 5781
Dist.: US-3747; CAN-1212; O'seas-822
North America: 50 States, 0 Provinces
Density: in TXFLCA
Projected New Units (12 Months): NR
Qualifications: 5, 5, 1, 1, 1, 4
FINANCIAL/TERMS:
Cash Investment: $65K
Total Investment: $133-182K
Minimum Net Worth: $100K
Fees: Franchise - $40K
Royalty - 6%; Ad. - 3%
Earnings Claims Statement: Yes
Term of Contract (Years): 10/5/5/
Avg. # Of Employees: 1 FT, 3-5 PT
Passive Ownership: Not Allowed
Encourage Conversions: No
Area Develop. Agreements: Yes/0
Sub-Franchising Contracts: No
Expand In Territory: Yes
Space Needs: 1,402 (avg.) SF
SUPPORT & TRAINING:
Financial Assistance Provided: Yes (D)
Site Selection Assistance: Yes
Lease Negotiation Assistance: Yes
Co-Operative Advertising: No
Franchisee Assoc./Member: No
Size Of Corporate Staff: 600
On-Going Support: A,,,D,E,F,G,H,I
Training: 1 Week On-Site in Local Corporate Store
SPECIFIC EXPANSION PLANS:
US: All United States
Canada: All CAN Exc. PQ
Overseas: All Countries

◀◀ ▶▶

GLORIA JEAN'S GOURMET COFFEES
28 Executive Pk., # 200
Irvine, CA 92614
Tel: (800) 354-JAVA (949) 260-6757
Fax: (949) 260-6745
E-Mail: nromero@gloriajeans.com
Web Site: www.gloriajeans.com
Ms. Norma Romero, Franchise Sales Administrator

American's largest retail gourmet coffee franchisor offers the highest-quality gourmet coffees, teas and accessories. Our unique store design and exclusive coffee bean counter are the focal points of our nationally honored company. Each store has up to 64 varieties of coffees.

BACKGROUND: IFA MEMBER
Established: 1979; 1st Franchised: 1986
Franchised Units: 97
Company-Owned Units: <u>10</u>
Total Units: 107
Dist.: US-136; CAN-0; O'seas-16
North America: 38 States, 0 Provinces
Density: in WIILCA
Projected New Units (12 Months): 20
Qualifications: 4, 4, 3, 3, 4, 5
FINANCIAL/TERMS:
Cash Investment: $125K
Total Investment: $182K-672K
Minimum Net Worth: $350K
Fees: Franchise - $16-32.5K
Royalty - 6%; Ad. - 2%
Earnings Claims Statement: No
Term of Contract (Years): 15/Lease
Avg. # Of Employees: 2 FT, 8 PT
Passive Ownership: Discouraged
Encourage Conversions: NA
Area Develop. Agreements: Yes/1
Sub-Franchising Contracts: No
Expand In Territory: Yes
Space Needs: 200-1,000 SF
SUPPORT & TRAINING:
Financial Assistance Provided: Yes (I)
Site Selection Assistance: Yes
Lease Negotiation Assistance: Yes
Co-Operative Advertising: No
Franchisee Assoc./Member: Yes/Yes
Size Of Corporate Staff: 150
On-Going Support: ,B,C,D,E,F,G,H,I
Training: 2 Weeks Corporate Training Store

SPECIFIC EXPANSION PLANS:
US: All United States
Canada: No
Overseas: All Countries

◀◀ ▶▶

THE HONEYBAKED HAM CO.
AND CAFÉ

HONEYBAKED HAM CO. & CAFE
5445 Triangle Pkwy., # 400
Norcross, GA 30022
Tel: (866) 968-7424 (678) 966-3238
Fax: (678) 966-3134
E-Mail: hbhdevelopment@hbham.com
Web Site: www.honeybakedfranchising.com
Mr. Jim Squire, Franchise Development Manager

The HONEYBAKED HAM CO. & CAFE is a truly exciting franchise opportunity with 50 years of experience building a strong brand. We are the original (and the world's largest) specialty retailer of high quality spiral-sliced glazed hams, turkeys and other special occasion center-of-the-table products complemented by a full service cafe.

BACKGROUND: IFA MEMBER
Established: 1957; 1st Franchised: 1998
Franchised Units: 122
Company-Owned Units: <u>284</u>
Total Units: 406
Dist.: US-380; CAN-0; O'seas-0
North America: 39 States, 0 Provinces
Density: 37 in GA, 43 in FL, 46 in CA
Projected New Units (12 Months): NR
Qualifications: 4, 3, 4, 3, 2, 4
FINANCIAL/TERMS:
Cash Investment: $100K-125K
Total Investment: $325K-375K
Minimum Net Worth: $350K
Fees: Franchise - $30K
Royalty - 5-6%; Ad. - 2%
Earnings Claims Statement: Yes
Term of Contract (Years): 7/7
Avg. # Of Employees: 1 FT, 7 PT
Passive Ownership: Discouraged
Encourage Conversions: Yes
Area Develop. Agreements: Yes/2
Sub-Franchising Contracts: No
Expand In Territory: Yes
Space Needs: 2,000 SF
SUPPORT & TRAINING:
Financial Assistance Provided: No
Site Selection Assistance: Yes

Lease Negotiation Assistance: Yes
Co-Operative Advertising: No
Franchisee Assoc./Member: No
Size Of Corporate Staff: 110
On-Going Support: ,,C,D,E,F,G,h,I
Training: 2 Weeks Atlanta, GA;
1 Week Franchise's Location
SPECIFIC EXPANSION PLANS:
US: 25 states
Canada: No
Overseas: NR

≪ ≫

IT'S A GRIND COFFEE HOUSE

6272 E. Pacific Coast Hwy., # E
Long Beach, CA 90803
Tel: (866) IAG-JAVA (562) 594-5600 +
256
Fax: (562) 594-4100
E-Mail: franchise@itsagrind.com
Web Site: www.itsagrind.com
Mr. Steve Olson, SVP Franchise Development

IT'S A GRIND is the fastest-growing coffee franchise in the U.S., with 267 franchises sold throughout the U.S. An upscale, neighborhood coffee house with a blues and jazz motif, our stores feature the highest-quality fresh micro-roasted specialty whole bean coffees, traditional, espresso and iced blended coffee drinks, tea and tea-based drinks, bagels, muffins, scones and assorted bakery items.

BACKGROUND: IFA MEMBER
Established: 1994; 1st Franchised: 2001
Franchised Units: 75
Company-Owned Units: 6
Total Units: 81
Dist.: US-81; CAN-0; O'seas-0
North America: 14 States, 0 Provinces
Density: in NVCAAZ
Projected New Units (12 Months): 75
Qualifications: NR
FINANCIAL/TERMS:
Cash Investment: $125K
Total Investment: $248-466K
Minimum Net Worth: $400K
Fees: Franchise - $36K
Royalty - 6%; Ad. - 1%
Earnings Claims Statement: Yes
Term of Contract (Years): 10/Varies

Avg. # Of Employees: 15 FT, PT
Passive Ownership: Not Allowed
Encourage Conversions: No
Area Develop. Agreements: Yes/1
Sub-Franchising Contracts: No
Expand In Territory: Yes
Space Needs: 1,200-6,000 SF
SUPPORT & TRAINING:
Financial Assistance Provided: No
Site Selection Assistance: Yes
Lease Negotiation Assistance: Yes
Co-Operative Advertising: No
Franchisee Assoc./Member: Yes/Yes
Size Of Corporate Staff: 26
On-Going Support: A,B,C,D,E,F,G,H,I
Training: 2 Weeks Long Beach, CA Headquarters
SPECIFIC EXPANSION PLANS:
US: Most States in US
Canada: No
Overseas: NR

≪ ≫

JO TO GO COFFEE

1263 Main St.
Green Bay, WI 54302
Tel: (866) 568-6461 (920) 884-6601 + 108
Fax: (920) 482-5623
E-Mail: franchise@jotogo.com
Web Site: www.jotogo.com
Mr. Jonathon Lukens, VP of Franchising

Full-service, gourmet double-drive-thru, serving premium coffee and espresso-based drinks, smoothies, tea, chai, fresh bakery. Run your business with as few as six employees. Have fun in a fast-growing industry that's immensely profitable.

BACKGROUND:
Established: 1998; 1st Franchised: 2001
Franchised Units: 9
Company-Owned Units: 5
Total Units: 14
Dist.: US-14; CAN-0; O'seas-0
North America: 1 States, 0 Provinces
Density: 13 in WI,
Projected New Units (12 Months): 20
Qualifications: 4, 5, 3, 3, 5, 5
FINANCIAL/TERMS:
Cash Investment: NA
Total Investment: $82.5-786K
Minimum Net Worth: NA
Fees: Franchise - $25K
Royalty - 7%; Ad. - 1%
Earnings Claims Statement: Yes
Term of Contract (Years): 5/5/5/5/
Avg. # Of Employees: 4 FT, 2 PT
Passive Ownership: Discouraged

Encourage Conversions: NA
Area Develop. Agreements: Yes/1
Sub-Franchising Contracts: No
Expand In Territory: Yes
Space Needs: 500 SF
SUPPORT & TRAINING:
Financial Assistance Provided: No
Site Selection Assistance: Yes
Lease Negotiation Assistance: Yes
Co-Operative Advertising: Yes
Franchisee Assoc./Member: No
Size Of Corporate Staff: 8
On-Going Support: ,,C,D,E,F,G,H,
Training: 15 Days Corporate Office & Local Store
SPECIFIC EXPANSION PLANS:
US: All U.S (Where Registered)
Canada: Yes
Overseas: NR

≪ ≫

P. B. LOCO

2124 University Ave., W.
Saint Paul, MN 55114
Tel: (651) 641-1422
Fax: (866) 729-1937
E-Mail: contact@pbloco.com
Web Site: www.pbloco.com
Ms. Jodene Jensen, CoPresident

P.B. Loco peanutbutterlicious cafes are the home of gourmet flavored peanut butter. P.B. Loco developed a line of proprietary flavored peanut butters around which its cafe menu is focused. With peanut butter flavors like Raspberry White Chocolate, Jungle Banana, Asian Curry Spice and European Cafe Mocha, P.B. Loco continues to wow its customers.

BACKGROUND:
Established: 2004; 1st Franchised: 2005
Franchised Units: 5
Company-Owned Units: 2
Total Units: 7
Dist.: US-7; CAN-0; O'seas-0
North America: 3 States, 0 Provinces
Density: 2 in ND, 2 in MN, 3 in AZ
Projected New Units (12 Months): NR
Qualifications: 3, 3, 3, 3, 3, 3
FINANCIAL/TERMS:
Cash Investment: Varies
Total Investment: $200-300K
Minimum Net Worth: $250K
Fees: Franchise - $22K
Royalty - 5%; Ad. - 1%
Earnings Claims Statement: No
Term of Contract (Years): 10/5
Avg. # Of Employees: 1-2 FT, 6-7 PT

Passive Ownership: Discouraged
Encourage Conversions: NA
Area Develop. Agreements: Yes/5
Sub-Franchising Contracts: No
Expand In Territory: No
Space Needs: 900-1,400 SF

SUPPORT & TRAINING:
Financial Assistance Provided: No
Site Selection Assistance: Yes
Lease Negotiation Assistance: Yes
Co-Operative Advertising: No
Franchisee Assoc./Member: No
Size Of Corporate Staff: 12
On-Going Support: ,,C,D,E,,,,
Training: 10 Days Bloomington, MN

SPECIFIC EXPANSION PLANS:
US: All United States
Canada: No
Overseas: NR

<< >>

P. J.'S COFFEE OF NEW ORLEANS

109 New Camellia Blvd., # 200
Covington, LA 70433
Tel: (800) 749-5547 (985) 792-5776
Fax: (985) 792-1201
E-Mail: tmareno@pjscoffee.com
Web Site: www.pjscoffee.com
Ms. Tonya Mareno, Dir. Franchise Operations

P. J.'S COFFEE & TEA has long been regarded as a leader in the specialty coffee industry in the southeast. Our neighborhood-based cafes are set apart from others because we roast and distribute only the highest-quality coffee and serve it in warm, comfortable settings. Our customer base is extremely varied. We provide an unusually high level of service to our franchisees because quality is of the utmost importance to us.

BACKGROUND: IFA MEMBER
Established: 1978; 1st Franchised: 1989
Franchised Units: 107
Company-Owned Units: 1
Total Units: 108
Dist.: US-108; CAN-0; O'seas-0
North America: 4 States, 0 Provinces
Density: 2 in MS, 17 in LA, 2 in FL
Projected New Units (12 Months): 7
Qualifications: 5, 5, 3, 3, 2, 3

FINANCIAL/TERMS:
Cash Investment: $100K-150K
Total Investment: $100K-150K
Minimum Net Worth: $120K
Fees: Franchise - $20K
Royalty - 5%; Ad. - 1%

Earnings Claims Statement: No
Term of Contract (Years): 10/10
Avg. # Of Employees: 1 FT, 6 PT
Passive Ownership: Allowed
Encourage Conversions: Yes
Area Develop. Agreements: Yes/1
Sub-Franchising Contracts: No
Expand In Territory: Yes
Space Needs: 1,200 SF

SUPPORT & TRAINING:
Financial Assistance Provided: No
Site Selection Assistance: Yes
Lease Negotiation Assistance: Yes
Co-Operative Advertising: No
Franchisee Assoc./Member: No
Size Of Corporate Staff: 74
On-Going Support: ,B,C,D,E,,G,h,I
Training: 2 Days Corporate Office;
10 Days Corporate Store; 3 Days On-
Location Sites

SPECIFIC EXPANSION PLANS:
US: Southeast
Canada: No
Overseas: NR

<< >>

PURIFIED WATER TO GO

5160 S. Valley View Blvd., # 102
Las Vegas, NV 89118-1778
Tel: (800) 976-9283 (702) 895-9350
Fax: (702) 895-9306
E-Mail: mike@watertogo.com
Web Site: www.watertogo.com
Ms. Stacy Beaudoin, President

PURIFIED WATER TO GO, recently featured on NBC nightly news, is a full-service or express retail outlet, selling purified water by the gallon, purified ice and related products. As the leader in water store franchises, PURIFIED WATER TO GO answers today's need for superior quality drinking water. Water is purified on store premises, and customers are drawn to the appeal of our sparkling clean, blue and white interior design.

BACKGROUND: IFA MEMBER
Established: 1991; 1st Franchised: 1995
Franchised Units: 65
Company-Owned Units: 2
Total Units: 67
Dist.: US-67; CAN-0; O'seas-0
North America: 12 States, 0 Provinces
Density: 12 in WA, 5 in NV, 5 in NM

Projected New Units (12 Months): 15
Qualifications: 4, 2, 1, 3, 4, 5

FINANCIAL/TERMS:
Cash Investment: $25-50K
Total Investment: $75-145K
Minimum Net Worth: $150K
Fees: Franchise - $23-29K
Royalty - 4-6%; Ad. - $150-200/Mo
Earnings Claims Statement: No
Term of Contract (Years): 10/10
Avg. # Of Employees: 1 FT, 1 PT
Passive Ownership: Discouraged
Encourage Conversions: NA
Area Develop. Agreements: Yes/1
Sub-Franchising Contracts: No
Expand In Territory: Yes
Space Needs: 500-1,000 SF

SUPPORT & TRAINING:
Financial Assistance Provided: Yes (D)
Site Selection Assistance: Yes
Lease Negotiation Assistance: Yes
Co-Operative Advertising: No
Franchisee Assoc./Member: Yes/Yes
Size Of Corporate Staff: 9
On-Going Support: ,B,C,D,E,F,G,H,I
Training: 5 Days Corporate Office in Las
Vegas, NV

SPECIFIC EXPANSION PLANS:
US: All United States
Canada: All Canada
Overseas: All Countries

<< >>

ROCKY MOUNTAIN CHOCOLATE FACTORY

265 Turner Dr.
Durango, CO 81301
Tel: (800) 438-7623 (970) 259-0554
Fax: (970) 259-5895
E-Mail: pope@rmcf.net
Web Site: www.sweetfranchise.com
Mr. Greg Pope, SVP Franchise Development

Retail sale of packaged and bulk chocolates, brittles, truffles, sauces, cocoas, coffees, assorted hard candies and related chocolate and non-chocolate items. In-store preparation of fudges, caramel apples and dipped fruits via interactive cooking demonstrations. Complete line of gift and holiday items. Supplemental retail sale of soft drinks, ice cream, cookies and brewed coffee.

BACKGROUND: IFA MEMBER
Established: 1981; 1st Franchised: 1982
Franchised Units: 227
Company-Owned Units: 8

Total Units: 235
Dist.: US-235; CAN-17; O'seas-1
  North America: 41 States, 3 Provinces
  Density: 22 in CO, 36 in CA, 12 in BC
Projected New Units (12 Months): 12-15
Qualifications: NR

FINANCIAL/TERMS:
Cash Investment: $50K
Total Investment: $113-213K
Minimum Net Worth: $250K
Fees: Franchise - $19.5K
  Royalty - 5%; Ad. - 1%
Earnings Claims Statement: No
Term of Contract (Years): 5/5
Avg. # Of Employees: 2 FT, 4 PT
Passive Ownership: Discouraged
Encourage Conversions: NA
Area Develop. Agreements: No
Sub-Franchising Contracts: No
Expand In Territory: Yes
Space Needs: 800-1,200 SF

SUPPORT & TRAINING:
Financial Assistance Provided: Yes (D)
Site Selection Assistance: Yes
Lease Negotiation Assistance: Yes
Co-Operative Advertising: No
Franchisee Assoc./Member: Yes/Yes
Size Of Corporate Staff: 12
On-Going Support: ,B,C,D,E,F,G,H,I
Training: 7 Days Durango, CO;
  5 Days Store Site

SPECIFIC EXPANSION PLANS:
US: All United States
Canada: No
Overseas: All Countries

≪ ≫

SANGSTER'S HEALTH CENTRES
2218 Hanselman Ave.
Saskatoon, SK S7L 6A4 Canada
Tel: (306) 653-4481 + 26
Fax: (306) 653-4688
E-Mail: franchise@sangsters.com
Web Site: www.sangsters.com
Ms. Wanda Wilson, Business Development Manager

Health and well being are part of today's lifestyle with an enormous demand for vitamins, minerals, sports nutrition, body care and aromatherapy. SANGSTER'S HEALTH CENTRES has over 30 years of market experience and aggressive growth both in Canada and internationally. SANGSTER'S has received many awards including the CFA's 2001 Marketing Award. SANGSTER'S complete franchise system includes: Exclusive Private Label Supplements, extensive training, on-going

support, and national advertising.

BACKGROUND:
Established: 1971; 1st Franchised: 1978
Franchised Units: 50
Company-Owned Units: 8
Total Units: 58
Dist.: US-0; CAN-58; O'seas-0
  North America: 0 States, 7 Provinces
  Density: 14 in SK, 11 in ON, 8 in AB
Projected New Units (12 Months): 8
Qualifications: 3, 3, 4, 2, 3, 4

FINANCIAL/TERMS:
Cash Investment: $30-50K
Total Investment: $120K-180K
Minimum Net Worth: $50K
Fees: Franchise - $25K
  Royalty - 5%; Ad. - 2%
Earnings Claims Statement: No
Term of Contract (Years): 5/2-5
Avg. # Of Employees: 2 FT, 1 PT
Passive Ownership: Discouraged
Encourage Conversions: Yes
Area Develop. Agreements: No
Sub-Franchising Contracts: No
Expand In Territory: Yes
Space Needs: 600-1,000 SF

SUPPORT & TRAINING:
Financial Assistance Provided: Yes (D)
Site Selection Assistance: Yes
Lease Negotiation Assistance: Yes
Co-Operative Advertising: No
Franchisee Assoc./Member: Yes/Yes
Size Of Corporate Staff: 13
On-Going Support: ,B,C,D,E,F,G,H,
Training: 2 Weeks Saskatoon, SK;
  Minimum of 1 Week Franchisee Location

SPECIFIC EXPANSION PLANS:
US: All United States
Canada: All Canada
Overseas: Europe, Asia

≪ ≫

SCHAKOLAD CHOCOLATE FACTORY
5966 Lakehurst Dr.
Orlando, FL 32819
Tel: (407) 248-6400
Fax: (407) 248-1466
E-Mail: franchise@schakolad.com
Web Site: www.schakolad.com
Mr. Edgar Schaked, President

Hand-made, fine chocolates made on premises for customers to watch. Over 30 years experience in chocolate making. Our goal is to become the premiere high quality chocolatier in the U.S. and international

markets.

BACKGROUND: IFA MEMBER
Established: 1995; 1st Franchised: 1999
Franchised Units: 33
Company-Owned Units: 0
Total Units: 33
Dist.: US-31; CAN-0; O'seas-2
  North America: 12 States, 0 Provinces
  Density: 2 in VA, 5 in TX, 9 in FL
Projected New Units (12 Months): 12
Qualifications: NR

FINANCIAL/TERMS:
Cash Investment: $110-150K
Total Investment: $110-150K
Minimum Net Worth: $200K
Fees: Franchise - $30K
  Royalty - 4%; Ad. - 1%
Earnings Claims Statement: No
Term of Contract (Years): 5/5/5/5
Avg. # Of Employees: 3 FT, 0 PT
Passive Ownership: Not Allowed
Encourage Conversions: No
Area Develop. Agreements: No
Sub-Franchising Contracts: No
Expand In Territory: Yes
Space Needs: 800-1,400 SF

SUPPORT & TRAINING:
Financial Assistance Provided: No
Site Selection Assistance: Yes
Lease Negotiation Assistance: Yes
Co-Operative Advertising: Yes
Franchisee Assoc./Member: Yes/Yes
Size Of Corporate Staff: 2
On-Going Support: ,B,C,D,E,F,G,H,
Training: 1-2 Weeks Orlando, FL

SPECIFIC EXPANSION PLANS:
US: Eastern United States
Canada: No
Overseas: NR

≪ ≫

SECOND CUP, THE
6303 Airport Rd.
Mississauga, ON L4V 1R8 Canada
Tel: (800) 569-6318 (905) 362-1818 + 1525
Fax: (905) 362-1121
E-Mail: franchising@secondcup.com
Web Site: www.secondcup.com
Ms. Teresa Patricio, Franchise Development Associate

As the largest retailer of specialty coffee in Canada with over 370 locations coast to coast, we are committed in attracting quality franchisees. Together, with outstanding location and store operations, we are dedicated to serving the best coffee in the world in an inviting atmosphere with uncompromising standards of customer service, quality and freshness.

BACKGROUND:
Established: 1975;   1st Franchised: 1980
Franchised Units: 360
Company-Owned Units: 0
Total Units: 360
Dist.:   US-0; CAN-360; O'seas-0
  North America: 0 States, 10 Provinces
  Density: 30 in QC, 170 in ON, 55 in AB
Projected New Units (12 Months):   40
Qualifications: 4, 5, 4, 4, 4, 5
FINANCIAL/TERMS:
Cash Investment: $90-140K
Total Investment: $100K-140K
Minimum Net Worth: NA
Fees: Franchise - $27K
  Royalty - 9%;   Ad. - 3%
Earnings Claims Statement: No
Term of Contract (Years):   Lease/
Avg. # Of Employees: 5 FT, 10 PT
Passive Ownership: Not Allowed
Encourage Conversions: Yes
Area Develop. Agreements: No
Sub-Franchising Contracts: No
Expand In Territory: Yes
Space Needs: 1,000-1,500 SF
SUPPORT & TRAINING:
Financial Assistance Provided: No
Site Selection Assistance: Yes
Lease Negotiation Assistance: Yes
Co-Operative Advertising: No
Franchisee Assoc./Member: Yes/Yes
Size Of Corporate Staff: 60
On-Going Support: A,B,C,D,E,F,G,h,I
Training: 3 Weeks Toronto, ON
SPECIFIC EXPANSION PLANS:
US: No
Canada: All Canada
Overseas: NR

◅◅ ▻▻

SUNOCO APLUS
1735 Market St., # LL
Philadelphia, PA 19130
Tel: (800) 777-6444 (215) 977-3000
Fax: (215) 246-8598
E-Mail: franchiseapplications@sunocoinc.com
Web Site: www.sunocoaplusfranchise.com
Ms Andrea Horos, Marketing Develop-

ment Manager

Sunoco APlus has identified the needs of busy consumers and provides quality and convenience merchandise to meet the needs of today's busy lifestyle. The APlus Franchise Program offers exceptional business systems, extensive training and quality marketing tools. We provide ongoing business support and are backed by the Sunoco brand, long recognized as an industry leader. We encourage you to review our program and consider how you may join our successful Franchise community.

BACKGROUND: IFA MEMBER
Established: 1886;   1st Franchised: 25
Franchised Units: 270
Company-Owned Units: 500
Total Units: 770
Dist.:   US-770; CAN-0; O'seas-0
  North America: 15 States, 0 Provinces
  Density:
Projected New Units (12 Months):   n/a
Qualifications: 3, 3, 3, 3, 3, 3
FINANCIAL/TERMS:
Cash Investment: Varies
Total Investment: $300-600K
Minimum Net Worth: Varies
Fees: Franchise - $30K
  Royalty - varies;   Ad. - varies
Earnings Claims Statement: No
Term of Contract (Years):   varies/varies
Avg. # Of Employees: Varies
Passive Ownership: Not Allowed
Encourage Conversions: Yes
Area Develop. Agreements: No
Sub-Franchising Contracts: No
Expand In Territory: No
Space Needs: NA
SUPPORT & TRAINING:
Financial Assistance Provided: No
Site Selection Assistance: No
Lease Negotiation Assistance: No
Co-Operative Advertising: No
Franchisee Assoc./Member: No
Size Of Corporate Staff: 5000
On-Going Support: ,,,,,,,,
Training: 4 weeks Philadelphia/Local
  Market
SPECIFIC EXPANSION PLANS:
US: Northeast
Canada: No
Overseas: NR

◅◅ ▻▻

SUPPER THYME USA
2536 S. 156th Cir.

Omaha, NE 68130
Tel: (866) 867-5001 (402) 933-4521
Fax: (402) 614-5900
E-Mail: keri.willenborg@supperthymeusa.com
Web Site: www.supperthymeusa.com
Ms. Keri Willenborg, Director Corporate Affairs

SUPPER THYME USA Franchise Services offers you the opportunity to operate a business, providing supplies, equipment, ingredients and instructions to prepare, on the premises, ready-to-cook entrees to take home, freeze and use as needed for family meals.

BACKGROUND:
Established: 2003;   1st Franchised: 2004
Franchised Units: 18
Company-Owned Units: 1
Total Units: 19
Dist.:   US-19; CAN-0; O'seas-0
  North America: 11 States, 0 Provinces
  Density: 3 in MN, 3 in MI, 3 in NE
Projected New Units (12 Months):   30
Qualifications: 3, 2, 1, 3, 5, 4
FINANCIAL/TERMS:
Cash Investment: $25-35K
Total Investment: $110-185K
Minimum Net Worth: NA
Fees: Franchise - $35K
  Royalty - 6.0%;   Ad. - 1%
Earnings Claims Statement: No
Term of Contract (Years):   5/5
Avg. # Of Employees: 1 FT, 2 PT
Passive Ownership: Not Allowed
Encourage Conversions: Yes
Area Develop. Agreements: No
Sub-Franchising Contracts: Yes
Expand In Territory: Yes
Space Needs: 1,500 SF
SUPPORT & TRAINING:
Financial Assistance Provided: Yes (I)
Site Selection Assistance: Yes
Lease Negotiation Assistance: Yes
Co-Operative Advertising: Yes
Franchisee Assoc./Member: No
Size Of Corporate Staff: 6
On-Going Support: 0,B,C,D,E,F,G,H,
Training: 1 Week Franchisee City;
  2 Weeks Omaha, NE
SPECIFIC EXPANSION PLANS:
US: All United States
Canada: No
Overseas: NR

◅◅ ▻▻

WHITE HEN PANTRY

700 E. Butterfield Rd. Suite 300
Lombard, IL 60148
Tel: (800) 726-8791 (630) 311-3100
Fax: (630) 366-3447
E-Mail: franchise@whitehen.com
Web Site: www.whitehen.com
Ms. Tangy McGee, Franchise Sales Facilitator

For nearly 40 years, White Hen has served as one of the premier convenience retailers in metropolitan Chicago and greater Boston. 275 stores serve more than a quarter million customers each day with a full line of distinctive products including national brands, fresh sliced-to-order deli items, custom-crafted sandwiches, fresh salads, gourmet soup, the country's best coffee, blended smoothies and shakes and more.

BACKGROUND: IFA MEMBER
Established: 1965;   1st Franchised: 1965
Franchised Units: 218
Company-Owned Units: 8
Total Units: 226
Dist.:   US-226; CAN-0; O'seas-0
 North America: 3 States, 0 Provinces
 Density: in MAINIL
Projected New Units (12 Months):   10
Qualifications: 2, 4, 3, 2, 3, 5
FINANCIAL/TERMS:
Cash Investment: $40-70K
Total Investment: $55-250K
Minimum Net Worth: NA
Fees: Franchise - $25K
 Royalty - 8%+;   Ad. - Included
Earnings Claims Statement: Yes
Term of Contract (Years):   5/5
Avg. # Of Employees: 2 FT, 12 PT
Passive Ownership: Not Allowed
Encourage Conversions: NA
Area Develop. Agreements: No
Sub-Franchising Contracts: No
Expand In Territory: Yes
Space Needs: 2,500 SF
SUPPORT & TRAINING:
Financial Assistance Provided: Yes (I)
Site Selection Assistance: NA
Lease Negotiation Assistance: NA
Co-Operative Advertising: Yes
Franchisee Assoc./Member: Yes/Yes

Size Of Corporate Staff: 120
On-Going Support: A,B,C,D,E,F,G,H,I
Training: 1 Week Corporate Office;
 2 Weeks On-Site
SPECIFIC EXPANSION PLANS:
US: IL, MA, NH, IN Only
Canada: No
Overseas: NR

≪ ≫

WINE NOT INTERNATIONAL

380 Spring Gate Blvd.
Thornhill, ON L4J 4K6 Canada
Tel: (888) 946-3668 (519) 599-7400
Fax: (519) 599-7300
E-Mail: sales@winenotinternational.com
Web Site: www.winenotinternational.com
Mr. Grant Cats, VP Franchise Sales

WINE NOT INTERNATIONAL is a franchise-based Custom Winery concept ideal for those with an entrepreneurial spirit and a passion for wine. WINE NOT INTERNATIONAL wineries are full-service, federally bonded wineries equipped with state-of-the-art fermentation equipment, professional tasting bar and lounge areas. We also provide both direct retail and wholesale sales, customized labeling and a unique customer participation experience.

BACKGROUND: IFA MEMBER
Established: 1993;   1st Franchised: 2002
Franchised Units: 8
Company-Owned Units: 0
Total Units: 8
Dist.:   US-8; CAN-0; O'seas-0
 North America: 8 States, 0 Provinces
 Density: 2 in TX, 2 in IL
Projected New Units (12 Months):   10
Qualifications: 4, 3, 2, 3, 3, 5
FINANCIAL/TERMS:
Cash Investment: $85-150K
Total Investment: $250-350K
Minimum Net Worth: $100-500K
Fees: Franchise - $50K
 Royalty - 5%;   Ad. - 0
Earnings Claims Statement: No
Term of Contract (Years):   10/10
Avg. # Of Employees: 2 FT, 2 PT
Passive Ownership: Discouraged
Encourage Conversions: Yes
Area Develop. Agreements: Yes/1

Sub-Franchising Contracts: Yes
Expand In Territory: Yes
Space Needs: 2,500-3,000 SF
SUPPORT & TRAINING:
Financial Assistance Provided: No
Site Selection Assistance: Yes
Lease Negotiation Assistance: Yes
Co-Operative Advertising: No
Franchisee Assoc./Member: Yes/Yes
Size Of Corporate Staff: 10
On-Going Support: A,B,C,D,E,F,G,H,I
Training: 1 Week On-Site Training
SPECIFIC EXPANSION PLANS:
US: All United States
Canada: No
Overseas: Caribbean

≪ ≫

FIVE LARGEST PARTICIPANTS IN SURVEY						
Company	# Fran-chised Units	# Co-Owned Units	# Total Units	Franchise Fee	On-Going Royalty	Total Investment
1. Ace Hardware	4,800	0	4,800	$5K		$400K-1.1M
2. Snap-On Tools	4,490	51	4,541	$5K	$50/Mo.	$16.7-278.4K
3. Matco Tools	1,507	0	1,507	$0	0%	$72-170K
4. Medicine Shoppe, The	1,287	25	1,313	$10-18K	2-5.5%	$77-152.5K
5. SIGNARAMA	905	0	905	$42.5K	6%	$150K

All of the data provided are proprietary and should not be quoted without acknowledging *Bond's Franchise Guide*.

7 VALLEYS CUSTOM BLENDS

47 N. Port Royal Dr.
Hilton Head Island, SC 29928
Tel: (800) 788-4367 (843) 681-3966
Fax: NA
E-Mail: franchise@customblends.com
Web Site: www.customblends.com
Ms. Frances Tucci, VP

7 Valleys Custom Blends Since 1993. At the forefront of a nationwide movement in tobacco for 15 years. 7 Valleys Custom Blends believes in providing their consumer the largest variety of make your own cigarette supplies. We offer our own brands of high quality blends developed just for us. We have a system that allows any consumer to switch tobaccos without the chemicals of pre-made cigarettes and without high cost. Pleasurable retail with regular consumers. Master Franchises and Area Developers available!

BACKGROUND:

Established: 1993; 1st Franchised: 2005
Franchised Units: 3
Company-Owned Units: 1
Total Units: 4
Dist.: US-4; CAN-0; O'seas-0
  North America: 1 States, 0 Provinces
  Density: 4 in PA
Projected New Units (12 Months): 1-3

Qualifications: 2, 3, 2, 2, 2, 5
FINANCIAL/TERMS:
Cash Investment: $85K
Total Investment: $122-205K
Minimum Net Worth: $200K
Fees: Franchise - $30K
  Royalty - 6%; Ad. - 1%
Earnings Claims Statement: Yes
Term of Contract (Years): 5/5
Avg. # Of Employees: 2 FT, 1 PT
Passive Ownership: Allowed
Encourage Conversions: Yes
Area Develop. Agreements: Yes/5
Sub-Franchising Contracts: Yes
Expand In Territory: Yes
Space Needs: 1000 SF
SUPPORT & TRAINING:
Financial Assistance Provided: Yes (D)
Site Selection Assistance: Yes

Lease Negotiation Assistance: Yes
Co-Operative Advertising: Yes
Franchisee Assoc./Member: No
Size Of Corporate Staff: 4
On-Going Support: „C,D,E,,,,I
Training: 10 Days York, PA
SPECIFIC EXPANSION PLANS:
US: All United States
Canada: No
Overseas: NR

◄◄ ►►

ACE HARDWARE

2200 Kensington Ct.
Oak Brook, IL 60523
Tel: (630) 990-6900
Fax: (630) 368-3394
E-Mail: myace@acehardware.com
Web Site: www.myace.com
Mr. Tim Knox, Corp. Manager Business
Development

ACE HARDWARE is a Fortune 500 company of over 5,100 retailers selling hardware and related home improvement products. ACE is now offering franchise opportunities in selected markets nationwide. Come grow in this new endeavor with the backing of a company possessing 84 years of success, along with outstanding purchasing power, brand recognition and retail practices.

BACKGROUND: IFA MEMBER
Established: 1924; 1st Franchised:
Franchised Units: 4800
Company-Owned Units: 0
Total Units: 4800
Dist.: US-4800; CAN-0; O'seas-328
North America: 50 States, 0 Provinces
Density:
Projected New Units (12 Months): 150
Qualifications: 5, 4, 3, 3, 3, 5
FINANCIAL/TERMS:
Cash Investment: $250K
Total Investment: $400K-1.1M
Minimum Net Worth: $400K
Fees: Franchise - $5K
  Royalty - ; Ad. -
Earnings Claims Statement: No
Term of Contract (Years): 20/5
Avg. # Of Employees: FT, 15-25 PT
Passive Ownership: Not Allowed

Encourage Conversions: Yes
Area Develop. Agreements: No
Sub-Franchising Contracts: No
Expand In Territory: Yes
Space Needs: 4,000-20,000 SF
SUPPORT & TRAINING:
Financial Assistance Provided: Yes (D)
Site Selection Assistance: Yes
Lease Negotiation Assistance: Yes
Co-Operative Advertising: No
Franchisee Assoc./Member: No
Size Of Corporate Staff: 5000
On-Going Support: A,B,C,D,e,F,G,,
Training: 6 Weeks Oak Brook, IL
SPECIFIC EXPANSION PLANS:
US: Selected markets in U.S.
Canada: No
Overseas: Selected countries

◄◄ ►►

BATTERIES PLUS

925 Walnut Ridge Dr.
Hartland, WI 53029-9389
Tel: (800) 274-9155 (262) 912-3000
Fax: (262) 912-3100
E-Mail: franchising@batteriesplus.com
Web Site: www.batteriesplus.com
Mr. Rod Tremelling, Franchise Development Executive

BATTERIES PLUS is America's Battery Experts (TM), providing 1,000s of batteries for 1,000s of items, serving both retail and commercial customers. The $19 billion battery market, growing 6.5% annually, is driven by technology and lifestyles. BATTERIES PLUS is a unique opportunity in this growth industry not yet saturated with competitors. Our turn-key program includes a unique store design, graphics, signage and product brands and proven operating methods.

BACKGROUND: IFA MEMBER
Established: 1988; 1st Franchised: 1992
Franchised Units: 308
Company-Owned Units: 17
Total Units: 325
Dist.: US-325; CAN-0; O'seas-0
North America: 40 States, 0 Provinces
Density: 16 in WI, 17 in MN, 8 in MI
Projected New Units (12 Months): 35
Qualifications: 5, 5, 2, 3, 2, 3
FINANCIAL/TERMS:
Cash Investment: $75K-150K
Total Investment: $143K-195K
Minimum Net Worth: $500K
Fees: Franchise - $30K
  Royalty - 4%; Ad. - 1%

Earnings Claims Statement: Yes
Term of Contract (Years): 10/10
Avg. # Of Employees: 3-4 FT, 0 PT
Passive Ownership: Not Allowed
Encourage Conversions: No
Area Develop. Agreements: Yes/1
Sub-Franchising Contracts: No
Expand In Territory: No
Space Needs: 1,800-2,000 SF
SUPPORT & TRAINING:
Financial Assistance Provided: Yes (D)
Site Selection Assistance: Yes
Lease Negotiation Assistance: Yes
Co-Operative Advertising: No
Franchisee Assoc./Member: No
Size Of Corporate Staff: 100
On-Going Support: „C,D,E,F,G,,I
Training: 2 Weeks On-Site Franchisee's
  Store; 3 Weeks Corporate Training
  Center
SPECIFIC EXPANSION PLANS:
US: All United States
Canada: No
Overseas: NR

◄◄ ►►

BEADNIKS

2700 Avenger Dr., #111
Virginia Beach, VA 23452
Tel: (757) 463-5564
Fax: (757) 463-5556
E-Mail: franchiseinfo@beadniks.com
Web Site: beadniks.com
Mr. Craig Sexton, Director of Franchising

Beadniks is more than a business opportunity,it's a lifestyle. Explore a world of exotic beads in this activity-based retail concept. Beadniks offers an exotic world theme store where customers create custom jewelry with beads from the far corners of the globe. Join the Beadniks family and become part of the number one bead store in the country and the fastest growing beading and craft concept in franchising. We offer exceptional training and support, national buying power and proven marketing programs.

BACKGROUND:
Established: 1990; 1st Franchised: 2006
Franchised Units: 8
Company-Owned Units: 0
Total Units: 8

Dist.: US-8; CAN-0; O'seas-0
North America: 7 States, 0 Provinces
Density: 1 in IL, 1 in FL, 1 in CA
Projected New Units (12 Months): 2
Qualifications: 3, 3, 2, 2, 5, 5

FINANCIAL/TERMS:

Cash Investment: $50-75K
Total Investment: $333-434K
Minimum Net Worth: $100K
Fees: Franchise - $40K
Royalty - 6%; Ad. - .6%
Earnings Claims Statement: No
Term of Contract (Years): 5/5
Avg. # Of Employees: 2 FT, 4 PT
Passive Ownership: Discouraged
Encourage Conversions: Yes
Area Develop. Agreements: Yes/0
Sub-Franchising Contracts: No
Expand In Territory: Yes
Space Needs: 1,500-2,000 SF

SUPPORT & TRAINING:

Financial Assistance Provided: Yes (I)
Site Selection Assistance: Yes
Lease Negotiation Assistance: Yes
Co-Operative Advertising: No
Franchisee Assoc./Member: No
Size Of Corporate Staff: 4
On-Going Support: ,,C,D,E,F,G,H,
Training:10 Days On Site; 2 Weeks Home Office

SPECIFIC EXPANSION PLANS:

US: All States
Canada: No
Overseas: NR

≪ ≫

CD WAREHOUSE

900 N. Broadway
Oklahoma City, OK 73102
Tel: (800) 641-9394 (405) 236-8742
Fax: (405) 949-2566
E-Mail:
Web Site: www.cdwarehouse.com
Mr. Matt Allen, Vice President

CD WAREHOUSE is a rapidly growing franchise, specializing in the sale of pre-owned CDs and DVDs. Our stores also buy and trade used CD's, sell top new CDs, and sell other music-related items. Our proprietary software makes it easy to buy and sell pre-owned CDs, even without prior music knowledge.

BACKGROUND:

Established: 1992; 1st Franchised: 1992
Franchised Units: 216
Company-Owned Units: 64
Total Units: 280

Dist.: US-263; CAN-7; O'seas-10
North America: 36 States, 3 Provinces
Density: 17 in CA, 21 in FL, 51 in TX
Projected New Units (12 Months): 15
Qualifications: 5, 3, 1, 2, 4, 4

FINANCIAL/TERMS:

Cash Investment: $40-60K
Total Investment: $122-162K
Minimum Net Worth: $150K
Fees: Franchise - $20K
Royalty - 5%/4%; Ad. - 1.75%
Earnings Claims Statement: No
Term of Contract (Years): 10/10
Avg. # Of Employees: 2-3 FT, 3-4 PT
Passive Ownership: Discouraged
Encourage Conversions: NA
Area Develop. Agreements: Yes/1
Sub-Franchising Contracts: No
Expand In Territory: Yes
Space Needs: 1,500-2,000 SF

SUPPORT & TRAINING:

Financial Assistance Provided: Yes (D)
Site Selection Assistance: Yes
Lease Negotiation Assistance: Yes
Co-Operative Advertising: No
Franchisee Assoc./Member: Yes/Yes
Size Of Corporate Staff: 25
On-Going Support: ,,C,D,E,,G,H,I
Training: 5-6 Days Oklahoma City, OK Training Center

SPECIFIC EXPANSION PLANS:

US: All United States
Canada: All Canada
Overseas: All Countries

≪ ≫

CERAMICS TO GO

31875 Corydon St. # 130
Lake Elsinore, CA 92530
Tel: (888) 951-8646 (951) 674-1166
Fax: (951) 674-5577
E-Mail: kelli@ceramicstogo.net
Web Site: www.ceramicstogo.com
Ms. Kelli Chandler, Administrator

A coffee house/art gallery environment where you can successfully paint ceramics. Add a consignment art gallery where you can sell finished consignment art pieces by local artists. We are the "Leader of the Line" providing thousands of pre-designed ceramic pieces that are fun and

easy to complete. Easy turn-key operation. Community based marketing programs designed to introduce thousands of potential customers to your studio. A business that is as much fun as it is a business.

BACKGROUND: IFA MEMBER

Established: 2006; 1st Franchised: 2008
Franchised Units: 0
Company-Owned Units: 2
Total Units: 2
Dist.: US-1; CAN-0; O'seas-0
North America: 1 States, 0 Provinces
Density: 1 in CA
Projected New Units (12 Months): 18
Qualifications: 3, 2, 2, 2, 2, 2

FINANCIAL/TERMS:

Cash Investment: $99.7-195.6K
Total Investment: $99.7-195.6K
Minimum Net Worth: NA
Fees: Franchise - $30K-40K
Royalty - 5%; Ad. - 3%
Earnings Claims Statement: No
Term of Contract (Years): 10/5
Avg. # Of Employees: 1 FT, 2 PT
Passive Ownership: Discouraged
Encourage Conversions: Yes
Area Develop. Agreements: No
Sub-Franchising Contracts: No
Expand In Territory: No
Space Needs: 1,000 SF

SUPPORT & TRAINING:

Financial Assistance Provided: No
Site Selection Assistance: Yes
Lease Negotiation Assistance: Yes
Co-Operative Advertising: No
Franchisee Assoc./Member: No
Size Of Corporate Staff: 12
On-Going Support: A,B,C,D,E,F,G,H,I
Training: 2 Weeks Lake Elsinore, CA

SPECIFIC EXPANSION PLANS:

US: SW, All United States
Canada: No
Overseas: NR

≪ ≫

CHRISTMAS DECOR

7602 University Ave., P.O. Box 5946
Lubbock, TX 79408
Tel: (800) 687-9551 (806) 772-1225
Fax: (806) 722-9627
E-Mail: info@christmasdecor.net
Web Site: www.christmasdecor.net
Mr. Glenn Lewis, Director of Franchise Relations

Holiday and event decorating services provided to homes and businesses. Fun, high-margin business that offers annual income by working only 4-6 months of the year. Also, an excellent add-on business for landscape, pool and spa, electrical and other seasonal service contractors. Landscape lighting franchise available also to create year round business.

BACKGROUND: IFA MEMBER
Established: 1986; 1st Franchised: 1996
Franchised Units: 375
Company-Owned Units: 0
Total Units: 375
Dist.: US-375; CAN-32; O'seas-0
 North America: 44 States, 2 Provinces
 Density: 23 in TX, 14 in OH, 13 in MI
Projected New Units (12 Months): 100
Qualifications: 2, 4, 2, 3, 3, 4
FINANCIAL/TERMS:
Cash Investment: $9K-17.9K
Total Investment: $11K-50K
Minimum Net Worth: NR
Fees: Franchise - $9.5-15.9K
 Royalty - 2-4.5%; Ad. - $180/Yr.
Earnings Claims Statement: No
Term of Contract (Years): 5/5
Avg. # Of Employees: 2-4 FT, 3-20 PT
Passive Ownership: Discouraged
Encourage Conversions: NA
Area Develop. Agreements: No
Sub-Franchising Contracts: No
Expand In Territory: No
Space Needs: Varies
SUPPORT & TRAINING:
Financial Assistance Provided: Yes (D)
Site Selection Assistance: Yes
Lease Negotiation Assistance: No
Co-Operative Advertising: No
Franchisee Assoc./Member: Yes/Yes
Size Of Corporate Staff: 18
On-Going Support: A,B,,D,,,G,h,I
Training: 3 Days Major Cities in US;
 2 Days Continuing Education in Major
 Cities
SPECIFIC EXPANSION PLANS:
US: All United States
Canada: All Canada
Overseas: All Christian Countries

◄◄ ►►

COLOR ME MINE
3722 San Fernando Rd.
Glendale, CA 91204
Tel: (888) 265-6764 (503) 254-2304
Fax: (818) 240-9712
E-Mail: maria@colormemine.com
Web Site: www.colormemine.com
Ms. Maria Baker, Exec. Dir. Franchise
 Develop.

COLOR ME MINE is the world's leader in contemporary ceramics and crafts studios. Our comprehensive training and support system includes studio operations, glazing, firing, design techniques, construction, marketing, business models, and licensed manufacturers to ensure consistency and supply.

BACKGROUND:
Established: 1992; 1st Franchised: 1996
Franchised Units: 124
Company-Owned Units: 1
Total Units: 125
Dist.: US-102; CAN-2; O'seas-21
 North America: 22 States, 2 Provinces
 Density: 8 in PA, 8 in NJ, 44 in CA
Projected New Units (12 Months): 34
Qualifications: 4, 3, 2, 3, 5, 5
FINANCIAL/TERMS:
Cash Investment: $40-50K
Total Investment: $146-195K
Minimum Net Worth: $150K
Fees: Franchise - $30K
 Royalty - 5%; Ad. - 1%
Earnings Claims Statement: Yes
Term of Contract (Years): 5/5
Avg. # Of Employees: 2 FT, 4 PT
Passive Ownership: Discouraged
Encourage Conversions: Yes
Area Develop. Agreements: No
Sub-Franchising Contracts: Yes
Expand In Territory: Yes
Space Needs: 1,100-2,000 SF
SUPPORT & TRAINING:
Financial Assistance Provided: No
Site Selection Assistance: Yes
Lease Negotiation Assistance: Yes
Co-Operative Advertising: No
Franchisee Assoc./Member: Yes/Yes
Size Of Corporate Staff: 15
On-Going Support: A,B,C,D,E,F,G,H,I
Training: 5 Days Franchised Location; 10
 Days Home Office in Glendale, CA
SPECIFIC EXPANSION PLANS:
US: All United States
Canada: All Canada
Overseas: All Countries

◄◄ ►►

COLORTYME
5501 Headquarters Dr.
Plano, TX 75024
Tel: (800) 411-8963 (972) 403-4905
Fax: (972) 403-4923
E-Mail: jdeering@colortyme.com
Web Site: www.colortyme.com
Mr. Jim Deering, Dir. Franchise Develop-

ment

The nation's oldest rental-purchase franchise company, specializing in electronics, furniture, appliances and computers.

BACKGROUND: IFA MEMBER
Established: 1979; 1st Franchised: 1982
Franchised Units: 215
Company-Owned Units: 0
Total Units: 215
Dist.: US-215; CAN-0; O'seas-0
 North America: 34 States, 0 Provinces
 Density: 12 in VA, 34 in TX, 19 in FL
Projected New Units (12 Months): 30
Qualifications: 4, 4, 4, 3, 3, 4
FINANCIAL/TERMS:
Cash Investment: $130K-150K
Total Investment: $151K-264K
Minimum Net Worth: $350K
Fees: Franchise - $25K
 Royalty - 5%; Ad. - $250/Mo.
Earnings Claims Statement: Yes
Term of Contract (Years): 5-10/5-10
Avg. # Of Employees: 6 FT, 0 PT
Passive Ownership: Discouraged
Encourage Conversions: Yes
Area Develop. Agreements: Yes/1
Sub-Franchising Contracts: No
Expand In Territory: Yes
Space Needs: 3,500 SF
SUPPORT & TRAINING:
Financial Assistance Provided: Yes (D)
Site Selection Assistance: Yes
Lease Negotiation Assistance: Yes
Co-Operative Advertising: No
Franchisee Assoc./Member: Yes/Yes
Size Of Corporate Staff: 21
On-Going Support: ,,C,D,E,F,G,H,
Training: 4 Weeks Varied Training
SPECIFIC EXPANSION PLANS:
US: All United States
Canada: No
Overseas: NR

◄◄ ►►

COMPAGNIA DEL MOBILE
4100 N. E. Second Ave., # 106
Miami, FL 33137
Tel: (305) 573-2500
Fax: (305) 573-2555
E-Mail: fdimise@compagiadelmobileusa.
com
Web Site: www.compagniadelmobileusa.
com
Mr. Francisco Di Mise, Director

Internationally famous home design/furnishing company establishing its presence in the United States with brand kitchen cabinet furniture, wardrobes, children's furniture and other design products. Stores operate in Europe, Asia, Middle East and America.

BACKGROUND:

Established: 1939; 1st Franchised: 1998
Franchised Units: 60
Company-Owned Units: 2
Total Units: 62
Dist.:   US-3; CAN-0; O'seas-59
  North America: 2 States, Provinces
  Density: 2 in FL, 1 in VA
Projected New Units (12 Months):   NR
Qualifications: NR

FINANCIAL/TERMS:

Cash Investment: $10-40K
Total Investment: $60-250K
Minimum Net Worth: $80K
Fees: Franchise - $5K
  Royalty - 2%;   Ad. - 5%
Earnings Claims Statement: No
Term of Contract (Years):   5/5
Avg. # Of Employees: 2 FT, 0 PT
Passive Ownership: Allowed
Encourage Conversions: No
Area Develop. Agreements: Yes/1
Sub-Franchising Contracts: Yes
Expand In Territory: Yes
Space Needs: 2,500 SF

SUPPORT & TRAINING:

Financial Assistance Provided: No
Site Selection Assistance: Yes
Lease Negotiation Assistance: No
Co-Operative Advertising: No
Franchisee Assoc./Member: No
Size Of Corporate Staff: 300
On-Going Support: A,B,c,D,E,F,,h,
Training: 2 Weeks Franchisee Location;
  1 Week Italy; 3 Days Miami, Fl

SPECIFIC EXPANSION PLANS:

US: All United States
Canada: NR
Overseas: NR

<< >>

CROWN TROPHY

9 Skyline Dr.
Hawthorne, NY 10532-1402
Tel: (800) 583-8228 +4 (914) 347-7700 +203
Fax: (914) 347-0211

E-Mail: scott@crowntrophy.com
Web Site: www.crownfranchise.com
Mr. Scott W. Kelly, Executive Vice President

The only franchise of its kind in America, CROWN TROPHY is the largest supplier and fastest growing retailer of trophies and awards in the country. Crown offers a full-service facility utilizing state-of-the-art equipment along with the most innovative product line in the industry. CROWN TROPHY is truly a one of a kind, unique franchise opportunity.

BACKGROUND: IFA MEMBER

Established: 1978; 1st Franchised: 1984
Franchised Units: 126
Company-Owned Units: 0
Total Units: 126
Dist.:   US-126; CAN-0; O'seas-0
  North America: 39 States, 0 Provinces
  Density: 11 in TX, 15 in NY, 8 in NJ
Projected New Units (12 Months):   12
Qualifications: 2, 2, 1, 3, 5, 5

FINANCIAL/TERMS:

Cash Investment: $30K-40K
Total Investment: $160K-190K
Minimum Net Worth: $75K
Fees: Franchise - $35K
  Royalty - 5%;   Ad. - 0%
Earnings Claims Statement: No
Term of Contract (Years):   5/5/5/
Avg. # Of Employees: 1 FT, 2 PT
Passive Ownership: Discouraged
Encourage Conversions: Yes
Area Develop. Agreements: No
Sub-Franchising Contracts: No
Expand In Territory: Yes
Space Needs: 1,600-1,800 SF

SUPPORT & TRAINING:

Financial Assistance Provided: Yes (I)
Site Selection Assistance: Yes
Lease Negotiation Assistance: Yes
Co-Operative Advertising: No
Franchisee Assoc./Member: Yes/Yes
Size Of Corporate Staff: 10
On-Going Support: ,,C,D,E,F,G,H,I
Training: 4 Days On-Site;
  8 Days Corporate Office

SPECIFIC EXPANSION PLANS:

US: All United States
Canada: No
Overseas: NR

<< >>

![DECK THE WALLS - Specialists in Art, Custom Framing and Design]

DECK THE WALLS

14300 Cornerstone Village Dr., # 321
Houston, TX 77014
Tel: (800) 543-3325
Fax: (714) 896-8598
E-Mail: anance@fcibiz.com
Web Site: www.dtwfraninfo.com
Ms. Ann Nance, Director Franchise Development

DECK THE WALLS is the nation's largest specialty retailer of art, custom framing & wall décor. Each store carries a large selection of limited & open edition prints, custom frame molding & mats. Easy to learn & operate; exceptional training & support; national buying power & proven marketing programs. Stores located in high-traffic regional malls & shopping centers. Rewarding business in a growing industry.

BACKGROUND: IFA MEMBER

Established: 1979; 1st Franchised: 1981
Franchised Units: 50
Company-Owned Units: 0
Total Units: 50
Dist.:   US-50; CAN-0; O'seas-0
  North America: 34 States, 0 Provinces
  Density: 17 in TX, 14 in PA, 12 in FL
Projected New Units (12 Months):   0
Qualifications: 4, 5, 1, 3, 3, 4

FINANCIAL/TERMS:

Cash Investment: $50K-60K
Total Investment: $156.8K-233.4K
Minimum Net Worth: $250K
Fees: Franchise - $30K
  Royalty - 6%;   Ad. - 2%
Earnings Claims Statement: No
Term of Contract (Years):   10/10
Avg. # Of Employees: 1 FT, 2 PT
Passive Ownership: Allowed
Encourage Conversions: Yes
Area Develop. Agreements: No
Sub-Franchising Contracts: No
Expand In Territory: Yes
Space Needs: 1,200-1,600 SF

SUPPORT & TRAINING:

Financial Assistance Provided: Yes (I)
Site Selection Assistance: Yes
Lease Negotiation Assistance: Yes
Co-Operative Advertising: Yes
Franchisee Assoc./Member: Yes/Yes
Size Of Corporate Staff: 26
On-Going Support: ,,C,D,E,F,G,H,I
Training: 4 Days Store; 2 Weeks St. Louis, MO

SPECIFIC EXPANSION PLANS:

US:	All United States
Canada:	No
Overseas:	NR

<< >>

DOLLAR DISCOUNT STORES OF AMERICA

1362 Naamans Creek Rd.
Boothwyn, PA 19061
Tel: (800) 227-5314 (888) 365-52 497-1991
Fax: (610) 485-6439
E-Mail: info@dollardiscount.com
Web Site: www.dollardiscount.com
Mr. Mitchel Insel, Franchise Director

Dollar stores.

BACKGROUND:	IFA MEMBER
Established: 1982;	1st Franchised: 1987
Franchised Units:	165
Company-Owned Units:	0
Total Units:	165
Dist.:	US-165; CAN-0; O'seas-0
North America:	States, Provinces
Density:	in MIPAWI
Projected New Units (12 Months):	40
Qualifications:	3, 2, 2, 3, 3, 5
FINANCIAL/TERMS:	
Cash Investment:	$20-30K
Total Investment:	$120-130K
Minimum Net Worth:	$100K
Fees: Franchise -	$18K
Royalty - 3%;	Ad. - 1%
Earnings Claims Statement:	No
Term of Contract (Years):	10/15
Avg. # Of Employees:	1-2 FT, 5-6 PT
Passive Ownership:	Discouraged
Encourage Conversions:	NA
Area Develop. Agreements:	No
Sub-Franchising Contracts:	No
Expand In Territory:	No
Space Needs:	2,000-4,000 SF
SUPPORT & TRAINING:	
Financial Assistance Provided:	Yes (D)
Site Selection Assistance:	Yes
Lease Negotiation Assistance:	Yes
Co-Operative Advertising:	No
Franchisee Assoc./Member:	Yes/Yes
Size Of Corporate Staff:	19
On-Going Support:	A,B,C,D,E,F,G,H,I
Training:	5 Days Boothwyn, PA

SPECIFIC EXPANSION PLANS:

US:	All United States
Canada:	No
Overseas:	NR

<< >>

ENGLISH BUTLER CANADA

39 King St., Brunswick Sq.
Saint John, NB E2L 4W3 Canada
Tel: (416) 966-9802
Fax: (416) 966-9803
E-Mail: nassad@englishbutler.com
Web Site: www.englishbutler.com
Mr. Nicholas Assad, Franchise Director

Elegant, traditional gifts and home decorating accessories. Merchandise ranges from printer to pictures, afghans to table linens and collectibles to seasonal giftware.

BACKGROUND:

Established: 1984;	1st Franchised: 1994
Franchised Units:	11
Company-Owned Units:	2
Total Units:	13
Dist.:	US-0; CAN-13; O'seas-0
North America:	0 States, 3 Provinces
Density:	15 in ON, 2 in NS, 3 in NB
Projected New Units (12 Months):	6-8
Qualifications:	4, 4, 3, 3, 4, 5
FINANCIAL/TERMS:	
Cash Investment:	$75K
Total Investment:	$75K-100K
Minimum Net Worth:	$100K
Fees: Franchise -	$25K
Royalty - 6%;	Ad. - 0.5%
Earnings Claims Statement:	No
Term of Contract (Years):	10/5
Avg. # Of Employees:	2 FT, 3-5 PT
Passive Ownership:	Discouraged
Encourage Conversions:	No
Area Develop. Agreements:	No
Sub-Franchising Contracts:	No
Expand In Territory:	Yes
Space Needs:	2,000 SF
SUPPORT & TRAINING:	
Financial Assistance Provided:	Yes (D)
Site Selection Assistance:	Yes
Lease Negotiation Assistance:	Yes
Co-Operative Advertising:	No
Franchisee Assoc./Member:	Yes/Yes
Size Of Corporate Staff:	7
On-Going Support:	,B,,D,E,F,,h,
Training:	3 Weeks Corporate Stores

SPECIFIC EXPANSION PLANS:

US:	No
Canada:	ON, PQ, AB
Overseas:	NR

<< >>

FAST-FIX JEWELRY AND WATCH REPAIRS

1300 N. W. 17th Ave., # 170
Delray Beach, FL 33445
Tel: (800) 359-0407 (561) 330-6060
Fax: (561) 330-6062
E-Mail: fastfix.ifa@mybrunno.com
Web Site: www.fastfix.com
Mr. Jason Mattes, Director of Franchise Development

With a 25-year track record, Fast-Fix Jewelry and Watch Repairs is the #1 national chain of dedicated jewelry and watch repair stores with more than 160 franchised locations operating in the United States and Canada. Fast-Fix stores operate only in major regional malls that afford customers "while-they-shop" jewelry and watch repair service. Prior jewelry experience is not necessary. Our full training program at Fast-Fix University along with our support system that includes national conventions and regiona

BACKGROUND:	IFA MEMBER
Established: 1984;	1st Franchised: 1987
Franchised Units:	157
Company-Owned Units:	3
Total Units:	160
Dist.:	US-153; CAN-2; O'seas-2
North America:	27 States, 2 Provinces
Density:	17 in TX, 24 in FL, 39 in CA
Projected New Units (12 Months):	15
Qualifications:	4, 5, 2, 2, 2, 5
FINANCIAL/TERMS:	
Cash Investment:	$75K-125K
Total Investment:	$142,750-$307,750
Minimum Net Worth:	$250K
Fees: Franchise -	$40K
Royalty - 5%;	Ad. - 2%
Earnings Claims Statement:	Yes
Term of Contract (Years):	10/10
Avg. # Of Employees:	3 FT, 2 PT
Passive Ownership:	Discouraged
Encourage Conversions:	No
Area Develop. Agreements:	Yes/1
Sub-Franchising Contracts:	Yes
Expand In Territory:	Yes
Space Needs:	250-850 SF
SUPPORT & TRAINING:	
Financial Assistance Provided:	Yes (I)
Site Selection Assistance:	Yes
Lease Negotiation Assistance:	Yes

Co-Operative Advertising:	No
Franchisee Assoc./Member:	Yes/Yes
Size Of Corporate Staff:	18
On-Going Support:	„C,D,E,,G,H,I
Training:	5 Days On-Site;

10 Days National Training Center in Delray Beach, FL

SPECIFIC EXPANSION PLANS:

US:	All United States
Canada:	All Canada
Overseas:	All Countries

◄◄ ►►

FASTFRAME

1200 Lawrence Dr., # 300
Newbury Park, CA 91320-1234
Tel: (800) 333-3225 (805) 498-4463
Fax: (805) 498-8983
E-Mail: brenda@fastframe.com
Web Site: www.fastframe.com
Ms. Breda Hales, Franchise Development
 Support

FASTFRAME is the largest and fastest-growing custom picture framing franchise in the world. With over 300 locations, we maintain our leadership in the industry by recruiting business partners who are both qualified and passionate about our industry. We strive to provide our franchisees with an all-inclusive and uncomplicated process whereby they can easily become a part of this very enjoyable business. FASTFRAME has built its reputation of high quality craftsmanship and customer satisfaction.

BACKGROUND:	**IFA MEMBER**
Established: 1986;	1st Franchised: 1987
Franchised Units:	271
Company-Owned Units:	0
Total Units:	271
Dist.:	US-271; CAN-0; O'seas-36
North America:	35 States, 0 Provinces
Density:	17 in TX, 19 in IL, 63 in CA
Projected New Units (12 Months):	40
Qualifications:	5, 4, 1, 1, 1, 5

FINANCIAL/TERMS:

Cash Investment:	$30K-45K
Total Investment:	$106K-150K
Minimum Net Worth:	$150K
Fees: Franchise -	$25K
Royalty - 7.5%;	Ad. - 3%
Earnings Claims Statement:	No
Term of Contract (Years):	10/10
Avg. # Of Employees:	1 FT, 2 PT

Passive Ownership:	Not Allowed
Encourage Conversions:	Yes
Area Develop. Agreements:	No
Sub-Franchising Contracts:	No
Expand In Territory:	Yes
Space Needs:	1,200-1,500 SF

SUPPORT & TRAINING:

Financial Assistance Provided:	Yes (D)
Site Selection Assistance:	Yes
Lease Negotiation Assistance:	Yes
Co-Operative Advertising:	No
Franchisee Assoc./Member:	Yes/Yes
Size Of Corporate Staff:	23
On-Going Support:	A,B,C,D,E,F,G,H,I
Training:	2 Weeks Newbury Park, CA;

1 Week On-Site

SPECIFIC EXPANSION PLANS:

US:	All United States
Canada:	No
Overseas:	NR

◄◄ ►►

FASTSIGNS

2542 Highlander Wy.
Carrollton, TX 75006-2333
Tel: (800) 827-7446 + 5616 (214) 346-5600
Fax: (972) 248-8201
E-Mail: bill.mcpherson@fastsigns.com
Web Site: franchise.fastsigns.com
Mr. William N. McPherson, VP Franchise
 Sales

FASTSIGNS centers use state-of-the-art computer technology to create custom signs, graphics, banners, trade show exhibits, vehicle graphics and much more. A pioneer in the sign industry, FASTSIGNS has continued to grow by optimizing our systems and expanding the scope of our products and services. Today, with a growing store network of over 550 centers in 6 countries, FASTSIGNS is an acknowledged leader in one of the world's most dynamic franchised industries. At FASTSIGNS, our primary goal is to help our franchisees build successful centers that achieve and maintain high sales volumes and maximum profits, year after year. And we're accomplishing our goal! Our average per store gross sales have increased 16 of the last 18 years to $612,000 in 2008 (Average gross sales for the period ending 12/31/08 as stated in our FDD).

BACKGROUND:	**IFA MEMBER**

Established: 1985;	1st Franchised: 1986
Franchised Units:	552
Company-Owned Units:	0
Total Units:	552
Dist.:	US-467; CAN-22; O'seas-63
North America:	45 States, 6 Provinces
Density:	35 in FL, 43 in CA, 58 in TX
Projected New Units (12 Months):	22
Qualifications:	5, 5, 1, 3, 4, 5

FINANCIAL/TERMS:

Cash Investment:	$75K
Total Investment:	$170,659-$316,673
Minimum Net Worth:	$250K
Fees: Franchise -	$27,500
Royalty - 8%;	Ad. - 2%
Earnings Claims Statement:	Yes
Term of Contract (Years):	20/10
Avg. # Of Employees:	5-6 FT, 0 PT
Passive Ownership:	Not Allowed
Encourage Conversions:	Yes
Area Develop. Agreements:	No
Sub-Franchising Contracts:	No
Expand In Territory:	Yes
Space Needs:	1,200 SF

SUPPORT & TRAINING:

Financial Assistance Provided:	Yes (I)
Site Selection Assistance:	Yes
Lease Negotiation Assistance:	Yes
Co-Operative Advertising:	Yes
Franchisee Assoc./Member:	Yes/Yes
Size Of Corporate Staff:	93
On-Going Support:	„C,D,E,,G,H,I
Training:	2 Weeks Dallas, TX; 1 Week

On-Site

SPECIFIC EXPANSION PLANS:

US:	All United States
Canada:	All Canada except Quebec
Overseas:	UK, New Zealand, Australia

◄◄ ►►

FRAMEMOBILE, THE

159 Santa Paula Ave.
Santa Barbara, CA 93111
Tel: (866) 372-6328 (805) 696-6878
Fax: (805) 504-2096
E-Mail: gballou@framestoyou.com
Web Site: www.framemobile.com
Mr. Greg Ballou, Founder

The FrameMobile will revolutionize the framing industry, by providing in-home custom framing with the highest quality materials and workmanship, convenience and affordability. The FrameMobile will reduce the high cost associated with custom framing by not having a store-front lease, eliminate the risk of transporting valuable art to and from framing, and allow our customers to make better framing material selections in the exact surroundings and lighting in which their art work will be displayed.

BACKGROUND:

Established: 2004;	1st Franchised: 2006
Franchised Units:	0
Company-Owned Units:	1
Total Units:	1
Dist.:	US-1; CAN-0; O'seas-0
North America:	1 States, 0 Provinces
Density:	1 in CA,
Projected New Units (12 Months):	NR
Qualifications:	3, 3, 3, 3, 3, 3

FINANCIAL/TERMS:

Cash Investment:	$40-50K
Total Investment:	$126.5-163.5K
Minimum Net Worth:	NR
Fees: Franchise -	$105K
Royalty - 5%;	Ad. - $50/mo.
Earnings Claims Statement:	No
Term of Contract (Years):	10/10
Avg. # Of Employees:	1 FT, 0 PT
Passive Ownership:	Allowed
Encourage Conversions:	NA
Area Develop. Agreements:	Yes/0
Sub-Franchising Contracts:	No
Expand In Territory:	Yes
Space Needs:	NA

SUPPORT & TRAINING:

Financial Assistance Provided:	No
Site Selection Assistance:	NA
Lease Negotiation Assistance:	NA
Co-Operative Advertising:	No
Franchisee Assoc./Member:	No
Size Of Corporate Staff:	0
On-Going Support:	,,,,,,,
Training:	1 Week Santa Barbara, CA

SPECIFIC EXPANSION PLANS:

US:	All United States
Canada:	No
Overseas:	NR

◄◄ ►►

FRAMING & ART CENTRE

3524 Mainway
Burlington, ON L7M 1A8
Tel: (800) 543-3325 (314) 719-8200 + 245
Fax: (713) 896-8598
E-Mail: ddahl@fcibiz.com
Web Site: www.framingartcentre.com
Mr. Dave Dahl, VP Franchise Development

FRAMING & ART CENTRE is Canada's only national art & custom framing store, specializing in a hands-on, artistic environment. Each store offers a large selection of design samples, prints and posters with custom framing in a creative atmosphere. Easy to learn and operate, exceptional training and support, national buying power and proven marketing programs. Air Miles offered.

BACKGROUND: IFA MEMBER

Established: 1974;	1st Franchised: 1977
Franchised Units:	51
Company-Owned Units:	0
Total Units:	51
Dist.:	US-0; CAN-51; O'seas-0
North America:	0 States, 5 Provinces
Density:	29 in ON, 12 in BC, 6 in AB
Projected New Units (12 Months):	5
Qualifications:	4, 3, 3, 3, 3, 5

FINANCIAL/TERMS:

Cash Investment:	$35-50K
Total Investment:	$118-179K
Minimum Net Worth:	$200K
Fees: Franchise -	$30K
Royalty - 6%;	Ad. - 1%
Earnings Claims Statement:	No
Term of Contract (Years):	10/10
Avg. # Of Employees:	2 FT, 2 PT
Passive Ownership:	Discouraged
Encourage Conversions:	Yes
Area Develop. Agreements:	Yes/1
Sub-Franchising Contracts:	No
Expand In Territory:	Yes
Space Needs:	1,200-1,400 SF

SUPPORT & TRAINING:

Financial Assistance Provided:	No
Site Selection Assistance:	Yes
Lease Negotiation Assistance:	Yes
Co-Operative Advertising:	Yes
Franchisee Assoc./Member:	No
Size Of Corporate Staff:	4
On-Going Support:	,,C,D,E,,G,H,I
Training:	10 Days Burlington, ON

SPECIFIC EXPANSION PLANS:

US:	No
Canada:	All Canada
Overseas:	NR

◄◄ ►►

FRANCHISEMART

2121 Vista Pkwy.
West Palm Beach, FL 33411
Tel: (877)757-6550 (561) 868-1390
Fax: (561) 478-4340
E-Mail: franchise@franchisemart.com
Web Site: www.franchisemart.com
Ms. Bernice Carley, Director Franchise Development

Now the company that helps match people with the right business opportunity could be the right business opportunity for you! When you invest in FranchiseMart, you are investing in one of the hottest ideas in franchising, but also one that was created by a team of experts with over 30 years of franchising experience. FranchiseMart was founded on the premise that there is a business opportunity out there for everyone. And now, the most innovative concept in franchising could be the business for you!

BACKGROUND: IFA MEMBER

Established: 2006;	1st Franchised: 2007
Franchised Units:	8
Company-Owned Units:	0
Total Units:	8
Dist.:	US-6; CAN-0; O'seas-2
North America:	4 States, 0 Provinces
Density:	
Projected New Units (12 Months):	50
Qualifications:	3, 3, 3, 3, 3, 3

FINANCIAL/TERMS:

Cash Investment:	$35
Total Investment:	$110-115
Minimum Net Worth:	$50
Fees: Franchise -	$29.5
Royalty - 7;	Ad. - 2
Earnings Claims Statement:	No
Term of Contract (Years):	35/0
Avg. # Of Employees:	2 FT, 0 PT
Passive Ownership:	Not Allowed
Encourage Conversions:	NA
Area Develop. Agreements:	No
Sub-Franchising Contracts:	No
Expand In Territory:	No
Space Needs:	1,200 SF

SUPPORT & TRAINING:

Financial Assistance Provided:	Yes (I)
Site Selection Assistance:	Yes
Lease Negotiation Assistance:	Yes
Co-Operative Advertising:	No
Franchisee Assoc./Member:	Yes/No
Size Of Corporate Staff:	150
On-Going Support:	,,,D,E,,G,H,
Training:	1 week Franchisee location; 1 week WPB HQ

SPECIFIC EXPANSION PLANS:

US:	All United States
Canada:	No
Overseas:	All Countries

◄◄ ►►

GRAND RENTAL STATION/ TAYLOR RENTAL

203 Jandus Rd.
Cary, IL 60013-2861
Tel: (800) 833-3004 (773) 695-5310
Fax: (847) 516-9921
E-Mail: hbrown@truserv.com
Web Site: www.truserv.com
Mr. Phil Agee, National Sales Manager

Complete equipment rental operation, specializing in light contractor, home owner and party/special occasion rentals. We provide a complete support program including market/site evaluation, store design, inventory customization, hands-on-training and on-going field and technical support.

BACKGROUND:

Established: 1910; 1st Franchised: 1985	
Franchised Units:	450
Company-Owned Units:	0
Total Units:	450
Dist.:	US-450; CAN-0; O'seas-0
North America:	42 States, 0 Provinces
Density:	in PANYMA
Projected New Units (12 Months):	60
Qualifications:	4, 4, 1, 1, 2, 4

FINANCIAL/TERMS:

Cash Investment:	$75-150K
Total Investment:	$225-250K
Minimum Net Worth:	$100K
Fees: Franchise -	$1.5K
Royalty - 1.3%;	Ad. - $30/Mo.
Earnings Claims Statement:	No
Term of Contract (Years):	10/10
Avg. # Of Employees:	3 FT, 3 PT
Passive Ownership:	Discouraged
Encourage Conversions:	Yes
Area Develop. Agreements:	No
Sub-Franchising Contracts:	No
Expand In Territory:	Yes
Space Needs:	5,000 SF

SUPPORT & TRAINING:

Financial Assistance Provided:	No
Site Selection Assistance:	Yes
Lease Negotiation Assistance:	Yes
Co-Operative Advertising:	No
Franchisee Assoc./Member:	Yes/Yes
Size Of Corporate Staff:	16
On-Going Support:	,B,C,D,E,F,G,H,I
Training:	1 Week Gary, IL

SPECIFIC EXPANSION PLANS:

US:	All United States
Canada:	All Canada
Overseas:	All Countries

≪ ≫

The Great Frame Up
Where Picture Framing is an Art™

GREAT FRAME UP, THE

14300 Cornerstone Village Dr., # 321
Houston, TX 77014
Tel: (800) 543-3325
Fax: (713) 896-8598
E-Mail: anance@fcibiz.com
Web Site: www.thegreatframeup.com
Ms. Ann Nance, Director Franchise Development

THE GREAT FRAME UP is part of the world's largest retail franchisor of affordable, high-quality custom framing. Specializing in custom framing in a hands-on, artistic environment featuring wide selections of custom frame moldings & mat styles, a proprietary framing system, superior design center & more. Easy to learn & operate; exceptional training & support; national buying power & proven marketing programs. Growth industry.

BACKGROUND: IFA MEMBER

Established: 1971; 1st Franchised: 1975	
Franchised Units:	181
Company-Owned Units:	0
Total Units:	181
Dist.:	US-181; CAN-0; O'seas-0
North America:	32 States, 0 Provinces
Density:	27 in IL, 20 in GA, 16 in CA
Projected New Units (12 Months):	30
Qualifications:	4, 5, 1, 3, 3, 4

FINANCIAL/TERMS:

Cash Investment:	$50-60K
Total Investment:	$157-233K
Minimum Net Worth:	$250K
Fees: Franchise -	$30K
Royalty - 6%;	Ad. - 2%
Earnings Claims Statement:	Yes
Term of Contract (Years):	10/10
Avg. # Of Employees:	1 FT, 2 PT
Passive Ownership:	Allowed
Encourage Conversions:	Yes
Area Develop. Agreements:	No
Sub-Franchising Contracts:	No
Expand In Territory:	Yes
Space Needs:	1,200-1,600 SF

SUPPORT & TRAINING:

Financial Assistance Provided:	Yes (I)
Site Selection Assistance:	Yes
Lease Negotiation Assistance:	Yes
Co-Operative Advertising:	Yes
Franchisee Assoc./Member:	Yes/Yes
Size Of Corporate Staff:	26
On-Going Support:	,,C,D,E,F,G,H,I
Training:	4 Days In Store;

2 Weeks St. Louis, MO

SPECIFIC EXPANSION PLANS:

US:	All United States
Canada:	No
Overseas:	NR

≪ ≫

GROWER DIRECT FRESH CUT FLOWERS

4220 - 98 St., # 301
Edmonton, AB T6E 6A1 Canada
Tel: (800) 567-7258 (780) 436-7774
Fax: (780) 436-3336
E-Mail: franchises@grower.com
Web Site: www.grower.com
Mr. Doug Munro, CEO

As the largest floral chain retailer, our independently operated franchise locations sell the world's highest-quality fresh cut roses and other flowers in a unique 'boutique-style' setting. Product is sourced directly from the finest producers known and transported weekly to our stores via GROWER DIRECT's distribution system. Rapid product sales translate into 50-60 inventory turns annually and help make the enjoyment of FRESH CUT FLOWERS an affordable and everyday event for our customers.

BACKGROUND:

Established: 1991; 1st Franchised: 1993	
Franchised Units:	68
Company-Owned Units:	3
Total Units:	71
Dist.:	US-0; CAN-71; O'seas-0
North America:	0 States, 10 Provinces
Density:	22 in ON, 15 in BC, 38 in AB
Projected New Units (12 Months):	12
Qualifications:	4, 4, 2, 2, 4, 4

FINANCIAL/TERMS:

Cash Investment:	$40K
Total Investment:	$55-75K
Minimum Net Worth:	$50K
Fees: Franchise -	$12.5K
Royalty - $240/Wk.;	Ad. - $15/Wk.
Earnings Claims Statement:	No
Term of Contract (Years):	10/10
Avg. # Of Employees:	1 FT, 2 PT
Passive Ownership:	Discouraged
Encourage Conversions:	Yes
Area Develop. Agreements:	No
Sub-Franchising Contracts:	Yes
Expand In Territory:	Yes
Space Needs:	400-1,000 SF

SUPPORT & TRAINING:

Financial Assistance Provided:	No
Site Selection Assistance:	Yes

Lease Negotiation Assistance: Yes
Co-Operative Advertising: No
Franchisee Assoc./Member: Yes/Yes
Size Of Corporate Staff: 14
On-Going Support: ,b,C,D,E,,G,H,I
Training: 5 Days Store; 5 Days Classroom; 5 Days Industry Tours
SPECIFIC EXPANSION PLANS:
US: No
Canada: All Canada
Overseas: NR

HOBBYTOWN USA
6301 S. 58th St.
Lincoln, NE 68516-3676
Tel: (800) 858-7370 (402) 434-5064
Fax: (402) 434-5078
E-Mail: nichole@hobbytown.com
Web Site: www.hobbytown.com
Ms. Nichole Ernst, Associate Vice President

HOBBYTOWN USA stores are full-line hobby stores, featuring trains, models, radio-controlled vehicles, games, collectible cards, gifts, accessories and much more! The HOBBYTOWN USA system provides store owners with a comprehensive package of systems and services to be competitive in the hobby and entertainment industries.

BACKGROUND: IFA MEMBER
Established: 1980; 1st Franchised: 1985
Franchised Units: 190
Company-Owned Units: 1
Total Units: 191
Dist.: US-192; CAN-0; O'seas-0
North America: 41 States, 0 Provinces
Density: 10 in TX, 14 in CA
Projected New Units (12 Months): 30
Qualifications: 4, 3, 2, 2, 2, 5
FINANCIAL/TERMS:
Cash Investment: $60-80K
Total Investment: $175-350K
Minimum Net Worth: $150K
Fees: Franchise - $19.5K
Royalty - 3-4%; Ad. - NA
Earnings Claims Statement: No
Term of Contract (Years): 10/10
Avg. # Of Employees: 1-2 FT, 2-3 PT
Passive Ownership: Discouraged
Encourage Conversions: Yes
Area Develop. Agreements: No
Sub-Franchising Contracts: No
Expand In Territory: Yes
Space Needs: 3,000 SF
SUPPORT & TRAINING:

Financial Assistance Provided: Yes (D)
Site Selection Assistance: Yes
Lease Negotiation Assistance: Yes
Co-Operative Advertising: No
Franchisee Assoc./Member: Yes/Yes
Size Of Corporate Staff: 40
On-Going Support: A,,C,D,E,F,G,H,I
Training: 1 Week Home Office;
3 Weeks On-Site
SPECIFIC EXPANSION PLANS:
US: All United States
Canada: All Canada
Overseas: NR

HOMETOWN HEARTH & GRILL
240 Rte. 10 W.
Whippany, NJ 07981-0206
Tel: (888) 298-0031 (954) 429-8602
Fax: (954) 429-1389
E-Mail: dlefevere@suburbanenergy.com
Web Site: www.suburbanfranchising.com
Mr. Dellray Lefevere, National Sales Manager

A HOMETOWN HEARTH & GRILL franchised retail location offers gas grills, outdoor products, fireplaces, hearth stoves, replacement parts and accessories that transform indoor and outdoor spaces with elegance, luxury and warmth. We offer a range of products and services few retailers can match. From broad selection to expert advice, consumers can shop our stores with the confidence that they are getting the best quality, the best service and the best value. 28 years of successful experience.

BACKGROUND: IFA MEMBER
Established: 1991; 1st Franchised: 2004
Franchised Units: 0
Company-Owned Units: 16
Total Units: 16
Dist.: US-13; CAN-0; O'seas-0
North America: 9 States, 0 Provinces
Density: 2 in WA, 2 in OR, 2 in NJ
Projected New Units (12 Months): 10
Qualifications: 4, 3, 2, 3, 4, 5
FINANCIAL/TERMS:
Cash Investment: $80-120K
Total Investment: $300-600K
Minimum Net Worth: $300K
Fees: Franchise - $39.5K

Royalty - 5%; Ad. - 2%
Earnings Claims Statement: Yes
Term of Contract (Years): 10/5/5/
Avg. # Of Employees: 3 FT, 1 PT
Passive Ownership: Not Allowed
Encourage Conversions: Yes
Area Develop. Agreements: No
Sub-Franchising Contracts: No
Expand In Territory: Yes
Space Needs: 2,500 SF
SUPPORT & TRAINING:
Financial Assistance Provided: Yes (D)
Site Selection Assistance: Yes
Lease Negotiation Assistance: Yes
Co-Operative Advertising: No
Franchisee Assoc./Member: Yes/Yes
Size Of Corporate Staff: 4500
On-Going Support: A,B,C,D,E,F,G,h,I
Training: 2 Weeks Whippany, NJ;
On-Going In-Store
SPECIFIC EXPANSION PLANS:
US: All United States
Canada: No
Overseas: NR

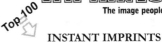

INSTANT IMPRINTS
9808 Waples St.
San Diego, CA 92121
Tel: (800) 542-3437 +856 (858) 642-4848
Fax: (858) 453-6513
E-Mail: instantimprints@franconnect.com
Web Site: www.instantimprints.com
Mr. Bruce C. Keller, Director of Franchise Development

INSTANT IMPRINTS is the first and only concept of its kind to combine Embroidery, Screen Printing, Signs & Banners, Heat Transfers and Promotional Products in one single location. These five industries combine over $50 billion in market revenues; our stores specialize in helping businesses and groups promote themselves and their brand by offering a full range of customized branding solutions. Whether working with a local sports team or a major corporation, our in-house capabilities give us the ability to provide quick service, quality products and complete customization while maintaining excellent margins. We have developed turn-key solutions for newcomers as well as created benefits for seasoned industry professionals looking to convert to a full service business.

BACKGROUND: IFA MEMBER

Established: 1992; 1st Franchised: 2002

Franchised Units:	57
Company-Owned Units:	0
Total Units:	57
Dist.:	US-85; CAN-7; O'seas-1
North America:	23 States, 2 Provinces
Density:	7 in MO, 11 in CO, 12 in CA
Projected New Units (12 Months):	20
Qualifications:	4, 3, 2, 3, 2, 4

FINANCIAL/TERMS:

Cash Investment:	$50-60K
Total Investment:	$168-194K
Minimum Net Worth:	$350K
Fees: Franchise -	$29,950
Royalty - 5%; Ad. - 3.5% - combined 2% nat - 1.5% local	
Earnings Claims Statement:	No
Term of Contract (Years):	10/10
Avg. # Of Employees:	2 FT, 1 PT
Passive Ownership:	Not Allowed
Encourage Conversions:	Yes
Area Develop. Agreements:	Yes/10
Sub-Franchising Contracts:	Yes
Expand In Territory:	No
Space Needs:	1,200 SF

SUPPORT & TRAINING:

Financial Assistance Provided:	Yes (I)
Site Selection Assistance:	Yes
Lease Negotiation Assistance:	Yes
Co-Operative Advertising:	Yes
Franchisee Assoc./Member:	No
Size Of Corporate Staff:	18
On-Going Support:	,,C,D,E,,G,H,I

Training: 2 Weeks Corporate (San Diego) Training; 1 Week Observational In-Store Training;1 Week Onsite Training

SPECIFIC EXPANSION PLANS:

US:	All United States
Canada:	All Canada

Overseas: UK, Australia, Mexico, Western Europe, Japan, Sing

◄◄ ►►

JOE LOUE TOUT RENT ALL

12912 rue Brault
Mirabel, QC J7J 1P3 Canada
Tel: (800) 361-2020 (450) 420-6268
Fax: (450) 430-7777
E-Mail: infojlt@bellnet.ca
Web Site: www.joelouetout.ca
Jacques Dubois, President

Equipment rental in 4 different options: tools, recreational vehicles, special events, motorcycles. Full operating support, including school. Buying group with central billing. Specific insurance plans. Own computer program.

BACKGROUND:

Established: 1982; 1st Franchised: 1982

Franchised Units:	80
Company-Owned Units:	0
Total Units:	80
Dist.:	US-0; CAN-80; O'seas-0
North America:	0 States, 3 Provinces
Density:	63 in QC, 11 in ON, 6 in NB
Projected New Units (12 Months):	8
Qualifications:	4, 4, 3, 3, 4, 3

FINANCIAL/TERMS:

Cash Investment:	$25-65K
Total Investment:	$200-500K
Minimum Net Worth:	$25K
Fees: Franchise -	$45K
Royalty - 5%;	Ad. - 3%
Earnings Claims Statement:	Yes
Term of Contract (Years):	5/5
Avg. # Of Employees:	4 FT, 2 PT
Passive Ownership:	Discouraged
Encourage Conversions:	Yes
Area Develop. Agreements:	No
Sub-Franchising Contracts:	Yes
Expand In Territory:	Yes
Space Needs:	2,000 SF

SUPPORT & TRAINING:

Financial Assistance Provided:	Yes (D)
Site Selection Assistance:	Yes
Lease Negotiation Assistance:	Yes
Co-Operative Advertising:	No
Franchisee Assoc./Member:	No
Size Of Corporate Staff:	5
On-Going Support:	,B,C,D,E,F,G,H,I
Training:	1 Week Head Office; 1 Month Store

SPECIFIC EXPANSION PLANS:

US:	As Master Franchisor
Canada:	Ontario
Overseas:	As Master Franchisor

◄◄ ►►

Just-A-Buck®

JUST-A-BUCK

301 N. Main St., # 5
New City, NY 10956
Tel: (800) 332-2229 (845) 291-7018
Fax: (845) 638-3878
E-Mail: rs@spyral.net
Web Site: www.just-a-buck.com

Mr. Ronald Sommers, Dir. Franchise Development

Merchandise that would sometimes cost as much as ten times more at any other store makes JUST-A-BUCK fun to shop and fun to run. America's premier franchised dollar store. Each location is neat and clean. It takes hard work but the concept is simple and it's made even easier with on-going support, training and help with everything from marketing to merchandising. IFA Member. Entrepreneur Top 500.

BACKGROUND: IFA MEMBER

Established: 1988; 1st Franchised: 1994

Franchised Units:	34
Company-Owned Units:	11
Total Units:	45
Dist.:	US-45; CAN-0; O'seas-0
North America:	7 States, 0 Provinces
Density:	21 in NY, 10 in NJ, 6 in CT
Projected New Units (12 Months):	15
Qualifications:	4, 3, 2, 2, 2, 4

FINANCIAL/TERMS:

Cash Investment:	$40-50K
Total Investment:	$137K-228K
Minimum Net Worth:	$150K
Fees: Franchise -	$25K
Royalty - 4%;	Ad. - 2%
Earnings Claims Statement:	No
Term of Contract (Years):	10/20
Avg. # Of Employees:	6 FT, 10 PT
Passive Ownership:	Not Allowed
Encourage Conversions:	Yes
Area Develop. Agreements:	Yes/1
Sub-Franchising Contracts:	No
Expand In Territory:	Yes
Space Needs:	3,000 SF

SUPPORT & TRAINING:

Financial Assistance Provided:	Yes (D)
Site Selection Assistance:	Yes
Lease Negotiation Assistance:	Yes
Co-Operative Advertising:	No
Franchisee Assoc./Member:	No
Size Of Corporate Staff:	18
On-Going Support:	A,B,C,D,E,F,G,H,I
Training:	10 Days NY State; 10 Days On-Site

SPECIFIC EXPANSION PLANS:

US:	All United States
Canada:	All Canada
Overseas:	All Countries

◄◄ ►►

LATEX CITY

1814 Franklin St., # 820
Oakland, CA 94612
Tel: (510) 839-5462

Fax: (510) 839-2104
E-Mail: angie@worldfranchising.com
Web Site: www.latexnovelty.com
Ms. Christina Kimmel, President

Unique ground-floor specialty retailing opportunity in booming latex novelty aid business. Complete line of proprietary products. Turn-key package includes lease negotiation, fully stocked inventory, in-store merchandising/display. On-going support. LATEX CITY is ideal for aggressive couples. This is not smut - but a highly profitable, high-margin, fully legal business.

BACKGROUND:

Established: 1972;   1st Franchised: 1986
Franchised Units: 26
Company-Owned Units: 4
Total Units: 30
Dist.:   US-25; CAN-2; O'seas-3
  North America: 17 States, 1 Provinces
  Density: 3 in CA, 3 in NY, 2 in OR
Projected New Units (12 Months):   10
Qualifications: NR

FINANCIAL/TERMS:

Cash Investment: $65K
Total Investment: $85-235K
Minimum Net Worth: NR
Fees: Franchise - $15K
  Royalty - 6%;   Ad. - 2%
Earnings Claims Statement: Yes
Term of Contract (Years):   10/10
Avg. # Of Employees: 2 FT, 0 PT
Passive Ownership: Discouraged
Encourage Conversions: Yes
Area Develop. Agreements: Yes/1
Sub-Franchising Contracts: No
Expand In Territory: No
Space Needs: 1,000-1,400 SF

SUPPORT & TRAINING:

Financial Assistance Provided: Yes (D)
Site Selection Assistance: Yes
Lease Negotiation Assistance: Yes
Co-Operative Advertising: No
Franchisee Assoc./Member: NR
Size Of Corporate Staff: 6
On-Going Support: A,B,C,D,,,G,H,
Training: 3 Weeks Headquarters;
  1 Week Plant; 2 Weeks On-Site

SPECIFIC EXPANSION PLANS:

US: All United States
Canada: Major Cities
Overseas: NR

LIVING LIGHTING

294 Walker Dr., # 2

Brampton, ON L6T 4Z2 Canada
Tel: (866) 463-4124 (905) 790-9023
Fax: (905) 790-7059
E-Mail:
Web Site: www.livinglighting.com
Ms. Ashley Loyst, Franchise Marketing

Living lighting is a unique retail concept featuring an extensive selection of stylish lighting fixtures, lamps, outdoor lighting and accessories.

BACKGROUND:

Established: 1968;   1st Franchised: 1970
Franchised Units: 34
Company-Owned Units: 0
Total Units: 34
Dist.:   US-0; CAN-34; O'seas-0
  North America: 0 States, 4 Provinces
  Density: 25 in ON, 2 in AB
Projected New Units (12 Months):   6
Qualifications: NR

FINANCIAL/TERMS:

Cash Investment: $80K
Total Investment: $200-350K
Minimum Net Worth: NR
Fees: Franchise - $25K
  Royalty - 5%;   Ad. - 1%
Earnings Claims Statement: No
Term of Contract (Years):   10/10
Avg. # Of Employees: Varies
Passive Ownership: Not Allowed
Encourage Conversions: NA
Area Develop. Agreements: Yes/0
Sub-Franchising Contracts: No
Expand In Territory: No
Space Needs: 2,000-3,000 SF

SUPPORT & TRAINING:

Financial Assistance Provided: No
Site Selection Assistance: Yes
Lease Negotiation Assistance: Yes
Co-Operative Advertising: Yes
Franchisee Assoc./Member: No
Size Of Corporate Staff: 20
On-Going Support: ,,C,D,E,,G,H,I
Training: NR

SPECIFIC EXPANSION PLANS:

US: No
Canada: All Canada
Overseas: NR

≺≺ ≻≻

MARAD FINE ART

23 Atlantic St.
Stamford, CT 06901
Tel: (203) 323-2200
Fax: (203) 323-8200
E-Mail: maradart@aol.com
Web Site: www.maradfineart.com

Mr. Dick Fierstein, President

MARAD FINE ART offers qualified individuals with a flair for sales and an appreciation of art the chance to operate their own commercial art business from their home or office. Product line contains over 15,000 of the world's best-loved art reproductions in quality, custom mattes and frames at the same low price for each piece. Comprehensive sales training, exclusive territories and a turnkey ordering/fulfillment system allow for easy start-up, operational efficiency, little overhead and NO INVENTORY.

BACKGROUND:

Established: 1938;   1st Franchised: 2002
Franchised Units: 3
Company-Owned Units: 1
Total Units: 4
Dist.:   US-4; CAN-0; O'seas-0
  North America: 1 States, 0 Provinces
  Density: 1 in CT,
Projected New Units (12 Months):   4
Qualifications: 3, 4, 2, 2, 3, 4

FINANCIAL/TERMS:

Cash Investment: $35-60K
Total Investment: $35-60K
Minimum Net Worth: $100K
Fees: Franchise - $35-60K
  Royalty - 4%;   Ad. - 2%
Earnings Claims Statement: No
Term of Contract (Years):   10/5
Avg. # Of Employees: 1 FT, 0 PT
Passive Ownership: Not Allowed
Encourage Conversions: NA
Area Develop. Agreements: No
Sub-Franchising Contracts: No
Expand In Territory: Yes
Space Needs: NA

SUPPORT & TRAINING:

Financial Assistance Provided: Yes (D)
Site Selection Assistance: NA
Lease Negotiation Assistance: NA
Co-Operative Advertising: No
Franchisee Assoc./Member: No
Size Of Corporate Staff: 1
On-Going Support: ,,,,,,,
Training: 1 Day Stamford CT;
  1 Day Hauppage, NY

SPECIFIC EXPANSION PLANS:

US: All United States
Canada: No
Overseas: All Countries

≺≺ ≻≻

MATCO TOOLS

4403 Allen Rd.
Stowe, OH 44224-1096
Tel: (888) 696-2826 (330) 926-5351
Fax: (330) 926-5325
E-Mail: richard.dayton@matcotools.com
Web Site: www.gomatco.com
Mr. Richard Dayton, National Franchise Sales Manager

Sales of automotive tools, equipment and computerized diagnostic equipment to professional automotive service technicians and repair center owners. MATCO TOOLS is a home-based franchise that is owner-operated. Our business features weekly sales and service via mobile distribution. We offer exclusive territories, outstanding initial and continuing training and personalized business consultation. MATCO TOOLS and/or SBA loan financing.

BACKGROUND: IFA MEMBER
Established: 1946; 1st Franchised: 1993
Franchised Units: 1507
Company-Owned Units: 0
Total Units: 1507
Dist.:   US-1507; CAN-18; O'seas-0
  North America: 50 States, 0 Provinces
  Density: 124 in TX, 89 in FL, 195 in CA
Projected New Units (12 Months): 251
Qualifications: 3, 2, 2, 2, 3, 5
FINANCIAL/TERMS:
Cash Investment: $30K-35K
Total Investment: $72K-170K
Minimum Net Worth: $75K
Fees: Franchise - $0
  Royalty - 0%;   Ad. - 0%
Earnings Claims Statement: Yes
Term of Contract (Years): 10/10
Avg. # Of Employees: 1 FT, 0 PT
Passive Ownership: Discouraged
Encourage Conversions: No
Area Develop. Agreements: No
Sub-Franchising Contracts: No
Expand In Territory: Yes
Space Needs: NA
SUPPORT & TRAINING:
Financial Assistance Provided: Yes (D)
Site Selection Assistance: NA
Lease Negotiation Assistance: NA
Co-Operative Advertising: No
Franchisee Assoc./Member: Yes/Yes
Size Of Corporate Staff: 400
On-Going Support: A,B,C,D,E,F,G,H,I
Training:3 Weeks On-Site/Field Training;
  10 Days Corporate Office
SPECIFIC EXPANSION PLANS:
US: All United States
Canada: Yes
Overseas: NR

◄◄ ►►

MEDICAP PHARMACY

4350 Westown Pkwy., # 400
West Des Moines, IA 50266-1061
Tel: (800) 445-2244 (515) 224-8400
Fax: (515) 224-8494
E-Mail: cjames@medicaprx.com
Web Site: www.medicap.com
Mr. Calvin C. Ames, SVP Franchise Development

MEDICAP PHARMACY - convenient, low-cost, professional pharmacies. The stores operate in an average of 1,500-2,000 square feet. We average 90% RX and the remaining 10% over-the-counter products, including MEDICAP-brand private label. We specialize in starting new stores and converting existing full-line drug stores and independent pharmacies to the MEDICAP concept. We teach independent pharmacists how to survive in today's marketplace.

BACKGROUND: IFA MEMBER
Established: 1971; 1st Franchised: 1974
Franchised Units: 225
Company-Owned Units: 12
Total Units: 237
Dist.:   US-237; CAN-0; O'seas-0
  North America: 38 States, 0 Provinces
  Density: 7 in SC, 23 in NC, 50 in IA
Projected New Units (12 Months): 25
Qualifications: 3, 1, 4, 5, 3, 5
FINANCIAL/TERMS:
Cash Investment: $20K-60K
Total Investment: $300K-325K
Minimum Net Worth: NR
Fees: Franchise - $8.5-15K
  Royalty - 2 or 3.9%; Ad. - 1%
Earnings Claims Statement: Yes
Term of Contract (Years): 20/10
Avg. # Of Employees: 2 FT, 0 PT
Passive Ownership: Allowed
Encourage Conversions: Yes
Area Develop. Agreements: No
Sub-Franchising Contracts: No
Expand In Territory: Yes
Space Needs: 1,500 SF
SUPPORT & TRAINING:
Financial Assistance Provided: Yes (D)
Site Selection Assistance: Yes
Lease Negotiation Assistance: Yes
Co-Operative Advertising: No
Franchisee Assoc./Member: NR
Size Of Corporate Staff: 62
On-Going Support: ,B,C,D,E,F,G,H,I
Training: 4 Days Headquarters;
  3 Days On-Site; 3 Days Computer
SPECIFIC EXPANSION PLANS:
US: All United States
Canada: All Canada
Overseas: All Countries

◄◄ ►►

MEDICINE SHOPPE, THE

1 Rider Plaza Dr., # 300
Earth City, MO 63045
Tel: (800) 325-1397 (314) 993-6000
Fax: (314) 872-5500
E-Mail: dlhota@medshoppe.com
Web Site: www.medicineshoppe.com
Mr. Daniel P. Lhota, SVP Franchise Sales/Devel.

Medicine Shoppe International is the largest and fastest growing chain of franchised pharmacies in the world. MSI offers its owners numerous ways to enter pharmacy ownership, i.e. acquisition of existing pharmacies, new store development, supermarkets clinic locations. Diversify your portfolio and participate in the graying of America.

BACKGROUND: IFA MEMBER
Established: 1970; 1st Franchised: 1970
Franchised Units: 1287
Company-Owned Units: 25
Total Units: 1313
Dist.:   US-1133; CAN-0; O'seas-180
  North America: 47 States, 0 Provinces
  Density: 121 in PA, 111 in FL, 71 in CA
Projected New Units (12 Months): 65
Qualifications: 3, 3, 4, 5, 2, 4
FINANCIAL/TERMS:
Cash Investment: $10-18K
Total Investment: $77K-152.5K
Minimum Net Worth: $50K
Fees: Franchise - $10-18K
  Royalty - 2-5.5%; Ad. - $200/Mo.
Earnings Claims Statement: Yes
Term of Contract (Years): 10/15
Avg. # Of Employees: 2 FT, 1 PT
Passive Ownership: Allowed
Encourage Conversions: Yes

Area Develop. Agreements:	Yes/1
Sub-Franchising Contracts:	No
Expand In Territory:	Yes
Space Needs:	1,200 SF

SUPPORT & TRAINING:

Financial Assistance Provided:	Yes (D)
Site Selection Assistance:	Yes
Lease Negotiation Assistance:	Yes
Co-Operative Advertising:	No
Franchisee Assoc./Member:	No
Size Of Corporate Staff:	240
On-Going Support:	A,B,C,D,E,F,G,H,I
Training:	6 Days St. Louis, MO

SPECIFIC EXPANSION PLANS:

US:	All United States
Canada:	Master License
Overseas:	All Countries

◄◄ ►►

MERKINSTOCK

P. O. Box 12488
Oakland, CA 94604
Tel: (510) 839-5462
Fax: (510) 839-2104
E-Mail: sourcebook@earthlink.net
Web Site: www.merkinstock.com
Mr. Jeffrey F. Elder, President

World's largest selection of merkins - both natural and synthetic. Over 35 models, 15 color selections. Custom fitting in discrete environment. Also custom dyeing. Guaranteed satisfaction. 15 stores in Far East and Europe prove that concept is ripe for aggressive expansion into the U. S. market. Looking for entrepreneurs with the desire to succeed.

BACKGROUND:

Established: 1992;	1st Franchised: 1995
Franchised Units:	52
Company-Owned Units:	7
Total Units:	59
Dist.:	US-42; CAN-2; O'seas-15
North America:	2 States, 1 Provinces
Density:	1 in NV, 2 in CA
Projected New Units (12 Months):	10
Qualifications:	3, 5, 4, 2, 3, 5

FINANCIAL/TERMS:

Cash Investment:	$90K
Total Investment:	$150K
Minimum Net Worth:	$250K

Fees: Franchise -	$20K
Royalty - 6%;	Ad. - 2%
Earnings Claims Statement:	Yes
Term of Contract (Years):	15/15
Avg. # Of Employees:	2 FT, 0 PT
Passive Ownership:	Not Allowed
Encourage Conversions:	Yes
Area Develop. Agreements:	Yes/1
Sub-Franchising Contracts:	Yes
Expand In Territory:	No
Space Needs:	1,200 SF

SUPPORT & TRAINING:

Financial Assistance Provided:	Yes (D)
Site Selection Assistance:	Yes
Lease Negotiation Assistance:	Yes
Co-Operative Advertising:	No
Franchisee Assoc./Member:	No
Size Of Corporate Staff:	4
On-Going Support:	a,B,C,D,E,f,G,,I
Training:	3 Weeks Headquarters;
	2 Weeks On-Site

SPECIFIC EXPANSION PLANS:

US:	All United States
Canada:	All Canada
Overseas:	All Countries

◄◄ ►►

**METAL SUPERMARKETS
INTERNATIONAL**

170 Wilkinson Rd., # 17-18
Brampton, ON L6T 4Z5 Canada
Tel: (800) 807-8755 (905) 459-0466 + 227
Fax: (905) 459-3690
E-Mail: aarminen@metalsupermarkets.com
Web Site: www.metalsupermarkets.com
Mr. Andrew Arminen, VP Franchise Division

METAL SUPERMARKETS is a highly specialized supplier of small quantities of virtually all types and forms of metal. Customers are maintenance departments of all types of industries. As 'convenience stores of the metals industry,' we have no minimum order We offer fast delivery, custom cutting and can source rare metals.

BACKGROUND: IFA MEMBER

Established: 1985;	1st Franchised: 1987
Franchised Units:	60
Company-Owned Units:	21
Total Units:	81
Dist.:	US-24; CAN-26; O'seas-31
North America:	24 States, 7 Provinces
Density:	1 in FL, 13 in ON, 2 in PA
Projected New Units (12 Months):	8
Qualifications:	5, 3, 3, 3, 3, 5

FINANCIAL/TERMS:

Cash Investment:	$125K
Total Investment:	$230-270K
Minimum Net Worth:	$350K
Fees: Franchise -	$39.5K
Royalty - 6%;	Ad. - 0%
Earnings Claims Statement:	No
Term of Contract (Years):	10/10
Avg. # Of Employees:	3 FT, 1 PT
Passive Ownership:	Discouraged
Encourage Conversions:	Yes
Area Develop. Agreements:	Yes/1
Sub-Franchising Contracts:	No
Expand In Territory:	Yes
Space Needs:	4,000 SF

SUPPORT & TRAINING:

Financial Assistance Provided:	No
Site Selection Assistance:	Yes
Lease Negotiation Assistance:	Yes
Co-Operative Advertising:	No
Franchisee Assoc./Member:	Yes/Yes
Size Of Corporate Staff:	15
On-Going Support:	,,C,D,E,F,G,h,I
Training:	1 Week Toronto, ON;
	2 Weeks Corporate Store; 2 Weeks
	Own Store

SPECIFIC EXPANSION PLANS:

US:	All United States
Canada:	PQ
Overseas:	Europe

◄◄ ►►

MUSIC GO ROUND

4200 Dahlberg Dr., # 100
Minneapolis, MN 55422-4837
Tel: (800) 269-4076 (763) 520-8582
Fax: (763) 520-8501
E-Mail: mgr-franchise-development@musicgoround.com
Web Site: www.musicgoround.com
, Franchise Development Department

MUSIC GO ROUND stores buy, sell and trade quality used and new instruments, equipment and accessories.

BACKGROUND: IFA MEMBER

Established: 1986;	1st Franchised: 1994
Franchised Units:	37
Company-Owned Units:	0
Total Units:	37
Dist.:	US-37; CAN-0; O'seas-0
North America:	25 States, 0 Provinces
Density:	3 in WI, 4 in TX, 3 in MI

Projected New Units (12 Months): 4
Qualifications: 5, 4, 3, 2, 1, 4
FINANCIAL/TERMS:
Cash Investment: $73K-96K
Total Investment: $242K-320K
Minimum Net Worth: $350K
Fees: Franchise - $20K
Royalty - 3%; Ad. -
Earnings Claims Statement: Yes
Term of Contract (Years): 10/10
Avg. # Of Employees: 2 FT, 2 PT
Passive Ownership: Not Allowed
Encourage Conversions: No
Area Develop. Agreements: No
Sub-Franchising Contracts: No
Expand In Territory: No
Space Needs: 2,500-3,000 SF
SUPPORT & TRAINING:
Financial Assistance Provided: No
Site Selection Assistance: Yes
Lease Negotiation Assistance: Yes
Co-Operative Advertising: No
Franchisee Assoc./Member: No
Size Of Corporate Staff: 97
On-Going Support: „C,D,E,F,G,,I
Training: 4 Days Minneapolis, MN;
;5 DaysMinneapolis, MN
SPECIFIC EXPANSION PLANS:
US: All United States
Canada: No
Overseas: NR

‹‹ ››

PINCH-A-PENNY

14480 62nd St., N.
Clearwater, FL 33760-2721
Tel: (727) 531-8913 + 237
Fax: (727) 536-8066
E-Mail: aheflin@pinchapenny.com
Web Site: www.pinchapenny.com
Mr. Adam S. Heflin, Franchise Development Manager

PINCH-A-PENNY is the nation's largest franchise retailer of swimming pool, spa and patio supplies.

BACKGROUND: IFA MEMBER
Established: 1975; 1st Franchised: 1976
Franchised Units: 200
Company-Owned Units: 2
Total Units: 202
Dist.: US-202; CAN-0; O'seas-0
North America: 4 States, 0 Provinces
Density: 1 in GA, 174 in FL, 2 in AL
Projected New Units (12 Months): 15
Qualifications: NR
FINANCIAL/TERMS:
Cash Investment: $150-350K

Total Investment: $150-350K
Minimum Net Worth: $250K
Fees: Franchise - $30K
Royalty - 6%; Ad. - 4%
Earnings Claims Statement: Yes
Term of Contract (Years): 5/20
Avg. # Of Employees: FT, 0 PT
Passive Ownership: Not Allowed
Encourage Conversions: No
Area Develop. Agreements: No
Sub-Franchising Contracts: No
Expand In Territory: Yes
Space Needs: 1,500-3,500 SF
SUPPORT & TRAINING:
Financial Assistance Provided: No
Site Selection Assistance: Yes
Lease Negotiation Assistance: Yes
Co-Operative Advertising: No
Franchisee Assoc./Member: No
Size Of Corporate Staff: 0
On-Going Support: A,B,C,D,E,,,H,I
Training: 4 Weeks Headquarters
SPECIFIC EXPANSION PLANS:
US: All United States
Canada: No
Overseas: NR

‹‹ ››

RAFTERS HOME STORES/ PANHANDLER

294 Walker Dr., # 2
Brampton, ON L6T 4Z2 Canada
Tel: (866) 463-4124 (905) 790-9023
Fax: (905) 790-7059
E-Mail: franchises@franchisebancorp. com
Web Site: www.livcan.com
Ms. Ashley Loyst, Franchise Marketing

An exciting home decor and giftware store filled to the rafters with the latest selection of stylish home fashions and unique gift giving ideas.

BACKGROUND:
Established: 1975; 1st Franchised: 1975
Franchised Units: 25
Company-Owned Units: 0
Total Units: 25
Dist.: US-0; CAN-25; O'seas-0
North America: 0 States, 7 Provinces
Density: 6 in ON, 6 in NS, 12 in AB
Projected New Units (12 Months): 6
Qualifications: NR
FINANCIAL/TERMS:
Cash Investment: $70K
Total Investment: $200K-350K
Minimum Net Worth: NR
Fees: Franchise - $25K

Royalty - 4-6%; Ad. - 1%
Earnings Claims Statement: No
Term of Contract (Years): 10/10
Avg. # Of Employees: Varies
Passive Ownership: Not Allowed
Encourage Conversions: NA
Area Develop. Agreements: Yes/0
Sub-Franchising Contracts: No
Expand In Territory: No
Space Needs: 2,000-6,000 SF
SUPPORT & TRAINING:
Financial Assistance Provided: No
Site Selection Assistance: Yes
Lease Negotiation Assistance: Yes
Co-Operative Advertising: Yes
Franchisee Assoc./Member: Yes/Yes
Size Of Corporate Staff: 20
On-Going Support: „C,D,E,,G,H,I
Training:
SPECIFIC EXPANSION PLANS:
US: No
Canada: All Canada
Overseas: NR

‹‹ ››

RAINSOFT

2080 E. Lunt Ave.
Elk Grove Village, IL 60007
Tel: (800) 724-6763 (847) 867-8941
Fax: (970) 663-5343
E-Mail: dmiller@aquion.com
Web Site: www.rainsoft.com
Mr. Don Miller, VP of Business Development

RAINSOFT Water Treament has enjoyed nearly constant expansion in its 51-year history. RAINSOFT provides clean, soft, luxurious great-tasting water to homes and businesses. With a lifetime warranty, one of the strongest in the industry, you know, like our one million plus clients, that you are in good hands. With Franchise-like programs and on-site support before, during and after opening, many dealers are now second-generation businesses with significant cash flow and both passive and active income.

BACKGROUND: IFA MEMBER
Established: 1953; 1st Franchised: 1959
Franchised Units: 190
Company-Owned Units: 0
Total Units: 190

Dist.: US-162; CAN-4; O'seas-24
North America: 36 States, 2 Provinces
Density: 22 in FL, 10 in MI, 14 in TX
Projected New Units (12 Months): 30
Qualifications: 4, 2, 1, 2, 3, 5

FINANCIAL/TERMS:

Cash Investment: $70-100K
Total Investment: $70-100K
Minimum Net Worth: $100K
Fees: Franchise - $0K
 Royalty - 0%; Ad. - 0%
Earnings Claims Statement: No
Term of Contract (Years): 2/2
Avg. # Of Employees: 15 FT, 4 PT
Passive Ownership: Not Allowed
Encourage Conversions: NA
Area Develop. Agreements: No
Sub-Franchising Contracts: No
Expand In Territory: Yes
Space Needs: 2,500 SF

SUPPORT & TRAINING:

Financial Assistance Provided: No
Site Selection Assistance: Yes
Lease Negotiation Assistance: Yes
Co-Operative Advertising: No
Franchisee Assoc./Member: No
Size Of Corporate Staff: 170
On-Going Support: ,B,C,D,E,,G,H,I
Training: 1 Week 14 Days;
 Up to 6 Weeks Before/during/after
 opening new store; twice a year Conventions/Meetings

SPECIFIC EXPANSION PLANS:

US: All United States
Canada: All Canada
Overseas: All Countries, Emphasis on
UK, France, Russia, China

‹‹ ››

RUSSELL WATERGARDENS & KOI

16515 Redmond Way, # 436-C
Redmond, WA 98052
Tel: (800) 844-9314 (425) 869-6700
Fax: (425) 869-6711
E-Mail: info@russellwatergardens.com
Web Site: www.russellwatergardens.com
Mr. John Russell, Director of Franchising

Russell Watergardens & Koi is the world's first professional pond and water feature equipment, Koi and supply galleria superstore franchise program! Our Benefit Advantage - Exclusive equipment and products • FUN franchise - Exclusivity that limits your competition - Destination format that draws customers from great distances - Retail/Wholesale/Install/Service - Filtration equipment, pumps, plumbing, underwater lighting, algae prevention, maintenance supplies, water plants, fish pharmacy, Koi & pond fish - Underserved market with outstanding growth potential - Exceptional training and support

BACKGROUND:

Established: 1997; 1st Franchised: 2008
Franchised Units: 0
Company-Owned Units: 1
Total Units: 1
Dist.: US-1; CAN-0; O'seas-0
North America: 1 States, 0 Provinces
Density: 1 in WA
Projected New Units (12 Months): 1-2
Qualifications: 4, 4, 3, 2, 4, 5

FINANCIAL/TERMS:

Cash Investment: $90K
Total Investment: $237 - 421.2K
Minimum Net Worth: $350K
Fees: Franchise - $35K
 Royalty - 6%; Ad. - 1%
Earnings Claims Statement: No
Term of Contract (Years): 5/5
Avg. # Of Employees: 4 FT, 4 PT
Passive Ownership: Discouraged
Encourage Conversions: Yes
Area Develop. Agreements: Yes/5
Sub-Franchising Contracts: No
Expand In Territory: No
Space Needs: 2,000 SF Interior Min;
 10,000 SF Exterior SF

SUPPORT & TRAINING:

Financial Assistance Provided: No
Site Selection Assistance: Yes
Lease Negotiation Assistance: Yes
Co-Operative Advertising: No
Franchisee Assoc./Member: No
Size Of Corporate Staff: 0
On-Going Support: ,,C,D,E,F,,h,I
Training: 2 weeks Franchise location;
 4 weeks Corporate headquaters

SPECIFIC EXPANSION PLANS:

US: Northwest primarily with other states possible
Canada: No
Overseas: NR

‹‹ ››

SHOEBOX
NEW YORK

SHOEBOX NEW YORK

1346 Oakbrook Dr., # 170
Norcross, GA 30093
Tel: (800) 524-6444 (770) 514-4500
Fax: (770) 514-4903
E-Mail: franchiseinfo@nexcenfm.com
Web Site: www.shoeboxny.com
Mr. Martin Amschler, Cheif Development Officer

Since 1954, Shoebox New York has been New York's top multi-branded women's retailer for luxury and designer footwear, handbags & accessories. Shoebox New York's reputation is built on its vast product assortment & trend-setting styles, offering women the latest fashions from top European & American designers. Shoebox New York's exceptional product offering, personalized customer experience & trendy new store design have gained a dedicated following of sophisticated women worldwide.

BACKGROUND: IFA MEMBER

Established: 1954; 1st Franchised: 2008
Franchised Units: 13
Company-Owned Units: 0
Total Units: 13
Dist.: US-9; CAN-0; O'seas-4
North America: 2 States, 0 Provinces
Density: 1 in FL, 8 in NY
Projected New Units (12 Months): 70
Qualifications: 5, 5, 4, 4, 4, 3

FINANCIAL/TERMS:

Cash Investment: $150,000
Total Investment: $390,450-840,900
Minimum Net Worth: $350,000
Fees: Franchise - $39,900
 Royalty - 5%; Ad. - 2%
Earnings Claims Statement: No
Term of Contract (Years): 10/5
Avg. # Of Employees: 10 FT, 5 PT
Passive Ownership: Discouraged
Encourage Conversions: NA
Area Develop. Agreements: Yes/10
Sub-Franchising Contracts: No
Expand In Territory: Yes
Space Needs: 1000-2000 SF

SUPPORT & TRAINING:

Financial Assistance Provided: No
Site Selection Assistance: Yes
Lease Negotiation Assistance: Yes
Co-Operative Advertising: No
Franchisee Assoc./Member: Yes/No
Size Of Corporate Staff: 135

On-Going Support: A,B,C,D,E,F,G,H,I
Training: Atlanta, GA
SPECIFIC EXPANSION PLANS:
US: Yes
Canada: Yes
Overseas: NR

‹‹ ››

SIGN-A-RAMA

2121 Vista Pkwy.
West Palm Beach, FL 33411
Tel: (800) 286-8671 (561) 640-5570
Fax: (561) 640-5580
E-Mail: signinfo@signarama.com
Web Site: www.signarama.com
Mr. Michael Prince, Director Franchise
   Development

World's largest full-service sign franchise.
Over 900 locations in 50 countries. Ranked
#1 in industry. No experience needed.
Full training, local back-up and support.
Financing available.

BACKGROUND: IFA MEMBER
Established: 1986;   1st Franchised: 1987
Franchised Units: 905
Company-Owned Units: 0
Total Units: 905
Dist.:   US-597; CAN-38; O'seas-270
   North America: 46 States, 5 Provinces
   Density: 34 in NJ, 61 in FL, 97 in CA
Projected New Units (12 Months):   100
Qualifications: 5, 4, 1, 1, 4, 5
FINANCIAL/TERMS:
Cash Investment: $48K
Total Investment: $150K
Minimum Net Worth: $60K
Fees: Franchise - $42.5K
   Royalty - 6%;   Ad. - 0%
Earnings Claims Statement: No
Term of Contract (Years):   35/35
Avg. # Of Employees: 3 FT, 0 PT
Passive Ownership: Discouraged
Encourage Conversions: Yes
Area Develop. Agreements: No
Sub-Franchising Contracts: Yes
Expand In Territory: Yes
Space Needs: 1,200 SF
SUPPORT & TRAINING:
Financial Assistance Provided: Yes (I)
Site Selection Assistance: Yes
Lease Negotiation Assistance: Yes
Co-Operative Advertising: Yes
Franchisee Assoc./Member: Yes/Yes
Size Of Corporate Staff: 180

On-Going Support: A,B,C,D,E,F,G,H,I
Training: 1 Week On-The-Job;
   2 Weeks On-Site; 2 Weeks West Palm
   Beach, FL
SPECIFIC EXPANSION PLANS:
US: All United States
Canada: All Canada
Overseas: All Countries

‹‹ ››

SIGNS BY TOMORROW

8681 Robert Fulton Dr.
Columbia, MD 21046
Tel: (800) 765-7446 (410) 312-3600
Fax: (410) 312-3520
E-Mail: sales@signsbytomorrow.com
Web Site: www.signsbytomorrow.com
Mr. Mike Cline, Franchise Sales Manager

Computer-generated, one day, signs and
graphics shop. Business-to-business, high
growth, high gross margins, service-oriented, multiples possible. Most extensive
training and support system. Aggressive R
& D program. High rate of franchisee success and satisfaction. No tech experience
necessary.

BACKGROUND: IFA MEMBER
Established: 1986;   1st Franchised: 1987
Franchised Units: 179
Company-Owned Units: 1
Total Units: 180
Dist.:   US-180; CAN-0; O'seas-0
   North America: 34 States, 0 Provinces
   Density: 15 in PA, 9 in NJ, 16 in MD
Projected New Units (12 Months):   20
Qualifications: 4, 5, 1, 4, 5, 5
FINANCIAL/TERMS:
Cash Investment: $50K
Total Investment: $19K-263K
Minimum Net Worth: $200K
Fees: Franchise - $28.5K
   Royalty - 3-6%;   Ad. - 1%
Earnings Claims Statement: Yes
Term of Contract (Years):   20/20
Avg. # Of Employees: FT, PT
Passive Ownership: Not Allowed
Encourage Conversions: No
Area Develop. Agreements: No
Sub-Franchising Contracts: No
Expand In Territory: No
Space Needs: 1,800 SF
SUPPORT & TRAINING:

Financial Assistance Provided: Yes (I)
Site Selection Assistance: Yes
Lease Negotiation Assistance: Yes
Co-Operative Advertising: Yes
Franchisee Assoc./Member: Yes/Yes
Size Of Corporate Staff: 27
On-Going Support: ,,C,D,E,F,G,H,I
Training: 3 Weeks Headquarters;
   2 Weeks Store
SPECIFIC EXPANSION PLANS:
US: All United States
Canada: No
Overseas: NR

‹‹ ››

SIGNS FIRST

813 Ridge Lake Blvd., # 495
Memphis, TN 38120
Tel: (800) 852-2163 (901) 682-2264
Fax: (901) 682-2475
E-Mail: franchise@signsfirst.com
Web Site: www.signsfirst.com
Ms. Peggy Cahoon, Office Manager

SIGNS FIRST is the only franchise with
over 25 years sign industry experience. We
specialize in computer-generated, one-day
temporary and permanent signs for retail,
professional and commercial businesses
on a cash and carry basis. Franchisee support is unparalleled with comprehensive
training, on-going technological support
and marketing assistance.

BACKGROUND:
Established: 1966;   1st Franchised: 1989
Franchised Units: 33
Company-Owned Units: 0
Total Units: 33
Dist.:   US-33; CAN-0; O'seas-0
   North America: 0 States, 0 Provinces
   Density: 13 in TN, 12 in MS, 3 in CO
Projected New Units (12 Months):   5
Qualifications: 3, 4, 3, 1, 3, 5
FINANCIAL/TERMS:
Cash Investment: $20K
Total Investment: $20-65K
Minimum Net Worth: $250K
Fees: Franchise - $10-15K
   Royalty - 6%;   Ad. - 0%
Earnings Claims Statement: No
Term of Contract (Years):   10/10
Avg. # Of Employees: 2 FT, 0 PT
Passive Ownership: Discouraged
Encourage Conversions: Yes
Area Develop. Agreements: Yes/1
Sub-Franchising Contracts: No
Expand In Territory: Yes
Space Needs: 1,500 SF

SUPPORT & TRAINING:

Financial Assistance Provided:	NR
Site Selection Assistance:	Yes
Lease Negotiation Assistance:	Yes
Co-Operative Advertising:	No
Franchisee Assoc./Member:	No
Size Of Corporate Staff:	6
On-Going Support:	,B,C,D,E,F,G,,I
Training:	2 Weeks Memphis, TN;
1 Week + Follow-Up Visit Store	

SPECIFIC EXPANSION PLANS:

US:	All United States
Canada:	No
Overseas:	NR

≪ ≫

Snap-on

SNAP-ON TOOLS

2801 80th St., P.O. Box 1410
Kenosha, WI 53143
Tel: (800) 786-6600 (877) 476-2766
Fax: (262) 656-5635
E-Mail: franchiseopportunities@snapon.com
Web Site: www.snaponfranchise.com
Mr. Mike Doweidt, Director of Franchising

The premier solutions provider to the vehicle service industry. Premium quality products, delivered and sold with premium service. We are proud of our heritage and are boldly addressing the future needs of our customers with improved efficiency, creating products and services from hand tools to data and management systems. Contact us today for discussion.

BACKGROUND: IFA MEMBER

Established: 1920;	1st Franchised: 1991
Franchised Units:	4490
Company-Owned Units:	<u>51</u>
Total Units:	4541
Dist.:	US-3622; CAN-357; O'seas-814
North America: 50 States, 12 Provinces	
Density:	245 in TX, 202 in PA, 373 in CA
Projected New Units (12 Months):	682
Qualifications:	3, 4, 2, 2, 5, 5

FINANCIAL/TERMS:

Cash Investment:	$16.7-52K
Total Investment:	$16.7-278.4K
Minimum Net Worth:	NR
Fees: Franchise -	$5K
Royalty - $50/Mo.;	Ad. - 0%
Earnings Claims Statement:	Yes
Term of Contract (Years):	10/5

Avg. # Of Employees:	1 FT, 0 PT
Passive Ownership:	Not Allowed
Encourage Conversions:	Yes
Area Develop. Agreements:	No
Sub-Franchising Contracts:	No
Expand In Territory:	Yes
Space Needs:	NR

SUPPORT & TRAINING:

Financial Assistance Provided:	Yes (D)
Site Selection Assistance:	NA
Lease Negotiation Assistance:	NA
Co-Operative Advertising:	No
Franchisee Assoc./Member:	No
Size Of Corporate Staff:	NR
On-Going Support:	A,B,C,D,E,F,G,h,I
Training: 1 Week Branch or Regional Office; 1 Week Branch; 3 Week On-the-Job	

SPECIFIC EXPANSION PLANS:

US:	All United States
Canada:	All Canada
Overseas: Japan, UK, Germany, Australia, New Zealand, S. Africa	

≪ ≫

STORK NEWS OF AMERICA

1305 Hope Mills Rd., # A
Fayetteville, NC 28304
Tel: (800) 633-6395 (910) 426-1357
Fax: (910) 426-2473
E-Mail: no2stork@earthlink.net
Web Site: www.storknews.com
Mr. John M. Young, VP Franchise Development

The number one and the original newborn yard display business. New mothers, fathers, grandmothers and grandfathers, or any family relations want to tell the world about their new arrival. Rated in many publications as the best buy in home-operated businesses. Almost all operators are Mom's and some Mr. Mom's that don't want to have to ship their kids to day care and then go to work. With a STORK NEWS franchise, kids can go along to work, too.

BACKGROUND:

Established: 1983;	1st Franchised: 1986
Franchised Units:	141
Company-Owned Units:	<u>1</u>
Total Units:	142
Dist.:	US-140; CAN-1; O'seas-1
North America: 33 States, 1 Provinces	
Density:	14 in VA, 12 in FL, 11 in CA
Projected New Units (12 Months):	12
Qualifications:	1, 4, 1, 1, 3, 5

FINANCIAL/TERMS:

Cash Investment:	$8-20K
Total Investment:	$14K
Minimum Net Worth:	NA
Fees: Franchise -	$7-10K
Royalty - $0.50-1K;	Ad. - NA
Earnings Claims Statement:	No
Term of Contract (Years):	Perpetual/
Avg. # Of Employees:	1 FT, 0 PT
Passive Ownership:	Allowed
Encourage Conversions:	NA
Area Develop. Agreements:	No
Sub-Franchising Contracts:	No
Expand In Territory:	Yes
Space Needs:	NA

SUPPORT & TRAINING:

Financial Assistance Provided:	No
Site Selection Assistance:	No
Lease Negotiation Assistance:	No
Co-Operative Advertising:	No
Franchisee Assoc./Member:	No
Size Of Corporate Staff:	10
On-Going Support:	,,D,,F,G,,I
Training:	Manual

SPECIFIC EXPANSION PLANS:

US:	All United States
Canada:	All Canada
Overseas:	NR

≪ ≫

STREET CORNER

2945 S.W. Wanamaker Dr.
Topeka, KS 66614
Tel: (800) 789-NEWS (785) 272-8529 + 103
Fax: (785) 272-2384
E-Mail: timothy@streetcorner.com
Web Site: www.streetcorner.com
Mr. Tim Leffert, Sales

STREET CORNER is the "Convenience Store in the Mall," offering the things that mall employees and mall patrons want during their shopping experiences: aspirin, fountain and bottled drinks, coffee and tea and newspapers, lottery, snacks, candy and gun, fax and copy services, cigarettes and cigars, souvenirs and gifts, office and desk supplies and other incidentals.

BACKGROUND:

Established: 1988;	1st Franchised: 1995
Franchised Units:	54
Company-Owned Units:	<u>0</u>
Total Units:	54

Dist.: US-54; CAN-0; O'seas-0
North America: 27 States, 0 Provinces
Density: 4 in TN, 4 in NY, 8 in NJ
Projected New Units (12 Months): 30
Qualifications: 4, 1, 1, 1, 1, 2

FINANCIAL/TERMS:
Cash Investment: $19.9K
Total Investment: $140-190K
Minimum Net Worth: $150K
Fees: Franchise - $19.9K
  Royalty - 4.5%; Ad. - 0%
Earnings Claims Statement: No
Term of Contract (Years): 7/7
Avg. # Of Employees: 1 FT, 2 PT
Passive Ownership: Allowed
Encourage Conversions: NA
Area Develop. Agreements: Yes/0
Sub-Franchising Contracts: Yes
Expand In Territory: Yes
Space Needs: 150-800 SF

SUPPORT & TRAINING:
Financial Assistance Provided: Yes (D)
Site Selection Assistance: Yes
Lease Negotiation Assistance: Yes
Co-Operative Advertising: No
Franchisee Assoc./Member: No
Size Of Corporate Staff: 8
On-Going Support: A,,C,D,E,F,G,h,I
Training: At least 40 Hours On-Site

SPECIFIC EXPANSION PLANS:
US: All United States
Canada: No
Overseas: NR

◄◄ ►►

TINDER BOX INTERNATIONAL
3 Bala Plz., E., # 102
Bala Cynwyd, PA 19004
Tel: (800) 846-3372 (610) 668-4220
Fax: (610) 668-4266
E-Mail: info@tinderboxinternational.com
Web Site: www.tinderboxinternational.
com
Mr. Wayne Best, President

The world's largest and oldest chain of premium cigar, tobacco, smoking accessory and gift stores, with 70 years' experience as the undisputed industry leader.

BACKGROUND: IFA MEMBER
Established: 1928; 1st Franchised: 1965

Franchised Units: 56
Company-Owned Units: 1
Total Units: 57
Dist.: US-57; CAN-0; O'seas-0
North America: 50 States, 0 Provinces
Density: 9 in OH, 9 in IL, 17 in CA
Projected New Units (12 Months): 25
Qualifications: 5, 3, 1, 2, 4, 5

FINANCIAL/TERMS:
Cash Investment: $90-130K
Total Investment: $240-350K
Minimum Net Worth: $250-300K
Fees: Franchise - $30K
  Royalty - 4-5%; Ad. - 3%
Earnings Claims Statement: No
Term of Contract (Years): 15/5
Avg. # Of Employees: 1-2 FT, 2-3 PT
Passive Ownership: Allowed
Encourage Conversions: Yes
Area Develop. Agreements: Yes/0
Sub-Franchising Contracts: No
Expand In Territory: Yes
Space Needs: 800-1,500 SF

SUPPORT & TRAINING:
Financial Assistance Provided: Yes (D)
Site Selection Assistance: Yes
Lease Negotiation Assistance: Yes
Co-Operative Advertising: No
Franchisee Assoc./Member: No
Size Of Corporate Staff: 10
On-Going Support: a,,C,D,E,F,G,H,I
Training: 5 Days Home Office;
  3-5 Days Franchisee's Store; Within 30
  Days Follow-Up Store Visit

SPECIFIC EXPANSION PLANS:
US: All United States
Canada: All Canada
Overseas: All Countries

◄◄ ►►

WICKS 'N' STICKS
P. O. Box 1965
Cypress, TX 77410-1965
Tel: (888) 873-3714 (713) 856-7442
Fax: (713) 856-8159
E-Mail: pparker@wicksnsticks.com
Web Site: www.wicksnsticks.com
Ms. Patty Parker, Franchise Development

Nation's largest and most respected franchised retailer of quality candles, fragrancing and related home decorative products. Franchisees are offered outstanding name recognition, comprehensive training and extensive start up and on-going support. Rated a top franchise by both Success Gold 200 and Income Opportunities Platinum 2000.

BACKGROUND:
Established: 1968; 1st Franchised: 1968
Franchised Units: 148
Company-Owned Units: 7
Total Units: 155
Dist.: US-155; CAN-0; O'seas-0
North America: 37 States, Provinces
Density: 14 in CA, 13 in FL, 14 in TX
Projected New Units (12 Months): 17
Qualifications: 5, 3, 3, 3, 3, 5

FINANCIAL/TERMS:
Cash Investment: $65K
Total Investment: $198.5-330.72K
Minimum Net Worth: $70K Liquid
Fees: Franchise - $35K
  Royalty - 2.5% (in 2002); Ad. - 0%
Earnings Claims Statement: No
Term of Contract (Years): 5+/
Avg. # Of Employees: 1 FT, 6 PT
Passive Ownership: Not Allowed
Encourage Conversions: NA
Area Develop. Agreements: No
Sub-Franchising Contracts: No
Expand In Territory: Yes
Space Needs: 1,000-1,700 SF

SUPPORT & TRAINING:
Financial Assistance Provided: No
Site Selection Assistance: Yes
Lease Negotiation Assistance: Yes
Co-Operative Advertising: No
Franchisee Assoc./Member: Yes/Yes
Size Of Corporate Staff: 21
On-Going Support: A,,C,D,E,F,G,H,I
Training: 8 Days Corporate Office,
  Houston, TX

SPECIFIC EXPANSION PLANS:
US: All United States
Canada: No
Overseas: NR

◄◄ ►►

WIRELESS ZONE
34 Industrial Park Pl.
Middletown, CT 06457
Tel: (860) 798-4473
Fax: (860) 632-9343
E-Mail: seanf@wirelesszone.com
Web Site: www.wirelesszone.com
Mr. Sean Fitzgerald, National VP Franchise Growth

WIRELESS ZONE stores are primarily retail, with strong emphasis on local ownership, networking and community involvement. Franchise provides local field support staff, centralized advertising and purchasing, initial and on-going training and strong commissions and residual income from Verizon Wireless phones, service, accessories, wireless email, etc. Join a winning team!

BACKGROUND: IFA MEMBER
Established: 1988; 1st Franchised: 1989
Franchised Units: 280
Company-Owned Units: 0
Total Units: 280
Dist.: US-280; CAN-0; O'seas-0
 North America: 13 States, 0 Provinces
 Density: 38 in PA, 23 in NY, 46 in CT
Projected New Units (12 Months): 65
Qualifications: 2, 4, 3, 2, 1, 5
FINANCIAL/TERMS:
Cash Investment: $50-100K
Total Investment: $65.3-193.5K
Minimum Net Worth: NA
Fees: Franchise - $8.5-25K
 Royalty - 10%; Ad. - $800/Mo.
Earnings Claims Statement: No
Term of Contract (Years): 7/7
Avg. # Of Employees: 2 FT, 1 PT
Passive Ownership: Discouraged
Encourage Conversions: Yes
Area Develop. Agreements: No
Sub-Franchising Contracts: Yes
Expand In Territory: Yes
Space Needs: 1,000 SF
SUPPORT & TRAINING:
Financial Assistance Provided: Yes (D)
Site Selection Assistance: Yes
Lease Negotiation Assistance: Yes
Co-Operative Advertising: No

Franchisee Assoc./Member: Yes/Yes
Size Of Corporate Staff: 64
On-Going Support: ,B,C,D,E,,G,H,
Training: 2 Days 3rd Party Trainer New
 Store; Up to 1 Week Executive Trainer
SPECIFIC EXPANSION PLANS:
US: FL and VA to ME
Canada: No
Overseas: NR

◄◄ ►►

YOUR DOLLAR STORE WITH MORE

102 - 1626 Richter St.
Kelowna, BC V1Y 2M3 Canada
Tel: (250) 860-4225
Fax: (250) 860-4215
E-Mail: ydswm@dollarstore.ca
Web Site: www.dollarstore.ca
Mr. Dave Uzelman, President

YOUR DOLLAR STORE WITH MORE targets a wide range of retail customers who are looking to purchase everyday products at a low prices. These customers want to save time and make their shopping dollars go farther. With a franchise that fits in with today's lifestyles, our franchisees are able to sell many $1 items, plus others priced higher, which allows them to create an exciting merchandise mix. We are also the only dollar store franchise in Canada that supports franchisees through a National Advert. Fund.

BACKGROUND:
Established: 1998; 1st Franchised: 1998
Franchised Units: 180

Company-Owned Units: 4
Total Units: 184
Dist.: US-0; CAN-184; O'seas-0
 North America: 11 States, 11 Provinces
 Density: 58 in AB, 62 in BC, 26 in SK
Projected New Units (12 Months): 25
Qualifications: 4, 3, 3, 3, 4, 4
FINANCIAL/TERMS:
Cash Investment: $75-200K
Total Investment: $150-400K
Minimum Net Worth: $100K
Fees: Franchise - $20K
 Royalty - 4%; Ad. - .5%
Earnings Claims Statement: Yes
Term of Contract (Years): 10/10
Avg. # Of Employees: 4 FT, 4 PT
Passive Ownership: Discouraged
Encourage Conversions: Yes
Area Develop. Agreements: Yes/1
Sub-Franchising Contracts: No
Expand In Territory: Yes
Space Needs: 3,000-10,000 SF
SUPPORT & TRAINING:
Financial Assistance Provided: No
Site Selection Assistance: Yes
Lease Negotiation Assistance: Yes
Co-Operative Advertising: No
Franchisee Assoc./Member: Yes/Yes
Size Of Corporate Staff: 15
On-Going Support: ,,C,D,E,,G,H,
Training: 1 Week (5 Business Days
 Franchisee's Store Location
SPECIFIC EXPANSION PLANS:
US: No
Canada: All Canada
Overseas: NR

◄◄ ►►

For a full explanation
of the data provided
in the Franchisor
Profiles, please refer to
*Chapter 2, "How to Use
the Data."*

	THREE LARGEST PARTICIPANTS IN SURVEY					
Company	# Fran-chised Units	# Co-Owned Units	# Total Units	Franchise Fee	On-Going Royalty	Total Investment
1. Sonitrol	178	34	212	$20-50K	2.5%	$250-600K
2. Interquest Detection Canines	38	2	40	$30K	6%	$30-70K
3. Shield Security Systems	10	1	11	$35K	5%	$39.5-66.7K

All of the data provided are proprietary and should not be quoted without acknowledging *Bond's Franchise Guide*.

INTERQUEST DETECTION CANINES

21900 Tomball Pkwy.
Houston, TX 77070-1526
Tel: (800) 481-7768 (281) 320-1231
Fax: (281) 320-2512
E-Mail: mferdi@interquestfranchise.com
Web Site: www.interquestfranchise.com
Mr. Michael P. Ferdinand, VP Franchise Operations

INTERQUEST provides a home-based business opportunity incorporating the use of scent-trained canines to detect the presence of contraband in schools and industry. Limited competition, with great territories available throughout the US.

BACKGROUND: IFA MEMBER
Established: 1988; 1st Franchised: 1999
Franchised Units: 38

Company-Owned Units: 2
Total Units: 40
Dist.: US-40; CAN-0; O'seas-0
  North America: States, Provinces
  Density: 7 in CA, 3 in LA, 8 in TX
Projected New Units (12 Months): 5
Qualifications: 3, 3, 2, 2, 4, 4
FINANCIAL/TERMS:
Cash Investment: $30-50K
Total Investment: $30-70K
Minimum Net Worth: $250K
Fees: Franchise - $30K
  Royalty - 6%; Ad. - 1%
Earnings Claims Statement: No
Term of Contract (Years): 10/10
Avg. # Of Employees: 1-3 FT, 0 PT
Passive Ownership: Discouraged
Encourage Conversions: NA
Area Develop. Agreements: No
Sub-Franchising Contracts: No
Expand In Territory: Yes

Space Needs: NA
SUPPORT & TRAINING:
Financial Assistance Provided: Yes (D)
Site Selection Assistance: Yes
Lease Negotiation Assistance: NA
Co-Operative Advertising: No
Franchisee Assoc./Member: No
Size Of Corporate Staff: 10
On-Going Support: a,b,C,d,,,G,h,I
Training: 2 Weeks Houston, TX
SPECIFIC EXPANSION PLANS:
US: Southeast, Northeast
Canada: No
Overseas: NR

◄◄ ►►

SHIELD SECURITY SYSTEMS
1690 Walden Ave.
Buffalo, NY 14225
Tel: (800) 474-4353 (866) 430-5878
Fax: (716) 636-8819
E-Mail: franchise@shieldsecurity.net
Web Site: www.shieldsecurity.net
Ms. Mary Jezioro, VP

Use your entrepreneurial skills to develop wealth and a secure future with recurring revenue and triple income streams from long term customers. Operate from your office or home with low inventory requirements, low overhead and high margins. Excellent opportunity for women and minorities. Serious, positive, motivated individuals only, please.

BACKGROUND:
Established: 1976;	1st Franchised: 2002
Franchised Units:	10
Company-Owned Units:	1
Total Units:	11
Dist.:	US-11; CAN-0; O'seas-0
North America:	0 States, 0 Provinces
Density:	3 in TX, 3 in GA, 2 in FL
Projected New Units (12 Months):	NR
Qualifications:	3, 3, 3, 3, 3, 3

FINANCIAL/TERMS:
Cash Investment:	$39.5-66.7K
Total Investment:	$39.5-66.7K
Minimum Net Worth:	$250K
Fees: Franchise -	$35K
Royalty - 5%;	Ad. - 2%
Earnings Claims Statement:	No
Term of Contract (Years):	10/10
Avg. # Of Employees:	1 FT, 3-4 PT
Passive Ownership:	Discouraged
Encourage Conversions:	NA
Area Develop. Agreements:	No
Sub-Franchising Contracts:	No
Expand In Territory:	Yes
Space Needs:	NA

SUPPORT & TRAINING:
Financial Assistance Provided:	No
Site Selection Assistance:	Yes
Lease Negotiation Assistance:	NA
Co-Operative Advertising:	No
Franchisee Assoc./Member:	No
Size Of Corporate Staff:	5
On-Going Support:	A,B,C,D,E,F,,H,I
Training:	3-4 Days Buffalo, NY

SPECIFIC EXPANSION PLANS:
US:	TX, MI, GA, FL, NJ, PA
Canada:	No
Overseas:	NR

SONITROL
211 N. Union, # 350
Alexandria, VA 22314-2643
Tel: (800) 328-5607 (703) 684-6606
Fax: (703) 684-6612
E-Mail: ccobb@sonitrol.com
Web Site: www.sonitrol.com
Mr. Todd Leggett, VP Business Development

SONITROL offers a broad line of security systems to commercial and residential subscribers. A majority of SONITROL products are sold to businesses which have typically been in operations for over a year. The signature system is based on a sound activated audio. This process allows for verification of alarms and has resulted in the apprehension of over 135,000 criminals.

BACKGROUND:
	IFA MEMBER
Established: 1964;	1st Franchised: 1965
Franchised Units:	178
Company-Owned Units:	34
Total Units:	212
Dist.:	US-209; CAN-1; O'seas-2
North America:	41 States, 0 Provinces
Density:	11 in NY, 14 in FL, 24 in CA
Projected New Units (12 Months):	3
Qualifications:	4, 5, 3, 2, 5, 4

FINANCIAL/TERMS:
Cash Investment:	$100-200K
Total Investment:	$250-600K
Minimum Net Worth:	$250K
Fees: Franchise -	$20-50K
Royalty - 2.5%;	Ad. - NA
Earnings Claims Statement:	No
Term of Contract (Years):	10/10
Avg. # Of Employees:	Varies
Passive Ownership:	Not Allowed
Encourage Conversions:	NA
Area Develop. Agreements:	No
Sub-Franchising Contracts:	No
Expand In Territory:	No
Space Needs:	NR

SUPPORT & TRAINING:
Financial Assistance Provided:	NR
Site Selection Assistance:	NA
Lease Negotiation Assistance:	No
Co-Operative Advertising:	No
Franchisee Assoc./Member:	Yes/Yes
Size Of Corporate Staff:	11
On-Going Support:	,,C,d,E,,G,h,I
Training:	Business Training On-Site;
	1 Week Technical Training in Orlando;
	1 Week Sales Tr. in Dallas

SPECIFIC EXPANSION PLANS:
US:	All United States
Canada:	No
Overseas:	NR

FIVE LARGEST PARTICIPANTS IN SURVEY						
Company	# Fran-chised Units	# Co-Owned Units	# Total Units	Franchise Fee	On-Going Royalty	Total Investment
1. UPS Store, The	5,982	0	5,982	$29,950	5%	$170.8-279.4K
2. Instant Tax Service	1,706	12	1,718	$34K		$39-89K
3. Merry Maids	1,256	194	1,454	$21-29K	5-7%	$24-57K
4. Maids Home Services, The	1,027	26	1,053	$10K + $.95 per QHH	3.9-6.9%	$175-225K
5. PostNet	850	0	850	$30K	5%	$174-196K

All of the data provided are proprietary and should not be quoted without acknowledging *Bond's Franchise Guide.*

1-800-DRYCLEAN
3948 Ranchero Dr.
Ann Arbor, MI 48108-2775
Tel: (866) 822-6115 (734) 822-6340
Fax: (734) 822-6666
E-Mail: tburns@1-800-dryclean.com
Web Site: www.1-800-dryclean.com
Mr./Ms. T. Burns, Licensing Coordinator

The $10 billion dry cleaning industry creates tremendous potential for 1-800-DRY-CLEAN when combined with the need of busy consumers looking for convenience. Our convenient, hassle-free dry cleaning pick-up and delivery system provides consumers exceptional dry cleaning and laundry service. Business formats include the single van opportunity, the multiple van fleet option and expansion of van opportunities to either the dry cleaning plant or drop store format.

BACKGROUND: IFA MEMBER
Established: 2000;   1st Franchised: 2000
Franchised Units: 109
Company-Owned Units: 0
Total Units: 109
Dist.:   US-109; CAN-0; O'seas-0
   North America: 23 States, 0 Provinces

Density: 4 in TX, 5 in IL, 16 in CA
Projected New Units (12 Months):   25
Qualifications: 4, 3, 1, 2, 1, 5
FINANCIAL/TERMS:
Cash Investment: $42.4K-$64.4K
Total Investment: $60K-$100K
Minimum Net Worth: $100K
Fees: Franchise - $15K
   Royalty - 7%;   Ad. - 1%
Earnings Claims Statement: Yes
Term of Contract (Years):   10/10
Avg. # Of Employees: 0 FT, 1 PT
Passive Ownership: Discouraged
Encourage Conversions: Yes
Area Develop. Agreements: No
Sub-Franchising Contracts: No

Expand In Territory: Yes
Space Needs: 200 SF
SUPPORT & TRAINING:
Financial Assistance Provided: No
Site Selection Assistance: Yes
Lease Negotiation Assistance: Yes
Co-Operative Advertising: No
Franchisee Assoc./Member: No
Size Of Corporate Staff: 10
On-Going Support: „C,D,E,,G,h,I
Training: 5 Days Franchise Location;
    5 Days Home Office; 4-6 Weeks
    Right-Start Program
SPECIFIC EXPANSION PLANS:
US: All United States
Canada: All Canada
Overseas: NR

≪ ≫

1-800-GOT-JUNK?
1055 W. Hastings St., 6th Fl.
Vancouver, BC V6E 2E9 Canada
Tel: (866) 920-5865 (800) 468-5865
Fax: (801) 751-0634
E-Mail: franopps@1800gotjunk.com
Web Site: www.1800gotjunk.com
Ms. Colleen Ryan, Franchise Recruitment
    Manager

1-800-GOT-JUNK? has revolutionized customer service in junk removal for over 10 years. By setting the mark for service standards and professionalism, an industry that once operated without set rates, price lists or receipts, now has top service standards. You will have the expert advice and support that is key to success. Our intensive training program will get you on track; our on-going support and continuing education will keep you there. Centralized call center allows you to focus on your business.

BACKGROUND: IFA MEMBER
Established: 1989; 1st Franchised: 1999
Franchised Units: 300
Company-Owned Units: 0
Total Units: 300
Dist.: US-236; CAN-36; O'seas-4
North America: 44 States, 9 Provinces
Density: 13 in NY, 20 in FL, 45 in CA
Projected New Units (12 Months): 100
Qualifications: 5, 5, 1, 2, 4, 5
FINANCIAL/TERMS:
Cash Investment: $70-100K
Total Investment: $90-300K

Minimum Net Worth: $150K
Fees: Franchise - $16K
    Royalty - 8%; Ad. - 1%
Earnings Claims Statement: Yes
Term of Contract (Years): 5/15
Avg. # Of Employees: 6 FT, 4 PT
Passive Ownership: Discouraged
Encourage Conversions: No
Area Develop. Agreements: No
Sub-Franchising Contracts: No
Expand In Territory: Yes
Space Needs: 350 SF
SUPPORT & TRAINING:
Financial Assistance Provided: Yes (D)
Site Selection Assistance: NA
Lease Negotiation Assistance: NA
Co-Operative Advertising: Yes
Franchisee Assoc./Member: Yes/Yes
Size Of Corporate Staff: 100
On-Going Support: a,B,C,D,,,G,H,I
Training: 5-10 Days Vancouver, BC; 3-5
    Days Assigned Territory
SPECIFIC EXPANSION PLANS:
US: All United States
Canada: Yes
Overseas: NR

≪ ≫

AIM MAIL CENTERS
15550-D Rockfield Blvd.
Irvine, CA 92618
Tel: (800) 669-4246 (949) 837-4151
Fax: (949) 837-4537
E-Mail: ssawitz@aimmailcenters.com
Web Site: www.aimmailcenters.com
Mr. Steve Sawitz, Franchise Development

AIM Mail Centers, based in Irvine, California, has developed a unique and AIM-azing opportunity designed especially for motivated professionals. AIM Mail Centers are complete postal and business service centers, offering a wide array of products and services to small business and the general customer. This includes shipping services with UPS, FEDEx and the US Postal Service. We provide packaging, stamps, faxing, notary, mailbox rentals, photocopies, office supplies and much much more. INDUSTRY OPPORTUNITY: The homebased business market is growing at a remarkable rate. Growing from a base

of 6 million home offices in 1980, more than one in four U.S. workers in 28 million households is now regularly working at home at least part of the week. For the past five years at a rate of one every 35 seconds, someone has begun a full or part time business in their home. With this, as well as residential and business customers, the demand for postal and business services continues to boom.

BACKGROUND: IFA MEMBER
Established: 1985; 1st Franchised: 1989
Franchised Units: 97
Company-Owned Units: 0
Total Units: 97
Dist.: US-97; CAN-0; O'seas-0
North America: 22 States, 0 Provinces
Density:
Projected New Units (12 Months): 15
Qualifications: 5, 1, 1, 3, 5, 5
FINANCIAL/TERMS:
Cash Investment: $5K
Total Investment: $160-210K (includes working capital)
Minimum Net Worth: $250K+
Fees: Franchise - $26.9K
    Royalty - 5%; Ad. - 2%
Earnings Claims Statement: Yes
Term of Contract (Years): 15/5
Avg. # Of Employees: 1 FT, 2 PT
Passive Ownership: Discouraged
Encourage Conversions: Yes
Area Develop. Agreements: No
Sub-Franchising Contracts: No
Expand In Territory: Yes
Space Needs: 800-1,200 SF
SUPPORT & TRAINING:
Financial Assistance Provided: Yes (I)
Site Selection Assistance: Yes
Lease Negotiation Assistance: Yes
Co-Operative Advertising: Yes
Franchisee Assoc./Member: Yes/Yes
Size Of Corporate Staff: 14
On-Going Support: „C,D,E,F,G,H,I
Training: 2 Weeks AIM National Support
    Center - Irvine, CA; 5 Days In Store;
    24 hour phone support/Store Visits
SPECIFIC EXPANSION PLANS:
US: All United States
Canada: No
Overseas: NR

≪ ≫

AIR BROOK LIMOUSINE
P. O. Box 123
Rochelle Park, NJ 07662
Tel: (201) 368-3974

Fax: (201) 368-2247
E-Mail: airbrook@erols.com
Web Site: www.airbrook.com
Mr. Jim Dziekonski, Franchise Director

Limousine Service / Ground Transportation.

BACKGROUND:
Established: 1969; 1st Franchised: 1971
Franchised Units: 73
Company-Owned Units: 0
Total Units: 73
Dist.: US-73; CAN-0; O'seas-0
North America: 1 States, Provinces
Density: 73 in NJ,
Projected New Units (12 Months): 10
Qualifications: 2, 2, 2, 2, 3, 4
FINANCIAL/TERMS:
Cash Investment: $5.5-11K
Total Investment: $10.5-20K
Minimum Net Worth: NA
Fees: Franchise - $7.5-12.5K
Royalty - 35%; Ad. - 0%
Earnings Claims Statement: No
Term of Contract (Years): 10/2
Avg. # Of Employees: 2 FT, 0 PT
Passive Ownership: Not Allowed
Encourage Conversions: NA
Area Develop. Agreements: No
Sub-Franchising Contracts: No
Expand In Territory: Yes
Space Needs: NA
SUPPORT & TRAINING:
Financial Assistance Provided: Yes (D)
Site Selection Assistance: NA
Lease Negotiation Assistance: NA
Co-Operative Advertising: No
Franchisee Assoc./Member: No
Size Of Corporate Staff: 112
On-Going Support: A,B,C,D,,,G,H,I
Training: 5 Days Rochelle Park, NJ
SPECIFIC EXPANSION PLANS:
US: NJ Only
Canada: No
Overseas: NR

⫷⫸

AIT FREIGHT SYSTEMS
P. O. Box 66730
Chicago, IL 60666
Tel: (800) 323-6649 + 405 (630) 766-8300
Fax: (630) 775-1410
E-Mail: pstrompolis@aitworldwide.com
Web Site: www.aitworldwide.com
Mr. Paul Strompolis, Corporate Development

Freight forwarder - international and domestic.

BACKGROUND:
Established: 1979; 1st Franchised: 1988
Franchised Units: 17
Company-Owned Units: 10
Total Units: 27
Dist.: US-27; CAN-0; O'seas-0
North America: 16 States, Provinces
Density: 1 in IL, 2 in NC, 2 in TX
Projected New Units (12 Months): 2
Qualifications: 4, 5, 5, 3, 4, 4
FINANCIAL/TERMS:
Cash Investment: $25-50K
Total Investment: $46K
Minimum Net Worth: $46K
Fees: Franchise - $13K
Royalty - 12.8%; Ad. - 1%
Earnings Claims Statement: Yes
Term of Contract (Years): 20/10
Avg. # Of Employees: 5 FT, 0 PT
Passive Ownership: Discouraged
Encourage Conversions: No
Area Develop. Agreements: Yes/1
Sub-Franchising Contracts: No
Expand In Territory: No
Space Needs: 10,000 SF
SUPPORT & TRAINING:
Financial Assistance Provided: Yes (D)
Site Selection Assistance: Yes
Lease Negotiation Assistance: No
Co-Operative Advertising: No
Franchisee Assoc./Member: No
Size Of Corporate Staff: 35
On-Going Support: A,,,D,E,,,,I
Training: 2 Days Chicago, IL
SPECIFIC EXPANSION PLANS:
US: Southwest, Northeast
Canada: All Canada
Overseas: NR

⫷⫸

**AMERICARE RESTROOM
HYGIENE & SUPPLY**
225 Laura Dr., # A
Addison, IL 60101
Tel: (800) 745-6191 (630) 458-1990
Fax: (630) 458-1994
E-Mail: richard@americarehygiene.com
Web Site: www.americarehygiene.com
Mr. Richard F. Gac, President

Aroma enhancement plus infection control systems for retail, commercial and industrial manufacturing, specializing in full line of high profit products and services for germ killing, restroom supplies and maintenance. Also, interior non-toxic power washing of kitchens, restrooms, delis, coolers, food prep areas, etc. to eliminate cross contamination of infectious diseases. Plus, exterior, environmentally-friendly high-heat power washing of sidewalks, grease pits and dumpster areas.

BACKGROUND:
Established: 1990; 1st Franchised: 1993
Franchised Units: 30
Company-Owned Units: 10
Total Units: 40
Dist.: US-40; CAN-0; O'seas-0
North America: 3 States, 0 Provinces
Density: 2 in WI, 3 in IN, 36 in IL
Projected New Units (12 Months): 12
Qualifications: 3, 2, 1, 2, 3, 5
FINANCIAL/TERMS:
Cash Investment: $2.5-9.5K
Total Investment: $9.5-95K
Minimum Net Worth: $50K
Fees: Franchise - $9.5K
Royalty - 8-13%; Ad. - 2%
Earnings Claims Statement: No
Term of Contract (Years): 10/10
Avg. # Of Employees: 1 FT, 0 PT
Passive Ownership: Not Allowed
Encourage Conversions: NA
Area Develop. Agreements: Yes/1
Sub-Franchising Contracts: Yes
Expand In Territory: Yes
Space Needs: NA
SUPPORT & TRAINING:
Financial Assistance Provided: Yes (D)
Site Selection Assistance: Yes
Lease Negotiation Assistance: NA
Co-Operative Advertising: No
Franchisee Assoc./Member: No
Size Of Corporate Staff: 10
On-Going Support: A,B,C,D,E,F,G,H,I
Training: 2 Weeks Addison, IL
SPECIFIC EXPANSION PLANS:
US: IL, IN, MI, WI
Canada: No
Overseas: NR

⫷⫸

Hottest New Franchise

CARING TRANSITIONS
Caring Transitions — Senior Moving • Downsizing • Estate Sales
10700 Montgomery Rd.
Cincinnati, OH 45242
Tel: (800) 647-0766 (513) 587-4988
Fax: (513) 563-2691
E-Mail: webinquiry@caringtransitions.net
Web Site: www.caringtransitions.net
Ms. Amber Kershaw, Sales Support Man-

ager

Ranked "Top 50 New Franchises" by Entrepreneur, 2009, this is a rewarding, home-based business helping Seniors and their families transition from their homes to retirement communities. You'll work with bank trustees, Realtors®, moving companies and other professionals to help ease relocation. Five days of extensive, on-site training on operating and growing a successful business. With six revenue streams and the Senior population expected to double by 2030, this is the next big wave in Senior Care.

BACKGROUND: IFA MEMBER
Established: 2006; 1st Franchised: 2006
Franchised Units: 40
Company-Owned Units: 0
Total Units: 40
Dist.: US-40; CAN-0; O'seas-0
  North America: 24 States, 0 Provinces
  Density: 3 in FL, 3 in OH, 4 in VA
Projected New Units (12 Months): 30
Qualifications: 3, 3, 1, 2, 3, 4
FINANCIAL/TERMS:
Cash Investment: $18.9K
Total Investment: $36.7K-64.4K
Minimum Net Worth: $20K
Fees: Franchise - $27.9K
  Royalty - 6% or $300; Ad. - $150/month
Earnings Claims Statement: Yes
Term of Contract (Years): 10/10
Avg. # Of Employees: 1 FT, 1 PT
Passive Ownership: Allowed
Encourage Conversions: NA
Area Develop. Agreements: No
Sub-Franchising Contracts: No
Expand In Territory: No
Space Needs: NA
SUPPORT & TRAINING:
Financial Assistance Provided: Yes (I)
Site Selection Assistance: NA
Lease Negotiation Assistance: NA
Co-Operative Advertising: Yes
Franchisee Assoc./Member: No
Size Of Corporate Staff: 50
On-Going Support: ,,C,D,,,,H,I
Training: 5 Business Days Cincinnati, OH
SPECIFIC EXPANSION PLANS:
US: All U.S.
Canada: All Canada
Overseas: All Countries

◄◄ ►►

CASH PLUS

3002 Dow Ave., # 120
Tustin, CA 92780-7233

Tel: (888) 707-2274 (714) 731-2274
Fax: (714) 731-2099
E-Mail: bblomstrom@cashplusinc.com
Web Site: www.cashplusinc.com
Ms. Brooke Blomstrom, Director of Franchise Development

We are meeting America's changing financial needs with tasteful, attractive retail stores that have proven to be appealing to customers across the socioeconomic spectrum. Our unique style shows genuine care for our customers - this is good for business. A powerful marketing program is designed to be cost-effective and offers support from major retailers. Shorter hours, fewer employees, computer management systems and training - it's all here for you.

BACKGROUND: IFA MEMBER
Established: 1985; 1st Franchised: 1988
Franchised Units: 85
Company-Owned Units: 2
Total Units: 87
Dist.: US-86; CAN-1; O'seas-0
  North America: 8 States, 1 Provinces
  Density: 5 in FL, 7 in OH, 46 in CA
Projected New Units (12 Months): 30
Qualifications: 4, 5, 1, 3, 4, 5
FINANCIAL/TERMS:
Cash Investment: $50-100K
Total Investment: $124-204K
Minimum Net Worth: $200K
Fees: Franchise - $22.5K
  Royalty - 6%; Ad. - 3%
Earnings Claims Statement: Yes
Term of Contract (Years): 10/5/5
Avg. # Of Employees: 2 FT, 2 PT
Passive Ownership: Allowed
Encourage Conversions: Yes
Area Develop. Agreements: Yes/5
Sub-Franchising Contracts: No
Expand In Territory: Yes
Space Needs: 1,000-1,200 SF
SUPPORT & TRAINING:
Financial Assistance Provided: Yes (D)
Site Selection Assistance: Yes
Lease Negotiation Assistance: Yes
Co-Operative Advertising: No
Franchisee Assoc./Member: Yes/Yes
Size Of Corporate Staff: 9
On-Going Support: 0,b,C,D,E,F,G,h,i
Training: 1 Week Franchisee Store;
  1 Week Tustin, CA
SPECIFIC EXPANSION PLANS:
US: West,SW,NW,Midwest,SE
Canada: No
Overseas: NR

◄◄ ►►

CHECKCARE SYSTEMS

8900 Greenway Commons Pl., # 200
Louisville, KY 40220
Tel: (800) 673-2435 (502) 719--295
Fax: (502) 719-0300
E-Mail: joe_caruso@checkcare.com
Web Site: www.checkcare.com
Mr. Joseph E. Caruso, President

CHECKCARE SYSTEMS is the fastest-growing check guarantee and verification company in the U.S. Proprietary software and hardware configuration included in total investment. Our national account base makes this opportunity a 'must investigate.'

BACKGROUND: IFA MEMBER
Established: 1982; 1st Franchised: 1984
Franchised Units: 42
Company-Owned Units: 0
Total Units: 42
Dist.: US-42; CAN-0; O'seas-0
  North America: 22 States, 0 Provinces
  Density: 5 in TX, 7 in GA, 6 in FL
Projected New Units (12 Months): 3
Qualifications: 4, 3, 2, 3, 3, 3
FINANCIAL/TERMS:
Cash Investment: $65-85K
Total Investment: $110-169K
Minimum Net Worth: $100K
Fees: Franchise - $12.5-45K
  Royalty - 5%; Ad. - 0.5%
Earnings Claims Statement: Yes
Term of Contract (Years): 7/7
Avg. # Of Employees: 13 FT, 2 PT
Passive Ownership: Discouraged
Encourage Conversions: Yes
Area Develop. Agreements: Yes/1
Sub-Franchising Contracts: No
Expand In Territory: No
Space Needs: 2,000 SF
SUPPORT & TRAINING:
Financial Assistance Provided: Yes (D)
Site Selection Assistance: Yes
Lease Negotiation Assistance: No
Co-Operative Advertising: No
Franchisee Assoc./Member: Yes/Yes
Size Of Corporate Staff: 20
On-Going Support: ,b,c,d,e,f,G,h,
Training: 2 Weeks Columbus, GA
SPECIFIC EXPANSION PLANS:
US: West Coast,Northeast
Canada: All Canada
Overseas: NR

◄◄ ►►

COLOR-GLO INTERNATIONAL

7111-7115 Ohms Ln.
Minneapolis, MN 55439-2158
Tel: (800) 333-8523 (952) 835-1338
Fax: (952) 835-1395
E-Mail: cgiinc@aol.com
Web Site: www.color-glo.com
Mr. Scott L. Smith, VP Franchise Sales

The leader in the leather and fabric restoration and repair industry. From automotive to marine to aircraft to all-leather furniture, COLOR-GLO leads the way with innovative products and protected application techniques. We serve all US and foreign car manufacturers.

BACKGROUND: IFA MEMBER
Established: 1976;   1st Franchised: 1984
Franchised Units: 112
Company-Owned Units: 0
Total Units: 112
Dist.:   US-112; CAN-1; O'seas-21
  North America: 0 States, 0 Provinces
  Density: 12 in OR, 15 in FL, 10 in CA
Projected New Units (12 Months):   50
Qualifications: 4, 4, 3, 4, 3, 3
FINANCIAL/TERMS:
Cash Investment: $39.5K
Total Investment: $41K-44.8K
Minimum Net Worth: $20K
Fees: Franchise - $7.5K
  Royalty - 2-4%;   Ad. - 0%
Earnings Claims Statement: Yes
Term of Contract (Years):   10/5
Avg. # Of Employees: 1 FT, 0 PT
Passive Ownership: Allowed
Encourage Conversions: NA
Area Develop. Agreements: Yes/1
Sub-Franchising Contracts: Yes
Expand In Territory: Yes
Space Needs: NA
SUPPORT & TRAINING:
Financial Assistance Provided: Yes (D)
Site Selection Assistance: NA
Lease Negotiation Assistance: NA
Co-Operative Advertising: No
Franchisee Assoc./Member: Yes/Yes
Size Of Corporate Staff: 20
On-Going Support: ,B,C,D,,,G,H,I
Training: 2 Weeks On-Location
SPECIFIC EXPANSION PLANS:
US: All United States
Canada: All Canada
Overseas: All Countries

◄◄   ►►

COMET ONE-HOUR CLEANERS

406 W. Division St.
Arlington, TX 76011
Tel: (817) 461-3555
Fax: (817) 861-4779
E-Mail: cometgodfrey@msn.com
Web Site: www.cometcleaners.com
Mr. Jack D. Godfrey, Jr., President

We offer a turn-key opportunity in the laundry and dry-cleaning business. Site evaluation, complete training and installation are just a few of the services that COMET offers. There is a franchise fee of $250 per month required, as opposed to other franchisors that require a percent of your gross income per year.

BACKGROUND:
Established: 1960;   1st Franchised: 1967
Franchised Units: 330
Company-Owned Units: 11
Total Units: 341
Dist.:   US-332; CAN-0; O'seas-9
  North America: 15 States, 0 Provinces
  Density: 206 in TX, 17 in IN, 30 in AR
Projected New Units (12 Months):   20
Qualifications: 4, 4, 1, 3, 3, 4
FINANCIAL/TERMS:
Cash Investment: $80-100K
Total Investment: $200-400K
Minimum Net Worth: $80K
Fees: Franchise - $25K
  Royalty - 0%;   Ad. - NA
Earnings Claims Statement: No
Term of Contract (Years):   5/5/5/
Avg. # Of Employees: 6 FT, 2-3 PT
Passive Ownership: Discouraged
Encourage Conversions: No
Area Develop. Agreements: No
Sub-Franchising Contracts: No
Expand In Territory: Yes
Space Needs: 1,800-2,000 SF
SUPPORT & TRAINING:
Financial Assistance Provided: Yes (D)
Site Selection Assistance: Yes
Lease Negotiation Assistance: Yes
Co-Operative Advertising: No
Franchisee Assoc./Member: Yes/Yes
Size Of Corporate Staff: 12
On-Going Support: ,,c,D,E,,G,H,I
Training: 1 Week Waco, TX; 1 Week Store
SPECIFIC EXPANSION PLANS:
US: All United States
Canada: No
Overseas: NR

◄◄   ►►

CRATERS & FREIGHTERS

331 Corporate Cir., # J
Golden, CO 80401
Tel: (800) 949-9931 (303) 399-8190
Fax: (303) 399-9964
E-Mail: bob@cratersandfreighters.com
Web Site: www.cratersandfreighters.com
Mr. Bob Molnar, COO

Craters & Freighters is the leader in specialty freight solutions, providing expert packaging, crating and shipping services from its network of locations nationwide. Unique to the transportation industry, Craters & Freighters builds customized shipping containers and wood crates engineered to ensure valuable shipments arrive safe, damage-free and on-time.

BACKGROUND: IFA MEMBER
Established: 1990;   1st Franchised: 1991
Franchised Units: 65
Company-Owned Units: 0
Total Units: 65
Dist.:   US-65; CAN-0; O'seas-0
  North America: 30 States, 0 Provinces
  Density: 5 in TX, 6 in FL, 6 in CA
Projected New Units (12 Months):   14
Qualifications: 5, 4, 2, 4, 3, 5
FINANCIAL/TERMS:
Cash Investment: NR
Total Investment: $90-130K
Minimum Net Worth: $150K
Fees: Franchise - $27K
  Royalty - 5%;   Ad. - 1%
Earnings Claims Statement: No
Term of Contract (Years):   15/15
Avg. # Of Employees: 4 FT, 0 PT
Passive Ownership: Discouraged
Encourage Conversions: NA
Area Develop. Agreements: No
Sub-Franchising Contracts: No
Expand In Territory: Yes
Space Needs: 3,000-5,000 SF
SUPPORT & TRAINING:
Financial Assistance Provided: No
Site Selection Assistance: Yes
Lease Negotiation Assistance: Yes
Co-Operative Advertising: Yes
Franchisee Assoc./Member: Yes/Yes
Size Of Corporate Staff: 10
On-Going Support: A,B,C,D,E,,G,h,I
Training: 10 Days Home Office in
  Golden, CO
SPECIFIC EXPANSION PLANS:

US: All United States
Canada: All Canada
Overseas: All Countries

‹‹ ››

DR. VINYL AND ASSOCIATES

201 N. W. Victoria Dr.
Lee's Summit, MO 64086-9381
Tel: (800) 531-6600 (816) 525-6060
Fax: (816) 525-6333
E-Mail: tbuckley@drvinyl.com
Web Site: www.drvinyl.com
Mr. Tom Buckley, Jr., Franchise Devel.
   Director

DR. VINYL is consistently ranked among the best in its industry by national, independent surveys. Not only do we provide top quality vinyl, leather, fabric, hard plastic, windshield and vinyl siding repair, but we offer extensive training, on-going support, research and development of new products and techniques, a national advertising program and more. Customize your business to suit the local market, add paint touch-up, upholstery, paintless dent removal.

BACKGROUND: IFA MEMBER
Established: 1972; 1st Franchised: 1981
Franchised Units: 289
Company-Owned Units: 5
Total Units: 294
Dist.: US-232; CAN-0; O'seas-62
   North America: 50 States, 0 Provinces
   Density: 15 in NC, 25 in MO, 17 in IL
Projected New Units (12 Months): 30
Qualifications: 3, 5, 2, 3, 3, 5
FINANCIAL/TERMS:
Cash Investment: $15-20K
Total Investment: $49-76.5K
Minimum Net Worth: $50K
Fees: Franchise - $34.9K
   Royalty - 7%; Ad. - 1%
Earnings Claims Statement: No
Term of Contract (Years): 10/10
Avg. # Of Employees: 11 FT, 0 PT
Passive Ownership: Not Allowed
Encourage Conversions: NA
Area Develop. Agreements: Yes/1
Sub-Franchising Contracts: No
Expand In Territory: Yes
Space Needs: NA

SUPPORT & TRAINING:
Financial Assistance Provided: Yes (D)
Site Selection Assistance: NA
Lease Negotiation Assistance: NA
Co-Operative Advertising: Yes
Franchisee Assoc./Member: No
Size Of Corporate Staff: 14
On-Going Support: ,,C,D,,,G,H,I
Training: 1 Week Franchisee's Location;
   2 Weeks Lee's Summit, MO
SPECIFIC EXPANSION PLANS:
US: All United States
Canada: All Canada
Overseas: All Countries

‹‹ ››

DRY CLEANING STATION

8301 Golden Valley Rd., # 230
Minneapolis, MN 55427
Tel: (800) 655-8134 (763) 541-0832
Fax: (763) 542-2246
E-Mail: johnca@franchisemasters.com
Web Site: www.drycleaningstation.com
Mr. John A. Campbell, Chief Executive
   Officer

A high-quality, lower priced dry cleaner and shirt laundry, offering a special niche in the industry, including environmentally efficient equipment, proprietary unique software/computer systems and attractively designed, high-traffic stores.

BACKGROUND:
Established: 1987; 1st Franchised: 1993
Franchised Units: 48
Company-Owned Units: 0
Total Units: 48
Dist.: US-48; CAN-0; O'seas-0
   North America: 7 States, 0 Provinces
   Density: 4 in NE, 5 in MN
Projected New Units (12 Months): 50
Qualifications: 5, 3, 1, 2, 2, 5
FINANCIAL/TERMS:
Cash Investment: $40-120K
Total Investment: $50-350K
Minimum Net Worth: $250K
Fees: Franchise - $22.5K
   Royalty - 2-5%; Ad. - 0%
Earnings Claims Statement: Yes
Term of Contract (Years): 15/2-5
Avg. # Of Employees: 4 FT, 2 PT
Passive Ownership: Discouraged
Encourage Conversions: No
Area Develop. Agreements: Yes/1
Sub-Franchising Contracts: No
Expand In Territory: Yes
Space Needs: 2,200-4,000 SF
SUPPORT & TRAINING:

Financial Assistance Provided: Yes (D)
Site Selection Assistance: Yes
Lease Negotiation Assistance: Yes
Co-Operative Advertising: No
Franchisee Assoc./Member: No
Size Of Corporate Staff: 5
On-Going Support: ,B,C,D,E,,G,H,I
Training: 10-15 Days Store and
   Headquarters
SPECIFIC EXPANSION PLANS:
US: All United States
Canada: All Canada
Overseas: All Countries

‹‹ ››

HEEL QUIK!

1730 Cumberland Point Dr., # 5
Marietta, GA 30067
Tel: (800) 255-8145 (770) 951-9440
Fax: (770) 953-6270
E-Mail: hqcorp@bellsouth.net
Web Site: www.heelquik.com
Ms. Betty Hubauer, Franchise Support

Personal services franchise opportunity with a range of services and investment levels, including shoe repair, dry cleaning, clothing alterations, monogramming, key cutting and knife and scissors sharpening.

BACKGROUND:
Established: 1983; 1st Franchised: 1984
Franchised Units: 743
Company-Owned Units: 0
Total Units: 743
Dist.: US-175; CAN-1; O'seas-567
   North America: 20 States, 1 Provinces
   Density: 8 in FL, 78 in GA, 58 in TX
Projected New Units (12 Months): 12
Qualifications: 3, 3, 1, 2, 3, 3
FINANCIAL/TERMS:
Cash Investment: $15-35K
Total Investment: $45-95K
Minimum Net Worth: $25-75K
Fees: Franchise - $15.5-17.5K
   Royalty - 4%; Ad. -
Earnings Claims Statement: No
Term of Contract (Years): 20/10/10/
Avg. # Of Employees: 2 FT, 1 PT
Passive Ownership: Allowed
Encourage Conversions: Yes
Area Develop. Agreements: Yes/1
Sub-Franchising Contracts: Yes
Expand In Territory: Yes

Space Needs: 500 SF

SUPPORT & TRAINING:

Financial Assistance Provided: Yes (D)
Site Selection Assistance: Yes
Lease Negotiation Assistance: Yes
Co-Operative Advertising: No
Franchisee Assoc./Member: No
Size Of Corporate Staff: 24
On-Going Support: „c,d,„G,„I
Training: 2 Weeks Marietta, GA

SPECIFIC EXPANSION PLANS:

US: All United States
Canada: All CAN Exc. AB
Overseas: All Countries

HESTER PAINTING & DECORATING

7340 N. Monticello Ave.
Skokie, IL 60076
Tel: (877) 437-8371 (847) 677-5103
Fax: (847) 677-5139
E-Mail: franchise@hesterdecorating.com
Web Site: www.hesterfranchising.com
Mr. Steve Hester, President

Join America's finest painting and faux finishing company! No painting experience is needed! Based on 40 years of experience, the Hester Painting & Decorating franchise program offers a great opportunity to own your own business. Our comprehensive training & support, estimating software, professional marketing system and exclusive faux finish showroom will give you a full palette of tools to run your own custom painting business. Contact us now to take the next step in painting your future with success!

BACKGROUND: IFA MEMBER
Established: 1968; 1st Franchised: 2007
Franchised Units: 0
Company-Owned Units: 2
Total Units: 2
Dist.: US-2; CAN-0; O'seas-0
North America: 1 States, 0 Provinces
Density: 2 in IL
Projected New Units (12 Months): 3-5
Qualifications: 3, 4, 1, 2, 1, 5

FINANCIAL/TERMS:

Cash Investment: $50K
Total Investment: $125.2-215.8K
Minimum Net Worth: NR
Fees: Franchise - $50K
Royalty - 6%; Ad. - 1.5%
Earnings Claims Statement: No
Term of Contract (Years): 5/5
Avg. # Of Employees: 6-12 FT, 1 PT

Passive Ownership: Allowed
Encourage Conversions: Yes
Area Develop. Agreements: No
Sub-Franchising Contracts: No
Expand In Territory: No
Space Needs: 1000 SF

SUPPORT & TRAINING:

Financial Assistance Provided: No
Site Selection Assistance: Yes
Lease Negotiation Assistance: No
Co-Operative Advertising: No
Franchisee Assoc./Member: No
Size Of Corporate Staff: 15
On-Going Support: „C,d,E,„G,h,
Training: 19 Days Chicago, IL - Painting/
Faux; 9 Days Chicago, IL - Management;4 DaysFranchisee Location

SPECIFIC EXPANSION PLANS:

US: All
Canada: No
Overseas: NR

INSTANT TAX SERVICE

1 S. Main St., # 1400
Dayton, OH 45402
Tel: (888) 870-1040 (888) 870-1040
Fax: (877) 822-9139
E-Mail: franchise@instanttaxservice.com
Web Site: www.instanttaxservicefranchise.com
Mr Brook Wise, VP Franchise Sales

Instant Tax Service is a retail income tax preparation firm serving citizens and residents of the United States in nearly 1,200 offices in 34 states. We specialize in professional tax preparation, expedited refunds, and refund anticipation loans. We're a fast, friendly alternative in the tax business. We pride ourselves on our outstanding customer service, community outreach programs, and the opportunities we give our franchising partners.

BACKGROUND:

Established: 2000; 1st Franchised: 2004
Franchised Units: 1706
Company-Owned Units: 12
Total Units: 1718
Dist.: US-1718; CAN-0; O'seas-0
North America: 0 States, 0 Provinces
Density:
Projected New Units (12 Months): NR
Qualifications: NR

FINANCIAL/TERMS:

Cash Investment: $39K-89K
Total Investment: $39K-89K
Minimum Net Worth: NR

Fees: Franchise - $34K
Royalty - ; Ad. -
Earnings Claims Statement: No
Term of Contract (Years): NR/
Avg. # Of Employees: FT, PT
Passive Ownership: Not Allowed
Encourage Conversions: No
Area Develop. Agreements: No
Sub-Franchising Contracts: No
Expand In Territory: No
Space Needs: NR

SUPPORT & TRAINING:

Financial Assistance Provided: No
Site Selection Assistance: No
Lease Negotiation Assistance: No
Co-Operative Advertising: No
Franchisee Assoc./Member: NR
Size Of Corporate Staff: NR
On-Going Support: „„„„„
Training: NR

SPECIFIC EXPANSION PLANS:

US: NR
Canada: NR
Overseas: NR

LAPELS DRY CLEANING

962 Washington St.
Hanover, MA 02339
Tel: (866) 695-2735 (781) 829-9935
Fax: (781) 829-9546
E-Mail: sales@lapelsdrycleaning.com
Web Site: www.lapelsdrycleaning.com
Ms. Laura Hurley, Franchise Administrator

With a Lapels Dry Cleaning franchise you can leave all the work of cleaning & processing garments to the professionals or take control of putting out a quality garment. Lapels' focus is on customer service & growing your business. There is a Lapels Franchise Program for everyone - Lapels Express -Protected pick-up & delivery route; Lapels Single-Unit Retail Store; Lapels Multi-Unit Retail Stores; Master Franchise; Lapels Earth-Friendly Plant - Provide retail & wholesale cleaning services.

BACKGROUND: IFA MEMBER
Established: 2000; 1st Franchised: 2001
Franchised Units: 43
Company-Owned Units: 0

Total Units: 43
Dist.: US-43; CAN-0; O'seas-0
  North America: 9 States, 0 Provinces
  Density: 4 in TX, 2 in RI, 22 in MA
Projected New Units (12 Months): 48
Qualifications: 5, 3, 1, 1, 3, 3
FINANCIAL/TERMS:
Cash Investment: $20K-1325K
(depending on program)
Total Investment:$33K-500K (depending on program)
Minimum Net Worth: $30-150K
(depending on program)
Fees: Franchise - $20-30K (depending on program)
  Royalty - 5%; Ad. - 0%
Earnings Claims Statement: No
Term of Contract (Years): 10/10
Avg. # Of Employees: FT, 3 PT
Passive Ownership: Discouraged
Encourage Conversions: Yes
Area Develop. Agreements: Yes/10
Sub-Franchising Contracts: No
Expand In Territory: Yes
Space Needs: 1,000-2,000 SF
SUPPORT & TRAINING:
Financial Assistance Provided: Yes (I)
Site Selection Assistance: Yes
Lease Negotiation Assistance: Yes
Co-Operative Advertising: Yes
Franchisee Assoc./Member: Yes/Yes
Size Of Corporate Staff: 5
On-Going Support: „C,d,E,„G,H,I
Training: 1 Day Corporate Office;
  5 Days Existing Location; 2-5 Days
  New Store
SPECIFIC EXPANSION PLANS:
US: NE
Canada: Yes
Overseas: NR

<< >>

MAID BRIGADE
4 Concourse Pkwy., # 200
Atlanta, GA 30328-5397
Tel: (800) 722-6243 + 102 (770) 551-9630
Fax: (770) 391-9092
E-Mail: franrec@maidbrigade.com
Web Site: www.maidbrigade.com
Ms. Donna Bohn, VP Franchise Development

Developing, owning and running a business shouldn't be a job. It should be a passion. At Maid Brigade, we pride ourselves on making sure it's so. Providing professional home cleaning with a focus on "Customers for Life," Maid Brigade franchisees are part of a company that is acutely focused on success and growth.

BACKGROUND: IFA MEMBER
Established: 1979; 1st Franchised: 1984
Franchised Units: 422
Company-Owned Units: 0
Total Units: 422
Dist.: US-73; CAN-50; O'seas-2
  North America: 36 States, 7 Provinces
  Density: 39 in VA, 21 in TX, 46 in CA
Projected New Units (12 Months): 40
Qualifications: 4, 3, 2, 3, 2, 5
FINANCIAL/TERMS:
Cash Investment: $34.5K+
Total Investment: $87K+
Minimum Net Worth: $150K
Fees: Franchise - $29.5K
  Royalty - 3.5-6.9%; Ad. - 2%
Earnings Claims Statement: Yes
Term of Contract (Years): 10/10
Avg. # Of Employees: 15 FT, 0 PT
Passive Ownership: Allowed
Encourage Conversions: Yes
Area Develop. Agreements: No
Sub-Franchising Contracts: No
Expand In Territory: Yes
Space Needs: 700-1,200 SF
SUPPORT & TRAINING:
Financial Assistance Provided: Yes (I)
Site Selection Assistance: Yes
Lease Negotiation Assistance: Yes
Co-Operative Advertising: Yes
Franchisee Assoc./Member: Yes/Yes
Size Of Corporate Staff: 13
On-Going Support: A,B,C,D,E,F,G,H,I
Training: 3 Days Follow-Up Visit;
  5 Days; 5 Days Atlanta, GA; at
  another MB location; 5 Days On-Site
  Week of Opening
SPECIFIC EXPANSION PLANS:
US: All United States
Canada: All Canada
Overseas: All Countries

<< >>

MAID TO PERFECTION
3465 W. Vine St.
Kissimmee, FL 34741
Tel: (800) 648-6243 (407) 870-2474
Fax: (407) 932-1746
E-Mail: maidsvc@aol.com
Web Site: www.maidtoperfectioncorp.com
Dr. Michael Katzenberger, CEO

MAID TO PERFECTION (R) is the only major cleaning franchise that provides access to every residential and commercial service dollar, within an exclusive territory. Ranked #1 for franchisee support/satisfaction in Success Magazine; cited as one of only 15 Great, Low-Investment franchises by Black Enterprise Magazine.

BACKGROUND: IFA MEMBER
Established: 1980; 1st Franchised: 1990
Franchised Units: 305
Company-Owned Units: 0
Total Units: 305
Dist.: US-295; CAN-10; O'seas-0
  North America: 24 States, 2 Provinces
  Density: 33 in PA, 50 in MD, 20 in CA
Projected New Units (12 Months): 50
Qualifications: 5, 5, 2, 4, 4, 5
FINANCIAL/TERMS:
Cash Investment: $56K-75K
Total Investment: $56K-75K
Minimum Net Worth: $150K
Fees: Franchise - $15K
  Royalty - 5-7%; Ad. - 0%
Earnings Claims Statement: No
Term of Contract (Years): 10/10
Avg. # Of Employees: 15 FT, 5 PT
Passive Ownership: Discouraged
Encourage Conversions: Yes
Area Develop. Agreements: Yes/5
Sub-Franchising Contracts: Yes
Expand In Territory: Yes
Space Needs: 400-800 SF
SUPPORT & TRAINING:
Financial Assistance Provided: Yes (D)
Site Selection Assistance: Yes
Lease Negotiation Assistance: Yes
Co-Operative Advertising: No
Franchisee Assoc./Member: No
Size Of Corporate Staff: 7
On-Going Support: „C,D,E,„G,H,I
Training: 7 Days On-Site;
  3 Days Corporate Headquarters
SPECIFIC EXPANSION PLANS:
US: All United States
Canada: All Canada
Overseas: All Countries

<< >>

MaidPro®

MAIDPRO
60 Canal St., 4th Fl.
Boston, MA 02114
Tel: (888) 624-3776 (617) 742-8787 + 222
Fax: (617) 720-0700

371

E-Mail: chuck@maidpro.com
Web Site: www.maidpro.com
Mr. Chuck Lynch, Director, Strategic Planning

MaidPro is setting the trend in the home and office cleaning industry. MaidPro has a contemporary approach to this high-growth service. With unmatched graphic design and marketing, a completely paperless office and the ability for clients to request service on the Internet, MAIDPRO's franchisees have become successful in running a larger business.

BACKGROUND: IFA MEMBER
Established: 1991;   1st Franchised: 1997
Franchised Units: 105
Company-Owned Units: 1
Total Units: 106
Dist.:   US-106; CAN-0; O'seas-0
  North America: 28 States, 0 Provinces
  Density: 9 in MA, 11 in FL, 6 in CA
Projected New Units (12 Months):   20
Qualifications: 3, 3, 1, 2, 4, 5
FINANCIAL/TERMS:
Cash Investment: $60K
Total Investment: $60-120K
Minimum Net Worth: $100K
Fees: Franchise - $7.9K
  Royalty - 3.5-6.5%;   Ad. - 1%
Earnings Claims Statement: No
Term of Contract (Years):   10/5
Avg. # Of Employees: 15 FT, 3 PT
Passive Ownership: Not Allowed
Encourage Conversions: Yes
Area Develop. Agreements: No
Sub-Franchising Contracts: No
Expand In Territory: Yes
Space Needs: 500-1,500 SF
SUPPORT & TRAINING:
Financial Assistance Provided: Yes (D)
Site Selection Assistance: Yes
Lease Negotiation Assistance: Yes
Co-Operative Advertising: No
Franchisee Assoc./Member: Yes/Yes
Size Of Corporate Staff: 22
On-Going Support: „C,D,E,,G,h,I
Training: 1 Week Onsite - Boston, MA;
  6 Weeks Self-Study
SPECIFIC EXPANSION PLANS:
US: All United States
Canada: All Canada
Overseas: NR

<< >>

Maids Etc.®
The Full Service People

MAIDS ETC.
4907 Hollendale Dr., # 208
Raleigh, NC 27616
Tel: (866) 578-6243 (919) 834-8215
Fax: (919) 834-7630
E-Mail: franchise@maidsetc.com
Web Site: www.maidsetc.com
Ms. LaVerne Artis, Vice President

It's time to clean up with MAIDS ETC. and create your own future in the residential and commercial cleaning industries, which are experiencing explosive growth. We are the "Full Service People," offering full-service residential and commercial Bulls-Eye Cleaning Systems. We provide our owner-operators with training, consultation, operational support and access to the latest advances in technology.

BACKGROUND:
Established: 1995;   1st Franchised: 2003
Franchised Units: 3
Company-Owned Units: 1
Total Units: 4
Dist.:   US-4; CAN-0; O'seas-0
  North America: 3 States, Provinces
  Density: 2 in NC, 1 in NY, 1 in SC
Projected New Units (12 Months):   25
Qualifications: 5, 3, 1, 3, 4, 5
FINANCIAL/TERMS:
Cash Investment: $19-25K
Total Investment: $36-56K
Minimum Net Worth: Varies
Fees: Franchise - $10K
  Royalty - 5-7%;   Ad. - 0-2%
Earnings Claims Statement: No
Term of Contract (Years):   5/5
Avg. # Of Employees: 2 FT, 6 PT
Passive Ownership: Discouraged
Encourage Conversions: Yes
Area Develop. Agreements: No
Sub-Franchising Contracts: No
Expand In Territory: Yes
Space Needs: 800+ SF
SUPPORT & TRAINING:
Financial Assistance Provided: Yes (D)
Site Selection Assistance: Yes
Lease Negotiation Assistance: NA
Co-Operative Advertising: No
Franchisee Assoc./Member: No
Size Of Corporate Staff: 2
On-Going Support: A,B,C,D,e,F,,H,I
Training:7 Days Headquarters in Raleigh, NC

SPECIFIC EXPANSION PLANS:
US: All United States
Canada: All Canada
Overseas: All Countries

<< >>

MARTINIZING DRY CLEANING
422 Wards Corner Rd.
Loveland, OH 45140-6950
Tel: (800) 827-0345 (513) 351-6211
Fax: (513) 731-0818
E-Mail: cleanup@martinizing.com
Web Site: www.martinizing.com
Mr. Jerald E. Laesser, Vice President

MARTINIZING is the most recognized brand name in dry cleaning. The # 1 Dry Cleaning Franchise: MARTINIZING has been ranked the # 1 dry cleaning franchise 19 out of the last 22 years by Entrepreneur Magazine.

BACKGROUND:
Established: 1949;   1st Franchised: 1949
Franchised Units: 591
Company-Owned Units: 0
Total Units: 591
Dist.:   US-389; CAN-19; O'seas-234
  North America: 38 States, 3 Provinces
  Density: 36 in WI, 92 in MI, 67 in CA
Projected New Units (12 Months):   25
Qualifications: 5, 4, 1, 3, 1, 5
FINANCIAL/TERMS:
Cash Investment: $125K
Total Investment: $363K-550.5K
Minimum Net Worth: $225K
Fees: Franchise - $35K
  Royalty - 4%;   Ad. - 0.5%
Earnings Claims Statement: Yes
Term of Contract (Years):   20/
Avg. # Of Employees: 2 FT, 4 PT
Passive Ownership: Discouraged
Encourage Conversions: Yes
Area Develop. Agreements: Yes/1
Sub-Franchising Contracts: Yes
Expand In Territory: Yes
Space Needs: 1,500-2,000 SF
SUPPORT & TRAINING:
Financial Assistance Provided: Yes (D)
Site Selection Assistance: Yes
Lease Negotiation Assistance: Yes
Co-Operative Advertising: No
Franchisee Assoc./Member: Yes/Yes
Size Of Corporate Staff: 16
On-Going Support: „C,D,E,,G,H,I

Training: 1 Week Classroom; 2 Weeks In-Store

SPECIFIC EXPANSION PLANS:

US:	All United States
Canada:	All Except AB,ON
Overseas:	Europe, Far and Middle East

⨞⨞ ⨞⨞

MERRY MAIDS

3839 Forest Hill-Irene Rd.
Memphis, TN 38125
Tel: (800) 798-8000 (901) 597-8100
Fax: (901) 597-8140
E-Mail: franchisesales@merrymaids.com
Web Site: www.merrymaids.com
Ms. Vickie Alexander, Franchise Sales Manager

MERRY MAIDS is the largest and most recognized company in the home cleaning industry. The company's commitment to training and on-going support is unmatched. MERRY MAIDS is highly ranked as an established and fast growing franchise opportunity according to leading national publications. We offer low investment, cross-selling promotions with our partner companies, research and development and excellent marketing support.

BACKGROUND:	**IFA MEMBER**
Established: 1979;	1st Franchised: 1980
Franchised Units:	1256
Company-Owned Units:	194
Total Units:	1454
Dist.:	US-951; CAN-70; O'seas-433
North America:	49 States, 7 Provinces
Density:	56 in TX, 54 in IL, 142 in CA
Projected New Units (12 Months):	32
Qualifications:	5, 3, 1, 3, 4, 5

FINANCIAL/TERMS:	
Cash Investment:	$24-29K
Total Investment:	$24-57K
Minimum Net Worth:	Varies
Fees: Franchise -	$21-29K
Royalty - 5-7%;	Ad. - 0.25-1%
Earnings Claims Statement:	No
Term of Contract (Years):	5/5
Avg. # Of Employees:	2 FT, 12 PT
Passive Ownership:	Discouraged
Encourage Conversions:	Yes
Area Develop. Agreements:	No
Sub-Franchising Contracts:	No
Expand In Territory:	Yes
Space Needs:	800 Minimum SF

SUPPORT & TRAINING:	
Financial Assistance Provided:	Yes (D)
Site Selection Assistance:	No
Lease Negotiation Assistance:	No
Co-Operative Advertising:	No
Franchisee Assoc./Member:	No
Size Of Corporate Staff:	65
On-Going Support:	„C,D,„G,H,I
Training: 8 Days Headquarters, Memphis, TN	

SPECIFIC EXPANSION PLANS:	
US:	All United States
Canada:	All Canada
Overseas:	All Countries

⨞⨞ ⨞⨞

MOLLY MAID

3948 Ranchero Dr.
Ann Arbor, MI 48108-2775
Tel: (800) 665-5962 (734) 822-6800
Fax: (734) 822-6888
E-Mail: tburns@mollymaid.com
Web Site: www.mollymaid.com
Mr. T. Burns, Licensing Coordinator

MOLLY MAID is # 1 in the industry in residential cleaning and home care service. Ranked in INC 500, Entrepreneur's Top 100, Platinum 200, Entrepreneur 509 and Business Start-Ups As Top 200 Hottest Franchises. MOLLY MAID's technology won The Windows Worldwide Open in 1995 sponsored by Bill Gates.

BACKGROUND:	**IFA MEMBER**
Established: 1979;	1st Franchised: 1979
Franchised Units:	744
Company-Owned Units:	0
Total Units:	744
Dist.:	US-744; CAN-167; O'seas-100
North America:	36 States, 3 Provinces
Density: 146 in ON, 25 in MI, 60 in CA	
Projected New Units (12 Months):	30
Qualifications:	3, 3, 1, 3, 4, 5

FINANCIAL/TERMS:	
Cash Investment:	$65K
Total Investment:	$150K-160K
Minimum Net Worth:	$250K
Fees: Franchise -	$15K
Royalty - 3.5-6.5%;	Ad. - $100/mo.
Earnings Claims Statement:	Yes
Term of Contract (Years):	10/10
Avg. # Of Employees:	12 FT, 0 PT
Passive Ownership:	Not Allowed
Encourage Conversions:	No
Area Develop. Agreements:	No
Sub-Franchising Contracts:	No
Expand In Territory:	Yes
Space Needs:	600 SF

SUPPORT & TRAINING:	
Financial Assistance Provided:	Yes (I)
Site Selection Assistance:	No
Lease Negotiation Assistance:	No
Co-Operative Advertising:	No
Franchisee Assoc./Member:	Yes/Yes
Size Of Corporate Staff:	25
On-Going Support:	„C,D,,F,G,h,I
Training: 6 Months Right Start Program; 5 Days Home Office; 5 Days Franchise Location	

SPECIFIC EXPANSION PLANS:	
US:	All United States
Canada:	All Canada
Overseas:	All Countries

⨞⨞ ⨞⨞

MTO CLEANING SERVICES

7100 E. Pleasant Valley Rd., # 300
Independence, OH 44131
Tel: (877) 392-6278 (216) 674-0645
Fax: (216) 674-0650
E-Mail: franchise@mtoclean.com
Web Site: www.mtoclean.com
Ms. Kylene Golubski, VP Business Development

Established in 1988, MTO Cleaning Services, formerly Maids to Order, now enables franchisees to offer carpet cleaning, floor care, air duct and power washing services for residential and commercial clients. On top of this exceptional revenue potential, MTO Cleaning Services gives its franchisees initial training and on-going support in marketing, technology and business planning.

BACKGROUND:	**IFA MEMBER**
Established: 1988;	1st Franchised: 1992
Franchised Units:	62
Company-Owned Units:	0
Total Units:	62
Dist.:	US-62; CAN-0; O'seas-0
North America:	19 States, 0 Provinces
Density:	4 in TX, 10 in OH, 3 in NH

Projected New Units (12 Months): 20
Qualifications: 3, 2, 1, 2, 2, 5
FINANCIAL/TERMS:
Cash Investment: $5-9.9K
Total Investment: $17.3-100.9K
Minimum Net Worth: $300K
Fees: Franchise - $5-9K
  Royalty - 3-6%; Ad. - 4.5%
Earnings Claims Statement: Yes
Term of Contract (Years): 15/15
Avg. # Of Employees: 3 FT, 12 PT
Passive Ownership: Not Allowed
Encourage Conversions: No
Area Develop. Agreements: No
Sub-Franchising Contracts: Yes
Expand In Territory: Yes
Space Needs: 500 SF
SUPPORT & TRAINING:
Financial Assistance Provided: No
Site Selection Assistance: Yes
Lease Negotiation Assistance: Yes
Co-Operative Advertising: No
Franchisee Assoc./Member: Yes/Yes
Size Of Corporate Staff: 10
On-Going Support: A,,C,D,E,,G,h,I
Training: 6 Weeks Independence, OH &
  On-Site
SPECIFIC EXPANSION PLANS:
US: All United States
Canada: All Canada, except ON and AB
Overseas: NR

≺≺ ≻≻

NAVIS PACK & SHIP
5675 DTC Blvd., # 280
Greenwood Village, CO 80111
Tel: (866) 738-6820 (303) 741-6626 +
6532
Fax: (303) 531-6530
E-Mail: franchiseinfo@gonavis.com
Web Site: www.gonavis.com
Ms. Lauren Johnson, Director of Franchise Licensing

NAVIS PACK & SHIP CENTERS, established in 2001, specialize in packaging, shipping and fulfillment of items that are fragile, large, awkward and valuable. NAVIS PACK & SHIP CENTERS is a B2B marketing-oriented concept that primarily services commercial clients, handling business equipment, computers, office furniture, art, and antiques. Locations are in light industrial or warehouse areas. Navis has been franchising since 1984 with Handle With Care Packaging Store, a retail entity.

BACKGROUND: IFA MEMBER
Established: 1980; 1st Franchised: 2002
Franchised Units: 85
Company-Owned Units: 0
Total Units: 85
Dist.: US-61; CAN-2; O'seas-0
  North America: 28 States, 1 Provinces
  Density: 6 in TX, 4 in IL, 6 in CA
Projected New Units (12 Months): 32
Qualifications: 5, 5, 2, 4, 5, 5
FINANCIAL/TERMS:
Cash Investment: $59.2-99.7K
Total Investment: $118.2-255.4K
Minimum Net Worth: $350K
Fees: Franchise - $45K
  Royalty - 6%; Ad. - 3%
Earnings Claims Statement: Yes
Term of Contract (Years): 10/5/5/
Avg. # Of Employees: 3-5 FT, 0 PT
Passive Ownership: Not Allowed
Encourage Conversions: Yes
Area Develop. Agreements: No
Sub-Franchising Contracts: No
Expand In Territory: Yes
Space Needs: 3,000 SF
SUPPORT & TRAINING:
Financial Assistance Provided: Yes (I)
Site Selection Assistance: Yes
Lease Negotiation Assistance: Yes
Co-Operative Advertising: Yes
Franchisee Assoc./Member: Yes/Yes
Size Of Corporate Staff: 30
On-Going Support: A,B,C,D,E,F,G,h,I
Training: 9 Weeks Online Pre-Training;
  2 Weeks Denver,CO; 1 Week Certified
  Training Facility
SPECIFIC EXPANSION PLANS:
US: All United States
Canada: All Canada
Overseas: All Countries

≺≺ ≻≻

NU-LOOK 1-HR. CLEANERS
5970 S.W. 18th St., # 331
Boca Raton, FL 33433-7197
Tel: (800) 413-7881 (561) 362-4190
Fax: (561) 362-4229
E-Mail: marketing@nu-look.com
Web Site: www.nulookcleaners.com
Mr. Karl N. Dickey, President/CEO

Retail dry cleaner.

BACKGROUND:
Established: 1967; 1st Franchised: 1967

Franchised Units: 50
Company-Owned Units: 3
Total Units: 53
Dist.: US-41; CAN-0; O'seas-12
  North America: 4 States, Provinces
  Density: 24 in FL, 12 in MD, 10 in VA
Projected New Units (12 Months): 25
Qualifications: 2, 4, 2, 2, 3, 4
FINANCIAL/TERMS:
Cash Investment: $45-75K
Total Investment: $125-200K+
Minimum Net Worth: $150K
Fees: Franchise - $20K
  Royalty - 2%; Ad. - 3%
Earnings Claims Statement: No
Term of Contract (Years): 20/10
Avg. # Of Employees: 2 FT, 2 PT
Passive Ownership: Discouraged
Encourage Conversions: Yes
Area Develop. Agreements: Yes/1
Sub-Franchising Contracts: Yes
Expand In Territory: Yes
Space Needs: 1,200-1,400 SF
SUPPORT & TRAINING:
Financial Assistance Provided: Yes (D)
Site Selection Assistance: Yes
Lease Negotiation Assistance: Yes
Co-Operative Advertising: No
Franchisee Assoc./Member: No
Size Of Corporate Staff: 4
On-Going Support: ,,C,D,E,,G,H,
Training: 4 Weeks Deerfield Beach, FL
SPECIFIC EXPANSION PLANS:
US: All United States
Canada: All Canada
Overseas: All Countries

≺≺ ≻≻

OXXO CARE CLEANERS
1874 N. Young Cir.
Hollywood, FL 33020
Tel: (866) G02-OXXO (954) 921-6111
Fax: (954) 924-6333
E-Mail: jremond@oxxousa.com
Web Site: www.oxxousa.com
Ms. Jaime Remond, National Sales Director

OXXO Care Cleaners offers an innovative concept in dry cleaning, 24 hours/7 days a week pickup service, environmentally safe cleaning process, no harsh chemicals, hand ironing, state of the art technology, air conditioned boutique type stores.

BACKGROUND:
Established: 2001; 1st Franchised: 2002
Franchised Units: 25
Company-Owned Units: 3

Total Units: 28
Dist.: US-28; CAN-0; O'seas-0
　North America: 2 States, 0 Provinces
　Density: 1 in NJ, 11 in FL
Projected New Units (12 Months): NR
Qualifications: 3, 3, 3, 3, 3, 3
FINANCIAL/TERMS:
Cash Investment: $25-150K
Total Investment: $100K-1MM
Minimum Net Worth: $800K
Fees: Franchise - $25K
　Royalty - 4%; Ad. - 1%
Earnings Claims Statement: No
Term of Contract (Years): 10/10
Avg. # Of Employees: 0 FT, 0 PT
Passive Ownership: Discouraged
Encourage Conversions: NA
Area Develop. Agreements: Yes/5
Sub-Franchising Contracts: No
Expand In Territory: Yes
Space Needs: 1,500 SF
SUPPORT & TRAINING:
Financial Assistance Provided: No
Site Selection Assistance: Yes
Lease Negotiation Assistance: Yes
Co-Operative Advertising: Yes
Franchisee Assoc./Member: Yes/Yes
Size Of Corporate Staff: 12
On-Going Support: „C,D,e,f,G,h,I
Training: 2 Weeks Store;
　2 Weeks Headquarters
SPECIFIC EXPANSION PLANS:
US: All United States
Canada: No
Overseas: NR

PACKAGING AND SHIPPING SPECIALISTS
5211 85th St., # 104
Lubbock, TX 79424
Tel: (800) 877-8884 (806) 794-9996
Fax: (806) 794-9997
E-Mail: mike@packship.com
Web Site: www.packship.com
Mr. Mike Gallagher, President

No Royalties! We are a complete copy shop with all shipping companies - UPS, FedEx and more. We are a combination of several businesses under one roof.

Copying, mailing, sign service, invitations and announcements, mail box rentals and much more. All with no royalties.

BACKGROUND:
Established: 1981; 1st Franchised: 1988
Franchised Units: 806
Company-Owned Units: 1
Total Units: 807
Dist.: US-804; CAN-2; O'seas-1
　North America: 37 States, 1 Provinces
　Density: 90 in TX, 10 in NM, 9 in LA
Projected New Units (12 Months): 60
Qualifications: 3, 2, 1, 2, 2, 2
FINANCIAL/TERMS:
Cash Investment: $20-40K
Total Investment: $91-138K
Minimum Net Worth: $150K
Fees: Franchise - $28.9K
　Royalty - 0%; Ad. - 0%
Earnings Claims Statement: Yes
Term of Contract (Years): 10/10
Avg. # Of Employees: 2 FT, 2 PT
Passive Ownership: Allowed
Encourage Conversions: Yes
Area Develop. Agreements: Yes/1
Sub-Franchising Contracts: Yes
Expand In Territory: Yes
Space Needs: 1,600 SF
SUPPORT & TRAINING:
Financial Assistance Provided: Yes (D)
Site Selection Assistance: Yes
Lease Negotiation Assistance: Yes
Co-Operative Advertising: No
Franchisee Assoc./Member: Yes/Yes
Size Of Corporate Staff: 18
On-Going Support: A,b,C,D,E,F,G,h,I
Training: 14 Days Ann Arbor, MI;
　14 Days Dallas, TX
SPECIFIC EXPANSION PLANS:
US: All United States
Canada: All Canada
Overseas: All Countries

PAK MAIL
7173 S. Havana St., # 600
Centennial, CO 80112-3891
Tel: (800) 833-2821 (303) 957-1000
Fax: (800) 336-7363
E-Mail: sales@pakmail.org
Web Site: www.pakmail.com
Mr. Evan Lasky, President/CEO

PAK MAIL is a convenient center for packaging, shipping and business support services, offering both residential and commercial customers air, ground, and ocean carriers, custom packaging and crat-

ing, private mailbox rental, mail services, packaging and moving supplies, copy and fax service and internet access and related services. We ship anything, anywhere.

BACKGROUND: IFA MEMBER
Established: 1983; 1st Franchised: 1984
Franchised Units: 430
Company-Owned Units: 0
Total Units: 430
Dist.: US-421; CAN-8; O'seas-22
　North America: 42 States, 0 Provinces
　Density: 41 in GA, 91 in FL, 22 in CA
Projected New Units (12 Months): 50
Qualifications: 3, 2, 2, 2, 2, 5
FINANCIAL/TERMS:
Cash Investment: $50K
Total Investment: $130-164K
Minimum Net Worth: $100K
Fees: Franchise - $29,950
　Royalty - 5% Sliding; Ad. - 2%
Earnings Claims Statement: Yes
Term of Contract (Years): 10/10
Avg. # Of Employees: 1 FT, 1 PT
Passive Ownership: Discouraged
Encourage Conversions: Yes
Area Develop. Agreements: Yes/1
Sub-Franchising Contracts: No
Expand In Territory: Yes
Space Needs: 1,200 SF
SUPPORT & TRAINING:
Financial Assistance Provided: Yes (D)
Site Selection Assistance: Yes
Lease Negotiation Assistance: Yes
Co-Operative Advertising: No
Franchisee Assoc./Member: Yes/Yes
Size Of Corporate Staff: 22
On-Going Support: ,B,C,D,E,F,G,H,I
Training: 10 Days Englewood;
　3 Days Existing Center; 3 Days New
　Center at Opening
SPECIFIC EXPANSION PLANS:
US: All United States
Canada: All Canada
Overseas: All Countries

PARCEL PLUS
12715 Telge Rd.
Cypress, TX 77429-2289
Tel: (888) 280-2053 (281) 256-4221
Fax: (281) 256-4178
E-Mail: franchisedevelopment@iced.net
Web Site: www.parcelplus.com

Mr. Donald Averitt, VP Franchise Sales

PARCEL PLUS centers offer packaging, freight, cargo, crating and international shipping in a retail setting. We provide a professional way to pack-and-ship everything from fragile antiques to large cargo items. An outside sales associate and/or the center owner utilize a consultative selling program to grow the freight and cargo segments.

BACKGROUND: IFA MEMBER
Established: 1986; 1st Franchised: 1988
Franchised Units: 100
Company-Owned Units: 0
Total Units: 100
Dist.: US-100; CAN-0; O'seas-0
North America: 20 States, 0 Provinces
Density: 30 in VA, 29 in TX, 18 in MD
Projected New Units (12 Months): NR
Qualifications: NR
FINANCIAL/TERMS:
Cash Investment: $47K
Total Investment: $152.2-198.4K
Minimum Net Worth: NR
Fees: Franchise - $30K
 Royalty - 6%; Ad. - 1%
Earnings Claims Statement: No
Term of Contract (Years): 15/
Avg. # Of Employees: 2 FT, 2 PT
Passive Ownership: Discouraged
Encourage Conversions: Yes
Area Develop. Agreements: No
Sub-Franchising Contracts: No
Expand In Territory: Yes
Space Needs: 1,200 SF
SUPPORT & TRAINING:
Financial Assistance Provided: Yes (D)
Site Selection Assistance: Yes
Lease Negotiation Assistance: Yes
Co-Operative Advertising: No
Franchisee Assoc./Member: Yes/Yes
Size Of Corporate Staff: NR
On-Going Support: A,B,C,D,E,F,G,H,I
Training: 2 Weeks Headquarters;
 1 Week On-Site
SPECIFIC EXPANSION PLANS:
US: All United States
Canada: No
Overseas: NR

PERMA-GLAZE
1638 S. Research Loop Rd., # 160
Tucson, AZ 85710
Tel: (800) 332-7397 (520) 722-9718
Fax: (520) 296-4393
E-Mail: permaglaze@theriver.com
Web Site: www.permaglaze.com
Mr. Dale R. Young, President/CEO

PERMA GLAZE specializes in multi-surface restoration of bathtubs, sinks, countertops, appliances, porcelain, metal, acrylics, cultured marble and more. PERMA GLAZE licensed representatives provide valued services to hotels/motels, private residences, apartments, schools, hospitals, contractors, property managers and many others.

BACKGROUND: IFA MEMBER
Established: 1978; 1st Franchised: 1981
Franchised Units: 64
Company-Owned Units: 1
Total Units: 65
Dist.: US-54; CAN-7; O'seas-16
North America: 36 States, 3 Provinces
Density: 4 in FL, 4 in AZ
Projected New Units (12 Months): 20
Qualifications: 4, 2, 1, 3, 4, 3
FINANCIAL/TERMS:
Cash Investment: $2.5-3K
Total Investment: $32.5
Minimum Net Worth: $29.5K
Fees: Franchise - $29.5K
 Royalty - 6/5/4%/$200 Min.; Ad. -
Earnings Claims Statement: Yes
Term of Contract (Years): 10/10
Avg. # Of Employees: 1 FT, 0 PT
Passive Ownership: Allowed
Encourage Conversions: NA
Area Develop. Agreements: Yes/1
Sub-Franchising Contracts: No
Expand In Territory: Yes
Space Needs: NA
SUPPORT & TRAINING:
Financial Assistance Provided: Yes (D)
Site Selection Assistance: Yes
Lease Negotiation Assistance: NA
Co-Operative Advertising: No
Franchisee Assoc./Member: Yes/Yes
Size Of Corporate Staff: 6
On-Going Support: ,,C,D,,,G,H,I
Training: 5 Days Tucson, AZ
SPECIFIC EXPANSION PLANS:
US: All United States

Canada: All Canada
Overseas: All Countries

PODS
6061 45th St., N.
St. Petersburg, FL 33714
Tel: (888) 776-7637 (727) 528-6303
Fax: (813) 354-4664
E-Mail: dlemay@podsusa.com
Web Site: www.podsusa.com
Mr. Don LeMay, Franchise Dewvelopment

Portable on demand storage. PODS utilizes a specially equipped truck and patented hydraulic lift technology to deliver, retrieve and store up to an 8x8x16 foot container. Revolutionizing the moving and storage industry

BACKGROUND: IFA MEMBER
Established: 1997; 1st Franchised: 1998
Franchised Units: 55
Company-Owned Units: 11
Total Units: 66
Dist.: US-66; CAN-0; O'seas-0
North America: 9 States, 0 Provinces
Density: in MN,NFL
Projected New Units (12 Months): 25
Qualifications: 5, 4, 1, 1, 3, 3
FINANCIAL/TERMS:
Cash Investment: $400K
Total Investment: $1.5MM+
Minimum Net Worth: $1MM
Fees: Franchise - $75K
 Royalty - 8%/$3.5K/Mo.; Ad. - 2%
Earnings Claims Statement: No
Term of Contract (Years): 20/10
Avg. # Of Employees: 5 FT, 0 PT
Passive Ownership: Allowed
Encourage Conversions: NA
Area Develop. Agreements: No
Sub-Franchising Contracts: No
Expand In Territory: No
Space Needs: 20,000 SF
SUPPORT & TRAINING:
Financial Assistance Provided: No
Site Selection Assistance: Yes
Lease Negotiation Assistance: No
Co-Operative Advertising: No
Franchisee Assoc./Member: Yes/Yes
Size Of Corporate Staff: 110
On-Going Support: A,b,,d,E,,G,H,I
Training: 2 Weeks St. Petersburg, FL
SPECIFIC EXPANSION PLANS:
US: NE, SE, Midwest
Canada: No
Overseas: NR

≪ ≫

POSTAL ANNEX+

7580 Metropolitan Dr., # 200
San Diego, CA 92108-4417
Tel: (800) 456-1525 (619) 563-4800
Fax: (619) 563-9850
E-Mail: ryan@postalannex.com
Web Site: www.postalannex.com
Mr. Ryan Heine, Director of Franchising

Retail business service center, providing: packaging, shipping, copying, postal, mail box rental, printing fax, notary, office supplies and more.

BACKGROUND: IFA MEMBER
Established: 1985; 1st Franchised: 1986
Franchised Units: 375
Company-Owned Units: 0
Total Units: 375
Dist.: US-374; CAN-0; O'seas-1
  North America: 25 States, 0 Provinces
  Density: 20 in OR, 17 in MI, 130 in CA
Projected New Units (12 Months): 36
Qualifications: 5, 3, 1, 1, 3, 3
FINANCIAL/TERMS:
Cash Investment: $50K
Total Investment: $128.8-190.1K
Minimum Net Worth: $200K
Fees: Franchise - $29.95K
  Royalty - 5%; Ad. - 2%
Earnings Claims Statement: Yes
Term of Contract (Years): 15/15
Avg. # Of Employees: 1 FT, 2 PT
Passive Ownership: Allowed
Encourage Conversions: Yes
Area Develop. Agreements: Yes/1
Sub-Franchising Contracts: No
Expand In Territory: Yes
Space Needs: 1,200 SF
SUPPORT & TRAINING:
Financial Assistance Provided: Yes (D)
Site Selection Assistance: Yes
Lease Negotiation Assistance: Yes
Co-Operative Advertising: No
Franchisee Assoc./Member: Yes/Yes
Size Of Corporate Staff: 21
On-Going Support: ,,c,d,E,,G,H,I
Training: 2 Weeks San Diego, CA;
  1 Week On-Site
SPECIFIC EXPANSION PLANS:
US: All United States
Canada: All Canada
Overseas: All Countries

≪ ≫

POSTAL CONNECTIONS OF AMERICA

1081 Camino del Rio S., # 109
San Diego, CA 92108
Tel: (800) 767-8257 (619) 294-7550
Fax: (619) 294-4550
E-Mail: dhurley@postalconnections.com
Web Site: www.postalconnections.com
Mr. David W. Hurley, VP Franchise Development

POSTAL CONNECTIONS OF AMERICA franchises are specialty postal and copy service centers offering a variety of services, including packing, shipping, mailbox rentals, fax, money transfer & money orders and notary services. Our newer outlets also include state-of-the-art technology features, such as computer work stations with high speed Internet access, e-mail address, video conferencing and meeting rooms, truly making our locations "virtual offices."

BACKGROUND: IFA MEMBER
Established: 1985; 1st Franchised: 1996
Franchised Units: 75
Company-Owned Units: 0
Total Units: 75
Dist.: US-75; CAN-0; O'seas-0
  North America: 24 States, 0 Provinces
  Density: 7 in OR, 29 in CA, 12 in AZ
Projected New Units (12 Months): 36
Qualifications: 4, 3, 1, 3, 1, 4
FINANCIAL/TERMS:
Cash Investment: $34-45K
Total Investment: $114-149K
Minimum Net Worth: $100K
Fees: Franchise - $21K
  Royalty - 4%; Ad. - 0
Earnings Claims Statement: No
Term of Contract (Years): 10/10
Avg. # Of Employees: 0 FT, 2 PT
Passive Ownership: Discouraged
Encourage Conversions: Yes
Area Develop. Agreements: Yes/10
Sub-Franchising Contracts: No
Expand In Territory: Yes
Space Needs: 1,200 SF
SUPPORT & TRAINING:
Financial Assistance Provided: Yes (I)
Site Selection Assistance: Yes
Lease Negotiation Assistance: Yes
Co-Operative Advertising: No

Franchisee Assoc./Member: No
Size Of Corporate Staff: 12
On-Going Support: ,,C,d,e,,,h,I
Training: 4 Days New Location;
  5 Days Store
SPECIFIC EXPANSION PLANS:
US: All United States
Canada: All Canada
Overseas: Asia, Europe, South America,
  Middle East, Australia

≪ ≫

POSTNET

1819 Wazee St.
Denver, CO 80202
Tel: (800) 841-7171 (303) 771-7100
Fax: (303) 771-7133
E-Mail: info@postnet.com
Web Site: www.postnet.com
Mr. Brian Spindel, Executive Vice President

PostNet Centers offer graphic design, digital printing and copying, computer rental stations and much more. Consumers count on PostNet for high quality printing services, digital copy services in black and white or full color, and a host of finishing services to professionally complete any project. And, when it's time to send or receive something, PostNet offers domestic and international parcel shipping with companies like UPS, FedEx and DHL, traditional postal services, packaging services and supplies, and private mailboxes. Create, Duplicate, Deliver. That's the PostNet advantage.

BACKGROUND: IFA MEMBER
Established: 1992; 1st Franchised: 1993
Franchised Units: 850
Company-Owned Units: 0
Total Units: 850
Dist.: US-438; CAN-26; O'seas-386
  North America: 41 States, 4 Provinces
  Density: 54 in TX, 44 in NV, 55 in CA
Projected New Units (12 Months): 100
Qualifications: 5, 3, 1, 3, 4, 5
FINANCIAL/TERMS:
Cash Investment: $50K
Total Investment: $174-196K
Minimum Net Worth: $300K
Fees: Franchise - $30K
  Royalty - 5%; Ad. - 2%
Earnings Claims Statement: No
Term of Contract (Years): 15/15

Avg. # Of Employees:	2 FT, 1 PT
Passive Ownership:	Not Allowed
Encourage Conversions:	Yes
Area Develop. Agreements:	Yes/1
Sub-Franchising Contracts:	No
Expand In Territory:	Yes
Space Needs:	1,200 SF

SUPPORT & TRAINING:

Financial Assistance Provided:	Yes (I)
Site Selection Assistance:	Yes
Lease Negotiation Assistance:	Yes
Co-Operative Advertising:	No
Franchisee Assoc./Member:	No
Size Of Corporate Staff:	30
On-Going Support:	„C,D,E,F,G,H,I
Training:	2 Weeks Denver, CO;

1 Week Store Opening; 2-3 Days
Follow-Up

SPECIFIC EXPANSION PLANS:

US:	All United States
Canada:	All Canada
Overseas:	All Countries Not Currently

Represented

<< >>

PRESSED 4 TIME

8 Clock Tower Pl., # 110
Maynard, MA 01754
Tel: (800) 423-8711 (978) 823-8300
Fax: (978) 823-8301
E-Mail: randy@pressed4time.com
Web Site: www.pressed4time.com
Mr. Randy Erb, Dir. Franchise Development

The nation's first and foremost dry-cleaning/shoe repair, pick-up and delivery franchise. Coast to coast, more than 50,000 customers smile when they see our franchisees. Dry-cleaning and shoe repair are performed by local merchants. Experience in the 7 billion-dollar dry-cleaning industry is not needed. If you like people and can work on your own, then this leading home-based, mobile franchise is probably for you!

BACKGROUND:

Established: 1987;	1st Franchised: 1990
Franchised Units:	180
Company-Owned Units:	0
Total Units:	180
Dist.:	US-172; CAN-1; O'seas-7

North America:	31 States, 2 Provinces
Density:	10 in CA, 13 in FL, 13 in PA
Projected New Units (12 Months):	30
Qualifications:	3, 1, 1, 2, 3, 5

FINANCIAL/TERMS:

Cash Investment:	$31-38K
Total Investment:	$31-38K
Minimum Net Worth:	NA
Fees: Franchise -	$25K
Royalty - 6%;	Ad. - 0%
Earnings Claims Statement:	No
Term of Contract (Years):	10/10
Avg. # Of Employees:	1 FT, 0 PT
Passive Ownership:	Discouraged
Encourage Conversions:	Yes
Area Develop. Agreements:	No
Sub-Franchising Contracts:	No
Expand In Territory:	Yes
Space Needs:	NA

SUPPORT & TRAINING:

Financial Assistance Provided:	No
Site Selection Assistance:	Yes
Lease Negotiation Assistance:	NA
Co-Operative Advertising:	No
Franchisee Assoc./Member:	No
Size Of Corporate Staff:	5
On-Going Support:	„C,D,E,,G,H,I
Training:	1 Day Franchise;

3 Days Franchise; 3 Days Corporate at
Maynard, MA

SPECIFIC EXPANSION PLANS:

US:	All United States
Canada:	All Canada
Overseas:	NR

<< >>

TWO MEN AND A TRUCK

3400 Belle Chase Way
Lansing, MI 48911
Tel: (800) 345-1070 (517) 394-7210
Fax: (517) 394-7432
E-Mail: franchiseinfo@twomenandatruck.com
Web Site: www.twomenandatruck.com
Ms. Pamela Batten, Franchise Sales Coordinator

TWO MEN AND A TRUCK is the nation's first and largest local moving franchise. Known as the "Movers Who Care," TWO MEN AND A TRUCK is committed to exceeding customers' expectations.

They offer a full range of residential and commercial moving services, as well as boxes and packing supplies.

BACKGROUND:	IFA MEMBER
Established: 1985;	1st Franchised: 1989
Franchised Units:	205
Company-Owned Units:	3
Total Units:	208
Dist.:	US-202; CAN-5; O'seas-1
North America:	29 States, 1 Provinces
Density:	18 in MI, 14 in GA, 20 in FL
Projected New Units (12 Months):	32
Qualifications:	3, 4, 1, 3, 5, 5

FINANCIAL/TERMS:

Cash Investment:	$50K
Total Investment:	$150-412.9K
Minimum Net Worth:	$300K+
Fees: Franchise -	$37K
Royalty - 6%;	Ad. - 1%
Earnings Claims Statement:	Yes
Term of Contract (Years):	5/5
Avg. # Of Employees:	5 FT, 3 PT
Passive Ownership:	Discouraged
Encourage Conversions:	Yes
Area Develop. Agreements:	Yes/5
Sub-Franchising Contracts:	No
Expand In Territory:	Yes
Space Needs:	800+ SF

SUPPORT & TRAINING:

Financial Assistance Provided:	No
Site Selection Assistance:	No
Lease Negotiation Assistance:	No
Co-Operative Advertising:	Yes
Franchisee Assoc./Member:	Yes/Yes
Size Of Corporate Staff:	55
On-Going Support:	„C,D,,,G,h,I
Training:	3 Weeks Lansing, MI at Stick

Men University

SPECIFIC EXPANSION PLANS:

US:	All United States, 30 units
Canada:	All Canada, 1 unit
Overseas:	South Africa, 1 unit

<< >>

UNISHIPPERS

746 E. Winchester St., # 200
Salt Lake City, UT 84107-8512
Tel: (800) 999-8721 (801) 708-5822
Fax: (801) 708-5922
E-Mail: chip.baranowski@unishippers.com
Web Site: www.unishippers.com/franchising
Mr. Chip Baranowski, Franchise Development Manager

UNISHIPPERS is an international shipping company that provides individual solutions and personalized customer service to our customers - all at discounted prices.

BACKGROUND: IFA MEMBER
Established: 1987; 1st Franchised: 1990
Franchised Units: 277
Company-Owned Units: 3
Total Units: 280
Dist.: US-279; CAN-0; O'seas-1
 North America: 50 States, 0 Provinces
 Density: 20 in TX, 20 in NY, 27 in CA
Projected New Units (12 Months): 4
Qualifications: 4, 5, 1, 1, 5, 5
FINANCIAL/TERMS:
Cash Investment: $40.8-382.4K
Total Investment: $40.8-382.4K
Minimum Net Worth: NA
Fees: Franchise - $10-50K
 Royalty - 16.5%; Ad. - 1% Gross
Earnings Claims Statement: Yes
Term of Contract (Years): 5/5
Avg. # Of Employees: 1 FT, 0 PT
Passive Ownership: Not Allowed
Encourage Conversions: NA
Area Develop. Agreements: No
Sub-Franchising Contracts: Yes
Expand In Territory: No
Space Needs: NR
SUPPORT & TRAINING:
Financial Assistance Provided: Yes (D)
Site Selection Assistance: Yes
Lease Negotiation Assistance: Yes
Co-Operative Advertising: No
Franchisee Assoc./Member: No
Size Of Corporate Staff: 60
On-Going Support: ,,,D,,,G,h,
Training: 1 Week Salt Lake City, UT;
 Time Varies Franchisee's Location
SPECIFIC EXPANSION PLANS:
US: No
Canada: All Canada
Overseas: Western Europe, Pacific Rim

UNITED CHECK CASHING
325 Chestnut St., # 3000
Philadelphia, PA 19106
Tel: (800) 626-0787 (215) 238-0300
Fax: (215) 238-9056
E-Mail: info@unitedfsg.com
Web Site: www.unitedfsg.com
Mr. Richard Morris, SVP Development

Owning a United Check Cashing business is the closest thing you can do in franchising to owning a bank. United Check Cashing centers provide a wide assortment of vital services, in addition to just check cashing, to the "underbanked" segment of consumers seeking an alternative to traditional banking relationships and the growing fees associated with banks. Our franchisees operate clean, bright, safe retail centers located in urban and suburban markets, and they pride themselves on building strong consumer r

BACKGROUND: IFA MEMBER
Established: 1977; 1st Franchised: 1992
Franchised Units: 150
Company-Owned Units: 0
Total Units: 150
Dist.: US-150; CAN-0; O'seas-0
 North America: 16 States, 0 Provinces
 Density: 48 in PA, 50 in NJ, 9 in FL
Projected New Units (12 Months): 20
Qualifications: 5, 5, 2, 2, 4, 5
FINANCIAL/TERMS:
Cash Investment: $70-100K
Total Investment: $200-300K
Minimum Net Worth: $350K
Fees: Franchise - $27.5K
 Royalty - 0.002% of Volume; Ad. - 3% Income
Earnings Claims Statement: Yes
Term of Contract (Years): 15/15
Avg. # Of Employees: 1 FT, 2 PT
Passive Ownership: Allowed
Encourage Conversions: Yes
Area Develop. Agreements: Yes/1
Sub-Franchising Contracts: No
Expand In Territory: Yes
Space Needs: 1,000 SF
SUPPORT & TRAINING:
Financial Assistance Provided: Yes (D)
Site Selection Assistance: Yes
Lease Negotiation Assistance: Yes
Co-Operative Advertising: No
Franchisee Assoc./Member: Yes/Yes
Size Of Corporate Staff: 16
On-Going Support: ,,C,D,E,F,G,H,I
Training:2 Weeks Corporate Headquarters
 Philadelphia, PA
SPECIFIC EXPANSION PLANS:
US: CA, CT, GA, KY, FL, MD, MI, OH, WA, TX
Canada: No
Overseas: NR

The UPS Store™

UPS STORE, THE
6060 Cornerstone Ct., W.
San Diego, CA 92121-3762
Tel: (877) 623-7253 (858) 597-8513
Fax: (858) 546-7493
E-Mail: usafranchise@mbe.com
Web Site: www.theupsstore.com
, MBE Sales Department

In April 2001, Mail Boxes Etc., Inc., the world's largest franchisor of retail shipping, postal and business service centers, became a subsidiary of UPS, the world's largest express carrier and package delivery company. In 2003, the company introduced The UPS STORE franchise opportunity to offer franchisees and customers the best of both businesses. With over 5,800 The UPS Store and Mail Boxes Etc. locations in more than 75 countries and territories, the network is the global leader in its market.

BACKGROUND: IFA MEMBER
Established: 1980; 1st Franchised: 1980
Franchised Units: 5982
Company-Owned Units: 0
Total Units: 5982
Dist.: US-4459; CAN-302; O'seas-1397
 North America: 50 States, 10 Provinces
 Density: 279 in TX, 411 in FL, 662 in CA
Projected New Units (12 Months): 183
Qualifications: 5, 4, 3, 3, 3, 5
FINANCIAL/TERMS:
Cash Investment: $15K
Total Investment: $170.8-279.4K
Minimum Net Worth: NA
Fees: Franchise - $29,950
 Royalty - 5%; Ad. - 3.5%
Earnings Claims Statement: No
Term of Contract (Years): 10/10
Avg. # Of Employees: 2 FT, 2+ PT
Passive Ownership: Discouraged
Encourage Conversions: Yes
Area Develop. Agreements: Yes/0
Sub-Franchising Contracts: No
Expand In Territory: No
Space Needs: 1,200-1,800 SF
SUPPORT & TRAINING:
Financial Assistance Provided: Yes (D)
Site Selection Assistance: Yes
Lease Negotiation Assistance: Yes
Co-Operative Advertising: Yes
Franchisee Assoc./Member: Yes/Yes
Size Of Corporate Staff: 400
On-Going Support: A,B,C,d,e,,G,h,I
Training: 2 Weeks Local Certified Franchise Training Center; 2 Weeks San Diego, CA
SPECIFIC EXPANSION PLANS:
US: All United States
Canada: All Canada

Overseas: All Countries

ZIPS DRY CLEANERS

7500 Greenway Center Dr.
Greenbelt, MD 20770
Tel: (877) 321-3277 (301) 313-0389
Fax: (301) 345-2895
E-Mail: franchise@321zips.com
Web Site: www.321zips.com
Mr. Andy Cucchiara, VP Franchise Operations

ZIPS® is 'America's One Price Dry Cleaner'. Our successful business model is based on the revolutionary concept of offering any garment dry cleaned for just $1.99 AND ready for pick-up the same day – that's less than half the price of today's industry average! ZIPS® is expanding, offering franchise opportunities to qualified individuals and groups. If selected, you may be part of the ZIPS® revolution with a ZIPS Dry Cleaners® franchise of your own!

BACKGROUND:	IFA MEMBER
Established: 2004;	1st Franchised: 2006
Franchised Units:	20
Company-Owned Units:	0
Total Units:	20
Dist.:	US-20; CAN-0; O'seas-0
North America:	4 States, 0 Provinces
Density:	11 in MD, 6 in VA, 3 in CA
Projected New Units (12 Months):	14
Qualifications:	5, 5, 1, 1, 4, 5

FINANCIAL/TERMS:

Cash Investment:	$150-225K
Total Investment:	$500-700K+
Minimum Net Worth:	$450
Fees: Franchise -	$50K
Royalty - 6%;	Ad. - 4%
Earnings Claims Statement:	Yes
Term of Contract (Years):	10/10

Avg. # Of Employees:	4-6 FT, 6-10 PT
Passive Ownership:	Discouraged
Encourage Conversions:	No
Area Develop. Agreements:	Yes/3
Sub-Franchising Contracts:	No
Expand In Territory:	Yes
Space Needs:	3,500 SF

SUPPORT & TRAINING:

Financial Assistance Provided:	No
Site Selection Assistance:	Yes
Lease Negotiation Assistance:	Yes
Co-Operative Advertising:	Yes
Franchisee Assoc./Member:	No
Size Of Corporate Staff:	5
On-Going Support:	A,B,C,D,E,,G,H,I
Training:	7 weeks Existing store; 1 week Corp Office

SPECIFIC EXPANSION PLANS:

US:	Mid-Atlantic
Canada:	No
Overseas:	No

FIVE LARGEST PARTICIPANTS IN SURVEY

Company	# Fran- chised Units	# Co- Owned Units	# Total Units	Franchise Fee	On-Going Royalty	Total Investment
1. The Athlete's Foot	558	0	558	$39.9K	5%	$200-525K
2. Kampgrounds Of America / KOA	450	27	477	$30/ 22.5/ 7.5K	8%	$200K-4MM
3. Play It Again Sports	395	0	395	$20K	5%	$190.2- 351.1K
4. American Poolplayers Association	290	2	292	Varies	20%	$12-14.8K
5. Pro Golf International	148	1	149	$49.5K	2.5%	$300K+

All of the data provided are proprietary and should not be quoted without acknowledging *Bond's Franchise Guide*.

AMERICAN POOLPLAYERS ASSOCIATION

1000 Lake St. Louis Blvd., # 325
Lake St. Louis, MO 63367-1340
Tel: (800) 372-2536 (636) 625-8611 + 5118
Fax: (636) 625-2975
E-Mail: ddavis@poolplayers.com
Web Site: www.poolplayers.com
Mr. Doug Davis, Franchise Development Assist.

APA franchisees operate recreational pool leagues utilizing "The Equalizer", a unique handicap system that equalizes play. The League, previously known as the Bud Light Pool League or the Camel pool League, and now known nationally as the "APA Pool League", currently consists of over 250,000 members who compete in year-round weekly play. Franchisees receive customized software, technical updates, complete training, marketing support and networking opportunities at the annual convention.

BACKGROUND: IFA MEMBER
Established: 1981; 1st Franchised: 1982
Franchised Units: 290
Company-Owned Units: 2
Total Units: 292
Dist.: US-275; CAN-19; O'seas-1

North America: 47 States, 6 Provinces
Density: 16 in TX, 28 in IL, 18 in FL
Projected New Units (12 Months): 20
Qualifications: 3, 3, 2, 2, 1, 5

FINANCIAL/TERMS:
Cash Investment: $12K-14.8K
Total Investment: $12K-14.8K
Minimum Net Worth: NA
Fees: Franchise - Varies
Royalty - 20%; Ad. - NA
Earnings Claims Statement: No
Term of Contract (Years): 2/5/10
Avg. # Of Employees: Varies
Passive Ownership: Not Allowed
Encourage Conversions: NA
Area Develop. Agreements: No

Sub-Franchising Contracts:	No
Expand In Territory:	No
Space Needs:	NA

SUPPORT & TRAINING:

Financial Assistance Provided:	No
Site Selection Assistance:	Yes
Lease Negotiation Assistance:	NA
Co-Operative Advertising:	No
Franchisee Assoc./Member:	Yes/Yes
Size Of Corporate Staff:	50
On-Going Support:	A,,,D,,,G,H,
Training:	5 Days APA Home Office

SPECIFIC EXPANSION PLANS:

US:	All United States
Canada:	All Canada
Overseas:	NR

◀◀ ▶▶

ATHLETE'S FOOT, THE
1346 Oakbrook Dr., # 170
Norcross, GA 30093
Tel: (800) 524-6444 (770) 514-4676
Fax: (770) 514-4903
E-Mail: franchiseinfo@theathletesfoot.com
Web Site: www.theathletesfoot.com
Mr. Martin Amschler, VP Franchise

THE ATHLETE'S FOOT, with more than 600 stores in 45 countries, is the leading international franchisor of name-brand athletic footwear. As a franchisee, you will benefit from headquarters' support, including training, advertising, real estate and product selection.

BACKGROUND: IFA MEMBER

Established: 1971;	1st Franchised: 1972
Franchised Units:	558
Company-Owned Units:	0
Total Units:	558
Dist.:	US-218; CAN-1; O'seas-339
North America:	34 States, 1 Provinces
Density:	24 in GA, 25 in IL, 27 in FL
Projected New Units (12 Months):	30
Qualifications:	4, 5, 3, 3, 2, 5

FINANCIAL/TERMS:

Cash Investment:	$85K
Total Investment:	$200-525K
Minimum Net Worth:	$250K
Fees: Franchise -	$39.9K
Royalty - 5%;	Ad. - 2%

Earnings Claims Statement:	No
Term of Contract (Years):	10/5
Avg. # Of Employees:	2 FT, 6 PT
Passive Ownership:	Discouraged
Encourage Conversions:	Yes
Area Develop. Agreements:	Yes/10
Sub-Franchising Contracts:	Yes
Expand In Territory:	Yes
Space Needs:	1,200-2,800 SF

SUPPORT & TRAINING:

Financial Assistance Provided:	No
Site Selection Assistance:	Yes
Lease Negotiation Assistance:	Yes
Co-Operative Advertising:	No
Franchisee Assoc./Member:	Yes/Yes
Size Of Corporate Staff:	135
On-Going Support:	,,C,D,E,f,G,H,I
Training:	On-Going Location; Headquarters in Atlanta

SPECIFIC EXPANSION PLANS:

US:	All United States
Canada:	All Canada
Overseas:	All Countries

◀◀ ▶▶

FIELD OF DREAMS
2 S. University Dr., # 325
Ft. Lauderdale, FL 33324
Tel: (800) 589-6648 (954) 377-0004
Fax: (954) 475-8785
E-Mail: franchiseinfo@fieldofdreams.com
Web Site: www.fieldofdreams.com
Ms. Roseann Rosario, Executive Assistant

FIELD OF DREAMS, the ultimate sports and celebrity gift store.

BACKGROUND:

Established: 1990;	1st Franchised: 1991
Franchised Units:	19
Company-Owned Units:	10
Total Units:	29
Dist.:	US-28; CAN-1; O'seas-1
North America:	18 States, 0 Provinces
Density:	2 in TX, 3 in GA, 3 in CA
Projected New Units (12 Months):	10
Qualifications:	5, 4, 5, 4, 4, 5

FINANCIAL/TERMS:

Cash Investment:	$70K-100K
Total Investment:	$183.3K-319.5K
Minimum Net Worth:	$150K
Fees: Franchise -	$32.5K
Royalty - 6%;	Ad. - 3%
Earnings Claims Statement:	No
Term of Contract (Years):	Lease/
Avg. # Of Employees:	1 FT, 2 PT
Passive Ownership:	Discouraged
Encourage Conversions:	NA
Area Develop. Agreements:	Yes/1

Sub-Franchising Contracts:	No
Expand In Territory:	Yes
Space Needs:	900-1,400 SF

SUPPORT & TRAINING:

Financial Assistance Provided:	Yes (D)
Site Selection Assistance:	Yes
Lease Negotiation Assistance:	Yes
Co-Operative Advertising:	No
Franchisee Assoc./Member:	No
Size Of Corporate Staff:	9
On-Going Support:	,,C,D,E,,,h,I
Training:	10 Days Orlando, FL

SPECIFIC EXPANSION PLANS:

US:	All United States
Canada:	All Canada
Overseas:	All Countries

◀◀ ▶▶

GOLF ETC. OF AMERICA
2201 Commercial Ln.
Granbury, TX 76048
Tel: (800) 806-8633 (817) 279-7888
Fax: (817) 579-1793
E-Mail: sales@golfetc.com
Web Site: www.golfetc.com
Mr. Don Willingham, Dir. Franchise Development

Total turn-key golf pro shop franchise. Retail center for golf equipment, accessories, gift items and furniture. Service center built inside for precision custom fitting and repair of golf clubs. Exciting and fun sports and entertainment industry.

BACKGROUND: IFA MEMBER

Established: 1993;	1st Franchised: 1995
Franchised Units:	66
Company-Owned Units:	0
Total Units:	66
Dist.:	US-66; CAN-0; O'seas-0
North America:	26 States, 0 Provinces
Density:	15 in TX, 5 in LA, 10 in FL
Projected New Units (12 Months):	24
Qualifications:	NR

FINANCIAL/TERMS:

Cash Investment:	$179.5K
Total Investment:	$350-425K
Minimum Net Worth:	$130-145K
Fees: Franchise -	$15K
Royalty - Call;	Ad. - NA
Earnings Claims Statement:	No
Term of Contract (Years):	NR/
Avg. # Of Employees:	1 FT, 2 PT
Passive Ownership:	Allowed

Encourage Conversions: No
Area Develop. Agreements: No
Sub-Franchising Contracts: No
Expand In Territory: No
Space Needs: 3,000 SF

SUPPORT & TRAINING:

Financial Assistance Provided: No
Site Selection Assistance: Yes
Lease Negotiation Assistance: Yes
Co-Operative Advertising: No
Franchisee Assoc./Member: No
Size Of Corporate Staff: 11
On-Going Support: ,b,,D,E,,G,H,I
Training: 1 Week Granbury, TX

SPECIFIC EXPANSION PLANS:

US: All United States
Canada: NR
Overseas: NR

≪ ≫

GOLF USA

7608 N. Harvey Ave.
Oklahoma City, OK 73116
Tel: (800) 488-1107 (405) 751-0015
Fax: (405) 755-0065
E-Mail: franchise@golfusa.com
Web Site: www.golfusa.com
Mr. Rick Benson, VP Franchise Sales & Operations

Discount golf retail stores, complete with name-brand, pro-line equipment, apparel and accessories. Indoor driving range/swing analyzer.

BACKGROUND: IFA MEMBER
Established: 1986; 1st Franchised: 1989
Franchised Units: 110
Company-Owned Units: 2
Total Units: 112
Dist.: US-80; CAN-7; O'seas-23
North America: 30 States, 5 Provinces
Density: 6 in TX, 6 in NE, 8 in FL
Projected New Units (12 Months): 20
Qualifications: 5, 4, 3, 3, 4, 5

FINANCIAL/TERMS:
Cash Investment: $75-100K
Total Investment: $300-400K
Minimum Net Worth: $300K
Fees: Franchise - $34-44K
Royalty - 2%; Ad. - 1%
Earnings Claims Statement: No
Term of Contract (Years): 15/15
Avg. # Of Employees: 2 FT, 1 PT
Passive Ownership: Discouraged
Encourage Conversions: Yes

Area Develop. Agreements: Yes/0
Sub-Franchising Contracts: Yes
Expand In Territory: Yes
Space Needs: 2,500-5,000 SF

SUPPORT & TRAINING:
Financial Assistance Provided: Yes (D)
Site Selection Assistance: Yes
Lease Negotiation Assistance: Yes
Co-Operative Advertising: Yes
Franchisee Assoc./Member: Yes/Yes
Size Of Corporate Staff: 30
On-Going Support: A,B,C,D,E,F,G,H,I
Training: 10 Days Europe;
10 Days Oklahoma City, OK

SPECIFIC EXPANSION PLANS:
US: All United States
Canada: All Canada
Overseas: All Countries

≪ ≫

HOMEGAMERS

400 N. Center St.
Westminster, MD 21157
Tel: (877) 9-GAMERS (216) 308-4298
Fax: (216) 393-0120
E-Mail: seth@homegamers.net
Web Site: www.homegamers.net
Mr. Seth Richards, Director of Franchise Sales

HomeGamers is a one-of-a-kind, mall based, franchise opportunity that cashes in on two growing industries. These hot industries are home entertainment products and licensed sports products. The products that you will sell include billiard tables and supplies, poker tables, juke boxes, casino games, slot machines, pinball and arcade games, neon signs, home theater furniture, thousands of licensed sports products, and much more! Who said work isn't fun? Please go to www. homegamers.net to see what we mean.

BACKGROUND: IFA MEMBER
Established: 2006; 1st Franchised: 2008
Franchised Units: 0
Company-Owned Units: 1
Total Units: 1
Dist.: US-1; CAN-0; O'seas-0
North America: 0 States, 0 Provinces
Density:
Projected New Units (12 Months): 4
Qualifications: 4, 4, 3, 2, 3, 4

FINANCIAL/TERMS:
Cash Investment: $50K
Total Investment: $286-528K
Minimum Net Worth: $0
Fees: Franchise - $25K
Royalty - 5%; Ad. - 1%
Earnings Claims Statement: No
Term of Contract (Years): 10/5
Avg. # Of Employees: 3 FT, 3 PT
Passive Ownership: Discouraged
Encourage Conversions: NA
Area Develop. Agreements: No
Sub-Franchising Contracts: No
Expand In Territory: Yes
Space Needs: 6000 SF

SUPPORT & TRAINING:
Financial Assistance Provided: Yes (I)
Site Selection Assistance: Yes
Lease Negotiation Assistance: Yes
Co-Operative Advertising: Yes
Franchisee Assoc./Member: No
Size Of Corporate Staff: 3
On-Going Support: ,,C,D,E,F,,H,
Training: 2 weeks Corporate
Headquarters; Westminster, MD;
1 week On-Site Training

SPECIFIC EXPANSION PLANS:
US: All
Canada: No
Overseas: NR

≪ ≫

I9 SPORTS

1723 S. Kings Ave.
Brandon, FL 33511
Tel: (800) 975-2937
Fax: (813) 662-9114
E-Mail: franchisesales@i9sports.com
Web Site: www.i9sportsfranchise.com
Mr. Jim Cherry, Chief Operating Officer

i9 SPORTS is the world's first complete amateur sports franchise for the 42 million youth athletes nationwide. i9 SPORTS offers franchise opportunities for people to own and operate local amateur sports leagues, tournaments, camps, clinics, special events and child development programs for kids of all ages. i9 SPORTS provides a low-investment, low-overhead, fully-computerized business that you can run from home. Turn your love of amateur sports into a rewarding home-based business.

BACKGROUND: IFA MEMBER
Established: 1995; 1st Franchised: 2003
Franchised Units: 117
Company-Owned Units: 0
Total Units: 117
Dist.: US-117; CAN-0; O'seas-0
North America: 26 States, 0 Provinces
Density: 10 in NY, 16 in FL, 9 in CA
Projected New Units (12 Months): 50
Qualifications: 4, 4, 4, 4, 4, 4

FINANCIAL/TERMS:
Cash Investment: $50K-60K
Total Investment: $46K-87K
Minimum Net Worth: $100K
Fees: Franchise - $12.5-18.5K
Royalty - 7.5%; Ad. - 1%
Earnings Claims Statement: Yes
Term of Contract (Years): 10/10
Avg. # Of Employees: 0-1 FT, 0-1 PT
Passive Ownership: Not Allowed
Encourage Conversions: No
Area Develop. Agreements: Yes/1
Sub-Franchising Contracts: No
Expand In Territory: Yes
Space Needs: NA

SUPPORT & TRAINING:
Financial Assistance Provided: Yes (I)
Site Selection Assistance: Yes
Lease Negotiation Assistance: NA
Co-Operative Advertising: Yes
Franchisee Assoc./Member: Yes/Yes
Size Of Corporate Staff: 10
On-Going Support: A,B,C,D,E,F,G,H,I
Training: 2 Days Territory Field Visit;
5 Days Tampa, FL

SPECIFIC EXPANSION PLANS:
US: All United States
Canada: All Canada
Overseas: NR

≪ ≫

**Great people.
Great camping.™**

**KAMPGROUNDS OF AMERICA /
KOA**
P.O. Box 30558
Billings, MT 59114
Tel: (800) 548-7239 (406) 248-7444
Fax: (406) 254-7414
E-Mail: phittmeier@koa.net

Web Site: www.koa.com
Mr. Patt Hittmeier, VP Franchise Development

KAMPGROUNDS OF AMERICA is North America's largest franchise system of open-to-the public campgrounds; no membership fees or annual dues are required. All KOA campgrounds offer RV and tent sites; 90% also offer Kamping Kabins. Nearly 2 million copies of the KOA directory are printed and distributed to campers. KOA campgrounds are located in 45 of the contiguous United States, 8 Canadian Provinces, Mexico and Japan.

BACKGROUND:
Established: 1962; 1st Franchised: 1962
Franchised Units: 450
Company-Owned Units: 27
Total Units: 477
Dist.: US-477; CAN-32; O'seas-8
North America: 45 States, 8 Provinces
Density: 27 in FL, 23 in CO
Projected New Units (12 Months): 8
Qualifications: 5, 3, 2, 3, 4, 4

FINANCIAL/TERMS:
Cash Investment: $150-500K
Total Investment: $200K-4MM
Minimum Net Worth: $300K
Fees: Franchise - $30/22.5/7.5K
Royalty - 8%; Ad. - 2%
Earnings Claims Statement: Yes
Term of Contract (Years): 5/
Avg. # Of Employees:5 (Varies) FT, 0 PT
Passive Ownership: Discouraged
Encourage Conversions: Yes
Area Develop. Agreements: No
Sub-Franchising Contracts: No
Expand In Territory: Yes
Space Needs: 10+ acres SF

SUPPORT & TRAINING:
Financial Assistance Provided: No
Site Selection Assistance: Yes
Lease Negotiation Assistance: No
Co-Operative Advertising: No
Franchisee Assoc./Member: Yes/Yes
Size Of Corporate Staff: 65
On-Going Support: A,B,C,D,E,F,G,h,I
Training: 5 Days Billings, MT

SPECIFIC EXPANSION PLANS:
US: All United States
Canada: All Canada
Overseas: NR

≪ ≫

LTS LEADERBOARD
21043 - 2591 Panorama Dr.

Coquitlam, BC V3E 2Y0 Canada
Tel: (800) 411-4448 (604) 468-2211 + 110
Fax: (604) 468-0101
E-Mail: info@ltsleaderboard.com
Web Site: www.ltsleaderboard.com
Mr. Robert Meister, Director Franchise Development

LeaderBoard Tournament Systems (LTS) is a system that enhances the entire fundraising experience for participants, sponsors and organizers, while also providing many tools to help RAISE MORE MONEY.

BACKGROUND: IFA MEMBER
Established: 1995; 1st Franchised: 2001
Franchised Units: 28
Company-Owned Units: 1
Total Units: 29
Dist.: US-24; CAN-2; O'seas-3
North America: 13 States, 2 Provinces
Density: 2 in IL, 4 in FL, 4 in CA
Projected New Units (12 Months): NR
Qualifications: 4, 3, 3, 3, 3, 4

FINANCIAL/TERMS:
Cash Investment: $49-173K
Total Investment: $49-173K
Minimum Net Worth: $200K
Fees: Franchise - Varies
Royalty - Varies; Ad. - 0%
Earnings Claims Statement: No
Term of Contract (Years): 5/5
Avg. # Of Employees: 2 FT, 0 PT
Passive Ownership: Not Allowed
Encourage Conversions: NA
Area Develop. Agreements: No
Sub-Franchising Contracts: No
Expand In Territory: No
Space Needs: NR

SUPPORT & TRAINING:
Financial Assistance Provided: No
Site Selection Assistance: NA
Lease Negotiation Assistance: NA
Co-Operative Advertising: No
Franchisee Assoc./Member: Yes/Yes
Size Of Corporate Staff: 9
On-Going Support: ,,C,D,,,G,H,I
Training: 2 Weeks Vancouver, BC

SPECIFIC EXPANSION PLANS:
US: All United States
Canada: Yes
Overseas: NR

≪ ≫

NEVADA BOB'S GOLF
2000, 335 Eighth Ave., S.W.

Calgary, AB T2P 1C9 Canada
Tel: (877) 222-GOLF (702) 451-3333
Fax: (702) 451-9378
E-Mail: franchise@nevadabobs.com
Web Site: www.nevadabobS.com
Ms. Tracey Pegler,

Join the leader in the retail golf industry! With a brand name spanning more than 25 years, NEVADA BOB'S has experience, innovation and an established track record as one of the world's largest golf specialty retailers. Entering a market with an instantly recognizable, established brand name provides you with a substantial advantage over the competition. We are positioned for growth! You can't afford to miss this opportunity!

BACKGROUND:

Established: 1974; 1st Franchised: 1974	
Franchised Units:	77
Company-Owned Units:	0
Total Units:	77
Dist.:	US-51; CAN-26; O'seas-0
North America:	15 States, 3 Provinces
Density:	12 in BC, 12 in CA, 6 in TN
Projected New Units (12 Months):	NR
Qualifications:	4, 4, 3, 3, 4, 4

FINANCIAL/TERMS:

Cash Investment:	$100K
Total Investment:	$300-722K
Minimum Net Worth:	NR
Fees: Franchise -	$50K
Royalty - 2%;	Ad. -
Earnings Claims Statement:	No
Term of Contract (Years):	10/10
Avg. # Of Employees:	2 FT, 3 PT
Passive Ownership:	Discouraged
Encourage Conversions:	Yes
Area Develop. Agreements:	Yes/1
Sub-Franchising Contracts:	No
Expand In Territory:	Yes
Space Needs:	~5,000 SF

SUPPORT & TRAINING:

Financial Assistance Provided:	No
Site Selection Assistance:	Yes
Lease Negotiation Assistance:	Yes
Co-Operative Advertising:	No
Franchisee Assoc./Member:	No
Size Of Corporate Staff:	10
On-Going Support:	,,C,D,E,,,H,I
Training:	Min 5 Days Calgary, AB

SPECIFIC EXPANSION PLANS:

US:	All United States
Canada:	All Canada
Overseas:	NR

≪ ≫

OUTDOOR CONNECTION

424 Neosho
Burlington, KS 66839
Tel: (888) 548-0636 (620) 364-5500
Fax: (620) 364-5563
E-Mail: info@outdoor-connection.com
Web Site: www.outdoor-connection.com
Mr. Marc Glades, President

OUTDOOR CONNECTION franchise owners market fishing and hunting travel. Over 200 lodges, guides and charter services have been pre-inspected to ensure quality. These destinations pay OUTDOOR CONNECTION 15-20% of their package rates for all bookings made. An excellent support system is in place for franchise owners to tap into.

BACKGROUND:

Established: 1988; 1st Franchised: 1990	
Franchised Units:	78
Company-Owned Units:	3
Total Units:	80
Dist.:	US-80; CAN-0; O'seas-0
North America:	33 States, 0 Provinces
Density:	8 in WI, 5 in MN, 5 in FL
Projected New Units (12 Months):	20
Qualifications:	3, 2, 2, 2, 3, 2

FINANCIAL/TERMS:

Cash Investment:	$10K
Total Investment:	$10-15.5K
Minimum Net Worth:	NA
Fees: Franchise -	$10K
Royalty - 4%;	Ad. - 1%
Earnings Claims Statement:	No
Term of Contract (Years):	5/5
Avg. # Of Employees:	1 FT, 1 PT
Passive Ownership:	Discouraged
Encourage Conversions:	NA
Area Develop. Agreements:	No
Sub-Franchising Contracts:	No
Expand In Territory:	Yes
Space Needs:	500 SF

SUPPORT & TRAINING:

Financial Assistance Provided:	Yes (D)
Site Selection Assistance:	No
Lease Negotiation Assistance:	No
Co-Operative Advertising:	Yes
Franchisee Assoc./Member:	No
Size Of Corporate Staff:	4
On-Going Support:	,,,D,E,,G,H,
Training:	2 Days Burlington, KS

SPECIFIC EXPANSION PLANS:

US:	All United States
Canada:	All Canada, except Quebec
Overseas:	NR

≪ ≫

PANDA FRANCHISES

305 Marc Aurele Fortin Blvd.
Laval, PQ H7L 2A3 Canada
Tel: (450) 622-4833 + 201
Fax: (450) 622-2939
E-Mail: info@pandashoes.com
Web Site: www.pandashoes.com
Ms. Linda Goulet, President

Children's shoe specialist - locations in major malls across Canada - 40 stores. Complete training program, including selling, merchandising, administration, etc. National advertising. Best selection of footwear for kids.

BACKGROUND:

Established: 1972; 1st Franchised: 1974	
Franchised Units:	31
Company-Owned Units:	1
Total Units:	32
Dist.:	US-0; CAN-32; O'seas-0
North America:	0 States, 4 Provinces
Density:	30 in QC, 5 in ON, 4 in BC
Projected New Units (12 Months):	0
Qualifications:	NR

FINANCIAL/TERMS:

Cash Investment:	$125K
Total Investment:	$200K-350K
Minimum Net Worth:	NR
Fees: Franchise -	$25K
Royalty - 4%;	Ad. - 0.5%
Earnings Claims Statement:	No
Term of Contract (Years):	5/Lease
Avg. # Of Employees:	3 FT, 2 PT
Passive Ownership:	Discouraged
Encourage Conversions:	Yes
Area Develop. Agreements:	No
Sub-Franchising Contracts:	No
Expand In Territory:	Yes
Space Needs:	800 SF

SUPPORT & TRAINING:

Financial Assistance Provided:	No
Site Selection Assistance:	Yes
Lease Negotiation Assistance:	Yes
Co-Operative Advertising:	No
Franchisee Assoc./Member:	NR
Size Of Corporate Staff:	8
On-Going Support:	,B,C,D,E,F,G,H,
Training:	2 Weeks Toronto, ON;
2 Weeks On-Site (at Opening)	

SPECIFIC EXPANSION PLANS:

US:	No
Canada:	All Canada
Overseas:	NR

≪ ≫

PLAY IT AGAIN SPORTS

4200 Dahlberg Dr., # 100
Minneapolis, MN 55422-4837
Tel: (800) 453-7752 (763) 520-8480
Fax: (763) 520-8501
E-Mail: pias-franchise-development@play
itagainsports.com
Web Site: www.playitagainsports.com
Franchise Development

Our retail stores blend the sale of used and new, name-brand sports equipment along with promoting trade-in discounts. This sales mix creates ultra-high value for the customer while providing significantly higher gross profit margins than traditional retailers.

BACKGROUND: IFA MEMBER
Established: 1983;   1st Franchised: 1988
Franchised Units: 395
Company-Owned Units: 0
Total Units: 395
Dist.:   US-349; CAN-44; O'seas-0
  North America: 47 States, 8 Provinces
  Density: 25 in ON, 40 in FL, 40 in CA
Projected New Units (12 Months):   15
Qualifications: 5, 4, 2, 2, 1, 4
FINANCIAL/TERMS:
Cash Investment: $57.1-105.3K
Total Investment: $190.2-351.1K
Minimum Net Worth: $350K
Fees: Franchise - $20K
  Royalty - 5%;   Ad. -
Earnings Claims Statement: Yes
Term of Contract (Years):   10/10
Avg. # Of Employees: 3 FT, 2 PT
Passive Ownership: Not Allowed
Encourage Conversions: No
Area Develop. Agreements: No
Sub-Franchising Contracts: No
Expand In Territory: No
Space Needs: 2,500-3,000 SF
SUPPORT & TRAINING:
Financial Assistance Provided: No
Site Selection Assistance: Yes
Lease Negotiation Assistance: Yes
Co-Operative Advertising: No
Franchisee Assoc./Member: No
Size Of Corporate Staff: 97
On-Going Support: ,,C,D,E,F,G,H,I
Training: 5 Days Minneapolis, MN;
  4 Days Minneapolis, MN
SPECIFIC EXPANSION PLANS:

US: All United States
Canada: All Canada
Overseas: NR

‹‹ ››

PRO GOLF INTERNATIONAL

37735 Enterprise Ct., # 600
Farmington Hills, MI 48331
Tel: (800) 776-4653 + 226 (248) 994-0553
+ 226
Fax: (248) 489-9334
E-Mail: pgaglio@progolfdiscount.com
Web Site: www.progolfamerica.com
Mr. Perry Gaglio, Franchise Director

PRO GOLF offers the best opportunity to make money among the golf franchise stores available today. We have the best training, the largest selection of private label and exclusive products to sell and the best name - PRO GOLF. Come visit PRO GOLF and learn how a successful retail golf store should operate.

BACKGROUND: IFA MEMBER
Established: 1962;   1st Franchised: 1974
Franchised Units: 148
Company-Owned Units: 1
Total Units: 149
Dist.:   US-123; CAN-22; O'seas-4
  North America: 30 States, 4 Provinces
  Density: 13 in MI, 9 in FL, 12 in CA
Projected New Units (12 Months):   20
Qualifications: 5, 4, 3, 4, NR, 5
FINANCIAL/TERMS:
Cash Investment: $100K
Total Investment: $300K+
Minimum Net Worth: $400K
Fees: Franchise - $49.5K
  Royalty - 2.5%;   Ad. - 0-1%
Earnings Claims Statement: No
Term of Contract (Years):   15/10
Avg. # Of Employees: 4 FT, 3 PT
Passive Ownership: Discouraged
Encourage Conversions: Yes
Area Develop. Agreements: Yes/1
Sub-Franchising Contracts: No
Expand In Territory: Yes
Space Needs: 4,000-6,000 SF
SUPPORT & TRAINING:
Financial Assistance Provided: Yes (D)
Site Selection Assistance: Yes
Lease Negotiation Assistance: Yes
Co-Operative Advertising: No

Franchisee Assoc./Member: No
Size Of Corporate Staff: 15
On-Going Support: ,B,C,D,E,F,G,H,I
Training: 8-12 Days Corporate Office in
  MI; 4-6 Days Your Location
SPECIFIC EXPANSION PLANS:
US: All United States
Canada: All Canada
Overseas: All That Have Golfers

‹‹   ››

PUTT-PUTT GOLF COURSES OF AMERICA

6350 Quadrangle Dr., # 210
Chapel Hill, NC 27517
Tel: (919) 493-9999 + 104
Fax: (919) 402-9902
E-Mail: bkastl@putt-putt.com
Web Site: www.putt-putt.com
Mr. Bob Kastl, Director of Sales

PUTT-PUTT GOLF is now in its 50th year of operation. It is the oldest and largest operator/franchisor of miniature golf and family entertainment centers in the world. PUTT-PUTT GOLF operates in 26 states and in 8 foreign countries and specializes in the development of PUTT-PUTT GOLF, gamerooms, batting cages, bumper cars, go-carts and laser tag.

BACKGROUND:
Established: 1954;   1st Franchised: 1955
Franchised Units: 132
Company-Owned Units: 0
Total Units: 132
Dist.:   US-110; CAN-1; O'seas-21
  North America: 26 States, 1 Provinces
  Density: 12 in NC, 13 in OH, 21 in TX
Projected New Units (12 Months):   12
Qualifications: 4, 5, 2, 3, 3, 4
FINANCIAL/TERMS:
Cash Investment: $35K-1MM
Total Investment: $1.5K-5MM
Minimum Net Worth: $500K
Fees: Franchise - $25-50K
  Royalty - 5%;   Ad. - 2%
Earnings Claims Statement: No
Term of Contract (Years):   20/
Avg. # Of Employees: FT, 0 PT
Passive Ownership: Allowed
Encourage Conversions: NA
Area Develop. Agreements: No
Sub-Franchising Contracts: No
Expand In Territory: No
Space Needs: 3-7 acres SF
SUPPORT & TRAINING:
Financial Assistance Provided: Yes (D)
Site Selection Assistance: Yes

Lease Negotiation Assistance: Yes
Co-Operative Advertising: No
Franchisee Assoc./Member: No
Size Of Corporate Staff: 6
On-Going Support: „C,D,,,G,H,I
Training: 1 Week Training Center;
3-7 Days Franchisee's

SPECIFIC EXPANSION PLANS:
US: All United States
Canada: All Canada
Overseas: South America

◂◂ ▸▸

SOCCER POST INTERNATIONAL
2903 Hwy., E. 138
Wall, NJ 07719
Tel: (732) 578-1377
Fax: (732) 578-1399
E-Mail: stunis@soccerpost.com
Web Site: www.soccerpost.com
Mr. Stephen Tunis, Franchise Director

A soccer specialty retail business, featuring top-of-the-line, cutting-edge soccer equipment from Adidas, Nike, Reebok, Xara, etc. Owner of store will become the center of soccer activity in the communities they serve. Must be soccer savvy!

BACKGROUND:
Established: 1978; 1st Franchised: 1991
Franchised Units: 25
Company-Owned Units: 7
Total Units: 32
Dist.: US-32; CAN-0; O'seas-0
North America: States, Provinces
Density: 2 in IL, 7 in NJ, 8 in PA
Projected New Units (12 Months): 12
Qualifications: 5, 3, 1, 3, 4, 5

FINANCIAL/TERMS:
Cash Investment: $190-250K
Total Investment: $190-250K
Minimum Net Worth: $300K
Fees: Franchise - $19.5K
Royalty - 3-5%; Ad. - 1.5-3%
Earnings Claims Statement: Yes
Term of Contract (Years): 5/5
Avg. # Of Employees: 1 FT, 2-4 PT
Passive Ownership: Allowed
Encourage Conversions: Yes
Area Develop. Agreements: Yes/1
Sub-Franchising Contracts: Yes
Expand In Territory: Yes
Space Needs: 3,200 SF

SUPPORT & TRAINING:
Financial Assistance Provided: Yes (D)
Site Selection Assistance: Yes
Lease Negotiation Assistance: Yes
Co-Operative Advertising: No

Franchisee Assoc./Member: No
Size Of Corporate Staff: 9
On-Going Support: „C,D,E,F,G,h,I
Training: 2 Weeks Plus Store, Voorhees, NJ

SPECIFIC EXPANSION PLANS:
US: All United States
Canada: No
Overseas: NR

◂◂ ▸▸

Hottest New Franchise

TOTAL GOLF ADVENTURES
390 N. Sepulveda Blvd., # 1060
El Segundo, CA 90245
Tel: (310) 333-0622
Fax: (310) 607-0055
E-Mail: info@totalgolfadventures.com
Web Site: www.totalgolfadventures.com
Mr. Steve Tanner, National Program Director / COO

Total Golf Adventures (TGA) has created a teaching method and program that grows the game of golf and a business model that brings golf to the students, parents and families. The cornerstone of the TGA organization and model is our creation of the first and only national Golf Enrichment Program for PK-8th grade students. TGA brings golf directly to the schools and other alternative facilities in the forms of pay-for-play programs and programs that are grant funded. These programs generally take place in the after school time period. Students advance through TGA's 5 Level Program at their schools and facilities and then transition to the golf course through TGA camps, tournaments, clinics, leagues and private lessons. TGA provides the infrastructure for success, on-site training, initial equipment/stationary/apparel packages, a website with a custom Content Management System, Database and online registration, and all of the ongoing support they need to succeed.

BACKGROUND:
Established: 2003; 1st Franchised: 2006
Franchised Units: 39
Company-Owned Units: 1
Total Units: 40
Dist.: US-40; CAN-0; O'seas-0
North America: 22 States, 0 Provinces

Density: 3 in MI, 3 in FL, 9 in CA
Projected New Units (12 Months): 8-12
Qualifications: 3, 4, 4, 4, 3, 4

FINANCIAL/TERMS:
Cash Investment: $5-40K
Total Investment: $13-57K
Minimum Net Worth: $50K
Fees: Franchise - $5-40K
Royalty - 8%; Ad. - 0
Earnings Claims Statement: No
Term of Contract (Years): 5/5
Avg. # Of Employees: 1 FT, 5-15 PT
Passive Ownership: Discouraged
Encourage Conversions: NA
Area Develop. Agreements: Yes/2
Sub-Franchising Contracts: No
Expand In Territory: No
Space Needs: NA

SUPPORT & TRAINING:
Financial Assistance Provided: No
Site Selection Assistance: Yes
Lease Negotiation Assistance: NA
Co-Operative Advertising: No
Franchisee Assoc./Member: Yes/Yes
Size Of Corporate Staff: 4
On-Going Support: A,B,C,D,,,G,H,
Training: 2-3 days In your territory

SPECIFIC EXPANSION PLANS:
US: All United States
Canada: No
Overseas: NR

◂◂ ▸▸

VELOCITY SPORTS PERFORMANCE
3650 Brookside Pkwy., # 300
Alpharetta, GA 30022
Tel: (866) 955-0400 (678) 990-2555
Fax: (678) 990-2560
E-Mail: info@velocitysp.com
Web Site: www.velocitysp.com
Ms. Chris Koestner, Director Franchise Development

VELOCITY SPORTS PERFORMANCE provides people who are passionate about kids and sports the opportunity to combine that with their passion for business. By investing in a VELOCITY SPORTS PERFORMANCE training center, franchise owners offer athletes of all ages and skill sets the chance to train in state-of-the-art facilities, under professional, certified coaches and ultimately give them the chance to take their athletic performance to the highest levels.

BACKGROUND: IFA MEMBER
Established: 1999; 1st Franchised: 2002
Franchised Units: 75
Company-Owned Units: 1
Total Units: 76
Dist.: US-73; CAN-3; O'seas-0
North America: 30 States, 2 Provinces
Density: 8 in TX, 5 in NJ, 11 in CA
Projected New Units (12 Months): 50
Qualifications: 5, 5, 2, 4, 3, 5
FINANCIAL/TERMS:
Cash Investment: $150K
Total Investment: $350-655K
Minimum Net Worth: $500-750K
Fees: Franchise - $54K
Royalty - 2-6%; Ad. - $2.5K/Mo.
Earnings Claims Statement: No
Term of Contract (Years): 10/10
Avg. # Of Employees: 8 FT, 0 PT
Passive Ownership: Discouraged
Encourage Conversions: NA
Area Develop. Agreements: Yes/1
Sub-Franchising Contracts: Yes
Expand In Territory: Yes
Space Needs: 15,000-20,000 SF
SUPPORT & TRAINING:
Financial Assistance Provided: Yes (I)
Site Selection Assistance: Yes
Lease Negotiation Assistance: Yes
Co-Operative Advertising: No
Franchisee Assoc./Member: Yes/Yes
Size Of Corporate Staff: 16

On-Going Support: a,B,C,D,E,,G,H,I
Training: 2 Weeks Alpharetta, GA
SPECIFIC EXPANSION PLANS:
US: All United States
Canada: All Canada
Overseas: Australia and others

≪ ≫

WORLD CLASS ATHLETE
1814 Franklin St., # 820
Oakland, CA 94612
Tel: (510) 839-5462
Fax: (510) 839-2104
E-Mail: sourcebook@earthlink.net
Web Site: www.worldclass.com
Mr. Chris F. Elders, President

WORLD CLASS ATHLETE offers a unique, specialty sporting goods concept. Product mix concentrates on athletic footwear, running, tennis and swimwear. Emphasis on race sponsorship, training programs and custom fitting. All major lines of footwear, accessories, warm-up suits and bags. Custom re-soling at Company-owned distribution centers. Founded by world class athlete Jeff Bond.

BACKGROUND:
Established: 1976; 1st Franchised: 1977
Franchised Units: 42
Company-Owned Units: 12
Total Units: 54
Dist.: US-41; CAN-9; O'seas-4
North America: 15 States, 2 Provinces

Density: 8 in WA, 7 in KY, 25 in CA
Projected New Units (12 Months): 14
Qualifications: 3, 5, 4, 2, 3, 5
FINANCIAL/TERMS:
Cash Investment: $90K
Total Investment: $150K
Minimum Net Worth: $250K
Fees: Franchise - $22K
Royalty - 6%; Ad. - 2%
Earnings Claims Statement: Yes
Term of Contract (Years): 15/15
Avg. # Of Employees: 2 FT, 4 PT
Passive Ownership: Not Allowed
Encourage Conversions: Yes
Area Develop. Agreements: Yes/1
Sub-Franchising Contracts: Yes
Expand In Territory: No
Space Needs: 1,800-2,200 SF
SUPPORT & TRAINING:
Financial Assistance Provided: Yes (D)
Site Selection Assistance: Yes
Lease Negotiation Assistance: Yes
Co-Operative Advertising: No
Franchisee Assoc./Member: No
Size Of Corporate Staff: 12
On-Going Support: a,B,C,D,E,f,G,,I
Training: 3 Weeks Headquarters;
2 Weeks On-Site
SPECIFIC EXPANSION PLANS:
US: All United States
Canada: All Canada
Overseas: Europe, U.K., Australia, New Zealand

≪ ≫

FIVE LARGEST PARTICIPANTS IN SURVEY

Company	# Fran- chised Units	# Co- Owned Units	# Total Units	Franchise Fee	On-Going Royalty	Total Investment
1. Results Travel	918	0	918	$1.5K (Currently Waived)	$600	$10.4-25K
2. UniGlobe Travel	750	0	750	$2-25K	$275-550	$5K
3. Carlson Wagonlit Travel Associates	669	2	671	$1.5K	Varies	$1.6-11.6K
4. CruiseOne	575	0	575	$9.8K	3%	$10-22K
5. Cruise Holidays	232	0	232	$30K	$750/mo.	$137-248K

All of the data provided are proprietary and should not be quoted without acknowledging *Bond's Franchise Guide.*

CarlsonWagonlit Travel

Your experience begins with ours.

**CARLSON WAGONLIT TRAVEL
ASSOCIATES**

701 Carlson Pkwy., MS 8206
Minneapolis, MN 55305
Tel: (800) 213-7295
Fax: (763) 212-2409
E-Mail: marc.moore@carlson.com
Web Site: www.carlsontravel.com
Mr. Marc Moore, Director of Franchise
  Sales

Start-up and conversion travel agencies available. Preferred supplier program; national and local marketing and advertising newsletters; brochures; assistance with commercial business development; regional meetings; participation in CARLSON Selling Systems; Associate consulting service; hotel programs; 24-hour service center; centralized support department; international rate desk; and professional development programs. Leading technology to maximize efficiency.

BACKGROUND: IFA MEMBER
Established: 1900;   1st Franchised: 1984
Franchised Units: 669
Company-Owned Units: 2

Total Units: 671
Dist.:   US-671; CAN-0; O'seas-0
  North America: 50 States, 0 Provinces
  Density: 44 in WI, 58 in TX, 62 in MI
Projected New Units (12 Months):   30
Qualifications: 3, 4, 5, 4, 3, 4
FINANCIAL/TERMS:
Cash Investment: $1.5K
Total Investment: $1.6-11.6K
Minimum Net Worth: NA
Fees: Franchise - $1.5K
  Royalty - Varies;   Ad. - Varies
Earnings Claims Statement: No
Term of Contract (Years):   5/5
Avg. # Of Employees: Varies
Passive Ownership: Discouraged

Encourage Conversions:	Yes
Area Develop. Agreements:	No
Sub-Franchising Contracts:	No
Expand In Territory:	Yes
Space Needs:	NR

SUPPORT & TRAINING:

Financial Assistance Provided:	No
Site Selection Assistance:	No
Lease Negotiation Assistance:	No
Co-Operative Advertising:	Yes
Franchisee Assoc./Member:	Yes/Yes
Size Of Corporate Staff:	160
On-Going Support:	,,,d,e,,g,h,i

Training: 3 Days Minneapolis/On-Site for Start-Ups; Minneapolis for Conversions

SPECIFIC EXPANSION PLANS:

US:	All United States
Canada:	No
Overseas:	NR

◄◄ ►►

Relax...you're with us

CRUISE HOLIDAYS
6442 City W. Pkwy.
Minneapolis, MN 55344-3245
Tel: (800) 824-1481 (952) 914-6743
Fax: (763) 219-4182
E-Mail: mwollak@ttfg.com
Web Site: www.cruiseholidays.com
Ms. Megan Wollak, Franchise Development

Cruise Holidays is the largest cruise-specialty franchise in North America offering retail and home-based franchises and career opportunities. Cruise Holidays is also a distinguished provider of all-inclusive resort and land tour vacation packages. It is our carefully crafted standards and brand positioning that set Cruise Holidays apart from the competition. Our name says it all . . . a focus on the cruise experience for our customers. If you are interested in the excitement and allure of the cruise industry, Cruise Holidays has the expertise to help you achieve your entrepreneurial dream.

BACKGROUND: IFA MEMBER
Established: 1984; 1st Franchised: 1984

Franchised Units:	232
Company-Owned Units:	0
Total Units:	232
Dist.:	US-202; CAN-30; O'seas-0

North America:	34 States, 4 Provinces
Density:	21 in ON, 18 in FL, 27 in CA
Projected New Units (12 Months):	40
Qualifications:	5, 5, 1, 1, 4, 5

FINANCIAL/TERMS:

Cash Investment:	$30K
Total Investment:	$137K-248K
Minimum Net Worth:	$250K
Fees: Franchise -	$30K
Royalty - $750/mo.;	Ad. - 0%
Earnings Claims Statement:	No
Term of Contract (Years):	3/3
Avg. # Of Employees:	1 FT, 0 PT
Passive Ownership:	Not Allowed
Encourage Conversions:	Yes
Area Develop. Agreements:	No
Sub-Franchising Contracts:	No
Expand In Territory:	Yes
Space Needs:	800-1000 SF

SUPPORT & TRAINING:

Financial Assistance Provided:	No
Site Selection Assistance:	Yes
Lease Negotiation Assistance:	No
Co-Operative Advertising:	Yes
Franchisee Assoc./Member:	Yes/Yes
Size Of Corporate Staff:	13
On-Going Support:	,,C,D,E,,G,h,I

Training: 3 weeks New Franchisee training in Minneapolis, MN

SPECIFIC EXPANSION PLANS:

US: All United States except Alaska
Canada: All Canada except Quebec, New Brunswick, Newfoundl

Overseas:	NR

◄◄ ►►

CRUISEONE
1415 NW 62nd St., # 205
Ft. Lauderdale, FL 33309-1955
Tel: (800) 892-3928 (954) 958-3700
Fax: (954) 958-3697
E-Mail: tcourtney@cruiseone.com
Web Site: www.cruiseonefranchise.com
Mr. Tim Courtney, Director of Franchise Sales

CRUISEONE is a nationwide, home-based cruise & travel franchise company representing all major cruise lines and tour operators. Franchisees are professionally trained in a 6-day comprehensive program. CruiseOne provides a heritage of excellence, unrivaled buying power, industry-leading technology solutions, pride of true business ownership, and access to a large corporate support team to help you grow. CruiseOne is a member of the International Franchise Association (IFA) and participates in the VetFran and Minor-

ityFran initiatives offering incentives and rebates to encourage business ownership.

BACKGROUND: IFA MEMBER

Established: 1991; 1st Franchised: 1992	
Franchised Units:	575
Company-Owned Units:	0
Total Units:	575
Dist.:	US-575; CAN-0; O'seas-0
North America:	45 States, 0 Provinces
Density:	40 in TX, 101 in FL, 63 in CA
Projected New Units (12 Months):	70
Qualifications:	3, 4, 2, 3, 5, 4

FINANCIAL/TERMS:

Cash Investment:	$9.8K
Total Investment:	$10-22K
Minimum Net Worth:	NR
Fees: Franchise -	$9.8K
Royalty - 3%;	Ad. - .25%
Earnings Claims Statement:	No
Term of Contract (Years):	5/
Avg. # Of Employees:	1 FT, 0 PT
Passive Ownership:	Not Allowed
Encourage Conversions:	NA
Area Develop. Agreements:	No
Sub-Franchising Contracts:	No
Expand In Territory:	Yes
Space Needs:	NA

SUPPORT & TRAINING:

Financial Assistance Provided:	Yes (D)
Site Selection Assistance:	NA
Lease Negotiation Assistance:	NA
Co-Operative Advertising:	Yes
Franchisee Assoc./Member:	No
Size Of Corporate Staff:	80
On-Going Support:	A,B,C,D,,F,,h,I

Training: 6 Days Ft. Lauderdale, FL

SPECIFIC EXPANSION PLANS:

US:	All United States
Canada:	10
Overseas:	2

◄◄ ►►

DISCOVERY MAP INTERNATIONAL
P. O. Box 1529
La Conner, WA 98257
Tel: (877) 820-7827 (360) 547-1374
Fax: (360) 466-2710
E-Mail: franchise@discoverymap.com
Web Site: www.discoverymap.com
Ms. Monica Whitmore, Director of Franchise Development

Discovery Map International is a business-to-business map and guide publishing business that caters to the multi-billion dollar travel and tourism industry. With home-based offices, our franchise owners provide cost-effective advertising solutions that help local business owners boost their sales via Discovery Map's beautiful hand-illustrated maps and in-room hotel guest directories.

BACKGROUND: IFA MEMBER
Established: 1987; 1st Franchised: 1999
Franchised Units: 31
Company-Owned Units: 15
Total Units: 46
Dist.: US-46; CAN-0; O'seas-0
North America: 12 States, 0 Provinces
Density: 5 in MT, 3 in FL, 4 in AZ
Projected New Units (12 Months): NR
Qualifications: 4, 3, 4, 3, 3, 4
FINANCIAL/TERMS:
Cash Investment: $60K
Total Investment: $53K-83K
Minimum Net Worth: $250K
Fees: Franchise - $25-40K
Royalty - NR; Ad. - 2% of product cost
Earnings Claims Statement: Yes
Term of Contract (Years): 10/10
Avg. # Of Employees: 13 FT, 0 PT
Passive Ownership: Not Allowed
Encourage Conversions: NA
Area Develop. Agreements: Yes/0
Sub-Franchising Contracts: No
Expand In Territory: Yes
Space Needs: NR
SUPPORT & TRAINING:
Financial Assistance Provided: No
Site Selection Assistance: NA
Lease Negotiation Assistance: NA
Co-Operative Advertising: No
Franchisee Assoc./Member: Yes/No
Size Of Corporate Staff: 13
On-Going Support: ,,C,D,,F,G,h,I
Training: Varies Field Training;
5-8 Days La Conner WA; Varies Franchise Owner's Home
SPECIFIC EXPANSION PLANS:
US: All United States except WA, RI, ND
Canada: No
Overseas: NR

≪ ≫

EXPEDIA CRUISESHIPCENTERS
400-1055 W. Hastings St.
Vancouver, BC V6E2E9

Tel: (888) 883-9033 (604) 678-3585
Fax: (604) 685-1245
E-Mail: franchise@cruisefranchise.com
Web Site: www.cruisefranchise.com
Mr. Michael Mutsaerts, VP Franchise Sales

Change Your Life. At Expedia CruiseShip-Centers, you'll get tools to create wealth -- time to create joy. With over 110 retail locations from coast to coast and a powerful internet strategy, our Franchise Partners enjoy a rewarding business and a great lifestyle. Proven, turn-key systems and support means no travel industry experience is required to launch your business. Enjoy the competitive advantage of the #1 travel brand, massive buying power, award-winning marketing and industry-leading technology.

BACKGROUND: IFA MEMBER
Established: 1987; 1st Franchised: 1988
Franchised Units: 110
Company-Owned Units: 2
Total Units: 112
Dist.: US-1; CAN-111; O'seas-0
North America: 1 States, 9 Provinces
Density: 10 in AB, 35 in BC, 53 in ON
Projected New Units (12 Months): 20
Qualifications: 4, 3, 2, 4, 4, 5
FINANCIAL/TERMS:
Cash Investment: $75K
Total Investment: $120K-150K
Minimum Net Worth: $250K
Fees: Franchise - $43K
Royalty - 9%; Ad. - $630/mo
Earnings Claims Statement: No
Term of Contract (Years): 10/5
Avg. # Of Employees: 2 FT, 12 PT
Passive Ownership: Discouraged
Encourage Conversions: Yes
Area Develop. Agreements: No
Sub-Franchising Contracts: No
Expand In Territory: Yes
Space Needs: 900 SF
SUPPORT & TRAINING:
Financial Assistance Provided: No
Site Selection Assistance: Yes
Lease Negotiation Assistance: Yes
Co-Operative Advertising: Yes
Franchisee Assoc./Member: No
Size Of Corporate Staff: 76
On-Going Support: ,,C,D,E,,,h,I
Training: 4 weeks self study International Cruise Academy (self-study);
1 week in-classroom Cruise Management Academy (Vancouver);2 days; 7 daysRegional Meetings (2 X per year) (Toronto & Vancouver)

SPECIFIC EXPANSION PLANS:
US: All
Canada: All
Overseas: NR

≪ ≫

RESULTS TRAVEL
701 Carlson Pkwy.
Minnetonka, MN 55305
Tel: (888) 523-2200
Fax: (763) 212-2302
E-Mail: admin@resultstravel.net
Web Site: www.resultstravel.com
Mr. John Risner, General Manager

Results Travel is the family of agencies where YOU matter. This is a means to achieve greater revenues for the sales you attain today, without requiring a multi-year commitment to join. Without requiring you to change your name or lose your identity. Benefit from override agreements and lucrative commission structures.

BACKGROUND:
Established: 1984; 1st Franchised: 2000
Franchised Units: 918
Company-Owned Units: 0
Total Units: 918
Dist.: US-918; CAN-0; O'seas-0
North America: 50 States, 0 Provinces
Density: 37 in TX, 42 in MN, 68 in IL
Projected New Units (12 Months): 100
Qualifications: 5, 4, 5, 3, 5, 5
FINANCIAL/TERMS:
Cash Investment: $200-250K
Total Investment: $10.4-25K
Minimum Net Worth: $300K
Fees: Franchise - $1.5K (Currently Waived)
Royalty - $600; Ad. - NA
Earnings Claims Statement: No
Term of Contract (Years): 1/1
Avg. # Of Employees: Varies
Passive Ownership: Allowed
Encourage Conversions: Yes
Area Develop. Agreements: No
Sub-Franchising Contracts: No
Expand In Territory: Yes
Space Needs: Varies
SUPPORT & TRAINING:
Financial Assistance Provided: No
Site Selection Assistance: No
Lease Negotiation Assistance: No
Co-Operative Advertising: Yes
Franchisee Assoc./Member: Yes/Yes
Size Of Corporate Staff: 22
On-Going Support: A,,C,D,,F,G,H,I
Training: 1 Day Ft. Lauderdale, FL;

1 Day Palm Beach Gardens, FL; 1 Day Philadelphia, PA

SPECIFIC EXPANSION PLANS:
US: All United States
Canada: No
Overseas: NR

≪ ≫

SEAMASTER CRUISES

701 Carlson Pkwy.
Minnetonka, MN 55305
Tel: (800) 824-1481 (763) 212-4590
Fax: (763) 212-5270
E-Mail: smcsupport@seamastercruises.com
Web Site: www.seamastercruises.com
Ms. Megan Slind, Sales Development Coord.

SeaMaster Cruises offers an exciting business specializing in selling cruise and cruise related vacations from your own home. SeaMaster Cruises is part of the Carlson Travel Franchise Group, the largest travel franchisor in the world today supporting over 1700 travel agencies in the U.S. alone. We provide the highest commissions available, marketing programs and proprietary technology. We'll show you how to build a successful business with travel perks and a lifestyle that allows you to be your own boss.

BACKGROUND:
Established: 2003;   1st Franchised: 2003
Franchised Units: 62
Company-Owned Units: 0
Total Units: 62
Dist.:   US-62; CAN-0; O'seas-0
North America: 25 States, 0 Provinces
Density: 5 in MN, 9 in FL, 11 in CA
Projected New Units (12 Months):   NR
Qualifications: 3, 3, 3, 3, 3, 3
FINANCIAL/TERMS:
Cash Investment: $9.5K
Total Investment: $10.3-16.9K
Minimum Net Worth: $100K
Fees: Franchise - $9.5K
Royalty - 3%;   Ad. - $100 flat after 12 Mo.
Earnings Claims Statement: No
Term of Contract (Years):   5/5
Avg. # Of Employees: 1 FT, 0 PT
Passive Ownership: Not Allowed
Encourage Conversions: NA
Area Develop. Agreements: No
Sub-Franchising Contracts: No
Expand In Territory: No
Space Needs: NA

SUPPORT & TRAINING:
Financial Assistance Provided: No
Site Selection Assistance: NA
Lease Negotiation Assistance: NA
Co-Operative Advertising: No
Franchisee Assoc./Member: Yes/Yes
Size Of Corporate Staff: 7
On-Going Support: A,B,C,D,,F,G,,I
Training: 7-10 Days At Sea Onboard
Training Cruise; 1 Week Minneapolis, MN
SPECIFIC EXPANSION PLANS:
US: All United States
Canada: No
Overseas: NR

≪ ≫

TRAVEL LINES EXPRESS

9858 Glades Rd., # 208
Boca Raton, FL 33434
Tel: (561) 482-9557
Fax:
E-Mail: tley2k@aol.com
Web Site: www.travellinesexpress.com
Mr. David Korn, Vice President

Home-based travel agency franchise program. Full-service travel agency, offering cruises, airline tickets, hotels, car rentals, vacation packages and tours. Lowest franchise fee $300 includes state-of-the-art reservation system. Complete internet training and Website development. Lowest monthly royalty fee of 1%.

BACKGROUND: IFA MEMBER
Established: 2003;   1st Franchised: 2003
Franchised Units: 15
Company-Owned Units: 1
Total Units: 16
Dist.:   US-16; CAN-0; O'seas-0
North America: 20 States, 0 Provinces
Density:
Projected New Units (12 Months):   NR
Qualifications: NR
FINANCIAL/TERMS:
Cash Investment: $10-50K
Total Investment: $10-50K
Minimum Net Worth: NA
Fees: Franchise - $10-50K
Royalty - 1%;   Ad. - 0%
Earnings Claims Statement: No
Term of Contract (Years):none/continual
Avg. # Of Employees: 1 FT, 0 PT
Passive Ownership: Discouraged
Encourage Conversions: No
Area Develop. Agreements: No
Sub-Franchising Contracts: No
Expand In Territory: Yes

Space Needs: NA
SUPPORT & TRAINING:
Financial Assistance Provided: No
Site Selection Assistance: NA
Lease Negotiation Assistance: NA
Co-Operative Advertising: No
Franchisee Assoc./Member: No
Size Of Corporate Staff: 7
On-Going Support: ,,,D,,,G,H,I
Training: Complete On-Line Training
SPECIFIC EXPANSION PLANS:
US: All United States
Canada: All Canada
Overseas: All Countries

≪ ≫

TRAVEL NETWORK

560 Sylvan Ave.
Englewood Cliffs, NJ 07632
Tel: (800) 669-9000 (201) 567-8500
Fax: (201) 567-4405
E-Mail: info@rezconnect.com
Web Site: www.travelnetwork.com
Mr. Michael Y. Brent, President

Join the exciting travel industry with the leading travel franchisor as the owner of a TRAVEL NETWORK full-service travel agency catering to the business and leisure traveler. A TRAVEL NETWORK VACATION CENTRAL agency focuses solely on the lucrative leisure travel markets, or, as the owner of a full-service agency, catering to the business traveler as well as the leisure traveler. Our program includes complete start-up assistance, site selection and more.

BACKGROUND:
Established: 1982;   1st Franchised: 1982
Franchised Units: 225
Company-Owned Units: 1
Total Units: 226
Dist.:   US-178; CAN-4; O'seas-44
North America: 35 States, 1 Provinces
Density: 14 in CA, 18 in FL, 26 in NJ
Projected New Units (12 Months):   30
Qualifications: 4, 4, 1, 2, 3, 4
FINANCIAL/TERMS:
Cash Investment: $80K
Total Investment: $120K
Minimum Net Worth: $50K
Fees: Franchise - $14.9K
Royalty - $350/Mo.;   Ad. - $50/Mo.
Earnings Claims Statement: No
Term of Contract (Years):   15/15
Avg. # Of Employees: 2 FT, 5 PT
Passive Ownership: Discouraged
Encourage Conversions: Yes

Area Develop. Agreements: Yes/1
Sub-Franchising Contracts: Yes
Expand In Territory: Yes
Space Needs: 600+ SF

SUPPORT & TRAINING:
Financial Assistance Provided: Yes (D)
Site Selection Assistance: Yes
Lease Negotiation Assistance: Yes
Co-Operative Advertising: No
Franchisee Assoc./Member: Yes/Yes
Size Of Corporate Staff: 18
On-Going Support: a,B,C,D,E,,G,H,I
Training: 1 Week NJ; 1 Week Orlando, FL

SPECIFIC EXPANSION PLANS:
US: All United States
Canada: All Canada
Overseas: All Countries

⪪ ⪫

UNIGLOBE TRAVEL
1199 W. Pender St., # 900
Vancouver, BC V6E 2R1 Canada
Tel: (800) 863-1606 (604) 718-2600
Fax: (604) 718-2678

E-Mail: info@uniglobetravel.com
Web Site: www.uniglobefranchise.com
Mr. Andrew Henry, VP US Operations

Entrepreneur has consistently awarded UNIGLOBE TRAVEL the #1 company in travel-agency franchising. All UNI-GLOBE travel agency franchisees benefit from programs and systems designed to handle the needs of both the corporate and leisure client. UNIGLOBE franchisees benefit from money-saving automation agreements and top-notch incentive commission programs with major airline, hotel, car rental, tour and cruise-line companies.

BACKGROUND: IFA MEMBER
Established: 1979; 1st Franchised: 1980
Franchised Units: 750
Company-Owned Units: 0
Total Units: 750
Dist.: US-342; CAN-128; O'seas-235
  North America: 50 States, 9 Provinces
  Density: 41 in OH, 45 in IL, 109 in CA
Projected New Units (12 Months): 100
Qualifications: 5, 4, 1, 3, 4, 5

FINANCIAL/TERMS:
Cash Investment: $1.5K
Total Investment: $5K

Minimum Net Worth: $60K
Fees: Franchise - $2-25K
  Royalty - $275-550; Ad. - $550
Earnings Claims Statement: No
Term of Contract (Years): 10/5
Avg. # Of Employees: 3 FT, 1 PT
Passive Ownership: Discouraged
Encourage Conversions: Yes
Area Develop. Agreements: Yes/1
Sub-Franchising Contracts: Yes
Expand In Territory: Yes
Space Needs: 1,200 SF

SUPPORT & TRAINING:
Financial Assistance Provided: Yes (I)
Site Selection Assistance: Yes
Lease Negotiation Assistance: Yes
Co-Operative Advertising: Yes
Franchisee Assoc./Member: Yes/No
Size Of Corporate Staff: 100
On-Going Support: ,,C,D,e,,G,h,I
Training: 3-5 Days Irvine, CA

SPECIFIC EXPANSION PLANS:
US: All United States
Canada: All Canada
Overseas: All Countries

⪪ ⪫

For a full explanation
of the data provided
in the Franchisor
Profiles, please refer to
*Chapter 2, "How to Use
the Data."*

123-AWARDS.COM

123-Awards.com
It's That Easy!

310 Shaw Rd., # H
South San Francisco, CA 94080
Tel: (888) 805-7253 (650) 588-1707
Fax: (650) 240-0699
Web Site: www.123-awards.com
E-mail: sales@123-awards.com
Contact: Rod Gilchrist, Owner
Other Offices In:

BUSINESS FOCUS
Retailer of plaques, awards and promotional products.

Major Areas of Concentration:

1) Retirement plaques and awards
2) Recognition plaques and awards
3) Incentives
4) Promotional products

BACKGROUND

Business Established In:	1999
Association Memberships:	
Full-Time Employees:	8
Full-Time Professionals:	8
Major Franchising Clients in Past 3 Yrs.:	

AREAS CONSULT IN
U.S.:
Canada:
Overseas:

◄◄ ►►

ACCURATE FRANCHISING, INC.

2121 Vista Pkwy.
West Palm Beach, FL 33411
Tel: (561) 868-1358
Fax: (561) 868-2637
Web Site: www.ufgservices.com
E-mail: sartony@aol.com
Contact: Mr. Tony Foley, President
Other Offices In:

BUSINESS FOCUS
Accurate Franchising, Inc. provides a complete, "concept to franchise" service backed by over 30 years of experience. We have used our expertise to create a program for those interested in taking the steps to franchising their business in standard or customizable packages depending on their needs. We provide tools to help through every step of the process. From legal documentation, franchise agreement preparation, Disclosure documents, strategic

394

planning, operations manuals, trade marking, complete marketin

Major Areas of Concentration:

1) Disclosure documents prepared
2) Manual of operations created
3) Franchise sales brochure created
4) Domestic franchise agreement

BACKGROUND
Business Established In: 2007
Association Memberships:
Full-Time Employees: 4
Full-Time Professionals: 6
Major Franchising Clients in Past 3 Yrs.: Popscorn, Palm Beach Puppies, Earth Graphics

AREAS CONSULT IN
U.S.: Yes
Canada: No
Overseas: Yes, Australia, South Africa, Spain, U.K., Nigeria, Canada, Italy, Kazakhistan, Croatia, Japan

AMERICAN ASSOCIATION OF FRANCHISEES AND DEALERS

P. O. Box 81887
San Diego, CA 92138-1887
Tel: (800) 733-9858 (619) 209-3775
Fax: (619) 209-3775
Web Site: www.aafd.org
E-mail: benefits@aafd.org
Contact: Mr. Robert L. Purvin, Chairman/CEO
Other Offices In: Sacramento, CA; Austin/Shamrock, TX; Indianapolis, IN

BUSINESS FOCUS
National non-profit trade association advocating the interests and rightss of owners of franchised businesses and independent dealers and promoting Total Quality Franhcising practices. At AAFD supports the growth and effectiveness of independent franchisee associations organized or affiliates as chapters of the AAFD. The AAFD provides a wide range of economic and legaal benefits for franchisee groups and individual members. The AAFD provides support of individuals who are investigating investent in a franchise or dealership opportunity.

Major Areas of Concentration:

1) The formation, promotion and support of effective independent franchisee associations (often organized as trademark chapters of the AAFD).
2) The development and promotion of AAFD's Fair Franchising Standards and the Accreditation of Franchisors who respect the AAFD's Standards to earn our prestigious Fair Franchising Seal.
3) Legal and economic support of individual franchisees and dealer businesses.

BACKGROUND
Business Established In: 1992
Association Memberships:
Full-Time Employees: 6
Full-Time Professionals: 2
Major Franchising Clients in Past 3 Yrs.: The AAFD has more than 45 existing chapters and affiliated chapters, including: North American Association of Subway Franchisees, Meineke Dealers Association, Denny's Franchisee Association, Domino's Franchisee Association

AREAS CONSULT IN
U.S.: Yes
Canada: Yes
Overseas: No

AMERICAN FRANCHISEE ASSOCIATION (AFA)

53 W. Jackson Blvd, Suite 1157
Chicago, IL 60604
Tel: (312) 431-0545
Fax: (312) 431-1469
Web Site: www.franchisee.org
E-mail: larrybeck@franchisee.org
Contact: Mr. Larry Beck, Office Manager
Other Offices In:

BUSINESS FOCUS
The American Franchisee Association (AFA) is a national trade association of franchisees and dealers founded in February 1993. Fifteen thousand individuals who own over 30,000 franchised outlets in 60 different industries are members of the AFA. The AFA was formed to improve the business conditions for franchising generally, while working diligently to protect the economic interests of franchisees. The AFA accomplishes this goal by providing two

additional avenues to resolve potential conflicts. First, the AFA constantly advocates the franchisee's position. Second, the AFA communicates with federal and state lawmakers about the inherent imbalance written into the contracts governing the franchisor-franchisee relationship.

Major Areas of Concentration:

1) Representation: The AFA represents the interests of franchisees to the media, the government and the public.
2) Communication: The AFA publishes the AFA E-Newsletter for its members to keep them informed on recent legal decisions and operational issues of importance to small business franchisees. AFA's Web Community provides an online forum for franchisees to communicate, buy and sell products and services, exchange ideas and post important notices.
3) Networking: AFA members can network AFA Franchisee Leadership Summits held in Chicago. At the Franchisee Leadership Summit, the leaders of independent franchisee associations are invited to spend a day sharing their experiences and discussing issues of concern. Franchisees can also network on AFA's Web Community through chat rooms, discussion forums and personal web sites.
4) Legal Referrals: AFA's Directory of Affiliate Members will put you in contact with some of the best franchisee lawyers in the country.
5) Health Insurance: AFA provides group health insurance for its members through either: 1) a Mini-Med program 2) a self-funded program; or 3) an individual program.

BACKGROUND

Business Established In:	1993
Association Memberships:	
Full-Time Employees:	3
Full-Time Professionals:	2

Major Franchising Clients in Past 3 Yrs.: Association of Kentucky Fried Chicken Franchisees, National Franchise Association (Burger King), National Coalition of 7-Eleven Franchisees, Denny's Franchisee Association, Dairy Queen Operators Association, International Organization of Little Ceasar's Franchisees, Roto Rooter Franchisee Association, National Association of Satellite Contract Owners (H&R Block) and Quizno's Franchisee Association.

AREAS CONSULT IN

U.S.:	Yes
Canada:	Yes
Overseas:	Yes - We consult internationally, specifically Canada, Australia, and China.

450 B Street, Suite 1950
San Diego, CA 92101
Tel: (866) 837-6063 (619) 692-3807
Fax: (619) 858-2996
Web Site: www.benetrends.com
E-mail: lfischer@benetrendsinc.com
Contact: Mr. Len Fischer, Esq., President
Other Offices In: 1180 Welsh Road, Suite 170M, North Wales, PA 19454

BUSINESS FOCUS

At BeneTrends, Inc., we help rainy day savers become rainmakers. Using our Rainmaker Plan, you can use the funds in your 401K, IRA, profit-sharing, or annuity plans to open a franchise--and become a rainmaker--without taxes or penalties.

Major Areas of Concentration:

1) Franchise Financing
2) Small Business Financing

BACKGROUND

Business Established In:	
Association Memberships:	
Full-Time Employees:	Confidential
Full-Time Professionals:	Confidential
Major Franchising Clients in Past 3 Yrs.:	Confidential

AREAS CONSULT IN

U.S.:	Yes
Canada:	No
Overseas:	No

670 N. Commercial St.
Manchester, NH 03101
Tel: (866) 623-5784 (603) 626-0333
Fax: (603) 218-6849
Web Site: www.bizunite.com
E-mail: hello@bizunite.com
Contact: Barth Getto, VP of Professional Development
Other Offices In:

BUSINESS FOCUS

BizUnite is a white label marketplace of business services designed specifically for cooperatives, franchises and other membership organizations. BizUnite was founded in 2007 by retail powerhouse CCA Global Partners. It's located in Manchster, New Hampshire. More information about the company can be found at http://www.bizunite.com

Major Areas of Concentration:
1) Cost Savings
2) Business Services
3) Professional Networking

BACKGROUND

Business Established In:	2007
Association Memberships:	IFA
Full-Time Employees:	11
Full-Time Professionals:	11

Major Franchising Clients in Past 3 Yrs.: Professional Carpet Systems, Flooring America, ProSource

AREAS CONSULT IN

U.S.:	Yes, All
Canada:	Yes, All
Overseas:	Yes, Australia, Africa

CANAM FRANCHISE DEVELOPMENT GROUP

"Franchising in Canada just got easier"

2607 McBain Ave.
Vancouver, BC V6L 2C7 Canada
Tel: (866) 730-5553 (604) 730-5553
Fax: (604) 876-6460
Web Site: www.canamfranchise.com
E-mail: rob@canamfranchise.com
Contact: Mr. Rob Lancit, President
Other Offices In:

BUSINESS FOCUS

CANAM Franchise Development Group helps U.S. franchisors sell franchises in Canada. We become your Canadian Franchise Sales Team. We provide franchise development services to companies wanting to franchise in Canada. With dedicated personal attention and concern for our clients, our team of experts offers a proven system that develops, packages, and launches franchise programs within the Canadian marketplace. And most importantly, we take responsibility for implementing our sales strategies and recommendations. CANAM Franchise Development Group can accelerate your company's expansion into Canada. Our vast knowledge of the Canadian marketplace and our extensive industry database, gives you immediate access to qualified individuals or corporations who are committed to franchising. We have solved the problems most franchisors are likely to experience in developing their concept in Canada. Our main goal is to make your franchise program lucrative, marketable and enduring. We believe your success is our success.

Major Areas of Concentration:

1) Sales & Marketing: 1) Provide a Canadian office 2) Planning, organizing and controlling all aspects of sales process 3) Lead Generating Programs 4) Recruitment and selection of the right franchises 5) Franchisee evaluation and profiles 6) Access to our database of corporations and entrepreneurs actively seeking franchise opportunities 7) Provide short term local management and operations services on initial stage of franchise development 8) Development of a marketing plan and budget incorporating unique, efficient, inexpensive cost strategies that yield optimum results 9) Brand awareness at Canadian exhibitions
2) Legal & Real Estate - Through our affiliation with leading franchise legal & real estate experts, CANAM offers: 1) Assistance with trademark registration 2) Advice on incorporating in Canada 3) Information about disclosure laws of Canada 4) Preparation of legal agreements and documentation 5) Lease negotiations 6) Store design and build out
3) Financing: 1) Assistance with obtaining third party financing for franchisees from finance companies that specialize in all types of financing for franchisees including start-up expenses, equipment and real estate

BACKGROUND

Business Established In:	2001
Association Memberships:	
Full-Time Employees:	2
Full-Time Professionals:	

Major Franchising Clients in Past 3 Yrs.: Discovery Computers, Precision Tune Auto Care, The Tan Company, Criterium Engineers, Quik Internet, Instant Imprints, Cleantastic International, Puckmasters, Computer Renaissance

AREAS CONSULT IN

U.S.:	Yes
Canada:	Yes
Overseas:	Yes - Australia, New Zealand, Singapore, United Kingdom, Italy, The Caribbean

COMPREHENSIVE LOYALTY

"Guiding the Loyalty Transformation Process"

862 E. Wildmere
Longwood, FL 32750
Tel: (407) 339-2612
Fax: (407) 339-7412

Web Site: www.comprehensiveloyalty.com
E-mail: petertravers@earthlink.net
Contact: Mr. Peter Travers, Founder
Other Offices In: San Francisco area and Virginia Beach, VA

BUSINESS FOCUS

Comprehensive Loyalty is a team of seasoned consultants and analysts specializing in site selection studies and customer loyalty development. The name Comprehensive Loyalty was chosen because of years of working with companies who have fragmented their customer development programs by ignoring site location and modern database marketing techniques. We specialize in a comprehensive approach that incorporates store development (site selection), loyalty-based data processing, database marketing and customer profiling (RFM scores, customer segments of highest lifetime value, attrition studies), market share analysis and incentive compensation. This approach leads to achieving Marketing Alignment (TM) and a "Loyalty Transformation Process. Computerized site selection: rigorous examination of your present customer base is carried out using regression models to determine predictive attributes. Distance decay models, competitive effect formulas, sister store or cannibalization formulas are all combined in a computer model. The model is cross-validated for accuracy (usually within + or - 5% to 8%m depending on sample sizes). Hundreds of potential sites are then evaluated using GIS software. Don't fly in the dark, use science to find your best location. Customer profiling for target marketing. Loyalty analysis for increased profits, and databased marketing services are all provided. Associates have combined 80 years of experience.

Major Areas of Concentration:

BACKGROUND

Business Established In:
Association Memberships:
Full-Time Employees:
Full-Time Professionals: 5
Major Franchising Clients in Past 3 Yrs.: Safeway, Certified Growers, Stater Bros., Premium Pet, Yardbirds, Gap, Home Depot, Ernst Home Centers, Wickes Furniture and Sportmart. Comprehensive Loyalty is also the #1 supplier of site selection studies for RV and marine industries.

AREAS CONSULT IN
U.S.:   Yes
Canada: Yes
Overseas: No

◀◀ ▶▶

Phoenix, AZ 85034
Tel: (866) 301-8050 (480) 302-3574
Fax: (866) 301-8051
Web Site: www.profitkeeper.com
E-mail: dion@profitkeeper.com
Contact: Mr. Dion Garner, VP Client Solutions
Other Offices In:

BUSINESS FOCUS

Core3 is the company that brings you the ProfitKeeperTM back office solutions -- real-time web-based accounting, reporting and payroll solutions; and profitability tools for franchises. Its proven solutions quantify lost profits and track critical trends, averages, benchmarks and performance indicators. With customized screens and themed sites, ProfitKeeper enhances brand identity for franchises. Its intuitive, easy-to-use solutions save time and money for both franchisees and franchisors. www.core3inc.com

Major Areas of Concentration:

1) Reporting: Our reporting services offer real-time web-based reporting of Key Performance Indicators (KPIs), Sales and Royalty calculations, and Financial statements.
2) Accounting: Both web-based and full-service accounting options are available, providing user-friendly interfaces and profitability tools to help members save time and money. No accounting or business experience is needed as our "To-Do" list guides members through the tasks needed to manage their books.
3) Payroll: ProfitKeeper has partnered with payroll partners to provide both web-based and full-service solutions that integrate seamlessly with the ProfitKeeper Accounting solution.
4) Tax Services: Sales, Property and Income Tax services are available.

BACKGROUND

Business Established In:	2001
Association Memberships:	IFA
Full-Time Employees:	32
Full-Time Professionals:	32

Major Franchising Clients in Past 3 Yrs.: Pearle Vision (Luxottica Retail), Kahala (Cold Stone Creamery, Blimpie, Great Steak, Johnnies Pizza, Samurai Sam's), Color Me Mine, Papa Murphy's, golfTEC, Cousins Subs, WingZone, Aim Mail Centers, Express Oil Change, Meineke (Driven Brands).

AREAS CONSULT IN
U.S.:   Yes, All US
Canada: Yes, English speaking areas for Reporting and Accounting Services only (not Payroll or Tax Services)
Overseas: Yes, English speaking countries

◀◀ ▶▶

CORE3

3600 E. University Dr., # D-1600

CUMMINGS, SUZANNE, LAW OFFICES OF

The Law Office of Suzanne C. Cummings

Two Main St., # 300
Stoneham, MA 02180
Tel: (800) 982-9636 (781) 481-9090
Fax: (781) 481-9191
Web Site: www.scummingslaw.com
E-mail: scummings@scummingslaw.om
Contact: Ms. Suzanne C. Cummings, President
Other Offices In:

BUSINESS FOCUS

We are a national franchise consulting organization providing a wide range of services to both start-up and established franchisors as well as prospective franchisees. Our services include franchise system development, franchise sales strategies, marketing/direct mail/advertising, press releases/publicity programs, franchisee relationship programs, operations manuals, business plans, document maintenance and more.

Major Areas of Concentration:

1) Franchise System Development
2) Franchise Sales Strategies
3) System Documentation Development
4) Franchise Document Maintenance

BACKGROUND

Business Established In: 1992
Association Memberships:
Full-Time Employees: NR
Full-Time Professionals: NR
Major Franchising Clients in Past 3 Yrs.: Hoop Mountain, Resort Maps, Gecko Hospitality, Ideal Image, Blackjack Pasta Bar

AREAS CONSULT IN

U.S.: Yes
Canada: Yes - Toronto
Overseas: Yes - United Kingdom

<< >>

DIAMOND FINANCIAL SERVICES (FRANCHISE FUNDING)

262 Highway 36
West Keansburg, NJ 07734
Tel: (877) 508-2274 (732) 787-9191
Fax: (732) 495-7058
Web Site: www.franchisefunding.net
E-mail: don@franchiseloans.com
Contact: Mr. Don Johnson, President
Other Offices In:

BUSINESS FOCUS

We specialize in franchise business lending nationwide as franchise finance specialists/consultants. We have close relationships and utilize only the most aggressive business/franchise lenders for loan sizes from $100K to $3 million. Loan programs include start-ups, expansion, business acquisition, real estate, and refinance. Our specialty is SBA (Small Business Administration) financing, lending programs that are guaranteed by SBA but provided by conventional leaders. SBA programs are offered to almost anyone! We help you evaluate the possibility of buying a Franchise, assist you through the application process, professionally package your loan application and work with you until loan closing.

Major Areas of Concentration:
SBA financing can be applied for:
1) Acquisition of Business (or Buyout of Partners)
2) Franchise Businesses and Fees (for start-up or multi-locations)
3) Equipment or Equipment Refinance
4) Working Capital
5) Debt Restructuring

BACKGROUND

Business Established In: 1999
Association Memberships:
Full-Time Employees:
Full-Time Professionals:
Major Franchising Clients in Past 3 Yrs.: Subway, Quiznos, UPS Store, Coldstone Creamery, The Coffee Beanery, Maggie Moos, Cottman Transmission, Midas, Cartridge World, Executive Tans

AREAS CONSULT IN

U.S.: Yes
Canada: No
Overseas: No

<< >>

DYNAMIC PERFORMANCE SYSTEMS, INC.

478 Valermo Dr.
Etobicoke, ON M8W 2M7 Canada
Tel: (800) 719-9993 (416) 201-0202
Fax: (416) 201-0808
Web Site: www.dynamicperformancesystems.com
E-mail: fred@franchise-profiles.com
Contact: Mr. Fred Berni, President
Other Offices In:

BUSINESS FOCUS

Looking for a way to select and train great franchisees? The FranchiZe Profile can help you do it with unparalleled accuracy. Unlike other selection tools and profiles, the FranchiZe Profile is concerned solely with predicting performance of your franchise candidate. Rather than describing a personality, it measures the 7 common core values all successful franchisees have in common. Then it compares your candidate to successful franchisees. It gives you pointers on what to watch out for during the selection process. Plus, to help ensure a candidate's success, it gives training recommendations. Also included in every report is an Interviewing Workbook.

Major Areas of Concentration:
1) Franchisee selection
2) Pre-employment testing and training for retail staff and managers

BACKGROUND
Business Established In: 1988
Association Memberships:
Full-Time Employees: 1
Full-Time Professionals: NR
Major Franchising Clients in Past 3 Yrs.: U.S. - H&R Block, Maui Wowi Fresh Hawaiian Blends, Yum Brands. Canada - Canadian Tire, M&M Meat Shops. U.K. - Horwath Franchising, Dollond & Aitchison Ltd. New Zealand - Video Ezy NZ, Stirling Sports. Australia - Cookie Man

AREAS CONSULT IN
U.S.: Yes
Canada: Yes
Overseas: Yes - U.K., New Zealand, Australia

ENTREPRENEUR AUTHORITY, THE

5800 Granite Pkwy., Suite 300
Plano, TX 75024
Tel: (866) 246-AUTH (972) 731-6766
Fax: (214) 585-0084
Web Site: www.eAuth.com
E-mail: info@eAuth.com
Contact: Mr. David Omholt, President
Other Offices In: North America

BUSINESS FOCUS
The Entrepreneur Authority is an international network of franchise advisors. Through our Franchise Center of Excellence (FCOE), our advisors are trained to create win-win business relationships between franchisors and franchisees. No other network combines the integrity, the dedication to client service and strong franchise acumen as T.E.A.

Major Areas of Concentration

1) Franchise and self-employment counseling to prospective franchisees
2) Matching qualified franchisees with pre-screened franchisors
3) Helping franchisors create franchisee-friendly franchise systems by adhering to fair franchising standards

BACKGROUND
Business Established In: 2002
Association Memberships:
Full-Time Employees: 3
Full-Time Professionals: 15
Major Franchising Clients in Past 3 Yrs.: AAMCO, D.O.T.I., Foot Solutions, Gotcha Covered, Honey Baked Ham Company, Interface Financial Group, Mega Wraps, One-Hour Martinizing, Speed Pro and Sport Clips

AREAS CONSULT IN
U.S.: Yes
Canada: Yes
Overseas: Yes - Mexico, Canada, Great Britain, Germany, Asia

ENTREPRENEUR'S SOURCE, THE

900 Main St. S., Bldg. #2
Southbury, CT 06488
Tel: (800) 289-0086 (203) 264-2006
Fax: (203) 264-3516
Web Site: www.franchiseexperts.com
E-mail: joe@thesource.com
Contact: Mr. Joe Mathewa, COO
Other Offices In: 19 States

BUSINESS FOCUS
By representing our clients' interests above all others, The Entrepreneur's Source has become America's leading independent franchise consulting organization. Our commitment continues to be helping people and businesses grow. We provide all of our clients with the most comprehensive, objective, unbiased and meaningful advice so they can achieve the American Dream of being in business for themselves. We apply these same win-win principles and energies to our franchise development efforts. We firmly believe there cannot be successful franchisors without successful franchisees.

Major Areas of Concentration:

1) The Entrepreneur's Source provides consulting, coaching and placement services to people exploring their options in business

ownership. Using a proven success system, developed by our founders who share over 40 years experience in all aspects of
2) franchising and business success, we have helped hundreds of people choose the right franchise.

BACKGROUND

Business Established In:	1984
Association Memberships:	
Full-Time Employees:	5
Full-Time Professionals:	30
Major Franchising Clients in Past 3 Yrs.:	NR

AREAS CONSULT IN

U.S.:	Yes
Canada:	Yes
Overseas:	No

FIRSTDATA DIRECT BUSINESS GROUP

4000 Coral Ridge Drive
Coral Springs, FL 33076
Tel: (800) 910-1654
Fax:
Web Site: www.firstdatadirect.com
E-mail: phil.krivacek@firstdata.com
Contact: Mr. Phil Krivacek,
Other Offices In: Atlanta, Denver, Coral Spring, Melville NY

BUSINESS FOCUS

First Data, through its financial partners, provides franchisors and franchisees with the highest quality, world class electronic payment acceptance program. We offer the scale, experience, resources, and technology required to help franchisors and franchisees grow and increase profitability. With more than a million merchant locations established, First Data understands merchants and their needs. With more than 30 years of processing experience, we deliver the reliability and stability that are essential to growing your business.

Major Areas of Concentration:
1) Credit card processing
2) Gift and loyalty cards
3) Debit and check card processing
4) Electronic check conversion and check guarantee

BACKGROUND

Business Established In:	1867
Association Memberships:	
Full-Time Employees:	30000
Full-Time Professionals:	

Major Franchising Clients in Past 3 Yrs.: Smoothie King, Gloria Jeans Coffee, Jimmy John's, Charleys Subs, Carvel, H&R Block, Athlete's Foot, and many more.

AREAS CONSULT IN

U.S.: Yes
Canada: We can refer you to another department in our company.
Overseas: Yes - 87 countries worldwide

FRANCHISE BUSINESS SYSTEMS, INC.

2319 N. Andrews Ave.
Fort Lauderdale, FL 33311
Tel: (800) 382-1040 (954) 563-1269
Fax: (954) 563-2153
Web Site: www.franchiseaccounting.com
E-mail: steve@franchiseaccounting.com
Contact: Mr. Steve Weil, President
Other Offices In:

BUSINESS FOCUS

Complete franchisor and franchisee accounting and accounting system design firm, from monthly accounting and bookkeeping to outsourcing your entire accounting function including royalty reporting and royalty collection. We are a complete financial management solution.

Major Areas of Concentration:

1) Accounting and Bookkeeping Services
2) Business Consulting and Fianancial Management Seminars
3) Royalty Reporting and Collection
4) Intranet Services

BACKGROUND

Business Established In:	1984
Association Memberships:	
Full-Time Employees:	25
Full-Time Professionals:	10

Major Franchising Clients in Past 3 Yrs.: Planet Smoothie, Alpha Graphics, PJs Coffee and Tea, ServiceMaster, Amoco, HouseMaster, DOTI

AREAS CONSULT IN

U.S.:	Yes
Canada:	Yes
Overseas:	No

FRANCHISE DISPUTE RESOLUTIONS (FARRELL LAW GROUP)

4900 Falls of the Neuse Rd., #212
Raleigh, NC 27609

Tel: (800) 447-3148 (919) 872-0300
Fax: (919) 872-0303
Web Site: www.farrell-lawgroup.com
E-mail: rfarrell@farrell-lawgroup.com
Contact: Mr. Richard W. Farrell, Senior Partner
Other Offices In:

BUSINESS FOCUS

FDR is a dispute resolution service dedicated, and directed solely, to resolving franchise system disputes nationwide. FDR was founded in 1985 by Richard W. Farrell and Mark A. La Mantia, who, as attorneys, have represented the interests of both franchisors and franchisees throughout the U.S. for a combined total of more than 40 years. They have been involved in every aspect of franchising, including the establishment of franchise systems and drafting of UFOC documents.

Major Areas of Concentration:

1) Franchise industry dispute resolution.

BACKGROUND

Business Established In: 1995
Association Memberships:
Full-Time Employees: 6
Full-Time Professionals: 3
Major Franchising Clients in Past 3 Yrs.: NR

AREAS CONSULT IN

U.S.: Yes
Canada: Yes
Overseas: Yes - United Kingdom, Denmark.

◄◄ ►►

FRANCHISE GREENHOUSE

2121 Vista Pkwy.
West Palm Beach, FL 33411
Tel: (561) 868-1358
Fax: (561) 868-2637
Web Site: www.ufgservices.com
E-mail: sartony@aol.com
Contact: Mr. Tony Foley, President
Other Offices In:

BUSINESS FOCUS

Franchise Greenhouse is your "domestic" sales team partner. We have the sales experience to take your system and grow it into a U.S. category leader. In today's fast-paced franchise environment, more and more companies are making the wise choice to "outsource"

their franchise sales growth so they can focus on other key issues within their company. Franchise Greenhouse is comprised of franchise sales professionals that have been in the industry for many years and have a reputation of success and integrity.

Major Areas of Concentration:

1) Domestic franchise sales
2) Lead generation consultation
3) Discovery day training
4) In-house support staff training

BACKGROUND

Business Established In: 2007
Association Memberships:
Full-Time Employees: 4
Full-Time Professionals: 6
Major Franchising Clients in Past 3 Yrs.: Fruit Flowers, Virginia Barbeque, Grins 2 Go, Tint World, Estate Group, Earth Graphics, Popscorn

AREAS CONSULT IN

U.S.: Yes
Canada: No
Overseas: Yes - Australia, South Africa, Spain, UK, Nigeria, Canada, Italy, Kazakhstan, Croatia, Japan

◄◄ ►►

FRANCHISE MATCH®

900 Main St. S., Bldg. #2
Southbury, CT 06488
Tel: (203) 405-2165
Fax:
Web Site: www.franchisematch.com
E-mail: pconley@franchisesource.com
Contact: Mr. Patrick Conley, Dir. Of Marketing & Technology
Other Offices In:

BUSINESS FOCUS

FranchiseMatch.com is the world's first Virtual Franchise Coaching portal, built upon 25 years of experience of helping people discover ideal business and franchise opportunities. Franchise Match® is a simple five-step process that engages visitors by asking questions about geography, investments, industries, priorities and timing. The results are then sent to an Entrepreneur's Source Coach for further discussion, education and coaching, resulting in an ideal Franchise Match®.

Major Areas of Concentration:

1) Franchise Placement
2) Lead Development
3) Virtual Coaching
4) Franchise Awareness

BACKGROUND

Business Established In: 2008
Association Memberships: TES has been a member of the IFA for over a decade.
Full-Time Employees: 12
Full-Time Professionals: 4
Major Franchising Clients in Past 3 Yrs.: Driven Brands, Snap Fitness, Spring-Green, Sandler Training, Aussie Pet Mobile, Puro Clean, Doctors Express, WSI, ICED, Molly Maids + 200 more.

AREAS CONSULT IN

U.S.: Yes
Canada: Yes
Overseas: Not yet - will begin consulting internationally in 2009

<< >>

FRANCHISE OPPORTUNITY SPECIALIST

13140 Colt Rd., # 211
Dallas, TX 75240
Tel: (972) 786-0017
Fax: (972) 783-1673
Web Site: www.franchiseopportunityspecialist.com
E-mail: abarr@franchiseopportunityspecialist.com
Contact: Ms. Anne Barr, Consultant/Owner
Other Offices In: .

BUSINESS FOCUS

We help potential franchisees narrow the field. We look at personality, skill sets, personal and financial goals, and exit strategies and introduce clients to franchises that will be a good fit. We also guide clients through the research process of buying a franchise. And best of all... there is no charge for our services to buyer clients.

Major Areas of Concentration:

1) Helping potential franchisees find their right fit in business/ franchise ownership.
2) Working nationally with Franchisors to expand their brand. We understand that every franchise has unique needs when it comes to expansion. Franchise Opportunity Specialist has the knowledge and experience necessary to develop a customized sales plan for each Franchisor

BACKGROUND

Business Established In: 2005
Association Memberships: IFA
Full-Time Employees: 2
Full-Time Professionals: 4
Major Franchising Clients in Past 3 Yrs.: Floppy's Mouse Club, Fantastic Sams, MosquitoNix, Hart Health, Huntington Learning Centers, All Over Media

AREAS CONSULT IN

U.S.: Yes
Canada: No
Overseas: No

<< >>

FRANCHISE VIDEO MAKERS

5120 Virginia Way, # B-23
Brentwood, TN 37027
Tel: (877) 476-9222
Fax: (877) 862-9323
Web Site: www.franchisevideomakers.com
E-mail: roi@franchisevideomakers.com
Contact: Mr. Greg George, Founder
Other Offices In: North Carolina

BUSINESS FOCUS

Franchise Video Makers produces high quality franchise sales videos for franchisors. Franchise Video Makers also offer franchise vidmail sales and tracking software so franchisors can track every step of the sales process.

Major Areas of Concentration:

1) Franchise Video Makers produces four high quality franchise sales videos
2) Franchise Video Makers offers franchise vidmail sales and tracking software
3) Franchise Video Makers offers Franchise Vid-Seo, video search engine optimization services
4) Franchise Video Makers does business domestically and internationally

BACKGROUND

Business Established In: 2008
Association Memberships:
Full-Time Employees: 6
Full-Time Professionals: 3

403

Major Franchising Clients in Past 3 Yrs.:

AREAS CONSULT IN
U.S.:	Yes
Canada:	Yes
Overseas:	No

FRANCHISE VIDEOS ONLINE, LLC

14502 N. Dale Mabry Hwy, # 200
Tampa, FL 33618
Tel: (800) 393-1066 (813) 514-2120
Fax: (800) 717-8698
Web Site: www.franchisevideos.com
E-mail: thom.sudol@gmail.com
Contact: Mr. Thom Sudol, VP Sales and Marketing
Other Offices In:

BUSINESS FOCUS
Most successful Franchisors today use the power of video to sell Franchises. Why? Because it is effective in clearly communicating every aspect of the concept from top to bottom. Videos bring much more pre-educated and qualified candidates to the negotiating table. We have developed this unique website that effectively and efficiently presents franchise opportunities to thousands of potential franchisees combining the power of video with the convenience of the internet.

Major Areas of Concentration:

1) Online Advertising and Lead Generation for Franchising and Business Opportunities.
2) Video Production specializing in Franchising.
3) Brochure Printing & Design Services
4) Web Site Design and Development specializing in Franchising.

BACKGROUND
Business Established In:	2004
Association Memberships:	
Full-Time Employees:	10
Full-Time Professionals:	4

Major Franchising Clients in Past 3 Yrs.: Subway, N-Hance, Chem Dry, Booster Juice, Cottman Transmission, EmbroidMe, Sign*A*Rama, Mathnasium, Theater Extreme, Franchise Growth Systems.

AREAS CONSULT IN
U.S.:	Yes
Canada:	Yes
Overseas:	Yes - UK, Argentina, Spain, France, Columbia, Italy, Venezuela, South Africa, Costa Rica, Chile

FRANCHISEADVANTAGE.COM

P.O. Box 420035
Atlanta, GA 30342
Tel: (770) 391-5054
Fax:
Web Site: www.franchiseadvantage.com
E-mail: mmaxwell@franchiseadvantage.com
Contact: Matt Maxwell, General Manager
Other Offices In:

BUSINESS FOCUS
FranchiseAdvantage is a leading website dedicated to generating quality sales leads for franchisors. Since 2000, we have been helping franchisors find new franchisees to grow their franchise! In addition to a large selection of franchises and business opportunities, FranchiseAdvantage.com also has a directory of over 30,000 businesses-for-sale, including 3,000 existing franchises for sale. It is a one-stop shop for people interested in owning their own business. Contact us today to learn more on how we can help you grow your business! We look forward to helping you.

Major Areas of Concentration:

1) Lead Generation for Franchisors - providing franchisors quality sales leads to help them identify quality franchisee prospects.
2) Resource Center - helping franchisors and business owners connect with needed suppliers and resources to run their business successfully
3) Business-For-Sale Listing Service - we help brokers and individual business owners market their businesses-for-sale and find buyers
4) Brand Promotion - franchises on our site have an opportunity to advertise their brand and promote their business

BACKGROUND
Business Established In:	2000
Association Memberships:	IFA
Full-Time Employees:	7
Full-Time Professionals:	7

Major Franchising Clients in Past 3 Yrs.: Any Lab Test Now, DVD Now, Fantastic Sam's Hair Salons, Gandolfo's, Money Mailer, Senior Helpers, Sylvan Learning

AREAS CONSULT IN
U.S.:	Yes
Canada:	Yes
Overseas:	No

FRANCHISEKNOWHOW, LLC

P.O. Box 714
Stony Brook, NY 11790
Tel: (631) 246-5782
Fax: (631) 689-6905
Web Site: www.franchiseknowhow.com
E-mail: ed@franchiseknowhow.com
Contact: Mr. Ed Teixeira, President
Other Offices In: Beijing and Guanpong, China; Contact: Ms. Fay Deng

BUSINESS FOCUS

FranchiseKnowHow is headed by Ed Teixeira, who has over 25 years of franchise industry experience. FKH provides a full range of services to companies who desire to begin a franchise operation. Other areas of expertise include international franchising, with offices in NY and China. FKH has established strong relationships in the Chinese market. Contact information for China office: Tel: 86-135-1079-2899; 86-10-86671155; 86-10-82783466; Fax: 86-10-82898040; Address: 1104 Chuang Ye Building; Cinxi Road, Shangdi Information Industry Baseaidian District, Beijing, China 100085

Major Areas of Concentration:

FranchiseKnowHow can service any franchisor needs. We have the knowledge and expertise.

1) New Franchise Start-ups
2) International Franchising
3) Franchisee Satisfaction Audits
4) Franchisor Dispute Resolution

BACKGROUND

Business Established In: 2003
Association Memberships:
Full-Time Employees: 3
Full-Time Professionals: 3
Major Franchising Clients in Past 3 Yrs.: Netspace, FranchiseMagazine China, Reading Transformations, Aqua200, NobleKnits, Wall Street Deli, Arthur Treachers Fish & Chips

AREAS CONSULT IN

U.S.: Yes
Canada: Yes
Overseas: Yes - Japan, Spain, Thailand, Indonesia, Brazil, Canada, UK, China

◄◄ ►►

FRANCHISOR DATABASE

Franchisor Database

1814 Franklin St., # 603
Oakland, CA 94612
Tel: (800) 841-0873 (510) 839-5471
Fax: (510) 839-2104
Web Site: www.FranchisorDatabase.com
E-mail: rob@worldFranchising.com
Contact: Rob Bond, President
Other Offices In:

BUSINESS FOCUS

When you invest valuable time, money and energy on mailings or sales calls, you need the most accurate and extensive data available. Our research staff is dedicated to building the data, verifying and updating it on an on-going basis to provide you with: - Over 3,000 active North American franchisors. - Over 5,000 individual contacts (President/CEO and/or primary contact for franchising). - Unlimited usage. - 20+ fields of information in each profile. - Primary email address designated by franchisor. - Guaranteed accuracy - $.50 rebate for each incorrect mailing address. - Custom sorts available - size, geographic area, industry group, etc. Minimum order is $400. - Optional quarterly updates - $150. - Data emailed in Excel format. - Mailing labels for entire database (Avery 14-Up Labels) - $800. Single use. - 20% discount for www.FranchisingSuppliers.com partners. - Complimentary listing on www.FranchisingSuppliers.com for new database subscribers.

Major Areas of Concentration:

BACKGROUND

Business Established In:
Association Memberships:
Full-Time Employees: 5
Full-Time Professionals: 3
Major Franchising Clients in Past 3 Yrs.: Over 100 franchise industry service providers.

AREAS CONSULT IN

U.S.:
Canada:
Overseas:

◄◄ ►►

FRANCORP, INC.

The Leader in Franchise Development and Consulting. Worldwide.

20200 Governors Drive
Olympia Fields, IL 60461
Tel: (800) 372-6244 (708) 481-2900

Fax: (708) 481-5885
Web Site: www.francorp.com
E-mail: info@francorp.com
Contact: Mr. Patrick Callaway, President
Other Offices In: Mexico City; Tokyo; Dubai; Kuala Lumpur; Santiago

BUSINESS FOCUS

Named among the "top 100 management consulting firms in North America" by Consultants News, FRANCORP is the nation's largest management consulting firm specializing in franchise development. FRANCORP is the only firm with all franchise services under one roof. FRANCORP has consulted with almost 10,000 companies and has developed over 2,000 franchises. A FRANCORP Franchise Development Program includes the strategic planning, legal, operational, marketing and sales tools a company needs to expand into franchi

Major Areas of Concentration:

1) Franchise Development Programs, including feasibility studies, business plans, legal documents, operations manuals, marketing and sales materials.
2) Consulting for established franchisors, including lead generation programs, franchise brochures, international brokerage, public relations and expert witness services.
3) International Franchise Consulting - FRANCORP has offices in 9 countries and a worldwide network of affiliates in the global expansion process.
4) Expansion Assessments - FRANCORP analyses the capabilities/resources of various business systems to assist both internal and external decision makers in assessing the feasibility of franchising, licensing, dealer conversion, venture capital funding, etc.

BACKGROUND

Business Established In: 1976
Association Memberships:
Full-Time Employees: 50
Full-Time Professionals: 36
Major Franchising Clients in Past 3 Yrs.: Texaco Express Lube, Ace Hardware, Amoco Oil Company, Pollo Campero International, Jimmy John's, Hurricane Wings.

AREAS CONSULT IN

U.S.: Yes
Canada: Yes
Overseas: Yes - Mex., Arg., Japan, Chile, DR, UAE, Phil.

Loft Building #2, Entrance D, #103, Dubai Media City
Dubai, United Arab Emirates
Tel: 00971 4 367 8290
Fax: 00971 4 367 2651
Web Site: www.franexcel.com
E-mail: michael@franexcel.com
Contact: Mr. Sary Hamawy, CEO
Other Offices In: Malaysia, Singapore, Kuwait

BUSINESS FOCUS

FranExcel is a leading international network of franchise consultancy and marketing professionals, offering results oriented franchise marketing services across five continents. FranExcel is a multi faceted global franchise service provider, which combines the resources of one of the leading franchise web portal, franchise publication, electronic media and promotion of major franchise events worldwide. FranExcel works with franchise concepts from across the world, helping them establish in new territories by finding them qualified investors. We work as partners with our clients and invest in them to minimize their risk and maximize their strategies providing the perfect match needed for success - - every time.

Major Areas of Concentration:

1) Representation, Marketing, and Promotion of Franchise Opportunities
2) Franchise Development and Expansion Programs
3) Franchise Publication. Web based and printed Advertising and Sponsorship packages.
4) Franchise Training and Education. Support Programs to Governments and Franchise Suppliers.

BACKGROUND

Business Established In: 2006
Association Memberships: International Franchise Association (IFA)
Full-Time Employees: 9
Full-Time Professionals: 12
Major Franchising Clients in Past 3 Yrs.: Al Hokair Group, KSA; Liwa Trading Enterprises, UAE; Jawad Business Group, Bahrain; Burger Fuel International Ltd., New Zealand; Trends International Franchising Company, Lebanon; High & Mighty Ltd., UK; Abbey Design Sdn Bhd, Malaysia; Bin Hendi Group, UAE; Tasty Limited, UAE; Arabian Oud, KSA, UAE

AREAS CONSULT IN

U.S.: Yes, All US

Canada:	Yes, All Canada
Overseas:	Yes,

Australia, Belgium, Brazil, Canada, France, India, Italy, Malaysia,
New Zealand, Singapore, UK, USA

◄◄ ►►

GRAPHIC BUSINESS SOLUTIONS

1912 John Towers Ave.
El Cajon, CA 92020
Tel: (800) 747-9529 (619) 258-4081
Fax: (619) 449-6248
Web Site: www.gogbs.com
E-mail: rita@gogbs.com
Contact: Ms. Rita Cannon, Director of Corporate Marketing
Other Offices In:

BUSINESS FOCUS

GBS is the leading manufacturer of full-color, custom designed and die-cut refrigerator magnets. Tailored to meet your franchise needs with a specific emphasis on custom imprinting for each franchise location, our magnets are of the highest quality at the most affordable pricing in the industry. From the implementation of your magnetic marketing plan to easy online ordering on a website designed specifically for you, our offering options are diverse. Call for a free marketing consultation.

Major Areas of Concentration:

Did you know the average American opens their refrigerator door 20 times a day? Magnetic marketing works by increasing your brand exposure and your revenue. At no cost to you, GBS will provide the following services:
1) Perform an in-depth consultation of your needs and offer magnetic marketing suggestions
2) Design a quality magnet specific to your franchise
3) Customize a website for your franchise featuring your -magnet, various marketing tips and an EASY one-click ordering process
4) Take and process all orders either directly with your franchisees, or through your corporate office

BACKGROUND

Business Established In:	1994
Association Memberships:	
Full-Time Employees:	42
Full-Time Professionals:	12

Major Franchising Clients in Past 3 Yrs.: Available Upon Request.

AREAS CONSULT IN

U.S.:	Yes

Canada:	Yes
Overseas:	Yes

◄◄ ►►

IFRANCHISE GROUP

905 W. 175th St., # 2 N
Homewood, IL 60430
Tel: (708) 957-2300
Fax: (708) 957-2395
Web Site: www.ifranchise.net
E-mail: jjanusz@ifranchise.net
Contact: Ms. Judy Janusz, VP of Administration
Other Offices In:

BUSINESS FOCUS

Franchise consulting for new and established franchisors. The iFranchise Group is comprised of the nation's leading professionals in the field of franchising. Senior consultants for the iFranchise Group bring over 250 years of experience to their clients. Services include franchise feasibility, franchise structure, legal documentation, operations and training materials and assistance with franchise sales and franchise feasibility. Franchise development for start-up franchisors. Franchise marketing and sales. Franchise implementation assistance.

Major Areas of Concentration:

BACKGROUND

Business Established In:	1998
Association Memberships:	
Full-Time Employees:	20
Full-Time Professionals:	14

Major Franchising Clients in Past 3 Yrs.: Ace Hardware, Bridgestone/Firestone, Crafter's Marketplace, Dippin' Dots, Hallmark, Harris Teeter, Horizon Pharmacy, Line-X, Van Heusen and Successories.

AREAS CONSULT IN

U.S.:	Yes
Canada:	Yes

Overseas: Yes - Japan, U.K., Argentina, Chile, Philippines, Spain

 ◄◄ ►►

IMPACT MARKETING SERVICES

15029 N. Thompson Peak Pkwy, #B 111-442
Scottsdale, AZ 85260
Tel: (800) 836-6625 (480) 767-1321
Fax: (866) 267-1255
Web Site: www.impactmarketingservices.com
E-mail: john@impactmarketingservices.com
Contact: Mr. John W. Lee, Principal
Other Offices In: Dallas, TX

BUSINESS FOCUS

IFA Member. Established in 1991. Full-service national marketing and advertising firm. Specialize in development and implementation of strategic marketing plans, local store marketing plans, grand opening and grand re-opening plans, marketing workshops, and store consultation services. Clients: Mail Boxes Etc/The UPS Store since 1991, The Great Frame Up, Pizza Hut. National franchise consumer and business-to-business and multi-regional franchise organizations.

Major Areas of Concentration:

1) Development of annual marketing plans and implementation - corporate and local store planning and consultation.
2) Grand opening/Grand re-opening programs - new stores achieve and exceed break-even faster.
3) Media planning and placement - complete services. Free standing newspaper inserts as low as $26 per thousand.
4) Marketing workshops, training and coaching - motivating field marketing training

BACKGROUND

Business Established In: 1991
Association Memberships:
Full-Time Employees: 4
Full-Time Professionals: 4
Major Franchising Clients in Past 3 Yrs.: Mail Boxes Etc/The UPS Store, The Great Frame Up, Audio-Visual Headquarters, MotoPhoto, Winfree Marketing & Sales Institute, Taco Casa

AREAS CONSULT IN

U.S.:   Yes
Canada: Yes
Overseas: Yes

KUSHELL ASSOCIATES, INC.

235 Fearrington Post
Pittsboro, NC 27312
Tel: (919) 542-3500
Fax: (919) 542-1156
Web Site: www.kushellassociates.com
E-mail: kushellassociates@msn.com
Contact: Mr. Robert Kushell,
Other Offices In: Partners in South America, Far East and Europe

BUSINESS FOCUS

Our Consulting Group advises multinational, entrepreneurial and Minority companies on how to develop well constructed Franchise Systems. There are 14 distinct modules that we create to convert an existing business into a market ready Franchise Program. We assist established Franchisors with domestic and international growth, marketing and sales strategies. We are very skilled in assisting Franchisors that have strained relations with their Franchisees to create a healthy and harmonious business climate for all parties. We have also focused our extensive Franchise and business knowledge and resources in assisting Minority business owners to convert their existing business into a Franchise Model.

Major Areas of Concentration:

1) Developing Franchise Programs for multi-national and entrepreneurial companies.
2) Assisting Minority owned businesses to become Franchisors.
3) Assisting Franchise Systems to create and maintain healthy relationships with their Franchisees as they focus increasingly on opening more new units.
4) Assisting Franchisors develop and implement a sound international sales and marketing program.

BACKGROUND

Business Established In: 1984
Association Memberships:
Full-Time Employees:
Full-Time Professionals: 4
Major Franchising Clients in Past 3 Yrs.: Volvo, Money Mailer, Smart House, Amorix, Sandler Sales Institute, Dynamark, Tuffy Muffler, USIC, Restaurant System Intl. And Saudi Fisheries Inc.

AREAS CONSULT IN

U.S.:   Yes
Canada: Yes

Overseas: Yes - Saudi Arabia, UAR, Egypt, Taiwan, Hong Kong, Philipines, Brazil, Argentina, Chile, England, Spain, Denmark, Mexico, and Canada

≪ ≫

THE LEASE COACH

Howard Hughes Center, 6080 Center Dr., 6th Floor PMB 10048
Los Angeles, CA 90045
Tel: (800) 738-9202 (780) 448-2645
Fax: (780) 448-2670
Web Site: www.theleasecoach.com
E-mail: dalewillerton@theleasecoach.com
Contact: Mr. Dale Willerton, President
Other Offices In:

BUSINESS FOCUS

The Lease Coach® is a network of Certified Commercial Lease Consultants who work exclusively for both franchisee and franchisor tenants across the United States and Canada. The Lease Coach wrote the book on leasing for tenants, "Negotiate Your Commercial Lease." The Lease Coach provides one-on-one coaching and consulting, lease negotiating, site selection, and document reviews for both new leases and renewals. For more information, consulting inquiries, self-help products, and IFA franchise show seminar dat

Major Areas of Concentration:

1) Coaching and Consulting -- We provide one on one consultation prior to your new lease deal or renewal beginning and throughout the process as it develops.
2) We will professionally negotiate your lease or renewal. There is simply no substitute for years of negotiating experience.
3) Site Selection -- Selecting the right property and even the right space for your company inside a building is like laying the first brick upon which every brick is laid. Our Site Selection expertise will help ensure you select the best location for you business.
4) Aside from avoiding the nasty clauses you will enjoy the peace of mind knowing what you are really agreeing to before signing.

BACKGROUND

Business Established In: 1993
Association Memberships: CFA, IFA, BBB
Full-Time Employees: 3
Full-Time Professionals: 3
Major Franchising Clients in Past 3 Yrs.: Subway, Quiznos, Gymboree Play & Music, Arby's, General Nutrition Centers (GNC), The UPS Store, Fantastic Sam's, Dairy Queen, Grower Direct Fresh Cut Flowers, Little Caesar's, Aaron's Sales & Lease Ownership

AREAS CONSULT IN
U.S.: Yes, all US
Canada: Yes, all Canada
Overseas: No

≪ ≫

MADDOX UNGAR SILBERSTEIN, PLLC

Maddox Ungar Silberstein, PLLC
CPAs and Business Advisors

30600 Telegraph Rd., # 2175
Bingham Farms, MI 48025
Tel: (248) 203-0080
Fax: (248) 281-0940
Web Site: www.maddoxungar.com
E-mail: rons@maddoxungar.com
Contact: Mr. Ronald N. Silberstein, Principal
Other Offices In:

BUSINESS FOCUS

CPA firm. We audit franchisors and we provide other services such as consulting, litigation support, and franchisee royalty audits to franchisors. One of our principals, Ron Silberstein was CFO and Chief Administrative Officer of a major franchisor for 4+ years – so, we have real world franchising experience.

Major Areas of Concentration:

1) Our specialty niches are audits of franchisors and audits of small-medium size publicly traded companies and companies readying to go public.
2) Our franchising experience sets us apart from most other CPA firms.
3) We have clients located throughout the US, Canada, and Asia.
4) We are an IFA supplier member and we attend the annual IFA convention.

BACKGROUND
Business Established In:
Association Memberships: IFA, AICPA, MACPA, PCAOB
Full-Time Employees: 7
Full-Time Professionals: 6
Major Franchising Clients in Past 3 Yrs.: Industries we have worked with include quick service restaurants, sit down restaurants, children's education, service, and retail.

AREAS CONSULT IN
U.S.: Yes
Canada: Yes
Overseas: No

≪ ≫

MANAGEMENT 2000

P.O. Box 69130
Oro Valley, AZ 85737
Tel: (800) 847-5763 (520) 818-9988
Fax: (520) 818-3277
Web Site: www.mgmt2000.com
E-mail: m2000@mgmt2000.com
Contact: Mr. Bob Gappa, President
Other Offices In:

BUSINESS FOCUS

What is your company slogan or motto? To be the premier franchise consulting company by giving people what they expect, and more. What makes your services unique to franchises? Management 2000 has been part of the franchise community for over 20 years. Over that time we have seen dramatic changes that affect our business. One of our goals has always been to identify changing conditions that affect the relationships between franchisors and franchisees. Once these have been identified, we structure our programs to specifically address these areas. What services do you provide for franchisors? Our services are designed to help our clients get, keep and create very satisfied customers. We do this by helping clients think through and define solutions to their strategic and operational problems and opportunities. We have designed training programs for all levels of corporate and franchisee personnel. Management 2000 conducts convention speeches and prepares Expert Witness reports for franchisors. Our primary focuses are in helping senior management understand the franchising business and how to enhance the customer experience. What services do you provide to franchisees? We provide franchisees with training programs as they come on board with a new company and subsequent programs with Leaders, Guides, and Participant Workbooks. Where is your company headed in the future? We continually strive to enhance what our customers want and need to successfully grow their businesses. Why do you think franchising is such a popular choice for entrepreneurs? Franchising gives entrepreneurs a way to create wealth. Becoming a franchisee provides the average and above-average worker an opportunity to enhance their lifestyle and secure their financial future.

Major Areas of Concentration:

1) Training/Education: Management 2000 develops & conducts training programs specifically for franchising. We conduct a regular schedule of seminars for franchise recruiters, field personnel and franchise executives. We customize & conduct these programs for our clients. We write training programs for initial franchisee training, convention workshops and other training to meet clients' specific needs. Our training leads participants to understand the power of franchising & their role in the strategic-partnership between franchisor and franchisee. Programs for field personnel include how to use the consultative approach as well as how to implement business planning & local store marketing with franchisees.

2) Manuals: Management 2000 writes manuals to document a variety of operating systems. Manuals are not boiler plated but are the result of on-site visits with unit and operations personnel. Manuals include pre-opening procedures; field operation guides, conducting audits and visitations, local store marketing, prospecting and sales, creating a customer-driven culture, and managing for profitability. For use throughout the organization by franchise development staff to recruit and select better franchisees, by field personnel for effective franchise consulting; and by franchisees, to insure faithful adherence to the operating system.

3) Consulting: Management 2000 products & services include: complete program for start-up companies, how to Close More Franchise Sales; how to get your franchisees to use business plans; convention speeches: strategic planning; customer acquisition/retention strategies; strategies to build average unit volumes; how to improve the effectiveness of your field consultants; customer service strategies; prospect profiling; franchise attitude survey; improving the effectiveness of your area developers; development of effective growth strategies; research, write & re-write operations manuals; design & write leader's guides and training manuals; customer tracking systems for improved profitability; and improving franchisor/franchisee relations.

BACKGROUND

Business Established In: 1981
Association Memberships:
Full-Time Employees:
Full-Time Professionals:
Major Franchising Clients in Past 3 Yrs.: GMAC Real Estate, GNC, H&R Block, Petland, Smoothie King, Pro Source, Link Staffing, Brinker Int'l, Epmark, Applebee's, Allied Domecq, Medicine Shoppe Int'l

AREAS CONSULT IN

U.S.:	Yes
Canada:	Yes
Overseas:	Yes

MICHAEL H. SEID & ASSOCIATES, LLC

94 Mohegan Drive
West Hartford, CT 06117
Tel: (860) 523-4257
Fax: (860) 523-4530
Web Site: www.msaworldwide.com
E-mail: mseid@msaworldwide.com
Contact: Mr. Michael H. Seid, Managing Director
Other Offices In: Atlanta, GA and San Rafael, CA

BUSINESS FOCUS

What is your company slogan or motto? To be the premier franchise consulting company by giving people what they expect, and more. What makes your services unique to franchises? Management 2000 has been part of the franchise community for over 20 years. Over that time we have seen dramatic changes that affect our business. One of our goals has always been to identify changing conditions that affect the relationships between franchisors and franchisees. Once these have been identified, we structure our programs to specifically address these areas. What services do you provide for franchisors? Our services are designed to help our clients get, keep and create very satisfied customers. We do this by helping clients think through and define solutions to their strategic and operational problems and opportunities. We have designed training programs for all levels of corporate and franchisee personnel. Management 2000 conducts convention speeches and prepares Expert Witness reports for franchisors. Our primary focuses are in helping senior management understand the franchising business and how to enhance the customer experience. What services do you provide to franchisees? We provide franchisees with training programs as they come on board with a new company and subsequent programs with Leaders, Guides, and Participant Workbooks. Where is your company headed in the future? We continually strive to enhance what our customers want and need to successfully grow their businesses. Why do you think franchising is such a popular choice for entrepreneurs? Franchising gives entrepreneurs a way to create wealth. Becoming a franchisee provides the average and above-average worker an opportunity to enhance their lifestyle and secure their financial future.

Major Areas of Concentration:

Established franchisors recognize MSA background as both franchisors and franchisees and our experience in branding, retailing, marketing and finance provide them with a team of advisors who have the practical experience necessary to implement leading edge strategies to improve their systems performance. We have been fortunate in the recognition that the franchising community has bestowed on us. Michael Seid, co-author with the late Dave Thomas, founder of Wendy's of Franchising for Dummies is the first and only professional service provider ever directly elected to the Board of the International Franchise Association.

1) Franchise system design and development
2) Strategic and tactical planning and execution
3) Domestic and international expansion growth strategies
4) Training and operations manuals
5) Restaurant consulting

BACKGROUND

Business Established In:	1987
Association Memberships:	IFA, American bar Association, Georgia Restaurant Association, American Institute of CPA.
Full-Time Employees:	
Full-Time Professionals:	
Major Franchising Clients in Past 3 Yrs.:	See website at www.MSAWorldwide.com

AREAS CONSULT IN

U.S.:	Yes
Canada:	Yes
Overseas:	Yes

◄◄ ►►

MUTUAL OF OMAHA COMPANIES

Mutual of Omaha Plaza, 10th Floor
Omaha, NE 68175
Tel: (800) 223-6927 (402) 351-2076
Fax: (402) 351-5829
Web Site: www.mutualofomaha.com
E-mail: pjenson@mutualofomaha.com
Contact: Mr. Paul Jenson, National Account Manager
Other Offices In:

BUSINESS FOCUS

The Mutual of Omaha Companies offer many discounted or enhanced individual association insurance products to members of the American Association of Franchisees and Dealers (AAFD), as well as to other national, state and local associations. Our nearly 50 years of working with associations and their members has provided us experience and insight on how to be more customer-driven/customer friendly and responsive. Contact your local Mutual of Omaha Companies representative or call 800-223-6927 for more information.

Major Areas of Concentration:

1) Major Medical, Major Hospital, Critical Illness,
2) Disability Income, Long Term Care,
3) Life, Annuities, Retirement Vehicles, Investment,
4) Products for Employers at the Worksite.

BACKGROUND

Business Established In:	1909
Association Memberships:	
Full-Time Employees:	NR
Full-Time Professionals:	NR
Major Franchising Clients in Past 3 Yrs.:	NR

AREAS CONSULT IN

U.S.:	Yes
Canada:	Yes
Overseas:	NR

◄◄ ►►

NEXSITE ONLINE SOLUTIONS

1000 Andover Park E.
Seattle, WA 98188
Tel: (206) 324-5644 + 246
Fax: (206) 324-8939
Web Site: www.nexsiteonline.com
E-mail: info@nexsiteonline.com
Contact: Mr. Steve Bergendoff, Director of Development
Other Offices In:

BUSINESS FOCUS

Nexsite Online Solutions is the powerful resource and operating system that enables companies to order branded items and conduct comprehensive print, email and Web marketing campaigns. Nexsite is an online service that eliminates the need to purchase, develop and maintain software with expensive IT personnel. We create a single intelligent portal for your entire system governed by headquarters that enables your franchisees with tools and capabilities to customize products and operate programs they simply could not accomplish on their own. It is a scalable, centrally organized, low cost, highly efficient enterprise solution to adopt advanced marketing technologies and succeed in today's challenging business climate. Nexsite Online is the front door to our set of marketing solutions ideally suited to franchise organizations. We are not only the marketing system we are:

Major Areas of Concentration:

1) Full service printers with web, sheetfed, digital and reprographics equipment.
2) Full service mailers with high speed ink jet equipment including source, develop and manage lists and databases.
3) Publishers of print and electronic magazines, directories and newsletters.
4) Producers of seminars and conferences. We contract strategy, planning, production and administration services for all types of events.

BACKGROUND

Business Established In: 2008
Association Memberships: Pacific Printing Industries, GraphicArt Technical Foundation, Printing Industries of America
Full-Time Employees: 35
Full-Time Professionals: 10
Major Franchising Clients in Past 3 Yrs.:

AREAS CONSULT IN

U.S.: Yes, All US
Canada: Yes, All Canada
Overseas: No

<< >>

PERMA-GLAZE

1638 S. Research Loop Rd., #160
Tucson, AZ 85710
Tel: (800) 332-7397 (520) 722-9718
Fax: (520) 296-4393
Web Site: www.permaglaze.com
E-mail: permaglaze@permaglaze.com
Contact: Mr. Dale R. Young, President
Other Offices In:

BUSINESS FOCUS

Perma-Glaze specializes in multi-surface refinishing and restoration, including bathroom/kitchen fixtures, such as bathtubs, tile, metal, fiberglass, appliances, countertops, floors, cabinets, etc. Investment provides 3 distinct profit opportunities in one all-inclusive package. No experience necessary, minimum investment is $19,500. The unique Perma-Glaze opportunity offers a challenging and rewarding career as well as a valued association with an internationally respected company. Call us at 800-332-7397 or visit our website: www.permaglaze.com.

Major Areas of Concentration:

1) Perma-Glaze is actively seeking motivated individual to join us and profit in this billion dollar industry. Our major areas of concetration are in the residential, institutional, commercial and government accounts.

BACKGROUND

Business Established In: 1978
Association Memberships:
Full-Time Employees: 10
Full-Time Professionals: 10
Major Franchising Clients in Past 3 Yrs.: NR

AREAS CONSULT IN

U.S.: Yes
Canada: Yes
Overseas: Yes - Malaysia, Singapore, Chile, Argentina, Venezuela

<< >>

PRECISION MAILERS, LLC

1701 River Run Rd., # 901
Fort Worth, TX 76107
Tel: (817) 299-8551
Fax: (817) 390-0500
Web Site: www.venturemanagersolution.com

E-mail: mark@precisionmailers.com
Contact: Mr. Mark Mauser, Owner
Other Offices In:

BUSINESS FOCUS

Precision Mailers has developed Venture Manager which is an easy to use, one-stop system that includes real time mailing list counts, printing and direct mail ordering, proofing, fulfillment, and secure online payments for franchised networks. Give your people more time to run their day-to-day operations by simplifying their marketing functions with Venture Manager. Franchisees can get counts, generate proofs, and order all of their products 24/7/365 days a year when it is convenient for them. No back and forth phone calls or emails, order in as little as 5 minutes, schedule monthly orders, while we fulfill all products from one of our (3) regional facilities. You control the brand and image you want in the marketplace while franchisees enjoy ease of use and save money by consolidating marketing materials. For more information, please also visit our corporate site at: http://www.precisionmailers.com.

Major Areas of Concentration:

1) Precision Mailers offers franchised organizations real time list counts, customization, online proofing, payment and fulfillment all in one place with Venture Manager
2) Precision Mailers also strategizes with our franchisors to insure list, creative, print, promotional items, and postal configuration is utilized effectively to maximize cost savings across their organization.
3) Each system is custom-built and includes password protection, order authorization hierarchy, custom reporting functions, unlimited users, live data feed and data upload features, real time PDF proof generation, and secure payment gateway.
4) Precision Mailers also offers a complete line of custom offline print jobs, client profiling, customer acquisition programs, and full back end campaign analysis.

BACKGROUND

Business Established In:	2005
Association Memberships:	IFA, DMA
Full-Time Employees:	14
Full-Time Professionals:	5

Major Franchising Clients in Past 3 Yrs.: MaidPro, Sport Clips, Sweet & Sassy, Great Clips, Nhance

AREAS CONSULT IN

U.S.:	Yes
Canada:	Yes
Overseas:	No

100 PFL Way
Livingston, MT 59741
Tel: (800) 930-6040 (406) 823-7047
Fax: (406) 222-4990
Web Site: www.printingforless.com
E-mail: bizdev@printingforless.com
Contact: Philip Naro, VP Business Development
Other Offices In:

BUSINESS FOCUS

PrintingForLess.com is the first and largest e-commerce commercial printer in the USA. PFL specializes in providing small to medium businesses with high-quality marketing materials including business cards, brochures, postcards, stationery, catalogs and more. PrintingForLess.com strives to consistently deliver a superior printing experience to every customer by providing award-winning customer service and delivering on every promise. The Wall Street Journal reported that PFL has succeeded in striking the best balance between human and online interaction with customers by investing in technology and people to become "easy to do business with." In addition, PFL provides a 100% customer satisfaction guarantee on both products and service.

Major Areas of Concentration:

1) PrintingForLess.com offers franchises custom-built private print shops where franchisees can choose, customize and order their marketing materials in just minutes.
2) A Private Print Shop makes local marketing fast, easy and convenient by providing an easy to use website for ordering franchise-approved, high quality customizable marketing materials.
3) Each customer is supported by their own dedicated customer service team to help them every step of the way.
4) In addition, PFL can handle any custom print job and offers a complete range of mailing services including sourcing targeted mailing lists.

BACKGROUND

Business Established In:	1996
Association Memberships:	IFA, California Association of Realtors
Full-Time Employees:	200
Full-Time Professionals:	

Major Franchising Clients in Past 3 Yrs.: Curves, Duct Tape Marketing, Fresh Fruit Bouquet, IM=X Pilates, Junga Juice, Kalologie, Mr. Sandless, Partner On Call Network, Oil & Vinegar and Sola Salon Studios

AREAS CONSULT IN

U.S.:	Yes
Canada:	Yes
Overseas:	No

<< >>

THE RAWLS GROUP

"Perpetuating Family Business Legacies Through the Next Generation"

1700 W. Colonial Dr.
Orlando, FL 32804
Tel: (800) 77-RAWLS (407) 578-4455
Fax: (407) 578-4480
Web Site: www.rawlsgroup.com
E-mail: info@rawlsgroup.com
Contact: Kendall Rawls, Marketing & Public Relations
Other Offices In: Atlanta, GA; New York, NY; Baltimore, MD; Des Moines, IA; Los Angeles, CA; Sacramento, CA

BUSINESS FOCUS

The Rawls Group is a nationally recognized succession planning firm specializing in working with privately -held franchisee business owners. By partnering with our clients and their other advisors, we work to develop a plan that will perpetuate the leadership, culture, performance, and relationships that are key to business success. Whether the goal is to perpetuate the business through a family member, a key executive or the choice is to sell to a third party; The Rawls Group is uniquely positioned to assist in addressing the issues that impact ongoing business success and value.

Major Areas of Concentration:

1) Developing a compatible exit strategy; Successor identification/preparation; Equitable estate distribution
2) Maintaining family/partner harmony; Enhancing Communication; Aligning the strategic goals of the family with the strategic goals of the business
3) Key manager retention & motivation; Integrating succession planning requirements of the franchisor with your plan
4) Leadership development; Management synergy and teamwork

BACKGROUND

Business Established In: 1973
Association Memberships: National Franchisee Association of Burger King, North American Association of Subway Franchisees
Full-Time Employees: 10
Full-Time Professionals: 13
Major Franchising Clients in Past 3 Yrs.: Available upon Request

AREAS CONSULT IN

U.S.: Yes, All US
Canada: Yes, All Canada
Overseas: No

<< >>

REGENCY COMPANIES

3300 Battleground Ave., # 410
Greensboro, NC 27410
Tel: (877) 388-9090 (336) 574-1970
Fax: (336) 553-1700
Web Site: www.regencycompanies.com
E-mail: info@regencycompanies.com
Contact: Mr. Julius Dizon, Chief Executive Officer
Other Offices In: Las Vegas, NV / Rochester, NY / Atlanta, GA

BUSINESS FOCUS

REGENCY'S three-fold mission is to assist businesses in reducing employee turnover, enhance employee loyalty, and promote administrative efficiency. This is accomplished through Regency's affordable Employee Health Insurance Program without employer contribution requirement, offering VISA Pay Cards for employees with no bank accounts, and Regency's web-based state-of-the-art payroll system. Regency's Health Insurance Program consists of medical, dental, and vision insurance coverage. Regency's VISA Pay Cards allow employees to have their net pay loaded on the card. Regency's proprietary payroll system can receive electronic files from a company's Point-of-Sale software or electronic time clock resulting in an error-free payroll processing through the Internet.

Major Areas of Concentration:

1) Affordable Comprehensive Employee Health Insurance Program with no employer contribution requirement.
2) VISA Pay Cards to load the net pay of employees who do not have bank accounts.
3) Proprietary web-based state-of-the-art payroll system that can accept electronic files from POS software and electronic time clocks.
4) Assist clients in processing Work Opportunity Tax Credits (WOTC), E-Verify, and background checks.

BACKGROUND

Business Established In: 2002
Association Memberships: NAPEO (National Association of PEO's), Better Business Bureau Nationwide, Multiple Chambers of Commerce, Denny's Franchise Association, Choice Hotels Preferred Vendors, AAHOA Preferred Vendors.
Full-Time Employees: 42
Full-Time Professionals: 15
Major Franchising Clients in Past 3 Yrs.: Choice Hotels Association, AAHOA (Asian American Hotel Owners Association), Denny's Franchise Association, Wienerschnitzel Franchise Association, McDonald's Franchise Association, Tortilleria Franchise, Strings Italian, Domino's Pizza

AREAS CONSULT IN

U.S.:	Yes, All
Canada:	No
Overseas:	No

≪ ≫

REMOTE DATA BACKUPS, INC.

P.O. Box 543
Fort Collins, CO 80522
Tel: (866) 722-2587 (970) 493-2466
Fax: (970) 493-4178
Web Site: www.RemoteDataBackups.com
E-mail: r_askew@remotedatabackups.com
Contact: Mr. Richard Askew, VP of Marketing & Operations
Other Offices In:

BUSINESS FOCUS

Remote Data Backups, Inc. is an industry leader in online backups. RDB has the most secure backup system on the market today featuring two separate underground data bunkers and highly expert 24/7 support. Remote Data Backups is much more than an online backup software as we have highly trained technicians who can restore lost data to pre-crash condition. It's not a matter of "if" you lose your data, but more a matter of "when." You will want the superior insurance which Remote Data Backups brings to yo

Major Areas of Concentration:

1) Remote Data Backups, Inc's primary focus is on training trusted professionals (IT Techs, Accountants, Business Consultants, Software Develpers) to sell the online backup system to their contacts with our FREE Partner Program. We provide all the branded marketing materials and support resources making it seamless to succeed in the Program. The single most important task which our affiliates need to focus on to succeed, is to simply "Just Install It!" Our Partners earn up to 40% commissions and when a disa
2) Remote Data Backups, Inc's secondary focus is backing up data for individual businesses who install our program directly from our website. We provide support with our highly credentialed technical talent.

BACKGROUND

Business Established In:	2000
Association Memberships:	IFA Supplier Forum
Full-Time Employees:	10
Full-Time Professionals:	10

Major Franchising Clients in Past 3 Yrs.: ServiceMaster, ServPro, PostNet, Lawn Doctor, Expectec, Padgett Business Services, Parcel Plus, Adventures in Advertising, CFO Today/Ledger Plus,

Mr. Rooter, Sign-A-Rama

AREAS CONSULT IN

U.S.:	Yes
Canada:	Yes
Overseas:	Yes

≪ ≫

RENAISSANCE FRANCHISE CONSULTING, INC.

4573 State Route 73 West
Wilmington, OH 45177
Tel: (937) 383-2520
Fax: (937) 383-2518
Web Site:
E-mail: jeffbevis@renaissancefranchising.com
Contact: Mr. Jeff Bevis, Principal
Other Offices In: Tulsa, OK

BUSINESS FOCUS

Our practice is focused on the areas of franchise development, sales, operations/field support and strategic planning. We work alongside small and medium-sized franchisors to accelerate their growth and improve operating results. We are also very experienced providing financial analysis of unit economics and demographic market analysis services at local, regional and national levels.

Major Areas of Concentration:

1) Evaluating current processes to improve and enhance sales results.
2) Review and align more effective operations/field support ROI.
3) Create and facilitate 3 and 5 year strategic plans to accelerate growth.
4) Perform field audits and financial analysis of franchisees for improvement in unit economics.

BACKGROUND

Business Established In:	2003
Association Memberships:	IFA through franchisor and client relationships
Full-Time Employees:	4
Full-Time Professionals:	3

Major Franchising Clients in Past 3 Yrs.: Comfort Keepers, INTERIORS by Decorating Den, The Growth Coach, Fresh Coat, Caring Transitions, International Franchise Holdings, Inc.

AREAS CONSULT IN

U.S.:	Yes, all U.S.
Canada:	Yes, all Canada
Overseas:	Yes, UK, Australia, Ireland, Portugal, Singapore

⤙⤙ ⤚⤚

RESTAURANT VALUES

1625 W. Elizabeth, Suite B-4
Ft. Collins, CO 80521
Tel: (877) 870-2650 (970) 484-6598
Fax: (866) 214-3869
Web Site: www.restaurantvalues.com
E-mail: gary@restaurantvalues.com
Contact: Mr. Gary Vette, Owner/Director
Other Offices In:

BUSINESS FOCUS

Restaurant Values provides a Restaurant Valuation Report with 3 to 5 nationally recognized income and/or market location approaches to the current business value -- independently (not real estate nor business brokers). We use restaurant market data from nationally recognized independent sources, plus support data from CBI's. Also provide a Market Analysis report to determine if a specific market is viable; plus a Fiscal Analysis to determine if the market makes economic sense. Restaurant Values also provides a Financial Review on an existing restaurant -- identifying the "red flags" in expenses and/or income flow.

Major Areas of Concentration:

1) Restaurant Business Valuations
2) Market Analysis
3) Financial Review of expenses on existing restaurants
4) Fiscal Analysis on a proposed restaurant

BACKGROUND

Business Established In:	1980
Association Memberships:	
Full-Time Employees:	
Full-Time Professionals:	

Major Franchising Clients in Past 3 Yrs.: VCM Ltd, IHOP, K&J Mgt, Harwood Int, Pizza Inn, Hooter's, KFC

AREAS CONSULT IN

U.S.:	Yes
Canada:	No
Overseas:	No

⤙⤙ ⤚⤚

SOURCE BOOK PUBLICATIONS

1814 Franklin St., # 603
Oakland, CA 94612
Tel: (800) 841-0873 (510) 839-5471
Fax: (510) 839-2104
Web Site: www.worldfranchising.com
E-mail: rob@worldfranchising.com
Contact: Mr. Robert E. Bond, Publisher
Other Offices In:

BUSINESS FOCUS

Source Book Publications is the pre-eminent provider of reliable, up-to-date information on franchising - books, databases, consulting services and Internet sites. Bond's Franchise Guide (20) Editions) is the industry bible. "How Much Can I Make?" includes ~100 recent earnings claim statements. Bond's Top 100 Franchise focuses on today's top franchises. Bond's Hottest New Franchises focuses on up-and-coming franchises with less than 50 operating units. Tips & Traps When Buying A Franchise provides in insigh

Major Areas of Concentration:

1) Exposure and lead generation for international franchisors through sophisticated directories and specialized publications promoting the 100 "best" franchises by each of 4 major industry groupings.
2) Maintainenance of highly accurate databases for those selling goods or services to the franchising industry.
3) Development of interactive websites that promote franchisors, franchise attorneys and franchise industry service providers.
4) Organizer of the National Minority Franchising Initiative, which includes a website (www.minorityfranchising.com), a book (the Minority Franchising Guide) and a series of intense 2-day weekend seminars throughout the country.

BACKGROUND

Business Established In:	1985
Association Memberships:	
Full-Time Employees:	4
Full-Time Professionals:	4

Major Franchising Clients in Past 3 Yrs.: Over 400 major franchising clients.

AREAS CONSULT IN

U.S.:	Yes
Canada:	Yes
Overseas:	Yes

⤙⤙ ⤚⤚

ST. JACQUES FRANCHISE MARKETING

18 Cattano Ave.
Morristown, NJ 07960
Tel: (800) 708-9467 +102 (973) 829-0858 + 102
Fax: (973) 644-4743
Web Site: www.franchisefame.com
E-mail: philip@st.jacques.com
Contact: Mr. Philip St. Jacques, President
Other Offices In:

BUSINESS FOCUS

St. Jacques Franchise Marketing specializes in marketing and advertising for franchise organizations. Marketing a franchise brand is different, requiring a delicate balance between franchisor and franchisee with communication between all parties paramount to the success of any campaign. We been constructing and executing marketing strategies for many world class franchised and traditional companies for over fifteen years. Current clients include CENTURY 21, COLDWELL BANKER COMMERCIAL, ADP, and GlaxoSmithKline among others. We invite you to www. franchisefame.com to find out more about what St. Jacques Franchise Marketing can do for your organization.

Major Areas of Concentration:

1) Franchise Marketing and Advertising Strategies
2) Organic Sales Growth
3) Lead Generation
4) Franchisee Communications

BACKGROUND

Business Established In: 1990
Association Memberships:
Full-Time Employees: 9
Full-Time Professionals: 9
Major Franchising Clients in Past 3 Yrs.: Century 21, Coldwell Banker, Coldwell Banker Commercial, Cendant Corporation, Western Union, Sears Music School

AREAS CONSULT IN
U.S.:   Yes
Canada: No
Overseas: No

STARTUPJOURNAL.COM

P.O. Box 300
Princeton, NJ 08543-0300
Tel: (800) 366-3975 (312) 750-4050
Fax: (312) 750-4052
Web Site: www.startupjournal.com
E-mail: jim.graf@dowjones.com
Contact: Mr. Jim Graf, Director of Franchisor Advertising
Other Offices In: 1 S. Wacker, #2100, Chicago, IL 60606

BUSINESS FOCUS

StartupJournal.com is the Web's center for entrepreneurs from The Wall Street Journal, the world's leading business publication. Content comes from the powerful editorial resources of The Wall Street Journal, as well as WSJ.com, industry experts and StartupJournal.com's editorial team. In addition, this highly focused collection of relevant information, resources and tools showcases businesses and franchises for sale. From food and auto services to retail and staffing, StartupJournal.com is a premier resource of franchise opportunities available. StartupJournal.com presents advertisers with a unique opportunity to reach entrepreneurs.

Major Areas of Concentration:

1) Exclusive news, columnists and features focused on starting or buying a business or franchise, plus "how to" information covering all aspects of business ownership.
2) Tools to help entrepreneurs and small-business owners make smarter decisions and better use of their time. For example, the site helps readers write a business plan and search for venture capital.
3) Extensive listings of business opportunities and franchises for sale.
4) Strong demographics for advertisers. StartupJournal.com provides advertisers a unique opportunity to reach readers who are poised to start their own business, and who have the means to do so.

BACKGROUND
Business Established In: 1999
Association Memberships:
Full-Time Employees:
Full-Time Professionals:
Major Franchising Clients in Past 3 Yrs.:

AREAS CONSULT IN
U.S.:   This site is available world-wide
Canada: NR
Overseas: NR

STRATEGIC ADVISORY GROUP, INC.

P. O. Box 773
Sag Harbor, NY 11963
Tel: (631) 725-7746
Fax: (631) 725-7739
Web Site: www.strategicadvisorygroup.com
E-mail: phance@strategicadvisorygroup.com
Contact: Mr. Pierce W. Hance, Managing Director
Other Offices In:

BUSINESS FOCUS

Strategic Advisory Group, Inc. is a specialist in corporate finance and investment banking services, with unique experience in the franchise industry. The services we provide stress innovative applications of finance techniques for creative solutions to client problems. We are uniquely qualified, with the experience and resources to execute sophisticated finance strategies. Our network of international and domestic capital sources is specifically directed toward investments in middle market and late early stage companies. Our experience with the public capital markets enables us to provide guidance and direction to companies targeting public offerings, selecting underwriters, or seeking corporate joint venture partners.

Major Areas of Concentration:

1) Merger and acquisition services,
2) agency services for private placements of equity and debt securities and
3) strategic corporate advisory services for valuations, recapitalizations, reorganizations and financial development.

BACKGROUND

Business Established In: 1992
Association Memberships:
Full-Time Employees: 2
Full-Time Professionals: 2
Major Franchising Clients in Past 3 Yrs.: Deck The Walls, BAB Holdings/My Favorite Muffin, Hugo Boss, USA, Cash Converters USA, R. J. Gator's, Golden Pear Group, Great Clips Regional Companies, Inches-A-Weigh, Pour-LaFrance!, Pudgies Famous Chicken.

AREAS CONSULT IN

U.S.:	Yes
Canada:	Yes
Overseas:	Yes - Brazil

◄◄ ►►

STRATEGIC FRANCHISE SERVICES

1431 Greenway Dr., # 250
Irving, TX 75038
Tel: (972) 812-8124
Fax: (866) 243-7004
Web Site: www.franchiseehealthbenefits.com
E-mail: benefits@strathealthcare.com
Contact: Mr. Richard Fuchs, President
Other Offices In:

BUSINESS FOCUS

SFS provides affordable health insurance benefits to major franchise networks, individual franchisees, and medium to small organizations. SFS has developed the only insurance programs that meet the specific needs of the franchise industry... small number of employees in each location, multi-state locations, and each franchise is an individual business. SFS develops specific programs for individual franchise concepts.

Major Areas of Concentration:

1) Individual & limited major medical health insurance programs
2) Discount medical benefits
3) Asset protection health insurance
4) Lifestyle & health newsletters

BACKGROUND

Business Established In: 1992
Association Memberships:
Full-Time Employees: 4
Full-Time Professionals: 3
Major Franchising Clients in Past 3 Yrs.: UPS Stores, MBE, Submarina, Subway, Senior Helpers, MetroMedia, Dunkin Donuts, County Place Living

AREAS CONSULT IN

U.S.:	Yes
Canada:	No
Overseas:	No

◄◄ ►►

SUREPAYROLL, INC.

SUREPAYROLL

Your Payroll. Our Passion.℠

2350 Ravine Way, #100
Glenview, IL 60025
Tel: 877-954-7873 847-676-8420 + 7230
Fax: 847-510-0800
Web Site: www.SurePayroll.com
E-mail: calvin.steinhoff@surepayroll.com
Contact: Mr. Calvin Steinhoff, VP, Business Development
Other Offices In:

BUSINESS FOCUS

SurePayroll is a simple and affordable online service that allows users to process payroll in minutes. By recommending SurePayroll, you can help your franchisees eliminate the time-intensive tasks and penalty risks that come with processing payroll. Not only does our system calculate wages and deductions, but we deposit and file payroll taxes on their behalves, and keep up with federal, state and local payroll tax regulations. All they have to do is enter payroll hours online — we handle the rest, including working with the IRS, if necessary. SurePayroll comes with support from friendly payroll experts and a 6-month, money-back guarantee.

Major Areas of Concentration:

1) Online Payroll with Tax Management: SurePayroll allows franchises to complete payroll in minutes. They simply go online, enter hours and our system automatically calculates wages and deductions, and deposits and files payroll taxes. Employees are paid through direct deposit, or the franchisee can print checks.
2) HR Services: Integrated with the franchisees' SurePayroll account, SureAdvisor is a suite of HR resources, including customized labor compliance posters, a complete library of pre-populated business forms, valuable best-practice guides, and a helpful alerts and reminders service.
3) 401K: Designed specifically for small businesses, SurePayroll's Sure401K is an affordable, easy-to-manage 401K plan that integrates with the franchisees' SurePayroll account.

BACKGROUND

Business Established In: 2000
Association Memberships:
Full-Time Employees: 130
Full-Time Professionals: 130
Major Franchising Clients in Past 3 Yrs.: Keller Williams, Kumon, Cartridge World, UPS, Jackson Hewitt, RE/MAX, Subway SERVPRO, Planet Beach, Rocky Mountain Chocolate Factory, Curves gyms

AREAS CONSULT IN

U.S.:   Yes
Canada: No
Overseas: No

UFOCS.COM

1814 Franklin St., # 603
Oakland, CA 94612
Tel: (800) 841-0873 (510) 839-5471
Fax: (510) 839-2104
Web Site: www.UFOCs.com
E-mail: info@ufocs.com
Contact: Ms. Blair Cavagrotti, Senior Editor
Other Offices In:

BUSINESS FOCUS

UFOCs.com is the definitive source of current and historical FDDs/UFOCs and Item 19s. Over 20,000 FDDs/UFOCs are available from an extensive library that dates back to 1990. Roughly 3,000 individual franchise concepts are listed in our FDD/UFOC Store. Whether you need a company's entire FDD/UFOC, including Franchise Agreement, or an individual FDD/UFOC item, we can meet your needs in an efficient and cost-effective manner. All FDDs/UFOCs are available in PDF format and are delivered via email. Over 1,700 earnings claims are also available, either as pre-selected packages or as individual statements. The vast majority of FDD/UFOC orders are processed within 2 - 3 hours..

Major Areas of Concentration:

BACKGROUND

Business Established In: 2005
Association Memberships:
Full-Time Employees: 4
Full-Time Professionals: 3
Major Franchising Clients in Past 3 Yrs.: Over 500 franchisor clients.

AREAS CONSULT IN

U.S.:   Yes
Canada: No
Overseas: No

UNIGLOBE TRAVEL

18662 MacArthur Blvd., #100
Irvine, CA 92612
Tel: (800) 863-1606 (949) 623-9000
Fax: (949) 623-9008
Web Site: www.uniglobetravel.com
E-mail: salesinfo@uniglobetravel.com
Contact: Mr. Andrew Henry, VP US Operations

Other Offices In:

BUSINESS FOCUS

Entrepreneur has consistently awarded UNIGLOBE TRAVEL the #1 company in travel-agency franchising. All UNIGLOBE travel agency franchisees benefit from programs and systems designed to handle the needs of both the corporate and leisure client. UNIGLOBE franchisees benefit from money-saving automation agreements and top-notch incentive commission programs with major airline, hotel, car rental, tour and cruise-line companies.

Major Areas of Concentration:

BACKGROUND

Business Established In:	1980
Association Memberships:	
Full-Time Employees:	85
Full-Time Professionals:	NR
Major Franchising Clients in Past 3 Yrs.:	NR

AREAS CONSULT IN

U.S.:	Yes
Canada:	Yes
Overseas:	Yes

VALUATION ASSOCIATES

732 N. Thornton Ave.
Orlando, FL 32803
Tel: (800) 926-4142 (407) 896-6300
Fax: (407) 896-0113
Web Site: www.valuationassociates.com
E-mail: valuation-assoc@worldnet.att.net
Contact: Mr. Ed Karabedian, Principal
Other Offices In:

BUSINESS FOCUS

VALUATION ASSOCIATES is a comprehensive valuation and consulting company serving the restaurant, hospitality and petroleum marketing industries.

Major Areas of Concentration:
1) Restaurant Finance Industry;
2) Hospitality and Resort Industry;
3) Petroleum Marketing Industry.

BACKGROUND

Business Established In:	1964
Association Memberships:	
Full-Time Employees:	NR
Full-Time Professionals:	NR
Major Franchising Clients in Past 3 Yrs.:	NR

AREAS CONSULT IN

U.S.:	Yes
Canada:	Yes
Overseas:	NR

VEGARD VEVSTAD FRANCHISE CONSULTING

24124 Lakeside Trail
Crete, IL 60417
Tel: (708) 828-0152
Fax: (708) 672-4473
Web Site: www.franchiseconsultingfirm.com
E-mail: vvevstad@franchiseconsultingfirm.com
Contact: Mr. Vegard Vevstad, President
Other Offices In:

BUSINESS FOCUS

Vegard Vevstad Franchise Consulting transforms entrepreneurial ventures into global enterprises through franchising and other dedicated channels of distribution. Our multi-cultural senior consultants with advanced degrees in law, management, finance, marketing, teaching, etc., and more than 15 years of worldwide franchise management, consulting, and teaching experience, spanning Fortune 500 companies and over 200 smaller franchise companies in most every industry, guarantee great value and fast, expert service.

Major Areas of Concentration:

We are a full service franchise consulting and development firm providing:

1) Prototype Development. We assess how to improve the profitability of the core business, plan and implement improvements, and document policies and procedures.
2) Enterprise Development. We develop and implement strategies for the entire enterprise, including channels of distribution, feasibility studies, business plans, due diligence investigations, mergers and acquisitions, etc.
3) Channel Development. We structure and document all channel relationships, using detailed pro forma analysis to test important assumptions.
4) Franchisee Development. We develop and implement a complete program to recruit and train channel partners, using a multi-faceted marketing and sales campaign and multi-media assessment and training programs.

BACKGROUND

Business Established In:	2000
Association Memberships:	
Full-Time Employees:	1
Full-Time Professionals:	1
Major Franchising Clients in Past 3 Yrs.: Cheeky Wadsworth (WI),	

The Ground Pat'I (LA), Max's of Manila (CO), The Coffee Cup (FL), Smart Start (TX), Floor Coverings Direct (IL), Cajun Boiler's (AR), Potato Valley Café (MD)

AREAS CONSULT IN

U.S.:	Yes
Canada:	Yes

Overseas: Yes - Scandinavia, Switzerland, Spain, Portugal, Kuwait, Philippines, Argentina, Chile, Guatemala, Dominican Republic

<< >>

VIDI EMI

2450 Washington Ave.
San Leandro, CA 94577
Tel: (510) 667-9999
Fax:
Web Site: www.vidiemi.com
E-mail: info@vidiemi.com
Contact: Mr. Robin Simmons, Client Services & Operations Manager
Other Offices In: Menlo Park, NV

BUSINESS FOCUS

Vidi Emi an E-Marketing agency with it's roots in email marketing. We give the highest quality sending, reporting and customer care that you can receive from a company that will know you on a first name basis. A full service firm, Vidi provides everything, from creative design, programming, QA, Testing, segmentation, consultation and deployment. We put our customer's success as our own and look to re-engage with every send.

Major Areas of Concentration:

1) Email Marketing.
2) Search Engine Marketing.
3) Database Management.
4) Strategic Consultation.

BACKGROUND

Business Established In:	2001
Association Memberships:	
Full-Time Employees:	
Full-Time Professionals:	
Major Franchising Clients in Past 3 Yrs.:	

AREAS CONSULT IN

U.S.:	All U.S.
Canada:	All Canada
Overseas:	UK, India

<< >>

WEB CONFERENCING CENTRAL

1539 Monrovia Ave., Suite 11
Newport Beach, CA 92663

Tel: 949-631-0274
Fax:
Web Site: www.web-conferencing-central.com
E-mail: knelson@web-conferencing-central.com
Contact: Mr. Kevin Nelson,
Other Offices In:

BUSINESS FOCUS

Provides a complete set of internet tools for running live online meetings, teleconferences, recorded presentations branded with your company info, web surveys and forms, transferring large files through a URL and more. One system that can be used for training, sales, tech support and collaboration.

Major Areas of Concentration:

BACKGROUND

Business Established In:	2004
Association Memberships:	
Full-Time Employees:	11
Full-Time Professionals:	5
Major Franchising Clients in Past 3 Yrs.:	

AREAS CONSULT IN

U.S.:	Yes, All US
Canada:	Yes, All Canada
Overseas:	No

<< >>

WOMEN IN FRANCHISING, INC. (WIF)

53 West Jackson Blvd, #1157
Chicago, IL 60604
Tel: (800) 222-4943 (312) 431-1467
Fax: (312) 431-1469
Web Site: www.womeninfranchising.com
E-mail: info@womeninfranchising.com
Contact: Mr. Larry Beck, Executive Assistant
Other Offices In:

BUSINESS FOCUS

Women In Franchising, Inc. (WIF) founded in Chicago, Illinois in

1987, offers franchise consulting services for women and minorities interested in becoming franchisees or franchisors. WIF's offers a number of consulting services including: presenting workshops and seminars that teach prospective franchisees the skills and knowledge needed to evaluate, finance, and purchase a franchise; providing one-on-one assistance to persons who are considering buying a franchise by conducting a UFOC (Uniform Franchise Offering Circular) Review; assisting entrepreneurs in expanding their business via franchising with a Feasibility Study to assess their readiness to franchise.

Major Areas of Concentration:
1) Education and Training: WIF offers expertise in the development, coordination and implementation of franchise business training seminars on a national basis.
2) Federal Contracts: WIF has been a federal contractor in the U.S.
3) Minority Business Development Agency (MBDA), under a program created to stimulate the growth of minority franchises and also with the U.S. Small Business Administration (SBA) to conduct research entitled, Women and Minorities in Franchising and Financing Practices.
4) Consulting Services: WIF provides a variety of tools and one-on-one assistance to prospective franchisees and franchisors including audio seminars, a detailed Operations Manual and sales guidance, and national public relations contracts for recruiting franchisees.
5) Specialized Service: WIF offers consulting services, workshops, and franchisor trade missons targeted to Native American entrepreneurs and tribal governments.

BACKGROUND
Business Established In: 1987
Association Memberships:
Full-Time Employees: 4
Full-Time Professionals: 3
Major Franchising Clients in Past 3 Yrs.: Verlo Mattress Factory Stores, Whitewater, Wisconsin; Shape Up Sisters, Aguas Buenas, Puerto Rico; We The People Forms & Service Centers, USA, Santa Barbara, California; Creative Colors International, Tinley Park, Illinois; United States Hispanic Chamber of Commerce, Washington, D.C.; Women's Business Development Center, Chicago, Illinois; The American Franchisee Association, Chicago, Illinois

AREAS CONSULT IN
U.S.: Yes
Canada: Yes
Overseas: Yes - China and India

◄◄ ►►

WORLD FRANCHISING NETWORK

1814 Franklin St., # 603
Oakland, CA 94612

Tel: (800) 841-0873 (510) 839-5471
Fax: (510) 839-2104
Web Site: WorldFranchising.com
E-mail: rob@worldfranchising.com
Contact: Mr. Rob Bond, President
Other Offices In:

BUSINESS FOCUS
Providing exposure and lead generation to the franchising community through over 10 websites that focus on specific areas of franchising. The portal website is www.WorldFranchising.com. Others include www.100TopFranchises.com, www.HottestNewFranchises.com, www.PickThePerfectFranchise.com, www.MinorityFranchising.com, www.SourceBookPublications.com, www.FranchisingResourceCenter.com, www.FranchisingSuppliers.com and www.FranchisingAttorney.com. four annual publications - Bond's Franchise Guide, Bond's Top 100 Franchises, How Much Can I Make?, and Bond's Hottest New Franchises. A listing on 3 - 4 websites and 3 - 4 websites is only $1,500 for 12 months. Give us a call at (800) 841-0873 for more information.

Major Areas of Concentration:

1) Lead generation through multiple websites and publications.
2) Consulting services provided to clients.

BACKGROUND
Business Established In:
Association Memberships:
Full-Time Employees:
Full-Time Professionals:
Major Franchising Clients in Past 3 Yrs.:

AREAS CONSULT IN
U.S.: Yes
Canada: Yes
Overseas: Yes

◄◄ ►►

WORLD FRANCHISORS

2121 Vista Pkwy.
West Palm Beach, FL 33411
Tel: (561) 868-1358
Fax: (561) 868-3637
Web Site: www.ufgservices.com
E-mail: sartony@aol.com
Contact: Mr. Tony Foley, President
Other Offices In:

BUSINESS FOCUS

World Franchisors is your "global" sales partner. We sell "master licenses" worldwide to expand your franchise globally in a fraction of the time and at a fraction of the cost. Selling master licenses can be a very time consuming and complicated process, especially in certain markets. We've already established relationships in more than 50 countries throughout the world. We know the territory and have actually sold dozens of master licenses for some very well known franchise brands. World Franchisors, exper

Major Areas of Concentration:

1) Selling of master licenses
2) Market consultation for expansion purposes
3) Economic and political demographics
4) Franchise agreement preparation consultation

BACKGROUND

Business Established In: 2004
Association Memberships:
Full-Time Employees: 4
Full-Time Professionals: 6
Major Franchising Clients in Past 3 Yrs.: PostNet, Fruit Flowers, Sign-A-Rama, EmbroidMe, Virginia Barbeque, Grins 2 Go, Tint World, Billboard Connection, FranchiseMart, Planet Beach International

AREAS CONSULT IN

U.S.: Yes
Canada: Yes
Overseas: Yes - Australia, South Africa, Spain, UK, Nigeria, Italy, Kazakhstan, Croatia, Japan

XPANSHEN MARKETING COMMUNICATIONS

731 N. Weber, Suite 202
Colorado Springs, CO 80903
Tel: (719) 599-7678
Fax: (719) 599-7751
Web Site: www.xpanshen.com
E-mail: info@xpanshen.com
Contact: Ms. Rhonda Bauer, Founder/CEO
Other Offices In:

BUSINESS FOCUS

We are business invigorators. Xpanshen was founded with one goal in mind -- to help businesses grow and expand. From consumer research to publicity and prospecting, from local store marketing to national advertising campaigns, we analyze the needs, develop

the solutions, execute the programs and measure the results. Throughout our process, we sharpen the focus and clarify the objectives. Time and time again we have produced growth for our clients; in traffic, sales and brand awareness. For those companies who recognize that the rules have changed -- call Xpanshen. We'll work right along side of you to meet your company's growth needs.

Major Areas of Concentration:

1) Marketing -- consumer research, competitive research, secret shopper services, strategic planning, stealth marketing programs, special promotions and consumer loyalty programs.
2) Public Relations -- talk shows, pitch and write articles, community involvement, employee communications, crisis communications, special events.
3) Advertising -- national, regional, local branding and sales advertising in the fields of TV, radio, outdoor, print, direct mail, interactive, coupons and other traditional and non-traditional media.
4) Media -- coop program development and management, planning, buying and analysis.

BACKGROUND

Business Established In: 1992
Association Memberships:
Full-Time Employees: 6
Full-Time Professionals: 2
Major Franchising Clients in Past 3 Yrs.: International Franchise Association, Lemar's Donuts, Domino's Pizza, Barkbusters, CinnaMonster

AREAS CONSULT IN

U.S.: Yes
Canada: No
Overseas: No

FRANCHISE & BUSINESS LAW GROUP

20 South Charles St., 3rd Fl.
Baltimore, MD 21201
Tel: (410) 986-0099
Fax: (410) 986-0123
Web Site: www.franbuslaw.com
Contact: Mr. David L. Cahn
Email: info@franbuslaw.com
Other Offices In:

PROFILE
Franchising, Dispute Resolution, Business Law

BACKGROUND
Firm Established In:	2004
Serving Franchising Community Since:	1997
% of Billable Hrs. to Franchise Clients:	90%
Full-Time Employees:	3
Full-Time Professionals:	2

Major Franchise Clients in Past 3 Yrs.:
David Cahn has represented franchisees or the franchisor in the following systems: Baskin Robbins, Dunkin' Donuts, TruePresence, Xpose Fitness, Medifast Weight Control Center, 360 Painting, The Grout Medic, UPS Stores, Maggie Moo's Ice Cream

MR. DAVID L. CAHN

PROFILE
Drafting and negotiating franchise agreements and real estate leases, preparing and registering franchise offering circulars; preparing LLC operating agreements or corporate by-laws; representing clients in franchisor-franchisee disputes

BACKGROUND
Year Admitted to the Bar:	1995
Licensed to Practice in:	Maryland and District of Columbia

Education/Honors: Stanford University, B.A. 1990; University of Pennsylvania, J.D. 1995; formerly associated with Piper Rudnick LLP, 1997 - 2001

Professional Assns./Membership: Chairperson, Maryland State Bar, Franchise Law Comm., Member, ABA Forum on Franchising and AAFD LegaLine

Publications: The Impact of the Uniform Commercial Code on Franchising, ABA Forum on Franchising, 2006; Post-Expiration Covenants Not To Compete, LJN's Franchising Business & Law Alert, 2002; Earnings Claims: The Disclosure Franchisors Should Try To Make, Franchise Law Journal, 2001

PROVIDE LEGAL SERVICES IN
U.S.:	Yes
Canada:	No
Overseas:	No

◄◄ ►►

FRIEDMAN, ROSENWASSER & GOLDBAUM P.A.

5355 Town Center Rd., # 801
Boca Raton, FL 33486
Tel: (561) 395-5511
Fax: (561) 368-9274
Web Site: www.franchiselaw.com
Contact: Mr. Ronald N. Rosenwasser
Email: rrosenwasser@franchiselaw.com

Other Offices In: Boston, MA; Lexington, KY

PROFILE

Experienced in all aspects of planning and executing domestic and international expansion through franchising and other expansion strategies; intellectual property protection; litigation and alternative dispute resolution; corporate matters involving all aspects of company formation, growth, financing and sale; lease and real estate matters; and general legal problem-solving

BACKGROUND

Firm Established In:	1976
Serving Franchising Community Since:	1976
% of Billable Hrs. to Franchise Clients:	Over 50%
Full-Time Employees:	8
Full-Time Professionals:	6

Major Franchise Clients in Past 3 Yrs.:
Jan-Pro Franchising International; Velocity Sports Performance; Shula's Steakhouses; Buy Owner International Real Estate; Colorall International Technologies; Fast-Fix Jewelry Repair; Pollo Tropical Restaurants; IHOP master franchise; Quiznos master franchise

MR. RONALD N. ROSENWASSER

Email: rrosenwasser@frglaw.com

PROFILE

Experienced in all aspects of planning and executing domestic and international expansion through franchising and other expansion strategies; intellectual property protection; corporate matters involving all aspects of company formation, growth, financing and sale; and general legal problem-solving

BACKGROUND

Year Admitted to the Bar:	1983
Licensed to Practice in:	Florida
Education/Honors:	AV rated.

Professional Assns./Membership: ABA; FL Bar; International Bar; International Trademark Association; International Franchise Association

Publications: "Understanding the Legal Environment for Franchising"; "International Franchising and Distribution"; "Federal Franchise Law - What is a Franchise and How is it Regulated"; "How to Franchise Your Business"; "Franchise Litigation: Causes of Action, Procedural Issues, Strategies and Ethical Considerations"; "Structuring Growth Via Distributorships/Dealerships, Company-Owned Outlets, Licensing Arrangements and Other Non-Franchise Alternatives"; "Twilight Zone: Regulated v. Unregulated Licensing, Dealership and

PROVIDE LEGAL SERVICES IN

U.S.:	Yes
Canada:	No
Overseas:	Yes. We also provide assistance to US companies

and individuals who desire to do business in all foreign countries.

THE RICHARD L. ROSEN LAW FIRM, PLLC

110 E. 59th St., 23rd Fl.
New York, NY 10022
Tel: (212) 644-6644
Fax: (212) 644-3344
Web Site: www.richardrosenlaw.com
Contact: Mr. Richard L. Rosen
Email: rlr@rosenlawpllc.com
Other Offices In:

PROFILE

While we are experienced in most business matters, including the areas of corporate law, real estate development, lease negotiations and dispute resolution, we have a long standing, special involvement in the franchising field. As long time practitioners in the field of franchise, we are familiar with virtually every franchise related issue that our clients may face, whether it be buying or selling a franchise, negotiating a lease, setting up a franchise program and preparing the necessary agreements and disclosure documents, forming or counseling a franchisee association or litigating, arbitrating, mediating (or negotiating) a dispute. Our experience enables us to guide and counsel our clients effectively and efficiently wherever they are located.

BACKGROUND

Firm Established In:	2005
Serving Franchising Community Since:	1971
% of Billable Hrs. to Franchise Clients:	50%
Full-Time Employees:	5
Full-Time Professionals:	3

Major Franchise Clients in Past 3 Yrs.: Franchisors: Little Scoops, Tilden Auto Care; Franchisees: Closets By Design Franchisee Association, Cold Stone Creamery, Dunkin Donuts, Exxon Mobil; Famous Famiglia, Five Guys Famous Hamburgers, Goddard Schools, Retro Fitness

MR. BRIAN D. PORCH, JR.

Email: bp@rosenlawpllc.com

PROFILE

Commercial litigation, Corporate transactions, Franchise litigation, Franchise and commercial transaction, Intellectual property and Entertainment law, Intellectual property litigation, Antitrust, Media, Government investigations, Commercial Real Estate litigation

BACKGROUND

Year Admitted to the Bar:	2002
Licensed to Practice in:	Connecticut, New York

Education/Honors: Emory University School of Law; University

of Connecticut

Professional Assns./Membership: NYC Bar Association; NY County Lawyers' Association; The Fairfield County Bar Association

Publications:

PROVIDE LEGAL SERVICES IN

U.S.:	Yes
Canada:	No
Overseas:	
	No

MR. RICHARD L. ROSEN

Tel: (212) 644-6644 +394
Email: rlr@rosenlawpllc.com

PROFILE
Richard L. Rosen has been actively engaged in the practice of franchise law in New York City for over 35 years during which time he has represented many franchisors and franchisees both as counsel and as a business advisor. Mr. Rosen has counseled and represented franchisors in the setting up of franchising systems and programs, has formed franchising entities, drafted and negotiated franchise agreements, registration statements, disclosure documents and other ancillary franchise documents; he has represented franchisees and franchisee associations, and has litigated (both in state and federal courts), arbitrated and mediated matters on behalf of both franchisors and franchisees.

BACKGROUND

Year Admitted to the Bar:	1968
Licensed to Practice in:	New York

Education/Honors: Cornell University; New York Law School; NYU Real Estate Institute; NYS Regents Scholar; Listed in Who's Who in America, Who's Who in American Law, The Best Lawyers in America, 100 Best Lawyers (Franchise Times), Super Lawyers; Lifetime Achievement Award (American Association of Franchisees and Dealers); Martindale Hubbell rating AV (Highest), and list of Preeminent Attorneys

Professional Assns./Membership: ABA; AAFD; CPR Panel of Neutrals; Franchise Lawyers Association; IFA; National Franchise Mediation Steering Committee; NYC Bar Association; and NYS Bar Association

Publications: Contributing author, "The Complete Guide to Evaluating, Buying and Growing your Franchise Business", The Association of Small Business Development Centers; "Renewal of your Franchise: Some Solutions", Franchise Times; "How to Franchise your Business", The Association of the Bar of the City of New York; and various other publications

PROVIDE LEGAL SERVICES IN

U.S.:	Yes
Canada:	No
Overseas:	Yes, various countries

MR. LEONARD S. SALIS

Email: ls@rosenlawpllc.com

PROFILE
Corporate law, Franchise law, Real estate, Trusts and estates, Commercial litigation

BACKGROUND

Year Admitted to the Bar:	1996
Licensed to Practice in:	New York

Education/Honors: Brooklyn Law School; State University of NY at Buffalo

Professional Assns./Membership: NYC Bar Association; NY County Lawyers' Association; ABA Forum Committee on Franchising

Publications:

PROVIDE LEGAL SERVICES IN

U.S.:	Yes
Canada:	No
Overseas:	No

SNELL & WILMER L.L.P.

350 S. Grand Ave., # 2600
Los Angeles, CA 90071
Tel: (213) 929-2543
Fax: (213) 929-2525
Web Site: www.swlaw.com
Contact: Ms. Susan Grueneberg
Email: sgrueneberg@swlaw.com
Other Offices In:

PROFILE
In addition to franchise law, the firm is known for its zealous representation in complex business litigation including class action defense, labor and employment counseling and defense and franchise litigation. The firm's full-service expertise also extends to real estate, intellectual property, mergers and acquisitions, securities, commercial lending, gaming and tax.

BACKGROUND

Firm Established In:	1938

Serving Franchising Community Since:
% of Billable Hrs. to Franchise Clients:
Full-Time Employees:
Full-Time Professionals:
Major Franchise Clients in Past 3 Yrs.: The firm represents numerous franchise clients in many areas, including restaurants and food service, transportation, real estate, home services, fit-

ness, recreation and health. The firm also represents non-franchised distribution systems.

MS. SUSAN GRUENEBERG

PROFILE
Ms. Grueneberg advises clients on laws affecting product and service distribution including franchise and business opportunity laws both domestically and internationally. This involves structuring distribution programs, regulatory compliance, preparation of disclosure documents, negotiations with franchisees, termination, nonrenewal and transfer issues, defense of enforcement actions and resolution.

BACKGROUND
Year Admitted to the Bar: 1980
Licensed to Practice in: CA

Education/Honors: BA cum laude, UCLA (1973); JD, UCLA (1979); US State Department Fellowship (1976-1978); US National Academy of Sciences Fellowship (1979-1981)

Professional Assns./Membership: Chair, ABA Forum on Franchising (2001-2003); Member, IFA Legal/Legislative Committee (1996-Present); Chair, Advisory Committee, NASAA Franchise Project Group

Publications: Numerous articles for publications of the America Bar Association Forum on Franchising, the International Franchise Association, the California State Bar, Continuing Education of the Bar and other groups.

PROVIDE LEGAL SERVICES IN
U.S.:   Yes
Canada: Yes
Overseas: Yes

WORLDFRANCHISING.COM

The Definitive Guide to the World of Franchising

FRANCHISOR QUESTIONNAIRE

FRANCHISOR INFORMATION

1. **Franchise Trade Name:** _____
2. **Address:** _____
   City: _____ , **State/Prov.** _____ **Zip/Postal Code:** _____
   Phone: (800) _____ **or (**) _____
   Fax: ( ) _____
   Internet: www._____ **General Email:** _____
   Expediter Email(s) (up to 3 email addresses we should use to notify you of franchisee leads):
   _____

3. **Contact Person:** _____ **Position:** _____
   Email*: _____

4. **President/CEO*:** _____ **Title*:** _____
   Email*: _____ (* Will not be published.)

BUSINESS DESCRIPTION

5. Please describe your business. Use the full space available to set your franchise apart from other franchising opportunities, i.e. sell your system to the potential franchisee.
   _____
   _____
   _____
   _____
   _____
   _____
   _____

FRANCHISOR BACKGROUND

6. Year company was founded _____.

7. First year as franchisor _____.

8. Actual number of Franchised Units   _____ Units
   Actual number of Company-Owned Units   _____ Units

9. Total Operating Units   _____ Units

10. Of Total Operating Units listed in # 9,
    _____ are in the U.S.   _____ are in Canada.   _____ are Overseas.

11. A) How many U.S. States have operating units?   _____
    B) How many Canadian Provinces have operating units?   _____
    C) How many Foreign Countries have operating units?   _____
    D) What 3 States/Provinces have the largest number of operating units?
       How many operating units are located in these States/Provinces?

	States/Provinces	# of Units
1.	_____	_____
2.	_____	_____
3.	_____	_____

12. How many new units do you plan to open in the next 12 months?   _____ Units

FRANCHISOR QUESTIONNAIRE (cont.)

13. In qualifying a potential franchisee, please rank the following criteria from Unimportant to Very Important. (Please circle.)

	Unimportant				Very Important
Financial Net Worth	1	2	3	4	5
General Business Experience	1	2	3	4	5
Specific Industry Experience	1	2	3	4	5
Formal Education	1	2	3	4	5
Psychological Profile	1	2	3	4	5
Personal Interview(s)	1	2	3	4	5

14. The following States/Province require a separate registration (or disclosure, indicated by an *) document. In which are you currently registered to franchise?

❑ All Below or ❑ IN ❑ ND ❑ WA
❑ CA ❑ MD ❑ OR* ❑ WI
❑ FL* ❑ MI* ❑ RI ❑ DC
❑ HI ❑ MN ❑ SD
❑ IL ❑ NY ❑ VA ❑ Alberta

15. Including the owner/operator, how many employees are recommended to staff the average franchised unit? _____ Full-Time _____ Part-Time

16. What square footage and type(s) of sites do most of your franchise units require? _____ sq. ft.
❑ Free-Standing Building (FS) ❑ Storefront (SF) ❑ Strip Center(SC) ❑ Regional Mall(RM)
❑ Home-Based (HB) ❑ Other _____ ❑ Not Applicable

17. Do you encourage conversions? ❑ Yes ❑ No ❑ Not Applicable

FINANCIAL REQUIREMENTS

18. Even though the cash investment may vary substantially by individual unit, what is the range of equity capital (up-front cash) required? $ _____

19. What is the range of total investment required? $ _____

20. What is the minimum net worth required of the franchisee? $ _____

21. How much is the initial franchise fee for a new franchisee? $ _____

22. How much is the on-going royalty fee? _____ % or _____

23. How much is the on-going advertising fee? _____ % or _____

24. Do you provide potential franchisees with an Earnings Claim Statement? ❑ Yes ❑ No

TERMS OF CONTRACT

25. What is the term of the original franchise agreement? _____ Years

26. What is the term of the renewal period? _____ Years

27. Passive ownership of the initial unit is ❑ Allowed ❑ Allowed, But Discouraged ❑ Not Allowed

28. Do you have Area Development Agreements? ❑ Yes ❑ No
If Yes, for what period? _____ Years

29. Do you have Sub-Franchisor Contracts covering specified territories? ❑ Yes ❑ No

30. Can the franchisee establish additional outlets within his/her area? ❑ Yes ❑ No

FRANCHISOR QUESTIONNAIRE (cont.)

FRANCHISOR SUPPORT AND TRAINING PROVIDED

31. Do you assist the franchisee in site selection? ☐ Yes ☐ No ☐ Not Applicable

32. Do you assist the franchisee in lease negotiations? ☐ Yes ☐ No ☐ Not Applicable

33. Is financial assistance available? ☐ Yes ☐ No ☐ N.A.; If Yes, ☐ Direct or ☐ Indirect

34. Do you participate in co-operative advertising? ☐ Yes ☐ No ☐ Not Applicable

35. Does your system have a franchisee association? ☐ Yes ☐ No
If Yes, are you a member? ☐ Yes ☐ No

36. How many full-time, paid personnel are currently on your corporate staff? _____

37. Which of the following on-going services do you provide to the franchisee?

Service	Included in Fees	At Additional Cost	N.A.
A. Central Data Processing	☐	☐	☐
B. Central Purchasing	☐	☐	☐
C. Field Operations Evaluation	☐	☐	☐
D. Field Training	☐	☐	☐
E. Initial Store Opening	☐	☐	☐
F. Inventory Control	☐	☐	☐
G. Franchisee Newsletter	☐	☐	☐
H. Regional Or National Meetings	☐	☐	☐
I. 800 Telephone Hotline	☐	☐	☐

38. Please note the location and duration of any initial training sessions included in the franchise fee?

Location	Duration
A. _____	_____
B. _____	_____
C. _____	_____

SPECIFIC EXPANSION PLANS

39. In which specific regions of the U.S. are you actively seeking new franchisees?
For example: All U.S., or NW & SW, or NJ Only.

_____

40. Are you actively seeking franchisees in Canada? ☐ Yes ☐ No
If Yes, in which Provinces? ☐ All or _____

41. Are you actively seeking franchisees Overseas? ☐ Yes ☐ No
If Yes, in which Provinces? ☐ All or _____

Name of Respondent: _____ **Phone:** (___) _____

SOURCE BOOK PUBLICATIONS
Serving the Franchising Industry
1814 Franklin Street, Suite 603, Oakland, CA 94612
(800) 841-0873 ❖ (510) 839-5471 ❖ Fax: (510) 839-2104 ❖ E-Mail: info@worldfranchising.com
www.franchisingsuppliers.com ❖ www.worldfranchising.com ❖ www.franchisingattorney.com

WORLDFRANCHISING.COM

The Definitive Guide to the World of Franchising

RESPONSE FORM

☐ **YES, we wish to participate on the www.worldfranchising.com website and in the 2010 (21st) Edition of *Bond's Franchise Guide*. I understand that we will be charged $1,500 and that the benefits include:**

- An immediate 12-month listing of company profile on www.worldfranchising.com, www.minorityfranchising.com and www.picktheperfectfranchise.com, including 4-color logo
- Website profile updates throughout the year at no charge
- Access to prospective franchisees via the Franchise Expediter™
- Detailed company profile in the 2010 (21st) Edition of *Bond's Franchise Guide*, including black-and-white logo
- Complimentary copy of *Bond's Franchise Guide* upon publication
- Consideration for inclusion in the 2010 (4th) Edition of *Bond's Top 100 Franchises* for companies with 50 or more operating units.

To participate, please do the following:

1. SUBMIT MATERIALS

☐ Page 1-3   Franchisor Questionnaire
☐ Page 4   Response Form
☐ Company Logo   Email high-quality (300 DPI, EPS, TIF or JPG format) 4-color logo to logos@worldfranchising.com

☐ Letterhead/Business Card (optional)

Fax or email materials to Source Book Publications at (510) 839-2104 or info@worldfranchising.com.

2. ENCLOSE PAYMENT

☐ Payment Included

☐ Charge My   ☐ Visa   ☐ MasterCard   ☐ American Express

Card #: _____ Expiration Date: _____

Name on Card: _____

☐ Invoice Us

_____   _____
Approved By   **Date**

_____
Company Name

SOURCE BOOK PUBLICATIONS
Serving the Franchising Industry
1814 Franklin Street, Suite 603, Oakland, CA 94612
(800) 841-0873 ❖ (510) 839-5471 ❖ Fax: (510) 839-2104 ❖ E-Mail: info@worldfranchising.com
www.franchisingsuppliers.com ❖ www.worldfranchising.com ❖ www.franchisingattorney.com

Alphabetical Listing of Franchisors

* Indicates Top 100 Franchise

** Indicates Hottest New Franchise

B

C

D

E

M

Alphabetical Listing of Franchise Industry Service Providers and Attorneys

Franchise Industry Service Providers

The Ultimate "Insider's Guide" to Actual Sales,
Expenses and/or Profit Data on 93 Major Franchise Systems

"How Much Can I Make?"

2009 (9th) Edition

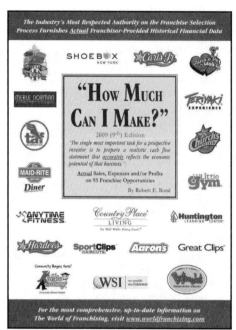

Key Features:

- 93 Earnings Claims Statements

- 4 Major Industry Categories

- 353 Pages

- Critical, Never-Before-Published Franchisor-Provided Information

PUBLISHED ANNUALLY

Yes, I want to order _____ copy(ies) of *"How Much Can I Make?"* at $34.95 each ($45.50 Canadian). Please add $8.50 per book for shipping* & handling ($12.00 Canada; international shipments at actual cost). California residents add appropriate sales tax.

Name_____Title_____

Company_____Telephone No. (_____) _____

Address _____

City _____ State/Prov. _____ Zip _____

Email Address_____

☐   Check Enclosed or

Charge my: ☐ MasterCard   ☐ Visa

Card#:_____Expiration Date:_____

Signature:_____Security Code:_____

Please send to: **Source Book Publications**, 1814 Franklin Street, Suite 603, Oakland, CA 94612

* Note: All books shipped by USPS Priority Mail.
Satisfaction Guaranteed. If not fully satisfied, return for a prompt, 100% refund.

**For faster service, please call (800) 841-0873, fax to (510) 839-2104
or email to info@worldfranchising.com**

Now's the time to be **in business for yourself,** but **not by yourself**. Own a Franchise.

Los Angeles Convention Center
October 2–4, 2009

Visit: **WCFExpo.com**

With today's unpredictable economy, and uncertain job market, there's never been a better time to take control of your financial future – by being in business for yourself

When you own a proven franchise, you have the support of a professional team to help you carry the load. That's why a franchise is a safer way to be in business for yourself.

At the West Coast Franchise Expo, you'll be able to see hundreds of the top franchises. Sample their products. Attend educational seminars. And get all the information you need to choose the right franchise for your interests, skills and investment level – all in one place.

Don't miss this opportunity to take control of your financial future.

SPONSORED BY

IFA 🌐 | **Franchising**™
INTERNATIONAL FRANCHISE ASSOCIATION | **Building** local businesses, one **opportunity** at a time.

Produced by MFV Expositions
For Exhibitor Info Call: Maryjane at 201.881.1666
or exhibit@mfvexpo.com

An In-Depth Analysis of Today's Top Franchise Opportunities

Bond's Top 100 Franchises

2009 (3rd) Edition

Key Features:

In response to the constantly asked question, *"What are the best franchises?"*, this book focuses on the top 100 franchises broken down into four major segments — food-service, lodging, retail and service-based franchises. Within each group, a rigorous, in-depth analysis was performed on over 500 systems. Many of the companies selected are household names. Others are rapidly-growing, mid-sized firms that are also strong national players. Still others are somewhat smaller systems that demonstrate sound concepts, exceptional management and an aggressive expansion system. Companies were analyzed on the basis of historical performance, brand identification, market dynamics, franchisee satisfaction, the level of training and on-going support, financial stability, etc. This book includes detailed four to five page profiles on each company, as well as key statistics and industry overview. All companies are proven performers and most have a national presence.

JUST PUBLISHED

Yes, I want to order _____ copy(ies) of *Bond's Top 100 Franchises* at $24.95 each ($32.50 Canadian). Please add $8.50 per book for shipping & handling ($12.00 Canada; international shipments at actual cost). California residents add appropriate sales tax.

Name_____Title_____

Company_____Telephone No. (_____) _____

Address_____

City_____ State/Prov. _____ Zip _____

Email Address_____

☐ Check Enclosed or

Charge my: ☐ MasterCard ☐ Visa

Card #:_____ Expiration Date: _____

Signature:_____Security Code:_____

Please send to: **Source Book Publications**, 1814 Franklin Street, Suite 603, Oakland, CA 94612

* Note: All books shipped by USPS Priority Mail.

Satisfaction Guaranteed. If not fully satisfied, return for a prompt, 100% refund.

For faster service, please call (800) 841-0873, fax to (510) 839-2104
or email to info@worldfranchising.com